T0135349

Lecture Notes in Computer Science 13777

More information about this series at https://link.springer.com/bookseries/558

Weizhi Meng · Rongxing Lu · Geyong Min ·
Jaideep Vaidya (Eds.)

Algorithms and Architectures for Parallel Processing

22nd International Conference, ICA3PP 2022
Copenhagen, Denmark, October 10–12, 2022
Proceedings

 Springer

Editors
Weizhi Meng 🆔
Technical University of Denmark
Kongens Lyngby, Denmark

Geyong Min 🆔
University of Exeter
Exeter, UK

Rongxing Lu 🆔
University of New Brunswick
Fredericton, NB, Canada

Jaideep Vaidya 🆔
Rutgers University
Newark, NJ, USA

ISSN 0302-9743   ISSN 1611-3349 (electronic)
Lecture Notes in Computer Science
ISBN 978-3-031-22676-2   ISBN 978-3-031-22677-9 (eBook)
https://doi.org/10.1007/978-3-031-22677-9

This Springer imprint is published by the registered company Springer Nature Switzerland AG
The registered company address is: Gewerbestrasse 11, 6330 Cham, Switzerland

Preface

The 22nd International Conference on Algorithms and Architectures for Parallel Processing (ICA3PP 2022) was held during October 10–12, 2022, and organized by the Technical University of Denmark. Due to the COVID-19 situation, it was held fully online.

ICA3PP 2022 was the 22nd in this series of conferences, which started in 1995, devoted to algorithms and architectures for parallel processing and computing. ICA3PP is now one of the most well-known international events that covers the many dimensions of parallel algorithms and architectures, encompassing fundamental theoretical approaches, practical experimental projects, and commercial components and systems. With the emerging demands of computing systems and applications, the power of computing systems has been remained a challenge. In recent years, various computing solutions such as parallel computing algorithms and architectures have been proposed. ICA3PP aims to bring together international academics and practitioners to exchange ideas and present research on improving the efficiency, performance, reliability, security, and interoperability of computing systems and applications.

This year, ICA3PP received 91 valid submissions, and each submission was reviewed by at least three reviewers in a single blind process. Based on their significance, novelty, technical quality, presentation, and practical impact, 33 full papers were accepted along with 10 short papers, giving an acceptance rate of 36.3%. In addition to the paper presentations, the program of the conference included five keynote speeches from esteemed scholars in the area:

1) Schahram Dustdar from TU Wien (Austria) with a talk on "Edge Intelligence - A Research Roadmap",
2) Zheng Yan from Xidian University (China) with a talk on "Trust, Security and Privacy of 5G Positioning",
3) Muttukrishnan Rajarajan from City, University of London (UK) with a talk on "Future of digital identity management in decentralised and distributed settings",
4) Ding Wang from Nankai University (China) with a talk on "How to Attack and Generate Honeywords", and
5) Song Guo from The Hong Kong Polytechnic University (China) with a talk on "Neural-enhanced Edge Perception Systems".

For the success of ICA3PP 2022, we would like to take this opportunity to express our sincere gratitude to the Program Committee members and reviewers for their dedicated and professional service. We were honored to have so many renowned scholars be part of this conference. Finally, we would like to thank all speakers, authors, and participants for their great contribution and support.

October 2022

Weizhi Meng
Rongxing Lu
Geyong Min
Jaideep Vaidya

Organization

General Co-chairs

Laurence T. Yang   Hainan University, China/St. Francis Xavier
University, Canada
Weijia Jia   Beijing Normal University and UIC, China
Vincenzo Piuri   Universita degli Studi di Milano, Italy

Program Chairs

Weizhi Meng   Technical University of Denmark, Denmark
Rongxing Lu   University of New Brunswick, Canada
Geyong Min   University of Exeter, UK
Jaideep Vaidya   Rutgers University, USA

Publicity Chairs

Tian Wang   Beijing Normal University and UIC, China
Aniello Castiglione   University of Naples Parthenope, Italy
Cheng Huang   University of Waterloo, Canada
Huawei Huang   Sun Yat-sen University, China

Publication Chair

Wenjuan Li   The Hong Kong Polytechnic University, China

Steering Committee

Yang Xiang (Chair)   Swinburne University of Technology, Australia
Weijia Jia   Beijing Normal University and UIC, China
Yi Pan   Georgia State University, USA
Laurence T. Yang   Hainan University, China/St. Francis Xavier
University, Canada
Wanlei Zhou   City University of Macau, China

Program Committee

Daniel Andresen	Kansas State University, USA
Danilo Ardagna	Politecnico di Milano, Italy
Silvio Barra	University of Naples, Italy
Siegfried Benkner	University of Vienna, Austria
Ladjel Bellatreche	LIAS, ISAE-ENSMA, France
Philip Brown	University of Colorado Springs, USA
George Bosilca	University of Tennessee, USA
Alfredo Cuzzocrea	University of Calabria, Italy
Chao Chen	James Cook University, Australia
Massimo Cafaro	University of Salento, Italy
Carmen De Maio	Universita degli Studi di Salerno, Italy
Zipei Fan	The University of Tokyo, Japan
Marc Frincu	Nottingham Trent University, UK
Jing Gong	Uppsala University, Sweden
Chunpeng Ge	Nanjing University of Aeronautics and Astronautics, China
Zonghua Gu	UMU, Sweden
Zhitao Guan	North China Electric Power University, China
Jinguang Han	Southeast University, China
Runchao Han	Monash University and CSIRO's Data61, Australia
Qiong Huang	South China Agricultural University, China
Xinyi Huang	Fujian Normal University, China
Houcine Hassan	Universitat Politecnica de Valencia, Spain
Peter Kropf	University of Neuchatel, Switzerland
Ioanna Kantzavelou	University of West Attica, Greece
Fagen Li	University of Electronic Science and Technology of China, China
Wenjuan Li	Hong Kong Polytechnic University, China
Zhiqiang Li	A10 Networks, USA
Xueqin Liang	Xidian University, China
Jingqiang Lin	University of Science and Technology of China, China
Laurent Lefevre	Inria, France
Paul Lu	University of Alberta, Canada
Francesco Palmieri	University of Salerno, Italy
Radu Prodan	University of Klagenfurt, Austria
Antonio Ruiz-Martinez	University of Murcia, Spain
Sokol Kosta	Aalborg University, Denmark
Susumu Matsumae	Saga University, Japan
Weizhi Meng	Technical University of Denmark, Denmark

Vincenzo Moscato	University of Naples, Italy
Weitian Tong	Georgia Southern University, USA
Ivan Rodero	Rutgers University, USA
Vladimir Voevodin	Lomonosov Moscow State University, Russia
Yong Yu	Shaanxi Normal University, China
Wei Wang	Beijing Jiaotong University, China
Yunling Wang	Xi'an University of Posts and Telecommunications, China
Tian Wang	Beijing Normal University and UIC, China
Roman Wyrzykowski	Czestochowa University of Technology, Poland
Qianhong Wu	Beihang University, China
Jun Shao	Zhejiang Gongshang University, China
Jordan Samhi	University of Luxembourg, Luxembourg
Ali Shoker	KAUST, Saudi Arabia
Tianze Sun	University of Toronto Scarborough, Canada
Massimo Torquati	University of Pisa, Italy
Zhe Xia	Wuhan University of Technology, China
Shigeng Zhang	Central South University, China
Fangguo Zhang	Sun Yat-sen University, China
Mingwu Zhang	Hubei University of Technology, China
Junlong Zhou	Nanjing University of Science and Technology, China

Subreviewers

Samira Afzal	Wanrong Gu	Hua Shen
Alexander Antonov	Bruno Guindani	Vadim Voevodin
Atakan Aral	Hamid Hadian	Muhammad Waleed
Enes Bajrovic	Dong Huang	Jinfeng Wang
Chao Chen	Lifeng Huang	Kun Wang
Haotian Chen	Huang Jianye	Minmei Wang
Jianxi Chen	Vladislav Kashansky	Tian Wang
Jianzhang Chen	Jianchang Lai	Yang Wang
Nestoras Chouliaras	Liying Li	Yuzhu Wang
Brandon Collins	Taous Madi	Bohang Wei
Yangguang Cui	Narges Mehran	Yang Yang
Mieszko Ferens	Andrey Nagiyev	Lu Yin
João Nuno Ferreira Alves	Dmitry Nikitenko	Liang Yun
Federica Filippini	Vassilis Papaspirou	Pingge Zhang
Andreu Fornos	Martin Sandrieser	Xiaotong Zhou
Qiyuan Gao	Hamta Sedghani	Konstantin Zhukov
Luis Garcia	Ahmad Sheikh	Ruozhou Zuo

Contents

Efficient Remote Memory Paging
for Disaggregated Memory Systems

Tao Wang, Haikun Liu$^{(\boxtimes)}$, and Hai Jin

National Engineering Research Center for Big Data Technology and System,
Services Computing Technology and System Lab, Cluster and Grid Computing Lab,
School of Computer Science and Technology, Huazhong University of Science and
Technology, Wuhan 430074, China
{twang_hust,hkliu,hjin}@hust.edu.cn

Abstract. Memory disaggregation has attracted increasing attention
in recent years because it is a cost-efficient approach to scale memory
capacity for applications in a data center. However, the latency of remote
memory access is a major concern in disaggregated memory systems.
This paper presents VANDI, a virtual memory paging mechanism that
allows applications to use remote memory pools transparently. VANDI
enables effective data caching and prefetching mechanisms to address
the problem of high access latency in disaggregated memory systems.
VANDI exploits a low-complexity cache replacement strategy to optimize the asynchronous staging queue so that the remote write latency
can be significantly reduced. VANDI can also prefetch data in multi-
granularity from a remote memory pool in an adaptive manner, and thus
further improves the hit rate of the local cache to reduce the read latency
of remote memory. Our extensive experiments using micro-benchmarks
show that VANDI can improve the performance of typical remote paging system–Infiniswap by up to 15×–102×. VANDI can also improve the
performance of state-of-the-art disaggregated memory system–Valet by
1.2×–2.7×. For typical machine learning workloads, VANDI can achieve
20% to 80% performance improvement compared with the state-of-the-
art Valet.

Keywords: Heterogeneous memory · Disaggregated memory · Virtual
memory · Cache replacement

1 Introduction

In cloud data centers, the memory requirement of applications are usually
dynamic due to the dynamics of cloud workloads. This often leads to imbalanced memory usage on different servers. The memory resource in some servers
may be underutilized, while other servers may be unable to satisfy the memory requirement of large data-centric applications. A previous study [17] has
observed that most servers in a cluster experience memory imbalance for more
than one half of operation time. Moreover, the utilization of allocated memory
is also rather low in most cases.

© Springer Nature Switzerland AG 2023
W. Meng et al. (Eds.): ICA3PP 2022, LNCS 13777, pp. 1–20, 2023.
https://doi.org/10.1007/978-3-031-22677-9_1

Recently, memory disaggregation [11] has been proposed to address the memory capacity wall problem by dynamically scaling computing and memory resource independently. Disaggregated memory systems enable servers to access remote memory like using the local memory. Typically, memory resource in remote servers is pre-allocated as memory pools. When a server node has not sufficient memory to execute a task, it allocates memory from a remote server node with free memory resource to satisfy applications' memory requirement. Although remote memory pools offer high scalability, the high latency and low bandwidth of remote memory accesses are major concerns of disaggregated memory systems.

The emergence of *Remote Direct Memory Access* (RDMA) [12] technology provides a promising approach to address the problem of remote memory accesses. RDMA technology can bypass the remote server's OS kernel and even CPUs to access the remote memory through an *RDMA Network Interface Controller* (RNIC). Since the remote CPU is often not aware of one-sided RDMA based memory accesses, RDMA can significantly reduce the CPU resource consumption on the remote server. In addition, RDMA provides extremely low latency and high bandwidth, which can alleviate the key concern of high latency for *distributed shared memory* (DSM) pools [6]. With the emergence of *Non-Volatile Memory* (NVM) [13] technologies, NVM has become increasingly popular to expand the capacity of main memory in a server. NVM has many good features such as byte-addressability, near-zero standby power consumption, high storage density, and low cost. Although it can offer rather fast memory accesses, its performance is still several times slower than that of *Dynamic Random Access Memory* (DRAM). Thus, it is more practical to exploit the advantages of both DRAM and NVM memories in a heterogeneous memory architecture, which not only enlarges the memory capacity, but also guarantees high-performance memory accesses and enhances the scalability of distributed shared memory systems.

Most DSM proposals focus on the scalability of memory capacity that disaggregated memory systems can offer to a cluster. A few studies propose new hardware/architecture [8,10], and new programming models [4,14] to implement disaggregated memory systems. However, these proposals often lack application-level transparency. Most applications need to be modified when they are going to migrate to disaggregated memory systems. A few proposals explore a remote memory paging mechanism [7,16,21] to use disaggregated memory transparently, without modifying legacy applications. However, these disaggregated memory systems still suffer from high latency of remote memory allocations and accesses.

In this paper, we present VANDI, a virtual memory paging mechanism based on distributed heterogeneous memory pools. VANDI aims to address the problem of high access latency of disaggregated memory systems. There are mainly three root causes of high latency. First, the software overhead of local staging queue is rather high, and thus increases the access latency of remote memory. Second, each remote read operation has to fetch a whole page in the remote memory pool, resulting in high data access latency. Third, the DRAM cache of the local server is often inefficiently utilized, leading to frequent page swapping between the local server and the remote server.

We design and implement hot data caching and prefetching technologies in VANDI to hide the high latency of remote memory accesses. First, we optimize the staging queue of the DRAM cache in the local server to support asynchronous remote memory paging. Second, we also design a simple and effective page prefetching mechanism to further improve the cache hit rate and alleviate the issue of DRAM cache pollution.

We evaluate VANDI with an I/O intensive workload FIO, and the big data benchmark–Hibench such as *Bayes, Kmeans Clustering, Logistic Regression* (LR) [9], and *Linear* workloads. Experimental results show that our caching and prefetching mechanisms in VANDI can improve the hit ratio of the local cache by 95%. VANDI can improve the performance of the typical remote paging system–Infiniswap [7] by up to 15×–102×. VANDI can also achieve 1.2×–2.7× performance improvement compared with the state-of-the-art disaggregated memory system–Valet [2]. For typical machine learning workloads, VANDI can achieve 20% to 80% performance improvement compared with the state-of-the-art Valet.

The remaining of this paper is organized as follows. Section 2 discusses the challenges of disaggregated memory systems. Section 3 and Sect. 4 introduce the design and implementation of VANDI in detail, respectively. Section 5 presents the evaluation of VANDI. Section 6 describes the related work. We conclude in Sect. 7.

2 Motivation

2.1 Remote Memory Access Latency

When we use RDMA technologies to access disaggregated memory, an RDMA connection channel between the client and the server should be established. Previous studies show that the data transmission of RDMA read and write operations account for only 0.3% of the end-to-end latency, while the RDMA connection setup and *memory region* (MR) mapping operations account for 29% and 9% of the end-to-end latency, respectively. In previous designs, RDMA connection operations are removed from the critical path of RDMA read/write operations, but the overhead of MR mapping operations is still significant. Valet [2] uses an asynchronous queue to hide the latency of dynamic MR mapping, and uses lock-free queues to cache data, and thus reduces the latency of data transmission. However, its local memory is only used as an on-demand data cache, without distinguishing the data access frequency (hotness), and thus often results in inefficient use of the local cache and wastes network bandwidth due to cache thrashing.

2.2 Expensive RDMA Read Operations

The local memory buffer is effective to hide the latency of RDMA write operations for applications because the writes can be staged in the buffer and then replicated to the remote MR asynchronously. However, since the RDMA read operation is often on the critical data path, applications often should suffer the high latency of remote memory accesses in disaggregated memory systems. Although Valet provides a local memory buffer on the client node, its data hit rate is relatively low as its LRU-based cache replacement strategy is not cost-effective in some cases. Most disaggregated memory systems use extremely high-speed RDMA networks for data transfer, but the remote memory access latency is still an order of magnitude higher than that of the local DRAM access. If the read request can hit the memory buffer locally as much as possible, the memory access latency and the cost of data transmission can be significantly reduced. To further improve the hit rate of the local cache, VANDI caches frequently-accessed data and pre-fetches data that may be accessed in the future.

3   Design

In this section, we describe the detailed designs of VANDI, mainly including an effective cache replacement strategy, a simple yet efficient data prefetching strategy, and the integration of these two strategies.

3.1   Architectural Overview

VANDI is a virtual memory paging mechanism designed for disaggregated memory systems. It mainly optimizes data caching and prefetching mechanisms to reduce the latency of remote memory accesses. Figure 1 shows the overall architecture of VANDI. The remote memory is accessed through a client/server model. VANDI provides a local memory cache in the client node for remote memory pools. Server nodes are classified into client and server modules according to the deployment of programs. The client module pre-allocates a local DRAM buffer as a memory pool, and write requests issued from the block device layer of the OS kernel are temporarily stored in this cache. The server module pre-allocates memory regions from the remote memory pool. To facilitate the remote memory allocation for client programs, the remote memory pool is divided into fixed size blocks (called REGION). The client's local cache is logically divided into two parts: the original cache and the prefetch cache. A *Radix Tree* (RT) is used to store the auxiliary structure (called entry) of the meta data. An entry is mapped with a data block (called element) in the local memory pool.

REGION actually divides a physically continuous memory space into many blocks which are 1 GB by default. This division is to facilitate the MR mapping between memory pools of the client and the server. For each RDMA operation, the program's local data is mapped to the remote REGION. When the read request misses the cache, it will be read from the corresponding REGION in the remote server. Each node can run different programs based on distributed memory pools. A program only needs to modify a configuration file to change the roles and dependencies of different nodes before running. Thus, it is easy to deploy a legacy program over the distributed memory pool.

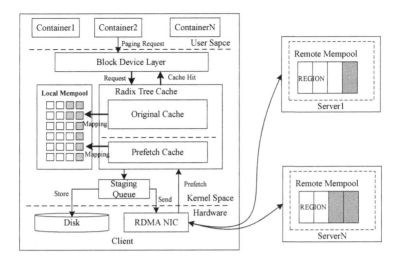

Fig. 1. An overview of VANDI architecture

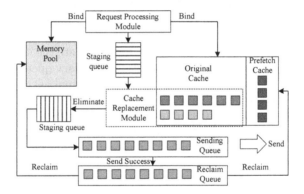

Fig. 2. The architecture of VANDI client module

VANDI Client Module. The VANDI client uses local DRAM as a cache to mitigate the performance degradation due to remote memory accesses. Figure 2 shows the structure of the VANDI client module. Similar to Infiniswap, VANDI creates a fix-sized block device that is mounted to a Linux swap partition. When the local memory is used up, a few recently-unused pages in the main memory will be swapped into the swap partition. We modify the page swapping mechanism and the major page fault handler in the Linux kernel to change the original data path, so that the data that will be written into the Linux swap partition is forwarded to the pre-allocated MR in the remote memory pool. When the program starts, the client registers the block device according to the configuration information, and pre-allocates a contiguous memory pool of appropriate size from the local DRAM. The memory pools in the client and the server are partitioned according to the granularity of the element (i.e., 4 KB page) in the

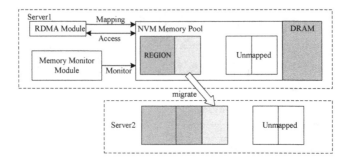

Fig. 3. The architecture of VANDI server module

memory pool. This paging granularity is consistent with the page size of the Linux OS. This is convenient for data storing and accessing, without splitting or coalescing the requested data.

The index of the local cache is implemented with a radix tree, which receives the request from the block device to extract a key and map to an element (a page) with a pointer. The radix tree is widely used for memory management because the data structure offers high-performance indexing for storage and data querying. The original cache and the prefetch cache share the same radix tree to reduce the overhead of querying. However, their auxiliary queues are separated, and the prefetched data will be promoted to the original cache if it is touched in the prefetch cache. When a page is evicted from the original cache, the data in the page will be added to the sending queue, and later will be written to the remote memory pool. At this time, this page is added into a recycling queue. A background program is responsible for reclaiming memory resource from the local cache.

VANDI Server Module. Since one-sided RDMA operations are remote CPU and OS kernel oblivious, the memory management at the server side should be as simple as possible. Like the client side, the server also pre-allocates MRs according to the configuration during the initialization. However, the difference is that the server can use both large-capacity NVM and fast DRAM as the remote memory pool.

Figure 3 shows the architecture of the server module of VANDI. The hybrid DRAM and NVM are architected in a *Non-Uniform Memory Access* (NUMA) machine. The memory pool at the server side is allocated through a NUMA allocation mechanism. NUMA can select different memory nodes to store data according to the relative position between the processor and the memory. Specifically, the server can choose the NVM node to pre-allocate a memory pool which is divided into multiple REGIONs according to the REGION size. Unlike the client side, the memory REGION allocated at the server side is not divided into 4 KB pages because the server node only needs to satisfy the memory access request from the client as much as possible and does not need to know how

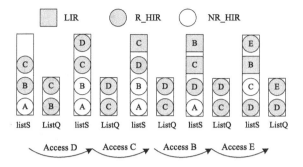

Fig. 4. An illustration of cache replacement

many pages are used. The client initiates an RDMA connection with the server through two-sided RDMA operations, and uses the local memory address to calculate the address offset in the remote memory pool. The client data address in the remote memory pool is determined by the index and offset of the memory REGION where the data is located. A REGION can only be mapped with one client. However, when a client's remote memory requirement exceeds the size of a REGION, the client can initiate another RDMA connection to map a new REGION. When the memory resource at the server side is used up, the server will migrate data to other server nodes through the memory monitoring module, and then update the mapping of the original REGION to the new server node.

3.2 Multi-level Cache

In this section, we will present the detailed design of the multi-level local cache at the client side.

Two Levels of Logical Cache. The local cache at the client server is logically divided into an original cache and a prefetch cache, and each cache uses an unique queue to store cache entries. However, these two caches use a single radix tree for data indexing. This can avoid querying two radix trees when VANDI checks whether data is hit in the two caches. Due to the potential cache pollution caused by data prefetching and the short lifetime of the prefetched data, the capacity of the prefetched cache is set much smaller than that of the original cache, and the capacity ratio of the two caches can be customized through a configuration file. In the original cache, there are two cache queues, namely the list-S for storing hot data and the linked list-Q for storing cold data. The capacity of the list-S is much larger than that of the list-Q, and the total capacity of the two lists is equal to the capacity of the local memory pool. This idea is derived from the *Low Inter-reference Recency Set* (LIRS) caching algorithm.

Efficient Cache Replacement Strategy. Our cache replacement strategy takes advantages of the data structure of the LIRS algorithm. There are two

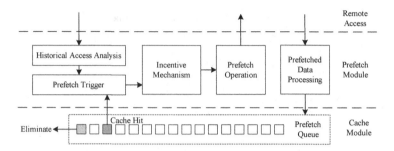

Fig. 5. The data prefetching module at the client server

important concepts, i.e., time interval *Recency* (R), and spatial interval *Inter-Reference Recency* (IRR). R represents the time interval between two consecutive data accesses, and IRR represents how many times other data have been accessed between two consecutive accesses of a given data. IRR can reflect both temporal and spatial locality. The data in our cache strategy has the following states: *Low Inter-reference Recency* (LIR, hot data) state, *High Inter-reference Recency* (HIR, cold data) state. The HIR state can be further divided into *Resident HIR* (R_HIR, resident cold data) state and *Non-Resident HIR* (NR_HIR, non-resident cold data) state. The data hotness of these states gradually decreases, and the hotness determines whether the data should be evicted when the free cache is not available. When a data will be evicted, the new data is placed in the head of the stack and the head of the queue at the same time, and its status is set as R_HIR. Figure 4 shows the status of the data in the stack and the queue during the cache replacement operation. In the original LIRS algorithm, even when the cache is not full, data may be still evicted. In contrast, our optimized replacement strategy only evicts data when the cache is full.

Prefetch Cache Promotion. Since the prefetched data may be never accessed, we choose the *First In First Out* (FIFO) replacement strategy for the prefetch cache. The prefetch cache is independent of the original cache. However, if the prefetched data is touched in the cache, that implies that the data prefetching is effective and the data may become hotter. The prefetched data will be promoted to the original cache upon a prefetch cache hit. Then, the data state is updated according to the cache replacement strategy for the original cache.

3.3 Adaptive Dynamic Prefetch

The principle of data prefetching is to fetch data blocks from the remote memory pool into the client's local cache in advance if the data is predicted to be accessed in the near future. Figure 5 shows the data prefetching module, which includes historical access analyzing, prefetch triggering mechanism, adaptive prefetch granularity adjustment, data prefetch operation, and prefetched data processing.

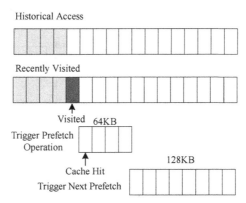

Fig. 6. Dynamic granularity adjustment for the prefetch triggering

Historical Access Analysis. Data prefetching is mainly exploited to accelerate RDMA read operations. In order to analyze the data access characteristics, it is necessary to extract the data request from the data path. Then, according to the address of the data, multiple data addresses are split or integrated to model the future access pattern via two schemes. The first one is a continuity judgment, i.e., if the adjacent access addresses are strictly continuous, there may be a sequential access pattern. In the second case, the accessed addresses are not strictly continuous but are very close (using variance as a criterion). Prefetching is triggered when these two conditions are met. Moreover, prefetching can be also triggered when the cache hits the prefetched data.

Adaptive Prefetching Threshold. The threshold for triggering the prefetch operation represents the difficulty of the current prefetch trigger, and the value is not fixed. The initial value is set when the program starts (the value is equal to 64 KB), and its value will increase or decrease according to the net benefit of the current prefetching strategy. The strategy only depends on the change of cache hit ratio and the prefetch coverage. The prefetch coverage reflects the proportion of prefetched data that is touched in the cache. VANDI monitors the cache hit rate and the prefetch coverage based on historical access information. When the cache hit rate decreases, the prefetch threshold decreases because it is easier to trigger prefetch and improve the hit rate. The prefetch coverage rate reflects the hit rate of the prefetched data. A higher prefetch coverage rate often implies lighter cache pollution. When the prefetch coverage rate declines, the prefetch threshold should increase so that it is harder to trigger the prefetching, and also reduce unnecessary prefetching.

Dynamic Adjustment of Data Prefetch Granularity. The default data prefetching granularity is 64 KB (16 pages) when the prefetching is triggered. Fine-grained data access can alleviate the cache pollution caused by wrongly

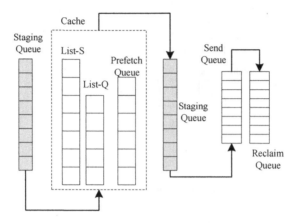

Fig. 7. The pipeline and staging queues of data flow

prefetching. Since the throughput of remote data accesses for large data granularity is much higher than that of multiple small granularity accesses, the data
granularity of prefetching has a significant impact on the performance of remote
memory accesses. First, if the historical access analysis indicates that the possibility of sequential accesses will increase, so the prefetching module will increase
the granularity of prefetching to prefetch larger data blocks. On the other hand,
if the subsequent memory access hits the prefetched data, the prefetch module also believes that the previous prefetching is effective, and then continues
to prefetch the subsequent data. Historical data access analysis can identify
sequential access patterns and trigger a basic prefetch operation (Fig. 6). When
the data is accessed immediately after fetching, the prefetch module will set the
granularity of the next prefetching to 64 pages (256 KB). If the subsequent access
hits continuously, the prefetch granularity will increase by 2 times again. The
maximum prefetch granularity can increase as large as 2 MB in VANDI.

4   Implementation

4.1   Redesign the Critical Data Path

VANDI uses a local memory pool to remove RDMA write operations from the
critical data path of client applications. All write operations can be temporarily
staged in the local cache, and then are written to the remote memory pool
asynchronously. VANDI focuses on the optimizations of the network bandwidth
utilization of RDMA operations and the cache hit rate at the client side.

The Pipeline and Staging Queues of Data Flow. Figure 7 shows a total
of seven queues in which data flows in the direction of the arrows. The first is a
staging queue for storing the original data temporarily. This queue is mainly used
to store data after encapsulating the *bio* structure of the dismantling request,

and waits for the data to be cached and replaced. There are three queues in the local cache, which are the list-S and list-Q of the original cache, and the prefetch queue of the prefetch cache. The data then flows to the staging queue (a linked list) in which the data is evicted by the FIFO replacement policy. Finally, the data is passed to the sending queue and the recycling queue which temporarily store the data to be sent to the remote memory pool, and the memory space of the data will be reclaimed once the data has been sent out. The whole pipeline adopts a producer-consumer model and uses a lock mechanism to avoid a large amount of data accumulated in the pipeline by throttling data traffic moderately.

Data Sending and Memory Reclaiming. Figure 8 shows that data is not sent immediately when it is picked up from the send queue. VANDI encapsulates data blocks with continuous memory addresses into a large page according to data indexes, and records the data length contained in the large page. This vectored I/O mechanism is convenient for batch processing. It reduces the number of RDMA operations and the corresponding software overhead. In VANDI, a context resource pool is used to reduce resource allocation overhead caused by frequent RDMA requests. The data structure of the context contains a buffer of temporary data, the information of the RDMA connection, and the cache prefetch strategy. When the data is successfully sent out, it moves to the recycling queue. A recycling thread continuously removes data entries from the recycling queue to avoid data accumulation. Since the data has been stored in the remote memory pool at this time, the local cache does have to retain the data. The memory reclaiming operation is performed as follows. First, the memory space of the local memory pool mapped to the data entry is reclaimed. Second, the data entry in the local cache is deleted.

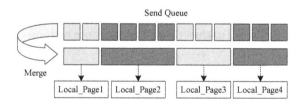

Fig. 8. Merge operation before data sending

4.2 Page Writes

In the block device layer, the bio of a write request is often disclosed to determine whether the data has been cached. If it is true, the data in the cache is updated. Otherwise, the data is added into the memory pool and its index is added to the radix tree. The data is then send to the staging queue and waits for an RDMA write operation. At this time, the write request has been completed locally and can be returned to applications. In the asynchronous RDMA write operation, the data is sent out from the staging queue, and VANDI also checks whether it is hit in the local cache and determines the status of the data. When the cache becomes full, cold data is evicted and sent to the remote memory pool.

4.3 Page Reads

For each read operation, VANDI first checks whether the data exists in the cache. If it is not found, an RDMA read operation should be performed to read the data from the remote memory pool, and then the data is stored in the original cache. Upon a read, the access information is recorded, and later the historical access analysis mechanism of the data prefetching module can analyze the memory access records. If the read operation hits the original cache, the status of the data is updated. If the read hits the prefetch cache, VANDI not only promotes the data from the prefetch cache to the original cache, but also prefetches more data from the remote memory pool.

5   Evaluation

Experimental Setup. We run experiments on physical servers connected with 56 Gbps Infiniband networks. Each server is equipped with Intel Xeon Gold 6230v2 processors (32 virtual cores 2.10 GHz), 64 GB memory, Mellanox Connect X-3, and 1 TB Intel Optane DC persistent memory. The Optane memory is used as main memory in a memory pool. We set the block I/O size to 4 KB, and set the capacity of one REGION to 1 GB. The default capacity of the local memory pool is 4 GB. We evaluate VANDI with FIO micro-benchmarks and seven popular memory intensive applications including six machine learning applications and one graph computing application, as shown in Table 1. We compare VANDI with the state-of-the-art disaggregated memory systems–Infiniswap and Valet.

Table 1. Benchmarks and performance metrics.

Benchmarks	Descriptions	Metrics
FIO	Caching scheme	Cache hit ratio
FIO	Data Prefetching scheme	Cache hit ratio
FIO	Adaptive granularity adjustment scheme	Coverage ratio
FIO	Using different sizes of the local memory pool	Bandwidth
PageRank	Graph computing workload in Ligra	Execution time
Hibench	Six ML workloads	Execution time

5.1   Effectiveness of Our Optimization Schemes

Caching Scheme. We evaluate the caching scheme using FIO which performs random data accesses with a zipfian distribution (i.e., a power-law probability distribution). In our experiments, different memory access patterns can be set

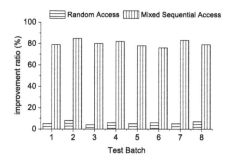 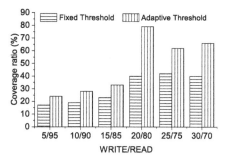

Fig. 9. The performance improvement of data prefetching compared with the non-prefetching approach

Fig. 10. The impact of adaptive prefetching threshold adjustment on the prefetching coverage rate

by changing a parameter theta of the zipfian distribution. A larger value of theta implies more memory accesses are concentrated on a few pages. We measure the cache hit rate under different data distributions. With the increase of theta, the cache hit rate gradually increases, and approximates 95% when theta is 1.2. This experimental result shows that the caching scheme in VANDI can effectively keep hot data in the local cache of the client server, and thus improve the cache hit rate.

Data Prefetching Scheme. In order to evaluate the effectiveness of the data prefetching scheme, two data access patterns are used in our experiments. The first is a random access pattern with a zipfian distribution, and the second is a mixed sequential access pattern with 25% write operations and 75% read operations. Figure 9 shows that the data prefetching scheme can only achieve about 7% performance improvement compared with the non-prefetching scheme for the random access pattern. However, the cache hit rate can be significantly improved by about 80% for the mixed sequential access pattern. This is because our data prefetching scheme can effectively identify the sequential access pattern according to historical memory access records, but is hard to predict the random access pattern.

Adaptive Prefetching Threshold Adjustment. In this experiment, the prefetch coverage is evaluated by FIO with different write-read ratios of the mixed sequential access pattern. The changes of the prefetch coverage rate can reflect the effectiveness of the adaptive prefetching threshold adjustment strategy when it is enabled or disabled. Figure 10 shows that the adaptive prefetching threshold adjustment generally delivers higher prefetching coverage rate than the fixed threshold, and the prefetching coverage rate is higher when the proportion of read operations becomes higher. Because the adaptive prefetching threshold adjustment can alleviate the cache pollution problem effectively. When the

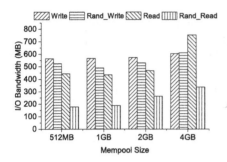

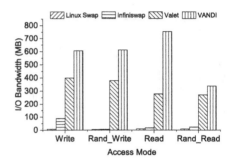

Fig. 11. Performance of different memory pool size

Fig. 12. Bandwidth performance of four access modes

threshold of prefetching increases, the data granularity and frequency of prefetching will decrease, and thus causes less cache pollution.

Size of the Local Cache. In order to evaluate the impact of the local memory pool size on the performance of VANDI, we exploit the FIO tool to measure the I/O throughput of workloads using four data access patterns. Figure 11 shows the FIO throughput is improved for the four workloads when the local cache (Mempool) size increases. Even for 512 MB local cache, VANDI still has very high I/O throughput relative to the larger cache. This implies that VANDI only needs to utilize a small amount of local memory to achieve high throughput of remote memory accesses.

5.2 Microbenchmarks

At first, we evaluate the performance of different disaggregated memory systems under different memory access patterns using FIO, and then we evaluate the performance improvement of different disaggregated memory systems using multithreaded FIO.

Memory Access Patterns. Figure 12 shows that the I/O throughput of different memory systems under different memory access modes. The native Linux swap mechanism shows the lowest performance because data needs to be frequently swapped between main memory and very slow *Hard Disk Drive* (HDD) when the main memory is used up. VANDI can improve the system throughput of both random and sequential access modes significantly. For the sequential write mode, VANDI outperforms Infiniswap and Valet by 6.8× and 1.5×, respectively. For the random write mode, VANDI outperforms Infiniswap and Valet by 102× and 1.6×, respectively. For the sequential and random read modes, VANDI outperforms Infiniswap by 44× and 15×, respectively, and outperforms Valet by 2.7× and 1.2×, respectively. These results demonstrate that our caching and prefetching schemes are beneficial for accelerating remote memory accesses.

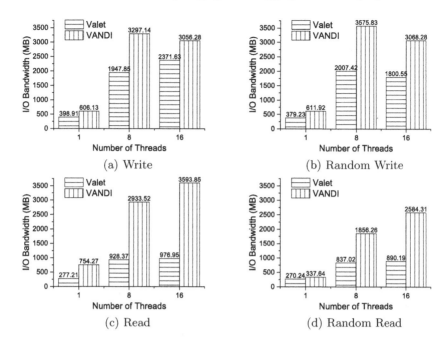

Fig. 13. The performance of four memory access modes under multithreading

Multithreading. Multi-threading can improve data parallelism and effectively increase the system throughput. We also evaluate the throughput of FIO with four memory access modes under the multithreading case, as shown in Fig. 13. The I/O throughput is significantly improved under the multi-threading cases for all memory access modes. The performance of Valet and VANDI using 8 and 16 FIO threads is much higher than that of single-threading. VANDI can improve the throughput by 4×–5× in the case of multi-threading. However, the performance does not increases linearly with the number of threads because the bandwidth contention of RDMA operations becomes intensive for more client threads. The software overhead caused by thread synchronization also offsets the performance improvement of multi-threading.

5.3 Performance of Graph Computing Workloads

We chose the PageRank algorithm under the Ligra graph computing framework as a real-world workload to evaluate the performance of VANDI. The Ligra graph computing framework can generate different types of graph datasets. In our experiments, we select the rMatGraph tool to generate an rMat graph with 223 million vertices, and the number of edges is 10 times more than the number of vertices. We first measure the total amount of memory resource required by the application, and then we limit the capacity of the local memory pool so that the client application has to use the remote memory pool for memory resource

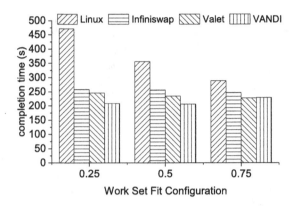

Fig. 14. Execution time of PageRank under different memory resource constraints

extension. We configure the available local memory capacity to only satisfy 25%, 50%, and 75% memory requirement of PageRank in our experiments.

Figure 14 shows the execution time of the PageRank algorithm for four systems under different satisfactory rates of memory resource requirements. When the satisfactory rate of the local memory resource required by the application is lower, the application runs longer. Because remote page swapping operations should be performed frequently due to insufficient memory resource, and thus the performance overhead becomes larger. Linux needs to swap pages between the main memory and the disk when the main memory is used up, and the execution time greatly increases when the local memory resource can only fit 25% of the applications' memory requirement. The three disaggregated memory systems can swap pages between the local memory and the remote memory pool, and achieve relatively high performance even when only 25% memory requirement is satisfied by the local memory.

5.4   Performance of Machine Learning Workloads

We choose six machine learning applications in Hibench to evaluate VANDI. Hibench is a big data benchmarking suite that can be use to evaluate the execution time, system throughput, and resource utilization of different big data applications. Hibench relies on Hadoop [19] and Spark [20] platforms in our experiments. The dataset in our experiments is generated by a dataset generator in Hibench.

Figure 15 shows the execution time of six machine learning workload in different memory systems. Since these machine learning applications are both memory-intensive and compute-intensive, we constrain the capacity of local memory at the client side to only satisfy 50% memory requirement of applications, and other memory requirement is satisfied by the remote memory pool. The performance of these applications in the native Linux is still the lowest. Since Infiniswap has not a local cache at the client side, it causes frequent page

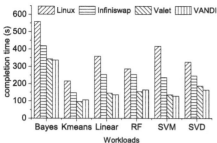
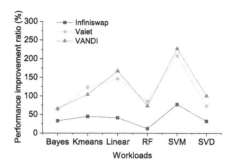

Fig. 15. Execution time of different machine learning workloads

Fig. 16. The performance improvement ratio of three systems relative to Linux

faults that trigger remote page swapping between the client and the remote memory pool. The cost of remote memory accesses has a significant impact on the application performance. In contrast, VANDI can prefetch data from the remote memory pool and store it in the local cache which can significantly reduce the amount of remote memory accesses, and thus achieves significant performance improvement compared with Infiniswap.

Figure 16 shows the performance improvement ratio of three disaggregated memory systems relative to the Linux system. We find that Valet and VANDI using a local cache can improve the application performance significantly by up to 2.2×. Although VANDI uses NVM as the remote memory pool while Valet uses all DRAM memory, Valet and VANDI generally achieve similar performance improvement. The reason is that the local memory of Valet is only used as an on-demand cache, with distinguishing the data hotness, and thus often results in inefficient use of the local cache and wastes network bandwidth due to cache thrashing.

6   Related Work

Distributed Shared Memory (DSM) [5] have long been studied in the past decades. With the development of high-performance RDMA network technologies, disaggregated memory systems [7,8,18] have attracted increasing attention in recent years. There are mainly three research directions on disaggregated memory systems:

- The first category is to trade a little increase of remote memory access latency for higher throughput, or to make a tradeoff between the system throughput and memory energy consumption. Infiniswap [7] is a typical disaggregated memory system that exploits the remote page swapping mechanism to use remote memory resource transparently, without modifying source codes of legacy applications. However, the remote memory access latency is extremely long due to the software overhead of page fault handling. The most recent work FastSwap [1] shares the same idea with Infiniswap, but exploits multiple work queues to achieve a high-throughput page swapping mechanism. The work zombieland [15] exploits a disaggregated memory system to reduce the energy consumption of cold data.

- The second category is to alleviate the problem of memory capacity wall and memory load imbalance in a cluster through memory disaggregation. Most disaggregated memory systems such as Infiniswap [7], Valet [2], and Gengar [3] offer these functionalities for data center applications.
- The third category is to provide disaggregated memory services with low latency similar to the local DRAM. AIFM [18] proposes a low-latency remote memory access scheme by providing simple programming APIs at the application level, avoiding the read-write amplification suffered by the remote paging mechanism. Gengar [3] also has the same design principle as AIFM. It offers high-performance user-level APIs to use remote memory resource. Gengar redesigns the RDMA write primitive to shorten the write latency of remote memory, and exploits a caching mechanism to reduce the read latency of remote memory. Recently, we have witnessed the rapid development of *Compute Express Link* (CXL) which is a high-performance cache-coherent interconnect for processors, memory expansion devices, and accelerators. It promises much lower latency and higher bandwidth relative to RDMA networks, and has a vast potential to build next-generation high-performance disaggregated memory systems.

7   Conclusion

Memory disaggregation has been a cost-efficient approach to share large-capacity memory resource among multiple servers in a data center. However, current memory disaggregation systems still suffer from high latency of remote memory access. This paper presents VANDI, a virtual memory paging mechanism that allows applications to use disaggregated memory resource efficiently and transparently. VANDI enables effective data caching and prefetching mechanisms to address the problem of high access latency in disaggregated memory systems. VANDI reduces the latency of RDMA write operations by redesigning the caching mechanism on the critical data path. VANDI also designs a simple and practical data prefetching mechanism to further improve the cache hit rate of read operations. In this way, VANDI can effectively hide remote memory access latency and the cost of data migration. Our extensive experiments using micro-benchmarks show that VANDI can improve the performance of the typical remote paging system–Infiniswap by up to $15\times$–$102\times$. VANDI can also improve the performance of state-of-the-art disaggregated memory system–Valet by $1.2\times$–$2.7\times$. For typical machine learning workloads, VANDI can achieve 20% to 80% performance improvement compared with the state-of-the-art Valet.

Acknowledgements. This work is supported jointly by National Natural Science Foundation of China (NSFC) under grants No. 62072198, 61832006, 61825202, 61929103.

References

1. Amaro, E., et al.: Can far memory improve job throughput? In: Proceedings of the Fifteenth European Conference on Computer Systems, pp. 1–16 (2020)
2. Bae, J., Su, G., Iyengar, A., Wu, Y., Liu, L.: Efficient orchestration of host and remote shared memory for memory intensive workloads. In: Proceedings of The International Symposium on Memory Systems, pp. 194–208 (2020)
3. Duan, Z., et al.: Gengar: an RDMA-based distributed hybrid memory pool. In: Proceedings of the 41st IEEE International Conference on Distributed Computing Systems, pp. 92–103 (2021)
4. Elmeleegy, K., Olston, C., Reed, B.: Spongefiles: mitigating data skew in mapreduce using distributed memory. In: Proceedings of the ACM SIGMOD International Conference on Management of Data, pp. 551–562 (2014)
5. Endo, W., Sato, S., Taura, K.: MENPS: a decentralized distributed shared memory exploiting RDMA. In: Proceedings of IEEE/ACM Fourth Annual Workshop on Emerging Parallel and Distributed Runtime Systems and Middleware, pp. 9–16 (2020)
6. Gao, P.X., et al.: Network requirements for resource disaggregation. In: Proceedings of 12th USENIX Symposium on Operating Systems Design and Implementation, pp. 249–264 (2016)
7. Gu, J., Lee, Y., Zhang, Y., Chowdhury, M., Shin, K.G.: Efficient memory disaggregation with infiniswap. In: Proceedings of 14th USENIX Symposium on Networked Systems Design and Implementation, pp. 649–667 (2017)
8. Guo, Z., Shan, Y., Luo, X., Huang, Y., Zhang, Y.: Clio: a hardware-software co-designed disaggregated memory system. In: Proceedings of the 27th ACM International Conference on Architectural Support for Programming Languages and Operating Systems, pp. 417–433 (2022)
9. Jia, Y., et al.: Caffe: convolutional architecture for fast feature embedding. In: Proceedings of the 22nd ACM International Conference on Multimedia, pp. 675–678 (2014)
10. Lim, K., et al.: System-level implications of disaggregated memory. In: Proceedings of IEEE International Symposium on High-Performance Computer Architecture, pp. 1–12 (2012)
11. Liu, L., Cao, W., Sahin, S., Zhang, Q., Bae, J., Wu, Y.: Memory disaggregation: research problems and opportunities. In: Proceedings of IEEE 39th International Conference on Distributed Computing Systems, pp. 1664–1673 (2019)
12. Magoutis, K.: Memory management support for multi-programmed Remote Direct Memory Access (RDMA) systems. In: Proceedings of IEEE International Conference on Cluster Computing, pp. 1–8 (2005)
13. Meena, J.S., Sze, S.M., Chand, U., Tseng, T.Y.: Overview of emerging nonvolatile memory technologies. Nanoscale Res. Lett. **9**(1), 1–33 (2014)
14. Nelson, J., et al.: Latency-tolerant software distributed shared memory. In: Proceedings of USENIX Annual Technical Conference, pp. 291–305 (2015)
15. Nitu, V., Teabe, B., Tchana, A., Isci, C., Hagimont, D.: Welcome to zombieland: practical and energy-efficient memory disaggregation in a datacenter. In: Proceedings of the Thirteenth European Conference on Computer Systems, pp. 1–12 (2018)
16. Oura, H., Midorikawa, H., Kitagawa, K., Kai, M.: Design and evaluation of page-swap protocols for a remote memory paging system. In: Proceedings of IEEE Pacific Rim Conference on Communications, Computers and Signal Processing, pp. 1–8 (2017)

17. Reiss, C., Tumanov, A., Ganger, G.R., Katz, R.H., Kozuch, M.A.: Heterogeneity and dynamicity of clouds at scale: google trace analysis. In: Proceedings of the Third ACM Symposium on Cloud Computing, pp. 1–13 (2012)
18. Ruan, Z., Schwarzkopf, M., Aguilera, M.K., Belay, A.: AIFM: high-performance, application-integrated far memory. In: Proceedings of the 14th USENIX Symposium on Operating Systems Design and Implementation, pp. 315–332 (2020)
19. Shvachko, K., Kuang, H., Radia, S., Chansler, R.: The Hadoop distributed file system. In: Proceedings of IEEE 26th Symposium on Mass Storage Systems and Technologies, pp. 1–10 (2010)
20. Zaharia, M., Chowdhury, M., Franklin, M.J., Shenker, S., Stoica, I.: Spark: cluster computing with working sets. In: Proceedings of USENIX Workshop on Hot Topics in Cloud Computing (2010)
21. Zhang, P., Li, X., Chu, R., Wang, H.: HybridSwap: a scalable and synthetic framework for guest swapping on virtualization platform. In: Proceedings of IEEE Conference on Computer Communications, pp. 864–872 (2015)

pCOVID: A Privacy-Preserving COVID-19 Inference Framework

Yinqiu Wang$^{(\boxtimes)}$, Yuchuan Luo, Lin Liu, and Shaojing Fu

College of Computer, National University of Defense Technology, Changsha, China
`yinqiuwang@nudt.edu.cn`

Abstract. Deep learning based medical image diagnosis systems are of increasing importance in the battle against COVID-19 epidemic. However, how to ensure patients' data privacy and model's privacy while maintaining high accuracy and efficiency is widely considered a huge challenge. In this work, we propose a privacy-preserving COVID-19 inference framework based on a modified additive secret sharing scheme. Most of the prior works achieve the secure inference scheme by designing a series of secure computing sub-protocols with respect to the operations involved in plaintext DNN execution. However, they do not consider the optimization of DNN model, which leads to poor performance in efficiency and/or accuracy. To speedup the secure inference while maintaining a high accuracy, we co-design the DNN model and the secure execution protocol and holistically optimize both aspects. Firstly, two optimization techniques named fixed-point quantization and layer fusion are applied to the well-trained model to obtain a secret sharing-friendly model. Then, based on the modified additive secret sharing scheme, we manage to design a series of interactive sub-protocols, such as secure convolution, secure ReLU, secure average pooling and secure truncation, which achieve the same or even higher security level with high efficiency. By using these new sub-protocols, we propose a secure and efficient COVID-19 inference system. In addition, users do not interact with the cloud except outsourcing data and receiving the inference result. Our security analysis shows that the scheme protects outsourced data security, model privacy as well as inference result privacy. Experimental results on real-world datasets indicate that our scheme is efficient and practical, and is expected to play a role in the fight against COVID-19 epidemic.

Keywords: Privacy-preserving · Deep neural network inference · Additive secret sharing · Covid-19 inference

1 Introduction

Thanks to the advent of the era of big data and the continuous improvement of the computing power of hardware, deep learning has been widely developed in

---

Y. Wang and Y. Luo—Contribute equally to the paper.

W. Meng et al. (Eds.): ICA3PP 2022, LNCS 13777, pp. 21–42, 2023.
https://doi.org/10.1007/978-3-031-22677-9_2

real-world applications such as speech recognition [1], image classification [16] and medical diagnosis [15]. At the meantime, the combination of cloud computing and deep learning has produced a new AI application paradigm-Deep learning as a service (DLaaS). There has been a mount of real world DLaaS productions such as Google Prediction API, Amazon ML, Azure ML Studio. In this scenario, the service provider holds the well-trained model. Users access the DL service by sending their data to the server to obtain the inference result through a well defined service interface and no need to concern with their limited computing resources.

One of the biggest beneficiaries in real world applications is the medical diagnosis. Since 2019 to now, COVID-19[1] caused by severe acute respiratory syndrome coronavirus 2 (SARS-CoV-2) has spread worldwide and leading to the COVID-19 pandemic, which has made a problematic situation for humans all over the world. It is vital to detect the patient earlier and accurately during the fight against the epidemic. In the period of pandemic, deep learning-assisted diagnosis can bring great convenience to doctors and patients. Many researchers have applied deep learning model to help medical institutions to detect the cases. For COVID-19 cases, there are some symptoms in the lungs, which could be identified by computed tomography(CT), magnetic resonance imaging(MRI) and X-rays radiography. In this condition, multiple hospitals hold a pre-trained DNN model for COVID-19 detection, they upload the model to the cloud to provide online-diagnosis service for users. Users could upload their chest X-ray images to the cloud for online diagnosis, thus eliminating the need for patients to travel long distances to medical institutions and further reducing the flow of personnel so as to avoid the risk of secondary propagation, which is vital especially during the COVID-19 pandemic.

However, it has some problems during the cloud-based COVID-19 inference. Firstly, the chest X-ray images contain patients' privacy information, uploading plaintext images directly to the cloud may violate the users' privacy by revealing their private data to the cloud. Moreover, the inference results could be exposed to the cloud service provider and other parties (e.g. attackers) during the communication between users and cloud, thus producing tremendous troublesome to the users since the positive diagnosis results may bring discrimination to the patients. Secondly, the pre-trained model is considered as an essential component of the model owners' intellectual property. Model owners (i.e. hospitals) invest a significant amount of resources to gather the massive training datasets and train the model. Hence, model owners will ensure their model privacy to guarantee their profitability and maintain their competitive advantage. In the medical diagnosis, the data of patients is considered to be sensitive and should be protected due to the health privacy regulations such as HIPAA [3]. Data anonymization is a commonly used method in the release of private data, but related research [24] has proved that data anonymization cannot protect the privacy of medical data in some scenarios. Boulila et al. [7] proposed a privacy-preserving COVID-19 classification framework based on Paillier homomorphic encryption. In this

---

[1] Coronavirus disease 2019.

framework, the data privacy was protected during the inference phase. The accuracy loss is less than 1% on the testing set. However, the computational overhead of homomorphic encryption is high and the depth of their model reached 53 layers, which implies a very huge computational overhead during the inference. Guo *et al.* [12] combined the Paillier homomorphic encryption with supervised learning to realize an efficient and accurate data-search based privacy-preserving medical image classification and searching system. However the intermediate result of the protocol may reveal some information about the query image to the cloud server, thus infringes the privacy of image data. Moreover, the computational overhead of homomorphic encryption is not negligible.

In this paper, we propose pCOVID, a novel privacy-preserving COVID-19 inference framework based on secure computing-friendly neural network optimization and modified additive secret sharing. We note that most of the existing schemes support the computations involved in the model by constructing corresponding secure computing protocols. However, due to the lack of collaborative design, deep learning model and secure computing mechanism cannot be well combined, which leads to inefficiency and reduced accuracy. To this end, we consider a synergistic complementary design of the model and secure computing protocol. Firstly, as the computational overhead of secure computing depends on the bit width of finite field, we propose to perform fixed-point quantization on the pre-trained model to reduce the bit width of the model parameters so as to reduce the bit length of finite field needed to hold the computation involved during the inference. Then, according to the structural characteristics of the model, a layer fusion process is carried out to further reduce the computational overhead of the secure execution. Thus, a secure computation-friendly model is obtained. Then, we design a series of efficient secure computing protocols for the optimized model based on the modified additive secret sharing scheme. Through the usage of optimized DNN model and efficient secure computing protocols, our scheme achieves efficient and accurate privacy-preserving COVID-19 detection while ensures the privacy of users' data, model parameters and inference results. We highlight our contributions as follows:

1. We proposed a practical privacy-preserving COVID-19 inference framework-pCOVID through the co-design of DNN model and modified additive secret-sharing based secure computing protocols. pCOVID maintains the privacy of both DNN model and users' data during the inference while achieves an accuracy of 95.2%
2. In view of that the computational and communication overhead of secure computation protocols are highly dependent on the bit length of finite field, we proposed to perform fixed-point quantization and layer fusion to optimize the pre-trained model in a secret sharing-friendly way, which greatly reduced the computational and communication overhead of secure inference phase and thus realized efficient privacy-preserving COVID-19 inference.
3. We redesigned a set of lightweight additive secret sharing based sub-protocols, which achieve the same security level but with higher efficiency compared with existing works. Then, combined with the optimized model, we achieved

the practical privacy-preserving inference of COVID-19 X-ray images. It is expected to be deployed in the future to help people fighting against the COVID-19 epidemic.

The remainder of this paper is as follows. In Sect. 2, we introduce the preliminaries. In Sect. 3, we describe the system overview and threat model. Section 4 presents the model optimization methods and the details of secure execution protocols are presented in Sect. 5. Section 6 presents the proposed privacy-preserving scheme. Section 7 gives the security analyses. Experimental evaluation is presented in Sect. 8, and Sect. 9 concludes the paper.

2   Preliminaries

In this section, we introduce some essential preliminary concepts, such as deep neural network, neural network based COVID-19 detection and additive secret sharing, which serve as the basis of our scheme.

2.1   COVID-19 Detection Using Convolutional Neural Network

Deep neural network (DNN) is a sequence of multiple computational layers that transform the input into output. These layers can be divided into two classes based on the type of operation: linear layers and non-linear layers. For linear layers, it mainly includes convolution (Conv) layers, fully-connected (FC) layers, average-pooling layers. For non-linear layers, it consists of activation layers and max-pooling layers. We briefly explain these commonly used layers as follows.

Conv and FC layer. Conv and FC layer only involve the linear operation during the inference phase. The Conv layer performs linear transformation over the feature maps (images for the first Conv layer).

A convolution layer consists of a weight tensor[2] $\mathcal{A} \in \mathbb{R}^{I \times O \times K \times K}$ Where I and O denote the channels of input and output respectively and K denotes the kernel size. The input of a Conv layer is a feature map represented as a multichannel tensor $\mathcal{X} \in \mathbb{R}^{B \times C \times H \times W}$ where B denotes the batch size and C is the number of channels. While H and W are the dimensions of feature map. The i-th channel of the output is computed by sliding the kernel over the corresponding channel of input and computing the convolution between the windowed input and kernel, and adding the bias term b_i to the result if the convolution layer contains a bias vector $\boldsymbol{b} \in \mathbb{R}^O$.

Fully-connected layer is another form of linear transformation that operates on the input vector. It contains a weight matrix $W \in \mathbb{R}^{M \times N}$. It takes a input vector $\boldsymbol{x} \in \mathbb{R}^N$ and conduct the matrix-vector product between W and $\boldsymbol{x}$ and generates the output vector $\boldsymbol{y} \in \mathbb{R}^M$. The formulation of this transformation of FC layer can be denoted as $\boldsymbol{y} = W \cdot \boldsymbol{x} + \boldsymbol{b}$ where $\boldsymbol{b}$ is a bias vector.

---

[2] Matrix and tensor are usually used interchangeably in this paper.

Pooling. Pooling layers operate on each channel of the feature map outputted by the preceding layer. The most commonly used pooling operations in DNN are max pooling and average pooling. These pooling layers partition the input feature map into a set of non-overlapping rectangles and compute the maximum or the average values in each rectangle as output. Typically, pooling layers reduce the size of feature map by a factor of k where k is the pooling window size.

Non-linear Activation. Non-linear activation layers introduce nonlinearity into neural networks and allow to bound inputs to a finite range. Element-wise non-linear transformation will be applied to the input during the inference. In this paper, we particularly utilize the Rectified Linear Unit (ReLU) as the activation function for each activation layer. The result of ReLU(x) can be denoted by max(x,0), where x is the element of feature map to be activated. It is easy to notice that ReLU only involves comparison computations between x and 0.

Since the convolutional neural network can be trained to extract feature automatically to learn the difference between various image categories, it also can be used to distinguish COVID-19 positive images from normal images. There are various CNN-based COVID-19 detection approaches have been proposed and the results have been shown to be promising in terms of accuracy. Wang *et al.* [25] proposed COVID-Net network architecture which achieved a test accuracy of 93.3%. Khan *et al.* [18] proposed CoroNet, a deep CNN model to perform image processing on X-ray images and classify them positively or negatively. Apostolopoulos *et al.* [2] evaluated the performance of five pre-trained networks regarding the detection of COVID-19 from chest X-ray images. The results showed that VGG19 and MobileNetv2 achieved a high accuracy at 93.48% and 92.85% respectively.

Note that the number of hidden layers is a significant aspect to be considered for obtaining good performance. Deeper model usually means better non-linear expression ability and can learn more complex relationships from datasets. But it is often prone to overfitting. Moreover, deep models with more parameters have huge computational overhead during inference phase. Therefore, the number of hidden layers must be well-defined for optimal performance. Based on the results of our pre-experiments, we chose ResNet-18 as our backbone network for its good performance.

2.2 Additive Secret Sharing

Additive secret sharing is one of the most important technologies in secure multiparty computation. During the sharing process, the secret value will be securely and randomly split into multi-shares and shared to multiple parties. The secret can be reconstructed only when enough number of shares are combined. In this paper, we only focus on the two-party involved situation. In this scenario, the secret value x is randomly split into two shares $\langle x \rangle^A$ and $\langle x \rangle^B$ over $\mathbb{Z}_q$ and sent to party A and party B respectively, where $\mathbb{Z}_q$ is the finite field with a negotiated modulus q. To reconstruct secret value x, one of the two parties sends his share to the other who calculates $x = \langle x \rangle^A + \langle x \rangle^B \bmod q$. We denote this reconstruction process as $x \leftarrow \text{Rec}(\langle x \rangle)$. In the following, for simplicity, we omit the "mod q".

In the following, we introduce three essential additive secret sharing based computation protocols, which are the foundation of our proposed secure sub-protocols.

1) **Secure Addition Protocol** (SAdd). It should be noted that each party can execute addition locally without any communication. For example, party A holds $\langle x \rangle^A$ and $\langle y \rangle^A$ and party B holds $\langle x \rangle^B$ and $\langle y \rangle^B$, and they want to compute $z = x + y$. Due to the linearity of addition, each party only needs to compute $\langle x \rangle + \langle y \rangle$ locally, and the result is naturally the corresponding share of $x + y$.

2) **Secure Multiplication Protocol** (SMul). Given the random shares of two inputs $(\langle x \rangle^A, \langle x \rangle^B)$ and $(\langle y \rangle^A, \langle y \rangle^B)$, it performs secure multiplication and outputs $(\langle z \rangle^A, \langle z \rangle^B)$, where $\langle z \rangle^A + \langle z \rangle^B = x \cdot y$. During execution, the Beaver's triple [4] is required to execute the secure multiplication protocol for shared values.

3) **Secure Comparison Protocol** (SCmp). The secure comparison protocol is one of the most fundamental building blocks in our scheme. Given two shared numbers $\langle x \rangle$ and $\langle y \rangle$, the SCmp returns $\langle z \rangle$. If $x < y$, $z = 1$, otherwise $z = 0$. We use the secure comparison protocol proposed by Chen *et al.* [9]. The details of SCmp are available in [9].

Note that the pre-computed arithmetic triples need be fresh for every multiplication. This generation process can be done off-line by the two parties through using the Oblivious Transfer (OT) [23] or a trusted third party [21]. More details about the pre-computed arithmetic triple generation can be found in reference [4]. In this work, we mainly consider the on-line computation and communication process.

3   System Model and Design Goal

3.1   System and Threat Model

As shown in Fig. 1, our privacy-preserving COVID-19 inference system involves two non-colluding clouds, the model owner, multiple data owners and a trusted third party.

- **Clouds**: There are two non-colluding clouds in our system, denoted as cloud A and cloud B. Both of them maintain the model outsourced by the model owner. They perform a series of secure protocols to execute secure inference for users' shared medical image data in a privacy-preserving way.
- **Model Owner**: There are multiple hospitals jointly trained a DNN model for COVID-19 detection utilizing their local medical data. After that, to reduce the execution overhead during the secure inference process, two model optimization methods named fixed-point quantization and layer fusion will be

performed on the well-trained model. And then, to preserve the private information of the model, the model owner split the model into two shares and sends them to cloud A and B respectively. The details of model optimization will be given later in this paper.

– **Data Owners**: The users are the owners of image data. To get the diagnostic results in a privacy-preserving way, users split their image data into two additive shares before uploading them to the clouds and receive the shares of inference results from cloud A and B respectively. It is easy to notice that only the user can recover the inference result, the privacy of both data and inference result are protected during the secure inference.

– **Trusted third party**: The trusted third party (T) is responsible for the generation of values needed during the secure execution. Note that the T is only involved in the offline phase, it is not involved in the online phase and thus does not receive any values from other parties.

It is easy to notice that, there is no communication between users and other entities during the secure inference except for the data outsourcing, which means the communication overhead for the users is negligible.

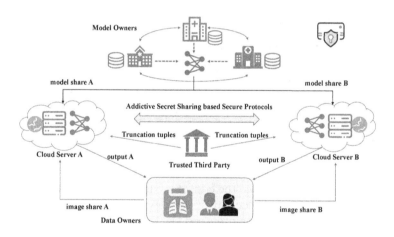

Fig. 1. System model

Our scheme is based on the semi-honest threat model, in which all the participants will strictly follow the designed protocols, but each of them may try to infer the private information of other parties based on their own data view. Additionally, we assume that there is no collusion in the scheme, that means each party will not collude with each other throughout the execution of protocols. We remark that the two non-colluding cloud servers model is easy to realize in the real world, in which cloud server A and B belong to different companies such as Google and Amazon, and any collusion will damage their interests and reputations if caught by users. Consistent with prior works, our scheme strives to keep the privacy of the users' medical data and model owners' DNN model weights and assumes the data-independent information such as layer types, kernel size of each layers, number of layers, and the additive secret sharing computation ring size can be public to both users and servers.

3.2   Design Goals

Our framework is expected to achieve the following design goals:

- **Accuracy**. The secure inference accuracy of our framework should be as high as possible and the loss of accuracy compared with plaintext inference should be negligible.
- **Confidentiality**. Our scheme should be secure under the semi-honest model. Both users' data and model weights have to remain confidential at any time and only the corresponding user is able to see the inference result.
- **Practicability**. Our framework should be efficient in order to be practical in real-world applications.

4   Secret Sharing Friendly Model Optimization

4.1   Fixed-Point Quantization

Deep neural network inference is a computationally intensive task, and the execution of neural network in secure domain will bring huger computational overhead. How to reduce the execution overhead of the model in the ciphertext domain is a challenging work.

There are some methods aim to reduce the DNN computational overhead in plaintext domain such as additive neural network [8] and network pruning [14]. While these methods increase the plaintext execution efficiency, they cannot be applied to reduce the execution overhead under the secure domain. Contemporary methods such as approximation of nonlinear layer and binarization of network parameters could reduce the cost of secure execution, but they come at the cost of reduced inference accuracy.

To approach this problem, we proposed the fixed-point quantization method that can reduce the secure execution overhead for both linear layers and nonlinear layers. The motivation to implement fixed-point quantization is two-fold. Firstly, the computational and communication overhead of secure execution is highly dependent on the computation bitwidth, lower computation bitwidth would significantly reduce the secure execution overhead. Secondly, the error resiliency and redundancy of neural network parameters are well-proved [22], thus we can replace the full-precision 32 bits float parameter format with low-bit fixed-point data format, and the loss of accuracy can be negligible compared with full-precision model.

We denote the fixed-point number as $[QI, QF]$ where QI denotes the integer part of the number and QF is the fractional part of the number. We use the notation $\langle IL, FL \rangle$ to denote a fixed-point representation where the bit width of integer part is IL while the bit width of fractional part is FL. The smallest positive number that can be represented in the given fixed-point format is denoted as $\delta = 2^{-FL}$. And we define $\lfloor x \rfloor$ as the largest integer multiple of δ less than or equal to x.

The conversion of 32 bits float numbers to low bit fixed-point numbers requires rounding operation. In this work, we use two rounding methods: (1) Nearest rounding which rounds the float number to the nearest corresponding fixed-point number; (2) Stochastic rounding [13] where the probability of rounding a real number to a fixed-point number is proportional to their difference. Stochastic rounding is an unbiased rounding scheme, which has the property that the expected rounding error is zero. Given a float number x and the target fixed-point representation $\langle IL, FL \rangle$, These two approximation schemes are denoted as follows:

1) Nearest rounding

$$
\text{Round}\,(x, \langle IL, FL \rangle) = \begin{cases} \lfloor x \rfloor, \lfloor x \rfloor \le x \le \lfloor x \rfloor + \dfrac{\delta}{2} \\ \lfloor x \rfloor + \delta, \lfloor x \rfloor + \dfrac{\delta}{2} < x \le \lfloor x \rfloor + \delta \end{cases} \tag{1}
$$

2) Stochastic rounding: The probability of rounding x to $\lfloor x \rfloor$ is proportional to their difference:

$$
\text{Round}(x, \langle IL, FL \rangle) = \begin{cases} \lfloor x \rfloor & , \text{ w.p. } 1 - \frac{x - \lfloor x \rfloor}{\delta} \\ \lfloor x \rfloor + \delta & , \text{ w.p. } \frac{x - \lfloor x \rfloor}{\delta} \end{cases} \tag{2}
$$

We compared the two approximate methods in the subsequent experiments, and the experimental results will be described in detail in the experiment section.

4.2   Layer Fusion

Recall that batch normalization is a commonly used operation in DNN models. It is mainly applied on the output of preceding convolution layer to adjust the range of numerical values by multiplying each row by α_i and adding β_i to the result. Implementing the batch normalization operation in secure domain would incur non-negligible computation cost. Thus, we consider to merge the batch normalization layer with the preceding linear layer so as to execute the combination of convolution layer and batch normalization via a single linear operation (i.e.,matrix-multiplication). For the merged layer, the new weight matrix rows are $\alpha_i \cdot \boldsymbol{w}_i$ and bias values are $\alpha_i \cdot \boldsymbol{b}_i + \beta_i$, thus the BN layer can be removed from the DNN model.

5   Additive-Secret-Sharing Based Protocols

5.1   Modified Additive Secret Sharing Scheme

The existing additive secret sharing schemes can only support the secure computation of unsigned integers, and there will be errors in the secure computation of signed integers. However, the mixed computation of both signed and unsigned integers will be involved during our secure computation protocols. To address the correctness problem during the secure execution, we use the modified additive secret sharing scheme proposed by Chen *et al.* [9]. In this scheme, the absolute value of any plain text integer x is less than p, where p is a power of 2. The split modulus q is set as $q = 4 \cdot p$. During the sharing process, we first compute $x' \leftarrow x \bmod q$ and then split x' over $\mathbb{Z}_q$ as the standard method introduced in 2.2. To recover x, we first compute $x'' \leftarrow \langle x' \rangle^A + \langle x' \rangle^B \bmod q$. If $x'' < q/4$, it implies the plain text number corresponding to x' is unsigned and we set $x \leftarrow x'$; if $x'' > 3q/4$, we set $x \leftarrow x'' - q$, which means x is a signed integer. Besides, if $x \in [q/4, 3q/4]$, it implies that an error has occurred and we set $x = error$ and terminate the following processes.

5.2   Secure Convolution Protocol (SConv)

Algorithm 1: Secure Convolution Protocol (SConv)

Input: A has $\langle W \rangle^A, \langle X \rangle^A$; B has $\langle W \rangle^B, \langle X \rangle^B$.
Output: A outputs $\langle \mathtt{Conv}(W, X) \rangle^A$; B outputs $\langle \mathtt{Conv}(W, X) \rangle^B$.
Offline Phase:
1. T generates matrix beaver triples $\{\langle A \rangle, \langle B \rangle, \langle C \rangle\}$ where A has the same dimension with W and B has the same dimension with X and sends shares of them to party A and party B respectively .
Online Phase:
2. A: $\langle E \rangle^A = \langle W \rangle^A - \langle A \rangle^A$; $\langle F \rangle^A = \langle X \rangle^A - \langle B \rangle^A$.
3. B: $\langle E \rangle^B = \langle W \rangle^B - \langle A \rangle^B$; $\langle F \rangle^B = \langle X \rangle^B - \langle B \rangle^B$.
4. $A \& B$ exchange the shares $\langle E \rangle$ and $\langle F \rangle$, recover $E \leftarrow Rec(\langle E \rangle)$; $F \leftarrow Rec(\langle F \rangle)$.
5. A: $\langle Z \rangle^A \leftarrow \mathtt{Conv}\left(F, \langle A \rangle^A\right) + \mathtt{Conv}\left(E, \langle B \rangle^A\right) + \langle C \rangle^A$.
6. B: $\langle Z \rangle^B \leftarrow \mathtt{Conv}\left(E, F\right) + \mathtt{Conv}\left(F, \langle A \rangle^B\right) + \mathtt{Conv}\left(E, \langle B \rangle^B\right) + \langle C \rangle^B$.

The secure convolution is one of the most fundamental protocols in our scheme. We notice that the convolution operation actually only involves element-wise multiplication and addition, thus we design our secure convolution protocol by incorporating the main idea of Beaver's triplet [4]. As illustrated in Algorithm 1, our secure convolution protocol is divided into an offline phase and an online phase. Since the offline phase is independent of the input, it can be executed by the trusted third party T before, thus leading to an efficient online phase that only involves interactions between cloud A and B.

Offline Phase. The trusted third party T generates the Beaver's triplet in matrix form (A, B, C) where A has the same dimension with W and B has the dimension with X, $C = A \cdot B$. Then A, B and C are split into two random shares and distributed to cloud server A and B respectively.

Online Phase. Party A and B first mask their weight and input data by computing $\langle E \rangle = \langle W \rangle - \langle A \rangle$ and $\langle F \rangle = \langle X \rangle - \langle B \rangle$. Then, they exchange shares of $\langle E \rangle$ and $\langle F \rangle$ with each other to recover E and F. Finally, party A and B compute $\langle Z \rangle^A = \text{Conv}\left(F, \langle A \rangle^A\right) + \text{Conv}\left(E, \langle B \rangle^A\right) + \langle C \rangle^A$ and $\langle Z \rangle^B = \text{Conv}\left(E, F\right) + \text{Conv}\left(F, \langle A \rangle^B\right) + \text{Conv}\left(E, \langle B \rangle^B\right) + \langle C \rangle^B$, where Conv denotes the convolution operation in plaintext domain.

5.3   Secure ReLU Protocol (SReLU)

In this subsection, inspired by main idea of the secure comparison protocol, we propose our secure ReLU protocol, which is one of the most commonly used sub-protocols in our scheme. It takes shares of preceding convolution layer's output as input and outputs the additive shares of ReLU(X).

This protocol is based on the following observations. Firstly, since ReLU only involves element-wise comparison computations between input X and O(i.e. zero matrix with the same dimension). The result of $max\,(x, 0)$ depends on the sign of x. In our modified additive secret sharing scheme, for any $|x| \in \mathbb{Z}_p$ and shared over $\mathbb{Z}_q$, we can observe that the most significant bit of x is 1 if and only if $x < 0$. Obliviously, the MSB reflects the relationship between x and 0. To correctly compute the ReLU function in secure domain, party A and B can firstly apply bitwise addition to calculate the shared MSB of X as Z in parallel, then the final result can be easily computed by invoking $\text{SMul}\,(\text{SAdd}\,(\langle 1 \rangle, -\langle Z \rangle), \langle X \rangle)$. The details of secure ReLU protocol are available in Algorithm 2. The bitwise

---

Algorithm 2: Secure ReLU Protocol (SReLU)

Input: A has $\langle X \rangle^A$; B has $\langle X \rangle^B$.

Output: A outputs $\langle \text{ReLU}(X) \rangle^A$; B outputs $\langle \text{ReLU}(X) \rangle^B$.

Offline Phase:

1:   T generates Beaver's triples the sub-protocol uses and sends shares of them to party A and B respectively.

Online Phase:

2:   **for** each element x in X **do**

3:      A: decomposes $\langle x \rangle^A$ into $u_{l-1}, \cdots, u_1$ in bits;

4:      B: decomposes $\langle x \rangle^B$ into $v_{l-1}, \cdots, v_1$ in bits;

5:      $A\&B$: $\{\langle c \rangle^A, \langle c \rangle^B\} \leftarrow \text{SMul}\,(\langle u_1 \rangle, \langle v_1 \rangle)$

6:      **for** $i = 2$ to $l - 2$ **do**

7:         $A\&B$: $\{\langle a \rangle^A, \langle a \rangle^B\} = \text{SMul}\,(\langle u_i \rangle, \langle v_i \rangle)$

8:         $A\&B$: $\{\langle b \rangle^A, \langle b \rangle^B\} = \text{SAdd}\,(\langle u_i \rangle, \langle v_i \rangle)$

9:         $A\&B$: $\{\langle c \rangle^A, \langle c \rangle^B\} = \text{SAdd}\,(\langle a \rangle, \text{SMul}\,(\langle b \rangle, \langle c \rangle))$

10:     **end for**

11:     A computes $\langle z \rangle^A \leftarrow \langle u_{l-1} \rangle^A + \langle v_{l-1} \rangle^A + \langle c \rangle^A$

12:     B computes $\langle z \rangle^B \leftarrow \langle u_{l-1} \rangle^B + \langle v_{l-1} \rangle^B + \langle c \rangle^B$

13:     A sets $\langle z \rangle^A = \langle z \rangle^A$, B sets $\langle z \rangle^B = -\langle z \rangle^B$

14:     $A\&B$: $\{\langle z' \rangle^A, \langle z' \rangle^B\} \leftarrow \text{SMul}\,(\langle z \rangle, \langle z \rangle)$

15:     $A\&B$: $\{\langle \text{ReLU}\,(x) \rangle^A, \langle \text{ReLU}\,(x) \rangle^B\} \leftarrow \text{SMul}\,(\text{SAdd}\,(\langle 1 \rangle, -\langle z' \rangle), \langle x \rangle)$

16:   **end for**

17:   A and B return $\langle \text{ReLU}\,(X) \rangle^A$ and $\langle \text{ReLU}\,(X) \rangle^B$ respectively.

---

addition is from step 2 to 12, after that, party A and B convert the shared MSB from $\mathbb{Z}_2$ to $\mathbb{Z}_q$.

Discussion. Recently, several additive secret sharing based secure ReLU protocols have been proposed. Huang's work [17] processes the ReLU function based on their secure comparison protocol which takes extra computational cost to convert shares from additive sharing to bit sharing. Additionally, they simply set the activated shares as 0 when the value to be activate is less than 0, which discloses the information about distribution of intermediate values. In Xia *et al.*'s work [26], the real value to be activated is masked by multiplying a positive number. Since the range of real value will be disclosed to servers, it poses security risks.

5.4   Secure Average Pooling Protocol (SAvgPool)

In this subsection, we introduce our secure average pooling protocol which will be used during the secure inference.

For each pooling window, party A and B first compute $\langle Sum \rangle = \sum_{i=1}^{N} \sum_{j=1}^{N} \langle x_{i,j} \rangle$ where $x_{i,j}$ is element in current pooling window. Then, A and B compute $\langle S \rangle \leftarrow$ SCmp$(\langle Sum \rangle, \langle 0 \rangle)$ and set $\langle S \rangle^A = 1 - 2 \cdot \langle S \rangle^A$, $\langle S \rangle^B = -2 \cdot \langle S \rangle^B$ to record the sign of Sum that if Sum < 0, $S = -1$ otherwise $S = 1$. Then A and B compute $\langle S' \rangle \leftarrow$ SMul$(\langle S \rangle, \langle Sum \rangle)$ to get the shared absolute value of Sum. Next, they attempt to get the division result $\langle Z \rangle$ between $\langle S' \rangle$ and N^2 where the pooling window size is N. Finally, the pooling result is computed as

---

Algorithm 3: Secure Average Pooling Protocol (SAvgPool)

Input: A has $\langle X \rangle^A$; B has $\langle X \rangle^B$, pooling window size N
Output: A outputs $\langle \text{AvgPool}(X) \rangle^A$; B outputs $\langle \text{AvgPool}(X) \rangle^B$.

1: **for** each pooling window **do**
2:    A computes $\langle Sum \rangle^A \leftarrow \sum_{i=1}^{N} \sum_{j=1}^{N} \langle x_{i,j} \rangle^A$
3:    B computes $\langle Sum \rangle^B \leftarrow \sum_{i=1}^{N} \sum_{j=1}^{N} \langle x_{i,j} \rangle^B$
4:    $A \& B$: $\{\langle S \rangle^A, \langle S \rangle^B\} =$ SCmp$(\langle Sum \rangle, \langle 0 \rangle)$
5:    A sets $\langle S \rangle^A = 1 - 2\langle S \rangle^A$, B sets $\langle S \rangle^B = -2\langle S \rangle^B$
6:    $A \& B$:$\{\langle S' \rangle^A, \langle S' \rangle^B\} =$ SMul$(\langle S \rangle, \langle Sum \rangle)$
7:    A choose a random number $r \in \mathbb{Z}_q$, sets $\langle u \rangle^A = \langle S' \rangle^A + r \bmod q$, sends $\langle u \rangle^A$ to B.
8:    B sets $\langle u \rangle^B = \langle S' \rangle^B$, recover $u \leftarrow$ Rec$(\langle u \rangle)$.
9:    A sets $\langle Z'_1 \rangle^A = -\lfloor r/N^2 \rfloor, \langle Z'_2 \rangle^A = -\lfloor r/N^2 \rfloor$.
10:   B sets $\langle Z'_1 \rangle^B = \lfloor u/N^2 \rfloor$, $\langle Z'_2 \rangle^B = \lfloor (u+q)/N^2 \rfloor$.
11:   $A \& B$: $\{\langle t \rangle^A, \langle t \rangle^B\} =$ SCmp$(\langle u \rangle, \langle r \rangle)$, where $\langle r \rangle^A = r$, $\langle r \rangle^B = 0$.
12:   $A \& B$: $\{\langle Z' \rangle^A, \langle Z' \rangle^B\} =$ SAdd$(\langle Z'_2 \rangle, -\langle Z'_1 \rangle)$
13:   $A \& B$: $\{\langle Z \rangle^A, \langle Z \rangle^B\} =$ SAdd$($SMul$(\langle t \rangle, \langle Z' \rangle), \langle Z'_1 \rangle)$.
14:   $A \& B$: $\{\langle \text{AvgPool}(x) \rangle^A, \langle \text{AvgPool}(x) \rangle^B\} =$ SMul$(\langle S \rangle, \langle Z \rangle)$
15: **end for**
16: A and B return $\langle \text{AvgPool}(X) \rangle^A$ and $\langle \text{AvgPool}(X) \rangle^B$ respectively.

$\langle AvgPool(x)\rangle \leftarrow \texttt{SMul}(\langle S\rangle, \langle Z\rangle)$. The division operation is based on the observation that $\left|\left((S'+r)/N^2 - r/N^2\right) - S'/N^2\right| < 1$ where r is a random number and N^2 is the public divisor. Thus the division result Z between $\langle S'\rangle$ and N^2 can be computed as $Z \leftarrow \left((S'+r)/N^2 - r/N^2\right)$. Party A first generates a random number r to mask S' and sends $\langle u\rangle^A$ to B. After receiving $\langle u\rangle^A$, B recover u by running $u \leftarrow \texttt{Rec}(\langle u\rangle)$. To deal with the overflow situation, A and B generates two candidates respectively for $\langle Z\rangle$ where $\langle Z_1'\rangle^A = -\lfloor r/N^2\rfloor$, $\langle Z_2'\rangle^A = -\lfloor r/N^2\rfloor$ and $\langle Z_1'\rangle^B = \lfloor u/N^2\rfloor$, $\langle Z_2'\rangle^B = \lfloor (u+q)/N^2\rfloor$. After that, A and B test whether $u < r$ by running $\langle t\rangle \leftarrow \texttt{SCmp}(\langle u\rangle, \langle r\rangle)$, where $\langle r\rangle^A = r$ and $\langle r\rangle^B = 0$. If $u < r$, it implies that an overflow has occurred and $\langle Z_2'\rangle$ is the corresponding result, otherwise $\langle Z_1'\rangle$ is the right one. Then they compute $\langle Z'\rangle \leftarrow \texttt{SAdd}(\langle Z_2'\rangle, -\langle Z_1'\rangle)$ and $\langle Z\rangle \leftarrow \texttt{SAdd}(\texttt{SMul}(\langle t\rangle, \langle Z'\rangle), \langle Z_1'\rangle)$, the final result is computed as $\langle AvgPool(x)\rangle \leftarrow \texttt{SMul}(\langle S\rangle, \langle Z\rangle)$.

Discussion. In [17], Huang _et al._ claimed that the secure average pooling operation can be performed locally. It is not tenable when the dividend is negative. Actually, applying division operation to the shares locally will lead to errors in reconstruction phase.

5.5   Secure Truncation Protocol (STrun)

In our modified additive secret sharing scheme, the secure multiplication of two fixed-point values of FL-bits precision results at a shared value of 2FL-bits precision. In order to execute subsequent secure computations, truncation is necessary to do to maintain the precision after secure convolution protocol. We design our secure truncation protocol with the help of the trusted third party.

Algorithm 4: Secure Truncation Protocol (STrun)

Input: A has $\langle X\rangle^A$ after secure convolution, B has $\langle X\rangle^B$ after secure convolution; number of bits FL needs to be truncated.

Output: A outputs $\langle X'\rangle^A$ after truncation; B outputs $\langle X'\rangle^B$ after truncation.

Offline Phase:

1: T generates a random float matrix R, where each element $r_{i,j} \in [0,1)$
2: T converts each element $r_{i,j}$ to fixed-point through stochastic rounding.
3: T computes $R' = R \cdot 2^{FL}$, $R'' = R' \cdot 2^{FL}$, shares R' and R'' to A and B respectively.

Online Phase:

4: $A\&B$: $\{\langle Z\rangle^A, \langle Z\rangle^B\} = \texttt{SAdd}(\langle X\rangle, -\langle R''\rangle)$
5: $A\&B$: exchange shares of $\langle Z\rangle$ to recover $Z = X - R''$, set $Z' = Z/2^{FL}$.
6: A and B return truncation results $\langle X'\rangle^A = \langle R'\rangle^A$ and $\langle X'\rangle^B = \langle R'\rangle^B + Z'$ respectively.

Offline Phase. The trusted third party T generates a random float matrix R where each element $r_{i,j} \in [0, 1)$ and converts it into fixed-point matrix R'. Then T transforms R' into integer and computes $R'' = R' \cdot 2^{FL}$. After that, T sends secret shares of R' and R'' to party A and B respectively.

Online Phase. After receiving $\langle R' \rangle$ and $\langle R'' \rangle$, party A and B compute $\langle Z \rangle$ as $\langle Z \rangle \leftarrow \mathsf{SAdd}\,(\langle X \rangle, -\langle R'' \rangle)$ and running $Z \leftarrow \mathsf{Rec}\,(\langle Z \rangle)$ to recover the masked value. Then, B truncates Z locally as $Z' = Z/2^{FL}$ and sets truncated share as $\langle X' \rangle^B = Z' + \langle R' \rangle^B$ and A sets its truncated share as $\langle X' \rangle^A = \langle R' \rangle^A$. Obliviously, X' is exactly the truncated value.

Discussion. The truncation protocol of [19] is designed to truncate locally after secure multiplication. But their truncation protocol will introduce two probability errors where the small error is at most 1 off from the desired result at the chance of $1/2$ and the harsh error is no more than q off from the desired result at the chance of x/q where x is the value after multiplication. In order to avoid the harsh error as much as possible, the finite field should be large enough, thus rendering a large overhead on secure protocols.

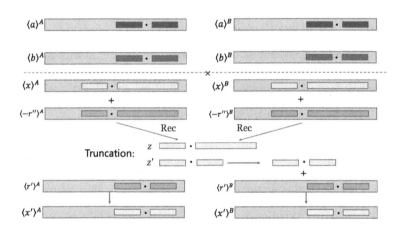

Fig. 2. Secure truncation

6 Privacy-Preserving COVID-19 Inference

Algorithm 5: Secure COVID-19 Inference Protocol (SCI)

Input: A has share of user's image data $\langle X \rangle^A$ and model weight share $\langle W \rangle^A$;
$\quad$ B has share of user's image data $\langle X \rangle^B$ and model weight share $\langle W \rangle^B$.
Output: A outputs the inference result $\langle Y \rangle^A$ and B outputs $\langle Y \rangle^B$.
1: **for** each layer i in W **do**
2: $\quad$ **if** layer i is convolutional layer **then**
3: $\quad\quad$ $A \& B$ execute SConv
4: $\quad\quad$ $A \& B$ execute STrun
5: $\quad$ **else if** layer i is ReLU layer **then**
6: $\quad\quad$ $A \& B$ execute SReLU
7: $\quad$ **else if** layer i is average pooling layer **then**
8: $\quad\quad$ $A \& B$ execute SAvgPool
9: $\quad$ **end if**
10: **end for**
11: $A \& B$ return $\langle Y \rangle^A = \langle W(X) \rangle^A$ and $\langle Y \rangle^B = \langle W(X) \rangle^B$ respectively.

The details of privacy-preserving COVID-19 inference are available in algorithm 5. Firstly, the model owner and users outsource the model weight W and image data X to the cloud servers respectively. Then, cloud A and B execute the corresponding sub-protocols according to the type of current layer. After that, cloud A and B send $\langle Y \rangle$ to the user. After receiving $\langle Y \rangle^A$ and $\langle Y \rangle^B$, the user recover the inference result by running $Y \leftarrow \text{Rec}(\langle Y \rangle)$. Note that only the user itself can recover the inference result, the privacy of diagnostic result is protected in our scheme.

7 Security Analysis

In this section, we analyze the security of the sub-protocols proposed including SConv, SReLU, SAvgPool and STrun. Then, we demonstrate that our privacy-preserving COVID-19 inference scheme can preserve the data confidentiality, model confidentiality and result privacy against a semi-honest attacker $\mathcal{A}$. The security analysis of our system is under the typical universal composability framework based on the semi-honest model, which relies on the following definition and lemmas.

Definition 1 (security under the semi-honest model [11]) *We say a protocol is secure if there exists a probabilistic polynomial-time simulator S that can generate a view for the adversary A in the real world and the view is computationally indistinguishable from its real view.*

Lemma 1. *A protocol is perfectly simulated if all its sub-protocols are perfectly simulated [5].*

Lemma 2. *[5] [6] If a random element r is uniformly distributed on $\mathbb{Z}_N$ and independent from any variable $x \in \mathbb{Z}_N$, then $r \pm x$ is also uniformly random and independent from x.*

The proofs of Lemma 1 and Lemma 2 are available in [5,6]. Since the sub-protocols performed locally can be perfectly simulated, we mainly prove the security for the ones that need interactions between cloud A and B in the following. The security proofs of SMul and SCmp are available in [9,17] respectively. Based on the proofs of SMul and SCmp, we can easily prove that the SConv and SReLU are secure under the semi-honest model in a similar way. Next, we prove the security of other sub-protocols.

Theorem 1. *The SAvgPool algorithm proposed is secure under the semi-honest model.*

Proof. In each loop of Algorithm 3, for step 2 and 3, the operations are performed locally. From steps 4 to 6, the interaction only occurs in SMul and SCmp, whose security has been proven. In step 7 and 8 of SAvgPool, cloud A's execution view can be denoted as $\Pi_{7-8}^A(\text{SAvgPool}) = \{r, \langle S'\rangle^A, \langle u\rangle^A\}$ where $r \in \mathbb{Z}_q$ is randomly chosen by cloud A, $\langle S'\rangle^A$ is obtained through SMul in step 6. $\langle u\rangle^A = \langle S'\rangle^A + r \bmod q$. $\Pi_{A7-8}^S(\text{SAvgPool})$ is computationally indistinguishable from $\Pi_{7-8}^A(\text{SAvgPool})$. Similarly, we can prove that cloud B's execution view is also computationally indistinguishable from simulator's view. For step 9 and 10 in SAvgPool, the operations are performed locally. In other steps of SAvgPool, the interaction only occurs in SCmp, SAdd and SMul, whose security has been proven. Thus, we draw a conclusion that both cloud A's execution view and cloud B's execution view can be perfectly simulated. Based on the above analyses, we conclude that SAvgPool is secure under the semi-honest model.

Theorem 2. *The STrun algorithm proposed is secure under the semi-honest model.*

Proof. The execution view of cloud A can be denoted as $\Pi_A(\text{STrun}) = \{\langle X\rangle^A, \langle Z\rangle^A, \langle R'\rangle^A, \langle R''\rangle^A, \langle Z\rangle^B\}$ where $\langle Z\rangle^B = \langle X\rangle^B - \langle R''\rangle^B$. It is trivial to see that all these values are uniformly random. Thus the execution view of cloud A in STrun is perfectly simulated. In a similar way, we can easily demonstrate that the cloud B's execution view can be perfectly simulated. Thus, we draw the conclusion that STrun is secure under the semi-honest model.

Theorem 3. *The privacy-preserving COVID-19 inference scheme is secure in the semi-honest model, and also can preserve the data confidentiality, the model confidentiality and inference result privacy against an active adversary.*

Proof. In a similar way, we can prove our privacy-preserving COVID-19 inference scheme is secure under the semi-honest model. For our SCI, the interactive information only occurs in SConv, SReLU, SAvgPool and STrun which all have been demonstrated secure under the semi-honest model. Based on these analyses, we can conclude that our privacy-preserving COVID-19 inference scheme is secure under the semi-honest model.

Next, we discuss that our scheme can protect the DNN model and data confidentiality as well as result privacy against an active adversary $\mathcal{A}$. If $\mathcal{A}$ eavesdrops the transmission link between cloud A and B, the intermediate values will be obtained by it. Since the model weights and user data as well as inference result are secret shared over $\mathbb{Z}_q$, they are uniformly random for $\mathcal{A}$. $\mathcal{A}$ cannot get the original value of them unless it comprises cloud A and B simultaneously, which is forbidden in our threat model. For the inference result, it is also random for these two clouds. Thus, we can claim that out privacy-preserving COVID-19 inference scheme can protect the model privacy, the user data privacy and the inference result privacy from the active adversary $\mathcal{A}$.

8   Evaluation

In this section, we first evaluate the performance of our additive secret sharing based secure protocols in theory. Then, to further assess the accuracy and efficiency of our scheme, we conduct experiments to evaluate the performance of our proposed sub-protocols and the privacy-preserving COVID-19 inference scheme.

8.1   Theoretical Analysis

8.1.1   Computational Overhead

The computational overhead of our proposed sub-protocols is illustrated in Table 1. Here, we suppose that the bit-length of the split modulus q is l, the runtime of SMul with two shared multipliers is T_{SMul}. We also suppose that the input matrices of SConv, SReLU, SAvgPool and STrun are of size $K \times K$ for simplicity, the pooling window size in SAvgPool is N.

Table 1. Computational and Communication overhead of Proposed Protocols

Protocol	Computational overhead	Communication overhead
SConv	$O(K^2)T_{\text{SMul}}$	$O(4K^2l)$
SReLU	$O(2K^2l)T_{\text{SMul}}$	$O(8K^2l)$
SAvgPool	$O(4K^2/N^2 \cdot l)T_{\text{SMul}}$	$O(28K^2/N^2 \cdot l)$
STrun	—	$O(2K^2l)$

For SConv, it runs SMul once for each element in input matrix, so it takes $O(K^2)T_{\text{SMul}}$ time. For SReLU, for each element in input matrix X, it runs once SMul from steps 1 to steps 5, twice in each iteration from steps 6 to 10 and once from steps 11 to 16. So it takes $O(1 + (l - 3) \cdot 2 + 1)T_{\text{SMul}}$ for each element, thus it takes $O(2K^2l)T_{\text{SMul}}$ time. For SAvgPool, it runs SMul three times and SCmp twice for each pooling operation in current pooling window, note that the pooling window size is N, thus it takes $O(4K^2/N^2 \cdot l)T_{\text{SMul}}$ time. For STrun, it only runs SAdd once for each element, thus the computational overhead of STrun is negligible.

8.1.2   Communication Overhead

For SConv, the communication overhead occurs in the exchange of $\langle E \rangle$ and $\langle F \rangle$ between two clouds. Since each element of $\langle E \rangle$ and $\langle F \rangle$ is $l - 1$ bits at most, the communication overhead of SConv is $O(4K^2l)$. For other protocols, the communication overhead mainly occurs in performing SMul where two multipliers are both shared. As illustrated before, in SMul, each party sends the share of $\langle e \rangle$ and $\langle f \rangle$ to each other, so the communication overhead is $4(l - 1)$ bits at most. For each element in SReLU, it operates SMul $O(2l)$ times, and each SMul is mainly operated over $\mathbb{Z}_2$ except for twice operated over $\mathbb{Z}_q$. So the communication overhead of SReLU is $O(4(2 - 1) \times (2K^2l)) = O(8K^2l)$. In a similar way, we can deduce the communication overhead of SAvgPool and STrun, which is available in Table 1.

8.2   Experimental Performance

Our experiments are performed on a laptop equipped with Intel(R) Core(TM) i7-10875H CPU @ 2.30 GHz (16 CPUs) and 16GB RAM. We use the pre-trained ResNet-18 as our backbone network which contains 17 convolution layers and 1 FC layer and train it with PyTorch. Our proposed sub-protocols were implemented in Python 3.8. The NumPy 1.19 package was used to implement secret-sharing based secure protocols in parallel.

The COVID-19 Radiography Database[3] is a stage released COVID-19 image dataset which is widely used in many deep learning based COVID-19 inference systems [10,20]. It contains 3616 COVID-19 positive cases along with 10,192 normal, 6012 lung opacity, 1345 viral pneumonia chest X-ray images up to now. We randomly selected 700 positive images, 2000 normal images and 400 viral pneumonia images to form the test dataset, and the rest of the image data corresponding to these three categories is used as the training set.

In this subsection, we use this dataset to construct the privacy-preserving COVID-19 inference system, and to show the performance of our secure inference system is comparable with the standard DNN inference system without privacy consideration. We first use this dataset to train a commonly used network ResNet-18 as our backbone network and the max pooling layers are replaced by average pooling layers for ease of implementation. The float baseline model achieves a accuracy of 95.2% in plaintext domain.

Accuracy. We first evaluate the accuracy of our system. Since the bit length of fractional part influences the inference accuracy, we evaluate the inference accuracy for these two rounding methods with different bit length of fractional part. We set the total bit length of fixed-point number as 16 and change the bit length of fractional part. The result is shown in Fig. 6. The red dotted line denotes the inference accuracy of the float model in plaintext domain. We can see that, in both cases, the inference accuracy increase with the number of fractional bits. This makes sense because during the rounding procedure the more bits the

---

[3] https://www.kaggle.com/tawsifurrahman/covid19-radiography-database.

fractional part allocated, the less decimal digits of the original value will be lost. The accuracy loss is negligible when the fractional part bits is more than 8. Also we can see that, the stochastic rounding method has smaller loss of accuracy, which is more obvious when the number of bits of fractional part is less than 7.

Then, to further explore the impact of different data rounding methods and number of fractional bits on the inference accuracy, we use the Mean Absolute Error (MAE) and Root Mean Squared Error (RMSE) to evaluate the inference accuracy. Their definitions are as follows:

$$\text{MAE} = (\Sigma|y_i' - y_i|/m) \ , \tag{3}$$

$$\text{RMSE} = \sqrt{(\Sigma(y_i' - y_i)^2)/m} \tag{4}$$

where y_i' denotes the inference result of fixed-point model and y_i denotes the corresponding inference vector of baseline model. Experimental results are available in Fig. 3 and Fig. 4. It is obvious to see that the stochastic rounding method has less inference error compared with the nearest rounding method especially when the number of fractional bits is less than 7. This is primarily because at reduced fractional precision, some of the model weights are rounded down to zero when using the nearest rounding. In contrast, the stochastic rounding preserves the weight information statistically.

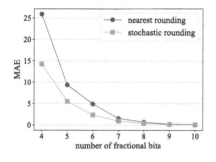

Fig. 3. MAE

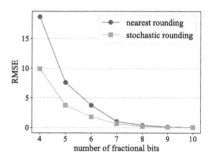

Fig. 4. RMSE

Efficiency. Then, we test the runtime of our privacy-preserving COVID-19 inference scheme. Since the split modulus q mainly influences the performance of runtime of sub-protocols, we evaluate the system runtime with different split modulus q, and the result is available in Fig. 5. We can see that even the bit length of q is set as 64, the total runtime of our system is no more than 80 s which is acceptable in practical application. Note that our experiments are conducted on one CPU core, it can achieve higher efficiency by using multiple CPU cores in parallel in the real-world cloud environments.

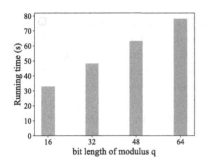

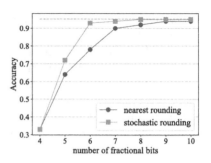

Fig. 5. Total runtime   **Fig. 6.** Inference accuracy

9   Conclusion

In this paper, we proposed a lightweight additive secret sharing based privacy-preserving COVID-19 inference scheme. We first optimize the DNN model in a secret sharing-friendly manner to reduce the computational and communication overhead in the secure inference phase. Then, based on the modified additive secret sharing scheme, we designed a series of efficient secure computing sub-protocols, with the help of these sub-protocols, we achieved the efficient privacy-preserving COVID-19 inference scheme. Our scheme maintains model privacy, data privacy and inference result privacy. The experimental results showed that our system achieves high efficiency and accuracy for COVID-19 X-ray image inference while ensuring the privacy requirements. This shows that our scheme has certain potential application value in the scenario of fighting against the COVID-19 epidemic.

Acknowledgment. This work is supported by the National Key Research and Development Program of China under Grant 2020YFC2003400, National Nature Science Foundation of China (No.62072466, No.62102430, No.62102429), Natural Science Foundation of Hunan Province (No.2021JJ40688), and the NUDT Grants (No. ZK19-38).

References

1. Abdel-Hamid, O., Mohamed, A.R., Jiang, H., Deng, L., Penn, G., Yu, D.: Convolutional neural networks for speech recognition. IEEE/ACM Trans. audio, speech, lang. process. 22(10), 1533–1545 (2014)
2. Apostolopoulos, Ioannis D.., Mpesiana, Tzani A..: Covid-19: automatic detection from X-ray images utilizing transfer learning with convolutional neural networks. Phys. Eng. Sci. Med. **43**(2), 635–640 (2020). https://doi.org/10.1007/s13246-020-00865-4
3. Assistance, H.C.: Summary of the HIPAA privacy rule. Office for Civil Rights (2003)

4. Beaver, D.: Efficient Multiparty Protocols Using Circuit Randomization. In: Feigenbaum, J. (ed.) CRYPTO 1991. LNCS, vol. 576, pp. 420–432. Springer, Heidelberg (1992). https://doi.org/10.1007/3-540-46766-1_34

5. Bogdanov, D., Laur, S., Willemson, J.: Sharemind: A Framework for Fast Privacy-Preserving Computations. In: Jajodia, S., Lopez, J. (eds.) ESORICS 2008. LNCS, vol. 5283, pp. 192–206. Springer, Heidelberg (2008). https://doi.org/10.1007/978-3-540-88313-5_13

6. Bogdanov, D., Niitsoo, M., Toft, T., Willemson, J.: High-performance secure multiparty computation for data mining applications. Int. J. Inf. Secur. **11**(6), 403–418 (2012)

7. Boulila, W., Ammar, A., Benjdira, B., Koubaa, A.: Securing the classification of covid-19 in chest x-ray images: a privacy-preserving deep learning approach. arXiv preprint arXiv:2203.07728 (2022)

8. Chen, H., et al.: AdderNet: do we really need multiplications in deep learning? In: Proceedings of the IEEE/CVF Conference on Computer Vision and Pattern Recognition, pp. 1468–1477 (2020)

9. Chen, J., Liu, L., Chen, R., Peng, W., Huang, X.: SecRec: a privacy-preserving method for the context-aware recommendation system. IEEE Trans. Dependable Secure Comput. 1 (2021)

10. Chowdhury, M.E., et al.: Can AI help in screening viral and Covid-19 pneumonia? IEEE Access **8**, 132665–132676 (2020)

11. Goldreich, O.: Foundations of cryptography: volume 2, basic applications. Cambridge University Press (2009)

12. Guo, C., Jia, J., Choo, K.K.R., Jie, Y.: Privacy-preserving image search (PPIS): Secure classification and searching using convolutional neural network over large-scale encrypted medical images. Comput. Secur. **99**, 102021 (2020)

13. Gupta, S., Agrawal, A., Gopalakrishnan, K., Narayanan, P.: Deep learning with limited numerical precision. In: International Conference on Machine Learning, pp. 1737–1746. PMLR (2015)

14. Han, S., Mao, H., Dally, W.J.: Deep compression: Compressing Deep Neural Networks with Pruning, Trained Quantization and Huffman Coding. arXiv preprint arXiv:1510.00149 (2015)

15. Hannun, A.Y., et al.: Cardiologist-level arrhythmia detection and classification in ambulatory electrocardiograms using a deep neural network. Nat. Med. **25**(1), 65–69 (2019)

16. Hu, W., Huang, Y., Wei, L., Zhang, F., Li, H.: Deep convolutional neural networks for hyperspectral image classification. J. Sens. **2015** (2015)

17. Huang, K., Liu, X., Fu, S., Guo, D., Xu, M.: A lightweight privacy-preserving cnn feature extraction framework for mobile sensing. IEEE Trans. Dependable Secure Comput. **18**(3), 1441–1455 (2019)

18. Khan, A.I., Shah, J.L., Bhat, M.M.: Coronet: A deep neural network for detection and diagnosis of covid-19 from chest X-ray images. Comput. methods programs biomed. **196**, 105581 (2020)

19. Mohassel, P., Zhang, Y.: SecureML: a system for scalable privacy-preserving machine learning. In: 2017 IEEE Symp. Secur. Priv(SP), pp. 19–38. IEEE (2017)

20. Rahman, T., et al.: Exploring the effect of image enhancement techniques on Covid-19 detection using chest X-ray images. Comput. Biol. Med. **132**, 104319 (2021)

21. Riazi, M.S., Weinert, C., Tkachenko, O., Songhori, E.M., Schneider, T., Koushanfar, F.: Chameleon: a hybrid secure computation framework for machine learning applications. In: Proceedings of the 2018 on Asia Conference on Computer and Communications Security, pp. 707–721 (2018)

22. Sarwar, S.S., Venkataramani, S., Raghunathan, A., Roy, K.: Multiplier-less artificial neurons exploiting error resiliency for energy-efficient neural computing. In: 2016 Design, Automation & Test in Europe Conference & Exhibition (DATE), pp. 145–150. IEEE (2016)

23. Thomas, S., Michael, Z.: GMW vs. Yao? Efficient Secure Two-Party Computation with Low Depth Circuits. In: Sadeghi, Ahmad-Reza. (ed.) FC 2013. LNCS, vol. 7859, pp. 275–292. Springer, Heidelberg (2013). https://doi.org/10.1007/978-3-642-39884-1_23

24. Sweeney, L.: Matching known patients to health records in Washington state data. arXiv preprint arXiv:1307.1370 (2013)

25. Wang, L., Lin, Z.Q., Wong, A.: Covid-net: A tailored deep convolutional neural network design for detection of Covid-19 cases from chest X-ray images. Sci. Rep. **10**(1), 1–12 (2020)

26. Xia, Z., Gu, Q., Xiong, L., Zhou, W., Weng, J.: Privacy-preserving image retrieval based on additive secret sharing. arXiv preprint arXiv:2009.06893 (2020)

Hierarchical Reinforcement Learning-Based Mobility-Aware Content Caching and Delivery Policy for Vehicle Networks

Le Zhang[1], Yongxuan Lai[1,3(✉)], and Fan Yang[2]

[1] School of Informatics/Shenzhen Research Institute, Xiamen University,
Xiamen 361005, China
zhangle@stu.xmu.edu.cn

[2] School of Aerospace Engineering, Xiamen University, Xiamen 361005, China
yang@xmu.edu.cn

[3] School of Mathematics and Information Engineering, Longyan University,
Longyan 364012, China
laiyx@xmu.edu.cn

Abstract. Mobile Edge Computing (MEC) has been regarded as a promising technology to satisfy the growing demand for resource-intensive applications in vehicle networks. Content caching and delivery, a critical problem in MEC, has attracted much research attention in the past decade. However, most existing caching schemes in the vehicle network scenario still confront two challenges: 1) High mobility of vehicles results in unstable connectivity; 2) Fairly massive state spaces of existing schemes have become their obstacles to good scalability. To address these challenges, we propose a hierarchical reinforcement learning (HRL)-based mobility-aware content caching and delivery policy for vehicle networks. First of all, we formulate the caching and delivery problem as a Markov decision process (MDP) problem. Our aim is to minimize the time-averaged transmission cost in the vehicle network scenario. To address the curse of dimensionality, we decompose the joint optimization of content caching and delivery into the vehicle side and RSU side subproblems. DDPG and Double-DQN are applied to address these two subtasks. Furthermore, an LSTM-based location prediction module is built to mine the mobility patterns of vehicles. Experimental studies and analysis, which are conducted on a real-world dataset, demonstrate that our approach outperforms other baseline schemes in terms of transmission cost and convergence speed.

Keywords: Mobile edge computing · Vehicle network · Content caching and delivery · Hierarchical reinforcement learning · Deep deterministic policy gradient

This work is partially supported by Longyan Industry-Education Integration Project of Xiamen University (20210302) and the Natural Science Foundation of Guangdong (2021A1515011578).

W. Meng et al. (Eds.): ICA3PP 2022, LNCS 13777, pp. 43–62, 2023.
https://doi.org/10.1007/978-3-031-22677-9_3

1   Introduction

The past decade has witnessed the widespread adoption of smart vehicles across Intelligent Transportation Systems (ITS). Meanwhile, the wide commercial roll-out of fifth-generation (5G) networks has facilitated a wide range of innovative vehicle applications, such as in-car entertainment, autonomous driving and live traffic monitoring [9]. However, there are some challenges in providing these applications with high quality of experience (QoE) in Vehicle Networks (VN). First of all, the emerging content will consume an extremely large data volume, such as video streaming and Virtual Reality/Augmented Reality (VR/AR). Secondly, many multimedia applications also involve live interaction between users, which requires low-latency content delivery [23]. These challenges are difficult to solve in the traditional centralized cloud-based computation. Fortunately, Mobile Edge Computing (MEC) has emerged as a promising paradigm to support these resource-demanding applications with stringent latency and reliability requirements. MEC moves computing and storage resources to close proximity to mobile users, such as Base Stations (BSs) and Road Side Units (RSUs), so that the latency to users will be remarkably reduced [1,4]. At the same time, cache nodes at the edge of networks can cache popular contents in advance, which alleviates strain on the backhaul links.

Content caching and delivery is a critical problem in mobile edge computing, which has attracted much research attention in recent years. Generally speaking, the storage space of edge nodes is often limited, which necessitates the careful design of an efficient content caching and delivery policy. Most existing caching schemes can be classified into two categories: reactive caching and proactive caching [8]. Firstly, Least Recently Used (LRU), Least Frequently Used (LFU), and their variants are examples of reactive caching. These caching schemes are driven by simple statistics of request history and mine user request patterns to guide the cache decision. They are easy to implement and widely used in Content Delivery Networks (CDNs). However, they are not suitable for the features of vehicle network scenarios, such as high mobility and dynamic content popularity. In contrast, proactive caching schemes predict content popularity in advance and cache the most popular contents which are possible to be accessed in the recent future. In proactive caching schemes, it is of vital importance to accurately predict content popularity. A large number of existing studies in the broader literature have investigated machine learning-based proactive caching schemes by utilizing deep learning [13,19], reinforcement learning [12,15,23] and federated learning [22], etc.

The advent of autonomous driving and demand for improved road safety and in-car entertainment have led to the development of vehicle-to-everything (V2X) technology and vehicle networks (VN). The integration of vehicle network and MEC will greatly promote the sensing and computing capability of vehicle network at the network edge. Despite recent advancements in Machine Learning(ML)-based proactive caching, utilizing ML approaches for edge caching in vehicle networks still confronts the following two challenges: 1) High mobility: High movement of vehicles results in unstable connectivity, and vehicles may not have enough time to download the entire requested content during the time staying in the area of one edge node. In order to improve the quality of experience, cache schemes must be mobility aware and enable multiple cache nodes to collaborate; 2) Scalability: Most of existing studies use end-to-end reinforcement learning techniques, which makes their state spaces very large and impairs their potential to scale. Specifically, the state space expands exponentially as the number of linked vehicles rises, delaying the model's convergence. This is so-called *the curse of dimensionality* [2].

In past decades, Hierarchical Reinforcement Learning (HRL) has been regarded as one of the promising technologies to alleviate the curse of dimensionality and scale reinforcement learning to the long-horizon tasks [10]. HRL decomposes a long-horizon(i.e., large state and action space) reinforcement learning task into a hierarchy of subproblems or subtasks. This inspired us to come up with our own solution for content caching and delivery for vehicle networks. Different from the existing schemes of HRL-based caching [7,11], our scheme focuses on the edge caching in vehicle network scenarios and applies a divide-and-conquer strategy to reduce the dimensions. In this paper, we propose a hierarchical reinforcement learning(HRL)-based mobility-aware content caching and delivery policy for vehicle networks, which has better scalability and universality. This caching scheme aims to minimize the time-averaged transmission cost in the scenario of vehicle networks with high mobility and dynamic content popularity. The content caching and delivery problem is formulated as an MDP problem and decomposed into vehicle side and RSU side subproblems. Deep deterministic policy gradient (DDPG) and double deep Q-network (Double-DQN) are applied to solve these two subproblems. The major contributions of this paper are as follows:

- We propose an HRL-based mobility-aware content caching and delivery policy for vehicle networks with high mobility and dynamic content popularity. The joint optimization of content caching and delivery is modeled as a Markov decision process (MDP) problem. This framework aims to minimize the time-averaged transmission cost in the scenario of vehicle networks.
- Borrowing ideas from HRL, we decompose the joint optimization of content caching and delivery into vehicle side and RSU side subproblems. DDPG and Double-DQN are used to address these two subtasks. Furthermore, a Long Short Term Memory(LSTM)-based location prediction module is built to mine the mobility patterns of vehicles. Through these efforts, we hope to achieve better scalability and generality.
- Experimental studies and analysis are conducted on a real-world taxi trajectory dataset, which demonstrates that our approach outperforms other baseline schemes in terms of transmission cost and convergence speed.

The rest of this paper is organized as follows. Section 2 summarizes the related work of this paper. Section 3 presents the system model. Section 4 formulates the content caching and delivery problem and reformulates it as an MDP problem. In Sect. 5, we introduce the detailed hierarchical reinforcement learning-based mobility-aware content caching and delivery policy for vehicle networks. Experimental studies and analysis are provided in Sect. 6. Finally, Sect. 7 concludes the paper and presents some future directions.

2 Related Work

Content Caching and Delivery in MEC. Mobile edge computing provides cloud computing and caching capabilities at the edge of cellular networks. A large number of recent works have been reported to investigate content caching and delivery in mobile edge networks. Jiang et al. [5] proposed a cooperative content caching and delivery framework to minimize average content downloading latency. The content caching problem is formulated as an integer-linear programming problem and solved by using the subgradient method. The content delivery policy is formulated as an unbalanced assignment problem and solved by using Hungarian algorithm. Yao and Ansari [21] jointly optimized the content placement and storage allocation for Internet of Things (IoT) to minimize the total network traffic cost. Two heuristic algorithms were proposed in order to reduce the computational complexity of the problem. Sun et al. [16] designed a cooperative content caching approach among small cells, for which the tradeoff between content delivery latency and storage cost was investigated.

Content Caching and Delivery in Vehicle Networks. The vehicle network, which is a promising paradigm to support diverse vehicular applications, has drawn much research attention with a wide range of works on content caching and delivery. In [3], a vehicle-based distributed storage scheme via local vehicle-to-vehicle (V2V) communications was proposed to cope with the vehicle mobility issue. Structured redundancy via erasure coding was also introduced in order to combat the volatile V2V links. In order to deal with the challenges of high mobility and privacy, Yu et al. [22] proposed a mobility-aware proactive edge caching scheme based on federated learning to leverage the private training data distributed on local vehicles for predicting content popularity. Context-aware adversarial autoencoder (C-AAE) was introduced to predict the highly dynamic content popularity.

Content Caching and Delivery with DRL. In the past decade, with the continuous enhancement of computing power brought by graphics processing units (GPUs), deep learning (DL) has aroused great interest and extensive research with fruitful outcomes in academia. Deep reinforcement learning (DRL), which combines the advantages of deep learning and reinforcement learning, is regarded as a powerful tool to solve sequential decision making problems. As a result, much effort has been made to utilize DRL to deal with content caching and delivery in vehicle networks. Qiao et al. [12] formulated the joint content caching and delivery optimization problem as a double timescale Markov decision process (DTS-MDP), and deep deterministic policy gradient (DDPG) was leveraged to obtain a suboptimal solution. However, its state space was fairly large and the method did not have good scalability. In [23], Zong et al. employed an ensemble of constituent caching policies and a DRL agent was trained to adaptively select the best-performing policy to control the cache. But the single cache node was its downside and the migration to the vehicle network scenario was difficult as a result. In [15], a QoE-driven edge caching method for the IoV was proposed to solve the RSU caching optimization problem. A class-based user interest model was established, which was more suitable for systems with a large number of small files. A deep reinforcement learning method was designed to address the QoE-driven RSU cache update issue effectively.

Most of the above-mentioned studies are end-to-end reinforcement learning approaches, which leads to their state spaces being fairly massive and having poor scalability. As the number of connected vehicles grows, the state space increases exponentially, which results in slow convergence of the model. A more systematic and theoretical analysis is required for the curse of dimensionality in content caching and delivery problem. This motivates us to propose a hierarchical reinforcement learning(HRL)-based mobility-aware content caching and delivery policy for vehicle networks, which has better scalability and universality.

3   System Model

In this section, we propose the content caching and delivery framework in vehicle networks including network model, communication model, mobility model and request model.

3.1   Network Model

We consider a general model of mobile edge computing in vehicle networks with different types of edge caching nodes, including a macro base station (MBS), several road side units (RSU) and content requesting vehicles (CRV), as shown in Fig. 1. Let $\mathbb{N} = \{0, 1, ..., N\}$ represent the index set of edge caching nodes, in which 0 is the index of MBS and $\{1, 2, ..., N\}$ is the index set of RSUs. Let $\mathbb{K} = \{1, 2, ..., K\}$ denote the index set of CRVs to make requests to access contents. The index set of all available contents is denoted by $\mathbb{F} = \{1, 2, ..., F\}$. We assume that the MBS is the centralized content provider and has the abundant storage capacity to cache all available contents. Furthermore, each RSU $n \in \mathbb{N}$ and each CRV $k \in \mathbb{K}$ are equipped with a limited caching storage capacity, which is represented by M_n and L_k respectively.

The MBS serves all the RSUs with all the contents and the connections between the MBS and RSUs use optical fibers. Vehicles traverse the coverage areas of several RSUs and each CRV communicates with only one RSU through wireless links at the same time. The system runs over an infinite period of time, which is divided into slots, denoted as $t = 0, 1, 2, ...$. During the content caching and delivery process, a CRV will require a desired content (e.g., navigation map update, video streaming, etc.). Then, the local cache of CRV will be checked first

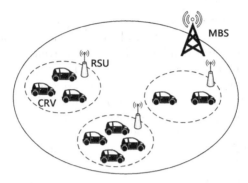

Fig. 1. The network model consists of a macro base station (MBS), several road side units (RSU) and content requesting vehicles (CRV).

to see whether the requested content is cached. The cache state of each content for CRV k is denoted by $\mathbb{CV}_k = \{CV_k^f \in \{0,1\}|f \in \mathbb{F}\}$, where $CV_k^f = 0$ means that content f is not cached and $CV_k^f = 1$ means that content f is cached. The CRV can receive immediate service if the content has already been cached. If not, the request will be sent to the RSU to which the CRV is connected. In the same way, the cache of RSU will be checked whether the requested content is cached. The cache state of each content for RSU n is indicated by $\mathbb{CR}_n = \{CR_n^f \in \{0,1\}|f \in \mathbb{F}\}$, where $CR_n^f = 0$ means that content f is not cached and $CR_n^f = 1$ means that content f is cached. If the content is located in the cache of RSU, it will be transmitted to the CRV with a certain communication cost. We call it *a cache hit* that the requested content could be available in the cache of CRV or RSU. Otherwise, the CRV has to fetch the desired content from the MBS (i.e., *a cache miss*), which will spend a higher communication cost. To sum up, the object of this caching framework is to provide content delivery services for smart vehicles with the communication cost as lower as possible.

Notably, the CRV may not be able to fetch all parts of the content in one time slot due to high mobility. Let $RE_k(t)$ denote the remaining size of the content requested by CRV k in the time slot t. When the CRV enters the coverage area of another RSU, the remaining part of the requested content will be transmitted subsequently.

3.2 Communication Model

In wireless communication, we consider that MBS and RSU allocate the orthogonal spectrum resources to CRVs such that there is no interference between wireless communications. The signal-to-noise ratio (SNR) between edge caching node i and CRV j at time slot t is given by

$$\gamma_{i,j}(t) = \frac{P_i g_{i,j}}{\sigma^2 + \sum_{v \in K \setminus \{j\}} P_i g_{i,v}}, \forall i \in \mathbb{N}, \forall j \in \mathbb{K} \qquad (1)$$

where P_i is the transmission power of edge caching node i, $g_{i,j}$ is the channel gain between edge caching node i and CRV j, σ^2 is the power of additive white Gaussian noise.

Based on the assumption that the available spectrum resource is denoted as W^{mbs} Hz for MBS and W_n^{rsu} Hz for RSU n, $w_{i,j}(t)$ can be allocated as the continuous bandwidth resource to CRV j by edge caching node i. According to Shannon Theory, the data rate to fetch a segment of content f between edge caching node i and CRV j is given by [14]

$$r_{i,j}(t) = w_{i,j}(t) * \log_2\left(1 + \gamma_{i,j}(t)\right), \forall i \in \mathbb{N}, \forall j \in \mathbb{K} \tag{2}$$

where $w_{i,j}(t)$ is the bandwidth resource allocated to CRV j and $\gamma_{i,j}(t)$ is the SNR at time slot t.

3.3 Request Model

The request of CRV k is denoted by $Q_k(t) = f \in \overline{\mathbb{F}}$, where $k \in \mathbb{K}, \overline{\mathbb{F}} = \mathbb{F} \cup \{0\}$. If there is no new request of CRV k, then $Q_k(t) = 0$. The vehicle will not submit a new request until the last request is served. We assume that the request history of one CRV follows a Markov chain and the next request only depends on the last request. We adopt the same vehicle request model as [17], where the request transition probability from content i to j of CRV k is given by

$$p_{i,j} = \begin{cases} P_0, & i \in \overline{\mathbb{F}}, j = 0 \\ (1 - P_0) \frac{\frac{1}{j^\beta}}{\sum_{j'=1}^{F} \frac{1}{j'^\beta}}, & i = 0, j \in \mathbb{F} \\ (1 - P_0) \frac{1}{H}, & i \in \mathbb{F}, j = (i+h) \bmod (F+1), h \in \{1, 2, \ldots, H\} \\ 0, & \text{otherwise.} \end{cases} \tag{3}$$

To be specific, P_0 indicates the probability that a vehicle does not have a new request in the current slot ($j = 0$). When the vehicle does not have a request in the last slot ($i = 0$), the request model depends on the content popularity, which follows a Zipf-like distribution, and β indicates the parameter of the distribution. Furthermore, each content $i \in \mathbb{F}$ has a set of H neighboring contents indicated as $\mathbb{H}_i = \{f \in \mathbb{F} : f = (i+h) \bmod (F+1), \ h \in \{1, 2, \ldots, H\}\}$, where H is the number of neighboring contents. The transition probability from content $i \in \mathbb{F}$ to its neighboring contents $j \in \mathbb{H}_i$ is modeled as a uniform distribution. In other words, the vehicle randomly selects a content from neighbor contents as the next request. Otherwise, the transition probability from $i \in \mathbb{F}$ to other contents $j \notin \mathbb{H}_i$ is zero.

For convenience of understanding, the notations used in this paper are summarized in Table 1.

Table 1. Summary of key notations.

Notation	Description
$\mathbb{N}$	Index set of edge caching nodes(MBS, RSUs)
$\mathbb{K}$	Index set of content requesting vehicles(CRVs)
$\mathbb{F}$	Index set of all available contents
M_n	Caching storage capacity of RSU $n \in \mathbb{N}$
L_k	Caching storage capacity of CRV $k \in \mathbb{K}$
$CR_n^f(t)$	Cache state of each content f for RSU n in time slot t
$CV_k^f(t)$	Cache state of each content f for CRV k in time slot t
$RE_k(t)$	Remaining size of the content requested by CRV k in time slot t
$r_{i,j}(t)$	Data rate to fetch a segment of content f between cache node i and CRV j
$Q_k(t)$	Request of CRV k at time slot t
$p_{i,j}$	Request transition probability from content i to j of CRV k
$Loc_k(t)$	Region index where CRV k is located at time slot t
$\Delta CR_n^f(t)$	Cache update action of RSU n for content f
$\Delta CV_k^f(t)$	Cache update action of CRV k for content f
$WM_{0,k}(t)$	Allocated bandwidth to CRV k by MBS 0
$WR_{n,k}(t)$	Allocated bandwidth to CRV k by RSU n
$c_{i,j}(t)$	Transmission cost from edge caching node i to CRV j at time slot t

4 Problem Formulation

In this section, we formulate the joint optimization of content caching and delivery as a Markov decision process (MDP) problem. The detailed definitions of MDP, including state space, action space and reward, will be given.

4.1 State Space

At the beginning of each time slot, the agent will receive environment state information, including request content index, caching state, remaining size of content and vehicle locations. Specifically, the state space contains the following:

1. $Q_k(t) \in \overline{\mathbb{F}}$: request of CRV k at time slot t
2. $CR_n^f(t) \in \{0,1\}$: cache state of each content f for RSU n at time slot t
3. $CV_k^f(t) \in \{0,1\}$: cache state of each content f for CRV k at time slot t
4. $RE_k(t) \leq S_{max}$: remaining size of the content requested by CRV k in time slot t, where S_{max} denotes the max size of all contents
5. $Loc_k(t) \in \{1,2,...,L\}$: location of CRV k at time slot t, which is represented by the region index the CRV is driving in. There will be more details about transport regions in Sect. 6.

The joint state space of the MDP process is denoted by $s(t) \in \mathbb{S}$:

$$s(t) = \{\mathbb{Q}(t), \mathbb{CR}(t), \mathbb{CV}(t), \mathbb{RE}(t), Loc(t)\}. \tag{4}$$

Thus, the size of the whole state space is $|\mathbb{S}| = (F+1)^K \times 2^{(N+K)F} \times S_{max}^K \times L^K$, which grows exponentially with the number of vehicles K and has poor scalability.

4.2 Action Space

After receiving the current environment state, the agent will decide which contents should be stored to which cache nodes and how to allocate the bandwidth resource, which would be done to the environment in order to achieve a lower communication cost. To be specific, the action space contains the following:

1. $\Delta CR_n^f(t) \in \{-1, 0, 1\}$: RSU cache update action, where -1 means deleting the content from the cache, 0 refers to maintaining the content cache states and 1 means inserting the content into the cache
2. $\Delta CV_k^f(t) \in \{-1, 0, 1\}$: CRV cache update action, which has the same meaning as $\Delta CR(t)$
3. $WM_{0,k}(t) \leq W^{mbs}$: allocated bandwidth to CRV k by MBS 0
4. $WR_{n,k}(t) \leq W_n^{rsu}$: allocated bandwidth to CRV k by RSU n.

The joint action space of the MDP process is denoted by $a(t) \in \mathbb{A}$:

$$a(t) = \{\Delta\mathbb{CR}(t), \Delta\mathbb{CV}(t), \mathbb{WM}(t), \mathbb{WR}(t)\}. \tag{5}$$

Thus, the size of the whole action space is $|\mathbb{A}| = 3^{(N+K)F} \times (W^{mbs})^K \times (W_n^{rsu})^{NK}$. Same as above, the size of action space grows exponentially with the number of vehicles K.

4.3 Reward

The objective of this content caching and delivery policy is to provide content delivery services for smart vehicles with the communication cost as lower as possible. Based on this assumption, we design the following cost function to represent the transmission cost from edge caching node i(i.e., MBS and RSUs) to CRV j in the scenario of vehicle networks:

$$c_{i,j}(t) = p_i^b * \min\left(RE_j(t), r_{i,j}(t) * \Delta t\right), \forall i \in \mathbb{N}, \forall j \in \mathbb{K} \tag{6}$$

where p_i^b means the price per unit bandwidth for edge caching node i, which is higher for the MBS and lower for RSUs on account of different distances to CRVs. We assume that the service provider adopts resource-usage-based pricing [12]. If the remaining size of the content in one time slot (i.e., $RE_j(t)$) is smaller than the maximum amount of data transmitted in one time slot (i.e., $r_{i,j}(t)*\Delta t$), it will be billed according to the actual amount of data transmitted.

Further, the objective function can be given by the time-averaged transmission cost:

$$\min \lim_{T \to \infty} \frac{1}{T} \sum_{t=1}^{T} \sum_{i=0}^{N} \sum_{j=1}^{K} c_{i,j}(t). \tag{7}$$

Considering that general reinforcement learning algorithms are designed to maximize cumulative reward and we need to minimize the transmission cost, we apply the negative exponential function of the transmission cost as the reward function:

$$R(t) = e^{-\sum_{i=0}^{N}\sum_{j=1}^{K} c_{i,j}(t)}. \tag{8}$$

According to the Bellman equation, we can obtain the optimal policy for environment state s:

$$\mu^*(s) = \arg\max_{a\in\mathbb{A}} \left[R + \sum_{s\prime\in\mathbb{S}} \Pr\left(s' \mid s, a\right) V\left(s'\right) \right] \tag{9}$$

where s and a are the current state and action at time slot t, $s\prime$ is the next state at time slot $t+1$ and $V(*)$ is the value function of state.

5   Hierarchical Reinforcement Learning-Based Caching and Delivery

In this section, we propose the hierarchical reinforcement learning (HRL)-based mobility-aware content caching and delivery policy for vehicle networks, in order to reduce the dimensions of state and action space and achieve better scalability and universality. In addition, we apply the LSTM algorithm to mine the mobility patterns of vehicles for the purpose of caching potential popular contents in advance.

According to the problem formulated in Sect. 4, the state space and action space are fairly massive and grow exponentially with the number of vehicles, which results in poor scalability. Convergence will take a long time if we simply apply traditional reinforcement learning algorithms, such as Q-learning and DQN. This leads to greatly reduced model scalability and actual application value. To address *the curse of dimensionality*, we apply the hierarchical reinforcement learning and divide the joint optimization of content caching and delivery into two subproblems (i.e., vehicle side and RSU side), as shown in Fig. 2.

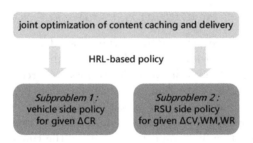

Fig. 2. The framework of hierarchical reinforcement learning(HRL)-based policy.

Subproblem 1: vehicle side policy.

For given cache action in RSUs $\Delta\mathbb{CR}(t)$

$$\mu_V^*(s) = \underset{\Delta\mathbb{CV}(t),\mathbb{WM}(t),\mathbb{WR}(t)}{\text{argmax}} \left[R + \sum_{s'\in\mathbb{S}} \Pr\left(s' \mid s,a\right) V\left(s'\right) \right]. \tag{10}$$

Subproblem 2: RSU side policy.

For given cache action in CRVs $\{\Delta\mathbb{CV}(t),\mathbb{WM}(t),\mathbb{WR}(t)\}$

$$\mu_R^*(s) = \underset{\Delta\mathbb{CR}(t)}{\text{argmax}} \left[R + \sum_{s'\in\mathbb{S}} \Pr\left(s' \mid s,a\right) V\left(s'\right) \right]. \tag{11}$$

Note that the agent decision for cache action $\Delta\mathbb{CR}(t)$ in RSU side only affects the state $\mathbb{CR}(t)$, which has no influence on the vehicle side. In other words, adjusting the RSU side policy has much less influence on the vehicle side. Hence, we first optimize the vehicle side policy in subproblem 1 with RSU side policy fixed. We will apply DDPG algorithm to solve subproblem 1 in Sect. 5.1. Then, we will optimize the RSU side policy in subproblem 2 with vehicle side policy fixed and use Double-DQN algorithm to address subproblem 2 in Sect. 5.2.

5.1   Vehicle Side Policy

In this section, we fix the RSU side policy and optimize the vehicle side policy. In this case, the state space is simplified to $s(t) = \{\mathbb{Q}(t),\mathbb{CV}(t),\mathbb{RE}(t),Loc(t)\}$ and the action space is simplified to $a(t) = \{\Delta\mathbb{CV}(t),\mathbb{WM}(t),\mathbb{WR}(t)\}$. Accordingly, the size of state space decreases to $(F+1)^K \times 2^{KF} \times S_{max}^K \times L^K$ and the size of action space decreases to $3^{KF} \times (W^{mbs})^K \times (W_n^{rsu})^{NK}$. Considering the massive action space, we choose the Deep Deterministic Policy Gradient (DDPG) algorithm [6] to address this MDP problem. Different from the value-based DQN, DDPG is policy-based (i.e., directly output actions) and absorbs the advantages of DQN, which makes it more suitable for high-dimensional continuous action spaces. The architecture of DDPG is shown in Fig. 3. In the following parts, we will discuss the detailed modules of DDPG.

Actor Network μ Update. Different from stochastic policy, the actor network μ learns a deterministic policy $a = \mu(s|\theta^\mu)$ with the actor network parameter θ^μ. The input is the current state s and its output is the deterministic action $\mu(s|\theta^\mu)$, which is used to update the actor network parameter with the output of critic network $Q(s,a)$:

$$\nabla_{\theta^\mu}\mu = \nabla_a Q(s,a)\nabla_{\theta^\mu}\mu(s|\theta^\mu). \tag{12}$$

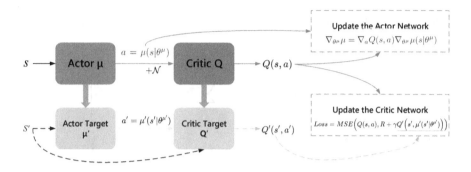

Fig. 3. The architecture of DDPG.

Critic Network Q Update. The critic network Q is responsible for evaluating policies based on the action-value function $Q(s, a)$ with the critic network parameter θ^Q. The input is the current state s and the actual action $a_t = \mu(s|\theta^\mu) + \mathcal{N}$ where $\mathcal{N}$ denotes the Ornstein-Uhlenbeck noise [18] that functions as the exploration of policy. The output is the value function $Q(s, a)$ which is used to update the actor network parameter and calculate the TD error $y_t - Q(s, a)$ where y_t is the target value generated by critic target network Q'. The critic network parameter θ^Q will be updated by minimizing the loss:

$$Loss = MSE(Q(s, a), y_t) \tag{13}$$

$$= MSE\left(Q(s, a), R + \gamma Q'\left(s', \mu'(s'|\theta^{\mu'})\right)\right). \tag{14}$$

Target Networks Update. The actor target network μ' and critic target network Q' are applied to calculate the target value y_t. Their architectures are consistent with the primary networks. However, they are updated slowly compared to the primary networks, which makes the learning performance stable and robust. Exponentially weighted moving average (EWAM) scheme is applied to update the target networks' parameters $\theta^{\mu'}$ and $\theta^{Q'}$:

$$\theta^{\mu'} \leftarrow \tau\theta^\mu + (1 - \tau)\theta^{\mu'} \tag{15}$$

$$\theta^{Q'} \leftarrow \tau\theta^Q + (1 - \tau)\theta^{Q'} \tag{16}$$

where $\tau \in [0, 1]$ is the weight parameter.

Experience Replay. DDPG draws on the experience replay of DQN. It constructs a replay memory to store a series of historical experiences $[s, a, c, s']$ to avoid sample-correlation during the training process. The network parameters can be updated by randomly choosing mini-batch samples from replay memory.

5.2 RSU Side Policy

In this section, we fix the vehicle side policy and optimize the RSU side policy. In this case, the state space is simplified to $s(t) = \{\mathbb{Q}(t), \mathbb{CR}(t), Loc(t)\}$ and the action space is simplified to $a(t) = \{\Delta\mathbb{CR}(t)\}$, which are only related to RSUs. The dimension of state space decreases to $(F+1)^K \times 2^{NF} \times L^K$ and the dimension of action space decreases to 3^{NF}. As can be seen, the dimensions of state and action are reduced tremendously compared to the vehicle side and the action space is discrete. For the purpose of accelerating the convergence, we adopt the Double-DQN algorithm to solve subproblem 2.

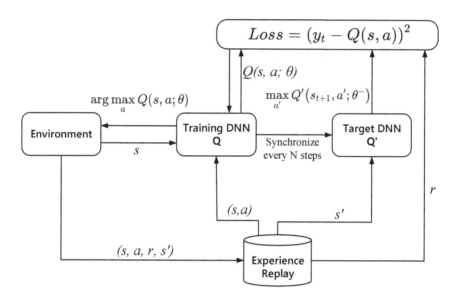

Fig. 4. The architecture of the DQN algorithm. The Double-DQN shares the same architecture and deep network as the DQN algorithm and differs from the DQN only in the calculation of the target value.

Double-DQN [20] is the variant of the DQN algorithm and has the same architecture and deep network as the DQN algorithm, as shown in Fig. 4. In the DQN scheme, the deep neural network (DNN) Q is applied to estimate the state-action reward $Q(s, a)$. If we simply use one DNN, there are two key challenges in the training step: 1) The target is unstable, where the objective function for optimizing the DNN parameters depends on these parameters themselves; 2) The training samples are strongly correlated instead of independent, which makes the gradient descent towards a deterministic direction and there is a considerable probability that the training process will not converge. To address these challenges, DQN takes two measures accordingly: 1) Freezing target DNN Q': The parameters of target DNN Q' are fixed during several training steps until the parameters of DDN Q are synchronized to the target DNN Q', in order to keep the learning objective steady; 2) Experience replay memory D, which consists of interactions between the client and the environment. In each training step, DQN samples a batch of data from the experience memory as the training data and calculates the target value as follows:

$$y_t = \begin{cases} R_t & \text{if episode terminates at step } t+1 \\ R_t + \gamma \max_{a'} Q'(s_{t+1}, a'; \theta^-) & \text{otherwise.} \end{cases} \quad (17)$$

The loss function is defined as the mean square error: $(y_t - Q(s, a))^2$.

However, due to the max operation, the state-action value $Q(s, a)$ would be overestimated and the entire evaluation is overestimated accordingly since we always tend to select the action $\arg\max_{a'} Q'(s_{t+1}, a'; \theta^-)$. To avoid this upward bias, Double-DQN decouples the calculation operation by applying the training DNN Q to select actions, while employing the target DNN Q' to evaluate actions. The only difference between Double-DQN and DQN is the calculation of the target value, which alleviates the overestimation and instability:

$$y_t = \begin{cases} R_t & \text{if terminate at step } t+1 \\ R_t + \gamma Q\left(s_{t+1}, \underset{a}{\arg\max} Q'(s_{t+1}, a; \theta); \theta^-\right) & \text{otherwise.} \end{cases}$$

$$(18)$$

6   Experiments

In this section, we first introduce the experiment setup and the baseline schemes. Then the performance of our proposed scheme is evaluated on a real-world dataset and simulation results are given.

6.1   Experiment Setup

The schemes are implemented in Python 3.6 and experiments are run on a desktop computer with AMD R5 3600X CPU, 3.8 GHz, 16G RAM under Ubuntu 18.04.5 LTS. Furthermore, we use the TensorFlow platform to implement the DDPG and Double-DQN algorithm of the content caching and delivery policy. The main parameters employed in the simulations are summarized in Table 2.

We apply the taxi trajectory dataset of the Xiamen island to simulate the mobility of vehicles, which consists of latitudes, longitudes and GPS times, etc. The road network of Xiamen island is used for the simulation, which contains 24,750 road nodes and 3,234 road segments. This road network covers the range of [118.0660E,118.1980E] × [24.4240N,24.5600N]. The Xiamen island is divided into 16 transport regions and a day is divided into 24 time slots.

Furthermore, we apply Long Short-Term Memory (LSTM) algorithm, which has proven to be an effective solution to time series prediction problems, to preprocess the trajectory data and mine vehicle mobility patterns before being fed to the RL agent. Specifically, we apply 24 units of LSTM to predict the

Table 2. Simulation Parameters.

Parameter	Value/Description
Number of RSUs	16
Number of CRVs	[30, 60]
Number of contents	[10, 40]
Size of contents	[20, 80] MB
Storage Capacity of RSU	200 MB
Storage Capacity of CRV	[80, 120] MB
Bandwidth of MBS, RSUs	[5, 20] MHz
Transmission Power of MBS	35 dBm
Transmission Power of RSU	33 dBm
Power of Gaussian Noise	−95 dBm

location in the next time slot. At the beginning of each time slot, the vector of the previous latitudes and longitudes would be given to the input of LSTM. The output of LSTM is the latitude and longitude where vehicles may be in this time slot. Then the latitude and longitude will be transferred into the index of transport region, which is served as the location of CRVs at time slot t (i.e., $Loc_k(t)$ in Sect. 4.1).

6.2   Baseline Schemes

For performance comparison, we present the baseline schemes as follows:

– *Random*: The contents cached in RSUs and CRVs are randomly selected from all of the available contents.
– *Least Recently Used (LRU)*: When the cache capacity of RSU or CRV is already full, the least recently used content will be evicted. In other words, the longest unrequested content will be removed.
– *Least Frequently Used (LFU)*: When the cache capacity of RSU or CRV is already full, the least frequently used content will be evicted. In other words, the content with the smallest request frequency will be removed.
– *Double Time-Scale DDPG (DTS DDPG)* [12]: The cooperative caching problem is modeled as a double time-scale Markov decision process (DTS-MDP). The content caching decision is made on the large time-scale while the joint decision of vehicle scheduling and bandwidth allocation is implemented on the small time-scale. The DDPG algorithm is implemented to obtain a suboptimal solution.

6.3   Simulation Results

Impact of the Number of Contents. As shown in Fig. 5, we compare the transmission cost for different numbers of contents. We vary the number of contents from 10 to 40. The capacity of CRVs is 100 MB and the number of CRVs

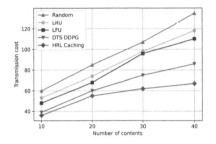
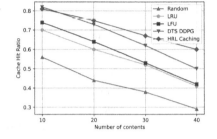

Fig. 5. Impact of the number of contents on the transmission cost.

Fig. 6. Impact of the number of contents on the cache hit ratio.

is 50. It can be observed that the transmission costs of five approaches all obviously increase with the increase of the number of contents. This is because the more contents there are, the more cache replacement is needed, which causes an increase in the transmission cost. As expected, the proposed HRL-based caching policy performs better with various numbers of contents compared to other baseline schemes. The line chart in Fig. 6 demonstrates that the cache hit ratio has a decreasing trend for all caching schemes as the number of contents increases. Our proposed approach still performs better than other baseline schemes and the advantage is even greater when the number of contents increases.

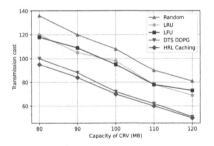
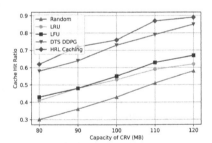

Fig. 7. Impact of the capacity of CRVs on the transmission cost.

Fig. 8. Impact of the capacity of CRVs on the cache hit ratio.

Impact of the Capacity of CRVs. Then, we compare the transmission cost and cache hit ratio for different cache capacities of CRVs. We change the cache capacity of CRVs from 80 MB to 120 MB. As we can see in Fig. 7, the increasing cache capacity has a positive impact on the transmission cost. The transmission cost decreases with the increase of cache capacity, especially for our proposed HRL-based caching policy. This is reasonable because a larger cache capacity enables CRVs to cache more popular contents simultaneously, which will reduce the number of wireless communications to the MBS or RSUs. In Fig. 8, as the cache capacity grows, our proposed approach is the best scheme and the Random scheme has the worst performance. This is because the Random scheme does not consider the content popularity and has no ability to predict the next request.

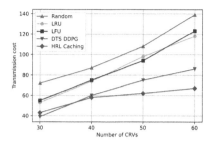
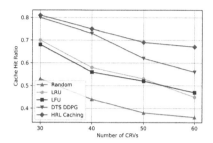

Fig. 9. Impact of the number of CRVs on the transmission cost.

Fig. 10. Impact of the number of CRVs on the cache hit ratio.

Impact of the Number of CRVs. In addition, we change the number of CRVs to compare the transmission cost and the cache hit ratio. We change the number of CRVs from 30 to 60 and the number of contents is set to 100. The capacity of CRVs is set to 100 MB. Figure 9 illustrates that our approach achieves the best performance and the gap between HRL-based caching policy and DTS DDPG policy becomes larger with the increasing number of CRVs. This reveals that our approach has better scalability than DTS DDPG and is more suitable for large-scale vehicle network scenarios. In Fig. 10, the cache hit ratio decreases with the increasing number of CRVs. This is because the cache capacity is limited and unable to satisfy all requests of vehicles. Furthermore, it is worth noting that the LRU and LFU schemes have similar performances, as they are both driven by simple statistics of request history and mine user request patterns to guide the cache decision.

The Convergence Performance. Figure. 11 shows the convergence performance of our proposed HRL approach and other baseline schemes. The number of contents is fixed as 100. The capacity of CRVs is set to 100 MB and the number of CRVs is 50. It can be observed that for HRL-based caching policy and DTS DDPG policy, the total content transmission cost of each episode decreases rapidly and gradually maintains a relatively stable value with the increase of training episodes. Meanwhile, there are no significant changes occurring in the transmission cost with the increase of episodes for Random, LRU and LFU schemes. This is consistent with the fact that they are not reinforcement learning-based schemes. In addition, the HRL-based caching policy converges at about 400 episodes, which is obviously faster than DTS DDPG. This shows that it has better scalability from another aspect.

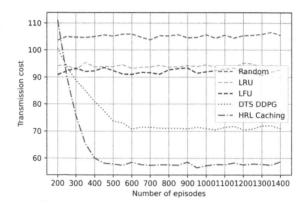

Fig. 11. The convergence performance.

7 Conclusion

In this paper, we focus on the main challenges in vehicle networks, including high mobility and scalability. An HRL-based mobility-aware content caching and delivery policy for vehicle networks is proposed to achieve better scalability and generality. The joint optimization of content caching and delivery is decomposed into two subproblems. DDPG and Double-DQN are adopted to deal with sequential decision problems. Experimental results demonstrate that our approach reduces the dimension of state space and outperforms other baseline schemes in terms of transmission cost and convergence speed. Our approach still has huge room for improvement. In the future, we will continue to improve our scheme in terms of more accurate location prediction and collaboration between edge caching nodes.

References

1. Abbas, N., Zhang, Y., Taherkordi, A., Skeie, T.: Mobile edge computing: a survey. IEEE Internet Things J. **5**(1), 450–465 (2018). https://doi.org/10.1109/JIOT.2017.2750180
2. Barto, A.G., Mahadevan, S.: Recent advances in hierarchical reinforcement learning. Discrete Event Dyn. Syst. **13**(1), 41–77 (2003). https://doi.org/10.1023/A:1022140919877
3. Hu, B., Fang, L., Cheng, X., Yang, L.: Vehicle-to-vehicle distributed storage in vehicular networks. In: 2018 IEEE International Conference on Communications (ICC), pp. 1–6 (2018). https://doi.org/10.1109/ICC.2018.8422220
4. Hu, Y.C., Patel, M., Sabella, D., Sprecher, N., Young, V.: Mobile edge computing - a key technology towards 5G. ETSI White Pap. **11**(11), 1–16 (2015)
5. Jiang, W., Feng, G., Qin, S.: Optimal cooperative content caching and delivery policy for heterogeneous cellular networks. IEEE Trans. Mob. Comput. **16**(5), 1382–1393 (2017). https://doi.org/10.1109/TMC.2016.2597851

6. Lillicrap, T.P., et al.: Continuous control with deep reinforcement learning. In: 4th International Conference on Learning Representations, ICLR 2016, San Juan, Puerto Rico, May 2–4, 2016, Conference Track Proceedings (2016). http://arxiv.org/abs/1509.02971

7. Majidi, F., Khayyambashi, M.R., Barekatain, B.: HFDRL: An intelligent dynamic cooperate cashing method based on hierarchical federated deep reinforcement learning in edge-enabled IoT. IEEE Int. Things J. 9(2), 1402–1413 (2022). https://doi.org/10.1109/JIOT.2021.3086623

8. Narayanan, A., Verma, S., Ramadan, E., Babaie, P., Zhang, Z.: Deepcache: a deep learning based framework for content caching. In: Proceedings of the 2018 Workshop on Network Meets AI ML, pp. 48–53 (2018). https://doi.org/10.1145/3229543.3229555

9. Nomikos, N., Zoupanos, S., Charalambous, T., Krikidis, I.: A survey on reinforcement learning-aided caching in heterogeneous mobile edge networks. IEEE Access 10, 4380–4413 (2022). https://doi.org/10.1109/ACCESS.2022.3140719

10. Pateria, S., Subagdja, B., Tan, A.h., Quek, C.: Hierarchical reinforcement learning: A comprehensive survey. ACM Comput. Surv. 54(5), 1-35 (2021). https://doi.org/10.1145/3453160

11. Qian, Y., Wang, R., Wu, J., Tan, B., Ren, H.: Reinforcement learning-based optimal computing and caching in mobile edge network. IEEE J. Sel. Areas Commun. 38(10), 2343–2355 (2020). https://doi.org/10.1109/JSAC.2020.3000396

12. Qiao, G., Leng, S., Maharjan, S., Zhang, Y., Ansari, N.: Deep reinforcement learning for cooperative content caching in vehicular edge computing and networks. IEEE Int. Things J. 7(1), 247–257 (2020). https://doi.org/10.1109/JIOT.2019.2945640

13. Qin, Z., Xian, Y., Zhang, D.: A neural networks based caching scheme for mobile edge networks: Poster abstract. In: Proceedings of the 17th Conference on Embedded Networked Sensor Systems, pp. 408–409 (2019). https://doi.org/10.1145/3356250.3361961

14. Rappaport, T.S., et al.: Wireless communications: principles and practice, vol. 2. prentice hall PTR New Jersey (1996)

15. Song, C., Xu, W., Wu, T., Yu, S., Zeng, P., Zhang, N.: QoE-driven edge caching in vehicle networks based on deep reinforcement learning. IEEE Trans. Veh. Technol. 70(6), 5286–5295 (2021). https://doi.org/10.1109/TVT.2021.3077072

16. Sun, Y., Chen, Z., Liu, H.: Delay analysis and optimization in cache-enabled multi-cell cooperative networks. In: 2016 IEEE Global Communications Conference (GLOBECOM), pp. 1–7 (2016). https://doi.org/10.1109/GLOCOM.2016.7841723

17. Sun, Y., Cui, Y., Liu, H.: Joint pushing and caching for bandwidth utilization maximization in wireless networks. IEEE Trans. Commun. 67(1), 391–404 (2019). https://doi.org/10.1109/TCOMM.2018.2858791

18. Szepesvári, C.: Joint pushing and caching for bandwidth utilization maximization in wireless networks. Synth. Lect. Artif. Intell. Mach. Learn. 4(1), 1–103 (2010). https://doi.org/10.2200/S00268ED1V01Y201005AIM009

19. Tsai, K.C., Wang, L., Han, Z.: Mobile social media networks caching with convolutional neural network. In: 2018 IEEE Wireless Communications and Networking Conference Workshops (WCNCW), pp. 83–88 (2018). https://doi.org/10.1109/WCNCW.2018.8368988

20. Van Hasselt, H., Guez, A., Silver, D.: Deep reinforcement learning with double q-learning. In: Proceedings of the AAAI conference on artificial intelligence. vol. 30 (2016). https://doi.org/10.1609/aaai.v30i1.10295

21. Yao, J., Ansari, N.: Joint content placement and storage allocation in c-rans for IoT sensing service. IEEE Int. Things J. **6**(1), 1060–1067 (2019). https://doi.org/10.1109/JIOT.2018.2866947

22. Yu, Z., Hu, J., Min, G., Zhao, Z., Miao, W., Hossain, M.S.: Mobility-aware proactive edge caching for connected vehicles using federated learning. IEEE Trans. Intell. Transp. Syst. **22**(8), 5341–5351 (2021). https://doi.org/10.1109/TITS.2020.3017474

23. Zong, T., Li, C., Lei, Y., Li, G., Cao, H., Liu, Y.: Cocktail edge caching: ride dynamic trends of content popularity with ensemble learning. In: IEEE INFOCOM 2021 - IEEE Conference on Computer Communications, pp. 1–10 (2021). https://doi.org/10.1109/INFOCOM42981.2021.9488910

Compromise Privacy in Large-Batch Federated Learning via Malicious Model Parameters

Shuaishuai Zhang[1], Jie Huang[1,2]([✉]), Zeping Zhang[1],
and Chunyang Qi[1]

[1] School of Cyber Science and Engineering, Southeast University,
Nanjing 211189, China
{sszhang,jhuang,zhangzp9970,chunyangqi}@seu.edu.cn
[2] Purple Mountain Laboratories, Nanjing 211111, China

Abstract. Federated Learning (FL) is a distributed learning paradigm, in which users share their gradients instead of local data to preserve privacy. Previous works have shown that the server in FL can reveal user's local data by inverting shared gradients. However, a large batchsize can defense against these attacks effectively by obfuscating gradients calculated on each data. In this paper, we propose a novel Gradient Inversion Attack which can compromise privacy in large-batch FL. Firstly, the server constructs malicious model parameters which can mitigate the confusion of gradients. Then users' model parameters are tampered purposely by the server. From users' shared gradients computed on malicious model parameters, the server can recover private local trainsets perfectly in large-batch FL. Experiments on CIFAR100 show that our method can recover 92%, 77% and 54% of the data points in a batch with batchsize 128, 256 and 512, respectively. Compared with previous works, our method has a higher performance and versatility.

Keywords: Federated learning · Gradient inversion · Privacy leakage · Malicious model parameters

1 Introduction

With the rapid development of electrical technology, Machine Learning is widely used in various institutions, such as hospitals, banks and goverments. Different institutions need to train a global model collaboratively while ensuring data privacy. Federated Learning (FL) [8,11,19] is proposed to solve the question. In FL, users train models on their local data and share gradients with a central server. The central server computes average gradients and sends it back to all participated users. People believe that privacy is preserved because their training data is kept local.

The privacy-preserving of Federated Learning is based on the assumption that shared gradients leak little privacy. However, recent works have overturned the assumption and proven that the server can compromise privacy by inverting

© Springer Nature Switzerland AG 2023
W. Meng et al. (Eds.): ICA3PP 2022, LNCS 13777, pp. 63–80, 2023.
https://doi.org/10.1007/978-3-031-22677-9_4

shared gradients. Generally, privacy attacks in FL can be divided into three categories: Membership-Inference [12,15], Property-Inference [3,10,12] and Gradient Inversion [4,6,7,14,16,20–22].

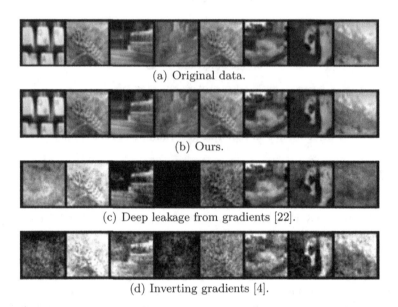

(a) Original data.

(b) Ours.

(c) Deep leakage from gradients [22].

(d) Inverting gradients [4].

Fig. 1. Examples of recovered data compared of two optimization-based methods and ours. The target model is a fully connected neural networks and the batchsize is 256.

Gradient Inversion is the most powerful attack of these three. Attackers can recover victim's private data directly by analyzing shared gradients. Hitaj *et al.* [6] firstly proposed an attack on distributed deep learning based on Generative Adversarial Networks (GAN) [5]. Attackers train a GAN with shared gradients to generate a prototypical sample of victim's private data. Zhu *et al.* [22] shows the feasibility of recovering original training data from gradients by formulating it as an optimization problem. Tremendous researches [4,7,20,21] have been made to improve this optimization-based attack.

However, a large batchsize can defense against optimization-based methods effectively. Because a large batchsize exacerbates the confusion of gradients, making it harder to recover data by solving optimization problem. Experiments in [4,20,22] show that these attack methods are effective only when the batchsize of training is no more than 48. Latest works [1,2,17] try to attack privacy in large-batch training by tampering architectures or parameters of the global model purposely. While these methods are limited to models using *ReLU* layers. In this study, we propose a novel Gradient Inversion Attack to compromise privacy in large-batch FL. We construct malicious model parameters to mitigate the confusion of gradients. Then private data can be recovered perfectly and quickly by analyzing shared gradients. Figure 1 represents some examples of recovered data with our method and optimization-based methods. We also summarizes previous methods in Table 1 and compare them with our method. The advantages of our method are as follows:

(1) Our attack method can recover more private data in a large batchsize such as 128, 256 and 512. While optimization-based methods require a small batchsize such as 1, 16 and 32.
(2) Our method is effective on models using different activation functions such as *ReLU*, *Tanh* and *Sigmoid*.
(3) Our method can recover data points perfectly and quickly instead of spending much time solving optimization problems.

Table 1. Comparison of previous works and our method. AD: Auxiliary data, RID: Recover individual data point, AF: Activation functions in target models, Opt: Optimization for recovering data points.

Method	Label-Free	AD-Free	RID	Batchsize $1 \longrightarrow larger$	AF-Free	Opt-Free
Hitaj et al., 2017 [6]		✓		✓	✓	
Zhu et al., 2019 [22]	✓	✓	✓	✓		
Geiping et al., 2020 [4]	✓	✓	✓	✓	✓	
Yin et al., 2021 [20]	✓		✓	✓	✓	
Schuster et al., 2022 [1]	✓	✓	✓	✓		✓
Ours	✓		✓	✓	✓	✓

In this paper, we assume the server owns auxiliary data that is independently and identically distributed with users' private trainsets. It could be testsets provided by users for validating model performance. And we should point out that recovered data points do not exist in auxiliary data. These are strong assumptions but can further reveal the great power of Gradient Inversion Attacks. Figure 2 demonstrates the main idea of our attack method. Firstly, the server constructs malicious model parameters with auxiliary data. Then tamper users' model parameters by sending malicious averaged gradients $\bar{g}$. Each user will compute gradients g_i on malicious model parameters and share them with the server. Finally, the server can recover users' private data by analyzing shared gradients g_i. Our attack is based on the direct data leakage [13] in the FC layer. However, gradient obfuscation in a batch hinders the data leakage effectively. So we utilize malicious model parameters to mitigate the obfuscation in shared gradients, making it possible to compromise privacy in large-batch FL. Figure 4 shows each recovered data point in a batch with our attack method. We successfully recover 59 of 64 data points in a batch perfectly.

Our main contributions are as follows:

(1) We analyze the direct data leakage in a FC layer theoretically in both one data training and mini-batch training. We confirm that large-batch training can not guarantee users' privacy in FL.

(2) We propose a novel Gradient Inversion Attack. Exploiting malicious model parameters, we can mitigate the obfuscation in shared gradients and compromise privacy in large-batch FL.
(3) We experimentally show that our method has a better performance and versatility compared with previous methods. We also explain the reasons for our outstanding performance on models using three different activation functions.

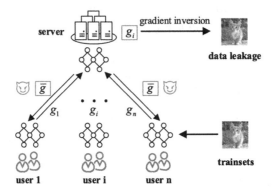

Fig. 2. The illustration of our attack method. The server tampers local models by delivering the malicious model parameters $\bar{g}$ to all users. Then the server can recover private trainsets successfully from shared gradients g_i which is computed on tampered local models.

2   Related Work

2.1   Federated Learning

Federated Learning [11] is a distributed learning paradigm which has gained much attention in recent years. Users cooperate to train a global machine learning model via a privacy-preserving way in which gradients are shared instead of private data. A central server trusted by most users coordinates the training process by iteratively aggregating users' gradients. In details, every user trains the global model with their local data (X_i, Y_i) in round k by optimizing the model parameters θ^k using a loss function $\mathcal{L}$. The server computes the average gradients $\frac{1}{N} \sum_{i=1}^{N} \nabla_\theta \mathcal{L}_{\theta^k}(X_i, Y_i)$ with N users' shared gradients. The latest average gradients are sent back to individual users and they can update local models according to Eq. (1). This process is called as federated SGD and will continue for many rounds until the global model converges.

$$\theta^{k+1} = \theta^k - \tau \frac{1}{N} \sum_{i=1}^{N} \nabla_\theta \mathcal{L}_{\theta^k}(X_i, Y_i) \tag{1}$$

2.2 Gradient Inversion Attack

GAN-Based Methods. Hitaj *et al.* [6] firstly propose a GAN-based method to compromise privacy in FL. The GAN procedure pits a discriminative deep learning network D against a generative deep learning network G. They use the global model in FL as network D to help network G generate victim's data. Wang *et al.* [16] proposed mGAN-AI which works "invisibly" on the server side. It enables a malicious server to target any client and compromise the client-level privacy. However, these GAN-based methods can only be used to generate class-wise data, not specific data points.

Optimization-Based Methods. The idea of optimization-based methods is to generate fake data which can produce the similar gradients with real data. To recover original data (x^*, y^*) from gradients $\nabla_\theta \mathcal{L}_\theta(x^*, y^*)$, DLG [22] formulates it as the problem of

$$\min_{x,y} ||\nabla_\theta \mathcal{L}_\theta(x, y) - \nabla_\theta \mathcal{L}_\theta(x^*, y^*)||^2 \qquad (2)$$

and solve this optimization problem with an L-BFGS solver. Zhao *et al.* [21] find that the ground truth label y^* can be directly obtained from gradients, making DLG more stable and efficient. However, DLG works poorly on neural networks with *ReLU* layers. As L-BFGS slover requires the model parameters are third order derivable while *ReLU* makes higher-order derivatives discontinuous. To make optimization-based methods more general, Geiping *et al.* [4] use the cosine similarity to calculate the distance between fake and true gradients and solve it with an Adam solver. The cosine similarity can compute both norm magnitude and direction of gradients and improves the effectiveness of attacks. The very recent work [7, 20] introduce prior knowledge to constrain the search space of the optimization problem and achieve a better result.

Malicious Parameters Methods. Different from two former methods, malicious parameters methods [1, 2, 17] introduce a dishonest server who can tamper gradients sent to users purposely. Fowl *et al.* [2] insert an *imprint module* into the global model as a special layer to reveal private data. Improved methods without modification of model architecture are proposed in [1]. They initialize users' model parameters adversarially to recover private data in large-batch training. However, their method only perform well on models using *ReLU* layers. In this study, we construct more effective malicious parameters with auxiliary data. We can recover more data than [1] on models using three different activation functions.

3   Method

3.1   Threat Model

In FL, users and a central server cooperate to train a global model according to the federated SGD. The server intends to recover users' local trainsets from shared gradients. We assume the server has auxiliary data such as users' testsets which is used to construct malicious model parameters $\hat{\theta}$. The server can tamper users' normal model parameters θ_u as $\hat{\theta}$ by sending malicious averaged gradients $\bar{g} = \hat{\theta} - \theta_u$. Then users train models on one batch of local data and share gradients with the server. From shared gradients, the server can recover many private data points. We will investigate the strength of Gradient Inversion attack via malicious model parameters.

3.2   The Direct Data Leakage from Gradients

Data Leakage in Single-Data Training. Firstly, we introduce the direct leakage of single data point in a biased FC layer. It was found in prior works [13,22] and inspires our method in this study.

For a biased FC layer followed by a *ReLU* activation function, we let $W \in \mathbb{R}^{m \times n}$ denote the weights and $B \in \mathbb{R}^m$ denotes the bias. The output y_i of ith neuron with the input $x \in \mathbb{R}^n$ is computed as

$$y_i = w_i^T x + b_i \tag{3}$$

where w_i and b_i are the ith row of W and B respectively. By back propagation, we obtain the gradients of loss function $\mathcal{L}$ w.r.t weights w_i and bias b_i as

$$\frac{\partial \mathcal{L}}{\partial w_i^T} = \frac{\partial \mathcal{L}}{\partial y_i} \cdot \frac{\partial y_i}{\partial w_i^T} = \frac{\partial \mathcal{L}}{\partial y_i} \cdot x \tag{4}$$

and

$$\frac{\partial \mathcal{L}}{\partial b_i} = \frac{\partial \mathcal{L}}{\partial y_i} \cdot \frac{\partial y_i}{\partial b_i} = \frac{\partial \mathcal{L}}{\partial y_i} \tag{5}$$

Joint Eq. (4) and Eq. (5), the single input x is recovered perfectly as

$$x = \frac{\partial \mathcal{L}}{\partial w_i^T} \cdot \left(\frac{\partial \mathcal{L}}{\partial b_i}\right)^{-1} \tag{6}$$

if there exists any neuron in this FC layer with $\frac{\partial \mathcal{L}}{\partial b_i} \neq 0$. For fully connected neural networks (FCNN), we can recover its single input from gradients of the first FC layer directly.

Data Leakage in Mini-Batch Training. In practical scenarios, the batchsize is usually set as 32, 64 or greater values. For mini-batch training, we find that

Proposition 1. *Consider a FC layer trained on a batch of data, the recovered data $\tilde{x}$ computed from aggregated gradients is a linear combination of each original input.*

Proof. When training on a batch of N data points, aggregated gradients $\frac{\partial \mathcal{L}}{\partial w_i^T}$ and $\frac{\partial \mathcal{L}}{\partial b_i}$ of the ith neuron are the average value of gradients computed on each data. The aggregated gradients can be written as

$$\frac{\partial \mathcal{L}}{\partial w_i^T} = \frac{1}{N} \sum_{j=1}^{N} \frac{\partial \mathcal{L}}{\partial y_{i,j}} \cdot \frac{\partial y_{i,j}}{\partial w_{i,j}^T} = \frac{1}{N} \sum_{j=1}^{N} \frac{\partial \mathcal{L}}{\partial y_{i,j}} x_j \tag{7}$$

$$\frac{\partial \mathcal{L}}{\partial b_i} = \frac{1}{N} \sum_{j=1}^{N} \frac{\partial \mathcal{L}}{\partial y_{i,j}} \cdot \frac{\partial y_{i,j}}{\partial b_{i,j}} = \frac{1}{N} \sum_{j=1}^{N} \frac{\partial \mathcal{L}}{\partial y_{i,j}} \tag{8}$$

So, the recovered data $\tilde{x}$ from gradients of the ith neuron can be computed as follows

$$\tilde{x} = \frac{\partial \mathcal{L}}{\partial w_i^T} \cdot \left(\frac{\partial \mathcal{L}}{\partial b_i}\right)^{-1} = \sum_{j=1}^{N} \alpha_j x_j \quad and \quad \alpha_j = \frac{\partial \mathcal{L}}{\partial y_{i,j}} \cdot \left(\sum_{n=1}^{N} \frac{\partial \mathcal{L}}{\partial y_{i,n}}\right)^{-1} \tag{9}$$

Here α_j is the factor of each data point x_j.

Equation (9) demonstrates that a large batchsize makes the recovered data more confusing and protects data privacy to a certain extent. It is a common solution applied in FL for defending against Gradient Inversion attacks and is useful for both GAN-based methods and optimization-based methods. However, the single-data-activated neuron (SDAN) in the FC layer still leaks privacy in large-batch training.

Definition 1. *(SDAN). Given a batch of training data $\{x_j | j = 1, 2, \cdots, N\}$. We call the ith neuron as an SDAN w.r.t data x_t if its output $y_{i,j} = w_i^T x_j + b_i \leqslant 0$ for all $j \neq t$ where w_i, b_i are the weights and bias of the ith neuron.*

If the ith neuron followed by a *ReLU* layer is an SDAN w.r.t x_t, the output $z_{i,j} = \max(y_{i,j}, 0) = \max(w_i^T x_j + b_i, 0) = 0$ for all $j \neq t$. And the gradients $\frac{\partial \mathcal{L}}{\partial y_{i,j}}$ will be 0 for all $j \neq t$. The *ReLU* layer blocks the gradients on the data with a negative output. So the aggregated gradients are only related with data x_t. The factor $\alpha_j = 0$ for all $j \neq t$ and Eq. (9) can be converted as $\tilde{x} = x_t$.

We find that data points can still be recovered perfectly via SDANs in large-batch training. As attackers, we expect more SDANs exist in the first FC layer. If every data point owns at least one SDAN in the first FC layer, we can recover the whole batch of data directly.

3.3 Constructing Malicious Model Parameters

SDANs can help us compromise privacy from aggregated gradients in large-batch training. However, there exists a small number of SDANs in a normal trained model. To amplify the leakage of private data, we find it is possible to generate more SDANs in the FC layer by constructing malicious model parameters.

Algorithm 1 shows our method of constructing malicious model parameters θ for the first FC layer. Firstly, we initialize the model parameters with Algorithm

3 proposed in [1]. It initializes parameters by sampling from the Gaussian distribution. This initialization can further improve the performance of our proposed method. In Sect. 4.3, we make comparative experiments to validate performances of our method with and without Algorithm 3.

Secondly, we train malicious parameters with auxiliary data to learn prior knowledge. The trained malicious parameters can generate more SDANs according to the feature distriubution of auxiliary data. In Algorithm 1, our objective is to make each data owns its SDAN and the locations of SDANs do not overlap with each other. To realize this objective, we select suitable neurons to be SDANs in each round of training. For the ith data x_i in one batch, compute its output $\mathbf{O}_i = Sigmoid(f(\theta, x_i)) \in \mathbb{R}^L$ passing through a FC layer f with L neurons followed by a $Sigmoid$ layer. The $Sigmoid$ layer scales the neuron outputs $f(\theta, x_i)$ in the range $(0, 1)$. If we want the tth neuron to be the SDAN w.r.t x_i, the output $f_t(\theta, x_i)$ of the tth neuron should be a big positive value and outputs $f_j(\theta, x_i)$ of other neurons should be small negative values. So $\mathbf{O}_{i,t}$ should be close to 1 and $\mathbf{O}_{i,j}$ for $j \neq t$ should be close to 0. For each data, we calculate the gradients $\nabla_\theta l(\mathbf{O}_i, t)$ of **negative log likelihood loss** function l to update malicious model parameters. The malicious model parameters θ can be expressed as

$$\theta \leftarrow \arg\min_\theta \mathbb{E}_{x_i \sim D_{aux}} \left[-log(Sigmoid(f_{t_i}(\theta, x_i))) \right] \tag{10}$$

where t_i is the index of the SDAN w.r.t each data x_i.

Comparing with artificial assignments of SDANs, we let each data choose their best SDANs automatically in the training process. Algorithm 2 *TopkIndex* shows the selection of SDANs of each data. The list $\mathbf{S}$ records the neurons those have already been chosen as SDANs by other data in the same batch. The list $\mathbf{C}$ records the number of times each neuron is selected. Firstly, we exclude neurons in list $\mathbf{S}$ and neurons with a selected times greater than $\bar{c}$ which is the average value of $\mathbf{C}$. Then select the tth neuron as the SDAN w.r.t x_i when $\mathbf{O}_{i,t}$ is the largest among the remaining neurons. Additionaly, we set a parameter k to let each data select multiple neurons as SDANs. A suitable value of k can generate more SDANs and help us recover more data.

4   Experiments

In this section, we validate the performance of our proposed Gradient Inversion attack. We introduce the metric **Recovery Ratio** R_{40dB} which is the percentage of recovered data in a batch. R_{40dB} is defined as

$$R_{40dB} = \frac{N_{40dB}}{B} \tag{11}$$

where N_{40dB} is the number of recoverd data with **PSNR** greater than $40dB$ and B is the number of data in a batch. The recovered data with a PSNR of $40dB$ can be considered to be the same as original data. As the mean square error between two figures is smaller than $1e - 4$.

Algorithm 1. Malicious Parameters Training

Input:

    θ: parameters of one FC layer f with L neurons

    k: the number of neurons to select per data

    η: learning rate

    D_{aux}: auxiliary data

    N: training batchsize

Output:

    θ: malicious model parameters

1: $\theta \leftarrow ParametersInitialization(\theta, \mathcal{N}(\mu, \sigma), s)$
2: $\mathbf{C} \leftarrow \mathbf{0}$ where $|\mathbf{C}| = L$
3: $\bar{c} \leftarrow \frac{1}{L} sum(\mathbf{C})$
4: **for** $r \leftarrow 1$ to $\lfloor \frac{|D_{aux}|}{N} \rfloor$ **do**
5:     $\mathbf{S} \leftarrow \emptyset$
6:     **for** $i \leftarrow 1$ to N **do**
7:         $\mathbf{O}_i = Sigmoid(f(\theta, x_i))$
8:         $\mathbf{T}_i = TopkIndex(\mathbf{O}_i, k, \mathbf{S}, \mathbf{C}, \bar{c})$
9:         $g_i \leftarrow (1/|\mathbf{T}_i|) \sum \nabla_\theta l(\mathbf{O}_i, t)$ where $t \in \mathbf{T}_i$
10:        $\mathbf{S} \leftarrow \mathbf{S} \cup \mathbf{T}_i$
11:        **for each** $t \in \mathbf{T}_i$ **do**
12:            $\mathbf{C}_t \leftarrow \mathbf{C}_t + 1$
13:        $\bar{c} \leftarrow \frac{1}{L} sum(\mathbf{C})$
14:     $\bar{g} \leftarrow \frac{1}{N} \sum_{i=1}^{N} g_i$
15:     $\theta \leftarrow \theta - \eta \bar{g}$
16: **return** θ

Algorithm 2. TopkIndex

Input:

    $\mathbf{O}_i$: the output computed on data x_i

    k: the number of neurons to select per data

    $\mathbf{S}$: indexes of neurons that has been selected in one batch training

    $\mathbf{C}$: the number of times each neuron is selected

    $\bar{c}$: the average value of elements in $\mathbf{C}$

Output:

    $\mathbf{T}_i$: indexs of neurons selected by data x_i

1: $\mathbf{T}_i \leftarrow \varnothing$
2: **for each** $s \in \mathbf{S}$ **do**
3:     $\mathbf{O}_{i,s} \leftarrow 0$
4: **for** $j \leftarrow 1$ to $|\mathbf{C}|$ **do**
5:     **if** $\mathbf{C}_j > \bar{c}$ **do**
6:         $\mathbf{O}_{i,j} \leftarrow 0$
7: **While** $k > 0$ **do**
8:     $t \leftarrow \arg\max \mathbf{O}_{i,t}$
9:     $\mathbf{T}_i \leftarrow \mathbf{T}_i \cup \{t\}$
10:     $\mathbf{O}_{i,t} \leftarrow 0$
11:     $k \leftarrow k - 1$
12: **return** $\mathbf{T}_i$

Algorithm 3. Parameters Initialization

Input:

    θ: weights (n dimensions) and bias of one FC layer with l neurons, $\theta \in \mathbb{R}^{l \times (n+1)}$

    $\mathcal{N}(\mu, \sigma)$: the Gaussian distribution with mean μ and std σ

    s: the scaling factor

Output:

    θ: initialized parameters of one FC layer

1: **for** $i \leftarrow 1$ to l **do**

2:     $\mathbf{N} \leftarrow \{j | j \sim \mathcal{U}(1, n)\}$ where $\mathcal{U}$ is the Discrete uniform distribution and $|\mathbf{N}| = \frac{n}{2}$

3:     $\mathbf{P} \leftarrow \{j | j \in \{1, 2, 3, \cdots, n\}, j \notin \mathbf{N}\}$

4:     $\mathbf{z}_- \sim \mathcal{N}(\mu, \sigma)$ and $|\mathbf{z}_-| = \frac{n}{2}$

5:     $\mathbf{z}_+ \leftarrow -s * \mathbf{z}_-$

6:     $\theta_i[\mathbf{N}] \leftarrow Shuffle(\mathbf{z}_-)$

7:     $\theta_i[\mathbf{P}] \leftarrow Shuffle(\mathbf{z}_+)$

8: **return** θ

Our method can be applied to attack both the fully connected neural network (FCNN) $\mathcal{M}1$ and the convolutional neural network (CNN) $\mathcal{M}2$. Two models used in experiments are listed in Table 2. We construct malicious parameters for the first FC layer according to Algorithm 1. If the model is $\mathcal{M}2$, we use the method in [1] to set the parameters of convolutional layers. It makes convolutional layers transmit data unaltered up to the first FC layer. Figure 3 shows the detailed parameters of first three filters of each convolutional layer. The first three channels stay the same as original data after the operation of CNN. Then we can recover original data from gradients of the first FC layer in models.

We use two different datasets, namely Fashion MNIST [18] and CIFAR100 [9]. In our experiments, the server as an attacker constructs malicious model parameters with auxiliary data (testsets of each datasets), trying to recover users' private data (trainsets of each datasets).

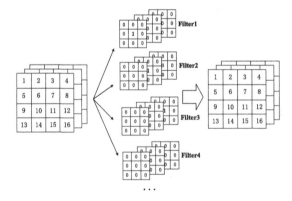

Fig. 3. Malicious model parameters of filters in convolutional layers in $\mathcal{M}2$.

4.1 Comparison with Previous Methods

We compare our method with work [1,13]. The performance of [13] is the baseline which represents the normal degree of data leakage in a FC layer. As the parameters of the FC layer in [13] are sampled from standard Gaussian distribution. For our method, we use the testsets to train malicious parameters with batchsize 64, $k = 4$ on CIFAR100 and with batchsize 64, $k = 1$ on Fashion MNIST. Fashion MNIST is used to train model $\mathcal{M}1$ and CIFAR100 is used to train model $\mathcal{M}2$. The training process runs for 300 epochs with the learning rate $\eta = 1e - 3$ in the first 200 rounds and $\eta = 1e - 4$ in last 100 rounds. For the method in [1], malicious model parameters are generated according to Algorithm 3 with mean $\mu = 0$, std $\sigma = 2$ and the scaling factor $s = 0.97$. Table 3 shows the recovery ratio R_{40dB} of three methods against gradients using different batchsize.

Table 2. The architectures of neural networks used in experiments. n: number of neurons, act: activation function, f: number of kernels, k: size of kernel, s: stride, p: size of padding.

$\mathcal{M}1$: FC NN Architecture	$\mathcal{M}2$:CNN Architecture
Dense(n=1024, act=relu)	Conv(f=6, k=3, s=1, p=1, act=relu)
Dense(n=2048, act=relu)	Conv(f=12, k=3, s=1, p=1, act=relu)
Dense(n=3072, act=relu)	Conv(f=24, k=3, s=1, p=1, act=relu)
Dense(n=2048, act=relu)	Flatten()
Dense(n=1024, act=relu)	Dense(n=1024, act=relu)
Dense(n=Number of classes, act=None)	Dense(n=Number of classes, act=None)

Table 3. Recovery-ratio $R_{40dB}(\%)$ of three methods against gradients using different training batchsize B.

	FashionMNIST			CIFAR100		
	[13]	[1]	Proposed	[13]	[1]	Proposed
$B = 64$	45.92 ± 4.98	66.10 ± 5.54	$\mathbf{99.58 \pm 0.86}$	59.46 ± 5.77	95.92 ± 2.75	$\mathbf{97.87 \pm 1.82}$
$B = 128$	27.47 ± 2.94	44.94 ± 4.09	$\mathbf{96.91 \pm 1.81}$	45.27 ± 4.21	85.08 ± 3.51	$\mathbf{91.98 \pm 2.66}$
$B = 256$	14.40 ± 1.84	31.04 ± 3.03	$\mathbf{81.40 \pm 2.91}$	26.74 ± 3.31	67.73 ± 4.00	$\mathbf{77.16 \pm 3.02}$
$B = 512$	8.08 ± 2.14	18.75 ± 3.78	$\mathbf{46.03 \pm 5.67}$	12.85 ± 1.47	43.06 ± 2.73	$\mathbf{53.96 \pm 2.54}$

Compared with two other methods, our method has advantages in two aspects:

High Recovery Ratio. In general, our method performs better that others in all cases. Figure 4 illustrates all images in a batch recovered by our proposed method. Results of [13] is the normal degree of direct data leakage in FC layers. With the batchsize B gets larger, the average data leakage of each batch in

[13] decreases from 45.92% to only 8.08% on Fashion MNIST. It demonstrates that a large batchsize can prevent privacy leakage. With the help of malicious parameters, our method and [1] both can recover more data points than [13]. Compared with [1], R_{40dB} of our method is about 30% higher on Fashion MNIST and 10% higher on CIFAR100 when $B = 512$. As the auxiliary data contain the prior knowledge of trainsets of users. The training process makes the malicious parameters adaptive to the distriubution of users' local data, generating more SDANs in the first FC layer. We further increase the upper bound of Gradient Inversion attacks via malicious model parameters.

High Stability. The standard deviation of our method is lower than others in most cases. As the training of malicious parameters in our method can get the maximum expected value of recovery ratios for different batches of data. It is an important feature for active attacks. Considering the victims have a possibility to detect the malicious parameters, we expect to recover more data points in a small rounds of attacks. The low deviation can ensure the success of our attacks. While work [1,13] sample parameters from Gaussian distriubution, it brings much instability.

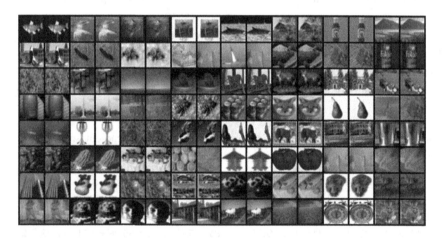

Fig. 4. The recovered data of our attack against gradients trained on one batch of 64 data points. The odd columns show the original figures and the even columns show the recoverd figures. We can reconstruct 59 of 64 data points perfectly.

4.2   Performance on Models Using Different Activation Functions

Methods in [1,13] and ours are all based on the direct data leakage caused by *ReLU*. However, our method can perform well on models using different activation functions which is challenging to other methods. We further improve the versatility of these Gradient Inversion attacks based on malicious parameters.

In this section, we validate the performance of three methods on the model $\mathcal{M}1$ using different activation functions, including *ReLU*, *Tanh* and *Sigmoid*. The results are shown in Table 4. As we can see, our method achieves a much higher recovery ratio than others when the model uses *Tanh* and *Sigmoid*.

Table 4. Recovery ratio $R_{40dB}(\%)$ of three methods on the model $\mathcal{M}1$ using different activation functions.

	Fashion MNIST			CIFAR100		
	[13]	[1]	Proposed	[13]	[1]	Proposed
ReLU	45.76 ± 4.99	66.88 ± 5.53	$\mathbf{99.55 \pm 0.91}$	63.50 ± 5.48	95.37 ± 2.84	$\mathbf{97.88 \pm 1.87}$
Tanh	20.04 ± 4.45	15.61 ± 4.59	$\mathbf{94.21 \pm 3.77}$	55.18 ± 6.01	16.66 ± 5.05	$\mathbf{88.85 \pm 3.89}$
Sigmoid	4.99 ± 2.10	4.15 ± 2.32	$\mathbf{73.22 \pm 6.96}$	39.93 ± 7.14	11.71 ± 4.85	$\mathbf{71.37 \pm 5.99}$

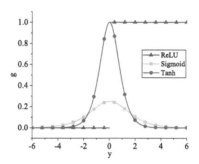

Fig. 5. The gradients of three activation functions.

To explain the reason why our method is more effective for different activation functions, we should analyze the outputs of neurons. In Sect. 3.2, we expect each neuron can output a positive value PO on one specific data (positive data points) and output negative values NO on other data (negative data points). Because *ReLU* truncats the gradients, the factors α of negative data points all equal 0 in Eq. (9). While gradients of *Tanh* and *Sigmoid* are continuous as shown in Fig. 5. In this case, we can still recover data of high quality if the factor of the positive data point is large enough and those of negative data points are small enough.

We denote the outputs of neurons as y and outputs of activation functions as $z = AF(y)$. From Eq. (9), we know $\alpha_{i,j} \propto \frac{\partial \mathcal{L}}{\partial y_{i,j}}$. Due to $\frac{\partial \mathcal{L}}{\partial y_{i,j}} = \frac{\partial \mathcal{L}}{\partial z_{i,j}} \frac{\partial z_{i,j}}{\partial y_{i,j}}$, we find that $\alpha_{i,j} \propto \frac{\partial \mathcal{L}}{\partial y_{i,j}} \propto \frac{\partial \mathcal{L}}{\partial z_{i,j}} \frac{\partial z_{i,j}}{\partial y_{i,j}} \propto \frac{\partial z_{i,j}}{\partial y_{i,j}}$. The gradients of activation functions $g_{i,j} = \frac{\partial z_{i,j}}{\partial y_{i,j}}$ have an important influence on performance of data recovery. Figure 5 shows the gradients g of three activation functions $w.r.t$ the input y. So PO should be small but positive to increase the gradient g and the factor α of positive data points will get larger. NO should be small enough to decrease g and the factor α of negative data points will get smaller.

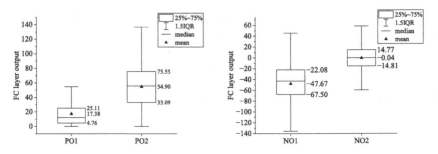

(a) The distribution of outputs on positive data points.

(b) The distribution of outputs on negative data points.

Fig. 6. The distribution of neuron outputs on positive and negative data points.

We trained the model $\mathcal{M}1$ on CIFAR100. On the first FC layer, we collected outputs of specific neurons from which we can recover data with PSNR greater than 40 dB. Figure 6 illustrates the distribution of PO and NO of our method ($PO1$, $NO1$) and the method in [1] ($PO2$, $NO2$). Obviously, $PO1$ are smaller positive values than $PO2$ for positive data points. $NO1$ are smaller negative values than $NO2$ for negative data points. So our method can make the factor of positive data larger than that of negative data. And we can recover more data points from aggregated gradients in the case of *Tanh* and *Sigmoid*.

From Fig. 5, we also find that the gradient of *Tanh* decreases much faster than that of *Sigmoid*. It makes more negative data points have a lower factor in recoverd data. So the recovery ratios in the case of *Tanh* are generally higher than those in the case of *Sigmoid*.

4.3 Factors Affecting the Performance of Our Method

Local Gradient Update. In practical FL, users will update their model parameters for several epochs and then send gradients to the central server. The local updates may change our malicious parameters and decrease the recovery ratio. Figure 7 shows the variation of recovery ratio with local training epochs. In each epoch, the user trains local models with 10 batches of data and the batchsize is 64. As we can see, the recovery ratio can remain the same if the user uses a small learning rate $1e-3$ or $5e-3$. The largest learning rate $5e-2$ makes the recovery ratio decrease from 0.98 to 0.52 only in one epoch. So the performance of our attack depends on the local learning rate and epochs. If local updates make small changes to the malicious parameters, our method can still recover much original data.

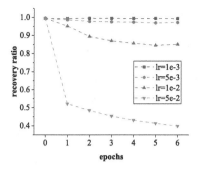

Fig. 7. The recovery ratio dependent on the local training epochs and learning rate in practical FL.

The Initialization of Malicious Parameters. In Algorithm 1, we use Algorithm 3 proposed by [1] to initialize parameters before training. Figure 8 shows the impact of parameter initialization on performance of our method. Without parameter initialization, our method can have the similar recovery ratio with [1] on *ReLU* in Fig. 8(a), but have higher recovery ratios on *Tanh* and *Sigmoid* in Fig. 8(b). In this study, we innovatively combine the method of sampling from Gaussian distriubution with the training of malicious parameters. Our method achieves the highest recovery ratios in cases of any batchsize and any activation functions. Overall, our work further improves the effectiveness and generality of Gradient Inversion Attacks based on malicious model parameters.

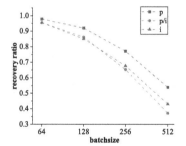
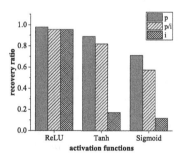

(a) Performances of three cases on models using *ReLU*.

(b) Performances of three cases on models using different activation functions.

Fig. 8. Impacts of parameters initialization on performance of our method. p: our proposed method, i: the parameters initialization in [1], p/i: our method without parameters initialization.

The Number of Neurons to Select Per Data. In Algorithm 2, we let each data select k neurons to be its SDANs. We make numerous experiments to investigate the impact of k on performance of our method. Figure 9 shows the recovery ratios R_{40dB} on different values of k. When $k = 1, 2, 4$, we can obtain high recovery ratios. The best value of k is 4 on CIFAR100 and 1 on Fashion MNIST. We think setting $k = 1$ is more suitable for datasets with a small interclass distance such as MNIST and Fashion MNIST. In these datasets, images of the same class are similar and more likely to activate the same neuron. So letting each data select only one neuron can achieve higher recovery ratios. For CIFAR100, the interclass distance is larger. Setting $k = 4$ can generate more SDANs for each data point and improve the performance of our Gradient Inversion Attack.

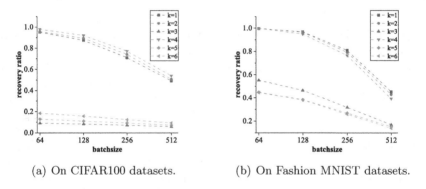

(a) On CIFAR100 datasets.   (b) On Fashion MNIST datasets.

Fig. 9. The impact of different k on recovery ratios R_{40dB}.

5   Conclusion

In this paper, we have proposed a novel Gradient Inversion Attack to compromise privacy in large-batch FL. Our attack is based on the direct data leakage from a FC layer. It is a common way to reveal privacy from gradients. However, we find that a large batchsize can obfuscate gradients and defense against this attack effectively. To mitigate the confusion of gradients, we design a method to construct malicious model parameters purposely. The server can tamper local model parameters before users compute gradients. From users' shared gradients, nearly the whole batch of private data can be recovered perfectly. Experiments show that our method performs better not only on large-batch trainings, but also on models using different activation functions. We can recover 97%, 77% and 54% of the data points in a batch with batchsize 64, 256 and 512, respectively. Our work further reveals the power of Gradient Inversion Attacks in FL.

Acknowledgements. This work was supported by the National Key Research and Development Program of China (No. 2018YFB2100400). We also thanks Southeast University and Purple Mountain Laboratory. Thanks the Big Data Computing Center of Southeast University for supporting computing resources.

References

1. Boenisch, F., Dziedzic, A., Schuster, R., Shamsabadi, A.S., Shumailov, I., Papernot, N.: When the Curious Abandon Honesty: federated learning is not private. arXiv:2112.02918 [cs] (2021)
2. Fowl, L., Geiping, J., Czaja, W., Goldblum, M., Goldstein, T.: Robbing the Fed: directly obtaining private data in federated learning with modified models. arXiv:2110.13057 [cs] (2022)
3. Ganju, K., Wang, Q., Yang, W., Gunter, C.A., Borisov, N.: Property inference attacks on fully connected neural networks using permutation invariant representations. In: Proceedings of the 2018 ACM SIGSAC Conference on Computer and Communications Security, pp. 619–633. CCS '18, Association for Computing Machinery, New York, NY, USA (2018)
4. Geiping, J., Bauermeister, H., Dröge, H., Moeller, M.: Inverting gradients-how easy is it to break privacy in federated learning? Adv. Neural. Inf. Process. Syst. **33**, 16937–16947 (2020)
5. Goodfellow, I., et al.: Generative adversarial nets. In: Advances in Neural Information Processing Systems, vol. 27. Curran Associates, Inc. (2014)
6. Hitaj, B., Ateniese, G., Perez-Cruz, F.: Deep Models Under the GAN: information leakage from collaborative deep learning. In: Proceedings of the 2017 ACM SIGSAC Conference on Computer and Communications Security, pp. 603–618. CCS '17, Association for Computing Machinery, New York, NY, USA (2017)
7. Jeon, J., Kim, j., Lee, K., Oh, S., Ok, J.: Gradient inversion with generative image prior. In: Advances in Neural Information Processing Systems, vol. 34, pp. 29898–29908. Curran Associates, Inc. (2021)
8. Konečný, J., McMahan, H.B., Yu, F.X., Richtárik, P., Suresh, A.T., Bacon, D.: Federated Learning: Strategies for Improving Communication Efficiency. arXiv:1610.05492 [cs] (2017)
9. Krizhevsky, A., Hinton, G., et al.: Learning multiple layers of features from tiny images (2009)
10. Mahloujifar, S., Ghosh, E., Chase, M.: Property inference from poisoning. In: 2022 IEEE Symposium on Security and Privacy (SP), pp. 1569–1569 (2022)
11. McMahan, B., Moore, E., Ramage, D., Hampson, S., y Arcas, B.A.: Communication-Efficient Learning of Deep Networks from Decentralized Data. In: Artificial Intelligence and Statistics, pp. 1273–1282. PMLR (2017)
12. Melis, L., Song, C., De Cristofaro, E., Shmatikov, V.: Exploiting unintended feature leakage in collaborative learning. In: 2019 IEEE Symposium on Security and Privacy (SP), pp. 691–706 (2019)
13. Phong, L.T., Aono, Y., Hayashi, T., Wang, L., Moriai, S.: Privacy-preserving deep learning: revisited and enhanced. In: Batten, L., Kim, D.S., Zhang, X., Li, G. (eds.) ATIS 2017. CCIS, vol. 719, pp. 100–110. Springer, Singapore (2017). https://doi.org/10.1007/978-981-10-5421-1_9
14. Shokri, R., Shmatikov, V.: Privacy-preserving deep learning. In: Proceedings of the 22nd ACM SIGSAC Conference on Computer and Communications Security, pp. 1310–1321. CCS '15, Association for Computing Machinery, New York, NY, USA (2015)
15. Shokri, R., Stronati, M., Song, C., Shmatikov, V.: Membership inference attacks against machine learning models. In: 2017 IEEE Symposium on Security and Privacy (SP), pp. 3–18 (2017)

16. Wang, Z., Song, M., Zhang, Z., Song, Y., Wang, Q., Qi, H.: Beyond inferring class representatives: user-level privacy leakage from federated learning. In: IEEE INFOCOM 2019 - IEEE Conference on Computer Communications, pp. 2512–2520 (2019)
17. Wen, Y., Geiping, J., Fowl, L., Goldblum, M., Goldstein, T.: Fishing for user data in large-batch federated learning via gradient magnification. arXiv preprint arXiv:2202.00580 (2022)
18. Xiao, H., Rasul, K., Vollgraf, R.: Fashion-MNIST: a novel image dataset for benchmarking machine learning algorithms (2017)
19. Yang, Q., Liu, Y., Chen, T., Tong, Y.: Federated machine learning: concept and applications. ACM Trans. Intell. Syst. Technol. **10**(2), 12:1–12:19 (2019)
20. Yin, H., Mallya, A., Vahdat, A., Alvarez, J.M., Kautz, J., Molchanov, P.: See through gradients: image batch recovery via gradinversion, pp. 16337–16346 (2021)
21. Zhao, B., Mopuri, K.R., Bilen, H.: iDLG: improved deep leakage from gradients. arXiv:2001.02610 [cs, stat] (2020)
22. Zhu, L., Han, S.: Deep leakage from gradients. In: Yang, Q., Fan, L., Yu, H. (eds.) Federated Learning. LNCS (LNAI), vol. 12500, pp. 17–31. Springer, Cham (2020). https://doi.org/10.1007/978-3-030-63076-8_2

PMemTrace: Lightweight and Efficient Memory Access Monitoring for Persistent Memory

Yushuqing Zhang, Kai Lu$^{(\boxtimes)}$, Zhenwei Wu, and Wenzhe Zhang

College of Computer, National University of Defense Technology, Changsha, China
{zhangyushuqing20,kailu,zhenweiwu,wenzhezhang}@nudt.edu.cn

Abstract. Persistent memory gains increasing popularity in recent years. Many persistent memory systems leverage memory access monitoring to achieve user-transparent crash consistency enforcement. However, traditional program analysis-oriented memory access monitoring mechanisms incur prohibitive performance overheads in persistent memory applications. Especially, for applications developed for systems with hybrid DRAM and persistent memory, existing memory tracking approaches cannot distinguish volatile and persistent memory writes, which leads to significant unnecessary runtime cost.

This paper describes PMemTrace, a lightweight and efficient memory access monitoring approach for persistent memory. PMemTrace conducts best-effort pointer analysis to speculatively reduce as many redundant instrumentations to volatile writes as possible at compile time. Besides, PMemTrace enforces thread-local memory access permission control with the Memory Protection Keys (MPK) hardware primitive in recent Intel processors to track the mistakenly filtered persistent writes.

The evaluation results show that PMemTrace substantially outperforms the state-of-the-art memory tracking systems.

Keywords: Memory access monitoring · Memory protection key · Compiler instrumentation · Pointer analysis

1 Introduction

Persistent memory (PMEM) is a new kind of memory which offers data durability, byte-addressability, disk-like capacity, and DRAM-like speed at the same time [1]. These novel properties of persistent memory make it possible for programs to directly access persistent data via CPU load and store instructions instead of traversing the legacy block-oriented storage stack. Intel and Micron have released commercial Optane DC persistent memory to the market in April 2019. Though byte-grained data persistence is promising, it is not easy to build correct and high-efficient persistent memory applications, especially to ensure the crash-consistency [2].

Modern processors typically involve multiple levels of caches to achieve higher memory performance. The hardware-controlled cache line eviction policy makes

© Springer Nature Switzerland AG 2023
W. Meng et al. (Eds.): ICA3PP 2022, LNCS 13777, pp. 81–97, 2023.
https://doi.org/10.1007/978-3-031-22677-9_5

memory stores reach the main memory layer out of the program order. Programs have to deliberately perform enforced cache line eviction and memory fence operations to ensure correct recovery. To ease crash-consistency enforcement, a large number of persistent memory systems, such as durable memory transactions, persistent threads, durable data structures, have been proposed in recent years. Many of these systems incorporate memory monitoring mechanisms to transparently collect persistent write trace [3].

However, traditional analysis-oriented memory monitoring techniques, such as page protection, compiler instrumentation, etc., introduce prohibitive performance overheads in persistent memory programs [4–12]. Page protection-based memory monitoring collects page-grained memory traces through page fault handling. The target pages are firstly specified as read only. Once the program writes to a write-protected page, a page fault will be triggered. The page fault handler records the page access, then remove write-protection from this page thus that the faulting write could be completed. Several inherent drawbacks make protection-based memory monitoring sub-optimal for persistent memory. Firstly, page-level monitoring cannot take full advantages of the byte-addressability of persistent memory. Besides, only the first write to a page will trigger a protection fault. The program have to re-protect the target pages to collect more detailed access records. This further constrains the flexibility of protection-based method. Moreover, frequent access permission changes lead to frequent translation lookaside buffer (TLB) flushes, making protection-based monitoring less efficient.

Compiler instrumentation inject function calls around each write operation during compiling, it supports byte-granularity trace, and is more flexible than protection-based monitoring. Due to processors access DRAM and persistent memory via same set of memory instructions, compiler instrumentation cannot distinguish durable writes to persistent memory and volatile writes to DRAM. Thus, compiler instrumentation has to consequently monitor volatile writes and durable writes together. However, tracing volatile writes to DRAM is pointless in persistent memory system. Given that volatile writes dominate real word persistent memory applications [6], the redundant instrumentations are non-negligible.

Based on previous observation, we propose PMemTrace, a lightweight and efficient memory access monitoring solution dedicated for persistent memory. In particular, PMemTrace leverages alias analysis to speculatively avoid instrumentation to DRAM writes. Addressing the best-effort feature of alias analysis techniques, PMemTrace also incorporates lightweight thread-local memory access permission control via the Memory Protection Keys (MPK) hardware primitive in recent Intel processors to ensure each single write to persistent memory could be monitored, no matter how accurate the alias analysis method is.

In comparison of the state-of-theart NVthreads and PMThreads systems, PMemTrace substantially outperforms in the stress test running with zero to forty threads. Using the 100,000-scale ycsb dataset, we investigate the efficiency and accuracy of PMemTrace. The results report negligible false positive rate

(0–0.288%) and false negative rate (3.84–4.14%) compared to the percentage of correct instrumentation.

In summary, we make the following contributions:

- We propose a lightweight and high-efficient memory monitoring method dedicated for persistent memory systems. It will potentially ease the programming of persistent memory.
- We investigate an approach to combine static and dynamic memory monitoring methods and manage to achieve a solution that is insensitive to alias analysis accuracy.
- We explore the possibility to make more use of the newly-released MPK extensions to achieve more lightweight and flexible protection-based memory monitoring.

2   Related Work

Memory Techniques Employed in Existing Persistent Memory Systems. NVthreads [13] is a programming model that adds persistence to legacy multi-threaded C/C++ programs, it performs user-transparent memory access monitoring through page protection. NVthreads leverages synchronization operations, such as lock acquire and release, to determine the boundaries of failure-atomic regions. Each time the program enters a failure-atomic region, the runtime needs to write-protect the whole persistent memory heap so that the persistent writes in this region could be tracked. For applications with fine-grained failure-atomic regions, NVthreads will suffer considerable performance degradation due to frequent page faults. Atlas [14] and PMthreads [15] monitor persistent memory access via compiler instrumentation. Atlas incorporates a LLVM pass that inserts a call to the access tracking function before each memory store instruction, with the address and value passed to that function. As the processor access persistent memory and DRAM with a same set of memory instructions, it is impossible for the LLVM pass to statically determine either a memory store will modify persistent memory or not. Consequently, the LLVM pass has to conservatively instrument each individual store instruction, which incurs significant redundant tracking over DRAM writes. PMThreads provides a page fault handler for memory monitoring in addition to compiler instrumentation.

Distinguishing Durable and Volatile Memory Stores. There have been efforts in the literature that try to statically discriminate durable writes to persistent memory and volatile writes to DRAM [4,16–20]. AGAMOTTO [21] is a crash-consistency bug detection framework for persistent memory applications. It adopts symbolic execution to explore the state space of its target program. To prioritize exploration towards program locations that access persistent memory heavily, AGAMOTTO adopts pointer analysis to identify instructions modifying persistent memory. The pointer analysis procedure maps each pointer in the program to a set of memory locations. Pointers have non-empty intersections between the sets of the memory locations they mapped to are regarded as *aliased*. Besides, pointers returned by persistent memory allocations are considered as persistent pointers. AGAMOTTO treats memory stores taking operands *aliased* with persistent memory pointers as persistent writes.

3   PMemTrace Design

3.1   Architecture Overview

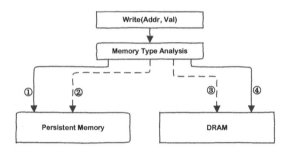

Fig. 1. PMemTrace architecture.

PMemTrace combines compiler instrumentation with page protection. The persistent heap is initially write-protected. The compiler pass incorporates a pointer analysis component that speculatively classifies memory write instructions into durable writes (solid arrows in Fig. 1) and volatile writes (dashed arrows in Fig. 1). For durable writes, a tracking function is inserted before the write instruction. Meanwhile, a durable write is surrounded with a pair of code snippets that respectively removes and recalls the write-protection over the persistent heap so that it could silently modify the write-protected persistent memory region without triggering a page fault (① in Fig. 1). Durable writes that are mis-predicted as volatile writes (② in Fig. 1) will be tracked in the page fault handler. Concerning volatile writes, mis-predictions (④ in Fig. 1) simply produce some redundant DRAM access records without affecting the correctness of PMemTrace.

3.2   Pointer Analysis

We employ the CFL-Steens algorithm for context-insensitive pointer alias analysis. The algorithm constructs a variable usage graph based on the CFL reachability formula proposed by Xin Zheng [22]. Each node is a memory location, and each edge is an action (dereference, reference, or assignment) that occurs at that memory location. Two variables are aliased if one value can reach another value's node through the graph, and the language formed by all actions conforms to a context-free grammar, as shown in Fig. 2.

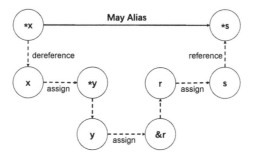

Fig. 2. Example of alias analysis.

CFL-Steens divides the alias types of two pointers into four types: `MustAlias`, `PartialAlias`, `MayAlias` and `NoAlias`. In order to avoid long-chain pointers that may exist in some persistent memory systems with epoch buffers, we use `MayAlias` to determine whether a write operation will access persistent memory objects. This method is more tolerant of the judgment criteria of aliases, which may cause false positives. However, false positives do not affect the correctness of memory traces compared to false negatives. The impact on performance is insignificant compared to the DRAM instrumentation overhead.

Through the algorithm outlined in Radu Rugina [23], CFL-Steens transforms the graph into a set of variables (n = variables) that may alias in $\mathcal{O}(n \log n)$ time, thus limiting the time of graph search for each query. The accuracy of this analysis is about the same as that of the first-level context-sensitive Steensgaard algorithm [24], with $\mathcal{O}(n)$ and $\mathcal{O}(n + m \log m)$ time complexity on trees and graphs, respectively, which is faster than the current Most alias analysis algorithms.

3.3 Lightweight Thread-Local Access Permission Control

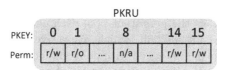

Fig. 3. PKRU register.

PMemTrace achieves lightweight thread-local access control leveraging the MPK extensions in recent Intel processors. MPK provides group-wise permission control via tagging memory pages with protection keys (`pkey`), it dedicates 4 previously unused bits in the page table entry (PTE) to a memory protection key, thus can provide up to 16 distinct page groups. Unlike traditional page protection mechanism, in which changing permissions involves expensive system calls and TLB invalidations, MPK inherently supports lightweight permission switching. In a MPK-capable CPU, each core has a userspace register PKRU with two separate bits (Access Disable and Write Disable) for each key, as shown in Fig. 3. User programs could access PKRU with the unprivileged RDPKRU and WRPKRU instructions to gain thread-local protection rights control.

Table 1. Linux kernel pkey-related system calls.

Syscall	Description
Pkey_alloc	pkey allocation
Pkey_free	pkey release
Pkey_mprotect	Tagging PTEs with pkey

4   Implementation

Linux has already incorporated system calls for interaction with the MPK hardware since kernel version 5.13 that deal with pkey allocation, pkey release, and pkey tagging.

```
1   int fd=open("/pmem/pool", O_RDWR);
2   void* pmem_pool=mmap(NULL, len, PROT_READ|PROT_WRITE, MAP_SHARED, fd, 0);
3   int pkey=pkey_alloc(0, PKEY_DISABLE_WRITE);
4   pkey_mprotect(pmem_pool, len ,PROT_READ|PROT_WRITE,pkey);
5   pkey_enable_write(pkey);
6   pkey_disable_write(pkey);
```

Fig. 4. Programming model.

Figure 4 shows how PMemTrace interacts with the MPK mechanism. More specifically, the code region from line 1 to 4 sets up the persistent memory pool, allocates a pkey, and tags the persistent pool with pkey. Line 5 and 6 in Fig. 4 give wrapper functions for WRPKRU, which respectively grants and withdraws WRITE permission to the pages tagged with pkey via modifying the PKRU register. In particular, line 3 sets the Write Disable bit of pkey in PKRU, indicates that the pkey-tagged pages are read only. Access flags passed into pkey_mprotect at line 4 (PROT_READ|PROT_WRITE) configures the corresponding page table entries of the persistent memory pool. The effective access permission is determined by the intersection of the ones specified in the page table entries and the PKRU register. Thus, Line 3 and 4 eventually write-protects the persistent memory pool.

As WRPKRU is a unprivileged instruction and the PKRU register is private to each core, permission control with pkey_enable_write and pkey_disable_write is extremely lightweight and inherently thread-local, which makes frequent fine-grained permission switching possible. In our evaluation, changing permission with `pkey_enable_write` and `pkey_disable_write` incurs less than almost 50% overhead (see details in Sect. 5).

We allocate a pkey to persistent memory at the same time as it is allocated. This process is implemented by changing the memory allocator hoard, and the user allocates and releases persistent memory through the two interface functions `xxmalloc` and `xxfree`.

With write-protection enforced, any write access to the persistent memory pool will violate the `pkey` restriction and send a `SIGSEGV` signal. Given the pointer analysis result, PMemTrace statically removes thus `pkey` restriction for the predicted durable writes that are expected to access persistent memory. Specifically, a `pkey_enable_write(pkey)` is inserted before each durable write instruction to make it execute silently without triggering a exception, with a `pkey_disable_write(pkey)` injected right after the durable write to re-protect the persistent memory pool.

The way to search for instrumented objects is given in Algorithm 1. Table 2 gives the notation descriptions in the pseudocode.

Table 2. Notation descriptions.

Notation	Descriptions
Ptr	The base address of PMEM
Need_trace	A boolean variable used to determine whether a function is worth tracing
AliasStores	The set of aliased instructions
NoAliasStores	The set of non-aliased instructions
StoreInst	Store instructions
CallInst	Call instructions

For durable writes omitted during best-effort pointer analysis, exceptions will be fired. PMemTrace registers a custom `SIGSEGV` signal handler to track the faulting write. To let the faulting instruction continue, the signal handler also clears the corresponding `Write Disable` bit of the `PKRU` value saved in the FPU context. When the signal handler returns, the value of the `PKRU` register is restored from the exception stack, the persistent memory pool becomes writable. To track subsequent uninstrumented modifications to the persistent memory pool, the memory pool has to be re-protected. Addressing this problem, PMemTrace conservatively inserts a `pkey_disable_write` on `pkey` after each write instruction that is considered as volatile write during pointer analysis.

Algorithm 1. Local Search Based Algorithm

Input: Function $\mathbb{F}$, global pointer ptr
Output: whether the function has been modified
1: need_trace ← false
2: **for** instruction $I \in \mathbb{F}$ **do**
3:    **if** I is a CallInst **then**
4:       **if** I calls xx_malloc **then**
5:          ptr ← I
6:       **else if** I is a memory call **then**
7:          need_trace ← true
8:       **end if**
9:    **end if**
10: **end for**
11: **for** instruction $I \in \mathbb{F}$ **do**
12:    **if** I is a StoreInst **then**
13:       **if** ptr && need_trace **then**
14:          **if** pointer of I and ptr is MayAlias **then**
15:             ++AliasStores
16:          **else**
17:             ++NoAliasStores
18:          **end if**
19:       **else**
20:          ++NoAliasStores.
21:       **end if**
22:    **else if** I is a CallInst **then**
23:       **if** I calls xx_free **then**
24:          ptr ← nullptr
25:       **end if**
26:    **end if**
27: **end for**
28: **return** false

---

5   Evaluation

5.1   Environment

All the experiments are executed on a dual-socket NUMA machine running Ubuntu 20.04, kernel 5.4.0. Each socket has an Intel(R) Xeon(R) Gold 6230 CPU @2.10 GHz, containing 20 physical cores, giving a system total of 40 physical cores (no hyperthreading). Each Xeon chip shares 55 MB of L3 cache between its 20 cores, and each core has 1.3 MB L1d cache, 1.3 MB L1i cache and 40 MB L2 cache. Each socket is populated with 32 GB of DRAM and 128 GB Optane DC persistent memory in App Direct mode, providing a total of 64 GB main memory and 256 GB persistent memory. All benchmarks are built with clang++ 6.0.1. The compiler instrumentation is implemented in LLVM 6.0.1. All figures report the average of 10 execution runs.

5.2 Performance

We first measure the overheads of memory tracking of PMemTrace, NVthreads and PMthreads on two different concurrent data structures. PMemTrace-F (PMemTrace without alias-analysis) and PMThreads-I tracks DRAM memory modifications at instruction-level. PMThreads-P that leverages page protection mechanisms to monitor DRAM writes PMThreads at page-level. The data structures considered are:

- FAST-FAIR, a concurrent persistent B+Tree. We instruct the tree node constructor (destructor) to allocate (release) tree nodes with xxmalloc (xxfree).
- Lock-Coupling List, a concurrent ordered linked list from synchrobench. Again, we replace malloc and free with xxmalloc and xxfree for persistent heap management of linked list nodes.

We analyse the scalability of PMemTrace via execution with the 1, 2, 4, 8, 10, 16, 20, 32, and 40 threads. For each read:write operations configuration(1:9, 1:1, 9:1), we run for a fixed number of operations and measure the throughput achieved by all the threads. For the B+tree, we generate 2,000,000 8-byte keys following the uniform distribution. The microbenchmark program dynamically generates 8-byte values for each insert. For all the evaluations towards B+tree, we insert 1,000,000 key-value pairs during the warming-up phase, and measure the aggregated throughput achieved in 1,000,000 operations under different read:write ratios. For the ordered linked list, the stress test program inserts 40,000 uniformly distributed elements to the list during warming up, and performs an extra 40,000 list operations with the configured read:write ratio.

Figure 5 and Fig. 6 give the aggregated throughput of all the threads. These figures demonstrate that, as parallelism increases, the throughput scales of PMemTrace surpasses all of others at close to 40 threads. Furthermore, the throughput results of PMemTrace-F and PMThreads-I show that MPK can reduce almost 50% overhead for instrumentation. Obviously less data is persisted in the linked list in comparison to the B+tree, leading to similar performance for PMemTrace, PMThreads and PMemTrace.

5.3 Efficiency

MPKs are applied in both trace paths, which enable page fault handlers to track memory total accurately with less overhead. We set up a pair of comparative versions, one that only uses the page fault handler setting MPK and one that instrumented every store instructions(Full-Instrumentation). Table 3 gives the overheads of Full-instrumentation and Only-Fault-handler for 100000, 200000, 400000, 800000, 1600000 storage operations (PM:DRAM = 1:1), concluding that even with a lightweight hardware protection mechanism, page fault handler is still inferior to Full-Instrumentation in performance.

Full-Instrumentation treats all store instructions in functions with memory calls as instrumentation objects and uses MPK to track them. Therefore, the

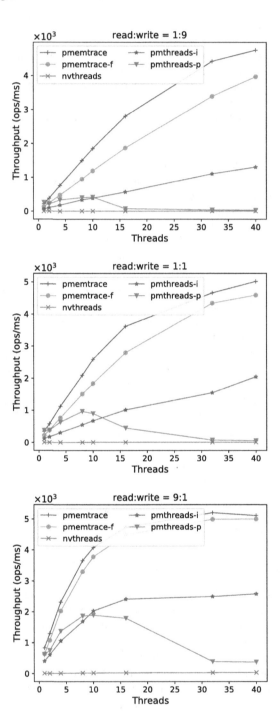

Fig. 5. Stress test B$^+$ tree.

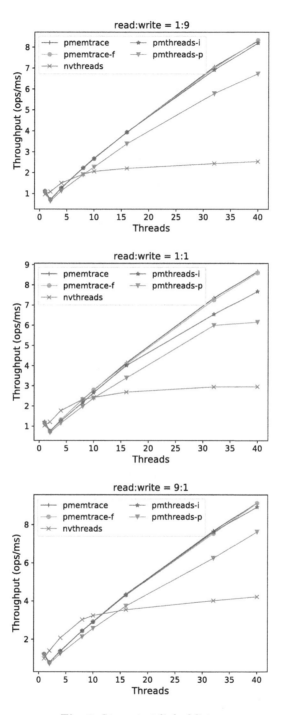

Fig. 6. Stress test linked list.

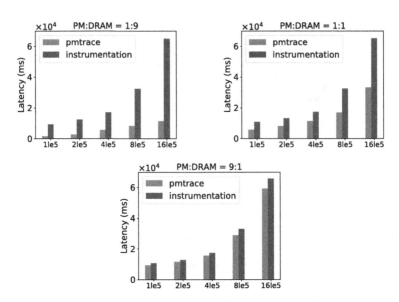

Fig. 7. Cost of different paths.

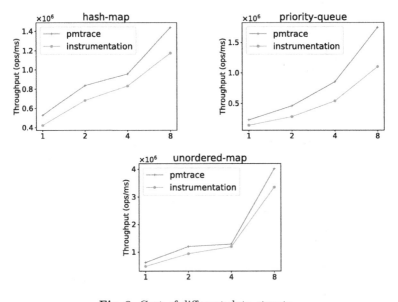

Fig. 8. Cost of different data structs.

Table 3. Latency at different operand sizes.

	100000	200000	400000	800000	1600000
Full-Instr.	16335	17164	28993	57549	116551
Only-Fault.	281901	542509	1079079	2150921	4299546

Table 4. Compile-phase alias pointers detection.

	Instructions	Percentage
May alias to PM	47	23.86%
No Alias to PM	150	76.14%

only performance difference between Full-Instrumentation and PMemTrace is due to alias analysis.

Table 4 lists the number of MayAlias store instructions and NoAlias store instructions found at the static compilation level. This result proves that PMem-Trace has a certain ability to distinguish writes to PMEM and DRAM at compile time, but does not reflect the actual overhead when the program has a large number of iterations. Therefore, we set three different PM/DRAM ratios (1:9, 1:1, 9:1), and adjusted the number of write operations to PMEM at data scales of 100,000, 200,000, 400,000, 800,000, and 1,600,000, and collect the runtime latencies of both. Figure 7 shows that PMemTrace results in lower latency as the proportion of writes to DRAM gradually increases, which is sufficient to demonstrate the benefit of alias analysis in filtering invalid instrumentation.

Since the effect of alias analysis is highly correlated with the proportion of persistent memory operations, we also tested the PMemTrace and Full-instrumentation overheads of of three common data structures hash map, priority queue, and out-of-order map persistence operations using 100,000-scale data in the yscb dataset. We evaluted the throughput of these three data structures executed by 1, 2, 4, and 8 threads. Figure 8 shows that operation scales of PMem-Trace are basically the same as the Full-instrumentation, but the performance is always better. We conclude that although MPK can greatly reduce latency, alias analysis is still necessary in the operation of general data structures.

5.4 Accuracy

This section will evaluate the accuracy of the two trace paths of PMemTrace while the program is running. We define PM_{true} to be PMEM store operations that are tracked and correctly detected, $DRAM_{false}$ to be falsely detected DRAM memory operations, and PM_{false} to be untracked but detected by our page fault Handler detected. Using the experimental conditions in the previous section, we select two data structures for one update corresponding to one persistence operation (vector) and multiple persistence operations (hash map), and measure the average of PM_{true}, $DRAM_{false}$ and PM_{false} under 1, 2, and 4 thread executions for them.

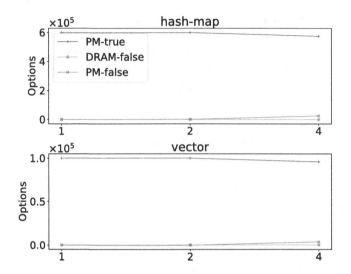

Fig. 9. Accuracy of hashmap and vector.

Figure 9 shows that as the parallelism increases, the average false positive rate of both data structures remains consistent, and the false negative rate increases slightly. We believe that alias analysis will lead to unavoidable instrumentation of some DRAM writes (e.g., prepare data) that are similar in time and space to PMEM writes. When the number of threads performing concurrent write operations increases, some instrumentation functions are not executed, and the corresponding write operations are tracked by the page fault handler.

Consider evaluation parameters as:

– False Positive Rate:

$$\frac{DRAM_{false}}{PM_{true} + DRAM_{false} + PM_{false}}$$

– False Negatives Rate:

$$\frac{PM_{false}}{PM_{true} + DRAM_{false} + PM_{false}}$$

Compared with uninstrumented persistent pointers, instrumentation of volatile pointers have no effect on the correctness of memory monitoring, therefore we used a wider standard of alias analysis. Table 5 shows that the false negative rate due to loose aliasing criteria is negligible, even 0% in single-threaded or dual-threaded execution.

Table 5. False positive & false negative rates.

HASH-MAP	False Positive Rate	False Negatives Rate
Thread-1	0%	0%
Thread-2	0%	0%
Thread-4	0%	4.144%
VECTOR	False Positive Rate	False Negatives Rate
Thread-1	0.288%	0%
Thread-2	0.288%	0%
Thread-4	0.288%	3.845%

6   Conclusion

This paper presents PMemTrace, a lightweight and efficient memory access monitoring approach optimized for persistent memory. The key insight of PMemTrace is to speculatively avoid redundant instrumentation on volatile memory writes. Leveraging the lightweight thread-local access permission control provided by the MPK hardware primitive in recent Intel CPUs, PMemTrace also captures the persistent memory accesses mistakenly omitted in the static analysis stage. Our evaluation results show that PMemTrace substantially outperforms existing memory access monitoring approaches and manages to save up to 76.14% unnecessary volatile writes instrumentation.

Acknowledgment. This work is supported by National High-level Personnel for Defense Technology Program (2017-JCJQ-ZQ-013), NSF 61902405, the National University of Defense Technology Foundation under Grant Nos. ZK20-09, the Natural Science Foundation of Hunan Province of China under Grant No. 2021JJ40692 and NUDT HPCL Research Fund 202101-04. Kai Lu is the corresponding author of this paper.

References

1. Zhang, W., Kai, L.U., Wang, X., Jian, J.: Fast persistent heap based on non-volatile memory. IEICE Trans. Inf. Syst. **100**(5), 1035–1045 (2017)
2. Baldassin, A., Barreto, J., Castro, D., Romano, P.: Persistent memory: a survey of programming support and implementations. ACM Comput. Sur. **54**, 1–37 (2021)
3. Fu, X., et al.: Witcher: systematic crash consistency testing for non-volatile memory key-value stores. In: Proceedings of the ACM SIGOPS 28th Symposium on Operating Systems Principles (2021)
4. Ly, D., Kosmatov, N., Signoles, J., Loulergue, F.: Soundness of a dataflow analysis for memory monitoring. ACM SIGAda Ada Lett. **38**(2), 97–108 (2019)
5. Wang, H. Zhai, J., Tang, X., Yu, B., Ma, X., Chen, W.: Spindle: informed memory access monitoring, in 2018 USENIX Annual Technical Conference (USENIX ATC 18). Boston, MA: USENIX Association, Jul. 2018, pp. 561–574. https://www.usenix.org/conference/atc18/presentation/wang-haojie

6. Nalli, S., Haria, S., Hill, M. D., Swift, M. M., Volos, H., Keeton, K.: An analysis of persistent memory use with whisper. In: Proceedings of the Twenty-Second International Conference on Architectural Support for Programming Languages and Operating Systems, ser. ASPLOS '17. New York, NY, USA: Association for Computing Machinery 45, pp. 135–148 (2017). https://doi.org/10.1145/3037697.3037730

7. Payer, M., Kravina, E., Gross, T. R.: Lightweight memory tracing. In: 2013 USENIX Annual Technical Conference (USENIX ATC 13). San Jose, CA: USENIX Association, pp. 115–126 (2013). https://www.usenix.org/conference/atc13/technical-sessions/presentation/payer

8. Laurenzano, M.A., Tikir, M.M., Carrington, L., Snavely, A.: PEBIL: efficient static binary instrumentation for Linux. In: IEEE International Symposium on Performance Analysis of Systems Software (2010)

9. Nethercote, N., Seward, J.: Valgrind: a program supervision framework. Electron. Notes Theoret. Comput. Sci. **89**(2), 44–66 (2003)

10. Luk, C.-K.: Pin: building customized program analysis tools with dynamic instrumentation, SIGPLAN Not., **40**(6), 190–200 (2005). https://doi.org/10.1145/1064978.1065034

11. Luk, C.-K.: Pin: building customized program analysis tools with dynamic instrumentation, ACM SIGPLAN notices, **40**(6), 190–200 (2005)

12. Kalbfleisch, S.,Werling, L., Bellosa, F.: Vinter: automatic non-volatile memory crash consistency testing for full systems. In: 2022 USENIX Annual Technical Conference (USENIX ATC 22). Carlsbad, CA: USENIX Association, pp. 933–950 (2022). http://www.usenix.org/conference/atc22/presentation/werling

13. Hsu, T. C.-H., Brügner, H., Roy, I., Keeton, K., Eugster, p.: Nvthreads: practical persistence for multi-threaded applications. In: Proceedings of the Twelfth European Conference on Computer Systems, ser. Euro Sys '17. New York, NY, USA: Association for Computing Machinery, pp. 468–482 (2017). https://doi.org/10.1145/3064176.3064204

14. Chakrabarti, D. R., Boehm, H.-J., Bhandari, k.: Atlas: leveraging locks for non-volatile memory consistency, SIGPLAN Not., **49**(10), 433–452 (2014). https://doi.org/10.1145/2714064.2660224

15. Wu, Z., Lu, K., Nisbet, A., Zhang, W., Luján, M.: PMThreads: persistent memory threads harnessing versioned shadow copies. In: Proceedings of the 41st ACM SIGPLAN Conference on Programming Language Design and Implementation, ser. PLDI 2020. New York, NY, USA: Association for Computing Machinery, pp. 623–637 (2020). https://doi.org/10.1145/3385412.3386000

16. Shang, L., Xie, X., Xue, J.: On-demand dynamic summary-based points-to analysis. In: Proceedings of the Tenth International Symposium on Code Generation and Optimization, ser. CGO '12. New York, NY, USA: Association for Computing Machinery, pp. 264–274 (2012). https://doi.org/10.1145/2259016.2259050

17. Sridharan, M., Bodík, R.: Refinement-based context-sensitive points-to analysis for java, SIGPLAN Not., **416**, 387–400 (2006). https://doi.org/10.1145/1133255.1134027

18. MSridharan, M., Gopan, D., Shan, L., Bodík, R.: Demand-driven points-to analysis for java, SIGPLAN Not., **40**(10), 59–76 (2005). https://doi.org/10.1145/1103845.1094817

19. Xu, G., Rountev, A., Sridharan, M.: Scaling CFL-reachability-based points-to analysis using context-sensitive must-not-alias analysis. In: Drossopoulou, S. (ed.) ECOOP 2009. LNCS, vol. 5653, pp. 98–122. Springer, Heidelberg (2009). https://doi.org/10.1007/978-3-642-03013-0_6

20. Yan, D., Xu, G., Rountev, A.: Demand-driven context-sensitive alias analysis for java. In: Proceedings of the 2011 International Symposium on Software Testing and Analysis, ser. ISSTA'11. New York, NY, USA: Association for Computing Machinery, pp. 155–165 (2011). https://doi.org/10.1145/2001420.2001440

21. Neal, I., et al.: AGAMOTTO: how persistent is your persistent memory application? In: 14th USENIX Symposium on Operating Systems Design and Implementation (OSDI 20). USENIX Association, pp. 1047–1064 (2020). https://www.usenix.org/conference/osdi20/presentation/neal

22. Zheng, X., Rugina, R.: Demand-driven alias analysis for C, SIGPLAN Not., **43**(1), 197–208 (2008). https://doi.org/10.1145/1328897.1328464

23. Zhang, Q., Lyu, M.R., Yuan, H., Su, Z.: Fast algorithms for DYCK-CFL-reachability with applications to alias analysis, SIGPLAN Not., **48**(6), 435–446 (2013). https://doi.org/10.1145/2499370.2462159

24. Steensgaard, B.: Points-to analysis in almost linear time. In: Proceedings of the 23rd ACM SIGPLAN-SIGACT Symposium on Principles of Programming Languages, ser. POPL'96. New York, NY, USA: Association for Computing Machinery, pp. 32–41 (1996). https://doi.org/10.1145/237721.237727

SeqTrace: API Call Tracing Based on Intel PT and VMI for Malware Detection

Zhenquan Ding[1,2], Yonghe Guo[3], Hui Xu[2(✉)], Longchuan Yan[3], Lei Cui[2], Yuanlong Peng[3], Feng Cheng[2], and Zhiyu Hao[2]

[1] School of Cyber Security, University of Chinese Academy of Sciences, Beijing, China
[2] Institute of Information Engineering, Chinese Academy of Sciences, Beijing, China
{dingzhenquan,xuhui,cuilei,chengfeng,haozhiyu}@iie.ac.cn
[3] State Grid Information and Telecommunication Branch, Beijing, China
372687651@qq.com, 49864286@qq.com, yuanlong-peng@sgcc.com.cn

Abstract. API-call sequence, a significant dynamic feature of the software, is widely applied to malware detection. Unfortunately, native approaches to API-call analysis are time-consuming and cause heavy performance penalties. To improve the efficiency of API-call analysis, this paper proposes a novel dynamic analysis approach named SeqTrace based on Intel Process Trace (PT) and Virtual Machine Introspection (VMI) technologies. First, we propose an API-call Tracing approach based on the Intel PT feature of the CPU. It leverages Intel PT to trace the execution of analyzed samples and logs relative information of their API calls with slight overhead. Then, to efficiently translate the semantics of API calls from logged information, we design Semantic Decoder based on VMI technology. Moreover, we implement a prototype API called SeqTrace on the QEMU/KVM platform and evaluate it through a set of experiments. Compared with previous approaches, the experimental results show that SeqTrace achieves API-call sequence tracing with fine-grained semantic information and reduces the tracing overhead by more than 80%.

Keywords: API call · Intel Process Trace · Virtual Machine Introspection · Malware analysis

1 Introduction

The API-call sequence is a significant dynamic feature of the software. Assisted by deep learning approaches [2–7], it is widely applied to malware detection. Most previous studies focus on improving the security and information accuracy of the API-call analysis. For example, CWSandbox [9] installs drivers or modules within a monitored OS to catch API-call sequences using API hooking and DLL injection. Within the same OS with malware, it is system-aware and easily bypassed. To solve the problem, Nitro [8] traces API using Virtual Machine

W. Meng et al. (Eds.): ICA3PP 2022, LNCS 13777, pp. 98–116, 2023.
https://doi.org/10.1007/978-3-031-22677-9_6

Introspection (VMI) technique. It is OS-agnostic because implemented on the virtual machine manager (VMM). However, it introduces heavy overhead for interpreting semantic information of processes in guest VM from raw data caught in the VMM layer. Unfortunately, more than 500 thousand malware are detected daily, according to the report [10]. Therefore, existing approaches are too time-consuming to analyze an increasing number of samples. Therefore, efficiency is as important as security and accuracy in malware analysis.

The critical challenge for achieving efficiency analysis is the semantic gap. Using existing approaches based on VMI, once catching an API in guest OS, it would suspend the VM, trapped into VMM and analyze semantic information in VMM. This trapping and analyzing mechanism is ineffective and introduces heavy performance penalty for guest VM. To solve this problem, some existing approaches deploy the analyzing system in guest OS to mitigate the semantic gap at the cost of security, which is fatal in malware detection. For timely and effective malware detection, we achieve an efficient and security approach for API-call analysis.

With this in mind, this paper proposes the dynamic analysis framework named SeqTrace. It first leverages hardware-based VMI to monitor the process creation and destruction behavior in guest VM. Once catching the creation behavior of the process we are concerned about, SeqTrace triggers CPU-embedded Intel PT to transparently and efficiently log the relative instruction sequence of the API call. Then, the logged instruction sequence is interpreted into an API-call sequence through a designed Intel PT decoder. Finally, Seq-Trace exports a serialized tree of API calls from the start to the end of one process, which can be used as an input feature of deep learning networks to distinguish whether it is malicious. To our knowledge, our proposed SeqTrace is the first system that combines Intel PT and VMI to trace API-calls sequence in VMM. Benefit from deployed in VMM, it is capable of tracking and analyzing malware in kernel space and user space with high security. With the assistance of Intel PT, it can capture and log malware behaviors with lower performance overhead. Specifically, the performance penalty of SeqTraces keeps below 15%. Especially, it is below 7% in CPU-intensive experiments. Moreover, compared to the Drakvuf approach, SeqTrace reduces the performance penalty by more than 80% in both IO-intensive and CPU-intensive experiments.

In summary, the main contributions of this paper are as follows:

First, we propose an IPT-based API-call Tracing approach, which leverages Intel PT to dynamically trace the execution of malware in real-time.

Second, to obtain API-call sequences, we design VMI-based Semantic Decoder to effectively translate the semantic information from the raw data caught by Intel PT component.

Last, we have implemented a prototype system named SeqTrace based on the QEMU-KVM virtualization platform and conducted a set of experiments to demonstrate its effectiveness.

The remaining of this paper is organized as follows. Section 2 introduces some background technologies. Section 3 describes the overview of our framework and shows how SeqTrace achieves API call analyzing with Intel PT and VMI. Section 4 illustrated the implementation details of our framework. We evaluate our SeqTrace in 5. Finally, Sect. 6 reviews related works and Sect. 7 conclude the work.

2   Background

2.1   Virtual Machine Introspection

Virtual Machine Introspection (VMI), which is first introduced in [11], provides a novel technique for tracing and analyzing the instantaneous state of the virtual machine in Virtual Machine Monitor (VMM). It leverages the advantage of hardware virtualization to silently intercepts semantic information of VM on-demand, such as the state of memory, I/O, and API call. It is OS-independent and OS-agnostic because it runs in the VMM. Therefore, it would not be compromised by malware running in guest OS except for VM escape, so it supports attacks analysis at the kernel level. Supported by hardware virtualization, VMI is to trigger VM trapping by setting some specific event registers, i.e., MSR, and then grabbing semantic information from VM. Unfortunately, the trapping mechanism would result in heavy performance overhead for VM because it could suspend VM for analysis. To capture more semantic information about VM execution, previous approaches usually sacrifice the VM's performance to catch more information.

2.2   Intel Processor Trace

As an embedded feature of the latest CPU hardware, Intel Process Trace (PT) [13] enables tracing the execution of processes with hardware assistance. It is able to fetch the complete control flows with a slight performance overhead. The flows traced by Intel PT are outlined and extracted in real-time and then stored in the forms of specific packets, including Taken/Not-Taken Packet (TNT), Target IP Packet (TIP), Flow Update Packet (FUP), and Page Information Packet (PIP). Each type of packet represents a different kind of branching information. For example, PIP packets record the switches of processes (i.e., change of CR3 registers) and the TIP packets indicate indirect call (i.e., call or ret) in process. The packets recorded by Intel PT are highly condensed and directly written to memory, so the performance overhead caused by Intel PT is slight. Due to this advantage, Intel PT has been widely used in control flow tracing and behavior analysis. However, packets captured by Intel PT are raw data, which is obscure and exists a semantic gap in VM behavior. Therefore, it requires semantic translation before application in the field of security analysis, which always depends on the information of the guest OS, such as kernel symbol.

3   Design of SeqTrace

This section will describe the design of SeqTrace. We start by presenting the architecture and the challenges to be addressed. Then, we propose an IPT-based API-call Catching Approach and VMI-based Semantic Decoder to tackle the challenges.

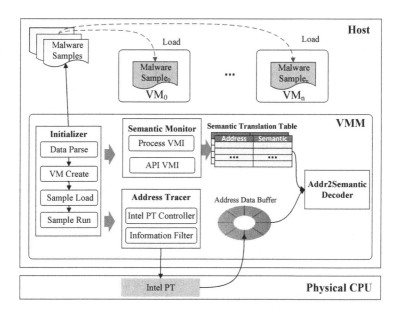

Fig. 1. The architecture of SeqTrace.

3.1   System Architecture

SeqTrace is an API-call analysis system for malware detection. It uses the technologies of VMI and Intel PT to effectively extract API-call sequences of malware samples. Its architecture consists of Initiator, Semantic Monitor, Process Tracer, and Addr2Semantic Decoder, as illustrated in Fig. 1. As the entrance to SeqTrace, Initializer is responsible for automatically creating virtual machine environments according to malicious samples and loading them into it for dynamical analysis. Then, Semantic Monitor, the semantics warehouse of SeqTrace, maintains a Semantic Translation Table of VM. It employs the VMI technology to monitor VM execution and seize process creation or API loading operations to dynamically update the Semantic Translation Table. To obtain the execution of a specific malware sample, Address Tracer is designed to catch API-call-related information by leveraging Intel PT technology. Meanwhile, a ring buffer named Address Data Buffer is created to store API information caught by Address Tracer. However, the data in Address Data Buffer is address sequences of procedure and API, and there is a semantic gap between these data and the execution feature of the malware sample, so it cannot be directly delivered into the analysis model for malware detection. Therefore, Addr2Semantic Decoder is designed to translate address sequences in Address Data Buffer into high-level semantic information according to the Semantic Translation Table.

There are two significant challenges in achieving SeqTrace and we will describe how to solve them in detail in the following subsections:

- Tracking the execution of process incurs a high-performance penalty for VM. To mitigate this penalty, we propose the IPT-based API-call Tracing Approach in Sect. 3.2.
- There is a semantic gap between the logged information and the behavior of the procedure. Therefore, we design a VMI-based Semantic Decoder to decode the logged information by Intel PT in Sect. 3.3.

3.2   IPT-Based API-Call Tracing Approach

The existing VMI-based API-call analysis approach is time-consuming because its trapping-and-analyzing mechanism causes a heavy performance penalty. To mitigate this problem, we introduce Intel PT technology to trace the API-call behavior of the procedure. As mentioned in Sect. 2.2, Intel PT could effectively trace execution and branch information of processes with negligible performance overhead. Unfortunately, it only logs address information of the process execution in the form of raw data. Therefore, it is a challenge to interpret the semantic data from logged raw data to get the API-call sequence.

To solve this problem, we propose the IPT-based API-call Tracing Approach. As illustrated in Sect. 2.2, it employs Intel PT to efficiently log the execution trace of the procedure and then extracts API-call-related information from logged information. However, hundreds of MB of data traced by Intel PT within one second lead to heavy pressure on Data Buffer and Decoder, which become a bottleneck in malware analysis. To narrow the data and reduces unnecessary computation, we introduce a VMI technology named Libvmi [14]. Specifically, by using information from VMI technology, Analysis Director can get the process information of running malware sample, including associated process id and which permission level it is running in. Then, Analysis Director dynamically adjusts the configuration of VM and setting of Intel-PT to trace specific processes at specific permission levels. Therefore, the data collected by Intel-PT would be strong pertinence.

As illustrated in Fig. 2, to achieve IPT-based API-call Tracing, the Analysis Director, QEMU-PT, and KVM-PT are running in user-land, QEMU, and KVM respectively. Firstly, the Analysis Director automatically probes the startup of VMs, obtains their information, and delivers the initial setting of Intel-PT to QEMU-PT. QEMU-PT runs in QEMU and listens to commands from user-land. Once receiving the settings of Intel-PT, it interacts with KVM-PT to set up Intel PT for execution tracing. During the malware execution, the Intel-PT would trace all procedures in the VM and store the data in Data Buffer. Meanwhile, Analysis Director gets the identifications of malware-associated procedures utilizing VMI data from the KVM-PT component and decoded by the QEMU-PT component. Then, Analysis Director targets the Intel-PT to specific malware procedures of VM. In this way, it minimizes the ranges of Intel-PT traces, thus mitigating the performance penalty caused by tracing and improving analysis performance.

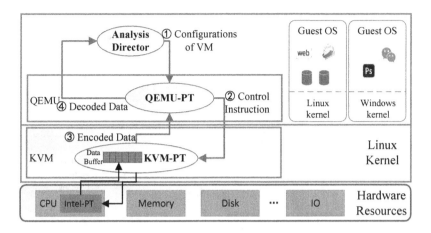

Fig. 2. The workflow of IPT-based API-call Tracing Approach.

3.3 VMI-Based Semantic Decoder

The data recorded by Intel PT are instructions with API addresses, thus there is a semantic gap between the recorded data and the behavior of malware. Therefore, it is difficult to recognize the feature of malware using the data recorded by Intel PT. Previous approaches utilize binary translation to obtain semantic information about malware. By Leveraging disassembled data, the analyzer can reconstruct a static API-call tree of the malware sample. However, there are two problems. Disassembled binary does not satisfy the requirements for dynamical analysis because it only provides the static feature. On the other hand, the approach of binary translation is unsuitable for non-binary malware samples. To accurately extract semantic information from dynamically recorded data by Intel PT, we propose a Semantic Decoder based on VMI technology.

The core idea of the VMI-based Semantic Decoder is to maintain semantic translation tables using VMI technology and then dynamically decode the logged address data into API-call sequences according to the semantic tables. As illustrated in Fig. 3, it mainly consists of three parts, i.e., data filtering, construction of semantic translation tables using VMI technology, and semantic decoding from address to API-call sequences. Next, we will introduce the workflow in detail.

Data Filtering. First of all, Intel PT traces the execution of malware samples and records their execution paths with several types of data packets. Because only two kinds of packets are relevant to API-call sequences, i.e., TIP and PIP packets, we should filter the recorded data by discarding any data other than these two types. Then, we catch switch operations of processes (i.e., change of CR3 registers) from PIP packets and get instructions about the indirect call (i.e., call or ret) from TIP packets. Specifically, PIP packets are produced when process switching and they record the value of CR3 registers (i.e., process address), so we can get the address of running processes from PIP packets. TIP packets

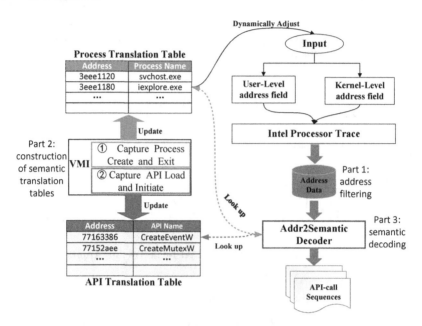

Fig. 3. The workflow of VMI-based Semantic Decoder.

indicate the call of an API function, so SeqTrace can obtain the API address from TIP packets.

Construction of Semantic Translation Tables. Since we have obtained the address sequences of Processes and APIs trigged by malware, we are only required to recognize what they are. Therefore, we build semantic translation tables to decode the address sequences leveraging VMI technology. Specifically, the APIs associated with Process switching, e.g., PspInsertProcess and PspExitProcess for Windows VM, are monitored by the VMI component to update the mapping between addresses and process names in the Process Semantic Translation Table. Meanwhile, the VMI component monitors the APIs associated with the indirect call, e.g., LdrpLoadDll and LdrpInitializeProcess, to dynamically maintain the API Translation Table.

Semantic Decoding. The address sequences of processes and APIs are stored in the Data Buffer. To decode the address sequences into semantic information, i.e., name of processes and APIs, we designed an Addr2Semantic Decoder. It reads the address from Data Buffer and looks up the Process Translation Table and API Translation Table to translate the address into Process name or API name. In this way, we obtain the malware sample's processes name and corresponding API-call sequences.

Assisted by VMI technology, SeqTrace precisely and effectively decodes the data traced by Intel PT into high-level semantic information for malware analysis. It makes full use of the advantages of both technologies and achieves better performance with lower overhead.

4   Implementation

We implement SeqTrace on the QEMU/KVM platform, adding 2800 LOCs in KVM for trapping API, 3900 LOCs in Qemu for decoding trapped raw data into API address and 800 LOCs in user space for loading samples automatically and interpreting API-call sequence. In the following section, we will present some key implementation details.

4.1   Semantic Recognition

As an analysis technology at the VMM layer, VMI triggers a VM-Exit event when trapping an API and pauses VM until the analysis is finished. Therefore, VMI would introduce significant performance overhead during the analysis process. To mitigate this problem, we propose an IPT-based API-call Tracing Approach to trace the execution of processes. As mentioned above, the addresses of processes and APIs have been recorded by Intel PT in the forms of TIP packets and PIP packets. To get the API-call sequences of a specific process, we only need to maintain semantic translation tables utilizing VMI and then translate the addresses sequences into corresponding semantical information, including process name and sequences of the API name. The detailed steps are as follows.

First of all, VMI technology is employed to maintain the semantic translation tables, i.e., the Process Translation Table and API Translation Table. It utilizes the Intel-x hardware feature to dig the semantic information by accessing and analyzing the entire memory space of the VM.

To maintain the Process Translation Table, the Decoder intercepts the action of process creation, acquires its CR3, and dynamically updates the table. By analyzing the workflow of process creation, we find that there is an EPROCESS struct to manage the process information, and a PsActiveProcess link to manage all processes in the kernel. Therefore, the Process Translation Table is initialized when SeqTrace boots by reading the information in the PsActiveProcess link. Specifically, SeqTrace access the chain of kernel Process according to the PsActiveProcess, walk through the process chain and analyze the information of every EPROCESS struct node to get the information of every process. It acquires the process name and process address by analyzing the ActiveProcessLinks in the EPROCESS struct. In this way, the initial mappings of process addresses and process names are obtained. Moreover, once a process is created, the PspInsert-Process, an API running in ring 0, is responsible for inserting or deleting the EPROCESS struct of the newly created process into the PsActiveProcess link. And the PspExitProcess is triggered to delete the corresponding EPROCESS struct from the PsActiveProcess link when the process dies. Consequently, both APIs are intercepted by SeqTrace to dynamically update the semantic information of the Process Translation Table.

To maintain the API Translation Table, Decoder not only needs to grab the semantic information of preloaded APIs but also has to intercept APIs loaded on demand. Specifically, the Decoder component walks through the list of running processes to acquire the semantic information of the preloaded APIs when Seq-Trace is booted up. Taking VM with Windows OS as an example, the PEB and PEB_LDR_DATA chain in the EPROCESS struct stores semantic information of APIs. Therefore, the Decoder walks through the chain of PEB_LDR_DATA, grabs the mapping of address and API name, and then stores them into API Translation Table. Next, Decoder tries to intercept the API call of LdrpLoadDll and LdrpInitializeProcess to be aware of the change of API call semantic information. For this purpose, Decoder walks through the running process chain from which we can find the base address of LdrpLoadDll and LdrpInitializeProcess. Then, the VMI component of Decoder utilizes HEMC [16] to intercept those APIs, i.e., LdrpLoadDll and LdrpInitializeProcess. In this way, the VM will be trapped into VMM once one of these APIs is loaded into memory. Next, Decoder reads the address from the ESP (Extended Stack Pointer) register or RSP (Rex prefix Stack Pointer) register and dynamically updates the semantic information into the API Translation Table.

By leveraging semantic mapping information from Process Translation Table and API Translation Table, we could effectively decode the address sequences of processes and APIs into corresponding semantic name sequences. Therefore, using the VMI technology, SeqTrace decouples the execution tracing and semantic analyzing. It does not need to acquire abundant semantics when tracing the execution of processes in VM and performs semantic recognition in parallel with VM running. Although a small number of APIs is monitored to maintain the semantic tables, it is triggered at a very low frequency compared to those long-running execution. Hence, the proposed approach would significantly reduce the performance overhead of the system.

4.2 Adaptive Configuration of Intel PT

This subsection describes how to effectively adaptively configure the Intel PT to support process tracing.

Firstly, the Analysis Director captures the VMs startup execution by monitoring the change of the /dev/KVM file, which is a device file created by QEMU. Then, it obtains the configurations of VM involving vCPUs with the help of VMI. Next, the Analysis Director would transfer the configurations of VMs and the privilege spaces (user-space or kernel-space) that would be monitored to QEMU-PT. As a bridge between Analysis Director and KVM-PT, QEMU-PT calls the IOCTL to deliver the configurations to KVM-PT once receiving that information and allocates memory space to store the traced address data.

Then, to configure the Intel PT, KVM-PT parses the configuration from QEMU-PT and sets a specific bit of the MSR register to enable process tracing on specific vCPUs. In addition, the Information Filter in KVM-PT would filter the traced data and save the required data (i.e., related to a particular process or permission space) in the Data Buffer of QEMU-PT.

Next, QEMU-PT would decode the recorded data in Data Buffer into process and API-call sequences. The specific workflow has been described in Sect. 4.1. Finally, QEMU-PT delivers the decoded data to the Analysis Director to conduct further analysis.

Based on Intel PT and VMI technology, SeqTrace is OS-independent and OS-agnostic because it is implemented in VMM and does not need to preinstall agents inside VM. Moreover, the Intel PT provides ways to efficiently trace the execution data of processes running inside the VM, then VMI technology achieves semantic translation to translate the traced data into semantic information, including process and API-call sequences. Therefore, it would be safer and more efficient to analyze malware leveraging our SeqTrace.

5 Experiment

In this section, we evaluate SeqTrace by a set of experiments. We first demonstrate the effectiveness of SeqTrace. Then, we measure the performance gain of SeqTrace approach compared to the native approach.

```
"WS2_32.dll": {
    "GetAddrInfoExA": 83611,
    "GetAddrInfoExW": 53738,
    "GetAddrInfoW": 18569,
    "GetNameInfoW": 26287,
    "WSAAsyncGetHostByName": 94826,
    "WSAConnect": 52287,
    "WSAConnectByNameA": 116918,
    "WSAConnectByNameW": 116015,
    "WSADuplicateSocketA": 90550,
    "WSADuplicateSocketW": 90408,
    "WSARecv": 28809,
    "WSARecvFrom": 52134,
    "WSASend": 17414,
    "WSASendMsg": 111563,
    "WSASendTo": 111372,
    "gethostbyname": 95859,
    "connect": 27613,
    "listen": 45057,
    "recv": 27406,
    "recvfrom": 46812,
    "send": 28417,
    "sendto": 13493
},
"wlanapi.dll": {
    "WlanConnect": 28697,
    "WlanEnumInterfaces": 23545,
    "WlanGetSecuritySettings": 40409,
    "WlanHostedNetworkForceStart": 41611,
    "WlanHostedNetworkForceStop": 41740,
    "WlanHostedNetworkInitSettings": 42913,
    "WlanHostedNetworkQueryProperty": 41869,
    "WlanHostedNetworkQuerySecondaryKey": 44217,
    "WlanHostedNetworkQueryStatus": 43171,
    "WlanHostedNetworkRefreshSecuritySettings": 43042,
    "WlanHostedNetworkSetProperty": 42377,
    "WlanHostedNetworkSetSecondaryKey": 43657,
    "WlanHostedNetworkStartUsing": 41353,
    "WlanHostedNetworkStopUsing": 41482,
    "WlanIhvControl": 26465,
    "WlanQueryAutoConfigParameter": 24444,
    "WlanQueryInterface": 25873,
    "WlanRegisterNotification": 29729,
    "WlanRegisterVirtualStationNotification": 44881,
    "WlanScan": 27073
},
```

Fig. 4. The excerpted RVA of Windows functions.

5.1 Experimental Setup

All experiments are conducted on physical servers configured with Intel Xeon 6230 processors and 256 GB DDR4 RAM running Red Hat 7.4 with a 64-bit 3.10.0 Linux Kernel and QEMU-2.9.0. We configure the VM with two vCPU and 4 GB RAM running Windows 7 with 32-bit.

We compare our SeqTrace with kAFL [15] and Drakvuf [38], both of which are existing approaches for API-call analysis. DRAKVUF [38] set specific addresses to achieve accurate interception of API calls. The kAFL utilizes Intel PT and disassembling to conduct analysis. In the following sections, we will conduct multiple experiments with these approaches to measure their performance.

5.2 Pretreatment

Before conducting experiments, SeqTrace grabs the relative virtual address (RVA) of APIs from the kernel of the guest OS preparing for semantic translation as mentioned in HEMC [16]. In Our experiments, we have gotten the RVA of more than 700 high-risk Windows APIs. As shown in Fig. 4, it is some RVA of APIs from Windows OS.

5.3 Effectiveness of SeqTrace

To prove the effectiveness of SeqTrace, we employ 1,000 malicious samples that are downloaded from VirusSign [39] to conduct our effectiveness evaluation. In the experiments, all malicious samples and specific malware are deployed in VM, and SeqTrace runs in VMM to acquire and analyze their behaviors. SeqTrace can directly obtain the running log outside VM and there is no need to install an agent inside VMs.

With the help of qemu-nbd, malicious samples and typical malware are dynamically loaded into VMs and automatically triggered to execute. During the execution, SeqTrace could get the API-call sequences in real-time by leveraging the IPT-based API-call Tracing Approach and VMI-based Semantic Decoder. As illustrated in Fig. 5, it is the log of API-call sequences in the form of XML, from which the API-call sequence for one operational action can be obtained. Furthermore, we can grab the complete API-call sequence of one process by in-depth filtering. These API-call sequences can be fed into the machine learning models to detect the malicious behaviors of samples. However, it is worth noting that the API-call sequence of some processes in Fig. 5 is missing and only 700 kinds of high-risk Windows APIs could be grabbed in advance. Therefore, some API addresses failed to be matched successfully. In this experiment, one thousand malicious samples are executed with the running of SeqTrace, and we get a series of log files that occupy more than 2 GB of disk space. We extract the complete API-call sequences from the log files, and then the API-call sequences are fed into the TextCNN model to recognize whether the samples are malicious. By analyzing those API-call sequences, SeqTrace can identify many malicious samples. The experiment results prove the effectiveness of SeqTrace.

```
<process name="iexplore.exe" addr="3eee1680">
    <api_list name="GetLogicalDrives" addr="77155986"/>
    <api_list name="GetDriveTypeW" addr="77163be6"/>
    <api_list name="CreateEventW" addr="77163386"/>
</process>
<process name="iexplore.exe" addr="3eee1680">
    <api_list name="GetTokenInformation" addr="7778431c"/>
    <api_list name="CreateFileMappingW" addr="77150a7f"/>
    <api_list name="MapViewOfFile" addr="7715899b"/>
    <api_list name="GetTokenInformation" addr="7778431c"/>
    <api_list name="CreateFileMappingW" addr="77150a7f"/>
    <api_list name="MapViewOfFile" addr="7715899b"/>
    <api_list name="MapViewOfFile" addr="7715899b"/>
    <api_list name="GetFileInformationByHandleEx" addr="771538ad"/>
    <api_list name="CreateEventW" addr="77163386"/>
</process>
<process name="explorer.exe" addr="3eee11e0">
</process>
<process name="iexplore.exe" addr="3eee1680">
    <api_list name="CreateEventW" addr="77163386"/>
</process>
<process name="iexplore.exe" addr="3eee1680">
    <api_list name="GetSystemWindowsDirectoryW" addr="7716451b"/>
    <api_list name="GetSystemWindowsDirectoryW" addr="7716451b"/>
    <api_list name="CreateEventW" addr="77163386"/>
    <api_list name="CreateMutexW" addr="77152aee"/>
    <api_list name="CreateEventW" addr="77163386"/>
    <api_list name="CreateMutexW" addr="77152aee"/>
    <api_list name="GetSystemWindowsDirectoryW" addr="7716451b"/>
    <api_list name="GetSystemWindowsDirectoryW" addr="7716451b"/>
</process>
<process name="svchost.exe" addr="3eee11c0">
</process>
<process name="iexplore.exe" addr="3eee1680">
    <api_list name="GetTokenInformation" addr="7778431c"/>
    <api_list name="GetTokenInformation" addr="7778431c"/>
    <api_list name="GetTokenInformation" addr="7778431c"/>
</process>
<process name="svchost.exe" addr="3eee1120">
    <api_list name="CreateEventW" addr="77163386"/>
    <api_list name="DuplicateHandle" addr="7715cdd9"/>
</process>
```

Fig. 5. The running behavioral log.

5.4   Overhead Evaluation

To evaluate SeqTrace thoroughly, we deploy the following workload in the VM to represent a variety of characteristics:

- HD Tune Pro benchmarks [17] is used to measure the driver's performance, which means an IO-intensive workload.
- Fritz Chess benchmarks [18] is a computer chess test program, and it is frequently used to test CPU performance.

To measure the gain of performance, we analyze 260 kinds of APIs and 700 kinds of APIs respectively leveraging SeqTrace, and comparing them against those of kAFL and Drakvuf. These high-risk APIs (e.g. APIs related to file operation or process operation) are obtained and summarized from engineering applications with millions of samples which may be increased or adjusted with the accumulation of engineering experience in the future. Figure 6 and Fig. 7 show the performance overhead in various configurations. Specifically, SeqTrace-260 and Drakvuf-260 explore 260 kinds of the same APIs at the user level. In addition, SeqTrace-700 and Drakvuf-700 analyze the 700 kinds of APIs involving user-level API and kernel-level API.

Overhead of IO-Intensive Application. HD Tune Pro is often used to measure the driver's performance as a hard disk utility with many functions. In this

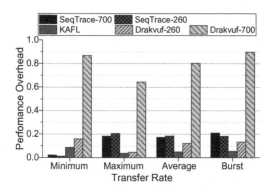

Fig. 6. Performance overhead of IO-intensive application.

experiment, HD Tune Pro is employed as an IO-intensive application to calculate the performance penalty caused by SeqTrace. As illustrated in Fig. 6, we obtain the performance of an application in terms of minimum transfer rate, maximum transfer rate, average transfer rate, and burst transfer rate. And then calculate the performance overhead by the ratio of performance degradation to performance value in normal execution without taking API-call tracing. As reported in Fig. 6, KAFL incurs the least performance penalty, i.e., 5.79%, but there is a semantic gap for behavior analysis. For Drakvuf, although only an 11.54% performance penalty is incurred in the Drakvuf-260 case, it incurs 80.43% penalty in the Drakvuf-700 case. Therefore, the performance overhead caused by Drakvuf is heavily influenced by the number of traced APIs. SeqTrace incurs 14.69% and 14.78% performance penalty for SeqTrace-260 and SeqTrace-700 respectively. Therefore, SeqTrace mitigates the performance penalty by 81.62% (i.e., $\frac{80.43\% - 14.78\%}{14.78\%}$) for 700 samples cases. Thus, the results prove that SeqTrace is almost unaffected by the variation of the API number for IO-intensive applications.

Overhead of CPU-Intensive Application. Fritz Chess Benchmark is a computer chess test program that is frequently used to measure CPU performance. In this experiment, Fritz Chess Benchmark is employed as a CPU-intensive application to measure the performance impact on the CPU when using SeqTrace. The experiment results are reported in Fig. 7. The contrast ratio and per thousand steps of CPU are used to evaluate the performance overhead of SeqTrace. As illustrated in Fig. 7, SeqTrace incurs stable performance overhead, i.e., 5.87% and 6.07% for SeqTrace-260 and SeqTrace-700 respectively, which is similar to the IO-intensive Application. As expected, Drakvuf is heavily influenced by the number of traced APIs, i.e., 32.24% and 50.51% for Drakvuf-260 and Drakvuf-700 respectively. It can be seen that SeqTrace reduces the performance penalty by 81.79% (i.e., $\frac{32.24\% - 5.87\%}{32.24\%}$) and 87.96% for 260 samples and 700 samples cases respectively. Compared to 3.94% of KAFL, SeqTrace introduces slightly more performance overhead, but it gets more ample semantic information. The results

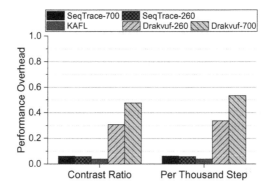

Fig. 7. Performance overhead of CPU-intensive application.

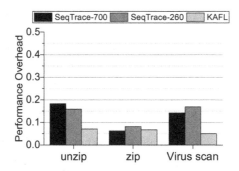

Fig. 8. Performance overhead of real-world application.

prove that the performance overhead of SeqTrace is independent of the number of analyzed APIs. The reason is that SeqTrace leverages Intel PT to trace API addresses and Process addresses with a low-performance penalty. Moreover, SeqTrace only requires intercepting four APIs(i.e., PspInsertProcess, PspExit-Process, LdrpLoadDll, and LdrpInitializeProcess) for semantic translation no matter how many APIs are analyzed. Therefore, the performance overhead of SeqTrace is little affected by the number of analyzed APIs.

Overhead of Comprehensive Application. In this subsection, we use some real-world applications, i.e., unzip, zip, and virus scan, to evaluate the performance of SeqTrace and report the performance overhead in Fig. 8.

As illustrated in Fig. 8, the performance overheads caused by SeqTrace-260 are 15.82%, 8.16%, and 14.13% for unzip, zip, and virus scan workload respectively. As expected, the results of SeqTrace-700 are similar to SeqTrace-260, which means that the number of traced APIs has little effect on the performance overhead. For KAFL, the performance overheads are 7.02%, 6.67%, and 4.99% respectively. It can be seen that SeqTrace introduces slightly higher performance overheads than kAFL. It is mainly due to SeqTrace employing VMI to trap some APIs. Although SeqTrace leads to a slightly higher performance penalty, it obtains specific semantic information of API-call sequences that kAFL cannot get.

Combining the experiments of CPU-intensive and IO-intensive applications, we find SeqTrace performs better on CPU-intensive applications than IO-intensive applications. Moreover, compared to existing approaches, SeqTrace significantly reduces the performance overhead and would be less affected by the workloads and configurations.

6 Related Work

API-call sequence analysis has been researched and applied in many fields. For example, Mamoun [30] designs an automatic system and employs the n-gram and reverse engineer to extract behavior features of malware. Ashkan Sami [31] directly extracted API calls from PE files, which are used to create an attribute set to detect malware programs. Cheng Wang [32] utilizes the decompile analysis to get the API sequence of malware and form them into the behavior characteristic. Then, they employ the Bayes algorithm to see suspicious programs according to those characteristics. However, these static analysis approaches extract API-call sequences from code segments, so they are unsuitable for unknown malware analysis.

CWSandbox [9] propose dynamic approaches for API-call analysis. It leverages API hooking and dynamic library injection techniques to hook functions into the malware programs, intercept relevant APIs, and automatically analyze malware. Cuckoo [33] employs API hooking to intercept all appropriate API calls and then generates API-call sequences. Based on Cuckoo Sandbox, UNVEIL [2] Leverage filesystem driver of window OS to intercept filesystem activity for ransomware detection. Unfortunately, the monitoring tools that run with the same privileges as malware are vulnerable to being compromised by malware. To solve this problem, Bin Shi proposes ShadowMonitor [34] approach. It consists of two compartments, i.e., the main compartment and shadow compartment, which are assigned to different access privileges and would not be discovered or accessed by malware running in VMs.

With the development of hardware virtualization technology, another dynamic analysis approach named external dynamic analysis is proposed. It is implemented in the hypervisor, so it does not need an agent in the guest OS. Therefore, the dynamic analysis tools are OS-independent. For example, XenAccess [35] accessed the memory and disk data to reconstruct the semantics of the API call using Xen's infrastructure. Ether [36] intercepted instruction, memory, and API-call information outside VMs and provided a transparent method for malware analysis. Bryan presents an open-source software named Libvmi [14] to get the entire memory of guest VMs and monitor their run-time internal state. Nitro [8] proposes an event-driven mechanism to trap kernel API calls and register sensitive events. It is triggered when registered events occur. NOR [37] presents an event-driven snapshot to get activities of VMs with lower performance overhead. To obtain the API address, DRAKVUF [38] traps specific addresses instead of some address pages to achieve accurate API interception.

As the new processor feature introduced in the fifth or above-generation Intel processors, Intel PT provides the ability to trace the execution branches of processes with a slight performance penalty. Most of researches utilize this technology in fuzzing [15,19–21] and integrity check of control-flow [22–25]. For example, PT-CFI [27] combines Intel PT and disassembling technology to detect control flow hijacking. Intel PT and disassembling are also employed in kAFL [15] to examine the security of kernel components. However, we find that Intel PT has not independently been used to accomplish one task in PT-CFI and kAFL. The reason is that Intel PT only traces the address data and has no semantic information. Therefore, data decoding is required before using for malware analysis. Disassembling is an approach employed to solve this problem in some researches [28,29], but it is not convenient and flexible. It is because we must obtain the binary code previously. If the binary code is not acquired or known, we cannot decode the traced data and get the semantic information.

Compared to previous works, our SeqTrace mitigates the performance overhead and improves the efficiency of API-call analysis by combining the technology of VMI and Intel PT. It first leverages the Intel PT to effectively trace the execution of malware and dynamically grab API-call data. Then, it utilizes VMI to translate the data with no semantic information into API-call sequences.

7 Conclusion

This paper presents SeqTrace, a novel dynamic API-call sequence tracing approach implemented in VMM for malware detection. SeqTrace first proposes an IPT-based API-call Tracing Approach, which takes full advantage of Intel PT's hardware feature to effectively record information of malware execution. Next, it designs a VMI-based Semantic Decoder to achieve semantic translation leveraging the abundant semantic features of VMI. A set of experiments proves that SeqTrace achieves a significant performance improvement in tracing API-call sequences and it would be helpful in practice malware analysis.

Due to the limitation of Intel PT technology, SeqTrace can only work on Intel 5th generation and above processors. It can obtain all execution streams under Linux and Windows operating systems and is not limited by application types in the operating system. Before using SeqTrace to achieve data, we need to obtain the corresponding address data in advance, such as the RVA address of the API. In the future, we can use SeqTrace for automated vulnerability mining and fuzzing.

Acknowledgments. This work is supported by the National Natural Science Foundation of China (grant no. 62072453, 61972392), Youth Innovation Promotion Association of the Chinese Academy of Sciences (no. 2020164).

References

1. Steven, H., Anil, S.: Intrusion detection using sequences of system calls. J. Comput. Secur. **6**(3), (1999)
2. Amin, K., Sajjad A., Collin, M., William, R., Engin, K.: UNVEIL: a large-scale, automated approach to detecting ransomware. In: 25th USENIX Security Symposium (USENIX Security 2016), pp. 757–772 (2016)
3. Thomas, N.-K., Max W.: Semi-supervised classification with graph convolutional networks. arXiv preprint, arXiv:1609.02907 (2016)
4. Rosenberg, I., Shabtai, A., Rokach, L., Elovici, Y.: Generic black-box end-to-end attack against state of the art API call based malware classifiers. In: Bailey, M., Holz, T., Stamatogiannakis, M., Ioannidis, S. (eds.) RAID 2018. LNCS, vol. 11050, pp. 490–510. Springer, Cham (2018). https://doi.org/10.1007/978-3-030-00470-5_23
5. Fadadu, F., Handa, A., Kumar, N., Shukla, S.K.: Evading API call sequence based malware classifiers. In: Zhou, J., Luo, X., Shen, Q., Xu, Z. (eds.) ICICS 2019. LNCS, vol. 11999, pp. 18–33. Springer, Cham (2020). https://doi.org/10.1007/978-3-030-41579-2_2
6. Bergenholtz, E., Casalicchio, E., Ilie, D., Moss, A.: Detection of metamorphic malware packers using multilayered LSTM networks. In: Meng, W., Gollmann, D., Jensen, C.D., Zhou, J. (eds.) ICICS 2020. LNCS, vol. 12282, pp. 36–53. Springer, Cham (2020). https://doi.org/10.1007/978-3-030-61078-4_3
7. Binghui, W., Zhenqiang, G.: Attacking graph-based classification via manipulating the graph structure. In: 2019 ACM SIGSAC Conference on Computer and Communications Security, pp. 2023–2040 (2019)
8. Pfoh, J., Schneider, C., Eckert, C., et al.: Nitro: hardware-based system call tracing for virtual machines. In: International Workshop on Security, pp. 96–112 (2011)
9. Holz, T., Freiling, F., Willems, C.: Toward automated dynamic malware analysis using CWSandbox. IEEE Secur. Priv. **5**(2), 32–39 (2007)
10. Bojan, J.: A Not-So-Common Cold: Malware Statistics in 2021. March 2021. https://dataprot.net/statistics/malware-statistics
11. Garfinkel, T., Rosenblum, M.: A virtual machine introspection based architecture for intrusion detection. In: 10th Network and Distributed System Symposium (NDSS 2003), San Diego, CA, USA (2003)
12. Bauman, E., Ayoade, G., Lin, Z.: A survey on hypervisor-based monitoring: approaches, applications, and evolutions. ACM Comput. Surv. **48**(1), 1001–1033 (2015)
13. Intel 64 and IA-32 architectures software developer's manual. (2016)
14. Payne, B.-D.: Simplifying virtual machine introspection using LibVMI. In: Technical Reports SAND2012-7818, Sandia National Laboratories (2012)
15. Sergej, S., Cornelius, A., Robert, G., Sebastian, S., Thorsten, H.: kAFL: hardware-assisted feedback fuzzing for OS kernels. In: 26th USENIX Conference on Security Symposium, Vancouver, BC, pp. 167–182. USENIX Association (2017)
16. Ding, Z., Cui, L., Fei, H., et al.: A high-efficiency and comprehensive dynamic behavior analysis system for malware based on hardware virtualization. In: 22nd International Conference on High Performance Computing and Communications; 18th International Conference on Smart City; 6th International Conference on Data Science and Systems (HPCC/SmartCity/DSS), IEEE (2020)
17. HD Tune Pro, www.hdtune.com
18. Fritz Chess, www.jens-hartmann.at/Fritzmarks/

19. Bohme, M., Pham, V.-T., Roychoudhury, A.: Coverage-based greybox fuzzing as markov chain. IEEE Trans. Software Eng. **45**(5), 489–506 (2019)
20. Cha, S.-K., Woo, M., Brumley, D.: Program-adaptive mutational fuzzing. In: IEEE Symposium on Security and Privacy, pp. 725–741. IEEE (2015)
21. Sanjay, R., Vivek, J., Ashish, K., Lucian, C., Cristiano, G., Herbert, B.: VUzzer: application-aware evolutionary fuzzing. In: 24th Network and Distributed System Symposium (NDSS 2017), San Diego, CA, USA (2017)
22. Ge, X., Talele, N., Payer, M., et al.: IEEE European Symposium on Security and Privacy. Fine-grained control-flow integrity for kernel software, IEEE (2016)
23. Vishwath, M., Per, L., Stefan, B., Kevin, W.-H., Michael, F.: Opaque control-flow integrity. In: 22th Network and Distributed System Symposium (NDSS 2015), San Diego, CA, USA (2015)
24. Carlini, N., Barresi, A., Payer, M., Wagner, D., Gross, T.-R.: Control-flow bending: on the effectiveness of control-flow integrity. In: 24th USENIX Conference on Security Symposium, Washington, D.C., pp. 161–176. USENIX Association (2015)
25. Payer, M., Barresi, A., Gross, T.R.: Fine-grained control-flow integrity through binary hardening. In: Almgren, M., Gulisano, V., Maggi, F. (eds.) DIMVA 2015. LNCS, vol. 9148, pp. 144–164. Springer, Cham (2015). https://doi.org/10.1007/978-3-319-20550-2_8
26. Wang, M., Yin, H., Bhaskar, A.-V., Su, P., Feng, D.: Binary code continent: finer-grained control flow integrity for stripped binaries. In: 31st Annual Computer Security Applications Conference (ACSAC 2015), Los Angeles, CA, USA, pp. 331–340 (2015)
27. Gu, Y., Zhao, Q., Zhang, Y., Lin, Z.: PT-CFI: transparent backward-edge control flow violation detection using intel processor trace. In: 7th ACM on Conference on Data and Application Security and Privacy, Scottsdale, Arizona, USA, pp. 173–184 (2017)
28. Ge, X., Cui, W., Jaeger, T.: GRIFFIN guarding control flows using Intel Processor Trace. In: 22nd International Conference on Architectural Support for Programming Languages and Operating Systems (ASPLOS 2017), Xi'an, China, pp. 585–598 (2017)
29. Wang, X.-R., Liu, Y.-T., Chen, H.-B.: Transparent protection of kernel module against ROP with Intel processor trace. J. Software **29**(5), 1333–1347 (2018)
30. Alazab, M., Layton, R., Venkataraman, S., Watters, P.: Malware detection based on structure detection based on structural and behaal and behavioural features of API calls. In: proceedings of the 2010 International Cyber Resilience Conference, pp. 1–10 (2010)
31. Sami, A., Yadegari, B., Rahimi, H., Peiravian, N., Hashemi, S., Hamze, A.: Malware detection based on mining API calls. In: proceedings of the 2010 ACM Symposium on Applied Computing (SAC 2010), New York, USA, pp. 1020–1025 (2010)
32. Wang, C., Pang, J., Zhao, R., Liu, X.: Using API sequence and Bayes algorithm to detect suspicious behavior. In: 2009 International Conference on Communication Software and Networks, pp. 544–548 (2009)
33. Oktavianto, D., Muhardianto, I.: Cuckoo Malware Analysis. Packt Publishing Ltd (2013)
34. Shi, B., Cui, L., Li, B., Liu, X., Hao, Z., Shen, H.: ShadowMonitor: an effective In-VM monitoring framework with hardware-enforced isolation. In: Research in Attacks, Intrusions, and Defenses, pp. 670–690 (2018)
35. Bryan, D.-P., Carbone, M., Lee, W., et al.: Secure and Flexible Monitoring of Virtual Machines. In: 23th Annual Computer Security Applications Conference, pp. 385–397, ACM (2007)

36. Dinaburg, A., Royal, P., Sharif, M., et al.: Ether: malware analysis via hardware virtualization extensions. In: 15th ACM conference on Computer and Communications Security, pp. 51–62 (2008)
37. Wang, C., Hao, Z., Yun, X.: NOR: towards non-intrusive, real-time and OS-agnostic introspection for virtual machines in cloud environment. In: Chen, X., Lin, D., Yung, M. (eds.) Inscrypt 2017. LNCS, vol. 10726, pp. 500–517. Springer, Cham (2018). https://doi.org/10.1007/978-3-319-75160-3_29
38. Tamas, K.-L., Steve, M., Bryan, D.-P., et al.: Scalability, fidelity and stealth in the DRAKVUF dynamic malware analysis system. In: 30th Annual Computer Security Applications Conference, pp. 386–395 (2014)
39. VirusSign, www.virussign.com/index.html

CP³: Hierarchical Cross-Platform Power/Performance Prediction Using a Transfer Learning Approach

Xinxin Qi, Juan Chen[✉], and Lin Deng

National University of Defense Technology, Changsha, China
{qixinxin19,juanchen,denglin}@nudt.edu.cn

Abstract. Cross-platform power/performance prediction is becoming increasingly important due to the rapid development and variety of software and hardware architectures in an era of heterogeneous multi-core. However, accurate power/performance prediction is faced with an obstacle caused by the large gap between architectures, which is often overcome by laborious and time-consuming fine-grained program profiling on the target platform. To overcome these problems, this paper introduces CP^3, a hierarchical Cross-platform Power/Performance Prediction framework, which focuses on utilizing architecture differences to migrate built models to target platforms. The core of CP^3 is the three-step hierarchical transfer learning approach, hierarchical division, partial transfer learning, and model fusion, respectively. CP^3 firstly builds a power/performance model on the source platform, then rebuilds it with the reduced training data on the target platform, and finally obtains a cross-platform model. We validate the effectiveness of CP^3 using a group of benchmarks on X86- and ARM-based platforms that use three different types of commonly used processors. Evaluation results show that when applying CP^3, only 1% of the baseline training data is required to achieve high cross-platform prediction accuracy, with power prediction error being only 0.65%, and performance prediction error being only 4.64%.

Keywords: Cross-platform prediction · Performance model · Power model · Transfer learning

1 Introduction

Power and performance prediction plays a critical role in parallel and distributed computing, especially for application development, energy-efficiency optimization, power-aware resource management, and job scheduling [1–3]. For the multi-core systems nowadays, the architecture evolves quickly and becomes increasingly heterogeneous. The diverse computation units (e.g., CPU and GPU) and Instruction Set Architectures (ISAs, e.g., X86 and ARM) further increase the complexity and heterogeneity of the systems, making it common for applications

© The Author(s) 2023
W. Meng et al. (Eds.): ICA3PP 2022, LNCS 13777, pp. 117–138, 2023.
https://doi.org/10.1007/978-3-031-22677-9_7

to run on different platforms. Despite the fact that the same application is running on two different CPU architectures, the application performance differs by a factor of 100. As a result, power and performance evaluations across different platforms are more challenging than ever [4–6].

Developing a power and performance model to determine the average power consumption and execution time of a program is a crucial part of power and performance evaluation since it is inexpensive, non-intrusive, and has few side effects. In cross-platform scenarios, however, it becomes more difficult due to the complexity of the applications and gaps between platforms. Previous works have focused on certain parts (basic blocks or phases) of programs rather than the whole application in order to reduce the complexity of problem-solving. These approaches were based on a belief that good cross-platform predictions are only possible through studying the behavior of machine-independent programs [5–7]. Programm phases that perform the same computation behave similarly across platforms, implying that their performance metrics display the same or similar trends, but their execution times differ. On the basis of this, they divide the program into multiple phases, and then match the phases, forecasting the power consumption and performance on the target platform.

Although phase-based approaches offer a solution for cross-platform prediction, there are two issues. Firstly, this assumption is not always valid due to the difference in computing and memory access capabilities across different platforms. Even if the same workload is performed, there is a large difference in program behavior, which leads to inaccuracy, as shown in Fig. 1 (c). Furthermore, this method requires running a small set of benchmarks offline and collecting performance data, such as performance monitoring counters (PMCs), in order to fully describe each machine's power and performance characteristics. After that, the neural network is trained to generalize the cross-platform relationships between program phases and phase characteristics. In order to achieve satisfactory accuracy with neural networks, a large amount of training data must be collected. This is a labor-intensive and time-consuming process. Considering both of these issues, we no longer focus on the phase similarity of the application itself, but rather on the differences between architectures. In our case, we make some adjustments to the power/performance model of the known platform using transfer learning to make it suitable for the target platform. Recent years have witnessed the widespread use of transfer learning in the field of performance prediction, which uses less training data by transferring knowledgeacross environments.

In this work, we propose CP^3, a $\underline{C}$ross-platform $\underline{P}$ower/$\underline{P}$erformance $\underline{P}$rediction framework, to achieve high model accuracy with as few training data as possible. The core of CP^3 is a three-step hierarchical transfer learning approach, which utilizes architecture differences to migrate the power/performance model on the known platform while reducing training data. There are three steps of CP^3. **Step 1. Hierarchical division.** We observed that application-related features that are closely relevant to the application but platform-independent make negligible impacts on the model accuracy. Based on this, we divide the

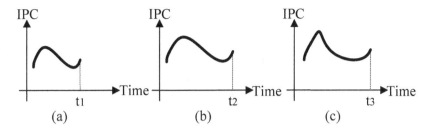

Fig. 1. The similarity of program phases that execute the same load varies by platforms. Sub-figures (a), (b) and (c) show that IPC variation on platforms A, B, and C. From (a) to (b), only the execution time changes, but the shape does not change. From (a) to (c), not only the execution time changes, but also the shape is different due to different computing and memory access capabilities.

features and still use the PMCs that are closely related to the application but not related to the platform when modeling on the target platform. In addition, we recollect platform-related features and combine them to complete the model training. **Step 2. Partial transfer.** On the basis of hierarchical division, we use transfer learning to learn the relationship between the source platform and the target platform and conduct model transfer. The transfer learning approach could significantly reduce the number of needed samples for satisfactory accuracy. The hierarchical division guides us to divide features into multiple layers, therefore reducing the number of features contained in a training sample; the transfer learning approach reduces the number of training samples. **Step 3. Model Fusion.** We further adopt a model fusion approach, by combining the application-layer model of the source platform with the platform-layer model of the target platform, and obtain the cross-platform model.

To summarize, we make the following contributions:

- We find great data reduction potentials by figuring out those features with nearly "zero" contributions to the prediction model. Specifically, we show that the application-related features have little impact on cross-platform power/performance modeling.
- We design CP^3 that achieves a high model accuracy while reducing the training data from the sample and feature dimensions simultaneously.
- We conduct extensive experimental evaluations on CP^3 in real-world cross-platform scenarios. The results demonstrate that CP^3 uses only 1% of the baseline training data while achieving prediction errors of 0.8% and 4.6% for power and performance prediction, respectively.

The rest of the paper is organized as follows. Section 2 discusses related work. Section 3 introduces the motivation. Section 4 proposes and details the design of CP^3. Section 5 presents the experimental environment and Sect. 6 evaluates CP^3. Finally, Sect. 7 concludes the paper.

2 Related Work

Cross-platform prediction, which predicts power and performance on an unknown platform using data from the known platform's power and performance statistics, has been an active study topic. The difficulty of creating an accurate and low-overhead power/performance model stems from how complicated software and hardware are. So far, three different types of approaches have been put forth: simulation-based, analytical modeling-based, and learning-based approaches.

Although accurate, simulation-based techniques like cycle-accurate instruction set simulations [8] have obvious performance issues. Traditional analytical modeling techniques, on the other hand, are accurate to a certain extent but are computationally inefficient. In order to do this, cross-platform prediction methods based on machine learning are suggested. Accuracy is maintained while speedups of orders of magnitude are offered via learning-based techniques (as shown in Table 1).

Table 1. Overview of existing cross-platform approaches.

	Target	Method	Granularity	Way
[9]	performance	linear regression	whole program	instrumentation
[7,10]	power & performance	convex optimization	basic block	instrumentation
[6]	performance	stochastic dynamic coupling	binary	sampling
[5]	power & performance	neural network	phases	sampling
[11]	performance	transfer learning	whole program	sampling
CP^3	power & performance	transfer learning	whole program	sampling

Currently, learning-based methods use settings where training and prediction are carried out at a finer granularity to attain high accuracy. These methods necessitate either instrumenting the source code to retrieve the basics [7,9,10], sampling the binary file [6], or extracting the application phase using hardware counters [5]. Zheng et al. successively introduced instrumentation-based and sampling-based approaches for power and performance prediction of the whole program as well as for different phases [6,7,9]. However, all these instrumentation-based methods are limited to predicting a single application where source code is available. In addition, instrumentation has a non-negligible execution overhead. In order to estimate power and performance across various hardware configurations, Kim et al. [5] developed P^4, a sampling-based framework that first performs offline characterization and then formulates the power/performance model. By concentrating on certain parts (basic blocks or phases) rather than the entire program, these techniques significantly reduce the difficulty of problem solving. Nonetheless, they made the assumption that program phases that carry out the same computation behave identically across platforms, but this assumption isn't necessarily the case because different platforms have varied computing and memory access capabilities. Apart from this, a large amount of training data is required to guarantee high model accuracy, which brings heavy data collection overhead.

Recent years have witnessed the widespread use of transfer learning in the field of performance prediction. It reduces learning costs (training data) by transferring knowledge about performance behaviors across environments. Sun et al. [12] modeled the correlation between the execution time and runtime features through automatically instrumenting an MPI program. Marathe et al. [13] introduced a deep learning technique augmented with domain transfer learning to identify high performing application configurations in static cross-platform modeling. Malakar et al. [14] proposed that for homogeneous platforms, using 1% of training data on the target platform to retrain the model on the source platform can predict the remaining 99% of the performance data on the target platform. Amit et al. [15,16] explored the transfer learning technique for cross-platform or cross-system prediction. Differently, they regarded hardware-related features, i.e. configurations as features to form dataset. Kumar et al. [11] used transfer learning to achieve performance prediction from simulated systems to physical systems and across different architectures. Meanwhile, they point out that prediction accuracy in memory-bound applications is higher than in compute-bound applications due to the variability of processor manufacturing. Although these studies have reduced training samples through transfer learning, they have not fully exploited the data reduction potential. Kumar's work is most similar to ours, but differs in that we achieve power/performance prediction for different architectures. Moreover, not only using off-the-shelf transfer learning approaches, we propose a hierarchical transfer learning method combined with feature characteristics, which greatly reduces the training data and ensures the model accuracy.

3   Motivation

The application-related features have little impact on cross-platform power/ performance modelling, which inspires us to consider hierarchical division. In this section, we test the correctness of this point.

Generally, the features required in modelling can be divided into three levels, i.e., application level, platform level, and intermediate level. Features at the intermediate level that are generated when a program runs on a certain platform are a mix of application-related and platform-related features. Here, we split the intermediate features into two parts and propose four cases. Table 2 describes four cases for comparisons. In four artificially presented cases, different levels of features are mixed to be used as inputs to CP^3 training. Case 1 uses all levels of feature for modelling, Case 2 uses all features except those at the application level, Case 3 uses some application-related features at the intermediate level, and Case 4, which is implemented by CP^3, uses all platform-related features. The MAPEs are tested under these cases and the experimental results are shown in the last two rows of Table 2.

We reach two important observations through Table 2, which inspires us to propose the hierarchical transfer learning approach.

1. One observation is that **application-related features do not significantly affect model accuracy in the cross-platform scenario**. Hence, removing the application-related features does not have a significant impact on the model's accuracy. For example, in Table 2, removing features causes the reduction of accuracy by less than 0.5%, which inspires us to propose CP^3.

2. Another very important observation is that **when only using input parameters for modelling, model accuracy will be greatly reduced**. This also illustrates the important role of platform-related features as opposed to application-related features in modelling, further demonstrating why removing application-related features is a rational decision.

Table 2. Feature levels involved in four cases.

	Case 1	Case 2	Case 3	Case 4
Application	✓		✓	
Inter. (app)	✓	✓	✓	
Inter. (plat)	✓	✓		✓
Platform	✓	✓		✓
$MAPE_{power}$	0.91%	0.91%	10.30%	0.97%
$MAPE_{perfromance}$	1.22%	1.52%	3.86%	1.54%

Inspired by the above two points, we consider to further stratify the intermediate features into platform-related and application-related, and propose a hierarchical transfer learning method.

4   Methodology

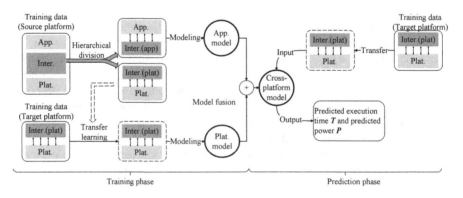

Fig. 2. Overview of the CP^3 framework.

Figure 2 gives the overview of the CP^3 framework, which has two phases, i.e., the training phase and prediction phase. In the training phase, CP^3 adopts the proposed three-step hierarchical transfer learning approach to construct the cross-platform model. In the prediction phase, collecting the required features on the target platform as the input to the cross-platform model, CP^3 outputs the execution time T and the average power consumption P.

The hierarchical transfer learning approach consists of three steps. In the first step, we split all features into two parts, that is, features with a three-level structure are further divided into four levels (two parts). In this way, it is no longer necessary to collect all the features on the target platform. In the second step, we consider reducing the sample size by applying partial transfer. Finally, we use the model fusion approach, to realize the combination of the application-layer model of the source platform and platform-layer model of the target platform and obtain the cross-platform model. The rest of this section elaborates the three-step hierarchical transfer learning approach.

4.1 Hierarchical Division

Figure 2 gives the schematic diagram of the hierarchical division approach. As we mentioned before, the features required in modeling can be divided into three levels, i.e., application level (App. in Fig. 2), platform level (Plat. in Fig. 2), and intermediate level (Inter. in Fig. 2). App. features refer to the input parameters of the application and the configuration parameters set by the user when submitting the job (as shown in Table 6). Plat. features refer to the hardware specifications , such as CPU frequency, memory capacity, and cache size (as shown in Table 5). Inter. features refer to power/performance statistics generated when a specific application runs on a specific platform. These features are a mix of application-related and platform-related features. Performance monitoring events are representative features at the intermediate level, which directly reflects the CPU activities caused by the interaction between applications and platforms. Each time the program is run, the above three types of features can be collected to form a vector $x_i(1 < i < N)$, N is the total number of samples.

Based on our observations, relying on existing three-level features will not be able to determine a minimum number of critical features on the target platform that will cover the training data in full. For this reason, we propose a hierarchical division method, an embedded feature selection method [17] that includes sparsity reduction, feature reduction, and feature division, allowing further selection of features at the intermediate level automatically.

Sparsity Reduction. First, LASSO [18] regression is used for sparsity reduction. The training data has strong sparseness because it is made up of input parameters from multiple applications, thus being different and rarely overlapping. It can be seen from Table 6 that the input parameters of Graph500 and SMG2000 do not overlap. LASSO regression is a data dimensionality reduction method, which adds $L1$ penalty term on the basis of linear regression model, which is shown in Eq. (1),

$$\frac{1}{N}\Sigma_{i=1}^{N}(\vec{w}^{\mathrm{T}} \cdot \vec{x}_i + b - \vec{y}_i)^2 + \lambda\|w\|_1 \tag{1}$$

where $\vec{x}_i$ is the eigenvector, $\vec{w}^{\mathrm{T}}$ is the corresponding weight vector, N is the total number of features containing in $\vec{x}_i$, $\vec{y}_i$ is the actual value on the target platform, b is the constant, $\lambda\|w\|_1$ is the $L1$ penalty term. The addition of the $L1$ penalty term completes the feature selection. By compressing the original coefficients, the originally small coefficients are directly compressed to 0, so that the features corresponding to these coefficients are regarded as insignificant features. The insignificant features are directly discarded, thereby reducing the sparsity. By applying LASSO regression, we select k features for subsequent processing.

Feature Reduction. Modern computing systems have more than 100 performance monitoring events, but they can only collect a few of them simultaneously because of monitoring overhead, which makes it crucial to select a small number of PMCs with the highest relevance. To pick out as few features as possible that have high relevance as possible, we quantify features' importance by introducing the Decision Tree [19] based feature selection method, therefore l pivot features are selected.

The construction process of Decision tree is actually the process of selecting the best features. Decision tree is usually a process of recursively selecting the optimal features, and splitting the features so that each sub-data set has the best fitting effect. Building a tree realizes feature selection and feature importance ranking. In a built decision tree, the features closer to the root node are more important. With Decision Tree, we select the pivot features that contribute a lot to the accuracy of the power or performance model on the given platform.

Feature Division. To minimize the number of features, we propose the idea of hierarchical division under the guidance of hierarchical thinking that further partitioning the current three-level features to form four feature levels. The core of hierarchical division is to divide features at the intermediate level into two types, i.e., features that are related to platforms and features that are related to applications. From top to bottom, the four levels of the source platform are the top application-level features, intermediate application-level features, intermediate platform-level features, and the bottom platform-level features.

Following the discovery of the l pivot features, we calculate the Pearson Correlation Coefficients [20] (PCCs) P_{app} and $P_{platform}$ for the the application-level pivot features and platform-level pivot features respectively as Eq. (2),

$$\rho_{X,Y} = \frac{cov(X,Y)}{\sigma_X\sigma_Y} = \frac{E[(X - \mu_X)(Y - \mu_Y)]}{\sigma_X\sigma_Y} \tag{2}$$

where $\rho_{X,Y}$ is the PCC, X represent the pivot feature set at the intermediate level and Y represent the feature set at the application level, $cov(X,Y)$ is the co-variance of X and Y, σ_X and σ_Y are variance of X and Y, μ_X and μ_Y are standard deviation of X and Y respectively, E represents expectation.

We choose $l - n$ ($l - n = 2$ in the paper) pivot features at the application level with ρ_{app} greater than the preset threshold as the application-related features at the intermediate level and select n ($n = 8$ in the paper) pivot features at the platform level with $\rho_{platform}$ greater than the preset threshold as the platform-related features at the intermediate level. The pivot features at the application level and the application-related features at the intermediate level are used as the upper two levels of training data, and the pivot features at the platform level and platform-related features at the intermediate level are used as the bottom two levels of training data. The feature size required for modeling reduces considerably after applying hierarchical division, and only the platform-related features are required in modeling.

Table 3. Pivot Features on platforms A, B, and C.

No.	A	B	C
1	cpu-migrations	L1-dcache-load-misses	BUS_ACCESS_LD
2	idq.ms_dsb_occur	branch-misses	ASE_SPEC
3	l1d_pend_miss.pending	cpu-migrations	VFP_SPEC
4	llc_misses.pcie_read	bus-cycles	EXC_DABORT
5	llc_references.pcie_read	iTLB-loads	EXC_TRAP_IRQ
6	major-faults	major-faults	BR_MIS_PRED_BTB_INDIR
7	page-faults	uncore_iio_free_running_0 /bw_out_port1/	BR_MIS_PRED_RETURN
8	offcore_requests.demand_rfo	uncore_iio_free_running_1 /bw_out_port2/	ETM_EXT_OUT0
9	offcore_response.pf_l2_rfo.llc _hit.any_response	uncore_iio_free_running_1 /util_out_port3/	L2_TLB_ACCESS_PF
10	uops_issued.flags_merge	uncore_iio_free_running_2 /util_out_port2/	L2_TLB_REFILL

4.2   Partial Transfer

Another big challenge faced in cross-platform modeling is how to overcome the huge gap between the source platform and the target platform. Owing to the completely different architectures, platform-related features are different on different platforms. This is generally overcome at the cost of a large number of samples for training on the target platform in previous studies. Different from previous studies, we apply partial transfer based on the structural correspondence learning (SCL) [21] algorithm.

SCL is an unsupervised learning framework, which makes use of the unlabeled data from the target domain to extract some relevant features that may reduce the difference between the domains. There are three steps of SCL. In the first step, we define a set of pivot features (the number of pivot features is denoted by n) on the unlabeled data from both domains. Although SCL has long been thought to be able to reduce the difference between domains, how to select the pivot features is difficult and domain-dependent. In this paper, we modify the way of selecting pivot features, and provide more details in Sect. 4.1, finally obtaining n pivot features after feature selection.

In the second step, we remove these pivot features from the data and treats each pivot feature as a new label vector. The n classification problems can be constructed. The adopted classifier in this paper is Decision Tree. By assuming each problem can be solved by the linear classifier, so SCL can learn a matrix $\boldsymbol{W}_s$. The goal of partial transfer is to minimize the loss function [22] L, namely

$$\min L(\langle \vec{w}_{is}^{\mathrm{T}} \cdot \vec{x}_{it} | 1 \leq i \leq m \rangle, \vec{y}_t) \tag{3}$$

where matrix $\boldsymbol{X}_t = [\vec{x}_{1t}, \vec{x}_{2t}, ..., \vec{x}_{mt}]$ represents n features and m samples of CP^3 on the target platform. Each sample vector $\vec{x}_{it}$ has n feature components. The corresponding weight matrix of $\boldsymbol{X}_s$ is $\boldsymbol{W}_s$. We use the matrix $\boldsymbol{W}_s$ on the source platform to make predictions. $\vec{w}_{is}^{\mathrm{T}} \cdot \vec{x}_{it}$ represents the ith sample predicted value $(1 \leq i \leq m)$ of CP^3 on the target platform, and y_{it} represents the i sample observed value of CP^3 on the target platform. For each i $(1 \leq i \leq m)$, Eq. (3) needs to satisfy the minimization of $|y_{it} - \vec{w}_{is}^{\mathrm{T}} \cdot \vec{x}_{it}|$.

Matrix $\boldsymbol{W}_s$ is shown as Eq. (4),

$$\boldsymbol{W}_s = [\vec{w}_{1s}, ..., \vec{w}_{ks}, \vec{w}_{(k+1)s}, ..., \vec{w}_{ms}] \tag{4}$$

where vectors $\vec{w}_{1s}, ..., \vec{w}_{ks}$ represent the weights corresponding to application-related feature vectors $\vec{x}_{1s}, ..., \vec{x}_{ks}$ on the source platform. And vectors $\vec{w}_{(k+1)s}, ..., \vec{w}_{ms}$ represent the weights corresponding to platform-related feature vectors $\vec{x}_{(k+1)s}, ..., \vec{x}_{ms}$.

In the third step, we apply singular value decomposition (SVD) [23] to matrix $\boldsymbol{W}_s$. Under the optimal goal as Eq. (3) shows, its corresponding weight vectors are $\vec{w}_{1s}, ..., \vec{w}_{ks}$, which become $\vec{w}_{1t}, ..., \vec{w}_{kt}$ through the iterative weighted method,

$$\boldsymbol{W}_t = [\vec{w}_{1t}, ..., \vec{w}_{kt}, \vec{w}_{(k+1)t}, ..., \vec{w}_{mt}] \tag{5}$$

$$\boldsymbol{W}_t^* \leftarrow \arg\min L \triangleq [\vec{w}_{1t}^*, ..., \vec{w}_{kt}^*, \vec{w}_{(k+1)s}^*, ..., \vec{w}_{ms}^*] \tag{6}$$

where the transformation from $\vec{w}_{(k+1)s}^*, ..., \vec{w}_{ms}^*$ to $\vec{w}_{(k+1)t}^*, ..., \vec{w}_{mt}^*$ adopts the modified SCL method. Let $\boldsymbol{W}_s = UDV^{\mathrm{T}}$, then $\theta = U^{\mathrm{T}}$ can be obtained, and finally the features $\vec{x}_{it}$ on the target platform can be transferred to new features $\theta \vec{x}_{it}$, achieving the alignment of the pivot features on the source platform and target platform.

4.3   Model Fusion

Figure 3 gives the flow chart of three-step cross-platform modeling based on the proposed hierarchical transfer learning. In the first step, with hierarchical division, the features at the intermediate level are further divided into two sub-levels, forming a four-level structure. The upper two levels are application-related features, which are used to construct the application-layer model S_u, and the lower two levels are platform-related features, which are used to construct the platform-layer model S_d. In the same manner, the application-layer model T_u and the platform-layer model T_d of the target platform can be developed. Models such as S_u and T_u, which use application-related features as their training data, do not change when applied in cross-platform scenarios, i.e., $S_u = T_u$, so there is no need to retrain T_u on the target platform. This observation will be verified in Sect. 6. In the second step, to migrate the built model from the source platform to the target platform quickly, the proposed partial transfer is applied to reduce the sample size, realizing the migration from S_d to T_d. In the third step, the model fusion algorithm is used to combine the application-layer model S_u on the source platform with the platform-layer model T_d of the target platform to produce the *cross-platform model* of the CP^3 framework. The rest of this section elaborates on this algorithm.

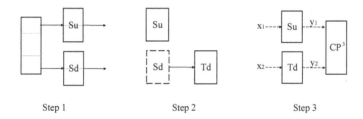

Fig. 3. Schematic of three steps of the hierarchical transfer learning approach.

The model fusion algorithm is essentially a layered weighted modeling method [24], which can be divided into two layers. As Fig. 3 shows, the first layer is the individual layer, which refers to the already-trained application-layer model of the source platform and the platform-layer model of the target platform, the second layer is the fusion layer, which refers to the cross-platform model that combines all the individual layers' models. The model fusion algorithm includes two steps. In the first step, we take the training data x_1 and x_2 as the individual layer's input, and obtain the models S_u and S_d. The outputs of the individual layer are the predicted values $\tilde{y}_1, \tilde{y}_2$. In the second step, we use $\tilde{y}_1$ and $\tilde{y}_2$ as the inputs of the fusion layer to obtain the output, $\mathbf{Y}$. Elements y_1 and y_2 are the actual values corresponding to $\tilde{y}_1$ and $\tilde{y}_2$.

Algorithm 1. Model fusion algorithm

Require:
　　Training datasets $D_1 = \{(x_1, y_1)\}$, $D_2 = \{(x_2, y_2)\}$;
　　Elementary learning algorithms ϱ_1, ϱ_2;
　　Secondary learning algorithm ϱ_3.
Ensure:
　　CP^3 Model H.
　　// construct models at the individual layer
1: $h_1 = \varrho_1(D_1)$;
2: $h_2 = \varrho_2(D_2)$;
3: $\tilde{y}_1 = h_1(x_1)$;
4: $\tilde{y}_2 = h_2(x_2)$;
　　// construct the fused model
5: $D_3 = \{([\tilde{y}_1, \tilde{y}_2], [y_1, y_2])\}$;
6: $H = \varrho_3(D_3)$.

The descriptions of the modeling process of CP^3 appear in Algorithm 1. The elements x_1 and y_1 form the training dataset D_1, and the elements x_2 and y_2 form the training dataset D_2. Elementary learning algorithms ϱ_1 and ϱ_2, such as gradient boosting tree [25], can be used to train models S_u and T_d. The final results of S_u and T_d are h_1 and h_2, respectively. $[\tilde{y}_1, \tilde{y}_2]$ and $[y_1, y_2]$ form the training dataset D_3. CP^3 adopts the secondary learning algorithm ϱ_3 to obtain the final result, H.

5   Experimental Setup

This section describes the platforms, benchmarks, training data and metrics used in this paper.

5.1   Platforms and Environment

The experiments are conducted on three different computing platforms, denoted as A, B, and C. Table 4 gives the hardware parameters of each platform. These three platforms have different characteristics. B with the latest model of Intel x86 processor has higher processor frequency, bigger DRAM capacity, and better performance than A. A is a 16-node cluster. C is a node with an ARM-based processor.

All three platforms support frequency scaling and three processor frequency levels (maximum, medium, minimum) are set for each platform, i.e., minimum frequency, medium frequency, and maximum frequency, which are detailed in Table 4. Different frequency levels can be set using the *cpufreq* governor [26] on platforms A and B. For C, three frequency levels can be set in the registers. Compilers used for compilation are GCC 5.4.0, GCC 4.8.5, and GCC 4.9.0 for A, B, and C, respectively. OpenMPI 4.0.5, OpenMPI 4.1.0, and OpenMPI 4.0.1 are used as MPI libraries on platforms A, B, and C, respectively.

Table 4. Configurations of three platforms.

	Platform A	Platform B	Platform C
Max. (frequency)	2.6 GHz	3.2 GHz	2.2 GHz
Mid. (frequency)	2.2 GHz	2.8 GHz	1.8 GHz
Min. (frequency)	1.8 GHz	2.2 GHz	1.4 GHz
#cores per CPU	10	8	64
#CPUs per node	2	2	1
Hyper-threading	Yes	Yes	No
Mem size per node	64 GB	384 GB	128 GB
Cache size per node	25 MB	24.75 MB	16 MB
#nodes	16	1	1
Network	InfiniBand	NA	NA

5.2 Benchmarks

We choose `Graph500` and `SMG2000` to evaluate the CP^3 framework. `Graph500` (version 3.0.0) [27] is a widely used benchmark for data-intensive computing. Its computing kernel is the breadth-first search (BFS) of the graph starting from a single source vertex. `SMG2000` [28] is a parallel semi-coarse multi-grid solver for linear systems, which is produced by finite difference, finite volume, or finite element discretization of diffusion equations. This solver is crucial to reach better scalability for simulating radiation diffusion. Table 6 gives the input parameters of `Graph500` and `SMG2000`, which are also regarded as features at the application level in the CP^3 framework.

5.3 Training Data

We collect training data by running benchmarks on three platforms three times or more until the 95% confidence bound under different configurations as shown in Table 5. As explained below, we use a variety of techniques to obtain different features, i.e., hardware parameters, application parameters, and runtime PMCs, and labels, i.e., performance and power consumption.

Table 5. Features at the platform level of CP^3

Parameter	Type	Range
Platform number	Numerical	[0, 1, 2]
#nodes	Numerical	[1, 16]
#processes	Numerical	[1, 640]
frequency	Numerical	[Min_freq, Mid_freq, Max_freq]
#threads / core	Numerical	[1, 2]
Mem size	Numerical	[64, 128, 384]
Cache size	Numerical	[25, 24.75, 16]

- The hardware parameters can be collected through reading the operating system, and the application parameters can be extracted via *shell* scripts from the log file to obtain fields related to input parameters and user configuration parameters.
- Performance monitoring events are collected by the *perf* [29] tool every 1000 ms on platforms A and B. Additionally, to access PMCs on platform C, we have developed our own Linux loadable kernel module (LLKM).
- We record the start time and end time of the program to obtain the execution time of the program.
- We use the *perf* tool on A and B to record the processor and memory power usage by reading performance monitoring events */power/energy-pkg/* and */power/energy-ram/* at 1000 ms interval. On platform C, cascading the I^2C interface of the power supply and the CPU enables us to read the real-time processor voltage and current by directly accessing the registers *0x8b* and *0x8c*, therefore the real-time CPU and DRAM power consumption are obtained at a sampling rate of 1000 ms. Using the real-time power consumption per second, we calculate the average power consumption of the program from all the instantaneous power consumption throughout its execution.

Every benchmark runs for more than 60 s and up to 60 min. Note that PMCs on three platforms are sampled in a fixed interval (1000 ms) when running benchmarks under different problem scales as Table 6 shows. To ensure the robustness of CP^3, we randomly select 10,000 samples of the source platform. Additionally, to reduce the profiling overhead, we only collect 1000 samples (or less) of the target platform to obtain the cross-platform model.

Table 6. Features at the application level of CP^3.

Benchmark	Parameter	Type	Range
Graph500	SCALE	Numerical (Integer)	[8–26]
	edgefactor	Numerical (Integer)	[8, 16, 32, 64]
SMG2000	nx / ny /nz	Numerical (Integer)	[100–250]
	Px / Py / Pz	Numerical (Integer)	[4, 8, 16, 64]
	cx / cy / cz	Numerical (Float)	[0.1–1.0]

5.4 Metrics

The Mean Absolute Percentage Error (MAPE) is used to evaluate the CP^3 framework. Eq. (7) gives the detailed representation of $MAPE$,

$$\text{MAPE} = \frac{100\%}{n} \sum_{i=1}^{n} |\frac{\hat{y}_i - y_i}{y_i}|, \text{MAPE} \geq 0 \tag{7}$$

where y_i represents the observed average power or execution time for the ith sample. $\hat{y}_i$ represents the predicted average power and execution time for the ith

sample. The closer the MAPE value is to zero, the higher the CP^3 accuracy. For the remainder of this paper, we use $MAPE_{power}$ and $MAPE_{perf}$ denote the MAPE of power and performance model.

The coefficient of determination (R^2) is used to determine the fit of the model as Eq. (8) shows,

$$R^2 = 1 - \frac{\sum_{i=1}^{n}(y_i - \hat{y}_i)^2}{\sum_{i=1}^{n}(y_i - \bar{y}_i)^2}, 0 \le R^2 \le 1 \tag{8}$$

where y_i and $\hat{y}_i$ are the same as those in Eq. (7). $\bar{y}_i$ represents the average of all samples i $(1 \le i \le n)$. The larger the value of R^2, i.e., the closer R^2 is to 1, the better the model fit.

6   Evaluation of CP^3

We conduct a group of experiments to evaluate the effectiveness of CP^3. Evaluation results show that CP^3 achieves high accuracy with only 1% of the baseline training data when i) across different architectures and (b) across different platforms belonging to the same architecture. We also explore the application-generality and hardware-generality of CP^3 with different benchmarks and different frequency levels. The rest of this section details the evaluation results.

6.1   Overall Results

Table 7. Overall results of CP^3

		Power		Performance	
		MAPE	R^2	MAPE	R^2
Same architecture	Platform $A \rightarrow$ Platform B	0.97%	0.99	2.54%	0.99
	Platform $B \rightarrow$ Platform$A$	0.62%	0.99	1.86%	0.99
Different architecture	Platform $A \rightarrow$ Platform C	0.52%	0.99	2.58%	0.98
	Platform $C \rightarrow$ Platform A	0.33%	0.99	1.33%	0.99
	Platform $B \rightarrow$ Platform C	1.13%	0.99	9.9%	0.84
	Platform $C \rightarrow$ Platform B	0.33%	0.99	9.63%	0.86

On the three platforms involved in this paper, we conduct a group of experiments in terms of power prediction and performance prediction, and calculated the MAPE and R^2 values. Table 7 presents the evaluation results in different scenarios. As shown in Table 7, the average MAPE value for all experiments of power prediction is 0.65% with CP^3, and the maximum MAPE value is only 1.13% (B $\rightarrow$ C). According to Table 7, all R^2 values of power prediction are all above 0.9, which illustrates the good fit of CP^3. The average MAPE value for all experiments of performance prediction is 4.64% and the maximum MAPE

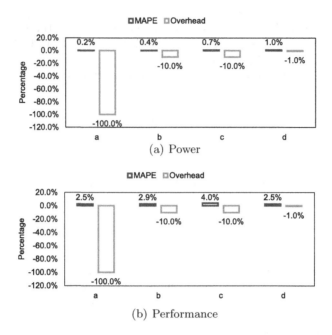

Fig. 4. Comparisons with the baseline in terms of accuracy and overhead

value is only 9.9% (B → C). The average R^2 value is 0.94 and all R^2 values are between 0.84 and 0.99.

Following the same data used in the paper, we set the baseline that a model trained with all the samples and all the features. In comparison with baseline, CP^3 only has a 1% data overhead. This is because CP^3 selects only 10 pivot features (less than 10%) from more than 100 PMCs provided by the platforms and only 1000 samples (10% of all the samples), so as to yield only 1% data overhead(10% x 10%). To illustrate CP^3's effectiveness, we set four cases in scenario A → B, i.e., (a) the baseline (with 100% overhead), (b) all the samples and 10% features (with 10% overhead), (c) 10% samples and all the features (with 10% overhead), and (d) 10% samples and 10% features (with 1% overhead). The MAPEs for case (a), (b), (c) and (d) are 0.2%, 0.4%, 0.7%, and 0.65% in power prediction, and 2.45%, 2.87%, 3.98%, and 4.67% in performance prediction. We plot the relationship between accuracy and overhead in Fig. 4. Note that the red bars represent the percentages of data when compared case (a)-(d) with the baseline. It can be observed that CP^3 (case (d)) offers a significant reduction in data overhead (only 1%) and a slight increase in MAPE (only 0.5% for power prediction and 2% for performance prediction) in comparison to the baseline.

6.2   Across Different Architectures

The most challenging problem in cross-platform modeling is how to achieve accurate prediction across different architectures. Different architectures, such as X86 and ARM, have significant differences in instructions such as branch and conditional jump, and etc.

Table 3 lists the pivot features of the three platforms. It is known that platforms A and B are X86-based platforms while C is an ARM-based platform. According to Table 3, platforms belonging to the same architecture have high similarities in the distribution of pivot features. However, a significant difference exists between X86-based platforms and ARM-based platforms. The pivot features of the X86-based platforms focus on the description of the CPU branches, CPU stalls, cache, offcore and uncore parts. In addition to focusing on bus access, memory access, and cache access, ARM-based platforms' pivot features mainly focus on exceptions and scheduling stalls, which is the main difference between the pivot features of X86-based platforms and ARM-based platforms. This difference in architectures often leads to lower accuracy of cross-architecture modeling.

This section uses platform A or B as the source platform (X86-based), C as the target platform (ARM-based) to carry out cross-architecture experiments, namely A → C, and B → C. Table 7 gives the overall power and performance prediction results. For all cross-architecture scenarios, CP^3 can achieve accurate power and performance prediction. Corresponding to A → C, C → A, B → C, and C → B, the MAPE values of power prediction are 0.52%, 0.33%, 1.13%, and 0.33%, respectively, and all R^2 values can reach 0.99. The average MAPE value is 0.58% and the average R^2 value is 0.99 when performing power prediction. For performance prediction results, the MAPE values are 2.58%, 1.33%, 9.9%, and 9.63%, respectively, and the R^2 values are 0.98, 0.99, 0.84, and 0.86, respectively. The average MAPE value is 5.86% and the average R^2 value is 0.92. It can be observed from Table 7 that when performing cross-architecture performance prediction, using B as the source platform leads to a relatively higher MAPE and lower R^2 value than other scenarios. The reason may be that platforms A and C can obtain fewer performance monitoring events than B due to hardware platforms' limitation, which describes CPU activities less specific, leads to lower accuracy of CP^3 in scenarios B → C and C → B.

The selection of the source platform does affect the model's prediction accuracy. All experimental results show that when the source platform supports fewer performance monitoring events and the target platform supports more performance monitoring events, the MAPE value of cross-platform prediction is lower. As shown in Table 7, after changing the source platform from A to C, the MAPE value becomes from 0.52% to 0.33%. Also, the MAPE value decreases from 1.13% to 0.33% when using C as the source platform rather than B. It's easy to observe that after exchanging the source platform and the target platform, the MAPE value becomes 2x to 4x of the original scenario. Table 7 also shows the similar trends for performance prediction. Different source platforms differ in specifications and performance monitoring events, making the prediction accuracy difference after exchanging the source platform and the target platform.

6.3   Across Same Architectures but Different Platforms

When the source platform and the target platform adopt the same architecture, the accuracy of CP^3 is higher than that of cross-architecture scenarios. This section evaluates the effectiveness of CP^3 when across different platforms belonging to the same architecture. Table 7 gives the power and performance prediction results of two sets of experiments. Corresponding to A → B and B → A, the MAPE values of power prediction are 0.97%, and 0.62%, respectively, and R^2 values are all 0.99. The average MAPE value is 0.8% and the average R^2 value is 0.99 when performing power prediction. For performance prediction results, the MAPE values of performance prediction are 2.54%, and 1.86%, respectively, and R^2 values are all 0.99.

As can be seen from Table 7, the prediction accuracy under the same architecture is improved compared to the accuracy under different architectures when performing performance prediction. This phenomenon occurs because experimental platforms with the same architecture have similarities in instructions and types of performance monitoring events. The similarity in instructions brings the likeness of various computing components' activities and provides higher accuracy for the model. The similarity of the types of performance monitoring events reduces transfer learning difficulty, making the model more accurate and better fitting.

6.4   Generality of CP^3

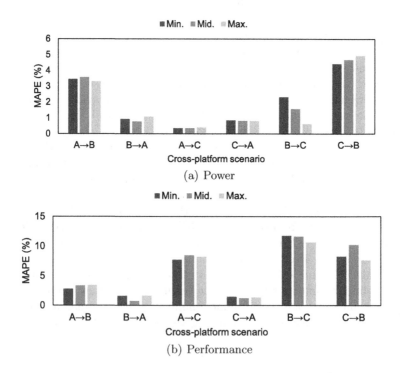

(a) Power

(b) Performance

Fig. 5. Impact of different frequency level on CP^3.

Different Frequency Levels. CPU frequency affects the accuracy of cross-architecture power prediction. As Fig. 5 shows, three frequency levels are set for each platform. Frequency does affect the accuracy of power/performance prediction, but its impact has no apparent law. As Fig. 5 shows, in some scenarios, such as B → C, and C → B, the higher the frequency, the higher the accuracy, while in other scenarios, such as A → C, C → A, the lower the frequency, the higher the accuracy. This result occurs because frequency can directly affect power consumption, so the frequency value plays an essential role in power prediction while having little effect on performance prediction.

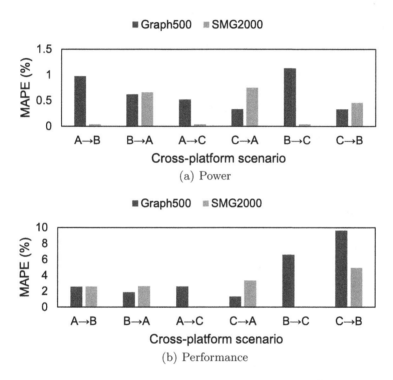

Fig. 6. Impact of different benchmarks on CP^3.

Different Benchmarks. CP^3 is suitable for power or performance prediction of a variety of applications, and the accuracy is related to the number of input parameters of the applications. The greater the number of input parameters, the higher the prediction accuracy. Figure 6 shows the experimental results of CP^3 for benchmarks Graph500 and SMG2000. From Fig. 6, it can be seen that in the six sets of experiments, no matter when performing performance prediction or power prediction, the MAPE values of SMG2000 are lower than that of Graph500, and the R^2 values are higher. The average MAPE value of Graph500 is 4.08% while the average MAPE value of SMG2000 is 2.28% when performing performance prediction. And the average MAPE value of Graph500 is 0.65% while the average MAPE value of SMG2000 is 0.49% when performing power prediction. SMG2000 can always achieve better prediction accuracy no matter in terms of performance or power consumption because SMG2000 has more input parameters. Table 6 shows there are three input parameters for Graph500 and nine input parameters for SMG2000. Having more input parameters makes the application-layer model more accurate, bringing higher prediction accuracy and lower MAPE value.

6.5   Comparisons

Table 2 describes comparison results between our approach and Kumar's work [11]. Similarly with Table 2, we split all features into four layers. As experimental results show, the two methods have the same error when predicting performance, and the accuracy of CP^3 is basically the same as that of Kumar's work when predicting power consumption, in which the former is slightly worse than the latter. But it is worth noting that the amount of data used by CP^3 is one-tenth of that of Kumar's work (Table 8).

Table 8. Feature levels involved in four cases.

	Kumar's work [11]	CP^3
Application	✓	
Inter. (app)	✓	
Inter. (plat)	✓	✓
Platform	✓	✓
$MAPE_{power}$	0.91%	0.97%
$MAPE_{perfromance}$	1.22%	1.54%

7   Conclusion

To reduce data overhead brought by time-consuming program profiling in learning-based cross-platform prediction, this paper presents CP^3, which focuses on utilizing architecture differences to migrate built models to target platforms with as little data as possible. Evaluation results show that CP^3 uses only 1% of the baseline training data to achieve only 0.65% of the prediction error for power prediction and 4.64% for performance prediction on average. Now CP^3 is only validated on multi-core general-purpose processors. Future research will explore other architectures. Additionally, by exploring the differences in different architectures, we aim to further improve the accuracy of CP^3 across different architectures.

Acknowledgements. This work is supported in part by the Key R&D project grant number No.2018YFB0204301, the Advanced Research Project of China under grant number 31511010203 and the Research Program of NUDT grant number ZK18-03-10.

References

1. Wang, R., et al.: Brief introduction of tianHe exascale prototype system. Tsinghua Sci. Technol. **26**, 361–269 (2021)
2. Top500 performance development. https://www.top500.org/statistics/perfdevel/ (2020)
3. Reed, D.A., Dongarra, J.: Exascale computing and big data. Commun. ACM **58**(7), 56–68 (2015)
4. Dongarra, J., Lastovetsky, A.L.: High Performance Heterogeneous Computing, volume 78. Wiley, Hoboken, NJ (2009)
5. Kim, Y., Mercati, P., More, A., Shriver, E., Rosing, T.: P4: phase-based power/performance prediction of heterogeneous systems via neural networks. In: 2017 IEEE/ACM International Conference on Computer-Aided Design (ICCAD), pp. 683–690 (2017)
6. Zheng, X., Vikalo, H., Song, S., John, L.K., Gerstlauer, A.: Sampling-based binary-level cross-platform performance estimation. In: Design, Automation Test in Europe Conference Exhibition (DATE), 2017, pp. 1709–1714 (2017)
7. Zheng, X., John, L.K., Gerstlauer, A.: Accurate phase-level cross-platform power and performance estimation. In: 2016 53nd ACM/EDAC/IEEE Design Automation Conference (DAC), pp. 1–6. IEEE Press (2016)
8. Binkert, N., et al.: The gem5 simulator. SIGARCH Comput. Archit. News **39**(2), 1–7 (2011)
9. Zheng, X., Ravikumar, P., John, L.K., Gerstlauer, A.: Learning-based analytical cross-platform performance prediction. In: 2015 International Conference on Embedded Computer Systems: Architectures, Modeling, and Simulation (SAMOS), pp. 52–59 (2015)
10. Zheng, X., John, L.K., Gerstlauer, A.: LACross: learning-based analytical cross-platform performance and power prediction. Int. J. Parallel Prog. **45**(6), 1488–1514 (2017)
11. Kumar, R., Mankodi, A., Bhatt, A., Chaudhury, B., Amrutiya, A.: Cross-platform performance prediction with transfer learning using machine learning. In: 2020 11th International Conference on Computing, Communication and Networking Technologies (ICCCNT), pp. 1–7. IEEE (2020)
12. Sun, J., Sun, G., Zhan, S., Zhang, J., Chen, Y.: Automated performance modeling of HPC applications using machine learning. IEEE Trans. Comput. **69**(5), 749–763 (2020)
13. Marathe, A., et al.: Performance modeling under resource constraints using deep transfer learning. In: Proceedings of the International Conference for High Performance Computing, Networking, Storage and Analysis, SC 2017, New York, USA (2017). Association for Computing Machinery
14. Malakar, P., Balaprakash, P., Vishwanath, V., Morozov, V., Kumaran, K.: Benchmarking machine learning methods for performance modeling of scientific applications. In: 2018 IEEE/ACM Performance Modeling, Benchmarking and Simulation of High Performance Computer Systems (PMBS), pp. 33–44 (2018)
15. Mankodi, A., Bhatt, A., Chaudhury, B., Kumar, R., Amrutiya, A.: Modeling performance and power on disparate platforms using transfer learning with machine learning models. In: Das, B., Patgiri, R., Bandyopadhyay, S., Balas, V.E. (eds.) Modeling, Simulation and Optimization. SIST, vol. 206, pp. 231–246. Springer, Singapore (2021). https://doi.org/10.1007/978-981-15-9829-6_18

16. Mankodi, A., Bhatt, A., Chaudhury, B.: Performance prediction from simulation systems to physical systems using machine learning with transfer learning and scaling. Concurrency Comput. Pract. Experience e6433 (2021)
17. Saeys, Y., Inza., et al.: A review of feature selection techniques in bioinformatics. Bioinformatics **23**(19), 2507–2517 (2007)
18. Li, F., Yang, Y., Xing, E.: From lasso regression to feature vector machine. In: Advances in Neural Information Processing Systems (2005)
19. Decision Tree. https://en.wikipedia.org/wiki/Decision_tree (2020)
20. Akoglu, H.: User's guide to correlation coefficients. Turk. J. Emerg. Med. **18**(3), 91–93 (2018)
21. Blitzer, J., McDonald, R., Pereira, F.: Domain adaptation with structural correspondence learning. In: Proceedings of the 2006 Conference on Empirical Methods in Natural Language Processing, EMNLP 2006, pp. 120–128, USA (2006). Association for Computational Linguistics
22. Loss function. https://www.educba.com/loss-functions-in-machine-learning (2020)
23. Golub, G.H., Reinsch, C.: Singular value decomposition and least squares solutions. Numer. Math. **14**(5), 403–420 (1970)
24. Wolpert, D.: Stacked generalization. Neural Networks **5**(2), 241–259 (1992)
25. Ke, G., et al.: Lightgbm: a highly efficient gradient boosting decision tree. In: Guyon, I. (eds.) Advances in Neural Information Processing Systems, vol. 30, pp. 3146–3154. Curran Associates Inc (2017)
26. CPU Frequency Governor. https://wiki.analog.com/resources/tools-software/linuxdsp/docs/linux-kernel-and-drivers/cpufreq/cpufreq (2020)
27. Graph 500 reference implementations. http://www.graph500.org/referencecode
28. The smg2000 benchmark. https://asc.llnl.gov/computingresources/purple/archive/benchmarks/smg
29. The Perf tool. http://www.brendangregg.com/perf.html

Effective Vehicle Lane-Change Sensing Using Onboard Smartphone Based on Temporal Convolutional Network

Junbo Hu[1], Kai Liu[1,3]([✉]), Feiyu Jin[1], Guozhi Yan[1], Hao Zhang[2], Songtao Guo[1], and Hu Min[3]

[1] Chongqing University, Chongqing 400044, China
{junbohu,liukai0807,fyjin,yanguozhiup,guosongtao}@cqu.edu.cn
[2] Chongqing University of Posts and Telecommunications, Chongqing 400065, China
zhanghao@cqupt.edu.cn
[3] Nanfang College Guangzhou, Guangzhou 510970, China
minh@nfu.edu.cn

Abstract. Lane-change sensing is one of the fundamental requirements to enable autonomous driving and safety-critical Intelligent Transportation System (ITS) applications. This work presents a deep-learning approach for detecting the lane changing of vehicles using onboard smartphone, aiming at achieving low-cost and scalable sensing and complementing computer vision-based solutions in special traffic conditions such as heavy fog weather. Specifically, we first present a lane-change sensing framework based on accelerometer and gyroscope readings from the onboard smartphone, which supports offline trajectory data collection and training, as well as online real-time lane-change sensing. Second, in light of the fact that Temporal Convolutional Network (TCN) is computational-efficiency for sequential tasks, we propose a TCN-based Lane-Change Sensing (TCN-LCS) algorithm, which consists of a dynamic sequence length adaptation method for offline training, and a sliding window inference strategy for online inference. Finally, we build the system prototype and give an extensive performance evaluation in real-world traffic environments. The experimental results conclusively demonstrate the feasibility and efficiency of the proposed framework and solution.

Keywords: Temporal convolutional network · Inertial sensors · Lane-change sensing · Performance evaluation

This work was supported in part by the National Natural Science Foundation of China under Grant No. 62172064, the Chongqing Young-Talent Program (Project No. cstc2022ycjh-bgzxm0039), the Venture & Innovation Support Program for Chongqing Overseas Returnees (Project No. cx2021063) and the Science and Technology Research Program of Chongqing Municipal Education Commission (Grant No.KJQN202100637).

W. Meng et al. (Eds.): ICA3PP 2022, LNCS 13777, pp. 139–153, 2023.
https://doi.org/10.1007/978-3-031-22677-9_8

1   Introduction

With the emerging of autonomous driving and rapid development of safety-critical Intelligent Transportation Systems (ITSs), such as cooperative intersection control [10], the lane-level tracking of vehicles has received great attention in both academia and industry. Currently, the most prevalent vehicle localization technologies are based on Global Navigation Satellite System (GNSS) [14,16], but they cannot support lane-level tracking because of ionospheric effects, satellite clock errors and multipath interferences, etc. Computer vision (CV) based lane detection is another mainstream technology to enable lane-level tracking [2,9,20]. Nevertheless, these solutions may not work in extreme weather conditions such as heavy fog and heavy rain, or in particular driving situations such as the blurred line of lanes, which may compromise system robustness. Some other studies have investigated the lane-level tracking based on laser ranging [12,24] or Wi-Fi fingerprinting [6,7,11,25,26], and even more some studies have consider the deployment and security of Wi-Fi AP [18,19]. However, these approaches require additional on-board hardware such as LiDAR (Light Detection and Ranging) or roadside infrastructures such as Wi-Fi APs, which may render system practicality and scalability.

To compensate for the limitations of aforementioned primary technologies, the lane-change sensing based on inertial sensors and data fusion have been explored in recent studies [8,15,22,27]. Zheng et al. [27] leveraged steering angel and vehicle speed from CAN-bus to detect lane-change with Hidden Markov Model (HMM) based classifier and k-nearest neighbor (KNN) classifier. Schle et al. [15] gave a comprehensive analysis on lane-change detection features including distance between the vehicle and left/right lane marking, orientation angel and lateral displacement, etc., and proposed a generative model based on Naïve Bayesian approach to detect lane-change. Klitzke et al. [8] proposed a lane-change detection framework based on unsupervised learning, which modelled the vehicle state as six driving primitives according to the distance to the lane line, and the vehicle driving primitive is unsupervised classified by HMM and the lane-change behavior is recognized by Dynamic Time Wrapping (DTW). Woo et al. [22] proposed a lane-change detection method based on vehicle-trajectory prediction, where the distance to the centerline, the lateral velocity and the potential feature are formulated as the feature vector, and the Support Vector Machine (SVM) is adopted as the classifier. However, these solutions require pre-deployment of infrastructure and additional hardware, or need to acquire data from on-board sensors, which is inconvenient and will incur extra costs.

Since smartphones have received increasing popularity over recent years, more and more smartphone-based vehicular applications are developed, some studies have investigated vehicle lane-change tracking using onboard smartphones [4,13,23]. Xu et al. [23] designed a pattern-based approach to detect lane-change behavior with lateral acceleration of onboard smartphone, which is obtained by empirical analysis of historical vehicle lane-change data. Chen et al. [4] proposed a system called VSense, where a bump-based steering detection algorithm based on gyroscope thresholds is designed, which can detect four types of vehicles steering behaviors. Ouyang et al. [13] further analyzed the smartphone gyroscope data under various vehicle behaviors (i.e., turn, lane-change and U-turn) to deal with continuous sensor waveforms and detect multiple vehicles steering behaviors. Nevertheless, these approaches are normally based on Dead-Reckoning (DR) and empirical threshold estimation, which may suffer from error accumulation over time and the inflexible/unpractical setting of the threshold. Therefore, some researchers try to infer vehicle behaviors with exploring sensor data on continuous time series, instead of discrete readings. In these studies, the technology of deep learning has gained more attention than traditional methods. Florian et al. [21] utilized Long Short-Term Memory (LSTM) network to estimate the point in time a lane change actually happens and performed a high accuracy. Shahverdy et al. [17] modeled the vehicle behavior inference problem as a classification problem and converted the sensor data into image, then fed it into a two-dimensional (2D) Convolutional Neural Network (CNN) for the identification of driving behaviors. However, these methods don't consider the limitations of mobile phone performance or the structural characteristics of the sensor data different from the images.

With above motivations, this work is dedicated to proposing an effective vehicle lane-change sensing architecture and a tailored algorithm based on onboard smartphone sensor readings. Specifically, the designed architecture will support the collection and processing of historical vehicle trajectories for the offline data training and the online lane-change sensing. On this basis, a Temporal Convolutional Network (TCN) [1] model is trained for detecting lane-change behaviors of vehicles. The rationale is that TCN performs convolution operation in time dimension, which is more suitable for the sequential task of inertial sensor data than 2D-CNN. And compared with mainstream Recurrent Neural Networks (RNNs) , TCN, which adopts one-dimensional convolution and dilated causal convolution, is more computation-effective on tasks with time sequential data and more suitable for being deployed onboard. The main contributions of this work are summarized as follows:

- We present an effective vehicle lane-change sensing system architecture based on onboard smartphone, which consists of an offline classifier training phase and an online lane-change sensing phase. Specifically, during offline classifier training phase, the system continuously collects the inertial data sequence of the onboard smartphone, which enables the training the lane-change sensing model. During the online lane-change sensing phase, the real-time obtained inertial data sequences are input into the trained classifier to infer the vehicle behavior (i.e., Left Lane-Change, Right Lane-Change and No Lane-Change).
- We propose a Temporal Convolutional Network based Lane-Change Sensing (TCN-LCS) algorithm. Specifically, a dynamic sequence length adaptation method is designed to align the inertial data sequence, and the Mini-Batch Gradient Descent (MBGD) is adopted for offline training. Further, the sensor data with corresponding labels are adopted to train the TCN model, which detects lane-change behavior of the vehicles in real-time. Finally, a sliding

window inference strategy is proposed to enhance the robustness and improve the accuracy of lane-change sensing.

– We build the system prototype and give an extensive performance evaluation in real-world traffic environments. Specifically, an android-based APP is implemented to collect inertial sensors' readings. Different types of mobile devices have been deployed in different models of vehicles. We have driven over 150 km under different traffic conditions, including highways, city roads, tunnels, flyovers, and campus roads for data collection, offline TCN training and online testing. The experimental results conclusively demonstrate the effectiveness of the proposed solution.

The rest of this paper is organized as follows. Section 2 presents the system architecture. Section 3 proposes the TCN-LCS algorithm. In Sect. 4, we build the system prototype and carry out real-world experiments. Finally, we conclude this paper in Sect. 5.

2   System Architecture

In this part, we propose a vehicle lane-change sensing system architecture, which utilizes only smartphone's inertial data to detect lane-change behavior. As shown in Fig. 1, the system architecture consists of the offline classifier training and the online lane-change sensing phases. In particular, during the offline classifier training phase, vehicles' driving data and corresponding labels are input into the designed model as the training set. On the other hand, during the online lane-change sensing phase, the onboard smartphone continuously collects the sensors' data sequences, which are input into the lane-change behavior classifier to obtain real-time vehicle behavior. Detailed designs are elaborated as follows.

Offline Classifier Training Phase: The goal of this phase is to train the vehicle lane-change behavior classifier based on the historical driving data. Specifically, a large number of historical vehicles driving data are collected, including onboard smartphone sensors data reflecting the vehicle driving behavior and auxiliary data used to identify accurate vehicle behavior, such as video recording for front view. After that, feature extraction is carried out on the raw sensor data to generate features called inertial sequence and corresponding labels are generated through auxiliary data processing. Finally, the training set composed of features and labels drives the training the lane-change behavior classification model.

Online Lane-Change Sensing Phase: It is designed to sense the vehicle lane-change behavior using trained classifier along with the real-time collected inertial sequence data from the onboard smartphones. First, a background process is implemented to collect the real-time inertial sensors' readings from the onboard smartphone, including acceleration and angular velocity. Second, the sensor data is preprocessed to form the inertial sequence to conform to the model input, and it is input into trained lane-change behavior classifier periodically. Finally, the classifier outputs the lane-change event, which is one of the three categories, i.e.,

No Lane-Change (No-LC), Left Lane-Change (Left-LC) and Right Lane-Change (Right-LC).

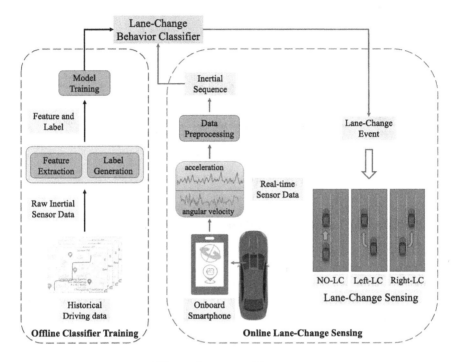

Fig. 1. System architecture

3   TCN-Based Lane-Change Sensing

In this section, we propose a TCN-LCS algorithm to enable the sensing of vehicle lane-change based on the sequence data of inertial sensors. TCN is an effective model for processing tasks with time sequential data, and it is also suitable for being developed at end devices such as smartphones due to its low overhead and computation-efficiency characteristics [1]. In general, the proposed TCN-LCS algorithm consists of an offline-training phase and an online-inference phase. As shown in Fig. 2, in the offline training phase, a data-preprocessing method is firstly designed to process the raw inertial sensor data, which includes a data deduplication mechanism to remove the redundant sensor readings and a sequence length adaptation mechanism to dynamically align the length of inertial data sequences. In the online inference phase, a sliding window inference strategy is proposed to accurately locate the period of a lane-change behavior and select corresponding sensor readings for model inference.

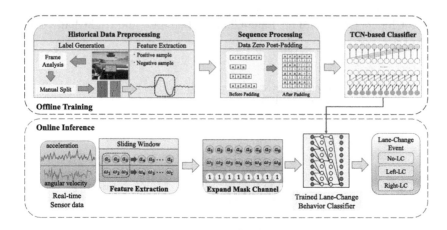

Fig. 2. Workflow of TCN-LCS

3.1   TCN-Based Lane-Change Behavior Classifier

The basic rationale is to exploit the sequential data of acceleration a_T and angular velocity ω_T to infer the vehicle lane-change behavior y_T, where T represents the length of time window. The goal of such a classifier is to find a mapping $f(a_T, \omega_T) \rightarrow y_T$ to minimize the differences between actual observations and corresponding predictions. Figure 3 shows the classifier architecture, where five TCN blocks are sequentially connected, and a slice layer and an FC (Fully Connected) layer are adopted to produce the output. Details of the classifier are elaborated as follows.

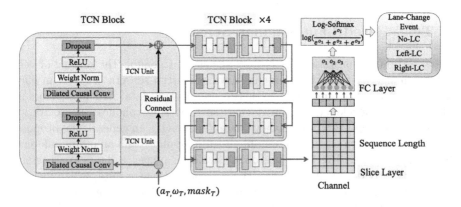

Fig. 3. TCN-based lane-change behavior classifier

TCN Blocks: Each TCN block consists of two TCN units and a residual connection. TCN units sequentially connect a weight normalization (WN), a rectified linear unit (ReLU) and a spatial dropout after a dilated causal convolution, which consists of causal convolution and dilated convolution. Specifically, the causal convolution is used for temporal data, which ensures the output at time t only derives from inputs at time t-1. In contrast, the dilated convolution only accesses every n-th element from inputs, which can expand the receptive field of the network output to historical data. Therefore, it reduces the number of network layers and the complexity of the model. Then, the WN is used to normalize the weight matrix for eliminating the dependence on batch distribution when training sequential data. ReLU and dropout are adopted to effectively avoid the gradient disappearance and overfitting. Finally, a residual connection is applied in each TCN block, which allows layers to learn modifications from the identify mapping rather than the entire transformation and it has been proved as a computation-efficient deep network architecture [5].

Slice Layer and FC Layer: Due to the characteristics of convolutional networks, the dimension of output features with TCN blocks is determined by the length of input sequence and the number of feature channels (i.e., the number of hidden units per layer). Recall that TCN leverages causal convolution to ensure that future data will not leak to the past (i.e., the data after time t will not be used to calculate the output at time t), and thus, after dilated causal convolution, only the output at the last timestamp contains the whole historical information of the input time sequence data. Since the goal is to identify whether the vehicle changes lanes from a sequential data of inertial sensors, a slice layer is added to slice the output features and only keep those of the last timestamp. Then, the feature vector obtained by slicing is input to the FC layer to produce the classification result. Finally, we utilize log-softmax function to enlarge the probability distance of each classification and speed up loss calculation.

Gradient Descent Strategy: The Mini-Batch Gradient Descent (MBGD) is adopted for model training, which can effectively avoid slow convergence and local optimum problems by using a set of samples for training at a time. Specially, we randomly select eight inertial data sequences as a mini-batch to train TCN every time.

3.2 Offline Training Procedures

For the offline training of TCN-LCS, two types of inertial sensors (i.e., accelerometer and gyroscope) are collected from the onboard smartphone. The set of sensor readings along the trajectory is denoted by $Traj = (A, \Omega)$, where $A = (a_1, a_2, a_3, \ldots a_{t-1}, a_t)$, which is the accelerometer's readings, a_t is the acceleration at the time t. The set of gyroscope's readings is denoted by $\Omega = (\omega_1, \omega_2, \omega_3, \ldots, \omega_{t-1}, \omega_t)$, where ω_t is the angular velocity at the time t. Due to the network congestion, the duplicated sensor data with the same timestamp might collected, which may undermine the model training. To deal with such a problem, we design a data deduplication mechanism by traversing sensor readings collected along the trajectory and deleting the duplicated data based on the sampling timestamp. On this basis, the raw sensor readings will be processed to generate training set by following two steps.

Historical Data Preprocessing: In order to train the TCN model, the collected inertial sensors readings are further divided into inertial data sequences, which is denoted by $IDS = (a_T, \omega_T)$, where a_T and ω_T represent acceleration and angular velocity in the time slice T, respectively. Each inertial data sequence can be considered as the input of TCN model and the corresponding label for each sequence has three categories, namely, Left-LC, Right-LC and No-LC, representing left, right and no lane-change, respectively. First, we separate the sensor data related to the lane-change behavior as the positive samples. Specifically, the start time and the end time of a lane-change behavior is determined based on the ground truth, which is manually labeled via the recorded video along the vehicle trajectory. Second, the labeled timestamps are used to segment the lane-change related sensor readings into the inertial data sequences. Third, the corresponding label (i.e., Left-LC, Right-LC) is determined by the vehicle's lane-change direction at the corresponding period. Finally, we separate the sensor readings according to the lane-change behavior, and split the rest inertial sensor data of the trajectory sequentially with a fixed length as the negative samples.

Sequence Processing: The separated positive samples may have different length since the duration of the lane-change behavior is affected by the complex traffic conditions and notably different driving behaviors. Figure 4 shows the statistical analysis of the duration of around 180 times lane-change behaviors. We observe that the mean duration for lane-change is around 4.5s, and the variance is about 0.82. In view of this, we design a sequence length adaptation mechanism to dynamically align the inertial data sequences in a mini batch during TCN model training.

Specifically, the sequence length adaptation mechanism consists of three steps. First, it determines the maximum length of inertial data sequence in current batch and sets it as the input data length. Second, it leverages zero post-padding to align the length of all the inertial data sequence in this batch by adding a certain number of zero values at the tail of inertial data sequences that have insufficient sensor readings. Third, since the zeros has their physical meaning when being processed as the inertial sensor data, an extra input channel called data-mask channel is added to distinguish the origin and padded value in inertial data sequences. Data-mask channel has the same length with the filled inertial sensor readings (i.e., acceleration data and angular velocity data) and it uses one bit value for each reading to indicate its validity.

Moreover, the training data set may suffer from the unbalance sample problem, since the time duration of lane-change may much shorter than that of driving along the same lane. To address such a problem, we further adopt an over-sampling method called SMOTE [3] to ensure that the number of positive and negative samples are approximately equivalent. Specifically, it first randomly selects n samples from the K-nearest neighbors of a sample from minority class. Then, new samples are randomly synthesized between the selected sample and its neighbors.

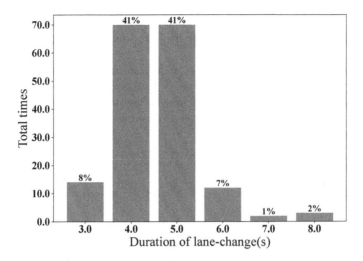

Fig. 4. Duration of lane-change

3.3 Online Inference Procedures

The online-inference stage consists of feature extraction, mask channel expansion and inference phases, in which the first two stages are used to generate the input of the classifier trained in the offline training phase. And during the feature extraction stage, when collected inertial sensors data are split with the fixed length for inference, the sensor readings related to one lane-change behaviors may be separated into two slices, which could undermine the inference accuracy. Therefore, we design a sliding window inference strategy to tackle such a problem. The general idea of the strategy is to increase the inference times with slide window so as to accurately locate the time period of lane-change. On this basis, the raw sensor readings will be processed through the following two steps to form the input of trained classifier.

Feature Extraction: Firstly, the sliding window is applied for real-time sensor data collection. Let L and T denotes the length and the step size of the sliding window, respectively. During online inference, every L inertial sensor readings are input into the TCN model for one lane-change behavior detection. Once a positive behavior (i.e., the output of classifier is Left-LC or Right-LC) is detected, the start point of the sliding window will be reset to the next timestamp when the lane-change is completed. Otherwise, we move forward T readings for the next detection. In addition, to tackle the problem of different durations of lane-change, the values of L and T are chosen based on the average lane-change duration trained based on the current road segments.

Expand Mask Channel: Recall that the trained TCN-based lane-change behavior classifier expects to receive three channels of data input, namely two inertial sequence channels (i.e., acceleration channel and angular velocity channel) and a data-mask channel. And the data-mask channel is used to distinguish the origin and padded value in inertial data sequences. Since there is no padded data existed for the real-time inertial sensor data, the mask channel for real-time inertial sensor data is set to 1.

After the above two steps, the preprocessed inertial sequences from real-time onboard smartphone inertial sensors along with the extended data-mask channel are input into the trained TCN-based lane-change behavior classifier, and the classifier outputs the prediction of current vehicle lane-change behavior.

4   Performance Evaluation

4.1   Experimental Setup

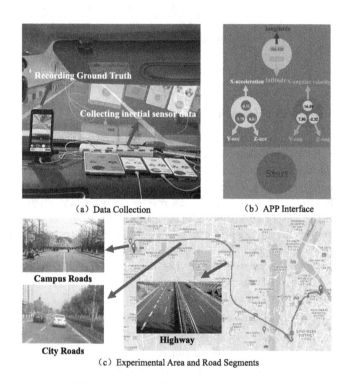

(a) Data Collection   (b) APP Interface

(c) Experimental Area and Road Segments

Fig. 5. Experimental setup

We have built the system prototype based on the architecture described in Sect. 2. In particular, an Android-based APP is developed for data collection, and the APP has been installed on 4 different types of smartphones (i.e., Huawei Pad BTV-DL09, MI note 3, RedMI K20 pro and OnePlus 7 pro), which are mounted in the front of the vehicle, as shown in Fig. 5(a). The APP interface is shown in Fig. 5(b), which enables real-time display of three-axis reading of accelerometer, gyroscope and GPS positioning results (i.e., longitude and latitude). We have driven over 150 km in both campus and urban areas in Chongqing, China for data collection. Specifically, we have driven along the route as shown in Fig. 5(c), crossing Shapingba District and Gaoxing District, for a number of rounds (the route is about 25 km), and the route contains a variety of road conditions including highways, city roads, tunnels, flyovers, and campus roads. Two different vehicle models (i.e., Ford Focus and Jeep Great Commander) are adopted for data collection. 80% of the collected data are used for offline training of the TCN-LCS model, 10% are used for model validation and the remaining 10% are used for online testing. To obtain the ground truth, we have shot the video during data collection and then analyzed the video frame by frame to detect the accurate timestamps for vehicles' current lane positions and lane-change behaviors.

4.2   Experimental Results

Effectiveness of TCN-LCS on lane-change detection: First, we conduct an experiment to evaluate the accuracy of TCN-LCS on lane-change detection. The fixed length of inertial data sequences related to No Lane-Change is set to 200, and the hyperparameters of TCN-LCS model are set as follows. The values of *epoch size* and *dropout* are set to 20 and 0.05, respectively. In the test data set, there are 359 No-LC samples, 40 Left-LC samples and 37 Right-LC samples (Table 1).

Table 1. Confusion matrix

Ground truth	Evaluation		
	No-LC	Left-LC	Right-LC
No-LC	354	3	2
Left-LC	0	38	2
Right-LC	1	1	35

The experimental results are summarized in Tabel 1. As shown, TCN-LCS identified 38 Left-LC and 35 Right-LC from the total of 40 Left-LC and 37 Right-LC, respectively, given the recall of 95% and 94.6%, respectively. On the other hand, 3 No-LC samples and 1 Right-LC samples were incorrectly identified as Left-LC, and thus the precision of Left-LC is 90.48%. On the other hand, 2 No-LC samples and 2 Left-LC samples were incorrectly identified as Right-LC, and thus the precision of Right-LC is 89.74%. Based on the above analysis, the F1 scores of lane-change detection, which is the harmonic mean of the precision and recall, are both 0.92 for Left-LC and Right-LC.

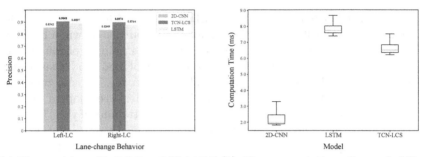

(a) The precision of Left-LC and Right-LC (b) The computation time of different
in different models   models

Fig. 6. Comparison with 2D-CNN and LSTM

Comparison with 2D-CNN and LSTM: In this part, we compared the proposed TCN-LCS with two baselines, which are 2D-CNN [17] and LSTM respectively. The precision of Left-LC and Right-LC and computation time are used as the evaluation metrics and the experimental results as shown in Fig. 6. As shown in Fig. 6(a), our model achieve the best precision in the lane-change detection, and LSTM acquires a very close precision, but its computation time is higher than TCN-LCS. The computation time of three methods are shown in Fig. 6(b), due to the "image" converted by inertial sensor data is too small, 2D-CNN can satisfy the size of receptive field with few layers, so its computation time is relative low. Realistically, although 2D-CNN has achieved great success in the field of image classification, converting time-series inertial sensor data into "images" may be not appropriate. On the contrary, TCN performs convolution operation in time dimension, which can achieve preferable performance.

Effect of Different Traffic Environments: In this part, we evaluate the online performance of TCN-LCS under different traffic environments, including campus roads, city roads and highways. The parameters of the sliding window inference strategy are configured as follows: the length of sliding window L is set to 300, 200 and 200 in campus roads, city roads and highways, respectively. The step size T is set to 50 in all the traffic environments. The experimental results are shown in Fig. 7. In the campus road scenario, TCN-LCS detected all the lane-change behaviors excepting the last continuous right lane-change, as shown in Fig. 7(a), given the accuracy of 100% and the recall of 80%. The primary reason is that due to continuous lane-change behaviors, the sensor data of the second lane-change might be incompletely processed. Similar issues also existed in the city road scenario. The lane-change detection results in city road environments are shown in Fig. 7(b), As noted, there were two incorrect identifications out of eight, given the accuracy of 75%. Finally, note that since there is no ominously lane-change on the highway, as shown in Fig. 7(c), all the lane-change behaviors were correctly detected in highway environments, given 100% accuracy and recall.

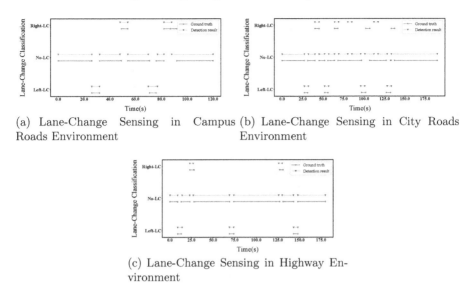

(a) Lane-Change Sensing in Campus Roads Environment

(b) Lane-Change Sensing in City Roads Environment

(c) Lane-Change Sensing in Highway Environment

Fig. 7. Evaluation under different traffic environments

5   Conclusion

This paper investigated an effective vehicle lane-change sensing approach using onboard smartphone inertial sensors. Firstly, a system architecture was proposed to enable low-cost and scalable lane-change sensing, which consists of an offline classifier training phase based on the historical vehicle driving data and an online lane-change sensing phase based on the real-time collected inertial sensor data. Further, a TCN-LCS algorithm was proposed. In particular, during the offline training phase, a data pre-processing method is designed to process the raw inertial sensor data, and a dynamic sequence length adaptation method is designed to address the inconsistency of inertial sequence length. During the online inference phase, a sliding window inference strategy is proposed to improve the robustness and accuracy of lane-changing behavior detection. Finally, we implemented the system prototype and collected the data for TCN model training by driving over 150 km in different traffic environments, including campus roads, city roads, highways, etc. A comprehensive experimental evaluation has been conducted in real-world environments, which conclusively demonstrated the effectiveness of the proposed solutions.

References

1. Bai, S., Kolter, J.Z., Koltun, V.: An empirical evaluation of generic convolutional and recurrent networks for sequence modeling. arXiv preprint arXiv:1803.01271 (2018)

2. Bhandari, R., Nambi, A.U., Padmanabhan, V.N., Raman, B.: Driving lane detection on smartphones using deep neural networks. ACM Trans. Sens. Netw. **16**(1), 1–22 (2020). https://doi.org/10.1145/3358797

3. Chawla, N.V., Bowyer, K.W., Hall, L.O., Kegelmeyer, W.P.: SMOTE: synthetic minority over-sampling technique. J. Artif. Intell. Res. **16**, 321–357 (2002). https://doi.org/10.1613/jair.953

4. Chen, D., Cho, K.T., Han, S., Jin, Z., Shin, K.G.: Invisible sensing of vehicle steering with smartphones. In: Proceedings of the 13th Annual International Conference on Mobile Systems, Applications, and Services (MobiSys), pp. 1–13 (2015). https://doi.org/10.1145/2742647.2742659

5. He, K., Zhang, X., Ren, S., Sun, J.: Deep residual learning for image recognition. In: 2016 IEEE Conference on Computer Vision and Pattern Recognition (CVPR), pp. 770–778 (2016). https://doi.org/10.1109/CVPR.2016.90

6. Jin, F., et al.: Toward scalable and robust indoor tracking: design, implementation, and evaluation. IEEE Internet Things J. **7**(2), 1192–1204 (2020). https://doi.org/10.1109/JIOT.2019.2953376

7. Jin, F., Liu, K., Zhang, H., Wu, W., Cao, J., Zhai, X.: A zero site-survey overhead indoor tracking system using particle filter. In: 2019 IEEE International Conference on Communications (ICC), pp. 1–7 (2019). https://doi.org/10.1109/ICC.2019.8761621

8. Klitzke, L., Koch, C., Köster, F.: Identification of lane-change maneuvers in real-world drivings with hidden markov model and dynamic time warping. In: 2020 IEEE 23rd International Conference on Intelligent Transportation Systems (ITSC), pp. 1–7 (2020). https://doi.org/10.1109/ITSC45102.2020.9294481

9. Lee, D., Kwon, Y.P., McMains, S., Hedrick, J.K.: Convolution neural network-based lane change intention prediction of surrounding vehicles for ACC. In: 2017 IEEE 20th International Conference on Intelligent Transportation Systems (ITSC), pp. 1–6 (2017). https://doi.org/10.1109/ITSC.2017.8317874

10. Liu, K., Lim, H.B., Frazzoli, E., Ji, H., Lee, V.C.S.: Improving positioning accuracy using GPS pseudorange measurements for cooperative vehicular localization. IEEE Trans. Veh. Technol. **63**(6), 2544–2556 (2014). https://doi.org/10.1109/TVT.2013.2296071

11. Liu, K., et al.: Toward low-overhead fingerprint-based indoor localization via transfer learning: design, implementation, and evaluation. IEEE Trans. Ind. Inform. **14**(3), 898–908 (2018). https://doi.org/10.1109/TII.2017.2750240

12. Maaref, M., Khalife, J., Kassas, Z.M.: Lane-level localization and mapping in GNSS-challenged environments by fusing lidar data and cellular pseudoranges. IEEE Trans. Intell. Veh. **4**(1), 73–89 (2019). https://doi.org/10.1109/TIV.2018.2886688

13. Ouyang, Z., Niu, J., Liu, Y., Rodrigues, J.: Multiwave: a novel vehicle steering pattern detection method based on smartphones. In: 2016 IEEE International Conference on Communications (ICC), pp. 1–7 (2016). https://doi.org/10.1109/ICC.2016.7511088

14. Park, S.G., Cho, D.J.: Smart framework for GNSS-based navigation in urban environments. Int. J. Satell. Commun. Network. **35**(2), 123–137 (2017). https://doi.org/10.1002/sat.1166

15. Schlechtriemen, J., Wedel, A., Hillenbrand, J., Breuel, G., Kuhnert, K.D.: A lane change detection approach using feature ranking with maximized predictive power. In: 2014 IEEE Intelligent Vehicles Symposium Proceedings (IV), pp. 108–114 (2014). https://doi.org/10.1109/IVS.2014.6856491

16. Schreiber, M., Königshof, H., Hellmund, A.M., Stiller, C.: Vehicle localization with tightly coupled GNSS and visual odometry. In: 2016 IEEE Intelligent Vehicles Symposium (IV), pp. 858–863 (2016). https://doi.org/10.1109/IVS.2016.7535488
17. Shahverdy, M., Fathy, M., Berangi, R., Sabokrou, M.: Driver behavior detection and classification using deep convolutional neural networks. Expert Syst. Appl. **149**, 113240 (2020). https://doi.org/10.1016/j.eswa.2020.113240
18. Wang, T., Jia, W., Xing, G., Li, M.: Exploiting statistical mobility models for efficient Wi-Fi deployment. IEEE Trans. Veh. Technol. **62**(1), 360–373 (2013). https://doi.org/10.1109/TVT.2012.2217159
19. Wang, T., et al.: Propagation modeling and defending of a mobile sensor worm in wireless sensor and actuator networks. Sensors **17**(1), 139 (2017). https://doi.org/10.3390/s17010139
20. Wei, Z., Wang, C., Hao, P., Barth, M.J.: Vision-based lane-changing behavior detection using deep residual neural network. In: 2019 IEEE Intelligent Transportation Systems Conference (ITSC), pp. 3108–3113 (2019). https://doi.org/10.1109/ITSC.2019.8917158
21. Wirthmüller, F., Klimke, M., Schlechtriemen, J., Hipp, J., Reichert, M.: Predicting the time until a vehicle changes the lane using LSTM-based recurrent neural networks. IEEE Robot. Autom. Lett. **6**(2), 2357–2364 (2021). https://doi.org/10.1109/LRA.2021.3058930
22. Woo, H., et al.: Lane-change detection based on vehicle-trajectory prediction. IEEE Robot. Autom. Lett. **2**(2), 1109–1116 (2017). https://doi.org/10.1109/LRA.2017.2660543
23. Xu, X., Yu, J., Zhu, Y., Wu, Z., Li, J., Li, M.: Leveraging smartphones for vehicle lane-level localization on highways. IEEE Trans. Mob. Comput. **17**(8), 1894–1907 (2018). https://doi.org/10.1109/TMC.2017.2776286
24. Yi, S., Worrall, S., Nebot, E.: Integrating vision, lidar and GPS localization in a behavior tree framework for urban autonomous driving. In: 2021 IEEE International Intelligent Transportation Systems Conference (ITSC), pp. 3774–3780 (2021). https://doi.org/10.1109/ITSC48978.2021.9564875
25. Zhang, H., Liu, K., Jin, F., Feng, L., Lee, V., Ng, J.: A scalable indoor localization algorithm based on distance fitting and fingerprint mapping in Wi-Fi environments. Neural Comput. Appl. **32**(9), 5131–5145 (2019). https://doi.org/10.1007/s00521-018-3961-8
26. Zhang, H., et al.: Dual-band wi-fi based indoor localization via stacked denosing autoencoder. In: 2019 IEEE Global Communications Conference (GLOBECOM), pp. 1–6. IEEE (2019). https://doi.org/10.1109/GLOBECOM38437.2019.9013872
27. Zheng, Y., Hansen, J.H.L.: Lane-change detection from steering signal using spectral segmentation and learning-based classification. IEEE Trans. Intell. Veh. **2**(1), 14–24 (2017). https://doi.org/10.1109/TIV.2017.2708600

A Web Service Recommendation Method Based on Adaptive Gate Network and xDeepFM

Zhi Tao[1], Buqing Cao[1(✉)], Hongfan Ye[1,2(✉)], Guosheng Kang[1], Zhenlian Peng[1], and Yiping Wen[1]

[1] School of Computer Science and Engineering and Hunan Key Laboratory of Service Computing and New Software Service Technology, Hunan University of Science and Technology, Xiangtan, Hunan, China
buqingcao@gmail.com
[2] School of Computer and Artificial Intelligence, Huaihua University, Huaihua, China

Abstract. With the rapid development of service computing technology, more and more companies and organizations are encapsulating and publishing their operational data or resources to the Internet in the form of Web services, resulting in an exponential increase in the number of Web services. To automatically generate or recommend a group of Web services according to the user's natural language requirements description, to build a Mashup application to meet the user's requirement is a hot topic in service computing. Some researchers enhance the quality of Web service recommendation by using auxiliary information into the recommendation system. However, they mainly focus on adding external information (e.g., pre-training of external corpora) to enhance semantic features, while some internal statistical features of the corpus such as word distribution on labels and frequency are not fully exploited. Compared to other exterior knowledge, statistical features are naturally compatible with Web service recommendation tasks. To fully exploit the statistical features, this paper proposes a Web service recommendation method based on adaptive gate network and xDeepFM model. In this method, firstly, the description document of Web services is taken as the basic corpus, the semantic and statistical information in the corpus are mined by utilizing the adaptive gate network, and the statistical features are encoded by a variational encoder. Secondly, the similarity between Web services is derived from the semantic features, at the same time the popularity and co-occurrence of Web services are calculated. Thirdly, the xDeepFM model is used to mine the explicit and implicit higher-order interactions in the sparse matrix which consists of the above information to recommend Web services for Mashup application. Finally, a multiple sets of experiments based on the dataset crawled from the ProgrammableWeb have been conducted to evaluate the proposed method and the experimental result shows that the proposed method has better performance in the *AUC* and *Logloss* compared with the state-of-art baseline methods.

Keywords: Service recommendation · Adaptive gate network · xDeepFM

© Springer Nature Switzerland AG 2023
W. Meng et al. (Eds.): ICA3PP 2022, LNCS 13777, pp. 154–169, 2023.
https://doi.org/10.1007/978-3-031-22677-9_9

1 Introduction

With the booming development of the Internet and its related technologies, the deep integration of information technology and service industry, represented by big data [1], has promoted far-reaching changes in the software industry, while accelerating the cross-field integration and innovative development of service computing technology [2]. As the most prospective technology based on service-oriented computing (SOC) [3], Web services are widely used in applications based on service-oriented architecture (SOA) by providing services through a typical Web services protocol to ensure that application services from different platforms can interoperate. Therefore, a growing amount of modern organizations and companies are encapsulating their business, data or resources into online services and publishing them on the Internet, which leads to a significant increase in the number of Web services [5]. Web services composition enables developers to create applications tailored to their needs and quickly build Mashup applications [6]. As it overcomes the problem of information island [4], it provides an efficient and fast solution for the integration of applications in the distributed heterogeneous environment, thus becoming the most critical aspect in facilitating the efficiency of service development.

The emergence of a large number of online services brings information overload. Therefore, recommendation systems are attracting more and more attention from researchers as an effective solution to the information overload problem. Traditional recommendation methods mainly include content-based, collaborative filtering and hybrid recommendation methods [6]. Among this, content-based recommendation is based on the item's content, which is simple and effective, but the content features are limited and only one kind of recommendation result can be returned. Collaborative filtering, on the other hand, makes recommendations based on the interaction between users and items, but it is limited by cold starts, data sparsity, and insufficient feature depth interaction capabilities. Hybrid recommendation methods [8] are expected to better improve the quality of recommendations, which usually combine the collaborative filtering recommendations and content-based recommendations to overcome the problems inherent in using a single approach.

In the process of recommendation, exploring different kinds of auxiliary information can promote the quality and performance of the recommendation system, and enable it to provide more relevant recommendation results based on the existing Web services description documents [9]. Nevertheless, how to effectively introduce complex and different kinds of auxiliary information into recommendation systems is an important issue faced by researchers [22]. Several researchers use deep recommendation models and techniques such as factorization machine (FM) [10], to extract wide range of relevant features from heterogeneous and multi-source information to enrich the deep feature representation of users and items. However, the above research works often tend to focus on describing the description documents of Web services when adding auxiliary information, while ignoring the original features such as word distribution and frequency, which are intrinsic, static, and easy to retrieve [25][26]. One of the most representative algorithms that utilizes statistical information is term frequency-inverse document frequency (TF-IDF) [25], which is a direct information retrieval technique for document modeling. However, due to the limitation of bag-of-words, TF-IDF is unable to capture fine-grained semantics using word location information, which makes TF-IDF less advantageous than other deep learning models.

Recently, some researchers have proposed the adaptive gate network (AGN) model [12]. This model is able to train in a corpus to obtain statistical information. It uses a novel adaptive gate network to add corpus-level statistical features (e.g., word frequency, word distribution on labels) to low-confidence semantic features to enrich the semantic features and thus improve the performance of model. Since the above statistical features are derived from the Web services description documents, which are naturally compatible with the recommendation task. So it can effectively enrich the knowledge of recommendation system and promote the performance of the recommendation accordingly. xDeepFM model, on the other hand, is capable of jointly learning both explicit and implicit higher-order interaction features. It completes the high-order explicit interaction between Web service features through compressed interaction network (CIN). In addition, xDeepFM uses DNNs to learn the implicit higher-order interactions between features. Thus, xDeepFM can fully exploit the explicit and implicit higher-order features in the Web service description documents. Inspired by the above researches, this paper proposes a Web services recommendation method based on AGN and xDeepFM [13], denoted as AGN-xDeepFM. In this method, firstly, it applies AGN to extract the semantic features of the Web service description document carrying statistical information. Then, it calculates the similarity, popularity and co-occurrence between Web services, and using them as the input of the xDeepFM model. Finally, xDeepFM mines the above information and recommends the most appropriate Web services for building Mashup application. To sum up, the main contributions of this paper are outlined as below:

- To our best knowledge, this is the first attempt by using deep learning technology to fully mine the statistical information of word frequency and labels distribution at corpus level to achieve efficient Web service recommendation.
- A new Web service recommendation method AGN-xDeepFM is proposed in this paper. It rises the accuracy of similarity calculation by adding the statistical information of word frequency and labels distribution to the semantic features in the description documents of Web services through the AGN model, and uses the xDeepFM model to fuse multi-dimensional features such as similarity, popularity and co-occurrence to recommend Web services.
- The experiments are conducted on real datasets of ProgrammableWeb platform and the experimental results show that the AGN-xDeepFM outperforms other popular Web service recommendation methods based on deep neural network and effectively improves the performance and quality of Web service recommendation.

The remainder of this paper is organized as follows. In Section II, the research work related to Web service recommendation is introduced in detail. Section III provides a detailed description of the AGN-xDeepFM proposed in this paper. Section IV analyzes and discusses the experimental results and variable parameters. Section V summarizes the work in the paper and presents the future work.

2   Related Work

Web services with various functionality are constantly emerging on the Internet, developers can create more complex, composable Web service applications, such as Mashup, by aggregating various Web services from diverse platforms through the typical Web protocols [14]. Effective Web service recommendation method can facilitate Web service discovery, composition and application. There are many research findings on Web service recommendation based on collaborative filtering algorithm, but the recommendation quality and effect are not satisfying due to the limitation of data sparsity and cold start. To overcome these problems, some researchers improve the performance of Web service recommendation by adding auxiliary information to the recommendation system [15].

Currently, many researchers study on the application of deep neural networks in Web service recommendation, such as CNN proposed by Conneau [16], which operates directly at the character level and can perform convolutional and pooling operations using smaller convolutional kernels. Shi et al. [17] proposes a recommendation system for mining Web services' functional description documents using LSTM. Wang et al. [18] presents a QoS prediction algorithm which utilizes LSTM to predict future reliability. Based on the Text-GCN model proposed by Yao et al. [23], the WSC-GCN model is designed by Ye et al. [24] to model and predict the network structure of word hiding in documents. These works show that using DNNs can achieve better results in Web service recommendation. Ye et al. [19] devises a Wide&Bi-LSTM method for Web service functionality description document modeling that fully exploits the content semantic information of Web service functionality description documents in both breadth and depth to achieve automatic Web services classification. Kang et al. [20] propose the NAFM method, which uses neural and attentional factorization machine for Web service recommendation. All the mentioned works achieve good results, which indicate that the proper using of external auxiliary information can effectively improve the performance of the recommendation model.

In recommendation systems, the interaction features of services and users are often discrete and sparse, so some researchers use logistic regression (LR) [21] to model these discrete, high-dimensional features. However, the LR ignores the relationship between different features, so some researchers propose the factorization machines (FM) [10] model, which alleviates the problems caused by sparse matrices by interacting with feature vectors. To explore the interactional features of services and users, many scholars apply deep neural networks to integrate the information between different features and utilize the DeepFM model [13], which mines the input sparse matrix by deep neural networks to integrate low-order feature interactions and high-order feature interactions, and consequently improves the efficiency and accuracy of the recommender system.

Recently, Li et al. [12] proposes the adaptive gate network approach in 2021, which uses a valve component to selectively add statistical information to semantic information for improving the performance of recommendation models. Lian et al. [13] designs a method called eXtreme deep factorization machine (xDeepFM) in 2018, which learns explicit and implicit higher-order feature interactions and lower-order feature interactions. Inspired by these works, this paper proposes a Web service recommendation method that fuses AGN and xDeepFM. In this method, firstly, it selectively integrates the statistical and semantic information of corpus-level Web service description documents to obtain more accurate similarity between Web services. Then, it uses xDeepFM to learn high-order and low-order feature interactions to fully explore the multi-dimensional information of Web service, such as similarity, popularity, co-occurrence, so as to obtain better Web service prediction and recommendation results. Finally, the experiments results show that the proposed method effectively improves the quality of Web service recommendation.

3   AGN-xDeepFM Method

The framework of AGN-xDeepFM method is shown in Fig. 1, which includes data processing, similarity calculation based on AGN model, Web service prediction based on xDeepFM, and Web service recommendation.

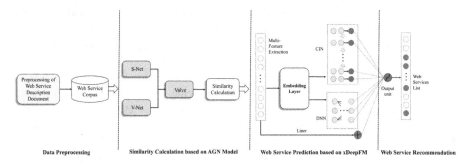

Fig. 1. The Framework of the Proposed Method

- Pre-processing. To eliminate the information which is unfavorable to the Web service recommendation, the pre-processing is performed.
- Similarity calculation based on AGN model. The AGN model is applied to explore the semantic and statistical features of the available APIs, and the similarity is calculated between Mashups and Mashups, APIs and APIs.
- Web service prediction based on xDeepFM. The xDeepFM is used to mine complex feature composition relationships and predict the probability of Web APIs that is called by Mashups. Meanwhile, Web service prediction is achieved in the modeling of xDeepFM by inputting the similarity between Mashups, the similarity between APIs, and the popularity and co-occurrence of APIs.
- Web service recommendation. As for users' Mashup requirement, the matched APIs are identified by using AGN model and the called probability is predicted by utilizing xDeepFM model. The predicted scores are ranked, the high-quality APIs are recommended for Mashup creation.

3.1 Data Preprocessing

Web service description document is composed of elements such as words, phrases, sentences, paragraphs, and as the length of the elements increases, the information contained in the documents becomes richer, but the number of feature compositions will also increase. It is necessary to eliminate meaningless information from the document corpus. This allows the model to perform semantic mining in a Web service corpus which contains Mashups and Web APIs with higher information density. The data preprocessing mainly includes the below steps:

- **Load the experimental data:** use pandas to load experimental data set and remove the data with incomplete information and messy code.
- **Tokenization:** apply NLTK (Natural Language Toolkit) in python to divide the Web service description documents into series of phrases or words according to space characters, i.e., divide Web service description document into the list of characters, and distinguish the punctuation marks from words.
- **Remove stop words and stemming:** exploit the deactivation word list in NLTK to percolate words and punctuation that are not useful for semantic mining. At the same time, the suffixes from words are removed such as "ing", "ly", "s", in a rule-based way. For instance, "betrayal" will be extracted as "betray" and "incentive" will be extracted as "incent". This process will effectively improve the accuracy of the subsequent similarity calculations.
- **One-hot encoding:** utilize the prefix array to build the dictionary space, the words in the dictionary space and Web service description documents are converted into one-hot vectors, which are used as the input data of AGN-xDeepFM model.

3.2 Similarity Calculation Based on AGN Model

The input of AGN model is consist of the description documents of Mashup and API. AGN is able to fuse content semantics and statistical information of Mashup and API.

AGN Model. The structural composition of the AGN model which comprises three main components, i.e., V-Net component, S-Net component (Bert base) and Valve component, is illustrated in detail in Fig. 2.

Global Information. TCoL is obtained directly from the corpus of Web service description document. These features are raw, but by identifying the relevance of words, extensive information can be mined and utilized for feature selection and information retrieval. That is to say, the importance of a word ω will increase if the distribution of that word is higher or lower in a particular category.

Definition 1: Given a word ω in Web service description and a Web service description document with c categories, the term-count-of-label (TCoL) vector for the word ω is:

$$C^\omega = [C_1, \ldots\ldots C_c] \tag{1}$$

where C_i is the number of words ω in category i. Now, given a sentence $s = \{\omega_i\}_{i=1}^m$ in Web service description, then the TCoL of the sentence is:

$$C^s = \left[C^{\omega 1}, \ldots\ldots C^{\omega_m}\right] \tag{2}$$

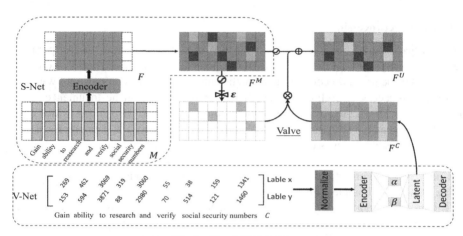

Fig. 2. The AGN Model.

V-Net. V-Net stands for variational encoding network. In V-Net, statistical information which is initially incompatible with the semantic features of the Web service description document will be converted to a valid representation. In this paper, variational autoencoder (VAE) is used to encode TCoL, which can restrict the latent space to a representation encoded by a multivariate gaussian distribution, thus obtaining a high-quality statistical feature matrix. Before fusing TCoL with the semantic features of Web service description document, it is necessary to generate TCoL from all sentences in the Web service description document, and obtain $A = \{C^s_{(i)}\}^M_{i=1}$. It is a composition of M discrete TCoL variables C with id i. Assume that the TCoL vector of all Web service description document is obtained by the process $p_\theta(C|a)$. In the process, there is a latent variable a of TCoL vector involved that is obtained by sampling from a prior distribution $p_\theta(a)$. Then, variational approximation $q_\varphi(a|C)$ is used to jointly learn the TCoL vector's variational parameters φ and θ as a way to solve the intractable problem of computing the posterior $p_\theta(a|C)$ of TCoL vector. Therefore, the model is optimized by maximizing the marginal likelihood which consists of the sum of the marginal likelihoods of individuals C.

$$logp_\theta(C) = D_{KL}(q_\varphi(a|C)||p_\theta(a|C)) + \mathcal{L}(\theta, \varphi; C) \tag{3}$$

Next, the likelihood term $L(\theta, \varphi; C)$ of TCoL vector can be derived to obtain a variational lower bound on the marginal likelihood, i.e.,

$$\mathcal{L}(\theta, \varphi; C) = -D_{KL}(q_\varphi(a|C)||p_\theta(a)) + E_{q_\varphi(a|C)}[logp_\theta(C|a)] \tag{4}$$

The variational framework is applied to the autoencoder by using the reparameterization, and two encoders are exploited to respectively generate two sets α and β as the mean value and standard deviation of the prior distribution. Since the approximate prior used in this paper as a multivariate gaussian distribution, the variational posterior is represented by the diagonal covariance:

$$logq_\theta(a|C) = logN(a; \alpha, \beta^2 I) \tag{5}$$

Thus, by training the unsupervised VAE model, the probabilistic encoder obtains the latent variable C^a, which is the global representation of the TCoL of the Web service description document. The training of V-Net is independent of the other components, C^a is generated at the beginning of the model and fused with the semantic information of the Web service description document through the Valve component.

S-Net. S-Net stands for semantic representation projection network, which can extract the semantic features from Web service description document and project them into an information space for evaluation. The input of S-Net is a fixed-length Web service description sentence s. Then the specific function of the component is described as follows:

Firstly, a pre-trained Bert base model is used for Web service feature map extraction:

$$M = Bert(s) \tag{6}$$

M denotes the Web service feature map extracted by the Bert model.

Next, the semantic features of the Web service description document are mapped into the information space through a dense layer:

$$F^M = W^M \cdot M + b^M \tag{7}$$

F^M denotes the semantic features of the Web service description document in the information space, which facilitates Valve components to perform information merging. Finally, input F^M into the sigmoid-activated function to obtain $F\prime^M = \sigma\left(F^M\right)$, where σ represents the sigmoid equation used to evaluate the confidence of the semantic features of the Web service description document.

Valve Components. Valve component can merge the semantic information and statistic information of Mashup and Web APIs. Since the TCoL representation C^a of the trained Web service description document is obtained offline. To utilize the statistical features of the Web service document effectively, this paper uses a dense layer to project C^a into the information space which is shared with the semantic features of the Web service description documents:

$$F^C = W^C \bullet C^a + b^C \tag{8}$$

The Valve component fuses F^M and F^C and outputs a statistically-informed content semantic feature F^U via an *AdaGate* function:

$$
\begin{aligned}
F^U &= AdaGate\left(F^M, F'^M, F^C, \varepsilon\right) \\
&= ReLU\left(F^M\right) + Valve(F'^M, \varepsilon) \odot F^C
\end{aligned}
\tag{9}
$$

where *ReLU* is the activation function. The values in F'^M are expressed as probabilities, and the purpose of the Valve function is to use the statistical features of Web service to strengthen the entries with low confidence ($\alpha \to 0.5$), in order to match the elements in F^C. Means that for each $m \in F'^M$:

$$Valve(m, \varepsilon) = \begin{cases} m, 0.5 + \varepsilon \geq \alpha \geq 0.5 - \varepsilon \\ 0, otherwise \end{cases} \tag{10}$$

where ε is a hyper-parameter that adjusts the confidence threshold. Therefore, using the *Valve*(m, ε) function as a filter is able to integrate the necessary statistical information of the Web service description document into the semantic features of it at the element level.

Similarity Calculation. After obtaining F^U that combines the statistical features with semantic features, a cosine similarity function is used to calculate the similarity of the feature vector for each Web service description document $f \in F^U$ with all the other feature vectors for Web services description documents:

$$Similarity(f, t) = \sum_{i=1}^{n} \frac{\sum_{j=1}^{n}(f_i \times t_j)}{\sqrt{f_i^2} \times \sqrt{\sum_{j=1}^{n} t_j^2}} \tag{11}$$

where f denotes the feature vector of the current Web service description document and t denotes all the other feature vectors for Web services description documents. $Similarity(f, t) \in [0, 1]$, its value more closes to 1 means the higher the similarity of the two Web services, and vice-versa.

3.3 Web Services Recommendation based on xDeepFM

xDeepFM Model. The input of the xDeepFM model is a discrete multi-dimensional information matrix which is composed of information such as one-hot codes, similarity scores of Web services, co-occurrence and popularity of Web service. This model will learn from the input matrix and predict the score or probability that the target Mashup will invoke Web API.

xDeepFM is composed of three components, i.e., CIN, DNN, and Linear part, which first reduces the discrete information in the input discrete multi-dimensional information matrix containing Web service features into a dense, low-dimensional, real-value vector by embedding layer, and then inputs it into CIN, DNN respectively. The CIN crosses the feature vectors by using vector-wise fashion. The embedding matrix is represented in CIN as $X^0 \in \mathbb{R}^{m \times D}$. The row i of X^0 denotes the embedding vector of Web service features corresponding to the i field, there are totally m real-value vector with D-dimension. Each layer of CIN will produce an intermediate results, and the output matrix of the k layer is denoted as $X^k \in \mathbb{R}^{H_k \times D}$, $H_0 = m$ and H_k denotes the number of feature vectors in the k layer, where the intermediate results are calculated as follows:

$$X_{h,*}^{k+1} = \sum_{i=1}^{H_k} \sum_{j=1}^{m} \Upsilon_{i,j}^{k+1,h} \left(X_{i,*}^k \circ X_{j,*}^0 \right) \tag{12}$$

where $\Upsilon_{i,j}^{k+1,h}$ denotes a scalar value that is a parameter on the position of row i and column j. $X_{i,*}^k$ denotes the feature vector in the i-th row of the output matrix at the k layer in the CIN, and $X_{h,*}^{k+1}$ denotes the feature vector in the h-th row in X^{k+1}.

After obtaining the output of each layer, all intermediate results in each layer of CIN will be pooled to transform X^k into a vector $v^k = [v_1^k, v_2^k, \ldots, v_{H_k}^k]$ with the length H_k, and stitched together to obtain $v^+ = [v^1, v^2, \ldots, v^k]$ and the output is the multidimensional discrete features $c = \frac{1}{1+exp((v^{k+})^T W^\circ)}$ of the Web service after feature vector crossover. Among this, the W° is a parameter vector with the length $\sum_{k=1}^{H_k}$.

DNN learns the implicit higher-order feature interaction, which is complementary to CIN and further enhances the effectiveness of the model for service recommendation. Linear takes the original Web service features without embedding as input, denoted as $y = \sigma(W_{linear}^{T}a)$, where a is the original Web service multidimensional discrete information matrix and σ is the activation function.

The above components are combined to obtain the final output $\hat{y}$ of the xDeepFM model, where $\hat{y} \in (0, 1)$. If $\hat{y} \geq 0.5$, then the Web API is recommended to the Mashup, and if $\hat{y} < 0.5$, then the Web API is not recommended to the Mashup:

$$\hat{y} = \sigma\left(W_{linear}^{T}a + W_{dnn}^{T}X_{dnn}^{k} + W_{cin}^{T}v^{+} + b\right) \tag{13}$$

where W_{linear}^{T}, W_{dnn}^{T}, and W_{cin}^{T} respectively correspond to the trainable parameters of the linear component, DNN component, and CIN component, b is a global bias item. Consequently, xDeepFM module effectively improves the effectiveness of Web service recommendations through above processing.

The Popularity and Co-occurrence of Web Service. The popularity of Web service represents the QoS information and users' preference, and its calculation formula is as follows:

$$pop(a_i) = \frac{Inv(a_i) - MinInv(Category(a_i))}{MaxInv(Category(a_i)) - MinInv(Category(a_i))} \tag{14}$$

where $Inv(a_i)$ indicates the number of the Web API "a_i" invoked by all Mashups, and $MinInv(\cdot)$ indicates the smallest number of the Web API invoked by Mashup in the history record, and $MaxInv(Category(a_i))$ indicates the maximum number of the Web API invoked in the history record, and $Category(a_i)$ indicates the Web APIs that belong to the same category as the Web API "a_i".

The co-occurrence of Web service refers the association relationship of Web service composition, which can be calculated by exploiting Jaccard similarity coefficient:

$$Co(a_i, a_j) = \frac{|a_i \cap a_j|}{|a_i \cup a_j|} \tag{15}$$

where $|a_i \cap a_j|$ indicates the total number that Web API "a_i" and Web API "a_j" are invoked by the same Mashup, $|a_i \cup a_j|$ indicates the total number of Web API "a_i" and Web API "a_j" are invoked by all Mashups.

4 Experimental Result and Analysis

4.1 Dataset and Experimental Setting

To evaluate the proposed method, this paper uses a real dataset of Web services crawled from the ProgrammableWeb platform. The dataset contains about 6000 Mashups and nearly 20,000 Web APIs, which includes detailed Web service description documents and their tag information. The top 30 categories with the highest quantity of Web services in this dataset is shown in Table 1. Moreover, the experimental data is divided into 60% training set, 20% validating set, and 20% testing set.

Table 1. Category Number Statistics of Top 30 Mobile Applications

Category	Number	Category	Number	Category	Number
Tools	850	Telephony	338	Games	240
Financial	758	Reference	308	Photos	228
Messaging	601	Security	305	Music	221
eCommerce	546	Search	301	Stocks	200
Payments	526	Email	291	Cloud	195
Social	501	Video	289	Data	187
Enterprise	472	Travel	284	Bitcoin	173
Mapping	437	Education	275	Other	165
Government	369	Transportation	259	Project Management	165
Science	368	Advertising	254	Weather	164

4.2 Evaluation Metrics

The evaluation metrics include *AUC* and *Logloss*, which are widely used in the recommendation system to evaluate the model performance from different aspects. The *AUC* is the area under the *ROC* curve:

$$AUC_i = \int_0^1 ROC_i(fpr)d(fpr) \tag{16}$$

In *ROC* space, the coordinates (*fpr*, *tpr*) represent the trade-off between false positive cases and true positive cases, fpr stands for false positive rate and tpr stands for true positive rate. $AUC \in (0, 1)$, when $0.5 < AUC < 1$, the model outperforms the random classifier, and the closer the value of *AUC* is to 1 indicates that the model is better for Web service recommendation.

Logloss measures the accuracy of the classifier by penalizing the incorrect classification. A smaller *Logloss* means that the model is more accurate in Web service recommendation, and the Logloss reflects the average bias of the sample:

$$Logloss = -\frac{1}{N}\sum_{i=1}^{N}\left(p_i\log\left(\widehat{p_i}\right)\right) + \log\left(1 - \widehat{p_i}\right) \times (1 - p_i) \tag{17}$$

Among this, N denotes the total sample quantity of mobile applications, $\widehat{p_i}$ denotes the predicted tag of the i-th sample, and p_i denotes the actual tag of the i-th sample.

4.3 Baselines

- **AGN-DeepFM:** The adaptive gate network is used to compute similarity and the DeepFM is applied to recommend Web services. The DeepFM learns both low-order and high-order feature interactions, reducing the usage of parameters and sharing the embedding of FM and DNN.

- **CNN-xDeepFM:** The convolutional neural network is used to compute similarity, and the xDeepFM is exploited to recommend Web services. CNN utilizes multiple kernels of different sizes to extract key information from Web service description document, thus enabling more efficient extraction of important features.
- **CNN-DeepFM:** The convolutional neural network is used to compute similarity, and the DeepFM is exploited to recommend Web services.
- **LSTM-xDeepFM:** The long short-term memory neural network is used to compute similarity, and the xDeepFM is exploited to recommend Web services. The LSTM can fully apply the historical context information in the Web service description document to enhance the performance of Web service recommendation.
- **LSTM-DeepFM:** The long short-term memory neural network is used to compute similarity, and the DeepFM is exploited to recommend Web services.
- **Transformer-xDeepFM:** The transformer is used to compute similarity, and the xDeepFM is exploited to recommend Web services. Transformer achieves better accuracy by using only encoder-decoder and attention mechanism.
- **Transformer-DeepFM:** The transformer is used to compute similarity, and the DeepFM is exploited to recommend Web services.

4.4 Experimental Results and Analysis

The experimental results are shown in Figs. 3 and 4, where the horizontal axis indicates the training size and the vertical axis indicates the performance metrics. In general, the proposed AGN-xDeepFM method has a better performance than other comparative methods in terms of *AUC* and *Logloss*.

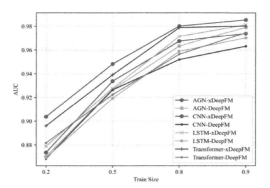

Fig. 3. AUC

- AGN-xDeepFM has the best performance compared to the baseline methods. The difference between AGN-xDeepFM and Transformer-xDeepFM is small when the training size is 0.8, and the difference in *AUC* is only 0.13% and the difference in *Logloss* is only 0.15%. However, the difference in *AUC* increases to 1.09% and the difference in *Logloss* increases to 1.1% when the training size is equal to 0.9. It shows

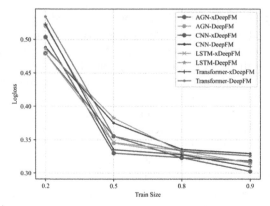

Fig. 4. Logloss

that the using the original corpus-level statistical information to deep learning for Web service recommendation can effectively raise its performance. And with the increasing of Web service data, the more significant the improvement of AGN-xDeepFM compared with other methods. It is clear that methods that use the xDeepFM have better recommendation quality compared to methods that use the DeepFM when the training size grows from 0.2 to 0.9. This is because the methods using xDeepFM consider both high-order and low-order items, and take into account both explicit and implicit combinations when recommending, thus effectively improving the performance of Web service recommendation.

- The recommendation performance of the AGN-xDeepFM gradually raises with the increasing of the experimental data. Especially, when the training size increases from 0.2 to 0.5, the recommendation performance of the AGN-xDeepFM raises the most. Among them, *AUC* increases by 4.45% and *Logloss* decreases by 35.29%. This is because as the experimental data adds, the hidden information of Web services mined by the AGN-xDeepFM is also increased, which effectively improves the performance of Web service recommendation. However, when the training size goes up from 0.8 to 0.9, the performance improvement of it is slower than that before. It is because in the increasing process of the experimental data, the information obtained by the recommendation system tends to be saturated and the information of the Web service contained in the categories with low ranking is less than that before, which is equivalent to the increase of "dirty" data to a certain extent, resulting in the performance degradation of Web service recommendation.

4.5 Hyper-parameter Analysis

- To prevent the AGN-xDeepFM model from over-fitting, this paper deeply investigates the effect of *dropoutrate* on the AGN part of the AGN-xDeepFM, as shown in Fig. 5(a) and (b), which demonstrate the change process of AUC and Logloss when the *dropoutrate* grows from 0.1 to 0.8 in steps of 0.1. It can be seen that the AGN-xDeepFM has the best performance when the *dropoutrate* is equal to 0.5, as well as the *AUC* value gradually increases and the *Logloss* value gradually decreases when the *dropoutrate* tends to 0.5. This verify that a suitable value of the *dropoutrate* in the AGN-xDeepFM improves the generalization ability of the model.

- To explore the effect of sentence length s in the AGN-xDeepFM, the value range of s is from 8 to 256. From Fig. 5(c) and (d), it can be seen that AUC shows an increasing trend and Logloss indicates a decreasing trend when $s <= 64$ and forms a stable and optimal performance when $s > 64$. That is to say, constantly increasing the value of s does not significantly improve the performance of the AGN-xDeepFM, but instead will consume more memory in the experiment. Thus, the length of sentence s is set to 64.

- It is noted that the hyperparameter ε in the Valve component defines the confidence interval for triggering information fusion. In the experiment, we use 0.1 as the step size and train with different ε values when growing from 0 to 0.5 to explore the effect of ε. From Fig. 5(e) and (f), we can see that the Valve component can effectively combine the information from different sources. Comparing to models without statistical information (i.e., $\varepsilon = 0$) or models that completely use statistical information (i.e., $\varepsilon = 0.5$), adaptively exploiting a part of statistical information can achieve better recommendation performance, and the AGN-xDeepFM has the best performance when $\varepsilon = 0.2$. This phenomenon effectively argues that it is useful to selectively integrate semantic and statistical information, not all statistical information, and some of them may bring noise to the model.

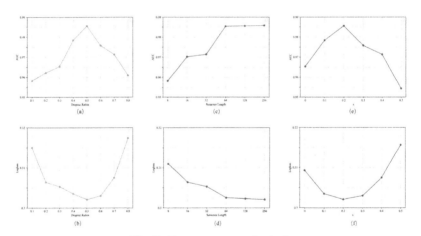

Fig. 5. Hyper-parameter Analysis

5   Conclusion

This paper focuses on the problem of how to recommend Web service efficiently and accurately, and proposes a Web service recommendation method AGN-xDeepFM by combining AGN model and xDeepFM model. In this method, it firstly fuses the corpus-level statistical and semantic information of Web service description document, which enriches the feature information of Web service description document. Then, it extracts the multi-dimensional features of Web service and uses xDeepFM to learn the explicit and implicit higher-order feature interactions for Web service recommendation. Finally, the experimental results show that the AGN-xDeepFM method is much better than other baseline methods in recommendation performance. In the future work, we will focus on exploring the using of federal learning models to Web service recommendation to further improve its performance on the premise of ensuring data privacy.

Acknowledgments. The authors thank the anonymous reviewers for their valuable feedback and comments. The work is supported by the National Natural Science Foundation of China (No. 61873316, 61872139, 61832014, and 61702181), Hunan Provincial Natural Science Foundation of China under grant No. 2021JJ30274, the Educational Commission of Hunan Province of China (No.20B244), and the Scientific Research Project of Huaihua University (No. HHUY2020-18). Buqing Cao and Hongfan Ye are the corresponding author of this paper.

References

1. Katal, A., Wazid, M., Goudar, R.H.: Big data: Issues, challenges, tools and good practices, ICCC2013 (2013)
2. Weerawarana, S., Curbera, F., et al.: Web Services Platform Architecture: SOAP, WSDL, WS-Policy, WS-Addressing, WS-BPEL, WS-Reliable Messaging and More. Prentice Hall PTR (2005)
3. Deng, S., Wu, H., Hu, D., Leon Zhao, J.: Service selection for composition with QoS correlations. IEEE Trans. Serv. Comput. **9**(2), 291–303 (2014)
4. Kim, G., Trimi, S., Chung, J.: Big-data applications in the government sector. Commun. ACM **57**(3), 78–85 (2014)
5. Milanovic, N., Malek, M.: Current solutions for web service composition. IEEE Internet Comput. **8**(6), 51–59 (2004)
6. Huang, L., Jiang, B., Lv, S., Liu, Y., Li, D.: Survey on deep learning-based recommender systems. Chin. J. Comput. **41**(7), 1619–1647 (2018)
7. Su, X., Khoshgoftaar, T.M.: A survey of collaborative filtering techniques. Adv. Artif. Intell. **29**(12), 426–434 (2009)
8. X. Wang, and Y. Wang, Improving content-based and hybrid music recommendation using deep learning, ACM Multim. 627–636 (2014)
9. Zeng, Z., et al.: Knowledge transfer via pre-training for recommendation: a review and prospect. Front. Big Data. **4**, 602071 (2021)
10. Rendle, S.: Factorization Machines. In: ICDM2010 (2010)
11. Guo, H., Tang, R., Ye, Y., Li, Z., He, X.: DeepFM: A factorization-machine based neural network for CTR prediction. In: IJCAI, pp. 1725–1731 (2017)
12. Li, X., Li, Z., Xie, H., Li, Q.: Merging statistical feature via adaptive gate for improved text classification. In: AAAI2021 (2021)
13. Lian, J., Zhou, X. et al.: xDeepFM: Combining explicit and implicit feature interactions for recommender systems. In: ACM SIGKDD2018 (2018)
14. Xia, B., Fan, Y., et al.: Category-aware API clustering and distributed recommendation for automatic mashup creation. IEEE Trans. Serv. Comput. **8**(5), 674–687 (2015)
15. Bobadilla, J., Ortega, F., et al.: Recommender systems survey. Know. Based Syst. **46**, 109–132 (2013)

16. Conneau, A., Schwenk, H., et al.: Very deep convolutional networks for text classification. In: ACL2017, pp. 1107–1116 (2017)
17. Shi, M., Tang, Y., Liu, J.: Functional and contextual attention-based LSTM for service recommendation in mashup creation. IEEE Trans. Parallel Distrib. Syst. **30**(5), 1077–1090 (2019)
18. Wang, H., Yang, Z., Yu, Q.: Online reliability prediction via long short-term memory for service-oriented systems. In: ICWS2017 (2017)
19. Ye, H., Cao, B., et al.: Web services classification based on wide & Bi-LSTM model. IEEE Access **7**, 43697–43706 (2019)
20. Kang, G., Liu, J., et al.: NAFM: Neural and attentional factorization machine for web API recommendation. In: ICWS2020 (2020)
21. Richardson, M., Dominowska, E., Ragno, R.: Predicting clicks: Estimating the click-through rate for new ads. In: WWW2007 (2007)
22. Yao, L., Mao, C., Luo, Y.: Graph convolutional networks for text classification. In: AAAI2019 (2019)
23. Ye, H., Cao, B. et al.: A web services classification method based on GCN. In: ISPA2019 (2019)
24. Aizawa, A.: An information-theoretic perspective of TF-IDF measures. Inf. Process. Manag. **39**(1), 45–65 (2003)
25. Yang, Y., Pedersen, J.O.: A comparative study on feature selection in text categorization. In: ICML1997, pp.412–420 (1997)
26. Ramos, J.: Using TF-IDF to determine word relevance in document queries. In: ICML2013 (2013)

PXCrypto: A Regulated Privacy-Preserving Cross-Chain Transaction Scheme

Yanran Zhang[1], Sheng Hu[1], Qin Wang[3], Bo Qin[1($\boxtimes$)], Qianhong Wu[2], and Wenchang Shi[1]

[1] Information School, Renmin University of China, Beijing, China
bo.qin@ruc.edu.cn
[2] School of Cyber Science and Technology, Beihang University, Beijing, China
[3] CSIRO Data61, Sydney, Australia

Abstract. The cross-chain technology is used to solve the problem of data islands between blockchains. Existing cross-chain techniques are challenging to resolve the conflict between transaction privacy and transaction regulation. Due to the decentralized nature of the blockchain, data on one chain are hard to get verified on another chain. Users cannot exchange across different heterogeneous chains without exposing transaction information. Also, cross-chain transactions increase the barrier to regulation from governments. To fill the gap, this paper proposes an innovative regulated privacy-preserving cross-chain transaction framework, called PXCrypto, which can achieve cross-chain transactions on any heterogeneous blockchain while regulating transactions and users' identities. PXCrypto maps heterogeneous tokens to the PXCrypto consortium chain by presenting cross-chain asset proofs, and then uses the corresponding wrapped tokens for trading. The scheme leverages a proxy multi-party computation mechanism to achieve cross-chain confidential transactions using an order matching mode to protect the bid prices on transaction orders. PXCrypto conducts transaction-related calculations through a pre-elected committee to regulate these transactions through the regulatory authority. We implement the scheme and accordingly conduct the evaluations. The results prove its security, efficiency, and practicality.

Keywords: Blockchain · Cross-chain · Privacy · Regulation

1 Introduction

Blockchain [1] is a distributed shared database that combines asymmetric encryption, digital signatures, hash functions, P2P networks, and other technologies. Thanks to its unique design, blockchain brings many advance properties covering openness, decentralization, accountability and transparency. It acts as the role of traditional reliable third parties but, surprisingly, without centralization risks.

Y. Zhang and S. Hu—Equal contribution.

W. Meng et al. (Eds.): ICA3PP 2022, LNCS 13777, pp. 170–191, 2023.
https://doi.org/10.1007/978-3-031-22677-9_10

Based on that, the blockchain technology has been vigorously developed during the past decades, and as a result, got widely used in many fields such as the Internet of things, medical treatment, finance, and other fields. However, we observe that several challenging barriers still exists, significantly hindering the further adoption of blockchain technologies.

In multiple business scenarios, the blockchain adopts different data structures, consensus mechanisms, and cryptographic algorithms. It is not easy for the chains with different purposes to be aggregated in one chain. The differences in the block structure, communication mode, and architectures make it difficult for one chain to parse the data on other chains. The great heterogeneity causes blockchains to be separated from each other, in which data cannot be circulated between chains. Meanwhile, on-chain data has uncertainty, and a legal block may be abandoned in the future. Most importantly, the blockchain relies on a decentralized architecture, and on-chain members rely on consensus to trust each other. This makes it difficult for users to trust the blocks from other chains.

Cross-chain technologies can effectively break the gap between heterogeneous blockchains, allowing data to smooth flow and get validated across chains. Existing cross-chain schemes use a large number of smart contracts for transactions, however, they lack corresponding smart contract privacy protection strategies. Users can freely view the cross-chain transactions, which increases the risk of private information disclosure and hinders the adoption of applications with privacy requirements. Meanwhile, the regulation of transactions is also worth discussing. At present, transactions on public chains such as Bitcoin [1] and Ethereum [2] are unsupervised. After many ICO projects have completed financing, it is difficult to regulate the landing of the project, resulting in huge risks for investors. If governments aim to regulate economic values behind digital currencies, they must strike a balance between transaction privacy and regulation.

- We propose a *regulated privacy-preserving cross-chain transaction* scheme, named PXCrypto, to achieve cross-chain transactions on any heterogeneous blockchain. The scheme can realize confidential cross-chain transactions (hiding order prices) as well as regulate the transactions and users' identities.
- We construct two modules to realize PXCrypto. The first module is the *cross-chain asset proof* scheme that can be used across any heterogeneous blockchains. The second is the *privacy-preserving proxy multi-party computation (PMPC)* protocol that realizes confidential transactions on blockchains. It uses an order matching mode for transactions to protect order prices and regulate transactions and users' identities. We formally prove its security.
- We further implement PXCrypto with comprehensive evaluations. Our implementation is built on the permissioned blockchain Hyperledger Fabric [3], to construct a stable and regulation-supported environment. The results prove that our scheme is satisfactorily efficient and feasible in practice.

Paper Structure: Section 2 gives the building block to construct PXCrypto. Section 3 introduces proposed system. Section 4 describes the cross-chain asset proof module and Sect. 5 describes the confidential transaction module. Section 6 analyzes PXCrypto in terms of security. Section 7 provide implementations and evaluations. Section 8 presents related work covering common cross-chain techniques and privacy schemes. Section 9 summarizes this work.

2   Building Block

In this section, we provide the preliminaries surrounding our proposed scheme. We introduce the concept of both *blockchain* and *secure multi-party computation*.

Blockchain Structure. Since the birth of Bitcoin [1], a large number of different types of blockchains have been proposed. Blockchain is a chain structure composed of a series of sequential blocks. Each block includes the block header and the block body. The block header mainly includes the hash of the previous block and the identification of the block, while the block body stores the detailed information of the block, such as transactions and transaction verification signatures. Researchers gradually found that the existing blockchain architecture is difficult to meet the requirements of users. In this way, Ethereum [2] has been introduced. Ethereum introduces smart contracts (SC) and utilizes them to realize state transitions. Various blockchain applications can be built on the top of the SC-supported platforms. At the same time, with the development of smart contracts, a suite of blockchain tokens based on ERC20/ERC721 [4,5] standards are created. The tokens can be easily exchanged within the same blockchain platform but are hard in heterogeneous platforms. In this paper, we aim to implement a scheme to support token transactions across different blockchains.

Secure Multi-party Computation. Secure multi-party computation was first proposed by Yao [6]. Secure multi-party computation protocols can meet the following two security requirements: (i) *input privacy:* Input privacy refers to that the secure multi-party computation protocol can protect participants' input and privacy; (ii) *computational correctness:* Computational correctness indicates that the secure multi-party computation protocol can obtain the correct execution results. At present, the mainstream secure multi-party computation framework can be divided into three categories: Yao's garbled circuit [7], SPDZ protocols [8] [9], and aby framework [10,11]. Secret sharing schemes [12,13] and oblivious transfer protocols [14] are widely used in these three schemes. In our system, we adopt the secret sharing scheme to protect the secret (e.g., the bid price) of users' orders. We ensure that the information on these orders cannot be disclosed to others. Meanwhile, we adopt SPDZ [8] to realize the order matching. In this way, no transaction information can be exposed during the matching process.

3   System Overview

In this section, we first present the system model and actors, as well as define the notations used in PXCrypto. Then, we introduce our system goals.

3.1 Actor

PXCrypto is a cross-chain asset trading scheme, allowing users to exchange different types of tokens on our relay chain. To operate these tokens, PXCrypto includes the following roles in the system:

– *User.* PXCrypto users are those who own digital assets on one chain and plan to exchange the assets on another chain.
– *Regulatory Authority.* The regulatory authority is responsible for the management of users' identities, providing registration services for users on the chain, and recording the related identity information. Disputes in cross transactions can be handled by the regulatory authority.
– *Asset Pledge Service Provider.* The asset pledge service provider can be undertaken by the official or chain users. The asset pledge service provider accepts the transfer of users in other chains and transfers the corresponding wrapped tokens in the relay chain to users in the chain.
– *Committee.* Committee undertakes the task of transaction matching. They receive the shares generated by users, execute the secure multi-party computing protocol with received fragments, and record the results on-chain.
– *Data Relayer.* The data relayer carries the node data from the source chain and transfers data to the relay chain.

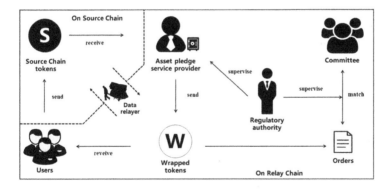

Fig. 1. Overall architecture

3.2 System Model

PXCrypto can establish communications between two different blockchains. We design a scheme that allows users to map the assets from the source chain to the relay chain and enable exchanges on the relay chain. Users can transfer the tokens from the source chain to the asset pledge service provider, and obtain the corresponding wrapped tokens in the relay chain. In this way, users can trade those tokens through orders on the relay chain. If the user wants to redeem his pledge deposit, he can also transfer the corresponding wrapped tokens back to the service provider, which will transfer the tokens from the source chain to the user's designated account. The overall system architecture is shown in Fig. 1. The regulatory authorities can view the asset pledge on the source chain and the order matching process on the relay chain. In contrast, users can only view their own order details, but they do not know other people's bids. Here, we provide the usage of each component. We also present notations in Table 1.

- *Source Chain.* The source chain refers to the blockchain from which the tokens are sent. It indicates the asset origination.
- *Relay Chain.* The relay chain refers to the blockchain to which the tokens are sent. It represents the transfer destination.
- *Source Token.* In our scheme, users can convert tokens on the source chain into the corresponding wrapped token on the relay chain, and then use the wrapped token to finish the trade on the relay chain.
- *Wrapped token.* A wrapped token is a token that represents a cryptocurrency from the source chain. The value of a wrapped token is worth the same as the original one. Tokens on different source chains are converted into different wrapped tokens on the relay chain.
- *Service smart contracts (SSC).* A smart contract subordinate to the asset pledge service provider. Users can input the number of tokens, the hash value of a transaction, and the address where the user wants to receive the wrapped token in SSC. After the service provider signs the contract, the user can publish the transaction on the source chain.

3.3 System Goals

Under this blockchain model, we derive the following goals for PXCrypto.

- *Privacy.* Ordinary blockchain users cannot view the bids and quantity of others in the order. Instead, they can only see the final transaction price.
- *Atomicity.* Users can atomically swap their tokens with other users in the relay chain. The trade either fully succeeds or fails followed by a rollback.
- *Auditability.* Regulatory authority should read any information about users and their orders. Meanwhile, the regulatory authority should also view all the asset pledge service provider's pledge information.
- *Decentralization.* Any user in PXCrypto can transfer and swap the corresponding wrapped tokens without any trusted third parties.
- *Efficiency.* PXCrypto uses an order matching mode. In a single order matching cycle, the matching of each order should take an average of one second to ensure the execution speed of cross-chain transactions.

Table 1. Notations

Symbol	Explanation
R	the relay chain
S	the source chain
H	hash value of the transaction
Tx	transactions proposed by users
u	users in PXCrypto
a	digital asset users pledge when they elect for committee
p	exchange rate price in orders
q	other order information besides p
pk_R, sk_R	the public key and private key of the regulatory authority
n	the size of the committee
t	the threshold value of secret sharing
E, D	the asymmetric encryption and decryption algorithm
SSS	the Shamir Secret Sharing scheme [12]
$(s_1, s_2, ..., s_n) \leftarrow \mathsf{SSS}(p, t, n)$	the protocols of the Shamir Secret Sharing scheme
$[s_i] = E_{pk_i}(s_i)$	encrypted shares
$o = \{[s_1], [s_2], ..., [s_n], q\}$	orders in the proposed PXCrypto
$o^R = \{[p], [q]\}$	backup order
MPC	multi-party computation program
T	order matching cycle

4   Cross-Chain Asset Proof Scheme

In this section, we will introduce the three phases to construct the cross-chain asset proof protocol, including *cross-chain asset proof*, *cross-chain asset redemption* and *appeal handling*. We provide details as follows.

Cross-Chain Asset Proof. We assume a user Alice controls a unit of tokens on the source chain S and hope to exchange tokens on the relay chain R, while an asset pledge service provider Bob controls a unit of wrapped tokens. Cross-chain asset proof scheme is shown in Fig. 2a PXCrypto completes the cross-chain asset proof scheme through the following steps.

- *Setup.* Alice obtains the public key of Bob on the source chain. She generates a transaction Tx on the source chain in advance and stores the hash value H. Alice enters the number of tokens, the hash value of the transaction, and the address where he wants to receive the wrapped token in the relay chain to SSC. If Bob is willing to undertake this contract, he can sign Alice's information and put the signature into SSC.
- *Transaction Publish.* After Alice receives and verifies Bob's signature, she can publish the transaction Tx.
- *Transaction Check.* Bob confirms whether the transaction Tx with a hash value H has been recorded on the source chain.
- *Receive.* Bob transfers the wrapped token with the quantity a to Alice's address on the relay chain R.

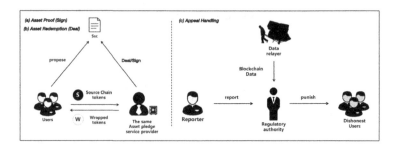

Fig. 2. Architectures for asset proof, asset redemption and appeal handling

Cross-Chain Asset Redemption. We assume a user Alice controls a unit of wrapped tokens on our relay chain R and wants to redeem those tokens on source chain S, while the issuer of those wrapped tokens belongs to Bob. The redemption scheme is shown in Fig. 2b PXCrypto completes the cross-chain asset redemption scheme through the following steps.

- *Setup.* Alice obtains the public key of Bob on the relay chain. Alice generates a transaction Tx on the relay chain in advance and stores the hash value H. Alice enters the number of wrapped tokens, the hash value of the transaction, and the address where he wants to receive tokens in the source chain to SSC. Bob must accept the redemption request within a limited time.
- *Transaction Publish.* Alice publish the transaction Tx.
- *Transaction Check.* Bob confirms whether the transaction Tx with a hash value H has been recorded on the relay chain.
- *Receive.* Bob transfers the token of quantity a to the address specified by Alice on source chain S.

Appeal Handling. Alice is the initiator in our process and also the first party to execute the transfer, meaning that she needs to bear additional risks. We require an asset pledge service provider to pledge a large number of digital assets in advance. The appeal handling scheme is shown in Fig. 2c If Alice has submitted the transaction and the asset pledge service provider fails to perform the corresponding transfer, Alice can apply to the regulatory authority for a ruling. PXCrypto completes the appeal handling scheme through the following steps.

- *Submit.* Alice submits the contract SSC and the published transaction Tx to the regulatory authority.
- *Judge.* Regulatory authority confirms the following conditions: (i) whether SSC contains Bob's signature; (ii) whether transaction Tx has been confirmed on-chain, (iii) whether the hash value of the transaction Tx is equal to the hash H that is recorded in SSC; (iv) whether asset pledge service provider Bob has submitted the corresponding transaction. If the above four conditions are met, the regulatory authority can transfer Bob's corresponding amount of pledge to Alice.

5   The Confidential Transaction Scheme

This section introduces the confidential transaction scheme on the consortium chain in PXCrypto. First, we describe the order matching mode adopted by PXCrypto for cross-chain transactions. Then, we propose a new mechanism called proxy multi-party computation (PMPC) for confidential transactions. At last, we give details on how to realize regulation for transactions and users' identities.

5.1   Order Matching Mode

According to the cross-chain asset proof scheme (Sect. 4), users can map the tokens from external blockchains to the PXCrypto consortium chain, and use the corresponding wrapped tokens for trading. PXCrypto uses an order matching mode for dealing with cross-chain transactions. Users submit an order in PXCrypto to declare the token types that they aim to exchange and then bid with their expected prices for the exchange rate. PXCrypto periodically collects users' orders and completes order matching according to a certain logic, so as to achieve efficient and reasonable cross-chain transactions. PXCrypto's order matching logic refers to Binance [15]. This allows multiple *buy* and *sell* orders to be matched at the same time, and the final transaction is carried out according to the unified transaction price. Here, we present a simple example of our order matching mode. For simplicity, assume that all orders trade the same token, the last deal price of that token is 100. There are two buy orders and three sell orders in the current order matching cycle. The prices of two buy orders are (100, 120), and the corresponding transaction volumes are (100, 200). The prices of three sell orders are (130, 140, 90) and the corresponding transaction volumes are (200, 100, 300). According to the order matching rule, the final deal price is 100, and the total volume is 300. As a result, all the buy orders are successfully traded, while only the sell order with a price of 90 is made the deal within this cycle.

As for the incentive mechanism of PXCrypto, although this is not the main focus of this paper, we can briefly introduce an idea according to the design of our order matching mode. After the order matching is completed, a certain percentage of the commission fees based on the transaction price and volume can be paid to the committee members as an incentive (Fig. 3).

5.2   Proxy Multi-party Computation (PMPC)

This section describes the proposed proxy multi-party computation protocol, which realizes users' cross-chain transactions while preserving their privacy.

Proxy Multi-party Computation. In addition to users and the regulatory authority, PXCrypto sets up a committee for order matching.

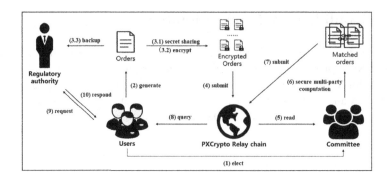

Fig. 3. PMPC modular design

- *Users.* Users can submit orders to buy and sell different wrapped tokens at any time. PXCrypto periodically matches users' orders through the PXCrypto committee. When the order matching is completed, users can query the result and conduct cross-chain transactions by atomic swapping.
- *Committee.* When PXCrypto is initialized, the committee elected by users will be formed. The committee is responsible for calculating matching results of transaction orders and earning fees. PXCrypto reads unmatched orders from the PXCrypto consortium chain and processes multi-party computations off-chain. Then, it submits matching results on-chain after calculation.
- *Regulatory Authority.* The regulatory authority reviews the transaction fairness and user identities and deals with transaction disputes in PXCrypto.

PMPC Protocol. The proposed PMPC protocol mainly consists of two algorithms and one protocol: the threshold secret sharing algorithm of order price Pshare, the order matching algorithm OrderMatching and the protocol for committee election ComElect. Most of the operations of these algorithms and protocols are on-chain, but a small number of off-chain operations are included. We give their concrete constructions as follows.

Protocol ComElect. Protocol ComElect describes how PXCrypto elects its committee members from all applied users. PXCrypto presets an integer n to specify the number of committee members. When PXCrypto initializes, m users will try to elect to become a committee member to gain benefits. For simplicity, we consider m is greater than or equal to n. We use $\{a_1, a_2, ..., a_m\}$ to represent the asset pledged by m users $\{u_1, u_2, ..., u_m\}$. Protocol ComElect will select the top n users with the most pledged assets as committee members.

- *Pledge.* Each user u_i pledges its asset a_i for the committee membership.
- *Sort.* PXCrypto sorts the assets $\{a_1, a_2, ..., a_m\}$ in descending order and obtains $\{a_{i_1}, a_{i_2}, ..., a_{i_n}, ..., a_{i_m}\}$.
- *Select.* PXCrypto chooses the users $\{u_{i_1}, u_{i_2}, ..., u_{i_n}\}$ as committee members.

Protocol ComElect

System Input: The size of committee n.

User Input: Assets $\{a_1, a_2, ..., a_m\}$ pledged by m users $\{u_1, u_2, ..., u_m\}$.

Output: Election result $\{u_{i_1}, u_{i_2}, ..., u_{i_m}\}$

1. Each user u_i pledge its asset a_i for PXCrypto committee membership.

2. $\{a_{i_1}, a_{i_2}, ..., a_{i_n}, ..., a_{i_m}\} \leftarrow$ sort descending$(a_1, a_2, ..., a_m)$.

3. Select user $\{u_{i_1}, u_{i_2}, ..., u_{i_m}\}$ as PXCrypto committee members.

Algorithm Pshare. Algorithm Pshare. describes how PXCrypto protects orders' prices submitted by users as private information. According to the number of committee members n in PXCrypto, PXCrypto sets up a threshold value t satisfying $t < n$. When a user generates an order, it first uses the (t, n)-Shamir threshold secret sharing protocol [12] to split the plaintext price into n shares, and use the public key of the current committee member to encrypt each share correspondingly. For regulatory needs, the user also uses the public key of the regulatory authority to encrypt the entire plaintext order and sent it to the regulatory authority as a backup.

Algorithm Pshare

User Input: Exchange rate price p, other order information q.

Public parameters: The public key of the regulator pk_R, the size of the committee n,

the threshold value t, public keys of each committee member $\{pk_1, pk_2, ..., pk_R\}$,

an asymmetric encryption algorithm E and decryption algorithm D.

Private parameters: Encrypted order o, backup order o^R.

Output: Matching results res.

1. The user performs (t, n)-SSS and obtains corresponding shares $\{s_1, s_2, ..., s_n\} \leftarrow \mathsf{SSS}(p, t, n)\}$.

2. For each s_i, the user calculates $[s_i] = E_{pk_i}(s_i)$, using committee members' public keys for encryption.

3. The user submits $o = \{[s_1], [s_2], ..., [s_n], q\}$ as encrypted orders to PXCrypto blockchain.

4. The user calculates $[p] = E_{pk_R}(p), [q] = E_{pk_R}(q)$, using the regulatory authority's public key for encryption.

5. The user submits $o^R = [p][q]$ as the backup order to the regulatory authority.

Algorithm OrderMatching. Algorithm OrderMatching describes how PXCrypto committee members periodically match orders. For simplicity, we consider all orders in OrderMatching to be an exchange between the same two tokens, and the first committee member is responsible for submitting the results to the chain. During each order matching cycle, the PXCrypto committee will read all orders from the blockchain that are not currently matched. According to the price shares contained in the encrypted order, the committee members will decrypt each order to obtain their share. After decryption, each committee member takes its share as private input and performs secure multi-party computation for order matching off-chain. The secure multi-party computation will output deal price and transaction volume. Then, the committee calculates the matching result and publishes it to the blockchain. Users can query the matching results of the current matching cycle on-chain after the order matching is completed. Users can obtain information including the purchase and sell orders, deal price, transaction volume, and transaction time. The buyer and seller complete the atomic asset swap and finally reach a confidential transaction.

Algorithm OrderMatching

Input: Encrypted order $\{o_1, o_2, ..., o_l\}$

Public parameters: Encrypted orders $\{o_1, o_2, ..., o_l\}$, an asymmetric encryption algorithm E and decryption algorithm D, a multi-party computation program MPC.

Private parameters: Private keys of the committee members $\{sk_1, ..., sk_n\}$.

Output: Matching results res.

1. For each member u_1 in the committee:

    a. Read $\{o_1, o_2, ..., o_l\}$ from PXCrypto consortium chain.

    b. For each $o_j = \{[s_1]_j, [s_2]_j, ..., [s_n]_j, q_j\}, j = (1, ..., l)$, calculates private input for the multi-party computation $input_i[j] = D_{sk_i}([s_i]_j)$.

    c. Takes array $input_i$ as u_i's private input.

2. The committee runs the program MPC off-chain, calculates $(dp, e, b_1, ..., b_l) \leftarrow \text{MPC}(input_1, ..., input_n)$, where dp is the deal price, e is the transaction volume and $b_j = \{0, 1\}$, where $b_j = 0, p_j \leq dp$ and $b_j = 1,, p_j \geq dp$, $(j, 1,, ..., l)$ is the comparison result between the secret price p and dp of each order.

3. The committee member u_1 clears buy/sell orders in chronological order, ensuring that each order is filled completely. Once the order o is fully filled, u_1 considers it is matched.

4. u_1 obtains res $= \{o^{j_1}, ..., o^{j_{l'}}\}||\{o^{j_{l'+1}}, ..., o^{j_l}\}$, where $\{o^{j_1}, ..., o^{j_{l'}}\}$ are l' matched orders and $\{o^{j_{l'+1}}, ..., o^{j_l}\}$ are $l - l'$ unmatched orders.

5. Committee member u_1 submit res to PXCrypto consortium chain.

Protocol **PMPC.** Based on the above algorithms and the protocol, we construct the proxy multi-party computation protocol as follows. The protocol can complete cross-chain confidential transactions and protect users' order prices.

- *Set-up.* PXCrypto execute protocol ComElect to form its committee.
- *Generate.* Users generate their buying or selling orders using algorithm Pshare, and submit $\{(o_1, o_1^R), (o_2, o_2^R), ..., (o_l, o_l^R)\} \leftarrow \text{Pshare}\{(p_1, q_1), ..., (p_l, q_l)\}$.
- *Match.* PXCrypto committee runs OrderMatching and submit the result res $= \{o^{j_1}, ..., o^{j_{l'}}\}||\{o^{j_{l'+1}}, ..., o^{j_l}\} \leftarrow \text{OrderMatching}(o_1, o_2, ..., o_l)$ on-chain.
- *Trade.* Users deal cross-chain transactions according to the matching results computed by PXCrypto committee.

5.3 Transaction Regulation Scheme

This section describes the transaction regulation scheme in PXCrypto. The regulation of transactions is carried out by the regulatory authority. In PXCrypto, the regulatory authority acts as a trusted party to certify the node assets on the chain, as well as regulates the order matching in PXCrypto. As the order matching of PXCrypto is completed by the committee, collusion may happen among the committee members to deliberately break the order matching processes to make profits. At this time, PXCrypto can regulate malicious transaction matching results. When an honest user on the blockchain finds that the calculation of the order matching result of a certain cycle is incorrect, i.e. a user submits a buying order with a higher price than the deal price of the matching result, users can pay a certain amount of tokens as a pledged deposit, and submit a transaction regulation request to the regulatory authority. The regulatory authority will accordingly verify whether the order matching result in this cycle is correct. Here, we introduce our transaction regulation module TXRegulation.

TXRegulation. Algorithm TXRegulation describes how the regulatory authority ensures the fairness of transactions. The honest user is called the *reporter* in the algorithm, the reporter will provide its own unmatched order as a part of the request. When a user submits an order in PXCrypto, in addition to performing threshold secret sharing of the plaintext price, it also encrypts the plaintext information of the order with the public key of the regulatory authority and sends it to the regulatory authority for backup. When the regulatory authority receives the transaction regulation request from the user, the regulatory authority decrypts the corresponding orders included in that cycle and recalculates them according to the order matching rules. The regulatory authority will generate an authoritative order matching result for comparison with the order matching results generated by the committee. We discuss two cases as follows.

- Case1 *False* ← TXRegulation: This indicates that the committee members have behaved evil. The pledge deposit of the user node will be refunded. All committee members will be punished, and the staked assets during the election from committee members will be frozen. Their membership qualifications will be accordingly canceled. Then, a new committee will be elected to perform subsequent order matching.
- Case2 *True* ← TXRegulation: This indicates that the user node has sent a malicious request. His pledge deposit will be frozen as punishment.

Through the above-mentioned regulation scheme, users can maintain their interests, the regulatory authority can ensure that the calculation results of order matching are correct. At the same time, such a mechanism increases the cost of evil behaviors for committee nodes and ensures the fairness of PXCrypto cross-chain transaction order matching.

Algorithm TXRegulation

Input: Reporter's unmatched order o'

Public parameters: Backup orders $\{o_1^R, ..., o_m^R\}$

Private parameters: Private key of the regulatory authority sk^R

Output: True or False

1. The regulatory authority find the certain order matching cycle T, where o' belongs to T.

2. The regulatory authority filter out the specified orders $\{o_1^R, ..., o_l^R\}$ belong to T in $\{o_1^R, ..., o_m^R\}$.

3. For each $o_i^R = \{[p_i][q_i]\}$, the regulatory authority decrypts $p_i = D_{sk^R}([p_i])$, $q_i = D_{sk^R}([q_i])$,

4. The regulatory authority calculates $(dp, e, b_1, ..., b_l)$, since the regulatory authority has known the plaintext (p, q) of each order.

5. The regulatory authority clears buy/sell orders in chronological order, ensuring that each order is filled completely.

6. The regulatory authority obtains $\{o_{j_1}^R, ..., o_{j_{l'}}^R\}||\{o_{j_{l'+1}}^R, ..., o_{j_l}^R\}$, where $\{o_{j_1}^R, ..., o_{j_{l'}}^R\}$ are l' matched orders
   and $\{o_{j_{l'+1}}^R, ..., o_{j_l}^R\}$ are $l - l'$ unmatched orders.

7. If $o' \in \{o_{j_1}^R, ..., o_{j_{l'}}^R\}$, output *False*, else output *True*.

5.4   Identity Regulation Scheme

This section describes the identity regulation scheme in PXCrypto. PXCrypto adopts the Idemix mechanism in Hyperledger Fabric. Idemix can effectively prove that one party owns the signature and corresponding attributes through zero-knowledge proof, without revealing the signature and the selected attribute value itself. This proof is also verifiable using the public key of the regulatory authority that originally signed the certificate and cannot be forged. Only users who know the secrets issued by the regulatory authority at the time of registration can generate proof about the secret and its attributes.

When a user on the chain registers in PXCrypto, the user applies to the regulatory authority. The regulatory authority will generate the user's identity certificate based on the attributes owned by the user, and provide the user's registration ID and a secret. The user executes the registration command with the registration ID and the secret, then obtains its public and private key assigned by the regulatory authority. When regulating transactions in PXCrypto, it is often necessary to establish a relationship between transaction data and users' identities. By binding transaction data with user registration IDs, it is possible to protect user privacy in PXCrypto through the Idemix mechanism while verifying which data is generated by which users. In this way, PXCrypto regulatory authority can regulate nodes' behaviors on the chain.

For regulated cross-chain confidential transactions, PXCrypto firstly sets up a regulatory authority and uses a notary-based cross-chain approach to map the tokens of other heterogeneous blockchains to the PXCrypto consortium chain. Through the cross-chain asset proof, the tokens on heterogeneous blockchains are exchanged for corresponding wrapped tokens. In the process of confidential transactions, PXCrypto proposes proxy multi-party computation. The user's plaintext price in the order is protected through asymmetric encryption and threshold secret sharing. Finally, the regulatory authority arbitrates the transaction results and regulates the identities of users on the chain, which ensures the security and fairness of transactions in PXCrypto.

6   Security and Property Analysis

This section analyzes PXCrypto in terms of *security* and *advanced properties*. We give our security analysis by adopting the real-ideal simulation paradigm [16]. To be noted, we merely present security proofs in sketch due to page limits.

6.1   Security Analysis

PXCrypto contains two major programs, namely the Shamir secret sharing algorithm (SSS) and the multi-party computation algorithm (MPC). For the SSS, it is not actually profitable for the committee members to collude with each other to restore the explicit price of the order, the committee would have to tamper with the result of the secure multi-party computation to make a profit. We follow the crux of real-ideal simulation proof systems [16] to demonstrate that our scheme is provably secure where the system can indistinguishably operate between the real scenario and the ideal scenario. As a sketch, we focus on the proofs of main programs, rather than surrounding primitives. Here are the details.

Definition 1 (PMPC). *The PMPC protocol can be denoted as a tuple with a series of elements as $(K, \mathsf{SSS}, \mathsf{MPC}, f_1, f_2)$, where K is a finite field, SSS is the Shamir secret sharing scheme in* Pshare, MPC *is the multi-party computation program in* OrderMatching. SSS *realizes a polynomial-time function f_1 by executing Lagrange interpolation for the secret recovery.* MPC *realizes a polynomial-time function f_2 by computing the order matching result.*

Definition 2 (Secure PMPC). *Let κ be the security parameter, x_i be the confidential input of committee member P_i, V_i denote the final view of P_i, y_i denote the final output of Π, and Π_j $(j = 1, 2)$ denote SSS and MPC of PMPC executed in real scenarios, respectively. We say that Π_j securely realizes f_j in the presence of semi-honest adversaries if there exist a simulator S_j such that, for every subset of corrupt parties C and all inputs $(x_1, ..., x_n)$, the distributions of*

$$\mathrm{Real}_{\Pi_j}(\kappa, C; x_1, ..., x_n) \overset{c}{\equiv} \mathrm{Ideal}_{f_j, S_j}(\kappa, C; x_1, ..., x_n)$$

are indistinguishable under κ, where $\mathrm{Real}_{\Pi_j}(\kappa, C; x_1, ..., x_n) := \{V_i | i \in C\}$, $(y_1, ..., y_n)$, and $\mathrm{Ideal}_{f_i, S_i}(\kappa, C; x_1, ..., x_n) := S_j(C, \{(x_i, y_i) | i \in C\}), (y_1, ..., y_n)$. For for every non-uniform polynomial-time algorithm $\mathcal{D}$ there exists a negligible function $\mu(\cdot)$ such that for every x and every κ,

$$|\Pr[\mathcal{D}(\mathrm{Real}_{\Pi_i}(\kappa, C; x)) = 1] - \Pr[\mathcal{D}(\mathrm{Ideal}_{f_i, S_i}(\kappa, C; x)) = 1]| \leq \mu(\kappa).$$

Lemma 1. *Given any t shares in* SSS, *the order price can be reconstructed by the committee whereas any $t - 1$ shares or less cannot reveal any useful information about the order price in* Pshare. *We refer to [17] for relevant proofs.*

Proof (Lemma 1). Pshare adopts the threshold Shamir secret sharing scheme. The security of Pshare follows the crux concept of Shamir's scheme. Let t denote the threshold value. The algorithm uses the polynomial $f(x)$ of degree $t - 1$ to share the secret where a_0 is the order price. Each share in Shamir's scheme is a result of substituting i in the polynomial function to obtain $f(i)$. The process will not leak any knowledge of a_0. For insufficient participants, the result fails since the polynomial $f(x)$ cannot be recovered at a degree less than $t - 1$.   □

Theorem 1. Π_1 *is secure against semi-honest adversaries under Definition 2.*

Proof (Theorem 1). In Π_1, each committee member P_i computes f_1 by a set of shares collecting from other committee members. Let $\mathcal{S}$ denote an adversary in the ideal world, $\mathcal{A}$ denote an adversary in the real world and α denote the secret shared in Π_1. Every output $y_i = \alpha$ obtained by committee member P_i should be identical. Considering totally m members exchange mutually their shares, we obtain $\text{Real}_{\Pi_1} = [x_{\mathcal{A}}, \{x_{i_k} \neq x_{\mathcal{A}} | k = 1, ..., m - 1\}, \alpha]$. Then, we present the behaviors of $\mathcal{S}$ in the ideal world as follows:

- $\mathcal{S}$ invokes $\mathcal{A}$ with its initial input denoted by $x_{\mathcal{A}}$.
- $\mathcal{S}$ adopts the Shamir secret sharing scheme and generates a total of $m - 1$ shares with the polynomial function corresponding to $x_{\mathcal{A}}$ and α.
- $\mathcal{S}$ sends the above $m-1$ shares to $\mathcal{A}$, simulating the communication conducted by $\mathcal{A}$ and other committee members. Hence, we have $\text{Ideal}_{f_1, \mathcal{S}_1} = [x_{\mathcal{S}}, \{x_{i_k}^{\mathcal{S}_1} \neq x_{\mathcal{S}} | k = 1, ..., m - 1\}, \alpha]$.

Since $\mathcal{S}$ uses the same secret sharing scheme (SSS in Pshare, proved secure in *Lemma 1*) as $\mathcal{A}$, the shares $\{x_{i_k}^{\mathcal{S}_1}\}$ simulated by $\mathcal{S}$ follow the same distribution as $\{x_{i_k}\}$. Thus, there exists a negligible function $\mu(\cdot)$ for SSS, such that

$$|\Pr[\mathcal{D}(\text{Real}_{\Pi_1}(\kappa, C; x_i)) = 1] - \Pr[\mathcal{D}(\text{Ideal}_{f_1, \mathcal{S}_1}(\kappa, C; x_i))) = 1]| \leq \mu_1(\kappa).$$

$\square$

Lemma 2. *For any arithmetic circuit* C *over* K, MPC *processed by committee members* $P_1, ..., P_n$ *in algorithm* OrderMatching *cannot reveal any information about the order price. We refer to this paper [18] for relevant proofs.*

Proof (Lemma 2). MPC in the PMPC protocol starts by letting each committee member share each of his inputs and send a share to each other. The arithmetic circuit C over K is then processed gate by gate, maintaining as invariant where all inputs and intermediate results are secret-shared, i.e., each value $a \in K$ is shared by $a_1, ..., a_n$, where P_i holds a_i. Assuming that the input values to a gate are a and b, determined by shares $a_1, ..., a_n$ and $b_1, ..., b_n$, respectively. We present the related operations, covering addition and multiplication as follows.

- **Addition.** For $i = 1, ..., n$, P_i computes $a_i + b_i$. The shares $a_1 + b_1, ..., a_n + b_n$ determine $a + b$ as required by the invariant.
- **Multiplication.** For $i = 1, ..., n$, P_i computes $a_i \cdot b_i = \tilde{c}_i$.
  - *Resharing step.* P_i parses the share $\tilde{c}_i$, resulting in shares of $c_{i1}, ..., c_{in}$ and sends c_{ij} to the committee member P_j.
  - *Recombination step.* For $j = 1, ..., n$, committee member P_j computes $c_j = \sum_{i=1}^{n} r_i c_{ij}$, where $(r_1, ..., r_n)$ is a fixed recombination vector [18]. The shares $c_1, ..., c_n$ determine c as required by the invariant.

The addition and multiplication operations can return correct results by the linearity of the secret sharing, and by the multiplication property. For privacy, the sharing of a result c during the multiplication operations starting from a, b is random and the corresponding results for addition are trivial. $\square$

Theorem 2. Π_2 *is secure against semi-honest adversaries under Definition 2.*

Proof (Theorem 2). Let $\mathcal{S}$ denote the adversary in ideal world, $\mathcal{A}$ denote the adversary in real world. By *Lemma 2*, input values a and b in every addition and multiplication gates are secretly shared in Π_2. f_2 computes the matching results gate by gate. Let a_i and b_i be the input of $\mathcal{A}$.

For addition, we have $\text{Real}_{\Pi_2} = [(a_i, b_i), \{a_j + b_j | j \neq i, j = 1, ..., n\}, a + b]$. We can simulate the behaviors of $\mathcal{S}$ as follows:

- $\mathcal{S}$ invokes $\mathcal{A}$ with its initial input a_i, b_i.
- $\mathcal{S}$ adopts corresponding SSS and generates $n - 1$ shares with the polynomial corresponding to (a_i, b_i) and $a + b$, denoted by $\{a_j^{\mathcal{S}_2} + b_j^{\mathcal{S}_2} | j \neq i, j = 1, ..., n\}$.
- $\mathcal{S}$ sends the above $n - 1$ shares to $\mathcal{A}$, simulating the communication executed by $\mathcal{A}$ and other committee members. Hence, we have $\text{Ideal}_{f_2, \mathcal{S}_2} = [(a_i, b_i), \{a_j^{\mathcal{S}_2} + b_j^{\mathcal{S}_2} | j \neq i, j = 1, ..., n\}, a + b]$. The shares $\{a_j^{\mathcal{S}_2} + b_j^{\mathcal{S}_2}\}$ simulated by $\mathcal{S}$ follow the same distribution as $\{a_j + b_j\}$.

For multiplication, We can simulate the behaviors of $\mathcal{S}$ as follows:

- $\mathcal{S}$ invokes $\mathcal{A}$ with its initial input a_i, b_i. $\mathcal{S}$ and $\mathcal{A}$ locally compute $a_i \cdot b_i = \tilde{c}_i$.
- During the *resharing* step, $\mathcal{S}$ follows $\mathcal{A}$ secretly parses $\tilde{c}_i$ into $c_{i1}, ..., c_{in}$.
- Then, $\mathcal{S}$ secretly shares c in $c_1^{\mathcal{S}_2}, ..., c_n^{\mathcal{S}_2}$, and reshares them in

$$\{c_{11}^{\mathcal{S}_2}, ..., c_{n1}^{\mathcal{S}_2}\}, ..., \{c_{1n}^{\mathcal{S}_2}, ..., c_{nn}^{\mathcal{S}_2},\}$$

respectively, where $c_{ij}^{\mathcal{S}_2} = c_{ij}, j = 1, ..., n$.
- During the *recombination* step, $\mathcal{S}$ sends $\mathcal{A}$ the set $\{c_{ji}^{\mathcal{S}_2} | j = 1, ...n\}$ to simulate the shares that $\mathcal{A}$ obtains. Then, $\mathcal{A}$ computes $c_i = \sum_{j=1}^{n} r_j c_{ji}^{\mathcal{S}_2}$.
- $\mathcal{S}$ sends $\mathcal{A}$ with the set $\{c_j^{\mathcal{S}_2} | j \neq i, j = 1, ..., n\}$ to simulate the shares that $\mathcal{A}$ gets for recovering c. Therefore, we have $\text{Real}_{\Pi_2} = [(a_i, b_i), \{c_{ji}, c_j | j \neq i, j = 1, ..., n\}, c]$ and $\text{Ideal}_{f_2, \mathcal{S}_2} = [(a_i, b_i), \{c_{ji}^{\mathcal{S}_2}, c_j^{\mathcal{S}_2} | j \neq i, j = 1, ..., n\}, c]$.

The shares $\{c_{ji}^{\mathcal{S}_2}, c_j^{\mathcal{S}_2}\}$ simulated by $\mathcal{S}$ follow the same distribution as $\{c_{ji}, c_j\}$. Hence, there a negligible function $\mu(\cdot)$ for MPC, such that

$$|\Pr[\mathcal{D}(\text{Real}_{\Pi_2}) = 1] - \Pr[\mathcal{D}(\text{Ideal}_{f_2, \mathcal{S}_2}) = 1]| \leq \mu_2(\kappa).$$

□

Theorem 3. *The proposed PMPC protocol is secure against semi-honest adversaries under Definition 1 and Definition 2.*

Proof (Theorem 3). Let Π_3 denote the PMPC protocol, the view in the real and ideal world of Π_3 is the combination of Π_1 and Π_2. We use R_{Π_i} as shorthand for $\Pr[\mathcal{D}(\text{Real}_{\Pi_i}) = 1]$ and I_{Π_i} for $\Pr[\mathcal{D}(\text{Ideal}_{f_i, S_i}) = 1]$. By integrating *Theorem 1* and *Theorem 2*, we can conclude that:

$$|R_{\Pi_3} - I_{\Pi_3}|$$
$$= |R_{\Pi_3} + (R_{\Pi_1} - I_{\Pi_1}) + (R_{\Pi_2} - I_{\Pi_2}) - (R_{\Pi_1} - I_{\Pi_1}) - (R_{\Pi_2} + I_{\Pi_2}) - I_{\Pi_3}|$$
$$\leq |R_{\Pi_1} - I_{\Pi_1}| + |R_{\Pi_2} - I_{\Pi_2}| + |R_{\Pi_3} - R_{\Pi_1} - R_{\Pi_2}| + |I_{\Pi_1} + I_{\Pi_2} - I_{\Pi_3}|$$
$$= |R_{\Pi_1} - I_{\Pi_1}| + |R_{\Pi_2} - I_{\Pi_2}|$$
$$\leq \mu_1(\kappa) + \mu_2(\kappa)$$

Therefore, we can observe that the PMPC protocol Π_3 can be distinguishable with a negligible probability, indicating that PMPC is proved to be secure against semi-honest adversaries under *Definition* 1 and *Definition* 2. □

6.2   Advanced Properties

Then, we give qualitative discussions of the enhanced properties.

- *Privacy.* We adopt an order matching mode to deal with users' cross-chain transactions. Its security is guaranteed by the secure multi-party computing protocol, and the user's order price is kept confidential during the process.
- *Atomicity.* The user's order is either fully matched and completed, or the order will be rolled back. PXCrypto does not make an incomplete deal.
- *Auditability.* The regulatory authority can inquire about all transactions. In the cross-chain asset proof scheme, the regulatory authority can handle the user's appeal and punish the asset pledge, or service provider. while in the confidential transaction scheme, the regulatory authority can maintain the fairness of transactions and regulate the identity of the user.
- *Decentralization.* There is no need for other trusted third parties in PXCrypto. If the asset pledge service provider refuses to execute subsequent transactions, it will be punished for the previously submitted pledge. If the Committee transmits mismatched data, the final result of the order matching is incorrect, which can be detected instantly.
- *Efficiency.* PXCrypto can effectively ensure that the average matching calculation time of each order is less than one second (evaluation details refer to Sect. 7). As the number of orders within a single order matching cycle increases, the total required calculation time will become longer. The efficiency of the scheme can be maintained by reasonably setting the upper limit of the orders that can be accommodated during a single order matching period.

7   Implementation and Evaluation

Experimental Configurations. We establish the experimental environments on the hardware laptop, equipped with 1 Core CPU and 2G memory. The operating system is Ubuntu 20.04 64-bit long-term version. Within the environment, we build the consortium blockchain on the top of Hyperledger Fabric, with specific versions of Fabric v2.3.1 and Fabric CA v1.4.9. The consortium chain is contained in the Docker version 20.10.7 with 20.10.7-0ubuntu1 20.04.1. Supporting components are Node.js v16.14.0 and NPM v7.14.0.

Implementation (Sketch). We emphasize two main algorithms in PMPC. For the algorithm Pshare, we adopt Python to generate the shares of order prices and use jsrsasign package in Node.js to implement RSA asymmetric encryption and decryption algorithms. For the algorithm OrderMatching, we use MP-SPDZ [19] to implement the *multi-party computation* (MPC) program, together with the Shamir Secret Sharing implementation [12,18]. The output of the MPC program

Fig. 4. Efficiency

in PMPC contains the *deal price*, *transaction volume*, and *comparison result* between order prices and deal prices. We provide the results of ten successful matched orders (OrderMatching in Fig. 5 at Appendix A). Here, the size of committee is 3.

Evaluation. We discuss the performance in terms of *efficiency* and *practicality*. Firstly, we demonstrate the efficiency of the PMPC protocol by analyzing the average order matching time. We measure the computation time required by the committee as the number of orders increases during a single order matching cycle (See Fig. 4). PXCrypto currently has acceptable efficiency in small-scale order matching, but in large-scale order matching, order matching rules need to be optimized to reduce the number of ciphertext operations in secure multi-party computation. Then, compared with mainstream cross-chain solutions such as Cosmos [20] and Polkadot [21], PXCrypto realizes the confidential transactions of users on the chain by hiding the order prices. At the same time, with the help of the nature of the consortium chain, PXCrypto can regulate the user's identity and the fairness of confidential transactions. Our scheme provides satisfactory practicability that can be practically applied to the actual management.

8   Related Work

This section provides the related work surrounding our scheme.

Cross-Chain Scheme. Blockchain is characterized by its decentralization where participants need to verify all the blocks on-chain. The cross-chain technique, thus, becomes a solution to enhance the scalability of blockchain. Ripple [22] proposed the Interledger scheme, designing connectors for users on different blockchain chains. Zamyatin et al. [23] proposed Xclaim and leverage chain relays to realize cross-chain transactions through verifiable smart contracts. Lightning network was proposed to deal with the transactions on Bitcoin in their sidechain. In the scheme, the hash-locked smart contract is adopted to ensure the atomic operation of both sides of the transaction. The Consensys team designed BTCRelay [24], which realized the data exchange between Ethereum and Bitcoin through a relay. Kwon et al. [20] proposed a cross-chain network: Cosmos, consisting of two major components: hub and zone. Cosmos adopt inter-blockchain communication (IBC) protocol for communication between hubs and zone and verify cross-chain data through the public key of relayers. Gavin et al. [21] introduced Polkadot, which includes the relay chain, parachains, and bridges. In Polkadot, parachains undertake different functions, while the relay chain as the hub processes the data across each parachain to provide cross-chain services. Bridges interact with existing chains as the interface.

Privacy Scheme. The pseudonym mechanism of addresses in blockchain has risks of being associated with the user's real identity under analytic tools. The total transparency feature makes all the transaction contents disclosed to the public. Researchers have widely discussed this problem. CryptoNote protocols [25] utilize the ring signature to hide the public key of the transaction initiator. The user's private key can connect multiple public keys to hide the transaction recipient. Several protocols, such as [26], adopt homomorphic encryption to hide the transaction contents. The scheme uses the Pedersen Commit to seal the plaintext values into ciphertext. At the same time, many researchers also employ zero-knowledge proof to hide the transaction information, such as Zerocoin [27], and Zerocash [28]. Other techniques like multi-party computation [29] and mixers [30] are also used to provide blockchain privacy. Besides the crypto-based solutions, the hardware-assisted technique [31] is another route to hide the transaction contents. Hawk [32] equipped the system with TEE to protect the confidentiality of contract states. Similarly, Ekiden et al. [33] also adopted TEE to protect state privacy. As in this work, we focus on the confidentiality of the order matching process, rather than the complete smart contract privacy.

9   Conclusion

In this paper, we provide a regulated privacy-preserving cross-chain transaction scheme called PXCrypto. PXCrypto contains two modules, namely the cross-chain asset proof scheme and the confidential transaction scheme. The former is responsible for the proof of cross-chain assets and provides users with conversion services between the tokens on the source chain and wrapped tokens on the relay chain. While the latter is responsible for token transactions and provides users with trading services for wrapped tokens. PXCrypto uses an order matching mode for token transactions. The implementation adopts threshold secret sharing and secure multi-party computing protocol to ensure privacy during the order matching process. At the same time, PXCrypto has introduced the regulatory authority, which can examine all transaction information and guarantee the fairness of cross-chain transactions. We accordingly implement both modules and present our evaluations. The results prove its efficiency and practicability.

Acknowledgements. This paper is supported by the National Key R&D Program of China through project 2020YFB1005600, the Natural Science Foundation of China through projects U21A20467, 61932011, 61972019, 72192801, the Beijing Natural Science Foundation through project M21031, the CCF-Huawei Huyanglin Foundation through project CCF-HuaweiBC2021009 and the fund for building world-class universities (disciplines) of Renmin University of China.

Appendix A

We give the screenshot (cf. Fig. 5) of ten matching orders. We conduct experiments using the MP-SPDZ's *Shamir-party* protocol. For simplicity, we run the computation program for three committee nodes in the same terminal. The order matching results consist of three parts: the deal price is 815, the transaction volume is 5409, and the price comparison outcomes between each order price and deal price (1 for *true* and 0 for *false*).

Fig. 5. Example output of the MPC program in PMPC

References

1. Nakamoto, S., Bitcoin, A.: A peer-to-peer electronic cash system. Bitcoin. https://bitcoin.org/bitcoin.pdf 4 (2008)
2. Wood, G., et al.: Ethereum: a secure decentralised generalised transaction ledger. Ethereum project yellow pap. **151**(2014), 1–32 (2014)
3. Androulaki, E., et al.: Hyperledger fabric: a distributed operating system for permissioned blockchains. In: EUROSYS, pp. 1–15 (2018)
4. Erc-20 token standard. https://ethereum.org/en/developers/docs/standards/tokens/erc-20 (2022)
5. Erc-721 token standard. https://ethereum.org/en/developers/docs/standards/tokens/erc-721 (2022)
6. Yao, A.C.: Protocols for secure computations. In: 23rd Annual Symposium on Foundations of Computer Science (SFCS), pp. 160–164. IEEE (1982)
7. Yakoubov, S.: A gentle introduction to yao's garbled circuits. preprint on webpage at https://web.mit.edu/sonka89/www/papers/2017ygc.pdf (2017)
8. Damgård, I., Pastro, V., Smart, N., Zakarias, S.: Multiparty computation from somewhat homomorphic encryption. In: Safavi-Naini, R., Canetti, R. (eds.) CRYPTO 2012. LNCS, vol. 7417, pp. 643–662. Springer, Heidelberg (2012). https://doi.org/10.1007/978-3-642-32009-5_38

9. Damgård, I., Keller, M., Larraia, E., Pastro, V., Scholl, P., Smart, N.P.: Practical covertly secure MPC for dishonest majority – or: breaking the SPDZ limits. In: Crampton, J., Jajodia, S., Mayes, K. (eds.) ESORICS 2013. LNCS, vol. 8134, pp. 1–18. Springer, Heidelberg (2013). https://doi.org/10.1007/978-3-642-40203-6_1

10. Demmler, D., Schneider, T., Zohner, M.: ABY-a framework for efficient mixed-protocol secure two-party computation. In: Network and Distributed System Security Symposium (NDSS) (2015)

11. Mohassel, P., Rindal, P.: ABY3: a mixed protocol framework for machine learning. In: Conference on Computer and Communications Security (CCS), pp. 35–52 (2018)

12. Shamir, A.: How to share a secret. Commun. ACM 22, 612–613 (1979)

13. Beimel, A., Chor, B.: Universally ideal secret-sharing schemes. IEEE Trans. Inf. Theory 40(3), 786–794 (1994)

14. Rabin, M.O.: How to exchange secrets with oblivious transfer. Cryptology ePrint Archive (2005)

15. Binance order matching examples. https://docs.binance.org/match-examples.html (2022)

16. Evans, D., et al.: A pragmatic introduction to secure multi-party computation. Found. Trends Priv. Secur. 2(2–3), 70–246 (2018)

17. Phiri, K.K., et al.: Linear (t, n) secret sharing scheme based on single polynomial. Int. J. Appl. Eng. Res. 13(14), 11600–11605 (2018)

18. Cramer, R., Damgård, I., Maurer, U.: General secure multi-party computation from any linear secret-sharing scheme. In: Preneel, B. (ed.) EUROCRYPT 2000. LNCS, vol. 1807, pp. 316–334. Springer, Heidelberg (2000). https://doi.org/10.1007/3-540-45539-6_22

19. Keller, M.: MP-SPDZ: a versatile framework for multi-party computation. In: Proceedings of the 2020 ACM SIGSAC Conference on Computer and Communications Security (CCS), pp. 1575–1590 (2020)

20. Kwon, J., et al.: Cosmos whitepaper. A Netw. Distrib, Ledgers (2019)

21. Wood, G.: Polkadot: vision for a heterogeneous multi-chain framework. White Paper 21, 2327–4662 (2016)

22. Bailie, A.H., Thomas, S.: Interledger: creating a standard for payments. In: Proceedings of the 25th International Conference Companion on World Wide Web (WWW), pp. 281–282 (2016)

23. Zamyatin, A., Harz, D., et al.: XCLAIM: trustless, interoperable, cryptocurrency-backed assets. In: 2019 IEEE Symposium on Security and Privacy (SP), pp. 193–210. IEEE (2019)

24. Btcrelay's documentation. http://btc-relay.readthedocs.io/en/latest (2022)

25. Saberhagen, N.V.: CryptoNote v 2.0 (2013)

26. Wang, Q., et al.: Preserving transaction privacy in bitcoin. FGCS 107, 793–804 (2020)

27. Miers, I., Garman, C., Green, M., Rubin, A.: Zerocoin: anonymous distributed e-cash from bitcoin. In: 2013 IEEE Symposium on Security and Privacy (SP), pp. 397–411. IEEE (2013)

28. Sasson, E.B., et al.: Zerocash: decentralized anonymous payments from bitcoin. In: 2014 IEEE Symposium on Security and Privacy (SP), pp. 459–474. IEEE (2014)

29. Bowe, S., Gabizon, A., Green, M.D.: A multi-party protocol for constructing the public parameters of the Pinocchio zk-SNARK. In: Zohar, A., et al. (eds.) FC 2018. LNCS, vol. 10958, pp. 64–77. Springer, Heidelberg (2019). https://doi.org/10.1007/978-3-662-58820-8_5

30. Zhang, R., et al.: Security and privacy on blockchain. CSUR **52**(3), 1–34 (2019)
31. Rujia Li et al.: Sok: TEE-assisted confidential smart contract. PETS **2022**, 711–731 (2022)
32. Kosba, A., et al.: Hawk: the blockchain model of cryptography and privacy-preserving smart contracts. In: 2016 IEEE Symposium on Security and Privacy (SP), pp. 839–858. IEEE (2016)
33. Cheng, R., et al.: Ekiden: a platform for confidentiality-preserving, trustworthy, and performant smart contracts. In: 2019 IEEE European Symposium on Security and Privacy (EuroSP), pp. 185–200. IEEE (2019)

CRFs for Digital Signature and NIZK Proof System in Web Services

Burong Kang[1,2,3], Lei Zhang[1,2(✉)], Yafang Yang[4], and Xinyu Meng[1,2]

[1] Engineering Research Center of Software/Hardware Co-design Technology
and Application, Ministry of Education, East China Normal University,
Shanghai 200062, China
{52174501012,52174501013}@stu.ecnu.edu.cn, leizhang@sei.ecnu.edu.cn
[2] Science and Technology on Communication Security Laboratory,
610041 Sichuan, China
[3] Research Institute of China Telecom Corporation Limited, Shanghai 200062, China
[4] School of Computer Science, Fudan University, Shanghai 200433, China
18110240046@fudan.edu.cn

Abstract. Web services are service-oriented computing technology
which allows computers running different operating domains to access
and share each other's databases. Each web service is an application
(like online business) which may require the private information of users.
Thus, it will be important to preserve these web users' individual privacy. The traditional approaches to achieve this goal in web security is
to use the cryptographic technologies, such as digital signature, NIZK
proof system. Whereas, some recent research results indicate that these
cryptographic technologies may suffer from the algorithm substitution
attack (ASA). ASA means that the cryptographic technology would be
embedded some backdoor in the process of its implementation by the
attacker, and with the backdoor information the attacker can steal the
user's private information. To address this problem, the concept of cryptographic reverse firewall (CRF) has been introduced, which could sanitize the messages inputting and outputting the user's computer. In this
paper, we construct the CRFs for the efficient Pointcheval-Sanders (PS)
signature as well as the NIZK proof system.

Keywords: Web security · Cryptographic reverse firewall · Digital
signature · Non-interactive zero knowledge proof system · Algorithm
substitution attack

1 Introduction

Web services are service-oriented computing technology which allows computers
running different operating domains to access and share each other's databases.
Each web service is an application (like online business) which may require the
private information of users [1–4]. Many current web services architectures are
based on the interaction of three types of entities: the *service requestor*, the *service provider* and the *service registry*. Generally speaking, the service provider

© Springer Nature Switzerland AG 2023
W. Meng et al. (Eds.): ICA3PP 2022, LNCS 13777, pp. 192–213, 2023.
https://doi.org/10.1007/978-3-031-22677-9_11

advertises its services in a service registry. The service requestor finds a suitable service from the service registry, and subsequently interacts with the associated service provider. In summary, there are two levels of security in web services. That is the transport-level security and the *message-level security*. The former is commonly provided by the SSL/TLS protocols. However, as mentioned in [5], the transport-level security is insufficient to the security of web services messages. For example, web services security requires integrity ensuring the message has not been tampered with [3,5]. This is generally accomplished with digital signatures. Thus, message-level security which could be achieved through the cryptographic technologies is an important aspect of web security.

The cryptographic technologies in the real world are commonly employed by users of web services under the assumption that they are implemented faithfully in the web system. However, the Snowden incident in 2013 revealed the fact to the world that the cryptographic technologies implemented in the machines of ordinary users are possibly suffered from the malicious *subversions* and *backdoors* conducted by some powerful attackers (e.g., NSA, manufacturers, supply-chain intermediaries), even though the underlying cryptographic primitives used to implement cryptographic technologies have been proven theoretically secure [6,7]. With the subverted or backdoored cryptographic implementations, the attacker can steal the user's private information (e.g., secret keys) without the awareness of users [8,9]. In practice, many significant instances of such attacks have been found out, such as the backdoor in the standardized Dual_EC_PRNG, the mass surveillance of NSA to the famous companies (e.g., Microsoft, Facebook, Apple, Google, etc.), so and so forth [10]. This kind of attack was originally termed as *kleptography* two decades ago [7]. Whereas, it was not paid more attention then. Motivated by Snowden revelations, it was reconsidered and redefined as the *algorithm substitution attack* (ASA) [11]. Various of cryptographic primitives, ranging from (public-key and private-key) encryptions, signatures, to protocols, proof systems, have been analysed to have the risk of ASAs [8–10,12]. Thus, ASA has been a major threat to cryptographic technologies.

Nowadays, to make cryptographic technologies defeat ASAs, some approaches have been proposed [12–16,18–20]. However, as summarized in [6], most of these approaches require various assumptions. Fortunately, it is also pointed out in [6] that the *cryptographic reverse firewall* (CRF) proposed in [12] is quite powerful since it could secure the fully black-box use of (possibly subverted) algorithms without complex detection mechanisms. CRF is an additional entity locating between the user's machine and the outside world [9,12,21,22]. The core idea of CRF is to modify the messages that user sends and receives as he/she engages in a cryptographic primitive potentially [12]. In such a way, the user's private information will not be leaked out, even if the user's machine is subverted. A well-designed CRF should satisfy three properties, i.e., *functionality maintaining*, *security preserving*, and *exfiltration resistance* [12]. The functionality maintaining requires that the CRF should not break the functionality of the underlying primitive when the user's machine is working correctly [12].

The security preserving guarantees that regardless of how the user's machine behaves, the presence of the CRF will provide the same security guarantees as the properly implemented primitive [12]. The exfiltration resistance means that regardless of how the user's machine behaves, the presence of the CRF will prevent the machine from leaking any information to the outside world [12]. The significant challenge is *how to design CRF for all kinds of existing cryptographic primitives?*

Until now, there have been the generic and instantiated constructions of CRFs applied to various cryptographic primitives, including message-transmission protocols, key agreement protocols, private function evaluations, public key encryptions, oblivious transfer protocols, interactive zero knowledge proof system, etc. *Digital signature* (DS) is one of the most fundamental cryptographic primitives and is not able to avoid ASAs which allow attacker to successfully extract the signing key of signer (i.e., service requestor) [8]. As a result of [8], two concrete ASAs (i.e., the biased-randomness attack and the small-randomness attack) are mounted on DS. The probability of the attacker to recover the signing key of the user is related to the length of the key and the randomness. Fortunately, a generic treatment to these ASAs on DS, as another significant result of [8], is that constructing CRFs in the signer's side for the re-randomizable DS schemes. In other words, the CRF could be deployed in the side of service requestors in the web system to achieve the goal of protecting their privacy. Whereas, no instantiation of DS scheme with CRF is given. Thus, we attempt to provide the instantiations of DS schemes with CRF.

Similarly, zero knowledge proof system is also a significant cryptographic technology in web services. It includes the *interactive zero knowledge* (IZK) proof system and the *non-interactive zero knowledge* (NIZK) proof system. The former requires that the prover and verifier interact with each other, the later only requires that there be some common public random string which the prover and verifier have access to. As demonstrated in [22] and [17], NIZK proof system could be used in web system by the user to request a legitimate service from the service provider. In [22], the authors first formalise the definitions of CRF for IZK proof system and its security properties (i.e., completeness preservation, strong soundness preservation, strong zero knowledge preservation and exfiltration resistance). As instantiations, they construct CRFs for a class of Sigma protocols-which are special types of IZK proof system-in the sides of both prover and verifier. Whereas, we find that *no CRF-based protection for NIZK proof system has been proposed so far*. Thus, there is no doubt that constructing CRFs for NIZK proof system schemes is meaningful.

1.1   Related Work

Nowadays, with the rapid development of the web systems, the web security has become a more and more crucial challenge. A common way to address the secure issues in web services is to use the cryptographic method, like the signature. From the aspect of practice, it will be a more efficient way to achieve the web security through specifying some standard signature algorithms. The standard *XML Signature* (including the traditional DSA and RSA-SHA1 signature algorithms) [23] is a fundamental building block for message-level security in web services which are based on XML. However, as noted in [23], the public keys of this standard algorithms are stored in standard X.509 certificates. This could result in the certificates management issue. To solve this issue, in 2007, Crampton et al. explored the application of identity-based cryptography in web services [5]. Their result stated that identity-based cryptography is naturally suitable for the message-level security needed by web services because it has some attractive properties. Whereas, as we all know, the identity-based cryptography is confronted with the key escrow problem. More recently, some research results indicate that signature algorithms would not avoid the ASAs.

In CCS 2015, Ateniese, Magri and Venturi initiated the formal study of ASA against DS [8]. Concretely, in their ASA model, a pseudorandom function with secret key-which could be regarded as a trapdoor embedded by attacker into signing algorithm-is used to bias the generation of randomness. As a result, each signature produced with biased randomness under signing key would leak one bit of signing key to attacker. In such a way, it will be possible for attacker to successfully recover a complete signing key and violate the security of signature scheme as long as he collects at least the same number of (sequential) signatures as the length of signing key. It is worth noting that their ASA against DS is stateful and is mounted on signature schemes in symmetric manner. Subsequently, Wang et al. proposed universal asymmetric (stateless) ASA against a certain class of signature schemes (i.e., splittable signatures) [24]. Unlike the symmetric ASA against DS in which the trapdoor key embedded into signing algorithm and the key used to extract signing key of users are actually the same one, in the asymmetric setting they are different. In other words, a pair of public/private keys is needed for attacker. The public key is inserted into the subverted signing algorithms, while secret key is used to recover signing key. In particular, Liu et al. showed that several existing signature schemes (e.g., DSA, Waters scheme, Paterson scheme, etc.) are subjected to their asymmetric ASA.

All these feasible ASAs on signature schemes encourage cryptographers to explore of effective countermeasures. In [8], Ateniese, Magri and Venturi considered this issue. Particularly, to protect signature schemes from the ASAs, they gave a generic construction of CRF for digital signature schemes. Briefly speaking, a CRF for a signature scheme is deployed in the side of signer and is an online external entity that could modify and sanitize the signature produced by the subverted signing algorithm before it is sent out from users machine to the outside world. Their results also show that every rerandomizable signature scheme is able to resist arbitrary ASAs with particular CRF. Moreover, they prove that such a CRF for rerandomizable signature scheme could maintain the correctness and will preserve the existential unforgeability under chosen message attack (EUF-CMA) of the original signature scheme. In practice, Ouyang et al. studied the possibility of CRF construction for identity-based signature (IBS) proposed in [10]. Whereas, as we all know, IBS has the problem of key escrow. We find that this problem is not avoidable in the CRF of IBS too. Thus, it will be meaningful to study that weather it is possible to construct CRF for some simpler signature scheme.

At present, the ASAs mounted on IZK and NIZK proof system and corresponding countermeasures are also studied. In [25], Bellare, Fuchsbauer and a Scafuro provided definitions and the securities of NIZK proof system in the presence of the subversion of common reference string (CRS). Later, Fuchsbauer studied the CRS subversion of succinct non-interactive arguments of knowledge (SNARK) [26]. In [27], Baghery amplified result of [25] and construct NIZK arguments that can achieve subversion zero-knowledge and simulation (knowledge) soundness at the same time. Whereas, we can find that these three researches mainly focus on the parameter subversion of primitives instead of ASAs of them. In [28], Berndt, Wichelmann, and Pott studied ASAs on cryptographic protocols. As they point out that ZK proof systems could be regarded as protocols and thus could be the attack aims of their ASAs against protocols. Subsequently, Ganesh et al. constructed CRFs for several IZK proof systems (i.e., sigma protocols) to make them resistant to ASAs [22]. Also, they researched the relations among the (possible) security definitions for the prover's CRF. Recently, Chakraborty considered CRF construction for strong simulation extractable NIZK (SSE-NIZK) argument systems when they aimed at building CRF for multiparty computation protocols [21]. Whereas, their construction is not a generic CRF construction for NIZK proof system. Thus, we provide a generic CRF construction for NIZK proof system and formolized its securities.

1.2 Our Contributions

Considering the above security threats of ASAs to DS and NIZK proof system, in this paper, we focus on making these cryptographic primitives resistent to ASAs with the constructions of CRFs. Briefly speaking, our contributions mainly contain the following two parts: 1) Since not any signature scheme could be built a CRF, it will be necessary to provide an efficient instantiation of CRF for digital signature. We build CRF for the wildly-used and efficient Pointcheval-Sanders's signature scheme (PS signature). The security proofs of this CRF are proven by the hybrid technique. The comparisons result show that our construction has lower theoretical computational cost than the existing CRF constructions for signatures. 2) Since there is no research result about the generic CRF construction for NIZK proof system at present, we formalize definitions of CRF for NIZK proof system and its securities. Then, we propose a generic CRF construction for NIZK proof system and prove its securities. Furthermore, we also point out that the CRF for Groth-and-Sahai's NIZK proof system could be referred to as an efficient instantiation.

The rest of this paper is organized as follows. Some preliminaries are given in Sect. 2. The CRF construction for digital signatures are stated in Sect. 3. We propose the generic construction of CRF for randomizable NIZK and give the corresponding proofs of securities in Sect. 4. Section 5 is the conclusion.

2 Preliminary

2.1 Notations and Definitions

Throughout this paper, we use λ to denote the security parameter. Let X be a finite set and A be an algorithm. We denote by $x \leftarrow_\$ X$ the random selection of an element x from X, by $y \leftarrow_\$ A(x_1, \ldots; r)$ the running of algorithm A with inputs $(x_1, \ldots; r)$ and output y. If a probabilistic algorithm's running time is polynomial in k, we call it probabilistic polynomial-time (PPT).

Definition 1 (Bilinear Groups [29]). *Bilinear groups are a set of three cyclic groups $\mathbb{G}_1, \mathbb{G}_2$ and $\mathbb{G}_T$ of prime order q, along with a bilinear map $\hat{e} : \mathbb{G}_1 \times \mathbb{G}_2 \to \mathbb{G}_T$ which satisfies the following properties:*

1. Bilineary : *For all $g \in \mathbb{G}_1$, $\tilde{g} \in \mathbb{G}_2$ and $a, b \in Z_q$, $\hat{e}(g^a, \tilde{g}^b) = \hat{e}(g, \tilde{g})^{a \cdot b}$.*
2. Non-degenerate : *For all $g \neq 1_{\mathbb{G}_1}$, $\tilde{g} \neq 1_{\mathbb{G}_2}$, $\hat{e}(g, \tilde{g}) \neq 1_{\mathbb{G}_T}$.*
3. Efficiently computability : *For all $g \neq 1_{\mathbb{G}_1}$, $\tilde{g} \neq 1_{\mathbb{G}_2}$, $\hat{e}(g, \tilde{g})$ can be computed efficiently.*

There are three types of pairings [29], in Type 1, $\mathbb{G}_1 = \mathbb{G}_2$; in Type 2, $\mathbb{G}_1 \neq \mathbb{G}_2$ but there is an efficiently computable homomorphism $\phi : \mathbb{G}_2 \to \mathbb{G}_1$; in Type 3, $\mathbb{G}_1 \neq \mathbb{G}_2$ and there is no efficiently computable homomorphism between $\mathbb{G}_1$ and $\mathbb{G}_2$.

Definition 2 (NP Relations [30]). *Proofs are related to the membership in an NP language L defined by an NP relation. Suppose $R : \{0,1\}^* \times \{0,1\}^* \to \{\text{ture}, \text{false}\}$. For all $x \in \{0,1\}^*$, let $R(x) = \{w : R(x, w) = \text{ture}\}$ be the witness for x. R is an NP relation if it is PPT. Let $L(R) = \{x : R \neq \emptyset\}$ be the language associated to R. an The fact that R is an NP relation means that $L(R) \in \text{NP}$.*

Definition 3 (Computational Indistinguishability [31]). *Two distributions X and Y are called (t, ε)-computationally indistinguishable (denoted by $\approx_c$) if for any distinguisher D running in time t, $|\Pr[D(X) = 1] - \Pr[D(Y) = 1]| \leqslant \varepsilon$.*

2.2 Digital Signature

A digital signature scheme $\mathcal{DS} = (\text{Setup}, \text{KGen}, \text{Sign}, \text{Verf})$ consists of the following algorithms associated with the security parameters λ [32].

- Setup : Takes as input the security parameters λ and outputs the system parameter Param.
- KGen : Takes as input the system parameter Param, outputs a signing/verification key pair $(sk, vk) \in \mathcal{SK} \times \mathcal{VK}$, where $\mathcal{SK}$ and $\mathcal{VK}$ denotes the space of signing and verification keys.
- Sign : Takes as inputs the signing key sk, a message $m \in \mathcal{M}$, and a random coin $r \in \mathcal{R}$, outputs a signature $\sigma \in \Sigma$, where $\mathcal{M}$ is the message space, $\mathcal{R}$ is the randomness space, Σ is the signature space.
- Verf : Takes as inputs the verification key vk and a message/signature pair (m, σ), outputs a decision bit that equals 1 iff σ is a valid signature for m.

Definition 4 (Correctness [32]). *Let $\mathcal{DS} = (\mathsf{Setup}, \mathsf{KGen}, \mathsf{Sign}, \mathsf{Verf})$ be a digital signature scheme. We say $\mathcal{DS}$ satisfies correctness if for all $\lambda \in \mathbb{N}$, for all $(sk, vk) \leftarrow_\$ \mathsf{KGen}(1^\lambda)$, and all message $m \in \mathcal{M}$, we have $\mathsf{Verf}(vk, (m, \sigma)) = 1$, where $\sigma \leftarrow_\$ \mathsf{Sign}(sk, m; r)$.*

Definition 5 (EUF-CMA [32]). *Let $\mathcal{DS} = (\mathsf{Setup}, \mathsf{KGen}, \mathsf{Sign}, \mathsf{Verf})$ be a digital signature scheme. We say $\mathcal{DS}$ is (t, q, ϵ)-existentially unforgeable if for all PPT adversaries $\mathcal{B}$ running in time t, it holds that $\Pr[\mathsf{Verf}(vk, (m^*, \sigma^*)) = 1 \wedge m^* \notin \mathcal{Q} : (vk, sk) \leftarrow_\$ \mathsf{KGen}(1^\lambda); (m^*, \sigma^*) \leftarrow_\$ \mathcal{B}^{\mathsf{Sign}(sk, \cdot(vk))}] \leq \epsilon$ where $\mathcal{Q} = \{m_1, \ldots, m_q\}$ denotes the records the messages which are queried to the Sign oracle.*

Definition 6 (Re-randomizable Signatures [32]). *Let $\mathcal{DS} = (\mathsf{Setup}, \mathsf{KGen}, \mathsf{Sign}, \mathsf{Verf})$ be a digital signature scheme. $\mathcal{DS}$ is efficiently re-randomizable if there is a PPT algorithm ReRan such that, for all $\lambda \in \mathbb{N}$, $(sk, vk) \leftarrow_\$ \mathsf{KGen}(1^\lambda)$, messages $m \in \mathcal{M}$, and all signatures σ such that $\mathsf{Verf}(vk, (m, \sigma)) = 1$, we have that the output distribution of ReRan is identical to that of $\mathsf{Sign}(sk, m)$.*

2.3 NIZK Proof System

Let R be an NP relation in NP language L. An NIZK proof system Π for relation R consists of three PPT algorithms ($\Pi.\mathsf{Setup}, \Pi.\mathsf{Prove}, \Pi.\mathsf{VerifyProof}$) specified as follows [30].

- $\Pi.\mathsf{Setup}$: Takes as input the security parameter 1^λ, and outputs a common reference string crs.
- $\Pi.\mathsf{Prove}$: Takes as input the 1^λ and parameter crs, an instance x, a witness $w \in \mathsf{R}(x)$ such that $\mathsf{R}(\mathsf{crs}, x, w)$ is hold, and outputs a proof π. This randomised algorithm is run by prover.
- $\Pi.\mathsf{VerifyProof}$: Takes as input the 1^λ and system parameter crs, an instance x, a proof π, and outputs $d \in \{\mathsf{ture}, \mathsf{false}\}$ indicating that weather π is a valid proof that $x \in L(\mathsf{R})$. The algorithm is deterministic and is run by the verifier.

For an NIZK proof system $\Pi = (\Pi.\mathsf{Setup}, \Pi.\mathsf{Prove}, \Pi.\mathsf{VerifyProof})$, it should satisfy some properties, i.e., completeness, soundness, zero knowledge, witness indistinguishability [25,30]. Informally, zero-knowledge captures the notion that a verifier learns nothing from the proof but the truth of the statement. Witness indistinguishability merely guarantees that different witnesses cannot be distinguished by malicious verifier. Soundness means an adversary cannot convince an honest verifier of a false statement. Completeness means all honest verifiers accept all correctly computed proofs. We recall the formal definitions of them in the following.

Definition 7 (Completeness). *For any $x \in L(\mathsf{R})$ and security parameter λ, the completeness requires that $\Pr[\Pi.\mathsf{VerifyProof}(1^\lambda, \mathsf{crs}, x, \pi) = \mathsf{ture}] = 1$ where $\mathsf{crs} \leftarrow_\$ \Pi.\mathsf{Setup}(1^\lambda), \pi \leftarrow_\$ \Pi.\mathsf{Prove}(1^\lambda, \mathsf{crs}, x, w)$ and the probability space is taken over the random coin tosses of prover and verifier.*

Definition 8 (Soundness). *For any* $x \notin L(\mathsf{R})$, *security parameter* λ *and any malicious prover, the soundness requires that there exists a negligible function* ε *such that* $\Pr[\Pi.\mathsf{VerifyProof}(1^\lambda, \mathsf{crs}, x, \pi) = \mathsf{ture}] \leq \varepsilon$, *where* $\mathsf{crs} \leftarrow_\$ \Pi.\mathsf{Setup}(1^\lambda), \pi \leftarrow_\$ \Pi.\mathsf{Prove}(1^\lambda, \mathsf{crs}, x, w)$ *and the probability space is the same as in the completeness.*

Definition 9 (Zero Knowledge). *This property requires that there exists a simulator* S *that could choose the common reference string by itself and produce a distribution space* $\{\mathsf{S}(x, \lambda)\}_{x \in L(\mathsf{R})}$ *for the output of proof, which is indistinguishable from the distribution space* $\{(\mathsf{crs}, \Pi.\mathsf{Prove}(1^\lambda, \mathsf{crs}, x))\}_{x \in L(\mathsf{R})}$, *where* $\mathsf{crs} \leftarrow_\$ \Pi.\mathsf{Setup}(1^\lambda)$.

Definition 10 (Witness Indistinguishability). *This property requires that for an adversary* $\mathcal{B} = (\mathcal{B}_1, \mathcal{B}_2)$, *there exists a negligible function* ε *such that* $\Pr[\mathsf{crs} \leftarrow_\$ \Pi.\mathsf{Setup}(1^\lambda), (x, w_1, w_2, state) \leftarrow \mathcal{B}_1(\mathsf{crs}), b \leftarrow_\$ \{0, 1\}, \pi \leftarrow_\$ \Pi.\mathsf{Prove}(1^\lambda, \mathsf{crs}, x, w_b), b' \leftarrow \mathcal{B}_2(state, \pi) : \mathsf{R}(x, w_1) = \mathsf{R}(x, w_2) = \mathsf{ture} \wedge b = b'] \leq 1/2 + \varepsilon$.

2.4 Randomizable NIZK Proof System

Let R be an NP relation in NP language L. A randomizable NIZK proof system Π for relation R consists of four PPT algorithms ($\Pi.\mathsf{Setup}, \Pi.\mathsf{Prove}, \Pi.\mathsf{VerifyProof}, \Pi.\mathsf{RandProof}$). The first three algorithms are the same as that in Sect. 2.3. We will specify the algorithm $\Pi.\mathsf{RandProof}$ in the following [33].

- $\Pi.\mathsf{RandProof}$: Takes as input the proof π for instance x in relation R, and produces a new proof π' for the same instance x. The updated proof π' must be indistinguishable from π.

The resulting proof produced by $\Pi.\mathsf{RandProof}$ must be indistinguishable from a new proof for an instance x. We allow the adversary to choose the instance x, the proof π that is used as input for $\Pi.\mathsf{RandProof}$, and the witness w that is used to form a new proof of the same instance. Formally:

Definition 11. *For* $\Pi = (\Pi.\mathsf{Setup}, \Pi.\mathsf{Prove}, \Pi.\mathsf{VerifyProof}, \Pi.\mathsf{RandProof})$, *we say that it is a* (t, ε)-*randomizable NIZK proof system if for all PPT adversary* $\mathcal{B} = (\mathcal{B}_1, \mathcal{B}_2)$ *running in time* t, *there exists a negligible function* ε *such that* $\Pr[\mathsf{crs} \leftarrow_\$ \Pi.\mathsf{Setup}(1^\lambda), (x, w, \pi, state) \leftarrow \mathcal{B}_1(\mathsf{crs}), b \leftarrow_\$ \{0, 1\}, \pi_0 \leftarrow_\$ \Pi.\mathsf{Prove}(1^\lambda, \mathsf{crs}, x, w), \pi_1 \leftarrow_\$ \Pi.\mathsf{RandProof}(\mathsf{crs}, x, \pi), b' \leftarrow \mathcal{B}_2(state, \pi_b) : \mathsf{R}(x, w) = \mathsf{ture} \wedge \Pi.\mathsf{VerifyProof}(1^\lambda, \mathsf{crs}, x, \pi)] \leq 1/2 + \varepsilon$.

The randomizable NIZK proof system has the same security properties as NIZK one. Here, we omit the formal definitions of these properties. We suggest readers seeing them in the Sect. 2.3.

3   Cryptographic Reverse Firewalls for Digital Signatures

3.1   Definitions of CRF for Digital Signatures

The subversion attacks for digital signatures and the formal treatment to this issue is firstly studied in [8]. Subversion attacks for digital signatures are modeled as the ability of the adversary $\mathcal{B}$ to replace the genuine signing algorithm with a different algorithm within a certain class $\mathcal{A}$ of ASAs. Let $\mathcal{DS}$ be a digital signature scheme. A subversion of $\mathcal{DS}$ is an algorithm $\tilde{\mathsf{A}} \in \mathcal{A}$. The algorithm $\tilde{\mathsf{A}}(\cdot, \cdot; \cdot)$ takes as input a signing key $sk \in \mathcal{SK}$, a message $m \in \mathcal{M}$, and a random coin $r \in \mathcal{R}_z$ and outputs a subverted signature $\tilde{\sigma} = \tilde{\mathsf{A}}(sk, m; r) \in \Sigma$. Note that algorithm $\tilde{\mathsf{A}}$ is completely arbitrary, with the only restriction that it should keep the same input-output interfaces as the original signing algorithm. In addition, subversions $\mathcal{A}$ for digital signatures is required to satisfy the verifiability and secret undetectability. The former means that the signatures produced using the subverted signing algorithm $\tilde{\mathsf{A}}$ (almost) always verify under the corresponding verification key vk. The latter captures the inability of ordinary users to tell whether signatures are computed using the subverted or the genuine signing algorithm.

Definition 12 (Cryptographic Reverse Firewalls w.r.t. DS). *Let $\mathcal{DS}$ be a digital signature scheme. The cryptographic reverse firewalls (CRFs) for $\mathcal{DS}$ is a tuple of algorithms $\mathcal{W}_{\mathcal{DS}} = (\mathcal{W}_{\mathcal{DS}}.\mathsf{Setup}, \mathcal{W}_{\mathcal{DS}}.\mathsf{Patch})$. $\mathcal{W}_{\mathcal{DS}}.\mathsf{Setup}$ takes as input the security parameters λ and a verification key $vk \in \mathcal{VK}$, outputs some initial public state $\delta \in \{0, 1\}^*$. $\mathcal{W}_{\mathcal{DS}}.\mathsf{Patch}$ takes as input the current state δ and a message/signature pair (m, σ), outputs a possibly modified signature σ' or the fault symbol $\perp$ and an updated state δ' (Fig. 1).*

Fig. 1. The framework of digital signature scheme with CRF for signer.

The CRFs for digital signature schemes denoted by $\mathcal{W}_{\mathcal{DS}}$ is a stateful algorithm. As demonstrated in [12], $\mathcal{CRF}$ is required to satisfy three basic properties, i.e., functionality-maintaining, weakly unforgeability-preserving, and weakly exfiltration-resistance. The functionality-maintaining property requires that the $\mathcal{W}_{\mathcal{DS}}$ should preserve the functionality of the underlying signature scheme, i.e., if a signature σ of message m is computed with the signing key sk, and the firewall is initialized by the corresponding verification key vk, the patched signature σ' should be a valid signatures for m under vk. The weakly exfiltration resistance property requires that the patched signatures are indistinguishable from real signatures to the eyes of an adversary. We review the formal definitions of them in the following.

Definition 13 (Functionality-Maintaining CRF w.r.t. DS). *Let $\mathcal{DS}$ be a digital signature scheme with cryptographic reverse firewall $\mathcal{W_{DS}} = (\mathcal{W_{DS}}.\mathsf{Setup}, \mathcal{W_{DS}}.\mathsf{Patch})$. We say that $\mathcal{W_{DS}}$ is functionality-maintaining for $\mathcal{DS}$, if for any polynomial $p(\lambda)$ and any vector of inputs $(m_1, \ldots, m_p) \in \mathcal{M}$, for any $(sk, vk) \leftarrow_\$ \mathsf{KGen}(1^\lambda)$, $\delta \leftarrow_\$ \mathcal{W_{DS}}.\mathsf{Setup}(1^\lambda, vk)$, $\sigma_1 \leftarrow_\$ \mathsf{Sign}(sk, m_1)$, $\ldots$, $\sigma_p \leftarrow_\$ \mathsf{Sign}(sk, m_p)$, $\sigma'_1 \leftarrow_\$ \mathcal{W_{DS}}.\mathsf{Patch}(m_1, \sigma_1, \delta)$, $\ldots$, $\sigma'_p \leftarrow_\$ \mathcal{W_{DS}}.\mathsf{Patch}(m_p, \sigma_p, \delta)$, there exists a negligible probability ε such that $\Pr[\mathsf{Verf}(vk, (m_i, \sigma'_i)) = 0] \leq \varepsilon$, where the probability is taken over the coin tosses of all involved algorithms.*

Definition 14 (Unforgeability-Preserving CRF w.r.t. DS). *Let $\mathcal{DS}$ be a digital signature scheme with cryptographic reverse firewall $\mathcal{W_{DS}} = (\mathcal{W_{DS}}.\mathsf{Setup}, \mathcal{W_{DS}}.\mathsf{Patch})$, $\mathcal{A}$ be some class of SAs for $\mathcal{DS}$. We say that $\mathcal{W_{DS}}$ is (t, n, q, ε)-unforgeability-preserving for $\mathcal{DS}$ against SAs if for all adversary $\mathcal{B}$ running in time t, we have that $\Pr[\mathcal{B} \text{ wins}] \leq \varepsilon$ in the following game.*

1. The challenger $\mathcal{C}$ runs $(sk, vk) \leftarrow_\$ \mathsf{KGen}(1^\lambda)$, computes $\delta \leftarrow_\$ \mathcal{W_{DS}}.\mathsf{Setup}(vk, 1^\lambda)$, gives (vk, δ) to $\mathcal{B}$.
2. The adversary $\mathcal{B}$ is allowed to have access to oracle $\mathsf{Sign}(sk, \cdot)$. Upon input the i-th query message m_i, this oracle returns $\sigma_i \leftarrow_\$ \mathsf{Sign}(sk, m_i)$. Let $\mathcal{Q} = \{m_1, \ldots, m_q\}$ be the list of all the messages queried signature oracle.
3. The adversary $\mathcal{B}$ can adaptively choose an algorithm $\tilde{\mathsf{A}}_j \in \mathcal{A}$ which meets the verifiability, and get the correspondingly $\mathcal{W_{DS}}.\mathsf{Patch}(\delta, (\cdot, \tilde{\mathsf{A}}_j(sk, \cdot)))$. Upon input the i-th query message $\tilde{m}_{i,j}$ for $i \in [q]$ and $j \in [n]$, the oracle returns $\sigma_{i,j} \leftarrow_\$ \mathcal{W_{DS}}.\mathsf{Patch}(\delta, (\tilde{m}_{i,j}, \tilde{\mathsf{A}}_j(sk, \tilde{m}_{i,j})))$ and updates the state δ. Let $\tilde{\mathcal{Q}}_j = \{\tilde{m}_{1,j}, \ldots, \tilde{m}_{q,j}\}$ be the list of all the messages queried for each $\tilde{\mathsf{A}}_j$.
4. Finally, $\mathcal{B}$ outputs a message/signature pair (m^*, σ^*); we say that adversary $\mathcal{B}$ wins the above game if and only if $\mathsf{Verf}(vk, (m^*, \sigma^*)) = 1$ and $m^* \notin \mathcal{Q} \cup \tilde{\mathcal{Q}}$, where $\tilde{\mathcal{Q}} = \bigcup_{j=1}^n \tilde{\mathcal{Q}}_j$.

Definition 15 (Exfiltration-Resistance CRF w.r.t. DS). *Let $\mathcal{DS}$ be a digital signature scheme with cryptographic reverse firewall $\mathcal{W_{DS}} = (\mathcal{W_{DS}}.\mathsf{Setup}, \mathcal{W_{DS}}.\mathsf{Patch})$. We say that $\mathcal{W_{DS}}$ is (t, n, q, ε)-exfiltration-resistance for $\mathcal{DS}$ if for all adversary $\mathcal{B}$ running in time t, we have that $|\Pr[\mathcal{B} \text{ wins}] - \frac{1}{2}| \leq \varepsilon$ in the following game.*

1. The challenger $\mathcal{C}$ runs $(sk, vk) \leftarrow_\$ \mathsf{KGen}(1^\lambda)$, computes $\delta \leftarrow_\$ \mathcal{W_{DS}}.\mathsf{Setup}(vk, 1^\lambda)$, samples $b \leftarrow_\$ \{0, 1\}$, gives (vk, δ) to $\mathcal{B}$.
2. The adversary $\mathcal{B}$ can adaptively choose an algorithm $\tilde{\mathsf{A}}_j \in \mathcal{A}$ for $j \in \mathbb{N}$ which meets the verifiability. Each of such algorithm implicitly defines an oracle that can be queried adaptively at most $q \in \mathbb{N}$ times.

- Upon input a query in of form $(j, m_{i,j})$ for $j \in [n]$ and $i \in [q]$, this oracle returns the i-th query message $\tilde{m}_{i,j}$ for $i \in [q]$ and $j \in [n]$, the oracle returns $\sigma_i \leftarrow_\$ \mathsf{Sign}(sk, m_i)$ if the challenge bit $b = 1$; otherwise, it returns $\sigma_{i,j} \leftarrow_\$ \mathcal{W}_{\mathcal{DS}}.\mathsf{Patch}(\delta, (m_{i,j}, \tilde{\mathsf{A}}_j(sk, m_{i,j})))$. In the case that $\tilde{\mathsf{A}}_j$ is not defined, this oracle outputs $\perp$.
- Note that $\mathcal{B}$ does not need to ask all q queries before choosing the next algorithm, i.e. the queries to each oracle $\tilde{\mathsf{A}}_j$ can be interleaved in an arbitrary manner.

3. Finally, $\mathcal{B}$ outputs a value $b' \in \{0, 1\}$; we say that $\mathcal{B}$ wins the game if and only if $b = b'$.

3.2   Review on the PS Signature Scheme

PS Assumption We denote by $\mathsf{Param} = (q, \mathbb{G}_1, \mathbb{G}_2, \mathbb{G}_T, g, \tilde{g}, \hat{e})$ the system parameter generated by the PSS.Setup algorithm. Let $y, x \in Z_q$, $\tilde{X} = \tilde{g}^x$, $\tilde{Y} = \tilde{g}^y$. For all PPT adversary $\mathcal{A}$ given the access to the $\mathcal{O}(\tilde{X}, \tilde{Y}, \cdot)$ oracle which inputs a value $m \in Z_q^*$ and outputs $(A = g^a, B = X^a \cdot g^{aym})$ where $a \in Z_q^*$ is chosen randomly, the probability $\Pr[x, y \in Z_q, \tilde{X} = \tilde{g}^x, \tilde{Y} = \tilde{g}^y, (m, A, B) \leftarrow_\$ \mathcal{A}^{\mathcal{O}(\tilde{X}, \tilde{Y}, \cdot)}(\mathsf{Param}, \tilde{X}, \tilde{Y}) : m \notin \mathcal{Q} \wedge m \in Z_q^* \wedge A \in \mathbb{G}_1 \wedge B = A^{x+ym}]$ is negligible, where $\mathcal{Q}$ is the list of queries that $\mathcal{A}$ made to $\mathcal{O}(\tilde{X}, \tilde{Y}, \cdot)$ oracle [32].

PS Signature. We construct a secure cryptographic reverse firewall for the pairing-based signature scheme proposed by Pointcheval and Sanders (PS signature). This signature scheme is provably secure under the LSRW assumption. The PS signature scheme $\mathcal{PSS}$ consists of algorithms (PSS.Setup, PSS.Gen, PSS.Sig, PSS.Ver) which are reviewed as below [32].

- PSS.Setup: Takes as input the security parameter 1^λ, and outputs the system parameter $\mathsf{Param} = (q, \mathbb{G}_1, \mathbb{G}_2, \mathbb{G}_T, g, \tilde{g}, \hat{e})$. We note that $\mathbb{G}_1 = \langle g \rangle$, $\mathbb{G}_2 = \langle \tilde{g} \rangle$ are two cyclic groups of prime order q, $\hat{e} : \mathbb{G}_1 \times \mathbb{G}_2 \to \mathbb{G}_T$ is a Type 3 bilinear map.
- PSS.Gen: Takes as input the system parameter Param, chooses x, y randomly from Z_q, computes $\tilde{X} = \tilde{g}^x$, $\tilde{Y} = \tilde{g}^y$, sets the verification key $vk = (\tilde{X}, \tilde{Y})$ and the signing key $sk = (x, y)$.
- PSS.Sig: Takes as input the message m and the signing key sk, chooses a randomness $A \in \mathbb{G}_1$, computes $B = A^{x+ym}$, sets and outputs the signature $\sigma = (A, B)$.
- PSS.Ver: Takes as input the verification key vk, the message m and purported signature σ, checks that weather the verification equation $\hat{e}(A, \tilde{X} \cdot \tilde{Y}^m) = \hat{e}(B, \tilde{g})$ holds. If it holds, the σ is a valid signature on message m.

The PS signature scheme is stated to be a re-randomizable signature scheme in [32]. That is, according to the Definition 6, there must be an algorithm PSS.ReRan which could re-randomize the signature σ produced from the PSS.Sig in the PS signature to generate an updated signature σ'. In the following, we give the algorithm PSS.ReRan.

- PSS.ReRan: Takes as inputs the signature $\sigma = (A, B)$ on message m, randomly chooses $\alpha \in Z_q^*$, computes and outputs $\sigma' = (A^\alpha, B^\alpha)$. The new signature σ' is also valid for message m.

3.3 The CRF Construction for PS Signature Scheme

Our CRF construction for PS signature is depicted in Fig. 2. Intuitively, the firewall uses the re-randomizable property of the underlying PS signature in order to "sanitizes" the signatures produced by the signer, in such a way that a functionality-maintaining subverted signer cannot signal information about the signing key through them. In the following, we present the CRF construction for PS signature in detail.

- PSS.Setup: Takes as input the security parameter 1^λ, and outputs the system parameter $\mathsf{Param} = (q, \mathbb{G}_1, \mathbb{G}_2, \mathbb{G}_T, g, \tilde{g}, \hat{e})$. We note that $\mathbb{G}_1 = \langle g \rangle$, $\mathbb{G}_2 = \langle \tilde{g} \rangle$ are two cyclic groups of prime order q, $\hat{e} : \mathbb{G}_1 \times \mathbb{G}_2 \to \mathbb{G}_T$ is a Type 3 bilinear map.
- PSS.Gen: Takes as input the system parameter Param, chooses x, y randomly from Z_q, computes $\tilde{X} = \tilde{g}^x$, $\tilde{Y} = \tilde{g}^y$, sets the verification key $vk = (\tilde{X}, \tilde{Y})$ and the signing key $sk = (x, y)$.
- $\mathcal{W}_{PSS}$.Setup: Takes as input the verification key $vk = (\tilde{X}, \tilde{Y})$, selects an element α from Z_q^*, and compute $\tilde{X}' = \tilde{X}^\alpha, \tilde{Y}' = \tilde{Y}^\alpha$. This algorithm outputs the re-randomised verification key $vk = (\tilde{X}', \tilde{Y}')$.
- PSS.Sig: Takes as input the message m and the signing key sk, chooses a randomness $A \in \mathbb{G}_1$, computes $B = A^{x+ym}$, sets and outputs the signature $\sigma = (A, B)$.
- $\mathcal{W}_{PSS}$.Patch: Takes as input the signature $\sigma = (A, B)$ and a randomness α, computes $A' = A^\alpha$ and $B' = B^{\alpha^2}$, outputs a re-randomised signature $\sigma' = (A', B')$.
- PSS.Ver: Takes as input the verification key vk', message m and signature σ', checks that weather the verification equation $\hat{e}(A', \tilde{X}' \cdot \tilde{Y}'^m) = \hat{e}(B', \tilde{g})$ holds. If it holds, the σ' is a valid signature on message m.

3.4 Security Proofs of the CRF for PS Signature Scheme

Theorem 1. *For the PS digital signature scheme $\mathcal{PSS} = (\mathsf{PSS.Setup}, \mathsf{PSS.Gen}, \mathsf{PSS.Sig}, \mathsf{PSS.Ver})$, which satisfies the correctness and existentially unforgeability, the CRF for the signer of $\mathcal{PSS}$ shown in Fig. 2 maintains the correctness and preserves the unforgeability for $\mathcal{PSS}$, moreover it is exfiltration resistance. We denote by $\mathcal{W}_{PSS} = (\mathcal{W}_{PSS}.\mathsf{Setup}, \mathcal{W}_{PSS}.\mathsf{Patch})$ the CRF for the signer of $\mathcal{PSS}$. In the following, we present the construction in detail.*

Proof. We will prove each property of the firewall below.

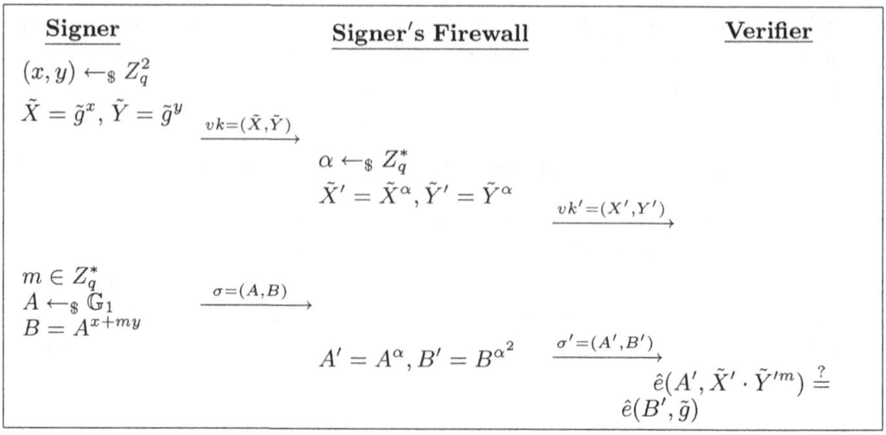

Signer	**Signer's Firewall**	**Verifier**

$(x, y) \leftarrow_\$ Z_q^2$

$\tilde{X} = \tilde{g}^x, \tilde{Y} = \tilde{g}^y$ $\xrightarrow{\quad vk=(\tilde{X},\tilde{Y}) \quad}$

$\alpha \leftarrow_\$ Z_q^*$

$\tilde{X}' = \tilde{X}^\alpha, \tilde{Y}' = \tilde{Y}^\alpha$ $\xrightarrow{\quad vk'=(X',Y') \quad}$

$m \in Z_q^*$

$A \leftarrow_\$ \mathbb{G}_1$ $\xrightarrow{\quad \sigma=(A,B) \quad}$

$B = A^{x+my}$

$A' = A^\alpha, B' = B^{\alpha^2}$ $\xrightarrow{\quad \sigma'=(A',B') \quad}$

$\hat{e}(A', \tilde{X}' \cdot \tilde{Y}'^m) \stackrel{?}{=}$

$\hat{e}(B', \tilde{g})$

Fig. 2. Signer's reverse firewall for the PS signature

(1) **Functionality-Maintaining**: This property can be proved very simply. The signer generates a pair of (sk, vk), then it computes the signature $\sigma = (A, B = A^{x+my})$ for message m. Next, the signer transfers the signature σ to the CRF. The CRF then updates the signature as $\sigma' = (A' = A^\alpha, B' = B^{\alpha^2})$ and sends it to the verifier. When the signer's CRF receives public key, it chooses a random secret $\alpha \in Z_q^*$, and sets $\tilde{X}' = \tilde{X}^\alpha, \tilde{Y}' = \tilde{Y}^\alpha$ and passes the re-randomized public key $vk' = (\tilde{X}', \tilde{Y}')$ to the verifier. As a result, the verifier could use the rerandomized public key and signature to verify the equation.

$$\hat{e}(A', \tilde{X} \cdot \tilde{Y}^m) = \hat{e}(A', \tilde{g}^{x\alpha+ym\alpha}) = \hat{e}(A^{\alpha(x\alpha+ym\alpha)}, \tilde{g}) = \hat{e}(B', \tilde{g}) \qquad (1)$$

(2) **Unforgeability-Preservation** and **Exfiltration-Resistance**: For any subverted implementation on the PS signature, the signer maintains the functionality. We will prove these securities using the game sequence. That is, prove the security game of PS signature with CRFs is indistinguishable from the original security game of PS signature in [32]. Next we consider the following games:

Game 0. It is identical to the security game of unforgeability-preserving CRF w.r.t. DS in Sect. 3.

Game 1. Same as **Game** 0 except that the generation of the verification key of users. That is, in **Game** 0 the verification key is vk' which is computed with algorithms PSS.Gen* and $\mathcal{W}_{PSS}$.Setup. Whereas, in **Game** 1 the verification key is vk that is actually computed with the honest (not be subverted) algorithm PSS.Gen.

Game 2. Same as **Game** 1 except that the generation of the signature of signers. That is, in **Game** 1 the signature $\sigma' = (A', B')$ of message m is computed with algorithms PSS.Sig* and $\mathcal{W}_{PSS}$.Patch. However, in **Game** 2 the signature is $\sigma = (A, B)$ that is computed with algorithm PSS.Sig.

Now, we will find that **Game** 2 is actually the security game of PS digital signature.

Then, we prove the indistinguishability between the pairs **Game** 0 and **Game** 1, **Game** 1 and **Game** 2 respectively. For the pair **Game** 0 and **Game** 1, verification key vk' in **Game** 0 is the re-randomized value of vk in **Game** 1 by the reverse firewall $\mathcal{W}_{\mathcal{PSS}}$.Setup. According to the key malleability, we could get that the distribution of vk' is identical to that of vk (i.e., both of them have the distribution $\mathbb{G}_2$). That is, **Game** 0 and **Game** 1 are indistinguishable. Further, we use the same way to prove the indistinguishability between **Game** 1 and **Game** 2. Concretely, we note that the signature σ' in **Game** 1 is the re-randomized value of original signature σ by the reverse firewall $\mathcal{W}_{\mathcal{PSS}}$.Patch. According to the signature malleability, we could obtain that the distribution of σ' is identical to that of σ (i.e., both of them have the distribution $\mathbb{G}_1$). That is, **Game** 1 and **Game** 2 are indistinguishable. As a result, the PS signature with CRF is unforgeability-preserving since the original PS signature scheme has been proven to be EUF-CMA secure.

3.5   Computation and Communication Cost

In this section, we compare our CRF for PS signature with both the simple signature scheme (S-CRF) and ID-based signature scheme (IBS-CRF) constructed in [10]. For simplicity of presentation, we denote these signatures by $DS = \{S, IBS, PSS\}$ in the following two tables. And, only expensive operations are considered. These two tables show that our CRF for PS signature is more suitable for being realized in the real life.

Table 1. Comparisons of computational cost.

Scheme	DS.Setup	$\mathcal{W}_{\mathcal{PKG}}$	DS.Gen	$\mathcal{W}_{\mathcal{DS}}$	DS.Sig	DS.Ver
S-CRF [10]	E	×	×	2E	$(l_m + 1)P_m + 3E$	3P
IBS-CRF [10]	E	3E	$(l_u + 1)P_m + 3E$	2E	$(l_u + l_m + 2)P_m + 5E$	4P
Our PS-CRF	0	×	2E	$4P_m$	P_m	2P

In Table 1, E denotes exponential operation, P_m denotes point multiplication operation, P denotes bilinear paring operation, l_u denotes the number of bit values of identity, l_m denotes the number of bit values of message. Note that Bit value indicates the total number where bit number equals 1 in a bit string. We use the symbol × to denote that no such an algorithm is involved in the corresponding CRF constructions. From Table 1, it is easy to see that our CRF for PS signature is the most efficient one because it needs the least computational cost than the other two CRF constructions.

Table 2. Comparisons of communication cost.

Scheme	DS.Setup	$\mathcal{W}_{PKG}$	DS.Gen	$\mathcal{W}_{DS}$	DS.Sig
S-CRF [10]	$(4+|m|)|\mathbb{G}_1|$	$\times$	$\times$	$4|\mathbb{G}_1|$	$2\mathbb{G}_1$
IBS-CRF [10]	$(5+|u|+|m|)|\mathbb{G}_1|$	$(10+2|u|+2|m|)|\mathbb{G}_1|$	$2|\mathbb{G}_1|$	$5|\mathbb{G}_1|$	$3|\mathbb{G}_1|$
Our PS-CRF	$|\mathbb{G}_1|+|\mathbb{G}_2|$	$\times$	$2|\mathbb{G}_2|$	$2(|\mathbb{G}_2|+|\mathbb{G}_1|)$	$2|\mathbb{G}_1|$

Table 2 compares our CRF construction for PS signature with the other two CRF constructions in the field of communication cost, where $|\mathbb{G}_1|$, $|\mathbb{G}_2|$ denote the length of an element in groups $\mathbb{G}_1$, $\mathbb{G}_2$, and $|m|$ denotes the length of a message, $|u|$ denotes the length of identity. Meanwhile, the content in the table represents the size of the parameters transferred in each operation, the operation DS.Ver only outputs "accept" or "reject", so there is no need to account its commutation cost because of its cost is ignoble. Also, we use the symbol $\times$ to denote that no such an algorithm is involved in the corresponding CRF constructions or its commutation cost is ignoble. From Table 2, we can learn that compared with other two constructions, our construction also has advantage to be employed in the practical web services system because its communication cost is not determined by the lengths of message and identity.

4   CRF Construction for NIZK Proof System

With the randomizability property of randomizable NIZK, it is feasible to construct a CRF in the side of prover. In the following, we will give the definitions of CRF for randomizable NIZK proof system and its security properties.

4.1   Definitions of CRF W.r.t. NIZK and Its Securities

In this section, we consider the scenario where a malicious verifier attacks either the ZK or the WI property of the underlying NIZK proof system. Meanwhile, the implementation of the prover's algorithm is subverted. In this case, the CRF is attached to the prover and sanitizes its incoming and outgoing messages. Of course, the most basic requirement is that the CRF should not ruin the protocol's functionality in case both parties are honest. This requirement is captured by the definition below. Note that even though we adopt the definition of NIZK proof system in common reference string model, it will be the same way in which the definitions and securities of CRF could be formalized for the one in random oracle model.

Definition 16 (Cryptographic Reverse Firewalls w.r.t. NIZK). *Let* Π *be an non-interactive zero knowledge proof system. The cryptographic reverse firewalls for* Π *is a tuple of algorithms* $\mathcal{W}_\Pi = (\mathcal{W}_\Pi.\text{Setup}, \mathcal{W}_\Pi.\text{Patch})$. $\mathcal{W}_\Pi.\text{Setup}$ *takes as input the security parameters* λ, *outputs some initial public state* $\delta \in \{0,1\}^*$. $\mathcal{W}_\Pi.\text{Patch}$ *takes as input the current state* δ *and a proof* π, *outputs a possibly modified proof* π' *or the fault symbol* $\perp$ *and an updated state* δ' *(Fig. 3).*

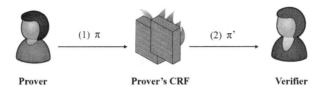

Prover   **Prover's CRF**   **Verifier**

Fig. 3. The framework of randomizable NIZK systems with CRF for Prover.

As for security, we consider three different properties for the CRF w.r.t. NIZK proof system, that is, the zero knowledge-preserving, witness indistinguishability-preserving, and exfiltration-resistance, as formally defined below. Looking ahead, since as we will show it is impossible to obtain any of these notions against an arbitrarily subverted prover, we formalize a weaker form of subversion where a tampered prover still needs to preserve the completeness property of the underlying NIZK proof system. A first natural requirement is to ask that a CRF should preserve the zero knowledge property of the underlying NIZK proof system, even when the prover's implementation has been tampered with. Similarly, it is natural to consider CRFs preserving the witness indistinguishability property of the underlying NIZK proof system, even when the prover's implementation has been tampered with. A different type of concern is exfiltration, in which a tampered prover's implementation attempts to leak secret information (e.g., about the witness) to the adversary. Following [22], we model exfiltration resistance of a CRF by asking that it should be hard to distinguish transcripts obtained by running the honest prover composed with the firewall from transcripts obtained by running a subverted prover composed with the firewall, even in case the verifier is malicious. Note that for the CRF w.r.t. NIZK proof system, it is impossible to investigate the soundness-preserving property because there will be a contradiction between the precondition of soundness and the subversion of prover. The former considers a malicious prover who aims to convince verifier of a tampered false statement, the latter might make an actually honest prover look like malicious. Thus, in the following we formalise the definitions of the above three properties.

Definition 17 (Completeness-Preserving CRF w.r.t. NIZK). *Let Π be an non-interactive zero knowledge proof system for relation R, satisfying completeness. We say that CRF $\mathcal{W}_\Pi = (\mathcal{W}_\Pi.\mathsf{Setup}, \mathcal{W}_\Pi.\mathsf{Patch})$ is completeness-preserving for the prover, if for any polynomial $p(\lambda)$ and any vector of inputs $(x_1, \ldots, x_p) \in L(R)$, for any $\mathsf{crs} \leftarrow_\$ \Pi.\mathsf{Setup}(1^\lambda)$, $\pi_1 \leftarrow_\$ \Pi.\mathsf{Prove}(1^\lambda, \mathsf{crs}, x_1, w_1)$, $\pi_p \leftarrow_\$ \Pi.\mathsf{Prove}(1^\lambda, \mathsf{crs}, x_p, w_p)$, $\delta \leftarrow_\$ \mathcal{W}_\Pi.\mathsf{Setup}(1^\lambda)$, $\pi'_1 \leftarrow_\$ \mathcal{W}_\Pi.\mathsf{Patch}(\pi_1, \delta)$, $\ldots$, $\pi'_p \leftarrow_\$ \mathcal{W}_\Pi.\mathsf{Patch}(\pi_p, \delta)$, there exists a negligible probability ε such that $\Pr[\Pi.\mathsf{VerifyProof}(1^\lambda, \mathsf{crs}, x_i, \pi_i) = \mathsf{ture}] \leq \varepsilon$, where the probability is taken over the coin tosses of all involved algorithms.*

Definition 18 (Zero Knowledge-Preserving CRF w.r.t. NIZK). *Let Π be an non-interactive zero knowledge proof system for relation R, satisfying zero* knowledge. We say that CRF $\mathcal{W}_\Pi = (\mathcal{W}_\Pi.\text{Setup}, \mathcal{W}_\Pi.\text{Patch})$ is zero knowledge-preserving for the prover, if there exists a simulator S that could choose the common reference string by itself and produce a distribution space $\{S(x, \lambda)\}_{x \in L(R)}$ for the output of proof, which is indistinguishable from the distribution space $\{(\text{crs}, \mathcal{W}_\Pi.\text{Patch}(\pi, \delta))\}_{x \in L(R)}$, where $\text{crs} \leftarrow_\$ \Pi.\text{Setup}(1^\lambda)$, $\delta \leftarrow_\$ \mathcal{W}_\Pi.\text{Setup}(1^\lambda)$, and $\pi \leftarrow_\$ \Pi.\text{Prove}(1^\lambda, \text{crs}, x, w)$.

Definition 19 (Witness Indistinguishability-Preserving CRF w.r.t. NIZK). *Let Π be an non-interactive zero knowledge proof system for relation R, satisfying witness indistinguishability. We say that CRF $\mathcal{W}_\Pi = (\mathcal{W}_\Pi.\text{Setup}, \mathcal{W}_\Pi.\text{Patch})$ is witness indistinguishability-preserving for the prover, if for an adversary $\mathcal{B} = (\mathcal{B}_1, \mathcal{B}_2)$, there exists a negligible function ε such that $\Pr[\text{crs} \leftarrow_\$ \Pi.\text{Setup}(1^\lambda), (x, w_1, w_2, state) \leftarrow \mathcal{B}_1(\text{crs}, x), b \leftarrow_\$ \{0, 1\}, \pi \leftarrow_\$ \Pi.\text{Prove}(1^\lambda, \text{crs}, x, w_b), \delta \leftarrow_\$ \mathcal{W}_\Pi.\text{Setup}(1^\lambda), \pi' \leftarrow_\$ \mathcal{W}_\Pi.\text{Patch}(\pi, \delta), b' \leftarrow \mathcal{B}_2(state, \pi') : R(x, w_1) = R(x, w_2) = \text{ture} \wedge b = b'] \leq 1/2 + \varepsilon$.*

Definition 20 (Exfiltration-Resistance CRF w.r.t. NIZK). *Let Π be an non-interactive zero knowledge proof system for relation R. We say that CRF $\mathcal{W}_\Pi = (\mathcal{W}_\Pi.\text{Setup}, \mathcal{W}_\Pi.\text{Patch})$ is exfiltration resistance for the prover, if for any adversary $\mathcal{B}$, it is hard for it to distinguish the distribution space $\{\pi : \pi \leftarrow_\$ \mathcal{W}_\Pi.\text{Patch}(\Pi.\text{Prove}(1^\lambda, \text{crs}, x, w), \delta)\}_{x \in L(R)}$ from the distribution space $\{\pi : \pi \leftarrow_\$ \mathcal{W}_\Pi.\text{Patch}(\widetilde{\Pi}.\text{Prove}(1^\lambda, \text{crs}, x, w), \delta)\}_{x \in L(R)}$, where $\text{crs} \leftarrow_\$ \Pi.\text{Setup}(1^\lambda)$, $\delta \leftarrow_\$ \mathcal{W}_\Pi.\text{Setup}(1^\lambda)$, and $\widetilde{\Pi}.\text{Prove}$ is the subverted algorithm producing proof.*

4.2 Generic Construction of CRF W.r.t. NIZK

Our generic construction of CRF $\mathcal{W}_\Pi = (\mathcal{W}_\Pi.\text{Setup}, \mathcal{W}_\Pi.\text{Patch})$ for NIZK proof system is depicted in Fig. 4. Intuitively, the firewall uses the re-randomizable property of the underlying NIZK proof system in order to "sanitizes" the proofs produced by the prover, in such a way that a completeness-preserving subverted prover cannot reveal the information about the witness through it. In the following, we present the CRF construction for NIZK proof system in detail.

- $\Pi.\text{Setup}$: Takes as input the security parameter 1^λ, and outputs a common reference string crs.
- $\mathcal{W}_\Pi.\text{Setup}$: Takes as input the security parameters λ, outputs some initial public state $\delta \in \{0, 1\}^*$. Note that this state value is allowed to be set as empty. It will depend on the concrete underlying NIZK proof system to determine whether set an empty state value. If the value of state value is not empty, the CRF construction is called to be stateful; otherwise, it is stateless.
- $\Pi.\text{Prove}$: Takes as input the 1^λ and parameter crs, an instance x, a witness $w \in R(x)$ such that $R(\text{crs}, x, w)$ is hold, and outputs a proof π. This randomised algorithm is run by prover.
- $\mathcal{W}_\Pi.\text{Patch}$: Takes as input the current state δ and a proof π, outputs a possibly sanitized proof π' or the fault symbol $\perp$ and an updated state δ'. Note that this algorithm could be realized through the $\Pi.\text{RandProof}$ algorithm in randomizable NIZK Proof System, i.e., $(\pi', \delta') \leftarrow_\$ \Pi.\text{RandProof}(\pi, \delta)$.

- Π.VerifyProof: Takes as input the 1^λ and system parameter crs, an instance x, a proof π, and outputs $d \in \{\text{ture}, \text{false}\}$ indicating that weather π is a valid proof that $x \in L(\mathsf{R})$. The algorithm is deterministic and is run by the verifier.

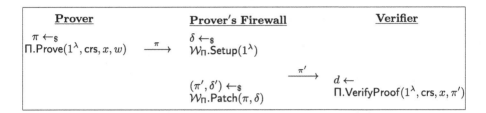

Fig. 4. Prover's reverse firewall for the randomizable NIZK proof system

4.3 Security Proof

Theorem 2. *Let* $\Pi = (\Pi.\mathsf{Setup}, \Pi.\mathsf{Prove}, \Pi.\mathsf{VerifyProof}, \Pi.\mathsf{RandProof})$ *be a randomizable non-inter-active zero knowledge proof system for relation* R, *satisfying completeness and zero knowledge. Then, the CRF* $\mathcal{W}_\Pi = (\mathcal{W}_\Pi.\mathsf{Setup}, \mathcal{W}_\Pi.\mathsf{Patch})$ *for the prover of* Π *(shown in Fig. 4) preserves completeness and is zero knowledge-preserving, witness indistinguishability-preserving, and weakly exfiltration-resistant for the prover.*

Proof. We will prove each property of the firewall in the following.

(1) **Completeness-Preserving**: It is obviously to see that the CRF $\mathcal{W}_\Pi$ constructed for NIZK proof system shown in Fig. 4 preserves the completeness property because the construction requires the proof sanitized by the reverse firewall $\mathcal{W}_\Pi$ in the side of prover should be verified by the verifier.

(2) **Zero Knowledge-Preserving**: Now, we show that the fact that Π satisfies the zero knowledge property implies that the sanitized Π with firewall $\mathcal{W}_\Pi$ satisfies zero knowledge too, i.e. there exists a PPT simulator $\widehat{\mathsf{S}}$ producing a distribution space $\{\widehat{\mathsf{S}}(x, \lambda)\}_{x \in L(\mathsf{R})}$ for the output of proof which is indistinguishable from the distribution space $\{(\mathsf{crs}, \mathcal{W}_\Pi.\mathsf{Patch}(\pi, \delta))\}_{x \in L(\mathsf{R})}$. More formally, there exists a PPT $\widehat{\mathsf{S}}$ such that:

$$\{(\mathsf{crs}, \mathcal{W}_\Pi.\mathsf{Patch}(\Pi.\mathsf{Prove}(1^\lambda, \mathsf{crs}, x, w), \delta))\}_{x \in L(\mathsf{R})} \approx_c \{\widehat{\mathsf{S}}(x, \lambda)\}_{x \in L(\mathsf{R})} \quad (2)$$

The latter can be explained as follows. By contradiction, assume that there exists a PPT distinguisher D and some polynomial $p(\lambda)$ such that for all PPT simulators $\widehat{\mathsf{S}}$ and $\mathsf{R}(x, w) = \text{ture}$, it holds:

$$\left| \Pr[\mathsf{D}(\mathsf{crs}, \mathcal{W}_\Pi.\mathsf{Patch}(\pi, \delta)) = 1] - \Pr[\mathsf{D}(\widehat{\mathsf{S}}(x, \lambda)) = 1] \right| \geq 1/p(\lambda).$$

We consider a simulator S for the underlying NIZK proof system Π, which could run the simulator $\widehat{\mathsf{S}}$ for the CRF $\mathcal{W}_\Pi$ of Π in the side of prover as an inner algorithm. Now, we find that the view of S perfectly emulates that of $\widehat{S}$. More formally, it holds:

$$\left|\Pr[D(\text{crs}, \Pi.\text{Prove}(1^{\lambda}, \text{crs}, x)) = 1] - \Pr[D(S(x, \lambda)) = 1]\right| \geq 1/p(\lambda),$$

which contradicts the zero knowledge property of Π.

(3) **Witness Indistinguishability-Preserving**: It is straightforward that the reverse firewall $\mathcal{W}_{\Pi}$ of Π satisfies this property because of the well-known fact that zero knowledge implies witness indistinguishability, but not viceersa [22]. Therefore, we conclude that if the CRF $\mathcal{W}_{\Pi}$ of Π in the side of prover satisfies zero knowledge, then $\mathcal{W}_{\Pi}$ of Π also satisfies witness indistinguishability.

(4) **Weakly Exfiltration-Resistance**: Since we have proved $\mathcal{W}_{\Pi}$ is zero knowledge preserving, there exists a PPT simulator $\widehat{S}$ such that the distribution of proofs sanitized by $\mathcal{W}_{\Pi}$ is indistinguishable from the ones outputted by $\widehat{S}$. More formally, we denote this as below.

$$\{(\text{crs}, \mathcal{W}_{\Pi}.\text{Patch}(\widetilde{\Pi}.\text{Prove}(1^{\lambda}, \text{crs}, x, w), \delta))\}_{x \in L(R)} \approx_c \{\widehat{S}(x, \lambda)\}_{x \in L(R)},$$

for any $\text{crs} \leftarrow_\$ \Pi.\text{Setup}(1^{\lambda}), \delta \leftarrow_\$ \mathcal{W}_{\Pi}.\text{Setup}(1^{\lambda})$, and any subverted proof generation algorithm $\widetilde{\Pi}.\text{Prove}$. As $\widehat{S}$ works for an arbitrarily subverted $\widetilde{\Pi}.\text{Prove}$, it works in particular for $\widetilde{\Pi}.\text{Prove} = \Pi.\text{Prove}$. Thus, the following holds:

$$\{(\text{crs}, \mathcal{W}_{\Pi}.\text{Patch}(\Pi.\text{Prove}(1^{\lambda}, \text{crs}, x, w), \delta))\}_{x \in L(R)} \approx_c \{\widehat{S}(x, \lambda)\}_{x \in L(R)}.$$

Combining the above two equations, we could obtain that for any subverted $\widetilde{\Pi}.\text{Prove}$, the following holds:

$$\{(\text{crs}, \mathcal{W}_{\Pi}.\text{Patch}(\widetilde{\Pi}.\text{Prove}(1^{\lambda}, \text{crs}, x, w), \delta))\}_{x \in L(R)}$$

$$\approx_c \{(\text{crs}, \mathcal{W}_{\Pi}.\text{Patch}(\Pi.\text{Prove}(1^{\lambda}, \text{crs}, x, w), \delta))\}_{x \in L(R)},$$

and thus $\mathcal{W}_{\Pi}$ is weakly exfiltration resistant for the prover.

4.4   Instantiation of CRF for NIZK Proof System

According to the above analyses, we find that to construct the CRF for the NIZK proof system, the premise is to choose the randomizable NIZK proof system. Therefore, to give the instantiation of the CRF construction for NIZK proof, we first need to find a randomizable NIZK proof system. Since Blum et al. initially proposed the original computable NIZK proof system in 1991 and Groth et al. constructed the first statistical NIZK proof system in 2006, various NIZK proof systems have been proposed up to now. However, by studying and comparing these NIZK schemes, we find that most of them are not randomizable. Fortunately, we can see in [33] that Belenkiy and Camenisch et al. first introduced the conception of randomizable NIZK proof system in order to construct an efficient entrustable anonymous credential system. The NIZK scheme proposed by Groth and Sahai in 2008 is extended to a randomizable NIZK proof system. For more detailed construction of randomization algorithm and correctness proof process of this system, we recommend to see [33]. We will omit it. It is not difficult to find that this instantiation construction can be completed by inserting the extended Groth-Sahai rerandom NIZK proof system in [34] into the CRF construction of the NIZK proof system shown in Fig. 4.

5   Conclusion

In this paper, to make the two wildly used cryptographic primitives in the web services resist to algorithm substitution attacks, we construct the cryptographic reverse firewalls for both of these primitives. The cryptographic reverse firewall is an additional entity and could sanitize the messages inputting and outputting the user's computer. In such a way, even though the cryptographic algorithms implemented in the user's computer might have been embedded some backdoor, the security of the messages sent and received by the user will be guaranteed. To provide an efficient instantiation of CRF for signature scheme, we construct CRF for the PS signature scheme. The comparison results show that our PS-CRF is more efficient than the existing S-CRF and IBS-CRF. Moreover, we provide a generic CRF construction for NIZK proof system and meanwhile formolize its security definitions. The security proofs are given in a rigorous way. We also consider using the Groth-Sahai's NIZK proof system could be referred to as an efficient instantiation of it.

Acknowledgement. This work is supported in part by the National Key R&D program of China (No. 2017YFB0802000); by the NSF of China under Grants 61972159; by the Foundation of Science and Technology on Communication Security Laboratory of China (No. 61421030108012104).

References

1. Boncella, R.J.: Web and web security. Commun. Assoc. Inf. Syst. **14**(1), 344–363 (2004)
2. Bertino, E., Martino, L., Paci, F., et al.: Security for Web Services and Service-Oriented Architectures. Springer, Heidelberg (2009). https://doi.org/10.1007/978-3-540-87742-4
3. Ra, G., Kim, T., Lee, I.: VAIM: verifiable anonymous identity management for human-centric security and privacy in the internet of things. IEEE Access **9**(2021), 75945–75960 (2021)
4. Xu, L., Jiang, C., Wang, J., et al.: Information security in big data: privacy and data mining. IEEE Access **2**(2014), 1149–1176 (2014)
5. Crampton, J., Lim, H.W., Paterson, K.G.: What can identity-based cryptography offer to web services? In: Proceedings of the 2007 ACM workshop on Secure Web Services, pp. 26–36 (2007)

6. Chen, R., Huang, X., Yung, M.: Subvert KEM to break DEM: practical algorithm-substitution attacks on public-key encryption. In: Moriai, S., Wang, H. (eds.) ASI-ACRYPT 2020. LNCS, vol. 12492, pp. 98–128. Springer, Cham (2020). https://doi.org/10.1007/978-3-030-64834-3_4

7. Young, A., Yung, M.: Kleptography: using cryptography against cryptography. In: Fumy, W. (ed.) EUROCRYPT 1997. LNCS, vol. 1233, pp. 62–74. Springer, Heidelberg (1997). https://doi.org/10.1007/3-540-69053-0_6

8. Ateniese, G., Magri, B., Venturi, D.: Subversion-resilient signature schemes. In: Proceedings of the 22nd ACM SIGSAC Conference on Computer and Communications Security, pp. 364–375 (2015)

9. Dodis, Y., Mironov, I., Stephens-Davidowitz, N.: Message transmission with reverse firewalls—secure communication on corrupted machines. In: Robshaw, M., Katz, J. (eds.) CRYPTO 2016. LNCS, vol. 9814, pp. 341–372. Springer, Heidelberg (2016). https://doi.org/10.1007/978-3-662-53018-4_13

10. Ouyang, M., Wang, Z., Li, F.: Digital signature with cryptographic reverse firewalls. J. Syst. Archit. **116**(2021), 102029 (2021)

11. Bellare, M., Paterson, K.G., Rogaway, P.: Security of symmetric encryption against mass surveillance. In: Garay, J.A., Gennaro, R. (eds.) CRYPTO 2014. LNCS, vol. 8616, pp. 1–19. Springer, Heidelberg (2014). https://doi.org/10.1007/978-3-662-44371-2_1

12. Mironov, I., Stephens-Davidowitz, N.: Cryptographic reverse firewalls. In: Oswald, E., Fischlin, M. (eds.) EUROCRYPT 2015. LNCS, vol. 9057, pp. 657–686. Springer, Heidelberg (2015). https://doi.org/10.1007/978-3-662-46803-6_22

13. Kang, B., Meng, X., Zhang, L., et al.: Nonce-based key agreement protocol against bad randomness. Int. J. Found. Comput. Sci. **30**(04), 619–633 (2021)

14. Kang, B., Huang, Z., Zhang, L.: Selective-opening security for public-key encryption in the presence of parameter subversion. In: Security and Communication Networks, 2021 (2021)

15. Meng, X., Zhang, L., Kang, B.: Fast secure and anonymous key agreement against bad randomness for cloud computing. IEEE Trans. Cloud Comput. (2020). https://doi.org/10.1109/TCC.2020.3008795

16. Zhang, L., Kang, B., Dai, F., et al.: Hybrid and hierarchical aggregation-verification scheme for VANET. IEEE Trans. Veh. Technol. (2022). https://doi.org/10.1109/TVT.2022.3189540

17. Baudet, M., Sonnino, A., Kelkar, M., et al.: Zef: low-latency, scalable, private payments. arXiv preprint arXiv:2201.05671 (2022)

18. Chow, S.S.M., Russell, A., Tang, Q., Yung, M., Zhao, Y., Zhou, H.-S.: Let a non-barking watchdog bite: cliptographic signatures with an offline watchdog. In: Lin, D., Sako, K. (eds.) PKC 2019. LNCS, vol. 11442, pp. 221–251. Springer, Cham (2019). https://doi.org/10.1007/978-3-030-17253-4_8

19. Russell, A., Tang, Q., Yung, M., et al.: Generic semantic security against a kleptographic adversary. In: Proceedings of the 2017 ACM SIGSAC Conference on Computer and Communications Security, pp. 907–922 (2017)

20. Fischlin, M., Mazaheri, S.: Self-guarding cryptographic protocols against algorithm substitution attacks. In: 2018 IEEE 31st Computer Security Foundations Symposium (CSF), pp. 76–90. IEEE (2018)

21. Chakraborty, S., Dziembowski, S., Nielsen, J.B.: Reverse firewalls for actively secure MPCs. In: Micciancio, D., Ristenpart, T. (eds.) CRYPTO 2020. LNCS, vol. 12171, pp. 732–762. Springer, Cham (2020). https://doi.org/10.1007/978-3-030-56880-1_26

22. Ganesh, C., Magri, B., Venturi, D.: Cryptographic reverse firewalls for interactive proof systems. Theoret. Comput. Sci. **855**(2021), 104–132 (2021)
23. Eastlake, D., Reagle, J., Solo, D., et al.: XML-signature syntax and processing. W3C recommendation, December 2002
24. Wang, Y., Chen, R., Liu, C., et al.: Asymmetric subversion attacks on signature and identification schemes. Pers. Ubiquitous Comput. 1–14 (2019)
25. Bellare, M., Fuchsbauer, G., Scafuro, A.: NIZKs with an untrusted CRS: security in the face of parameter subversion. In: Cheon, J.H., Takagi, T. (eds.) ASIACRYPT 2016. LNCS, vol. 10032, pp. 777–804. Springer, Heidelberg (2016). https://doi.org/10.1007/978-3-662-53890-6_26
26. Fuchsbauer, G.: Subversion-zero-knowledge SNARKs. In: Abdalla, M., Dahab, R. (eds.) PKC 2018. LNCS, vol. 10769, pp. 315–347. Springer, Cham (2018). https://doi.org/10.1007/978-3-319-76578-5_11
27. Baghery, K.: Subversion-resistant simulation (knowledge) sound NIZKs. In: Albrecht, M. (ed.) IMACC 2019. LNCS, vol. 11929, pp. 42–63. Springer, Cham (2019). https://doi.org/10.1007/978-3-030-35199-1_3
28. Berndt, S., Wichelmann, J., Pott, C., et al.: ASAP: algorithm substitution attacks on cryptographic protocols. In: Proceedings of the 2022 ACM on Asia Conference on Computer and Communications Security, pp. 712–726 (2022)
29. Galbraith, S.D., Paterson, K.G., Smart, N.P.: Pairings for cryptographers. Discret. Appl. Math. **156**(16), 3113–3121 (2008)
30. Kilian, J., Petrank, E.: An efficient noninteractive zero-knowledge proof system for NP with general assumptions. J. Cryptol. **11**(1), 1–27 (1998)
31. Dodis, Y., Ganesh, C., Golovnev, A., Juels, A., Ristenpart, T.: A formal treatment of backdoored pseudorandom generators. In: Oswald, E., Fischlin, M. (eds.) EUROCRYPT 2015. LNCS, vol. 9056, pp. 101–126. Springer, Heidelberg (2015). https://doi.org/10.1007/978-3-662-46800-5_5
32. Pointcheval, D., Sanders, O.: Short randomizable signatures. In: Sako, K. (ed.) CT-RSA 2016. LNCS, vol. 9610, pp. 111–126. Springer, Cham (2016). https://doi.org/10.1007/978-3-319-29485-8_7
33. Belenkiy, M., Camenisch, J., Chase, M., Kohlweiss, M., Lysyanskaya, A., Shacham, H.: Randomizable proofs and delegatable anonymous credentials. In: Halevi, S. (ed.) CRYPTO 2009. LNCS, vol. 5677, pp. 108–125. Springer, Heidelberg (2009). https://doi.org/10.1007/978-3-642-03356-8_7
34. Groth, J., Sahai, A.: Efficient non-interactive proof systems for bilinear groups. In: Smart, N. (ed.) EUROCRYPT 2008. LNCS, vol. 4965, pp. 415–432. Springer, Heidelberg (2008). https://doi.org/10.1007/978-3-540-78967-3_24

SPAC: Scalable Pattern Approximate Counting in Graph Mining

Ruini Xue[1,3]($\boxtimes$) (iD), Yijun Wang[1], Shengbo Liu[1], Yunxiang Li[1],
Wenhong Tian[1] (iD), and Weimin Zheng[2,3]

[1] University of Electronic Science and Technology of China, Chengdu, China
{xueruini,tian_wenhong}@uestc.edu.cn,
{201921080206,2019021415031,202052080613}@std.uestc.edu.cn
[2] Tsinghua University, Beijing, China
zwm-dcs@tsinghua.edu.cn
[3] Peng Cheng Lab (PCL), Shenzhen, China

Abstract. Pattern counting is a crucial task in graph pattern mining. Accurate counting is not affordable as the datasets grow larger and larger, and approximate counting is getting popular to provide an estimated answer quickly. However, current approximate counting approaches are still time-consuming and not scalable for extra-large graphs. This paper proposes SPAC, a fast and flexible pattern approximate counting method, based on the observation that pattern number distribution to degrees also follows power-law as the vertices, the common feature in graph datasets. By leveraging the distribution, SPAC can efficiently choose a small number of degrees as samples, fit the coefficients, and then calculate the pattern frequency directly. To provide flexibility for different use-cases, SPAC supports both accurate and approximate counting in the sampling phase. Moreover, edge weighting and interpolation techniques are adopted to emphasize the sample tail to improve fitting accuracy. The prototype of SPAC is implemented with GraphX on Spark, and is evaluated against various well-known graphs. The experimental results show that SPAC is up to 10x faster than accurate counting, keeping the same error level below 10%. Compared to existing approximate counting, SPAC is 1.4x–9x faster in general, while the error could be reduced to 20% of the current systems.

Keywords: Graph mining · Graph pattern mining · Graph pattern counting · Approximate calculation · Power-law distribution

1 Introduction

Along with the exponential increment of Internet data recently, the development of big data technology has been promoted drastically. It is crucial to process different kinds of data efficiently. A large part of the massive data is generated from the connection and interaction between separate entities like individuals. Intrinsically, such data could be organized into graph data structure [5]. A graph is composed of

© Springer Nature Switzerland AG 2023
W. Meng et al. (Eds.): ICA3PP 2022, LNCS 13777, pp. 214–232, 2023.
https://doi.org/10.1007/978-3-031-22677-9_12

vertices and edges, in which entity information is usually stored as vertices and the relationship between them is translated into edges. Therefore, it is straightforward to explore the correlation among the data by investigating the topology and metrics of the graph. Typical graph computing applications, like social networks [27] and webpage links [9], have been conducted successfully. For example, by modeling "*users*" and "*follow*" relation as vertices and edges respectively, graph algorithms could be applied to find out answers to many interesting questions, like "shortest paths between friends", "the largest community" and so on.

As one of the most widely adopted graph processing approaches, graph pattern mining (GPM) seeks for subgraphs (known as the "*pattern*") identical with the query graph structure expected by the users from the graph data. Typical GPM use-cases include finding motifs [24], frequent subgraph mining (FSM) [37] and clique mining [6]. The key algorithm in graph pattern mining is "pattern counting", the ability to compute pattern frequencies. However, this is a very hard computational task. In fact, determining if one subgraph exists at all in another larger network (i.e., subgraph isomorphism) is an NP-Complete problem [8]. Determining the exact frequency is even harder, and millions or even billions of subgraph occurrences are typically found even in relatively small networks. Existing algorithms for accurate counting can take hours [10,36]. For example, in a cluster of 20 nodes, the distributed GPM framework Arabesque needs more than 10 h to count triangles in a graph of 1 billion edges [33], which is unacceptable for many scenarios.

With the rapid increase of graph data, for example, large social network maps such as Twitter and Facebook, it is challenging to count patterns accurately. In the meanwhile, it is reported that exact results are not necessary for many applications [19,27]. For example, FSM only concerns which patterns are more frequent or whose counting is above a threshold. Therefore, recent systems turn to approximation theory and techniques to estimate the pattern occurrence for an acceptable balance between efficiency and accuracy [2,4]. Compared to Arabesque, ASAP [17] proposes an approximate method based on edge sampling, which improves the performance by two orders of magnitude, while only resulting in error below 5%.

Most approximate counting algorithms use sampling to reduce the graph size before processing. However, there are still expensive edge search operations in the sampling process. Additionally, in order to guarantee the accuracy level for large-scale graphs, ASAP needs to instantiate many more *estimators* for sampling, whose overhead might be the same as accurate calculation eventually. These issues indicate that it is challenging to design efficient GPM approximate algorithms considering performance, accuracy, and computational complexity.

Actually, most real-world graphs follow the power-law distribution [34], in which the distribution function f of a key variable x is a power function, $f(x) \sim x^{-k}$. To be specific, d (vertex degree) and $v_{\#}(d)$ (vertex number of degree d) in many graph comply with the law: $v_{\#}(d) = c \cdot d^{-k}$. Many different graph algorithms leverage the distribution feature for various improvement [1,7,20]. With respect to pattern counting, we observe that the contribution of vertices of different degrees to pattern counting varies a lot: the low-degree and a small number of medium-degree vertices account for much more than that of the high-degree ones. Unfortunately, most current approaches do not consider the power-law distribution, and uniformly process all vertices and edges. That means some calculations are useless in terms of estimation. Gao [12] samples uniform random graph according to degrees and deduced the relationship between the degree sequence and triangle number by strictly limiting $2 \leq k \leq 3$.

To address these challenges, we propose SPAC (**S**calable **P**attern **A**pproximate **C**ounting), a fast and flexible pattern counting method for power-law graphs. SPAC is devised based on the observation that pattern number and degree sequence follow the power-law distribution in power-law graphs. Therefore, it makes sense to fit the distribution by sampling a small number of degrees and then directly calculate the pattern number in the whole graph. Since SPAC avoids estimating in the entire dataset, it is much faster. To further reduce the sampling overhead, on the one hand, SPAC efficiently picks up sample points according to the power-law feature. And on the other hand, SPAC could use current approximate algorithms in the sampling phase in case of large datasets. Otherwise, accurate algorithms is applied by instead. These are the *APP* and *ACC* modes. Moreover, SPAC allows users to choose the samples manually, providing flexibility for real-world applications. The prototype of SPAC is implemented with GraphX on Spark, and is evaluated against various well-known graph datasets. The experimental results show that SPAC is up to 10x faster than accurate counting, keeping the same error level below 10%. Compared to existing approximate counting, SPAC is 1.4x–9x faster in general, while the error could be reduced to 20% of theirs. Basically, *APP* is 2x–5x faster than *ACC*. These results indicate that SPAC is scalable for extra-large scale graphs.

A summary of our contributions is as follows:

- We reveal that pattern number and degree also follow the power-law distribution in power-law graphs.
- Based on the above observation, we propose SPAC, a lightweight, fast and flexible pattern counting solution. It is a complementary of certain approximate approaches.
- We conduct extensive experiments with various well-known datasets. SPAC brings up to 9 times speedup overall.

The rest of this paper is organized as follows. Section 2 discusses the related work including accurate counting and approximate counting. Then, Sect. 3 introduces the design of SPAC as well as optimization details. The implementation of the prototype is described in Sect. 4 briefly, and Sect. 5 evaluates the prototype and presents the experimental results. Finally, we conclude this paper and describe the future plans in Sect. 6.

2   Related Work

Basically, pattern counting algorithms can be classified into two categories: *accurate counting* and *approximate counting*.

2.1 Accurate Counting

Accurate counting determines the exact frequency of the queried pattern. Given a k-size (k vertices) pattern, the classical algorithm first enumerates all connected subgraphs with k vertices, then uses graph isomorphism algorithms to classify the subgraphs to find a specific pattern. MFinder [24] applies the following steps to each edge of the network: the edge is initially stored into an empty set S, which recursively grows with edges that are not in S but share an endpoint with at least one edge in S; when $|S| = k$, checks whether the subgraph induced by S is found for the first time by maintaining a hash table of the found subgraphs.

Grochow and Kellis [16] propose an efficient single pattern search method. The vertex backtracking algorithm is applied to each vertex. It tries to build a partial mapping from the pattern to the target graph by building all possible assignments based on the number of neighbors.

Encapsulation methods leverage the common topological features of the pattern or extract the pattern features to avoid repeated calculations for isomorphism. For example, Ribeiro and Silva [28] design a prefix tree of the graph. Each node of the tree represents a different graph, in which the parent node and its child nodes share a common substructure. Then, it searches all isomorphic patterns from the root of the prefix tree.

Instead of static graphs, DOTTT [26] counts temporal triangles in graphs where edges come with timestamps. DOTTT extends the idea of degeneracy orientations from static graph triangle counting to temporal triangle counting, and runs twice as fast as existing state-of-the-art temporal triangle counters.

2.2 Approximate Counting

Due to the unacceptable computational complexity and low necessity of accurate counting, a variety of approximate counting methods are proposed for large graphs [3]. The main idea is to generate a reduced subgraph with sampling, accurately count on the subgraphs and then scale the subgraph result to estimate the final result.

Lim et al. [22] samples the edges with a constant probability, and checks the pattern once an edge is selected. It does not needs any other prior knowledge of the graph, and uses a Bloom filter to check duplicated edges. It takes more than 5 min to process 4 million vertices by a 60% sampling probability, and the error reaches as high as 20% on a server with 3.5 GHz Intel CPUs and 32 GB RAM.

FURL [18] and PartitionCT [35] assign ranks to edges and hash them to a large number of buckets. Each bucket only keeps the smallest edge. Once a new edge is stored, they search whether it can form a pattern with edges in other buckets. After all edges are processed, the subgraph result is scaled with HyperLogLog [11] to estimate the real pattern number in the entire graph. Although the hash sampling process is lightweight, the total execution is still time-consuming. On the graph with 1.13 million vertices, PartitionCT runs 100 s with 8×10^6 buckets and the error is 10% on a computer with a Quad-Core Intel Xeon E3-1226 v3 @ 3.30 GHz.

SWTC [15] proposes a sliding window-based algorithm to count triangles approximately in streaming graphs with duplicate edges. The core of SWTC is a fixed-length slicing strategy that addresses both unbiased sampling and cardinality estimation issues with a bounded memory usage. Given memory bound, SWTC outperforms Bounded-Priority-Sampling [13] in terms of estimation accuracy.

ASAP [17] launches a great number of *estimators* in parallel to sample the graph uniformly. Each estimator executes the neighborhood sampling algorithm and estimates the pattern number with Bayesian probability. Finally, ASAP aggregates the results of all estimators. The more estimators are created, the better the accuracy will be. ASAP provides ELP (error-latency-profile) to allow users to balance the calculation cost and result accuracy. In a graph of 3 million vertices, ASAP takes 40 s with 5% error in a cluster of 16 Amazon EC2 r4.2x large instances.

All approximate counting methods do some sort of sampling, and all of them consider the vertices and edges equally. That is, the graph is sampled uniformly, which does not actually take into account the power-law feature of most graphs. This is how SPAC behaves differently from the existing methods. Moreover, SPAC calculates with equations instead of counting (sampling indeed) one by one in traditional approaches, which makes SPAC faster and more scalable for extra-large graphs.

3   Design

This section first describes the key observation based on which SPAC is designed, then the workflow in detail, including the optimization techniques and policies used by SPAC.

3.1   Pattern Number Distribution to Degrees

Without loss of generality, the probability of each edge appearing in the pattern is equal: the more edges, the greater the probability of forming the pattern. Therefore, it is very likely that the distribution between degree and pattern number should be similar to the one between degree and edge number.

As aforementioned, the power-law distribution applies to many graph datasets, showing the relation between distinct degree (d) and vertex number of this degree ($v(d)$), i.e., $v(d) = C \cdot d^{-k}$. Then, we could get the mapping from a particular degree to the number of the edges ($e(d)$) connected to all vertices of this degree as in Eq. 1, which apparently also follows power law.

$$e(d) = v(d) \cdot d = C \cdot d^{-k} \cdot d = C \cdot d^{-k+1} \tag{1}$$

Therefore, we make the hypothesis that the pattern number $p(d)$ of degree d (i.e., patterns formed by the edges of the vertices of the degree), also satisfies the power law as in Eq. 2.

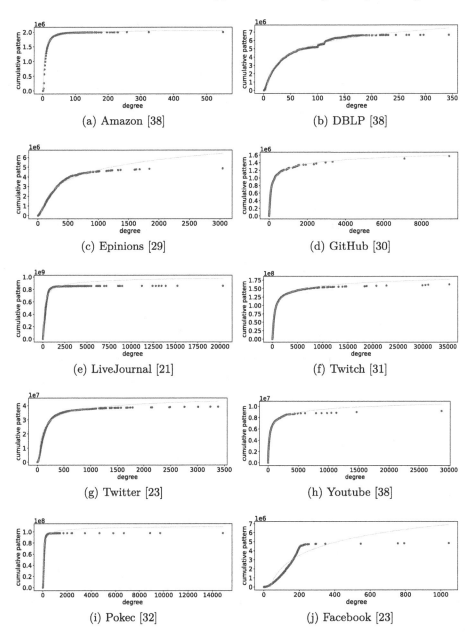

Fig. 1. Pattern number distribution to the degrees. All experiments use `TriangleCounting` function provided by GraphX [14], which is an accurate counting algorithm.

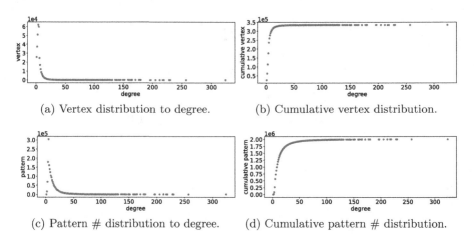

(a) Vertex distribution to degree.   (b) Cumulative vertex distribution.

(c) Pattern # distribution to degree.   (d) Cumulative pattern # distribution.

Fig. 2. Distributions of vertex and pattern number to degrees as well as their cumulative distributions for Amazon dataset [38]. 3-motifs (triangles) as the patterns are counted. All of them follows the power law.

$$p(d) = C_0 \cdot d^{-\alpha} + C_1, \quad (C_0 > 0, C_1 > 0) \tag{2}$$

We tested Eq. 2 against several typical graph datasets as Fig. 1. These graph datasets are very representative, from social networks to e-commerce, and range from 4 thousand to 4 million vertices. Except "Facebook", all other graphs follow the power-law distribution.

For the pattern counting problem, the final result is the total occurrence of the pattern in the entire graph, which could be calculated by the cumulative distribution function $P(d)$ as in Eq. 3. Similarly, it is also a power function.

$$P(d) \approx \int_1^d p(x)\mathrm{d}x = \frac{C_0}{-\alpha + 1}d^{-\alpha + 1} + C_2$$
$$= Ad^{-\beta} + B \quad (A < 0, B > 0, \beta > 0) \tag{3}$$

Figure 2 illustrates the equations with Amazon dataset [38]. Figure 2a is the original power-law distribution for degree and vertex number, and the cumulative function is presented in Fig. 2b. For the sake of simplicity, taking triangles as the patterns, Fig. 2c shows triangles frequency for vertices of distinct degrees, and Fig. 2d depicts the cumulative results. Apparently, the y-value of the rightmost point in Fig. 2d is the final result of pattern counting.

Based on Eq. 3, SPAC is designed to use formula fitting with pretty lightweight sampling to *calculate* the final result, which is more efficient than existing methods. The workflow of SPAC is illustrated in Fig. 3, and the following sections will introduce each phase in detail.

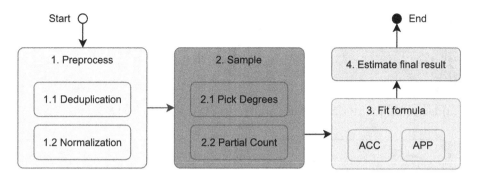

Fig. 3. SPAC workflow.

3.2 Preprocess

Partial Count. SPAC needs the graph to be power-law, otherwise the pattern computed is biased. Before confirming its distribution, we have to preprocess the dataset: *deduplicate* and *normalize* edges.

SPAC can not count patterns for directed graphs currently. For example, in directed graphs, 3 vertices may contribute more than 1 triangle considering edge directions. Fortunately, most typical pattern counting applications do not care about the directions, so directed datasets could be converted to undirected graphs. However, this conversion may lead to duplicated edges, therefore, SPAC needs to dedupliacate edges to keep the dataset as a simple graph. Additionally, SPAC normalizes the edge identification by taking the smaller vertex id as the edge source and the bigger one the sink. This is just for edge reference but not direction. Finally, SPAC collects the degree and vertex number information to verify its distribution by checking the R^2 in fitting $v(d) = c \cdot d^{-k}$. Though R^2 is an insufficient measure for nonlinear regression, it is good enough in many cases [25]. Table 1 lists the R^2 values of several datasets. For power-law obeyed graphs, their R^2 are very close to 1, while the outlier "Facebook" is very small. SPAC will stop in case a dataset's R^2 is below 0.7, a recommended threshold.

Table 1. R^2 of power-law distribution fitting for various graph datasets.

Dataset	R^2	Dataset	R^2	Dataset	R^2	Dataset	R^2	Dataset	R^2
Amazon	0.893	DBLP	0.955	Epinions	0.976	Youtube	0.926	LiveJournal	0.897
Pokec	0.787	Twitch	0.774	Twitter	0.856	GitHub	0.900	Facebook	**0.112**

3.3 Sample

The sampling phase consists of two steps: first, select some degrees (vertices indeed) as the samples and then count the pattern frequency for each sample.

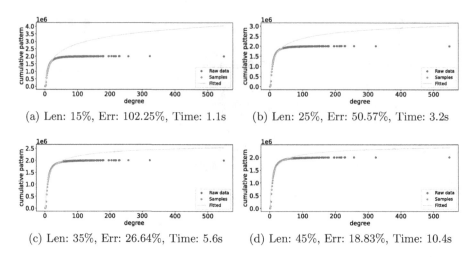

Fig. 4. Fitting results of different sample sequence length, 15%, 25%, 35% and 45% of total degrees, respectively. **Len** is the sample sequence length, **Err** is the error rate and **Time** is the run time.

Determine Degrees. There are two principles to select sample points: (1) no more than enough, and (2) no repeated counting. As Fig. 2d illustrated, the curve goes up in low degree area very quickly, and then maintains quite a long flat tail. So, in order to fit Eq. 3 precisely, it is better to keep enough low degree samples until the bend part, where the curve starts to go flat. Since Eq. 3 is the cumulative distribution, all patterns in a smaller degree will also appear in a larger degree. To avoid repeated calculation, SPAC counts incrementally. For example, to count the patterns for degree $d + 1$, SPAC incrementally introduces edges of all $d + 1$ degree vertices into the subgraph during counting degree d. To further simplify the calculation, all edges from $d + 1$ degree vertices to higher degrees are included as well. Because the pattern is counted starting from every vertex, a k-size pattern will be counted for k times in total, so the results should be divided by k. Only new edges involved patterns will be searched, and those founded before will not be recomputed. Therefore, SPAC picks up continuous subsequence from the begin the degree list as samples. The remaining challenge is *how to determine the length of the sample sequence*. It is actually a trade-off between sampling overhead and fitting accuracy.

Figure 4 shows the influence of different sample sequence lengths for Amazon dataset. It is clear that the bigger the sample (the longer the sequence), the more accurate the result. However, 25% is a better balance than the others considering the computing overhead. The turning points are different for different graphs, and SPAC searches them with a heuristic method.

We define fitting error in Eq. 4. E_l is the error rate with sample sequence length l, $d_{\max}$ the largest degree of the graph, P_l the fitted cumulative function formula, $P_l(d_{\max})$ the calculated final pattern number with the fitted formula, and P_{true} the real pattern number.

$$E_l = \frac{|P_l(d_{\max}) - P_{\text{true}}|}{P_{\text{true}}} \qquad (4)$$

The heuristic is based on the property presented in Fig. 4. As a convex curve, the gradient of the cumulative distribution gradually decreases: the initial steep part until the turning point contributes more to error rate reduction, compared to the degrees afterward. Theoretically, the turning point is where the gradient drops suddenly to a small value near 0. From the smallest degree, SPAC counts the pattern, extends to the next degree in the sample, and repeats until the gradient reaches a threshold. In this way, the sample sequence length is determined. Usually, the sampled vertices only take a small portion of the entire dataset, which benefits the counting process in Sect. 3.2.

The above approach counts the pattern accurately for each degree, while sometimes it is acceptable to use approximate results for quick investigation. The former mode is called ACC and the latter APP in SPAC. Due to the larger variance of estimated counts in APP mode, the gradient threshold should be smaller than that of ACC, and it is affordable to enlarge the sample sequence length because APP is much faster than ACC.

SPAC is flexible in choosing the threshold manually for a particular error rate. Moreover, SPAC prototype also allows the user to set the sample sequence length directly: the larger the sample, the more accurate the result as Fig. 4.

Now it is time to count the pattern frequency for each sample degree. As discussed before, ACC works in an incremental style to prevent redundant calculation, while APP uses the ASAP algorithm [17] to estimate. Our experiment results show that APP runs much faster than ACC, but its error does not increase significantly. It depends on the major objective to decide which one to choose. For better accuracy, ACC is preferred, while for rapid screening, APP stands out. SPAC leaves this flexibility decision to users.

The directly computed pattern frequency in APP mode needs to be adjusted to align with the incremental counting in ACC. Figure 5 shows that only the patterns (triangles) whose vertices all appear in the sampled subset could be counted, like $\Delta(1,2,3)$, $\Delta(2,5,6)$, but those crossing the boundaries are ignored, like $\Delta(3,A,B)$ and $\Delta(3,B,6)$. SPAC estimates them by a "scaling factor" f. Given the total edges in the sampled subset and the remaining one are a and b, respectively, the probability that all edges of a pattern located in the sampled subset (or, the probability a pattern can be scanned) is $(\frac{a}{a+b})^K$, where K is the number of pattern edges. Similarly, the probability in the remaining set, like $\Delta(A,B,D)$, $\Delta(D,F,G)$ is $(\frac{b}{a+b})^K$. If APP finds n triangles, the estimated real number including the crossing boundaries ones is Eq. 5, so the scaling factor is $f = (|E|^K - b^K)/a^K$, where $|E| = a + b$.

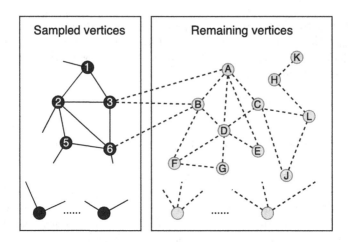

Fig. 5. Vertex 3 and 6 are newly added as the new degree, thus $\Delta(3, A, B)$ and $\Delta(3, B, 6)$ should be estimated by the scaling factor f.

$$n' = \frac{n}{\left(\frac{a}{a+b}\right)^K} \cdot \left(1 - \left(\frac{b}{a+b}\right)^K\right)$$
$$= n \cdot \frac{(a+b)^K - b^K}{a^K} = n \cdot \frac{|E|^K - b^K}{a^K} \tag{5}$$

3.4 Fit Formula

After obtaining the necessary samples, it is almost ready to fit Eq. 3. According to Sect. 3.2, most samples are from the lower degree part and very few from the high degree part, so the curve tail might not be fitted well, leading to a big fitting error. To address this potential issue, SPAC adopts two optimization policies to augment the sampled data: *sample weighting* and *sample interpolation*.

It is possible to use the classic nonlinear least square methods like Gauss Newton iteration to fit the coefficients. However, these methods treat all samples equally, and the fitted curve tail will departure from the truth in case of few samples in the flat part. SPAC improves this with weighted least square method, in which sample points are assigned different weights to emphasize certain ones in the curve. Specifically, SPAC weights the sample with its degree, so the high degree samples will have heavier weights. This is reasonable because they are near the turning points and have a significant impact on the curve shape. In this way, they could still affect the fitting error even though there are just a few such samples.

Another sample argument technique is to interpolate the end part of the samples, especially for ACC mode. The degrees of a graph are often non-continuous. Especially at the high degree part, the distribution is very dispersed. As we know, the end part of the samples is very flat and relatively stable in the curve,

Table 2. Graph datasets.

Datasets	Vertices	Edges
LiveJournal [21]	4,847,571	68,993,773
Pokec [32]	1,632,803	30,622,564
Youtube [38]	1,134,890	2,987,624
Amazon [38]	334,863	925,872
DBLP [38]	317,080	1,049,866
Twitch [31]	168,114	6,797,557
Twitter [23]	81,306	1,768,149
Epinions [29]	75,879	50,8837
GitHub [30]	37,700	28,9003
Facebook [23]	4,039	88,234

so it is safe to interpolate the missing degrees, which to some extent increases the weights of these samples. This is helpful in maintaining the shape of the curve tail during fitting. In the meanwhile, SPAC does not do interpolation for *APP* mode by default. This is because, for some datasets, the high degree samples are very scattered, and too many interpolated points are needed, which will amplify the errors introduced by *APP* itself.

With sample weighting and interpolation, SPAC can greatly improve the fitting result as discussed in Sect. 5.

4   Implementation

The prototype of SPAC is implemented with GraphX [14], Apache Spark [39] and SciPy package. GraphX loads datasets from the disk, and transforms them into vertices and edges. Then SPAC conducts operations of preprocessing and sampling phases in Fig. 3 with Spark, and finally fits Eq. 3 with SciPy. SPAC consists of about 2300 lines of Scala code and 200 lines of python. In order to compare with ASAP, we also reimplemented ASAP's core algorithm according to [17].

5   Evaluation

In this section, we first describe the experiment environment and datasets, then evaluate SPAC with existing accurate and approximate solutions, and finally show its limitation on a non-power-law graph.

5.1   Experiment Setup

We evaluate SPAC with many real-world graphs as in Table 2. The datasets are selected to cover different scenarios. First, they are of different scales, as small

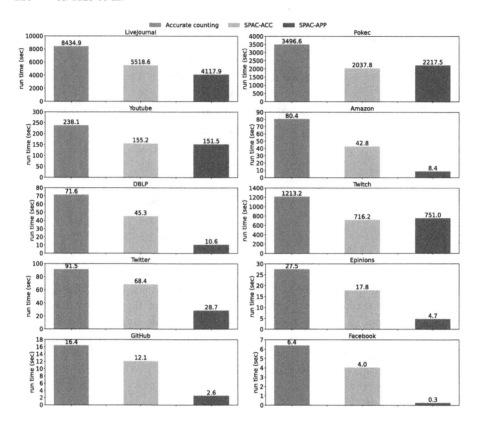

Fig. 6. Run time of SPAC and accurate counting.

as thousands of vertices and as large as millions of vertices. Second, the non-power-law graph "Facebook" is also tested to show how SPAC performs with unexpected datasets. All experiments are tested with 3-motif (triangle) pattern on an Aliyun r7 ECS: Intel Xeon (Ice Lake) Platinum 8369B CPU, 128G RAM and 100G SSD, equipped with Ubuntu 20.04 LTS and openJDK 8.

5.2   SPAC and Accurate Counting

Figure 6 presents the run times of SPAC, including APP and ACC, and the typical accurate counting method. SPAC can finish the tasks much more quickly than accurate counting. The speedup for ACC and APP are about 1.5x–2x and 3x–10x, respectively. This is primarily due to the small sequence lengths (percentage of sampled vertices), ranging from 20% to 65%, with an average of 47%, detected by SPAC automatically. Moreover, all the error rates are below 10%, an acceptable threshold for real-world applications, i.e., the final result is in the same magnitude as the actual number. Since the error rate of accurate counting is always 0, errors are not illustrated in the figure. Generally, APP runs faster than ACC, especially for Amazon, DBLP, Twitter, Epinions and GitHub.

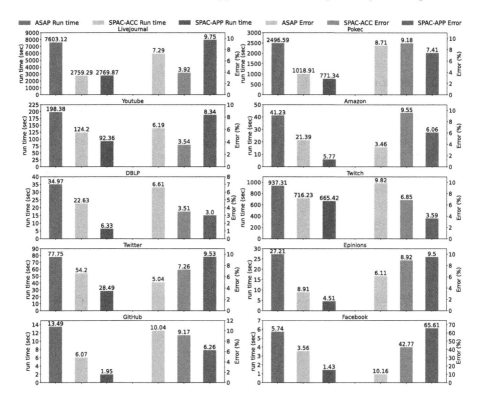

Fig. 7. Run time and error of SPAC and approximate counting (our implemented ASAP).

5.3   SPAC and Approximate Counting

As a new approximate counting method, SPAC should be compared with similar systems. However, we can not access the source codes of any existing approximate counting systems publicly. ASAP is regarded as the state of the art method, so we reimplemented its estimation part according to [17] to evaluate SPAC. For the sake of simplicity, ASAP is used directly to refer to our implementation.

Figure 7 illustrates the run time as well as the errors of SPAC and ASAP. Compared to ASAP, the run time of SPAC is reduced greatly, ranging from 1.4x to 9x. This is mainly because ASAP uses a huge number of estimators to sample over the entire graph, while SPAC stops sampling very early at the turning point, usually only including 30%–50% vertices. Additionally, *APP* is still the fastest. In terms of error, ASAP and SPAC does not surpass each other always. This is because the automatically sought turning points might lead to different fitting accuracies for different datasets.

Figure 8 presents how error rate varies along with the sample sequence length (in run time) for SPAC. The curves are basically the ELP model for ASAP. Not surprisingly, the error decreases as the run time increases, while SPAC can mostly deliver better results than ASAP. Due to the larger variance of *APP*, the *ACC* curve is more stable, but *APP* still reaches compelling accuracy.

5.4 Exception: Facebook

As mentioned in Table 1 and Fig. 1j, the "Facebook" dataset does not strictly satisfy the power-law distribution. In Fig. 6, the errors of "Facebook" for *ACC* and *APP* are 37.8% and 82.4%, respectively, much higher than the threshold. All "Facebook" sub-figures in Fig. 7 and Fig. 8 also show the worst results. According to the design principle of SPAC, it might not work as expected with non-power-law graphs. This will be further investigated in the future.

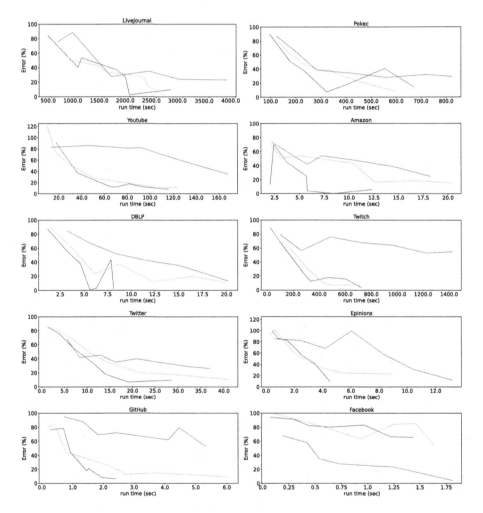

Fig. 8. The ELP of SPAC: how error changes with sample sequence length (in run time).

6   Conclusion and Future Work

Pattern counting, which computes the number of target pattern in a graph, is a very important problem with wide applications in social network analysis, anomaly detection, web mining, and the like. In this paper, we propose SPAC for fast and flexible pattern counting based on the observation that pattern number distribution to degrees also follows power-law. By leveraging the distribution, SPAC can efficiently choose a small number of degrees as samples, fit the coefficients, and then calculate the final result directly. To provide flexibility for different use-cases, SPAC supports both accurate and approximate counting in the sampling phase, the *ACC* and *APP* modes. Moreover, edge weighting and interpolation techniques are adopted to emphasize the sample tail to improve fitting accuracy. The design enables SPAC to support extra-large scale graphs.

The prototype of SPAC is implemented with GraphX on Spark, and is evaluated against various well-known graph datasets. The experimental results show that SPAC is up to 10x faster than accurate counting, keeping the same error level below 10%. Compared to existing approximate counting, SPAC is 1.4x–9x faster in general, while the error could be reduced to 20% of the current systems.

In the future, we will first investigate SPAC to support non-power-law graphs. In addition, SPAC can only count undirected graphs currently, we plan to extend it to deal with directed graphs as well as larger and more complicated patterns.

Acknowledgement. This research is partially supported by National Key Research and Development Program of China with ID 2018AAA0103203 and PCL Peng Cheng Cloud Brain with ID PCL2021A13. We thank Yingchun Ma for valuable comments on early versions and we thank the reviewers for their insights.

References

1. Abou-Rjeili, A., Karypis, G.: Multilevel algorithms for partitioning power-law graphs. In: Proceedings of the 20th International Conference on Parallel and Distributed Processing. IPDPS 2006, p. 124. IEEE Computer Society, USA (2006)
2. Agarwal, S., Mozafari, B., Panda, A., Milner, H., Madden, S., Stoica, I.: BlinkDB: queries with bounded errors and bounded response times on very large data. In: Proceedings of the 8th ACM European Conference on Computer Systems. EuroSys 2013, pp. 29–42. Association for Computing Machinery, New York (2013). https://doi.org/10.1145/2465351.2465355
3. Ahmed, N.K., Duffield, N., Neville, J., Kompella, R.: Graph sample and hold: a framework for big-graph analytics. In: Proceedings of the 20th ACM SIGKDD International Conference on Knowledge Discovery and Data Mining. KDD 2014, pp. 1446–1455. Association for Computing Machinery, New York (2014). https://doi.org/10.1145/2623330.2623757
4. Ananthanarayanan, G., Hung, M.C.C., Ren, X., Stoica, I., Wierman, A., Yu, M.: GRASS: trimming stragglers in approximation analytics. In: 11th USENIX Symposium on Networked Systems Design and Implementation (NSDI 14), pp. 289–302. USENIX Association, Seattle, April 2014. https://www.usenix.org/conference/nsdi14/technical-sessions/presentation/ananthanarayanan

5. Barabási, A.L., Pósfai, M.: Network Science. Cambridge University Press, Cambridge (2016). http://barabasi.com/networksciencebook/
6. Bron, C., Kerbosch, J.: Algorithm 457: finding all cliques of an undirected graph. Commun. ACM **16**(9), 575–577 (1973). https://doi.org/10.1145/362342.362367
7. Chung, F., Lu, L., Vu, V.: Eigenvalues of random power law graphs. Ann. Comb. **7**(1), 21–33 (2003)
8. Cook, S.A.: The complexity of theorem-proving procedures. In: Proceedings of the Third Annual ACM Symposium on Theory of Computing. STOC 1971, pp. 151–158. Association for Computing Machinery, New York (1971). https://doi.org/10.1145/800157.805047
9. Danisch, M., Balalau, O., Sozio, M.: Listing k-cliques in sparse real-world graphs*. In: Proceedings of the 2018 World Wide Web Conference. WWW 2018, pp. 589–598. International World Wide Web Conferences Steering Committee, Republic and Canton of Geneva, CHE (2018). https://doi.org/10.1145/3178876.3186125
10. Elseidy, M., Abdelhamid, E., Skiadopoulos, S., Kalnis, P.: Grami: frequent subgraph and pattern mining in a single large graph. Proc. VLDB Endow. **7**(7), 517–528 (2014). https://doi.org/10.14778/2732286.2732289
11. Flajolet, P., Fusy, É., Gandouet, O., Meunier, F.: HyperLogLog: the analysis of a near-optimal cardinality estimation algorithm. In: Jacquet, P. (ed.) AofA: Analysis of Algorithms. DMTCS Proceedings, vol. DMTCS Proceedings, vol. AH, 2007 Conference on Analysis of Algorithms (AofA 2007), pp. 137–156. Discrete Mathematics and Theoretical Computer Science, Juan les Pins, France, June 2007. https://doi.org/10.46298/dmtcs.3545, https://hal.inria.fr/hal-00406166
12. Gao, P., van der Hofstad, R., Southwell, A., Stegehuis, C.: Counting triangles in power-law uniform random graphs (2018). https://doi.org/10.48550/ARXIV.1812.04289, https://arxiv.org/abs/1812.04289
13. Gemulla, R., Lehner, W.: Sampling time-based sliding windows in bounded space. In: Proceedings of the 2008 ACM SIGMOD International Conference on Management of Data. SIGMOD 2008, pp. 379–392, Association for Computing Machinery, New York (2008). https://doi.org/10.1145/1376616.1376657
14. Gonzalez, J.E., Xin, R.S., Dave, A., Crankshaw, D., Franklin, M.J., Stoica, I.: GraphX: graph processing in a distributed dataflow framework. In: 11th USENIX Symposium on Operating Systems Design and Implementation (OSDI 2014), pp. 599–613. USENIX Association, Broomfield, October 2014. https://www.usenix.org/conference/osdi14/technical-sessions/presentation/gonzalez
15. Gou, X., Zou, L.: Sliding window-based approximate triangle counting over streaming graphs with duplicate edges. In: Proceedings of the 2021 International Conference on Management of Data. SIGMOD 2021, pp. 645–657. Association for Computing Machinery, New York (2021). https://doi.org/10.1145/3448016.3452800
16. Grochow, J.A., Kellis, M.: Network motif discovery using subgraph enumeration and symmetry-breaking. In: Speed, T., Huang, H. (eds.) RECOMB 2007. LNCS, vol. 4453, pp. 92–106. Springer, Heidelberg (2007). https://doi.org/10.1007/978-3-540-71681-5_7
17. Iyer, A.P., Liu, Z., Jin, X., Venkataraman, S., Braverman, V., Stoica, I.: ASAP: fast, approximate graph pattern mining at scale. In: 13th USENIX Symposium on Operating Systems Design and Implementation (OSDI 2018), pp. 745–761. USENIX Association, October 2018. https://www.usenix.org/conference/osdi18/presentation/iyer
18. Jung, M., Lim, Y., Lee, S., Kang, U.: FURL: fixed-memory and uncertainty reducing local triangle counting for multigraph streams. Data Min. Knowl. Disc. **33**(5), 1225–1253 (2019). https://doi.org/10.1007/s10618-019-00630-6

19. Kashtan, N., Itzkovitz, S., Milo, R., Alon, U.: Efficient sampling algorithm for estimating subgraph concentrations and detecting network motifs. Bioinformatics **20**(11), 1746–1758 (2004). https://doi.org/10.1093/bioinformatics/bth163
20. Koutra, D., Jin, D., Ning, Y., Faloutsos, C.: Perseus: an interactive large-scale graph mining and visualization tool. Proc. VLDB Endow. **8**(12), 1924–1927 (2015). https://doi.org/10.14778/2824032.2824102
21. Leskovec, J., Lang, K.J., Dasgupta, A., Mahoney, M.W.: Community structure in large networks: natural cluster sizes and the absence of large well-defined clusters. Internet Math. **6**(1), 29–123 (2009). https://doi.org/10.1080/15427951.2009.10129177
22. Lim, Y., Jung, M., Kang, U.: Memory-efficient and accurate sampling for counting local triangles in graph streams: from simple to multigraphs. ACM Trans. Knowl. Discov. Data **12**(1) (2018). https://doi.org/10.1145/3022186
23. McAuley, J., Leskovec, J.: Learning to discover social circles in ego networks. In: Proceedings of the 25th International Conference on Neural Information Processing Systems. NIPS 2012, vol. 1, pp. 539–547. Curran Associates Inc., Red Hook (2012)
24. Milo, R., Shen-Orr, S., Itzkovitz, S., Kashtan, N., Chklovskii, D., Alon, U.: Network motifs: simple building blocks of complex networks. Science **298**(5594), 824–827 (2002). https://doi.org/10.1126/science.298.5594.824
25. Montgomery, D.C., Peck, E.A., Vining, G.G.: Introduction to Linear Regression Analysis, 4th edn. Wiley, Hoboken (2006)
26. Pashanasangi, N., Seshadhri, C.: Faster and generalized temporal triangle counting, via degeneracy ordering. In: Proceedings of the 27th ACM SIGKDD Conference on Knowledge Discovery and Data Mining. KDD 2021, pp. 1319–1328. Association for Computing Machinery, New York (2021). https://doi.org/10.1145/3447548.3467374
27. Pržulj, N., Corneil, D.G., Jurisica, I.: Modeling interactome: scale-free or geometric? Bioinformatics **20**(18), 3508–3515 (2004). https://doi.org/10.1093/bioinformatics/bth436
28. Ribeiro, P., Silva, F.: G-tries: an efficient data structure for discovering network motifs. In: Proceedings of the 2010 ACM Symposium on Applied Computing. SAC 2010, pp. 1559–1566. Association for Computing Machinery, New York (2010). https://doi.org/10.1145/1774088.1774422
29. Richardson, M., Agrawal, R., Domingos, P.: Trust management for the semantic web. In: Fensel, D., Sycara, K., Mylopoulos, J. (eds.) ISWC 2003. LNCS, vol. 2870, pp. 351–368. Springer, Heidelberg (2003). https://doi.org/10.1007/978-3-540-39718-2_23
30. Rozemberczki, B., Allen, C., Sarkar, R.: Multi-scale attributed node embedding (2019). https://doi.org/10.48550/ARXIV.1909.13021, https://arxiv.org/abs/1909.13021
31. Rozemberczki, B., Sarkar, R.: Twitch gamers: a dataset for evaluating proximity preserving and structural role-based node embeddings (2021). https://doi.org/10.48550/ARXIV.2101.03091, https://arxiv.org/abs/2101.03091
32. Takac, L., Zábovský, M.: Data analysis in public social networks. In: International Scientific Conference and International Workshop Present Day Trends of Innovations, pp. 1–6, January 2012
33. Teixeira, C.H.C., Fonseca, A.J., Serafini, M., Siganos, G., Zaki, M.J., Aboulnaga, A.: Arabesque: a system for distributed graph mining. In: Proceedings of the 25th Symposium on Operating Systems Principles. SOSP 2015, pp. 425–440. Association for Computing Machinery, New York (2015). https://doi.org/10.1145/2815400.2815410

34. Vázquez, A., Pastor-Satorras, R., Vespignani, A.: Large-scale topological and dynamical properties of the internet. Phys. Rev. E **65**, 066130 (2002). https://doi.org/10.1103/PhysRevE.65.066130, https://link.aps.org/doi/10.1103/PhysRevE.65.066130

35. Wang, P., Qi, Y., Sun, Y., Zhang, X., Tao, J., Guan, X.: Approximately counting triangles in large graph streams including edge duplicates with a fixed memory usage. Proc. VLDB Endow. **11**(2), 162–175 (2017). https://doi.org/10.14778/3149193.3149197

36. Wu, M., et al.: Gram: scaling graph computation to the trillions. In: Proceedings of the Sixth ACM Symposium on Cloud Computing. SoCC 2015, pp. 408–421. Association for Computing Machinery, New York (2015). https://doi.org/10.1145/2806777.2806849

37. Yan, X., Han, J.: GSPAN: graph-based substructure pattern mining. In: 2002 IEEE International Conference on Data Mining, Proceedings, pp. 721–724 (2002). https://doi.org/10.1109/ICDM.2002.1184038

38. Yang, J., Leskovec, J.: Defining and evaluating network communities based on ground-truth. Knowl. Inf. Syst. **42**(1), 181–213 (2013). https://doi.org/10.1007/s10115-013-0693-z

39. Zaharia, M., Chowdhury, M., Franklin, M.J., Shenker, S., Stoica, I.: Spark: cluster computing with working sets. In: Proceedings of the 2nd USENIX Conference on Hot Topics in Cloud Computing. HotCloud 2010, p. 10. USENIX Association, USA (2010)

Haica: A High Performance Computing & Artificial Intelligence Fused Computing Architecture

Zhengbo Chen[1(✉)], Fang Zheng[2], Feng Guo[2], Qi Yu[2], and Zuoning Chen[3]

[1] Information Engineering University, Zhengzhou, China
chenzb1996@163.com
[2] State Key Laboratory of Mathematical Engineering and Advanced Computing, Wuxi, China
[3] Chinese Academy of Engineering, Beijing, China

Abstract. In recent years, HPC and AI fusion, which refers to applying AI technology to traditional HPC applications, has become a new trend. HPC and AI fusion requires supports for multiple precisions used in both domains. While, supporting multiple precisions in a single computing unit is not easy. Prior research typically targets on modifying a high-precision FMA to support low precisions. However, such efforts suffer from disadvantages of increased latency and limited compute throughput for low-precision operations, high area and power overhead, and limited support of new data formats appeared in AI domain. To address this issue, we propose Haica, a double-precision FMA and low-precision systolic array fused architecture, to achieve HPC and AI fusion. Our work has two innovations. First, we propose a low-cost multiple-low-precision FMA by taking advantage of the commonality among FP16, BF16, and TF32. Second, inspired by the idea of splicing high precision with low precision, we replace the multiply and merge modules in a double-precision FMA with a modified systolic array that is composed of the proposed low-precision FMAs. We implement the logic design of Haica using RTL and evaluate its overhead. Results show that compared to the naive combination of a double-precision FMA and single-half-mixed-precision systolic array, Haica provides extra support for BF16 and TF32 with only 7.87% area and 33.26% power overhead. This demonstrates that Haica achieves HPC and AI fusion in a cost-effective manner.

Keywords: Artificial intelligence · High performance computing · Fused multiply add · Systolic array

1 Introduction

Due to the significant advantages of Artificial Intelligence (AI) technology, recent years have seen a widespread adoption of AI technology in many application domains, such as computer vision [11], natural language processing [4], time series classification [19], human activity recognition [20], Malware detection [15], etc.

© Springer Nature Switzerland AG 2023
W. Meng et al. (Eds.): ICA3PP 2022, LNCS 13777, pp. 233–252, 2023.
https://doi.org/10.1007/978-3-031-22677-9_13

Applying AI technology to traditional High Performance Computing (HPC) applications, known as HPC and AI fusion, has become a new trend. HPC and AI fusion is a generalized concept, it includes but not limited to running HPC applications using lower precisions. For example, HPL-AI [5], a benchmark suite that appeared in recent years, converts the major computation in Linpack from double precision to half precision, which significantly accelerates the computation while preserving the accuracy. Such a fusion also includes using AI algorithms or models to solve problems in HPC applications. For instance, Han *et al.* used ResNet to perform moist physics parameterization [6]. Prior research [8,13] also illustrated the benefits of HPC and AI fusion.

To achieve this fusion, supports for multiple precisions are required since different precisions are used in HPC and AI domains. In traditional HPC domain, double precision (FP64) that follows IEEE-754 standard [16] is used. However, in AI domain, low precisions are desired. For example, in training scenarios, in addition to the commonly-used FP32 and FP16 formats that follow IEEE-754 standard, several new formats, such as BF16 (BFloat16) [10] and TF32 (Tensor Float32) [3], have also emerged; in inference scenarios, FP16 and low-precision integer (e.g., INT8) are common data formats.

However, supporting multiple precisions in a single computing unit is not easy because different precisions differ a lot in data formats, especially between high precision and low precision. In industry, Tensor Processing Unit (TPU)[9] released by Google and A100 [3] released by NVIDIA are two representative products that aim at providing tremendous computing power for AI applications. TPU organizes its computing units in form of systolic array [12], which is a regular and array-based architecture. The latest systolic array supports $INT8 \times INT8 + INT16$ and $BF16 \times BF16 + FP32$ matrix operations. A100 organizes its computing units in form of a tree-based architecture called Tensor Core [3]. A100 supports multiple precisions, including INT8, FP16, BF16, TF32, and FP64. Although Tensor Core covers mainstream precisions used in HPC and AI domains, its details are not publicly available; thereby, preventing researchers from conducting detailed analysis.

In the academic community, research usually targets on modifying the floating-point Fused Multiply Add (FMA) [7,14], the key computing unit of processors, to support two or more precisions. Arunachalam *et al.* [1] proposed an FMA component that supports two precisions. Chen *et al.* [2] proposed an FMA component that supports multiple precisions. Zhang *et al.* [21] extends a quadruple-precision FMA to provide support for double/single/half/mixed precision and dot-product operations. However, prior research suffers from four major shortcomings. **First**, sharing a common pipeline by high-/low-precision operations increases the latency of low-precision operations, because high-precision operations require more pipeline stages than low-precision operations. **Second**, supporting low-precision operations by modifying a high-precision FMA limits the compute throughput of low-precision operations due to limitations on input data width. **Third**, they incur high area and power overhead because of the giant difference between high-precision and low-precision data formats. **Last but not**

least, they do not support new data formats appeared in AI domain, e.g., BF16 and TF32.

To this end, we propose Haica, a double-precision FMA and low-precision systolic array fused architecture, to support HPC and AI fusion. Different from prior research that adopts a high-to-low routine, i.e., supporting low precisions by modifying a high-precision FMA, we follow a low-to-high manner. We first propose a low-cost multiple-low-precision FMA by taking advantages of the commonality among multiple low precisions. Inspired by the idea of splicing high precision with low precision, we propose Haica, which uses a 4×4 systolic array (composed of the proposed low-precision FMAs) to replaces the multiply and merge modules in a double-precision FMA. We implement the logic design of Haica using Register Transfer Level (RTL) and verify its correctness. We use Synopsys Design Compiler (DC) tool to evaluate its overhead. Results show that, compared to the baseline, the naive combination of a double-precision FMA and a 4×4 systolic array (composed of single-half-mixed-precision FMAs), Haica provides extra supports for BF16 and TF32 at the expense of 7.87% area overhead and 33.26% power overhead.

This paper makes the following contributions:

- We propose a low-cost multiple-low-precision FMA component by taking advantages of the commonality among multiple low precisions, including FP16, BF16, and TF32.
- We construct a 4×4 systolic array using 16 proposed FMAs to support multiple-low-precision operations with higher operation rate and lower overhead.
- We propose Haica, a double-precision FMA and low-precision systolic array fused architecture to support HPC and AI fusion. Evaluation result shows that Haica supports multiple precisions in a cost-effective manner.

The rest of this paper is organized as follows. Section 2 discusses related work. Section 3 introduces background on data formats, FMA, and systolic array. Section 4 motivates the need for an efficient multiple-low-precision computing architecture. Section 5 presents the detailed architecture of Haica. Section 6 evaluates Haica and analyzes its overhead. Section 7 concludes this paper.

2   Related Work

To our knowledge, this is the first work to provide supports for mainstream precisions used in HPC and AI domains by fusing FMA and systolic array. In this section, we discuss previous research related to HPC and AI fusion, and architecture for multiple-precision support.

2.1   HPC and AI Fusion

One representative case of HPC and AI fusion is running HPC applications with lower precision. HPL-AI is such an instance. By converting the major computation from double precision to half precision, the computing speed is improved significantly. Haidar *et al.* [5] evaluated HPL-AI using V100 GPU, results showed that the performance of mixed-precision operations is improved by 3× with acceptable accuracy loss. Another representative case of HPC and AI fusion is using AI technology to solve problems in HPC applications. Han *et al.* [6] proposed a new moist physics parameterization scheme based on deep learning. Compared to traditional HPC approach, the new scheme speedups the computing considerably and improves determination coefficients significantly. Kurth *et al.* [13] proposed "exascale deep learning" for climate data analysis, which achieved 1.1 EFLOPS peak performance by taking advantage of GPU's excellent single-/half-precision performance. Jia *et al.* [8] achieved parallelized deep learning simulation on Summit. On this basis, the performance of molecular dynamic simulations is improved significantly by combining double-precision operations with mixed-/half-precision operations. Our proposal—Haica, a computing unit that supports multiple-precision operations, can be used to facilitate HPC and AI fusion.

2.2   Architecture Support for Multiple Precisions

In the academic community, the architecture supports for multiple precisions are typically based on FMA unit used in HPC processors. Wu *et al.* [18] proposed an FMA component that supports double-/single-precision multiply-add operations and single-precision complex operations. Tannenbaum *et al.* [17] proposed a configurable FMA component that supports single-/half-precision multiply-add operations, half-precision multiplication and accumulation operations, which has been applied to V100 GPU. Arunachalam *et al.* [1] proposed an FMA component that supports two precisions, which reduces area by 48% and power by 49% with fusing technology, compared to a double-precision FMA. Chen *et al.* [2] proposed an FMA component that supports multiple precisions, including double-/single-/half-precision floating-point operations and 64-/32-/16-bit integer operations with 51% area overhead and 32% power overhead relative to a double-precision FMA. Zhang *et al.* [21] extends a quadruple-precision FMA to provide supports for double/single/half/mixed precision and dot product operations at the expense of 10.6% area overhead. Zhang *et al.* [22] proposed a flexible 16-bit floating-point/fixed-point FMA architecture, where the bit width of exponent and mantissa can be flexibly exchanged.

The above research has two major shortcomings. First, the proposed FMAs do not support new data formats appeared in AI applications, such as BF16 and TF32. Second, due to the giant difference between high-precision data formats and low-precision data formats, these proposals suffer from high hardware overhead. Instead of supporting high precisions and low precisions in a single FMA, our work first proposes an FMA that only supports low precisions and then replaces the multiply and merge modules in a double-precision FMA with a systolic array that is built on the proposed FMA. Compared to the above research, our work supports more precisions with lower hardware overhead.

3 Background

Section 3.1 describes commonly-used data formats that follow IEEE-754 standard and new data formats appeared in AI domain. Section 3.2 describes the architecture of a classical FMA. Section 3.3 introduces the architecture of systolic array.

3.1 IEEE Floating-Point Standard and New Data Formats

IEEE-754 [16] is a standard for binary floating-point arithmetic. Three commonly-used floating-point formats are specified in the standard: half precision, single precision, and double precision, which are 16-bit, 32-bit, and 64-bit, respectively. IEEE-754 has three basic components: sign, exponent, and mantissa. The sign represents a number is positive or negative, exponent determines the range of a number, while mantissa determines the precision. The relationship between the representation and true value is shown in Eq. (1).

$$X = (-1)^s \times 2^{e-bias} \times (1.f) \tag{1}$$

where, s, e, f, $bias$ represent sign, exponent, mantissa, and exponent offset, respectively. Exponent offsets of half, single, and double precision are 15, 127, and 1023, respectively.

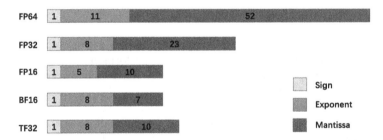

Fig. 1. Encoding formats of commonly-used precisions.

In recent years, some new data formats, e.g., BF16 and TF32, appear in AI applications. The encoding formats of BF16, TF32, and three IEEE-754 representations are shown in Fig. 1. It can be seen that these formats differ in exponent and mantissa length. BF16 has the same exponent length as FP32, making it easier to accumulate with FP32 after multiplication. TF32 reduces mantissa to 10 bits but keeps exponent as 8 bits, which helps to reduce overhead for multiplication. Both BF16 and TF32 have 8-bit exponent (the same as FP32). This makes it easy to support in an FMA with fusing technology. In this paper, we regard the same exponent length between BF16 and TF32, and the same mantissa length between FP16 and TF32 as commonality.

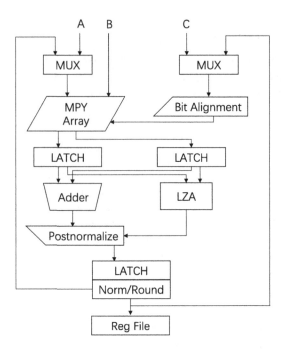

Fig. 2. Architecture of a classical floating-point FMA [7].

3.2 FMA Architecture

The floating-point FMA is the key computing unit in a processor. Its performance has a non-negligible impact on processor performance. In 1990, Hokenek *et al.* from IBM proposed the concept of FMA [7], which merged the multiply instruction and add instruction into one instruction to reduce overhead and delay. The architecture of classical FMA is shown in Fig. 2. In the first stage of pipeline, multiply, exponent calculation, and product alignment are processed in parallel; thereby, the data alignment is overlapped. The intermediate result (refers to mantissa multiply-add) is obtained by the end of first stage. In the second stage, an Leading Zero Anticipator (LZA) is used to predict the number of zeros. The introduction of LZA allows paralleled post-normalization and addition operations, which converts the mantissa of result to standard format. Combined with exponent and sign processing, the final result is obtained after normalizing and rounding. This is the mainstream floating-point FMA architecture, which is used in IBM's Power series processors, Intel's Itanium series processors, and other processors.

To reduce the delay of classical FMA, Lang *et al.* [14] proposed an optimized design, whose key idea include 1) combining the addition and rounding within a dual adder, and 2) the normalization is performed before the addition. Besides, they modified the design of LZA so that the leading bits of its output are produced first and can be used in normalization. Compared to the classical FMA, the latency-optimized FMA reduces delay by 15–20% at the expense of incurring higher hardware overhead. In this paper, we base our work on the classical FMA due to its widespread adoption and lower overhead. However, our proposal, Haica, can also be built on the latency-optimized FMA.

3.3 Architecture of Systolic Array

Systolic array is the major computing unit in Google's TPU [9], whose architecture is shown in Fig. 3. In systolic array, weight is transferred from top to bottom, and activation is transferred from left to right. The output of each column is summed by the accumulators. Systolic array achieves high data reuse and low requirement for memory access by taking advantages of data flow inside the array. The systolic array in the first generation of TPU supports $INT8 \times INT8 + INT16$ matrix operations, while in the second and third generation, the systolic array is extended to support $BF16 \times BF16 + FP32$ matrix operations. Since then, an increasing number of AI processors adopted array-based computing architecture.

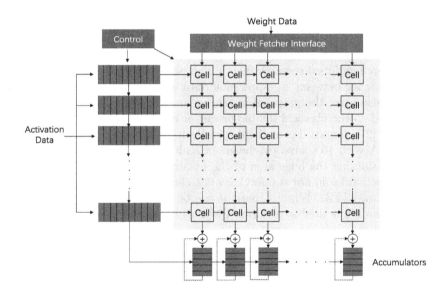

Fig. 3. The architecture of systolic array.

4 Motivation

The requirements for various precisions in HPC and AI domains have driven the supports of multiple precisions in FMA. To satisfy these requirements, the academia has made considerable efforts. We summarize relevant work in Table 1. The research listed in this table adopted a high-to-low routine, more specifically, supporting lower precisions by modifying a higher-precision FMA. However, we find that all works listed in Table 1 suffer from the following shortcomings.

Table 1. Related work comparison

Work	Supported precision	Architecture
[18]	FP64/FP32	Double-precision FMA
[1]	FP32/FP16	Single-precision FMA
[2]	FP64/FP32/FP16/INT	Double-precision FMA
[21]	QP128/FP64/FP32/FP16/mixed	Quadruple-precision FMA
[22]	flexible 16-bit floating-point and fixed-point	Half-precision FMA

First, sharing a common pipeline by high-/low-precision operations increases the latency of low-precision operations, because high-precision operations require more pipeline stages than low-precision operations. For example, the latency of FP16 operations will increase from 1 cycle (in a half-precision FMA) to 7 cycles (in an FMA proposed in [2]).

Second, supporting low-precision operations by modifying a high-precision FMA limits the compute throughput (in other words, operations-per-cycle) of low-precision operations due to limitations on input data width. For example, when FP16 operations are executed in a double-precision FMA, the compute throughput of FP16 is only 4x of FP64, which is far behind the 16x achieved by systolic array or tensor core.

Third, aforementioned research incurs high area and power overhead due to the giant difference between high-precision data formats and low-precision data formats. For example, the proposal in [2] increased area by 51% and power by 32% compared to the classical double-precision FMA (introduced in Sect. 3.2). Zhang *et al.* [21] proposed a multiple-precision FMA based on a quadruple-precision FMA with 10% area overhead. In reality, 10% area overhead is non-negligible considering the huge area of the quadruple-precision FMA. Last but not least, these works do not support new data formats appeared in AI domain, such as BF16 and TF32. What is more, it can be inferred that supporting these new data formats in a double-precision FMA will be ineffective in terms of area and power.

We identify two reasons for this high hardware overhead. First, the difference between high precision (e.g., FP64) and low precision (e.g., FP16) is significant, thereby, the modules in a double-precision FMA cannot be reused directly by low-precision FMA, and considerable efforts are involved in modifying these modules. Second, the area cost and power consumption in a double-precision FMA is dominated by multiply and merge modules. Therefore, it is not easy to reduce hardware overhead without considerable optimization to these two modules. To confirm this, we implemented the classical double-precision FMA using RTL, and evaluated its overhead using Synopsys DC tool with a commercial 28 nm standard cell library. The frequency is set to 2.5 GHz. The area and power breakdown are shown in Fig. 4(a) and 4(b), respectively. It can be seen that the multiply and merge modules incur more than 70% area and power overhead, demonstrating that the multiply and merge modules are two area-hungry and power-hungry modules in the double-precision FMA.

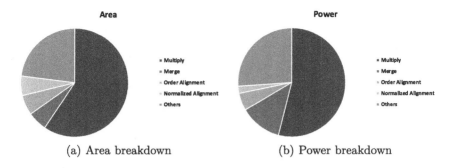

(a) Area breakdown   (b) Power breakdown

Fig. 4. Overhead of each module in a double-precision FMA.

Therefore, to support multiple precisions in a single computing unit, an efficient architecture is important and urgent. In this paper, we follow a low-to-high manner to implement the multiple-precision FMA. Two key insights are utilized to reduce hardware overhead. First, supporting multiple low precisions by modifying a single-half-mixed-precision FMA (rather than a double-precision FMA) can significantly reduce hardware overhead and implementation complexity by taking advantages of the commonality among FP16, BF16, and TF32. Second, splicing high precision with low precision (rather than extending high precision to support low precision), i.e., organizing multiple-low-precision FMAs in the form of systolic array and replacing the multiply and merge modules in a double-precision FMA with the systolic array, is more cost-effective and achieves higher compute throughput for low-precision operations. In the next section, we will describe the architecture of our proposal in detail.

5   Haica: An HPC and AI Fusion Architecture

Based on the analysis in Sect. 4, supporting high and low precision by simply modifying FMA is ineffective. To address this issue, we propose Haica, an multiple-precision computing architecture, to support HPC and AI fusion. The key ideas of Haica are as follows. Haica first modifies a single-half-mixed-precision FMA to provide extra supports for BF16 and TF32 (Sect. 5.1). The modified FMA incurs less hardware overhead by taking advantages of the commonality among FP16, BF16, and TF32. Then Haica replaces the multiply and merge modules in a double-precision FMA with a systolic array that is composed of the modified FMAs (Sect. 5.2). With such a design, Haica provides supports for INT16, FP16, BF16, TF32, and FP64 operations in a cost-effective manner. Finally, we discuss additional issues related to Haica (Sect. 5.3).

5.1   Multiple-Low-Precision FMA

The commonality among FP16, BF16, and TF32 makes it a better choice to support these data formats in a single-half-mixed-precision FMA. In this section, we propose a multiple-low-precision FMA to support the following operations: FP16 × FP16 + FP32, BF16 × BF16 + FP32, TF32 × TF32 + FP32, and INT16 × INT16 + INT32.

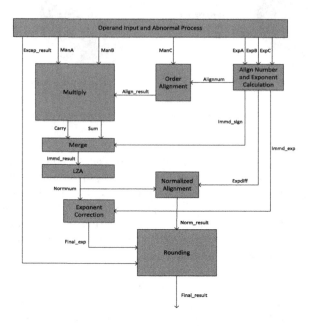

Fig. 5. The architecture of multiple-low-precision FMA.

The architecture of multiple-low-precision FMA is shown in Fig. 5, which is mainly composed of data preprocessing module (Operand Input and Abnormal Process in Fig. 5), exponent processing module (Align Number and Exponent Calculation), order alignment module (Order Alignment), multiply module (Multiply), merge module (Merge), and post-processing module (LZA, Normalized Alignment, Exponent Correction, Rounding). The input of this FMA is split into exponent and mantissa. The mantissa of two multiplication operands is sent to the multiplier to get the intermediate result. Each input's exponent is sent to exponent processing module to calculate the order difference, and then the addend is aligned according to order difference. The aligned addend and the intermediate result are added up. Next, rounding and index correction is performed after alignment. Finally, the output is selected, and overflow is checked. To reduce hardware overhead, fusing technology is applied to exponent processing, order alignment, and post-processing modules.

Data preprocessing module is responsible for splitting the input into sign, exponent, and mantissa, and checking abnormal input and result. As shown in Fig. 1, FP16 has a 5-bit exponent, while BF16 and TF32 have an 8-bit exponent; BF16 has a 7-bit mantissa, while FP16 and TF32 have a 10-bit mantissa. Therefore, the exponent of FP16/BF16/TF32 is 5-bit or 8-bit, and the mantissa is up to 10 bits. For mantissa that is less than 10-bit, zero padding, i.e., adding zeros, is performed.

Exponent processing and order alignment modules do the following work: calculating the amount of alignment, aligning the addend, predicting the sign and exponent of the final result. The order alignment is shown in Fig. 6. The major difference among the three data formats lies in the calculation of order difference and the number of alignment.

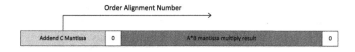

Fig. 6. Order alignment.

The multiply-add calculation is shown in Eq. (2), where $manA$, $manB$, $manC$ and Ea, Eb, Ec represent mantissa and exponent of operand A, B and C, respectively. d and q represent order difference and common factor, respectively. $p0$ and $p1$ represent exponent offset, which are 15 and 127, respectively. Under FP16, the order difference d is $Ec-Ea-Eb+2p0-p1 = Ec-Ea-Eb+2\times15-127 = Ec-Ea-Eb-97$, the common factor q equals $Ea+Eb-2\times15+27 = Ea+Eb-3$, and the alignment number equals $d-27$. Under BF16 and TF32, the order difference d is $Ec-Ea-Eb+2\times127-127 = Ec-Ea-Eb+127$, the common factor q is $Ea+Eb-2\times127+27 = Ea+Eb-227$, and the number of alignment is still $d-27$.

The reason for selecting $d-27$ as the number of alignment is as follows. Mantissa width of addend C is 24-bit (1 bit ahead of decimal point), and the mantissa multiply result of A × B is 48-bit (2 bits ahead of decimal point). If two zeros are filled for rounding, we have to align C for $24+2+2-1 = 27$ bits without considering order difference, so the final number of alignment is $d-27$. Therefore, we can calculate the order difference and number of alignment according to data format. In the order alignment module, the highest number is 76. Thus, it can be implemented through three levels. The first level aligns 0 to 7 bits according to $alignnum[2 : 0]$; the second level aligns 0 to 48 bits with a stride of 8 bits through $alignnum[5 : 3]$; and the third level determines whether aligning 64 bits.

$$A \times B + C = manA \times 2^{Ea-p0} \times manB \times 2^{Eb-p0} + manC \times 2^{Ec-p1}$$
$$= manA \times manB \times 2^{Ea+Eb-2p0} + manC \times 2^{Ec-p1} \qquad (2)$$
$$= 2^q \times (manA \times manB \times 2^{-27} + manC \times 2^{Ec-p1-q})$$

Multiply and merge modules are two key modules of an FMA, which are responsible for performing mantissa multiplication and merging the result with addend. We use 4-based Booth coding to generate partial products and use 4-2 CSA compression tree to merge them. Merge module first adds the sum and carry (output of the multiply module) up and then merges with the aligned addend mantissa to get the intermediate result. Note that, under three formats, the mantissa length of multiplication operand is 10-bit. However, to support INT16 × INT16+INT32 operation in the FMA, both multiply and merge modules use 16-bit inputs.

Once the intermediate result is ready, post-processing, including LZA, normalization alignment, exponent correction, and rounding, is performed. Since the addend and final result is single precision, we can directly use the post-processing module of single-precision FMA without modification. The post-processing module includes several sub-modules. LZA module predicts normalization number of alignment according to intermediate result. Normalization alignment module aligns the result to ensure that the highest bit of mantissa is 1. Exponent correction and rounding module correct and round the final exponent and mantissa. The final result is obtained after merging with the abnormal result.

In particular, we integrate integer multiplication and addition operation (INT16 × INT16+INT32) in the multiple-low-precision FMA, which is performed by specific individual sub-components. As the logic for supporting integer operation is very simple, we will not describe its logic in detail. In Sect. 6, for fairness, the single-half-mixed-precision FMA uses the same logic as the multiple-low-precision FMA to implementation INT16 operations.

5.2 Haica: A Double-Precision FMA and Low-Precision Systolic Array Fused Architecture

Inspired by the idea of splicing high precision with low precision, we can perform expensive double-precision operations in a low-precision systolic array. In this section, we propose Haica, a double-precision FMA and low-precision systolic array fused architecture, to support high and low precision with lower overhead. Before describing the architecture of Haica, we first present necessary modifications to the systolic array cell when the multiple-low-precision FMA is integrated.

The architecture of the modified systolic array cell is shown in Fig. 7. The systolic array cell comprises of an FMA and five registers, including two north data registers, a west data register, a sum data register, and a control register. Compared to single-half-mixed-precision FMA, the multiple-low-precision FMA increases the width of register and input data. This is because if the width of west and north data remains 16 bits, the input data with TF32 format will be loaded in two cycles; as a result, it takes two cycles to perform one operation. This causes severe power jitter. To address this issue, we increase the width of north and west data to 19 bits, and south output remains 32 bits. With this change, TF32 operation can be performed in one cycle, and power jitter is avoided. We use the modified cell to construct systolic array.

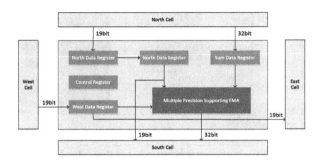

Fig. 7. The architecture of modified systolic array cell.

The overall architecture of Haica is shown in Fig. 8. It is modified on basis of a double-precision FMA. Haica consists of Data Pre-process, Exponent Process, Order Alignment, a modified 4×4 systolic array, LZA, Exponent Correction, Normalized Alignment, Rounding and Abnormal Process modules. Instead of implementing a double-precision FMA and low-precision systolic array separately, we use the systolic array to replace the multiply and merge modules, two most expensive modules in a double-precision FMA. In this way, the major computation involved in FP64 operation is performed by the systolic array. Totally, Haica supports INT16, INT64, FP16, BF16, TF32, and FP64 operations.

We first discuss the width of Haica's input data and output data. Haica supports FP64 operations, where multipliers A and B, addend C, and output D are 64 bits. Meanwhile, Haica supports 16 parallel mixed-low-precision operations. Both BF16 and FP16 are 16 bits, and FP32 is 32 bits, thereby the width of A and B are still 64 bits, but the width of C and D must be 128 bits. Therefore, the width of A and B remain unchanged, and we modify the width of addend and output to 128 bits. As the systolic array takes 19-bit TF32 inputs, Haica can perform 4 parallel TF32 × TF32+FP32 operations under current configuration.

The key idea of splicing high precision with low precision is shown in Fig. 9. According to IEEE-754 standard, FP64 has a 52-bit mantissa. To equally split the mantissa, we extend the 52-bit mantissa to 64-bit with zero padding. Then each extended input of the multiplier is split to four inputs, that is, $a1$-$a4$ and $b1$-$b4$ in Fig. 9, each with 16-bit mantissa. On this basis, the 64-bit mantissa multiplication can be completed with 16 INT16 multiplication. This split makes it feasible to implement the double-precision operations in a 4×4 systolic array.

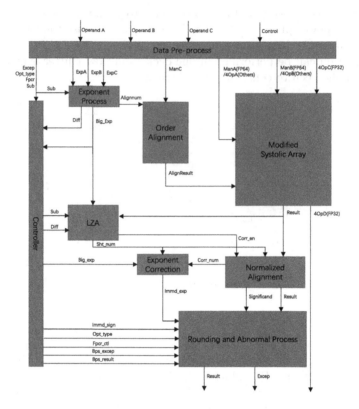

Fig. 8. The architecture of Haica.

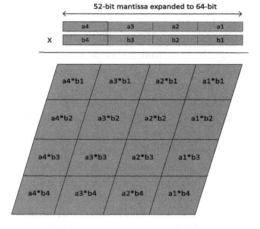

Fig. 9. Splicing high precision with low precision.

To achieve this goal, the data width inside the systolic array is adjusted. More specifically, the width of west data and north data is still 19-bit; while, the width of the sum varies correspondingly. For instance, the width of sum in the first to the last row is 32-bit, 48-bit, 64-bit, and 80-bit, respectively. Finally, four 80-bit output data are merged into one 128-bit product through the merge unit. The modified systolic array is shown Fig. 10(a) and the rule of data flow in the systolic array is shown in Fig. 10(b). As we clarified, to adapt to TF32, zero padding is used to convert the width of west and north data from 16-bit to 19-bit.

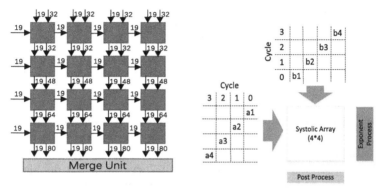

(a) Architecture of systolic array.   (b) Data flow in the systolic array.

Fig. 10. Architecture and data flow of systolic array.

According to Fig. 9 and Fig. 10(a), $a1 \times b1$ is performed in the first cell of the first row with 32-bit product. Similarly, $a1 \times b2$, $a1 \times b3$, and $a1 \times b4$ are performed in the second to fourth cell of the first row, respectively. Therefore, all products of the first row are 32-bit. $a2 \times b1$ is performed in the first cell of the second row and is accumulated with result of $a1 \times b1$. According to the multiplication rule in Fig. 9, the accumulation result is 48-bit. Similarly, the output of other cells in the second row is also 48-bit. Thus, the output of cells in the third and fourth row are 64-bit and 80-bit, respectively.

To achieve the 16-bit mantissa multiplication, only minor modification is required. More specifically, the data width inside the systolic array needs widen correspondingly. We take the first cell of the second row as an example. The FMA takes 16-bit multiplication operand and 32-bit addend as input. To get the result of $a2 \times b1$, the lower 16 bits of $a1 \times b1$ are directly taken as the lower 16 bits of $a2 \times b1$, which have been calculated by the first cell of the first row. Similarly, the merge unit takes four 80-bit adders instead of 128-bit adders as input. This design reduces unnecessary modification.

Except for modifications to systolic array and merge module, the other modules of Haica are similar to the double-precision FMA. For example, modules such as Exponent Process, Order Alignment, LZA, and Normalized Alignment remain the same as original double-precision FMA, while certain control logic is added to Data Pre-process, Rounding and Abnormal Process modules to adapt to a variety of operation modes. As the modification is minor, we do not describe corresponding logic in detail.

5.3 Discussion

In this section, we discuss additional issues related to Haica, including the pipeline cycles, the compute performance of supported operations, and requirement for data access.

As Haica is a fully-pipelined architecture, we briefly analyze the pipeline cycles of Haica. For low-precision operations, it performs INT16, FP16, BF16, and TF32 operations in the 4×4 systolic array, which can complete 16 multiply-add operations in one cycle. For FP64 operations, we use the classical 7-stage double-precision FMA for analysis, where multiply and merge modules are in stage 2 and stage 3, respectively. Eight cycles are taken to complete the multiplication operations in systolic array due to data dependence, i.e., the data stage starts from the top leftmost cell and ends at the bottom rightmost cell. In contrast, it takes only two cycles to complete the multiplication operations in the double-precision FMA. Consequently, it takes 13 cycles to complete an entire FP64 operation in Haica rather than 7 cycles in the double-precision FMA. The extra cycles are caused by larger startup overhead. However, from pipeline perspective, Haica is still able to generate one output per cycle if there are enough FP64 multiply-add operations. In addition, increasing pipeline stages (from 7-stage to 13-stage) requires more registers to store intermediate results, this may have an impact on processor's FP64 performance due to increased register consumption. However, this impact is minor for low-precision-dominated applications.

To adapt to TF32 operations, the width of north data and west data is increased to 19-bit, which causes instruction and memory access issues. To address this issue, we regard TF32 as 32-bit because it is stored as 32-bit data in memory with 13-bit zeros. Before sending to systolic array, the 32-bit input is tailored to 19-bit for calculation. This method can effectively address the irregular data width issue at the expense of limiting input data width to 32-bit, which is twice of 16-bit precision formats, e.g., BF16 and FP16. For TF32 format, two west inputs are sent to the third and fourth row, and two north inputs are sent to the third and fourth column, leaving other inputs being zeros. Therefore, only four cells perform the computation in reality, achieving 25% peak performance of FP16 operations.

In general, Haica can perform one INT64 × INT64 operation, one FP64 × FP64 +FP64 operation, 4 parallel TF32 × TF32+FP32 operations, and 16 parallel FP16 × FP16+FP32, BF16 × BF16+FP32, INT16 × INT16+INT32 operations. Although Haica differs A100 Tensor Core [3] in microarchitecture, they support similar operations and achieve similar operation rate, except that TF32 achieves 25% peak performance of FP16 in Haica.

6   Experiment

We implement the logic design of Haica using RTL. Then we verify its correctness using test signal method. We perform module-level test, function point test, and random number test. Results show that our proposed fusion architecture satisfies the correctness requirement. Finally, we evaluate the overhead of Haica using the physical synthesis method. Synopsys DC tool is utilized to analyze the frequency, area, and power consumption. The result is based on a commercial 28nm standard cell library.

Table 2. The overhead of multiple-low-precision FMA.

	Single-half-mixed-precision FMA	Single-precision FMA	Proposed FMA
Supported operations	FP16 × FP16+FP32 INT16 × INT16+INT32	FP32 × FP32+FP32	FP16 × FP16+FP32 BF16 × BF16+FP32 TF32 × TF32+FP32 INT16 × INT16+INT32
Highest frequency	1.35 GHz	1.08 GHz	1.2 GHz
Area (1 GHz)	3632.90 μm² (100%)	5701.72 μm² (156.95%)	4727.94 μm² (130.14%)
Power (1 GHz)	3.9542 mW (100%)	5.5734 mW (140.95%)	6.5702 mW (166.16%)

We first evaluate multiple-low-precision FMA by comparing it against single-precision FMA and single-half-mixed-precision FMA, because 1) our proposed FMA is based on a single-half-mixed-precision FMA, 2) TF32 is supported by the single-precision FMA since TF32 is an alternative to FP32. Note that the single-half-mixed-precision FMA supports INT16 × INT16+INT32, as described in Sect. 5.1. Because our proposed FMA is a component-level design, we use the highest frequency as the metric for performance, as [22] did. Area and power under 1 GHz are used for overhead analysis, and results are normalized to single-half-mixed-precision FMA. The result is shown in Table 2. It can be seen that the frequency of our proposed FMA reaches up to 1.2 GHz, which is slightly lower than single-half-mixed-precision FMA (1.35 GHz), while slightly higher than single-precision FMA (1.08 GHz). Compared to single-half-mixed-precision FMA, our proposed FMA increases area by 30% and power by 66%. Compared to single-precision FMA, the proposed FMA incurs less area overhead but more power overhead because our proposed FMA adds certain control logic to support BF16 and TF32. Experimental results demonstrate that our proposal provides extra supports for BF16 and TF32 with reasonable overhead by taking advantages of fusing technology.

Then we analyze the overhead of the proposed 4 × 4 systolic array (shown in Fig. 7) by comparing it against a basic 4 × 4 systolic array that is composed of 16 single-half-mixed-precision FMAs. Area and power under 1 GHz are used for overhead analysis. The result is shown in Table 3. It shows that our proposed

Table 3. The overhead of proposed systolic array.

	4 × 4 Systolic array	Proposed Systolic array
Supported operations	FP16 × FP16+FP32 INT16 × × INT16+INT32	FP16 × FP16+FP32 BF16 × BF16+FP32 TF32 × TF32+FP32 INT16 × INT16+INT32
Area (1 GHz)	60926.01 μm² (100%)	78462.51 μm² (128.78%)
Power (1 GHz)	53.9944 mW (100%)	83.5463 mW (154.73%)

systolic array increases area by 29% and power by 55% compared to the basic systolic array. The overhead increment is similar to a single FMA scenario (our proposed FMA relative to a single-half-mixed-precision FMA) because FMA is the major unit of a systolic array. Note that we make minor modifications (data width) to the proposed systolic array to make it compatible with other components in Haica. However, the major computing unit—the proposed multiple-low-precision FMA remains unchanged. Thus, the overhead of the systolic array in Haica (result is not shown) is similar as the reported result in Table 3.

Table 4. The overhead of Haica.

	Double-precision FMA +4 × 4 systolic array	Non-fused Haica	Haica
Supporting operations	FP16 × FP16+FP32 FP64 × FP64+FP64 INT64 × INT64 INT16 × INT16+INT32	FP16 × FP16+FP32 BF16 × BF16+FP32 TF32 × TF32+FP32 FP64 × FP64+FP64 INT64 × INT64 INT16 × INT16+INT32	FP16 × FP16+FP32 BF16 × BF16+FP32 TF32 × TF32+FP32 FP64 × FP64+FP64 INT64 × INT64 INT16 × INT16+INT32
Area (1 GHz)	87239.01 μm² (100%)	104775.50 μm² (120.10%)	94106.84 μm² (107.87%)
Power (1 GHz)	58.8452 mW (100%)	88.4068 mW (150.24%)	78.4200 mW (133.26%)

Finally, we evaluate the overhead of Haica by comparing it against a baseline (naive combination of a double-precision FMA and the basic systolic array in Table 3) and a non-fused Haica (naive combination of a double-precision FMA and the proposed systolic array without fusion). For fairness, the double-precision FMA is extended to support INT64 operation. The result is shown in Table 4. It shows that, compared to the baseline, Haica provides extra supports for BF16 and TF32 at the expense of 7.87% area overhead and 33.26% power overhead. Such an overhead is acceptable because the baseline will incur more than 50% area and power overhead if the baseline supports the exact same operations as Haica. Compared to the non-fused Haica, Haica reduces area by 10.18% and power by 11.3% by taking advantages of fusing technology.

Although the above analysis shows that Haica incurs certain area and power overhead than a single FMA, we think that Haica is still cost-effective because modern processors typically integrate multiple FMAs with different precisions to satisfy applications' requirements for varied precisions and exploit component-level parallelism. While, Haica has the capability of supporting mainstream precisions and achieving considerable operation parallelism using just one modified FMA. Compared to multiple independent FMAs, Haica incurs significantly less area and power overhead. For fairness, we do not compare Haica against relevant work listed in Table 1 because aforementioned research supports different precisions as Haica. It is not easy to compare them in a fair manner. In addition, despite tensor core supports similar precisions as Haica, we are still unable to compare Haica with tensor core due to a lack of publicly available documents.

7 Conclusion

To achieve HPC and AI fusion, supporting multiple precisions in a single computing unit is desired. Academia typically aims at modifying a single FMA to support two or more precisions. However, prior works suffer from non-negligible hardware overhead and limited supports for new data formats appeared in AI domain. To address this issue, we propose Haica, a double-precision FMA and low-precision systolic array fused architecture, to support HPC and AI fusion. Evaluation result shows that, compared to the baseline, a naive combination of a double-precision FMA and a basic systolic array, Haica provides extra supports for BF16 and TF32 with only 7.87% area and 33.26% power overhead.

References

1. Arunachalam, V., Raj, A.N.J., Hampannavar, N., Bidul, C.: Efficient dual-precision floating-point fused-multiply-add architecture. Microprocess. Microsyst. **57**, 23–31 (2018)
2. Chen, Z., Wu, T., Liu, X., Zheng, F., Ding, Y., Li, H.: Design and implementation of a multi-precision mixed floating point fused multiply add component. In: Proceedings of HPC China (2018). (in Chinese)
3. Choquette, J., Gandhi, W., Giroux, O., Stam, N., Krashinsky, R.: Nvidia a100 tensor core GPU: performance and innovation. IEEE Micro **41**(2), 29–35 (2021)
4. Dong, L., Wei, F., Xu, K., Liu, S., Zhou, M.: Adaptive multi-compositionality for recursive neural network models. IEEE/ACM Trans. Audio Speech Lang. Process. **24**(3), 422–431 (2015)
5. Haidar, A., Tomov, S., Dongarra, J., Higham, N.J.: Harnessing GPU tensor cores for fast FP16 arithmetic to speed up mixed-precision iterative refinement solvers. In: SC18: International Conference for High Performance Computing, Networking, Storage and Analysis, pp. 603–613. IEEE (2018)
6. Han, Y., Zhang, G.J., Huang, X., Wang, Y.: A moist physics parameterization based on deep learning. J. Adv. Model. Earth Syst. **12**(9), e2020MS002076 (2020)
7. Hokenek, E., Montoye, R.K., Cook, P.W.: Second-generation risc floating point with multiply-add fused. IEEE J. Solid-State Circuits **25**(5), 1207–1213 (1990)

8. Jia, W., et al.: Pushing the limit of molecular dynamics with ab initio accuracy to 100 million atoms with machine learning. In: SC20: International Conference for High Performance Computing, Networking, Storage and Analysis, pp. 1–14. IEEE (2020)

9. Jouppi, N.P., et al.: In-datacenter performance analysis of a tensor processing unit. In: Proceedings of the 44th Annual International Symposium on Computer Architecture, pp. 1–12 (2017)

10. Kalamkar, D., et al.: A study of bfloat16 for deep learning training. arXiv preprint arXiv:1905.12322 (2019)

11. Krizhevsky, A., Sutskever, I., Hinton, G.E.: ImageNet classification with deep convolutional neural networks. In: Advances in Neural Information Processing Systems, vol. 25 (2012)

12. Kumar, V.P., Tsai, Y.C.: Designing linear systolic arrays. J. Parallel Distrib. Comput. **7**(3), 441–463 (1989)

13. Kurth, T., et al.: Exascale deep learning for climate analytics. In: SC18: International Conference for High Performance Computing, Networking, Storage and Analysis, pp. 649–660. IEEE (2018)

14. Lang, T., Bruguera, J.D.: Floating-point fused multiply-add with reduced latency. In: Proceedings. In: IEEE International Conference on Computer Design: VLSI in Computers and Processors, pp. 145–150. IEEE (2002)

15. Mohammadi, F.G., Shenavarmasouleh, F., Amini, M.H., Arabnia, H.R.: Malware detection using artificial bee colony algorithm. In: Adjunct Proceedings of the 2020 ACM International Joint Conference on Pervasive and Ubiquitous Computing and Proceedings of the 2020 ACM International Symposium on Wearable Computers, pp. 568–572 (2020)

16. Rajaraman, V.: IEEE standard for floating point numbers. Resonance **21**(1), 11–30 (2016)

17. Tannenbaum, D.C., Iyer, S.: Logic circuitry configurable to perform 32-bit or dual 16-bit floating-point operations, uS Patent 9,465,578 (11 October 2016)

18. Wu, T.: The research and implementation of high performance vector FMAC unit for LTE. Ph.D. thesis, National University of Defense Technology (2011). (in Chinese)

19. Xiao, Z., Xu, X., Xing, H., Luo, S., Dai, P., Zhan, D.: RTFN: a robust temporal feature network for time series classification. arXiv preprint arXiv:2011.11829 (2020)

20. Xiao, Z., Xu, X., Xing, H., Song, F., Wang, X., Zhao, B.: A federated learning system with enhanced feature extraction for human activity recognition. Knowl.-Based Syst. **229**, 107338 (2021)

21. Zhang, H., Chen, D., Ko, S.B.: Efficient multiple-precision floating-point fused multiply-add with mixed-precision support. IEEE Trans. Comput. **68**(7), 1035–1048 (2019)

22. Zhang, H., Chen, D., Ko, S.B.: New flexible multiple-precision multiply-accumulate unit for deep neural network training and inference. IEEE Trans. Comput. **69**(1), 26–38 (2019)

AOA: Adaptive Overclocking Algorithm on CPU-GPU Heterogeneous Platforms

Zhixin Ou, Juan Chen$^{(\boxtimes)}$, Yuyang Sun, Tao Xu, Guodong Jiang, Zhengyuan Tan, and Xinxin Qi

National University of Defense Technology, Changsha, China
{ouzhixin16,juanchen,sunyuyang,xt.0320,jiangguodong,tanzhengyuan, qixinxin19}@nudt.edu.cn

Abstract. Although GPUs have been used to accelerate various convolutional neural network algorithms with good performance, the demand for performance improvement is still continuously increasing. CPU/GPU overclocking technology brings opportunities for further performance improvement in CPU-GPU heterogeneous platforms. However, CPU/GPU overclocking inevitably increases the power of the CPU/GPU, which is not conducive to energy conservation, energy efficiency optimization, or even system stability. How to effectively constrain the total energy to remain roughly unchanged during the CPU/GPU overclocking is a key issue in designing adaptive overclocking algorithms. There are two key factors during solving this key issue. Firstly, the dynamic power upper bound must be set to reflect the real-time behavior characteristics of the program so that algorithm can better meet the total energy unchanging constraints; secondly, instead of independently overclocking at both CPU and GPU sides, coordinately overclocking on CPU-GPU must be considered to adapt to real-time load balance for higher performance improvement and better energy constraints. This paper proposes an *Adaptive Overclocking Algorithm* (AOA) on CPU-GPU heterogeneous platforms to achieve the goal of performance improvement while the total energy remains roughly unchanged. AOA uses the function F_k to describe the variable power upper bound and introduces the load imbalance factor W to realize the CPU-GPU coordinated overclocking. Through the verification of several types convolutional neural network algorithms on two CPU-GPU heterogeneous platforms (Intel®Xeon E5-2660 & NVIDIA®Tesla K80; Intel®Core™i9-10920X & NIVIDIA®GeForce RTX 2080Ti), AOA achieves an average of 10.7% performance improvement and 4.4% energy savings. To verify the effectiveness of the AOA, we compare AOA with other methods including automatic boost, the highest overclocking and static optimal overclocking.

Keywords: Heterogeneous platform · Overclocking · Performance optimization · Energy consumption

W. Meng et al. (Eds.): ICA3PP 2022, LNCS 13777, pp. 253–272, 2023.
https://doi.org/10.1007/978-3-031-22677-9_14

1   Introduction

Almost all kinds of convolutional neural network algorithms and scientific computing programs generally use GPU for acceleration [4,8]. CPU-GPU heterogeneous platforms are becoming more and more widely used. Both CPU and GPU provide overclocking mechanisms, and moderate overclocking brings opportunities for further performance improvement. Although the CPU has the Intel Turbo Boost Technology [15], and the GPU has the Nvidia GPU Boost Technology [22], automatic overclocking through the system has certain limitations. It is meaningful to consider the goal that how to improve the performance by adaptively overclocking on CPU-GPU heterogeneous platforms while constraining the total energy consumption unchanged.

Existing researches on overclocking algorithms have targeted both homogeneous and heterogeneous platforms. One of the state-of-art algorithms for homogeneous platforms is to set a static frequency upper bound [38], which overclocks the frequency to the given upper bound in active state. Another existing method is overclocking under power constrain [14]. When the processor utilization is high and current power does not reach the power upper bound, the frequency keeps increasing. However, how to control the overall energy consumption of a certain task or program is a problem, especially for heterogeneous platforms with fewer overclocking algorithms [31]. A common way to improve CPU-GPU energy efficiency is to adjust CPU and GPU frequency on heterogeneous platforms. During the entire frequency adjustment process, the CPU and GPU are usually regarded as a whole for consistent frequency adjustment [36]. When it comes to CPU-GPU frequency adjustment on heterogeneous platforms, load balance between CPU and GPU is one of the key issues to consider. Frequency adjustment brings greater challenges to load balance.

For overclocking on CPU-GPU heterogeneous platforms, a commonly used method is overclocking under a given power upper bound, which achieves the purpose of improving performance while satisfying the total energy constraint. How to effectively keep the total energy unchanged during the CPU/GPU overclocking process is a key issue, which mainly includes two key factors.

- The static power upper bound is difficult to reflect the individual differences in performance and power of programs' behavior, which brings problems to improving program performance and the accuracy of power control. In addition to CPU/GPU frequency, the real-time usage of the program on the processor (such as instructions per cycle, processor core utilization, etc.) can also affect instantaneous processor power. Therefore, *power upper bound must be dynamic, not static.*
- Overclocking may cause or even aggravate the load imbalance of CPU-GPU heterogeneous platforms, thereby affecting performance improvement and total energy constrain. Independent overclocking of the CPU and GPU may cause the originally balanced load to become unbalanced, which is detrimental to our goals. When the CPU-GPU load imbalance increases, the performance has room for improvement, because the performance of heterogeneous

computing depends on the side with longer running time. Also, additional energy is consumed due to waiting. Therefore, *CPU-GPU overclocking must be coordinated, considering real-time load balance.*

Based on the two key factors in the design of overclocking algorithms, the solutions in this article are as follows.

- For the first key factor, turn the *static* power upper bound of overclocking into the adaptive *variable* power upper bound. The overclocking algorithm sets the initial power upper bound k_0 by calculating the expected power upper bound according to the characteristics of the usage of various programs on a given platform. In the dynamic overclocking process, the power upper bound k is adaptively adjusted to achieve precise real-time power control for individual program characteristics, according to the real-time usage of the current program on the CPU and GPU.
- For the second key factor, the load imbalance factor W is used to characterize whether the program is in the load balance state or load imbalance state, and to further adjust the overclocking range after normal overclocking for a further performance improvement.

In summary, this paper has the following three contributions.

1. Aiming at the challenge of constraining the total energy in overclocking, we find two key factors that affect adaptive overclocking: dynamic variable power upper bound k and coordinated overclocking (load imbalance factor W) at both sides of the CPU and GPU.
2. We propose an Adaptive Overclocking Algorithm on CPU-GPU Heterogeneous platforms (AOA), which first adjusts the dynamic power upper bound k of CPU and GPU separately according to the real-time operation of the current program on the CPU-GPU heterogeneous platforms; and introduce load imbalance factor W to coordinate overclocking range by improving load imbalance phenomenon for further performance improvement and better total energy constrain.
3. AOA is implemented and verified on two heterogeneous platforms (Intel®Xeon E5-2660 & NVIDIA®Tesla K80; Intel®Core™i9-10920X & NIVIDIA®GeForce RTX 2080Ti) using convolutional neural network algorithms. The experimental results show that the AOA improves the performance by 10.7% on average and 4.4% energy savings. To verify the effectiveness of the AOA, we compared AOA with methods including automatic boost, the highest overclocking and static optimal overclocking.

The structure of this article is as follows: Sect. 2 introduces the background and related work of overclocking methods on heterogeneous platforms. Section 3 illustrates the design ideas of overclocking algorithms and the description of AOA. Section 4 introduces the experimental platform and the experimental results of AoA on two heterogeneous platforms. Section 5 discusses the impact of two key factors on AOA effect. Section 6 is the concluding remarks.

2   Related Work

2.1   DNN in CPU-GPU Platforms

The heterogenous architecture becomes widely used in high performance computing [18,35], which is inseperable from the requirement for boost performance (high accuracy and fast training speed) of DNNs. While convolutional neural network (CNN) is one of the most successful deep neural network (DNN) models and have been applied in various fields such as computer vision and speech recognition [12,20], the cost of high power and energy attracts widespread attention [21,26,32].

Th inspires researches on energy efficiency of DNN models on CPU-GPU platforms. Sun et al. study the performance, power and energy characteristics of CNNs when running on CPU and GPU [29]. Rodrigues et al. [25] propose an evaluation framework that combines standard deep learning frameworks such as Caffe [17] and cuDNNv5 [8] to measure the performance and energy of DNNs. Mittal et al. [21] survey on methods for analyzing and improving GPU energy efficiency.

2.2   Energy Efficiency Optimization Methods

Existing energy efficiency optimization methods for heterogeneous platforms mainly have two types of ideas. One type of methods to improve energy efficiency is to reduce power or energy consumption while maintaining performance, which is realized by dynamic voltage frequency scaling (DVFS, usually frequency reduction). Yao [37] study the energy efficiency of CNN on high performance GPUs. Through a large number of comparative experiments on GPU architecture, DVFS settings and DNN configuration, they studied the impact of GPU DVFS on deep learning energy consumption and performance based on experience. Tang et al. [30] also research on the impact of GPU DVFS on the energy and performance of deep learning. However, reduced frequencies sometimes mean slower system configurations, which to some extent violate latency and throughput requirements of heterogeneous platforms in the context of high performance computing.

Another type of methods is to improve performance while controlling power and energy consumption, which is mainly achieved by overclocking. Existing works research on the effect of overclocking on performance [31]. Sasikala et al. [24] exploit the techniques of overclocking and throttling to enhance the performance while maintaining the system reliability. Wu et al. [33,34] improves energy efficiency by processor overclocking and memory frequency scaling. Yang et al. [36] treat the CPU and GPU as a whole for consistent frequency modulation. However, there are significant imbalance in both frequency and computing ability of CPUs and GPUs, which is ignored by consistent frequency modulation.

Researches show that load imbalance between CPU and GPU in some programs (such as BFS) also has important impact on performance [10]. Acun et al. [5] agree that performance inhomogeneity in power constrained environments drastically limits supercomputing performance. Chen et al. [7] investigate the optimization possibilities of the performance of parallel systems utilizing the time-dimension communication features. Chasapis et al. [6] research on the effect of manufacturing variability on computing ability. Gholkar et al. [11] show that a power capped job suffers from performance variation of otherwise identical processors leading to overall sub-optimal performance.

3   AOA Design

3.1   Key Issue and Key Factors in AOA

Key Issue - Energy Constraint. Overclocking brings performance improvement together with inevitable increase in instantaneous power, which makes the total energy likely to increase or decrease. If the total energy can be restrained from increasing during the overclocking process, it will not only save the energy consumption of the task ($E = P \cdot t$), but also improve the energy efficiency ($EDP = E \cdot t$). *How to effectively constrain the total energy unchanged in the overclocking process is a key issue in the overclocking algorithm design.*

Furthermore, dynamic overclocking is more beneficial to meet the constant total energy constraint than static overclocking, so we adopt dynamic overclocking instead of static overclocking.

The algorithm is designed with the total energy unchanged as the constraint. There are usually three control conditions: controlling the total energy unchanged, controlling frequency not exceed the max frequency, and controlling power not exceed the power upper bound.

There are some problems in designing dynamic overclocking by controlling the total energy unchanged. Since the total energy is the accumulation of power over a period of time, the total energy consumption of the program cannot be obtained before the program finishes running. Therefore, it is not possible to design dynamic overclocking by controlling the total energy unchanged in the algorithm. Setting the power upper bound for overclocking can avoid the above problem. The power can be obtained in real-time during the running of the program. Compared with the total energy, power upper bound can be directly used as a constraint that is easier to control dynamic overclocking.

There are also some problems in controlling the frequency not to exceed the upper bound. Although the performance improvement goal can be achieved by using frequency as the control condition, it is difficult to meet the constraint condition of constant total energy. The reason is that in addition to frequency, the real-time occupation factors of the processor by the program (such as instructions per cycle, processor core utilization, etc.) also affect instantaneous power. The formula (1) reflects the relationship between the processor clock frequency f and the instantaneous processor power P:

$$P_{total} = \alpha C V^2 f + P_{static} \tag{1}$$

where α is the CMOS circuit switching factor that reflects the busyness of the processor. As shown in Table 1, taking platform A as an example, when the CPU frequency f is at 2.6 GHz, the power values under 10% and 88% utilization are 60W and 140W respectively, with a difference of 133%. Compared with controlling frequency not exceeding max frequency, controlling instantaneous power not exceeding a given power upper bound is more helpful to achieve the goal of remaining the total energy unchanged.

Key Factors - Power Upper Bound and Load Balance

Key factor 1: The power upper bound must be dynamic, not static.

In the process of dynamic overclocking, if the upper bound of power is fixed to a value, that is not the most appropriate because it will bring difficulties to the control of total energy. We define a variable upper bound of dynamic power kP that is a variable parameter and different from the hardware power capping. Among them, P is the power value of the processor at the default frequency f_0. Considering that the value of P has a certain fluctuation relative to the same frequency f_0 under actual conditions, we take the typical power value of the processor as P. k is the Power Upper Bound Factor, which satisfies $1 \leq k \leq 1.2$. When $k = 1$, it means no overclocking; when $k = 1.2$, it means that the processor power after overclocking cannot be greater than 1.2 times of P. 1.2 is an empirical value obtained from historical experiments on the platform, and the value setting varies slightly on different platforms.

The design of the dynamic power upper bound is based on two considerations. One is the determination of the initial value of the overclocking power coefficient, and the other is the dynamic change process of the overclocking power coefficient.

Define k_0 as the initial value of variable power upper bound factor. By running various test programs on a given hardware platform (considering the balance of program feature distribution), the power and energy results of the processor under different occupancy conditions can be obtained, and then the power upper bound under the constraint of constant total energy can be obtained. The overclocking power coefficient k_0 is determined from this.

On the basis of k_0, the variable overclocking power coefficient k_t at time t is calculated by the function F_k.

$$k_t \leftarrow F_k(k_0, U_t) \tag{2}$$

where U_t represents the real-time processor occupancy of the program at time t, which is calculated according to processor utilization *utilization_percentage*, i.e. $U_t = utilization\_percentage \times f$.

Particularly, on the GPU side, the function of overclocking power coefficient is as follows.

$$k_t^{GPU} \leftarrow F_k^{GPU}(k_0, U_t^{GPU}) \tag{3}$$

On the CPU side, the function of overclocking power coefficient is as follows.

$$k_t^{CPU} \leftarrow F_k^{CPU}(k_0, U_t^{CPU}) \tag{4}$$

Key factor 2: Overclocking at both sides of the CPU and GPU must be coordinated, and real-time load balancing must be considered.

In order to judge whether the program is in a load balance state during the running process, the Load Imbalance Factor W and the threshold γ are introduced. Load imbalance factor at time t is denoted as W_t where $W_t = \frac{U^{GPU} - U^{CPU}}{U^{GPU} + U^{CPU}}$. As shown in Fig. 1, the program running on the CPU-GPU heterogeneous platform may be in the load balance state (slash fill area, $|W_t| \leq \gamma$) or in the load imbalance state (color fill area, $|W_t| > \gamma$).

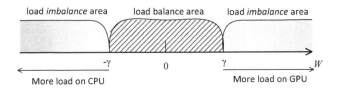

Fig. 1. Introduce load imbalance factor W to describe load balance area and load imbalance area (Color figure online)

When the program is in the load imbalance area, adjust the CPU and GPU frequencies according to the load balance adjustment function F_f to make the program in the load balance area again.

$$(f^{CPU}, f^{GPU}) \leftarrow F_f(f^{CPU}, f^{GPU}, W_t) \tag{5}$$

When $W > \gamma$, the workload on GPU side is heavier, the function F_f increases the GPU frequency f^{GPU} or decreases the CPU frequency f^{CPU}, where $f_{base}^{GPU} \leq f^{GPU} \leq f_{max}^{GPU}$, $f_{base}^{CPU} \leq f^{CPU} \leq f_{max}^{CPU}$, as follows.

$$\begin{cases} f^{GPU} \leftarrow f^{GPU} + \Delta f^{GPU}, & if \ (f^{GPU} + \Delta f^{GPU} \leq f_{max}^{GPU}) \\ f^{CPU} \leftarrow f^{CPU} - \Delta f^{CPU}, & else \ if \ (f^{CPU} - \Delta f^{CPU} \geq f_{base}^{CPU}) \\ (f^{CPU}, f^{GPU}) \ unchanged, & else \end{cases} \tag{6}$$

When $W < \gamma$, the workload on CPU side is heavier, the function F_f increases the CPU frequency f^{CPU} or decreases the GPU frequency f^{GPU}. The overclocking range is the same as before and the details are as follows.

$$\begin{cases} f^{CPU} \leftarrow f^{CPU} + \Delta f^{CPU}, & if \ (f^{CPU} + \Delta f^{CPU} \leq f_{max}^{CPU}) \\ f^{GPU} \leftarrow f^{GPU} - \Delta f^{GPU}, & else \ if \ (f^{GPU} - \Delta f^{GPU} \geq f_{base}^{GPU}) \\ (f^{CPU}, f^{GPU}) \ unchanged, & else \end{cases} \tag{7}$$

3.2 Description of AOA

The flowchart of the Adaptive Overclocking Algorithm (AOA) is shown in Fig. 2. Among them, the variable power upper bound factors on CPU and GPU are denoted as $(k_{t+1}^{CPU}, k_{t+1}^{GPU})$. Based on the tth overclocking cycle CPU and GPU usage ratio U_t^{CPU} and U_t^{GPU}, k_{t+1}^{CPU} and k_{t+1}^{GPU} are updated on CPU and GPU, respectively. (corresponding to Factor 1, represented by blue and yellow colors in Fig. 2).

The gray box part is dynamic overclocking under variable power upper bound power control. On the basis of the normal CPU and GPU overclocking (represented by blue and yellow colors respectively), the frequency values at both CPU and GPU are further updated according to the load balance factor W_t (f_{t+1}^{CPU}, f_{t+1}^{GPU}), that is, CPU-GPU cooperative overclocking (corresponding to Factor 2, blue and yellow mixed colors).

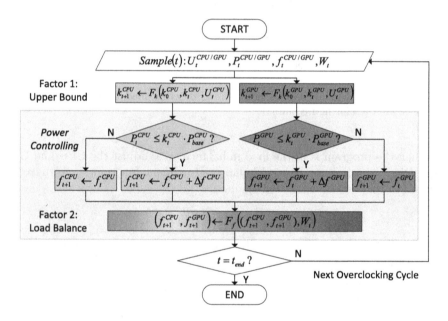

Fig. 2. Flow graph of the adaptive overclocking algorithm. (Color figure online)

The detailed description of the algorithm sees Algorithm 1.

Dynamic overclocking will cause additional time overhead. We evaluate the time overhead incurred by one overclocking operation or frequency scaling operation. Manually insert N times of overclocking or frequency scaling operations, then run the same program, and get the execution time of the program with the N times of overclocking, denoted as T. The default time of the program without overclocking is denoted as T_0. Comparing T and T_0 can obtain the additional time overhead due to the N times of overclocking or frequency scaling operations. Finally, the time overhead for a single overclocking or frequency scaling is calculated that is about 4 ms.

Algorithm 1. Adaptive Overclocking Algorithm

Input: program, k_0, $P_{base}^{CPU/GPU}$, $f_{base}^{CPU/GPU}$, $f_{max}^{CPU/GPU}$, $\Delta f^{CPU/GPU}$.
Output: k_t, $f_t^{CPU/GPU}$ $(t = 1, 2, 3..., t_{end})$.
  1: $t \leftarrow 1, k_t \leftarrow k_0$;
  2: **for** each overclocking cycle t $(t = 1, 2, 3, ..., t_{end})$ **do**
  3:    Sample data: $U_t^{CPU/GPU}$, $P_t^{CPU/GPU}$, $f_t^{CPU/GPU}$, W_t;
  4:    Output k_t and $f_t^{CPU/GPU}$;
  5:    Update   Power   Upper   Bound   Factor $k_{i+1}^{CPU/GPU}$ $\leftarrow$
        $F_k(k_0^{CPU/GPU}, k_t^{CPU/GPU}, U_t^{CPU/GPU})$;
  6:    **if** $(P_t^{CPU/GPU} \leq k_t^{CPU/GPU} \times P_{base}^{CPU/GPU})$ **then**
  7:        $f_{t+1}^{CPU/GPU} \leftarrow f_t^{CPU/GPU} + \Delta f^{CPU/GPU}$;
  8:    **else**
  9:        $f_{t+1}^{CPU/GPU} \leftarrow f_t^{CPU/GPU}$;
 10:    **end if**
 11:    $(f_{t+1}^{CPU}, f_{t+1}^{GPU}) \leftarrow F_f((f_t^{CPU}, f_t^{GPU}), W_t)$;
 12: **end for**
 13: **return** k_t, $f_t^{CPU/GPU}$

4   Experimental Results and Analysis

4.1   Experiment Environment

Heterogeneous Platform Hardware Environment. The experiments are carried out on two CPU-GPU heterogeneous platforms, called platform A and platform B, respectively. The specific configuration is shown in Table 1.

Table 1. Configuration parameters of platforms A and B

Environment	Platform A		Platform B	
	CPU	GPU	CPU	GPU
Processor type	Intel® Xeon E5-2600 v3	NVIDIA® Tesla K80	Intel® Core™ i9-10920X	NVIDIA® GeForce RTX 2080Ti
Frequency	2.6 GHz	575 MHz	3.5 GHz	1455 MHz
Power	105 W	150 W	165 W	285 W
#cores	10	2496	12	4352
#CPU (#GPU)	2	4	1	2
Hyperthreading	Disable	–	Disable	–
Auto-boost	Supported	Supported	Supported	Not available

Software Environment

Dataset and Benchmark. As for data set, this article uses ImageNet [9], a very famous data set in the field of image vision (CV). ImageNet is a recognition system that simulates human beings and is currently the world's largest database in the field of image recognition. After being proposed in 2009, ImageNet triggered the ILSVRC (ImageNet Large-Scale Visual Recognition Challenge), the most influential competition in the field of deep learning in the following years.

As for benchmark, this article has selected several classic CNN models [27] that have won the previous ILSVRC competitions, including alexnet [19], resnet [13] and vgg [28]. The specific program code is officially provided by pytorch on GitHub [23].

Monitoring Tools. On heterogeneous platforms, the power and performance indicators on CPU and those on GPU need to be monitored separately.

The power of the CPU is monitored by the `dstat` [1] tool. `dstat` allows users to view all your system resources in real time, and provides detailed and selective information, such as power/energy-pkg. The performance monitoring counters (PMC) of the CPU is monitored by `perf` [2]. `perf` is an analyzer tool that can abstract CPU hardware differences in Linux performance measurement and provides a simple command line interface based on the perf_events interface exported by the latest version of the Linux kernel.

The performance and power of the GPU are monitored through the NVIDIA System Management Interface (`nvidia-smi` [3]). `nvidia-smi` is a command line utility, based on the NVIDIA Management Library (NVML), designed to help manage and monitor NVIDIA GPU devices.

Parameter Settings. According to the AOA in Fig. 2, the parameters involved in the paper mainly include the variable power upper bound factor k, the load imbalance threshold γ and the frequency gear Δf. In the experiment, $k_0 = 1.1$, and $\gamma = 0.2$.

Table 2. Frequency gear settings of platforms A and B

Gears	Platform A (MHz)				Platform B (MHz)			
	CPU	Δf^{CPU}	GPU	Δf^{GPU}	CPU	Δf^{CPU}	GPU	Δf^{GPU}
0	2100	–	575	–	2700	–	1350	–
1	2200	100	614	39	2800	100	1365	15
2	2300	100	653	39	3000	200	1380	15
3	2400	100	692	39	3200	200	1395	15
4	2500	100	732	40	3300	100	1410	15
5	2600	100	771	39	3500	200	1425	15
6	–	–	810	39	–	–	–	–
7	-	–	849	39	–	–	–	–

The setting of frequency gear depends on the support of CPU and GPU hardware platform (see Sect. 4.1). For CPU frequency modulation, Intel provides the official overclocking tool XTU [16] for Intel Turbo Boost Technology.

However, the manual mentions that XTU only supports consumer-level products, not enterprise-level servers. The CPU frequency is set by the 'cpupower frequency-set' command.

For CPU frequency setting, Platform A uses 1350 MHz as the default CPU frequency, and sets up five CPU frequencies at 100 MHz intervals as overclocking options; Platform B uses 2.7 GHz as the default CPU frequency, and sets it upwards [2.8 GHz, 3.0 GHz, 3.2 GHz, 3.3 GHz, 3.5 GHz] as CPU overclocking options.

For GPU frequency setting, nvidia-smi provides a list of core frequencies supported by the GPU. Platform A uses 575 MHz as the default GPU frequency, and sets up seven GPU frequencies at an interval of about 39 MHz as overclocking options; Platform B uses 1350 MHz as the default GPU frequency, and sets up seven frequencies at 15 MHz intervals as overclocking options.

In summary, we set the CPU/GPU frequency modulation gear Δf in the experiment as shown in Table 2.

Comparisons. Other methods compared to the AOA method are shown below.

default: The default frequency is fixedly set to gear 0 in Table 2.
static$_{max}$: The static$_{max}$ frequency is fixedly set to the max gear in Table 2.
static$_{best}$: The static$_{best}$ frequency is fixedly set by running the program at each frequency combination once, and selecting the configuration corresponding to the result with the best energy efficiency as the static$_{best}$ frequency.
auto: The automatic frequency is set by official overclocking tools, XTU [16] for Intel Turbo Boost Technology and nvidia-smi for GPU overclocking.

4.2 AOA Overall Result

This section compares the results of AOA and default, and gives the AOA on utilization $U^{CPU/GPU}$, power $P^{CPU/GPU}$, and frequency $f^{CPU/GPU}$ result of platform A. In this chapter, the default CPU and GPU frequency is set to gear 0 in Table 2.

On platform A, the result of alexnet is shown in Fig. 3, the result of resnet is shown in Fig. 4, and the result of vgg is shown in Fig. 5. The two semi-axes of the vertical axis in the figure are both positive axes, the upper half represents the result on the GPU side, and the lower half represents the result on the CPU side.

Taking resnet as an example in Fig. 3. From the perspective of change trend, due to the design of epoch in the CNN algorithm, its utilization and power reflect periodicity in the time dimension. Comparing the results of AOA (solid black line) and default (dashed gray), we can find that the utilization value of a single epoch in alexnet has little change (in Fig. 3-a); but in terms of running time, AOA is overall shorter than default. From Fig. 3-b, it can be further seen that the change trend of power and utilization is consistent, and the power curve of AOA is slightly higher than the default. This increase in power is caused by the increase in frequency.

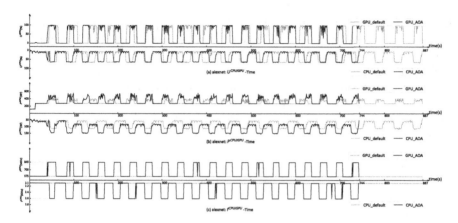

Fig. 3. $U^{CPU/GPU}$, $P^{CPU/GPU}$ and $f^{CPU/GPU}$ for alex in default frequency and AOA on platform A.

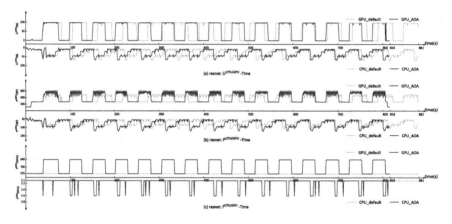

Fig. 4. $U^{CPU/GPU}$, $P^{CPU/GPU}$ and $f^{CPU/GPU}$ for resnet in default frequency and AOA on platform A.

Figure 3-c shows the adaptive dynamic adjustment effect of AOA on frequency. Corresponding to the utilization rate and power diagram, it can be found that when the utilization rate and power increase, AOA automatically increases the frequency according to the algorithm flow (Fig. 2). When the utilization rate and power decrease, the AOA automatically increases the frequency. Adapt to lower frequency.

On platform A, comparing AOA and default, the performance of alexnet is increased by 7.8%, and the energy is reduced by about 11%; the performance of resnet is increased by 8.3%, and the energy is increased by about 0.2%; the performance of vgg is increased by 16.1%, and the energy is reduced by 2.5%. The experimental results have reached the expected goal of the algorithm design, which is to improve the performance under the constraint of constant total

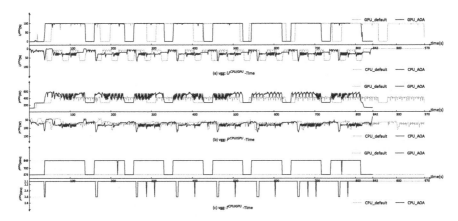

Fig. 5. $U^{CPU/GPU}$, $P^{CPU/GPU}$ and $f^{CPU/GPU}$ for vgg in default frequency and AOA on platform A.

energy. It is worth noting that the reduced energy can actually be used to further improve performance, and the overclocking frequency supported by the platform in the experiment has reached the upper bound.

Due to space limitations, the results on platform B are shown in Table 4. On platform B, it is difficult to increase energy efficiency because the power of NVIDIA GeForce RTX 2080Ti increases rapidly when the frequency overclocks slightly. Comparing AOA with default, even though the average performance is increased by 1.5%, and the average energy is increased by about 3.5%, AOA performs better in constraining total energy compared to max frequency.

4.3   Comparison with Other Methods

Platform a Comparison Results. This section compares the energy and performance between AOA and other methods, including default (frequency with gear 0), static max frequency (static$_{max}$), static best frequency (static$_{best}$) and automatic overclocking (auto).

The detailed comparison result on platform A is shown in Table 3. The calculation of Energy 'savings' and Time 'improvement' in Table 3 is as follow: $savings = \left(1 - \frac{E_{method}}{E_{default}}\right) \times 100\%$; $improvement = \left(1 - \frac{T_{method}}{T_{default}}\right) \times 100\%$.

As for comparison with the maximum frequency, the method for determining the maximum frequency is to set the maximum frequency on the CPU side and GPU side respectively.

As for comparison with the static optimal frequency, the method for determining the static optimal frequency is: according to setting multiple sets of static CPU-GPU frequencies, a set of results with the best performance under the constraint of not increasing the total energy is obtained. According to experimental results, in static frequency modulation, when the frequencies on both CPU and

GPU are set to the maximum value, the performance improvement goal can be best met under the energy constraint.

Moreover, we compares the energy efficiency of AOA and automatic over-clocking technology of CPU-GPU heterogeneous platforms. The method of automatic overclocking is: turn on Intel Turbo Boost Technology [16] on CPU, and turn on Nvidia GPU Boost Technology [22] on GPU.

Table 3. Comparison of AOA and other methods on platform A

AOA vs Others		alexnet	resnet	vgg	AVE
Energy (J) [savings]	Default	366068.37	403126.65	438716.4	402637.14
		[0.00%]	[0.00%]	[0.00%]	[0.00%]
	$static_{max}$	339484.11	430984.6	448662.53	406377.08
		[7.26%]	[−6.91%]	[−2.27%]	[−0.64%]
	$static_{best}$	339484.11	403126.65	431870.19	391493.65
		[7.26%]	[0.00%]	[1.56%]	[2.94%]
	auto	358028.78	419412.02	460568.18	412669.66
		[2.20%]	[−4.04%]	[−4.98%]	[−2.27%]
	AOA	326077.16	403948.64	428037.8	386021.20
		[10.92%]	[−0.20%]	[2.43%]	[4.38%]
Time (s) [improvement]	Default	888	908	1002	932.67
		[0.00%]	[0.00%]	[0.00%]	[0.00%]
	$static_{max}$	728	822	779	776.33
		[18.02%]	[9.47%]	[22.26%]	[16.58%]
	$static_{best}$	728	908	832	822.67
		[18.02%]	[0.00%]	[16.97%]	[11.66%]
	auto	723	755	779	752.33
		[18.58%]	[16.85%]	[22.26%]	[19.23%]
	AOA	819	833	841	831.00
		[7.77%]	[8.26%]	[16.07%]	[10.70%]
Freq (MHz) $[f^{CPU}, f^{GPU}]$	Default	[2100,575]	[2100,575]	[2100,575]	–
	$static_{max}$	[2600,849]	[2600,849]	[2600,849]	–
	$static_{best}$	[2600,849]	[2100,575]	[2400,771]	–
	Auto	[Turbo Boost, GPU Boost]			
	AOA	Dynamic adjust			

Platform B Comparison Results. The detailed comparison result on platform B is shown in Table 4.

Table 4. Comparison of AOA and other methods on platform B

AOA vs Others		alexnet	resnet	vgg	AVE
Energy (J) [savings]	Default	140507.8	172697.6	329068	214091.13
		[0.00%]	[0.00%]	[0.00%]	[0.00%]
	static$_{max}$	141491.1	186065.9	338351	221969.33
		[−0.70%]	[−7.74%]	[−2.82%]	[−3.75%]
	auto	Not available			
	AOA	143051.8	179545.8	342651	221749.53
		[−1.81%]	[−3.97%]	[−4.13%]	[−3.30%]
Time (s) [improvement]	default	606	532	1106	748.00
		[0.00%]	[0.00%]	[0.00%]	[0.00%]
	static$_{max}$	588	522	1069	726.33
		[2.97%]	[1.88%]	[3.35%]	[2.73%]
	auto	Not available			
	AOA	600	533	1077	736.66667
		[0.99%]	[−0.19%]	[2.62%]	[1.14%]
Freq (MHz) [f^{CPU}, f^{GPU}]	Default	[2700,1350]			
	static$_{max}$	[3500,1455]			
	Auto	Not available			
	AOA	Dynamic adjust			

Similar to the experimental setup of platform A, we also compared the effects of default, auto, static$_{max}$ and AOA of CNNs on platform B. We got the best results when using vgg as a neural network model. Compared with the benchmark setting, AOA has a performance improvement of 2.62% but caused a 4.13% increase in energy consumption; on the alexnet network, AOA reduces energy by 1.81%, but it brings a 1% performance loss; AOA does not work well on resnet and does not cause performance improvement, but it increases energy consumption by 3.97%.

As a result, the energy efficiency optimization effect of the AOA algorithm on platform A is better than that on platform B. Besides CPU itself, there are many factors that determine the performance of the CPU, such as the speed of the hard disk, the size of the memory, and the data throughput of the interconnection network, are all important factors that restrict the performance of the processor. As a server platform, platform A has higher reliability and performance of matching facilities than platform B, which is a computer host. Therefore, the performance improvement from overbanding is better than that of platform B. And the CPU and GPU power consumption of platform A is lower than that of platform B, as shown in the Table 1, the impact of overclocking on power consumption is lower than that of platform B. Therefore, the energy efficiency optimization effect of platform B is not as good as that of platform A.

5 Discussion for Key Factors

This section considers the evaluation of the key factors involved in AOA (see Sect. 3.1). Consider the energy constraint and performance improvement effect of the AOA algorithm when the dynamic power upper limit factor k and the load imbalance factor W change.

5.1 Impact of Factor 1: The Power Upper Bound Must Be Dynamic, Not Static

This section shows that the dynamic variable power upper limit k is necessary to meet the constraint of no increase in total energy. The variable power upper limit factor defined by AOA is based on the initial value k_0, and changes within a certain range according to the variable power upper bound function F_k according to the U_t obtained during the sampling period. The result is shown in Table 5.

Table 5. Evaluation on Parameter k

Parameter k		alexnet	resnet	vgg
Energy(J) [savings]	Default	366068.4	403126.6	438716.4
		[0.00%]	[0.00%]	[0.00%]
	k = 1.1	382594.0	437027.9	457669.4
		[−4.51%]	[−8.41%]	[−4.32%]
	k = 1.15	362765.6	436204.3	458734.5
		[0.90%]	[−8.20%]	[−4.56%]
	aoa	326077.2	403948.6	428037.8
		[11.92%]	[−0.20%]	[2.44%]
Time(s) [improvement]	Default	888	908	1002
		[0.00%]	[0.00%]	[0.00%]
	k = 1.1	862	861	825
		[2.70%]	[4.19%]	[16.67%]
	k = 1.15	819	833	841
		[2.93%]	[5.18%]	[17.66%]
	aoa	837	835	816
		[7.77%]	[8.26%]	[16.07%]

5.2 Impact of Factor 2: Overclocking at both Ends of the CPU and GPU Must Be Coordinated, and Real-Time Load Balancing Must be Considered

The load imbalance factor W defined by AOA mainly affects the result of AOA frequency modulation through the function F_f. According to the formula 5 of the function F_f, when the maximum/small frequency changes, it will affect the frequency modulation direction of AOA for load imbalance. In the experiment, the default frequency is always used as $f_{min}^{CPU/GPU}$. When $f_{max}^{CPU/GPU}$ is set to a small value, $f_t^{CPU/GPU}$ is easier to reach the upper limit judgment condition, and then the direction of further frequency modulation is changed from increasing the local frequency value to decreasing Frequency value at the other end. The influence of the maximum frequency change is shown in Table 6.

Table 6. Evaluation on parameter f_{max}

Parameter $[f_{max}^{CPU}, f_{max}^{GPU}]$		alexnet	resnet	vgg
Energy(J) [savings]	Default	366068.4	403126.6	438716.4
		[0.00%]	[0.00%]	[0.00%]
	AOA[2400,771]	395969.9	432592.5	454511.72
		[−8.16%]	[−7.31%]	[−3.60%]
	AOA[2600,849]	326077.2	403948.6	428037.8
		[11.02%]	[−0.20]	[2.44%]
Time(s) [improved]	Default	888	908	1002
		[0.00%]	[0.00%]	[0.00%]
	AOA[2400,771]	898	867	824
		[−1.13%]	[4.51%]	[17.76%]
	AOA[2600,849]	819	833	841
		[7.77%]	[8.25%]	[16.07%]

6 Conclusion

Although GPUs have been used to accelerate various convolutional neural network algorithms with good performance, the demand for performance improvement is still continuously increasing. CPU/GPU overclocking brings opportunities for further performance improvement in the CPU-GPU heterogeneous platform. How to effectively constrain the total energy to remain roughly unchanged during the CPU/GPU overclocking is a key issue in designing adaptive overclocking algorithms.

This paper proposes an *Adaptive Overclocking Algorithm (AOA)* on the CPU-GPU heterogeneous platform to achieve the goal of performance improvement while the total energy remains roughly unchanged. AOA uses the function F_k to describe the variable power upper bound, which embeds real-time CPU and GPU usage information of the program, and introduces a load imbalance factor W to realize the CPU-GPU coordinated overclocking. Through the verification of a convolutional neural network program on two CPU-GPU heterogeneous platforms, AOA achieved an average of 10.7% performance improvement, while 4.4% energy saved on platform A. Also, we compared AOA with other three methods, including programs with static max frequency, programs with static best frequency and automatic overclocking. The comparison results show that AOA performs the best with regard to the goal of improving performance while constraining total energy.

References

1. OL. http://dag.wiee.rs/home-made/dstat/. Accessed Dec 2021
2. Linux kernel profiling with perf. OL. https://perf.wiki.kernel.org/index.php/Tutorial. Accessed Dec 2021
3. Nvidia system management interface. OL. https://developer.nvidia.com/nvidia-system-management-interface. Accessed Dec 2021
4. Abadi, M., et al.: Tensorflow: large-scale machine learning on heterogeneous distributed systems. arXiv abs/1603.04467 (2016)
5. Acun, B., Miller, P., Kale, L.V.: Variation among processors under turbo boost in HPC systems. In: Proceedings of the 2016 International Conference on Supercomputing. ICS 2016. Association for Computing Machinery, New York (2016). https://doi.org/10.1145/2925426.2926289, https://doi-org-s.nudtproxy.yitlink.com/10.1145/2925426.2926289
6. Chasapis, D., Moretó, M., Schulz, M., Rountree, B., Valero, M., Casas, M.: Power efficient job scheduling by predicting the impact of processor manufacturing variability. In: Proceedings of the ACM International Conference on Supercomputing. ICS 2019, pp. 296–307. Association for Computing Machinery, New York (2019). https://doi.org/10.1145/3330345.3330372, https://doi-org-s.nudtproxy.yitlink.com/10.1145/3330345.3330372
7. Chen, J., et al.: Analyzing time-dimension communication characterizations for representative scientific applications on supercomputer systems. Front. Comp. Sci. **13**(6), 1228–1242 (2019)
8. Chetlur, S., et al.: CUDNN: efficient primitives for deep learning. arXiv abs/1410.0759 (2014)
9. Deng, J., Dong, W., Socher, R., Li, L.J., Li, K., Fei-Fei, L.: ImageNet: a large-scale hierarchical image database. In: 2009 IEEE Conference on Computer Vision and Pattern Recognition, pp. 248–255 (2009). https://doi.org/10.1109/CVPR.2009.5206848
10. Gad, E.A.: A work-stealing for dynamic workload balancing an CPU-GPU heterogeneous computing platforms. Thesis (2017). http://www.pqdtcn.com.nudtproxy.yitlink.com:80/thesisDetails/46952B07E4A7CC0D8C9AB6B408B99235
11. Gholkar, N., Mueller, F., Rountree, B.: Power tuning HPC jobs on power-constrained systems. In: 2016 International Conference on Parallel Architecture and Compilation Techniques (PACT), pp. 179–190 (2016). https://doi.org/10.1145/2967938.2967961
12. guassic: Text classification with CNN and RNN. https://github.com/gaussic/text-classification-cnn-rnn
13. He, K., Zhang, X., Ren, S., Sun, J.: Deep residual learning for image recognition. In: 2016 IEEE Conference on Computer Vision and Pattern Recognition (CVPR), pp. 770–778 (2016). https://doi.org/10.1109/CVPR.2016.90

14. Inadomi, Y., et al.: Analyzing and mitigating the impact of manufacturing variability in power-constrained supercomputing. In: Proceedings of the International Conference for High Performance Computing, Networking, Storage and Analysis. SC 2015. Association for Computing Machinery, New York (2015). https://doi.org/10.1145/2807591.2807638, https://doi-org-s.nudtproxy.yitlink.com/10.1145/2807591.2807638

15. Intel®: Overclocking: Maximizing your performance. OL. https://www.intel.com/content/www/us/en/gaming/overclocking-intel-processors.html. Accessed Dec 2021

16. Intel®: Release notes (xtu-7.5.3.3-releasenotes.pdf). OLhttps://downloadmirror.intel.com/29183/XTU-7.5.3.3-ReleaseNotes.pdf. Accessed Dec 2021

17. Jia, Y., et al.: Caffe: convolutional architecture for fast feature embedding. arXiv abs/1408.5093 (2014)

18. Kodama, Y., Odajima, T., Arima, E., Sato, M.: Evaluation of power management control on the supercomputer Fugaku. In: 2020 IEEE International Conference on Cluster Computing (CLUSTER), pp. 484–493 (2020). https://doi.org/10.1109/CLUSTER49012.2020.00069

19. Krizhevsky, A., Sutskever, I., Hinton, G.E.: Imagenet classification with deep convolutional neural networks. Commun. ACM **60**(6), 84–90 (2017). https://doi.org/10.1145/3065386

20. LeCun, Y., Kavukcuoglu, K., Farabet, C.: Convolutional networks and applications in vision. In: Proceedings of 2010 IEEE International Symposium on Circuits and Systems, pp. 253–256 (2010). https://doi.org/10.1109/ISCAS.2010.5537907

21. Mittal, S., Vetter, J.S.: A survey of methods for analyzing and improving GPU energy efficiency. ACM Comput. Surv. **47**(2) (2014). https://doi.org/10.1145/2636342, https://doi.org/10.1145/2636342

22. NVIDIA®: GPU boost. OL. https://www.nvidia.com/en-gb/geforce/technologies/gpu-boost/. Accessed Dec 2021

23. PyTorch: Imagenet training in PyTorch. OL. https://github.com/pytorch/examples/tree/master/imagenet. Accessed Dec 2021

24. Ravichandran, D.S.M.R.M.E.C.S.: Processor Performance Enhancement Using Self-adaptive Clock Frequency, vol. 3, July 2010

25. Rodrigues, C.F., Riley, G., Luján, M.: Fine-grained energy profiling for deep convolutional neural networks on the Jetson tx1. In: 2017 IEEE International Symposium on Workload Characterization (IISWC), pp. 114–115 (2017)

26. Rouhani, B.D., Mirhoseini, A., Koushanfar, F.: Delight: adding energy dimension to deep neural networks. In: International Symposium on Low Power Electronics and Design (2016)

27. Russakovsky, O., et al.: ImageNet large scale visual recognition challenge. Int. J. Comput. Vision **115**(3), 211–252 (2015). https://doi.org/10.1007/s11263-015-0816-y

28. Simonyan, K., Zisserman, A.: Very deep convolutional networks for large-scale image recognition. Comput. Sci. (2014)

29. Sun, Y., et al.: Evaluating performance, power and energy of deep neural networks on CPUs and GPUs. In: Cai, Z., Li, J., Zhang, J. (eds.) NCTCS 2021. CCIS, vol. 1494, pp. 196–221. Springer, Singapore (2021). https://doi.org/10.1007/978-981-16-7443-3_12

30. Tang, Z., Wang, Y., Wang, Q., Chu, X.: The impact of GPU DVFs on the energy and performance of deep learning: an empirical study. In: Proceedings of the Tenth ACM International Conference on Future Energy Systems. e-Energy 2019, pp. 315–325. Association for Computing Machinery, New York (2019). https://doi.org/10.1145/3307772.3328315
31. Thomas, D., Shanmugasundaram, M.: A survey on different overclocking methods. In: 2018 Second International Conference on Electronics, Communication and Aerospace Technology (ICECA), pp. 1588–1592 (2018). https://doi.org/10.1109/ICECA.2018.8474921
32. Wang, Y., et al.: E2-train: training state-of-the-art CNNs with over 80% energy savings. In: NeurIPS (2019)
33. Wu, F., Chen, J., Dong, Y., Zheng, W., Pan, X., Sun, Y.: Improve energy efficiency by processor overclocking and memory frequency scaling. In: 2018 IEEE 20th International Conference on High Performance Computing and Communications; IEEE 16th International Conference on Smart City; IEEE 4th International Conference on Data Science and Systems (HPCC/SmartCity/DSS), pp. 960–967 (2018)
34. Wu, F., et al.: A holistic energy-efficient approach for a processor-memory system. Tsinghua Sci. Technol. **24**(4), 468–483 (2019). https://doi.org/10.26599/TST.2018.9020104
35. Yang, C., et al.: Adaptive optimization for petascale heterogeneous CPU/GPU computing. In: 2010 IEEE International Conference on Cluster Computing, pp. 19–28 (2010). https://doi.org/10.1109/CLUSTER.2010.12
36. Yang, F., Xu, Y., Meng, X., Gao, W., Mai, Q., Yang, C.: Nvidia tx2-based CPU, GPU coordinated frequency modulation energy-saving optimization method. Patent (2019). Patent Application Number: 201910360182.6. Publication Patent Number: CN 110308784 A
37. Yao, C., et al.: Evaluating and analyzing the energy efficiency of CNN inference on high-performance GPU. Concurrency and Computation: Practice and Experience (2020)
38. Zamani, H., Tripathy, D., Bhuyan, L., Chen, Z.: SAOU: safe adaptive overclocking and undervolting for energy-efficient GPU computing. In: Proceedings of the ACM/IEEE International Symposium on Low Power Electronics and Design. ISLPED 2020, pp. 205–210. Association for Computing Machinery, New York (2020). https://doi.org/10.1145/3370748.3406553, https://doi.org/10.1145/3370748.3406553

GEM: Execution-Aware Cache Management for Graph Analytics

Mo Zou[1,2(✉)], Mingyu Yan[1], Wenming Li[1], Zhimin Tang[1,2], Xiaochun Ye[1],
and Dongrui Fan[1]

[1] State Key Lab of Processors, Institute of Computing Technology, CAS,
Beijing, China
zoumo@ict.ac.cn
[2] University of Chinese Academy of Sciences, Beijing, China

Abstract. Graph analytics plays a significant role in various application domains. However, the performance of graph analytics is limited by the inefficiencies of the cache hierarchy. In recent years, plenty of works focus on eliminating the irregular data accesses to accelerate graph analytics. However, we find that even regular data accesses cannot fully utilize cache hierarchy because current cache management is independent of execution characteristics. To this end, we propose GEM, a Graph-specialized Execution-aware cache Management at the L1D cache. GEM perceives from execution patterns in graph analytics and exploits customized cache management for regular data accesses without any preprocessing phase. More specifically, GEM identifies when the regular data accesses will occur and employs a length-aware fetch and reuse-aware replacement accordingly. We implement GEM on a popular multi-core simulator and evaluate the performance on various algorithms using several large real-world graphs. The result shows that GEM outperforms the state-of-the-art graph-specialized cache management by 21.1% on average and up to 44.5% in the best case, with up to 66% reduction of expensive off-chip memory accesses.

Keywords: Graph analytics · Cache management · Fetch · Replacement

1 Introduction

Graph analytics is a vital component in many application domains such as social network analysis [16,23,31,43,45] and computational biology [8,34]. For example, there exist an average of 1.45 billion active users on Facebook every day [20]. By encoding each user as a vertex and the relationship between users as an edge, Facebook has established a super-large social network graph and provided several interfaces to complete graph-relevant analysis such as friend recommendation [39], advertisement promotion [1], and purchase intention prediction [12]. For another example, in the biological field, Boolean model [27] expresses each gene as a vertex, encodes the attributes carried within the gene into the vertex

© Springer Nature Switzerland AG 2023
W. Meng et al. (Eds.): ICA3PP 2022, LNCS 13777, pp. 273–292, 2023.
https://doi.org/10.1007/978-3-031-22677-9_15

state value, and connects genes following their causation. In this way, Boolean model predicts the connections between unknown gene points.

However, graph analytics suffers from poor performance due to the under-utilized cache hierarchy. On the one hand, graph processing algorithms produce one data access, which usually reads or writes 4− or 8−byte data, less than every ten instructions [32]. Such a low compute-to-computation ratio makes the performance of graph analytics limited by the efficiency of the cache hierarchy. On the other hand, on-chip caches cannot store real-world graphs which contain millions of vertices and edges. Intensive irregular memory accesses existing in graph applications magnify the impact of frequent cache misses. According to [4], during 45% of the total execution cycles, the core has to stall and wait for data to be returned from DRAM, indicating that cache hierarchy is underutilized and thus hurts the graph analytics performance.

Hardware-based optimization has always been a hot topic in the field of graph analytics. Most prior schemes [3,14,32,33,35,44,46,47] focus on eliminating the irregular data accesses, improving their locality, and reducing expensive off-chip memory traffic. For example, GRASP [14] and P-OPT [3] evict the cachelines in LLC with a lower reuse possibility. PHI [33] and GraphPulse [35] coalesce multiple irregular data accesses if they target to the same vertex. However, they paid less attention to other data accesses, which were always thought to be cache-friendly.

In our work, we observe that the cache hierarchy is not perfect-performed for regular data accesses because current cache management is unaware of the execution characteristics in graph analytics. The execution can be classified into three phases: the Neighbor-Locating phase, the Neighbor-Scanning phase, and the State-Update phase. Although data accesses during the Neighbor-Scanning phase are regular, current cache hierarchy can be further optimized by learning from the Neighbor-Locating phase and performing execution-aware cache management.

To this end, we propose GEM, a Graph-specialized Execution-aware cache Manegement, which learns from execution patterns in graph analytics and exploits the synergy between cache managements and execution characteristics. GEM contains a length-aware fetch policy and a reuse-aware replacement policy. The length-aware fetch policy first recognizes the number of cachelines that will be required in the future. Then the policy sends a memory request with a required number to DRAM directly, which loads the specified number of cachelines from DRAM to L1D. The reuse-aware replacement policy initializes the *reuse times* when inserting a cacheline and updates *reuse times* upon each L1D hit. When evicting a cacheline, the replacement policy chooses the cacheline whose *reuse times* is 0, which indicates that this cacheline will no longer be accessed.

To summarize, our contributions are as follows:

- We quantity the inefficiencies of current cache management for regular data accesses and analyze the reasons.
- We propose GEM, a graph-specialized execution-aware cache management strategy. GEM contains an L1D fetch and replacement policy that collabo-

rates with graph application execution details, which reduces DRAM accesses and improves cache hierarchy utilization.
- We implement GEM on a simulator and evaluate the performance on various graph applications. GEM improves the performance by 21.1% on average (and by up to 44.5%) compared with the state-of-the-art cache management, and reduces expensive off-chip memory traffic by 17.8% on average (and by up to 66%).

The rest of the paper is organized as follows. In Sect. 2, we introduce the background of graph analytics. Sect. 3 discusses the motivation of our work. Sect. 4 illustrates the schemes of our proposed GEM. In Sect. 5, we characterize the methodology used in GEM. The performance and related analysis are provided in Sect. 6. Several related works are introduced in Sect. 7. Finally, we conclude our work in Sect. 8.

2   Background

2.1   Graph Processing Models

Most graph analytics adopts *pull-* [6,40] or *push-based* [7,38] processing models to traverse the entire graph and update one vertex's state value according to its neighbors' state values under specific functions.

In *push-based* models, one source vertex broadcasts its own state value S to its outgoing neighbors. Then each outgoing neighbor performs a user-defined function ϕ utilizing S and its previous state value N' to generate a new state value N, as illustrated in Eq. 1. In *pull-based* models, one destination vertex collects the state values of all incoming neighbors. Then the destination vertex modifies its state value upon the accumulated influence.

$$N = \phi(S, N') \tag{1}$$

The only difference between the two models is that *push-based* model updates destinations' state values following outgoing edges while *pull-based* model updates sources' state values following incoming edges. Both the models run iteratively until convergence. We will take the *push-based* computation model as an example in our next discussion.

2.2   Graph Representation

As the scale of the real-world graphs becomes larger and the sparsity becomes higher, Compressed Sparse Row (CSR) format becomes a widely used storage-efficient representation to encode graphs [6,14,28,32,38].

As shown in Fig. 1, one graph allocates three arrays, i.e., Offset array, Neighbor array, and State array, to maintain outgoing neighbors and information carried by each vertex. For each vertex, the Offset array holds an 8-byte pointer pointing to its first outgoing neighbor in the Neighbor array, which records an edge from source to destination. The Neighbor array stores all edges in the form

Fig. 1. Compressed sparse row representation.

of destination vertex IDs, and edge-weighted values are stored here as well for weighted graphs. The State array holds the current state value for each vertex, which usually occupies 4- or 8-byte storage space. In the rest of the paper, we call cachelines from the Offset array as the offset cachelines, cachelines from the Neighbor array as the neighbor cachelines, and cachelines from the State array as the state cachelines.

2.3   Graph Analytics Execution Phases

Corresponding to three arrays in Fig. 1, the execution of graph analytics can be classified into three phases: the Neighbor-Locating phase, the Neighbor-Scanning phase, and the State-Update phase. The Neighbor-Locating phase identifies the start and end addresses for Neighbor-Scanning phase. Then the Neighbor-Scanning phase obtains all outgoing neighbor IDs locating within the start and end addresses. Finally, the State-Update phase updates outgoing neighbor's state value according to neighbor IDs one by one.

Taking v_2 as a source vertex, during the Neighbor-Locating phase, the graph application reads v_2 and v_3 in the Offset array to identify the first and last outgoing neighbors of v_2 (i.e., the fourth and the sixth entries in the Neighbor array). Then during the Neighbor-Scanning phase, the graph application reads the adjacent elements in the Neighbor array to obtain all outgoing neighbor IDs of v_2 (i.e., 0, 3, and 4). Finally, during the State-Update phase, the graph application updates the state values of outgoing neighbors (i.e., v_0, v_3, and v_4) in the State array following Eq. 1.

3   Motivation

In this section, we first explore data accesses contributions caused by the three phases mentioned above. Then we investigate the under-utilization of current cache management and make an in-depth analysis. Finally, we propose two opportunities to guide GEM. The experimental platform and more graph-relevant details can be found in Sect. 5.

3.1   Data Accesses Breakdown

We classify data accesses into three types based on which phase it occurs. Noticing that during the Neighbor-Locating phase, all data accesses target to the

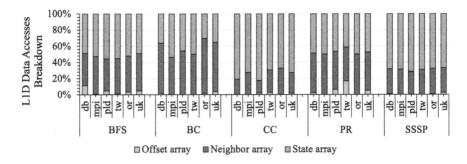

Fig. 2. Data access breakdown from different phases in L1D.

Offset array, we name them offset accesses. The other two types are neighbor accesses and state accesses accordingly.

Figure 2 illustrates the data accesses breakdown in L1D. It is obvious that neighbor accesses and state accesses take the most portion of the total L1D accesses, which are about 41.4% and 58.1% separately. On the other hand, offset accesses occupy only 0.5% of the total L1D accesses averaging across all data points. This is because that the average degrees (i.e., the average neighbor numbers) in the real-world graphs are generally large. Once determining the neighbor IDs' range of one source vertex, graph processing algorithms generate a large amount of neighbor accesses and state accesses without any further offset accesses until updating all neighbors' state values.

Because of the huge percentage gap between different data accesses, it is worth to focus on neighbor accesses and state accesses instead of offset accesses.

3.2 Underutilized Cache Hierarchy

If a graph is stored in the CSR format, the locality characteristics of neighbor accesses and state accesses are distinct. Neighbor accesses appear to exhibit a high spatial locality because the neighbor IDs are stored contiguously and sequentially in the Neighbor array. However, state accesses are much more random and suffer from poor locality in the cache hierarchy. Therefore, plenty of works [3,14,32,33,35,44,46,47] focus on eliminating the irregular state accesses and hence accelerating graph analytics.

To investigate cache hierarchy utilization for regular data accesses, we profile cache miss ratio of neighbor accesses. As indicated in Fig. 3, about 6.8% of the total neighbor accesses are missed in L1D. In the worst case of application SSSP, L1D neighbor accesses miss ratio is as high as 13.4% averaging across all input graphs, resulting in significant performance loss. Moreover, the average miss ratios of neighbor accesses in L2 and LLC are all more than 99%, denoting that once the neighbor data cannot be found in L1D, it will be hardly found in L2 and LLC.

The reason is that, although neighbor accesses are sequential within each cacheline, there does not exist an efficient way to fetch enough cachelines from

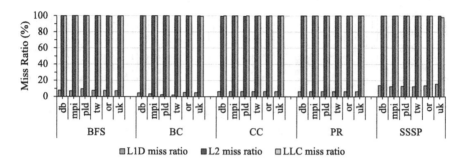

Fig. 3. Cache hierarchy miss ratio for neighbor accesses.

lower-level storage. For example, in Fig. 1, assuming that in the Neighbor array, v_0 and v_3 are stored in one cacheline while v_4 is stored in the next cacheline. To access v_4, one L1D miss occurs because the core does not know how many cachelines will be required to obtain all neighbor IDs of the source vertex v_2, and the cacheline maintaining v_4 cannot be found in L2 or LLC neither. It is more attractive to fetch all neighbor data that will be accessed before entering the Neighbor-Scanning phase, motivating us to design an intelligent fetch policy to improve the utilization of cache hierarchy for neighbor accesses.

Another problem with current cache management comes from the replacement policy. As introduced in Sect. 2.3, the core reads neighbor IDs during the Neighbor-Scanning phase for one-time, which means that once one neighbor cacheline is read out, that cacheline will not be used again. On the contrary, state cachelines may be accessed multiple times because one destination vertex may have several neighbors. In such a case, an efficient replacement policy should know exactly which cacheline will not be accessed and evict that cacheline immediately. However, the conventional LRU cache replacement policy just records the history of each cacheline, but cannot predict the future. To avoid cache pollution and save space for highly-reused cachelines (i.e., state cachelines), we intend to propose a replacement policy based on future reuse times.

3.3 Opportunity

Motivated by the inefficiencies of current cache management, combining with the execution characteristics of graph analytics, we propose the following two opportunities in GEM for neighbor accesses:

– A length-aware fetch policy for L1D. Through perceiving the Neighbor-Locating phase, we can calculate *how many cachelines* will be required during the Neighbor-Scanning phase to obtain all neighbor IDs. A required number of cachelines should be fetched from lower-level storage by one memory request. Moreover, because neighbor cachelines can not be found in L2 or LLC once missed in L1D, there should exist a direct path between L1D and DRAM to allow neighbor data be fetched quickly and enable L2 and LLC maintaining other highly-reused data.

- A reuse-based replacement policy for L1D. Because neighbor cachelines are accessed only once, an intelligent replacement policy should identify when a neighbor cacheline has been read out. When evicting a cacheline, the replacement policy should select finished neighbor cachelines to save space for highly-reused cachelines.
- Both the fetch and replacement policies are connected with the execution characteristics of graph applications. Overall, GEM learns necessary information from the execution patterns and guides the cache management.

4   GEM Design

4.1   Length-Aware Fetch Policy

To reduce the high L1D miss ratio and improve the cache utilization during the Neighbor-Scanning phase, we propose a length-aware fetch policy in GEM. First, the policy learns *how many neighbor cachelines will be required to obtain all neighbor IDs of current source vertex* from the Neighbor-Locating phase. Then, all neighbor cachelines are packed into one super-block and returned to L1D, avoiding frequent L1D misses and abundant data accesses. In addition, motivated by the observation that neighbor cachelines can hardly be found in L2 or LLC once missed in L1D, the length-aware fetch policy enables super-block to be fetched from DRAM directly instead of inserting in L2 or LLC, eliminating the considerable energy consumption for lower-level cache tag lookups. Next, we will describe the implementation details.

Identification. To complete the perception, the length-aware fetch policy is supposed to classify data access types (i.e., offset access, neighbor access, and state access) and execution phases instantly. Fortunately, the two identifications are bounded together (e.g., offset accesses only occur during the Neighbor-Locating phase).

In our design, we utilize the CSR storage format to track which array a data access targets to. In the graph software framework, we insert multiple interfaces at the location where the framework allocates memory space for the three arrays. Once the framework loads an input graph, the interfaces sends the start and end addresses to the core and the core records addresses in several 64-bit registers. As a result, the core maintains six addresses before the application execution. During the graph analytics execution, when the core sends a memory request, it compares the target address with the six registers to find which array the request targets to. Such a comparison is quickly because it is completed by the core. Then each data access are classified based on its target address and thus the core identifies the execution phases as well.

Perception. To perceive *where* and *how many cachelines* to fetch, GEM learns from offset accesses which have been identified. As introduced in Sect. 2.3, offset data determines the start and end locations of neighbor accesses. Once the cacheline required by one offset access is loaded into L1D, the core reads two consecutive pointers stored in that cacheline and knows *where* and *how many cachelines* easily.

For example, in Fig. 4, to perceive necessary knowledge of v_2's neighbor cachelines, the core: ❶ reads v_2 in the Offset array and gets the start address of v_2's neighbors (i.e., the fourth element in the Neighbor array); ❷ reads v_3 in the Offset array and gets the start address of v_3's neighbor (i.e., the seventh element in the Neighbor array); ❸ calculates the number of v_2's neighbors by subtraction (i.e., three neighbors). For now, by perceiving the offset data, the core learns significant information including the first neighbor address (i.e., the fourth element in the Neighbor array) and the number of neighbors of v_2 (i.e., three neighbors).

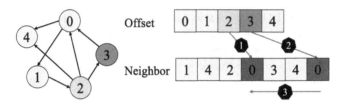

Fig. 4. Perception of *where* and *how many cachelines* are required for v_2's neighbor cachelines.

M-Fetch. To efficiently fetch multiple neighbor cachelines, we introduce *M-Fetch*, a new memory request with a starting address and cacheline number knowledge. Because the cache utilization of L2 and LLC is extremely low for neighbor accesses, we add a direct path between L1D and DRAM to send *M-Fetch* request and return neighbor cachelines from DRAM to L1D.

The starting address comes from the perception of offset data. However, the cacheline numbers are counted by an additional computation, which depends on neighbor numbers and each neighbor ID's storage occupancy. For example, each neighbor ID occupies 8-byte storage and one source vertex has 16 neighbors, requiring 2 cachelines to maintain all neighbor IDs in the Neighbor array. The core finishes the calculation, generates the corresponding *M-Fetch* request, and sends the request to DRAM.

Insertion. After DRAM receives a request *M-Fetch* request, it reads the required number of cachelines from the row buffer and packs them into one super-block, then sends the super-block back to L1D directly. In such a case, L1D receives a super-block containing multiple cachelines. L1D inserts each cacheline into the corresponding set separately based on our reuse-based replacement policy, which will be introduced in Sect. 4.2.

Architecture and Workflow. Figure 5 and Fig. 6 demonstrate the architecture and workflow of our length-aware fetch policy. First, there exist six address registers in the core to identify offset accesses through a quick address comparison. Once an offset access is identified and the corresponding offset cacheline is loaded into L1D, the core reads two consecutive data in the cacheline and sends the information to ReqGen module. The ReqGen module is responsible to generate a *M-Fetch* request carrying *where* and *how many cachelines* knowledge. Then the ReqGen module sends the *M-Fetch* request to DRAM directly following path ❷ in Fig. 5. After DRAM receives a *M-Fetch* request, it reads the required number of cachelines from the starting address and packs them into one super-block, then returns the super-block to L1D directly following path ❷ in Fig. 5. To simplify the architecture design, the bandwidth of direct path ❷ is set the same as the original path ❶, so cachelines from one super-block are transferred sequentially following a fixed bandwidth. Moreover, we set a maximum number of neighbor cachelines in one super-block (64 shows the best performance in our experiments). If the total neighbor cachelines of one source vertex exceed the limitation, the remaining neighbor cachelines will be processed following path ❶ as normal requests.

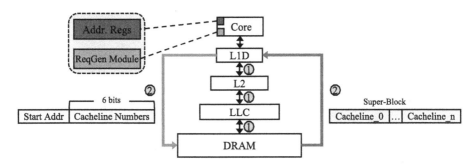

Fig. 5. Length-aware fetch policy architecture

4.2   Reuse-Based Replacement Policy

To improve L1D cache efficiency, we propose a reuse-based replacement policy in GEM. The key insight behind the policy is that *a neighbor cacheline will not be used again once all elements are read out*. In such a case, a smart replacement policy should know whether a neighbor cacheline has been finished and evict it immediately to avoid cache pollution. Moreover, an accurate eviction will also save space for cachelines that have a chance to be accessed in the future (e.g., state cachelines). Figure 7 demonstrates the required bits and workflow of the reuse-based replacement policy.

Cacheline Identification. Because the reuse-based policy is only valid for neighbor cachelines, we add an additional bit, *Neighbor Bit* (as shown in Fig. 7 ❶), in L1D tag array to record whether a cacheline is a neighbor cacheline or not. The *Neighbor Bit* is set as 1 if the cacheline comes from a super-block. Otherwise, the *Neighbor Bit* is set as 0, indicating a non-neighbor cacheline.

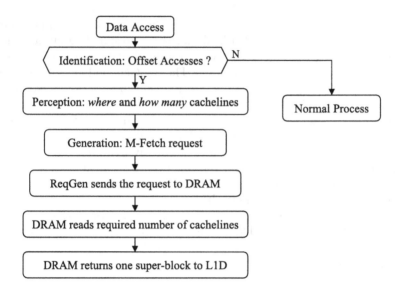

Fig. 6. Length-aware fetch policy workflow

Initialization and Update. For each neighbor cacheline, the reuse-aware replacement policy initializes its reuse times when inserting into L1D and updates the remaining reuse times upon each L1D hit. An additional field is added in L1D tag array, named *Reuse Times* (as shown in Fig. 7 ❶).

As shown in Fig. 7 ❷, if a neighbor cacheline is not the last cacheline in a super-block, it will be accessed totally. For example, if one neighbor ID occupies 8-byte storage, one 64-byte cacheline will be accessed up to 8 times. Such a neighbor cacheline's *Reuse Times* is initialized as 8. The situation is a little different for the last neighbor cacheline in a super-block. To simplify the replacement logic and minimize the hardware overhead, we initialize the *Reuse Times* of the last neighbor cacheline as 4. During the execution, upon each hit access, L1D reads its *Neighbor Bit* in the tag array. If this is a neighbor cacheline hit, L1D reduces its *Reuse Times* by 1 and updates its last accessed time. Otherwise, L1D only updates its last accessed time, as shown in Fig. 7 ❸.

Eviction. When needs to evict a cacheline, L1D first searches whether there exists a neighbor cacheline (i.e., *Neighbor Bit* is 1) that will not be accessed (i.e., *Reuse Times* is 0). If finds out, L1D evicts that cacheline. Otherwise L1D performs the LRU-based replacement policy. In such a scheme, even if we initialize the *Reuse Times* of the last neighbor cacheline from one super-block as 4, it still will be evicted based on the LRU policy, as shown in Fig. 7 ❹.

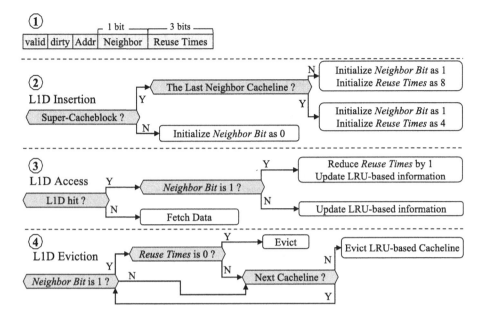

Fig. 7. Reuse-based replacement policy workflow.

5   Evaluation

5.1   Profiling Platform

We use Zsim [37], an execution-driven simulator, to measure performance with 4 OoO cores clocked at 4GHz and a 8MB shared LLC. To simulate memory behaviors accurately, we extend Zsim with DRAMsim3 [26], a detailed and cycle-accurate memory model supporting DDR4 protocol. Table 1 lists more configuration parameters. We fast forward the graph loading phase and run 100 million instructions to warm up cache. Then we mark the *Region of Interest (ROI)* in the code covering only *pull-* and *push-based* iterations. We collect status in *ROI* for 600 million instructions across all cores, similar to prior work [4].

5.2   Applications

We use five graph algorithms, Breadth-First Search (BFS), Betweenness Centrality (BC), Connected Component (CC), PageRank (PR), Single-Source Shortest Path (SSSP), covering both *push-* and *pull-based* computation models, from the widely used GAP [6] benchmark for our evaluation. Table 2 summarizes all applications.

5.3   Datasets

For our profiling, we use six real-world graphs detailed in Table 3. These graphs vary in size and degree distributions but all exceed the LLC capacity. As inputs to the graph algorithms, all graphs are encoded in CSR format. We combine the six real-world graphs with the five classic algorithms, producing 30 workloads in total, to be used in all evaluations mentioned in this research.

Table 1. System configurations

Core	4 OoO cores, 4GHz clock frequency, 128-entry ROB, 4-wide issue width, 16 MSHRs per core
L1-I/D Cache	private, 8-way 32KB per core, 64B cache line, 4 cycles access latency
L2 Cache	private, 8-way 256KB per core, 64B cache line, 12 cycles access latency
LLC	shared, 32-way 8MB, 64B cache line, 32 cycles access latency
Memory Controller	64-entry read/write queue, FR-FCFS [36] scheduling policy, Open-Page, address interleaving: rochrababgco
DRAM	4 channels, 2 ranks/channel, 4 bankgroups/rank, 4 banks/bankgroup, 16Gb DDR4-2400 × 8 chips, 8KB row buffer size [19], tRCD/tRAS/tWR 17/39/18 cycles, peak bandwidth 76.8 GB/s

Table 2. Graph applications

Application	Brief description	Model
BFS [5]	Traverses a graph from one root vertex until all neighbors are accessed and returns a distance array	Push
BC [7, 29]	Creates an array containing the centrality scores of each vertex to find the center	Push
CC [41]	Labels vertices into disjoint subsets to calculate how many components exist in the graph	Both
PR	Ranks all vertices based on incoming neighbors round by round until convergence or hit iteration limitation	Pull
SSSP [48]	Finds the shortest paths from one source vertex to all other vertices in a weighted graph	Push

Table 3. Graph datasets

Dataset	Abbrv.	|V|	|E|	Ave. Degree
Orkut [25]	*or*	9M	327M	36
Dbpedia [2]	*db*	18M	136M	8
PLD [24]	*pld*	43M	623M	14
Mpi [9]	*mpi*	53M	1963M	37
Twitter [23]	*tw*	62M	1468M	24
uk-2002 [11]	*uk*	134M	261M	2

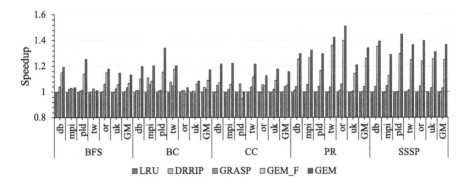

Fig. 8. Comparison of Performance. The results are normalized to the baseline design with LRU cache replacement policy. GEM_F means the application speedup when only adopting the length-aware fetch policy while GEM utilizes both the length-aware fetch policy and reuse-based replacement policy.

6 Result

In order to evaluate the effectiveness of GEM, we first show the experimental results of GEM individually for better comparison. Their performance are compared with existing state-of-the-art hardware optimizations [14,21]. Then, we quantitatively analyze how GEM effectively improves the performance.

6.1 Performance

We use the Instructions Per Cycle (IPC) to denote the system performance. Figure 8 summarizes the normalized performance improvement of DRRIP[1] [21], GRASP[2] [14], and GEM over the LRU baseline. To prove the performance improvements of length-aware fetch and reuse-aware replacement separately, GEM_F denotes the application speedups when only adopting the length-aware fetch policy while GEM denotes the application speedups when applying both fetch and replacement managements.

As shown in Fig. 8, using the length-aware fetch policy alone outperforms the LRU baseline with average speedups for BFS, BC, CC, PR, and SSSP are 6.7%, 9.1%, 5.3%, 26%, and 25.1%, respectively. Overall, the length-aware fetch policy yields 14.4% average speedup and up to 39.7% in the best case (on PR-*or*) over the LRU baseline. On the other hand, using the reuse-aware replacement policy alone provides an average speedup of 6.6% for BFS, 8.1% for BC, 10.3% for CC, 7.9% for PR, and 11.5% for SSSP. Among all of the 30 workloads, the reuse-aware replacement policy yields 8.3% speedup on average and up to 18.7% in the best case (on BC-*pld*) over the LRU baseline. Finally, GEM with integrated the length-aware fetch and the reuse-aware replacement policy achieves

---

[1] source code from https://github.com/ChampSim/ChampSim/blob/master/replacement/drrip.llc_repl.

[2] source code from https://github.com/faldupriyank/grasp.

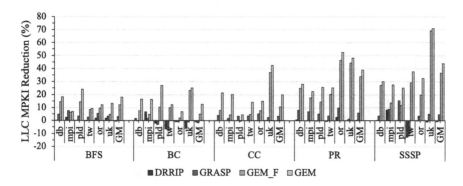

Fig. 9. LLC MPKI reduction for DRRIP, GRASP, GEM_F, and GEM over the LRU baseline. GEM_F means the application speedup when only adopting the length-aware fetch policy while GEM utilizes both the length-aware fetch policy and reuse-based replacement policy.

the performance improvement of 13.3% for BFS, 17.3% for BC, 15.6% for CC, 33.9% for PR, and 36.5% for SSSP. Benefiting from the two optimizations, GEM yields an average speedup of 25% (max 44.8%) over the LRU baseline. Compared with the state-of-the-art graph-specialized cache management GRASP, GEM improves the performance by 21.1% on average and up to 44.5% in the best case. As for prior techniques, DRRIP only slightly improves performance by 2%, and GRASP yields an average speedup of 5% over the baseline. This is mainly because DRRIP and GRASP can not capture information from the execution patterns of graph analytics.

6.2   LLC MPKI Reduction

To analyze the reason of performance improvements brought by GEM, we collect LLC MPKI (Misses Per Kilo Instructions) of different schemes and show the result in Fig. 9.

Figure 9 demonstrates that the length-aware fetch policy reduces the LLC MPKI by 12.3%, 5%, 10.9%, 33.9%, and 36.7% on average for BFS, BC, CC, PR, and SSSP separately. Overall, the length-aware fetch policy reaches an average of 13.4% LLC MPKI reduction compared with the LRU baseline and up to 69.3% in the best case (on SSSP-*uk*). The reuse-aware replacement policy reduces the LLC MPKI by 5.8% for BFS, 7.7% for BC, 9.2% for CC, 5.3% for PR, and 7.3% for SSSP. As a result, GEM integrated with the length-aware fetch and the reuse-aware replacement policy reduces the expensive LLC MPKI by 22% on average over the LRU baseline. When compared with the state-of-the-art GRASP, GEM also reduces LLC MPKI by 17.8% on average and up to 66% in the best case (SSSP-*uk*).

LLC misses reduction indicates a more efficient cache hierarchy. The reasons behind the LLC misses reduction can be summarized in two aspects:

- The length-aware fetch policy perceives the number of cachelines that will be accessed and fetch all neighbor cachelines in one packed super-block. Unlike prior works [4,42], the length-aware fetch policy focuses on regular accesses and learns from the execution characteristics. The length-aware fetch policy is accurate, which will not cause cache pollution. Because one DRAM access fetches multiple neighbor cachelines, the length-aware fetch policy reduces the expensive DRAM accesses significantly.
- The reuse-Aware Replacement policy is an intelligent replacement policy for neighbor cachelines. It initializes each neighbor cachelines reuse times and updates the times during the execution. So reuse-aware replacement policy identifies which neighbor cacheline will not be accessed accurately. In such a way, neighbor cachelines will only occupy a few number of cachelines in L1D, saving space for cachelines that have a chance to be accessed in the future.
- Overall, the design of GEM is bounded with the execution characteristics of graph analytics closely. It achieves significant performance improvements without any pre-processing phase and prediction behaviors. Through perceiving important knowledge from the execution phases, GEM outperforms the state-of-the-art schemes.

6.3   Limitations

Although GEM shows significant performance improvements, there exists one main limitation of GEM. GEM is based on CSR storage format to identify different access patterns fast and accurately. If a graph is stored in other format (e.g., sparse matrix), GEM will require a more complex mechanism such as history table to predict which memory access will trigger GEM. We leave it in our future work.

7   Related Work

7.1   Architectural Optimizations

GRASP [14] classifies the memory space as the hot vertices region and the cold vertices region after reordering and guarantees the cachelines from the hot vertices region to stay longer in cache. P-OPT [3] evicts cachelines based on the re-reference information of vertices. GRASP and P-OPT reduce cache misses to improve the application performance. DepGraph [47] dispatches different dependency-chains to different cores, allowing efficient asynchronous vertex state updates on multi-core processors. In this way, DepGraph improves the locality in private cache. PHI [33] coalesces multiple state updates in cache if they target to the same vertex and applies the merged state value to the memory controller together. GraphPulse [35] proposes a graph-specialized accelerator to coalesce updates in a FIFO queue. PHI and GraphPulse exploit temporal locality and reduce memory traffic through the coalescence. However, they mainly focus on eliminating the irregular accesses (i.e., state accesses) to speedup the graph applications. In our work, we prove that optimizing regular accesses (i.e., neighbor accesses) can also enhance the performance.

7.2 Software Optimizations

Software optimizations pre-process the storage space of a graph input instead of modifying the hardware architecture. Reordering is one of the most popular and effective scheme to make the graph analytics behavior more friendly to hardware architectures. The significant basis of reordering is the power law distribution [15,17], which means that in real-world graphs, a small fraction of vertices occupy most connections. Reordering schemes re-place these vertices in continuous memory space to make better use of cache hierarchy. Most reordering schemes utilize the average degree (i.e., edge number / vertex number) to classify vertices deserving reordered. HubSort [49] only reorders vertices whose degree is greater than the average degree while maintains vertices whose degree is lower than the average degree in there original memory location. Degree-Based Grouping (DBG) [13] divides multiple groups and set the degree range for each group. Then DBG inserts vertices one by one to its corresponding group. Although reordering scheme shows performance improvements, it requires additional pre-processing overhead. Moreover, when the graph is too large, the storage space of reordered vertices exceeds the cache capacity, limiting the effectiveness.

7.3 Cache Bypassing

Adaptive Cache Bypassing [18], Annex Cache [22], and LMP [30] utilize a predictor to determine whether a memory access should bypass the cache. AMB [10] tracks the history access information for cache blocks, skipping specific cache layers or bypassing memory requests to DRAM based on the recorded knowledge. Our proposed GEM outperforms the prior works in two ways. On the one hand, GEM directly utilizes the execution characteristics of graph applications according to simplified address comparison, and determines whether to send the requests to DRAM directly or not, which is accurate and avoids the unnecessary history tracking latency. On the other hand, GEM learns necessary knowledge from the execution phases and knows how many cachelines will be required in the future. GEM fetches multiple cachelines in one DRAM accesses, improving hardware resource utilization.

8 Conclusion

Graph processing plays an essential role in big data applications and is becoming more and more important. However, prior works mainly focus on eliminating the irregular memory accesses. In this work, we prove that even regular data accesses have an optimization space. We propose GEM, which contains a length-aware fetch policy and a reuse-aware replacement policy. GEM perceives the execution patterns in graph analytics and learns necessary information from the execution. The length-aware fetch policy fetches a required number of cachelines from DRAM directly to avoid frequent L1D misses. The reuse-aware replacement policy identifies which cacheline will not be accessed in the future and evicts it immediately. On a set of graph workloads, GEM improves the performance by 21.1% on average and up to 44.5% over the existing state-of-the-art hardware optimization.

Acknowledgements. This work was supported by CAS Project for Young Scientists in Basic Research (Grant No. YSBR-029), the National Natural Science Foundation of China (Grant No. 61732018, and 61872335), Austrian-Chinese Cooperative R&D Project (FFG and CAS) (Grant No. 171111KYSB20200002), and CAS Project for Youth Innovation Promotion Association.

References

1. Andreou, A., Silva, M., Benevenuto, F., Goga, O., Loiseau, P., Mislove, A.: Measuring the facebook advertising ecosystem. In: NDSS 2019-Proceedings of the Network and Distributed System Security Symposium, pp. 1–15 (2019)
2. Auer, S., Bizer, C., Kobilarov, G., Lehmann, J., Cyganiak, R., Ives, Z.: DBpedia: a nucleus for a web of open data. In: Aberer, K. (ed.) ASWC/ISWC -2007. LNCS, vol. 4825, pp. 722–735. Springer, Heidelberg (2007). https://doi.org/10.1007/978-3-540-76298-0_52
3. Balaji, V., Crago, N., Jaleel, A., Lucia, B.: P-OPT: practical optimal cache replacement for graph analytics. In: 2021 IEEE International Symposium on High-Performance Computer Architecture (HPCA), pp. 668–681. IEEE (2021)
4. Basak, A., et al.: Analysis and optimization of the memory hierarchy for graph processing workloads. In: 2019 IEEE International Symposium on High Performance Computer Architecture (HPCA), pp. 373–386. IEEE (2019)
5. Beamer, S., Asanovic, K., Patterson, D.: Direction-optimizing breadth-first search. In: SC'12: Proceedings of the International Conference on High Performance Computing, Networking, Storage and Analysis, pp. 1–10. IEEE (2012)
6. Beamer, S., Asanović, K., Patterson, D.: The gap benchmark suite. arXiv preprint arXiv:1508.03619 (2015)
7. Brandes, U.: A faster algorithm for betweenness centrality. J. Math. Sociol. **25**(2), 163–177 (2001)
8. Caetano, T.S., McAuley, J.J., Cheng, L., Le, Q.V., Smola, A.J.: Learning graph matching. IEEE Trans. Pattern Anal. Mach. Intell. **31**(6), 1048–1058 (2009)
9. Cha, M., Haddadi, H., Benevenuto, F., Gummadi, K.: Measuring user influence in twitter: The million follower fallacy. In: Proceedings of the International AAAI Conference on Web and Social Media. vol. 4 (2010)
10. Collins, J.D., Tullsen, D.M.: Hardware identification of cache conflict misses. In: MICRO-32. Proceedings of the 32nd Annual ACM/IEEE International Symposium on Microarchitecture, pp. 126–135. IEEE (1999)
11. Davis, T.A., Hu, Y.: The university of florida sparse matrix collection. ACM Trans. Math. Softw. (TOMS) **38**(1), 1–25 (2011)
12. Dehghani, M., Tumer, M.: A research on effectiveness of facebook advertising on enhancing purchase intention of consumers. Comput. Hum. Behav. **49**, 597–600 (2015)
13. Faldu, P., Diamond, J., Grot, B.: A closer look at lightweight graph reordering. In: 2019 IEEE International Symposium on Workload Characterization (IISWC), pp. 1–13. IEEE (2019)

14. Faldu, P., Diamond, J., Grot, B.: Domain-specialized cache management for graph analytics. In: 2020 IEEE International Symposium on High Performance Computer Architecture (HPCA), pp. 234–248. IEEE (2020)
15. Faloutsos, M., Faloutsos, P., Faloutsos, C.: On power-law relationships of the internet topology. ACM SIGCOMM Comput. Commun. Rev. **29**(4), 251–262 (1999)
16. Fan, W.: Graph pattern matching revised for social network analysis. In: Proceedings of the 15th International Conference on Database Theory, pp. 8–21 (2012)
17. Gonzalez, J.E., Low, Y., Gu, H., Bickson, D., Guestrin, C.: {PowerGraph}: Distributed {Graph-Parallel} computation on natural graphs. In: 10th USENIX Symposium on Operating Systems Design and Implementation (OSDI 2012), pp. 17–30 (2012)
18. Gupta, S., Gao, H., Zhou, H.: Adaptive cache bypassing for inclusive last level caches. In: 2013 IEEE 27th International Symposium on Parallel and Distributed Processing, pp. 1243–1253. IEEE (2013)
19. Hassan, H., et al.: Crow: A low-cost substrate for improving dram performance, energy efficiency, and reliability. In: Proceedings of the 46th International Symposium on Computer Architecture, pp. 129–142 (2019)
20. Ho, J.C.T.: How biased is the sample? Reverse engineering the ranking algorithm of facebook's graph application programming interface. Big Data Soc. **7**(1), 2053951720905874 (2020)
21. Jaleel, A., Theobald, K.B., Steely, S.C., Jr., Emer, J.: High performance cache replacement using re-reference interval prediction (RRIP). ACM SIGARCH Comput. Archit. News **38**(3), 60–71 (2010)
22. John, L.K., Subramanian, A.: Design and performance evaluation of a cache assist to implement selective caching. In: Proceedings International Conference on Computer Design VLSI in Computers and Processors, pp. 510–518. IEEE (1997)
23. Kwak, H., Lee, C., Park, H., Moon, S.: What is twitter, a social network or a news media? In: Proceedings of the 19th International Conference on World Wide Web, pp. 591–600 (2010)
24. Lehmberg, O., Meusel, R., Bizer, C.: Graph structure in the web: aggregated by pay-level domain. In: Proceedings of the 2014 ACM Conference on Web Science, pp. 119–128 (2014)
25. Leskovec, J., Krevl, A.: SNAP Datasets: stanford large network dataset collection. http://snap.stanford.edu/data (Jun 2014)
26. Li, S., Yang, Z., Reddy, D., Srivastava, A., Jacob, B.: DRAMsim3: a cycle-accurate, thermal-capable dram simulator. IEEE Comput. Archit. Lett. **19**(2), 106–109 (2020)
27. Lovrics, A., et al.: Boolean modelling reveals new regulatory connections between transcription factors orchestrating the development of the ventral spinal cord. PLoS ONE **9**(11), e111430 (2014)
28. Maass, S., Min, C., Kashyap, S., Kang, W., Kumar, M., Kim, T.: Mosaic: processing a trillion-edge graph on a single machine. In: Proceedings of the Twelfth European Conference on Computer Systems, pp. 527–543 (2017)
29. Madduri, K., Ediger, D., Jiang, K., Bader, D.A., Chavarria-Miranda, D.: A faster parallel algorithm and efficient multithreaded implementations for evaluating betweenness centrality on massive datasets. In: 2009 IEEE International Symposium on Parallel and Distributed Processing, pp. 1–8. IEEE (2009)
30. Malkowski, K., Link, G., Raghavan, P., Irwin, M.J.: Load miss prediction-exploiting power performance trade-offs. In: 2007 IEEE International Parallel and Distributed Processing Symposium, pp. 1–8. IEEE (2007)

31. Mislove, A., Marcon, M., Gummadi, K.P., Druschel, P., Bhattacharjee, B.: Measurement and analysis of online social networks. In: Proceedings of the 7th ACM SIGCOMM Conference on Internet Measurement, pp. 29–42 (2007)
32. Mukkara, A., Beckmann, N., Abeydeera, M., Ma, X., Sanchez, D.: Exploiting locality in graph analytics through hardware-accelerated traversal scheduling. In: 2018 51st Annual IEEE/ACM International Symposium on Microarchitecture (MICRO), pp. 1–14. IEEE (2018)
33. Mukkara, A., Beckmann, N., Sanchez, D.: PHI: architectural support for synchronization-and bandwidth-efficient commutative scatter updates. In: Proceedings of the 52nd Annual IEEE/ACM International Symposium on Microarchitecture, pp. 1009–1022 (2019)
34. Navlakha, S., Schatz, M.C., Kingsford, C.: Revealing biological modules via graph summarization. J. Comput. Biol. **16**(2), 253–264 (2009)
35. Rahman, S., Abu-Ghazaleh, N., Gupta, R.: GraphPulse: an event-driven hardware accelerator for asynchronous graph processing. In: 2020 53rd Annual IEEE/ACM International Symposium on Microarchitecture (MICRO), pp. 908–921. IEEE (2020)
36. Rixner, S., Dally, W.J., Kapasi, U.J., Mattson, P., Owens, J.D.: Memory access scheduling. ACM SIGARCH Comput. Archit. News **28**(2), 128–138 (2000)
37. Sanchez, D., Kozyrakis, C.: ZSim: fast and accurate microarchitectural simulation of thousand-core systems. ACM SIGARCH Comput. Archit. News **41**(3), 475–486 (2013)
38. Shun, J., Blelloch, G.E.: Ligra: a lightweight graph processing framework for shared memory. In: Proceedings of the 18th ACM SIGPLAN Symposium on Principles and Practice of Parallel Programming, pp. 135–146 (2013)
39. Spiliotopoulos, T., Pereira, D., Oakley, I.: Predicting tie strength with the facebook API. In: Proceedings of the 18th Panhellenic Conference on Informatics, pp. 1–5 (2014)
40. Sundaram, N., et al.: GraphMat: high performance graph analytics made productive. arXiv preprint arXiv:1503.07241 (2015)
41. Sutton, M., Ben-Nun, T., Barak, A.: Optimizing parallel graph connectivity computation via subgraph sampling. In: 2018 IEEE International Parallel and Distributed Processing Symposium (IPDPS), pp. 12–21. IEEE (2018)
42. Talati, N., et al.: Prodigy: improving the memory latency of data-indirect irregular workloads using hardware-software co-design. In: 2021 IEEE International Symposium on High-Performance Computer Architecture (HPCA), pp. 654–667. IEEE (2021)
43. Tang, L., Liu, H.: Graph mining applications to social network analysis. In: Aggarwal, C., Wang, H. (eds.) Managing and Mining Graph Data. Advances in Database Systems, vol. 40. Springer, Boston (2010)
44. Yan, M., et al.: Alleviating irregularity in graph analytics acceleration: a hardware/software co-design approach. In: Proceedings of the 52nd Annual IEEE/ACM International Symposium on Microarchitecture, pp. 615–628 (2019)
45. Yang, J., Leskovec, J.: Defining and evaluating network communities based on ground-truth. Knowl. Inf. Syst. **42**(1), 181–213 (2015)
46. Zhang, D., Ma, X., Thomson, M., Chiou, D.: Minnow: Lightweight offload engines for worklist management and worklist-directed prefetching. ACM SIGPLAN Not. **53**(2), 593–607 (2018)
47. Zhang, Y., et al.: DepGraph: a dependency-driven accelerator for efficient iterative graph processing. In: 2021 IEEE International Symposium on High-Performance Computer Architecture (HPCA), pp. 371–384. IEEE (2021)

48. Zhang, Y., et al.: Optimizing ordered graph algorithms with graphit. arXiv preprint arXiv:1911.07260 (2019)
49. Zhang, Y., Kiriansky, V., Mendis, C., Amarasinghe, S., Zaharia, M.: Making caches work for graph analytics. In: 2017 IEEE International Conference on Big Data (Big Data), pp. 293–302. IEEE (2017)

EnergyCIDN: Enhanced Energy-Aware Challenge-Based Collaborative Intrusion Detection in Internet of Things

Wenjuan Li[1]([envelope]) [ORCID], Philip Rosenberg[2], Mads Glisby[2], and Michael Han[3]

[1] Department of Electronic and Information Engineering,
The Hong Kong Polytechnic University, Hong Kong, China
`wenjuan.li@polyu.edu.hk`
[2] Department of Electronic Systems, Aalborg University, Aalborg, Denmark
[3] KOTO Research Center, Macao SAR, China

Abstract. With cyber attacks becoming more complex and advanced, a separate intrusion detection system (IDS) is believed to be insufficient for protecting the whole computer networks. Thus, collaborative intrusion detection networks (CIDNs) are proposed aiming to improve the detection performance by allowing various nodes to share required information or messages with other nodes. To defeat insider threats during the sharing process (e.g., malicious information), trust management is a necessary security mechanism for CIDNs, where challenge-based CIDNs are a typical example that sends a special kind of message, called *challenge*, to evaluate the reputation of a node. The previous work has proven that challenge-based CIDNs can defeat most common insider threats, but it may still suffer from some advanced insider threats, e.g., passive message fingerprint attack (PMFA). In this work, we develop EnergyCIDN, an enhanced challenge-based CIDN by adopting an energy-aware trust management model against advanced insider attacks. In the evaluation, we study the performance of EnergyCIDN under both simulated and practical Internet of Things (IoT) environments. The results demonstrate that EnergyCIDN can perform better than many similar schemes in identifying advanced malicious nodes.

Keywords: Intrusion detection · Collaborative network · Insider attack · Energy consumption · Trust management

1 Introduction

The Internet of Things (IoT) is a network system consisted of sensors, software and many interrelated computing devices. Various organizations are gradually adopting IoT devices for more efficient operations, enhanced customer service, and increased decision-making process [4,5]. The IoT market is expected to rise to 1.39 trillion by 2026, based on the report from Mordor Intelligence [1]. Such increase is partially caused by the COVID-19 pandemic, e.g., the need of remote monitoring, Internet-enabled devices.

© Springer Nature Switzerland AG 2023
W. Meng et al. (Eds.): ICA3PP 2022, LNCS 13777, pp. 293–312, 2023.
https://doi.org/10.1007/978-3-031-22677-9_16

On one hand, the wide adoption of IoT can benefit people's daily lives and increase the service quality, such as checking the precise quantity of supplies in the house. On the other hand, IoT has become one main target platform for cyber hackers. For instance, a report from VentureBeat revealed that more than 0.9 billion IoT related attacks have been happened in 2021, including DDoS and phishing [2]. Hence the IoT security market, which aims to promote IoT security devices and software, is expected to grow from 3.86 billion in 2021 to 5.09 billion in 2022, and finally achieve 15.06 billion by 2026 [3].

In the current security market, an intrusion detection system (IDS) is one of the essential security solutions used to protect IoT environments. An IDS often identifies security threats via either signature-based detection or anomaly-based detection. The former relies on the signature database while the latter depends on the accuracy of pre-established normal profile [44]. However, an IDS is often isolated, which is considered as insufficient when existing cyber attacks become more complex. For this sake, collaborative intrusion detection networks (CIDNs)[1] are proposed to improve the detection performance by allowing IDS nodes to share required information/data with other nodes [51].

Unfortunately, CIDNs may suffer from the same insider threats as a distributed network, where a malicious node can share false information to influence the network performance. To defend against such kind of attack, trust management is an important mechanism. As a typical example, challenge-based CIDNs can measure the trustworthiness of a node through sending a special type of message, called *challenge*, and judging the received feedback [12]. A line of research has shown the effectiveness of challenge-based trust management against most common insider attacks (e.g., newcomer attack, betrayal attack), but it was also found to be susceptible to advanced insider attacks [25], such as Passive Message Fingerprint Attacks (PMFA) [21] and Bayesian Poisoning Attacks (BPA) [40].

- *PMFA:* This is a type of collusion attack, in which several malicious insider nodes can share the information with each other, and then attempt to respond maliciously to selected messages.
- *BPA:* This is a kind of collusion attack, which enables several malicious nodes to exchange information and model received messages. Then these nodes can only send a malicious response to those messages whose aggregated appearance probability of normal requests is above the selected threshold.

Contributions. By analyzing these advanced attacks above, we identify that most of them require the malicious nodes to exchange the received messages for determining the target message. However, such interactions may increase the power consumption in an IoT environment. Hence analyzing the power consumption can be helpful for enhancing the performance of challenge-based CIDNs. Motivated by this observation, in this work, we propose an energy-aware trust management scheme for challenge-based CIDNs, named *EnergyCIDN*. Our contributions can be summarized as below.

---

[1] It is also known as distributed intrusion detection system (DIDS) or collaborative intrusion detection system (CIDS).

- To enhance the robustness of challenge-based trust management against advanced insider attacks, we design and develop *EnergyCIDN*, an energy-aware challenge-based CIDNs, which can measure the reputation of a node by considering energy consumption. This is because most malicious nodes need to send more messages with each other.
- Under *EnergyCIDN*, we introduce a hybrid trust management model consisting of challenge-based trust, packet-based trust and energy-aware trust. The hybrid trust model aims to evaluate the trustworthiness of a target node more accurately and efficiently.
- In the evaluation, we investigate the performance of *EnergyCIDN* in the aspects of trust computation and alarm aggregation, under both simulated and practical network environments. Our experimental results demonstrate that *EnergyCIDN* can be more robust against advanced insider attacks, compared with similar trust management schemes.

Paper Organization. Section 2 describes our proposed energy-aware challenge-based CIDNs with major components and hybrid trust management. Section 3 introduces our experimental setup under both simulated and practical network, and analyzes the collected results. Section 4 overviews similar research studies on collaborative intrusion detection. We discuss open challenges and future work in Sect. 5 and conclude the work in Sect. 6.

2 Our Proposed Approach

This section aims to introduce the energy-aware challenge-based CIDN framework, e.g., the major components and the hybrid trust model including challenge-based trust, packet-based trust and energy-aware trust.

2.1 Energy-Aware Challenge-Based CIDN Framework

Figure 1 illustrates the high-level view of our energy-aware challenge-based CIDNs, which consists of several major components: *IDS module, collaboration component, trust management component* and *P2P communication.*

- *IDS module* can perform the actual detection of various cyber attacks, by using either signature-based, anomaly-based or hybrid detection methods.
- *Collaboration component* is mainly responsible for assisting a node in measuring the reputation of a target node by sending out *normal requests* or *challenges*, and collecting the corresponding *feedback*. As shown in Fig. 1, node *A* can send a *normal request* or a *challenge* to node *B* and node *C*, and then receive the relevant feedback.
- *Trust management component* is responsible for evaluating the reputation of other nodes via a specific trust approach. Challenge-based mechanism is a kind of trust approach that computes the trust values through comparing the received feedback with the expected answers. Each node can send out

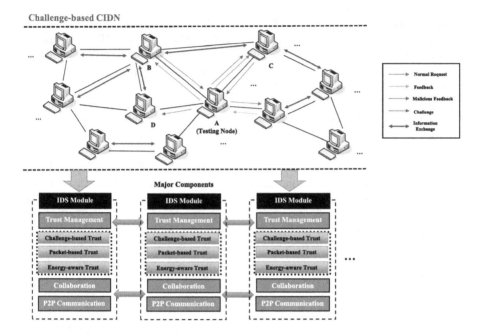

Fig. 1. The framework of energy-aware challenge-based CIDN.

either normal requests or challenges for alert (or alarm) ranking. To further protect challenges, the original work [12] assumed that challenges should be sent out in a random manner and in a way that makes them difficult to be distinguished from a normal alarm-ranking request.

- *P2P communication.* This component is responsible for connecting with other IDS nodes physically and providing network organization, management and communication among IDS nodes.

Network Interactions. In a CIDN environment, each IDS node can select its own partners according to defined policies, and construct a *partner list*. When a node wants to join the network, it should firstly apply and get a unique proof of identity (e.g., a public and a private key pair) via a trusted certificate authority (*CA*). In practice, if a node asks for joining the network, it has to send a request to one nearby CIDN node. Then, a decision can be made based on the acceptance policy, and a temporary *partner list* will be available. More specifically, a CIDN node can send two major types of messages: *normal request* and *challenge*.

- A *challenge* mainly contains a set of IDS alarms, where a testing node can send these alarms to the tested nodes for labeling the severity of alarms. Since the testing node knows the alarm severity in advance, a satisfaction level can be calculated for the tested node, based on the received feedback.
- A *normal request* is sent by a node, which can be used for performing alarm aggregation in improving the detection performance of a single detector. The

aggregation process usually only considers the feedback from highly trusted nodes. As a response, the corresponding IDS node should send back alarm ranking as their feedback.

Threat Model. In this work, we focus on two types of insider attacks: 1) common insider attacks, such as newcomer attack (a malicious node registers a new identity) and betrayal attack (a trusted node suddenly becomes malicious), which adopt a maximum harm model (by always trying to send false information); and 2) advanced insider attacks, such as PMFA (a type of collusion attack where several malicious nodes can identify normal request by exchanging received messages) and Bayesian Poisoning Attacks (a type of collusion attack where several malicious nodes can identify normal request via Bayesian modelling).

2.2   Hybrid Trust Management

Challenge-Based Trust. In practice, a CIDN node with the challenge-based trust management model can send a challenge in an average rate of ε, according to the requirements. Usually, the rate should be small for those nodes who have a very high or low trust value. For other nodes, the rate should be high in order to provide superior confidence in whether the target node is trusted or not. To ensure the effectiveness of such model, a pseudo random generation process can be used to send challenges.

Node Expertise. Different detectors may have their own detection superiority. This work thus accepts three levels of expertise: low (0.1), medium (0.5) and high (0.95), which can be formed by using the following functions [12,19].

$$f(p|\alpha, \beta) = \frac{1}{B(\alpha, \beta)} p^{\alpha-1}(1-p)^{\beta-1}$$
$$B(\alpha, \beta) = \int_0^1 t^{\alpha-1}(1-t)^{\beta-1}dt \tag{1}$$

where p ($\in [0,1]$) indicates how much it is possible to figure out an intrusion, $f(p|\alpha, \beta)$ describes how to compute the possibility by considering expertise level of el and difficulty level of dl ($\in [0,1]$). Intuitively, a bigger el can result in a higher possibility, whereas a bigger dl can decrease the possibility. Generally, α and β can be computed as below.

$$\alpha = 1 + \frac{el(1-dl)}{dl(1-el)} r$$
$$\beta = 1 + \frac{el(1-dl)}{dl(1-el)}(1-r) \tag{2}$$

where $r \in \{0,1\}$ represents the prospective result. Given a fixed dl, the detection performance of a node should depend on its particular level of proficiency. That is, an expert node should perform better than a non-expert node.

Node Trust Evaluation. As explained earlier, the ultimate trust value should rely on how much the received answers satisfy the expected feedback. Based on former work [12,22], the trust value of a node i according to node j can be derived as below.

$$T_{ft}^{i,j} = (w_s \frac{\sum_{k=0}^{n} F_k^{j,i} \lambda^{tk}}{\sum_{k=0}^{n} \lambda^{tk}} - T_s)(1 - x)^{dc} + T_s \tag{3}$$

where n indicates how many responses (or answers) are received, λ is a factor to allocate more weight on the recent response, $F_k^{j,i} \in [0,1]$ represents the satisfaction level on the received answer of k (number), and w_s is an adaptive weight: a) $w_s = \frac{\sum_{k=0}^{n} \lambda^{tk}}{m}$ if the received answers are less than a threshold of m; and b) $w_s = 1$ if the received answers are larger than m. Then x counts the percentage of "don't know" answers received within a given time slot, and dc is a parameter to control how much punishment should be given.

Packet-Based Trust. This type of trust is computed based on the received benign packets and the total packets from the target node. It is relatively objective as compared to the *feedback-based trust* and is helpful for determining a trusted route and identifying malicious nodes.

Similar to previous work [30], suppose N packets are sent from an IP address, of which k packets are proven to be *normal*. Our main objective is to estimate the possibility of $P(V_{N+1} = 1|n(N) = k)$: the status of $(N+1)$th packet when we know N packets are normal. Based on the *Bayesian Inference*, we can have the following:

$$P(V_{N+1} = 1|n(N) = k) = \frac{P(V_{N+1} = 1, n(N) = k)}{P(n(N) = k)} \tag{4}$$

We then apply the marginal probability distribution[2] and have the following:

$$P(n(N) = k) = \int_0^1 P(n(N) = k|p)f(p) \cdot dp \tag{5}$$

$$P(V_{N+1} = 1, n(N) = k) = \int_0^1 P(n(N) = k|p)f(p)p \cdot dp \tag{6}$$

As no prior information about p is given, we can assume that p is governed by a uniform prior distribution $f(p) = 1$, where $p \in [0,1]$. Hence in terms of Eq. (2) to Eq. (5), we can have the following:

$$P(V_{N+1} = 1|n(N) = k) = \frac{\int_0^1 P(n(N) = k|p)f(p)p \cdot dp}{\int_0^1 P(n(N) = k|p)f(p) \cdot dp} = \frac{k+1}{N+2} \tag{7}$$

---

[2] Marginal distribution of a subset of random variables is the probability distribution of the variables contained in the subset.

Then the packet-based trust of node i according to node j (denote $T_{pt}^{i,j}$) can be written as:

$$T_{pt}^{i,j} = \frac{k+1}{N+2} \tag{8}$$

where k is the amount of received benign packets and N is the total amount of received packets.

Energy-Aware Trust. Followed by the previous studies [15, 46], in this work, we consider that the energy consumption of node i by sending s-bits of data to node j at a distance d can be computed as follows:

$$Esend_j = \begin{cases} s \times E_{bit} + s \times \varepsilon_{fs} \times d^2, & d < d_0 \\ s \times E_{bit} + s \times \varepsilon_{mp} \times d^4, & d \geq d_0 \end{cases} \tag{9}$$

Then the energy consumption of node j by receiving s-bits data sent from node i is shown as below:

$$Ersv_j = s \times E_{bit} \tag{10}$$

where E_{bit} denotes energy consumption of transmitting *one* bit by the transmitter; ε_{fs} and ε_{mp} denote the energy consumption of the free-space and the multi-path fading model. d_0 is the threshold value for an amplifier to adjust its power, which can be calculated as below.

$$d_0 = \sqrt{\frac{\varepsilon_{fs}}{\varepsilon_{mp}}} \tag{11}$$

For node j, the energy consumption of aggregating s-bits data can be computed as below:

$$Eagr_j = s \times E_{fuse} \tag{12}$$

where E_{fuse} means the energy consumption of fusing *one* bit of data. Assume that the initial energy of each node is E_0, then the remaining energy of a node can be derived as:

$$RE_j^t = RE_j^{t+1} - Esend_j - Ersv_j - Eagr_j \tag{13}$$

Hence the energy-aware trust value (T_{et}) at node j can be calculated based on the above equations, as below:

$$T_{et} = \frac{RE_j^t}{E_0} \tag{14}$$

Single Fused Metric. We develop a single fused metric, named *total trust* (T_{total}), to facilitate the trust evaluation as below:

$$T_{total} = W_1 \times T_{fd} + W_2 \times T_{pt} + W_3 \times T_{et} \tag{15}$$

where W_1, W_2 and W_3 are weight values, and $W_1 + W_2 + W_3 = 1$. If given a threshold of t, we can measure the status of a node as below.

- If $T_{total} \geq t$, then the node is regarded as a trusted one.
- If $T_{total} < t$, then the node is regarded as a malicious one.

2.3   Alarm Aggregation

This is an important and critical process for a CIDN to enhance the detection performance by aggregating alarms and making a detection result. That is, a node can send a normal request for alarm rankings from other trusted nodes based on T_{total}. As an example, node j can aggregate the feedback $F_i(a)$ from node i and judge the current network status, e.g., the aggregated rank of alert a, by using a weighted majority approach as below.

$$R_j(a) = \frac{\sum_{T \geq r} T_{total}^i D_i^j F_i(a)}{\sum_{T \geq r} T_{total}^i D_i^j} \tag{16}$$

where $R_j(a)(\in [0,1])$ indicates the aggregated rank of alert a by node j. Then r is the trust threshold where node j only accepts the alarm rankings from those nodes whose reputation is higher than this threshold. $T_{total}^i(\in [0,1])$ indicates the total trust value of node i. $D_i^j(\in [0,1])$ describes how many *hops* between these two nodes.

3   Evaluation

In this section, we provide two experiments to study the performance of EnergyCIDN under both a simulated and a practical network environment.

- *Experiment-1.* This experiment set up a simulated IoT environment, and explored the performance of EnergyCIDN in the aspects of trust evaluation and aggregation error, under both common and advanced insider attacks.
- *Experiment-2.* This experiment collaborated with an IT organization, and investigated the performance of EnergyCIDN in a practical IoT network, under both common and advanced insider attacks. Figure 2 illustrates the high-level view of the practical network.

3.1   Experiment-1

CIDN Settings. In the simulated environment, we deployed a total of 50 nodes that were randomly distributed in a 50×50 grid area. The open-source IDS – Snort [47] was implemented in every CIDN node, as IDS module. Each node can detect nearby nodes and build a list of partner nodes after a period of time. To measure the reputation of partner nodes, each node can send out challenges randomly to its partners with an average rate of ε. There are two levels of request frequencies: ε_l and ε_h. For the nodes that have an unclear trust value around the threshold, the frequency should be set as high ε_h.

Table 1 summarizes the parameters for the simulated environment, i.e., the initial trust value was set as 0.5. All the parameters are selected based on prior work [11,19,22].

Table 1. Parameter settings in the simulated environment.

Parameters	Value	Description
λ	0.9	Forgetting factor
m	10	Lower limit of received feedback
d	0.3	Severity of punishment
ε_l	10/day	Low request frequency
ε_h	20/day	High request frequency
r	0.8	Trust threshold
T_s	0.5	Trust value for newcomers

Satisfaction Measurement. To simulate the satisfaction, let $Pe \in [0,1]$ denote the prospective response and $Pr \in [0,1]$ denote the received response. Then we can use the following function FL ($\in [0,1]$) to measure the satisfaction level.

$$FL = 1 - (\frac{Pe - Pr}{max(c_1 Pe, 1 - Pe)})^{c_2} \quad Pe > Pr \tag{17}$$

$$FL = 1 - (\frac{c_1(Pr - Pe)}{max(c_1 Pe, 1 - Pe)})^{c_2} \quad Pe \leq Pr \tag{18}$$

where c_1 manages the severity of punishment for incorrect estimates, and c_2 manages the satisfaction sensitivity. A larger c_2 means that the satisfaction is more sensitive to the feedback. In this work, we adopted $c_1 = 1.5$ and $c_2 = 1$, based on prior work [11,22].

Trust Convergence. Figure 3 depicts the convergence of trust values under the original challenge-based CIDN and our proposed EnergyCIDN. It is found that the convergence trend was dependent on the expertise level of a node.

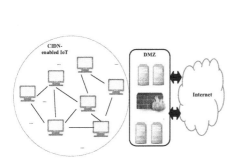

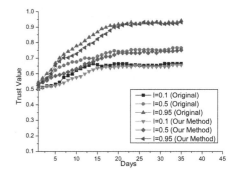

Fig. 2. The high-level architecture of the practical network: CIDN-enabled IoT with the deployed DMZ.

Fig. 3. Convergence of trust values between the original challenge-based CIDN and our method regarding different expertise nodes.

Generally, the more senior the node, the higher the trust value. In addition, our EnergyCIDN could result in a slower increase of trust values compared with the original one, which is more robust to newcomer attacks, as malicious nodes cannot obtain a high reputation value in a short time. It is figured out that the trust value will become stable after 30–35 days.

Trust Evaluation Under Common Insider Attacks. According to our threat model, we consider two types of common insider attacks: newcomer attack and betrayal attack. However, in practice, the ultimate goal of newcomer attack is to obtain a high reputation and then start sending malicious traffic or data, which can be considered as the first phase of betrayal-attack life circle. In addition, newcomer attack can be mitigated by the original challenge-based CIDNs, as each node has to register and get a valid identity. Hence, in this work, we only present the performance of detecting betrayal attacks.

We then randomly selected two expert nodes ($I = 0.95$) to perform the betrayal attack. Figure 4 and Fig. 5 describe the average trust values of malicious nodes and the error rate between the original challenge-based CIDNs and our proposed EnergyCIDN.

- Figure 4 shows that both the original challenge-based CIDN and our EnergyCIDN could keep decreasing the trust values of malicious nodes, while our method can decrease the reputation faster, i.e., the original scheme needed 4 days but our method only required 2 days to reduce the trust values of malicious nodes below the trust threshold. This is because our method utilized a hybrid trust model, which can be more sensitive to traffic changes.
- Figure 5 shows the error rate caused during the alarm aggregation. It is visible that the original scheme has an error rate of around 15% and 19% for false positive and false negative. By contrast, our EnergyCIDN could reduce the rate to 6.9% and 10%. This is because our method can identify the malicious nodes faster, and then exclude them from the alarm aggregation process.

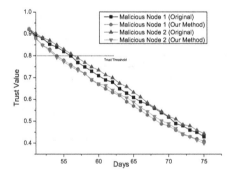

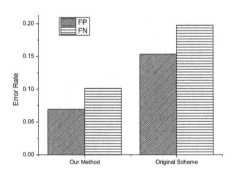

Fig. 4. Trust values of malicious nodes under betrayal attack between the original challenge-based CIDNs and our method.

Fig. 5. Error rate under betrayal attack during the alarm aggregation.

Trust Evaluation Under Advanced Insider Attack. To investigate the effect of advanced insider attacks, we mainly consider two attack types: Passive Message Fingerprint Attacks (PMFA) and Bayesian Poisoning Attacks (BPA). As they are a type of collusion attack, we randomly selected three expert nodes to perform the corresponding attack. Figure 6 and Fig. 7 depict the reputation of malicious nodes and the error rates under the original challenge-based CIDNs and our EnergyCIDN.

- As shown in Fig. 6, the trust value of PMFA/BPA malicious nodes could be maintained above the trust threshold, because the malicious nodes could identify normal requests by exchanging the received messages. In addition, it is found that BPA malicious nodes could maintain a higher trust value than PMFA malicious nodes, as BPA nodes could identify normal requests more precisely. By contrast, our method could detect all these malicious nodes quickly, though one additional day was required to decrease the reputation of BPA nodes below the threshold. This is because our method adopts packet-based trust and energy-aware trust, which could identify anomalies if a node exchanges an unusual amount of packets.
- Figure 7 shows the average error rate caused by PMFA/BPA malicious nodes under the original challenge-based CIDNs and our EnergyCIDN. It is found that these attacks could cause a roughly 35% error rate under the original scheme, but our method could reduce the rate to 11% for both false positive and false negative. This is because our method can detect malicious nodes, the slight increase is due to the one-day delay compared with the detection of betrayal attacks.

Based on the collected results, our proposed energy-aware method is viable to enhance the robustness of challenge-based CIDNs in the aspects of both trust evaluation and alarm aggregation.

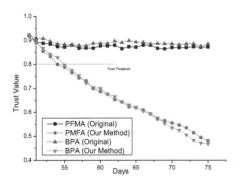

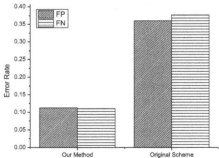

Fig. 6. Trust values of malicious nodes under PMFA and BPA between the original challenge-based CIDNs and our method.

Fig. 7. Average error rate under PMFA and BPA during the alarm aggregation.

3.2   Experiment-2

To explore the performance in a practical environment, we conducted a study in a CIDN-enabled IoT environment by collaborating with an IT organization. By balancing the security and privacy policies, the deployed environment includes 70 CIDN nodes, which can communicate with outside network via a DMZ. The security administrators from the participating organization were responsible for the environmental setup and audit. Similar to our experiment in the simulated environment, we also explored the effect of common insider attack (betrayal attack) and advanced insider attacks.

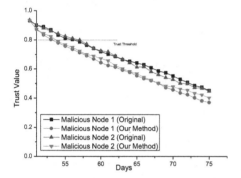
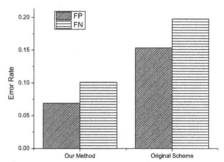

Fig. 8. Trust values of malicious nodes under betrayal attack between the original challenge-based CIDNs and our method.

Fig. 9. Error rate under betrayal attack during the alarm aggregation.

Trust Evaluation Under Common Insider Attacks. We randomly selected two expert nodes ($I = 0.95$) to perform a betrayal attack. Figure 8 and Fig. 9 describe the average trust values of malicious nodes and the error rates under the original challenge-based CIDNs and our EnergyCIDN.

- Figure 8 validates that both the original challenge-based CIDN and our proposed EnergyCIDN could identify malicious nodes under betrayal attack. It is observed that the original scheme required four days while our method only needed two days to confirm the malicious nodes. Further, we found that energy-aware trust is beneficial in the practical environment, as a real IoT node is more sensitive to power consumption than a simulated environment. This resulted in a more rapid decrease of trust values compared with that in the simulated environment.
- Figure 9 describes the error rate caused during the alarm aggregation. It is found that the error rate is around 16% and 18% for false positives and false negatives, but the rate could be decreased to around 5% and 8% with our method. The results validate that our method could achieve a lower error rate by identifying the malicious nodes faster.

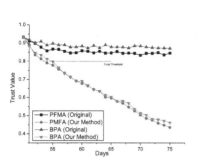 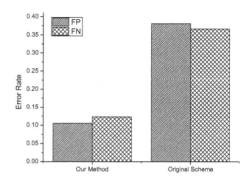

Fig. 10. Trust values of malicious nodes under PMFA and BPA between the original challenge-based CIDNs and our method.

Fig. 11. Average error rate under PMFA and BPA during the alarm aggregation.

Trust Evaluation Under Advanced Insider Attack. In this experiment, we explored the effect of Passive Message Fingerprint Attacks (PMFA) and Bayesian Poisoning Attacks (BPA). Figure 10 and Fig. 11 present the trust values of malicious nodes and the error rates under the original challenge-based CIDNs and our EnergyCIDN.

- Figure 10 validates the observations in the simulated experiment: that is, the original challenge-based CIDN could not identify PMFA and BPA malicious

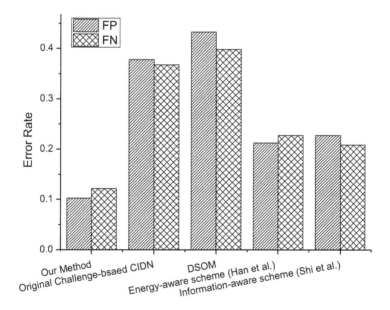

Fig. 12. The comparison with the state-of-the-art regarding error rates.

nodes, where BPA malicious nodes could have a higher reputation than the PMFA nodes. In the comparison, our method could decrease the trust values of both PMFA and BPA malicious nodes steadily. Also, we found that energy-aware trust is very helpful in a practical IoT environment, by analyzing the anomalies in power consumption against advanced malicious nodes.

– Figure 11 demonstrates that PMFA/BPA malicious nodes could cause an error rate of 38% and 36% under original challenge-based CIDNs. By contrast, our method could reduce the error rate to 10% and 12% respectively. This is because our EnergyCIDN could decrease the reputation of malicious nodes steadily to below the threshold and remove the negative impact.

Figure 12 further compares the error rates among several similar trust schemes, including energy-aware scheme [15] and information-aware scheme [46]. It is found that our proposed method could outperform these relevant schemes by leveraging the composed benefits from the challenge-based, packet-based and energy-aware trust.

On the whole, our practical results validate the observations in the simulated environment. It is proved that our method can provide enhanced performance against advanced insider attacks, in the aspects of detection efficiency and alarm aggregation.

4   Related Work

In real-world applications, a separate IDS often has no information about its deployed and protected environment, opening a chance for attackers and cyber-criminals. Due to the lack of contextual information, it becomes very hard for an IDS to figure out complicated attacks. Motivated by this issue, there is a great need for building a distributed system or collaborative network to enhance the detection performance [53].

Distributed Systems. Distributed systems have been widely used in various domains over the past years. For example, Porras *et al.* [43] introduced a system of EMERALD (Event Monitoring Enabling Responses to Anomalous Live Disturbances) with the aim to examine malicious actions in a large network (e.g., different layers). It used conventional IDS techniques to model and correlate distributed high-volume events. Snapp *et al.* [45] described a distributed intrusion detection system (DIDS), which could improve the examination process by refining and analyzing data in a centralized way. To mitigate the influence of DDoS attacks, COSSACK system [42] could work intelligently without the support and inputs from humans. Based on the actual scenarios, it could automatically create rules and signatures for detection. Yegneswaran *et al.* [55] described DOMINO (Distributed Overlay for Monitoring InterNet Outbreaks) with the aim to enhance the collaboration process in the distributed network. DOMINO system is believed to be heterogeneous, scalable, and robust.

Collaborative Intrusion Detection. A collaborative system encourages an IDS node to collect and exchange information with other nodes. Li *et al.* [17]

found that most distributed intrusion detection architectures could not be scalable under different communication mechanisms. Thus, they proposed a distributed detection system by means of a decentralized routing infrastructure. However, one big limitation is that all nodes in their approach should be intra trusted. This may lead to insider attacks, which are one common threat for various distributed systems and collaborative networks.

To protect distributed/collaborative systems against insider attacks, it is very important to design suitable trust mechanisms to measure the reputation in such systems and networks [28]. As an example, an overlay IDS was proposed by Duma et al. [8], aiming to defeat insider threats. It consists of a trust-aware engine for correlating alarms and an adaptive trust mechanism for handling trust. Tuan [50] explored the impact of game theory on detection improvement in a P2P network. They observed that: if a trust system was not designed with a proper incentive mechanism, then the more nodes within the system, the less likely that a suspicious node could be pointed out.

Fung et al. [11] proposed a kind of challenge-based CIDNs, aiming to evaluate the trustworthiness of an IDS node based on the received answers. They firstly proposed a collaboration framework for host-based detection and then designed a method to highlight the recent behavior of a node. To enhance such challenge mechanisms, Li et al. [18] defined a concept of *intrusion sensitivity* that can measure the detection sensitivity of an IDS. Generally, the intrusion sensitivity of an IDS can be varied according to attack types. They then introduced an *intrusion sensitivity-based trust management model* [19], which could allocate the value of intrusion sensitivity by using various machine learning algorithms, such as KNN classifier [35]. For pollution attacks in which a set of malicious nodes can collaborate to send fake information and influence alarm rankings, Li et al. [20] conducted a study and found that intrusion sensitivity can be used to figure out malicious nodes quickly. The results demonstrated that the use of intrusion sensitivity can be beneficial to distributed intrusion detection. Other related work regarding how to improve the performance of intrusion detection can refer to [9, 10, 31–34, 37, 38, 52].

Blockchain-Based Intrusion Detection. The application of blockchain technology in the intrusion detection domain has become popular in recent years. Meng et al. [39] provided the first insights on how to combine these two (IDS and blockchain) and discussed the potential challenges and future directions. More specifically, they argued that blockchain technology can be beneficial in improving an IDS in the aspects of data sharing, trust computation and alarm aggregation. For rule-based detection, Li et al. [24] discussed how to design a rule-based IDS with blockchain technology by establishing a verifiable rule database. This idea was followed their former work [49]. For anomaly-based detection, Golomb et al. [13] introduced a detection framework called CIoTA, which used blockchain technology to assist anomaly detection by sharing a machine learning model with each other. For firewall construction, Steichen et al. [48] designed ChainGuard, an OpenFlow-based firewall that could safeguard blockchain-based SDN and confirm malicious events / behavior within the network. Chiu and

Meng [7] developed BlockFW, a blockchain-based rule-sharing Firewall, which could provide validation and monitoring from multiple nodes. BlockFW could perform better than a traditional central-managed security solution as it can continue to serve correctly under a stressful network condition. Other related work can be referred to [6,14,16,26,27,41,54].

5   Discussion and Future Directions

Our EnergyCIDN showed promising results in both simulated and practical IoT environment, while as it adopts a hybrid trust model, some topics have to be discussed in our future work.

- *The effect of each trust.* Due to the page limit, the main focus of this work is to study the feasibility and the practicality of our proposed EnergyCIDN. We consider the composed benefits from all trust types in the experiments, but it is an important topic to explore the effect of each trust type, which can help better understand the detection effectiveness.
- *Diverse advanced insider attacks.* In this work, we mainly focus on Passive Message Fingerprint Attacks (PMFA) and Bayesian Poisoning Attacks (BPA), which are two major advanced threats to CIDNs. Our results figured out that analyzing the power consumption is an effective approach for detection. While some other advanced insider attacks can be considered such as special on-off attack (SOOA) [22,23] and random poisoning attack [36].
- *Blockchain-based trust type.* In this work, we adopt a hybrid trust model by considering challenge-based, packet-based and energy-aware trust. Currently, with blockchain technology being developed very fast, incorporating a blockchain-based trust could be helpful to enhance the existing trust evaluation. Such idea has been studied in the literature (e.g., [29]), and can be explored in our future work.

6   Conclusion

In this work, we developed EnergyCIDN, an energy-aware challenge-based CIDN that adopts a hybrid trust management model including challenge-based, packet-based and energy-aware trust. With a single fused metric, in the evaluation, we explored its performance in the aspects of trust evaluation (trust value) and alarm aggregation (error rate), under both simulated and practical IoT environment. Our results indicated that our EnergyCIDN could decrease the reputation of betrayal malicious nodes much faster than the original challenge-based CIDNs, and could identify advanced insider attacks (Passive Message Fingerprint Attacks and Bayesian Poisoning Attacks) effectively. For this sake, our method could have a much lower false rate (false positive and false negative) as compared with similar trust schemes. Overall, the results demonstrate the feasibility and the effectiveness of our proposed EnergyCIDN. This work aims to stimulate more research on the enhancement of collaborative intrusion detection.

Acknowledgments. This work was partially supported by the start-up fund in the Department of Electronic and Information Engineering, The Hong Kong Polytechnic University.

References

1. IoT Trends To Drive Innovation For Business In 2022 - MobiDev. https://mobidev.biz/blog/iot-technology-trends. Accessed 1 June 2022
2. Report: More than 1B IoT attacks in 2021. https://venturebeat.com/2022/04/25/report-more-than-1b-iot-attacks-in-2021/. Accessed 1 June 2022
3. IoT Security Global Market Report 2022. https://www.globenewswire.com/news-release/2022/03/22/2407932/0/en/IoT-Security-Global-Market-Report-2022.html. Accessed 3 May 2022
4. Ma, Z., Liu, L., Meng, W.: Towards multiple-mix-attack detection via consensus-based trust management in iot networks. Comput. Secur. **96**, 101898 (2020)
5. Paniagua, C., Delsing, J.: Industrial frameworks for internet of things: a survey. IEEE Syst. J. **15**(1), 1149–1159 (2021)
6. Cao, S., Dang, S., Zhang, Y., Wang, W., Cheng, N.: A blockchain-based access control and intrusion detection framework for satellite communication systems. Comput. Commun. **172**, 216–225 (2021)
7. Chiu, W.Y., Meng, W.: BlockFW - towards blockchain-based rule-sharing firewall. In: Proceedings of the 16th International Conference on Emerging Security Information, Systems and Technologies (SECURWARE), IARIA 2022 (2022)
8. Duma, C., Karresand, M., Shahmehri, N., Caronni, G.: A trust-aware, P2P-based overlay for intrusion detection. In: DEXA Workshop, pp. 692–697 (2006)
9. Fadlullah, Z.M., Taleb, T., Vasilakos, A.V., Guizani, M., Kato, N.: DTRAB: combating against attacks on encrypted protocols through traffic-feature analysis. IEEE/ACM Trans. Network. **18**(4), 1234–1247 (2010)
10. Friedberg, I., Skopik, F., Settanni, G., Fiedler, R.: Combating advanced persistent threats: from network event correlation to incident detection. Comput. Secur. **48**, 35–47 (2015)
11. Fung, C.J., Baysal, O., Zhang, J., Aib, I., Boutaba, R.: Trust management for host-based collaborative intrusion detection. In: De Turck, F., Kellerer, W., Kormentzas, G. (eds.) DSOM 2008. LNCS, vol. 5273, pp. 109–122. Springer, Heidelberg (2008). https://doi.org/10.1007/978-3-540-87353-2_9
12. Fung, C.J.; Zhu, Q., Boutaba, R., Basar, T.: Bayesian decision aggregation in collaborative intrusion detection networks. In: NOMS, pp. 349–356 (2010)
13. Golomb, T., Mirsky, Y., Elovici, Y.: CIoTA: collaborative IoT anomaly detection via blockchain. In: Proceedings of Workshop on Decentralized IoT Security and Standards (DISS), pp. 1–6 (2018)
14. Khan, A.A., Khan, M.M., Khan, K.M., Arshad, J., Ahmad, F.: A blockchain-based decentralized machine learning framework for collaborative intrusion detection within UAVs. Comput. Netw. **196**, 108217 (2021)
15. Han, Y., Hu, H., Guo, Y.: Energy-aware and trust-based secure routing protocol for wireless sensor networks using adaptive genetic algorithm. IEEE Access **10**, 11538–11550 (2022)
16. Hu, B., Zhou, C., Tian, Y.C., Qin, Y., Junping, X.: A collaborative intrusion detection approach using blockchain for multimicrogrid systems. IEEE Trans. Syst. Man Cybern. Syst. **49**(8), 1720–1730 (2019)

17. Li, Z., Chen, Y., Beach, A.: Towards scalable and robust distributed intrusion alert fusion with good load balancing. In: Proceedings of the 2006 SIGCOMM Workshop on Large-Scale Attack Defense (LSAD), pp. 115–122 (2006)

18. Li, W., Meng, Y., Kwok, L.-F.: Enhancing trust evaluation using intrusion sensitivity in collaborative intrusion detection networks: feasibility and challenges. In: Proceedings of the 9th International Conference on Computational Intelligence and Security (CIS), pp. 518–522. IEEE (2013)

19. Li, W., Meng, W., Kwok, L.-F.: Design of intrusion sensitivity-based trust management model for collaborative intrusion detection networks. In: Zhou, J., Gal-Oz, N., Zhang, J., Gudes, E. (eds.) IFIPTM 2014. IAICT, vol. 430, pp. 61–76. Springer, Heidelberg (2014). https://doi.org/10.1007/978-3-662-43813-8_5

20. Li. W., Meng, W.: Enhancing collaborative intrusion detection networks using intrusion sensitivity in detecting pollution attacks. Inf. Comput. Secur. **24**(3), 265–276 (2016). Emerald

21. Li, W., Meng, W., Kwok, L.F., Ip, H.H.S.: PMFA: toward passive message fingerprint attacks on challenge-based collaborative intrusion detection networks. In: Proceedings of the 10th International Conference on Network and System Security (NSS 2016), pp. 433–449 (2016)

22. Li, W., Meng, W., Kwok, L.F.: SOOA: exploring special on-off attacks on challenge-based collaborative intrusion detection networks. In: Proceedings of GPC, pp. 402–415 (2017)

23. Li, W., Meng, W., Kwok, L.-F.: Investigating the influence of special on-off attacks on challenge-based collaborative intrusion detection networks. Future Internet **10**(1), 1–16 (2018)

24. Li, W., Tug, S., Meng, W., Wang, Y.: Designing collaborative blockchained signature-based intrusion detection in IoT environments. Future Gener. Comput. Syst. (in Press). Elsevier

25. Li, W., Kwok, L.-F.: Challenge-based collaborative intrusion detection networks under passive message fingerprint attack: a further analysis. J. Inf. Secur. Appl. **47**, 1–7 (2019)

26. Li, W., Wang, Y., Li, J., Au, M.H.: Toward a blockchain-based framework for challenge-based collaborative intrusion detection. Int. J. Inf. Secur. **20**(2), 127–139 (2021)

27. Li, W., Wang, Y., Li, J.: Enhancing blockchain-based filtration mechanism via IPFS for collaborative intrusion detection in IoT networks. J. Syst. Archit. **127**, 102510 (2022)

28. Li, W., Meng, W., Kwok, L.-F.: Surveying trust-based collaborative intrusion detection: state-of-the-art, challenges and future directions. IEEE Commun. Surv. Tutor. **24**(1), 280–305 (2022)

29. Li, W., Meng, W.: BCTrustFrame: enhancing trust management via blockchain and IPFS in 6G era. IEEE Netw. **36**(4), 120–125 (2022)

30. Meng, Y., Kwok, L.F., Li, W.: Towards designing packet filter with a trust-based approach using Bayesian inference in network intrusion detection. In: Proceedings of the 8th International Conference on Security and Privacy in Communication Networks (SECURECOMM), pp. 203–221 (2012)

31. Meng, Y., Kwok, L.F.: Enhancing false alarm reduction using voted ensemble selection in intrusion detection. Int. J. Comput. Intell. Syst. **6**(4), 626–638 (2013). Taylor & Francis

32. Meng, Y., Li, W., Kwok, L.F.: Towards adaptive character frequency-based exclusive signature matching scheme and its applications in distributed intrusion detection. Comput. Netw. **57**(17), 3630–3640 (2013). Elsevier

33. Meng, W., Li, W., Kwok, L.-F.: An evaluation of single character frequency-based exclusive signature matching in distinct IDS environments. In: Proceedings of the 17th International Conference on Information Security (ISC), pp. 465–476 (2014)

34. Meng, W., Li, W., Kwok, L.-F.: EFM: enhancing the performance of signature-based network intrusion detection systems using enhanced filter mechanism. Comput. Secur. **43**, 189–204 (2014). Elsevier

35. Meng, W., Li, W., Kwok, L.-F.: Design of intelligent KNN-based alarm filter using knowledge-based alert verification in intrusion detection. Secur. Commun. Netw. **8**(18), 3883–3895 (2015). Wiley

36. Meng, W., Luo, X., Li, W., Li, Y.: Design and evaluation of advanced collusion attacks on collaborative intrusion detection networks in practice. In: Proceedings of the 15th IEEE International Conference on Trust, Security and Privacy in Computing and Communications (TrustCom 2016), pp. 1061–1068 (2016)

37. Meng, W., Li, W., Xiang, Y., Choo, K.K.R.: A Bayesian inference-based detection mechanism to defend medical smartphone networks against insider attacks. J. Netw. Comput. Appl. **78**, 162–169 (2017). Elsevier

38. Meng, W., Li, W., Kwok, L.-F.: Towards effective trust-based packet filtering in collaborative network environments. IEEE Trans. Netw. Serv. Manag. **14**(1), 233–245 (2017)

39. Meng, W., Tischhauser, E.W., Wang, Q., Wang, Y., Han, J.: When intrusion detection meets blockchain technology: a review. IEEE Access **6**(1), 10179–10188 (2018)

40. Meng, W., Li, W., Jiang, L., Choo, K.K.R., Su, C.: Practical Bayesian poisoning attacks on challenge-based collaborative intrusion detection networks. In: Proceedings of the ESORICS, pp. 493–511 (2019)

41. Meng, W., Li, W., Yang, L.T., Li, P.: Enhancing challenge-based collaborative intrusion detection networks against insider attacks using blockchain. Int. J. Inf. Secur. **19**(3), 279–290 (2020)

42. Papadopoulos, C., Lindell, R., Mehringer, J., Hussain, A., Govindan, R.: COSSACK: coordinated suppression of simultaneous attacks. In: Proceedings of the 2003 DARPA Information Survivability Conference and Exposition (DISCEX), pp. 94–96 (2003)

43. Porras, P.A., Neumann, P.G.: Emerald: event monitoring enabling responses to anomalous live disturbances. In: Proceedings of the 20th National Information Systems Security Conference, pp. 353–365 (1997)

44. Scarfone, K., Mell, P.: Guide to Intrusion Detection and Prevention Systems (IDPS). NIST Special Publication 800-94 (2007)

45. Snapp, S.R., et al.: DIDS (distributed intrusion detection system) - motivation, architecture, and an early prototype. In: Proceedings of the 14th National Computer Security Conference, pp. 167–176 (1991)

46. Shi, Q., Qin, L., Ding, Y., Xie, B., Zheng, J., Song, L.: Information-aware secure routing in wireless sensor networks. Sensors **20**(1), Article 165 (2020)

47. Snort: An an open source network intrusion prevention and detection system (IDS/IPS). http://www.snort.org/

48. Steichen, M., Hommes, S., State, R.: ChainGuard - a firewall for blockchain applications using SDN with OpenFlow. In: Proceedings of International Conference on Principles, Systems and Applications of IP Telecommunications (IPTComm), pp. 1–8 (2017)

49. Tug, S., Meng, W., Wang, Y.: CBSigIDS: towards collaborative blockchained signature-based intrusion detection. In: Proceedings of The 1st IEEE International Conference on Blockchain (Blockchain) (2018)

50. Tuan, T.A.: A game-theoretic analysis of trust management in P2P systems. In: Proceedings of ICCE, pp. 130–134 (2006)
51. Vasilomanolakis, E., Karuppayah, S., Muhlhauser, M., Fischer, M.: Taxonomy and Survey of Collaborative Intrusion Detection. ACM Computing Surveys 47(4), pp. 55:1–55:33 (2015)
52. Wang, Y., Meng, W., Li, W., Liu, Z., Liu, Y., Xue, H.: Adaptive machine learning-based alarm reduction via edge computing for distributed intrusion detection systems. Concurr. Comput. Pract. Exp. (2019). Wiley
53. Wu, Y.-S., Foo, B., Mei, Y., Bagchi, S.: Collaborative intrusion detection system (CIDS): a framework for accurate and efficient IDS. In: Proceedings of the 2003 Annual Computer Security Applications Conference (ACSAC), pp. 234–244 (2003)
54. Yenugunti, C., Yau, S.S.: A blockchain approach to identifying compromised nodes in collaborative intrusion detection systems. In: Proceedings of DASC/PiCom/CBDCom/CyberSciTech, pp. 87–93 (2020)
55. Yegneswaran, V., Barford, P., Jha, S.: Global intrusion detection in the DOMINO overlay system. In: Proceedings of the 2004 Network and Distributed System Security Symposium (NDSS), pp. 1–17 (2004)

Federated Learning-Based Intrusion Detection on Non-IID Data

Yongfei Liu[1,2], Guangjun Wu[1,2(✉)], Wenyuan Zhang[1,2]📵, and Jun Li[1,2]

[1] Institute of Information Engineering, Chinese Academy of Sciences, Beijing 100093, China
{liuyongfei,wuguangjun,zhangwenyuan,lijun}@iie.ac.cn
[2] School of Cyber Security, University of Chinese Academy of Sciences, Beijing 100049, China

Abstract. Intrusion detection is an effective means to deal with network attacks. Currently, the commonly used detection methods are based on machine learning. However, traditional machine learning-based methods are centralized architectures that require uploading data to cloud servers, which face serious latency and data security issues. Federated learning (FL) can collaboratively train a machine learning model with good performance while the data is kept locally on the client, which can effectively make up for the shortcomings of the centralized architecture. Most of the current research on using FL methods in machine learning-based intrusion detection ideally consider the data to be independent and identically distributed (IID), which doesn't conform to real scenarios. In the real world, due to the different environment of the client, the types of attacks contained in the data owned by each client may be different. Therefore, we study the effects of various non-independent and identically distribution (non-IID) settings on FL in detail and give specific partitioning methods. In addition, we also propose a FL data rebalancing method based on auxiliary classifier generative adversarial networks (ACGAN), which is experimentally validated on the UNSW-NB15 dataset. Experiments show that the proposed data augmentation method can well improve the impact of non-IID data on FL.

Keywords: Federated learning · Intrusion detection · Non independent identically distributed · Data augmentation · ACGAN

1 Introduction

With the rapid development of information technology, a large number of network services and applications have been applied to our daily life. While the network brings us convenience, it also faces huge security challenges. Traditional Internet security technologies such as firewalls and user authentication can't comprehensively protect networks and systems from increasingly complex attacks [4].

Intrusion detection [9] is an effective means to deal with network attacks. It can not only monitor malicious behaviors from outside the network, but also

© Springer Nature Switzerland AG 2023
W. Meng et al. (Eds.): ICA3PP 2022, LNCS 13777, pp. 313–329, 2023.
https://doi.org/10.1007/978-3-031-22677-9_17

monitor malicious behaviors inside the network, and provide real-time detection of malicious in the networks. Intrusion detection methods are mainly divided into the following three kinds [22]: methods based on statistical information, methods based on rules and methods based on machine learning. At present, the most commonly used method is based on machine learning [14].

In the past decade, various machine learning-based intrusion detection methods have been proposed. A popular approach is to use deep learning techniques to identify network anomalies [6]. Deep learning can learn complex patterns from high-dimensional data, which makes it a suitable solution for detecting network attacks. However, traditional deep learning-based approaches are centralized architectures. The data needs to be centralized in a cloud or data center before the intrusion detection model can be trained. Due to the huge amount of data and the need for centralized processing, this brings great challenges to the performance of the server. Data transmission also brings a lot of communication overhead, causing delay problems. In addition, the data contains sensitive information, and there is a risk of privacy leakage [21].

These limitations can be overcome by federated learning methods. Federated learning [16] is a new device-based distributed machine learning method. FL adheres to the ideal of "sending the code to the data end instead of sending the data to the code end", which avoids the transmission and centralized storage of user data and ensures that user privacy data is not uploaded. FL allows a large number of device to collaboratively training a machine learning model, which can train a machine learning model with good performance based on the local data of the device to improve the performance of intrusion detection.

Most of the current research on intrusion detection combined with FL ideally believe that the data on the client is IID [1,11,17]. However, in a real-world setting, due to the different environment of the client, the data collected varies from device to device, and the types of attacks contained in the data owned by each client may be different. In addition, the number of anomalies usually accounts for only a small part of the whole training set, which poses great challenges for FL training.

In order to make up for the shortcomings of existing research, we study FL-based intrusion detection on non-IID settings. We investigate the impact of non-IID settings on model training by setting different non-IID data partitions. Taking advantage of ACGAN's ability to generate corresponding category data according to specified label, rebalance the data with the help of FL to improve the impact of non-IID data. From the experimental results, our algorithm performs better than other state-of-the-art rebalancing techniques in the extreme non-IID case. The contributes of our work are as follows:

1) We consider more comprehensive non-IID data scenarios and give detailed partitioning methods.
2) We introduce a data rebalancing method for non-IID data, ACGAN-based federated learning data augmentation method.
3) We conduct extensive experiments on the UNSW-NB15 dataset to show the impact of the non-IID data setting on FL, and demonstrate that the

proposed data augmentation method can well improve the impact of non-IID data on FL.

The rest of this paper is organized as follows. Section 2 presents related work. Section 3 introduces the background knowledge of FL, data augmentation and so on. Section 4 details the non-IID data setting, ACGAN-based federated learning data augmentation method. Section 5 experiments show the impact of non-IID data setting on FL, and verify the performance of ACGAN-based federated learning data augmentation algorithm under non-IID data setting. Finally, we conclude this paper in Sect. 6.

2 Related Work

Currently, there are many research papers on the use of FL methods in deep learning-based intrusion detection. The related work can be divided into two categories: without considering data distribution and considering data distribution.

Without considering data distribution. Zhao [27] et al. proposed a FL-based multi-task neural network MT-DNN-FL to simultaneously perform anomaly detection tasks and traffic classification tasks. Popoolao [20] et al. proposed a FL method for zero-day botnet attack detection to avoid data privacy leakage issues in IoT edge devices, using a deep neural network architecture for network traffic classification. Man [15] et al. proposed an intelligent intrusion detection mechanism FedACNN, which assists the deep learning model CNN to complete intrusion detection through the FL mechanism. Liu [12,13] et al. proposed a FL-based CNN-LSTM model to detect anomalies. The CNN-LSTM model uses CNN units to capture fine-grained features and retains the advantages of LSTM units in predicting time series data. Yodav [25] et al. proposed an unsupervised deep learning method based on FL, which uses an autoencoder to learn from unlabeled data. The data distributions considered in these studies are all IID under ideal conditions. Although the detection effect is good, they can't reflect the real situation.

Considering data distribution. Campos [2] et al. evaluated a federated IDS method based on multi-class classifiers, considering different data distributions, for detecting different attacks in IoT scenarios. Chen [5] et al. proposed FedA-GRU, an intrusion detection algorithm for wireless edge network, aiming at the risk of network attack faced by wireless edge networks. These studies consider the case of non-IID, but don't give a division method, artificially specify the data owned by each client, and the number of clients is fixed, so it's not easy to study multi-client scenarios. Only experiments were conducted on non-IID data, but no improvement method was proposed for optimization based on poor performance under unbalanced conditions. Wang [23] et al. proposed a novel peer-to-peer algorithm P2PK-SMOTE for training supervised anomaly detection deep learning models in non-IID scenarios, including rebalancing the local training dataset by synthesizing data points in the minority class mechanism. Weinger [24] et al. pointed out that non-IID data would limit the effectiveness of deep learning model, and proposed to improve classification performance through data augmentation, including random sampling, SMOTE and ADASYN. These studies have made some improvements to quantity skew scenes, but due to the data augmentation method used is oversampling, it can only generate data of existing categories, and can't solve the situation of label skew.

Overall, there are still many deficiencies in current research on FL-based intrusion detection under non-IID settings. Therefore, we consider various non-IID scenarios in detail, give a specific division method, and propose an improved method according to the poor performance of FL under non-IID data.

3 System Model

In this section, we introduce the basic concepts of federated learning, Dirichlet distribution and data augmentation.

3.1 Federated Learning

In federated learning, it is generally considered that it consists of a central server and K clients. Each client has a local dataset $D_k = \{x_j, y_j\}_{j=1}^{|D_k|}$, where $|D_k|$ represents the total number of data samples for client k, x_j is the jth sample, y_j is corresponding label. $y_j \in \{1, 2, ..., C\}$, C represents the number of labels. The local loss of client k can be defined as:

$$\mathcal{L}_k(\omega_k) = \frac{1}{|D_k|} \sum_{j \in D_k} \ell(x_j, y_j; \omega_k) \tag{1}$$

where $\ell(x_j, y_j; \omega_k)$ is the loss corresponding to the data $\{x_j, y_j\}$, ω_k is the local model parameters of client k. The global loss for K clients can be denoted as:

$$\mathcal{L}(\omega) = \frac{\sum_{k=1}^{K} |D_k| \mathcal{L}_k(\omega_k)}{\sum_{k=1}^{K} |D_k|} \tag{2}$$

where ω is the global model parameters aggregated by the central server. The goal of FL is to find the optimal model parameters ω^*:

$$\omega^* = arg \min_{\omega} \mathcal{L}(\omega) \tag{3}$$

In order to obtain ω^*, the server and clients need to conduct T rounds of communication. Each round of communication requires the following steps:

Step 1 (Initialization): In the tth round of training, the server randomly selects a subset S_t from K clients, then the global model parameters ω^{t-1} are distributed to them.

Step 2 (Local training): The selected client use the local data D_k to train the received global model ω^{t-1}, then send the model parameters ω_k^t obtained by training to the server.

Step 3 (Aggregation): The server collects the local model parameters uploaded by the client, and runs an aggregation algorithm (e.g., FedAvg) to get the aggregation model ω^t.

3.2 Dirichlet Distribution

In order to generate non-IID data sets in different cases, we assisted the implementation by the Dirichlet distribution [8,26]. Dirichlet distribution is an important multi-dimensional continuous distribution in probability statistics, often referred to as $Dir(\alpha)$, and its distribution is controlled by the parameters of the positive real vector α. The definition of Dirichlet distribution can be formalized as the following description, let $\theta = [\theta_1, ..., \theta_m]$ be an m-dimensional vector, for any $i \in [1, 2, ..., m]$, there are $\theta_i \geq 0$ and $\sum_{i=1}^{m} \theta_i = 1$. Let k-dimensional vector $\alpha = [\alpha_1, ..., \alpha_k]$, for any $i \in [1, 2, ..., k]$, $\alpha_i > 0$. If $\theta \sim Dir(\alpha_1, ..., \alpha_k)$, then the following Dirichlet distribution probability density function exists:

$$P(\theta_1, .., \theta_m) = \frac{\Gamma(\sum_k \alpha_k)}{\prod_k \Gamma(\alpha_k)} \prod_{k=1}^{m} \theta_k^{\alpha_k - 1} \tag{4}$$

$$\Gamma(\alpha_k) = \int_0^{+\infty} x^{\alpha_k - 1} e^{-x} dx (x > 0) \tag{5}$$

The parameter α can control the skew degree of the generated data distribution. The smaller α, the higher the non-IID level of each client's data distribution; otherwise, the client's data distribution tends to the IID settings. For example, as shown in Fig. 1, we show the data distribution for 10 labels and 10 clients when $\alpha = [0.5, 100]$. When $\alpha = 0.5$, the amount of data in the same category varies greatly between clients. When $\alpha = 100$, the amount of data in the same category has little difference between clients.

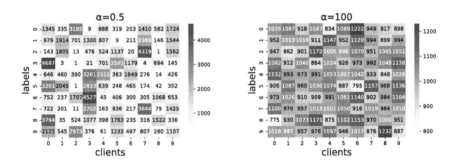

Fig. 1. Heatmap of data distribution under different α parameters.

3.3 Data Augmentation

SMOTE. Synthetic Minority OverSampling Technique (SMOTE) [3] is a commonly used data oversampling technique, which is an improved scheme of random oversampling algorithm. Random oversampling adopts the strategy of simply copying samples to increase the data, which is prone to the problem of model overfitting. The basic idea of the SMOTE algorithm is to analyze a few samples

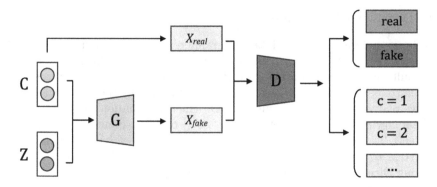

Fig. 2. ACGAN structure diagram.

and artificially synthesize new samples to add to the dataset according to the few samples. Specifically, SMOTE first applies K-Nearest Neighbors (KNN) to each $x_i \in D$ to compute its neighbors, and then randomly selects a x_i^j from its neighbors to apply linear interpolation, a newly synthesized instance x_{syn} can be denoted as:

$$x_{syn} = x_i + (x_i - x_i^j) \times \delta \quad (6)$$

where x_i and x_i^j both come from D, x_i^j is a randomly selected one from the k neighbors of x_i, and δ is a random number in the range $[0, 1]$. Synthesized data points x_{syn} are added to the dataset for training.

ACGAN. ACGAN [19] is a data generation model, which can generate corresponding categories of data according to labels. As shown in Fig. 2, ACGAN consists of a generator and a discriminator. The input of the generator consists of noise data z and corresponding class labels c, which are used to generate sufficiently realistic fake data. The discriminator has two functions: one is to distinguish the real and fake data, and the other is to classify the data. The objective function of ACGAN is:

$$\min_G \max_D V(D, G) = E_{x \sim p_{data}(x)}[\log D(x|y)] + E_{z \sim p_z(z)}[\log(1 - D(G(z|y)))] \quad (7)$$

where G is the generator, D is the discriminator, $x \sim p_{data}(x)$ represents the distribution obeyed by the real data, $z \sim p_z(z)$ represents the distribution obeyed by the noise data, $\log(\cdot)$ is the logarithmic function, $E(\cdot)$ represents the excepted value. The goal of the discriminator is that the discriminant result $D(x|y)$ for real data tends to 1, while the discriminant result $D(G(z|y))$ for the fake data generated by the generator tends to 0. The goal of the generator is to make the discriminator result $D(G(z|y))$ of the discriminator tend to 1.

Algorithm 1 describes the training process of the ACGAN model. The ACGAN model is trained by iterative training generator G and discriminator D.

Algorithm 1: ACGAN training algorithm

Input: Number of iterations E, D training steps S_d, G training steps S_g, batch size m, real data distribution p_{data}, noisy data distribution p_z, G model parameters ω_g, D model parameters ω_d, learning rate η;

Output: Data generator G, data discriminator D;

1   **for** $e = 1, 2, ..., E$ **do**

2   **phase 1: Train the discriminator**

3   **for** $s = 1, 2, ..., S_d$ **do**

4   Sample m samples from p_{data} : $\{(x_1, y_1^{real}), ..., (x_m, y_m^{real})\}$;

5   Sample m noise samples from p_z : $\{(z_1, y_1^{fake}), ..., (z_m, y_m^{fake})\}$;

6   Fixed parameters of G to prevent updating of G;

7       $\mathcal{L}_S = \frac{1}{m}\sum_{i=1}^{m}(\ell_s(D(x_i), 1) + \ell_s(D(G(z_i)), 0))$;

8       $\mathcal{L}_C = \frac{1}{m}\sum_{i=1}^{m}(\ell_c(D(x_i), y_i^{real}) + \ell_c(D(G(z_i)), y_i^{fake}))$;

9   Discriminator parameters update : $\omega_d \leftarrow \omega_d - \eta\nabla(\mathcal{L}_S + \mathcal{L}_C)$;

10   **end**

11   **phase 2 : Train the generator**

12   **for** $s = 1, 2, ..., S_g$ **do**

13   Sample m noise samples from p_z : $\{(z_1, y_1^{fake}), ..., (z_m, y_m^{fake})\}$;

14   Fixed parameters of D to prevent updating of D;

15       $\mathcal{L}_S = \frac{1}{m}\sum_{i=1}^{m}\ell_s(D(z_i), 1), \mathcal{L}_C = \frac{1}{m}\sum_{i=1}^{m}\ell_c(D(G(z_i)), y_i^{fake})$;

16   Generator parameters update : $\omega_g \leftarrow \omega_g - \eta\nabla(\mathcal{L}_S + \mathcal{L}_C)$;

17   **end**

18 **end**

---

4   Algorithm and System Design

In this section, we first introduce the non-IID setting implemented on the data. Then we introduce a federated learning data augmentation method based on ACGAN. Finally, we introduce an intrusion detection architecture based on federated learning.

4.1   Non-IID Data Setting

We consider three non-IID data [10] cases: 1) Quantity skew: different clients have the same category, but the number of samples in the same category varies greatly. 2) Label skew: different clients have very different categories, but the number of samples in the same category is almost the same. 3) Mixed skew: consider both quantity skew and label skew.

The non-IID division of data is shown in Table 1. When we divide the data, the data is divided into two classes: normal class and attack class, and consider their division separately. For normal class data, since there is only one class and each client generally has a large amount of such data, there is no label skew, and only the quantity skew needs to be considered. For the attack class, since there are multiple categories of attack classes, both label skew and quantity skew need to be considered. The Dirichlet distribution is used to simulate the quantity skew among different clients. c is used to denote the number of attack classes the client has.

Quantity skew. For normal class data, since each client has a large amount of such data, set the parameter $\alpha\_norm=0.5$. For attack class data, each client has all attack categories. Since the amount of attack data owned by each client is uncertain, five cases are considered, and the parameter α_att is set to 10,1,0.5,0.1 and 0.01, respectively.

Label skew. Since when the parameters of Dirichlet distribution are large, the data distribution will tend to IID, so set the parameters of normal class and attack class $\alpha\_norm=\alpha\_att=100$. For the number of attack categories each client has, consider two cases. One is that the number of categories owned by the client is fixed, but the specific categories owned are random. The other is the number of categories owned by the client is random, as is the class that has owned. For the first case, set the client to have 1,3,5 and 7 attack categories. For the second case, $random(1,8)$ is used to randomly select the number of attack categories possessed by the client.

Mixed skew. Consider both quantity skew and label skew. For normal class data, set $\alpha\_norm=0.5$. For attack class data, set $\alpha\_att=0.5$ when the number of classes owned by the client is fixed. Set α_att to 10,1,0.5,1,0.01 in the case that the number of categories owned by the client is random.

Table 1. Non-IID data partitioning

Non-IID scenarios	Normal class (quantity)	Attack class	
		Category	Quantity
Quantity skew	$\alpha\_norm = 0.5$	$c = 8$	$\alpha\_att = 10,1,0.5,0.1,0.01$
Label skew	$\alpha\_norm = 100$	$c = 1,3,5,7$	$\alpha\_att = 100$
		$c = random(1,8)$	
Mixed skew	$\alpha\_norm = 0.5$	$c = 1,3,5,7$	$\alpha\_att = 0.5$
		$c = random(1,8)$	$\alpha\_att = 10,1,0.5,0.1,0.01$

4.2 Federated Learning Data Augmentation Based on ACGAN

Non-IID data can make the trained aggregate model deviate from the optimal model. Research shows [7]: under non-IID data, by adding a small amount of data to the client, the performance of the FL algorithm can be improved. Therefore, data augmentation is a good way to improve the poor performance under non-IID data. Generative adversarial network (GAN) is a commonly used method of data augmentation, which can generate a large number of various fake data, and the generated fake data can effectively avoid the user's private information. As an improvement of GAN, ACGAN can generate data with specified labels. Therefore, we propose ACGAN-based federated learning data augmentation.

The proposed ACGAN-based federated learning data augmentation framework is shown in Fig. 3. The FL server trains to generate an ACGAN model,

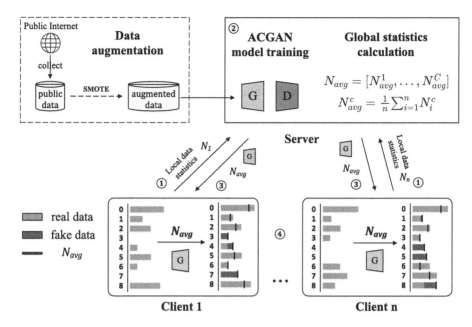

Fig. 3. Framework of federated learning data augmentation based on ACGAN.

and then distributes the generated model to clients, and each client uses the generated model to augment local data. Specific steps are as follows:

Phase 1: The client uploads the distribution information of the local sample data to the FL server. Let $S_1, ..., S_n$ represents n clients participating in federated learning, N_i^c represents the number of data samples of the cth class of the ith clients S_i, $c \in [1, ..., C]$, C represents the total number of data classes. Each client uploads its own local data statistics information $N_i = [N_i^1, ..., N_i^C]$ to the server.

Phase 2: The server computes global statistics information and trains the ACGAN model. After the server receives the statistical information N_i sent by the client i, it needs to process it to obtain the global statistical information N_{avg}. $N_{avg} = [N_{avg}^1, ..., N_{avg}^C]$, N_{avg}^c represents the average data volume of the cth class of all clients. $N_{avg}^c = \frac{1}{n} \sum_{i=1}^{n} N_i^c$. Since the server can only collect a small amount of training data, it is difficult to use this data to train an ACGAN model with good performance, so we use the SMOTE method to augment data and use the augmented data to train the ACGAN model.

Phase 3: The server distributes data generation model G and global statistics N_{avg}. The client needs to use G to augment local data, and decide whether to augment it and the amount of data augmented according to N_{avg}.

Phase 4: The client augments local data with G and N_{avg} sent by the server. The client compares the difference between its own local data statistics information and the global statistics information sent by the server. If the client S_i has samples of the cth class, it needs to compare the sizes of N_i^c and N_{avg}^c. If N_i^c is smaller than N_{avg}^c, $N_{avg}^c - N_i^c$ samples of the ith class need to be generated by the generator. If N_i^c is greater than N_{avg}^c, it remains unchanged. If the client S_i does not have the samples of the ith class, N_{avg}^c samples of the ith class are generated by the generator. Algorithm 2 describes the implementation of the above four steps.

Algorithm 2: Federated learning data augmentation algorithm based on ACGAN

Input: Client local data statistics information $N = [N_1, ..., N_n]$, category statistics information $[N^1, ..., N^C]$, client set S, total number of clients n, total number of data categories C;

Output: The trained ACGAN generator G, augmented dataset;

1 **Server :**
2 Initialization $N^c = 0, c \in [1, ..., C]$;
3 Get client local data statistics information N;
4 **for** $c = 1, 2, ..., C$ **do**
5   **for** $i = 1, 2, ..., n$ **do**
6          $N^c = N^c + N_i^c$;
7   **end**
8      $N_{avg}^c = \frac{1}{n}N^c$;
9   Add N_{avg}^c to N_{avg};
10 **end**
11 Train the ACGAN model;
12 Distribute the generative model G and global statistics N_{avg} to all clients;
13 **Client :**
14 **for** $i = 1, 2, ..., n$ **do**
15   Client S_i sends $N_i = [N_i^1, ..., N_i^C]$ to server;
16 **end**
17 Receive generative model G and global statistics information N_{avg};
18 **for** $i = 1, 2, ..., n$ **do**
19   **for** $c = 1, 2, ..., C$ **do**
20   **if** $N_i^c < N_{avg}^c$ **then**
21   Use G to expand the amount of data in this category to N_{avg}^c;
22   **end**
23   **end**
24 **end**

4.3   Intrusion Detection Based on Federated Learning

The flow chart of intrusion detection based on federated learning is shown in Fig. 4. The input training data first goes through the ACGAN-based federated learning data augmentation module to obtain an augmented dataset with relatively balanced data distribution among clients. The client uses this dataset as a local dataset and participates in FL to collaboratively train an intrusion detection model. Afterwards, the client uses the trained intrusion detection model to classify the test data to distinguish whether the data belongs to the normal class or the attack class. If the data belongs to the attack class, the specific attack class is given.

The federated learning data augmentation module based on ACGAN can effectively augment client data and improve the impact of non-IID on federated learning intrusion detection. The data augmented by the client does not need to be generated by the FL server, avoiding the communication overhead required for data transmission. Each client generates augmented samples based on different random inputs, so that the augmented data samples have high diversity.

Intrusion detection technology based on federated learning can help break the problem of data silos, enabling each client to train intrusion detection model with the help of other client's private dataset. It can better learn the pattern and distribution of attack and normal samples, improve the detection rate of attacks, and can also protect the privacy and security of the dataset.

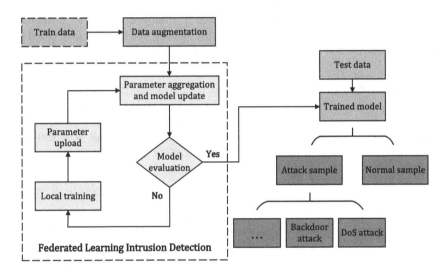

Fig. 4. Flow chart of intrusion detection based on federated learning.

5   Performance Evaluation

In this section, we conduct simulation experiments on representative public dataset to demonstrate the impact of the non-IID data setting on federated learning and verify the performance of the ACGAN-based federated learning data augmentation algorithm under the non-IID data setting.

5.1   Experimental Setup

Dataset Introduction. The raw network packets of the UNSW-NB15 [18] dataset were created by the IXIAPerfectStom tool of the Network Scope Lab of the Australian Centre for Cyber Security. The dataset has a total of 2540044 records, and each record has 49 features. There are a total of 9 types of attacks in the dataset, namely: *Fuzzers, Analysis, Backdoors, DoS, Exploits, Generic, Reconnaissance, Shellcode, Worms*.

Data Preprocessing. Since the classification uses the CNN model, the timestamp data is of little significance for the classification, so we choose to delete the *times-tamp* feature. Since the data features have both numerical type and string type characteristics, and the CNN model can only handle numerical types, the LabelEncoder vectorized encoding is performed on the *srcip, destip, proto, state, service, attack-cat* feature columns, and the String are converted to numeric types. Since the data value ranges of different columns of the data are quite different, *Z-score* standardization is performed on the data so that the mean value of the data is 0 and the standard deviation is 1. In addition, considering that the amount of data in *Worms* attack is too small, it is not conducive to non-IID data division, so this kind of attack is removed from the data set. In order to better verify the training effect of the model, the dataset is divided into training set and test set, and the ratio of training set to test set is 7:3.

Hyperparameter Settings. In the experimental setup, a total of $K = 100$ clients participate in federated learning. In each round, we choose 10% of the clients to participate in the training (i.e., $C = 0.1$). Each client trains on its local dataset D_k for 5 epochs with a batch size of 100 (i.e., $E = 5$ and $B = 100$). The number of communication rounds between the client and the server is 50, that is, $T = 50$.

5.2   Results of Running on Non-IID Data

First, we evaluate the performance of the intrusion detection model on the dataset under centralized, federated learning IID and non-IID. Our experimental results are shown in Fig. 5. From the figure, we can clearly observe that the accuracy of FL on IID data is not different from that of centralized learning. However, the accuracy of FL on non-IID data is significantly different from that of centralized. Convergence of FL on IID data is as stable as centralized. Compared to centralized, FL has relatively poor convergence on non-IID data. The experiment well verifies our previous analysis. On non-IID data, the accuracy and convergence of FL will be greatly affected.

In order to better study the accuracy and convergence of FL on non-IID data, we conducted more detailed experiments, as shown in Fig. 6. Experiments show that quantity skew has a greater impact on the accuracy of FL, label skew has a greater impact on the convergence of FL, and label skew is more serious than quantity skew.

Figure 6(a) shows the accuracy of FL under different quantity skew. It is not difficult to see from the figure that the degree of quantity skew has little impact on the convergence of FL, but has a great impact on the accuracy of FL. As the

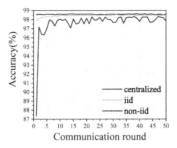

Fig. 5. Accuracy on centralized, federated learning IID and non-IID.

degree of quantity skew increases, the accuracy of FL gradually decreases, and the convergence also begins to deteriorate.

Figure 6(b) shows the accuracy of FL under different label skew. It is not difficult to see from the figure that the label skew has little effect on the accuracy of FL, but has a great impact on the convergence of FL. As the degree of label skew increases, the convergence of FL gradually deteriorates. In particular, when each client has only one attack class data, FL don't converge.

Figure 6(c) and 6(d) show the accuracy of FL under different mixed skew. Comparing Fig. 6(c) and 6(b), it is not difficult to find that in the case where the degree of quantity skew is not very extreme, the situation displayed under the mixed skew is more similar to the label skew. Comparing Fig. 6(d) and 6(a), it is not difficult to find that the convergence under mixed skew is worse than that under quantity skew. Under the action of label skew, extreme quantity skew don't converge.

5.3 Performance of Federated Learning Data Augmentation Algorithm Based on ACGAN

In this subsection, we show the performance of ACGAN-based federated learning data augmentation and compare our method with the SMOTE method in [23, 24].

Figure 7(a) shows the performance of our method under severe quantity skew and label skew. It can be clearly seen from the figure that our method has high robustness. After the data is augmented by our method, the FL training not only has high accuracy, but also has good convergence.

Figure 7(b) shows the performance of our method and the comparison method SMOTE under mixed skew. It can be seen from the figure that compared with the SMOTE method, our method is slightly higher than SMOTE in accuracy, but significantly better than SMOTE in convergence. Since the SMOTE method can only augment the existing category data of the client, this method can only solve the quantity skew, not the label skew. Since our method adopts ACGAN, it can solve both quantity skew and label skew.

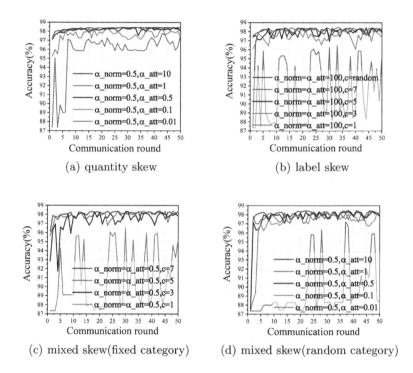

Fig. 6. Accuracy on non-IID data.

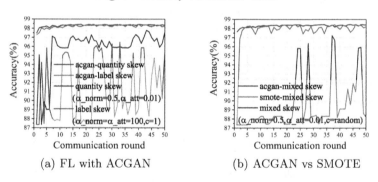

Fig. 7. Performance of FL data augmentation algorithm based on ACGAN.

5.4 Hyperparameter Analysis

In this subsection, we investigate the impact of different hyperparameter settings on our algorithm. We mainly study the effect of different client participation ratio C, different client training epochs E, and client batch size B on the accuracy and convergence of the algorithm.

Figure 8(a) shows the effect of client participation ratio C on our algorithm. As can be seen from the figure, with the increase of the C, the accuracy of our algorithm is not improved, but the convergence is improved. This shows that the C only affects the convergence of our algorithm.

Figure 8(b) shows the impact of client local training epochs E on our algorithm. As can be seen from the figure, with the increase of the E, the convergence of our algorithm is not improved, but the accuracy is improved. This shows that the E only affects the accuracy of our algorithm.

Figure 8(c) shows the impact of client batch size B on our algorithm. As can be seen from the figure, with the decrease of the B, the accuracy of our algorithm decreases and the convergence also deteriorates. This shows that the B not only affects the accuracy of our algorithm but also affects the convergence.

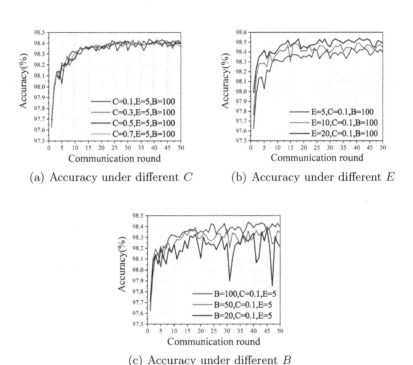

(a) Accuracy under different C (b) Accuracy under different E

(c) Accuracy under different B

Fig. 8. Performance of our algorithm under different hyperparameters.

6 Conclusion

We investigate FL-based intrusion detection on non-IID data. The effects of various non-IID setting on FL are considered in detail, and specific partitioning methods are given. In addition, a data rebalancing method for FL based on ACGAN is also proposed. We conduct extensive experiments on the UNSW-NB15 dataset, and the experiments show that non-IID data affects the accuracy

328 Y. Liu et al.

and convergence of FL, and in extreme cases, the model fails to converge. The proposed data augmentation method can well improve the impact of non-IID data on FL, and our algorithm performs better than other state-of-the-art data rebalancing methods.

References

1. Ayed, M.A., Talhi, C.: Federated learning for anomaly-based intrusion detection. In: 2021 International Symposium on Networks, Computers and Communications (ISNCC), pp. 1–8. IEEE (2021)
2. Campos, E.M., et al.: Evaluating federated learning for intrusion detection in internet of things: review and challenges. Comput. Netw. 108661 (2021)
3. Chawla, N.V., Bowyer, K.W., Hall, L.O., Kegelmeyer, W.P.: Smote: synthetic minority over-sampling technique. J. Artif. Intell. Res. **16**, 321–357 (2002)
4. Chen, G., Zheng, J., Yang, S., Zhou, J., Wu, W.: Fsafa-stacking2: an effective ensemble learning model for intrusion detection with firefly algorithm based feature selection. In: Lai, Y., Wang, T., Jiang, M., Xu, G., Liang, W., Castiglione, A. (eds.) ICA3PP 2021. LNCS, vol. 13156, pp. 555–570. Springer, Cham (2021). https://doi.org/10.1007/978-3-030-95388-1_37
5. Chen, Z., Lv, N., Liu, P., Fang, Y., Chen, K., Pan, W.: Intrusion detection for wireless edge networks based on federated learning. IEEE Access **8**, 217463–217472 (2020)
6. Ding, J., Lin, F., Lv, S.: Temporal convolution network based on attention for intelligent anomaly detection of wind turbine blades. In: Lai, Y., Wang, T., Jiang, M., Xu, G., Liang, W., Castiglione, A. (eds.) ICA3PP 2021. LNCS, vol. 13155, pp. 193–209. Springer, Cham (2021). https://doi.org/10.1007/978-3-030-95384-3_13
7. Duan, M., et al.: Astraea: self-balancing federated learning for improving classification accuracy of mobile deep learning applications. In: 2019 IEEE 37th International Conference on Computer Design (ICCD), pp. 246–254. IEEE (2019)
8. Hsu, T.M.H., Qi, H., Brown, M.: Measuring the effects of non-identical data distribution for federated visual classification. arXiv preprint arXiv:1909.06335 (2019)
9. Javaid, A., Niyaz, Q., Sun, W., Alam, M.: A deep learning approach for network intrusion detection system. EAI Endorsed Trans. Secur. Saf. **3**(9), e2 (2016)
10. Kairouz, P., et al.: Advances and open problems in federated learning. Found. Trends® Mach. Learn. **14**(1–2), 1–210 (2021)
11. Kim, S., Cai, H., Hua, C., Gu, P., Xu, W., Park, J.: Collaborative anomaly detection for internet of things based on federated learning. In: 2020 IEEE/CIC International Conference on Communications in China (ICCC), pp. 623–628. IEEE (2020)
12. Liu, Y., et al.: Deep anomaly detection for time-series data in industrial IoT: a communication-efficient on-device federated learning approach. IEEE Internet Things J. **8**(8), 6348–6358 (2020)
13. Liu, Y., Kumar, N., Xiong, Z., Lim, W.Y.B., Kang, J., Niyato, D.: Communication-efficient federated learning for anomaly detection in industrial internet of things. In: GLOBECOM 2020–2020 IEEE Global Communications Conference, pp. 1–6. IEEE (2020)
14. Lv, P., Xie, L., Xu, J., Li, T.: Misbehavior detection in VANET based on federated learning and blockchain. In: Lai, Y., Wang, T., Jiang, M., Xu, G., Liang, W., Castiglione, A. (eds.) ICA3PP 2021. LNCS, vol. 13157, pp. 52–64. Springer, Cham (2021). https://doi.org/10.1007/978-3-030-95391-1_4

15. Man, D., Zeng, F., Yang, W., Yu, M., Lv, J., Wang, Y.: Intelligent intrusion detection based on federated learning for edge-assisted internet of things. Secur. Commun. Netw. **2021** (2021)
16. McMahan, B., Moore, E., Ramage, D., Hampson, S., Arcas, B.A.: Communication-efficient learning of deep networks from decentralized data. In: Artificial intelligence and statistics, pp. 1273–1282. PMLR (2017)
17. Mothukuri, V., Khare, P., Parizi, R.M., Pouriyeh, S., Dehghantanha, A., Srivastava, G.: Federated learning-based anomaly detection for IoT security attacks. IEEE Internet Things J. (2021)
18. Moustafa, N., Slay, J.: Unsw-nb15: a comprehensive data set for network intrusion detection systems (unsw-nb15 network data set). In: 2015 Military Communications and Information Systems Conference (MilCIS), pp. 1–6. IEEE (2015)
19. Odena, A., Olah, C., Shlens, J.: Conditional image synthesis with auxiliary classifier GANs. In: International Conference on Machine Learning, pp. 2642–2651. PMLR (2017)
20. Popoola, S.I., Ande, R., Adebisi, B., Gui, G., Hammoudeh, M., Jogunola, O.: Federated deep learning for zero-day botnet attack detection in IoT edge devices. IEEE Internet Things J. (2021)
21. Rahman, S.A., Tout, H., Talhi, C., Mourad, A.: Internet of things intrusion detection: centralized, on-device, or federated learning? IEEE Netw. **34**(6), 310–317 (2020)
22. Ren, G., Zhang, Y., Zhang, S., Long, H.: Edge DDoS attack detection method based on software defined networks. In: Lai, Y., Wang, T., Jiang, M., Xu, G., Liang, W., Castiglione, A. (eds.) ICA3PP 2021. LNCS, vol. 13155, pp. 597–611. Springer, Cham (2021). https://doi.org/10.1007/978-3-030-95384-3_37
23. Wang, H., Muñoz-González, L., Eklund, D., Raza, S.: Non-IID data re-balancing at IoT edge with peer-to-peer federated learning for anomaly detection. In: Proceedings of the 14th ACM Conference on Security and Privacy in Wireless and Mobile Networks, pp. 153–163 (2021)
24. Weinger, B., Kim, J., Sim, A., Nakashima, M., Moustafa, N., Wu, K.J.: Enhancing IoT anomaly detection performance for federated learning. Digit. Commun. Netw. (2022)
25. Yadav, K., Gupta, B., Hsu, C.H., Chui, K.T.: Unsupervised federated learning based IoT intrusion detection. In: 2021 IEEE 10th Global Conference on Consumer Electronics (GCCE), pp. 298–301. IEEE (2021)
26. Yurochkin, M., Agarwal, M., Ghosh, S., Greenewald, K., Hoang, N., Khazaeni, Y.: Bayesian nonparametric federated learning of neural networks. In: International Conference on Machine Learning, pp. 7252–7261. PMLR (2019)
27. Zhao, Y., Chen, J., Wu, D., Teng, J., Yu, S.: Multi-task network anomaly detection using federated learning. In: Proceedings of the Tenth International Symposium on Information and Communication Technology, pp. 273–279 (2019)

Long-Term Fairness Scheduler for Pay-as-You-Use Cache Sharing Systems

Zhongyu Zhou[1], Shanjiang Tang[1(✉)], Hao Fu[2], Wanqing Chang[1], Ce Yu[1], Chao Sun[1], Yusen Li[3], and Jian Xiao[1]

[1] College of Intelligence and Computing, Tianjin University, Tianjin, China
{zhongyu_zhou999,tashj,wanqingchang,yuce,sch,xiaojian}@tju.edu.cn
[2] National Supercomputer Center in Tianjin, Tianjin, China
fuhao@nscc-tj.cn
[3] College of Computer Science, Nankai University, Tianjin, China
liyusen@nbjl.nankai.edu.cn

Abstract. Currently, pay-as-you-go cache systems have been widely available as storage services in cloud computing, and users usually purchase long-term services to obtain higher discounts. However, users' caching needs are not only constantly changing over time, but also affected by workload characteristics, making it difficult to always guarantee high efficiency of cache resource usage. Cache sharing is an effective way to improve cache usage efficiency. In order to incentivize users to share resources, it is necessary to ensure long-term fairness among users. However, the traditional resource allocation strategy only guarantees instantaneous fairness and is not thus suitable for pay-as-you-go cache systems. This paper proposes a long-term cache fairness allocation policy, named as FairCache, with several desired properties. First, FairCache encourages users to buy and share cache resources through group purchasing, which not only allows users to get more resources than when they buy them individually, but also encourages them to lend free resources or resources occupied by low-frequency data to others to get more revenue in the future. Second, FairCache satisfies pay-as-you-go fairness, ensuring that users' revenue is proportional to the cost paid in a long term. Furthermore, FairCache satisfies truthfulness property, which ensures that no one can get more resources by lying. Finally, Fair-Cache satisfies pareto efficiency property, ensuring that as long as there are tasks in progress, the system will maximize resource utilization. We implement FairCache in Alluxio, and the experimental results show that FairCache can guarantee long-term cache fairness while maximizing the efficiency of system resource usage.

Keywords: Long-term resource fairness · Efficiency · Cache sharing

© Springer Nature Switzerland AG 2023
W. Meng et al. (Eds.): ICA3PP 2022, LNCS 13777, pp. 330–350, 2023.
https://doi.org/10.1007/978-3-031-22677-9_18

1   Introduction

Data caching in today's big data era has been widely available in various data centers [1] and supercomputers [2], which generally takes memory devices as cache storage and has become an indispensable part of big data parallel processing frameworks [3,4] and distributed file systems [5–7]. It affects not only the execution performance of the program, but also the quality of services (QoS) provided to users.

Every moment, tens of thousands of users submit a large number of cache requests to the cloud servers. Cloud service providers will charge fees based on users' use of resources. To meet the demands of different types of users, cloud service providers propose various pricing strategies based on the length of use. When a user has short-term needs (e.g., an hour or a day), she can choose to pay per unit of time, which is a common way of charging for short-term services. The final fee is the price of a unit resource multiplied by the total usage. Conversely, when a user wants to obtain long-term usage rights (e.g., several months or years), she should opt for a paid subscription, as there will be a certain discount. This method not only saves user costs (compared to hourly payment), but also encourages users to always use cloud services and establish long-term friendly cooperative relationships.

However, since users' needs are time-varying, even if they purchase long-term services, there is no guarantee that these resources will always be fully utilized. This not only leads to higher costs, but also raises two problems: 1) *Resource Fragmentation Problem*. When users' demands are not enough to occupy all the space, the remaining capacity cannot be used by others, resulting in a waste of idle resources. 2) *Cache Inefficiency Problem*. Even if user demands occupy the entire capacity, these demands may be low frequency data, which can lead to a reduction in the system global efficiency.

To solve these problems, users can group purchase [8] resources and share them with each other. Firstly, compared with purchasing resources individually, group purchasing can get more resources for the same cost. Second, cache sharing can improve system global efficiency allowing users to obtain more benefits. Since different users have different needs at the same time, and the needs of the same user are also time-varying, users can lend their temporarily idle or inefficient cache resources to other users who are more in need through cache sharing, and take it back when needed in the future. Although there are security issues involved in cache sharing, there are mechanisms to ensure user privacy, which is not within the scope of this paper. However, in practice, users can be selfish and wants to cache as much data as possible into the memory, regardless of the popularity of the data. A problem then comes out that how to incentivize users to share cache given that users can be selfish, and improve the utilization and efficiency of cache resources while guaranteeing the long-term fairness for users.

The traditional Max-Min Fairness (MMF) [9] aims to maximize the minimum share of resources obtained by users to achieve fairness, which has been widely used in various data processing frameworks [10–12]. However, the implementation of such a MMF policy in these frameworks does not consider historical allocations of users, which is considered by us as Memoryless Cache Allocation Fairness (MCAF). With the following three problems, we argue that MCAF can not be applied to a pay-as-you-go cache sharing system.

Resource Inefficiency Problem. Consider a cache sharing system consisting of three users A, B and C. During Δt, S_1^A, S_1^B, S_1^C are the fair resource shares obtained by user A, B and C, and S_2^A, S_2^B, S_2^C are their actual cache demands. Assume that user A's $S_1^A > S_2^A$, user B's $S_1^B < S_2^B$ and C's $S_1^C < S_2^C$, user C's data is hotter than user B's. In an ideal situation, both user A and B will lend some resources to user C to cache more hot-data. However, since MCAF is to maximize the minimum needs of users, user B preempts user A's idle resources together with user C, resulting in inefficiency for cache resources.

Truthfulness Problem. In practice, users in the shared system may not be honest and we should have a robust policy to guarantee that users can not get benefits when cheating. However, we argue that MCAF can not guarantee this. Consider a sharing system consisting of three users A, B and C. Assume that user A is a liar who caches cold data, user B and C are honest and cache hot data. During Δt, due to user C's $S_1^C > S_2^C$, $(S_1^C - S_2^C)$ should be lent to user B for cache efficiency improvement. But user A will preempt user C's resources with user B by falsely reporting demands without being punished, violating truthfulness property (see the *Truthfulness* in Sect. 2). Furthermore, if all users are dishonest, vicious competition will be formed, which not only reduces the system resource usage efficiency, but also breaks the sharing incentive.

Pay-as-You-Use Fairness Problem. According to the pay-as-you-use rule, the total amount of resources a user receives over time t should be proportional to the cost she pays (see the *Pay-as-you-use Fairness* property in Sect. 2). Since users' needs are time-varying, there should be an adaptive policy to adjust the resource share allocated to each user for pay-as-you-use fairness in the long run, but MCAF can not guarantee it. Consider user A and B sharing a system. During Δt_1, suppose $S_1^A < S_2^A$ and $S_1^B > S_2^B$, then MCAF will lend user B's $(S_1^B - S_2^B)$ to user A. In the next time period Δt_2, $S_1^A < S_2^A$ and $S_1^B < S_2^B$. Since MCAF does not take into account the user's historical behaviors, user B can not take back the resources lent in Δt_1 from user A, but can only obtain S_1^B. Therefore, during $(\Delta t_1 + \Delta t_2)$, user B should be able to get the resources of $2 \cdot S_1^B$, but in fact only get the resources of $(S_1^B + S_2^B)$. In a long term, user B can not get the amount of resources that she should get, which is unfair to her.

We propose FairCache to solve the above three problems, which is a policy to guarantees a fair allocation of resources in the long run. FairCache satisfies four desired sharing properties, including Sharing Incentive, Truthfulness, Pay-as-you-use Fairness and Pareto Efficiency. First, considering that users' needs are time-varying, FairCache encourages users to share cache resources, and ensures that users get more benefits in a sharing environment through adaptive cache replacement policy than that of nonshared case. Second, FairCache satisfies truthfulness, it guarantees that no user can get more benefits by cheating. Furthermore, FairCache encourages users to sacrifice current fairness in exchange for future benefits. So in a long-term, pay-as-you-go fairness can be satisfied. Finally, FairCache can maximize the utilization and efficiency of cache resources, and no one can obtain more resources without reducing the resource share of other users.

Organization. Section 2 proposes four desirable properties of resource allocation in a sharing environment. Section 3 gives a motivation example to illustrate the differences among different allocation policies and emphasizes the importance of cache sharing. Section 4 proposes FairCache and points out that it satisfies four desired properties. We then improve the performance of FairCache with a knob θ to ensure that users maximize resource usage efficiency as much as possible while guaranteeing fairness in a long-term. Section 5 shows our evaluation results. First, by describing the details of resource allocation under FairCache and MCAF, we show that FairCache can guarantee the long-term fairness of users, while MCAF always suffers from sharing loss. We then show how Fair-Cache adjusts the knob to balance fairness and efficiency. We also evaluate the performance and overhead of FairCache, and the results show that FairCache is a lightweight scheduler suitable for multi-users. In Sect. 6 we review the related work. Finally, we conclude the paper in Sect. 7.

2   Desired Properties for Cache Sharing

In this section, we present four desired properties that we believe a nice cache allocation policy should satisfy, which are necessary for cache sharing systems in the long run.

Sharing Incentive: Sharing incentive not only enable each user to obtain more cache resources through group-purchasing with others than purchasing independently, but also improve cache resource utilization and efficiency. Otherwise, users are not willing to share resources. $\forall i \in [1, n]$, if user i satisfies the following equation, the policy is sharing incentive,

$$R_i(t) > \widetilde{R_i}(t), \tag{1}$$

where $R_i(t)$ and $\widetilde{R_i}(t)$ denote the total resources obtained by user i in time period t under shared and non-shared, respectively.

Pay-as-You-Use Fairness: The total resources that users obtain over a period of time t should be proportional to the cost they pay. Otherwise, users will be not willing to yield resources to other users even though they do not need. Pay-as-you-use fairness is a necessary condition to ensure sharing incentive. $\forall i \in [1, n]$, $R_i(t)$ purchased by user i should satisfy the following condition,

$$R_i(t) = R_i(\Delta t_1) + R_i(\Delta t_2) + \cdots + R_i(\Delta t_m), \tag{2}$$

where $t = \Delta t_1 + \Delta t_2 + \cdots \Delta t_m$, and each allocation $R_i(\Delta t_j)$ for user i may be greater than, equal to, or less than $\frac{R_i(t)}{m}$.

Truthfulness: We should have a robust policy to ensure that no one can harm others by lying about cache demands. Otherwise, it will reduce system efficiency and be unfair to other honest users. The policy is truthfulness when the following holds,

$$\forall i \in [1, n], \ R_i(t) \geq \overline{R_i}(t), \tag{3}$$

where $R_i(t)$ and $\overline{R_i}(t)$ denote the resources obtained by user i in honesty and cheating, respectively.

Pareto Efficiency: In a cache sharing system, it is not possible to make any-one obtain more cache resources without reducing the resource allocation of others. This property can maximize the utilization of the cache resource and prevent the waste of fragmented resources. If another allocation scheme $\widehat{R}(t)$ can not be found such that any two users i and j satisfy simultaneously, 1) $\forall i \in [1, n], \ R_i(t) \leq \widehat{R_i}(t)$, 2) $\exists j \in [1, n], \ R_j(t) < \widehat{R_j}(t)$, then the Pareto Efficiency is optimal.

3   Background and Motivation

Since the workload characteristics of users change over time, unbalanced cache demands among users often occur. Ideally, in a pay-as-you-go sharing system, users can balance their respective needs by sharing resources, thereby improving resource utilization and efficiency. However, sharing cache is risky because some users will definitely lose in the short-term. If the system cannot guarantee the long-term fairness of users, users will not be willing to share. To be able to describe the problem more clearly, we give a motivation example as follows.

Example 1. Consider a cache sharing system with two users User 1 and User 2 of 100GB DRAM. Each user maintains a file access queue, and their cache demands (i.e., file size and access frequency) change over time, as shown in Table 1. The time interval between two resource allocation operations is denoted as Δt ($\Delta t_1 = \Delta t_2 = \Delta t_3$).

Table 1. Changes in the cache demands of User 1 and User 2 during $\Delta t_1 \sim \Delta t_3$.

Time	User 1	User 2
Δt_1	$D_{1,1}$: 40G, 25times/s	$D_{2,1}$: 20G, 16times/s
	$D_{1,2}$: 50G, 20times/s	$D_{2,2}$: 50G, 12times/s
Δt_2	$D_{1,1}$: 20G, 30times/s	$D_{2,1}$: 50G, 40times/s
	$D_{1,2}$: 10G, 25times/s	$D_{2,2}$: 40G, 35times/s
Δt_3	$D_{1,1}$: 30G, 50times/s	$D_{2,1}$: 30G, 80times/s
	$D_{1,2}$: 50G, 40times/s	$D_{2,2}$: 40G, 60times/s

Figure 1a is the allocation result under isolation status. Although this policy can guarantee users' fairness, the resources are not fully utilized. It can be seen that during Δt_2, User 1 does not use her cache resources completely, resulting in a waste of 20G resources. Each user obtains 150G of accumulated resources, but in fact User 1 only uses 130G. Under this policy, the global efficiency (see the definition in Sect. 4.3) of system resources is $10630 (= 40 \cdot 25 + 10 \cdot 20 + 20 \cdot 30 + 10 \cdot 25 + 30 \cdot 50 + 20 \cdot 40 + 20 \cdot 16 + 30 \cdot 12 + 50 \cdot 40 + 30 \cdot 80 + 20 \cdot 60)$.

Under the MCAF policy of Fig. 1b, User 1 can lend her temporary free resources to User 2 during Δt_2, which nicely solves the problem of resource waste in isolation. However, during Δt_3, User 2's demands are greater than the resources she gets, User 2 will not return the resources borrowed from User 1 during Δt_2 due to the memoryless of MCAF. Although the global efficiency is increased to $11330 (= 40 \cdot 25 + 10 \cdot 20 + 20 \cdot 30 + 10 \cdot 25 + 30 \cdot 50 + 20 \cdot 40 + 20 \cdot 16 + 30 \cdot 12 + 50 \cdot 40 + 20 \cdot 35 + 30 \cdot 80 + 20 \cdot 60)$, this comes at the expense of fairness for User 1.

The FairCache allocation policy in Fig. 1c considers the long-term fairness of users, it solves the problem of MCAF borrowing but not returning, thereby incentivizing users to share caches. It can be seen that User 2 returns 20G resources to User 1 during Δt_3, which maintains absolute fairness for both users and increases the global efficiency to $10930 (= 40 \cdot 25 + 10 \cdot 20 + 20 \cdot 30 + 10 \cdot 25 + 30 \cdot 50 + 40 \cdot 40 + 20 \cdot 16 + 30 \cdot 12 + 50 \cdot 40 + 20 \cdot 35 + 30 \cdot 80)$.

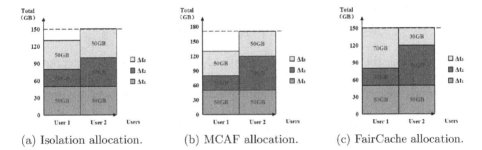

(a) Isolation allocation.   (b) MCAF allocation.   (c) FairCache allocation.

Fig. 1. A motivation example with two users in a long-term cache sharing systems for a comparison of Isolation, MCAF, FairCache allocation policies.

In summary, cache sharing is beneficial to users in the long-term, it not only allows users to obtain more resources but also improves the utilization and efficiency of resources. However, cache sharing must ensure the fairness of all users. If a policy like MCAF hurts some users' fairness, users are unwilling to share. Therefore, it is a challenge to motivate users to share caches and maximize resources utilization and usage efficiency while ensuring long-term user fairness.

4   Long-Term Cache Fairness Framework

We first present the overall definition of FairCache policy, and then prove that the proposed policy satisfies the four desired allocation properties mentioned above. Following that, we further propose an optimization scheme on the basis of FairCache to improve the global efficiency. Finally, we also give a brief analysis of the proposed optimization strategy.

4.1   FairCache Allocation

FairCache Allocation Model Definition. Consider a long-term cache sharing system, n users $U = \{u_1, u_2, ..., u_n\}$ share R cache resources, where u_i denotes the i-th user. Each user u_i needs to process a set of m files $F_i = \{f_{i,1}, f_{i,2}, ..., f_{i,m}\}$, where $f_{i,j}$ represents the j-th file to be accessed by user u_i. In real-world applications, a single file $f_{i,j}$ may be visited multiple times, i.e. $freq_{i,j}$, and the access frequencies of different files can vary a lot. We denote the access frequencies of all files as $Freq = \{freq_{1,1}, freq_{1,2}, ..., freq_{n,m}\}$. The cache system can periodically decide whether to cache or evict a caching file according to its access frequency. The time interval between two resource allocation operations is denoted as Δt. Hence the theoretical fair resources $r_i(\Delta t)$ reserved for user u_i in a specified time period Δt can be formulated as Eq. (4),

$$r_i(\Delta t) = \frac{R \cdot w_i}{\sum_{j=1}^{n} w_j}, \tag{4}$$

where w_i is the weight for user u_i. Therefore, the cumulative theoretical fair resources $R_i(t)$ group-purchased by user u_i in a period of time t can be represented as Eq. (5),

$$R_i(t) = \int_0^t r_i(\Delta t)\, d(\Delta t). \tag{5}$$

In addition, the cache resources currently demanded by user u_i is denoted as $g_i(\Delta t)$. If one user has abundant resources, idle resources will be preempted by other users (i.e., $r_i(\Delta t) - g_i(\Delta t)$). Consequently, the resource obtained by user u_i actually in each time period Δt is $a_i(\Delta t)$, and total resources $A_i(t)$ assigned to user u_i in t time in real cases should be formulated as Eq. (6),

$$A_i(t) = \int_0^t a_i(\Delta t)\, d(\Delta t). \tag{6}$$

In this situation, the target resource allocator can temporally violate the resource fairness across multiple users in a specified time period Δt (i.e., $r_i(\Delta t) > a_i(\Delta t)$ or $a_i(\Delta t) < r_i(\Delta t)$). In return, it can turn to guarantee the pay-as-you-use fairness under the constraint of the max-min fairness, which can be formulated as Eq. (7),

$$\frac{A_1(t)}{R_1(t)} = \frac{A_2(t)}{R_2(t)} = \cdots = \frac{A_n(t)}{R_n(t)}. \tag{7}$$

FairCache Analysis. FairCache can achieve a long-term fairness in a cache sharing environment. The core idea of FairCache is to restore resources from user u with the largest cumulative resources $A_i(t)$ by evicting files cached, and reassign the cache space to user u' with the smallest $A_j(t)$. Consequently, the difference in accumulated resources obtained among users can be continuously narrowed, and fairness can be guaranteed in the long-term. As shown in Algorithm 1, when user u' wants to access file f', the system will first check if there is enough cache space to keep it. If there is not enough space, FairCache will evict

---

Algorithm 1. The naive implementation of FairCache.

1: **function** FAIRCACHEALLOCATION(u', f')
2:    **while** $f'.size > DRAM.availableSize$ **do**
3:   ▷ DRAM does not have enough space.
4:        Select $f_{i,j}$ with the lowest priority cached by user u_i with the largest $A_i(t)$.
5:        $u = U.getLargestAllocationUser()$.
6:        $f = u.getLowestPriorityFile()$.
7:        **if** $f'.getFreq \leq f.getFreq$ **AND** $u' = u$ **then**
8:            **return CACHE_ABORT**.
9:        **else**   ▷ f' replaces the f.
10:            $DRAM.evict(f)$.
11:            $DRAM.availableSize+ = f.size$.
12:            $DRAM.availableSize- = f'.size$.
13:            $u'.cumulativeAllocation+ = f'.size$
14:            **return CACHE_SUCCEED**.
15:        **end if**
16:    **end while**
17: $DRAM.add(f')$.   ▷ DRAM has enough space to cache f'.
18: $DRAM.availableSize- = f'.size$.
19: $u'.cumulativeAllocation+ = f'.size$.

---

the file in the cache to reserve space for f' (*Line 2–16*). In this case, candidate files to be removed are from user u with the largest cumulative resources $A_i(t)$ (*Line 4–6*). Note that, candidate files are determined by the cache replacement strategy adopted. In LRU, priority is negatively correlated with time interval, and in LFU files with a low access frequency will have a low priority. Under the max-min fariness strategy, files priority are prioritized according to the decreasing order of the resource allocation. For the same user, we do not consider the priority relationship between file f' and file f, as long as f' is not accessed more frequently than f no replacement occurs, since user will not benefit from it (*Line 7–8*). There are two cases where system can evict a cache file (*Line 9–15*). For the same user, when the access frequency of f' is greater than f, f is replaced by f'. The other case is when $u' \neq u$, whenever f' has a higher priority than f, a replacement is to be made. Specifically, this is to ensure fairness among multiple users, even if f is accessed more frequently than f', forced file eviction can be triggered because $f'.getPriority > f.getPriority$. Otherwise, files can be directly cached while there are enough free resources (*Line 17–19*).

4.2   FairCache Property Proof

Theorem 1. *FairCache is sharing incentive.*

Proof. Assuming that there are a group of k users assigned with the same weight purchases R GB cache resources with a cost M. Consequently, each user could obtain $\frac{R}{k}$ cache resources at the cost of $\frac{M}{k}$. When one user try to purchase cache resources individually with the same budget, she will receive r GB ($r < \frac{R}{k}$)

Table 2. List of properties for Isolation, MCAF and FairCache.

Property	Allocation policy		
	Isolation	*MCAF*	*FairCache*
Sharing incentive			✓
Pay-as-you-use fairness	✓		✓
Truthfulness	✓		✓
Pareto efficiency		✓	✓

resources, as group-buying often has a larger discount. Hence, one user can only gain $\Delta t \cdot r$ resources in a period of time Δt. In contrast, she can receive $\Delta t \cdot \frac{R}{k}$ in total with the proposed FairCache policy and the group-buying method. Likewise, these resources can improve caching efficiency. It can be proved that FairCache conforms to the sharing incentive property.

Theorem 2. *FairCache satisfies pay-as-you-use fairness.*

Proof. In a cache sharing system, since user's own cache demands will change over time, and the demands among users are unbalanced, if there are unused resources, others will preempt them. However, users do not have to worry about short-term fairness loss. Because FairCache finds user i with the smallest $\frac{A_i(t)}{R_i(t)}$ every time and allocates resources to her first, the gap in total resources among users is continuously narrowed to ensure long-term fairness for users. Thus, Fair-Cache can guarantee the pay-as-you-use fairness in a long-term sharing system.

Theorem 3. *FairCache satisfies the truthfulness.*

Proof. According to Theorem 2, users can preempt idle resources in the system. Suppose user u_i artificially increases the frequency of file $f_{i,j}$ from $freq_1$ to $freq_2$ by fake access during Δt_1, thereby obtaining more resources m than user u_j. Then during Δt_2, no matter whether the $freq_3$ of $f_{i,j}$ is high or low, m should be returned to u_j. There must exist $freq_3 > freq_1$, such that $m \cdot (freq_1 - freq_3) < 0$, i.e., u_i loses her own benefits after cheating, users won't cheat because they don't benefit from cheating. Hence, FairCache satisfies the truthfulness property.

Theorem 4. *FairCache satisfies the pareto efficiency.*

Proof. FairCache encourages users to share unused cache resources to improve cache utilization, which means that cache can always be fully utilized as long as there are enough demands. In other words, no one can acquire more resources without reduce the amount resources obtained by others. Therefore, FairCache meets the pareto efficiency property.

Finally, we summarize the properties satisfied by Isolation, MCAF and Fair-Cache in Table 2. Since the isolation policy is non-shared, resources unused by users are wasted, thus, it violates the sharing incentive and pareto efficiency.

Both MCAF and FariCache are allocation policies designed for the sharing system. However, due to the memoryless of MCAF, it can only guarantee pareto efficiency. The proposed policy FairCache can achieve all those properties.

4.3 Efficiency Optimization for FairCache Policy

Although FairCache has high resource utilization, it still suffers from cache inefficiency problem. Cache efficiency $\phi_{f_{i,j}}(\Delta t)$ is formulated as Eq. (8). It refers to as $f_{i,j}$'s contribution to the system in each round,

$$\phi_{f_{i,j}}(\Delta t) = freq_{i,j} \cdot size(f_{i,j}), \tag{8}$$

where $size(f_{i,j})$ is the size of $f_{i,j}$. Hence, the cumulative global efficiency generated by system resources over a time period t can be expressed as,

$$\phi(t) = \int_0^t \sum_{i=1}^n \sum_{j=1}^m \phi_{f_{i,j}}(\Delta t) \, d(\Delta t). \tag{9}$$

Let's review Fig. 1c in the motivation example in Sect. 3. During Δt_3, User 2 gives up caching 20G $D_{2,2}$ and returns these resources to User 1 to cache $D_{1,2}$. Although the result guarantees users' fairness, the system loses $400(= 20 \cdot 60 - 20 \cdot 40)$ efficiency in this round because the frequency of $D_{1,2}$ is lower than that of $D_{2,2}$. In the long run, due to the time-varying needs of users, sometimes users will cache lots of cold data. Although her cache utilization is high, the cache efficiency is low. In fact, a resource allocation system should not only guarantee fairness constraints in many practical situations, but should also be sensitive to data popularity. For the user herself, whether these cold data are cached will not have much impact on the user's current benefits (e.g., eviction of 5G data accessed once per second will only lose efficiency 5). However, from the perspective of the global system, if these resources are used by users who need them more, it will not only benefit others, but also improve the cache efficiency. In addition, since FaiCache guarantees long-term fairness, users do not need to worry about not being able to get these resources back in the future.

In practice, there is no universal rules to distinguish hot and cold data prior to execution. According to the characteristic that file access follows the Zip distribution [21,22], generally speaking, 20% of the data occupies 80% of the access time. We should improve FairCache to make it sensitive to hot and cold data, so that in each round of resource allocation it will restrict users to cache only 20% of the hot data and encourage everyone to share the remaining capacity with others. By this means, it can not only help guarantee the long-term fairness across users, but also improve the global cache efficiency. We introduce an efficiency knob θ to solve the problem of the naive FairCache. θ represents the threshold of the replacement frequency of a file, which can be adjusted by the user by considering characteristics of current workloads. Files satisfying the criteria controlled by θ will be filtered out first, and the max-min fairness is applied otherwise. In order to measure users' fairness in resource allocation, we define $\gamma_i(t)$ as Fairness Degree (FD) for u_i as follows,

$$\gamma_i(t) = \frac{\int_0^t a_i(\Delta t)\, d(\Delta t)}{\int_0^t r_i(\Delta t)\, d(\Delta t)}. \tag{10}$$

When $\gamma_i(t) < 1$, it represents that the resource allocation for u_i does not meet the pay-as-you-go fairness within this time period, and the resource fairness is satisfied in other instances. Since cache resources are shared across multiple users in the pay-as-you-go sharing systems, if $\gamma(t)$ of some users are larger than 1, there must be a set of users whose fairness are violated. To describe the fairness of multiple users, two additional metrics, sharing loss $\Phi(t)$ and sharing benefit $\Theta(t)$, are introduced. They can be formulated as Eqs. (11) and (12),

$$\Phi(t) = \sum_{i=1}^{n} min\left\{\gamma_i(t) - 1, 0\right\}, \tag{11}$$

$$\Theta(t) = \sum_{i=1}^{n} max\left\{\gamma_i(t) - 1, 0\right\}, \tag{12}$$

where we can deduce that $\Phi(t)$ is less than 0 and $\Theta(t)$ is greater than 0. Our objective is to guarantee $\gamma(t)$ for all users should be equal to 1 under a specified time period t, i.e., each user should get a fair resource distribution.

FairCache with Efficiency Optimization. As shown in Algorithm 2, Fair-Cache maintains two additional file sets termed as $FileSet_{efficiency}$ and $FileSet_{fairness}$ (*Line 2–3*). $FileSet_{efficiency}$ contains files can be safely evicted with the LFU policy, which are all low-frequency, while $FileSet_{fairness}$ stands for a set of files in the cache whose access frequency values are larger than a given threshold θ. When user u' wants to access f', FairCache first checks whether there is enough free cache space for it. If it is satisfied, f' will be cached directly (*Line 44–46*). Otherwise, the eviction operation will be executed (*Line 4–43*). FairCache is a two-stage cache allocation policy. The first stage $FileSet_{efficiency}$ is designed to enhance the efficiency of cache resource usage (*Line 9–19*), which adopts the LFU strategy to assign cache resources to users, and the objective of the other stage $FileSet_{fairness}$ is to guarantee the long-term fairness across users in an efficient way (*Line 20–42*). When $f \in FileSet_{efficiency}$, it means that f needs to be replaced by a file that is accessed more frequently than it (*Line 10–15*), otherwise f will continue to occupy cache resources (*Line 16–18*). When $f \in FileSet_{fairness}$, the process of resource allocation depends not only on the frequency of file access, but also on the cumulative resource share of users. When $f'.getFreq \leq f.getFreq$, the file can not be replaced under normal circumstances (*Line 21–23*), because the user does not profit from it. However, there is a special case where f' can replace f when user u' has less total resources than user u and u' and u are not the same user. This is done to guarante fairness for user u' (*Line 24–29*). When $f'.getFreq > f.getFreq$, the normal replacement

---

Algorithm 2. FairCache with Efficiency Optimization.

1: **function** FAIRCACHEALLOCATION(u', f')
2:     $FileSet_{efficiency} = \{f_{i,j} | i \in [1, n], j \in [1, m], freq_{i,j} < \theta\}$.
3:     $FileSet_{fairness} = \{f_{i,j} | i \in [1, n], j \in [1, m], freq_{i,j} \geq \theta\}$.
4:     **while** $f'.size > cache.availableSize$ **do**
5:   ▷ DRAM does not have enough space.
6:         Select $f_{i,j}$ with the lowest priority cached by user u_i with the largest $R_i(t)$.
7:         $u = U.getLargestAllocationUser()$.
8:         $f = u.getLowestPriorityFile()$.
9:         **if** $f \in FileSet_{efficiency}$ **then**   ▷ Efficiency stage.
10:             **if** $f'.getFreq > f.getFreq$ **then**
11:                 $cache.evict(f)$.
12:                 $cache.availableSize+ = f.size$.
13:                 $cache.availableSize- = f'.size$.
14:                 $u'.totalAlloc+ = f'.size$
15:                 **return CACHE_SUCCEED.**
16:             **else if** $f'.getFreq \leq f.getFreq$ **then**
17:                 $u.totalAlloc+ = f.size$
18:                 **return CACHE_ABORT.**
19:             **end if**
20:         **else if** $f \in FileSet_{fairness}$ **then**   ▷ Fairness stage.
21:             **if** $f'.getFreq \leq f.getFreq$ **then**
22:                 **if** $u' = u$ **OR** $u' \neq u$ **AND** $u'.totalAlloc > u.totalAlloc$ **then**
23:                     **return CACHE_ABORT.**
24:                 **else if** $u' \neq u$ **AND** $u'.totalAlloc \leq u.totalAlloc$ **then**
25:                     $cache.evict(f)$.
26:                     $cache.availableSize+ = f.size$.
27:                     $cache.availableSize- = f'.size$.
28:                     $u'.totalAlloc+ = f'.size$
29:                     **return CACHE_SUCCEED.**
30:                 **end if**
31:             **else if** $f'.getFreq > f.getFreq$ **then**
32:                 **if** $u' = u$ **OR** $u' \neq u$ **AND** $u'.totalAlloc \leq u.totalAlloc$ **then**
33:                     $cache.evict(f)$.
34:                     $cache.availableSize+ = f.size$.
35:                     $cache.availableSize- = f'.size$.
36:                     $u'.totalAlloc+ = f'.size$
37:                     **return CACHE_SUCCEED.**
38:                 **else if** $u' \neq u$ **AND** $u'.totalAlloc > u.totalAlloc$ **then**
39:                     **return CACHE_ABORT.**
40:                 **end if**
41:             **end if**
42:         **end if**
43:     **end while**
44:     $cache.add(f')$.   ▷ Cache has enough space to cache f'.
45:     $cache.availableSize- = f'.size$.
46:     $u'.totalAlloc+ = f'.size$.

strategy should be executed (*Line 32–37*). However, when the total resources of user u' are greater than user u ($u' \neq u$), the system does not allow f to be replaced by f' even though there will be some efficiency loss (*Line 38–39*). In this case, cache resources should be allocated to user u in preference to reduce the fairness loss.

FairCache with Efficiency Optimization Analysis. θ acts as an efficiency knob for the resource allocator, which can be flexibly adjusted by the user based on workload characteristics to achieve a trade-off between the long-term fairness and the overall efficiency. Actually, although the system can guarantee the fairness of users in a long term under FairCache policy, different θ represent different degrees of sacrifice that users are willing to make in each round of allocation (i.e., tolerating temporary unfairness). Because the value of θ will be affected by the size and distribution of data access frequency, there are three situations as follows: 1) When $\theta = 0$, it means that no file in DRAM will enter into $FileSet_{efficiency}$, then FairCache will degenerate into Max-Min Fairness Fair-Cache. 2) When $\theta \to +\infty$, it means that all files will enter into $FileSet_{efficiency}$, and every round of resource allocation will replace all data in the cache, then FairCache becomes LFU. 3) When $\theta \in [0, +\infty)$, there is always another θ' that makes the resource allocation of users whose frequencies range from θ to θ' unchanged, we call it θ Invalid Range (θ–IR).

5   Evaluation

To evaluate the performance of the proposed algorithm, we implement FairCache with Alluxio-1.4.0 and conduct experiments on multiple macro-benchmarks and micro-benchmarks.

5.1   Experimental Setup

Alluxio Cluster. We build a ten nodes Alluxio cluster with one master node and nine slave nodes. Each node has 16 GB of memory and 8 CPU cores. We allocate 6 GB of DRAM resources to each node.

Macro-benchmark. We run three real-world macro-benchmarks: 1) *Synthetic Facebook Workload:* We pick one of the all-day workloads (i.e., FB2010_samples_24_times_1hr_0.tsv) [25] from SWIM and synthesize a new workload based on the data fields (i.e., job submission duration, time interval and frequency of job submissions, and job submission size). These jobs come from the Hive benchmark [24], which consists of four types of select queries, rankings-uservisits join, rankings selection, uservisits aggregation and grep select. 2) *Purdue Workload:* We choose five benchmarks (i.e., Grep, Ranked Inverted Index, Word-count, Inverted-index and Term-vector) from Purdue MapReduce Benchmarks Suite [26] and use 40 GB of data generated from the Wikipedia data [27] as the input for these benchmarks. 3) *TPC-H Workload:* TPC-H [28] is a benchmark that provides decision support by querying and analyzing user behavior records. To simulate continuous queries, we generate 400 datasets. Each dataset is about 200 MB and contains 8 tables ranging from 5 KB to 80 MB.

Micro-benchmark. Assume that four users share a cache system equally and each user has an access list of 20 files. We assume that the access demands of users are independent of each other and will not access the same files.

In the following section, we use macro-benchmarks to generate four access queues for users to describe the variation of user cache demands and FairCache resource allocation in a long-term sharing environment, while evaluating the results of user fairness degree and the performance and overhead of the FairCache policy. We then use micro-benchmarks to show that users have the flexibility to balance fairness and efficiency by changing θ.

5.2   Testbed Experimental Results

FairCache Resource Allocation. Figure 2 describes the resource allocation of four users under FairCache. Figure 2a and 2b show the users' current demands and allocated cache, while Fig. 2c shows the users' accumulated cache resources. We set up an access window of size 1000 to update the access frequency and track the cache allocation of four users running the macro-benchmarks over 20 windows, where users' demands can change or not between any two windows.

 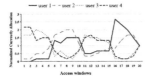 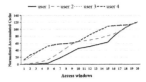

(a) Users' normalized current cache demands. (b) Users' normalized current allocated cache. (c) Users' normalized accumulated cache.

Fig. 2. Detailed description of the FairCache resource allocation process with four users.

During windows 1–5 in Fig. 2a, there are many unused cache resources due to insufficient demands of user 1 and 2. The system reserves a small amount of resources for user 1 and 2 and gives the remaining resources to user 3 and 4. Then, user 1 and 2's cache demands increase rapidly in windows 6–10, and everyone's demands exceed their fair share. Although user 3 and 4 still have lots of demands, they release some cache occupied by cold-data and give them back to user 1 and 2. When user 1 and 2's demands decrease again in windows 11–15, the resources that unused or occupied by cold-data will be fully utilized by user 3 and 4 again. Finally, when user 1's cache demands increase sharply in windows 16–20, other users will return resources to ensure cache efficiency. However, due to the fairness guarantee of FairCache, cache resources that user 1 gets in Fig. 2b are decreasing, despite she maintains high demands. Conversely, user 3's cache

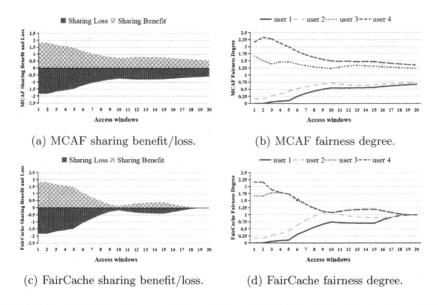

(a) MCAF sharing benefit/loss.

(b) MCAF fairness degree.

(c) FairCache sharing benefit/loss.

(d) FairCache fairness degree.

Fig. 3. (a) and (c) show the overall benefit/loss of MCAF and FairCache. (b) and (d) show the fairness degree of each user in MCAF and FairCache.

demands has not changed, but the resources she obtains are constantly increasing. In Fig. 2c, eventually the total amount of resources obtained by each user reaches equilibrium (i.e. the curve gets closer and closer).

Sharing Fairness Degree. We show in Sect. 4.3 that reducing sharing loss and ensuring pay-as-you-go fairness as much as possible in a long-term is an effective way to incentivize users to share cache resources. Figure 3a and 3c show the sharing benefit and loss of four users under MCAF and FairCache policies. Figure 3b and 3d describe the variation of the fairness of each user over time in more detail. We can find the difference between MCAF and FairCache.

First, because both allocation policies are enforced in a shared environment, this will result in more benefits for some users (compared to the isolated status). For example, both user 3 and 4 in Fig. 3b and 3d get more resources.

Second, FairCache is much better than MCAF. As shown in Fig. 3c, users can tolerate temporary unfairness in order to get more benefits in the future, because FairCache will definitely guarantee fairness to users in the long run. In contrast, the sharing loss problem of MCAF in Fig. 3a remains until all tasks are completed (i.e., ≈ -0.58). This is due to the memoryless nature of MCAF, which makes it impossible for users who lend unused resources at the moment to recover the same amount of resources when needed in the future, resulting in long-term unfairness.

Finally, when resource allocation is just starting, FairCache also has the problem of sharing loss in Fig. 3c, which is actually unavoidable. Because the

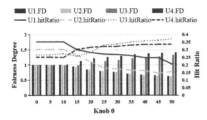
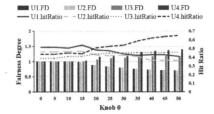

(a) Each user has 20 files with size 1GB each. All users' access to their files follows a Zipf distribution.

(b) Each user has 20 files with size from 0.25~1GB. All users' access to their files follows a Zipf distribution.

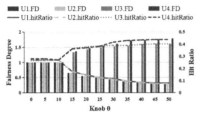
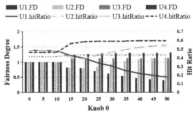

(c) Each user has 20 files with size 1GB each. Access to the files by user 1 and 2 follows a uniform distribution, while access to the files by the other two follows a Zipf distribution.

(d) Each user has 20 files with size from 0.25~1GB. Access to the files by user 1 and 2 follows a uniform distribution, while access to the files by the other two follows a Zipf distribution.

Fig. 4. A long-term cache sharing system under different knobs consisting of four users, each user has 6 GB DRAM. We emphasize that the sensitivity of θ to the balance of fairness and efficiency is influenced by the distribution of file size and access frequency.

purpose of FairCache is to ensure a long-term sharing fairness for users, some users will temporarily sacrifice current fairness in order to obtain more benefits in the future, without worrying about not being able to recover the lent resources in the future at all.

Fairness vs. Efficiency. First, FairCache can balance fairness and efficiency by adjusting θ. Since cache efficiency is positively correlated with hit ratio, hit ratio is used to represent the efficiency defined in Sect. 4.3. In Fig. 4, users can flexibly adjust θ according to the actual allocation. When θ is small, cache allocation is more biased towards fairness, and conversely the system will consider cache hit ratio improvement more. When θ exceeds a certain threshold, the resource allocation policy will become global LFU, when fairness is minimized. In addition, since $\theta-IR \in [0, 10]$, changing θ will not affect the cache hit ratio.

Second, different file sizes and access frequency distributions also affect the resource allocation of users in the shared system. In Fig. 4a, although the access frequency of user 3 and 4 is much higher than that of user 1 and 2, since users access to files follows the Zipf distribution, when θ increases, user 1 and 2 can still cache some popular files that are accessed frequently. As shown in Fig. 4c, the hit ratio of user 1 and 2 decreases when their access to files follows the uniform distribution compared to Fig. 4a. This is because user 1 and 2 lack the high frequency files in the Zipf distribution to grab more resources. Nevertheless, user 3 and 4 still have some cold-data accessed less frequently than user 1 and 2 in the uniform distribution. We change the size of the files accessed by the users in Fig. 4b and 4d, which are compared with Fig. 4a and 4c, respectively. Since some files have become smaller in size, users can write more data to the cache and therefore the hit ratio per user has increased. This illustrates that not only the file access frequency distribution, but also the difference in file size accessed by users can affect the cache allocation and hit ratio of system.

FairCache Performance and Overhead. Seven allocation policies are given in Fig. 5a to evaluate the performance of the system, including isolated states under non-shared, MCAF, LFU, Max-Min Fairness, and three different θ for FairCache.

First, as can be seen from Fig. 5a that allocating resources under isolated status has the lowest performance, with only 46% of the data having an average response time of 1000 ms. This is because unused resources can not be fully utilized in a non-shared environment. In contrast, due to other allocation policies all have different degrees of cache sharing, the average response time for 55%–62% of the data is within 1000 ms, which improves the system performance.

Moreover, although LFU is the global efficiency optimal policy, its CDF curve is slightly lower than that of the Max-Min Fairness policy. This is because many small-sized and low-frequency files present in the system are cached under the Max-Min Fairness policy, so the CDF curve of Max-Min Fairness accounts for a large proportion of the low response time. In fact, the low response time of the file does not mean that the cache resources are used efficiently, because the cache efficiency is determined by both the file size and the access frequency.

Finally, when $\theta \to 0$, its CDF curve will be more and more close to a Max-Min Fairness curve, and when $\theta \to +\infty$, its CDF curve will be more and more close to an LFU curve. This shows that in different scenarios, users can flexibly balance fairness and efficiency by adjusting θ.

We conduct 100 trials in Fig. 5b to evaluate the overhead of FairCache. Overhead refers to the time it takes for FairCache to decide whether and how to cache files for different numbers of users. We use the TPC-H dataset and consider a number of users from 10 to 100, each accessing 20 files, 0.25–1 GB in size. First, the result shows that the overhead time increases linearly with the number of users. Furthermore, the overhead of FairCache is lower compared to the generally read/write time of files in Fig. 5a. In summary, FairCache is a lightweight scheduler suitable for multi-users pay-as-you-go cache sharing systems.

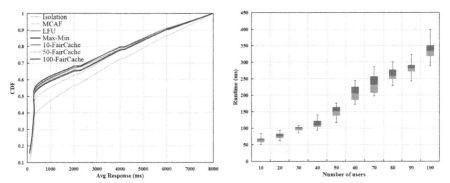

(a) Average file response time CDF under (b) The overhead of FairCache under differ-
different cache allocation policies.   ent number of users.

Fig. 5. Performance and overhead of FairCache in the cache sharing system.

6   Related Work

Cache Resource Allocation. Traditionally, efficiency first replacement strategies (e.g., LRU and LFU) and their improved versions [29,30] are widely adopted
in the allocation of cache resources. To improve LRU, Nathan et al. [19] proposed
the concept of least hit density and applied it to a key-value caching strategy,
which strictly filters objects that contribute little to the cache hit rate based on
conditional probability. Rodriguez et al. [31] designed a new class of adaptive,
machine-learned caching algorithms, CACHEUS, to address four workload primitive types by utilizing a combination of experts. Two new experts, SR-LRU and
CR-LFU, are used to handle scan and churn workload primitive types. However,
the above work is aimed at improving the hit rate under non-shared, and can not
be applied to the cache sharing system, otherwise it will lead to poor resource
fairness across users. An allocation mechanism using Cobb-Douglas preferences is
given in [33] to determine each user's fair share of hardware resources, while introducing modest performance penalties. For big data processing systems, Kunjir
et al. [20] developed a cache management platform ROBUS by using randomization over small time batches. A proportionally fair allocation mechanism is
adopted to satisfy the core property. Both FairRide [21] and OpuS [22] are based
on the max-min fairness [9]. They can be applied scenarios where multiple users
share cache files by using delay blocking to prevent users from "free-riding" to
achieve fairness and efficiency in the target system. Tang et al. [23] proposed a
new cache allocation policy ElastisSEM for DRAM and SSD, which contains a
knob to achieve a balance between fairness and efficiency. Although the above
methods can guarantee users' fairness in a shared environment, they do not consider the time-varying needs of users due to memoryless, and can not be applied
to a pay-as-you-go cache sharing system. The work of Choi et al. [32] is similar to
ours, which addresses the problem of cache allocation in a long-term shared environment. They predict users' data access patterns by a learning-based regression

method to improve the cache hit rate. However, this method does not guarantee users' fairness, and users are not willing to share in practice.

Fairness and Efficiency Scheduling Policy. Jian et al. [13] proposed a new method to quantify fairness and introduced Index of Fairness ranging from 0 to 1. Zukerman et al. [14] discussed the trade-off between efficiency metrics, such as utilization, throughput, revenue and fariness in telecommunication networks, and introduced the concept of α-fairness. Joe-Wong et al. [15] proposed a unified mathematical framework to better quantify the fairness in a multi-resource allocation environment, and developed two fairness functions to achieve a trade-off between fairness and efficiency. However, these works are limited to theoretical discussions and can not be directly used for verification in practical systems. In contrast, the FairCache policy proposed in this paper can be implemented in Alluxio. Niu et al. [16] proposed a meta-scheduler FLEX to aggregate existing schedulers, which can dynamically select the most suitable scheduler according to characteristics of current workloads and users' SLA. Both Tetris [17] and Qknober [34] are heuristic fairness-efficiency schedulers that control resource allocation through knobs On the basis of the CPU-GPU coupled architecture, Tang et al. [18] proposed an elastic multi-resource fair allocation strategy EMRF to balance between fairness and efficiency. However, due to the different characteristics of computing resources and cache resources, the cache resources we focus on have new challenges, such as resource inefficiency problem, truthfulness problem and pay-as-you-use fairness problem, which can not be solved by directly adopting the above methods. Moreover, the above methods can only guarantee part of the fairness of users, while our proposed method can guarantee the long-term fairness of users.

7   Conclusion

Pay-as-you-go cache sharing systems have been widely adopted in cloud computing, and cache fairness in such environments directly affects the experience of users, which is our primary consideration. However, we found that existing resource fairness policies, which are applied in frameworks such as YARN and Mesos, can not be directly applied in pay-as-you-go cache sharing systems due to three serious problems, i.e., resource inefficiency problem, truthfulness problem and pay-as-you-use fairness problem. In this paper, we proposed a long-term cache fairness allocation policy, FairCache, to solve the problems above. We also proposed four properties as metrics to measure fairness policies in a pay-as-you-go cache sharing system. FairCache can help improve the overall cache resources utilization and achieve a long-term fairness by permitting users to lead resources to others and get more revenue in the future. To further promote global cache efficiency, we propose an efficiency knob θ for FairCache. It allows users to adjust θ setting to achieve a tradeoff between fairness and efficiency. Finally, we provided an implementation of the proposed FairCache in Alluxio. Experiment results demonstrated that the proposed fairness policy could efficiently achieve long-term fairness across multiple users in a cache sharing system while maximizing the utilization and efficiency of system cache resources.

Acknowledgements. This work was funded by National Key Research and Development Program of China (2020YFC1522702) and National Natural Science Foundation of China (61972277).

References

1. Wang, G., Ng, T.S.E.: The impact of virtualization on network performance of amazon ec2 data center. In: 2010 Proceedings IEEE INFOCOM, pp. 1–9 (2010)
2. Wu, J., et al.: A benchmark test of boson sampling on Tianhe-2 supercomputer. Natl. Sci. Rev. **5**, 715–720 (2018)
3. Zaharia, M., Chowdhury, M., Franklin, M.J., Shenker, S., Stoica, I.: Spark: cluster computing with working sets. In: 2nd USENIX Workshop on Hot Topics in Cloud Computing (HotCloud 10) (2010)
4. Apache.Hadoop. https://hadoop.apache.org/
5. Palankar, M.R., Iamnitchi, A., Ripeanu, M., Garfinkel, S.: Amazon S3 for science grids: a viable solution. In: Proceedings of the 2008 International Workshop on Data-Aware Distributed Computing, pp. 55–64, June 2008
6. Carlson, J.: Redis in Action. Simon and Schuster (2013)
7. Li, H., Ghodsi, A., Zaharia, M., Shenker, S., Stoica, I.: Tachyon: reliable, memory speed storage for cluster computing frameworks. In: Proceedings of the ACM Symposium on Cloud Computing, pp. 1–15, November 2014
8. Cleverley, W.O., Nutt, P.C.: The effectiveness of group-purchasing organizations. Health Serv. Res. **19**, 65 (1984)
9. Ghodsi, A., Zaharia, M., Hindman, B., Konwinski, A., Shenker, S., Stoica, I.: Dominant resource fairness: fair allocation of multiple resource types. In: 8th USENIX Symposium on Networked Systems Design and Implementation (NSDI 2011) (2011)
10. Ghodsi, A., Zaharia, M., Shenker, S., Stoica, I.: Choosy: max-min fair sharing for datacenter jobs with constraints. In: Proceedings of the 8th ACM European Conference on Computer Systems, pp. 365–378, April 2013
11. Apache.YARN. https://hadoop.apache.org/docs/current2/index.html/
12. Hindman, B., et al.: Mesos: a platform for fine-grained resource sharing in the data center. In: 8th USENIX Symposium on Networked Systems Design and Implementation (NSDI 2011) (2011)
13. Jain, R.K., Chiu, D.M.W., Hawe, W.R.: A quantitative measure of fairness and discrimination. Eastern Research Laboratory, Digital Equipment Corporation, Hudson, May 1984
14. Zukerman, M., Tan, L., Wang, H., Ouveysi, I.: Efficiency-fairness tradeoff in telecommunications networks. IEEE Commun. Lett. 643–645 (2005)
15. Joe-Wong, C., Sen, S., Lan, T., Chiang, M.: Multiresource allocation: fairness-efficiency tradeoffs in a unifying framework. IEEE/ACM Trans. Network. **21**, 1785–1798 (2013)
16. Niu, Z.J., Tang, S.J., He, B.S.: An adaptive efficiency-fairness meta-scheduler for data-intensive computing. IEEE Trans. Serv. Comput. **12**, 865–879 (2016)
17. Grandl, R., Ananthanarayanan, G., Kandula, S., Rao, S., Akella, A.: Multi-resource packing for cluster schedulers. ACM SIGCOMM Comput. Commun. Rev. **44**, 455–466 (2014)

18. Tang, S.J., He, B.S., Zhang, S., Niu, Z.J.: Elastic multi-resource fairness: balancing fairness and efficiency in coupled CPU-GPU architectures. In: SC 2016: Proceedings of the International Conference for High Performance Computing, Networking, Storage and Analysis, pp. 875–886. IEEE, November 2016

19. Beckmann, N., Chen, H., Cidon, A.: LHD: improving cache hit rate by maximizing hit density. In: 15th USENIX Symposium on Networked Systems Design and Implementation (NSDI 2018), pp. 389–403 (2018)

20. Kunjir, M., Fain, B., Munagala, K., Babu, S.: ROBUS: fair cache allocation for data-parallel workloads. In: Proceedings of the 2017 ACM International Conference on Management of Data, pp. 219–234, May 2017

21. Pu, Q., Li, H., Zaharia, M., Ghodsi, A., Stoica, I.: FairRide: near-optimal, fair cache sharing. In: 13th USENIX Symposium on Networked Systems Design and Implementation (NSDI 2016), pp. 393–406 (2016)

22. Yu, Y., Wang, W., Zhang, J., Weng, Q., Letaief, K.B.: Opus: fair and efficient cache sharing for in-memory data analytics. In: 2018 IEEE 38th International Conference on Distributed Computing Systems (ICDCS), pp. 154–164. IEEE (2018)

23. Tang, S.J., Chai, Q.F., Yu, C., Li, Y.S., Sun, C.: Balancing fairness and efficiency for cache sharing in semi-external memory system. In: 49th International Conference on Parallel Processing (ICPP), pp. 1–11, August 2020

24. Apache Hive performance benchmarks. https://issues.apache.org/jira/browse/HIVE-396/

25. SWIM. https://github.com/SWIMProjectUCB/SWIM/

26. Ahmad, F., Lee, S., Thottethodi, M., Vijaykumar, T.N.: Puma: purdue mapreduce benchmarks suite (2012)

27. PUMA. http://web.ics.purdue.edu/fahmad/benchmarks/datasets.htm/

28. TPC-H. https://issues.apache.org/jira/browse/HIVE-600/

29. Matani, D., Shah, K., Mitra, A.: An O (1) algorithm for implementing the LFU cache eviction scheme. arXiv preprint arXiv:2110.11602 (2021)

30. Hasslinger, G., Heikkinen, J., Ntougias, K., Hasslinger, F., Hohlfeld, O.: Optimum caching versus LRU and LFU: comparison and combined limited look-ahead strategies. In: 2018 16th International Symposium on Modeling and Optimization in Mobile, Ad Hoc, and Wireless Networks (WiOpt), pp. 1–6. IEEE, May 2018

31. Rodriguez, L.V., et al.: Learning cache replacement with CACHEUS. In: 19th USENIX Conference on File and Storage Technologies (FAST 2021), pp. 341–354 (2021)

32. Choi, J., Gu, Y., Kim, J.: Learning-based dynamic cache management in a cloud. J. Parallel Distrib. Comput. **145**, 98–110 (2020)

33. Zahedi, S.M., Lee, B.C.: REF: resource elasticity fairness with sharing incentives for multiprocessors. ACM SIGPLAN Not. **49**, 145–160 (2014)

34. Tang, S.J., Yu, C., Li, Y.S.: Fairness-efficiency scheduling for cloud computing with soft fairness guarantees. In: IEEE Trans. Cloud Comput. (2020)

MatGraph: An Energy-Efficient and Flexible CGRA Engine for Matrix-Based Graph Analytics

Long Tan[1,2], Mingyu Yan[1(✉)], Duo Wang[1,2], Wenming Li[1], Xiaochun Ye[1], and Dongrui Fan[1]

[1] State Key Laboratory of Processors, Institute of Computing Technology, Chinese Academy of Sciences, Beijing, China
{tanlong,yanmingyu,wangduo18z,liwenming,yexiaochun,fandr}@ict.ac.cn
[2] School of Computer Science and Technology, University of Chinese Academy of Sciences, Beijing, China

Abstract. Graph analytics is increasingly important for solving problems in various fields. Matrix-based graph analytics has obtained much attention due to its high performance and ease of optimization. In the general architecture, due to the extremely high sparsity and complex connectedness of graphs, matrix-based graph analytics suffers from the deep and heavy pipeline as well as the low efficiency of the memory subsystem. Meanwhile, lots of accelerators based on application-specific integrated circuits (ASICs) for graph analytics are not flexible enough to support various matrix operations of diverse matrix-based graph algorithms, which have different graph semantics and dataflow.

In this paper, we present MatGraph, an energy-efficient and flexible architecture to support matrix-based graph analytics efficiently. MatGraph is based on coarse-grained reconfigurable architectures (CGRAs) which have both high energy efficiency and flexibility. According to the matrix operations on graphs, we conduct an abstract from the operators to define reduced instructions and design a lightweight pipeline to achieve high parallelism of instructions in CGRAs. To eliminate the impact of the highly sparse graph data, we design a bitmap-aware instruction filtering unit to filter out invalid instructions for each PE and increase the on-chip reuse of instructions. Furthermore, we propose a bidirectional data-aware sparsity removing scheme to eliminate the sparsity and redundant off-chip data accesses. Overall, MatGraph achieves 9.35x, 2.28x speedup, and 11.17x, 7.15x energy savings on average compared to state-of-the-art (SOTA) CPU-based and GPGPU-based solutions respectively. Compared to the SOTA graph analytics accelerator, MatGraph also achieves 1.59x speedup and 1.61x less energy.

Keywords: Graph analytics · Matrix-based programming model · CGRA · Energy-efficient · Flexible

© Springer Nature Switzerland AG 2023
W. Meng et al. (Eds.): ICA3PP 2022, LNCS 13777, pp. 351–372, 2023.
https://doi.org/10.1007/978-3-031-22677-9_19

1   Introduction

In the big data era, studying relationships among data demonstrated in the form of graphs has gained considerable attention. Graph analytics has become vital for solving problems in various scenarios including bioinformatics [16], social network analysis [19], autonomous vehicles [26] and brain science [3].

Therefore, lots of graph analytics software frameworks [4,21,28] and hardware accelerators [7,13,27,30,34] have been proposed to deal with various situations in recent years. The programming models of these works mainly can be divided into vertex-centric model [21], edge-centric model [28] and matrix-based model [4]. Vertex-centric model is widely used by recent works [13,34] due to its high productivity, but it's limited by unpredictable vertex behaviors and difficult to optimize the efficiency of memory accesses.

Matrix-based model is known for its high performance mentioned in [29,31] and good mathematical theory making it easier to analyze program behaviors than the vertex-centric model. However, because graphs are characterized by irregular connectedness and extremely high sparsity, matrix-based graph analytics suffers from the low efficiency of the memory subsystem and the low energy efficiency on general architectures including CPUs and GPGPUs owing to their complex and redundant pipelines. Many hardware accelerators based on ASICs for graph analytics are not flexible enough to support various generalized matrix operations in matrix-based graph analytics.

In this paper, we propose MatGraph, an energy-efficient and flexible architecture for matrix-based graph analytics. To flexibly support various matrix operations defined for different matrix-based graph algorithms based on semirings [4], we conduct an abstraction from the different semirings and define dozens of reduced instructions according to our abstraction of operators of semirings. We design a lightweight pipeline in processing elements (PEs) of CGRA to efficiently support the execution of reduced instructions. Utilizing the coarse-grained dataflow parallelism in CGRAs, we can achieve high parallelism of instructions to support various matrix operations in matrix-based graph analytics with high energy efficiency.

Due to the high sparsity of graph data, a CGRA accelerator for graph analytcis still confronts the following two challenges. **(1) Owing to massive irregular sparse graph data, the instructions among PEs cannot be reused, resulting in a large amount of instruction off-chip movement overhead, (2) Massive irregular sparse data produces a large number of invalid computations and redundant off-chip memory accesses.** Therefore, to address the two challenges above, **(1)** We propose a bitmap-aware instruction filtering strategy to filter out invalid instructions for each PE while increasing the on-chip reuse of instructions among PEs and alleviating the instructions off-chip movements caused by highly sparse graph data. **(2)** To further reduce the invalid computations and redundant memory accesses, we propose a bidirectional data-aware sparsity removing mechanism to eliminate the sparsity of graph data.

Our contributions are summarized as follows:

- We conduct an operator's abstraction from the various matrix operations for matrix-based graph analytics and define the reduced instructions for these operators to flexibly support distinctive matrix-based graph algorithms.
- We propose a flexible and energy-efficient architecture named MatGraph based on CGRA. It has lightweight pipelines to support the reduced instructions we propose while leveraging the dataflow execution model to achieve high parallelism of instructions.
- We design a bitmap-aware instruction filtering unit to filter out invalid instructions for each PE while increasing the on-chip reuse of instructions among PEs and alleviating the off-chip instruction movements. Additionally, we propose a bidirectional data-aware sparsity removing mechanism to further reduce the redundant off-chip data accesses and eliminate the sparsity of graph data.
- We implement MatGraph in RTL to attain its area and energy consumption and evaluate MatGraph using a detailed microarchitectural simulation to show improved performance compared to the state-of-the-art framework and accelerators.

2 Backgrounds

In this section, we first introduce common graph representations. Then, we make a brief description of the matrix-based graph analytics. Finally, we introduce the characteristics of CGRAs.

2.1 Graph Representation

A graph could be intuitively considered as an adjacency matrix, where the rows refer to the vertices and the matrix elements represent the edges. Figure 1(a) depicts an example graph $G < V, E >$. As shown in Fig. 1(c), it's the out-degree adjacency matrix of the example graph G, where the row index represents source nodes and the column index represents destination nodes. However, real-world graphs are highly sparse, which means that there would be many zero values in the adjacency matrix. These zero values incur the waste of both storage and computing resources. Thus, lots of other representations, which are suitable for highly sparse graph data, like the compressed sparse row (CSR), and compressed sparse column (CSC) have spawned. As presented in Fig. 1(b), we can express graph G using compressed formats to reduce storage like the compressed sparse row (CSR). The CSR consists of three arrays, containing a row array, edge array, and property array. The row array stores the first pointer of its neighborhood list in the edge array for each vertex. The edge array stores neighborhood lists for all vertices and the property array stores the property value of each vertex. Compressed sparse column (CSC) is similar to CSR except for its edge array stores the ingoing edges of each vertex.

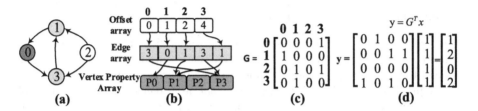

Fig. 1. (a) graph G, (b) graph adjacency matrix, (c) CSR representation for graph G, (d) shows computing vertex in-degrees of graph G using matrix multiplication. Vector x is all ones and the output vector y indicates the number of incoming edges of each vertex.

2.2 Matrix-Based Graph Analytics

Various graph analytics frameworks come with a variety of programming models, mainly falling into three categories: vertex-centric model [21], edge-centric model [28] and matrix-based model [4]. Of these models, vertex-centric model and edge-centric model are widely used due to ease of use, but it is difficult to optimize because of their unpredictable program behavior.

Matrix-based model have gained more attention because it's based on strong mathematical theory and can achieve good performance. Based on the graph theory of Denes Konig, operations on the adjacency matrix of a graph are equal to conducting graph analytics [18]. To illustrate this theory, a simple example of calculating in-degrees is shown in Fig. 1(d). Multiplying the graph adjacency matrix (unweighted graph) with a vector of all ones produces a vector of vertex in-degrees. Matrix-based model are based on the theory that graph algorithms can be described as matrix operations on different semirings [4] which are the basic mathematical definitions of matrix-based graph algorithms. The semirings of four well-known graph analytics algorithms, i.e., Breadth-First Search (BFS), Single Source Shortest Path (SSSP), Triangle Counting (TC), and PageRank (PR) are shown in Table 1. For different matrix-based graph algorithms, diverse generalized "multiply ($\otimes$)" and "add ($\oplus$)" matrix operations are used to represent miscellaneous graph semantics. As shown in Algorithm 1, we take BFS as an example of matrix-based graph algorithms.

Table 1. Semirings for different algorithms.

Semirings	Domain	$\oplus$	$\otimes$	0	Graph semantics	Algorithms
lor-land	{F, T}	$\vee$	$\wedge$	F	Connectivity	BFS
min-plus	$\mathbb{R} \cup \{+\infty\}$	min	+	$+\infty$	Shortest path	SSSP
integer arithmetic	$\mathbb{N}$	+	$\cdot$	0	Number of paths	TC
real arithmetic	$\mathbb{R}$	+	$\cdot$	0	Strength of paths	PR

Algorithm 1: An Example of Matrix-based Graph Analytics: BFS

---

    input   : Adjacency Matrix A
    output: Property Vector Y
1 **for** $i = 1$ to MaxIterations **do**
2   **for** $v = 1$ to MaxVertex **do**
3   **if** v is active **then**
4   create sparse vector X
5      $y = \mathrm{SpMV}(A, X, \mathrm{semirings}(\oplus.\otimes))$
6   **for** $j = 1$ to length(y) **do**
7         $v = \mathrm{getVertex}(j)$
8   **if** getNewProperty(v)$\neq$oldVertexProperty(v) **then**
9   set v is active
10            $Y[v] = \mathrm{getNewProperty}(v)$

11 return Y

2.3 Coarse-Grained Reconfigurable Architectures

CGRAs have been developing rapidly stemming from 1990s [6,14]. This architecture is a natural coarse-grained implementation based on the concept of reconfigurable computing proposed in 1960s [10]. It has gained much attention because it not only has high energy efficiency and performance like ASICs but also has great programmability [9,32].

CGRAs have a close relationship with dataflow architecture [5,12] because they often integrate with the dataflow mechanism. The operations of CGRAs can be driven by configuration flow or dataflow. The configuration of CGRAs defines PE's operations and interconnections. CGRAs can utilize efficient dataflow between PEs via interconnections, which is not supported in conventional CPUs. With the combination of dataflow and control flow, CGRAs can avoid over-serialized execution among PEs and exploit coarse-grained parallelism. Meanwhile, CGRAs can further support explicit data communication among PEs which can reduce the energy overhead of data movement among PEs. Therefore, this hybrid mode with dataflow and control flow is the important reason for CGRAs' high performance and energy efficiency. In this paper, we design a graph analytics engine based on CGRAs which combines the control flow and dataflow model to enable high performance without sacrificing energy efficiency and programmability.

3 Motivations

In this section, we motivate our work by recognizing the challenges of graph analytics and the constraints of prior work.

3.1 Challenges of Graph Analytics

The vertex-centric model is popular for graph analytics due to its high productivity. However, real-world natural graphs usually are highly sparse and follow power-law distribution wherein a small set of vertices are with a large fraction of all connections in the graph. The features of real-world graphs lead to a poor locality for data accesses and unpredictable vertex behaviors in vertex-centric graph analytics. Thus, vertex-centric model is difficult to optimize for better performance.

While for matrix-based graph analytics, more regular matrix operations substitute lots of random memory accesses which often happen in vertex-centric model. Regular and predictable matrix operations often lead to a better locality and regular memory access. Matrix-based model based on a solid mathematical theory [4] often shows high performance [29]. In our opinion, the matrix-based model could be a feasible approach to achieve better performance.

Unfortunately, in general architectures like CPUs, their complex pipelines are too deep and redundant for matrix-based graph analytics resulting in low performance and energy efficiency. Furthermore, graphs often show extremely high sparsity and this makes the performance of graph analytics on general architectures poor [15]. As shown in Fig. 2(a), we use LAGraph [23], which is a representative framework for matrix-based graph analytics, to run the BFS algorithm on the Intel Xeon CPU as an example. The datasets we use in the example are the RMAT Graph [25] listed in Table 4. Specifically, we use RMAT graphs with a vertex scale of 21 and the average vertex degrees ranging from 4 to 256 in this example. We can see the overall IPC is still very low, less than 0.25, which means running matrix-based graph algorithms on the general architecture is inefficient. At the same time, we observe that as the density of the dataset increases, the sparsity decreases, and the IPC increases, it shows that the overall efficiency is closely related to the sparsity of the dataset. Additionally, the density of the graph dataset is very low, and the sparsity is very high, up to 99.999%. Such high sparsity of graph data poses a great challenge to matrix-based graph analytics.

Recently, lots of accelerators based on the ASICs for vertex-centric graph analytics are proposed. Their architectures based on ASICs are often fixed and cannot be changed or reconfigured. However, matrix-based graph algorithms consist of different matrix operations which have distinguished execution behaviors and dataflow [22]. As depicted in Fig. 2(b), different algorithms have diverse computing kernels. These computing kernels have different dataflows, the precisions of operations, data access patterns, and reusability. For instance, the SpMV kernel of BFS works on bool values, while the SpMM kernel of TC operates on integer values. They differ more in the precision requirements and data access patterns of the graph data. It is challenging to design an architecture with fixed dataflow for matrix-based graph analytics. Thus, we need a lightweight and flexible matrix-based graph analytics engine to achieve high performance and energy efficiency.

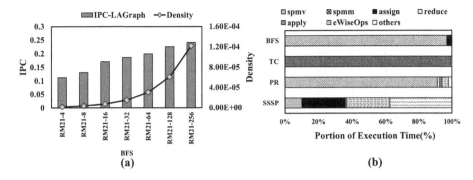

Fig. 2. (a) The IPC of BFS changes with the density of the data set, (b) Execution time breakdown of diverse computing kernels in different matrix-based graph algorithms.

3.2   Overcoming Challenges

As mentioned in Sect. 3.1, it's clear to find that the drawbacks of the programming models and general architectures conflict with each other and cannot be solved easily.

Opportunities. We observe that the important operators of matrix-based graph analytics are often no more than 20 operations. It's a better choice for us to design an energy-efficient accelerator with lightweight pipelines for matrix-based graph analytics with few reduced instructions which are necessary for graph operations. Additionally, as mentioned in Sect. 3.1, assorted matrix-based graph algorithms show great demands for hardware flexibility. According to Sect. 2.3, CGRA is popular because it can be used to achieve both high performance and flexibility. Thus, CGRA is an ideal base platform for us to accelerate matrix-based graph analytics. Based on these observations, we proposed MatGraph, a flexible and energy-efficient CGRA engine with reduced instructions for matrix-based graph analytics to tackle the challenges described above.

Challenges. However, as shown in Fig. 2, The sparsity of each graph dataset is more than 99.999%. Due to the high sparsity of graph data, a CGRA accelerator still confronts the following two challenges. **(1) Due to massive irregular sparse graph data, the instructions of different PEs cannot be reused, resulting in a large amount of instruction off-chip movement overhead, (2) Immense irregular sparse graph data produces a large number of invalid computations and redundant off-chip memory accesses.** Therefore, to address the two challenges above, **(1)** we propose a bitmap-aware instruction filtering strategy to increase the on-chip reuse of instructions and filter invalid computations caused by highly sparse graph data. **(2)** To further reduce the invalid computations and redundant memory accesses, we propose a data-aware bidirectional sliding window mechanism to eliminate the sparsity of graph data.

4 Design

4.1 Overview Architecture

In this section, we introduce our proposed architecture named MatGraph based on CGRA.

Hardware Implementation. Our proposed architecture is shown in Fig. 3(a), it is mainly composed of many tiled PEs, on-chip Scratchpad Memory (SPM), controllers, networks on chip (NoCs), and a prefetcher. As demonstrated in Fig. 3(b), each PE consists of an instruction filtering unit, dispatcher, instructions and operands buffer, routers, as well as a pipelined and lightweight computing unit without data hazards. It performs like a pipelined in-order core to execute instructions in a dataflow manner. Figure 3(c) depicts the organization of on-chip memory, which is in the form of a ping-pong buffer. In this way, the memory latency can be overlapped with the computing phase.

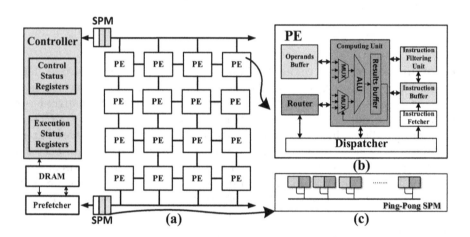

Fig. 3. (a) Overall architecture, (b) PE architecture, (c) Ping-Pong on-chip SPM.

Execution Model. To improve the parallelism of instructions and achieve high utilization of computing units of PEs, we adopt a codelet model as an execution model. The codelet model is inspired by a dataflow parallel execution model [11]. In this model, the total codes of an application are split into several codelets. A codelet contains a sequence of hardware instructions. There exist some dependencies among the codelets. As shown in the Fig. 4, according to the relationships of codelets, we can express the program of an application as a Codelets Dataflow Graph (CDG) and then map this CDG into the PEs. The execution of the codelet should follow the sequence in the CDG. A codelet will not issue until all conditions are met: 1) the data it depends on is available. 2) hardware resources it will use are idle. In this dataflow model, we can achieve high instruction and data-level parallelism.

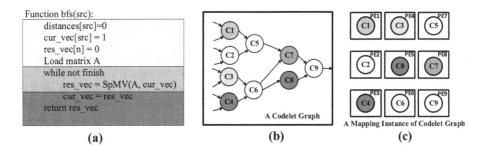

Fig. 4. Codelet execution model.

4.2 Reduced Instructions Based on Semirings

It's very challenging to flexibly support various matrix-based graph algorithms because they consist of different matrix operations meaning different execution patterns. To achieve this goal, we design a set of reduced instructions based on semirings [22]. As shown in Table 1, different semirings can express different graph semantics. According to different semirings, we design a set of reduced instructions from different matrix operations. As shown in Table 2, our defined instructions include 15 fixed-length instructions which are formatted as [FUNC, RS3, RS2, RS1, OPCODE] where OP is the operation code of the instructions, RS1-RS3 are three operands and FUNC is an additional field for other extendable functions.

Table 2. Reduced instructions and their functions.

Instructions	Functions
ADD	PeRAM[RS3] = PeRAM[RS1] + PeRAM[RS2]
MUL	PeRAM[RS3] = PeRAM[RS1] + PeRAM[RS2]
MADD	PeRAM[RS3] = PeRAM[RS1] * PeRAM[RS2] + PeRAM[RS3]
AOR	PeRAM[RS3] = (PeRAM[RS1] && PeRAM[RS2]) || PeRAM[RS3]
MIN	PeRAM[RS3] = min{PeRAM[RS1], PeRAM[RS2]}
MAX	PeRAM[RS3] = max{PeRAM[RS1], PeRAM[RS2]}
AND	PeRAM[RS3] = PeRAM[RS1] && PeRAM[RS2]
OR	PeRAM[RS3] = PeRAM[RS1] || PeRAM[RS2]
XOR	PeRAM[RS3] = PeRAM[RS1] $\oplus$ PeRAM[RS2]
AND-Bitwise	PeRAM[RS3] = PeRAM[RS1] & PeRAM[RS2]
OR-Bitwise	PeRAM[RS3] = PeRAM[RS1] | PeRAM[RS2]
XOR-Bitwise	PeRAM[RS3] = PeRAM[RS1] $\oplus$ PeRAM[RS2]
LOAD	PeRAM[RS3] = DRAM[$Base\_addr$ + {$RS1, RS2$}]
STORE	DRAM[$Base\_addr$ + {$RS1, RS2$}] = PeRAM[RS3]
MOVE	{PE[RS2], PeRAM[RS3]} = PeRAM[RS1]

There are a total of 15 instructions that can be categorized into three types. The details of the instructions are as follows.

Load and Store Instructions. We use the load and store instructions to transfer data between the on-chip memory and the local memory inside the PEs. They adopt the base-offset addressing mode to access the data residing in the memory. The base address of load and store usually are respectively specified in the dispatcher of each PE. With the base plus the offset value in the instructions, we can access the data residing in the on-chip or off-chip memory.

Computational Instructions. There are 12 computational instructions in total. These instructions work on the data reading from the local PE RAM. By combining these computational instructions, various matrix operations of matrix-based graph algorithms can be flexibly supported.

Move Instruction. The move instruction is the key point to achieving the dataflow models described in Sect. 4.1. It is responsible for transferring data from the source PE to the destination PE. This enables PEs to share on-chip instructions and operands easily.

4.3   Bitmap-Aware Instruction Filtering

To resolve the invalid instructions for each PE and reduce instruction off-chip movements caused by highly sparse graph data, we designed an instruction filtering unit in each PE called Bitmap-aware Instruction Filtering (BIF). The BIF design is driven by two key factors: (1) By dividing the matrix data into uniformly sized sub-matrices, all PE can share a set of instructions to reduce the overhead of lots of instruction movements, although the valid values in each matrix block are different, only the invalid values of the corresponding instructions need to be filtered out to complete the execution. (2) Storing matrix data

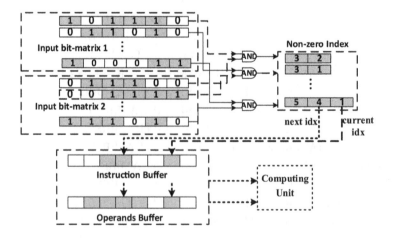

Fig. 5. Bitmap-aware instruction filtering unit.

in the form of a bitmap sacrifices smaller storage in exchange for greater performance gains, and a bitmap can also be directly used for computation in the graph traversal algorithm when checking connectedness such as BFS.

Figure 5 presents an overview of the structure of the BIF. The BIF repeatedly collects the valid index of non-zero values and instructions and transfers them to the computing unit. First, BIF obtains the non-zero index of each vector by reading the bitmap of the input matrix data that participates in the computations. The bitmap values of the two vectors from different input bit-matrix are performed with the AND operation to get the index of non-zero values in the results vector further. Then, BIF utilizes the non-zero index of the corresponding instruction and operands buffer to fetch the corresponding valid instructions and operands. Finally, it sends the fetched valid instructions and operands to the computing unit to complete the computations. In summary, using BIF, we can achieve the sharing of a set of instructions among PEs to increase on-chip reuse of instructions and reduce off-chip instructions movements. Besides, we can filter out invalid instructions for each PE, avoiding invalid computations.

4.4   Sparsity Removing with Bidirectional Sliding Window

Even if we convert the matrix data into a bitmap to guide the filtering of instructions and data shown in Sect. 4.3, there still be a lot of redundant data accesses and superfluous storage of the bitmap. The overhead of storing bitmaps and redundant data accesses is still not to be overlooked. In order to further reduce the impact of highly sparse graph data, we propose a bidirectional data-aware sliding window to remove data sparsity.

Graph Partition. Graph partitioning is an important method to process large graphs and achieve good scalability of graph analytics. We use the method of [20,34] to partition graph data, which is the basis of our bidirectional data-aware sparsity removing scheme in the next subsection. A graph adjacency matrix is divided into intervals (I) and shards (S) which are not disjoint. As the example Graph G shows in Fig. 6 (a), we group the 4 vertices as an interval and group the 4 * 4 edges as a shard. There are 4 intervals (from I_1 to I_4) and 4 * 44 shards (from S (1,1) to S (4,4)) in total. As shown in Fig. 6 (c) and (d), we call the two matrices of graph matrix multiplication row matrix A and column matrix B respectively. The row matrix A is stored in CSR format and the column matrix B is stored in CSC format.

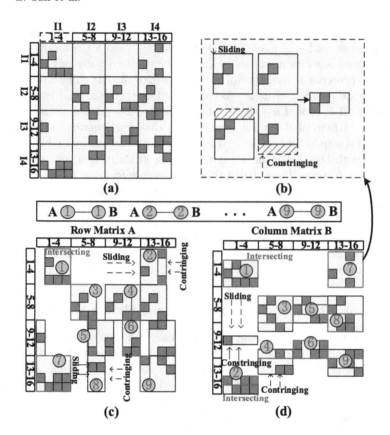

Fig. 6. Static partition and bidirectional data-aware sparsity removing to reduce redundant accesses. (a) Graph partition, (b) Window sliding and constringing, (c) Row matrix sliding window, (d) Column matrix sliding window.

Bidirectional Data-Aware Sparsity Removing (BSR). Finding the common valid part of two matrices when performing matrix multiplication can effectively reduce redundant data accesses and superfluous storage of the bitmap, but it is also time-consuming. To eliminate the sparsity and find the common valid part efficiently, we propose a bidirectional data-aware sparsity removing mechanism. For the column matrix, we firstly set the window size as the same as edge shards and slide the window down until getting an edge in the top row. Then, we constring the window size by moving the bottom row upward until an edge is met. The row matrix is similar to the process of the column matrix but it slides and constringes in the horizontal direction. After the row matrix and column matrix finish the process of window sliding and constringing, we make intersecting effectual shards of the row matrix and column matrix to get the common valid part. The detailed processes of window sliding, constringing, and intersecting are demonstrated in Algorithm 2.

Algorithm 2: GetOneCommonValidShard

---

input : Row Matrix A, Column Matrix B, Intervals I, Shards S, Vertex v
output: I_{valid}

$\triangledown$ **Window Sliding**

1 //For Column Matrix B
2 **while** $edge(row_{start}, v) == \emptyset$ **do**
3     $\lfloor$ $row_{start} \leftarrow row_{start} + 1;$

4 $row_{end} \leftarrow row_{start} + Window_{hight};$
5 $row_{start} \leftarrow row_{end} + 1;$
6 //For Row Matrix A
7 **while** $edge(column_{start}, v) == \emptyset$ **do**
8     $\lfloor$ $column_{index} \leftarrow column_{index} + 1;$

9 $column_{end} \leftarrow column_{start} + Window_{width};$
10 $column_{start} \leftarrow column_{end} + 1;$

$\triangledown$ **Window Contringing**

11 //For Column Matrix B
12 **while** $edge(row_{end}, v) == \emptyset$ *&&* $\forall$ v *in* I_i **do**
13    $\lfloor$ $row_{end} \leftarrow row_{end} - 1;$

14 //For Row Matrix A
15 **while** $edge(column_{end}, v) == \emptyset$ *&&* $\forall$ v *in* I_i **do**
16    $\lfloor$ $column_{end} \leftarrow column_{end} - 1;$

$\triangledown$ **Window Intersecting**

17 **if** $row_{end} \geq column_{start} \| column_{end} \geq row_{start}$ **then**
18    $\lfloor$ $I_{valid_{start}} \leftarrow max\{row_{start}, column_{start}\};$
19    $\lfloor$ $I_{valid_{end}} \leftarrow min\{row_{end}, column_{end}\};$

20 **else** $row_{end} < column_{start} \| column_{end} < row_{start}$
21    $\lfloor$ $I_{valid_{start}} \leftarrow 0;$ //common shard does not exist.
22    $\lfloor$ $I_{valid_{end}} \leftarrow 0;$

23 $I_{valid} \leftarrow I[I_{valid_{start}}, I_{valid_{end}}];$
24 **return** $I_{valid};$

Window Sliding. Figure 6 (b) shows the flow of window sliding. For each vertex interval, the top edge blocks window gradually slides downward and it stops when meets an edge on its top row. After that, a new window with the same size starting from the bottom row of its previous window slides down and stops with the same criterion. All the positions where windows stop are valid shards. As presented in Fig. 6 (c), for row matrix A, the window slides in the horizontal direction (i.e. sliding rightward). Figure 6 (d) shows column matrix B uses the same mechanism but the window slides in the vertical direction (i.e. sliding downward).

Window Constringing. Figure 6 (b) also depicts the process flow of window constringing. The window sliding can only filter the sparse area on the top size, however, sparsity still exists on the bottom side. To reduce the sparsity remaining on the bottom side, for column matrix B, the bottom row of each window moves upward until it meets an edge, and the window is constringing. For row matrix A, its window constringing in the horizontal direction (i.e. sliding leftward).

Window Intersecting. After the row matrix and column matrix obtain their valid effectual shards, we compare the upper bound and bottom bound of the horizontal shards in the row matrix and vertical shards in the column matrix respectively to get the common valid edges. Figure 6 (c)(d) shows the process of finding the common effectual part of the row matrix and the column matrix. The edges in the red color box (labeled with 1, 2, etc. in row matrix A and column matrix B) are the common valid part in each shard.

5   Methodology

5.1   Experimental Setup

To evaluate the effectiveness of MatGraph, we implement it in Verilog and synthesize it utilizing Synopsys Design Compiler with TSMC 12 nm GP standard VT library to evaluate its's power and area accurately. For the performance evaluation, we build an in-house cycle-accurate simulator and integrate the Ramulator [17] as its memory subsystem. The area, power, and access latency for the on-chip SRAM are estimated using Cacti 6.5 [24]. The energy for DDR4-2400 is estimated using 38 pJ/bit as in [2].

5.2   Baselines and System Configuration

We choose the LAGraph [23], which is a representative matrix-based graph analytics framework on CPU and a GPU-based matrix-based graph analytics framework GraphBLAST [35], to compare the performance and energy consumption of MatGraph. Besides, we evaluate Graphicionado [13], a state-of-the-art graph analytics accelerator, to compare the performance and energy savings with MatGraph. Table 3 lists the system configuration in details.

Table 3. System configuration for evaluation.

	LAGraph	GraphBLAST (V100)	Graphicionado	MatGraph
Compute Unit	2x Intel Xeon Silver 16 Cores @ 2.1 Ghz	5120x Cores @ 1.25 Ghz	128x Streams @ 1 Ghz	128x PEs @ 1 Ghz
On-chip Memory	40 MB	34 MB	40 MB	40 MB
Off-chip Memory	12 * 19.2 GB/s DDR4	900 GB/s HBM 2.0	12 * 19.2 GB/s DDR4	12 * 19.2 GB/s DDR4

5.3   Graph Algorithms and Datasets

We use BFS, SSSP, PR, and TC algorithms to evaluate MatGraph. Table 4 shows the graph datasets used for our evaluation. Random integer weights between 0 and 255 are assigned for the unweighted real-world graphs. We have both small and large graphs, which have diverse average vertex degrees. FR has the smallest average vertex degree, while the average vertex degree of HO is the largest, which means a better locality.

Table 4. Datasets used in the evaluation.

Graph	Vertices	Edges	Brief explanation
Flickr (FR) [8]	0.82M	9.84M	Flickr Crawl
Soc-Pokec (PK) [8]	1.63M	30.62M	Social Pokec Network
LiveJournal (LJ) [8]	4.00M	68.99M	LiveJournal Follower
Hollywood-2009 (HO) [8]	1.14M	113.90M	Movie Actors Social
Indochina-2004 (IN) [8]	7,41M	194.11M	Crawl of Indochina
Com-Orkut (OR) [8]	3.07M	234.37M	Orkut Social Network
RMAT scale 21 (RM21) [25]	2.1M	33.55M	Synthetic graph

6   Results

In this section, we first compare the results of our work (MatGraph) with LAGraph, GraphBLAST, and Graphicionado in terms of speedup and energy efficiency and provide analysis. Then, the area breakdowns of RFU and PE are presented.

6.1   Overall Results

SpeedUp. We first compare the performance speedup of MatGraph normalized to LAGraph, GraphBLAST, and Graphicionado in Fig. 7. The geometric mean across all algorithms is labeled as GM in the last set of bars. Overall, MatGraph achieves 9.35x, 2.28x, and 1.59x speedup over LAGraph, Graph-BLAST, and Graphicionado. MatGraph's main performance advantage comes from highly effective memory bandwidth utilization and reduction of off-chip memory access. Then, we analyze the performance improvement of each application in detail. Compared to LAGraph, the highest speedup achieved by Mat-Graph is 15.71x which happens on PR on the OR dataset. The lowest speedup MatGraph achieved is 5.38x on TC using the FR dataset. The speedup of the TC algorithm is smaller than other algorithms since the preprocessing of LAGraph efficiently improves the locality of memory accesses by sorting the vertices according to their degrees. On the other hand, compared to Graph-BLAST, MatGraph achieves higher speedup on the PR algorithm due to fewer random accesses to off-chip memory. For BFS and SSSP, it's because most of the active vertices have an edge list smaller than off-chip memory access vertices causing the low utilization of bandwidth.

Overall, MatGraph has an efficient lightweight pipeline without data hazards to execute instructions with high instruction parallelism. Besides, using a bitmap-aware instruction filtering unit, all PEs can share the same instructions and the off-chip memory accesses of instructions brought by highly sparse matrix data are further avoided. On the other hand, by utilizing the bidirectional data-aware sparsity removing, redundant memory accesses are further eliminated.

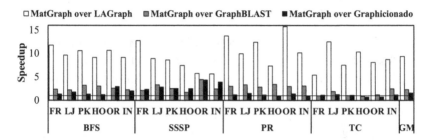

Fig. 7. MatGraph performance speedup over LAGraph, GraphBLAST, and Graphicionado.

Thus, MatGraph has higher bandwidth utilization to upgrade the performance than others.

Energy Efficiency. Figure 8 demonstrates the energy savings of MatGraph over LAGraph, GraphBLAST, and Graphicionado. Overall, the energy savings of all algorithms over LAGraph is 11.17x. While average energy savings across all algorithms over GraphBLAST is 7.15x because GPU consumes much more energy for the irregular off-chip memory accesses and low bandwidth utilization, especially in the case of BFS on HO dataset and SSSP on IN dataset. Compared to Graphicionado, MatGraph achieves 1.61x energy savings. The energy savings mainly comes from (1) less off-chip memory access due to higher on-chip instruction and data reuse and exact prefetch, and (2) the more efficient execution of instructions due to more lightweight instructions and pipeline.

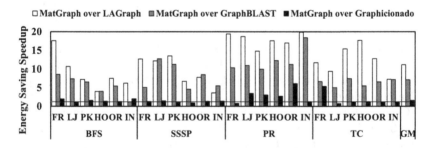

Fig. 8. Energy savings of MatGraph over LAGraph, GraphBLAST, and Graphicionado.

Off-Chip Memory Accesses. Figure 9 presents the total off-chip memory accesses reduction ratio of MatGraph over LAGraph, GraphBLAST, and Graphicionado during runtime. Overall, MatGraph reduces off-chip memory accesses by 61%, 43%, and 25% on average compared to LAGraph, GraphBLAST, and Graphicionado respectively. The main reasons are as follows: (1) Using our proposed instruction filtering scheme, MatGraph enables PEs to share the same instructions, which increases the reuse of on-chip instructions and reduces off-chip movements of instructions. (2) Utilizing bidirectional data-aware sparsity removing, MatGraph further reduces redundant off-chip data accesses to alleviate the severe off-chip memory accesses.

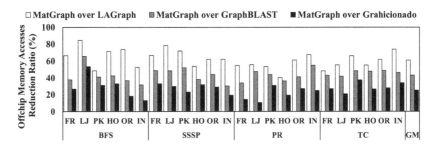

Fig. 9. Memory accesses of MatGraph normalized over LAGraph, GraphBLAST, and Graphicionado.

Utilization of Memory Bandwidth. As depicted in the Fig. 10, MatGraph achieves 53% memory bandwidth utilization on average. Graphicionado has similar bandwidth utilization to MatGraph due to its large on-chip memory and a good locality to access edge data. A large amount of random accesses causes low bandwidth utilization of 23%, and 36% for LAGraph, and GraphBLAST respectively. PageRank and TC have static task vectors and incur more regular memory accesses for instructions and graph data. Therefore, MatGraph, LAGraph, and GraphBLAST all have higher bandwidth utilization. However, BFS and SSSP, all have lower bandwidth utilization and MatGraph have 1.5x–2x bandwidth utilization over LAGraph and GraphBLAST. Since the bidirectional data-aware sparsity removing scheme brings better graph matrix data access locality for MatGraph.

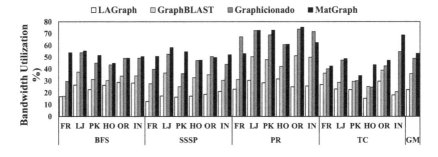

Fig. 10. Memory bandwidth utilization.

Area. Figure 11 shows the area breakdown of MatGraph except for off-chip memory and a single PE in MatGraph. The total area of MatGraph is 20.71 mm^2 and a PE in MatGraph takes 0.18 mm^2. The whole PE array consumes 47% of the whole chip area which is the majority. After that, SPM is used as the on-chip memory which consumed 36% overall. Such an architecture with a large on-chip SPM confronts our design of exact prefetching and hiding the latency of instruction and data access with computing. In a single PE, the operand buffer and instruction buffer consume up to 74% which dominates the majority of the area. With a large memory within PE, our design principle of increasing the on-chip instruction and data reuse among PEs works well to reduce off-chip memory access.

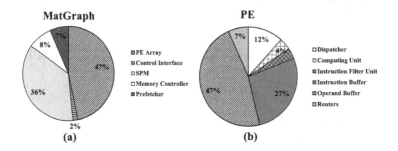

Fig. 11. (a) Area breakdown of MatGraph, (b) Area breakdown of a PE.

6.2 Effects of Optimizations

Figure 12 shows the detailed effects of the different optimizations. The leftmost bar represents the baseline case, which is without optimizations. Then, the optimization includes bitmap-aware instruction filtering (BIF), and bidirectional data-aware sparsity removing (BSR). As depicted, enabling BSR achieves 2.23x speedup on average. Applying BIF with BSR for MatGraph provides a total

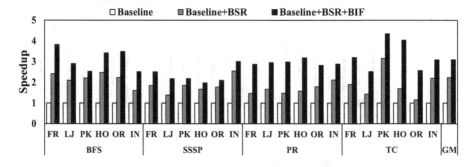

Fig. 12. Effects analysis of BSR and BIF optimizations.

3.10x speedup on average. BSR has a great impact on BFS and SSSP due to dynamic task vectors with different sparsity, which leads to lots of off-chip memory accesses. While PR and TC have less improvement with BSR optimization because it has fixed task vector and fewer off-chip memory accesses. All algorithms have performance improvement with BIF optimization, especially PR and TC, which demonstrates it's essential for MatGraph to increase the on-chip reuse of instructions and filter invalid computations and memory accesses.

7   Related Works

CPU-Based Graph Analytics Frameworks. Lots of vertex-centric graph analytics frameworks are proposed due to ease of use like Pregel [21]. Similar edge-centric graph analytics is proposed by X-stream [28] to optimize the irregular memory access in the vertex-centric model. Both vertex-centric and edge-centric models lack a strong mathematical theory and are difficult to optimize for better performance. CombBLAS [4] is the pioneering framework of matrix-based graph analytics offering a set of linear algebra primitives to graph analytics. Previous work [29] demonstrates the performance benefits of matrix-based graph analytics. To make matrix-based graph analytics programming easier, GraphBLAS [22] is proposed to simplify the programming of the matrix-based model. Hence, in terms of performance, we conclude that matrix-based models are a good choice for graph analytics.

GPU-Based Graph Analytics Frameworks. With the hundreds of CUDA cores and high bandwidth memory on GPU, GPU-based graph frameworks [33] achieve great performance improvement over CPU solutions. However, they need expensive preprocessing to transform irregularity to be regular to take advantage of its architecture and it also consumes a lot of energy to support a large number of threads. Nevertheless, our work achieves 2.28x speedup and 7.15x energy savings compared to GraphBLAST [35] which is the state-of-the-art matrix-based graph analytics framework on GPGPU.

Hardware Accelerator of Graph Analytics. There are lots of customized graph analytics accelerators. First, GraphR [30] targets to leverage the efficient compute capacity of ReRAM to accelerate the matrix operations of graph applications. Nevertheless, ReRAM technology is still not widely applied. Our work presents a practical solution by leveraging the off-the-shelf DDR4 and flexible CGRA architecture. On the other hand, many vertex-centric model-based graph analytics accelerators were explored. Graphicionado [13] uses specified on-chip memory to reduce random off-chip memory and pipelined data path to optimize vertex-centric graph analytics. GraphDyns [34] adds dynamic work distribution to further address irregularities in graph applications.

FPGA-based accelerators [7] utilize the high bandwidth of on-chip memory in FPGA to reduce irregular memory access but are limited by hardware resources in FPGA. Finally, recent works [1] offload the workloads into the logic layer of 3D memory technology like Hybrid Memory Cube (HMC) to accelerate graph applications with high bandwidth. However, the logic layer has a limited area budget and frequency. Unlike the above architecture, our work utilizes mature CGRAs to accelerate matrix-based graph analytics which has both high performance and flexibility.

8 Conclusion

In this paper, we present an energy-efficient and flexible hardware accelerator for matrix-based graph analytics named MatGraph. We use CGRAs as our base which are famous for their good performance and high flexibility. We define reduced instructions and design a lightweight pipeline to efficiently support matrix operations. To eliminate the impact of high sparsity of graphs, we propose an instruction filtering scheme to reduce invalid computations and increase the reuse of instructions. In addition, we design bidirectional data-ware sparsity removing based on the static partitions mechanism to reduce the redundant data accesses and further reduce the sparsity of graph data. Compared to LAGraph, GraphBLAST, and Graphicionado, Mat achieves 11.17x, 7.15x, and 1.61x less energy on average.

Acknowledgements. This work was supported by CAS Project for Young Scientists in Basic Research (Grant No. YSBR-029), the National Natural Science Foundation of China (Grant No. 61732018, and 61872335), Austrian-Chinese Cooperative R&D Project (FFG and CAS) (Grant No. 171111KYSB20200002), and CAS Project for Youth Innovation Promotion Association.

References

1. Ahn, J., Hong, S., Yoo, S., Mutlu, O., Choi, K.: A scalable processing-in-memory accelerator for parallel graph processing. In: Proceedings of the 42nd Annual International Symposium on Computer Architecture, pp. 105–117 (2015)
2. Association, J.S.S.T., et al.: Jedec standard: Ddr4 sdram. JESD79-4, September 2012
3. Bullmore, E., Sporns, O.: Complex brain networks: graph theoretical analysis of structural and functional systems. Nat. Rev. Neurosci. **10**(3), 186–198 (2009)
4. Buluç, A., Gilbert, J.R.: The combinatorial BLAS: design, implementation, and applications. Int. J. High Perform. Comput. Appl. **25**(4), 496–509 (2011)
5. Carter, N.P., et al.: Runnemede: an architecture for ubiquitous high-performance computing. In: 2013 IEEE 19th International Symposium on High Performance Computer Architecture (HPCA), pp. 198–209. IEEE (2013)
6. Chen, D.C., Rabaey, J.M.: A reconfigurable multiprocessor IC for rapid prototyping of algorithmic-specific high-speed DSP data paths. IEEE J. Solid-State Circuits **27**(12), 1895–1904 (1992)
7. Dai, G., Huang, T., Chi, Y., Xu, N., Wang, Y., Yang, H.: Foregraph: exploring large-scale graph processing on multi-FPGA architecture. In: Proceedings of the 2017 ACM/SIGDA International Symposium on Field-Programmable Gate Arrays, pp. 217–226 (2017)

8. Davis, T.A., Hu, Y.: The University of Florida sparse matrix collection. ACM Trans. Math. Softw. (TOMS) **38**(1), 1–25 (2011)

9. DeHon, A.: Fundamental underpinnings of reconfigurable computing architectures. Proc. IEEE **103**(3), 355–378 (2015)

10. Estrin, G.: Organization of computer systems: the fixed plus variable structure computer. In: Papers Presented at the May 3–5, 1960, Western Joint IRE-AIEE-ACM Computer Conference, pp. 33–40 (1960)

11. Gao, G.R., Suetterlein, J., Zuckerman, S.: Toward an execution model for extreme-scale systems-runnemede and beyond. Technical Memo (2011)

12. Giorgi, R., et al.: Teraflux: harnessing dataflow in next generation teradevices. Microprocess. Microsyst. **38**(8), 976–990 (2014)

13. Ham, T.J., Wu, L., Sundaram, N., Satish, N., Martonosi, M.: Graphicionado: a high-performance and energy-efficient accelerator for graph analytics. In: 2016 49th Annual IEEE/ACM International Symposium on Microarchitecture (MICRO), pp. 1–13. IEEE (2016)

14. Hartenstein, R.W., Hirschbiel, A.G., Riedmuller, M., Schmidt, K., Weber, M.: A novel ASIC design approach based on a new machine paradigm. IEEE J. Solid-State Circuits **26**(7), 975–989 (1991)

15. Huang, G., Dai, G., Wang, Y., Yang, H.: Ge-SPMM: general-purpose sparse matrix-matrix multiplication on GPUs for graph neural networks. In: SC20: International Conference for High Performance Computing, Networking, Storage and Analysis, pp. 1–12. IEEE (2020)

16. Ideker, T., Ozier, O., Schwikowski, B., Siegel, A.F.: Discovering regulatory and signalling circuits in molecular interaction networks. Bioinformatics **18**(suppl_1), S233–S240 (2002)

17. Kim, Y., Yang, W., Mutlu, O.: Ramulator: a fast and extensible dram simulator. IEEE Comput. Archit. Lett. **15**(1), 45–49 (2015)

18. König, D.: Graphen und matrizen, mat. Lapok **38**, 116–119 (1931)

19. Kwak, H., Lee, C., Park, H., Moon, S.: What is Twitter, a social network or a news media? In: Proceedings of the 19th International Conference on World Wide Web, pp. 591–600 (2010)

20. Kyrola, A., Blelloch, G., Guestrin, C.: Graphchi: large-scale graph computation on just a {PC}. In: 10th {USENIX} Symposium on Operating Systems Design and Implementation ({OSDI} 12), pp. 31–46 (2012)

21. Malewicz, G., et al.: Pregel: a system for large-scale graph processing. In: Proceedings of the 2010 ACM SIGMOD International Conference on Management of Data, pp. 135–146 (2010)

22. Mattson, T., et al.: Standards for graph algorithm primitives. In: 2013 IEEE High Performance Extreme Computing Conference (HPEC), pp. 1–2. IEEE (2013)

23. Mattson, T., et al.: Lagraph: a community effort to collect graph algorithms built on top of the graphblas. In: 2019 IEEE International Parallel and Distributed Processing Symposium Workshops (IPDPSW), pp. 276–284. IEEE (2019)

24. Muralimanohar, N., Balasubramonian, R., Jouppi, N.P.: Cacti 6.0: a tool to model large caches. HP laboratories 27, 28 (2009)

25. Murphy, R.C., Wheeler, K.B., Barrett, B.W., Ang, J.A.: Introducing the graph 500. Cray Users Group (CUG) **19**, 45–74 (2010)

26. Paden, B., Čáp, M., Yong, S.Z., Yershov, D., Frazzoli, E.: A survey of motion planning and control techniques for self-driving urban vehicles. IEEE Trans. Intell. Veh. **1**(1), 33–55 (2016)

27. Rahman, S., Abu-Ghazaleh, N., Gupta, R.: Graphpulse: an event-driven hardware accelerator for asynchronous graph processing. In: 2020 53rd Annual IEEE/ACM International Symposium on Microarchitecture (MICRO), pp. 908–921. IEEE (2020)

28. Roy, A., Mihailovic, I., Zwaenepoel, W.: X-stream: edge-centric graph processing using streaming partitions. In: Proceedings of the Twenty-Fourth ACM Symposium on Operating Systems Principles, pp. 472–488 (2013)

29. Satish, N., et al.: Navigating the maze of graph analytics frameworks using massive graph datasets. In: Proceedings of the 2014 ACM SIGMOD International Conference on Management of Data, pp. 979–990 (2014)

30. Song, L., Zhuo, Y., Qian, X., Li, H., Chen, Y.: GrapHR: accelerating graph processing using reram. In: 2018 IEEE International Symposium on High Performance Computer Architecture (HPCA), pp. 531–543. IEEE (2018)

31. Sundaram, N., et al.: GraphMAT: high performance graph analytics made productive. arXiv preprint arXiv:1503.07241 (2015)

32. Tessier, R., Pocek, K., DeHon, A.: Reconfigurable computing architectures. Proc. IEEE **103**(3), 332–354 (2015)

33. Wang, Y., Davidson, A., Pan, Y., Wu, Y., Riffel, A., Owens, J.D.: Gunrock: a high-performance graph processing library on the GPU. In: Proceedings of the 21st ACM SIGPLAN Symposium on Principles and Practice of Parallel Programming, pp. 1–12 (2016)

34. Yan, M., et al.: Alleviating irregularity in graph analytics acceleration: a hardware/software co-design approach. In: Proceedings of the 52nd Annual IEEE/ACM International Symposium on Microarchitecture, pp. 615–628 (2019)

35. Yang, C., Buluc, A., Owens, J.D.: Graphblast: A high-performance linear algebra-based graph framework on the GPU. arXiv preprint arXiv:1908.01407 (2019)

D-IOCost: Dynamic Cost-Aware Fair Queueing for Better I/O Proportionality and Performance

Yachun Liu, Dan Feng, Jianxi Chen$^{(\boxtimes)}$, and Chao Guo

Huazhong University of Science and Technology, Wuhan, China
{lycspring,dfeng,chenjx,guopro}@hust.edu.cn

Abstract. As high-speed SSDs supporting multi-queue interfaces are widely used in shared storage systems, scheduling strategies should ensure fair sharing of device resources. However, when facing the workload of different I/O characteristics, service time-based schedulers cannot achieve proportional bandwidth sharing totally, while sector-based schedulers often lead to insufficient resource utilization. Therefore, it is a great challenge to simultaneously achieve fair bandwidth sharing without compromising resource utilization.

This paper proposes a dynamic cost-aware fair queueing I/O scheduler (D-IOCost), guaranteeing fair bandwidth sharing while maximizing resource utilization for multi-queue systems. D-IOCost dynamically updates the weights of the I/O flows according to the service time of sector-sized requests to ensure fairness and adjusts the request dispatch parallelism based on I/O characteristics to maximize resource utilization.

Experimental results show that the I/O proportionality of D-IOCost is improved more than 10-times higher than the Linux latest I/O schedulers IOCost under the mixed workloads. Meanwhile, D-IOCost achieves more than 30% performance improvement over MQFQ, the state-of-the-art multi-queue fair queueing scheduler, especially for small read requests.

Keywords: Fair sharing scheduler · Performance · SSD

1 Introduction

Shared storage has become a popular solution in recent decades due to its lower hardware and management cost. With improved SSD performance, NVMe SSD based on the PCIe interface provides a multi-queue I/O structure to maximize the performance, enabling it to support parallel I/O of multiple applications. For example, the Samsung 980 Pro can perform one million I/O operations per second [1,2]. Therefore, achieving fairness and maximizing resource utilization is the primary concern when multiple applications access high-performance SSD.

Fair queueing schedulers [4,6,7,9–11] are a class of algorithms to schedule the I/O resource fairly among multiple applications. Due to its work-conserving nature, fair queueing schedulers support higher performance than budget-based

© Springer Nature Switzerland AG 2023
W. Meng et al. (Eds.): ICA3PP 2022, LNCS 13777, pp. 373–391, 2023.
https://doi.org/10.1007/978-3-031-22677-9_20

I/O schedulers [5,8]. Device-level schedulers [6,7,11] implemented in the SSD firmware allow for device-side parallelism at the cost of flexibility and feasibility. The latest device-level fair queueing scheduler D2FQ [11] is designed on top of the NVMe weighted round robin with the urgent priority class (WRR) feature, but it can not apply to all SSDs. Consequently, the host-level fair queueing scheduling schedulers implemented at the block layer are widely used for fairness, which fall into sector-based and service time-based fair queueing schedulers.

The sector-based fair queueing schedulers [10,21] take the sector-based size of the request as the I/O cost to share the bandwidth resources fairly. The latest sector-based I/O scheduler MQFQ [10] in the multi-queue block layer introduces the constant parallelism value D (the number of outstanding requests) and the throttling threshold value T to achieve the trade-off between resource utilization and fairness. However, they are affected by the characteristic of the workload, leading to decreased resource utilization and unfairness.

According to the workload characteristics, the service time-based fair queueing schedulers [4,9,12] use the request service time as I/O cost, realizing the fair sharing of device time, not bandwidth. When the workload characteristics of the flows[1] are different, the sector-sized I/O costs of the flows are various. Consequently, the number of sectors served by the flow in a period is disproportionate to its target weight, so bandwidth sharing is unfair. Target weights are set via quality of service parameters. I/O proportionality [3] refers to the bandwidth observed by I/O flows competing for I/O resources in a shared storage environment. I/O is said to be proportional if each flow's bandwidth is proportional to the relative target weight of the total bandwidth.

This paper proposes a dynamic cost-aware fair queueing I/O scheduler (D-IOCost) for multi-queue shared storage systems, guaranteeing fair bandwidth sharing while maximizing resource utilization. It takes the request service time as I/O cost and reallocates the flow's resource management parameters (i.e., weight) for fair bandwidth sharing. The dispatch parallelism is dynamically adjusted according to the workload characteristics to maximize resource utilization in this scheduler. Meanwhile, the time window is updated in real-time to guarantee the accuracy of the dispatch parallelism.

The D-IOCost scheduler is implemented at the Linux Cgroup layer [12], which supports fair bandwidth while maximizing the SSD throughput sharing on multi-queue storage. Implementing an I/O scheduler in the multi-queue block layer can be expensive because per-process I/O scheduling queues are necessary. Since adding a new policy at the Linux Cgroup layer is more accessible to implement by reusing most of the existing throttling layer code.

The D-IOCost scheduler is evaluated under the FIO workloads and realistic workloads. Due to the cost-aware characteristic of D-IOCost, it adjusts the flows' weights for fair bandwidth sharing. As a result, the fairness of D-IOCost is improved more than 10-times higher than the latest service time-based I/O schedulers IOCost [9] under the mixed workloads. Since D-IOCost adjusts the

---

[1] An I/O flow refers to a series of I/O requests issued by a resource principal, such as a container, virtual machine, or application.

request dispatch parallelism based on the I/O characteristics, it achieves more than 30% performance improvement over MQFQ [10], the state-of-the-art sector-based multi-queue fair queueing scheduler, especially for small read requests. This paper has the following contributions:

1. We successfully demonstrate building a dynamic cost-aware fair queueing I/O scheduler (D-IOCost), guaranteeing fair bandwidth sharing while efficiently maximizing resource utilization with various workloads on multi-queue systems.
2. In D-IOCost, the flow's weight and the request dispatch parallelism are adjusted dynamically according to the workload I/O characteristics for fair bandwidth sharing while maximizing resource utilization.
3. The detailed experimental results show that D-IOCost can provide better I/O proportionality and higher resource utilization.

The rest of this paper is structured as follows: the background and motivation are explained in Sect. 2 and the design of our method is introduced in Sect. 3. Experimental results are shown in Sect. 4. Finally, Sect. 5 concludes with a summary and future work.

2 Background and Motivation

With the rapid increase in the performance and capacity of SSDs, a single SSD storage device can simultaneously serve requests from multiple I/O flows. Then, fair sharing of SSD bandwidth is critical to meeting the service level agreements (SLAs) [13–15].

Offloading the I/O scheduling function to a device is a device-level approach for fair-sharing, but it is unsuitable for all SSDs and flows. FlashBlox and FLIN [6,7] partition SSD channels which allow for hardware-enforced isolation at the cost of flexibility in the number of flows. D2FQ [11] is designed to implement fairness on top of the device-side I/O scheduling feature (i.e., NVMe WRR), but it is not applied to the SSDs lacking WRR support.

Hence, the host-level schedulers [5,9,10,16,25] implemented at the block layer of the I/O stack are widely used for fairness. M. Bjørling et al. proposed a new multi-queue I/O architecture [16,25] to accommodate parallel I/O requests from multiple flows. After that, many fair sharing schedulers, such as BFQ [5] and MQFQ [10], were proposed for multi-queue shared storage systems. They can be categorized as budget-based I/O schedulers and fair queueing I/O schedulers.

2.1 Budget-Based I/O Scheduler

Budget-based I/O schedulers provide an independent scheduling queue for each flow. They allocate the budgets of the flows based on the target weights so that the bandwidth sharing is weight-based proportional. Hence, the Linux resource control architecture Cgroup [12] has become an attractive technology for fair bandwidth sharing due to its support for the weights (priorities) control.

In current Linux systems, the BFQ [5,8] scheduler and WDT [17] throttler are the typical budget-based I/O schedulers that support Cgroup on the multi-queue storage system. BFQ preserves a per-process queue for each flow and allocates the budget based on the target weight. It uses the budget to choose the next process to schedule. When a process is scheduled, the next budget increases if it consumes its allocated budget, negatively affecting the I/O proportionality. Meanwhile, per-process I/O scheduling queues introduce significant overhead in the multi-queue block layer. To guarantee the I/O proportionality matches the target weight and reduces the overhead, Ahn and Min propose the WDT [17] throttler at the Linux Cgroup layer. WDT describes a workload-dependent IO scheduler that distributes the bandwidth via target weights but can't occupy the whole bandwidth. Since the budget-based schedulers do not support work-conserving, storage devices may remain idle even for pending requests. As a result, storage device resources can not be fully utilized.

2.2   Fair Queueing I/O Scheduler

The proportional fair queueing schedulers [4,9,10,20] distribute the performance proportionally to the target weights of the application. Target weights are set via quality-of-service (QoS) parameters. Since it supports work-conserving, it has become an attractive solution for the fair sharing of storage resources. The fair queueing scheduling schedulers assign resources (e.g., bandwidth or device time) according to a system notion of virtual time unit (e.g., sector or service time). Consequently, fair queueing schedulers are divided into sector-based and service time-based fair queueing schedulers.

The sector-based fair queueing schedulers take the number of sectors served as the virtual time to improve I/O proportionality guarantees. SFQ [20] uses a single central queue to control the dispatch of requests. SFQ assigns a start tag and a finish tag when each request arrives and dispatches requests according to the increasing order of the start tag. Due to the central queue dispatching requests in order, SFQ cannot fully utilize the high-concurrency device. To solve this problem, SFQ(D) [21] allows up to D requests to be dispatched simultaneously. However, SFQ(D) still cannot support high resource utilization on multi-queue systems because of out-of-order request completion for the busy server case.

To address the above problem, MQFQ [10] proposes the latest sector-based fair queueing approach for multi-queue SSDs. It assigns a separate priority queue to each CPU core for high performance and maintains fairness by keeping track of the minimum virtual time of the process. It uses the dispatch parallelism parameter D to control the number of outstanding requests for better I/O efficiency in devices with internal parallelism. Fairness is achieved by the threshold parameter T, which limits the amount of service a flow can receive over its share. However, D is affected by the platform latency $(T_{platform})$[2], which is the most critical factor affecting request latency in low-latency SSDs. Consequently, MQFQ can not maximize resource utilization.

---

[2] The platform latency refers to the latency caused by software (I/O issue and completion, DMA) and hardware (e.g., chipsets) [18,23]. Wooseong [19] enables the reduction of the DMA latency to minimize overall system latency.

The service time-based fair queueing schedulers (e.g., Flashfq [4], FIOs [22], and VSSD [24]) compute the I/O cost according to an offline calibration for high resource utilization. It employs the normalized accumulated service time of the I/O flow to define its virtual time, which realizes the fair sharing of device time resources for a single-queue storage system. After that, Linux version 5.2 proposes a work-conserving multi-queue I/O fair sharing scheduler IOCost [9], which uses the request service time as the I/O cost based on Flashfq. It recovers the loss of total bandwidth when it misestimates the service received by flows, resulting in unfairness.

The service time-based fair queueing schedulers support fair bandwidth sharing with the same workloads but not for the different workloads. The sector-sized I/O costs of the flows are consistent with the same workloads. When the service time of the flow is in proportion to its target weight, so does the flow's number of sectors served, sharing the bandwidth fairly. It can't support the I/O proportionality with the different workloads due to the inconsistent sector-sized I/O costs. Therefore, a cost-aware scheduler that can maximize resource utilization while supporting fair bandwidth sharing with the different workloads is necessary for the multi-queue shared storage system.

3   Design and Implementation

This paper proposes a dynamic cost-aware fair queueing I/O scheduler (D-IOCost) on the multi-queue system, supporting fair bandwidth sharing while maximizing resource utilization. The D-IOCost scheduler consists of three parts: 1) the weights of the I/O flows are dynamically reallocated based on the sector-sized request's service time to achieve fair bandwidth sharing; 2) the dispatch parallelism is adjusted dynamically according to the I/O characteristics for maximizing resource utilization; 3) the time window is adjusted to guarantee the

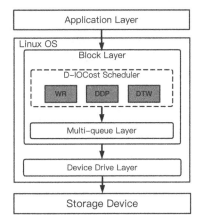

Fig. 1. Structure of D-IOCost scheduler

accuracy of the dispatch parallelism. It is implemented on the Linux Cgroup layer, as shown in Fig. 1.

Figure 2 shows the overview of D-IOCost's process. We assume that n tasks with different I/O target weights run concurrently. Flow-x represents a flow with the target weight x. The process of D-IOCost is logically separated into the Fairness Path and the High-performance Path. D-IOCost dynamically adjusts resource allocation parameters (i.e., weight and dispatch parallelism) based on I/O characteristics and historical running information to ensure fairness and high performance.

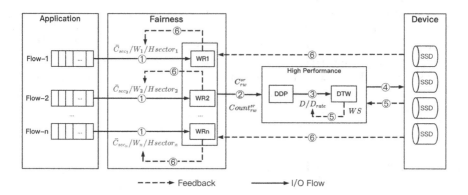

Fig. 2. Overview of D-IOCost's process

The Fairness Path makes the number of sectors served by the flow i (i=1...n) proportionate to its target weight (W_{target_i}) in a period. First, D-IOCost extracts the feature from the bios of flow i and calculates the sector-sized I/O cost ($\bar{C}_{sec_i}$). D-IOCost reallocates the resource management parameter weight (W_i) of the flow i based on its sector-sized I/O cost and target weight to achieve fair bandwidth sharing, as described in Sect. 3.1. Meanwhile, to reduce the impact of aggressive tasks on fairness, D-IOCost adjusts the $\bar{C}_{sec_i}$ according to the history of bandwidth resource usage information ($Hsector_i$) in step ⑥.

The High-performance Path periodically adjusts the dispatch parallelism to ensure high resource utilization. In step ②, D-IOCost collects the read/write average I/O cost ($\bar{C}_{rw}^{sr}$) and request count ($Count_{rw}^{sr}$) to adjust the dispatch parallelism parameter (D) and virtual time dispatch rate (D_{rate}) to maximize resource utilization, as described in Sect. 3.2. In step ③, D-IOCost adopts the dynamic time window algorithm to guarantee the accuracy of the D value, according to the feedback of the previous D in step ⑤. We further discuss the algorithm in Sect. 3.3. In step ④, D-IOCost flushes the bios to the SSDs.

3.1 Weight Reallocation

D-IOCost takes the service time as the I/O cost, and the virtual time in D-IOCost reflects device time usage. For each flow, its virtual time is defined as the start tag of its first backlogged request. Assuming the flow has multiple pending requests, dispatching this first request would increase the flow's virtual time by s/w, where w is the flow's weight and s is the service time of the request. The global virtual time progresses along with the wall clock at a rate specified by the virtual time dispatch rate (D_{rate}). D-IOCost provides fairness between only active flows, and it throttles a flow if its virtual time is far ahead of the global virtual time.

D-IOCost assigns a start and finish tag to each request when it arrives and dispatches requests in increasing order of start tags. The start tag for a request is set to be the maximum of the global virtual time and the last finish tag of the flow. The finish tag for a request is its start tag plus its cost, normalized to the weight of the flow. Table 1 lists variables used in the weight reallocation module (WR) for fairness: per-flow parameters and descriptions.

Table 1. Per-flow parameters and descriptions

Parameters	Descriptions
C_i^r	The I/O cost of the request r
$C_{sec_i}^r$	The sector-sized I/O cost of the request r
$\bar{C}_{sec_i}$	The average sector-sized I/O cost of flow i
$Hsector_i$	The historical sector numbers served by flow i
$prp_{ideal}(f_i)$	The idel I/O proportionality of f_i
$prp_{result}(f_i)$	The obtained I/O proportionality of f_i
R_i	The ratio of historical information to the average I/O cost in f_i
$Sector_i^r$	The sector-based size of the request r
VT_i	The virtual time of flow i
W_{target_i}	The QoS target weight of flow i
W_i	The resource management weight of flow i

The absolute I/O cost of request r in the flow i $(i = 1...n)$ is indicated as C_i^r $(r = 1...m)$ according to an offline calibration, which is divided by the flow's weight (W_i) to derive the relative I/O cost. The W_i is expressed as the resource allocation proportion of the flow among its siblings, as shown in Eq. (1). Each flow tracks its virtual time, which advances on each IO by the IO's relative cost. For example, a flow with W_i of 0.5 has a 50% share of the device time, and the relative cost of the IO is C_i^r/W_i. Then the virtual time of the flow i $(i = 1...n)$ in the interval $[t1,t2]$ can be expressed as $VT_i(t1,t2)$ in Eq. (2):

$$\sum_{k=1}^{n} W_i = 1 \tag{1}$$

$$VT_i(t1, t2) = \frac{\sum_{r=1}^{m} C_i^r}{W_i} \tag{2}$$

If flows have the same virtual time, their I/O resource usages are proportional to weights (W_i), and the fairness is satisfied. An allocation for flows i ($i = 1...n$) is fair if for every time interval $[t1,t2]$, we have:

$$VT_i(t1, t2) - VT_n(t1, t2) = 0; \qquad (3)$$

The service timed-based D-IOCost scheduler can directly use the wall-clock time to calculate the global virtual time GVT_i without tracking the minimum per-flow virtual times in real time. The global virtual time progresses along with the wall clock at a rate specified by the virtual time dispatch rate (D_{rate}). The D_{rate} is the virtual time against the wall clock and is updated periodically, which controls how fast or slow the global virtual time runs compared to the wall clock. For example, if D_{rate} is at 150%, the global virtual time runs at the 1.5x speed of the wall clock and generates 1.5x more IO service than the device cost model specifies. Comparing the flow's virtual time and the global virtual time will decide whether to throttle the flows' requests or not. The requests of the flow i are throttled only when its start tag exceeds the global virtual time.

To guarantee better I/O proportionality, the weight reallocation module (WR) in D-IOCost reallocates the weight (W_i) of the flow i ($i = 1...n$) separately based on its average sector-sized I/O cost ($\bar{C}_{sec_i}$) and target weight (W_{target_i}) (shown as the step ① in Fig. 2). To make the number of sectors served by the flow i proportional to the target weight, the I/O cost of the request k in the flow can be made of sector-sized I/O cost ($C_{sec_i}^r$), and the request size is expressed as ($Sector_{sec_i}^r$) ($r = 1...m$). The average I/O cost of flow i ($\bar{C}_{sec_i}$) is calculated according to Eq. (4), and the ratio of historical information to the I/O cost (R_i) is initialized to 1. We are substituting the target weights (W_{target_i}) and I/O cost ($\bar{C}_{sec_i}$) of the current time window into Eqs. (2) and (3), deriving Eq. (5). When all flows are backlogged, and the weights' distribution meets Eq. (5), D-IOCost can guarantee the fair bandwidth sharing on the different workloads.

$$\bar{C}_{sec_i} = \frac{\sum_{r=1}^{m} Sector_i^r * C_{sec_i}^r}{\sum_{r=1}^{m} Sector_i^r} * R_i \qquad (4)$$

$$W_i = \frac{W_{target_i} * \bar{C}_{sec_i}}{\sum_{k=1}^{n} W_{target_k} * \bar{C}_{sec_k}} \qquad (5)$$

To reduce the impact of aggressive tasks on fairness, the D-IOCost uses the history of bandwidth resource usage information in reallocating the sector-sized I/O cost of flow. Step ⑥ in Fig. 2 shows that when the difference between the flow's actual bandwidth usage proportion and the ideal I/O proportionality is more than the threshold value H (initialized to 5%), the average I/O cost ($\bar{C}_{sec_i}$) of flow i will be changed.

As shown in Eqs. (6) and (7), $prp_{ideal}(f_i)$ is the target weight share among the whole target weights, and $prp_{result}(f_i)$ is the obtained bandwidth share of the entire bandwidth. R_i is the ratio of historical information to the average I/O cost in f_i, representing the fairness of the current flow, shown as Eqs. (8). When the $prp_{result}(f_i)$ is smaller than the $prp_{ideal}(f_i)$, we need to improve the bandwidth share. Therefore, the average I/O cost of the flow i ($\bar{C}_{sec_i}$) in Eqs. (4) is reduced proportionally according to the R_i to increase the bandwidth share of the flow. Otherwise, the average I/O cost is increased.

$$prp_{ideal}(f_i) = \frac{W_{target_i}}{\sum_{k=1}^{n} W_{target_k}} \tag{6}$$

$$prp_{result}(f_i) = \frac{H sector_i}{\sum_{k=1}^{n} H sector_k} \tag{7}$$

$$R_i = \frac{prp_{result}(f_i)}{prp_{ideal}(f_i)} \tag{8}$$

3.2 Dynamic Dispatch Parallelism

The dispatch parallelism parameter D in D-IOCost controls the number of outstanding requests and is a trade-off between high resource utilization and fairness, similar to MQFQ. While a larger D may better utilize the device, it can be unfair because of the higher request waiting time. Therefore, D-IOCost will stop dispatching once there are D outstanding requests in the saturated device, as shown in step ④ of Fig. 2. Table 2 lists primary global variables and relative descriptions used in the following modules to maximize performance.

Table 2. Global parameters and descriptions

Parameters	Descriptions
$\bar{C}_{rw}^{sr}$	The average I/O cost in different I/O format
$Count_{rw}^{sr}$	The request counts in different I/O format
D	The dispatch parallelism
D_{rate}	The virtual time dispatch rate
D_T	The error threshold value of dispatch parallelism
H	The percentage error of I/O proportionality
P	The percentage error of the D_{rate}
$T_{platform}$	The latency caused by software and hardware
TW	The time window size
V_D	The dispatch parallelism amplitude ratio
V_{LastD}	The V_D based on the last statistical period
V_{max}	The max threshold of V_D
V'	The error threshold value of trend of V_D

To ensure fairness and maximize resource utilization, the D-IOCost scheduler minimizes the latency caused by software (I/O issue and completion) and hardware (e.g., chipsets), which refers to $T_{platform}$. The D-IOCost extracts the following features from a bio request: 1) read or write, 2) random or sequential, and 3) request size. It indicates that the I/O cost of request r in flow i (C_i^r) consists of two parts: one is the platform time $T_{platform}$, based on the $4\,KB$ sequential and random IO per second ($IOPS_{4KB}$) for reads and writes, and the other is the data transfer time $T_{transfer}$ according to the 4KB-based request size ($Size_{4KB}$) and read/write byte per second (Bps):

$$T_{transfer} = \frac{1sec}{Bps} * 4KB * Size_{4KB} \tag{9}$$

$$T_{platform} = \frac{1sec}{IOPS_{4KB}} - \frac{1sec}{Bps} * 4KB \tag{10}$$

$$C_i^r = T_{platform} + T_{transfer} \tag{11}$$

The D-IOCost proposes that D is adjusted dynamically according to the C_i^r and $T_{transfer}$ of different workloads (as shown in Eq. (12)). The $Depth$ is initialized to 64, and D is modified to maximize resource utilization when the workload changes, as shown in step ② of Fig. 2.

$$D = \frac{C_i^r * Depth}{T_{transfer}} \tag{12}$$

The dynamic dispatch parallelism module (DDP) is shown in Algorithm 1. Due to the different performance of read and write in sequential and random format on the SSD, D is adjusted dynamically considering the different I/O characteristics. The I/O characteristics parameters rw means read or write I/O type, and sr means sequential or random I/O access format. DDP must determine whether it is a read-intensive, write-intensive, sequential, or random format. It is evaluated by the average I/O cost ($\bar{C}_{rw}^{sr}$) and request count ($Count_{rw}^{sr}$). Because the D is related to the IO per second (IOPS), it is updated by the one whose request counts are the most, as shown in Eq. (12).

Algorithm 1. The Dynamic Dispatch Parallelism Algorithm

Input: $\bar{C}_{rw}^{sr}, Count_{rw}^{sr}, \bar{D}, D_{rate}, D_T, P$
Output: D
  $(rw, sr) \leftarrow max(Count_{rw}^{sr})$
  $D \leftarrow \frac{C_{rw}^{sr} * Depth}{T_{transfer}}$
  if $(abs(D - \bar{D}) > D_T)$ **then**
    if $(D > \bar{D})$ **then**
      $D_{rate} \leftarrow D_{rate} * (1 + P)$
    else
      $D_{rate} \leftarrow D_{rate} * (1 - P)$
    end if
  end if

According to the device saturation, the D-IOCost adjusts the virtual time dispatch rate (D_{rate}) by the parameter D. The $\bar{D}$ is the average D. When the

D deviates from the $\bar{D}$ more than D_T, we need to judge the state of the device saturation. If the $\bar{D}$ is lower than D, the device is not saturated, and D_{rate} will be increased by the threshold value P. Otherwise, the device is saturated, and D_{rate} is adjusted downwards. D-IOCost uses the percentage threshold P to change D_{rate} gradually, which is initialized to a binary index table to prevent aggressive flows. It over-provisions the parameter D_T for the maximum throughput of the device can always be met, D_T is initialized to 8.

3.3   Dynamic Time Window

Since parameter D is updated periodically in the time window (TW), a suitable TW is critical to guarantee the accuracy of D. The shorter the TW, the better I/O control timeliness, i.e., higher frequency tuning, which helps reduce control errors. However, the number of I/O requests sampled in a small TW may not be sufficient to provide accurate statistics, leading to inaccurate D and D_{rate} and performance fluctuations. Therefore, choosing an appropriate TW is critical to the fine-grained tuning of D to realize the trade-off between the timeliness of I/O control and the statistical accuracy of the information.

This paper uses the dispatch parallelism amplitude ratio (V_D) to evaluate the stability of the dispatch parallelism in the microsecond to provide the timeliness of I/O control. The smaller the value of V_D, the more accurate the parameter D, and the better timeliness of I/O control. Let D_k be D measured in the kth second of the microsecond period $(t1, t2)$. Let $T = [t2 - t1]$, and $\bar{D}$ is the average D, then the V_D in this period can be calculated by the Eq. (13):

$$V_D(t1, t2) = \frac{\sum_{k=t1}^{t2} \frac{|D_k - \bar{D}|}{\bar{D}}}{T} \tag{13}$$

The Dynamic time window module (DTW) is shown in Algorithm 2. The DTW algorithm aims to find a suitable solution to TW, provided that V_D is less than the predefined thresholds V_{max}, which is initialized to H. The DTW algorithm will operate if the V_D is larger than the threshold V_{max}. When the current V_D is ahead of the last dispatch parallelism amplitude ratio V_{LastD} by the threshold V', the DTW algorithm sets the lower limit of the time window (TW_{min}) to TW. Otherwise, TW will become the upper limit of the time window (TW_{max}). The function of the threshold V' is to reduce the influence of different I/O characteristics interference on the amplitude ratio measurements, which is initialized to H^*V_{LastD}.

As a heuristic optimization algorithm, the time complexity of the DTW algorithm is low. Assuming that the initial search space size of time window size (TW) is N in the first iteration, this value will be $N/2$ in the second iteration. According to the above logic, the DTW algorithm's time complexity can be computed as $O(logN)$. The average values of TW_{max} and TW_{min} will be used as the input parameters for the next round of optimization. The DTW algorithm will continue to optimize TW until V_D is less than the threshold value V_{max} or the difference between TW_{max} and TW_{min} is less than the minimum search range

MIN_R (initialed as 32 ms). The DTW algorithm returns TW and configures it as the time window size to achieve the accurate D and D_{rate} in the DDP module, as shown in steps ③, ④, and ⑤ of Fig. 2.

Algorithm 2. The Dynamic Time Window algorithm

Input: $TW_{max} = 512ms, TW_{min} = 32ms, TW = TW_{max}, V_D, V_{LastD}, V', V_{max}$
Output: TW, V_{LastD}
  while $(V_D > V_{max})$ and $(TW_{max} - TW_{min} > MIN\_R)$ **do**
    if $((V_D - V_{LastD}) < V')$ **then**
      $TW_{max} \leftarrow TW$
    else
      $TW_{min} \leftarrow TW$
    end if
    $TW \leftarrow (TW_{min} + TW_{max})/2$
  end while

---

4   Experimental Evaluation

This section evaluates the D-IOCost scheduler in terms of fairness and performance. The D-IOCost scheduler is implemented in the 5.6 Linux kernel at the Cgroup layer. Table 3 shows our experimental configuration, and we use a 24-core server with an Intel(R) Xeon(R) CPU E5-2643 v3 @3.40 GHz processor. A PCIe-attached Intel P3700 NVMe SSD fulfills nearly 0.5M IOPs for 4 KB requests in the D-IOCost setup.

Table 3. Experimental configuration

Hardware	Cpu	Intel(R) Xeon(R) CPU E5-2643 v3 @ 3.4 GHz
	Memory	DDR4 128 GB
	Storage	Intel DC P3700 series 800 GB SSD
Software	OS	Ubuntu 18.04 LTS
	Kernel	Linux 5.6.13
	FIO	libaio, random, read, direct I/O

We measure the impact of D-IOCost on realistic workloads(described in Table 4) and workloads with known characteristics generated by FIO [26]. We choose four realistic enterprise workloads. Financial1 and Financial2 were collected from OLTP applications running at two large financial institutions [27]. MSR-web_2 and MSR-proj_0 are block I/O traces collected from enterprise servers at Microsoft Research Cambridge [28]. These traces represent various environments, including a write-intensive pattern (e.g., MSR-proj_0), a read-intensive pattern (e.g., MSR-web_2), small-sized request patterns (e.g., Financial1 and Financial2), large-sized request patterns (e.g., MSR-web_0 and MSR-proj_0), a sequential pattern (e.g., MSR-web_2) and random patterns (e.g.,

MSR-proj_0, Financial1, and Financial2). Table 4 lists the workload traces' characteristics, and the request data size unit is KB. In our experiments, workloads are executed by 12 concurrent threads with a queue depth of 32.

Table 4. Feature of realistic workloads

Workloads	Workload characteristics		
	Read ratio	Av.W.Size (KB)	Av.R.Size (KB)
MSR-web_2	99.2%	21.1	53.8
MSR-proj_0	12.5%	41.0	17.8
Financial1	23.2%	3.8	2.3
Financial2	82.4%	2.8	2.3

Then, we compare D-IOCost to the two latest schedulers in the block layer: 1) MQFQ [10], the state-of-the-art sector-based multi-queue fair-queueing I/O scheduler. It introduces a dispatch parallelism value $D = 64$ and a threshold value $T = 45K$ to find a design point that provides most of the fairness of traditional fair queueing with most of the performance of fully independent queues. 2) Linux IOCost scheduler [9], the latest service time-based proportional share I/O scheduler included for the Cgroup layer since Linux 5.2, which is designed for containerized environments and provides scalable, work-conserving, and low-overhead IO control for storage devices. However, D2FQ [11] is designed to implement fairness on top of the device-side NVMe WRR I/O scheduling feature, but it is not applied to the SSDs lacking WRR support. As a result, we do not compare D2FQ with D-IOCost, which is implemented at the block layer and suitable for all SSDs.

Providing fairness is the primary goal of fair queueing schedulers when multiple flows contend on a storage device. We evaluate the schedulers on a host system by concurrently running four flows (denoted Flow-x, where x is the target weight) with different workloads. I/O proportionality [3] refers to the bandwidth observed by flows competing for I/O resources, which is normalized I/O bandwidth. To accurately quantify the I/O proportionality, a new metric called proportionality variation (PV) [3] is present by Eq. (14). N is the number of flows considered, $prp_{ideal}(f_i)$ and $prp_{result}(f_i)$ are the ideal I/O proportionality and the obtained I/O proportionality of f_i. Essentially, PV captures how much the actual I/O proportionality digresses from the ideal I/O proportionality. Hence, a lower PV means I/O proportionality is better matched.

$$PV = \frac{1}{N} * \sum_{i=1}^{N} |prp_{ideal}(f_i) - prp_{result}(f_i)| \qquad (14)$$

4.1 Fairness and Performance on Different I/O Request Size

Figure 3 and Fig. 4 show the fairness and performance of three schedules under the FIO workloads with different I/O request sizes. The x-axis denotes the workloads with different sizes: 4 KB, 8 KB, 32 KB, 64 KB, and the three schedulers we measure, while the y-axis represents the I/O proportionality (i.e., normalized bandwidth) and total bandwidth.

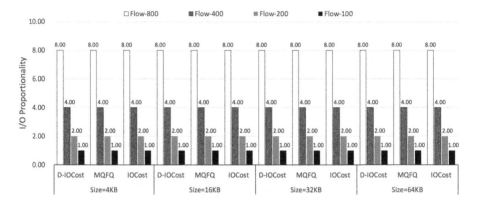

Fig. 3. I/O proportionality of schedulers with FIO workloads

The results in Fig. 3 show that as the request size increases, D-IOCost and IOCost can almost achieve fair bandwidth sharing like the MQFQ. Because the sector-sized I/O costs of the flows are consistent with the same workloads, the service received by the flows is weight-based proportional. D-IOCost and IOCost can always keep fairness without weight adjustment under the same FIO workloads. Meanwhile, MQFQ uses sector-based resource management to guarantee I/O proportionality efficiently.

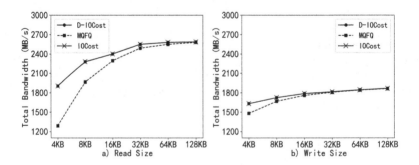

Fig. 4. Total bandwidth of schedulers with FIO workloads

As shown in Fig. 4, we observe that D-IOCost and IOCost can always ensure high performance under FIO workloads except for MQFQ. D-IOCost can dynamically update resource allocation parameters based on I/O characteristics. IOCost modifies the latency target to support the work-conserving feature. The resource utilization of MQFQ is low under the workload with a small request size owing to the inaccurate dispatch parallelism. Especially in 4 KB read request testing, the performance of the D-IOCost is more than 30% higher than MQFQ.

4.2 Fairness and Performance on Different I/O Type and Access Format

This section first discusses schedulers' fairness and total bandwidth with the same realistic workloads. In Fig. 5, the x-axis denotes the workloads with the same realistic workloads and the three schedulers we measure, while the y-axis represents the I/O proportionality. This result shows that the three schedulers almost guarantee fair bandwidth sharing under the same realistic workloads.

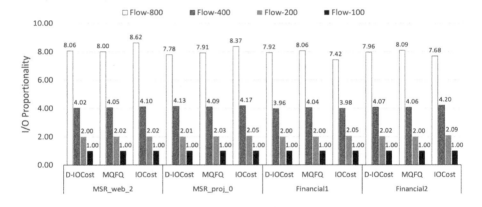

Fig. 5. I/O proportionality of schedulers with same realistic workloads

To quantify how well proportionality coincides with the given target weights, Fig. 6 (a) shows the *PV* values of the I/O schedulers. We can see that D-IOCost and MQFQ do a little better than IOCost in fair bandwidth sharing. Because with the same realistic workloads, IOCost supports the work-conserving properties mainly by updating the latency target leading to some unfairness.

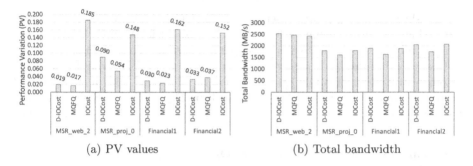

(a) PV values   (b) Total bandwidth

Fig. 6. PV values and total bandwidth of schedulers with same realistic workloads

Figure 6 (b) shows the total bandwidth of three schedulers with the same realistic workloads. The D-IOCost scheduler shows higher total bandwidth than MQFQ by up to 16% on average, especially 20% with the Financial2 and MSR-proj_0 workloads. It is due to MQFQ failing to update the request dispatch parallelism parameter D when the request size is small. However, D-IOCost can adjust the D based on the I/O characteristics.

Finally, We discuss the fairness and total bandwidth of three schedulers with different realistic workloads. To verify the effect of our dynamic adjustment strategy, we build mixed workloads with four realistic workloads with various I/O characteristics (as shown in Table 5).

Table 5. Experimental configuration of mixed workloads

	Weight = 800	Weight = 400	Weight = 200	Weight = 100
Workload1	MSR-web_2	Financial1	Financial2	MSR-proj_0
Workload2	MSR-proj_0	MSR-web_2	Financial1	Financial2
Workload3	Financial2	MSR-proj_0	MSR-web_2	Financial1
Workload4	Financial1	Financial2	MSR-proj_0	MSR-web_2

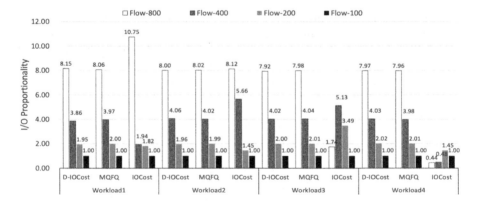

Fig. 7. I/O proportionality of schedulers with mixed workloads

The I/O proportionality of three schedulers with mixed workloads is shown in Fig. 7. The I/O proportionality of D-IOCost and MQFQ are close to the target weights, while IOCost deviates more than those. The *PV* value of D-IOCost and MQFQ are far less than IOCost in Fig. 8 (a). Especially in workload3 and workload4, the bandwidth of flows in IOCost observed is disproportionate to the target weight. The I/O proportionality of D-IOCost and MQFQ is improved more than 10-times higher than IOCost. Due to the cost-aware characteristic, the service time-based D-IOCost scheduler does well as the sector-based MQFQ scheduler in fair bandwidth sharing. Unfortunately, updating the latency target does not guarantee the work-conserving feature of IOCost under the latency-sensitive mixed workloads such as workload3 and workload4. IOCost needs to modify the weight to counter the compromising of bandwidth caused by wrong estimates, leading to unfairness. The results demonstrate that D-IOCost and MQFQ support better I/O proportionality than IOCost.

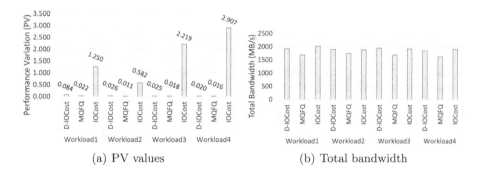

(a) PV values   (b) Total bandwidth

Fig. 8. PV values and Total bandwidth of schedulers with mixed workloads

Figure 8 (b) shows the total bandwidth of these three schedulers with mixed workloads. We observe that D-IOCost and IOCost outperform the MQFQ by up to 13% on average. Due to the workload-adaptive characteristic of D-IOCost, it adjusts the request dispatch parallelism based on the I/O characteristics for maximizing resource utilization. Meanwhile, the work-conserving IOCost scheduler supports high performance by configuring the weight and latency targets. MQFQ fails to update the dispatch parallelism value D and the throttling threshold T according to the workload, leading to low resource utilization.

The D-IOCost provides I/O resources management that is low overhead, work-conserving, cost-aware, and allows for QoS proportional configuration. D-IOCost can ensure no noticeable overhead due to its split between the issue path and the planning path, just like the IOCost [9]. From this, the overhead of D-IOCost (e.g., I/O cost analysis, weight reallocation) is always negligible. However, the overhead of MQFQ is high under the workload with a small request size owing to the inaccurate dispatch parallelism.

5 Summary

With the advent of modern SSDs that can deliver one million I/O operations per second, it has become increasingly difficult for the operating system to fulfill its responsibility for fairness without compromising the total bandwidth.

This paper proposes D-IOCost, a cost-aware, high-performance fair-queueing I/O scheduler on multi-queue systems. With judicious use of historical usage information and workload I/O characteristics, D-IOCost dynamically modifies the weights for fair bandwidth sharing and the request dispatch parallelism for maximizing resource utilization. Experiments confirm that the fairness of D-IOCost is enhanced more than 10-times compared to the Linux IOCost schedule, and the performance of D-IOCost is significantly improved by up to 30% compared to MQFQ. In conclusion, the D-IOCost can simultaneously maintain fair bandwidth sharing while maximizing resource utilization. In the future, we plan to extend our scheme to leverage different kinds of I/O cost computation for a better quality of service (e.g., request latency, IOPS, or bytes per second).

References

1. Jin, Y.T., Ahn, S., Lee, S.: Performance analysis of NVME SSD-based all-flash array systems. In: 2018 IEEE International Symposium on Performance Analysis of Systems and Software (ISPASS), pp. 12–21. IEEE (2018)
2. Liu, X., Lu, Y., Yu, J., et al.: Optimizing read and write performance based on deep understanding of SSD. In: 2017 3rd IEEE International Conference on Computer and Communications (ICCC), pp. 2607–2616. IEEE (2017)
3. Kim, J., Lee, E., Noh, S.H.: I/o scheduling schemes for better i/o proportionality on flash-based SSDs. In: 2016 IEEE 24th International Symposium on Modeling, Analysis and Simulation of Computer and Telecommunication Systems (MASCOTS), pp. 221–230. IEEE (2016)
4. Shen, K., Park, S.: FlashFQ: a fair queueing i/o scheduler for flash-based SSDs. In: 2013 USENIX Annual Technical Conference (USENIXATC 2013), pp. 67–78 (2013)
5. Valente, P., Avanzini, A.: Evolution of the BFQ Storage-I/O scheduler. In: 2015 Mobile Systems Technologies Workshop (MST), pp. 15–20. IEEE (2015)
6. Huang, J., Badam, A., Caulfield, L., et al.: FlashBlox: achieving both performance isolation and uniform lifetime for virtualized SSDs. In: 15th USENIX Conference on File and Storage Technologies (FAST 2017), pp. 375–390 (2017)
7. Tavakkol, A., Sadrosadati, M., Ghose, S., et al.: FLIN: enabling fairness and enhancing performance in modern NVMe solid state drives. In: 2018 ACM/IEEE 45th Annual International Symposium on Computer Architecture (ISCA), pp. 397–410. IEEE (2018)
8. Oh, K., Park, J., Eom, Y.I.: H-BFQ: supporting multi-level hierarchical Cgroup in BFQ scheduler. In: 2020 IEEE International Conference on Big Data and Smart Computing (BigComp), pp. 366–369. IEEE (2020)
9. Heo, T., Schatzberg, D., Newell, A., et al.: IOCost: block IO control for containers in datacenters (2022)
10. Hedayati, M., Shen, K., Scott, M.L., et al.: Multi-queue fair queueing. In: 2019 USENIX Annual Technical Conference (USENIXATC 2019), pp. 301–314 (2019)

11. Woo, J., Ahn, M., Lee, G., et al.: D2FQ: device-direct fair queueing for NVMe SSDs. In: 19th USENIX Conference on File and Storage Technologies (FAST 2021). pp. 403–415 (2021)
12. Cgroups v1. https://www.kernel.org/doc/Documentation/cgroup-v1/cgroups.txt
13. Kang, J.U., Hyun, J., Maeng, H., et al.: The multi-streamed solid-state drive. In: 6th USENIX Workshop on Hot Topics in Storage and File Systems (HotStorage 2014) (2014)
14. Kim, J., Lee, D., Noh, S.H.: Towards SLO complying SSDs through OPS isolation. In: 13th USENIX Conference on File and Storage Technologies (FAST 2015). pp. 183–189 (2015)
15. Chang, H.P., Yu, Y.C., Chung, P.Y.: Design and implementation of a shared multi-tiered storage system. In: 2018 3rd International Conference on Computer and Communication Systems (ICCCS), pp. 94–98. IEEE (2018)
16. Bjørling, M., Axboe, J., Nellans, D., et al.: Linux block IO: introducing multi-queue SSD access on multi-core systems. In: Proceedings of the 6th International Systems and Storage Conference, pp. 1–10 (2013)
17. Ahn, S., La, K., Kim, J.: Improving i/o resource sharing of Linux CGroup for NVME SSDs on multi-core systems. In: 8th USENIX Workshop on Hot Topics in Storage and File Systems (HotStorage 2016) (2016)
18. Caulfield, A.M., De, A., Coburn, J., et al.: Moneta: a high-performance storage array architecture for next-generation, non-volatile memories. In: 2010 43rd Annual IEEE/ACM International Symposium on Microarchitecture, pp. 385–395. IEEE (2010)
19. Cheong, W., Yoon, C., Woo, S., et al.: A flash memory controller for 15μ s ultra-low-latency SSD using high-speed 3D NAND flash with $3\mu s$ read time. In: 2018 IEEE International Solid-State Circuits Conference-(ISSCC), pp. 338–340. IEEE (2018)
20. Goyal, P., Vin, H.M., Cheng, H.: Start-time fair queueing: a scheduling algorithm for integrated services packet switching networks. IEEE/ACM Trans. Network. **5**(5), 690–704 (1997)
21. Greenberg, A.G., Madras, N.: How fair is fair queueing. J. ACM (JACM) **39**(3), 568–598 (1992)
22. Park, S., Shen, K.: FIOS: a fair, efficient flash I/O scheduler. In: FAST, vol. 12, p. 13 (2012)
23. Mao, B., Wu, S., Duan, L.: Improving the SSD performance by exploiting request characteristics and internal parallelism. IEEE Trans. Comput. Aided Des. Integr. Circuits Syst. **37**(2), 472–484 (2017)
24. Chang, D.W., Chen, H.H., Su, W.J.: VSSD: performance isolation in a solid-state drive. ACM Trans. Des. Autom. Electron. Syst. (TODAES) **20**(4), 1–33 (2015)
25. Axboe, J.: Linux block IO-present and future. In: Ottawa Linux Symposium, pp. 51–61 (2004)
26. Axboe, J: Flexible I/O Tester (2021). https://github.com/axboe/fio
27. UMass Trace Repository. http://traces.cs.umass.edu/index.php/Storage/Storage
28. MSR Cambridge Traces. http://iotta.snia.org/traces/388

Automated Binary Analysis: A Survey

Zian Liu[1,2(✉)], Chao Chen[3], Ahmed Ejaz[2], Dongxi Liu[2], and Jun Zhang[1]

[1] Swinburne University of Technology, Melbourne, Australia
102516622@student.swin.edu.au, junzhang@swin.edu.au
[2] Data6 61, CSIRO, Clayton, Australia
{ejaz.ahmed,dongxi.liu}@data61.csiro.au
[3] Royal Melbourne Institute of Technology, Melbourne, Australia
chao.chen@jcu.edu.au

Abstract. *Binary code analysis* is a process of analyzing the software or operating system when source code is inaccessible. This scenario occurs when one needs to analyze malware, a compiled software, or a closed-sourced operating system such as Windows, IOS, etc. In these scenarios, the source codes are deliberately made inaccessible by the vendor or programmer for various reasons. Binary analysis contains a wide range of analysis aims, techniques and methodologies. We concluded the methodologies into two categories: data-driven analysis and software-engineering-based analysis. Each category has a similar process in their methodology. We also concluded their limitation and summaries the challenges and future work.

1 Introduction

Binary code analysis is to perform various analyses on software or operating system at the binary code level when source code is unavailable. This survey focuses on binaries in popular platforms, including 1)common personal computer platforms (i.e., Windows and Linux), 2)Android, and 3)IOS.

The current research on binary analysis can be divided into two categories: 1) data-driven binary analysis and 2) software-engineering-based binary analysis. **Data-driven binary analysis** automatically learns the model through training. The model can be used for prediction, signature inference, etc. **Software-engineering-based binary analysis** requires various traditional static (offline), dynamic (online) program analysis techniques, and other automated program analysis methods to address specific research questions. Generally, **Software-engineering-based binary analysis** can be divided into 1) **offline analysis, online analysis**, and **hybrid analysis**. **Offline analysis** does not require the program to execute with concrete inputs. It statically or symbolically analyzes the program. It consists of two steps: 1) Preprocessing, which prepares the binary code by abstracting it to higher-level representation

W. Meng et al. (Eds.): ICA3PP 2022, LNCS 13777, pp. 392–411, 2023.
https://doi.org/10.1007/978-3-031-22677-9_21

or graph representation or finding initial points of interest, and 2) static analysis which uses static and symbolic analysis to analyze the prepared binary. **Online analysis** requires the program to be executed dynamically with concrete inputs. It contains two steps: 1) dynamic tracing, which records run time information, and 2) trace processing which further analyzes the traced dynamic information. **Hybrid analysis** uses both offline analysis and online analysis. It contains four steps: 1) preprocessing that prepares the binary code (i.e., abstract to higher-level representation or graph representation, or find initial points of interest), 2) static analysis which uses static and symbolic analysis to analyze the prepared binary, 3) dynamic tracing that records run time information, and 4) trace analysis to further analyze the traced dynamic information.

We surveyed the works across a wide range of topics, including malware classification and detection, program maliciousness detection, binary code similarity detection, reverse engineering, binary code exploitation, binary code rewriting, binary code vulnerability detection, etc. Existing surveys only focus on one or several topics of binary code analysis. [38] surveyed PDF-based adversarial malware detection, [2] surveyed dynamic analysis evasion techniques utilized by malware, [5] concluded the symbolic execution techniques utilized by program analysis, [7] introduced state-of-the-art attacks on Android platforms, [50] surveyed binary rewriting problems. However, there lacks a survey concluding the general binary code analysis.

The contribution of this survey paper include:

– We reviewed recent years' high-quality conference papers on binary analysis and concluded their common methodology and techniques, as well as limitations.
– We concluded the challenges and future trends for binary code analysis.

The survey is organized as follows: Sect. 2 introduces data-driven methodology techniques. Section 3 introduces software-engineering-based methodology and techniques. Section 4 discusses the challenge and possible future trend of binary analysis. Section 5 concludes the survey.

2   Data-Driven Binary Code Analysis

The data-driven binary analysis includes traditional machine-learning-based algorithms (e.g., k-Nearest Neighbor (k-NN), Support Vector Machines (SVM), Random Forests (RF), etc.) and deep learning algorithms (e.g., recurrent neuron network (RNN), Deep neuron network (DNN), and their variations). We categorize all the data-driven works by their platform, features extracted, and learning model in Table 1.

2.1   Feature Engineering for Binary Representation

Graph-Based Features. Mamadroid [41] uses call-graph-based features. Firstly, the call graph of the app's API calls was extracted. Then, the sequences of

Table 1. Data-driven category. IF shorts for Instruction Features. MSCS shorts for Maximally Suspicious Common Subgraph

	Windows or Linux	Android	IOS	Call Graph	Control Flow Graph	Data Dependency Graph	Condition-path Graph	Attribute Control Flow Graph	Dependency Graph	Segment Graph	MSCS	API Calls	Instruction Embedding	Markov Chain	Support Vector Machine	Discrete Finite Automaton	Spectral Clustering	Extremely Randomized Trees	Conditional Random Field	PV-DM	Recurrent Neuron Network	Graph Embedding Network	Long Short-Term Memory	Other
	Platform			Graph-based Features								IF		Learning Model										
Mamadroid [41]		✓		✓										✓										
HSOMINER [43]		✓			✓	✓	✓							✓										
Genius [21]	✓							✓									✓							
Gemini [55]	✓							✓														✓		
DEBIN [28]	✓								✓									✓	✓					
SAD THUG [11]	✓	✓	✓							✓					✓									
Astroid [23]	✓										✓													✓
Drebin [3]	✓											✓			✓									
EKLAVYA [18]	✓												✓								✓			
Asm2Vec [19]	✓												✓							✓				
DeepVSA [27]	✓												✓										✓	

API calls were categorized into two different levels, package name (e.g., java.lang) and family name (e.g., java, android, google). They further capture the frequency of the transition between every two calls by using Markov Chain.

HSOMINER [43] converts the code to an intermediate language (IR), builds a global control flow graph (CFG), and a backward data dependency graph (DDG). HSOMINER locates the basic blocks containing sensitive activities and uses CFG and DDG to produce condition-path graph (CPG). Then, HSOMINER extract features such as 1) trigger conditions leading to invoking the hidden activities, 2) behaviour differences between the paths with and without hidden activities, and 3) condition-path relation such as data dependency between some operation or variable with other variables within the condition.

Genius [21] extracts features based on a Attribute Control Flow Graph (ACFG). The features include statistical features and structural features. Statistical features include string constants, numeric constants, number of transfer instructions, number of calls, number of instructions, and number of arithmetic instructions. Structural features include the number of offspring and betweenness centrality, which measures a node's centrality in a graph. Gemini [55] also uses the ACFG-related features proposed in Genius. The difference lies in the processing and learning of the ACFG features.

DEBIN [28] lifts the assembly code into an intermediate representation called BAP-IR and builds a dependency graph. Then it extracts various program elements, including functions, register variables, memory offset variables, types, flags, instructions, constants, locations, and unary operations from the graph as the feature.

SAD THUG [11] decomposed the input image file into a sequence of segments and abstracted it to a directed graph. Then they capture possible transitions from one segment to another as a benign feature. They regard the segment order and length within those transitions as features. Because of the imbalance of malicious and benign image files, they only train on features extracted from benign images.

Astroid [23] extracts maximally suspicious common subgraph (MSCS) for all the samples in each malware family. They capture the MSCS's features such as node type, node metadata, control flow between nodes, etc.

Instruction Feature and Embedding. Drebin [3] extracts disassembled code features such as the existence of restricted API calls, used permissions, suspicious API calls, and network IP addresses. Some other works learn instructions' semantics by using Natural Language Processing (NLP) methods and models. EKLAVYA [18] uses the skip-gram negative sampling method and word embedding technique to learn the embedding of each instruction. They also consider each instruction's contextual information in the embedding. Asm2Vec [19] uses the PV-DM model to learn the embedding representation of each instruction from assembly code using unsupervised learning. DeepVSA [27] uses Long-Short-Term-Memory (LSTM) to learn a one-hot embedding of each instruction.

2.2 Model Training for Binary Analysis

In this step, the extracted features are fed to the model in order to train a model for different tasks such as malware prediction, vulnerability detection, etc., according to the research problem. Both traditional machine learning methods deep learning models, and sometimes, self-defined learning model are used.

MAMADroid [41] builds the Markov Chain based on the API call sequences to learn the frequency of the transition between every two calls. The frequency of the API call sequences indicates the maliciousness of the app.

Drebin [3] converts all the features to a one-hot vector and uses Support Vector Machines (SVM) to learn the model classifying malware based on these features.

HSOMINER [43] takes the trigger condition and their corresponding paths related features, as well as the label indicating whether the instance is HSO or not to train an SVM classification model.

SAD THUG [11] uses all the training samples' segment graphs to feed the training algorithm to construct a discrete finite automaton, which captures possible transitions from one segment to another in common image files.

[21] uses the extracted ACFG and calculates raw feature similarity. Then it clusters the features based on spectral clustering in order to generate a codebook representing image file bugs.

DEBIN [28] extracts program elements to build a dependency graph. DEBIN uses the Extremely Randomized Trees (ET) model and some other rules to predict which element is known (and should not be predicted), and which is not (thus should be predicted). DEBIN uses a Conditional Random Field (CRF) model to represent the conditional probability distribution and performs a Maximum a Posterior (MAP) inference to decide the most likely assignments for unknown elements.

Asm2vec [19] uses the PV-DM model (an extension to word2vec model) to learn the vector representation from assembly code. The vectors to be learnt are the repository function vector, each token's lexical semantic vector and its prediction vector. Later, the learnt assembly code vectors can be used for binary code similarity detection.

EKLAVYA [18] trains recurrent neuron network (RNN) models for four tasks: counting each function's arguments based on instructions from the caller, counting each function's arguments based on instructions from the callee, recovering arguments' types based on instructions from the caller, and recovering arguments' types based on instructions from the callee. The trained model can be later used for recovering disassembled binary code function types.

Gemini [55] uses the Basic Structure2vec Approach to aggregate graph topology and vertex-wise features recursively. Next, [55] uses Siamese architecture to learn parameters in the network, by taking pairs of ground truth similar ACFGs as input and optimizing an objective function. The trained model can be used later for predicting whether the two given binary functions are similar or not.

DEEPVSA [27] uses a bidirectional LSTM model for each instruction to generate an individual instruction embedding. The forward and backward networks are used in this step. It also uses a sequence-to-sequence model that takes the instruction embeddings as input and predicts the label, such as memory access regions for each instruction.

Astroid [23] learns the signature from the samples (i.e., generate the common subgraph from several input malicious family ICCGs). They designed and optimized their customized objective function, which encodes the scale of vertex coverage and the suspiciousness of the produced common subgraph.

2.3   Model Prediction, Evaluation, and Explanation

To test the performance of the trained machine learning model, one should test the model on binaries collected from the wild. However, generally, there is no available ground truth data (and labels) for the binary code in the wild. Thus it is common practice to divide the collected ground truth binary code with labels into training and testing datasets and use the testing set to validate the model performance and measure the model efficiency.

Various measurements can be applied to evaluate the model performance, including Accuracy, Recall, Precision and F1-score. Specifically, MAMADroid

[41] evaluates F-measure, precision, and recall on the malware classification result. Drebin [3] evaluates accuracy and false positive rate on the malware classification result. HSOMINER [43] evaluates precision and a recall of the HSO prediction result. SAD THUG [11] measures the true positive ratio and the true negative ratio of the malicious image file prediction. [21] measures the true positive rate and accuracy of the image file bug prediction. DEBIN [28] measures accuracy, precision, recall, and F1 on the program element prediction. Asm2vec [19] measures true positive ratio, recall, false positive, and precision on the similarity prediction result. EKLAVYA [18] measures the accuracy of function information predictions. Gemini [55] measures accuracy and ROC curve on the similarity prediction result. DEEPVSA [27] measures the precision, recall, and F1 on the VSA information prediction results. Astroid [23] measures the accuracy and false positive rate of the malicious app prediction.

Model efficiency can refer to both the prediction time and training time. However, prediction time is of more importance since the training process can be executed beforehand and directly deployed on the user side. A good model means good performance with minimal prediction time.

3 Software-Engineering-Based Binary Code Analysis

Software-engineering-based binary analysis is widely used to analyze binary code. The methods can be divided into 1) Offline analysis, which analyzes the binary code without actually executing the program, 2) Online analysis, which requires executing the program with concrete value; and 3) Hybrid analysis which combines both offline and online methods.

3.1 Offline Analysis

Offline analysis statically analyzes the program. It contains two steps in the methodology, including 1) Preprocessing, which prepares the binary code, and 2) Program analysis which performs the actual static analysis. Through preprocessing, binary codes are abstracted to higher-level representation (e.g., binary code to Intermediate Representation (IR)), or graph-based representation. Sometimes the preprocessing extracts initial instructions of interest. In Program analysis, traditional static program analyzing methods (i.e., code slicing, taint analysis, data-flow analysis, boolean satisfiability reasoning) and symbolic execution are widely used. Some other methods, such as calculating feature geometric centre and Natural Language Processing (NLP) based methods, can also be included (Table 2).

Prepossessing. Certain works prepossess the binary code by finding the desired instructions of interest. BATE [8] uses pattern matching to find Control Flow Guard (CFG) related code gadgets called PR gadgets and S gadgets as vulnerable primitive gadgets. KEPLER [53] firstly statically identifies five kinds of code gadgets as candidate vulnerable primitive gadgets.

Table 2. Offline Analysis category. HR shorts for Higher-level Representations. BSR shorts for Boolean Satisfiability Reasoning.

	Windows or Linux	Android	IOS	Instructions of Interest	HR	Graph Representation	Symbolic Execution	Data-flow Analysis	Code Slicing	Taint Analysis	BSR	Others
	Platform			Preprocessing			Program Analysis					
BATE [8]	✓			✓			✓					
KEPLER [53]	✓			✓			✓					
OOAnalyzer [45]	✓					✓	✓					
NORAX [14]	✓					✓		✓				
UROBOROS [48]	✓					✓						✓
RAMBLR [47]	✓				✓	✓		✓				
TriggerScope [24]		✓				✓	✓					
XPMChecker [57]		✓				✓		✓				
Flowdroid [4]		✓				✓				✓		
IccTA [36]		✓			✓	✓		✓				
Arcade [1]		✓				✓				✓		
Apposcopy [22]		✓				✓				✓		
MassVet [12]		✓		✓								✓
CoP [37]	✓				✓	✓	✓					
Bingo [10]	✓					✓		✓			✓	
Cruiser [34]			✓			✓						✓

Some other works preprocess the binary code by abstracting the binary code into higher-level representations. OOAnalyzer [45] firstly disassembles the binary and lifts the assembly instructions to a semantic presentation. It partitions the binary code into separate functions. NORAX [14] converts an input binary from machine code to assembly code in linear sweep fashion. UROBOROS [48] also linearly disassembles the binary and uses a validator to check the disassembled result. RAMBLR [47] disassemble each basic block. It also classifies binary code content into code, pointers, arrays, etc. TriggerScope [24] unpacks the Android APK and lifts it into a custom Intermediate Representation (IR). IccTA [36] transforms the Dalvik bytecode into Jimple and extracts Inter-Component Communication (ICC) links along with the collected data (e.g., ICC call parameters or Intent Filter values). MassVet [12] disassembled into a SMALI representation. CoP [37] firstly disassembles the binary code and lifts it to an intermediate representation.

Also, some work preprocesses binary code by translating binary code into a graph representation. XPMChecker [57] parses APK files and builds the inter-procedure control flow graph (ICFG). Flowdroid [4] unzips APK file and parses its layout XML file, DEX file, and manifest file. Afterwards, Flowdroid generates the dummy main method out of the list of lifecycle and callback methods and produces the inter-procedural control-flow graph (ICFG). IccTA [36] uses the modified FlowDroid [4] to build a complete control flow graph of the app. Arcade [1] builds a CFG after identifying public entry points or APIs. It also produces an Access-Control Flow Graph (AFG) from the built CFG, and transforms it into the protection map. Apposcopy [22] firstly performs pointer analysis and constructs the inter-component call graph (ICCG). Cruiser [34] finds View Controllers (VCs) with conditionally triggered UIs. To do so, Cruiser builds two labelled view controller graphs (LVCGs) from binaries and other layout files. CoP [37] construct CFG and call graphs (CG). Bingo [10] disassembles the given binary and builds the CFG. RAMBLR [47] recovers Control-flow Graph (CFG).

Program Analysis. Symbolic execution emulates the execution with abstract values rather than concrete values. It abstracts each operand as a symbolic formula after symbolic execution. Because of its semantic-preserving nature, it is wildly used as a program analysis method with diverse purposes. BATE [8] and KEPLER [53] use symbolic execution to validate the exploitability of stitching the candidate vulnerable code gadgets. OOAnalyzer [45] uses symbolic execution to represent low-level instruction behaviour as entity fact. CoP [37] uses symbolic execution to represent the semantics of each basic block. Bingo [10] extracts semantic features by using symbolic expressions to capture the relationship before and after a partial trace. TriggerScope [24] uses symbolic execution to extract block predicate.

Data-flow analysis takes some initial instructions as input and extracts all possible instructions to which the input instruction can be propagated. IccTA [36] uses a precise data-flow analysis to detect Inter-Component Communication (ICC)-based privacy leaks.

Code slicing takes some initial instructions as input and extracts all the data-flow or control-flow relevant instructions within the binary. NORAX [14] uses code slice to help transform the binary code. RAMBLR [47] uses program slicing to perform data identification and type recognition. XPMChecker [57] uses backward slicing along the ICFG to collect all instructions necessary to construct the URL. It also uses the program slice to reconstruct the string-related operations.

Taint analysis takes some untrustworthy instructions that might introduce malicious user inputs and extract the possible sink instructions (i.e., the instructions derive value from the potential malicious user input) by analyzing the information flow (i.e., data flow and control flow) of the program. Flowdroid [4] implemented both forward and backward taint analysis. Apposcopy [22] uses taint-analysis to construct an inter-component call graph (ICCG) and data flow (Table 3).

Table 3. Online Analysis category. BSR shorts for Boolean Satisfiability Reasoning.

	Windows or Linux	Android	IOS	Dynamic Instruction	CPU States	Memory States	System and API call	Other	Compare and Infer	Taint Analysis	Concolic Execution	Deobfuscation	Symbolic Execution	Code Slicing	BSR	Program Synthesis	Machine Learning	Other
	Platform			Dynamic Tracing					Trace Processing									
Tartarus [33]	✓			✓	✓	✓												✓
BareCloud [32]	✓						✓	✓	✓	✓								
Droidunpack [20]		✓		✓														✓
VMHunt [54]	✓			✓				✓					✓	✓	✓			
Syntia [9]	✓			✓												✓		
BB-DSE [6]	✓			✓									✓					
Binsim [40]	✓			✓			✓		✓				✓	✓				
RAZOR [44]	✓			✓			✓	✓						✓				✓
BinUnpack [16]	✓			✓		✓												✓
Malgene [31]	✓						✓		✓									
Malton [56]		✓					✓	✓		✓	✓							
[26]	✓			✓													✓	
TAINTINDUCE [17]	✓			✓														✓

Boolean satisfiability reasoning is a technique to solve the Boolean satisfiability problem (or SAT problem). It determines whether there exists an interpretation satisfying a given Boolean formula. In program analysis, this technique can be used to check whether the condition at some point of the program holds as the preconditions of the point can be represented in the form of boolean formulas. Arcade [1] uses Boolean satisfiability reasoning to extract the least privileged permission(s) the app needs to hold. Bingo [10] uses the Z3 constraint solver to generate input/output samples from symbolic expressions and feed them to the machine learning module to find the semantically similar functions.

Some works use other program analyses after processing. MassVet [12] calculates the geometric centres of the view graphs and control flow graphs. Cruiser [34] uses Natural Language Processing (NLP) techniques to identify inconsistency within the app text information. UROBOROS [48] identifies the symbol reference in the binary code and symbolizes them.

3.2   Online Analysis

Online analysis requires the program to be executed with concrete inputs. During execution, run time information is traced (e.g., memory or CPU states, executed instructions, system and API call, etc.). Then based on the traced information, various analyses are performed (e.g., traditional program analyzing methods, machine learning, program synthesizing, etc.).

Dynamic Tracing. Dynamically executed instructions can reveal adequate semantic information. Tracing the memory or CPU states before and after executing each instruction can retrieve more information. Tartarus [33] uses shadow memory to log the malware execution trace along with memory and CPU states. BareCloud [32] traces the execution of some pre-computed memory addresses. Droidunpack [20] traces instructions on Linux and DVM and supports Android Runtime (ART) tracing using hooking techniques. VMHunt [54] dynamically runs virtualized binary and logs the trace, including memory addresses of instruction, instruction name, source and destination operands, run time information, etc. Syntia [9] traces the dynamically executed instructions. Backward-Bounded Dynamic Symbolic Execution (BB-DSE) [6] also traces dynamically executed instructions. Binsim [40] records executed instruction with their opcode and operands. It also records memory access addresses. RAZOR [44] traces the executed instructions with their memory addresses and raw bytes. [26] generates execution traces. TAINTINDUCE [17] records dynamic execution trace. Specifically, this contains the memory addresses and complete registers states before and after each instruction. BinUnpack [16] traces the malware dynamic execution instruction using kernel-level DLL hijacking techniques. This technique substitutes the DLL in the standard DLL loading with a new version with monitoring functionality embedded. BinUnpack also dumps processes' memory.

System and API calls are also two tracing objects as they can demonstrate code behaviour to a certain extent. BareCloud [32] uses bare-metal analysis hosts and three malware analysis systems for dynamic tracing. It traces Windows API calls and system calls. Malgene [31] produces two sequences of system call under two different execution environments (i.e., Malware has evasive behaviour in one environment and does not have evasive behaviour in another environment). Malton [56] generates logs by instrumenting the native code and Android Runtime (ART). The logs contain the method invocations information. Binsim [40] record invoked system calls and their data flow dependencies. RAZOR [44] traces indirect jumps and calls targets.

Some other objects containing important execution information can be traced. BareCloud [32] also traces network traffic, user environment data (e.g., browser history, user document files, etc.), and disk-level state changes. Malton [56] also traces different layers' taint propagations and the results of the concolic executions. RAZOR [44] traces conditional branches that are both taken or non-taken.

Trace Processing. Comparing different traces can help infer important information. BareCloud [32] extracts malware behaviour by diffing the traced malware logs and a normal program log. Malgene [31] applies sequence alignment algorithms borrowed from bioinformatics to align the system call sequences to find the evasive behaviour and extract the evasion signature. Binsim [40] matches traces by using the system call alignment methods from MalGene [31] to check binary code similarity.

Existing program analysis techniques can be utilized to analyze the traced instructions further. Typical techniques include code slicing, taint analysis, symbolic execution, concolic execution etc. Malton [56] characterizes malware behaviours by taint analysis, the path exploration technique, and concolic execution. VMHunt [54] locates virtualized codes and deobfuscates the virtualized codes by using a backward slicing algorithm and Multiple Granularity Symbolic Execution. Binsim [40] performs dynamic slicing to check similarity. RAZOR [44] also uses basic block symbolization to extract debloat code.

Boolean satisfiability (or SAT) reasoning at a certain point in the program can help check the reachability of a branch and can be used to compare similarities. Backward-Bounded Dynamic Symbolic Execution (BB-DSE) [6] reasons whether execution flow can not reach some instruction address. This was done by backward and bounded reasoning that goes from some point in the program backwards and uses the SMT solver to decide whether all the predecessor conditions are satisfied. Binsim [40] uses the weakest precondition (a kind of boolean formula) to check similarity.

Program synthesis from the trace can help simplify the program's semantic information and thus deobfuscate the program. Syntia [9] randomly derives input and output pairs as the semantic of that trace window and uses the Monte Carlo Tree Search method to synthesize the program.

Machine learning can also be used for analyzing traces. [26] learns the developer-intended but costumer-unwanted codes using machine learning-based methods.

Some work implements their analysis patterns into scripts for automation. BinUnpack [16] extracts the imported address table (IAT) and compares it with the unpacking routine IAT to discover any rebuilt IAT at run time. Tartarus [33] finds all the dynamically generated code (also known as code waves) by comparing the instruction's shadow table and the shadow table of the process current instruction is within. Tartarus also finds the code injection by constructing the code injection graph. Droidunpack [20] analyzes Android packer behaviour, including Hidden OAT/DEX code extraction, Self-modifying code detection, Multi-layer unpacking detection, and Java native interface inspection. RAZOR [44] collects all the relevant paths that might be missed in tracing by using heuristic rules. TAINTINDUCE [17] learns taint rules by systematically generating seed states and mutating them to generate different input values. TAINTINDUCE learns the rule by identifying 1) a set of input bits which can influence the specific output bit and 2) the pre-conditions by tracking both direct dependencies and conditional dependencies (Table 3).

3.3 Hybrid Analysis

Hybrid analysis both requires online analysis and offline analysis. It contains four steps: 1) Preprocessing that abstracts binary code into higher-level representation or graph-based representation, or extract initial points of interest. 2) Static analysis that uses traditional static and symbolic analysis, 3) Dynamic tracing, which executes the program with concrete value and traces run time information;

Table 4. Hybrid Analysis category. BSR shorts for Boolean Satisfiability Reasoning. DEI shorts for Dynamically Executed Instructions. PCI shorts for Provide Complementary Information. HR shorts for Higher-level Representation.

	Windows or Linux	Android	IOS	Find Points of Interest	HR	Graph Representation	Other	Taint Analysis	Code Slicing	Data-flow Analysis	Control-flow Analysis	Symbolic Analysis	Deobfuscation	BSR	Other	DEI	Program Output	System or API call	Other	Infer	Futther Analyze Program	PCI
	Platform			Preprocessing				Static Analysis								Dynamic Tracing				Trace Analysis		
K-Hunt [35]	✓					✓		✓								✓		✓		✓		
Tiger [15]		✓		✓	✓	✓		✓								✓				✓		
CACOMPARE [29]	✓					✓											✓	✓	✓	✓		
RootExplorer [25]	✓					✓							✓					✓			✓	
Angr [46]	✓				✓	✓		✓	✓	✓	✓	✓				✓					✓	
WARDroid [39]		✓		✓				✓					✓			✓					✓	
IntelliDroid[51]		✓		✓						✓	✓					✓						✓
FlowCog [42]		✓		✓				✓								✓						✓
[49]		✓		✓								✓						✓		✓		
TIRO[52]		✓				✓										✓		✓			✓	

and 4) Trace analysis that performs diverse analysis (e.g., traditional program analysis methods, etc.).

Preprocessing. Abstracting the original binary code into graph representation is widely used for preprocessing. K-Hunt [35] disassembles the binary code and recovers the CFG to generate basic blocks. Tiger [15] constructs this app's call graphs (CG). CACOMPARE [29] preprocesses the binary through disassembling and generating CFG. RootExplorer [25] uses IDA Pro to disassemble the binary code and recover the CFG. Angr [46] can transform binary code into CFG.

Lifting binary code into higher-level representations can help further static analysis. Tiger [15] disassembles the app's DEX bytecode to the SMALI Intermediate Representation (IR). Angr [46] is a binary analysis framework. It supports translating to intermediate representation from multiple architectures using libVEX, and PyVEX.

Finding initial points of interest within the binary code is also a preprocessing purpose. Tiger [15] locates all of the app's network sinks (i.e., the messages-sending APIs). WARDroid [39] identifies points of interest (POIs) in the APK by extending FlowDoroid [4]. IntelliDroid [51] firstly identifies targeted API invocations by abstracting API calls. FlowCog [42] finds special statements (i.e., activation event and guarding condition) for each data flow. [49] first identifies message handling functions.

Static Analysis. Traditional program analysis techniques are widely used, including taint analysis, data-flow analysis, code slicing, and symbolic execution. WARDroid [39] uses backward taint propagation to track the data flow relating to web API. It then reconstructs the app's program dependence graph (PDG) by constructing a call-graph, points-to analysis, def-use chains analysis, and taint analysis. Tiger [15] performs backwards slicing to find the statements sent out through the sink. IntelliDroid [51] extracts call path constraints by using a forward control- and data-flow analysis. FlowCog [42] associates Android views with data flow or the activation event and guarding condition of the data flow by using a set of data flow analyses. Angr [46] supports static vulnerability discovery (e.g., recovering control flow, vulnerability detection with data modelling, and vulnerability detection with flow modelling). [49] uses symbolic analysis to infer response messages with symbolic constraints. K-Hunt [35] uses taint analysis to detect vulnerable cryptography implementation.

Boolean satisfiability (or SAT) reasoning at a certain point in the program is critical in understanding preconditions. WARDroid [39] also builds a template in the form of Z3-compliant formulas (i.e., a boolean formula) and regular expressions. It generates potential vulnerable inputs and requests by solving the boolean formula. RootExplorer [25] identifies feasible execution paths leading to successful root exploit execution by symbolic execution. RootExplorer uses an SMT solver to solve the preconditions that need to be met.

Some works use other analyzing techniques. K-Hunt [35] computes the ratio of x86/64 arithmetic and bitwise instructions (e.g., mul, xor, etc.) for each block and consider the block as a candidate crypto basic block if the ratio reaches some threshold. TIRO [52] detects potential obfuscation location and deobfuscate the code by using IntelliDroid [51]. CACOMPARE [29] traverses the CFG to recognize arguments needed for the execution by observing their behaviour on stacks. It also detects switch statements that include all the possible destination addresses of the indirect jumps.

Dynamic Tracing. Dynamically executed instructions and buffers used can reveal adequate information. K-Hunt [35] uses Intel PIN to trace dynamic executed instructions and buffers relevant to key generation and key propagation. Angr [46] supports dynamic execution tracing.

Program output can be dynamically traced to retrieve information extremely challenging to retrieve statically. WARDroid [39] sends the forged valid and invalid HTTP request to the server and gets the response. IntelliDroid [51] dynamically extracts the concrete values at runtime that satisfy the constraints. FlowCog [42] has an optional dynamic analysis module to output certain strings and view IDs which can not be resolved statically. Tiger [15] uses partial execution on the Dalvik virtual machine (VM) to record output traffic tokens.

System call or API call can demonstrate program semantics. TIRO [52] statically instruments the ART runtime and the application for both language-based obfuscation and runtime-based obfuscation. The tracing object is the caller method, the invocation site, and the actually executed method. CACOMPARE [29] traces library function calls. RootExplorer [25] traces system calls.

Some works trace other dynamic information. K-Hunt [35] traces execution statistics (e.g., the number of executions for a basic block, data bundles randomness). CACOMPARE [29] emulates the execution with randomly produced inputs. The semantic signature it collects includes function input and output values, comparison operands and condition codes. [49] records the execution stack of the app when the app is dynamically executing.

Trace Analysis. Some works use dynamic traces to infer information. K-Hunt [35] uses inputs of different size magnitudes to test basic blocks' data sensitivity. K-Hunt also measure the randomness of the collected data bundle, with both Chi-Square distribution and Monte Carlo π approximation tests. WARDroid [39] uses an edit distance algorithm to infer whether the server accepts the invalid request. Tiger [15] compares input and output traffic tokens to test the impact of each input on the invariant portion of the output. CACOMPARE [29] uses input and output relations as a signature to calculate the similarity between two signature sequences.

Some works use the traced information further analyzes the program. TIRO [52] uses the observed information (e.g., the executed caller method, the invocation site, and the actually executed method) to build the static call graph and deobfuscate the obfuscated code. Angr [46] supports dynamic vulnerability discovery (e.g., dynamic concrete execution), and exploitation (e.g., crash reproduction, exploit generation, exploit hardening). RootExplorer [25] uses the traced system calls to form a behaviour graph. [49] uses the traced stack execution information to pair the app's requests and responses.

Some works use the dynamic trace as a complementary method to acquire information that is hard to retrieve statically. Thus the traced information is provided directly to the static analyzing module. IntelliDroid [51] applies the recorded runtime concrete value to forge inputs that lead to the invocation of the targeted API. FlowCog [42] uses the dynamically resolved strings and view IDs to assist semantic extraction.

4   Challenge and Future Work

4.1   Binary Optimization and Obfuscation

Binary optimization poses a challenge for automatic binary analysis. The compiler usually performs binary optimization to speed up the speed of the binary executable. For example, whole program optimization, linker reusing identical function implementations, and function inlining can make binary code very complex, thus significantly increasing the difficulty of binary analysis [45]. Analyzing the optimized binary code, such as compiled with inlining, needs new research. Binary obfuscation refers to transforming a program into another executable one with the same functionality, with an unreadable code implementation. Like optimization, obfuscation also makes binary code complex and hard to analyze. Some existing anti-obfuscation tools can deal with simple obfuscation, but special obfuscation techniques still can bypass the tools, such as x86 obfuscation and hooking techniques [52]. A possible countermeasure is to explore the separation of application and run-time memory. Some recent obfuscation even transforms part of the original executable binary code into another low-level language. For example, on Windows and Linux platforms, the code virtualizer transforms part of the binary code into Virtual Code only understood by the specific virtual machine. Also, When analyzing mobile APK, sometimes unsupported code formats can be encountered, such as native code and JNI code [39], native code, and Javascript code [42]. This remains to be future work.

4.2   Adversarial Binary Analysis

In machine learning-based binary analysis, machine learning technology can be the target of a cyberattack to evade detection. Typical adversarial machine learning for binary analysis includes poisoning attack, trojan and backdoor attack, reprogramming, inference attack, and evasion attack. Poisoning attack could inject carefully crafted binary samples into the training set to degrade the performance of machine learning methods. It has demonstrated its effectiveness in worm signature generation, DoS attack detection and PDF malware classification [30]. Trojan and back door attacks aim to maintain the model's behaviour under regular input while misbehaving under particular triggers. Reprogramming attack aims at reprogramming the model to perform the task chosen by the attacker instead of performing the original task. Evasion attack occurs when the model is fed with the adversarial example that seems to belong to a category by humans but is classified to be another category by the model. Examples are adversarial work in [13] against malware detection and evading [43] by mimicking legitimate branches. Evasion attack can even evade domain knowledge-based works. For example, the security technique proposed in [42] is vulnerable to click-jacking attacks and UI redress attacks. The binary analysis method develops in [57] is vulnerable to the Java reflection attack that hides the invocation of Web resource manipulation API, as well as the attack on identifiers for recognizing Web principals and app principals through obfuscation. Another binary analysis method proposed in [34] is vulnerable to crowdturfing UI hiding techniques. As a countermeasure, Optical Character Recognition (OCR) tool can be used to extract the texts from images in the resource files. As a result, it is possible to identify enough UI semantics.

4.3   Advanced Dynamic Attacks

Advanced dynamic attacks can evade static and dynamic binary analysis. For example, the binary analysis technique proposed in [41] cannot handle attacks like reflection, dynamic code loading, or native code. For example, the static analysis tool developed in [43] has poor accuracy due to Android's Inter-Component Communications (ICC). Dead code remains a challenge [15] for dynamic analysis because the sinks are not executed at runtime. A possible countermeasure is to build a reachability test to reduce the impact of the dead code. There exist some advanced anti-dynamic techniques to prevent dynamic analysis. For example, several custom packers can evade dynamic analysis by monitoring the movement of the mouse cursor [16]. The countermeasure may create a more realistic environment that simulates user interaction. Moreover, a general countermeasure to anti-emulator evasion is to make the dynamic analysis environment more transparent. Furthermore, advanced dynamic attacks can generate or self-modify code in runtime, bypassing current dynamic binary analysis [14]. Dynamic linking in programming is also an unsolved problem for binary analysis [45]. A potential solution is to load the executable in conjunction with all of the required dynamic libraries for analysis.

5   Conclusions

In this survey, different categories of binary analysis are reviewed. These categories include data-driven and software-analysis-based binary code analysis. We reviewed the works with many different application scenarios and aims such as exploitation, malicious behaviour and malware detection, code clone detection, vulnerability detection, etc. We introduced them based on the common methodology. We compared the different and similar techniques used in each category. We also concluded the limitations of existing works and possible future directions.

References

1. Aafer, Y., Tao, G., Huang, J., Zhang, X., Li, N.: Precise android API protection mapping derivation and reasoning. In: Proceedings of the 2018 ACM SIGSAC Conference on Computer and Communications Security. CCS 2018, pp. 1151–1164. Association for Computing Machinery, New York (2018). https://doi.org/10.1145/3243734.3243842
2. Afianian, A., Niksefat, S., Sadeghiyan, B., Baptiste, D.: Malware dynamic analysis evasion techniques: a survey. ACM Comput. Surv. **52**(6) (2019). https://doi.org/10.1145/3365001
3. Arp, D., Spreitzenbarth, M., Hubner, M., Gascon, H., Rieck, K.: Drebin: effective and explainable detection of android malware in your pocket. In: NDSS. The Internet Society (2014). https://dblp.uni-trier.de/db/conf/ndss/ndss2014.html#ArpSHGR14
4. Arzt, S., et al.: Flowdroid: precise context, flow, field, object-sensitive and lifecycle-aware taint analysis for android apps. In: Proceedings of the 35th ACM SIGPLAN Conference on Programming Language Design and Implementation. PLDI 2014, pp. 259–269. Association for Computing Machinery, New York (2014). https://doi.org/10.1145/2594291.2594299
5. Baldoni, R., Coppa, E., D'Elia, D.C., Demetrescu, C., Finocchi, I.: A survey of symbolic execution techniques. ACM Comput. Surv. (CSUR) **51**, 1–39 (2018)

6. Bardin, S., David, R., Marion, J.Y.: Backward-bounded DSE: targeting infeasibility questions on obfuscated codes. In: 2017 IEEE Symposium on Security and Privacy (SP), pp. 633–651 (2017)
7. Bhat, P., Dutta, K.: A survey on various threats and current state of security in android platform. ACM Comput. Surv. **52**(1) (2019). https://doi.org/10.1145/3301285
8. Biondo, A., Conti, M., Lain, D.: Back to the epilogue: evading control flow guard via unaligned targets. In: NDSS (2018)
9. Blazytko, T., Contag, M., Aschermann, C., Holz, T.: Syntia: synthesizing the semantics of obfuscated code. In: Proceedings of the 26th USENIX Conference on Security Symposium. SEC 2017, pp. 643–659. USENIX Association, USA (2017)
10. Chandramohan, M., Xue, Y., Xu, Z., Liu, Y., Cho, C.Y., Tan, H.B.K.: Bingo: cross-architecture cross-OS binary search. In: Proceedings of the 2016 24th ACM SIG-SOFT International Symposium on Foundations of Software Engineering, p. 678–689. FSE 2016, Association for Computing Machinery, New York (2016). https://doi.org/10.1145/2950290.2950350
11. Chapman, J.P.: Sad thug: structural anomaly detection for transmissions of high-value information using graphics. In: Proceedings of the 27th USENIX Conference on Security Symposium. SEC 2018, pp. 1147–1164. USENIX Association, USA (2018)
12. Chen, K., et al.: Finding unknown malice in 10 seconds: mass vetting for new threats at the google-play scale. In: USENIX Security, pp. 659–674 (2015)
13. Chen, X., et al.: Android HIV: a study of repackaging malware for evading machine-learning detection. IEEE Trans. Inf. Forensics Secur. **15**, 987–1001 (2020)
14. Chen, Y., et al.: Norax: enabling execute-only memory for cots binaries on aarch64. In: 2017 IEEE Symposium on Security and Privacy (SP), pp. 304–319 (2017)
15. Chen, Y., You, W., Lee, Y., Wang, K.C.X., Zou, W.: Mass discovery of android traffic imprints through instantiated partial execution. In: Proceedings of the 2017 ACM SIGSAC Conference on Computer and Communications Security (CCS 2017), pp. 815–828. Association for Computing Machinery, New York (2017). https://doi.org/10.1145/3133956.3134009
16. Cheng, B., et al.: Towards paving the way for large-scale windows malware analysis: generic binary unpacking with orders-of-magnitude performance boost. In: Proceedings of the 2018 ACM SIGSAC Conference on Computer and Communications Security (CCS 2018), pp. 395–411. Association for Computing Machinery, New York (2018). https://doi.org/10.1145/3243734.3243771
17. Chua, L.Z., Wang, Y., Baluta, T., Saxena, P., Liang, Z., Su, P.: One engine to serve 'em all - inferring taint rules without architectural semantics. In: NDSS (2019)
18. Chua, Z.L., Shen, S., Saxena, P., Liang, Z.: Neural nets can learn function type signatures from binaries. In: Proceedings of the 26th USENIX Conference on Security Symposium. SEC 2017, pp. 99–116. USENIX Association, USA (2017)
19. Ding, S.H.H., Fung, B.C.M., Charland, P.: ASM2VEC: boosting static representation robustness for binary clone search against code obfuscation and compiler optimization. In: 2019 IEEE Symposium on Security and Privacy (SP), pp. 472–489 (2019)
20. Duan, Y., et al.: Things you may not know about android (un)packers: a systematic study based on whole-system emulation. In: NDSS (2018)
21. Feng, Q., Zhou, R., Xu, C., Cheng, Y., Testa, B., Yin, H.: Scalable graph-based bug search for firmware images. In: ACM Conference on Computer and Communications Security (CCS 2016) (2016)

22. Feng, Y., Anand, S., Dillig, I., Aiken, A.: Apposcopy: semantics-based detection of android malware through static analysis. In: FSE, pp. 576–587 (2014)

23. Feng, Y., Bastani, O., Martins, R., Dillig, I., Anand, S.: Automated synthesis of semantic malware signatures using maximum satisfiability. In: NDSS. The Internet Society (2017). https://dblp.uni-trier.de/db/conf/ndss/ndss2017.html#FengBMDA17

24. Fratantonio, Y., Bianchi, A., Robertson, W.K., Kirda, E., Krügel, C., Vigna, G.: TriggerScope: towards detecting logic bombs in android applications. In: 2016 IEEE Symposium on Security and Privacy (SP), pp. 377–396 (2016)

25. Gasparis, I., Qian, Z., Song, C., Krishnamurthy, S.V.: Detecting android root exploits by learning from root providers. In: Proceedings of the 26th USENIX Conference on Security Symposium. SEC 2017, pp. 1129–1144. USENIX Association, USA (2017)

26. Ghaffarinia, M., Hamlen, K.W.: Binary control-flow trimming. In: Proceedings of the 2019 ACM SIGSAC Conference on Computer and Communications Security. CCS 2019, pp. 1009–1022. Association for Computing Machinery, New York (2019). https://doi.org/10.1145/3319535.3345665

27. Guo, W., Mu, D., Xing, X., Du, M., Song, D.: DeepVSA: facilitating value-set analysis with deep learning for postmortem program analysis. In: Proceedings of the 28th USENIX Conference on Security Symposium. SEC 2019, pp. 1787–1804. USENIX Association, USA (2019)

28. He, J., Ivanov, P., Tsankov, P., Raychev, V., Vechev, M.: Debin: predicting debug information in stripped binaries. In: Proceedings of the 2018 ACM SIGSAC Conference on Computer and Communications Security. CCS 2018, pp. 1667–1680. Association for Computing Machinery, New York (2018). https://doi.org/10.1145/3243734.3243866

29. Hu, Y., Zhang, Y., Li, J., Gu, D.: Binary code clone detection across architectures and compiling configurations. In: Proceedings of the 25th International Conference on Program Comprehension. ICPC 2017, pp. 88–98. IEEE Press (2017). https://doi.org/10.1109/ICPC.2017.22

30. Jagielski, M., Oprea, A., Biggio, B., Liu, C., Nita-Rotaru, C., Li, B.: Manipulating machine learning: poisoning attacks and countermeasures for regression learning. In: 2018 IEEE Symposium on Security and Privacy (SP), pp. 19–35 (2018)

31. Kirat, D., Vigna, G.: Malgene: automatic extraction of malware analysis evasion signature. In: Proceedings of the 22nd ACM SIGSAC Conference on Computer and Communications Security. CCS 2015, pp. 769–780. Association for Computing Machinery, New York (2015). https://doi.org/10.1145/2810103.2813642

32. Kirat, D., Vigna, G., Kruegel, C.: Barecloud: bare-metal analysis-based evasive malware detection. In: 23rd USENIX Security Symposium (USENIX Security 2014), pp. 287–301. USENIX Association, San Diego, August 2014. https://www.usenix.org/conference/usenixsecurity14/technical-sessions/presentation/kirat

33. Korczynski, D., Yin, H.: Capturing malware propagations with code injections and code-reuse attacks. In: In Proceedings of the 2017 ACM SIGSAC Conference on Computer and Communications Security (CCS 2017), pp. 1691–1708. Association for Computing Machinery, New York (2017). https://doi.org/10.1145/3133956.3134099

34. Lee, Y., et al.: Understanding IoS-based crowdturfing through hidden UI analysis. In: 28th USENIX Security Symposium (USENIX Security 2019), pp. 765–781. USENIX Association, Santa Clara, August 2019. https://www.usenix.org/conference/usenixsecurity19/presentation/lee

35. Li, J., Lin, Z., Caballero, J., Zhang, Y., Gu, D.: K-hunt: pinpointing insecure cryptographic keys from execution traces. In: Proceedings of the 2018 ACM SIGSAC Conference on Computer and Communications Security (CCS 2018), pp. 412–425. Association for Computing Machinery, New York (2018). https://doi.org/10.1145/3243734.3243783

36. Li, L., et al.: ICCTA: detecting inter-component privacy leaks in android apps. In: 2015 IEEE/ACM 37th IEEE International Conference on Software Engineering, vol. 1, pp. 280–291 (2015)

37. Luo, L., Ming, J., Wu, D., Liu, P., Zhu, S.: Semantics-based obfuscation-resilient binary code similarity comparison with applications to software plagiarism detection. In: Proceedings of the 22nd ACM SIGSOFT International Symposium on Foundations of Software Engineering. FSE 2014, pp. 389–400. Association for Computing Machinery, New York (2014). https://doi.org/10.1145/2635868.2635900

38. Maiorca, D., Biggio, B., Giacinto, G.: Towards adversarial malware detection: lessons learned from pdf-based attacks. ACM Comput. Surv. **52**(4) (2019). https://doi.org/10.1145/3332184

39. Mendoza, A., Gu, G.: Mobile application web API reconnaissance: web-to-mobile inconsistencies & vulnerabilities. In: 2018 IEEE Symposium on Security and Privacy (S&P 2018) (2018). https://doi.org/10.1109/SP.2018.00039

40. Ming, J., Xu, D., Jiang, Y., Wu, D.: Binsim: trace-based semantic binary diffing via system call sliced segment equivalence checking. In: Proceedings of the 26th USENIX Conference on Security Symposium (SEC 2017), pp. 253–270. USENIX Association, USA (2017)

41. Onwuzurike, L., Mariconti, E., Andriotis, P., Cristofaro, E.D., Ross, G., Stringhini, G.: Mamadroid: detecting android malware by building Markov chains of behavioral models (extended version). ACM Trans. Priv. Secur. **22**(2) (2019). https://doi.org/10.1145/3313391

42. Pan, X., et al.: Flowcog: context-aware semantics extraction and analysis of information flow leaks in android apps. In: 27th USENIX Security Symposium (USENIX Security 2018), pp. 1669–1685. USENIX Association, Baltimore, August 2018. https://www.usenix.org/conference/usenixsecurity18/presentation/pan

43. Pan, X., Wang, X., Duan, Y., Wang, X., Yin, H.: Dark hazard: learning-based, large-scale discovery of hidden sensitive operations in android apps. In: 24th Annual Network and Distributed System Security Symposium, NDSS 2017, San Diego, California, USA, 26 February–1 March 2017. The Internet Society (2017). https://www.ndss-symposium.org/ndss2017/ndss-2017-programme/dark-hazard-learning-based-large-scale-discovery-hidden-sensitive-operations-android-apps/

44. Qian, C., Hu, H., Alharthi, M., Chung, P.H., Kim, T., Lee, W.: Razor: a framework for post-deployment software debloating. In: Proceedings of the 28th USENIX Conference on Security Symposium (SEC 2019), pp. 1733–1750. USENIX Association (2019)

45. Schwartz, E.J., Cohen, C.F., Duggan, M., Gennari, J., Havrilla, J.S., Hines, C.: Using logic programming to recover C++ classes and methods from compiled executables. In: Proceedings of the 2018 ACM SIGSAC Conference on Computer and Communications Security (CCS 2018), pp. 426–441. Association for Computing Machinery, New York (2018). https://doi.org/10.1145/3243734.3243793

46. Shoshitaishvili, Y., et al.: Sok: (state of) the art of war: offensive techniques in binary analysis. In: 2016 IEEE Symposium on Security and Privacy (SP), pp. 138–157 (2016)

47. Wang, R., et al.: Ramblr: making reassembly great again, January 2017. https://doi.org/10.14722/ndss.2017.23225

48. Wang, S., Wang, P., Wu, D.: Reassembleable disassembling. In: Proceedings of the 24th USENIX Conference on Security Symposium. SEC 2015, pp. 627–642. USENIX Association, USA (2015)

49. Wang, X., Sun, Y., Nanda, S., Wang, X.: Looking from the mirror: evaluating IoT device security through mobile companion apps. In: 28th USENIX Security Symposium (USENIX Security 2019), pp. 1151–1167. USENIX Association, Santa Clara, August 2019. https://www.usenix.org/conference/usenixsecurity19/presentation/wang-xueqiang

50. Wenzl, M., Merzdovnik, G., Ullrich, J., Weippl, E.: From hack to elaborate technique - a survey on binary rewriting. ACM Comput. Surv. **52**(3) (2019). https://doi.org/10.1145/3316415

51. Wong, M.Y., Lie, D.: Intellidroid: a targeted input generator for the dynamic analysis of android malware. In: NDSS (2016)

52. Wong, M.Y., Lie, D.: Tackling runtime-based obfuscation in android with tiro. In: Proceedings of the 27th USENIX Conference on Security Symposium (SEC 2018), pp. 1247–1262. USENIX Association, USA (2018)

53. Wu, W., Chen, Y., Xing, X., Zou, W.: Kepler: facilitating control-flow hijacking primitive evaluation for Linux kernel vulnerabilities. In: Proceedings of the 28th USENIX Conference on Security Symposium (SEC 2019), pp. 1187–1204. USENIX Association, USA (2019)

54. Xu, D., Ming, J., Fu, Y., Wu, D.: VMHunt: a verifiable approach to partially-virtualized binary code simplification. In: Proceedings of the 2018 ACM SIGSAC Conference on Computer and Communications Security (CCS 2018), pp. 442–458. Association for Computing Machinery, New York (2018). https://doi.org/10.1145/3243734.3243827

55. Xu, X., Liu, C., Feng, Q., Yin, H., Song, L., Song, D.X.: Neural network-based graph embedding for cross-platform binary code similarity detection. In: Proceedings of the 2017 ACM SIGSAC Conference on Computer and Communications Security (2017)

56. Xue, L., Zhou, Y., Chen, T., Luo, X., Gu, G.: Malton: towards on-device non-invasive mobile malware analysis for ART. In: 26th USENIX Security Symposium (USENIX Security 2017), pp. 289–306. USENIX Association, Vancouver, August 2017. https://www.usenix.org/conference/usenixsecurity17/technical-sessions/presentation/xue

57. Zhang, X., et al.: An empirical study of web resource manipulation in real-world mobile applications. In: 27th USENIX Security Symposium (USENIX Security 2018), pp. 1183–1198. USENIX Association, Baltimore, August 2018. https://www.usenix.org/conference/usenixsecurity18/presentation/zhang-xiaohan

LTNoT: Realizing the Trade-Offs Between Latency and Throughput in NVMe over TCP

Wenhao Gu, Xuchao Xie$^{(\boxtimes)}$, and Dezun Dong$^{(\boxtimes)}$

College of Computer, National University of Defense Technology,
Changsha 410073, China
{guwenhao16,xiexuchao,dong}@nudt.edu.cn

Abstract. NVMe over Fabrics (NVMeoF) is a new emerging storage disaggregation protocol specially designed for datacenters with high-performance NVMe SSDs and interconnection networks. However, existing NVMeoF implementations cannot meet the differentiated I/O demands of the diverse applications running in datacenters. This is because the applications usually show significantly different I/O characteristics and requirements, e.g., some applications (L-apps) are sensitive to latency while other applications (T-apps) show high throughput demands to storage systems. When L-apps and T-apps access remote NVMe SSDs via a same NVMeoF storage network, the I/O requests issued from these applications are equally treated and handled following the same I/O path in state-of-the-art NVMeoF implementations. This will finally incur severe I/O interference between L-apps and T-apps.

In this paper, we propose LTNoT, an end-to-end packet processing scheme with dedicated I/O pipelines for L-apps and T-apps in NVMe over TCP (NoT) implementation. Specifically, LTNoT separates T-apps and L-apps resources in each NVMeoF queue pair to achieve inter-queue I/O isolation, transfers capsule and data in batch along with the T-app pipeline to achieve interrupt-coalescing, and introduces immediate-delivery and workqueue-priority to optimize L-app request process. We implemented LTNoT in Linux Kernel and evaluated it using real-world benchmarks and applications. Our experimental results demonstrate that LTNoT can achieve 48.13% and 53.38% lower L-apps latency than i10 and NoT respectively, increase bandwidth by up to 33.31% than NoT on average, thus LTNoT can effectively alleviate the I/O interference issue in NVMe over TCP without introducing any negative performance impacts on either L-apps or T-apps.

Keywords: NVMe over fabrics · Inter-queue I/O Isolation · LTNoT

1 Introduction

For decades, all the hardware components needed by a datacenter server are physically packaged to run user programs [1]. With the trend towards cloud computing and storage, the ever-increasing number of deployed servers incurs

© Springer Nature Switzerland AG 2023
W. Meng et al. (Eds.): ICA3PP 2022, LNCS 13777, pp. 412–432, 2023.
https://doi.org/10.1007/978-3-031-22677-9_22

serious issues in datacenters [3,13], such as inefficient resource utilization, poor hardware elasticity, coarse failure domain, and bad heterogeneity support, etc. [4,36]. These issues can be potentially alleviated by the new emerging resource disaggregation architecture that separates hardware resources of servers into network-attached components, manages all the components remotely, and allocates resources for applications elastically. Currently widely used storage disaggregation technology separates computing and storage into different nodes [13], and connects them through a storage network to achieve independent expansion and on-demand allocation of storage resources.

As flash-based SSDs perform superior performance and are widely used in large-scale storage systems, the software overhead of traditional SCSI storage interface protocol prevents SSDs from exposing their high performance to upper-layer applications [24]. The novel NVMe protocol leverages the high throughput PCIe interconnect to utilize the internal parallelism of SSDs to the maximum. NVMe allocates a large number of deep paired submission and completion queues based on host memory. These paired parallel queues are the interface between the NVMe driver and the NVMe controller, through which they cooperate to manage queues and complete I/O operations. NVMe enables users to take full advantage of the performance potential of concurrent high-speed storage devices by efficiently supporting more processor cores, channels per device, I/O threads, and I/O queues.

In terms of disaggregated storage systems, the software overhead of iSCSI prevents NVMe SSDs from exposing their high performance to remote compute nodes. Just as extending SCSI to iSCSI on top of Ethernet protocol, NVMe over Fabrics (NVMeoF) is the latest extension of NVMe for remote storage access which allows remote access to NVMe controllers through high-speed RDMA, FC [7,18], and TCP networks [11]. NVMeoF eliminates the unnecessary protocol conversion initially required in the I/O path from host to remote NVMe SSDs and provides ultra-low remote access latency [32,37], thus realizing high-performance storage area networks. NVMeoF has been replacing iSCSI as the dominant remote storage interface protocol of disaggregated storage systems.

Although providing high-performance network transmission, deploying the RDMA-enabled or FC-enabled network infrastructure of the datacenter on a large scale is not feasible, since which will bring unacceptable expenses [9,10]. Given this problem, Intel, Cisco and other companies have jointly developed the NVMe-over-TCP (NoT) protocol standard, which has been approved as a new NVMeoF transport layer standard [22]. NoT standard allows using the existing common network infrastructure in datacenter to realize the NVMeoF storage network, while inheriting the defects of the TCP/IP stack. With the throughput supported by network and storage hardware technology reaching the order of millions of magnitude, its performance bottleneck has shifted to the processing efficiency for NVMeoF command message and data message in the software layer.

However, existing NVMeoF implementations cannot meet the differentiated I/O demands of the diverse applications running in datacenters. This is because the applications usually show significantly different I/O characteristics and requirements, e.g., some applications (L-apps) are sensitive to latency such as web search and image services, while other applications (T-apps) show high throughput demands to storage systems. When L-apps and T-apps access remote NVMe SSDs via a same NVMeoF storage network, the I/O requests issued from these applications are equally treated and handled following the same I/O path in state-of-the-art NVMeoF implementations [20,35,38]. This will finally incur severe I/O interference between L-apps and T-apps. Typically, i10 proposed by Hwang et al. which is NVMeoF interrupt-coalescing method optimized for NoT can not meet the I/O requirements of L-apps, and even cause inflated latency problem. NoT is even worse that it falls short of the system throughput demand. Therefore, how effectively avoid the I/O interference between multiple applications running simultaneously on the CPU is a dominant challenge yet.

In this paper, we propose LTNoT, an end-to-end packet processing scheme with dedicated I/O pipelines for L-apps and T-apps in NVMe over TCP implementation, to alleviate the I/O interference between multiple simultaneous applications in the CPU. Overall, our key insight are as follows:

- Inter-Queue I/O Isolation. We propose to set two dedicated I/O critical paths for each core by separating latency-sensitive and throughput-oriented resources between LTNoT queue pairs to achieve inter-queue I/O isolation.
- Specific Pipeline. LTNoT always transfers NoT PDUs in different policy along with specific L-apps or T-apps I/O pipeline to achieve isolated interrupt-coalescing or immediate-delivery.
- Workqueue Priority. LTNoT further introduces differentiated weight of iowork thread in L-apps and T-apps NoT queue to achieve preliminary priority scheduling.

We implemented LTNoT in Linux Kernel and evaluated it by FIO benchmarks and applications [2,29]. Our experimental results demonstrate that LTNoT can achieve 48.13% and 53.38% lower L-apps latency than i10 and NoT respectively, increase bandwidth by up to 33.31% than NoT on average, thus LTNoT can effectively alleviate the I/O interference issue in NVMe over TCP without introducing any negative performance impacts on either L-apps or T-apps.

The rest of the article is organized as follows. Section 2 presents the background and motivation. Section 3 and 4 provide an overview of LTNoT and describe the detailed design, respectively. We evaluate the performance of LTNoT in Sect. 5 and discuss the related work in Sect. 6. Finally, we make a summary of this paper.

2   Background and Motivation

2.1   NVMe-over-TCP

Benefiting from the continuous upgrading of network card devices, the proportion of network delay in remote storage access is reduced. The processing overhead of I/O has gradually become the main reason for the performance degradation when accessing NVMe SSD through NVMeoF in storage disaggregation

[17, 21, 39]. The overhead is not only the necessary time for I/O processing on the storage block device, but also a series of performance interference items such as context switching, redundant operation and data replication. The latter is the mitigable performance interference of the NVMeoF layer. NoT is a recent transport extension of NVMeoF released in 2019 [28, 34], which provides regulations of how the queue pairs of host and remote NVMe controller are mapped to TCP connections and CPU cores. NoT specifically defines how command capsule, response capsule, and data are encapsulated within TCP PDUs. Despite using TCP transmission will lose performance to a certain extent, it can compensate for the potential performance loss using offloading, smart NIC, or FPGA.

NoT host initially needs to establish a connection to remote NVMe controller in target to enable message transfers. The process of connection is to create multiple one-to-one mappings between host-based queues and controller-based queues. Each host-based queue pair and its associated controller-based queue pair will be mapped to a specific TCP connection and an individual CPU core. And each CPU core will only handle the transfers between its associated queue pairs. As long as the connection remains, NoT host and target drivers encapsulate the NVMe commands, response, and data into fabric-neutral capsules which are further encapsulated within TCP PDUs and transferred on top of standard TCP/IP protocol stack [30]. Generally, there are five kinds of PDUs used in NoT implementation, i.e., CMD (Command) PDU, R2T (Ready to Transfer) PDU, H2CData (Host to Controller Data) PDU, C2HData (Controller to Host Data) PDU, and Resp (Response) PDU.

2.2 NoT-Inherent CPU Overhead

NoT has promoted NVMeoF deployment scenarios to the most common Ethernet infrastructures in datacenters [31]. Meanwhile, the CPU overhead for I/O processing in NoT has become one of the main bottlenecks to keep NoT performance growing continuously along with the high-speed network technologies. Specifically, in the standard NoT implementation, when an I/O request from blk-mq attempts to access a remote NVMe device, NoT will take over the I/O request and encapsulate it into a CMD PDU, after which NoT ring the doorbell immediately to signal host driver to transfer the PDU. In the following I/O critical path, both NoT host and target will incur several interrupt requests to inform CPU to handle received PDUs. The number and type of PDUs generated by a single I/O request vary depending on the type and size of the I/O request. Different from NoT, NVMe-over-RDMA eliminates CPU-involved data transfers and only needs CPU to handle command and response capsules. Both NoT host and target will endure severe context-switching overhead introduced by diverse PDUs under I/O intensive workloads [5].

Fortunately, it has been proved that delaying ringing doorbells to accumulate multiple requests in each NoT queue and process the requests in batch can significantly reduce CPU overheads and amortize the software overhead of TCP/IP stack, which is exactly what i10 primarily does [19, 23]. Compared with standard

NoT implementation, i10 delays the time of ringing doorbell in the I/O critical path by temporarily gathering multiple PDUs transferred by the same NoT queue into a jumbo packet. Once the threshold is satisfied, i10 just wakes up the send thread of the NoT queue and sends all these packaged PDUs to the remote NoT queue as only one TCP transmission message. In this way, all the PDUs transferred in a same batch will incur only one interrupt request to CPU and the context switch overhead of NoT can be reduced. However, accumulating PDUs from the requests with differentiated I/O demands will be difficult to abstract the I/O request-level interference between L-apps and T-apps in NoT.

2.3   Blk-Switch

blk-switch is a newly proposed Linux blk-mq that applications use to access data on local or remote servers [20], which is mainly modified in the block layer of the Linux kernel. Its main contribution is to rebuild the block layer queues conceptually similar to a network switch. In the original storage stack, each core is bound with a blk-mq and a unique NVMeOF or NVMe local queue [5]. However, blk-switch decouples it and introduces a block layer architecture of multi ingress blk-mqs and multi egress NVMe queues mapping for the Linux storage stack. For a certain blk-mq, the number of multi egress queues is the number of NUMA nodes, since the queue mapping is only established in its corresponding core and the same numbered cores of adjacent NUMA nodes. Based on this, blk-switch applies the classical technologies in computer network literature (request scheduling, load balance and application scheduling) to the Linux storage stack. This multi exit queue design enables blk-switch to direct the requests submitted in the ingress queue on the core to the egress queue on any core according to the application performance objectives (T-app and L-app) and CPU load.

blk-switch counts the outstanding requests size on each egress queue at the block layer, thus observing the relatively idle and non-idle cores. Accordingly, it executes request or application scheduling on the core to achieve latency improvement and load balancing. The two scheduling methods can effectively handle the transient load and persistent load unbalance on a single core respectively. Thus blk-switch can maintain low latency and high throughput when multiple L-apps and T-apps compete for host resources at the computing, storage and network layer. However, compared with such loadable modules as NVMeOF, modifications at the block level require recompiling the entire kernel and will introduce extra processing overhead for the whole system. Moreover, in practical implementation, blk-switch divides the original NVMeOF or NVMe local queues into two parts: half of them are used to process L-app requests, and others to process T-app requests. blk-switch adopts the i10 queue for batch as the NVMeOF queue, which is not suitable to further improve the latency performance of the L-app. It leverages the redundant queues and resources in exchange for the latency performance of the L-app, rather than optimizing the per-core Linux queue.

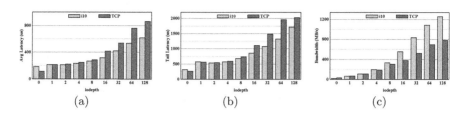

Fig. 1. L-app latency and Per-core Bandwidth performance with varying workloads.

2.4 Motivation

As shown in Fig. 1, we simulate the workload with different intensity by varying the iodepth of the T-app (16 KB read fio thread). Apparently, the L-app (4 KB read fio thread with iodepth=1) latency performance of i10 and NoT gets worse with the increase of workload intensity and cannot meet the user's demand for low latency. While NoT even shows bandwidth performance deteriorations compared with i10. Therefore, we need to reconsider the request sending strategy of NoT implementation. The exploration of request processing flow and details of NVMe-over-TCP and i10 help us design the latency-sensitive requests (L-reqs) and throughput-oriented requests (T-reqs) separation system. We highlight four key observations that guide LTNoT design decisions.

- Different types of requests require isolated processing mechanisms. We propose to separate L-req and T-req resources in each LTNoT core to achieve isolated L-app and T-app queue pairs, thus realizing the exclusive processing pipeline to carry custom-designed optimization.
- The latency overhead of L-req can be appropriately mitigated by instantaneous forwarding. Once the NVMeoF controller receives the L-req, the request processing queue will immediately submit it to the socket sending thread, thus mitigating the extra overhead of processing delays.
- The throughput of T-req can be effectively improved through batch processing. Aggregating multiple T-reqs into a jumbo packet transmission can amortize the overheads from network processing and TCP/IP software stack, thus the throughput performance of NoT can be improved.
- The priority of different pipelines should be considered. Giving the L-app queue a higher priority can further improve the latency performance of L-req, thus further alleviating the I/O interference between multiple applications.

3 System Overview

In this section, we provide an overview of the high-level design and insightful ideas of LTNoT. As shown in Fig. 2, LTNoT generally manages the data between the block layer and the TCP stack layer, transparent to any file system and application. As the end-to-end path between the host application and the target

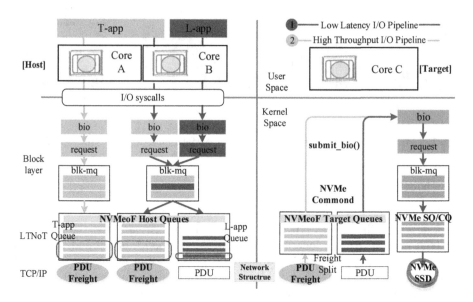

Fig. 2. System overview of LTNoT

NVMe storage device, LTNoT hardly affects the operation of the application, just modifies the processing pipeline throughout the Linux kernel.

Firstly, applications with different requirements (T-app or L-app) are automatically divided onto specific cores by the operating system. And read/write request generated by applications is interpreted into bio and transferred to the block layer through an I/O system call. The block layer performs operations such as bio merging and converts the bio into the request to add it into the blk-mq per-core.

The request of blk-mq is through calling queue_rq() function transmitted to the underlying NVMeoF layer, where L-reqs and T-reqs enter the corresponding (CPU, target, type) NVMeoF sending queues – L-app queue and T-app queue respectively. The two types of requests are processed and transmitted in an isolated and custom-designed way in the individual pipeline, and finally sent to the paired NVMeoF receiving queue at the target side through the TCP network. And this reconstructed NVMeoF queue is named as LTNoT queue, which will be discussed in detail in Sect. 4. After that, the LTNoT queue at the target receives data from the TCP receiving buffer according to the granularity of the request, and then parses the request, regenerates the bio, and uploads it to the block layer.

At this time, the request temporarily leaves the L-app and T-app pipeline. The block layer performs the same steps as accessing the local NVMe storage device. Then NVMeoF layer obtains the request result returned from the NVMe SSD, reentering the L-app or T-app pipeline. After that, the LTNoT queue pair sends the result back to the host side in the same way as aforementioned, thus accomplishing one I/O processing.

We design specific processing strategies for the T-app and L-app pipelines depicted in Sect. 4.2 to meet different I/O demands. In addition, we also set different priority weights for the two types of LTNoT queues, to speed the I/O path of L-reqs to achieve further latency optimization. Simultaneously, we describe how we modify the data structure to exhibit the priority and I/O demand in the whole kernel. We describe this ingenious technique in Sect. 4.3.

4 LTNoT Design

LTNoT mainly designs three modules - inter-Queue I/O isolation, T-app and L-app pipelines and LTprio. In this section, we will describe their implementation in detail.

4.1 Inter-Queue I/O Isolation

The implementation of LTNoT L-app and T-app isolated queue pairs mainly depends on three holistic mechanisms: first, each CPU allocates two dedicated queues corresponding to latency-sensitive and throughput-oriented applications and establishes one-to-one queue matching between host and target, which enables logically isolation; second, T-app and L-app queues apply for two sets of dedicated resources respectively, particularly the two socket resources to establish an individual TCP connection, which enables physically isolation; third, T-app and L-app queues are initialized as two work individuals and added to the CPU workqueue to ensure that the I/O processing and communication in queue pair can run in parallel. The application-type-aware inter-queue I/O isolation avoids the trouble caused by high contention and mutex. And it can exploit the benefits of designing dedicated strategies for T-reqs and L-reqs, which sheddings the performance limitation of the unified processing pipeline. Each queue pair is responsible for the I/O of one type of application and do not affect each other, providing a great dependency for batch or immediate-delivery. Next, we will introduce some intriguing implementation details.

LTNoT interface with blk-mq and NVMe queue. Whether accessing storage on remote or local, it will call queue_rq function to transmit the request on the host side. The difference is that one enters the NVMeoF layer and the other enters the NVMe device layer. LTNoT queue uses this NVMeoF interface to connect to blk-mq, which ensures that we can effectively obtain and analyze the I/O requests from the upper block layer originating from different applications. Here LTNoT enables a judgment function to determine the demand type of request, and wakes up L-app or T-app workqueue accordingly. On the contrary, after LTNoT receives the data or command returned by the opposite end of the queue, the final processing results can be fed back to the upper layer as before. On the target side, after receiving and parsing the request, LTNoT queue transfers the processed request to the block layer to regenerate the bio. After the NVMe SSD returns the I/O processing results to the NVMe completion queue (CQ), it also calls the queue_rq interface to transfer the request from the NVMe device

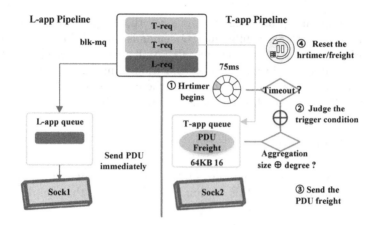

Fig. 3. T-app and L-app Pipelines

layer to the NVMeoF layer. Here LTNoT performs the same operation as the host side, thus the processing results of different types of requests can reenter the corresponding L-app or T-app pipeline and finally be transmitted to the host.

Communication over individual sock. LTNoT queues execute data interaction by creating sockets and maintaining long-term TCP connections between queue pairs. Due to the separation of T-app and L-app requests, the originally shared single sock is no longer applicable to the modified LTNoT pipelines with significant discrepancy. Therefore, we create a socket for L-app and T-app pipeline respectively, and manually change the socket settings according to the request demand, such as buffer size and function selection introduced in Sect. 4.2.

We mainly consider two schemes of L-app and T-app separation processing (1) intra-queue I/O isolation and (2) inter-queue I/O isolation. The former scheme can simplify the I/O classification and processing operations since requests and resource classification can be performed directly in one NVMeoF queue. Nevertheless, due to the chaotic and complicated data transmission, it is difficult to run the two dedicated pipelines in parallel and easy to cause competition trap or even result in performance deteriorations. On the contrary, the latter strategy can solve the problems and achieve good performance improvement through parallelism and targeted design. Notably, we adopt the method of inter-queue I/O isolation, and implement it on both the host side and the target side.

4.2   T-app and L-app Pipelines

As shown in Fig. 3, after the T-req wakes up the T-app queue, it firstly is temporarily packaged and encapsulated in PDU freight, which is a newly established container for accumulating PDUs. The queue then enters the quiesce state, waiting to be waked up again. In this process, the T-app queue ceaselessly aggregates the corresponding requests until triggering the sending condition, and then sends freight to the other end of queue pairs through the T-app queue sock. LTNoT merges multiple NVMeoF requests in PDU freight to realize interrupt-coalescing. A single interrupt can process more requests and send a jumbo packet, so as to improve throughput by reducing context switching and using TCP hardware acceleration such as TSO and GRO.

The trigger condition is that freight reaches the preset PDU-group size or the number of PDUs, or a high-precision timer with the goal of forcibly sending exceeds the timeout threshold. Whenever the freight receives the first request, the corresponding high-precision timer will be waked up and in turn, whenever the freight is sent, the timer thread will be canceled. The PDU-group size is set to 64KB which is the partition upper limit of TSO technology, and the time-out threshold is 75ms (a high-quality setting obtained from experiments). The number of PDUs is set loosely as 16 to avoid aggregating too many requests. Due to the aggregation of T-requests, the buffer originally dynamically adjusted by Linux Kernel is not suitable for sending the jumbo packet. Therefore, we manually set the TCP static buffer with an upper limit of 8MB through set-sockopt(). Moreover, since the freight is typically 64KB PDU group in batch, we use kernel_sendmsg() function rather than the kernel_sendpage(), because the performance of the former is much better than that of the latter for sending long flow data. kernel_sendmsg() can copy the kernel I/O vector to the socket buffer as a function parameter, which significantly improves the throughput in the presence of freight.

On the receiving side of the queue pair, it receives the header first from the sock receiving buffer, then parses the header information, analyzes the length of subsequent data, and finally receives data according to the parsed length. The T-app queue repeats the process of receiving requests, which not only realizes the unpacking of freight but also parses each I/O request. Subsequently, either submitting the regenerated bio or returning the results to the upper application, the request gets off the T-app pipeline.

After entering the L-app queue, L-req is immediately forwarded to the other end of queue pairs through the L-app queue sock without aggregation, so as to improve latency performance. After the request is sent through the sending thread, the L-app queue enters a quiesce state, waiting for the return of the request result or a new I/O request to be waked up again. The receiving thread of the queue pair works like T-app. Given that one L-req is forwarded instantly at a time, the setting of sock buffer dynamically adjusted by Linux Kernel is suitable. Moreover, we choose kernel_sendpage() instead of kernel_sendmsg() as the sending function in the L-app pipeline, since it behaves better than the latter for sending short flow data. kernel_sendpage() avoids data replication on the transmission side when sending data per page.

4.3   LTprio and Priority

Under the trade-off between acceptable latency and bandwidth, giving a higher priority for L-app queue work benefits the whole system since the L-req can be sent for processing faster. Since we have achieved inter-queue I/O isolation of

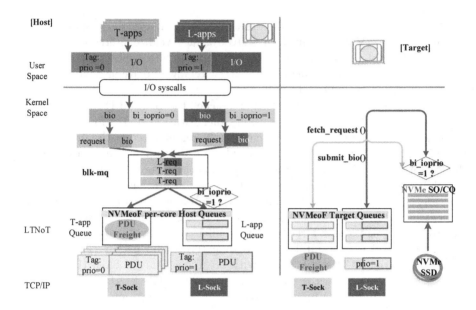

Fig. 4. System overview of LTNoT

the host side and the target, interestingly, we can actively change the priority weights of the L-app/T-app pipeline when allocating work-queue. In order to avoid starvation due to LTNoT priority, the NVMeoF driver will force sending to exhaust the requests if the aforementioned PDU group size falls short of the threshold and the high-precision timer timeout for the T-app pipeline.

In the Linux kernel, it is vastly challenging to infer the workload requirements of user layer applications and predict the priority of I/O requests. On the contrary, we can extend the LTNoT characteristic in the kernel by observing the priority parameter 'ioprio'. Figure 4 illustrates how the LTNoT system refers to the workload attribute in the whole storage stack. The user API of FIO has a 'prioclass' parameter, through which it can pass the request with the tag 'prio' to the kernel space. When the I/O request generates a bio, the block layer will modify the tag 'io_ioprio' to inherit the request 'prio'. After that, the blk-mq request is transferred to the NVMeoF controller by calling the queue_rq interface with the NVMeoF layer, where LTNoT modifies the request structure by adding a flag bit to mark the type of request (T-req or L-req). For this purpose, the LTNoT system provides a named LT_set_iotype thread, which allows the LTNoT queue to configure and dynamically change the properties of each request. At this time, the flag is set to latency-sensitive or throughput-oriented by judging the ioprio, so as to realize the design of request type/urgency, adapting to the workload attribute of the application. In addition, it is necessary for the NVMeoF driver and underlying layer to inherit this workload attribute. Therefore, we maintain the flag for the NVMeoF host and target queue to penetrate the whole storage stack. Therefore, LTNoT can capture attributes for each application in the kernel and populate the NVMeoF request with the flag 'prio'. If the incoming I/O request has an unspecified attribute, it is assigned as a throughput-oriented request by default.

5   Performance Evaluation

In this section, we evaluate the detailed behavior of LTNoT using realistic workloads.

5.1   System Implementation

We implement LTNoT as a loadable kernel module of Linux 4.20.0 by adding 1,221 lines of C codes based on the standard NoT implementation. Specifically, LTNoT extends the NVMeoF request structure (a tag for marking the request type) and defines two types of data structures, i.e., freight and hrtimer. We add several flags for recording the parameters used by freight and hrtimer. The hrtimer thread works with the help of the existing high-precision timer function in the Linux source code. By judging the flag 'prio' in the request, NVMeoF realizes the category determination of T-req and L-req, so as to enter the corresponding processing pipeline. Through flags 'nr_req' and 'fgt_timer' recorded in the T-app queue, LTNoT determines a freight should be transferred in time or delayed for more aggregation. The detailed implementation of LTNoT can be reached at https://github.com/jackey-gu/LTNoT.

5.2   Experimental Setup

We build an LTNoT prototype using two 2-socket servers that are equipped with Mellanox CX-5 EX. The two network interface cards (NICs) are directly connected through an optical fiber link and only enabled the Ethernet port in the experiments. Besides, we do not make any special changes to the NICs to demonstrate that LTNoT is general to common Ethernet infrastructures. NVMe SSD and RAM are configured with large redundancy. FIO and RocksDB are used as benchmarks to evaluate the performance of LTNoT. To comprehensively evaluate the behavior of LTNoT, we compared LTNoT with standard NoT implementation in the Linux kernel and the recently proposed i10 implementation. The detailed hardware and software configurations are described in Table 1. Unless otherwise specified, our test sets up a T-app thread and an L-app thread (a 4 KB read FIO thread with 'prio' = 1) on the NVMe SSD device.

5.3   Evaluation Results

We use the L-app latency and the system total bandwidth as the metrics to measure the effectiveness of LTNoT in alleviating I/O interference between multiple applications, since these are exactly the performance demands for different types of services.

Table 1. Hardware and software configurations

	Host	Target
CPU	2-socket Intel (R) Xeon (R) CPU E5-2692v2@2.20 GHz 12cores per socket, NUMA enabled (2 nodes)	2-socket Intel (R) Xeon (R) CPU E5-2660v2@2.60 GHz 10cores per socket, NUMA enabled (2 nodes)
MEM	125 GB of DRAM	64 GB of DRAM
NIC	Mellanox CX-5 EX (100 G) TSO/GRO = on, LRO = off, DIM disabled Jumbo frame enabled (4096 B)	
SSD	N/A	1.6 TB DERA D5457 NVMe SSD
IRQ	N/A	irqbalance enabled
OS	Centos 7 (kernel 4.20.0)	
FIO	version = fio–3.7, rw = randrw, size = 15 G cpus_allowed = 0–23, runtime = 300, engine = libaio gtod_reduce = off, Direct I/O = on CPU affinity enabled, group_reporting = 1	

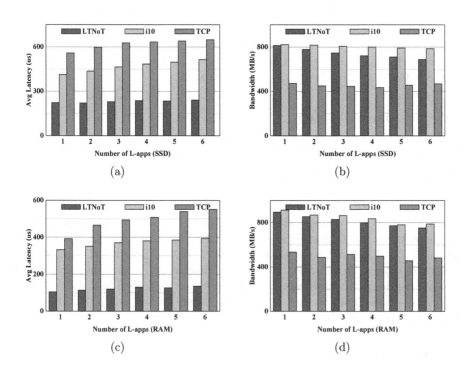

Fig. 5. Latency and bandwidth comparison with varying number of L-apps.

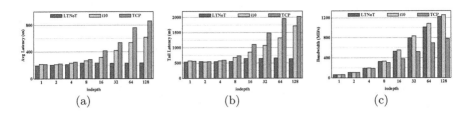

Fig. 6. Latency and bandwidth comparison with varying iodepth.

Performance with Varying Number of Threads. Figure 5 depicts the average latency and bandwidth performance with different number of L-apps in a single core. The experiments that the FIO threads access remote RAM and NVMe SSD of target show similar results, which proves the scalability of LTNoT on SSDs with better performance in the future. Figure 5(a) and (b) shows that in the SSD device test, LTNoT experiences a 50.74% and 62.68% reduction in latency performance on average compared with i10 and NoT. And it improves the NVMeoF bandwidth by 64.03% in comparison to NoT. With the increase of the number of L-apps, the bandwidth of LTNoT, NoT and i10 will decrease. This is because as the proportion of requests with 4KB block size increases, the IOPS increases but the overall bandwidth decreases. However, since LTNoT will preferentially process the L-app requests, the bandwidth deterioration is more than that of i10.

LTNoT achieves similar performance trends when evaluated with RAM, as shown in Fig. 5(c) and (d). However, the overall performance improvements of RAM are higher than that of NVMe SSD. This is because the I/O processing overhead of SSD devices is worse than that of RAM devices, which limits the demonstration of the performance benefits of LTNoT at the software level. Nevertheless, LTNoT has a 67.22% and 75.28% latency improvement over i10 and NoT, respectively, and a 64.97% throughput improvement compared with NoT.

Performance with Varying Iodepth. Figure 6 plots the average and tail I/O latencies and bandwidth with different T-app iodepth configurations. Compared with i10, both the average latency and tail latency of LTNoT can be significantly reduced by 26.76% on average and by up to 62.54% when the iodepth is set to 128. Besides, the latency reduction shows an obvious upward trend as the iodepth increases. When iodepth is low, LTNoT has slightly lower I/O latency than i10 and NoT. This is because the number of I/O requests from T-app is relatively sparse, and the delay mainly comes from the inherent overhead of CPU request processing and network data transmission. L-req is less disturbed by T-req, thus the income of LTNoT is weakened. On the contrary, when we use the I/O workloads with much higher iodepths, L-req can exploit the performance benefits of inter-queue I/O isolation well by amortizing the unnecessary overhead from waiting for T-reqs and request aggregation.

As the L-app and T-app resources are isolated and the requests with different attributes are handled differently, LTNoT can always achieve better performance

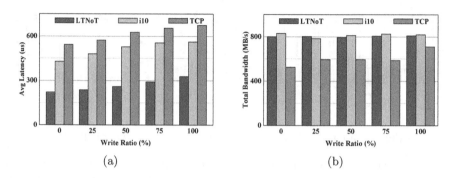

Fig. 7. Latency and Bandwidth comparison with varying write ratio.

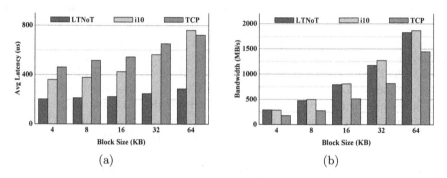

Fig. 8. Latency and Bandwidth comparison with varying block sizes.

than NoT with various I/O workloads. As shown in Fig. 6(c), LTNoT can get 25.32% higher bandwidth than NoT on average and it is nearly the same as i10. The bandwidth improvement of LTNoT shows a trend of continuous growth with the increase of iodepth compared with NoT. This is mainly because increasing iodepth will speed up the PDU aggregation in freights in the T-app pipeline, thus sending the 64KB jumbo packet continuously.

Performance with Varying Read/Write Ratios. In this experiment, we evaluate the impact of inter-queue I/O isolation by setting different read/write IO request ratios in FIO benchmarks. As shown in Fig. 7, compared with NoT, LTNoT shows obvious advantages in average latency and bandwidth. Compared with i10 and NoT, LTNoT decreases the average latency by 47.73% and 56.63% on average respectively. In the test of read-only and write-only, LTNoT presents up to 48.1% latency reduction and 41.57% latency improvement than i10. No matter how the read/write ratio changes, LTNoT maintains a stable improvement for the latency performance of L-app. In terms of bandwidth performance, LTNoT shows about 34.61% improvement in comparison to NoT.

Performance with Varying Block Sizes. We further evaluate the performance of LTNoT using the workloads with different request sizes, i.e., configuring

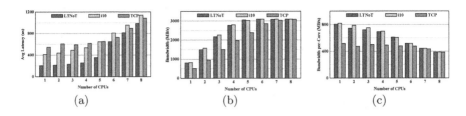

Fig. 9. Latency and Bandwidth comparison with number of cores.

different block sizes in FIO benchmarks. Figure 8 shows the latency and bandwidth comparisons with varying I/O request sizes to access remote NVMe SSD block devices. Apparently, the latency performance of LTNoT is much better than NoT and i10 and improves by 50.77% and 59.32% on average respectively. In addition, LTNoT can provide a bandwidth improvement of 52.31% than NoT. As shown in the experiment, the improvement of latency and throughput by LTNoT remain steady as the block size increases.

Scalability with Number of Cores. To further understand the performance scalability of LTNoT in the systems with multiple CPU cores, we evaluate the performance of LTNoT with different numbers of CPU cores from 1 to 8. Notably, as shown in Fig. 9(a) and 9(b), 6 cores is a dividing point of latency and total bandwidth performance, where the trend lines of the three tested systems change dramatically. This is because when accessing remote storage with 6 cores, the bandwidth of the whole system has reached the upper limit. In this case, the system cannot provide higher bandwidth as the number of cores increases. Thus the isolated queue design in LTNoT can not significantly mitigate the system performance loss caused by network congestion. When the number of cores is less than 6, both i10 and LTNoT present better total bandwidth performance than NoT and it is almost proportional to the number of CPU cores. And the bandwidth of LTNoT is steadily 45.37% improved than NoT. Besides, for a fixed number of CPU cores involved in this experiment, LTNoT always performs better than i10 and NoT in latency, 37.69% and 40.29% respectively. This indicates that LTNoT will not incur any performance loss compared with i10 and NoT before congestion. Different from bandwidth, the per-core bandwidth of i10 and LTNoT is obviously reduced as the number of CPU cores is used in this experiment as shown in Fig. 9(c).

RocksDB Performance. We use RocksDB, a widely-deployed key-value storage system, as a real application to evaluate the performance of LTNoT. With Ext4 filesystem to format the SSD block device and the default db_bench tool, we populate a 55 GB database containing 1,000,000,000 pieces of data. The RocksDB is deployed on both the host side and the target side. In order to minimize the impact of all the cache layers in the kernel, we enable direct I/O in the experiments. After mounting the remote SSD device on the host side, we

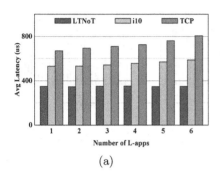 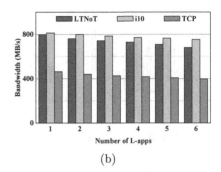

(a)   (b)

Fig. 10. Latency and Bandwidth comparison with RocksDB test.

generate a readrandom workload as the L-app to test single thread performance of single core with the block size of 4 KB. We generate an FIO thread as the T-app whose iodepth is set to 32 with the block size of 16 KB in this experiment.

Figure 10 shows the evaluation results of average latency performance and bandwidth performance. In terms of latency performance, LTNoT gains about a 36.78% improvement over i10 and has a greater 51.81% improvement compared with NoT. Compared with the FIO tests, due to the high application layer overhead of RocksDB, the latency performance improvement of LTNoT is slightly reduced. As the RocksDB test is to operate on the file system while FIO is to directly read the block device, thus the additional operation overhead in RocksDB leads to this latency performance difference. Since the application layer and filesystem increase the delay by 100μs, the benefits obtained from the modification of the kernel software layer are partially overshadowed. While the bandwidth performance of the T-app generated by FIO is negligibly impacted in the RocksDB test. The throughput of LTNoT is almost 0.73 times higher than that of NoT.

6   Related Work and Discussion

Resource Disaggregation. There have been many resource disaggregation proposals from industry in the past few years, such as the Machine of HP [12] and the composable system of IBM [8]. In addition, several key technologies have been well studied in academia. Lim et al. proposed disaggregating memory that can be used as network swap device and accessed through memory instructions transparently [26,27]. Shan et al. proposed LegoOS to manage disaggregated systems. InfiniSwap disaggregates memory from host CPU and swaps local memory to remote memory via RDMA [14]. These remote memory systems significantly promote the development of high-speed network technologies, which simultaneously mitigate the communication overhead for disaggregated storage systems.

Storage Disaggregation. Accessing remote storage through networks is a common practice in production systems. As the novel NVMe protocol leverages the high throughput PCIe interconnect to utilize the internal parallelism of SSDs to the maximum, the software overhead of iSCSI significantly prevents NVMe SSDs from exposing their high performance to remote hosts. Disaggregating NVMe SSDs is a more challenging task and have been studied in ReFlex [25], Decibel [33], and PolarFS [6]. Their basic design is to tightly integrate network and storage layers to minimize the software overhead in the I/O path, thus the high performance of the storage devices can be fully utilized by remote hosts.

NVMe over Fabrics. In recent years, NVMeoF has been replacing iSCSI as the dominant remote storage interface protocol of disaggregated storage systems. As the latest extension of NVMe for remote storage access which allows remote access to NVMe controllers through high-speed networks, NVMeoF can eliminate the unnecessary protocol conversion initially required in the I/O path from host to remote NVMe SSDs and provides ultra-low remote access latency. NVMeoF can dramatically reduce network and processing overheads, thus achieving negligible performance degradation for remote storage access.

There have been a few studies for improving the I/O management strategies in NVMeoF. Guz et al. characterized the overhead of NVMe over RDMA and concluded that NVMeoF only causes negligible performance degradation while iSCSI decreases I/O throughput by 20% [15]. Gao et al. proposed i10 that allows unmodified applications to operate directly on the kernel's TCP/IP stack and saturates a 100Gbps link for remote accesses using CPU utilization similar to SPDK and NVMe over RDMA [19]. Besides, several studies have presented the effectiveness of NVMeoF on real storage systems for big data and deep learning platforms. Choi et al. have evaluated the performance of NVMeoF with shared-disk file systems. Zhu et al. explore the use of NVMe storage disaggregation for support of deep neural networks [40]. Han et al. have improved the performance of the most popular Hadoop filesystem with NVMeoF [16].

7   Conclusion

In this paper, we introduce the design, implementation and evaluation of LTNoT, an inter-queue I/O isolated NVMe-over-TCP design that only modifies in the Linux kernel. LTNoT proposes the specific I/O process policy of latency-sensitive path and throughput-oriented path, thus alleviating the I/O interference between multiple simultaneous applications in the CPU. We implemented LTNoT in Linux Kernel and evaluated it by realistic benchmarks. Our experimental results demonstrate that LTNoT can the good trade-offs between latency and throughput compared with NVMe over TCP or i10.

Acknowledgements. We would like to thank the ICA3PP reviewers for their insightful feedback. This work was supported in part by Excellent Youth Foundation of Hunan Province under Grant No. 2021JJ10050 and the Science Foundation of NUDT under grant ZK21–03.

References

1. Al-Fares, M., Loukissas, A., Vahdat, A.: A scalable, commodity data center network architecture. ACM SIGCOMM Comput. Commun. Rev. **38**(4), 63–74 (2008)
2. Axboe, J.: Fio-flexible IO tester (2014). http://freecode.com/projects/fio
3. Barroso, L.A., Hölzle, U.: The datacenter as a computer: an introduction to the design of warehouse-scale machines. Synth. Lect. Comput. Archit. **4**(1), 1–108 (2009)
4. Belay, A., Prekas, G., Klimovic, A., Grossman, S., Kozyrakis, C., Bugnion, E.: Ix: a protected dataplane operating system for high throughput and low latency. In: 11th USENIX Symposium on Operating Systems Design and Implementation (OSDI 2014), pp. 49–65 (2014)
5. Cai, Q., Chaudhary, S., Vuppalapati, M., Hwang, J., Agarwal, R.: Understanding host network stack overheads. In: Proceedings of the 2021 ACM SIGCOMM 2021 Conference (SIGCOMM 2021), pp. 65–77 (2021)
6. Chapin, J., Rosenblum, M., Devine, S., Lahiri, T., Teodosiu, D., Gupta, A.: Hive: fault containment for shared-memory multiprocessors. In: Proceedings of the Fifteenth ACM Symposium on Operating Systems Principles (SOSP 1995), pp. 12–25 (1995)
7. Cherkasova, L., Kotov, V., Rokicki, T.: Fibre channel fabrics: evaluation and design. In: Proceedings of HICSS-29: 29th Hawaii International Conference on System Sciences (HICSS 1996), pp. 53–62 (1996)
8. Chung, I.H., Abali, B., Crumley, P.: Towards a composable computer system. In: Proceedings of the International Conference on High Performance Computing in Asia-Pacific Region (HPC Asia 2018), pp. 137–147 (2018)
9. Cobb, D., Huffman, A.: Nvm express and the PCI express SSD revolution. In: Intel Developer Forum (2012)
10. Cohen, D., Talpey, T., Kanevsky, A., Cummings, U., Krause, M.: Remote direct memory access over the converged enhanced ethernet fabric: evaluating the options. In: 2009 17th IEEE Symposium on High Performance Interconnects (HOTI 2009), pp. 123–130 (2009)
11. Dragojević, A., Narayanan, D., Castro, M., Hodson, O.: Farm: fast remote memory. In: 11th USENIX Symposium on Networked Systems Design and Implementation (NSDI 14), pp. 401–414 (2014)
12. Faraboschi, P., Keeton, K., Marsland, T., Milojicic, D.: Beyond processor-centric operating systems. In: 15th Workshop on Hot Topics in Operating Systems (HotOS XV) (2015)
13. Gao, P.X., Narayan, A., Karandikar, S., Carreira, J., Han: Network requirements for resource disaggregation. In: 12th USENIX Symposium on Operating Systems Design and Implementation (OSDI 2016), pp. 249–264 (2016)
14. Gu, J., Lee, Y., Zhang, Y., Chowdhury, M., Shin, K.G.: Efficient memory disaggregation with infiniswap. In: 14th USENIX Symposium on Networked Systems Design and Implementation (NSDI 2017), pp. 649–667 (2017)
15. Guz, Z., Li, H., Shayesteh, A., Balakrishnan, V.: NVMe-over-fabrics performance characterization and the path to low-overhead flash disaggregation. In: Proceedings of the 10th ACM International Systems and Storage Conference (SYSTOR 2017), pp. 1–9 (2017)
16. Han, D., Nam, B.: Improving access to HDFS using NVMeoF. In: 2019 IEEE International Conference on Cluster Computing (CLUSTER 2019), pp. 1–2 (2019)
17. Hellwig, C.: High performance storage with blkmq and scsi-mq (2014)

18. Hoff, B.: RDMA interconnects paving the way for NVMe over fabrics technology (2016)
19. Hwang, J., Cai, Q., Tang, A., Agarwal, R.: Tcp≈rdma: cpu-efficient remote storage access with i10. In: 17th USENIX Symposium on Networked Systems Design and Implementation (NSDI 2020), pp. 127–140 (2020)
20. Hwang, J., Vuppalapati, M., Peter, S., Agarwal, R.: Rearchitecting linux storage stack for μs latency and high throughput (2021)
21. Jeong, E., et al.: mTCP: a highly scalable user-level TCP stack for multicore systems. In: 11th USENIX Symposium on Networked Systems Design and Implementation (NSDI 2014), pp. 489–502 (2014)
22. Kaufmann, A., Stamler, T., Peter, S., Sharma: TAS: TCP acceleration as an OS service. In: Proceedings of the Fourteenth EuroSys Conference 2019 (EuroSys 2019), pp. 1–16 (2019)
23. Kim, S., Kim, H., Lee, J., Jeong, J.: Enlightening the i/o path: a holistic approach for application performance. In: 15th USENIX Conference on File and Storage Technologies (FAST 2017), pp. 345–358 (2017)
24. Klimovic, A., Kozyrakis, C., Thereska, E., John, B., Kumar, S.: Flash storage disaggregation. In: Proceedings of the Eleventh European Conference on Computer Systems (EuroSys 2016), pp. 1–15 (2016)
25. Klimovic, A., Litz, H., Kozyrakis, C.: Reflex: remote flash local flash. ACM SIGARCH Comput. Archit. News 45(1), 345–359 (2017)
26. Lim, K., Chang, J., Mudge, T., Ranganathan, P., Reinhardt, S.K., Wenisch, T.F.: Disaggregated memory for expansion and sharing in blade servers. ACM SIGARCH Comput. Archit. News 37(3), 267–278 (2009)
27. Lim, K., et al.: System-level implications of disaggregated memory. In: IEEE International Symposium on High-Performance Comp Architecture (HPCA 2012), pp. 1–12 (2012)
28. Lin, X., et al.: Scalable kernel TCP design and implementation for short-lived connections. ACM SIGARCH Comput. Archit. News 44(2), 339–352 (2016)
29. Love, R.: Linux kernel development. Pearson Education (2010)
30. Marinos, I., Watson, R.N., Handley, M.: Network stack specialization for performance. ACM SIGCOMM Comput. Commun. Rev. 44(4), 175–186 (2014)
31. Marty, M., Gribble, S., Kidd, N., Kononov, R., Evans, W.C.: Snap: a microkernel approach to host networking. In: 27th ACM Symposium on Operating Systems Principles (SOSP 2019), pp. 399–413 (2019)
32. Minturn, D.: Nvm express over fabrics. In: 11th Annual OpenFabrics International OFS Developers' Workshop (2015)
33. Nanavati, M., Wires, J., Warfield, A.: Decibel: isolation and sharing in disaggregated rack-scale storage. In: 14th USENIX Symposium on Networked Systems Design and Implementation (NSDI 17), pp. 17–33 (2017)
34. Prekas, G., Kogias, M., Bugnion, E.: Zygos: achieving low tail latency for microsecond-scale networked tasks. In: Proceedings of the 26th Symposium on Operating Systems Principles (SOSP 17), pp. 325–341 (2017)
35. Qiao, X., Xie, X., Xiao, L.: Load-aware transmission mechanism for NVMeoF storage networks. In: International Conference on High Performance Computing and Communication (HPCCE 2021), vol. 12162, pp. 105–112 SPIE (2022)
36. Shan, Y., Huang, Y., Chen, Y., Zhang, Y.: LegoOS: a disseminated, distributed OS for hardware resource disaggregation. In: 13th USENIX Symposium on Operating Systems Design and Implementation (OSDI 2018), pp. 69–87 (2018)

37. Son, Y., Kang, H., Han, H., Yeom, H.Y.: An empirical evaluation of nvm express SSD. In: International Conference on Cloud & Autonomic Computing (ICCAC 15), pp. 275–282 (2015)
38. Tai, A., Smolyar, I., Wei, M., Tsafrir, D.: Optimizing storage performance with calibrated interrupts. In: Proceedings of the 15th USENIX Symposium on Operating Systems Design and Implementation (OSDI 2021), pp. 129–145 (2021)
39. Yu, Y., et al.: Optimizing the block i/o subsystem for fast storage devices. ACM Trans. Comput. Syst. **32**(2), 1–48 (2014)
40. Zhu, Y., Yu, W., Jiao, B., Mohror, K., Moody, A., Chowdhury, F.: Efficient user-level storage disaggregation for deep learning. In: 2019 IEEE International Conference on Cluster Computing (CLUSTER 2019), pp. 1–12 (2019)

AS-cast: Lock Down the Traffic of Decentralized Content Indexing at the Edge

Adrien Lebre[1], Brice Nédelec[1(✉)], and Alexandre Van Kempen[2]

[1] Nantes Université, École Centrale Nantes, IMT Atlantique, CNRS, INRIA, LS2N,
UMR 6004, 44000 Nantes, France
{adrien.lebre,brice.nedelec}@ls2n.fr
[2] Qarnot Computing, 40/42 rue Barbès, 92120 Montrouge, France
alexandre.vankempen@qarnot-computing.com

Abstract. Although the holy grail to store and manipulate data in Edge infrastructures is yet to be found, state-of-the-art approaches demonstrated the relevance of replication strategies that bring content closer to consumers: The latter enjoy better response time while the volume of data passing through the network decreases overall. Unfortunately, locating the closest replica of a specific content requires indexing *every live* replica along with its *location*. Relying on remote services for such a aim enters in contradiction with the properties of Edge infrastructures as locating replicas may effectively take more time than actually downloading content. At the opposite, maintaining such an index at every node would prove overly costly in terms of memory and traffic.

In this paper, we propose a decentralized implementation of content indexing called AS-cast. Using AS-cast, every node only indexes its closest replica; and all connected nodes with a similar index compose a *partition*. AS-cast is (i) efficient, for it uses partitions to lock down the traffic generated by its operations to relevant nodes, yet it (ii) guarantees that every node eventually acknowledges its closest replica despite concurrent operations. Our prototype, implemented on PeerSim, shows that AS-cast scales well in terms of generated messages and termination time.

As such, AS-cast can constitute a novel building block for geo-distributed services in need of efficient resource sharing in the vicinity of regions.

Keywords: Edge infrastructures · Decentralized content indexing · Scoped broadcast · Logical partitioning protocol

1 Introduction

The data storage paradigm shifted from centralized in the cloud to distributed at the edges of the network. This change aims at keeping the data close to (i) its producers since data may be too expensive or sensitive to be transmitted through the network; and (ii) its consumers so data may quickly and efficiently reach them [13,16,35]. To favor this transition, new designs for data management across Edge infrastructures have been investigated [9,10,17,19]. They

© Springer Nature Switzerland AG 2023
W. Meng et al. (Eds.): ICA3PP 2022, LNCS 13777, pp. 433–454, 2023.
https://doi.org/10.1007/978-3-031-22677-9_23

enable strategies to confine traffic by writing data locally and replicating content according to effective needs. However, locating content remains challenging. Retrieving a content location may actually take more time than retrieving the content itself. Indeed, these systems, when not using a centralized index hosted in a Cloud, rely on distributed hash tables (DHT) spread across different nodes composing the infrastructure [29]. When a client wants to access specific content, it requests a remote node to provide at least one node identity to retrieve this content from. After retrieving the content, the client can create another replica to improve the performance of future accesses, but it must recontact the indexing service to notify of the creation of this new replica.

Such approaches are in contradiction with the objectives of Edge infrastructures that aim at reducing the impact of latency as well as the volume of data passing through the network. First, accessing a remote node to request content location(s) raises hot spots and availability issues. But most importantly, it results in additional delays [3,12] that occur even before the actual download started. Second, the client gets a list of content locations at the discretion of content indexing services. Without information about these locations, it often ends up downloading from multiple hosts, yet only keeping the fastest answer. In turn, clients either waste network resources, or face slower response time.

To address the aforementioned limitations, every node that might request or replicate content must also host its own content indexing service in a fully decentralized fashion [25]. At any time, it can immediately locate the closest replica of specific content. A naive approach would be that every node indexes and ranks *every live* replica along with its *location* information. When creating or destroying a replica, a node would notify all other nodes by broadcasting its operation [7,18]. Unfortunately, this also contradicts Edge infrastructure objectives, for such a protocol does not confine the traffic generated to maintain its indexes. A node may acknowledge the existence of replicas at the other side of the network while there already exists a replica next to it.

To mitigate the broadcasting overhead, a node creating a replica should notify all and only nodes that have no closer replica in the system. This would create interconnected sets of nodes, or *partitions*, gathered around a *source* being their respective replica. A node deleting its replica should notify all members of its partition so they can rally their new closest partition. Some periodic advertisement protocols [20,36] already provide both creation and deletion. Yet, their functioning requires (i) to generate traffic even when the system is quiescent, and (ii) the use of synchronous communications [36] or physical-time-based intervals tuned according to network topology parameters such as network diameter [20]. In this paper, we address the content indexing challenge as a distributed partitioning problem. Our contribution is threefold:

- We highlight the properties that guarantee decentralized consistent partitioning in dynamic infrastructures. We demonstrate that concurrent creation and removal of partitions may impair the propagation of control information crucial for consistent partitioning. Yet, nodes are able to purge stale information forever using only neighbor-to-neighbor communication, hence leaving room for up-to-date information propagation, and eventually consistent partitioning.

(a) Node R efficiently advertises its content by epidemic propagation. Every node requests R if needed.

(b) Node G creates a second replica by splitting the red set in two. Nodes request their closest replica host.

(c) Node B creates another replica. Node B needs to notify only a small subset of nodes.

(d) G destroys its replica. Nodes that belonged to its partition must find the closest partition they are in.

Fig. 1. Partitions grow/shrink depending on creations/removals of replicas.

- We provide an implementation entitled AS-cast that uses aforementioned principles to adapt its partitioning to creations and deletions of partitions even in dynamic systems where nodes can join, leave, or crash at any time. AS-cast's efficiency relies on a communication primitive called scoped-broadcast that enables epidemic dissemination of messages as long as receiving nodes verify an application-dependent predicate.
- We evaluate AS-cast through simulations using PeerSim [30]. Results empirically show that (i) AS-cast manages to quickly disseminate messages to the subset of relevant nodes; (ii) AS-cast's overhead decreases when the number of partitions increases; (iii) AS-cast does not generate traffic in quiescent systems; and (iv) AS-cast operates even in networks subject to physical partitioning.

The rest of this paper is organized as follows. Section 2 illustrates the motivation and problem behind our proposal. Section 3 describes dynamic consistent partitioning and its implementation. Section 4 presents our evaluations. Section 5 reviews related work. Section 6 concludes and discusses future work.

2   Motivation and Problem

Numerous studies addressed content indexing in geo-distributed infrastructures ranging from centralized services to fully decentralized approaches [23]. We advocate for the latter where nodes host the service themselves so they do not need to request remote – possibly far away third-party – entities to retrieve content locations. More precisely, we propose to consider the content indexing issue as a dynamic logical partitioning problem. This section motivates our positioning and explains the shortcomings of existing implementations.

Dissemination: Figure 1 depicts an infrastructure comprising 17 interconnected nodes spread across France. In Fig. 1a, a single Node R hosts the content, so every other node downloads from this node when it needs it. In that regard, Node R only needs to disseminate a message notifying all other nodes of its new content. Node R can use uniform reliable broadcast [18] and epidemic propagation [14] to guarantee that every node eventually knows the content location by efficiently using neighbor-to-neighbor communication.

Location: Then, in Fig. 1b, another Node G creates a replica of this content. Similarly to Node R, it notifies other nodes of this new replica. However, to avoid that north nodes request its replica, and south nodes request the northern one, nodes hosting a replica must add *location information* along with their notifications. As a consequence, every node eventually knows every replica location and can download from its closest host. Red nodes would request Node R while green nodes would request Node G.

Scoped Broadcast: Then, in Fig. 1c, another Node B creates a replica of this content. Similarly to Node R and Node G, Node B can notify other nodes of this new replica. However, the set of nodes that could actually use this new replica is actually much smaller than the network size. Uniform reliable broadcast is not designed for such a context and would generate a lot of unnecessary traffic. Instead, nodes need a communication primitive that propagates notifications within a scope by evaluating a predicate, starting at its broadcaster (the *source*). In other terms, nodes propagate notifications as long as they consider them useful based on location information they carry. We call such a primitive *scoped broadcast* (see Sect. 3.1), for messages transitively reach a subset of interconnected nodes (the *scope*). Using this primitive, nodes can lock down the traffic of content indexing to relevant nodes.

Logical Partitioning: Every node ends up with at least one known replica that is its closest. The set of interconnected nodes with the same closest replica is a *partition*. Every node belongs to one, and only one, partition (see Sect. 3.2). In Fig. 1c, there are three logical partitions.

Dynamic Partitioning: In Fig. 1d, Node G destroys its replica. Every node that belonged to its green partition must choose another partition to be in. While it makes sense for Node G to scoped broadcast its removal, Node B and Node R cannot afford to continuously advertise their replica to fill the gap left open by Node G. A better approach would consist in triggering scoped broadcast at bordering nodes of red and blue partitions once again. In other words, the scope of scoped broadcast changes over receipts by nodes. This dynamic partitioning raises additional challenges related to concurrent operations where removed partitions could block the propagation of other partitions (see Sect. 3.3). Next Section details the properties of scoped broadcast and dynamic partitioning, and provides an implementation called AS-cast.

3   Adaptive Scoped Broadcast

To provide dynamic logical partitioning using scoped broadcast, all live nodes must collaborate to disseminate messages that notify new or removed sources to

Table 1. Summary of notations.

Notation	Short	Description
G	Graph	Represents a network
V	Vertices	Represents the set of nodes, or processes
E	Edges	Represents the set of asynchronous communication links
w_{xy}	weight	Positive weight of the edge $\langle x, y \rangle$
π_{xz}/Π_{xz}	path/best Path	List of contiguous edges from Node x to Node z
$|\pi_{xz}|/|\Pi_{xz}|$	Sum of weights	Positive sum of weights of the path
σ_x	state	The local state of Node x
$b_x(m)$	broadcast	Node x creates a new message m that must be delivered by all nodes
$d_x(m)$	deliver	Node x delivers the message m
$r_y(m)/r_{yx}(m)$	receive	Node y receives the message m from any neighboring node/Node x
$s_{xy}(m)$	send	Node x sends the message m to Node y
$f_x(m)$	forward	Node x forwards the message m to its neighbors
$m \oplus \sigma$	Aggregator	Aggregates σ into the metadata of message m
$\phi(\mu, \sigma)$	Predicate	Checks the metadata μ using the state σ
$\Diamond P$	Eventually	Eventually predicate P is true
$e_1 \rightarrow e_2$	Happens before	The event e_1 happened before the event e_2. d, s, r etc. are events
D_x	Delivered	Set of delivered messages by Node x.
α_x^d or $\alpha_{\pi_{xz}}^d$	add source	Message that notifies the adding of Source x in the network
δ_x	Source deletion	Message that notifies the possible deletion of Source x by Node x
$\mathcal{S}(m)$	Stale message	Message m conveys stale control information

all and only interested nodes. This section reviews step-by-step the properties that allow nodes to converge to the desired state together. It first defines scoped broadcast, then uses it to guarantee consistent partitioning when a node can only become a new source in the system. It highlights the issue when a node can also remove its status of source. It shows that using local knowledge and scoped broadcast, nodes can still reach dynamic consistent partitioning when they are able to detect possible blocking conditions in the dissemination of required notifications, even in dynamic networks where nodes join, leave, or crash at any time. For convenience, Table 1 summarizes the notations used throughout the paper.

3.1 Scoped Broadcast

In this paper, we consider Edge infrastructures as a set of interconnected autonomous systems comprising heterogeneous nodes interconnected by communication links. Nodes involved in the management of content may crash but are not byzantine. Nodes can reliably communicate through asynchronous message passing to other known nodes called neighbors. We define scoped broadcast as a communication primitive that propagates a message around its broadcaster within an application-dependent scope.

Definition 1 (Autonomous system). *An autonomous system is a network comprising nodes and communication links that we represent as a graph of* *vertices and edges:* $G = \langle V, E \rangle$ *with* $E \in V \times V$. *A path* π_{xz} *from Node* x *to Node* z *is a sequence of contiguous edges* $[\langle x, y_1 \rangle, \langle y_1, y_2 \rangle, \ldots, \langle y_n, z \rangle]$.

Definition 2 (Scoped broadcast). *When Node* x *scoped broadcasts* $b_x(m)$ *a message* m, *every correct node* y *within a scope receives* $r_y(m)$ *and delivers it* $d_y(m)$. *The scope depends on the state* σ *of each node, the metadata* μ *piggybacked by each message, and a predicate* ϕ *verified from node to node:* $(b_x(m) \wedge r_y(m)) \implies \exists \pi_{xy} : \forall z \in \pi_{xy}, \phi(\mu_z, \sigma_z)$.

This definition encompasses more specific definitions of related work [22, 28, 38]. It underlines the transitive relevance of messages. It also highlights that the functioning of epidemic propagation is well-aligned with the objectives of scoped broadcast. As consequence, we assume implementations relying on the forwarding of messages from neighbor-to-neighbor.

Definition 3 (Forwarding). *When* x *forwards* $f_x(m)$ *a message* m, *it sends it* $(s_{xy}(m))$ *to all its neighbors* y *accumulating and aggregating* $(\oplus)$ *metadata that depends on its local knowledge* σ_x: $f_x(m) \implies \forall \langle x, y \rangle \in E : s_{xy}(m \oplus \sigma_x)$.

We use scoped broadcast to efficiently modify the state of each node depending on the partitions that exist in the system to reach consistent partitioning.

3.2   Consistent Partitioning

At any time, a node can decide to become a *source*, hence creating a new partition in the system by executing an `Add` operation. This partition includes at least its source plus neighboring nodes that are closer to this source than any other one. Such a distance (or *weight*) is application-dependent: in the context of maintaining distributed indexes, this would be about link latency that nodes could monitor by aggregating `pings`; or operational costs when dealing with multiple tenants.

Definition 4 (Consistent partitioning (CP)). *Assuming a set of sources* $S \subseteq V$, *a positive weight* w_{xy} *associated with each edge* $\langle x, y \rangle \in E$, *we define consistent partitioning as a set of logical partitions* $P_{s \in S}$ *where each node* x *belongs to the partition of its closest source* s, *i.e., there exists a path* π_{sx} *with a sum of weights* $|\pi_{sx}| = \sum \{w_{pq} | \langle p, q \rangle \in \pi_{sx}\}$ *smaller than any other path, with* $|\pi_{xx}|$ *being* x*'s greatest lower bound.*

Unfortunately, nodes do not share a common global knowledge of the network state. For nodes to eventually ($\Diamond$) reach consistent partitioning (CP), each source s must send `Add` notifications α_s to all nodes that are closer to it than any other source, along with enough metadata to allow them to decide of their closest source. Based on Definition 2 and Definition 3, this consists in ensuring that each node x eventually receives $\alpha_s^{|\Pi_{sx}|}$ where Π_{sx} is the *best* path from any source to it; the best value $|\Pi_{sx}|$ being built over forwarding along this path.

Theorem 1 (Forwarding of Best (FB) $\implies$ **$\Diamond$CP).** *Assuming that each node x stores its outgoing weights ($\forall \langle x, y \rangle \in E : w_{xy} \in \sigma_x$), a total order on messages based on weights ($m_s^d < m_{s'}^{d'}$ when $d < d' \vee (d = d' \wedge s < s')$), reliable communication links ($s_{xy}(m) \iff \Diamond r_{yx}(m)$), nodes eventually reach consistent partitioning if each node delivers its best (i.e., smallest) message among received messages R_x, and forwards its best message among delivered messages D_x such that $f_x(\alpha_s^d) \implies \forall \langle x, y \rangle \in E : s_{xy}(\alpha_s^{d \oplus w_{xy}})$, i.e., by accumulating the respective weight of used edges.*

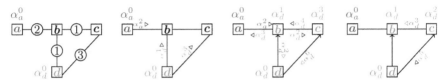

(a)   Both a and (b) Messages transit (c) b and c receive, (d) a and b discarded
d become sources. through links and deliver, and forward their received mes-
$w_{ab}=2$; $w_{bc}=w_{bd}=1$; carry   increasing α_d^1 and α_d^3 respec- sages. c improved
$w_{cd}=3$.   weights.   tively.   with α_d^2.

Fig. 2. Efficient consistent partitioning using S-cast. Partition P_a includes a while Partition P_d includes b, c, and d. Node c and Node d never acknowledge the existence of Source a, for Node b stops the propagation of the latter's notifications.

Proof. Whenever a node s becomes a source, it broadcasts hence delivers its own message $d_s(\alpha_s^{|\pi_{ss}|})$. Whatever its set of received messages, it acknowledges that it belongs to its own partition P_s since $\alpha_s^{|\pi_{ss}|} = \min D_s$ and it remains forever since $|\pi_{ss}|$ is its greatest lower bound. Such a source forwards its notification to its neighbors. Every neighbor eventually receives its notification since communication links are reliable. Whatever the order of received messages R_x at neighboring node x, total order ensures that it delivers notifications α_s^d when $d = |\pi_{ss}| + w_{sx} = \min |\pi_{s'x}|$ where $\min |\pi_{s'x}|$ is the lightest weight of x to any source s', s' being s in this case. Among these neighbors, at least those that fulfill the latest condition forward their respective notification. By transitivity, the message originating from s reaches all nodes that belong to P_s at least through their respective lightest path: $\forall y \in V, s, s' \in S : \min |\pi_{sy}| < \min |\pi_{s'y}| \implies \Diamond d_y(\alpha_s^{\min |\pi_{sy}|})$. When the system becomes quiescent, i.e., no node becomes source anymore, every node eventually acknowledges the partition it belongs to, i.e., nodes eventually reach consistent partitioning together. In addition, the protocol terminates: a node never delivers hence forwards a message after it received, delivered, and forwarded the message of its closest source from its lightest path.

Algorithm 1 shows the instructions that implement a *reactive* forwarding of best to reach consistent partitioning in a static network where nodes never join, crash, nor leave the system. As soon as a node receives a better message, it delivers and forwards it. The trade-off consists in decreasing termination time

---

Algorithm 1: Add-only CP protocol at Node p.

1 O_p, W_p	// set of neighbors and weights
2 $A_s^d \rightarrow \alpha_\varnothing^\infty$	// smallest distance d to Source s
3 **func** Add( ) receiveAdd($\varnothing, \alpha_p^0$)	// become source
4 **func** receiveAdd($q, \alpha_{s'}^{d'}$)	// notification from q
5 **if** $\alpha_{s'}^{d'} < A_s^d$ **then**	// check predicate (ϕ)
6 $A_s^d \leftarrow \alpha_{s'}^{d'}$	// deliver and update (σ)
7 **foreach** $n \in O_p$ **do** send$_n(\alpha_{s'}^{d'} \oplus^{w_{pn}})$	// forward to neighbors

---

at cost of increased traffic. Figure 2 illustrates the behavior of this algorithm on a system comprising 4 nodes a, b, c, and d. Both a and d become sources. They scoped broadcast notifications α_a^0 and α_d^0. They initialize their own state with the lowest value 0 (see Line 3), and send a message to each of their neighbors by accumulating the corresponding edge weight (see Line 7). In Fig. 2c, b receives α_d^1. Since it improves its own partition distance, it keeps it and forwards it to its neighbors. In Fig. 2d, b discards α_a^2, for it does not improve its partition distance. Neither c nor d will ever acknowledge that Source a exists. The protocol lacks of obvious traffic optimization, e.g., grey messages are useless in this scenario. Nevertheless, the system discards last transiting messages after it reached consistent partitioning.

Adding logical partitions to a static network is straightforward and lightweight. Unfortunately, removing partitions or introducing dynamic network membership increases complexity and costs caused by concurrent operations.

3.3 Dynamic Consistent Partitioning

At any time, a source can revoke its status of source by executing a Del operation, hence deleting its partition from the system. All nodes that belong to this partition must eventually choose another partition to belong to.

Definition 5 (Dynamic consistent partitioning (DCP)). *A DCP protocol enables nodes to join or leave the set of sources at any time while ensuring eventual consistent partitioning.*

Delete operations bring a new notion of order between events, and most importantly between message deliveries. A node s that performs a Del operation implicitly states that its preceding Add operation becomes obsolete. Their results – scoped broadcast in the form of Add notifications α_s – should be canceled by the corresponding Del notifications of staleness δ_s. We focus on the last delivery of each node, since the best is also the last, as highlighted by Algorithm 1.

Definition 6 (Happens-before ($\rightarrow$) [27]). *The transitive, irreflexive, and antisymmetric happens-before relationship defines a strict partial order between events. Two messages are concurrent if none happens before the other.*

Definition 7 (Stale messages). *Only the latest broadcast of a node matters. A message m conveys stale control information $\mathcal{S}(m)$ as soon as its broadcaster broadcasts another message: $\mathcal{S}(\alpha_x) = \exists \delta_x : b_x(\alpha_x) \rightarrow b_x(\delta_x)$. A node only delivers or sends messages that it assumes up-to-date. For convenience, we define $last(D) = \alpha_s \in D : \nexists \alpha_{s'} \in D : d_x(\alpha_s) \rightarrow d_x(\alpha_{s'})$.*

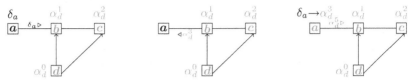

(a) a deletes its partition. It notifies all nodes that belong to its partition.

(b) δ stops when it encounters another partition. b answers with its partition.

(c) a receives, delivers, and forwards the message α_d^3. Every node belongs to P_d.

Fig. 3. Efficient removal of a partition using scoped broadcast.

A naive attempt at implementing DCP resembles echoes in acoustics: a sound propagates in the air before crashing into surrounding walls to finally come back altered. Following the principles of scoped broadcast as stated in Definition 2, a node x that receives a staleness notification δ_s forwards it only if the latter targets its current partition α_s. These messages propagate as long as they remain in the deleted partition. When they reach the bordering nodes of the deleted partition, it creates an echo of bordering partitions that will go backward to fill the gap left open by removals using forwarding of best (FB) as stated by Theorem 1.

Definition 8 (Forwarding of staleness (FS)). *Any source can broadcast a staleness notification at any time. Every node x delivers and forwards a received staleness notification δ_s if it targets its best up-to-date delivered message: $(last\ D_x = \alpha_s \wedge d_x(\alpha_s) \rightarrow r_x(\delta_s)) \implies d_x(\delta_s) \rightarrow f_x(\delta_s)$.*

Definition 9 (FB$^+$: echos). *In addition to FB, a node x that receives but does not deliver a staleness notification δ_s replies by – or echoes – its best up-to-date delivered message: $(last\ D_x = \alpha_{s'}^d \wedge \delta_{s'} \notin D_x \wedge d_x(\alpha_{s'}^d) \rightarrow r_{xy}(\delta_s)) \implies r_{xy}(\delta_s) \rightarrow s_{xy}(\alpha_{s'}^d \oplus^{w_{xy}})$.*

Figure 3 illustrates the behavior of this implementation (FB$^+$ $\wedge$ FS). Two partitions initially exist: P_a and P_d that respectively include $\{a\}$, and $\{b, c, d\}$. In Fig. 3a, a deletes its partition. FS in Definition 8 states that a must notify all its neighbors – here only b – that may belong to its partition. In Fig. 3b, b receives but does not deliver δ_a since δ_a does not target its current partition P_d. FB$^+$ in Definition 9 states that b must echo back its own best up-to-date message α_d^3, for it may be the best for a. Figure 3c shows that every node eventually belongs to P_d, therefore reaching consistent partitioning. Unfortunately, this protocol does not ensure consistent partitioning in every scenario.

Lemma 1 (FB$^+$ ∧ FS ⇏ DCP). *Forwarding best up-to-date, staleness, and echoes is not sufficient to guarantee dynamic consistent partitioning.*

Proof. Stale control information (see Definition 7) may impair the propagation of both (i) notifications about actual sources, and (ii) notifications about deleted partitions. In Fig. 4, a, b, c are chained with FIFO links, i.e., nodes receive the messages in the order of their sending. In Fig. 4a, a and c become sources, sending their respective notification message to b. In Fig. 4b, a and c delete their partition while b receives, delivers, and forwards α_a^2. In Fig. 4c, b receives, delivers, and forwards α_c^1, for it improves its best partition. Then it receives and discards δ_a, for its best partition does not match the deleted one. It echoes back α_c^3 to a. In Figs. 4d and 4e, a and b handle transiting notifications. Finally, Fig. 4f shows that c is stuck in the deleted P_a for not having received δ_a that b blocked earlier. The system does not reach consistent partitioning.

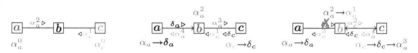

(a) Both a and c become sources. $w_{ab}=2$; $w_{bc}=1$.   (b) a and c delete their partition while b delivers and forwards α_a.   (c) b blocks the only transiting δ_a while b delivers and forwards α_c.

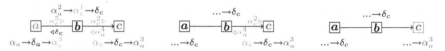

(d) a receives, delivers, and forwards α_c^3.   (e) a receives, delivers, and forwards δ_c.   (f) c is stuck in a stale partition P_a.

Fig. 4. The naive propagation of messages is insufficient to guarantee consistent partitioning. If c had children, they would stay in the wrong partition too.

The issue is that each node trusts its parent to forward all staleness notifications relevant to it. When this fails, as in Fig. 4, not only a node (c) may wrongfully stay in a partition (P_a) when its source (a) already deleted it, but it may contribute to its inconsistency by not forwarding farther but up-to-date messages from live sources.

A first step to avoid staying in inconsistent state is to extend the behavior of each node so nodes such as c, that would remain in a wrong partition, use their history of receipt and delivery to detect the possible blocking of staleness notifications that can hinder reaching consistent partitioning. In Fig. 4, b blocked the staleness notification δ_a that c needs since it belongs to a ephemeral partition P_c that c acknowledges to be stale before b does. Therefore, c can detect the possible blocking of δ_a since it acknowledges that its parent b received, delivered, and forwarded the stale notification α_c^1. In other terms, Node c acknowledges that between the delivery of α_c^1 and the delivery of δ_c, Node b blocked all other δ messages and therefore, it could have blocked the most important staleness notification: δ_a.

Lemma 2 ($\mathbf{FB^+} \wedge \mathbf{FS} \implies$ Detector existence). *Assuming FB^+ and FS, a chain of delivery on π_{xz} of α_x with $\alpha_x = last\ D_z$, if x broadcasts a staleness notification δ_x, either (A) z eventually delivers it, or (B) a node y in such a chain of delivery π'_{xz} eventually detects the possible blocking of δ_x.*

Proof. Assuming a chain of delivery $\pi_{xz} = [x, \dots, z]$ of α_x with $\alpha_x = last\ D_z$ and $d_x(\delta_x)$, we must prove that whatever the possible states of nodes that belong to this chain, it either leads to outcome (A) or (B).

(I) **Same last partition:** $\forall y \in \pi_{xz} : \alpha_x = last\ D_y$, with forwarding of staleness (Definition 8), $f_{\pi_{xz}[k]}(\delta_x) \implies \Diamond d_{\pi_{xz}[k+1]}(\delta_x)$ except if $\delta_x \in D_{\pi_{xz}[k+1]}$ meaning that $\pi_{xz}[k+1]$ already delivered and forwarded δ_x following another delivery chain. Therefore, z eventually receives, hence delivers δ_x (outcome A).

(II) **Different last partitions:** $\exists y \in \pi_{xz} \setminus \{x, z\} : \alpha_s = last\ D_y$, by (I), the staleness notification reaches the first of such a node $y = \pi_{xz}[k]$. Forwarding of staleness (Definition 8) states that the forwarding stops when y already delivered δ_x ($\delta_x \in D_y$ covered by (I)) or delivered a better message $\alpha_s = last\ D_y$. With $y' = \pi_{xz}[k+1]$, forwarding of best (Definition 9) implies three possible results:

   (i) y' **equivalent to y:** $\alpha_{s'} = last\ D_{y'}$ with $\alpha_{s'} \neq \alpha_x$ hence $y' \iff y$ which leaves two possible results as follows:

   (ii) y' **in P_x from another parent:** $r_{y'}(\alpha_s) \wedge \alpha_x = last\ D_{y'} \wedge \alpha_x < \alpha_s$ which means that a shorter path of delivery π'_{xz} exists that either forwards appropriate staleness notifications (covered by (I)) or detects a possible blocking of the latter as follows:

   (iii) y' **in P_x with y as parent).** but does not deliver the y's last partition for it already delivered the corresponding staleness notification: $r_{y'}(\alpha_s) \wedge \delta_s \in D_{y'} \wedge \alpha_x = last\ D_{y'}$ which detects a possible blocking of δ_x (outcome (B)). Without global knowledge, y' assumes it belongs to the shortest and only path of delivery of α_x thus it cannot further delegate the detection to another node.

As a second step, detecting nodes must proactively purge the system from their forwarded notifications. For instance in Fig. 4f, c detects the blocking of the staleness notification δ_a. It could broadcast δ_a in order to acknowledge the staleness of its own α_a^3 and inform neighboring nodes that delivered it as well. Unfortunately, there exists false positive in the blocking detection. Lemma 2's proof shows that the detection at y' does not depend on δ_x. Therefore δ_x may not exist but y' still receives α_s after the delivery of δ_s from the path it received and delivered α_x. Figure 5 highlights this behavior. In Fig. 5b, a does not delete its partition. In Fig. 5f and because of scoped broadcast, c received the same series of messages as in Fig. 4f. Yet, c must assume the existence of δ_a and act accordingly by forcing the staleness of its best delivered message and disseminate this information to its neighbors. To avoid flooding the system with false positive staleness notifications, we reduce the scope of staleness notifications by including only downstream nodes. In Fig. 5f, false positives would generate traffic at c and in turns, to its children if it had any. Nevertheless, this would not affect a nor b.

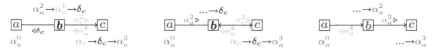

(a) a and c become sources. $w_{ab}=2$; $w_{bc}=1$.

(b) c deletes its partition but a does not. b delivers and forwards α_a.

(c) b delivers + forwards α_c.

(d) b delivers + forwards δ_c.

(e) a echoes back α_a^2 to b.

(f) a, b, c belong to P_a.

Fig. 5. From c's perspective, Fig. 4e and Fig. 5e are similar in terms of received messages, but the outcomes eventually differ. Yet, c must act on Fig. 5e, and acknowledge then propagate the *possible* staleness of Partition P_a.

Definition 10 (FS$^+$: forwarding staleness downstream). *Any node can broadcast a staleness notification at any time. A child node x delivers and forwards a received staleness notification if it comes from the path of delivery of its best up-to-date delivered message.*

It is worth noting that forwarding of staleness as stated in Definition 8 becomes a specific case of Definition 10 where the source itself forwards a staleness notification downstream. The notification must reach all nodes in its partition since the source has no nodes upstream, and belongs to the delivery path of all nodes that delivered this message.

Theorem 2 (FB$^+$ ∧ FS$^+$ ⟹ DCP). *A protocol guarantees dynamic consistent partitioning if it implements forwarding of best up-to-date messages with echos, forwarding of staleness messages downstream, and the detection of possible blocking triggers the forwarding of staleness notifications downstream.*

Proof. Detection triggers forwarding of staleness downstream which completes the case study of Lemma 2 by ensuring that, when a source broadcasts its staleness notification, all nodes that belong to its partition eventually deliver such a staleness notification. All downstream bordering nodes also eventually receive such a staleness notification and echo back their best delivered message. This triggers another competition as in Theorem 1 for the nodes that delivered the staleness notification.

Algorithm 2 shows the instructions of our implementation called AS-cast that enables dynamic consistent partitioning. It implements forwarding of best (see Line 13) and echos (see Line 21). To implement forwarding of staleness downstream as stated in Definition 10: (A) each node maintains a vector of versions that associates the respective known local counter of each known source, or has-been source. It constitutes a summary of known progress of other nodes; (B) each notification message α carries the list of identifier and counter of each node that forwarded it. In the worst case, both these structures grow linearly with the number of nodes in the system $\mathcal{O}(V)$. Nevertheless, following the principles of scoped broadcast, we expect that nodes only acknowledge a small subset of sources and messages; (C) each staleness notifications δ only carry the identifier and counter of the node – source or detector – that generated it. Only downstream nodes may deliver such message, since they carry the identifier of the generator. To implement the detection as stated in Lemma 2, each node only

---

Algorithm 2: AS-cast: DCP protocol at Node p.

```
1  O_p, W_p                                    // set of neighbors and weights
2  A_π^d ← α_∅^∞                               // best α so far
3  V ← ∅;  V[p] ← 0                            // vector of versions

4  func Add( )                          7  func Del( )
5  │  V[p] ← V[p] + 1                    8  │  V[p] ← V[p] + 1
6  │  receiveAdd(p, α_∅^0)               9  │  receiveDel(p, δ_{p,V[p]})

10 func receiveAdd(q, α_{π'}^{d'})              // notification of source creation
11 │  if α_{π'}^{d'} < A_π^d and ¬isStale(α_{π'}^{d'}) and ¬isLoop(α_{π'}^{d'}) then
12 │  │  A_π^d ← α_{π'}^{d'} ∪ ⟨p,V[p]⟩
13 │  │  foreach n ∈ O_p do  send_n(A_π^d ⊕ w_{pn})
14 │  else if isParent(q) and isStale(α_{π'}^{d'}) then
15 │  │  receiveDel(q, δ_{p,V[p]+1})            // detection of possible inconsistency
16 │  updateVersions(π')

17 func receiveDel(q, δ_{s,c})          // notification of a possible source removal
18 │  if ∃⟨s,c'⟩ ∈ π : c' < c then
19 │  │  A_π^d ← α_∅^∞
20 │  │  foreach n ∈ O_p \ q do  send_n(δ_{s,c})
21 │  else if A_s^d ≠ α_∅^∞ then  send_q(A_π^d ⊕ w_{pq})
22 │  updateVersions([⟨s,c⟩])

23 func onEdgeUp(q)                             // new communication link to q
24 │  if A_π^d ≠ α_∅^∞ then  send_q(A_π^d ⊕ w_{pq})
25 func onEdgeDown(q)                           // link to q removed (crash or leave)
26 │  if isParent(q) then  receiveDel(q, δ_{p,V[p]+1})

27 func isStale(α_{π'}^{d'})  return ∃⟨q,c⟩ ∈ π' : c < V[q]
28 func isLoop(α_{π'}^{d'})  return ⟨p,_⟩ ∈ π'
29 func isParent(q)  return ⟨q,_⟩ = π[|π| − 1]
30 func updateVersions(π')  for ⟨q,c⟩ ∈ π' do  V[q] ← max(V[q],c)
```

requires to know the direct parent of its best delivered message which is already included in the piggybacked path of this message. Receiving a message known to be stale from this parent triggers the generation of staleness notifications that can only be delivered by downstream nodes (see Line 14).

By reusing AS-cast's default behavior of echos and downstream staleness, Algorithm 2 also enables dynamic consistent partitioning even in dynamic networks subject to physical partitioning where nodes can join, leave, or crash at any time. Adding a node is equivalent to add as many edges as necessary. Since adding an edge may improve shortest paths, the protocol triggers a competition using echos of Definition 9. Removing a node is equivalent to removing all its edges. Removing an edge between two nodes may invalidate the shortest path of one of involved nodes plus downstream nodes, or impair the propagation of staleness notifications. Therefore, the protocol reuses its detectors of Lemma 2 to remove irrelevant messages from the system.

AS-cast follows the principles of scoped broadcast to efficiently and consistently propagate notifications to nodes that need them despite concurrent operations. Next Section aims at providing the empirical evidence of scalability and properties of the proposed approach.

4   Experimentation

In this section, we discuss the evaluations of AS-cast we conducted on top of PeerSim, a simulator to evaluate and assess distributed algorithms in large scale networks [30]. All the code of this experimentation section is available at: https:// gitlab.inria.fr/STACK-RESEARCH-GROUP/as-cast.

4.1   Scalability and Trade-Off of AS-cast

Description: We build a network comprising 10k nodes. First, we chain nodes together, then we add another link per node to another random node. Since links are bidirectional, each node has 4 communication links on average. We set the latency of links between 20 and 40 ms at random following a uniform distribution. To favor more concurrent operations, we set weights and latency to different values: each link has a weight between 5 and 15 set randomly using a uniform distribution. This allows nodes to receive messages in different orders, therefore generating more messages to reach consistent partitioning.

To evaluate dynamic consistent partitioning, we first create 100 partitions one at a time: nodes reach consistent partitioning before we create each new partition. Second, we remove every partition one at a time, in the order of their creation, hence starting from the first and oldest partition that had been added.

We measure the average number of messages per node per second; and the time before reaching consistent partitioning after adding or removing a partition.

Results: Figure 6 shows the results of this experiment. The top part shows the average traffic per node per second divided between α and δ messages. The bottom part shows the time before reaching consistent partitioning.

Figure 6 confirms that AS-cast's overhead depends on the size of partitions. This corresponds to a complexity in terms of number of messages of $\mathcal{O}(\frac{|E|}{|V| \cdot |P|})$ where E is the number of links, V is the number of nodes, and P is the number of partitions. In other terms, the pth partition contains $1/p$ nodes and reduces the size of closest partitions so every partition has $1/p$ nodes on average.

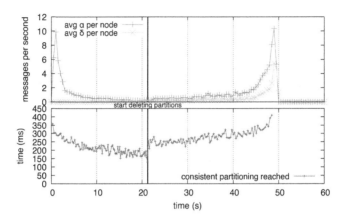

Fig. 6. Dynamic consistent partitioning overhead of AS-cast.

Therefore, the first partition is the most expensive, for α messages must reach every node which takes time and generate more traffic. AS-cast quickly converges towards consistent partitioning in 350 ms. The last and 100th partition added around 21 s is the least expensive. By using scoped broadcast, control information only reaches a small subset of the whole network.

Figure 6 also confirms that AS-cast's delete operations are roughly twice as expensive as creation ones. Indeed, the top part of the figure shows that after 21 s, when the experiment involves removals, traffic includes both α and δ messages. The latter aims at removing stale information and triggering competition while the former aims at updating shortest paths. As corollary, the convergence time increases, for δ messages must reach the partition borders before sound competitors propagate their partition. This delete operation involves concurrency: removals still propagate while the competition has started.

Figure 6 shows that the overhead of adding the 1st partition does not correspond to the overhead of deleting this 1st partition. When adding it, messages must reach all nodes while when removing it, messages must reach a small subset of this membership. AS-cast's overhead actually depends on current partitions as opposed to past partitions.

Finally, Fig. 6 highlights that after 49 s, i.e., after the 100 creations and the 100 deletes, nodes do not generate traffic anymore. Being reactive, AS-cast has no overhead when there is no operation in the system. AS-cast's overhead actually depends on its usage.

4.2   Traffic Containment in Dynamic Inter-autonomous Systems

Description: We build a network by duplicating the GÉANT topology [26] – an infrastructure of 271 nodes spanning across Europe – and we link these two clusters with a high latency link: 200 ms simulating cross-continental communications such as Europe-America. The experiments comprise $2 \times 271 = 542$ nodes and we derive intra-cluster latency from their nodes' geographic location.

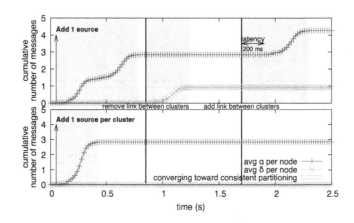

Fig. 7. Partitioning overhead of 2 clusters connected by a long distance link.

We evaluate the traffic of AS-cast by measuring the average number of messages per node over the experiments. In the first experiment, at 50 ms, only one node becomes source, hence there is only one partition for the whole distributed system. In the second experiment, at 50 ms, two nodes become sources, one per cluster. Afterwards both scenarios are identical. At 850 ms, we remove the link between the two clusters. At 1.7 s, we insert back this link.

Results: Figure 7 shows the results of this experimentation. The top part displays the results with one source while the bottom part displays the results with one source per cluster.

Figure 7 confirms that concurrent Adds may reach consistent partitioning faster. In particular, the top part of Fig. 7 depicts a slow down in traffic around 300 ms due to the high latency inter-continental link. The first plateau shows the source's autonomous system acknowledging this source, while the second shows the other autonomous system catching up. The inter-continental link is a bottleneck that does not exist when each cluster has its own source.

Figure 7 highlights that AS-cast operates well even when *physical* partitions appear. Indeed, the disconnection of the inter-continental link existing between the two clusters either leads to (i) additional traffic when the nodes do not have any source in their cluster because nodes need to purge all indexes about the remote unreachable source until reaching consistent partitioning; or (ii) a status

Table 2. Related work summary.

Approaches	Without Third-party	Update	Eventually Consistent	Reactive or Cyclic
Centralized [1,2,17,33]	✗	One	✓	R
DHT [6,11,23]	✗	Few	✓	R
Vector-based routing [21,32]	✓	all	✓	R/C
Replicated store [34]	✓	all	✓	R/C
Timeout-based [15,20]	✓	Scope	✗	C
Random walks [36]	✓	Scope	✓	C
Spanning Forest [4]	✓	Scope	✓	C
This paper	✓	**scope**	✓	**R**

quo as nodes of each cluster already target the source in their respective cluster. Finally, Fig. 7 shows that, when adding back the inter-continental link, the two clusters can communicate again. In the experiment involving one source for two clusters, it generates traffic. After a 200 ms delay corresponding to the inter-continental link latency, the cut off cluster starts to communicate α messages again. Eventually, all nodes belong to the same partition. However, in the experiment involving one source *per* cluster, the new link does not trigger noticeable traffic, for nodes already know their closest source in their cluster.

Overall, these experiments highlight the scalability of AS-cast in dynamic networks such as Edge infrastructures. Next Section reviews state-of-the-art approaches that can index content in geo-distributed infrastructures.

5 Related Work

Content indexing services in geo-distributed infrastructures allow nodes to retrieve specific content while leveraging the advantages of replication. These systems mostly rely on dedicated location services hosted by possibly remote third-party nodes; but cutting out the middleman requires that each node maintains its own index in a decentralized fashion. Table 2 summarizes the pros and cons of state-of-the-art approaches.

Third-party: Dedicated services are popular, for they propose the simplest mean to deploy such a service. They must maintain (i) the list of current replicas along with their respective location; and (ii) the network topology to determine the closest replica for every requesting node.

A central server that registers both these information facilitates the computation, for it gathers all knowledge in one place [1,2,17,33]. However, it comes with well-known issues such as load balancing, or single point of failure.

Distributing this index among nodes circumvents these issues [5,6,11,23, 37,39], but still raises locality issues where nodes (i) request to possibly far away location services the content location, and then (ii) request the actual content from possibly far away replicas. For instance, using distributed hash tables (DHT) [6,11,23], each node stores a part of the index defined by an interval between hash values. Hash values are keys to retrieve the associated content location. Before downloading any content, a node requests its location using its key. After round-trips between possibly distant DHT servers, the node gets available replicas. Contrarily to AS-cast, such services do not ensure to include the closest replica.

In addition, they often do not include distance information along with replica location. Determining where resides the closest replica for every requesting node necessarily involves some knowledge about the *current* topology. Maintaining a consistent view of an ever changing topology across a network is inherently complicated [8,32]. As a consequence, the requesting node ends up downloading from multiple replica hosts, yet only keeping the fastest answer. Nodes either waste network resources, or face lower response time.

Fully Decentralized: Cutting out the middleman by hosting a location service on each and every node improves response time of content retrieval. However, it still requires every node to index every live replica as well as their respective distance in order to rank them. Named Data Networking (NDN) [21] broadcasts information about cache updates to all nodes in the system. Having the entire knowledge of all the replica locations along with distance information carried into messages, each node easily determine where the closest copy of specific content resides, without contacting any remote service. In a routing context, distance-vector routing protocols such as BGP or OSPF [32] similarly broadcast information to all other nodes to infer a topology map of the network and derive routing tables. Conflict-free replicated datatype (CRDT) [34] for set data structures could also implement such a location service. Nodes would eventually have a set of all replicas, assuming eventual delivery of messages. Such solutions imply that every node receives every message, which contradicts the principles of Edge infrastructures that aim at reducing the volume of data passing through the network. On the opposite, each node running AS-cast only registers its closest replica. This allows AS-cast to use scoped broadcast as a communication primitive to lock down the traffic generated by content indexing based on distances.

Scoped Flooding: Some approaches also confine the dissemination of messages. Distance-based membership protocols such as T-Man [24] make nodes converge to a specific network topology depending on targeted properties. Following periodic exchanges, they add and remove communication links to other nodes to converge towards a topology ensuring the targeted properties. While membership protocols and AS-cast share common preoccupations, AS-cast does not aim at building any topology and never modifies neighbors of nodes.

The most closely related approaches to AS-cast come from information-centric networking (ICN) [15,20] and distributed clustering [36]. The sources advertise themselves periodically. Advertisements either stop as soon as they reach uninterested nodes [15,20], or propagate through most likely interested nodes [36]. However their cyclic operation requires that (i) they constantly generate traffic even in quiescent systems where nodes do not add nor destroy replicas; and (ii) they either operate in synchronous systems [4,36] or must define physical-clock-based timeouts the value of which depends on network topology properties such as network diameter [15,20]. Unfitting timeouts lead to premature removals of live replicas; or slow convergence where nodes wrongly believe that their closest replica is live while it was destroyed. On the opposite, AS-cast quickly informs each node of its closest replica even in large and dynamic networks with asynchronous communications; and has no overhead in quiescent systems.

6 Conclusion

With the advent of the Edge and IoT era, major distributed services proposed by our community should be revised to mitigate as much as possible traffic between nodes. In this paper, we addressed the challenge of content indexing as a dynamic logical partitioning problem where partitions grow and shrink to reflect content locations, and infrastructure changes. Using an efficient communication primitive called scoped broadcast, each node composing the infrastructure eventually knows the node hosting the closest replica of a specific content. The challenge resides in handling concurrent operations that may impair the propagation of messages, and in turn, lead to inconsistent partitioning. We highlighted the properties that solve this problem and proposed an implementation called AS-cast for Adaptive Scoped broadcast. Simulations confirmed that nodes quickly reach consistent partitioning together while the generated traffic remains locked down to partitions.

As future work, we plan to leverage the hierarchical properties of interconnected autonomous systems [31] to further limit the propagation of indexes within interested systems only. We expect that such an improvement would greatly benefit the autonomous systems, and particularly those hosting a large number of contents. Indeed, AS-cast ensures that every node eventually acknowledges its closest content replica. This feature unfortunately becomes an issue when each node is only interested by a small portion of content.

We also plan to evaluate our proposal within a concrete storage system such as InterPlanetary File System (IPFS) [6]. This would assess the relevance of AS-cast in real systems subject to high dynamics, and compare it against its current DHT-based indexing system that does not include distance in its operation. More generally, we claim that AS-cast and its extension can constitute novel building blocks for geo-distributed services. For instance, AS-cast could complement content delivery infrastructures [37] by efficiently sharing between nodes attached to the same CDN server the locations of web objects that have already been downloaded. This would further improve the containment of web traffic in our networks, and in turns, reduce the overall traffic footprint.

Acknowledgements. Most of the material presented in this article such as our prototype are available on the STACK Research Group. Activities have been done within the framework of Inria/QarnotComputing Défi, an initiative to *push carbon-neutral services towards the edge.*

References

1. Afanasyev, A., Yi, C., Wang, L., Zhang, B., Zhang, L.: SNAMP: secure namespace mapping to scale NDN forwarding. In: IEEE Conference on Computer Communications Workshops (2015)
2. Aggarwal, V., Feldmann, A., Scheideler, C.: Can ISPS and P2P users cooperate for improved performance? In: SIGCOMM Computer Communication Review (2007)
3. Asrese, A., Eravuchira, S., Bajpai, V., Sarolahti, P., Ott, J.: Measuring web latency and rendering performance: method, tools & longitudinal dataset. IEEE Trans. Netw. Serv. Manage. **16**, 535–549 (2019)
4. Barjon, M., Casteigts, A., Chaumette, S., Johnen, C., Neggaz, Y.M.: Maintaining a spanning forest in highly dynamic networks: the synchronous case. In: International Conference on Principles of Distributed Systems (2014)
5. Beaumont, O., Kermarrec, A.M., Marchal, L., Rivière, E.: VoroNet: a scalable object network based on Voronoi tessellations. In: IEEE International Parallel and Distributed Processing Symposium (2007)
6. Benet, J.: IPFS - content addressed, versioned, P2P file system. CoRR abs/1407.3561 (2014)
7. Birman, K.P., Hayden, M., Ozkasap, O., Xiao, Z., Budiu, M., Minsky, Y.: Bimodal multicast. ACM Trans. Comput. Syst. **17**, 41–88 (1999)
8. Breitbart, Y., Garofalakis, M., Martin, C., Rastogi, R., Seshadri, S., Silberschatz, A.: Topology discovery in heterogeneous IP networks. In: IEEE INFOCOM. Conference on Computer Communications (2000)
9. Confais, B., Lebre, A., Parrein, B.: An object store service for a fog/edge computing infrastructure based on IPFS and a scale-out NAS. In: IEEE International Conference on Fog and Edge Computing (2017)
10. Confais, B., Lebre, A., Parrein, B.: Performance analysis of object store systems in a fog and edge computing infrastructure. In: Transactions on Large-Scale Data-and Knowledge-Centered Systems (2017)
11. D'Ambrosio, M., Dannewitz, C., Karl, H., Vercellone, V.: MDHT: a hierarchical name resolution service for information-centric networks. In: ACM SIGCOMM Workshop on Information-centric Networking (2011)
12. Doan, T.V., Pajevic, L., Bajpai, V., Ott, J.: Tracing the path to YouTube: a quantification of path lengths and latencies toward content caches. IEEE Commun. Mag. **57**, 80–86 (2019)
13. Drolia, U., Guo, K., Tan, J., Gandhi, R., Narasimhan, P.: Cachier: edge-caching for recognition applications. In: IEEE 37th International Conference on Distributed Computing Systems (ICDCS) (2017)
14. Eugster, P.T., Guerraoui, R., Kermarrec, A.M., Massoulié, L.: Epidemic information dissemination in distributed systems. Computer **37**, 60–67 (2004)
15. Garcia-Luna-Aceves, J.J., Martinez-Castillo, J.E., Menchaca-Mendez, R.: Routing to multi-instantiated destinations: principles, practice, and applications. IEEE Trans. Mobile Comput. **17**, 1696–1709 (2018)

16. Guo, P., Hu, B., Li, R., Hu, W.: FoggyCache: cross-device approximate computation reuse. In: Annual International Conference on Mobile Computing and Networking. MobiCom (2018)
17. Gupta, H., Ramachandran, U.: Fogstore: a geo-distributed key-value store guaranteeing low latency for strongly consistent access. In: ACM Conference on Distributed and Event-based Systems. DEBS (2018)
18. Hadzilacos, V., Toueg, S.: A modular approach to fault-tolerant broadcasts and related problems. Technical report, USA (1994)
19. Hasenburg, J., Grambow, M., Bermbach, D.: Towards a replication service for data-intensive fog applications. In: ACM Symposium on Applied Computing (2020)
20. Hemmati, E., Garcia-Luna-Aceves, J.J.: A new approach to name-based link-state routing for information-centric networks. In: Proceedings of the 2nd ACM Conference on Information-Centric Networking. ICN (2015)
21. Hoque, A.K.M.M., Amin, S.O., Alyyan, A., Zhang, B., Zhang, L., Wang, L.: NLSR: named-data link state routing protocol. In: ACM SIGCOMM Workshop on Information-centric Networking (2013)
22. Hsiao, H.C., King, C.T.: Scoped broadcast in dynamic peer-to-peer networks. In: International Computer Software and Applications Conference (2005)
23. Iyer, S., Rowstron, A., Druschel, P.: Squirrel: a decentralized peer-to-peer web cache. In: Symposium on Principles of Distributed Computing. PODC (2002)
24. Jelasity, M., Babaoglu, O.: T-Man: gossip-based overlay topology management. In: Brueckner, S.A., Di Marzo Serugendo, G., Hales, D., Zambonelli, F. (eds.) ESOA 2005. LNCS (LNAI), vol. 3910, pp. 1–15. Springer, Heidelberg (2006). https://doi.org/10.1007/11734697_1
25. Kermarrec, A.M., Taïani, F.: Want to scale in centralized systems? Think P2P. J. Internet Serv. App. **6**, 16 (2015). https://doi.org/10.1186/s13174-015-0029-1
26. Knight, S., Nguyen, H.X., Falkner, N., Bowden, R., Roughan, M.: The internet topology zoo. IEEE J. Sel. Areas Commun. **29**, 1765–1775 (2011)
27. Lamport, L.: Time, clocks, and the ordering of events in a distributed system. Commun. ACM **21**(7), 558–565 (1978)
28. Lue, M.Y., King, C.T., Fang, H.: Scoped broadcast in structured P2P networks. In: Conference on Scalable Information Systems (2006)
29. Maymounkov, P., Mazières, D.: Kademlia: a peer-to-peer information system based on the XOR metric. In: Druschel, P., Kaashoek, F., Rowstron, A. (eds.) IPTPS 2002. LNCS, vol. 2429, pp. 53–65. Springer, Heidelberg (2002). https://doi.org/10.1007/3-540-45748-8_5
30. Montresor, A., Jelasity, M.: PeerSim: a scalable P2P simulator. In: Proceedings of the 9th International Conference on Peer-to-Peer (2009)
31. Nur, A.Y., Tozal, M.E.: Geography and routing in the internet. ACM Trans. Spatial Algorithms Syst. **4**(4), 1–6 (2018)
32. RFC2328: OSPF Version 2 (1998). https://tools.ietf.org/html/rfc2328
33. Seedorf, J., Kiesel, S., Stiemerling, M.: Traffic localization for P2P-applications: the ALTO approach. In: 2009 IEEE 9th International Conference on Peer-to-Peer Computing, pp. 171–177, September 2009
34. Shapiro, M., Preguiça, N., Baquero, C., Zawirski, M.: Conflict-free Replicated Data Types. Research Report RR-7687, July 2011
35. Shi, W., Cao, J., Zhang, Q., Li, Y., Xu, L.: Edge computing: vision and challenges. IEEE Internet Things J. **3**(5), 637–646 (2016)
36. Sohier, D., Georgiadis, G., Ere, S., Papatriantafilou, M., Bui, A.: Physarum-inspired self-biased walkers for distributed clustering. In: International Conference on Principles of Distributed Systems (2012)

37. Triukose, S., Wen, Z., Rabinovich, M.: Measuring a commercial content delivery network. In: Conference on World Wide Web (2011)
38. Wang, L., Bayhan, S., Ott, J., Kangasharju, J., Sathiaseelan, A., Crowcroft, J.: Pro-Diluvian: understanding scoped-flooding for content discovery in information-centric networking. In: ACM Conference on Information-Centric Networking (2015)
39. Xie, J., Qian, C., Guo, D., Wang, M., Shi, S., Chen, H.: Efficient indexing mechanism for unstructured data sharing systems in edge computing. In: IEEE Conference on Computer Communications (2019)

Heterogeneous Graph Based Long- And Short-Term Preference Learning Model for Next POI Recommendation

Shiyang Zhou, Jinghua Zhu$^{(\boxtimes)}$, Heran Xi, and Hongjun An

School of Computer Science and Technology, Heilongjiang University,
Harbin 150080, China
zhujinghua@hlju.edu.cn

Abstract. The next POI recommendation aiming at recommending the venues that people are likely interested in has become a popular service provided by location-based social networks such as Foursquare and Gowalla. Many existing methods attempt to improve the recommendation accuracy by modeling the long- and short-term preferences of people. However, these methods learn users' preferences only from their own historical check-in records, which leads to bad recommendation performance in sparse dataset. To this end, we propose a novel approach named long- and short-term preference learning model based on heterogeneous graph convolution network and attention mechanism (LSPHGA) for next POI recommendation. Specifically, we design a heterogeneous graph convolution network to learn the higher-order structural relations between User-POI-Categories and obtain the long-term preferences of users. As for the short-term preference, we encode the recent check-in records of users through self-attention mechanism and aggregate the short-term preference by spatio-temporal attention. Finally, the long- and short-term preference is linearly combined into a unified preference with personalized weights for different users. Extensive experiments on two real-world datasets consistently validate the effectiveness of the proposed method for improving recommendation.

Keywords: POI recommendation · Long- and short-term preference · Graph neural network · Attention mechanism · Spatio-temporal context

1 Introduction

With the rapid growth of Location-Based Social Networks (LBSNs), such as Foursquare, Yelp and Gowalla, the next Point-of-Interest (POI) recommendation which aims at providing personalized location recommendations to a user based on her/his historical check-in sequence has attracted wide attention from both academia and industry. The next POI recommendation not only helps users find their interested places from a large number of POIs, but also brings profits to the business to attract more potential customers [3,5,24,25]. Both long-term

© Springer Nature Switzerland AG 2023
W. Meng et al. (Eds.): ICA3PP 2022, LNCS 13777, pp. 455–470, 2023.
https://doi.org/10.1007/978-3-031-22677-9_24

and short-term preferences of users play an important role in deciding which POI they want to visit. The long-term preferences denoting the user's general interests are stable, while the short-term preferences learned from the recent check-in records represent user's recent interests and usually tend to change over time. The user's long-term and short-term preferences co-determine the next POI they will check-in [21].

Recently, several methods for POI recommendation by learning the user's long- and short-term preferences have been proposed. Early study proposed combining Markov chains with matrix factorization method [3] to learn the long- and short-term preference of users. Later on, recurrent neural networks (RNNs) with memory mechanism have produced excellent results in various sequential learning problems. Many studies [4,15,19,22,26] extended classic RNNs structure to make them have the ability to capture the long- and short-term preference.

Among these existing methods, two important challenges are not well addressed. First, high-order structure information in check-in data is still not effectively utilized. High-order structural information is ubiquitous in LBSN. For example, if two users have check-in records in many of the same POIs, it indicates that they have similar preferences and are more likely to visit POIs which the other has checked-in. When a user visits many POIs in the same category multiple times, he/she prefers to visit other POIs in this category. Due to the sparsity of user check-in data, the high-order structure information, such as similar users and same category of POIs, is indispensable for learning user preference. However, most current methods focus on learning user's preference only depend on their own check-in record while ignoring high-order structure information in check-in data. Second, existing methods based on RNNs do not take full advantage of the rich spatio-temporal context information in the user's trajectory. From a temporal perspective, these methods ignore the temporal periodicity of user mobility. Specifically, the periodicity of human activities is universal. Users tend to go to restaurants for breakfast in the morning. In the evening, they prefer shopping malls or gymnasiums. From a spatial perspective, these methods cannot effectively learn the spatial correlations between non-contiguous visits. For example, given a user's POI check-in sequence $\{l_1, l_2, l_3\}$, suppose l_1 is the user's home, l_2 is a play ground, l_3 is a restaurant near l_1. In this case, the user's movement from l_2 to l_3 is mainly determined by the short distance between l_1 and l_3, rather than the visit order between l_2 and l_3. However, most existing methods are difficult to capture it duo to they only consider the spatial distance between adjacent visits.

To this end, we propose a novel long- and short-term preference learning model based on heterogeneous graph convolution network and attention mechanism (LSPHGA for short) for the next POI recommendation. To thoroughly model users' long-term preferences, we construct a heterogeneous user-POI-category graph from the users' check-ins and use heterogeneous graph convolution network to learn the higher-order relationships among users, POIs, and categories through the message propagating between nodes. In modeling users' short-term preferences, we encode users' current trajectory through self-attention networks, and propose a spatio-temporal attention mechanism to aggregate users short-term preferences. Finally, we fuse the users' long- and short-term preferences and use the results for the final POI recommendation. Experimental results on real-world datasets show that our model significantly outperforms state-of-the-art methods on next POI recommendation.

The main contributions of this paper are summarized as follows:

1) We propose LSPHGA, a long- and short-preference learning model based on heterogeneous graph convolution network and attention mechanism for next POI recommendation.
2) We construct a heterogeneous user-POI-category graph and design a heterogeneous graph convolution network to learn user long-term preference with high-order information to mitigate the influence of data sparsity for the next POI recommendation.
3) We use self-attention mechanism to capture the correlation between users' historical check-ins, and propose a new attention mechanism to aggregate users' short-term preference through spatio-temporal contextual information.
4) We conduct extensive experiments on two public datasets to evaluate the performances of the proposed method. Our method is superior to the advanced method on next POI recommendation.

2   Related Works

Early studies use Markov chains [16] to predict the probability of the next behavior via a transition matrix. FPMC [17] introduces matrix factorization model to deal with the sparsity of check-in data. Based on FPMC, FPMC-LR [3] has been proposed to learn transition regularities with localized spatial constraint. NLPMM [2] combines the personalized Markov chain with the global Markov chain to capture global behavioral patterns.

Although these Markov chain based models partly address data sparsity, they do not understand the relationship among the check-in records of the user's entire trajectory. Challenged by the defects of Markov models, the recurrent neural network model has received extensive attention. STRNN [11] captures temporal cyclic effect and geographical influence by adding a time-specific and distance-specific transition matrix, respectively. HST-LSTM [8] proposes a hierarchical model that captures users' historical trajectory in an encoder and decoder manner. DeepMove [4] proposes a historical attention model that captures the multi-level periodicity of user check-in. PLSPL [22] combines attention mechanism for learning user's long-term preference with LSTM for learning user's short-term preference and uses user-based linear combination unit to learn the weight of long- and short-term preferences. STGN [26] modified basic LSTM by adding spatiotemporal gates to capture long- and short-term preference. CAPRE [1] encodes user-generated textual contents into content embedding to capture user interests. LSTPM [19] uses a context-aware nonlocal network to model user's long-term preferences, and a geo-delated RNN to conquer the limitation of RNNs in short-term user preference modeling. ATCA-GRU [13] proposes a category-aware model by combining the attention mechanism with GRU.

Due to its high efficiency and effectiveness, self-attention mechanism [20] has been widely applied in the field of natural language processing and has achieved excellent results in many tasks. In recent years, it was also used in next POI recommendation to capture the relationships between the user's check-ins. GeoSAN [10] uses the self-attention encoder to capture long-term sequential dependence and proposes the self-attention based geography encoder to represent the exact GPS positions of locations. STAN [14] first uses the self-attention mechanism to aggregate spatiotemporal correlation with linear interpolation and then though the attention matching layer recalls the target by considering personalized item frequency.

In the above-mentioned research, only partially of them learn both the long-term and short-term preferences of users. And all of them ignore high-order structure information in the user check-in data. Thus, in this paper, we propose LSPHGA, which not only captures high-order information in the user's long-term preference learning, but also utilizes spatio-temporal information to learn the user's short-term preference.

3   Preliminaries

In this section, we give problem formulations and term definitions. Let $U = \{u_1, u_2, \ldots, u_M\}$ be a set of users, $L = \{l_1, l_2, \ldots, l_N\}$ be a set of POI, $C = \{c_1, c_2, \ldots, c_O\}$ be a set of categories of POI, where M, N, and O are the numbers of users, POIs, and categories, respectively.

Definition 1 (historical trajectory). *The trajectory of user u is temporally ordered check-ins. Each check-in is a four-tuple (u, t, l, p) that represents the context of the interactions, which means that the user u at time t visited POI l that is located in the GPS coordinate $p = (lon_l, lat_l)$.*

Definition 2 (user-POI-category graph). *In this paper, we utilize the check-in sequences of all users to construct a user-POI-category graph $G = (V, E)$, as*

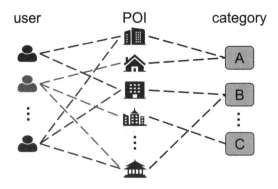

Fig. 1. Heterogeneous user-POI-category graph

shown in Fig. 1, which is a heterogeneous undirected graph. V is the node set in the graph, which is construct by including the user set U, the POI set L, and the category set C. E represents the edge set in the graph, which contains two types of edges: user-POI and POI-category. The edge of user-POI $e_{i,j}$ represents the user u_i has been to the POI l_j. Particularly if user u_i has visited POI l_j several times, there will be multiple edges between i and j. The edge of location-category $e_{i,j}$ represents the c_i is the category of l_j.

Definition 3 (current trajectory). *Given the historical trajectory of user u, we take the most recent n check-in records of u as the current trajectory. We set the current trajectory of user u as $S^u = \{s_1^u, s_2^u, \ldots, s_n^u\}$. If user's trajectory length $m < n$, we pad zeros to the right until the length grows to n and mask off the padding items during calculation.*

Definition 4 (next POI recommendation). *Given the heterogeneous user-POI-category graph G and the current trajectory S^u of user u, the task of the next POI recommendation is to predict the possibility of the candidate POI $l_c \in L$ that user will visit at the time t_{n+1}.*

4 Our Model

In this section, we introduce our model. As illustrated in Fig. 2, our model contains four main parts: the embedding layer, the long-term preference learning module, the short-term preference learning module, and the prediction layer. We first describe each part in detail in the following sections. Then we give the objective function and the training algorithm of our approach.

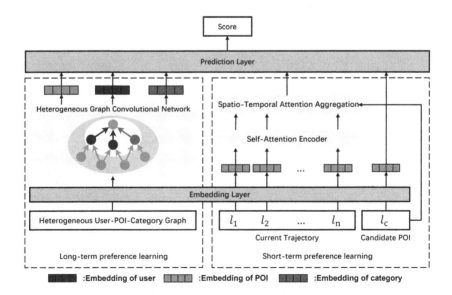

Fig. 2. The architecture of our model.

4.1 Embedding Layer

The embedding layer is used to encode user, POI, and category into latent representations. For user, POI, and category, we denote their embedded representations as $e^u \in R^d$, $e^l \in R^d$, and $e^c \in R^d$, respectively, where d represents the dimension of embedding space. For long-term preference learning, the output of embedding layer is latent representation of nodes in the heterogeneous graph. For short-term preference learning, the embedding of each user current trajectory S^u can be denoted as $E(u) = \{e^{l_1}, e^{l_2}, \ldots, e^{l_n}\} \in R^{n \times d}$. Since the self-attention encoder cannot capture relative positions in the sequence like RNN, we follow [7] to add positional embedding into $E(u)$.

4.2 The Long-Term Preference Learning Module

This module aims to learn the long-term preference of users by capturing the high-order structure information from the user-POI-category graph. Inspired by RGCN [18], we design a heterogeneous graph convolution network (HGCN), which first samples neighbor nodes for each node, and then updates its representation by aggregating the information from sampled neighbour nodes.

Graph neural networks typically update the representation of the node with all of its neighbors. However, user check-ins usually have long tail effects, where there are some POIs visited by many people and some POIs visited by few people [12]. In other words, the neighbor number of the nodes in the graph exists a huge difference, which makes it difficult for our model to update the representation of the node efficiently. To reduce computational overhead and improve computational efficiency, we follow [6] to uniformly sample a fixed number of neighbors for each node instead of using its entire neighbors.

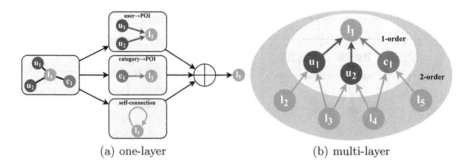

(a) one-layer   (b) multi-layer

Fig. 3. The structure of HGCN. Taking the POI node updating as example.

After neighbour sampling, we use HGCN to learn the representation of each node. A single layer of HGCN can be divided into two stages: information propagation and information aggregation. In the stage of information propagation, each node propagates information to their sampled neighbor nodes and meanwhile gathers the representations of them. As shown in Fig. 3(a), the POI node though relations user $\rightarrow$ POI and category $\rightarrow$ POI gathers the representations of users visited in it and own category, respectively. To preserve the original representation of the node, we add a relation of self-connection to each node. In the stage of information aggregation, each node aggregates the information from its neighbors and updates its representation. We calculate the updated representation of nodes by:

$$h_i' = W_0 h_i + \sum_{r \in R} \sum_{j \in N_i^r} \frac{1}{|N_i^r|} W_r h_j \tag{1}$$

where h_i' is the updated representation of node i, h_i is the original representation of node i, N_i^r is the set of sampled neighbors of node i under relation r, W_r is the transformation matrix assigned for relation r.

A single layer of HGCN can only capture the relationship between each node and its immediate neighbor nodes. To capture high-order relationships in graph, we extend the HGCN from one layer to multiple layers and utilize high-order propagation to gather information from high-order neighbor nodes. Taking the 2-order propagation path $l_2 \rightarrow u_1 \rightarrow l_1$ and $l_5 \rightarrow c_1 \rightarrow l_1$ in Fig. 3(b) as an example. The user u_1 and category c_1 respectively gather the embedding of l_2 and l_5 to update their representation and then propagate their representation to l_1. Through 2-order propagation, the POI l_1 can receive the information from 2-order neighbor l_2 and l_5. After the propagation in the l-th layer, each node updates its representation as follows:

$$h_i^{(l)} = \sigma(W_0^{(l)} W_i^{(l-1)} + \sum_{r \in R} \sum_{j \in N_i^r} \frac{1}{|N_i^r|} W_r^{(l-1)} h_j^{(l-1)}) \tag{2}$$

where h_i^l is the representation of node i at l layer, $W_r^{(l)}$ is the transformation matrix assigned for relation r at l-th layer, which is different for each layer. And the σ is the activation function.

4.3 The Short-Term Preference Learning Module

Self-Attention Encoder. To capture the interdependence in the user's trajectory, we use self-attention encoder [20] to update the representation of each check-in in the user's trajectory. The self-attention encoders contains multiple self-attention blocks, each of which consists of a self-attention layer and a feedforward network (FFN). Given the representation matrix E of the user's current trajectory, self-attention layer computes a new representation matrix A after converting them through distinct transformation matrices of query, key, and value $W_Q, W_K, W_V \in R^{d \times d}$ as follows:

$$A = Attention(EW_Q, EW_K, EW_V) \tag{3}$$

$$Attention(Q, K, V) = softmax(\frac{QK^T}{\sqrt{d}})V \tag{4}$$

After each self-attention layer, we apply the FFN layer, which is a two-layer feed-forward network, to endow model with non-linearity:

$$F = ReLU(AW_1 + b_1)W_2 + b_2 \tag{5}$$

where $W_1, W_2 \in \mathbb{R}^{d \times d}$ and $b_1, b_2 \in \mathbb{R}^{d \times 1}$.

For stabilizing and speeding up the training process, the residual connection and layer normalization are applied in the self-attention layer and the FNN layer.

Spatio-Temporal Attention Aggregation. To leverage the spatio-temporal context more effectively, we propose a spatio-temporal attention mechanism to aggregate the representation updated by the self-attention encoder. We first compute the spatio-temporal attention weight $W_{i,j}$ of the historical check-in s_i with respect to the candidate POI lj. The weight of spatio-temporal attention can be calculated as follows:

$$W_{i,j} = W_P(\Delta T_{i,j}) \cdot W_T(\Delta T_{i,j}) \cdot W_D(\Delta D_{i,j}) \tag{6}$$

$$W_P(\Delta T_{i,j}) = \frac{\cos(2\pi \Delta T_{i,j}) + 1}{2} \tag{7}$$

$$W_T(\Delta T_{i,j}) = e^{-\alpha \Delta T_{i,j}} \tag{8}$$

$$W_D(\Delta D_{i,j}) = e^{-\beta \Delta D_{i,j}} \tag{9}$$

where $\Delta T_{i,j} = |t_i - t_j|$ is temporal interval(in days) between check-in time t_i and prediction time t_j, $\Delta D_{i,j} = Haversine(p_i, p_j)$ is spatial distance between check-in POI l_i and candidate POI l_j. $W_P(\Delta T_{i,j})$ is temporal periodic weight with outputs bounded in $[0, 1]$ and when the temporal interval is close to an integer day, the temporal periodic weight is close to 1. $W_T(\Delta T_{i,j})$ and $W_D(\Delta D_{i,j})$ are temporal interval weight and spatial distance weight, respectively. The check-in which position near the candidate POI or time close to predict time tend to have stronger predictive power. Thus, we use exponential decay to model those factor. α and β are temporal decay rate and spatial decay rate, controlling how fast the weight decreases over time $\Delta T_{i,j}$ and spatial distance $\Delta D_{i,j}$.

Then, we learn user's short-term preference by fusing the output of self-attention encoder with different weights:

$$u_j^{short} = \sum_i \frac{exp(W_{i,j})}{\sum_i exp(W_{i,j})} \cdot l_i \tag{10}$$

where u_j^{short} is user's short-term preference for candidate POI l_j, l_i is the updated representation of i-th check-in.

4.4   Prediction Layer

The aim of the prediction layer is to calculate the preference score of each candidate POI in the POI set. To better integrate the user's long- and short-term preferences, we compute the preference score of candidate POI l_j for user u_i as follows:

$$y_{i,j} = \lambda_{u_i} \cdot h_{u_i} \cdot h_{l_j} + \mu_{u_i} \cdot h_{u_i} \cdot h_{c_k} + \gamma_{u_i} \cdot u_{i,j}^s \cdot e^{l_j} \tag{11}$$

where h_{u_i}, h_{l_j}, and h_{c_k} is the representation of user u_i, candidate POI l_j, and the category of candidate POI c_k at the last layer of the heterogeneous graph convolution network, respectively. $u_{i,j}^s$ is the vector of the short-term preference of user u_i for candidate POI l_j. e^{l_j} is the embedding of candidate POI l_j. λ_{u_i}, μ_{u_i}, and γ_{u_i} are the weight of the long-term POI preference, long-term category preference, and short-term preference for user u_i, which can be learned by our model.

4.5   Model Optimization

Most existing methods use binary cross-entropy loss to optimize their model. However, for each positive sample, the binary cross-entropy loss only samples one negative item from unvisited locations, which can not make fully effective use of the large number of unvisited locations. To this end, we adopt a negative sampler that samples K negative items from unvisited locations for each positive sample. In particular, after each training step, we will sample a new set of negative items. The loss is calculated as:

$$\mathcal{L} = - \sum_{S_u \in S} \left(log\big(\sigma(y_{u,p})\big) + \sum_{k=1}^{K} log\big(1 - \sigma(y_{u,n_k})\big) \right) \tag{12}$$

where S is the training set of user check-in, p is the target POI, n_k is the negative sample, which is not in the set of visited locations by user u.

5   Experiments

5.1   Datasets

We evaluate our model on two public Foursquare check-in datasets collected from New York City (NYC) and Tokyo (TKY) [23]. Each check-in record of datasets contains user ID, POI ID, category name, GPS coordinate and timestamp. We remove users with fewer than 5 check-ins and POIs which have been visited fewer than 5 times. Then we take the first 80% check-ins of each user as the training set, the latter 20% as the test set. The overall statistics of both datasets after preprocessing are shown in Table 1.

Table 1. Dataset statistics.

	NYC	TKY
Number of users	1083	2293
Number of POIs	9989	15177
Number of categories	382	362
Number of check-ins	157806	494807

5.2 Baseline Models

We compare our method with the following baselines:

- **STRNN** [11]: This model extends the RNN structure by applying time-specific transition matrices and distance-specific transition matrices to model spatio-temporal contexts.
- **TMCA** [9]: This model employs LSTM-based encoder-decoder network and introduces multi-level context attention and temporal attention mechanisms to select relevant historical and contextual factors.
- **STGN** [26]: This model improves LSTM architecture by adding two pairs of time and distance gates to model users' long-term and short-term preference respectively.
- **DeepMove** [4]: This model utilizes GRU to model long-range and complex dependencies in historical sequence and capture the multi-level periodicity of human mobility by an attention mechanism.
- **PLSPL** [22]: This model learns users' long-term preference with the attention mechanism and learns short-term preference by two parallel LSTM from location-level and category-level.
- **LSTPM** [19]: This model uses context-aware non-local network structure to model users' long-term preference and utilizes geo-dilated RNN to model users' short-term preference.
- **GeoSAN** [10]: This model uses geography encoder to represent the geographical location of the POI and applies self-attention network to capture long-term sequential dependence of user's trajectory.

5.3 Evaluation Matrices

To evaluate the next POI recommendation performance, we adopt two widely-used metrics of ranking evaluation, i.e., Recall@k and NDCG@k. Recall@K counts the fraction of correct POIs which can emerge in the top-k recommended lists. NDCG measures the quality of top-K ranking list by the position of correct POIs. The two evaluation metrics are higher, and the recommendation performance is better.

5.4 Settings

We set the embedding dimension to 60 and the training epoch to 50 for all methods, the other parameters of the baselines to the default values. In the long-term preference learning module, we set the number of the neighbours to 20 in neighbours sampling and the layer of heterogeneous graph convolution networks to 2. In the short-term preference learning module, we user three layers of self-attention modules for self-attention encoder, and the temporal decay rate α and the spatial decay rate β are set to 0.1 and 1000 respectively. We train our model using the Adam optimizer with a learning rate of 0.003 and set the dropout ratio to 0.5. When calculating the loss function, for each positive record, we randomly sample 10 negative samples.

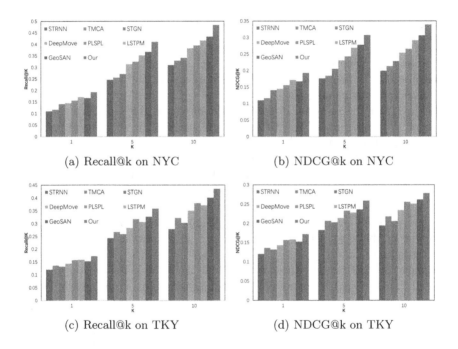

(a) Recall@k on NYC   (b) NDCG@k on NYC

(c) Recall@k on TKY   (d) NDCG@k on TKY

Fig. 4. Performance comparison of models on two datasets.

5.5 Comparison with Baselines

In this section, we analyze the performance of our proposed model and compare it with other baselines, as shown in Fig. 4. We can observe that our proposed method consistently outperforms all the baselines on two datasets and in terms of all evaluation metrics. Our proposed method archives average 11.2% and 10.1% improvements over the best-performing baseline in terms of Recall@5 and NDCG@5. This obviously indicates the superior effectiveness of our method.

Among baseline models, the self-attention model GeoSAN outperforms RNN-based models in most cases, which demonstrates the advantage of the self-attention network in modeling users' trajectory. Among RNN-based models, LSTPM and PLSPL have relatively better performances, due to their consideration of users' long- and short-term preference. Compared with other methods, TMCA and PLSPL have better performance in TKY than NYC. The main reason may be that the number of POI in TKY is more than NYC and as the number of POI increases, category information plays a more important role in learning users' preferences.

5.6 Ablation Study

In this section, we conduct a series of ablation experiments to analyze the effectiveness of the different components in our model. We drop different components and form the following variants of our model.

- Remove STP(Short-Term Preference): We remove the short-term preference learning components of LSPHGA and only utilize the long-term preference of user to recommend POI.
- Remove LTP(Long-Term Preference): We remove the long-term preference learning components of LSPHGA and only utilize the short-term preference of user to recommend POI.
- Remove HSI(High-order Structure Information): We remove the high-order structure information though using only one layer of heterogeneous graph convolution network, which makes nodes in the graph can only propagate information with their 1-order neighbour node.
- Remove TPW(Temporal Periodic Weight): We remove the temporal periodic weight in the spatio-temporal attention aggregation, ignoring the effect of periodicity of time.
- Remove TIW(Temporal Interval Weight): We remove the temporal interval weight in the spatio-temporal attention aggregation, ignoring the effect of time interval.
- Remove SDP(Spatial Distance Weight): We remove the spatial distance weight in the spatio-temporal attention aggregation, ignoring the effect of spatial distance.

Table 2 shows the results of the ablation study. We found that -LTP performs better than -STP. We suppose that -LTP can capture complicated spatio-temporal information and sequential patterns, which is crucial for next POI recommendation. Meanwhile, compared with -STP and -LTP, which only use users' long-term or short-term preferences, the complete method has better performance. This evidence that both users' long- and short-term preferences have positive impacts on their choice POI which they will go next. The experimental results of -HSI show that learning high-order structure information from the heterogeneous graph is crucial for improving the recommendation performance. And the results of the last three variants show that adding temporal periodic

Table 2. Performance comparison of different variants of LSPHGA.

Dataset	Variants	Rec@1	Rec@5	Rec@10	NDCG@5	NDCG@10
NYC	LSPHGA	0.1903	0.4111	0.4838	0.3076	0.3391
	-STP	0.1457	0.3514	0.4093	0.2653	0.2830
	-LTP	0.1678	0.3762	0.4387	0.2824	0.3073
	-HSI	0.1806	0.3902	0.4569	0.2926	0.3218
	-TPW	0.1874	0.4025	0.4724	0.3023	0.3324
	-TIW	0.1743	0.3868	0.4495	0.2864	0.3149
	-SDW	0.1705	0.3809	0.4427	0.2825	0.3095
TKY	LSPHGA	0.1725	0.3591	0.4352	0.2678	0.2921
	-STP	0.1358	0.3094	0.3844	0.2248	0.2589
	-LTP	0.1523	0.3263	0.4011	0.2437	0.2760
	-HSI	0.1630	0.3409	0.4162	0.2585	0.2867
	-TPW	0.1687	0.3524	0.4286	0.2622	0.2878
	-TIW	0.1621	0.3376	0.4136	0.2513	0.2784
	-SDW	0.1589	0.3317	0.4081	0.2481	0.2734

weight, temporal interval weight, and spatial distance weight all can improve the recommendation performance. Overall, the performance of our model is better than all variants, and it also proves the effectiveness of different components of the model.

5.7   Influence of Hyper-parameters

Influence of Embedding Dim. We vary the dimension of embedding d in the embedding layer from 10 to 90 with step 10. Figure 5 shows that our model achieves the best performance at $d = 60$, indicating that such dimension setting can best represent the information of user, POI, and category. And the performance of our model first increases with the growth of d and then lightly declines when d further increases. The reason is that the larger dimension has better expressive ability, but too large dimension also leads to the decrease of generalization performance and causes over-fitting issues.

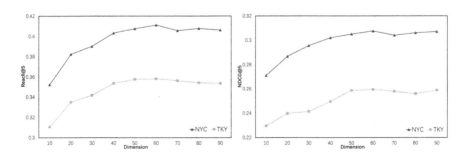

Fig. 5. Impact of embedding dimension.

Influence of Spatio-Temporal Decay Rate. We experiment a series of temporal decay rate $\alpha = [10^0, 10^{-1}, 10^{-2}]$ and spatial decay rate $\beta = [10^2, 10^3, 10^4, 10^5]$ in the spatio-temporal attention aggregation. Figure 6 shows the results. When increasing the temporal decay α and the spatial decay factor β, we observe that the prediction performance increases, and then decrease after $\alpha = 10^{-1}$ and $\beta = 10^4$. This reflects that both spatial distance and temporal interval are very important factors for predicting the next location, but too large α and β will make model ignore the role of temporal periodic.

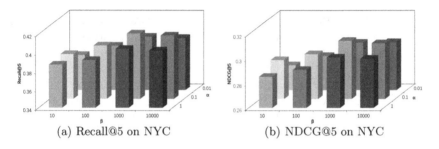

(a) Recall@5 on NYC   (b) NDCG@5 on NYC

Fig. 6. Results of different decay rate.

6   Conclusion

In this paper, we propose a novel model named LSPHGA for the next POI recommendation problem by learning the long- and short-term preferences of users. To learn the long-term preferences of users, we first construct a heterogeneous graph to represent the information of users' check-in, and use the heterogeneous graph neural network to learn the higher-order structural relationships in the heterogeneous graph through information propagation and information aggregation. We further use the self-attention mechanism to learn the correlation of users' recent check-in, and propose a spatio-temporal attention aggregation mechanism to effectively aggregate users' recent trajectory through spatio-temporal context information. The experimental results demonstrate that our proposed approach significantly improves the recommendation accuracy compared with the state-of-the-art methods. Besides, through ablation study, we show the importance of each part of our model at improving recommendation performance.

References

1. Chang, B., Koh, Y., Park, D., Kang, J.: Content-aware successive point-of-interest recommendation. In: Proceedings of the 2020 SIAM International Conference on Data Mining, pp. 100–108. SIAM (2020)
2. Chen, M., Liu, Y., Yu, X.: NLPMM: a next location predictor with Markov modeling. In: Tseng, V.S., Ho, T.B., Zhou, Z.-H., Chen, A.L.P., Kao, H.-Y. (eds.) PAKDD 2014. LNCS (LNAI), vol. 8444, pp. 186–197. Springer, Cham (2014). https://doi.org/10.1007/978-3-319-06605-9_16

3. Cheng, C., Yang, H., Lyu, M.R., King, I.: Successive point-of-interest recommendation. In: Twenty-Third International Joint Conference on Artificial Intelligence, Where You Like to Go Next (2013)

4. Feng, J., et al.: Deepmove: predicting human mobility with attentional recurrent networks. In Proceedings of the 2018 World Wide Web Conference, pp. 1459–1468 (2018)

5. Feng, S., Li, X., Zeng, Y., Cong, G., Chee, Y.M., Yuan, Q.: Personalized ranking metric embedding for next new poi recommendation. In: Twenty-Fourth International Joint Conference on Artificial Intelligence (2015)

6. Hamilton, W., Ying, Z., Leskovec, J.: Inductive representation learning on large graphs. In: Advances in Neural Information Processing Systems, vol. 30 (2017)

7. Wang-Cheng Kang and Julian McAuley. Self-attentive sequential recommendation. In: 2018 IEEE International Conference on Data Mining (ICDM), pp. 197–206. IEEE (2018)

8. Kong, D., Fei, W.: HST-LSTM: a hierarchical spatial-temporal long-short term memory network for location prediction. In IJCAI **18**, 2341–2347 (2018)

9. Li, R., Shen, Y., Zhu, Y.: Next point-of-interest recommendation with temporal and multi-level context attention. In: 2018 IEEE International Conference on Data Mining (ICDM) (2018)

10. Lian, D., Wu, Y., Ge, Y., Xie, X., Chen, E.: Geography-aware sequential location recommendation. In Proceedings of the 26th ACM SIGKDD International Conference on Knowledge Discovery & Data Mining, pp. 2009–2019 (2020)

11. Liu, Q., Wu, S., Wang, L., Tan, T.: Predicting the next location: a recurrent model with spatial and temporal contexts. In: Thirtieth AAAI Conference on Artificial Intelligence (2016)

12. Chen, M., Liu, Y., Yu, X.: NLPMM: a next location predictor with Markov modeling. In: Tseng, V.S., Ho, T.B., Zhou, Z.-H., Chen, A.L.P., Kao, H.-Y. (eds.) PAKDD 2014. LNCS (LNAI), vol. 8444, pp. 186–197. Springer, Cham (2014). https://doi.org/10.1007/978-3-319-06605-9_16

13. Liu, Y., et al.: An attention-based category-aware GRU model for the next poi recommendation. Int. J. Intell. Syst. **36**(7), 3174–3189 (2021)

14. Luo, Y., Liu, Q., Liu, Z.: Stan: Spatio-temporal attention network for next location recommendation. In: Proceedings of the Web Conference 2021, pp. 2177–2185 (2021)

15. Manotumruksa, J., Macdonald, C., Ounis, I.: A deep recurrent collaborative filtering framework for venue recommendation. In: Proceedings of the 2017 ACM on Conference on Information and Knowledge Management, pp. 1429–1438 (2017)

16. Rendle, S.: Factorization machines. In: 2010 IEEE International Conference on Data Mining, pp. 995–1000. IEEE (2010)

17. Rendle, S., Freudenthaler, C., Schmidt-Thieme, L.: Factorizing personalized Markov chains for next-basket recommendation. In: Proceedings of the 19th International Conference on World Wide Web, pp. 811–820 (2010)

18. Schlichtkrull, M., Kipf, T.N., Bloem, P., van den Berg, R., Titov, I., Welling, M.: Modeling relational data with graph convolutional networks. In: Gangemi, A., et al. (eds.) ESWC 2018. LNCS, vol. 10843, pp. 593–607. Springer, Cham (2018). https://doi.org/10.1007/978-3-319-93417-4_38

19. Sun, K., Qian, T., Chen, T., Liang, Y., Nguyen, Q.V.H., Yin, H.: Where to go next: modeling long-and short-term user preferences for point-of-interest recommendation. In: Proceedings of the AAAI Conference on Artificial Intelligence, vol. 34, pp. 214–221 (2020)

20. Vaswani, A., et al.: Attention is all you need. In: Advances In Neural Information Processing Systems, vol. 30 (2017)
21. Wu, Y., Li, K., Zhao, G., Qian, X.: Long-and short-term preference learning for next poi recommendation. In: Proceedings of the 28th ACM International Conference on Information and Knowledge Management, pp. 2301–2304 (2019)
22. Wu, Y., Li, K., Zhao, G., Qian, X.: Personalized long-and short-term preference learning for next poi recommendation. IEEE Trans. Knowl. Data Eng. **34**, 1944–1957 (2020)
23. Yang, D., Zhang, D., Zheng, V.W., Yu, Z.: Modeling user activity preference by leveraging user spatial temporal characteristics in LBSNS. IEEE Trans. Syst. Man Cybern. Syst. **45**(1), 129–142 (2014)
24. Yin, H., Zhou, X., Shao, Y., Wang, H., Sadiq, S.: Joint modeling of user check-in behaviors for point-of-interest recommendation. In: Proceedings of the 24th ACM International on Conference on Information and Knowledge Management, pp. 1631–1640 (2015)
25. Zang, H., Han, D., Li, X., Wan, Z., Wang, M.: Cha: Categorical hierarchy-based attention for next poi recommendation. ACM Trans. Inf. Syst. (TOIS) **40**(1), 1–22 (2021)
26. Zhao, P., et al.: Where to go next: a spatio-temporal gated network for next poi recommendation. IEEE Trans. Knowl. Data Eng. (2020)

SMTWM: Secure Multiple Types Wildcard Pattern Matching Protocol from Oblivious Transfer

Shuang Ding, Xiaochao Wei[(✉)], Lin Xu, and Hao Wang

School of Information Science and Engineering,
Shandong Normal University, Jinan, China
`wxc@sdnu.edu.cn`

Abstract. Secure wildcard pattern matching (SWPM) involves both sender and receiver entities, where the sender holds long text and the receiver holds short pattern containing wildcard characters. The receiver only learns the position information which the short pattern string appears in the long text string, and does not disclose any information to either party other than the input length. However, standard SWPM considers single kind of wildcard which is not suitable in many scenarios, e.g., normal genes mutate into different kinds of mutated genes in the gene matching scenario.

In our study, to better address the above problem, we construct an extended SWPM variant called secure multiple types wildcard pattern matching (SMTWM). In SMTWM functionality, the pattern contains multiple types of wildcard characters, such as (*, #). Besides, wildcards of each type can match special and different characters in the text. Considering the DNA sequence which contains 'AGCT' as example, the wildcard '*' can match A and G, and the whidcard '#' can match C and T. We propose a SMTWM protocol based on the oblivious transfer (OT) and the private equality test (PEQT) protocol in semi-honest model. Furthermore, the protocol simply needs a few number of public key operations and some fast symmetric key primitive using OT extension technique. Our experiments have shown that when the length of pattern is 2^8 and the length of text is 2^{16}, the running time is less than 0.4 and 2.5 s in the LAN and WAN.

Keywords: Secure wildcard pattern matching · Secure multiple types wildcard pattern matching · Oblivious transfer · Private equality test · Oblivious transfer extension

1 Introduction

Pattern matching is a basic algorithmic problem that attempts to locate the position of short pattern in longer text, and one of the most important variant

This work was supported by the China Postdoctoral Science Foundation (2018M632712), the National Natural Science Foundation of China for Young Scientists (61802235) and the National Natural Science Foundation of China (62071280).

W. Meng et al. (Eds.): ICA3PP 2022, LNCS 13777, pp. 471–489, 2023.
https://doi.org/10.1007/978-3-031-22677-9_25

of that is the wildcard pattern matching (WPM), and a wildcard character means that can be replaced by any character in the character sets. Wildcard pattern matching has been intensively studied and is widely used in various life scenarios. Secure wildcard pattern matching (SWPM) [1] involves both sender and receiver entities, where the sender holds long text and the receiver holds short pattern containing wildcard characters. The receiver only learns the position information which the short pattern string appears in the long text string, and does not disclose any information to either party other than the input length. Secure wildcard pattern matching could be applied in a number of domains, such as database queries [2], Bio-genetics [3] and information retrieval [4]. Two types of adversarial models are commonly considered: the malicious model and the semi-honest model. In the malicious model, the adversary can follow any polynomial-time strategy. In the semi-honest model, the adversary is assumed to comply with the protocol while trying to learn information from the protocol text. The protocols constructed in this paper can be used against semi-honest adversaries.

Traditional SWPM only considers single kind of wildcard, however, since patterns may contain incorrect characters and gaps, handing such issues in the pattern is essential. Especially, in the case of DNA sequences where a patient's DNA sequence has errors and cannot be matched to DNA sequences in the national gene bank, we can deal with them by inserting multi wildcards ('*', '#') into the pattern. It is well known that the DNA sequence consists of four types of nitrogenous bases: adenine(A), guanine(G), cytosine(C) and thymine(T). For generality and simplicity, we consider the wildcard '*' used in the pattern to replace 'A' and 'G', and the wildcard '#' to replace 'C' and 'T'. Therefore, the essential problem is finding where $p \in \{A, G, C, T, *, \#\}^m$ occurs in the text $t \in \{A, G, C, T\}^n$. According to whether the pattern string contains wildcards, we divide pattern matching into the following categories, i.e. pattern without wildcards (ACT), pattern with a single wildcard (AC*), pattern with multiple types wildcard patterns (AC*TG#T). Most early works in secure computing dealt with patterns without wildcards [5] or with single wildcards [6]. Patterns with multiple types wildcard provide the user with more flexibility in searching than patterns with a single wildcard. It is easy to see that pattern matching and its variants are widely used, but there are increasing threats to the privacy of data. For example, a hospital querying a national database for a patient's DNA sequence does not want patient's DNA sequence information to be leaked to national database, and the information in the national database cannot be leaked to the hospital. Therefore, we consider secure multiple types wildcard pattern matching (SMTWPM) problem in semi-honest model.

We focus on the following application scenario: the national gene bank stores human genetic data, when a human genetic disease occurs(nitrogenous base is mutated), the gene bank is searched for mutated genes similar to those of the patient, and the better the gene sequence match, the more accurate the diagnosis of the patients condition and the more efficient the treatment. Concretely, the national gene bank holds a text $t \in \{A, G, C, T\}^n$ and the hospital holds a pattern $p \in \{A, G, C, T, *, \#\}^m$, that is, the pattern p includes multiple types of wildcard. In particular, the wildcard * can only match the characters (A,G) and wildcard # can only match the characters (C,T) in the wildcard pattern matching. We proposed a SMTWM protocol that expects the hospital to receive the location of pattern p in the text t, while the national gene bank does not receive any information. That is, two security properties should be satisfied: 1) The pattern p is kept secret from the national gene bank, and 2) The hospital does not know any information about the text t other than the location of p. The model figure is shown in Fig. 1.

1.1   Related Works

There are two methods to ensure pattern matching computation. The first is a particular protocol, while the latter is a common protocol. In this paper, we mainly pay attention to particular protocol. According to our knowledge, the first person to considered secure pattern matching in secure computation was Troncoso-Pastoriza [7], they constructed a privacy preserving query protocol based on oblivious automata evaluation. Blanton [8] dealt with secure pattern matching in outsourcing scenario through techniques such as finite automaton and oblivious transfer, and applied it into DNA search problem. To address the private DNA matching problem, Katz et al. [9] constructed SPM protocols built on Yao's garbled circuit, the protocol improves the pattern matching efficiency with new keyword search and is resistant to malicious adversaries. Work on the above, these articles did not refer anything about pattern matching with wildcards. So far, we have observed that Baron et al. [10] first constructed a SPM protocol for solving the SPM problem with single character wildcards. The protocol was used to match patterns containing a single wildcard character with substring patterns of an arbitrary alphabet. Kerschbaum and Beck [11] constructed a new protocol for pattern matching with additional homomorphic encryption schemes with Bloom filters. Since then, Defrawy's [12] comparative experiments with some pattern matching protocols, showed the essential role of pattern matching in the fields of data sharing, private data protection, etc. To solve variants of the SPM problem, Hazay et al. [13] constructed some new protocols, which were more useful than earlier solutions. Yasuda et al. [4] conducted

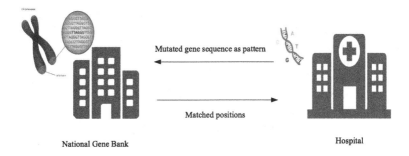

Fig. 1. Secure wildcard pattern matching in gene matching

a protocol to the SPM issue by using [14]'s ring-LWM based SWHE to analyse individual DNA sequences, but the solution is suitable for cloud computing. Recent developments in the field have been dominated by functional extensions to secure pattern matching, including approximate pattern matching, outsourcing pattern matching and wildcard pattern matching.

Wildcard pattern matching means that wildcard bits in a pattern can be replaced by any characters in the set of characters, and setting wildcard bits in a pattern can act as a bulk lookup. Hazay and Toft [15] transformed wildcard matches into exact matches by secretly replacing wildcards by two parties and resisting malicious adversaries. The protocol has communication complexity and computational complexity cost of $O(n + m)$ and $O(nm)$, respectively. This paper [4] constructed a security belt SPM protocol that is suitable for non-binary data and had been experimentally tested on real DNA sequences to query a gene sequence of length 16,500 in one second. In recent years, Kolesnikov et al. [16] solved the SPM problem by constructing a new security belt SPM protocol. Their protocol first used the OT protocol, where the two parties jointly input their data information and the receiver gets the output information, and then invokes the private equality test protocol to determine if the computed values are equal, if the values are equal it means pattern match successful. The protocol has a communication complexity and computational complexity cost of $O(nm)$ and $O(k)$, respectively. In 2020, Wei et al. [17] proposed a secure extended wildcard pattern matching protocol based on the cut-and-choose OT protocol. They first proposed extended wildcard pattern matching, which allows a client to obtain the entire set of substrings matching its pattern string, instead of the corresponding positions. Saha et al. [18] proposed a symmetric SPM-RW protocol and a public-key SPM-CW protocol to solve the pattern matching problem of repeated wildcard (RW) and compound wildcard (CW), using homomorphic encryption, polynomial packing and other techniques, respectively. The final calculation of the Hamming distance and the Squared Euclidean distance was used to determine whether the patterns match.

Approximate pattern matching is successful as long as the different information of the substrings and pattern strings in the text meets a given threshold. In real life, since many data are collected with varying degrees of variation and are not absolutely consistent, so approximate matching is widely used in fields such as face recognition, data mining and computational biology. In 2009, Jarrous and PIinkas [19] constructed an approximate pattern matching protocol that is resistant to malicious adversaries, using mainly oblivious polynomial evaluation techniques to solve the Hamming distance problem for functions of two inputs only. The communication complexity and computational complexity of protocol are $O(nm)$, respectively. After that, other works [20–23] also used some tools to address the approximate pattern matching issues, such as Fast Fourier transform (FFT) techniques, threshold secret sharing and the oblivious transfer (OT) protocol. In addition to the above works, which are all constructed under the standard model, the cloud-based security model matching issue is also considered. In 2018, Faust et al. [24] constructed the first SPM protocol in an outsourcing scenario, which is built on subset sum issues, while the protocol is secure in malicious adversary and semi-honest adversary models. In recent years, [25–27] and others have also done research related to the secure pattern matching problem with cloud assistance, and improved the efficiency and security of the protocol.

1.2   Our Contributions

Our specific contributions in this paper are as follows.

1. We construct a new protocol denoted as secure multiple types wildcard pattern matching (SMTWM) protocol based on OT and PEQT, which is used to address traditional SWPM problem in which the pattern string contains multiple types wildcards. Furthermore, in the pattern wildcards of each type can match special character. The SMTWM protocol is secure against semi-honest adversaries. More precisely, the protocol allows two parties (one holding a text string t and the other holding a pattern string p including multiple types wildcard) to determine whether t contains p, at the same time, without revealing either t or p to the other party.
2. We will show how to use this protocol to address the multiple types wildcard pattern matching issues. In this case, the two parties involved in the protocol, the sender holds text string t and the receiver holds the pattern string p. Especially, the string p contains two types of wildcard * and #, the wildcard * is used to replace AT and the wildcard # is used to replace CG. They perform the protocol to determine whether p can be found in t without disclosing their strings. Our experiments have shown that when the length of pattern is 2^8 and the length of text is 2^{16}, the running time is less than 0.4 and 2.5s in the LAN and WAN.

1.3   Paper Organization

Our paper consists of six sections. In Sect. 2, we focus on the preliminaries and definitions essential to our protocol. Second, in Sect. 3 we constructed a SMTWM protocol by using OT and PEQT. In Sect. 4, we focus on efficiency of the SMTWM protocol. Then, in Sect. 5 we focus on the experiment of secure SWTWM protocol. The conclusion is drawn in last section of our paper.

2   Preliminaries and Definitions

2.1   Oblivious Transfer

The Oblivious Transfer (OT) protocol as far back as 1981 Rabin [28] work, is a universal cryptographic primitive that is extensively applied to secure two-(multi-)party computing. In the OT protocol introduced by Rabin, the sender transmits a information to the receiver and the receiver has a 1/2 probability of receiving the message. After executing the OT, the sender does not know if the receiver has received the information, while the receiver does. In the 1-out-of-2 OT, the sender has two secret inputs (x_0, x_1) and the receiver has a choice bit b. After the protocol is executed, the receiver obtains the output x_b and the sender obtains no output. In this paper, we use the extended case 1-out-of-4(OT_4^1), where the sender has 4 secret inputs (x_1, x_2, x_3, x_4) and the receiver has a choice value $b \in \{1, 2, 3, 4\}$, and the receiver learns the output x_b from the 4 values at the end of the protocol. Figure 2 gives a detailed description of the functional function of the OT_4^1 protocol. We emphasize that OT extension technique of Kolesnikov [16] can be used to improve the efficiency OT protocols, such that only 128 base OTs can achieve the execution of 10^6 OTs. Therefore, the computational complexity of OT extension protocol is just $O(k)$, where k is security parameter which is 128.

PARAMETERS: two parties sender S and receiver R FUNCTIONALITY:

- Wait for input $\{x_1, x_2, x_3, x_4\} \in \{0, 1\}^*$ from the sender S.
- Wait for input $b \in \{1, 2, 3, 4\}$ from the receiver R.
- Give the receiver R output x_b .

Fig. 2. Oblivious transfer functionality OT_4^1

2.2 Privacy Equality Test

Private Equality Test (PEQT) allows two parties to input strings x_0 and x_1 respectively. Then, the receiver only learns 0 or 1 to show whether x_0 and x_1 are equal and the sender learns nothing. A detailed description of the functionality of PEQT protocol is given in Fig. 3. As shown in Kolsenikov [33], PEQT protocol can be constructed using efficient OT extension technique, such that the computational complexity of PEQT is also $O(k)$ which is the same as OT extension.

2.3 Secure Multiple Types Wildcard Pattern Matching Functionality

The pattern in wildcard pattern matching contains multiple types wildcard information, so a successful match implies that the non-wildcard positions have equal values and wildcard values can match the particular character. The meaning of the symbol $\preceq$ is as follows, if $p \preceq t$ we say that t matches pattern p. For simplicity, we consider our secure multiple types wildcard pattern matching functionality over DNA sequence consists of 'AGCT'. Besides, we only consider two wildcard '*' and '#', where '*' matches only the characters A and G, and '#' matches only the characters C and T. We emphasize that our propose functionality can be extended to general case where the alphabet of the text and the types of wildcards can be arbitrary. Figure 4 gives a detailed description of our secure multiple types wildcard pattern matching functionality.

PARAMETERS: Two parties sender S and receiver R FUNCTIONALITY:

- Wait for input $x_0 \in \{0,1\}^*$ from the sender S.
- Wait for input $x_1 \in \{0,1\}^*$ from the receiver R.
- Give the receiver R output 1 if $x_0 = x_1$ and 0 otherwise.

Fig. 3. Private equality test functionality $\mathcal{F}_{peqt}$

PARAMETERS: A text t with length n, a pattern p with length m, and two parties: text owner $\mathcal{DO}$ and pattern owner $\mathcal{U}$
FUNCTIONALITY:

- Wait for text $t \in \{A, G, C, T\}^n$ from the text owner $\mathcal{DO}$.
- Wait for pattern $p \in \{A, G, C, T, *, \#\}^m$ from the pattern owner $\mathcal{U}$.
- Give the pattern owner $\mathcal{U}$ output $\{i \in [n - m + 1] | p \preceq t_{[i,i+m-1]}\}$

Fig. 4. Secure wildcard types pattern matching functionality $\mathcal{F}_{smtwm}$

As shown above, the function $\mathcal{F}_{smtwm}$ involves two parties, the National Gene bank DO inputs the text information $t \in \{A, G, C, T\}^n$ and the integer m, and the hospital U inputs the pattern information $p \in \{A, G, C, T, \#, *\}^m$ and the integer n. The wildcard * matches only the characters AG, and the wildcard # matches only the characters CT. The hospital U outputs the starting position of the pattern p occurs in the text t. In other words, the protocol of the functionality $\mathcal{F}_{smtwm}$ is used to find out if the pattern containing multiple types wildcard is the match of $(n - m + 1)$ substrings of length m in text t. In particular, U can only learn the position of the start of the matching substring based on the function, however, U does not have information about the matching wildcard for substring of length m in text t.

2.4 Computationally Indistinguishability

Assume that $X = \{X(a,n)\}_{a \in \{0,1\}^*; n \in N}$ and $Y = \{Y(a,n)\}_{a \in \{0,1\}^*; n \in N}$ are 2 distributional overall and for any non-uniform polynomial-time algorithm D, the following inequality holds if there exits a negligible function $\xi(.)$ for each $a \in \{0,1\}^*$ and each $n \in \mathbb{N}$:

$$|P_r[D(X(a,n)) = 1)] - P_r[D(Y(a,n)) = 1)]| \leq \xi(n) \tag{1}$$

Then we say that the 2 distribution ensembles are computationally indistinguishable, denoted as $X \equiv Y$.

2.5 Security Definition

The protocol in this paper considers its security mainly in the context of a secure two-party computational model under semi-honest adversaries, using the ideal/realistic simulation paradigm to provide a formal definition of security [29–31], with the formal definition as follows:

Definition 1. Let $f : \{0,1\}^* \times \{0,1\}^* \rightarrow \{0,1\}^*$ be a two-input single-output function, π be a real protocol, and we say that the protocol π is safe to compute f in a semi-honest model, for every polynomial-time algorithm $\mathcal{A}$ in π, there is a corresponding algorithm $\mathcal{S}$ in the ideal world simulation that satisfies the following equation, where $i \in \{1,2\}$,

$$\{IDEAL_{f,\mathcal{S}(z),i}(x,y,z,n)\} \overset{c}{\equiv} \{REAL_{\pi,\mathcal{A}(z),i}(x,y,z,n)\} \tag{2}$$

x, y is the secret input for both sides, z is the auxiliary input, and $n \in \mathbb{N}$.

3   Secure Multiple Types Wildcard Pattern Matching Protocol

In the section, we propose a secure multiple types wildcard pattern matching protocol for the above functionality $\mathcal{F}_{smtwm}$ in semi-honest adversary model. The protocol is constructed using oblivious transfer protocol and private equality test protocol. Through the oblivious transfer, the hospital U (receiver) learns without knowing the text information each value corresponding to a certain value of the quadruple. Through the privacy equality test protocol, the hospital obtains where its pattern appears in the text of the National Gene Bank. In the following, we firstly show the main idea of our proposed protocol, and then give the concrete construction and security proof of the protocol.

3.1   The Idea of Protocol

In this subsection we use an example to show the whole idea of the protocol. Especially, the pattern p contains two types of wildcard * and #, the wildcard * is used to matching AG and the wildcard # is used to matching CT. For example, the National Gene bank DO has a string $t = (AGGCTCT)$ and Hospital U has a pattern containing wildcards $p = AG * CT\#$. For simplicity and convenience, we denote A,G,C,T as 1,2,3,4, such that $t = 1223434$ and $p = 12 * 34\#$. Besides, the text t contains two substrings $t'_1 = (122343)$ and $t'_2 = (223434)$ with the same length as the pattern.

Firstly, the hospital U (pattern owner)represent each value in $p = 12 * 34\#$ using a quadruple in which each value $S_i^j \in (0,1)^*$ is randomly chosen with the length of a security parameter (such as 40 bits), where $j \in (1,2,3,4)$ and $i \in [1, m]$. The purpose is to reduce the error probability to be negligible when two un-matched strings match successfully. Concretely, the pattern owner executes as follows:

– for non-wildcard, the quadruple contains four different values $\in (0,1)^*$ like $(S_i^1, S_i^2, S_i^3, S_i^4)$.

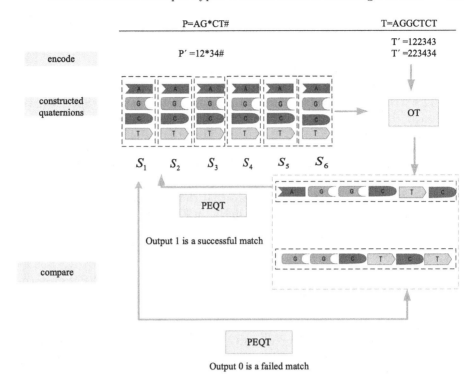

Fig. 5. The main ideas of the protocol

- for wildcard '*', the quadruple contains values $\in (0,1)^*$ like $(S_i^1, S_i^1, S_i^3, S_i^4)$ where the first two values are equal.
- for wildcard '*', the quadruple contains values $\in (0,1)^*$ like $(S_i^1, S_i^2, S_i^3, S_i^3)$ where the last two values are equal.

According to the above rules, the pattern $p = 12 * 34\#$ is represented as

$$\begin{bmatrix} (S_1^1, & S_1^2, & S_1^3, & S_1^4) \\ (S_2^1, & S_2^2, & S_2^3, & S_2^4) \\ (S_3^1, & S_3^2, & S_3^3, & S_3^4) \\ (S_4^1, & S_4^2, & S_4^3, & S_4^4) \\ (S_5^1, & S_5^2, & S_5^3, & S_5^4) \\ (S_6^1, & S_6^2, & S_6^3, & S_6^3) \end{bmatrix}$$

Besides, the pattern owner will act as sender in 1-out-of-4 OT protocols using these values as inputs. Then the National Gene bank DO will act as receiver in 1-out-of-4 OT protocols using $t_1' = (122343)$ and $t_2' = (223434)$ as the choice values. Concretely,

- for $t_1' = (122343)$, the National Gene bank DO learns $(S_1^1, S_2^2, S_3^1, S_4^3, S_5^4, S_6^3)$ and sets $S_1 = S_1^1 \oplus S_2^2 \oplus S_3^2 \oplus S_4^3 \oplus S_5^4 \oplus S_6^3$.

- for $t_2' = (223434)$, the National Gene bank DO learns $(S_1^2, S_2^2, S_3^3, S_4^4, S_5^3, S_6^4)$ and sets $S_2 = S_1^2 \oplus S_2^2 \oplus S_3^3 \oplus S_4^4 \oplus S_5^3 \oplus S_6^4$.

Afterwards, the hospital U and the National Gene bank DO run PEQT protocol in which the hospital U computes a value S according to its pattern $p = 12 * 34\#$ and the values chosen to represent the pattern. Specially, the hospital U chooses $S_1^1, S_2^2, S_3^1, S_4^3, S_5^4$ and S_6^3 for each value in $p = 12 * 34\#$, and sets $S = S_1^1 \oplus S_2^2 \oplus S_3^2 \oplus S_4^3 \oplus S_5^4 \oplus S_6^3$. Then the hospital U uses the above value S as its input to the PEQT protocol where the National Gene bank DO inputs S_1 and S_2 separately. Finally, the hospital U outputs 1 for the value S_1 which means that the sub-string t_1' matches the pattern p successfully, however, U outputs 0 for the value S_2 which means that the sub-string t_2' does not match the pattern p. The detailed drawing is shown in Fig. 5.

3.2 Protocol Construction

In this subsection, we propose the whole construction of our SMTWPM protocol. The propose protocol mainly contains the following steps:

1. Hospital U constructs the quadruple $(S_j^1, S_j^2, S_j^3, S_j^4)$, $j \in [1, m]$, where $(1,2,3,4)$ represents the value of (A,G,C,T) after encoding. For each value in p we construct a quadruple in which each value $S_i^j \in (0, 1)^*$ is randomly chosen with the length of a security parameter (such as 40 bits), where $j \in (1, 2, 3, 4)$ and $i \in [1, m]$. Specifically, when a position corresponds to the wildcard character *, the quadruple for that value is constructed as $(S_j^1, S_j^1, S_j^3, S_j^4)$, and when a position corresponds to the wildcard character #, the quadruple for that value is constructed as $(S_j^1, S_j^2, S_j^3, S_j^3)$, when the character at a position is a non-wildcard value, the quadruple for that value is constructed as $(S_j^1, S_j^2, S_j^3, S_j^4)$. These values will be used in OT protocols as the inputs of the sender (actually is the hospital U).
2. The National Gene bank DO runs a 1-out-of-4 oblivious transfer protocol with Hospital U, where U is the sender of the OT, and the input is the m quadruples chosen randomly and DO acts as the receiver of OT whose input is the encoded text message $t_{i,j}' = (t_{i,1}, t_{i,2}......t_{i,m})$ in which $i \in [1, n-m+1]$. After the OT protocol is executed with U, the DO as receiver learns a certain value of S_j^σ for each value of the quadruples, where σ is the choice value in each sub-strings, $\sigma \in \{1, 2, 3, 4\}$, $j \in [1, m]$. Then, DO sets $S_i = S_1^\sigma \oplus S_2^\sigma \oplus ...... \oplus S_m^\sigma$ where $i \in [1, n - m + 1]$.
3. The National Gene bank DO runs the Private Equality Test (PEQT) protocol with the hospital U. The DO acts as the sender of the PEQT, and the inputs are the values S_i, and U is the receiver of the PEQT with input is S, where $S = S^{p_1} \oplus S^{p_2} \oplus ...... \oplus S^{p_m}$ and p_i is each value of the pattern p. After the PEQT protocol is executed and the hospital U output 0 or 1. Specifically, if the national gene bank DO and hospital U inputs are equal, the receiver U outputs 1, otherwise it outputs 0. Figure 6 gives a detailed description of the multiple wildcard pattern matching protocol:

Correctness. The correctness of the protocol means that after a successful run of the protocol, Hospital U must end up with the correct result. Specifically, if there is a substring in the data t of the National Gene bank DO that is equal to the pattern string in Hospital U, then Hospital U must output a match of 1. On the contrary, if there is no substring in t that is equal to the pattern string, then Hospital U outputs 0. To illustrate the above two situations:

1. If the match is correct, it is shown that among the $(n-m+1)$ substrings with length m in the text t, there exists at least one substring of length m that is exactly equal to the pattern p. For this matched substring, the DO obtains the same values corresponding to pattern p chosen by the Hospital U, as a result, both the two parties input same values in PEQT protocol. Therefore, the Hospital U outputs 1 which means that the above substring matches the pattern successfully.

2. For a substring that fails, it means that at least one value in the substring does not match the corresponding value in the pattern p, we assume that $t_j \neq p_j$. As a result, the National Gene bank DO will obtain a different value

---

PARAMETERS:

1. Two parties: the National Gene bank $\mathcal{DO}$ and Hospital $\mathcal{U}$
2. A length n of text, a length m of pattern. Wildcard * only matches 'A' or 'G', wildcard # only matches 'C' or 'T'.
3. Ideal OT_4^1 $F_{OT_4^1}$ and PEQT F_{peqt} in Figure 1 and Figure 2, respectively.

INPUT OF $\mathcal{DO}$: a text $\boldsymbol{x} \in \{A, G, C, T\}^n$ encoded $\{1, 2, 3, 4\}^n$

INPUT OF $\mathcal{U}$: a pattern $\boldsymbol{p} \in \{A, G, C, T, *, \#\}^m$ encoded $\{1, 2, 3, 4, *, \#\}^m$.

PROTOCOL:

- **Pretreatment** :
  1. $\mathcal{U}$ constructs a quadruple for each $S_i^j \in \{0, 1\}^*$ with length of a security parameter (40 bits) where $j \in (1, 2, 3, 4)$ and $i \in [1, m]$, and then represents each value of his pattern p:
     - if the bit is non-wildcard, the representation is $(S_i^1, S_i^2, S_i^3, S_i^4)$;
     - if the bit is *, the representation is $(S_i^1, S_i^1, S_i^3, S_i^4)$;
     - if the bit is #, the representation is $(S_i^1, S_i^2, S_i^3, S_i^3)$;
     $\mathcal{U}$ uses these quadruples as her input in the following OT_4^1 protocols (as a sender). For simplicity, each quadruple is represented as $\boldsymbol{X}_i^\delta$, when $1 \leq i \leq m$ and $\delta \in \{1, 2, 3, 4\}$.

- **OT_4^1**
  1. The two parties execute a secure OT_4^1 protocol in which $\mathcal{U}$ inputs $\boldsymbol{X}_i^\delta$ and $\mathcal{DO}$ inputs encoded text information $\boldsymbol{t}_{i,j}' = t_{i,1}', t_{i,2}' \ldots t_{i,m}'$ where $j \in (1, 2, 3, 4)$ and $i \in [1, m]$.
  2. After executing the OT_4^1 protocols, $\mathcal{DO}$ (the receiver) receives outputs $(S_{i,1}^\sigma, S_{i,2}^\sigma \ldots S_{i,m}^\sigma)$, $\sigma \in \{1, 2, 3, 4\}$.

- **PEQT**
  1. The two parties execute a secure $PEQT$ protocol for each $1 \leq i \leq n - m + 1$, in which $\mathcal{DO}$ inputs $S_i = S_{i,1}^\sigma \oplus S_{i,2}^\sigma \oplus \ldots \oplus S_{i,m}^\sigma$ and $\mathcal{U}$ inputs $S = S^{p_1} \oplus S^{p_2} \oplus \ldots \oplus S^{p_m}$.
  2. After executing the $PEQT$ protocol, $\mathcal{U}$ (the receiver) receives outputs i if F_{peqt} outputs 1.

Fig. 6. SMTWM: secure multiple type wildcard pattern matching protocol

from OT protocol in position i, which is not the value corresponding p_j in the pattern p. Therefore, in the following PEQT protocol, the two parties inputs two different values and the Hospital U outputs 0 which indicates that the above substring fails to match the pattern p.

Security. Intuitively speaking, the security of the 1-out-of-4 OT protocol ensures that the National Gene bank DO cannot discover the pattern information of the hospital U. Note that the DO's message records contain only the information received from the U in the 1-out-of-4 OT protocol, so the privacy of the DO's input is protected. Considering the security of the U, in case the pattern string cannot match the substring in text string. The values obtained by the DO are random, so the DO does not know which value is relevant to the U input. In addition to this, all values in all positions are chosen at random. Therefore, DO has no ability to distinguish between wildcards and non-wildcard values, nor does it distinguish between random values and the original pattern information. Therefore, if the values do not match, DO cannot obtain any information other than the failed match result.

Theorem 1. *Assume the oblivious transfer protocol and the privacy equality test protocol are secure under semi-honest model, then $\mathcal{F}_{SMTWM}$ function can be safely computed through the π_{SMTWM} protocol in semi-honest model.*

Proof. The π_{SMTWM} protocol is shown to be secure, assuming that the oblivious transfer protocol primitive is implemented using an ideal functional function, and the following two scenarios are confirmed, the National Gene bank DO is corrupted or the Hospital U is corrupted.

Simulating U. Assuming that in the real protocol U is corrupted by adversary $\mathcal{A}$, we construct a polynomial-time simulator $\mathcal{S}$, which calls the input of $\mathcal{A}$ and uses it to simulate the protocol.

1. $\mathcal{S}$ receives the input $p \in \{A, G, C, T, *, \#\}^m$ and n from $\mathcal{A}$, and uses them as input to the function $\mathcal{F}_{SMTWM}$, $\mathcal{S}$ that learns all the matching positions.
2. Suppose the matching result contains matching positions $i_1, i_2......i_r$ and the substring $t_{i_1}, t_{i_2}......t_{i_i}$, which means that a string of m bits starting from i successfully matches pattern p.
3. For $i = i_1, i_2......i_r$, $\mathcal{S}$ chooses random values $S_{i,j}$, $j \in [1, m]$, and generates a quadruple for each bit in the order of protocol step 1. However, for other unmatched substrings, $\mathcal{S}$ randomly selects a quadruple. Note that since $\mathcal{S}$ is unknown to anything about the unsuccessful substrings, the values corresponding to these quadruples are arbitrary.
4. Using the above quadruple, $\mathcal{S}$ simulates the execution of the OT protocol with the aim of sending output to the adversary $\mathcal{A}$. Next, it needs to be shown that the joint output distribution of the simulated execution is computationally

indistinguishable from the distribution of the actual protocol. Specifically, we must proof the following equation.

$$\{IDEAL_{F_{MWPM},S(1^k),DO}((t,m),(p,n))\} \stackrel{c}{\equiv}$$
$$\{HYBRID^{OT^1_4}_{\pi_{MWPM},A(1^k)DO}((t,m),(p,n))\}$$

(3)

The two distributions only differ in that the simulator S randomly selects the quadruples that it should have been received from the DO after the oblivious transfer, while the adversary A receives the values of the quadruples directly from the DO after the oblivious transmission in the real protocol. However, since the simulator S knows the final matching result, the values it randomly selects are equivalent to the information derived from the values received by the adversary. Therefore, we consider the above simulation process to be indistinguishable from realistic protocol computation.

Simulating DO. Assuming that DO is corrupted by adversary A under the real protocol, we construct a polynomial-time simulator S where S calls the input of A and uses it to simulate the protocol.

1. S calls A with the input integer m and text $t \in \{AGCT\}^n$.
2. S simulates the oblivious transfer protocol and receives a quadruple which is produced by A according to its own input. S does not have access to the actual input of U during the simulation, so the oblivious transfer function's receiver is that it selected at random a pattern p of equal length.
3. S sends the adversary A's input to the function F_{SMTWM}. We are aware that the function F_{SMTWM} is a function in which only U learns an output, so it is necessary to show that there is no difference between the computation distribution generated by the ideal simulation and the actual implementation. In particular, we are supposed to prove the equation below:

$$\{IDEAL_{F_{MWPM},S(1^k),U}((t,m),(p,n))\} =$$
$$\{HYBRID^{OT^1_4}_{\pi_{MWPM},A(1^k)U}((t,m),(p,n))\}$$

(4)

We note that when we simulate protocol π, S selects a random pattern p to be used as an input to U. Still, U has its own text t in actual protocol π, and this is the only difference between the ideal world simulation process and the actual protocol implementation. Given that the oblivious transfer protocol we use it secure against semi-honest adversaries, S is computationally indistinguishable with respect to U's input. This security property assures that the emulation of S is non-differentiable from the execution of the real protocol. In general we have completed the proof of Theorem 1.

4   Protocol Efficiency

We will focus our efficiency analysis on three aspects of the protocol: round complexity, computational complexity and communication complexity, and give a comparison with the efficiency of related work.

1) Round Complexity. The secure multiple types wildcard pattern matching protocol we constructed requires a total of 4 rounds of interaction. Among them, 2 rounds are required in the oblivious transfer protocol. In the privacy equality test protocol, 2 interactions are required.

2) Computational complexity. In a multiple types wildcard pattern matching protocol $m(n-m+1)$ 1-out-of-4 OT and $n-m+1$ PEQT instance operations are required, so the computational complexity is $O(mn')$ and $n' = n-m+1$. Luckily, the OT extension in [32] can further reduce this overhead. One way to reduce the amount of OT instances required in an encryption protocol is offered by the OT extension protocol. Firstly, the two parties involves in the protocol run some instances of the basic OT. Then some symmetric key operations are computed locally. We would like to emphasise the number of basic OTs as a security parameter k, $k \ll nm$. Considering our protocol, which requires nm OT operations, some base OTs could be reduced from nm to k, $k \ll nm$ using OT extensions.

3) Communication complexity. Firstly, in the secure multiple types wildcard pattern matching protocol, an OT extension protocol needs to be executed once to achieve the $(n-m+1) \times m$ matrix effect. Secondly, a single execution of the privacy equality test also requires $(n-m+1) \times m$. Therefore, the communication complexity of the secure multiple types wildcard pattern matching protocol is $O(nm)$.

In Table 1, we present the results of the comparison between the protocols constructed in the paper and the relevant pattern matching protocols. Specifically, we compare the efficiency of the protocols in terms of three aspects: round complexity, computational complexity, and communication complexity, where n and m are the input lengths of the national gene pool and hospital in the pattern matching protocol, respectively, and k is the security parameter.

Table 1. Results of the comparison of some existing related protocols.

Protocol	Rounds	Computation	Communication	Security model	Wildcard types
[13]	$O(1)$	$O(nm)$	$O(nm)$	Malicious	Single wildcard
[20]	$O(1)$	$O(nlogm)$	$O((m+n)k^2)$	Malicious	Single wildcard
[10]	2	$O(m+n)$	$O(nk)$	Semi-honest	Single wildcard
Ours	4	$O(k)$	$O(nm)$	Semi-honest	Multiple types wildcard

Table 2. Total time in seconds of our protocol in different settings.

Setting	Pattern length m	Text length n				
		2^{16}	2^{18}	2^{20}	2^{22}	2^{24}
LAN	2^8	0.31(s)	0.81(s)	1.84(s)	8.15(s)	32.12(s)
	2^{10}	0.42(s)	0.95(s)	2.42(s)	10.43(s)	32.23(s)
	2^{12}	0.73(s)	1.95(s)	6.82(s)	25.05(s)	103.16(s)
	2^{14}	2.04(s)	7.81(s)	30.29(s)	120.21(s)	492.34(s)
WAN	2^8	2.07(s)	3.81(s)	10.22(s)	35.69(s)	140.91(s)
	2^{10}	2.54(s)	5.63(s)	17.21(s)	62.53(s)	255.86(s)
	2^{12}	4.57(s)	12.92(s)	43.32(s)	169.10(s)	762.14(s)
	2^{14}	12.23(s)	44.50(s)	171.98(s)	626.84(s)	2765.13(s)

5 Experiments

In this section, we use experimental results to measure the performance of a secure multiple types wildcard pattern matching protocol. Our protocol is constructed based on OT as well as PEQT. In the OT phase, we use the OT extension technique, which requires only a small number of basic OT protocols and some symmetric operations to achieve a large number of OT protocols, significantly reducing the number of OT protocols. The efficient PEQT protocol also achieves the effect of many PEQT protocol executions with a basic OT protocol and cheap symmetric operations. We ran the experiments on a PC running Windows 10 with an Intel(R) Core(TM) i5 CPU and 16 GB RAM. We run each side as a single thread on the same machine, communicating over the local host network, using the Linux tc command to emulate a network connection, setting the LAN to 10 Gbps network bandwidth and the WAN to 400 Mbps network bandwidth.

In this experiment, the length of text information is n and pattern information is m. We take pattern length to be $m = 2^8, 2^{10}, 2^{12}, 2^{14}$ and text length to be $n = 2^{16}, 2^{18}, 2^{20}, 2^{22}, 2^{24}$ respectively, the running time of the protocol in LAN and WAN is shown in Table 2. Our experiments have shown that when 2^8 is length of pattern string and 2^{16} is length of text string, the running time spent less than 0.4 and 2.5 s in the LAN and WAN.

We show the results of experimental in Fig. 7 and Fig. 8. As Fig. 7 shows, when the length of the text is 2^{16} and the length of the pattern is 2^8, the protocol takes is 0.31 s to execute, and it increases significantly when the text length is larger than 2^{20}. As Fig. 8 shows, when the length of the text is 2^{16} and the length of pattern is 2^8, the protocol takes is 2.07 s to execute and it increases significantly when the text length is larger than 2^{22}.

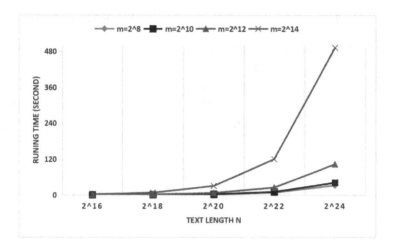

Fig. 7. Total running time in LAN setting

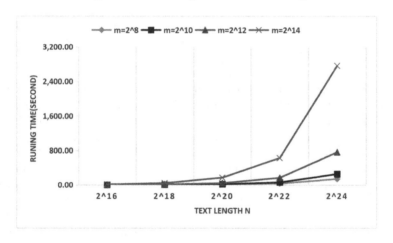

Fig. 8. Total running time in WAN setting

6   Conclusion

Our work focuses on constructing a secure SMTWM protocol in a semi-honest adversary model. The protocol is mainly designed and constructed based on oblivious transfer and privacy equality test techniques. We allow the hospital (the schema holder) to obtain information about the location of the short schema string in the long text string, with particular attention to the fact that the short schema string contains multiple types wildcard bits. The overall communication complexity of the protocol is $O(nm)$ and the computational complexity is $O(k)$, where n and m are the input lengths of the national gene bank and the hospital, and k is the security parameter.

References

1. Kim, M., Lee, H.T., Ling, S., Tan, B.H.M., Wang, H.: Private compound wildcard queries using fully homomorphic encryption. IEEE Trans. Dependable Secur. Comput. **16**(5), 743–756 (2019)
2. Chase, M., Shen, E.: Substring-searchable symmetric encryption. Proc. Priv. Enhancing Technol. **2015**(2), 263–281 (2015)
3. Faber, S., Jarecki, S., Krawczyk, H., Nguyen, Q., Rosu, M., Steiner, M.: Rich queries on encrypted data: beyond exact matches. In: Pernul, G., Ryan, P.Y.A., Weippl, E. (eds.) ESORICS 2015, Part II. LNCS, vol. 9327, pp. 123–145. Springer, Cham (2015). https://doi.org/10.1007/978-3-319-24177-7_7
4. Yasuda, M., Shimoyama, T., Kogure, J., Yokoyama, K., Koshiba, T.: Secure pattern matching using somewhat homomorphic encryption. In: Juels, A., Parno, B. (eds.) CCSW 2013, Proceedings of the 2013 ACM Cloud Computing Security Workshop, Co-located with CCS 2013, Berlin, Germany, 4 November 2013, pp. 65–76. ACM (2013)
5. Yasuda, M., Shimoyama, T., Kogure, J., Yokoyama, K., Koshiba, T.: Privacy-preserving wildcards pattern matching using symmetric somewhat homomorphic encryption. In: Susilo, W., Mu, Y. (eds.) ACISP 2014. LNCS, vol. 8544, pp. 338–353. Springer, Cham (2014). https://doi.org/10.1007/978-3-319-08344-5_22
6. Frikken, K.B.: Practical private DNA string searching and matching through efficient oblivious automata evaluation. In: Gudes, E., Vaidya, J. (eds.) DBSec 2009. LNCS, vol. 5645, pp. 81–94. Springer, Heidelberg (2009). https://doi.org/10.1007/978-3-642-03007-9_6
7. Troncoso-Pastoriza, J.R., Katzenbeisser, S., Celik, M.U.: Privacy preserving error resilient DNA searching through oblivious automata. In: Ning, P., di Vimercati, S.D.C., Syverson, P.F. (eds.) Proceedings of the 2007 ACM Conference on Computer and Communications Security, CCS 2007, Alexandria, Virginia, USA, 28–31 October 2007, pp. 519–528. ACM (2007)
8. Blanton, M., Aliasgari, M.: Secure outsourcing of DNA searching via finite automata. In: Foresti, S., Jajodia, S. (eds.) DBSec 2010. LNCS, vol. 6166, pp. 49–64. Springer, Heidelberg (2010). https://doi.org/10.1007/978-3-642-13739-6_4
9. Katz, J., Malka, L.: Secure text processing with applications to private DNA matching. In: Al-Shaer, E., Keromytis, A.D., Shmatikov, V. (eds.) Proceedings of the 17th ACM Conference on Computer and Communications Security, CCS 2010, Chicago, Illinois, USA, 4–8 October 2010, pp. 485–492. ACM (2010)
10. Baron, J., El Defrawy, K., Minkovich, K., Ostrovsky, R., Tressler, E.: 5PM: secure pattern matching. In: Visconti, I., De Prisco, R. (eds.) SCN 2012. LNCS, vol. 7485, pp. 222–240. Springer, Heidelberg (2012). https://doi.org/10.1007/978-3-642-32928-9_13
11. Beck, M., Kerschbaum, F.: Approximate two-party privacy-preserving string matching with linear complexity. In: IEEE International Congress on Big Data, BigData Congress 2013, Santa Clara, CA, USA, 27 June 2013–2 July 2013, pp. 31–37. IEEE Computer Society (2013)
12. Defrawy, K.E., Faber, S.: Blindfolded data search via secure pattern matching. Computer **46**(12), 68–75 (2013)
13. Hazay, C., Toft, T.: Computationally secure pattern matching in the presence of malicious adversaries. In: Abe, M. (ed.) ASIACRYPT 2010. LNCS, vol. 6477, pp. 195–212. Springer, Heidelberg (2010). https://doi.org/10.1007/978-3-642-17373-8_12

14. Naehrig, M., Lauter, K.E., Vaikuntanathan, V.: Can homomorphic encryption be practical? In: Cachin, C., Ristenpart, T. (eds.) Proceedings of the 3rd ACM Cloud Computing Security Workshop, CCSW 2011, Chicago, IL, USA, 21 October 2011, pp. 113–124. ACM (2011)
15. Hazay, C., Toft, T.: Computationally secure pattern matching in the presence of malicious adversaries. J. Cryptol. **27**(2), 358–395 (2014)
16. Kolesnikov, V., Rosulek, M., Trieu, N.: SWiM: secure wildcard pattern matching from OT extension. In: Meiklejohn, S., Sako, K. (eds.) FC 2018. LNCS, vol. 10957, pp. 222–240. Springer, Heidelberg (2018). https://doi.org/10.1007/978-3-662-58387-6_12
17. Wei, X., Xu, L., Zhao, M., Wang, H.: Secure extended wildcard pattern matching protocol from cut-and-choose oblivious transfer. Inf. Sci. **529**, 132–140 (2020)
18. Saha, T.K., Rathee, D., Koshiba, T.: Effcient protocols for private wildcards pattern matching. J. Inf. Secur. Appl. **55**, 102609 (2020)
19. Jarrous, A., Pinkas, B.: Secure hamming distance based computation and its applications. In: Abdalla, M., Pointcheval, D., Fouque, P.-A., Vergnaud, D. (eds.) ACNS 2009. LNCS, vol. 5536, pp. 107–124. Springer, Heidelberg (2009). https://doi.org/10.1007/978-3-642-01957-9_7
20. Vergnaud, D.: Efficient and secure generalized pattern matching via fast fourier transform. In: Nitaj, A., Pointcheval, D. (eds.) AFRICACRYPT 2011. LNCS, vol. 6737, pp. 41–58. Springer, Heidelberg (2011). https://doi.org/10.1007/978-3-642-21969-6_3
21. Wei, X., Zhao, M., Xu, Q.: Efficient and secure outsourced approximate pattern matching protocol. Soft. Comput. **22**(4), 1175–1187 (2018)
22. Liu, N., Xie, F., Wu, X.: Suffx array for multi-pattern matching with variable length wildcards. Intell. Data Anal. **25**(2), 283–303 (2021)
23. Vaiwsri, S., Ranbaduge, T., Christen, P., Ng, K.S.: Accurate and efficient suffix tree based privacy-preserving string matching, CoRR abs/2104.03018 (2021). arXiv:2104.03018
24. Faust, S., Hazay, C., Venturi, D.: Outsourced pattern matching. Int. J. Inf. Secur. **17**(3), 327–346 (2018)
25. Li, D., Dong, X., Cao, Z.: Secure and privacy-preserving pattern matching in outsourced computing. Secur. Commun. Netw. **9**(16), 3444–3451 (2016)
26. Zhang, T., Wang, X., Chow, S.S.M.: Privacy-preserving multi-pattern matching. In: Deng, R., Weng, J., Ren, K., Yegneswaran, V. (eds.) SecureComm 2016. LNICST, vol. 198, pp. 199–218. Springer, Cham (2017). https://doi.org/10.1007/978-3-319-59608-2_11
27. Zhou, J., Choo, K.R., Cao, Z., Dong, X.: PVOPM: verifiable privacy-preserving pattern matching with efficient outsourcing in the malicious setting. IEEE Trans. Dependable Secur. Comput. **18**(5), 2253–2270 (2021)
28. Rabin, M.O.: How to exchange secrets with oblivious transfer. IACR Cryptology ePrint Archive 450/187 (2005)
29. Goldreich, O.: The Foundations of Cryptography - Volume 2: Basic Applications. Cambridge University Press, Cambridge (2004)
30. Goldreich, O., Micali, S., Wigderson, A.: How to play any mental game or A completeness theorem for protocols with honest majority. In: Aho, A.V. (ed.) Proceedings of the 19th Annual ACM Symposium on Theory of Computing, New York, USA, pp. 218–229. ACM, New York (1987)
31. Hazay, C., Lindell, Y.: Efficient protocols for set intersection and pattern matching with security against malicious and covert adversaries. J. Cryptol. **23**(3), 422–456 (2010)

32. Ishai, Y., Kilian, J., Nissim, K., Petrank, E.: Extending oblivious transfers efficiently. In: Boneh, D. (ed.) CRYPTO 2003. LNCS, vol. 2729, pp. 145–161. Springer, Heidelberg (2003). https://doi.org/10.1007/978-3-540-45146-4_9
33. Kolesnikov, V., Kumaresan, R., Rosulek, M.: Efficient batched oblivious PRF with application to private set intersection. In: Proceedings of the 23rd ACM SIGSAC Conference on Computer and Communications Security, pp. 818–829. ACM, New York (2016)

A Label Flipping Attack on Machine Learning Model and Its Defense Mechanism

Qingru Li[1,2] ⓘ, Xinru Wang[2] ⓘ, Fangwei Wang[1,2(✉)] ⓘ,
and Changguang Wang[1,2(✉)] ⓘ

[1] Key Laboratory of Network and Information Security of
Hebei Province, Hebei Normal University, Shijiazhuang 050024, China
{fw_wang,wangcg}@hebtu.edu.cn
[2] College of Computer and Cyberspace Security, Hebei Normal University,
Shijiazhuang 050024, China

Abstract. Recently, the robustness of machine learning against data poisoning attacks is widely concerned. As a subclass of poisoning attack, the label flipping attack can poison training data resulting in reducing the classification performance of training model. This attack poses a more serious threat in complex network or high-noise environments, such as in the environment of Internet of Things. In this paper, a new label flipping attack method and its defense strategy are proposed. First, a label flipping attack based on agglomerative hierarchical clustering is proposed. The attack uses agglomerative hierarchical clustering to identify vulnerable samples in training data and then carries out label flipping on them. To defend against this attack, a TrAdaBoost-based label correction defense method is proposed. This method uses the TrAdaBoost algorithm to update the weight of the contaminated data, and then uses the updated weight value to judge and remark the contaminated training samples. The contaminated samples are cleaned and used to retrain the classifier. Compared with the state-of-the-art methods, the proposed attack strategy can reduce the accuracy of the model more effectively and the proposed defense method can better protect the classification model.

Keywords: Machine learning · Label flipping attack · TrAdaBoost · Agglomerative hierarchical clustering

1 Introduction

In recent years, Machine Learning (ML) technology has performed well in classification problems and model prediction, becoming an effective tool for solving classification problems and prediction problems, and is widely used in sensor networks[1], verification code recognition, image classification, recommendation system [2] and Internet of Things (IoT) environment [3]. Data used in Machine learning usually comes from an unreliable or unbelievable environment, which enables attackers to exploit this vulnerability to carry out poisoning attacks and cause huge and irreversible losses [4]. For example, in an IoT environment, devices can communicate with each other and attackers can access IoT devices and inject poison samples or maliciously modify training data

W. Meng et al. (Eds.): ICA3PP 2022, LNCS 13777, pp. 490–506, 2023.
https://doi.org/10.1007/978-3-031-22677-9_26

to carry out poisoning attacks, which may eventually cause irreversible damage, such as large-scale user information leakage, life, and property loss. A threat model of data poisoning attack in an IoT environment is shown in Fig. 1. In Fig. 1, some IoT devices run on the Android operating system, and we assume that the attacker can access certain IoT devices. The attacker then has the opportunity to manipulate the data being transmitted to and from each other. The machine learning algorithm is then exposed to the attacker, and the attacker may add poison samples or maliciously flip labels to fool the ML algorithm. Thus, the training data set is contaminated. If the attacker uses contaminated data to retrain the ML-based classification model, the classifier will perform an incorrect classification. Therefore, it is very important to study poisoning attack methods and the corresponding defense strategies against machine learning models. In recent years, more and more researchers have focused on machine learning-oriented poisoning attacks and their defense methods. As a subclass of poisoning attacks, label flipping attacks and their defense method are also key research directions.

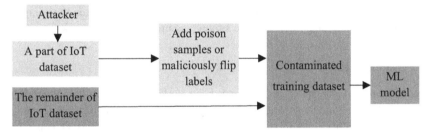

Fig. 1. A data poisoning attack threat model in an IoT environment

With the increasing demand for ML models, the security of models is widely concerned. Similar to most studies on poisoning attacks and their defense methods [5], this study focuses on poisoning attacks and their defense strategy under the condition of black-box ML [6], and proposes a framework of label flipping attacks and their defense strategy. On the one hand, potential security vulnerabilities of ML-based model in IoT environment is found, and a label flipping attack strategy based on agglomerative hierarchical clustering is proposed to reduce model accuracy. On the other hand, a label correction defense method based on TrAdaBoost is proposed to resist interference from the proposed attack on the classification model.

Our contributions are as follows.

1. A framework of label flipping attack on machine learning model and its defense method is proposed.
2. A label flipping attack method based on agglomerative hierarchical clustering is proposed. First, the training data is aggregated and hierarchically clustered, then the labels of the training data are flipped according to the clustering results, and finally the obtained contaminated training set is used to train the classification model.
3. A label correction defense method based on TrAdaBoost is proposed. First, the TrAdaBoost algorithm was used to update the weights of the contaminated training

set, and then the poisoned samples were identified and relabeled according to the weight values of the obtained samples. Finally, the new training set after being cleaned was used to retrain the classification model.

The remaining parts are organized as follows: Sect. 2 introduces the related work on label-flipping attack and defense methods. Section 3 describes the framework of the label flipping attack and its defense in detail, including a label flipping attack on machine learning model and its defense method. Section 4 verifies the effectiveness of the label flipping attack based on agglomerative hierarchical clustering and the performance of the proposed label correction defense method based on TrAdaBoost through experiments on real datasets. Section 5 is a summary of the entire paper.

2   Related Work

Domestic and foreign scholars have conducted a lot of research on poisoning attacks and their defense method. This section will elaborate related work from the perspective of poisoning attack strategy and defense strategy against poisoning attack.

2.1   Poisoning Attack

In recent years, industry and academia have been exploring the potential vulnerabilities of machine learning models brought by uncertainty and instability of training data, and based on this, effective poisoning attack strategies have been proposed. Data poisoning attacks on machine learning models mainly include maliciously modifying training data and injecting poison samples [7]. Liu et al. [8] implemented a poisoning attack by injecting poisoning samples into the training set. In the proposed method, enhanced conditional DCGAN produced image data with poisonous labels and injected it into the training set, and then the poisoning attack was executed by retraining the model. This attack has a good attack effect, but the time complexity of poisoning sample generation is high. Some researchers implemented attacks by maliciously modifying training data labels. For the problem of the distance between unbalanced samples, Paudice et al. [9] flipped the labels of the points far from the decision boundary to get a better attack effect. This method could reduce classification accuracy; however, it could not carry out targeted poisoning attacks. Taheri R.et al. [10] proposed a label flipping attack algorithm based on contour clustering, which was based on the distance between samples and did not apply to data with poor classification boundaries between samples. All of the attacks mentioned above are based on the distance between samples, which makes the time complexity of the algorithm high.

To solve the problem of uneven sample distribution, Zhang et al. [11] proposed a label flipping attack based on a naive Bayes classifier. This attack method selects the samples to be attacked and performs label flipping by calculating the entropy of training samples, which can reduce the classification accuracy more effectively compared with existing machine learning algorithms. All the above attacks are aimed at specific models. To solve the problem of adopting specific attack methods on different models, Vasu et al. [12] proposed an attack method that is not limited to model categories, that is, a binary label flip attack based on gradient. The proposed attack method is not limited by model categories, that is, it can be applied to different binary models and has good portability. However, this attack is computationally inefficient in small datasets. For data of a special type, effective attack methods are also proposed in the literature [13, 14]. Ma et al. [13] proposed a poisoning attack of the pair-comparison estimation, which can significantly reduce the performance of the collator. The defense method proposed in this paper can be applied to any type of data poisoning attack. However, in the case of large datasets with many feature types, it will be difficult to extract data features and the defense effect is reduced. The poisoning attack methods above are all attacks on offline data. To solve the problem of detecting online data poisoning attacks, Pang et al. [13] proposed a cumulative poisoning attack method for real-time data. This attack has a good effect on two typical real-time data flow models. However, the attack is not universal. At present, a variety of attack methods are highly dependent on the training data used. The literature [11] proposed a data-independent poisoning attack method, namely, a neural network structural space poisoning attack. The proposed attack method overcomes the dependence of traditional data poisoning attacks on training data. However, the attack is limited only to the search space of a certain neural network structure, which is not applicable to neural networks with other structure types. Aiming at the problems of low attack success rate and limited classification model in existing poisoning attack strategies, this study proposes a label flipping attack strategy which is suitable for multiple classification models and can effectively reduce the classification accuracy of models.

2.2 Defense Against Poisoning Attack

Existing research usually implements the defense against poisoning attacks by improving the robustness of the classification model or identifying and processing abnormal data points. For example, in the literature [15], the authors completed the defense against poisoning attacks by enhancing the robustness of the model. The author proposed a defense method based on data complexity that can effectively distinguish contaminated data and identify attacked samples, greatly improving the robustness of the classification model. In this paper, a random smoothing approach, which is not limited to point-to-point defense, is used to defend against label flipping attacks.

Some literatures defend poisoning attacks by recognizing and dealing with abnormal data points in training sets. Paudice et al. [9] adopted the outlier detection method to detect and remove outliers for correct classification. However, due to the small space between the sample data, benign data may be mislabeled, resulting in misclassification of the sample data. To solve the problem that edge data is prone to be misclassified, the author proposed a semi-supervised defense method based on clustering [10, 16], which effectively improved the classification accuracy of the training model, but it costs a lot of time. For the deficiency of existing methods only in defending against attacks for a specific classification model, some researchers put forward the poison attack defense strategy for multiple classification models. Ppkc et al.[17] proposed a defense method applicable to various algorithms by combining transfer learning with a defense algorithm. The proposed framework reduces the influence of contaminated data sets on the training model and significantly improves the robustness of the classification model. The defense method proposed by Elan et al. [18] can be applied to any type of data poisoning attack. However, in the case of large datasets with a large number of feature types, data features are difficult to extract, and the defense effect will be reduced. Tavallali et al. [19] proposed a label flipping attack method based on synthetic reduced nearest neighbors and proposed a corresponding defense method, which could identify malicious samples up to 80%. To solve the problem of label noise, Cheng et al. [20] proposed a data sterilization framework based on semi-supervised learning technology, which has a good defense effect against label flipping attacks based on the entropy method, but classification accuracy is still to be improved. In our paper, aiming at the problems of low model classification accuracy of existing defense methods and unable to apply to different classification models, we propose a new defense method, which can not only apply to a variety of classification models but also improve the robustness of the classification model under label flipping attack.

3   Label Flipping Attack and Its Defense Method

3.1   The Overall Block Diagram

With the wide application of machine learning in various fields, a variety of methods of poisoning attacks on machine learning models was proposed one after another. Therefore, it is increasingly important to study the robustness of machine learning models against poisoning attacks. To solve the problem of model robustness under poisoning attack, this paper explores a label flipping attack and studies its defense method. In the attack stage, a label flipping attack based on agglomerative hierarchical clustering is proposed. In the defense stage, we have proposed a label correction defense method based on TrAdaBoost algorithm. The overall block diagram of the system is shown in Fig. 2.

3.2   Label Flipping Attack Based on Agglomerative Hierarchical Clustering

A label flipping attack is a subclass of data poisoning attacks. The attacker implements the label flipping attack by maliciously modifying training data or injecting poison samples into the training set to reduce model performance. In this paper, we assumed that the distance between samples in the same class (benign or malicious) is small, and the distance between samples in a different class is large. Based on this assumption, we first use an agglomerative hierarchical clustering algorithm to classify the training samples, then a label flipping attack is performed. Since the samples on the classification boundary are away from the clustering center, they belong to the ambiguous category. If the labels of these samples are flipped, it is not easy to find them. Therefore, we flip the labels on the classification boundary to perform a label flipping attack.

Figure 3 shows the label flipping process. First, the training data is classified into benign and malicious clusters by agglomerative hierarchical clustering. Then, the silhouette clustering value [21, 22] of the sample is calculated according to the clustering results to select the sample data that are vulnerable to pollution. Finally, the label flip attack is carried out on the selected susceptible data to obtain a contaminated training set, and the contaminated training set is used to train the classification model to poison it.

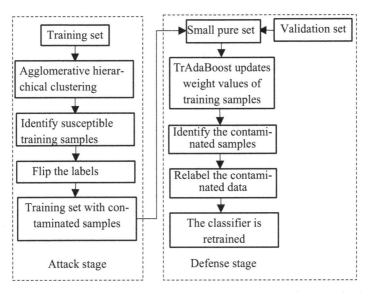

Fig. 2. The block diagram of the label flipping attack and its defense mechanism

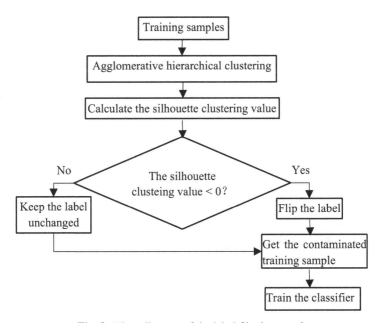

Fig. 3. Flow diagram of the label flipping attack

The steps of label flipping attack based on agglomerative hierarchical clustering are as follows:(1) An agglomerative hierarchical clustering algorithm is used to cluster the training data and the training data is clustered into benign samples and malicious samples. (2) According to the clustering results, the samples vulnerable to contamination are selected, that is, the samples with a fuzzy clustering boundary. These samples have no obvious attribution category and are suitable for label-flipping attack. Set L_i as the label of i-th sample in the dataset, that is:

$$L_i = \begin{cases} (x_i, y_i), & SV > 0 \\ (x_i, |1 - y_i|), & \text{otherwise} \end{cases}. \tag{1}$$

If the Silhouette clustering Value (SV) of a training sample is greater than 0, it indicates that the sample is correctly clustered. If the clustering silhouette value is less than or equal to 0, it indicates that the classification boundary of the sample is fuzzy and is suitable for label flipping attack. (3) Label flipping is performed on selected susceptible training data samples, that is, samples whose silhouette value is less than or equal to 0. Label flipping means that the label value 1 is converted to 0, that is, malicious data labels are labeled as benign data labels. Thus, the attacked training set had a large number of false negative data. (4) After labels are flipped, a contaminated training set will be obtained, and this contaminated data set will be used to train the classification model to perform label flipping attacks.

The attack process is shown in Algorithm 1.

Algorithm1 Label flipping attack based on agglomerative hierarchical clustering

Input: Training set samples X_train,   the labels of training samples Y_train
Output: The labels of   poisoned training sample   Poisoned_Y_train
   1:The training set is divided into two classes by agglomerative hierarchical clustering algorithm.
   2: S←The silhouette value S of cluster boundary sample is calculated according to clustering result.
   3: **for** each x_i ∈ X_train **do**
   4:     **if** $(S[x_i]<0)$then
   5:         Poisoned_Y_train$[x_i]$=abs(1-Y_train$[x_i]$)
   6:     **end if**
   7: **end for**
   8: **return** Poisoned_Y_train

In this paper, we assumed that the training data are separated into two classes (benign and malicious). In practice, malware can also be further classified, that is, the training data can be clustered into multiple classes.

3.3   Label Correction Defense Method Based on TrAdaBoost

In this section, we propose a TrAdaBoost-based label correction defense method for label flipping attacks based on agglomerative hierarchical clustering.

Figure 4 shows the defense process of a label-flipping attack. First, a source domain dataset (pure) and an auxiliary domain dataset (contaminated) are combined as input to the TrAdaBoost algorithm, and the TrAdaBoost algorithm initializes [23] and updates the weights of the training data. After several iterations, the training samples will be assigned a new weight. In the process of updating weight, if a sample from the contaminated dataset is misclassified, its weight will be reduced; otherwise, its weight will increase. If the sample from the pure set is misclassified, its weight will be increased; otherwise, its weight will be reduced. A training sample whose weight value is greater than a certain threshold is considered to be attacked and its label is relabeled, then a relabeled training set is obtained. Finally, the relabeled training set is used to retrain the classification model.

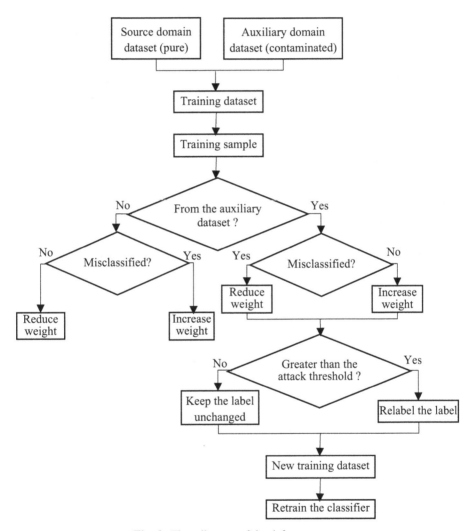

Fig. 4. Flow diagram of the defense process

The principle and the specific steps for updating weights are as follows:

Step 1: The source domain data set, which is composed of a small pure data set, and the auxiliary data set, which is composed of the contaminated training set, are combined into a new data set as the input for the TrAdaBoost algorithm. The weights of the training samples are initialized as follows:

$$w_i^1 = \begin{cases} 1/n, & i = 1,...,\, n \\ 1/m, & i = n+1,...,\, n+m \end{cases} \tag{2}$$

where, w_i^1 is the initial weight value of the contaminated training set and the pure set, n represents the sample number of the pure set and m represents the sample number of the contaminated training set.

Step 2: The initial weight in Step 1 is updated by the TrAdaBoost algorithm for many times, and finally a new weight is obtained. In the process of updating the weight, if the contaminated samples are misclassified, the weights of the sample will be reduced, which shows that the distribution of the sample is not in accordance with the data distribution of the trained model. In contrast, if the sample label in the contaminated training is judged correctly, the sample weight will be increased, which shows the distribution of the sample in accordance with the distribution of the trained model. However, if a sample in the pure set is misclassified, the weight of the sample will increase, indicating that the information of the training sample has not been well learned in the training process. Therefore, a larger weight should be assigned to the sample in the model-training process. On the contrary, if a sample in the pure set is correctly judged, it means that the sample is well learned and a smaller weight can be assigned to the sample. The weight update formula is as follows:

$$w_i^{t+1} = \begin{cases} w_i^t \beta^{|h_t(x_i)-c(x_i)|}, & i = 1,\,...,\, n \\ w_i^t \beta_t^{-|h_t(x_i)-c(x_i)|}, & i = 1,\,...,\, m \end{cases} \tag{3}$$

where w_i^{t+1} represents the weight of the contaminated training set and the pure set after t iteration, x_i represents the i-th sample, $c(x_i)$ represents the real category to which the sample belongs and h_t represents the classifier obtained by invoking the Learner in the TrAdaBoost algorithm. β and β_t are the weight coefficient, and $\beta = 1/(1+\sqrt{2(\ln n)/N})$, $\beta_t = \epsilon_t/(1-\epsilon_t)$. N represents the maximum number of iterations. The error rate of h_t in the auxiliary datasets is $\epsilon_t = \sum_{i=n+1}^{n+m} \frac{w_i^t |h_t(x_i)-c(x_i)|}{\sum_{i=n+1}^{n+M} w_i^t}$.

By the TrAdaBoost algorithm, the attacked samples and the unattacked samples will have completely different weight values after N iterations. Therefore, the weights can be used to distinguish attacked training samples from unattacked samples. The pseudo-code of the proposed defense algorithm is shown in Algorithm 2.

Algorithm2   Label correction defense method based on the TrAdaBoost

Input: The sample in the contaminated training set X_train, the label of the sample in the contaminated training set Poisoned_Y_train

Output: The label of relabeled training data Relabel_Y_train

   1:   Initializing the weight of i-th sample W_i^l in the training set

   2:   Setting weight parameter β

   3:   **For** t=1,...,N

        (1)   Setting the weight distribution P^t

        (2)   Invoking Learner and getting a classifier h_t

        (3)   Calculating the error rate ϵ_t of the classifier h_t on the source domain training set

        (4)   Calculating the weight parameter β_t according to ϵ_t

        (5)   Calculating the new weight w_i^{t+1} according to β_t

   4:   Relabeling the attacked training sample according to the obtained new weight

   5:   **Return**   the label of relabeled training set Relabel_Y_train

In Algorithm 2, the TrAdaBoost algorithm is used to update the weights of the training samples. Because the weight of poisoned data is different from that of clean training data, we can distinguish poisoned data from unattacked data according to the updated weights.

4   Experimental Evaluation

In this section, we evaluate the effectiveness of the proposed label-flipping attack and its defense mechanism through experiments. Drebin's Permission datasets and Genome's Permission datasets were used in the experiment. Drebin dataset comes from Android resources [24], and Genome is also an Android dataset [25]. The training set, the test set, and the validation set are divided in a proportion of 8:1:1.

4.1   Experimental Results of Label Flipping Attack

In this section, we evaluate the proposed label flipping attack based on agglomerative hierarchical clustering under different attack rates on Drebin and Genome datasets.

The Drebin datasets contain 5560 applications from 179 different malware families [24]. A sample in the Drebin dataset includes three features, and they are Permission, Intent, and API. Since Permission is directly related to the specific functions of the application, we think that Permission is a more important feature than API and Intent. Therefore, in this paper, we focus on the effect of flipping Permission features on classification results. The Genome dataset [25] is an Android sample data set supported by a National Science Foundation (NSF) project, which contains 1260 applications from 49 different families. A sample in the Genome dataset consists of three features: Permission, Intent, and API. Similarly to the Drebin dataset, for a sample in the Genome dataset, we also focus on its Permission feature.

The attacked classifiers are the Random Forest classifier (RF), Support Vector Machine classifier (SVM), Decision Tree classifier (DT), Multilayer Perceptron classifier (MLP), AdaBoost and Logistic Regression classifier (LR), and the performance index are classification accuracy and F1-score.

In the experiment, a label of Permission feature in Drebin dataset was flipped according to agglomerative hierarchical clustering. The classification results under different flipping rate are shown in Figs. 5 and 6.

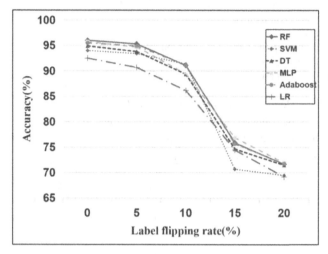

Fig. 5. Classification accuracy of the classifiers under different attack rates (Drebin)

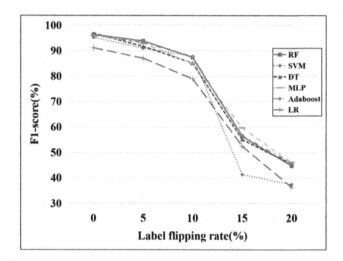

Fig. 6. F1-score of the classifiers under different attack rates (Drebin)

As seen from Figs. 5 and 6, with the increase in label flipping rate, classification accuracy and F1-score values of different classifiers decrease continuously, indicating that the performance of the classifiers is damaged, that is, the proposed attack method is effective for different classifiers. It can also be seen from Figs. 5 and 6 that, under the same flipping rate, different classifiers got different degrees of decrease; the reason is that the structure and the principles of these classifiers are different. Compared with attack effects under other flipping rates, the attack effect is the best when the flipping rate is 20%, which illustrates that the attack effect increases with increasing label flipping rate, and this is easy to understand.

For Genome dataset, we attack the Permission feature and evaluate the attack effect on different classifiers. The attack effects under different label flipping rates are shown in Figs. 7 and 8.

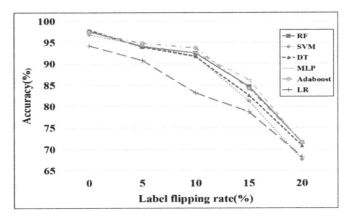

Fig. 7. Classification accuracy of the classifiers under different attack rates (Genome)

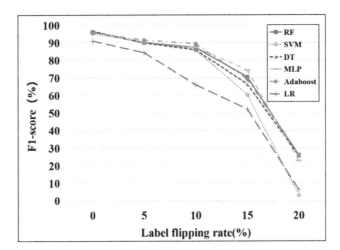

Fig. 8. F1-score of the classifiers under different attack rates (Genome)

It can be seen from Figs. 7 and 8 that the classification accuracy and F1-score of the classifiers decrease continuously with the increase of label flipping rate, which indicates that the proposed attack effectively reduces the classifier performance and achieves a good attack effect. It can also be seen from Figs. 7 and 8 that under the same flipping rate, the attack effect on different models is different. When the label flipping rate was 20%, the F1-score of different classifiers decreased to below 50%, indicating that the proposed attack method achieved good results on the Genome data set.

To verify the effectiveness of the proposed attack method, the classification accuracy of the proposed attack method is compared with the random flipping attack, label flipping attack based on density clustering, and k-means-based label flipping attack on RF, SVM, DT, MLP, AdaBoost, and LR classifiers on Drebin dataset. The results are shown in Table 1.

Table 1. Performance comparison of different attack algorithms (under flipping rate 20%)

Attack algorithm	Accuracy				
	RF	SVM	DT	LR	MLP
Random label flipping attack	92%	93%	88.6%	90.4%	91%
Label flipping attack based on K-means[10]	74.97%	75.38%	76.23%	-	-
Label flipping attack based on density clustering	76.6%	76.7%	76.7%	76.2%	76.8%
Label flipping attack based on agglomerative hierarchical clustering	**71.7%**	**69.5%**	**71.5%**	**69.2%**	**72%**

As can be seen from Table 1, the effect of the proposed label flipping attack based on agglomerative hierarchical clustering is significantly better than the random label flipping attack, the label flipping attack based on K-means and the label flipping based on density clustering, which indicates the effectiveness of the proposed attack method. The results in Table 1 show that, under the attack rate of 20%, the proposed attack method can reduce the classification accuracy of all used model to less than 72%.

4.2 Experimental Results of Defense

In this section, we evaluate the proposed label correction defense method based on TrAdaBoost, and we test the classification accuracy and F1-score on RF, SVM, DT, MLP, AdaBoost, LR, and other classifiers. The results on the Drebin dataset are shown in Figs. 9 and 10.

It can be seen from Figs. 9 and 10 that, with the increase in label flipping rate, the classification accuracy and F1-score of the classifiers almost remain stable and are significantly better than the results under label flipping attack, indicating that the proposed defense method can defend the label flipping attack. It can also be seen from Fig. 9 that, when the label flipping rate is at a ratio of 20%, the classification accuracy of the classifier remains at 88.5% or greater, and the maximum can reach 90%, indicating that the defense method has achieved a good effect on Drebin dataset.

We also evaluated the proposed defense method on the RF, SVM, DT, MLP, AdaBoost, and LR classifiers on Genome dataset. Experimental results under different label flipping proportions are shown in Figs. 11 and 12.

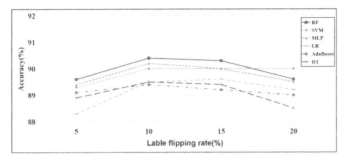

Fig. 9. Accuracy after defensive measures under different attack rates (Drebin)

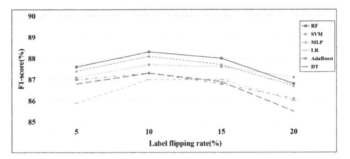

Fig. 10. F1-score after defensive measures under different attack rates (Drebin)

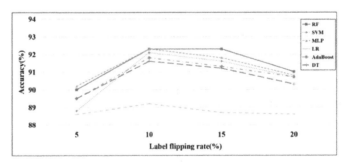

Fig. 11. Accuracy after defensive measures under different attack rates (Genome)

As can be seen from Figs. 11 and 12, with the increase in label flipping rate, the accuracy and F1-score of the classifiers are both stable at around 85%, indicating that the proposed defense method can defend against label flipping attacks and achieve a good effect. It can also be seen from Figs. 11 and 12 that at the same flipping rate, different classifiers have different defense effects, partly because different classifiers have different classification structures. Additionally, when the label flipping rate was 20%, the F1-score of different classifiers remained at approximately 85%, indicating that the proposed defense method achieved good results on Genome dataset.

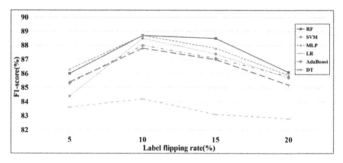

Fig. 12. F1-score after defensive measures under different attack rates (Genome)

To verify the superiority of the proposed defense method, the proposed method is compared with the Label-based Semi-supervised Defense method (LSD), the Clustering based Semi-supervised Defense method (CSD), the KNN-based Semi-Supervised Defense method (KSSD), and the AdaBoost-based Semi-Supervised defense method (AdaSSL) in the literature [20] on Drebin dataset. The experimental results are shown in Table 2.

Table 2. Comparison of different defense methods (under attack rate 20%)

Defense algorithm	Accuracy				
	RF	SVM	DT	LR	MLP
LSD[10]	85.85%	86.26%	85.9%	-	-
CSD[10]	86.59%	87%	87.52%	-	-
KSSD[26]	79.31%	79.72%	80.7%	-	-
AdaSSL[20]	-	84.69%	-	83.82%	85.23%
Label correction defense algorithm based on TrAdaBoost	**89.6%**	**90%**	**88.5%**	**89.2%**	**89.5%**

As shown in Table 2, the proposed TrAdaBoost-based label correction defense algorithm is superior to the LSD, CSD, KSSD and AdaSSL defense methods, indicating the superiority of the proposed defense method. As can be seen from Table 2, when the attack rate is 20%, the proposed defense method can achieve an accuracy of 88.5% or better on RF, SVM, DT, LR, and MLP, indicating that the proposed defense method can effectively protect attacked classifiers.

In this paper, we only study the effect of flipping Permission feature on classification results. In the future, we will use the SHapley Additive exPlanations (SHAP) technique to explore the effect of flipping the labels of other features on the classification results.

5   Conclusions and Limitations

In this paper, we propose a label flipping attack strategy based on agglomerative hierarchical clustering. Meanwhile, to defend the proposed label flipping attack method, we propose a TrAdaBoost-based label correction defense method. Finally, we verified the effectiveness of the proposed attack and defense methods on Drebin and Genome's Permission datasets. Extensive experimental results show that our proposed attack and defense methods achieve better results than the state-of-the-art methods.

Our method has some disadvantages. The proposed label flipping attack and its defense strategy are only for the binary classification problem, the problem of multiple classifications is not involved in this paper. The paper only studied the effect of the flipping Permission feature on the classification results, and the effect of flipping other features on classification results needs to be explored further. In the defense stage, a small clean dataset is also not easy to obtain. Moreover, the computational complexity of the algorithm is high because the pairwise distances of all samples in every class must be calculated each time. These disadvantages may limit the application of the proposed method in real world.

In the future, we will evaluate our proposed methods on the latest datasets. We will also focus on applying our proposed defense method to the multi-classification problem. And we will explore a new poisoning attack method, and the attacked models will be extended to deep learning models such as graph neural networks. We hope that the robustness of the machine model can be improved by studying the poisoning attack and its defense methods.

Acknowledgement. This work was supported by NSFC under Grants No. 61572170, Natural Science Foundation of Hebei Province under Grant No. F2021205004, Science and Technology Foundation Project of Hebei Normal University under Grant No. L2021K06, Science Foundation of Hebei Province Under Grant No. C2020342, Science Foundation of Department of Human Resources and Social Security of Hebei Province under Grant No. ZD2021062, and Foundation of Hebei Normal University under Grant No. L072018Z10.

References

1. Springborg, A. A., Andersen, M. K., Hattel, K. H., et al.: Towards a secure API client generator for IoT devices (2022)
2. Naumov, M., Mudigere, D., Shi, H. J. M., Huang, J., Sundaraman, N., et al.: Deep learning recommendation model for personalization and recommendation systems. (2019)
3. Baracaldo, N., Chen, B., Ludwig, H., Safavi, A., Zhang, R.: Detecting poisoning attacks on machine learning in IoT environments. In: 2018 IEEE International Congress on Internet of Things (ICIOT), pp. 57–64 (2018)
4. Schwarzschild, A., Goldblum, M., Gupta, A., Dickerson, J. P., Goldstein, T.: Just how toxic is data poisoning? a unified benchmark for backdoor and data poisoning attacks. In: International Conference on Machine Learning (PMLR), pp. 9389–9398 (2021)
5. Chen, J.Y., Zou, J.F., Su, M.M., Zhang, L.Y.: A review of deep learning model for poison attack and defense. J. Cyber Sec. **5**(04), 14–29 (2020)

6. Ren, Y., Zhou, Q., Wang, Z., Wu, T., Wu, G., Choo, K.K.R.: Query-efficient label-only attacks against black-box machine learning models. Comput. Sec. **90**, 101698–101707 (2020)

7. Bootkrajang, J.: A generalised label noise model for classification in the presence of annotation errors. Neuro Comput. **192**, 61–71 (2016)

8. Liu, H., Li, D., Li, Y.: Poisonous label attack: black-box data poisoning attack with enhanced conditional DCGAN. Neural Process. Lett. **53**(6), 4117–4142 (2021)

9. Paudice, A., Munoz-Gonzalez, L., Lupu, EC.: Label sanitization against label flipping poisoning attacks. In: Joint European Conference on Machine Learning and Knowledge Discovery in Databases. Springer, pp. 5–15 (2018)

10. Taheri, R., Javidan, R., Shojafar, M., Pooranian, Z., Miri, A., Conti, M.: On defending against label flipping attacks on malware detection systems. Neural Comput. Appl. **32**(18), 14781–14800 (2020). https://doi.org/10.1007/s00521-020-04831-9

11. Wu, R., Saxena, N., Jain, R.: Poisoning the search space in neural architecture search (2021)

12. Vasu, R. K., Seetharaman, S., Malaviya, S., Shukla, M., & Lodha, S.: Gradient-based data subversion attack against binary classifiers. (2021)

13. Ma, K., Xu, Q., Zeng, J., Cao, X., Huang, Q.: Poisoning attack against estimating from pairwise comparisons. IEEE Trans. Pattern Anal. Mach. Intell. (2021)

14. Tianyu, P., Xiao, Y., Yinpeng, D., Hang, S., Jun, Z.: Accumulative poisoning attacks on real-time data. Adv. Neu. Inf. Process. Syst. **34** (2021)

15. Chan, P.P.K., He, Z., Hu, X., Tsang, E.C.C., Yeung, D.S., Ng, W.W.Y.: Causative label flip attack detection with data complexity measures. Int. J. Mach. Learn. Cybern. **12**(1), 103–116 (2020). https://doi.org/10.1007/s13042-020-01159-7

16. Ishaq, N., Howard, T. J., Daniels, N. M.: Clustered hierarchical anomaly and outlier detection algorithms. In: 2021 IEEE International Conference on Big Data (Big Data), pp. 5163–5174, IEEE (2021)

17. Ppkc, A., Fl, A., Zca, B., Ying, S.A., Dsy, C.: Transfer learning based countermeasure against label flipping poisoning attack. Inform. Sci. **548**, 450–460 (2021)

18. Rosenfeld, E., Winston, E., Ravikumar, P., Kolter, Z.: Certified robustness to label-flipping attacks via randomized smoothing. In: International Conference on Machine Learning, pp. 8230–8241. PMLR (2020)

19. Tavallali, P., Behzadan, V., Tavallali, P., Singhal, M.: Adversarial poisoning attacks and defense for general multi-class models based on synthetic reduced nearest neighbors (2021)

20. Cheng, N., Zhang, H., Li, Z.: Data sanitization against label flipping attacks using AdaBoost-based semi-supervised learning technology. Soft. Comput. **25**(23), 14573–14581 (2021). https://doi.org/10.1007/s00500-021-06384-y

21. Xie, Y., Shekhar, S., Li, Y.: Statistically-robust clustering techniques for mapping spatial hotspots: a survey. ACM Comput. Surv. **55**(2), 1–38 (2022)

22. Rousseeuw, P.J.: Silhouettes: a graphical aid to the interpretation and validation of cluster analysis. J. Comput. Appl. Math. **20**, 53–65 (1987)

23. Antunes, J., Bernardino, A., Smailagic, A., et al.: Weighted multisource TrAdaBoost. In: Iberian Conference on Pattern Recognition and Image Analysis, pp. 194–205. Springer, Cham (2019)

24. Arp, D., Spreitzenbarth, M., Hubner, M., Gascon, H., Rieck, K., Siemens, C. E. R. T.: Drebin: effective and explainable detection of android malware in your pocket. In: Proceedings of the 21st Annual Network and Distributed System Security Symposium (NDSS), Vol. 14, pp. 23–26 (2014)

25. Zhou, Y., Jiang, X.: Dissecting android malware: characterization and evolution. In: 2012 IEEE Symposium on Security and Privacy, pp. 95–109. IEEE (2012)

26. Zhang, H., Cheng, N., Zhang, Y., Li, Z.: Label flipping attacks against naive Bayes on spam filtering systems. Appl. Intell. **2**, 4503–4514 (2021)

Astute Approach to Handling Memory Layouts of Regular Data Structures

Adam Šmelko[1], Martin Kruliš[1(✉)], Miroslav Kratochvíl[2], Jiří Klepl[1], Jiří Mayer[1], and Petr Šimůnek[1]

[1] Department of Distributed and Dependable Systems, Charles University, Prague, Czech Republic
{smelko,krulis}@d3s.mff.cuni.cz
[2] Luxembourg Centre for Systems Biomedicine, University of Luxembourg, Esch-sur-Alzette, Luxembourg
miroslav.kratochvil@uni.lu

Abstract. Programmers of high-performance applications face many challenging aspects of contemporary hardware architectures. One of the critical aspects is the efficiency of memory operations which is affected not only by the hardware parameters such as memory throughput or cache latency but also by the data-access patterns, which may influence the utilization of the hardware, such as re-usability of the cached data or coalesced data transactions. Therefore, a performance of an algorithm can be highly impacted by the layout of its data structures or the order of data processing which may translate into a more or less optimal sequence of memory operations. These effects are even more pronounced on highly-parallel platforms, such as GPUs, which often employ specific execution models (lock-step) or memory models (shared memory).

In this work, we propose a modern, astute approach for managing and implementing memory layouts with first-class structures that is very efficient and straightforward. This approach was implemented in Noarr, a GPU-ready portable C++ library that utilizes generic programming, functional design, and compile-time computations to allow the programmer to specify and compose data structure layouts declaratively while minimizing the indexing and coding overhead. We describe the main principles on code examples and present a performance evaluation that verifies our claims regarding its efficiency.

Keywords: Memory layout · Data structure · Cache · Parallel · Performance · Reusable

1 Introduction

This paper aims to tackle memory-related performance issues, which represent one of the most crucial performance optimization topics. In hardware, memory access is optimized by providing faster memories closer to the chip (like HBM2), multi-level caches and transfer buffers, and even specialized explicit near-core

© Springer Nature Switzerland AG 2023
W. Meng et al. (Eds.): ICA3PP 2022, LNCS 13777, pp. 507–528, 2023.
https://doi.org/10.1007/978-3-031-22677-9_27

memories (such as AVX512 registers or shared memory in Nvidia GPUs). Software developers benefit from these features by creating specialized, cache-aware algorithms, often tailored for a particular architecture.

The design of the way that the program data is laid out in memory is one of the crucial steps that ensures memory access performance. Even simple design choices like row- or column-major matrix storage impact the performance within the complex memory cache models by simplifying address translations, improving cache hit ratio and prefetching, or ensuring the alignment required for coalesced SIMD operations [7,14]. For parallel algorithms, the complexity of the problem becomes much broader because of cache-line collisions, false-sharing, non-uniform memory architectures, a variety of synchronization issues [3,11,18], and other factors. Many-core platforms (GPUs in particular) only amplify this by enforcing specific data access patterns in lockstep execution, advocating the use of programmer-managed caches (like shared memory), and having a significantly lower cache-to-core ratio in comparison to the CPUs [13].

The best layout is quite often elusive and needs to be discovered empirically. Furthermore, it often differs even among the utilized cache levels [10,12,17]. Consequently, the optimal implementations are often complicated, and most of the optimization-relevant code is not portable between hardware architectures. Enabling simple implementations of layout-flexible data structures and algorithms would improve the code portability (and value); however, systematic approaches are quite rare, often over-complicating the code logic and making the algorithm implementation not maintainable or usable beyond the community of specialists.

1.1   Motivational Example

To explain the motivation, objectives, and contributions of our research, we have selected a matrix multiplication problem widely known in computer science. For the sake of simplicity, we use the most straightforward implementation with $\mathcal{O}(N^3)$ complexity (computing $C = A \times B$ of square matrices N^2):

```
for (size_t i = 0; i < N; ++i)
    for (size_t j = 0; j < N; ++j) {
        C[i][j] = 0;
        for (size_t k = 0; k < N; ++k)
            C[i][j] += A[i][k] * B[k][j];
    }
```

Having a fixed algorithm structure (i.e., order of the operations), the memory layout of the matrices is the main issue affecting the performance. In this context, the layout is defined by transforming the abstract indices (i, j) into an offset, subsequently used to compute the actual memory address. For instance, the most common matrix layout is row-major, which computes the offset as $i*W+j$ (where W is the width of the matrix). A few examples of possible layouts are depicted in Fig. 1.

The aforementioned code sample used traditional C notation A[i][j] which enforces the row-major layout, which is sub-optimal for this algorithm. Having the second matrix in a col-major layout or using a z-curve for all matrices will

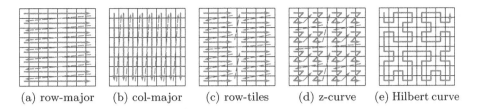

(a) row-major   (b) col-major   (c) row-tiles   (d) z-curve   (e) Hilbert curve

Fig. 1. Examples of common matrix layouts

improve cache utilization, and the algorithm would run several times to several orders of magnitude faster, depending on the platform. Therefore, we need to introduce layout flexibility into the code.

A typical object-oriented solution would be to create a class abstraction that would define a uniform interface for accessing matrix elements whilst enabling different implementations through derived classes. A slightly better and more reusable solution would be to separate the offset computation into a policy class that would be injected into the matrix as a template parameter:

```
class RowMajor {
    static size_t offset(size_t i, size_t j, size_t W, size_t H) {
        return i*W + j;
    }
};

template<typename T = float, class Layout = RowMajor>
class Matrix {
    /* ... */
    T& at(size_t i, size_t j) {
        return _data[Layout::offset(i, j, _W, _H)];
    }
};
```

The policy class makes the matrix implementation flexible (in terms of selecting the proper layout) and efficient (since the compiler can inline the static method). However, several drawbacks make this solution imperfect. The interface between the `Matrix` class and its layout policy (`RowMajor`) is created ad-hoc by the author of the main class, which complicates the code reusability of the layout policies in potentially compatible situations. The interface also prevents efficient constant propagation and caching of intermediate values. Furthermore, the strong encapsulation may prevent low-level optimizations, portability to other architectures (e.g., GPUs), and complicate data structure composition (e.g., when matrices in an array need to be interleaved).

We aim to design a more straightforward, more programmer-friendly solution to implementing *layout-agnostic* algorithms, focusing on enabling performance optimizations and parallel processing.

1.2 Objectives and Contributions

Our main objective was to create a library that allows the users to quickly adapt their algorithms and data structures for different memory layouts, with a particular focus on the following targets:

- Once an algorithm is adapted, it becomes layout-agnostic—i.e., no subsequent internal code modifications should be required to change the layout of the underlying data structures.
- The layout representation should not be coupled with memory allocation so that it could be used in different scenarios and different memory spaces (i.e., directly applicable with memory-mapped files or GPU unified memory).
- The interface should define an easily comprehensible abstraction for *indexing* (offset computation) that would hide its (possibly complex) nuances.
- The indexing mechanism should enable the compiler to evaluate constant expressions at compile time (e.g., fold constant dimensions of a structure into the generated code).
- The code overhead should be minimal, preferably smaller than with well-established practices, such as providing template policy classes to govern layout or allocation.

We have implemented Noarr header-only library[1] for C++ as a prototype that achieves the outlined objectives. C++ was chosen as a widely-used mainstream language that provides complete control over memory layout and allocation and is widely used for programming performance-critical applications, including parallel HPC systems and GPGPU computing. Its fundamental features, like the templating system and operator overloading, open possibilities for generic programming, compile-time optimizations, and the design of a functional-like interface, which simplifies the use of the library. Furthermore, the separation of indexing from (CPU-specific) memory management allowed us to directly utilize the library with Nvidia CUDA code, easily porting the layout-agnostic code on contemporary GPUs.

We believe that Noarr will make a significant contribution to simplifying the coding process and increasing performance in many scenarios, especially:

- Empirical exploration of possible layouts—i.e., finding the optimal combination of layouts for given data structures and algorithms by measuring the performance of all possible implementations.
- Implementing applications and libraries in which the optimal layout of data structures needs to be selected at runtime (e.g., based on the size of the problem or the best available architecture).
- Allowing simple yet efficient (semi)automatic layout transformations in case the input or output layouts differ from the optimal layouts for the computation.

Although the issues mentioned above can be identified in a large variety of data structures and algorithms, we are focusing mainly on regular data structures such as nested multi-dimensional arrays and structures (in the C/C++ sense). However, despite this narrow scope, we have identified that this problem is quite challenging, especially regarding optimizations for massively parallel environments like GPUs.

---

[1] Noarr is available as open-source on GitHub under MIT license: https://github.com/ParaCoToUl/noarr-structures.

The paper is organized as follows. Section 2 explains the key principles and benefits of the layout-agnostic algorithm design. The performance aspects of offset computation overhead are summarized in Sect. 3. In Sect. 4, we provide insights into the current implementation of the Noarr library. Related work and main conclusions are summarized in Sects. 5 and 6.

2   Extensible Memory Layout Structures

One of the most significant challenges of the outlined problem is to create an indexing abstraction that would follow the fundamental code design principles (especially in object-oriented programming, which is one of the most widely adopted paradigms), thus allowing the programmer to write neat and maintainable code, whilst minimizing performance overhead and making heavy use of the compile-time optimizations.

In this work, we propose using first-class indexing structures which can be detached entirely from the allocated memory and the data structures themselves. The indexing structure has a specific type (templated class) composed of predefined base types and a corresponding instance (object). This way, the information being passed to the layout-agnostic algorithm is divided into two parts:

- the data type passed via (inferred) template parameter, which bears the structure and constant parameters,
- and the object, which bears all dynamic parameters (such as sizes of non-constant dimensions of the data structure).

Before we focus on the benefits, let us emphasize the C++ cornerstones of Noarr that are pretty important for understanding the main principles (details are provided in Sect. 4).

- The indexing structure type composition is straightforward as the user merely combines predefined Noarr templated classes. Furthermore, thanks to the templating system, it is easy to create partially-defined structures, thus promoting code reusability. The construction of derived or augmented types (like binding the constant dimensions) is implemented in a functional manner, which is quite comprehensive and easy to write. Finally, modern C++ constructs like `auto` or template type inference make these type modifications easier to handle since only the instance object is passed down.
- The dimensions of the data structure are denoted using chars (typically letters), which are much more mnemonic than numbers or the order of definition. Furthermore, they can be used to define additional abstraction so that structures with the same set of named dimensions can be treated as compatible, regardless of the order of their definition or their actual layout representation.
- Finally, the implementation makes heavy use of `constexpr` functions which allow the compiler to be inlined, resolve, and even precompute many pieces of the layout-related code, thus making it more efficient. For instance, the

```
1    template <char I, char J, class struct_lhs_t, class struct_rhs_t, class struct_out_t>
2    __global__ float matmul_tile(const float* lhs_in, const float* rhs_in, float* out, const
  ↪  struct_lhs_t lhs_s, const struct_rhs_t rhs_s, struct_out_t out_s) {
3        constexpr size_t tile_w = 16;
4        constexpr auto tile_s = noarr::array<I, tile_w, noarr::array<J, tile_w,
  ↪      noarr::scalar<float>>>();
5        __shared__ float l_tile[tile_w * tile_w];
6        __shared__ float r_tile[tile_w * tile_w];
7        const uint32_t x = blockIdx.x * tile_size + threadIdx.x;
8        const uint32_t y = blockIdx.y * tile_size + threadIdx.y;
9
10       float acc = 0.f;
11       for (uint32_t i = 0; i < lhs_s.get_length<J>(); i += tile_w) {
12           tile_s.get_at<I, J>(l_tile, threadIdx.y, threadIdx.x) =
13               lhs_s.get_at<I, J>(lhs_data, y, threadIdx.x + i);
14           tile_s.get_at<I, J>(r_tile, threadIdx.y, threadIdx.x) =
15               rhs_s.get_at<I, J>(rhs_data, threadIdx.y + i, x);
16           __syncthreads();
17
18           for (uint32_t j = 0; j < tile_w; j++)
19               acc += tile_s.get_at<I, J>(l_tile, threadIdx.y, j)
20                   * tile_s.get_at<J, I>(r_tile, threadIdx.x, j);
21           __syncthreads();
22       }
23       out_s.get_at<I, J>(output_data, y, x) = acc;
24   }
```

Listing 1: CUDA matrix multiplication kernel based on Noarr library

constant dimensions can be translated into the expressions where the actual memory offsets are being computed, which may allow optimizations like pre-computing constant subexpressions.

Utilizing memory layouts as first-class objects can introduce some flexibility into the code. In this section, we demonstrate the two main ideas of the proposed approach: The ability to easily *decouple memory allocation from its interpreted layout* and the possibility of writing *memory-layout-agnostic functions*. Listing 1 presents an example that employs both these ideas using Noarr library.

2.1   Decoupling the Memory Management

In C++, memory is usually acquired following one of two scenarios—either it is allocated internally by a wrapping data structure (the 'owning' semantics), or it is provided by the caller (the 'borrowing' semantics). When the indexing structure is decoupled from the memory allocation and combined with the borrowing semantics, it can cover many elaborate memory management scenarios, such as file memory-mapping or sharing memory among threads (this also includes CUDA unified memory or shared memory).

In Noarr, the layout objects are entirely independent of memory management. To simplify the situation for programmers, it also provides a wrapper structure bag, which binds the layout structure with any pointer, acting as a smart pointer with borrowing semantics. The layout can be used alone to compute linearized offsets from input indices, which is also applicable in hypothetical scenarios beyond pointer-based memory addressing.

We present an example of a matrix multiplication kernel implemented in CUDA (Listing 1) to demonstrate the possibilities opened by proper decoupling. In the code, a GPU kernel performs the multiplication in tiles where each 16×16 tile of the output matrix is computed by one thread block, and each element is handled by one thread. A thread block cooperatively fetches a pair of tiles from the input matrices (one pair at a time) into the shared memory; all threads of the block then use the cached tiles to update their intermediate scalar products (which are kept in their registers) before iteratively loading successive pairs of tiles. Once all tiles are processed, each thread writes its aggregated result into the output matrix.

The example focuses on a typical pattern in GPU programming—a manual caching of data in the *shared memory*. Unlike global memory (accessible by all threads), the shared memory is an integral component of a streaming multiprocessor; thus, it is dedicated to the threads within the same thread block. Unsurprisingly, the two types of memory are allocated and managed in slightly different ways, albeit both use pointer-based addressing. The global memory is usually allocated before the execution of a kernel (i.e., by the host) and passed to a kernel as an argument (`lhs_in`, `rhs_in`, and `out` on line 2 of Listing 1). The shared memory is acquired inside the kernel by defining a C array with `__shared__` prefix (`l_tile` and `r_tile` on lines 5–6).

Considering also the host memory (where a copy of matrices also needs to reside), the programmer must manage three (partial) copies in three different memory spaces. A uniform abstraction (that supports owning and borrowing semantics) streamlines the code significantly. Furthermore, in this particular instance, we could also take advantage of having a different layout for different matrices—e.g., the optimum is reached if the left-side matrix is in the row-major while the right-side matrix is in the column-major format.

Listing 1 demonstrates, how the problem is solved using Noarr. The tiles are loaded into the shared memory on lines 12–15. The variables `lhs_s` and `rhs_s` represent the layout objects, which are bound with global memory pointers (`lhs_in` and `rhs_in` respectively) to read data from input matrices (lines 13 and 15). Another layout object `tile_s` is used for two shared memory pointers representing the cached tiles (lines 12 and 14). With these layout objects, different types of memory could be accessed using the same interface. Additionally, the code is ready for future layouts modifications and promotes the reusability of the existing layout structures.

2.2   Layout-Agnostic Functions

Formally, we may define the layout-agnostic property as a unique form of polymorphism. Layout-agnostic functions are implemented in a way that does not require altering their code when the layout of the used data structures needs to be changed. As hinted in the introduction, the layout selection may significantly affect performance. In extreme cases, the relative performance improvement achieved by optimal layout selection can reach orders of magnitude.

To demonstrate this effect, we show how the layout choice changes the performance of the matrix multiplication kernel from Listing 1, which is already written as layout-agnostic. Running the kernel with different layout configurations for each matrix is implemented by simply passing different function arguments (and corresponding template parameters, which the compiler can automatically infer in typical cases). We utilize this flexibility to find a layout combination that exhibits the best performance quickly.

For the sake of this example, we coded the following matrix layouts:

- *Row-major* layout (labeled **R**, which we use as a baseline)
- *Column-major* (**C**, a transposition of row-major layout)
- **R** *tiles in* **C** *order* (**RC**), which divides the matrix logically into 16×16 sub-matrices (tiles); data in each sub-matrix is stored with row-major layout, while the sub-matrices are organized in column-major layout
- **C** *tiles in* **R** *order* (**CR**) is analogical to **RC** layout, but the tiles use column-major layout internally, and are ordered in row-major fashion
- *CC* and *RR* are defined analogically

The layout of all inputs and outputs of the matrix multiplication is thus expressed as a triplet of individual matrix layouts. For example, **R** $\times$ **C** = **R** denotes a multiplication where the left and the output matrices are in row-major, and the right-side input matrix is in the column-major layout. Since the kernel 1 already caches tiles explicitly in the shared memory, we expect the tiled layouts to perform better. Likely, the **RR** $\times$ **RC** = **R** should exhibit the best performance (given the properties of the algorithm).

We have created a benchmark that tested the performance of the presented algorithm using all layout combinations possible. In each test, the input matrices were loaded to the GPU global memory already transformed into the selected matrix layouts, the kernel was executed, and its execution time was measured and recorded. A relevant selection of the experimental results is shown in Fig. 2. The graphs present the normalized times (in picoseconds and femtoseconds)—i.e., kernel execution times divided by the asymptotical amount of work (N^3 in this case). Details regarding our experimental setup can be found in Appendix A, and the complete set of results can be found in our replication package[2].

The result verified that **RC** is superior to the baseline row-major layout in both input positions. Furthermore, the $R \times C = R$ configuration (often praised on sequential architectures) exhibits worse than the baseline on massively parallel hardware. While this was expected, the primary outcome of this benchmark is methodological: A selection of input and output layouts can be tested systematically without reimplementation effort, while the larger exploration size of the selection (enabled by low coding overhead) provides a solid guarantee that the best-identified solution is indeed a good choice for a high-performance software.

---

[2] https://github.com/asmelko/ica3pp22-artifact.

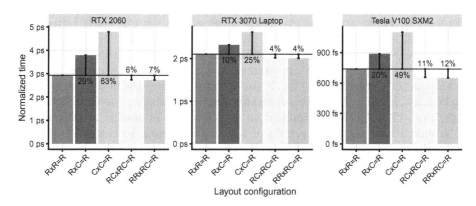

Fig. 2. Speedups of selected layout combinations relative to (row-major) baseline

```
1    template <char X, char Y, typename bag_in_t, typename bag_out_t>
2    static void transform(const bag_in_t& input_bag, bag_out_t& output_bag) {
3        for (size_t i = 0; i < input_bag.get_length<X>(); i++)
4            for (size_t j = 0; j < input_bag.get_length<Y>(); j++)
5                output_bag.at<X, Y>(i, j) = input_bag.at<X, Y>(i, j);
6    }
```

Listing 2: Key part of transformation routine for 2-index (2D) arrays

2.3 Transformations

The layout-agnostic algorithms can benefit from performance gains achieved by choosing the best layout for a given problem configuration and architecture. However, in real-world scenarios, the layout of the input and output data structures is often prescribed as an inherent part of the algorithm interface or selected by the caller (in the case of generic interfaces).

If the algorithm is complex enough and the performance gap between the prescribed layouts and optimal layouts is high, the data structures may be copied and transformed into their optimally organized counterparts to speed up the algorithm. With Noarr, the transformation can be handled in a generic way. Following our examples with matrices, Listing 2 presents the central part of a generic transformer for 2D structures.

In fact, we are currently extending Noarr to handle the transformations in a generic way for any-dimensional structures, and we are exploring techniques how to select the best way of iterating the structures (e.g., selecting the best ordering of nested loops) in order to optimize memory transfers and caching. However, this research is well beyond the scope of this paper.

Transformation Overhead Assessment. Employing transformations may be beneficial only under specific circumstances. Simply put, the algorithm must save more execution time than how long it takes to transform all the necessary data.

We want to demonstrate the overhead assessment on the previously introduced matrix multiplication example.

We have analyzed the layout transformation overhead for various matrix sizes and layouts. The key results are summarized in Fig. 3. We have observed that in the case of larger matrices ($N > 10,000$), the overhead is negligible, primarily because of the asymptotic complexity difference between the transformation algorithm ($\mathcal{O}(N^2)$) and the multiplication ($\mathcal{O}(N^3)$). For smaller matrices (with N around 1000), the relative ratio of the transformation to computation time expectably increased, and the transformation overhead caused the baseline to perform the best.

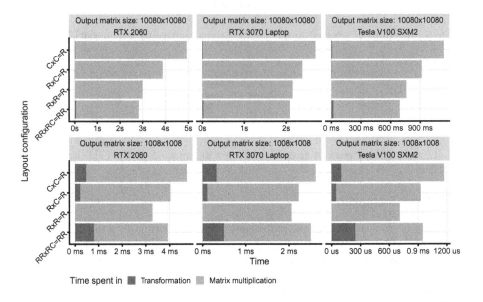

Fig. 3. Layout transformation times compared to actual matrix multiplication times

As demonstrated, deciding whether or when a layout transformation can be beneficial may be complicated; however, with Noarr, both the experiments and the actual decision to apply or not to the transformation can be implemented very quickly.

3   Performance Impact of Constant Expressions

One of the essential features of Noarr is that the first-class structures propagate along with their templated types, allowing us to embed statically defined properties (most importantly, the constant dimensions of the structure) into the type itself. Therefore, the compiler can employ optimizations like compile-time evaluation of constant expressions or exact-sized loop unrolling, which might lead to more efficient execution or even automated vectorization. These optimizations rarely produce a game-changing improvement in performance; thus, the programmers often overlook them. However, utilization of Noarr structure will introduce them naturally so the result code could run faster without any additional effort whilst maintaining other benefits like memory allocation decoupling or coding in a layout-agnostic manner.

To present the main idea, let us have an array A of N vectors in $\mathbb{R}^D$ where N is a variable, and D is a constant[3]. We want to compute the Euclidean distance between every vector in the array and given vector q (e.g., to find k nearest vectors, which is quite a typical task in many data-processing problems):

```
for (size_t i = 0; i < N; ++i) {
  float dist = 0.0f;
  for (size_t d = 0; d < D; ++d) {
    float diff = A[i*D + d] - q[d];
    dist += diff * diff;
  }
  dist = std::sqrtf(dist); // ...
}
```

When D is a constant, the compiler could unroll the loop entirely without additional branches. It might even attempt to unroll the outer loop if D is sufficiently small. The speedup achieved by having constant D may easily reach factor $3\times$ for very small values of D (e.g., $D = 2$)[4].

3.1 Indexing Performance

To demonstrate the impact of Noarr structures, we have selected a 3D stencil problem as an example. Stencil is a simple function computed iteratively for every element of a regular grid. We have used an averaging stencil executed on a 3D grid which could be used as an approximative simulation of gas diffusion, for instance. Our objective is to emphasize the difference between situations when the grid dimensions are constant (at compile time) and when they are determined at runtime.

The main code of the stencil is in Listing 3. Run-time variables size_x, size_y, and size_z denote the dimensions of the cube. The first part of this experiment aims at exposing only the compile-time optimizations of index computations, so we ensure that no optimizations related to constant dimensions are performed. Please note that the loops do not visit points residing on the faces of the grid so that we can ignore the border cases of the stencil function; thus, there are no branches in the code which leads to simpler and more stable measurement.

A naïve C-like implementation of the internal stencil function is presented in Listing 4. It uses the same variables in the loop to index the data pointers,

---

[3] If the code needs to handle several different dimensionalities D, it will be compiled for each D independently thanks to the power of C++ templates.

[4] If we measure only the Euclidean distance computation.

```
1   template <typename... Args> void run_stencil_grid(Args&&... args) {
2       for (size_t x = 1; x < size_x - 1; x++)
3           for (size_t y = 1; y < size_y - 1; y++)
4               for (size_t z = 1; z < size_z - 1; z++)
5                   stencil(std::forward<Args>(args)..., x, y, z);
6   }
```

Listing 3: Main stencil for-loop

preventing the compiler from doing more elaborate compile-time optimizations. This code is used as a baseline for the performance comparison.

```
1    inline void stencil(const float* in, float* out, size_t x, size_t y, size_t z) {
2        float sum = in[x * size_y * size_z + y * size_z + z];
3        sum += in[(x + 1) * size_y * size_z + y * size_z + z];
4        sum += in[(x - 1) * size_y * size_z + y * size_z + z];
5        sum += in[x * size_y * size_z + (y + 1) * size_z + z];
6        sum += in[x * size_y * size_z + (y - 1) * size_z + z];
7        sum += in[x * size_y * size_z + y * size_z + z + 1];
8        sum += in[x * size_y * size_z + y * size_z + z - 1];
9        out[x * size_y * size_z + y * size_z + z] = sum / 7;
10   }
```

Listing 4: Naïve implementation of stencil function

Making the dimensions constant may help the compiler to generate more optimal code. In C++, this can be achieved simply by defining the **size_*** variables as **constexpr**; however, such constants need to be declared at the global level, which significantly undermines any encapsulation or reusability of the code. Better way is to use fix-sized containers like **std::array** and make the stencil code templated so it can be used with any compatible containers (including **std::vector**).

```
1    using cube = noarr::array<'x', 1048576, noarr::array<'y', 32, noarr::array<'z', 32,
  ↪    noarr::scalar<float>>>>;
2    using bag = noarr:bag<cube, noarr::helpers::bag_policy<std::unique_ptr>>;
3
4    inline void stencil(const bag& in, bag& out, size_t x, size_t y, size_t z) {
5        float sum = in.at<'x', 'y', 'z'>(x, y, z);
6        sum += in.at<'x', 'y', 'z'>(x + 1, y, z);
7        sum += in.at<'x', 'y', 'z'>(x - 1, y, z);
8        sum += in.at<'x', 'y', 'z'>(x, y + 1, z);
9        sum += in.at<'x', 'y', 'z'>(x, y - 1, z);
10       sum += in.at<'x', 'y', 'z'>(x, y, z + 1);
11       sum += in.at<'x', 'y', 'z'>(x, y, z - 1);
12       out.at<'x', 'y', 'z'>(x, y, z) = sum / 7;
13   }
```

Listing 5: Noarr implementation of stencil with constant-sized **array**

Noarr provides a fixed layout structure `array`, which fulfills a similar role, but it can be easily integrated into more complex nested structures (even with custom layouts). Listing 5 presents the internal `stencil` rewritten for Noarr. The dimensions of the grid are no longer passed as variables, but they are embedded in the type of the `bag` structure as constants. Line 1 shows the assembling of the layout structure using a predefined `array` template.

To evaluate the performance, we have selected a grid of a specific size ($2^{20} \times 32 \times 32$) which confines the meaning of the diffuse simulation for a specific environment (e.g., gas in a pipe). The main reason is that the performance improvement caused by the compile-time optimizations is difficult to measure on regular structures since it takes only a small portion of overall time (especially when the computation causes many cache misses). This shape requires more index computations relative to other operations, making the difference more pronounced in the measurements.

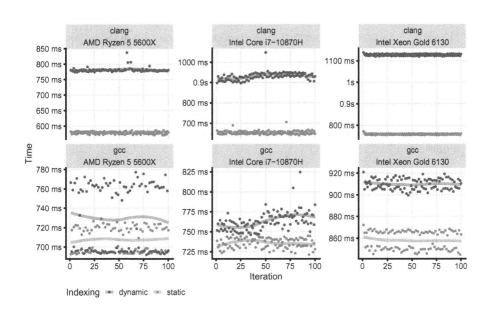

Fig. 4. Wall times of 100 stencil iterations (plotted lines represent the local regression of the measured times)

Figure 4 shows the comparison results of the two presented stencil implementations on three platforms using two compilers. The benefits of compile-time optimizations are visible on every platform and with both tested compilers, albeit there is only a small difference in some configurations. The details regarding the experimental methodology are summarized in Appendix A.

3.2   Constant-Loops Optimizations

The second part of this experiment extends the compile-time optimizations to the nested stencil grid loops. It requires replacing `size_*` variables in the main loops (Listing 3) with constants (i.e., `constexpr` or template arguments) so the compiler has enough information to perform exact loop-unrolling and better vectorization-related optimizations.

```
1    template <typename bag_t> constexpr void run_stencil_grid(bag_t in, bag_t out) {
2        for (size_t x = 1; x < in.get_legth<'x'>() - 1; x++)
3            for (size_t y = 1; y < in.get_legth<'y'>() - 1; y++)
4                for (size_t z = 1; z < in.get_legth<'z'>() - 1; z++)
5                    stencil(in, out, x, y, z);
6    }
```

Listing 6: Updated stencil for-loop with `bag` structure

However, converting these variables to constants may be quite tedious, especially if we want the code to be generic for both constant and non-constant scenarios. This particular issue can be easily overcome by utilization of Noarr `bag` structures. Having the layout information encoded both in the structure type and the object, method `get_length` can query dimension sizes and returns a constant or variable based on the layout specification, all this being decided at compile time. The grid loop function from Listing 3 needs to be rewritten as demonstrated in Listing 6.

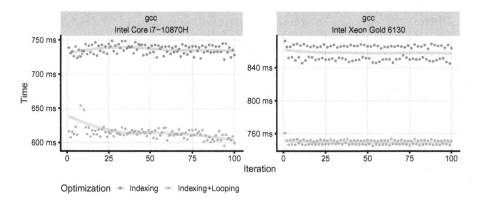

Fig. 5. Stencil execution times of two optimizations—compile-time *indexing* and the addition of constant-induced loop unrolling (*indexing+looping*)

Figure 5 presents the performance improvements of exposing constant variables to the grid iteration loop. We have included only measurements of programs compiled by `gcc` since `clang` was not able to take advantage of the constant values when they are passed through the `bag` structure interface.

4   Implementation and Technical Insights

The Noarr library[5] is logically divided into three levels, each building on top of the previous one: *structures*, *functions*, and *object wrappers*. The first two layers provide a rather low-level functional approach, while the last one encapsulates the first two into a more traditional C++ object-oriented design.

4.1   Structures

A *structure* is an object that stores information about a data layout. It exposes the information via a simple interface, providing its size in bytes (`size()`), the range of indices it supports (`length()`) and a current offset from the beginning of the structure in bytes (`offset()`).

The most trivial structure is `scalar` (Listing 7), which wraps the 'base' values to be used in more complex layouts. Scalar often wraps simple types like `float`, but it can also wrap any fixed-size C++ type (such as `struct` or `std::tuple`). The methods `length()` and `offset()` of `scalar` always return 0 because `scalar` represents only a single element.

```
1    template<class T>
2    struct scalar : contain<> {
3      static constexpr size_t size() noexcept { return sizeof(T); }
4      static constexpr size_t offset() noexcept { return 0; }
5      static constexpr size_t length() noexcept { return 0; }
6    };
```

Listing 7: A core part of the `scalar` structure used for wrapping simple values

The `array` structure (Listing 8) is more complicated: Like `std::array`, it represents a fixed-size array with a named dimension and statically defined number of elements of a given *substructure* type. Unlike `scalar` which wraps a *trivial type*, `array` is contains a Noarr *structural type*.

An important aspect of the structures is their ability to be combined and nested to create a *structure tree*. For instance, the composition of `scalar` and `array` is quite straightforward:

- `array<'a', 10, scalar<float>>` defines an array of 10 `float`s,
- `array<'i', 4, array<'j', 8, scalar<int>>>` represents a 4×8 row-major integer matrix layout,
- `array<'j', 8, array<'i', 4, scalar<int>>>` represents the same matrix in a column-major layout.

---

[5] https://github.com/ParaCoToUl/noarr-structures.

```
1   template<char Dim, size_t L, class T>
2   struct array : contain<T> {
3     constexpr size_t size() const noexcept {
4       return contain<T>::template get<0>().size() * L;
5     }
6     constexpr size_t offset(size_t i) const noexcept {
7       return contain<T>::template get<0>().size() * i;
8     }
9     static constexpr size_t length() noexcept { return L; }
10  };
```

Listing 8: Noarr **array** structure (some methods are omitted for brevity)

All structures inherit from class **contain**, which has several purposes: It serves as recursive storage for the wrapped structure, holds some useful meta-information about the nested substructures, and stores possible additional data for the structure, such as dynamic dimension length or the current offset index. Querying for various properties, which is its main purpose, is demonstrated in Listing 8. The **array** implements the **size()** function using the information (size) from its immediate substructure (line 4). In the example, queries work recursively on subsequent immediate substructures until the recursion is halted in **scalar::size()**. Using this mechanism, **contain** allows us to create the nested hierarchy of the structure tree easily.

There are several other built-in structures in Noarr library, such as **vector** and **tuple** (analogical to **std::vector** and **std::tuple**), which provide sufficient arsenal for composing memory layouts of many regular-shaped data structures. Moreover, the library design makes it open for extensions, and programmers may implement additional custom layout structures.

4.2   Functions

Noarr *functions* are C++ **constexpr** functions that serve as an expressive tool for obtaining complex information from the structure trees. They are used to compute offsets for memory pointers to provide indexation, transform structures, and query dimension lengths using a single, extensible functional interface.

Calling function **f** on a structure **s** is achieved using the (overloaded) 'pipe' operator |. Expression **s | f** denotes that **f** is applied on **s** (note this may sometimes differ from **f(s)** as detailed later in this section).

For example, the function **get_length()** traverses structure tree and calls **length()** on a substructure with the given dimension name:

```
size_t i_len = a_structure | get_lenght<'i'>();
```

The function **set_length()** proceeds similarly, but when a matching substructure is found, the whole structure is reconstructed to carry the new length. The following example shows that functions can be additionally chained one after another. Notably, all structures are immutable, which allowed us to ensure that **unsized_s** does not carry any unnecessary data:

```
auto unsized_s = vector<'i', vector<'j', scalar<float>>>();
auto sized_s = unsized_s | set_length<'i'>(4) | set_length<'j'>(8);
```

A function application on a structure may fail, such as when querying a length of a non-existing dimension. We say the function is *not applicable* on a structure. Taking the aforementioned two functions into account and the fact that every structure forms a structure tree, it is possible that a function is not *directly applicable* on the topmost structure but is applicable on some structures in the structure tree. For this reason, we distinguish three *piping mechanisms* that govern different means of the function-structure application:

- *Top application* (or *direct application*). This is the simplest form of piping, where s | f is equivalent to f(s). In other words, the function is applied directly to the topmost structure.
- *Get application.* Given the piping s | f, if f(s) is not applicable the piping mechanism attempts to apply f to the substructures of s recursively. It fails if f does not apply to any of the substructures or if it applies to more substructures. The trivial representative being get_length(), because there should be exactly one node in a structure tree with a specified dimension.
- *Transform application.* s | f either results in top application when f(s) is applicable or f is transformatively applied on all *direct* substructures of s. If the latter, the structure is reconstructed with these changes to the substructures.

The piping mechanism is implemented using C++ constexpr functions and metaprogramming. Together with the static nature of substructure hierarchies that encompasses the structure layer, the implementation is very efficient since it provides the necessary space for compiler optimizations. We can demonstrate this by precisely describing the operations executed when a function with the get application is applied to a structure. Let us have the following structure and function:

```
auto v4 = vector<'a', vector<'b', vector<'c', vector<'d', scalar<int>>>>>();
auto f = get_length<'d'>();
```

Expression v4 | f must perform a traversal of the structure tree to find the matching dimension. Fortunately, the way the structures and functions are implemented ensures that there is no run-time loop in the implementation. Because all substructures are known in compile-time, the traversal loop is unrolled using metaprogramming techniques. Furthermore, because the values are also known at compile-time, the result can be partially evaluated and, in turn, *no run-time code is generated*. In summary, applying v4 | f produces four unrolled function applications, three of which produce no operation at all (and usually get discarded by a compiler), and only one results in calling length() on a substructure that can be evaluated by the compiler.

4.3   Object Wrappers

Object wrappers provide object-oriented management of structures, functions, and the actual data. Noarr library offers two kinds of such objects—structure *wrappers* and `bags`.

A `wrapper` simplifies the work with structures by bundling the applications of the most common Noarr functions into member methods. That way, with a wrapper w of a structure s we can directly write `w.get_length<'d'>()` instead of `s | get_length<'d'>()`.

A `bag` provides the same interface as a `wrapper` but also contains a pointer to the underlying memory. To work with the data, it implements a member method `at<Dims...>(idxs...)` that is used to index the data pointer with respect to the enveloping structure layout. This method is a wrapper for the library function `get_at`. Without using a `bag`, the indexing might look like this:

```
auto s = array<'j', 8, array<'i', 4, scalar<float>>>();
float* ptr = allocate_memory_bytes(s.size());
float x = s | get_at<'i', 'j'>(ptr, 2, 3);
```

The `bag` binds the layout together with data, systematizing the computation on the last line as follows:

```
auto b = bag(s, ptr);
float x = b.at<'i', 'j'>(2, 3);
```

Furthermore, to manage an explicitly bound external pointer, `bag` can also allocate the underlying memory automatically if no pointer is given (i.e., it also carries the semantics of a smart pointer). Technically, `bag` can belong to either one of two semantic groups according to the way it acquires data:

- *Owning semantics.* The bag is constructed only with a structure to envelop. The data pointer of exact length is automatically allocated using standard memory management (e.g., by `unique_ptr`), and the length is determined by calling `size()` on the wrapped structure.
- *Borrowing semantics.* The bag is constructed with both structure and data pointer. In this case, the deallocation, as well as ensuring the proper data-block length, has to be enforced by the caller.

5   Related Work

A significant group of works that touch the problem of memory layouts are parallel programming languages such as X10 [5], Chapel [4] or Legion [2]. Apart from providing syntax for simple parallel code expression, these languages allow for data decomposition into regions that can be mapped within the same memory space or more complex non-uniform memory spaces. Hence, the memory layout expression addressed by these works is only researched to the point of high-level data distribution among processing elements.

Application-specific library generators, or *active libraries*, also utilize memory layouts. The most known representatives are ATLAS [19], SPIRAL [15] and FFTW [9] specializing in linear algebra, signal processing, and Fast Fourier Transform, respectively. They are trying to mitigate portability issues of manually optimized programs by selecting the best interprocedural optimizations for the hosting system using autotuning. Usually, these optimization strategies include some form of memory layout selection. It is important to note that active libraries target different stages in programming than Noarr; rather than performing the layout selection from the hardcoded set of layouts, Noarr provides means to *implement* such layout selections in a more extensible and object-oriented way.

The most related works we found are Kokkos [16], and GridTools [1]. These libraries allow the coupling of arbitrary data structures with memory layouts which can be either selected from a set of predefined layouts or programmatically customized.

GridTools specialize in block-structured grid applications such as combustion, seismic, and weather simulations, working with generalized stencil-like patterns. The library defines a storage infrastructure component that controls the layout, alignment, and padding of stored data fields. A layout is specified in code at compile time by selecting one of the predefined target backends, each well suited for a specific use case, such as vector instructions or GPU kernels. The library can be extended with new programmer-specified backends, but the layout can be altered only by permuting dimension order in a regular n-dimensional array.

An interesting approach is taken in the Kokkos library, which specifies the `View` class that couples the definition of data memory space, allocation, and layout altogether using C++ policy classes, yielding an object of similar functionality as our `bag`. The memory resource and allocation mechanism are abstracted and defined by the template argument. Kokkos provides multiple memory spaces such as `HostSpace`, `CudaSpace`, `CudaHostPinnedSpace`, thus representing CPU and GPU physical memory and their combinations.

In Kokkos, the memory layout is either implicitly deduced from the memory space or explicitly specified as another template parameter. The library implements row and column-major layouts together with the layout with strides with custom sizes. Kokkos allows user-defined memory layouts by defining a new layout policy and implementing a function that defines a bijective mapping between index space and memory addresses. However, this mapping must be defined on a regular n-dimensional array, using a minimal API that fits the `View` class.

Language-wise, our approach is similar to (and inspired by) known concepts from functional programming. Materialized, first-class composable references to sub-structures uncoupled from data have been extensively studied as optics [8]. In particular, the internal structures that implement the selection of array slices at certain indexes are similar to the concept of indexed lenses—kind of references that transparently provide information about the current index in a complicated structure, as summarized by Clarke et al. [6] In the future, it might be interesting to examine whether more advanced optics may be modeled in C++ for array accesses, e.g., expressing repeated data accesses similarly to lens-based traversals or reconstructing the user-facing indexes from known offsets using isomorphisms.

6 Conclusion

We have presented a new high-performance approach for managing the complexity of offset computation in array-like data structures in modern C++. We introduced first-class layout structures that can be used to describe complex array layouts and run the required offset computations. The implementation is based on C++ template metaprogramming, exposing a rich interface for manipulating the structures with index mnemonics while enabling many compiler optimizations by properly separating static compile-time parameters and known constants from dynamic data.

The technique promotes complete decoupling of array indexing from memory allocation, which makes it applicable for many scenarios, including direct processing of memory-mapped files or re-using the same data structure layout in various memory spaces (e.g., offloading computations to GPUs). We showed that the layout structures, combined with the C++ templating system, make it easier to create layout-agnostic algorithms and functions, leading to a simpler selection of optimal layouts for a given hardware platform and problem configuration. Additionally, the utilization of layout structures makes it easier to create semi-automated layout transform routines, which can improve the performance of many algorithms.

We have implemented the proposed ideas in Noarr, a prototype library demonstrating the viability of the approach. We demonstrated the benefits in several examples and experiments; most importantly, we showcased the ability to write shorter program source code that promotes easier experimentation and compilation into faster solutions. The library is publicly available as an open-source portable to all mainstream compilers, including CUDA `nvcc`, and may be readily used in designing new libraries that consider performance a priority. We expect that the approach will simplify the research focusing on optimizations and automatic tuning of the performance of complex parallel algorithms.

Acknowledgements. This work was supported by Charles University institutional funding SVV 260451.

A Experimental Methodology

The main objective of the benchmarking was to measure the speedups achieved by different layout combinations to support the claims mentioned in the work[6]. A more complex performance evaluation is beyond the scope of this paper and is planned in future work.

---

[6] More details and the data are in the replication package https://github.com/asmelko/ica3pp22-artifact.

A.1   GPU Benchmarking Setup

In the results, we present mainly the kernel execution times measured by the high-precision system clock, which is available on all platforms. The relative standard deviations in 20 collected measurements of each result were less than 5% of the mean value in all cases, so we report only the mean values.

Due to the page limit, the presented results were limited to matrices of sizes (1008×1008) and $(10,080 \times 10,080)$. However, more extensive testing on other problem instances, including a broader range of matrix sizes and non-square matrices, exhibited similar results.

The results were collected on the following platforms:

- NVIDIA Tesla V100 SXM2 (Volta, CC 7.0, 1.3 GHz), Rocky Linux 8
- NVIDIA GeForce RTX 2060 (Turing, CC 7.6, 1.7 GHz), Windows 10
- NVIDIA GeForce RTX 3070 laptop (Ampere, CC 8.6, 1.6 GHz), Windows 11

All platforms used CUDA toolkit 11.6 with an up-to-date driver. These devices represent three of the most recent Nvidia architectures and three typical hardware platforms (server, desktop PC, and laptop). Hence, we claim that the measurements sufficiently represent contemporary CUDA-enabled GPUs.

A.2   CPU Benchmarking Setup

We ran the kernel in 100 iterations for the stencil benchmark, plotted the local regression outlining the mean value, and distinguished the outliers. The measurements were conducted using the following CPUs:

- AMD Ryzen 5 5600X (hi-end desktop CPU, 3.70 GHz), Windows 10
- Intel Core i7-10870H (laptop CPU, 2.20 GHz), Windows 11
- Intel Xeon Gold 5218 (server CPU, 2.3 GHz), Rocky Linux 8.

Due to the fact that some compilers may optimize `constexpr` expressions better than others, we compiled the benchmark using `clang++` v12 and `g++` v11 compilers with `-O3` flag. We also compiled the stencil benchmark using the MSVC C++ compiler, but the results showed that it could not sufficiently optimize Noarr code in the current version; hence, MSVC results are not included.

All benchmarking datasets were synthetic, with data sampled randomly from the same uniform distribution. We consider synthetic validation sufficient since the performance of the benchmarked algorithms is not data-dependent.

References

1. Afanasyev, A., et al.: GridTools: a framework for portable weather and climate applications. SoftwareX **15**, 100707 (2021). https://doi.org/10.1016/j.softx.2021. 100707. https://www.sciencedirect.com/science/article/pii/S2352711021000522
2. Bauer, M., Treichler, S., Slaughter, E., Aiken, A.: Legion: expressing locality and independence with logical regions. In: Proceedings of the International Conference on High Performance Computing, Networking, Storage and Analysis, SC 2012, pp. 1–11. IEEE (2012)

3. Bethel, E.W., Camp, D., Donofrio, D., Howison, M.: Improving performance of structured-memory, data-intensive applications on multi-core platforms via a space-filling curve memory layout. In: 2015 IEEE International Parallel and Distributed Processing Symposium Workshop, pp. 565–574. IEEE (2015)
4. Chamberlain, B.L., Callahan, D., Zima, H.P.: Parallel programmability and the chapel language. Int. J. High Perform. Comput. Appl. **21**(3), 291–312 (2007)
5. Charles, P., et al.: X10: an object-oriented approach to non-uniform cluster computing. ACM SIGPLAN Not. **40**(10), 519–538 (2005)
6. Clarke, B., et al.: Profunctor optics, a categorical update. arXiv preprint arXiv:2001.07488 (2020)
7. Clauss, P., Meister, B.: Automatic memory layout transformations to optimize spatial locality in parameterized loop nests. ACM SIGARCH Comput. Archit. News **28**(1), 11–19 (2000)
8. Foster, J.N., Greenwald, M.B., Moore, J.T., Pierce, B.C., Schmitt, A.: Combinators for bidirectional tree transformations: a linguistic approach to the view-update problem. ACM Trans. Program. Lang. Syst. (TOPLAS) **29**(3), 17-es (2007)
9. Frigo, M., Johnson, S.G.: FFTW: an adaptive software architecture for the FFT. In: Proceedings of the 1998 IEEE International Conference on Acoustics, Speech and Signal Processing, ICASSP 1998 (Cat. No. 98CH36181), vol. 3, pp. 1381–1384. IEEE (1998)
10. Hawick, K.A., Playne, D.P.: Hypercubic storage layout and transforms in arbitrary dimensions using GPUs and CUDA. Concurr. Comput. Practice Exp. **23**(10), 1027–1050 (2011)
11. Heinecke, A., Bader, M.: Parallel matrix multiplication based on space-filling curves on shared memory multicore platforms. In: Proceedings of the 2008 Workshop on Memory Access on Future Processors: A Solved Problem, pp. 385–392 (2008)
12. Kruliš, M., Kratochvíl, M.: Detailed analysis and optimization of CUDA k-means algorithm. In: 49th International Conference on Parallel Processing-ICPP, pp. 1–11 (2020)
13. NVIDIA: CUDA C best practices guide (2013)
14. Panda, P.R., Semeria, L., De Micheli, G.: Cache-efficient memory layout of aggregate data structures. In: Proceedings of the 14th International Symposium on Systems Synthesis, pp. 101–106 (2001)
15. Püschel, M., et al.: Spiral: a generator for platform-adapted libraries of signal processing algorithms. Int. J. High Perform. Comput. Appl. **18**(1), 21–45 (2004)
16. Trott, C.R., et al.: Kokkos 3: programming model extensions for the exascale era. IEEE Trans. Parallel Distrib. Syst. **33**(4), 805–817 (2022). https://doi.org/10.1109/TPDS.2021.3097283
17. Weber, N., Goesele, M.: MATOG: array layout auto-tuning for CUDA. ACM Trans. Archit. Code Optim. (TACO) **14**(3), 1–26 (2017)
18. Weidendorfer, J., Ott, M., Klug, T., Trinitis, C.: Latencies of conflicting writes on contemporary multicore architectures. In: Malyshkin, V. (ed.) PaCT 2007. LNCS, vol. 4671, pp. 318–327. Springer, Heidelberg (2007). https://doi.org/10.1007/978-3-540-73940-1_33
19. Whaley, R.C., Dongarra, J.J.: Automatically tuned linear algebra software. In: Proceedings of the 1998 ACM/IEEE Conference on Supercomputing, SC 1998, p. 38. IEEE (1998)

SparG: A Sparse GEMM Accelerator for Deep Learning Applications

Bo Wang[✉], Sheng Ma[✉], Yuan Yuan, Yi Dai, Wei Jiang, Xiang Hou, Xiao Yi, and Rui Xu

National University of Defense Technology, Changsha, China
{bowang,masheng,Yuanyuan,daiyi,jiangwei,houxiang,yixiao,
xurui16a}@nudt.edu.cn

Abstract. Deep learning has become a hot field of research. Previously, the deep learning algorithms were mainly run by the CPU and GPU. With the rapid development of deep learning, it has been found that the previous processors can no longer carry the specific large-scale calculations of deep learning, and customized accelerators of deep learning have become popular. The main workload of most deep learning is the General Matrix-matrix Multiplication (GEMM), and emerging GEMM are highly sparse and irregular. The TPU and SIGMA are state-of-the-art GEMM accelerators in recent years, but the TPU does not support sparsity, and the SIGMA has insufficient utilization in some Processing Elements (PEs). In this paper, we design and implement the SparG, a flexible sparse GEMM accelerator. The SparG has a specific PE structure, a flexible distribution network, and an efficient reduction network. For sparse and irregular GEMMs, the SparG can maintain high utilization of PEs while taking advantage of sparsity. We run sparse and irregular GEMMs in the TPU, SIGMA, and SparG. The experimental results show that the performance of the SparG is the highest (30x better than the TPU, and 3.6x better than the SIGMA), and the SparG brings only a small amount of additional hardware overhead (~20% more than the TPU, and ~10% more than the SIGMA).

Keywords: Deep learning · GEMM · Accelerators

1 Introduction

In recent years, deep learning has become very popular. Different deep learning models are widely used in several important fields, including data mining [1], machine translation [2], recommendation [3], natural language processing [4], and search technology. Before the appearance of dedicated neural network processors, the running of deep learning algorithms mainly used the CPU and GPU. The explosion of big data applications have propelled the development of deep learning, but it also poses serious challenges to the data processing speed and scalability of traditional computer systems [5]. Traditional Von Neumann computer architectures are relatively inflexible, with separate processing

---

B. Wang, S. Ma and Y. Yuan—Contributed equally to this research.

© Springer Nature Switzerland AG 2023
W. Meng et al. (Eds.): ICA3PP 2022, LNCS 13777, pp. 529–547, 2023.
https://doi.org/10.1007/978-3-031-22677-9_28

and data storage components. Frequent data movement between traditional architecture processors and off-chip memory limits the system performance and energy efficiency. Hardware accelerators are customized with flexible architectures to run tensor computations efficiently for machine learning models. Deep learning accelerators are usually composed of a large number of highly parallel computing and storage units, which can accelerate the computing tasks in deep learning. Therefore, the design of dedicated chips of deep learning has gradually begun to rise.

The core computational task of most deep learning models in training and inference is the General Matrix-matrix Multiplication (GEMM). Accelerating the GEMM has become a major goal of hardware accelerator design. State-of-the-art GEMM accelerators include Google's TPU and the SIGMA [6, 7]. The TPU uses a systolic array as its hardware structure. A systolic array is a two-dimensional array composed of PEs, and the data flows only between PEs. Systolic array can reduce the exchange of data with the global cache and can reduce the data loading time, so it can reduce energy consumption and speed up the GEMM. Systolic arrays can efficiently compute the dense GEMM, but cannot take advantage of sparsity. Compared to accelerators that support sparsity, the TPU introduces additional computation time and energy consumption when running sparse GEMMs. The SIGMA is the latest sparse GEMM accelerator, which uses the Bitmap format for sparse data encoding and uses the Benes network for data routing. It proposes a FAN tree for accumulating irregular data, which accumulation time can reach $O(\log_2 N)$. The PE array utilization of the stationary matrix of SIGMA is high. However, in the SIGMA, the sparsity of the streaming matrix is not fully exploited, so its PE array utilization of the streaming matrix is insufficient.

We propose the SparG, a novel GEMM accelerator that supports sparsity. The SparG has a simpler and more efficient architecture than the SIGMA. The SparG can fully exploit the sparsity of both the streaming matrix and the stationary matrix. Therefore, both the streaming matrix and the stationary matrix have a high PE utilization. An irregular addition tree, Pipelined Adder Tree (PAT), that supports pipelined accumulation is used in the SparG. The accumulation time of irregular data can reach $O(1)$.

In summary, this paper makes the following contributions.

1. We design a novel architecture of the SparG for irregular and sparse GEMM, and the PE utilization of both the streaming matrix and the stationary matrix can achieve close to 100%.
2. We propose a flexible distribution network PE Bus, and a pipelined reduction network PAT. The time of PE Bus for data loading is $O(1)$, and the time of the PAT for accumulating irregular data is $O(1)$.
3. Experimental results show that the performance of SparG is 30x better than TPU and 3.6x better than SIGMA. The hardware overhead of SparG is ~20% more than TPU and ~10% more than SIGMA.

The rest of the paper is organized as follows. Section 2 introduces the background. Section 3 describes the disadvantages of TPU and SIGMA. Section 4 describes the architecture of SparG. Section 5 evaluates the SparG through experiments. Section 6 describes the related work. Section 7 summarizes the conclusion.

2 Background

2.1 Matrix Multiplication in Deep Learning Workloads

The CNN (Convolutional Neural Network) is one of the most successful algorithms of deep learning [8]. The CNN usually includes the convolutional layer, the ReLU layer, the pooling layer, and the fully connected layer. The main workload of CNN is the convolution operation of the convolution layer and the matrix multiplication operation of the fully connected layer. At present, the neural network processor usually converts the convolution operation into the matrix multiplication. Im2col is a traditional method that converts 3D convolution operations into matrix multiplications. Therefore, the GEMM operation is the core computing operation of deep learning training and inference. In particular, the GEMM operation can account for more than 70% of the computing cycle [7]. Thus, accelerating the GEMM is the main goal of hardware acceleration.

2.2 Sparsity in Deep Learning Workloads

Tensors in deep learning are always sparse. Multiple factors induce the sparsity to the tensors in deep learning models.

CNN uses the ReLU activation function to turn negative values to zeros [9]. The sparsity of input activations can reach 40% in CNN [10]. Max pooling also amplifies the sparsity [11]. Neural networks use drop-out layers to avoid overfitting. With drop-out, only partial activations are kept, which leads to the sparsity as well [12].

The weight pruning technique removes unimportant weights. The widely used pruning algorithms introduce significant sparsity. For example, more than 60% weights in the convolutional layer and 90% weights in the fully connected layer can be removed [13].

Pruning of input activations also leads to the sparsity [14]. The MASR reconstructs batch normalization [15], achieving about 60% input activation sparsity of RNN. For attention-based NLP models, SpAtten prunes unimportant tokens and heads [16]. It reports that the computation and DRAM accesses can be reduced by up to 3.8 times and 1.1 times respectively, while maintaining the model accuracy.

GANs use transposed convolutions in degenerate networks, where the input data is first amplified by inserting zeros between values. For the transposed convolution layers in GANs, there is 60% sparsity on average [17].

The design of deep learning accelerators needs to take into account the sparsity of tensors. Accelerators taking advantage of sparsity can eliminate inefficient computations and improve performance. By processing only operations involving non-zero values, the execution time and energy consumption of computations can be reduced. Meanwhile, by storing only non-zero values, the memory requirements can be reduced, reducing both on-chip and off-chip memory access counts [18].

3 Inefficiency of TPU and SIGMA

3.1 TPU

Google's TPU is designed for data center applications [6]. The main computing component of the TPU is the Matrix Multiply Unit, which is a systolic array composed of 256

× 256 computing units. The TPU passes the data between the computing units so that each data is processed multiple times. Thus, the TPU can significantly reduce the I/O operations. The TPU applies the weight stationary dataflow. The weight matrices are fixed in the systolic array, and the input matrices are transmitted and processed between the computing units in a certain order. Not only the input matrix is passed between the systolic array computing units, but also the partial sum is passed between the systolic array computing units. The calculated results are streamed out of the systolic array and stored in the result accumulator.

The systolic array is efficient for dense GEMMs, but not for sparse GEMMs. When computing a sparse matrix, the systolic array sends zeros into the multiplier for multiplication, resulting in additional computing time and energy consumption.

3.2 SIGMA

The SIGMA is a GEMM accelerator that supports sparsity [7]. The basic building block in the SIGMA architecture is a processor called the Flexible Dot Product Engine (Flex-DPE). Several Flex-DPEs are connected via a simple NoC to create the full SIGMA compute fabric. Each GEMM operation uses a contiguous set of Flex-DPEs. SIGMA uses the Benes network to support flexibility in data loading. Benes is an N-input N-output multi-level non-blocking network. Benes has $2\log(N) + 1$ stages, and each stage has N tiny 2*2 switches. Benes allows communication between any source and any destination without any contention [19]. The data communication time of the Benes network is $O(1)$. The SIGMA uses the Bitmap scheme to encode sparse data and supports the calculation of sparse matrices without decompression. For sparse irregular workloads, the performance of the SIGMA is 5.7x higher than the TPU. Although the SIGMA supports sparsity well, it has the problem of insufficient PE utilization for the streaming matrix, which will be discussed in detail later in Sect. 3.3.

3.3 Mapping of Sparse Irregular GEMM

In this section, we map a sparse irregular GEMM to the systolic array, SIGMA, and SparG, respectively. Figure 1a shows a sparse irregular GEMM. The MK matrix is the streaming matrix and the KN matrix is the stationary matrix.

Figure 1b shows the mapping of the sparse and irregular GEMM in the systolic array. The systolic array has 16 PEs. Due to the rigid structure of systolic array, only half of the PEs can be used, and zeros need to be filled into the systolic array as well. Only half of the KN matrix can be calculated each time. Once the calculation of the streaming matrix is complete, the second half of the KN matrix must be loaded and calculated again, which results in poor PE utilization and performance.

Similar to the discussion in the SIGMA paper [7], for the SIGMA and SparG, we focus on two different types of PE utilization. Namely, the StrUtil, which represents the PE array utilization of the streaming matrix, and the StaUtil, which represents the PE array utilization of the stationary matrix.

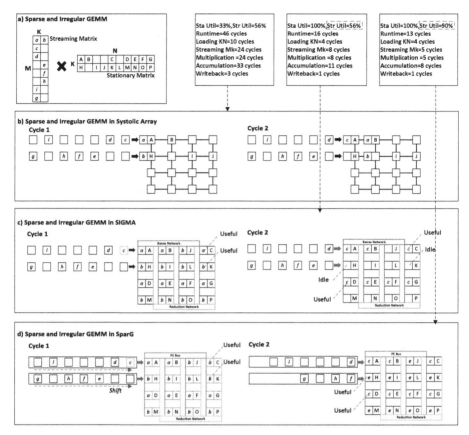

Fig. 1. The mapping of the sparse irregular GEMM in the systolic array, SIGMA, and SparG.

Figure 1c shows the mapping of the sparse irregular GEMM in the SIGMA which includes 16 PEs. Due to the flexible distribution and reduction network, the SIGMA only maps non-zero elements of the stationary matrix. The StaUtil of the SIGMA can reach 100%. However, when the streaming matrix enters the array, insufficient StrUtil occurs. In Fig. 1c, element '*c*' and '0' are in the same column. When '*c*' enters the array, '0' does not enter the array, so element '*c*' enters the array alone. Since '*c*' only uses part of the PEs, other PEs will be idle. In the Fig. 1c (Cycle 2), the PE containing the values (A, B, C, D, E, F, G) are used by '*c*', so they are useful. While the PEs containing the values (H, I, J, K, L, M, N, O, P) are not used by any element, so they are idle. Similarly, when '*d*' enters the array, the PEs containing the values (A, B, C, D, E, F, G) are useful, while the PEs containing the values (H, I, J, K, L, M, N, O, P) are idle. Therefore, the StrUtil of the SIGMA is insufficient (only 56% in this example).

Figure 1d shows the mapping of sparse irregular GEMM in the SparG which includes 16 PEs. Similar to the SIGMA, the SparG only maps non-zero elements of the stationary matrix to the PEs, The StaUtil of the SparG can reach 100%. Unlike the SIGMA, the streaming matrix in the SparG is shifted. When the streaming matrix flows in, the zero elements are skipped, and the nearest non-zero element flows into the PE. In the Fig. 1d, when element 'c' enters the array, element 'e' enters the array simultaneously. Similarly, when element 'd' enters the array, element 'f' enters the array simultaneously. In this way, all PEs are effectively utilized. Therefore, the StrUtil of the SparG is 90% in this example, which is much higher than that of the SIGMA.

4   The SparG Architecture

In this section, we propose the architecture of the SparG. As shown in Fig. 2a, the SparG contains the Global Buffer, PE Array, Accumulator, and Controller. The Global Buffer is used to store the block matrix in a Bitmap format, the PE Array is used to calculate the block GEMM, the Accumulator is used to accumulate the block matrix, and the Controller controls the progress of the SparG.

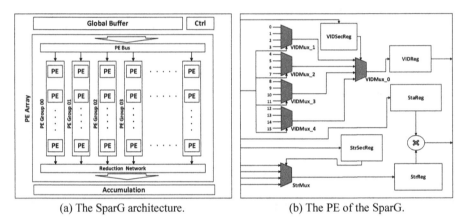

(a) The SparG architecture.   (b) The PE of the SparG.

Fig. 2. The architecture of SparG and the component of PE in the SparG.

4.1   Microarchitecture

PE and PE Groups
As shown in Fig. 2a, the SparG consists of several PE groups. Each PE group consists of several PEs. As shown in Fig. 2b, the PE contains five registers, which are VIDSecReg, VIDReg, StrSecReg, StrReg, and StaReg. The value ID (VID) indicates accumulation group of the multiplication result of streaming data and stationary data. Multiplication results of the same VID need to be added together. The value in the VIDSecReg is used to select the VID to the VIDReg. The VIDReg is used to store the VID. The value in the StrSecReg is used to select data on the PE Bus as the streaming data. StrReg is used to store the streaming data. StaReg is used to store the stationary data. The values in the VIDSecReg, the StrSecReg, and the StaReg are filled when loading the stationary data and do not change when loading the streaming data. The StrReg and the VIDReg

are filled when loading the streaming data. The PE contains several multiplexers. When loading the streaming data, according to the signal on the PE Bus and the value in the VIDSecReg, VIDMux_0 to VIDMux_4 select a VID and send it to the VIDReg (more details are shown in Fig. 5 (Step vi-b)). According to the value in the StrSecReg, the StrMux selects the data of the PE Bus and send it to the StrReg (more details are shown in Fig. 5 (Step vi-a)). There is a multiplier in PE, which is used to calculate the multiplication of stationary data and streaming data. The multiplication result and the VID are output to the reduction network simultaneously.

If a PE group contains K PEs, the large size N × N matrix is divided into small matrices of the size of K × N or N × K to perform block matrix operations. Several PE groups are used to compute a block matrix multiplication. As shown in Fig. 5 (Step iii), the number of PE groups required is determined when loading the stationary data.

Distribution Network

The distribution network is to load the stationary data and stream the other data. In systolic array, the distribution network consists of horizontal and vertical forwarding links between PEs. The data loading time of the systolic array is $O(K)$ for a K × K systolic array. The SIGMA uses the Benes network as the distribution network, and its data loading time can be reduced to $O(1)$. However, the Benes network requires additional logic to generate the routing information.

The SparG uses PE Bus as the distribution network. Each PE group is connected to a single PE bus, and the data loading time can reach $O(1)$. Compared with the Benes network, the bus structure is simpler, the wiring cost is less. In addition, data routing is implemented through multiplexers in the PE, so the SparG do not require additional logic to generate the routing information.

Reduction Networks

The reduction network is used to accumulate the multiplication results from the PE array. The reduction network of the systolic array is rigid, and it can only accumulate the same numbers of elements each time. Unlike the systolic arrays, flexible reduction networks usually require to accumulate different numbers of elements. As shown in Fig. 3b,c, the VID of 'a' has three elements that need to be added together. While the VID of 'b' has four elements to be added together.

The ART is a reduction network used in the MAERI [20]. The ART is an adder tree augmented with additional links. These additional links are used to forward the adder output to other nodes of the same level, instead of the parent node. The ART is built with three input adders, and two inputs are from the child nodes and one input is from the sibling node. This induces a high hardware overhead.

The FAN is a reduction network used in the SIGMA [7]. The FAN is based on a traditional binary adder tree. It places forwarding links between adders at different levels. The average accumulation time of the ART or the FAN is $O(\log_2 N)$. However, neither the ART nor the FAN can support pipelined accumulation, which significantly limits the performance.

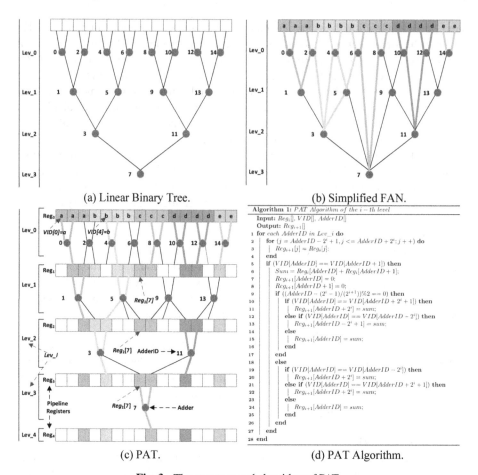

(a) Linear Binary Tree.

(b) Simplified FAN.

(c) PAT.

(d) PAT Algorithm.

Fig. 3. The structure and algorithm of PAT.

In this section, we proposed the Pipelined Adder Tree (PAT) as the reduction network, which is a linear addition tree with pipeline registers. Similar to the FAN, the PAT is based on the linear binary tree in Fig. 3a. By adding forwarding links on the linear binary tree, the simplified FAN can be obtained in Fig. 3b. Then adding pipeline registers between the stages of the simplified FAN can get the PAT in Fig. 3c. The value on the original forwarding link is temporarily stored in the pipeline register and passed backward by the pipeline register. For example, in Fig. 3b, 'adder 6' and 'adder 7' have a forwarding link. In Fig. 3c, after adding the pipeline register, 'adder 6' is connected to the 'Reg_1 [7]' of the next stage and is passed down stage by stage, and finally reaches the 'adder 7'.

The PAT runs in a pipelined manner, in which the input of each stage is the output of the previous stage. Figure 3d presents the algorithm for the i-th level of PAT. The input to the algorithm is the value of the pipeline register of this stage, the VID and AdderID. And the output is the value of the pipeline register of the next stage. Line 1 of the algorithm traverses the *AdderID* in *Lev_i*. The *Lev_i* in line 1 of the algorithm corresponds to the number of pipeline stages in Fig. 3c. For example, if i is '2', the *AdderID* in *Lev_i* contains '3' and '11'. Lines 2–4 of the algorithm assign initial values to the output registers. Line 5 judges whether an add operation needs to be performed according to the VID value. If an add operation is performed, lines 7–8 clear the two registers to remove the two added elements. Then lines 9–26 determine which register to put the sum into. The condition of line 9 to hold is that if the adder with this *AddID* is on the left side of the parent node in the linear binary. If all *AdderID* in *Lev_i* are traversed, the algorithm ends.

To show the advantage of PAT, we implement the linear binary tree, ART, FAN, and PAT with the RTL Verilog. We use the Xilinx Vivado Design Suite to evaluate their performance and hardware overhead. Each of these adder trees contains 31 adders. The values of different batches are used for accumulation. As shown in Fig. 4, the PAT has the highest performance due to pipelined accumulation. The PAT is about 3x faster than the FAN or the ART. The hardware overhead of PAT is the largest due to the additional pipeline registers. It is 2x more than the FAN or ART.

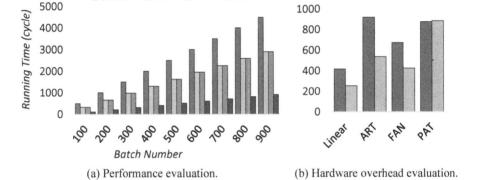

(a) Performance evaluation.   (b) Hardware overhead evaluation.

Fig. 4. The performance and hardware overhead of Linear, ART, FAN, and PAT.

4.2 Example

The following steps (corresponding to Fig. 5) describe a walk-through example of the SparG. In this example, each PE group contains four PEs (N_{PE} is 4).

Step i) Read two block matrices encoded in the Bitmap format. In this example, the MK matrix is stationary and the KN matrix is streaming.

Step ii) Row-wise OR operation on the streaming bitmap, and take the output as the valid bits of the column of the stationary bitmap. Then, the invalid elements are removed from the stationary bitmap.

Step iii) The number of ones in the stationary bitmap corresponds to the number of useful stationary values (N_{sta}). Since N_{sta} is 8 and N_{PE} is 4, two PE groups are required in this example.

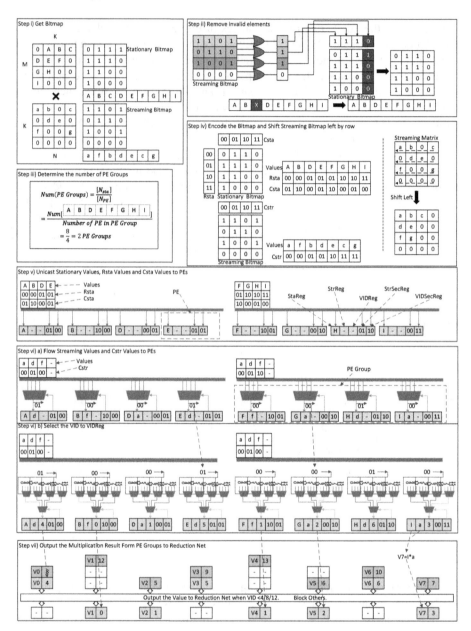

Fig. 5. An example of running the GEMM in the SparG.

Step iv) Encode the stationary bitmap and the streaming bitmap. For the stationary bitmap, get the column number and row number of the value from the bitmap and put them into the C_{sta} and R_{sta} arrays. For the streaming bitmap, the column number is put into the C_{str} array. The values of the streaming matrix need to be shifted left by row as

Fig. 5 (Step iv) shows. The column number and row number in the example only cost 2 bits.

Step v) Unicast the stationary value to each PE in the PE group. The stationary data is put into the StaReg. The corresponding values in the R_{sta} and C_{sta} arrays are also allocated to the PE. The data in the R_{sta} array is put into the VIDSecReg. The data in the C_{sta} array is put into the StrSecReg.

Step vi) Broadcast the streaming value to each PE group by column. PEs need to select a correct streaming value, and routing is required at this step. In the previous step, there is already a value in the StrSecReg. This value is used as the control signal for the multiplexer in Fig. 5 (Step vi-a). The multiplexer selects the value on the PE Bus and stores it in the StrReg. When the streaming data enters the StrReg, the corresponding C_{str} value is also put into the PE. The C_{str} value and the VIDSecReg value are taken as the control signal of the multiplexer in the Fig. 5 (Step vi-b). The multiplexer selects the corresponding VID and sent to the VIDReg.

The StaReg and the StrReg in the PE are connected to a multiplier. The multiplication result is generated after the stationary data and the streaming data are multiplied. The multiplication result and the value in the VIDReg are sent to the reduction network simultaneously.

Step vii) Since the streaming matrix is out of order (after shifted), the multiplication results with the same VID may be generated in different cycles. It is necessary to add a block FIFO before the reduction network. The value of the VID greater than or equal to 4 is blocked first, and the value of the addition ID greater than or equal to 8 is blocked in the next cycle. Then the unblocked VID and multiplication result are send into the PAT.

The above unicast, broadcast, multiply and add operations are all performed in a pipelined manner. A GEMM operation is complete once all non-zero values of the streaming matrix have flowed in and the output has been generated.

5 Evaluation

5.1 Experimental Methodology

We have compared the SparG with state-of-the-art GEMM accelerators, the TPU and SIGMA. To ensure evaluating the performance and hardware overhead with the same experimental platform, we use RTL Verilog HDL to implement the TPU, SIGMA, and SparG of the same scale. In our experiments, the systolic array of the TPU contains 8 × 8 PEs; the SIGMA contains 8 Flex-DPEs, and each Flex-DPE contains 8 PEs; the SparG contains 8 PE groups, and each PE group contains 8 PEs. The data width is 8 bits. We use the Xilinx Vivado Design Suite for logic simulation and synthesis. The clock cycle during simulation is set to 8ns, and the main frequency during synthesis is set to 125MHz. Additionally, we implement the TPU, SIGMA and SparG with 16 × 16 PEs for scalability analysis.

We have evaluated the GEMM with different sizes and different sparsities on the TPU, SIGMA, and SparG. In our experiments, the sparsity of MK and NK matrices are set to be the same. The TPU, SIGMA, and SparG all use the weight stationary dataflow. That is, when calculating the GEMM of dimension M-K-N, the KN matrix is stationary, and the MK matrix is streaming. Other dataflows have similar performance trends to the weight stationary dataflow, and we omit them for brevity.

5.2 Dense Regular and Dense Irregular GEMM

Figure 6 shows the performance and array utilization of the TPU, SIGMA, and SparG of the 8 × 8 scale when running dense regular GEMMs. The performance is measured as the count of cycles. The utilization is measured as the average of the StaUtil and StrUtil. Since there is no sparsity and the matrix is regular, every matrix element in the GEMM must be mapped. The array utilization of TPU, SIGMA and SparG are all 100%. The TPU has O(SqrtN) distribution and reduction. The SIGMA has O(1) distribution and O(Log$_2$N) reduction. The SIGMA is ~10% faster than the TPU. The SparG uses the PAT which has O(1) reduction. So the SparG is ~20% faster than the TPU and ~10% faster than the SIGMA.

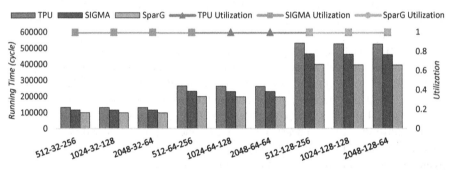

Fig. 6. The performance and array utilization of the TPU, SIGMA, and SparG when running dense regular GEMMs. The three numbers in the horizontal axis represent the size of GEMMs (M-K-N).

Figure 7 shows the performance and array utilization of the TPU, SIGMA, and SparG of the 8 × 8 scale when running dense irregular GEMMs. Since the array size of TPU, SIGMA and SparG in our experiments is 8 × 8, the GEMM is irregular when the size of K dimension is less than 8. For dense and irregular GEMMs, the PEs in the TPU systolic array cannot be fully filled, so the array utilization of the TPU cannot reach 100%. The Underutilization of TPU array results in additional time cost. The SIGMA and SparG use flexible distribution networks. All elements can be filled into PE, so the array utilization of both can reach 100%. The high utilization brings high performance to the SIGMA and SparG. In this experiment, the SIGMA and SparG are up to 10x faster than the TPU. The SparG is ~10% faster than the SIGMA due to the more efficient pipelined reduction network.

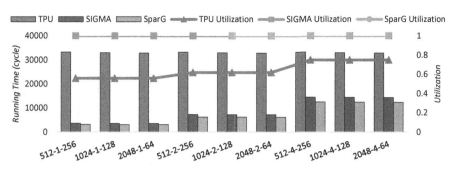

Fig. 7. The performance and array utilization of the TPU, SIGMA, and SparG when running dense irregular GEMMs.

5.3 Sparse Regular GEMM

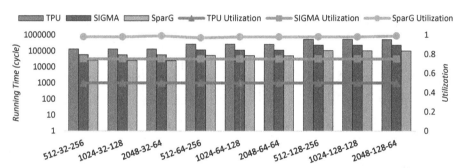

Fig. 8. The performance and array utilization of the TPU, SIGMA, and SparG when running 50%-sparse regular GEMMs.

Figures 8, 9 and 10 show the performance and array utilization of the TPU, SIGMA, and SparG of the 8 × 8 scale when running regular GEMMs with different sparsities. The vertical axis is on a logarithmic scale. Due to the introduction of sparsity, the TPU must map zeros to the systolic array, resulting in an insufficient array utilization. As shown in Fig. 1c, in the SIGMA, the StaUtil can be close to 100, but the StrUtil is low. So the average utilization of the SIGMA is low as well. In the SparG, both the StaUtil and the StrUtil are close to 100%, so the utilization of the SparG is the highest. Due to insufficient utilization, the performance of the TPU is the worst. Due to the highest utilization, the performance of the SparG is the best. In our experiments, for the sparse regular GEMMs, the performance of the SparG is 10x better than the TPU and 3.6x better than the SIGMA. With the sparsity increases, the performance difference between the SparG, SIGMA and TPU becomes larger.

5.4 Sparse Irregular GEMM

Figure 11, 12 and Fig. 13 show the performance and array utilization of the TPU, SIGMA, and SparG of the 8 × 8 scale when running irregular GEMMs with different sparsity.

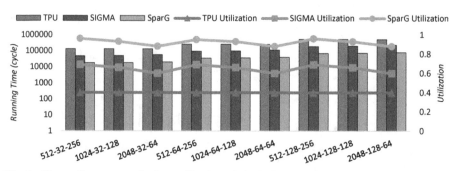

Fig. 9. The performance and array utilization of the TPU, SIGMA, and SparG when running 60%-sparse regular GEMMs.

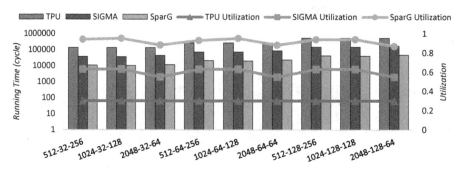

Fig. 10. The performance and array utilization of the TPU, SIGMA, and SparG when running 70%-sparse regular GEMMs.

The ordinate is on a logarithmic scale. The sparsity and irregularity lead to worse array utilization of the TPU, while that of the SparG is always the highest, and that of the SIGMA is modest. The TPU performs the worst when dealing with sparse and irregular GEMMs. Due to its low StrUtil, the performance of the SIGMA is worse than the SparG. In our experiments, the performance of SparG is 30x better than TPU and 3.6x better than SIGMA. As the increase of sparsity, the performance difference between the SparG, SIGMA, and TPU becomes larger. On sparse and irregular GEMMs, the advantage of SparG is very obvious.

5.5 Scalability Analysis

We implement the SparG with 256 PEs for scalability analysis. The design of PEs and PE groups is fixed. If a larger-scale SparG needs to be implemented, it is only necessary to add additional PE bus and PE groups. And there is no need to change the original PE and PE group. Figure 14 shows the performance and array utilization of the TPU, SIGMA, and SparG with 256 PEs when running sparse and irregular GEMMs. Experimental results show that the array utilization of SparG is the highest. And the performance of the SparG is >30x better than TPU and 3.6x better than the SIGMA. Compare to the 8

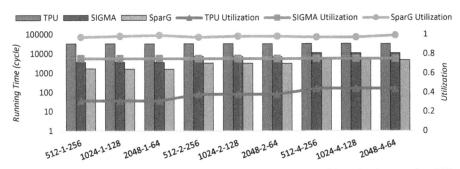

Fig. 11. The performance and array utilization of TPU, SIGMA, and SparG when running 50%-sparse irregular GEMMs.

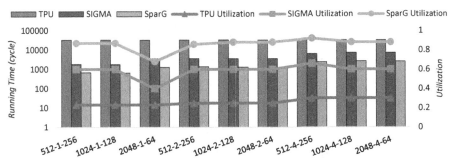

Fig. 12. The performance and array utilization of TPU, SIGMA, and SparG when running 60%-sparse irregular GEMMs.

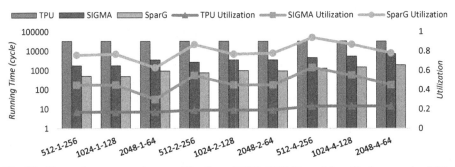

Fig. 13. The performance and array utilization of TPU, SIGMA, and SparG when running 70%-sparse irregular GEMMs.

× 8 scale SparG, the larger-scale SparG has high performance and utilization similarly. Therefore, SparG has better scalability.

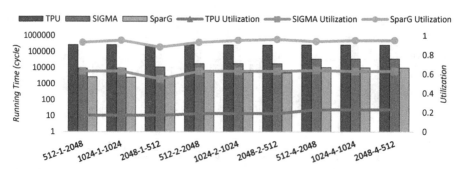

Fig. 14. The performance and array utilization of the TPU, SIGMA, and SparG with 256 PEs when running 70%-sparse irregular GEMMs.

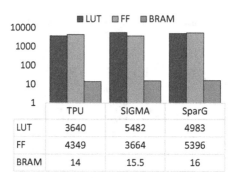

Fig. 15. The hardware overhead of the TPU, SIGMA, and SparG.

5.6 Hardware Cost Analysis

We evaluate the TPU, SIGMA, and SparG with 64 PEs. Figure 15 shows the hardware overhead of the TPU, SIGMA, and SparG. The TPU requires fewer hardware resources than the SparG due to its regular systolic array and simple distribution and reduction network. Compared with the SIGMA, the distribution network of the SparG is simpler, so the SparG requires less LUT (Look-up Tables) resources. Since the PE array and reduction network require more register resources, the demand for FF (Flip-Flops) resources of the SparG is larger. The external BRAM (Block Random Access Memory) resources of the three arrays are similar. On average, the hardware overhead of the SparG is ~20% more than the TPU and ~10% more than the SIGMA. Due to the large performance improvement, we consider that the additional hardware overhead of the SparG is acceptable.

6 Related Work

6.1 Sparsity

Single-Sided Sparsity
The Eyeriss gates the multiplier when it sees an input activation of zero, but it does not gate the multiplier on zero weights [21]. This gating approach can save energy, but not save execution time. The Cnvlutin is a value-based approach to hardware acceleration that eliminates most of the ineffectual operations about zero, improving performance and energy with no accuracy loss [14]. The Cnvlutin compresses activation values based on the ReLU operator, but it does not employ pruning to exploit weight sparsity. The Cambricon-X exploits weight sparsity, keeping only non-zero weights in its buffer [22]. The Cambricon-X exploits the sparsity and irregularity of NN models for increased efficiency, but it does not exploit activation sparsity. Unlike the Eyeriss, Cnvlutin, and Cambricon-X, the SparG exploits both activation and weight sparsity.

Double-Sided Sparsity
The SCNN and SparTen are recent sparse CNN accelerators that utilize both activation and weight sparsity [23, 24]. Specifically, SCNN employs a novel dataflow that enables maintaining the sparse weights and activations in a compressed encoding, which eliminates unnecessary data transfers and reduces storage requirements. The SparTen achieves efficient inner join operations by providing supporting for native two-sided sparse execution and memory storage. The EIE performs inference on compressed network model and accelerates the resulting sparse matrix-vector multiplication with weight sharing [25]. The EIE uses the packed representation of weights and activations, passing only non-zero operands to multipliers. The Extensor finds the intersection of weights and activations in compressed data, operating only on useful computations [26]. Our work also exploits double-sided sparsity, but the SparG mainly targets sparse and irregular GEMMs.

6.2 Flexible Interconnect

Eyeriss v2 is a DNN accelerator architecture designed for running compact and sparse DNNs [27]. To deal with the widely varying layer shapes and sizes, it introduces a highly flexible on-chip network, called hierarchical mesh, that can adapt to the different amounts of data reuse and bandwidth requirements of different data types, which improves the utilization of the computation resources. Furthermore, Eyeriss v2 can process sparse data directly in the compressed domain for both weights and activations and therefore is able to improve both processing speed and energy efficiency with sparse models. Eyeriss v2 uses a flexible NoC to support sparsity but targets small mobile CNNs instead of large GEMMs. MAERI is a DNN accelerator built with a set of modular and configurable building blocks that can easily support myriad DNN partitions and mappings by appropriately configuring tiny switches [20]. MAERI uses a tree-based interconnection network to achieve flexible mapping, but it cannot support the sparsity of input features. FlexFlow can leverage the complementary effects among feature map, neuron, and synapse parallelism to mitigate the mismatch [28]. FlexFlow develops a flexible dataflow architecture for different types of parallelism, but it is not for GEMMs. SIGMA proposes a flexible non-blocking interconnect [7], SIGMA can support double-sided sparsity in the GEMM but with the problem of insufficient utilization. The SparG proposed in this paper adopts efficient and flexible distribution network PE Bus and reduction network PAT.

7 Conclusion

In this paper, we design, implement and evaluate the SparG, a state-of-the-art GEMM accelerator for sparse deep learning applications. The SparG has a specific PE structure, a flexible distribution network, and a pipelined reduction network. And the SparG achieves high array utilization to support high performance. For sparse and irregular GEMMs, our experiments show that the performance of the SparG is 30x better than the TPU and 3.6x better than the SIGMA. In addition, the SparG brings only a small amount of additional hardware overhead.

Acknowledgments. This work is supported in part by the National Key R&D Project No.2021YFB0300300, the NSFC (62172430, 61872374, 62272476), the NSF of Hunan Province (2021JJ10052, 2022JJ10064).

References

1. Nguyen, G., et al.: Machine Learning and Deep Learning frameworks and libraries for large-scale data mining: a survey. Artif. Intell. Rev. **52**(1), 77–124 (2019). https://doi.org/10.1007/s10462-018-09679-z
2. Yang, S., Wang, Y., Chu, X.: A survey of deep learning techniques for neural machine translation. arXiv preprint arXiv:2002.07526 (2020)
3. Acun, B., Murphy, M., Wang, X., et al.: Understanding training efficiency of deep learning recommendation models at scale. In: HPCA2021, pp. 802–814. IEEE (2021)
4. Otter, D.W., Medina, J.R., Kalita, J.K.: A survey of the usages of deep learning for natural language processing. IEEE Trans. Neural Netw. Learn. Syst. **32**(2), 604–624 (2020)
5. AI and Compute, https://openai.com/blog/ai-and-compute/, last accessed 2022/04/01
6. Jouppi, N.P., et al.: In-datacenter performance analysis of a tensor processing unit. In: Proceedings of the 44th Annual International Symposium on Computer Architecture, pp 1–12. (2017)
7. Qin, E., Samajdar, A., Kwon, H., et al.: Sigma: a sparse and irregular gemm accelerator with flexible interconnects for dnn training. In: HPCA2020, pp. 28–70. IEEE (2020)
8. Gu, J., Wang, Z., Kuen, J., et al.: Recent advances in convolutional neural networks. Pattern Recogn. **77**, 354–377 (2018)
9. Krizhevsky, A., Sutskever, I., et al.: Imagenet classification with deep convolutional neural networks. Adv. Neural. Inf. Process. Syst. **25**, 1097–1105 (2012)
10. Li, J., Jiang, S., Gong, S., Wu, J., et al.: Squeezeflow: a sparse CNN accelerator exploiting concise convolution rules. IEEE Trans. Comput. **68**(11), 1663–1677 (2019)
11. Cao, S., Ma, L., Xiao, W., Zhang, C., et al.: Seernet: predicting convolutional neural network feature-map sparsity through low-bit quantization. In: Proceedings of the IEEE Conference on Computer Vision and Pattern Recognition, pp. 11216–11225 (2019)

12. Srivastava, N., Hinton, G., et al.: Dropout: a simple way to prevent neural networks from overfitting. J. Mach. Learn. Res. **15**(1), 1929–1958 (2014)
13. Han, S., Pool, J., Tran, J., et al.: Learning both weights and connections for efficient neural network. Adv. Neural. Inf. Process. Syst. **28**, 1135–1143 (2015)
14. Albericio, J., Judd, P., Hetherington, T., et al.: Cnvlutin: Ineffectual-neuron-free deep neural network computing. ACM SIGARCH Comput. Arch. News **44**(3), 1–13 (2016)
15. Gupta, U., Reagen, B., Pentecost, L., Donato, M., et al.: Masr: a modular accelerator for sparse rnns. In: 2019 28th International Conference on Parallel Architectures and Compilation Techniques (PACT), pp. 1–14. IEEE (2019)
16. Wang, H., Zhang, Z., Han, S.: Spatten: efficient sparse attention architecture with cascade token and head pruning. In: HPCA2021, pp. 97–110. IEEE (2021)
17. Yazdanbakhsh, A., Samadi, K., Kim, N.S., et al.: Ganax: a unified mimd-simd acceleration for generative adversarial networks. In: ISCA2018, pp. 650–661. IEEE (2018)
18. Horowitz, M.: 1.1 computing's energy problem (and what we can do about it). In: 2014 IEEE International Solid-State Circuits Conference Digest of Technical Papers (ISSCC), pp. 10–14. IEEE (2014)
19. Chakrabarty, A., Collier, M., Mukhopadhyay, S.: Matrix-based nonblocking routing algorithm for Beneš networks. In: 2009 Computation World: Future Computing, Service Computation, Cognitive, Adaptive, Content, Patterns, pp. 551–556. IEEE (2009)
20. Kwon, H., Samajdar, A., et al.: Maeri: enabling flexible dataflow mapping over dnn accelerators via reconfigurable interconnects. ACM SIGPLAN Notices **53**(2), 461–475 (2018)
21. Chen, Y.-H., Krishna, T., Emer, J.S., Sze, V.: Eyeriss: an energy-efficient reconfigurable accelerator for deep convolutional neural networks. IEEE J. Solid-State Circuits **52**(1), 127–138 (2017)
22. Zhang, S., Du, Z., Zhang, L., et al.: Cambricon-X: an accelerator for sparse neural networks. In: MICRO2016, pp. 1–12. IEEE (2016)
23. Parashar, A., Rhu, M., et al.: SCNN: An accelerator for compressed-sparse convolutional neural networks. ACM SIGARCH Comput. Arch. News **45**(2), 27–40 (2017)
24. Gondimalla, A., Chesnut, N., Thottethodi, M., et al.: Sparten: a sparse tensor accelerator for convolutional neural networks. In: MICRO2019, pp. 151–165 (2019)
25. Han, S., Liu, X., Mao, H., et al.: EIE: Efficient inference engine on compressed deep neural network. ACM SIGARCH Comput. Arch. News **44**(3), 243–254 (2016)
26. Hegde, K., Asghari-Moghaddam, H., Pellauer, M., et al.: Extensor: an accelerator for sparse tensor algebra. In: MICRO2019, pp. 319–333 (2019)
27. Chen, Y.H., Yang, T.J., Emer, J., et al.: Eyeriss v2: A flexible accelerator for emerging deep neural networks on mobile devices. IEEE J. Emerg. Sel. Top. Circuits Syst. **9**(2), 292–308 (2019)
28. Lu, W., Yan, G., Li, J., et al.: Flexflow: a flexible dataflow accelerator architecture for convolutional neural network. In: HPCA2017, pp. 553–564. IEEE (2017)

An Efficient Transformer Inference Engine on DSP

Kangkang Chen[1], Huayou Su[1(✉)], Chaorun Liu[1], and Xiaoli Gong[2]

[1] National University of Defense and Technology, Changsha, Hunan, China
chenkangkang20@outlook.com, {shyou,liuchaorun}@nudt.edu.cn
[2] Nankai University, Tianjin, China
gongxiaoli@nankai.edu.cn

Abstract. The transformer is one of the most important algorithms in the Natural Language Processing(NLP) field and widely used in computer vision recently. Due to the huge computation requirements, the current transformer acceleration work is mainly focused on GPUs of the data center, away from signal sources such as voice and video. Digital Signal Processor(DSP) is the traditional signal processing device and is usually deployed on the edge. Therefore, it can effectively reduce the processing time of the entire task by deploying deep learning models on edge devices like DSP. However, there are several challenges to deploying transformer models on DSP efficiently. Firstly, the transformer is too computationally intensive for DSP. Secondly, there is a lack of efficient transformer operator libraries on DSP. In addition, the input sequence's variable length makes it difficult for optimization methods such as batching to work. To solve these challenges, we proposed a DSP accelerated transformer inference engine, which consists of three components, an efficient transformer operator library based on a very long vector and Very Long Instruction Word(VLIW) architecture; an efficient memory optimization strategy to manage large amounts of intermediate results and alleviates data traffic problems due to insufficient on-chip memory; and a sequence warp method that packs varied sequences to a large one based on the sliding window and greedy algorithm. Experimental results show that the proposed DSP transformer engine's performance is comparable with that of the mainstream NVIDIA GPU, while the DSP's bandwidth is only 1/20 of that of the GPU.

Keywords: Transformer · DSP · Acceleration engine · Deep learning optimization

1 Introduction

In the early days of the rise of deep learning technology, researchers mainly used deep models such as Recurrent Neural Network (RNN), LSTM [11], and GRU [4]

K. Chen and H. Su—These authors contributed equally to this work.

© Springer Nature Switzerland AG 2023
W. Meng et al. (Eds.): ICA3PP 2022, LNCS 13777, pp. 548–567, 2023.
https://doi.org/10.1007/978-3-031-22677-9_29

to deal with problems in the NLP field. However, due to the inherent sequential nature, these methods are not friendly to the parallel processing of tasks. In addition, they are not good at dealing with long-term dependencies, which limits the application of deep learning techniques in the NLP field. In recent years, the transformer models represented with BERT [12] have achieved overwhelming results in NLP tasks [13,17] (such as reading comprehension, translation, etc.). In addition, more and more works apply transformers to computer vision [2,6, 9,25,28]. Currently, most transformer models are deployed on the GPU server, which is far from the signal source. The data needs to be transmitted from the signal acquisition terminal. In contrast, the DSP is closer to the signal, and using deep learning methods to process the data on DSP will improve the efficiency of the entire data processing chain. However, there are several challenges to optimize the inference of transformer models on DSP.

First of all, transformer models bring massive challenges to the computing platform in terms of computational requirements and memory traffic. For example, in a BERT(Large) model with seq_length of 384, the inference computation is about 229.5GFlops when considering General Matrix Multiplication (GEMM) component only. While the 24-layer LSTM [11] and GRU [4] network with 1024 units and feature dimension of 384, the computation is about 0.26GFlops and 0.19GFlops respectively. It makes it difficult for general DSPs to meet the requirements.

Secondly, though the multi-head structure of the transformer is suitable for parallel processing, the variable-length sequences make traditional deep neural network optimization methods ineffective, such as batching. When extending short sequences to fixed-length by zero-padding, an amount of extra computation will be introduced. In addition, the uncertainty of the intermediate data results from the variable length of the sequence, which makes memory optimization difficult.

Nowadays, the typical deep learning frameworks such as TVM [3], PyTorch [21], and Tensorflow [1] could perform transformer model inference. However, they focus on training or the traditional Convolutional Neural Network (CNN). There are also some works of optimization of the inference of transformer models, such as NVIDIA's FasterTransformer [20], Tencent's TurboTransformer [7], and ByteDance's Lightseq [24]. These optimization methods are oriented to NVIDIA's GPU and achieve good performance by designing new operators for the transformer and fusing kernels for the inference. However, the architecture of DSP is very different from that of GPU, such as the VILW and long vector feature. The existing deep learning framework and deep learning acceleration library are inefficient or unusable on DSP. A new transformer operator library needs to be built for DSP.

To solve the challenges, we proposed the first transformer inference engine based on DSP. This engine consists of three parts: a high efficient operator library for transformer on long vector architecture, a memory optimization strategy, and a sequence warp scheduler. We optimized all the operators of the transformer encoder with assembly code to fit DSP's long vector architecture. In addition, we fuse operators to reduce memory footprint. The memory optimization strategy manages the expensive on-chip memory at runtime, keeping recently used data and replacing invalid data based on the lifecycle. To overcome the inefficiency of zero-padding when batching varied length sequences, we proposed a sequence warp approach to pack several sequences into a longer one and submit it to the fixed-length issuer. Experimental results show that the performance of the proposed DSP transformer engine is comparable with that of GPU [20], while the bandwidth of DSP is 20 times lower than that of GPU. The innovative contributions of this paper are as follows:

(1) We implement the first transformer inference engine on DSP. Through building a high efficient operator library for transformer on long vector architecture, the proposed acceleration engine can achieve comparable performance to that of FasterTransformer [20] on the GPU of RTX3090.
(2) We propose a memory optimization strategy to efficiently use the limited on-chip memory based on variable lifetime. This method is significant for a bandwidth-constrained processor with DDR.
(3) We propose a sequence warp method, which packs several sequences into a very long and longer sequence based on a sliding window and a greedy algorithm.

The rest of the paper is structured as follows: Sect. 2 and Sect. 3 will introduce the background and related work on transformer; Sect. 4 will explain the proposed DSP-based transformer engine in detail; Sect. 5 will present and analyze our experimental results; Sect. 6 will share some conclusions.

2   Background

2.1   Transformer

The transformer [23] is widely used in the NLP field and has also brought revolutionary progress to the computer vision field. Attention is the key idea of the transformer, which can process different positions of the input sequence to calculate the representation of the sequence. The transformer uses self-attention layers (rather than RNN or CNN to handle inputs). Figure 1(a) shows the transformer architecture with encoder and decoder parts. In this paper, we only discuss the encoder parts. We firstly profile the structure of the typical transformer model and extract functions as fine-grained as possible, as shown in Fig. 1(b) and Fig. 1(c), H in the figure represents *num_heads*, L in the figure represents *num_layer*. We divided the encoder part into four parts, XW, SelfAttention, SelfOutput, and FFN, omitting the residual structure and incorporating layernorm into the previous part. The first one is the calculation of the matrix Q, K, and V from the embedding vector, corresponding to three linear operators with the same input embedding vector, where the matrix Q can be understood as a matrix for querying other words. The matrix K can be understood as a matrix queried by other words. The matrix V can be understood as the matrix of the information of the extracted words. Then matrix Q, K, and V will be split into several small ones by permute operation, and a transpose will be employed on the split K_i, the resulting Q_i, K_i, and V_i are the inputs of the multi-head attention part. The second part is SelfAttention, which focuses on calculating the similarity between tokens by performing matrix multiplication operations on the split Q_i and K_i. Before multiplying with the split V_i, a softmax operation is applied on the intermediate results of $Q_i \times K_i$ to strengthen attention on the related words. It should be emphasized that the memory footprint will increase. The third part is SelfOutput, which concatenates the results of SelfAttention and collects information captured by different heads, and then a linear and a layernorm operator will be applied. The last part is an FFN network, including two linear operators, an activation operator, and a layernorm operator. It will increase the vector space of the sequence, and an activation operator such as Gaussian Error Linear Units(GELU [10]) is usually applied between the two linear operators and apply a layernorm operator at the end.

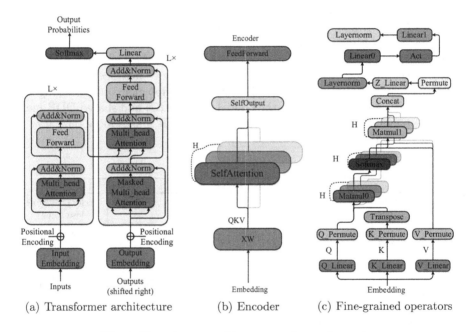

(a) Transformer architecture   (b) Encoder   (c) Fine-grained operators

Fig. 1. Transformer architecture and encoder part.

2.2 Brief Introduction to the Processor

The processor is a high-performance floating-point multicore vector processor for high-density computing, which integrates 22 vector processor cores. The processor's single-core architecture is shown in Fig. 2. The processor core consists of a Scalar Processing Unit (SPU) and a Vector Processing Unit (VPU). The SPU is responsible for the scalar calculation and flow control, and a shared register is designed between the SPU and the VPU to exchange data. The SPU provides broadcast instructions to broadcast the data of scalar registers to the vector registers of the VPU. The vector processor core supports the simultaneous transmission of 11 variable-length VLIW instructions, and the instruction execution packet supports up to 5 scalar instructions and 5 vector instructions. The instruction dispatch unit identifies the instruction execution packet and dispatches it to the corresponding functional unit for execution. The VPU provides the major vector computing capability, integrating 16 Vector Processing Elements (VPE). Each VPE includes a local register file of 64-bit registers, and at the same time, all the local registers of the same number of the VPE logically constitute a 1024-bit vector register. Each VPE includes 3 FMAC operation units, 1 BP unit, and 2 L/S data access units. The vector instructions assigned to each VPE are executed independently simultaneously, and each clock cycle supports concurrent execution of 3 FMAC operations. 2 vector L/S data access units simultaneously support two-way 2048-bit vector data load and store. The scalar memory of the processor includes the L1 Program Cache (L1P) and the L1 Data Cache (L1D), of which L1D can be configured as full cache, full Static Random-Access Memory (SRAM), and a mixture of both. The processor provides 768K large-capacity Array Memory (AM) for vector data access and provides Direct Memory Access (DMA) modes to achieve fast access to all levels of storage space. The 22 cores of the processor implement data sharing and exchange between cores through the Global Cache (GC) and shared DDR memory. The bandwidth difference between GC and DDR makes more data flow on GC while improving computational efficiency.

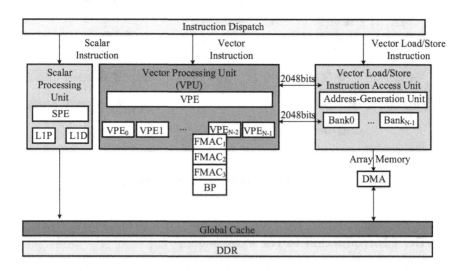

Fig. 2. Single-core architecture of the processor.

3   Related Works

At present, the optimization direction of transformer inference acceleration is mainly on GPU, CPU, and FPGA.

Acceleration on GPU. The acceleration is mainly on the GPU platform. For example, Yuxin Wang [26] discussed the factors affecting transformer inference through energy efficiency and throughput, concluded that similar length sequences should be batched, and finally proposed an alignment scheduling scheme for optimization. However, the work is hardly optimized at the kernel level. NVIDIA's TensorRT [19], which is usually responsible for model inference, improves performance by reconstructing the network structure and integrating some operations and also supports INT8 and FP16 precision computing. The computational graph and operator optimization used by TVM [3] also significantly improve the transformer inference performance. NVIDIA has proposed a library named FasterTransformer [20], which integrates a large number of operators to reduce GPU kernel scheduling and memory access, selects and optimizes matrix multiplication that performs a large number of calculations simultaneously, and also provides the low-precision operators. ByteDance proposes a high-performance training and inference library named Lightseq [24], which improves performance by kernel fusion and dynamic GPU memory reuse. They use hierarchical auto-regressive search instead of beam search for sentence-level and token-level classification applications. Most of the above works are only optimized at inference runtime and cannot handle variable-length sequences. Tencent's Turbo-Transformer [7] proposes an engine that includes an inference runtime and server system, optimizes edge operators such as softmax and layernorm, and adopts an efficient memory management scheme during inference runtime. It also solves the variable-length sequence problem that most libraries and frameworks do not support on server systems. Gongzheng Li et al. [15] proposed EET, which optimizes the sequence input by pre-filling decoding and thread block folding, mainly to solve the long sequence length problem.

Acceleration on CPU. There is also a large number of great work on transformer inference based on CPU platforms. For example, Amir Ganiev et al. [8] proposed a solution to improve the inference speed of offline batch jobs in Apache Spark by using service-based concurrency. Wu et al. [27] optimize the BERT through the MKL library and quantization based on the MXNET framework. Dave Dice and Alex Kogan [5] mainly study matrix multiplication operations in the transformer, perform relevant tests on whether weights are transposed, and improve performance by reducing order overhead and optimizing strategies for matrix multiplication microkernels.

Acceleration on FPGA. There is also a lot of work in hardware acceleration of transformer using FPGA, which is generally optimized through optimization methods such as quantization or clipping, compression, etc. For example, Zejian Liu et al. [18] improved performance-per-watt through quantizing weights, activations, softmax, layer normalization, and all the intermediate results; Bingbing

Li et al. [14] proposed an enhanced BCM-based compression method, optimized the overall transformer computing process, and finally designed an FPGA architecture to support these. Panjie Qi et al. [22] used block-balanced pruning to compress the model and developed the CBR format for block balanced sparse matrices. Li et al. [16] proposed an FPGA-aware automatic ViT acceleration framework, which can automatically find the best combination of quantization based on the proposed mixed-scheme quantization.

4   Transformer Inference Engine on DSP

In this paper, we proposed a DSP accelerated transformer inference engine, as shown in Fig. 3. This engine consists of three components, a high-efficiency operator library for transformer operators on long vector architectures, a software-managed memory optimization strategy, and a sequence warp method. We build microkernels to adapt long vector architectures by manually arranging assembly instructions. Focusing on the transformer inference, we design an on-chip memory allocation strategy based on variable lifecycle, which can reduce data transmission between off-chip memory and on-chip memory. Referencing the VLIW idea, our engine packs several sequences into a longer one and submits it to the fixed-length issuer, which avoids the extra computation of the padding method.

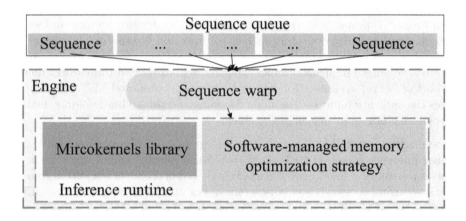

Fig. 3. DSP accelerated transformer models engine.

4.1   High-efficiency Operator Library on Long Vector Architectures

Here, we illustrate the optimization of matrix multiplication (the most time-consuming operation in the transformer) on the target DSP. We mainly focus on task decomposition and memory optimization.

Efficient Microkernels. For matrix multiplication of $A \times B = C$ in the transformer, we assume that A represents the embedding matrix of input sequence X of size $m \times k$, B represents the weights of $k \times n$ while C represents the output of the size $m \times n$. As shown in Fig. 2, the target processor has a small software-managed GC marked *gcs* MB shared by all cores, and the basic idea is to utilize the GC for data reuse and matrix blocking. Considering that the size of B is usually larger than A or C, for example, when *seq_length* $= 384$, when performing FP32 BERT(Large) model inference, the size of B is 4MB, while A the size is only 1.5MB. In addition, the matrix A and C will be used by other functions, and C will be set as the input for the next operation. We put A and C in GC while B is in DDR memory space. According to the basic principle, we design an adaptive blocking strategy for matrix multiplication of the transformer model based on the size of the matrix and GC.

We partition the original matrix in a row-first manner and offload the computation of different rows of matrix C to different kernels. Assuming that the number of cores is nc, we divide the matrices A and C into nc blocks, labeled A_i and C_i. The number of rows computed by each kernel is $cr = m/nc$ (assuming m is a multiple of nc).The matrix B will not be split because all kernels need to use the matrix B.

As mentioned in the Sect. 2.2, L1D and AM are smaller in size than GC and DDR. The data in GC (A and C) or DDR (B) should be divided into several blocks and sent to L1D and AM to facilitate SPU and VPU operations. For $A \times B = C$, if we put the matrices A and B from DDR or GC to AM, an extra transpose is required to pass a column of elements of the original matrix, so we transform the typical matrix multiplication formula as shown in the Equation(1).

$$c_i = a_{i0} \times b_0 + a_{i1} \times b_1 + ... + a_{ik-1} \times b_{k-1}$$
$$while \quad i = 0, 1, ..., m - 1 \tag{1}$$

Figure 4(a) shows the row-wise GEMM vectorization algorithm. The sload instruction means to load a a_{ij} element to scalar registers. The vload instruction means to load b_j vector to vector registers. The svmuladd instruction means to multiply and add the element a_ij and all elements of the vector b_j in the registers to get c_j. The vstore instruction means to store c_j to AM. According to the delay, we can execute the sload, the vload, and the svmuladd instructions in one cycle through the VLIW instruction.

Figure 4(b) shows the GEMM microkernel algorithm based on VLIW. The symbol & indicates that the instruction is executed on the same cycle as the previous instruction. Assume that the instruction delay cycles of sload, vload, svmuladd, and goto are 2, 1, 2, and 1. We load the first element of the first of the matrix A to register R0 in the first cycle by sload instruction. We load the first element of the second row of matrix A to the register R0 and the first row of the matrix B to vector registers VR0, VR1, and VR2 by sload and vload instruction in the second cycle. According to the delay period of sload, the value of the register R0 is the first element of the first row of the matrix A in the third cycle, and we multiply and add the first element of the first row of the matrix

A and the first row of the matrix B by the svmuladd instruction and store the result in registers VR4, VR5, and VR6, while j needs to be decremented. We need to do something similar to the third cycle and jump the loop label if $j > 0$ in the fourth cycle. The GEMM of the first two rows of matrix C is completed when $j = 0$, and we transfer the values of the registers VR4-VR9 to AM in the fifth and the sixth cycle. This pipelining technique takes full advantage of the MACs, and the utilization rate reaches the highest level.

Considering the memory space and the size of the matrix, we design an adaptive blocking strategy to load the data blocks of the matrices A, B, and C. The basic idea is to maximize the data reuse and bandwidth of on-chip memory. Depending on the matrix size, we implement two blocking methods. One is tiling on the dimension of m and n, and the other is tiling on all m, n, and k dimensions.

Input: Matrix A B;
Input: $m \leftarrow$ rows of matrix A,C
Input: k $\leftarrow$ cols of matrix A and rows of matrix B
Input: n $\leftarrow$ cols of matrix B,C
Output: Matrix C
1: for i< $m - 1$ do
2: for j< k $- 1$ do
3:    sload a_{ij} from l1d
4:    vload b_j from am
5:    svmuladd a_{ij} , b_j , c_j
6: end
7: vstore c_i to am
8: end

1. sload l1DR0+[0], R0
2. sload l1DR1+[cols], R0
    &vload am++[1],VR0,VR1,VR2
3.loop_label:
    svmuladd.MAC1 VR0,R0,VR4,VR4
    &svmuladd.MAC2 VR1,R0,VR5,VR5
    &svmuladd.MAC3 VR2,R0,VR6,VR6
    &sload ++l1DR0[1],R0
    &j=j-1
4. svmuladd.MAC1 VR0,R0,VR7,VR7
    &svmuladd.MAC2 VR1,R0,VR8,VR8
    &svmuladd.MAC3 VR2,R0,VR9,VR9
    &sload ++l1DR1[1],R0
    &vload am++[1],VR0,VR1,VR2
    &j>0 goto: loop_label
5. vstore VR4,VR5,VR6,am_out++[1]
6. vstore VR7,VR8,VR9,am_out++[1]

(a) Row-wise GEMM vectoriza- (b) GEMM microkernel algorithm based on VLIW
tion algorithm

Fig. 4. Row-wise GEMM vectorization method and GEMM microkernel algorithm based on VLIW.

For the tiling on m and n dimensions, from the perspective of the single-core of the DSP, we block the matrix according to the size of L1D and AM of a single-core. We split A_i into lp blocks in m dimension and split B into ap blocks in n dimension. Correspondingly, since C_i is the result of multiplying A_i by B, C will be split into lp blocks in the m dimension.

From the perspective of the multicore, the data blocking method and data flow are shown in Fig. 5. A big block of A is transferred to GC with DMA, then we divide this block into nc slices and scatter a slice for each core, as shown

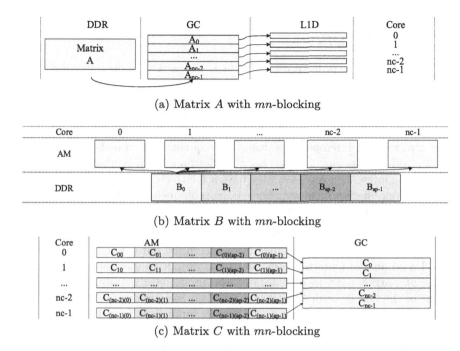

(a) Matrix A with mn-blocking

(b) Matrix B with mn-blocking

(c) Matrix C with mn-blocking

Fig. 5. Matrix A, B, C with mn-blocking method based on multicore.

in Fig. 5(a). To improve the memory efficiency, we broadcast one block of B marked as B_i from DDR to AM for all cores, as shown in Fig. 5(b). By iterating all blocks of B(from B_0 to B_{ap-1}), we can get the final result of C_i for all cores, as shown in Fig. 5(c). We design a GEMM microkernel with $m = 8$ to better use L1D and pipeline, tiling in the m dimension when the matrix A has more than 8 rows. Since the result of C will be set as the input of the next operator, we keep C in the GC. However, this method is only suitable for the cols of A is small, that $8 \times k \times 4$ byte data from A can be resident in L1D. When k is large enough, we adaptive to choose the other block method: tiling in all mkn dimensions. From the perspective of single-core, the mkn-blocking method means tiling the row of A and column of B based on the mn-blocking method. We divide the data of matrix A and C in k dimension according to the size of L1D and AM and split it into kp blocks. For each processing, the sub-block A_{ij} of the slice of A_i is multiplied by B_{ij} of the slice of B_i to obtain the partial result of C_{ij} and accumulates on the divided dimensions to get the final C_{ij}. According to the above strategy, for a matrix multiplication operation with $m = 8$, $k = 768$, $n = 768$, the single-core utilization is as high as 99.05%.

In addition, we use the kernel fusion optimization method, such as the fusion of GELU, softmax, and layernorm with the previous operator, which effectively reduces the transmission of data.

4.2   Software-managed Memory Optimization Strategy Based on Variable Lifecycle

From the perspective of flexibility, the current mainstream deep learning frameworks(such as PyTorch and TensorFlow) support both training and inference processing. Their memory allocation strategy mainly focuses on training and is inefficient for inference without backpropagation. For training, due to the need to retain intermediate results for backward processing, the lifecycle of data is often longer than inference, resulting in frequent data transfers between on-chip and off-chip memory. Observing that data are often read-only at the fixed layer during inference processes, they have a relatively short lifecycle and can be removed from on-chip memory after use. Specific memory allocations should be considered to improve inference performance.

Memory Optimization Strategy. For the inference of deep learning models, the memory footprints are mainly from the input data, weights, and output data. Based on the following considerations, we put the weights in DDR while the input/output data in GC. Firstly, the input data mainly come from the output of the last layer(or function), and when keeping output data in GC can avoid the time-consuming operator of loading input data from DDR to on-chip. Secondly, we can reuse the data, and storing it on GC can effectively improve bandwidth utilization, such as reusing the initial input X of the encoder when computing Q, K, and V. The question is how to effectively use the GC to reduce off-chip memory accesses. The basic idea is to keep recently used data on GC and replace invalid data based on the lifecycle. Combining fine-grained task merge strategies, the overall data distribution is shown in Fig. 6.

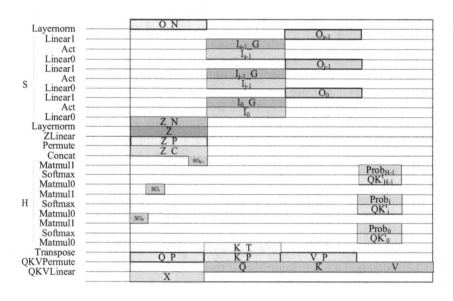

Fig. 6. Data allocation distribution of the transformer encoder on GC.

Fine-Grained Task Merging to Reduce Intermediate Compute Result Space Requirements. When processing the inference of transformer on GPU, the current frameworks usually perform the same kernel on data by using massive parallelism for high-efficiency throughput. For example, parallel processing can be done on the heads of multi-head attention. Although this massively parallel method can improve the utilization of GPU, it requires lots of space to save intermediate results. For on-chip space-limited architecture, massive parallelism may not be the best choice. In this paper, we propose two approaches to reduce intermediate space requirements.

The first one is to reshape the execution process to reduce on-chip storage requirements. The SelfAttention part includes three operators, namely MatMul0, Softmax, and Matmul1. When parallel computing is performed on all heads on Matmul0, taking BERT(Large) as an example, assuming $batch\_size=1$ and $seq\_length=384$, an intermediate result of 9MB will be generated. When seq_length is increased, the size of the intermediate result may be larger than GC and will have to be stored in DDR, which makes additional data transfer between DDR and on-chip memory. To solve this problem, we reshape the execution process and merge the three operators of MatMul0, Softmax, and Matmul1 into one. We first perform the process of one head from MatMul0, Softmax to Matmul1, then serialize on the multi-head. In this way, the intermediate result generated by the MatMul0 and Softmax operators is only 0.5625MB, which reduces GC requirements from 9MB to 0.5625MB. In addition, when executing MatMul, it is also possible to parallelize the m dimension of the matrix.

The second one is to block large operators into small ones and fuse them. In the FFN part, which includes three operators, namely Linear0, GELU, and Linear1, after executing Linear0, the n dimension size of its weight is expanded by four times, resulting in the expansion of the output by four times to 6MB if taking a typical BERT(Large) model with $seq\_length=384$ as an example. To reduce the on-chip memory requirement, we block the operators of Linear0 and Linear1 on the k dimension. Since the operations of GELU are organized element-wise, it will not increase the memory footprint. The total on-chip memory will be reduced by np times if we block the FFN on the k dimension with the factor of np. In our engine, if we divided the FFN into four blocks in the k dimension, the intermediate result generated by the operator reduces GC requirements from 6MB to 1.5MB.

4.3   Sequence Warp

Reusing data can reduce memory access pressure, which is one of the ways to affect performance. For deep learning models, weights can usually be reused by increasing the batch size, but if the batch size increases, the space required for input and output also increases with the batch size. According to the previous strategy, we store intermediate results such as the inputs and the outputs in the GC. Due to the limited space of the GC, increasing the $batch\_size$ may cause some data to be transferred to the DDR, so this method may not effectively improve the inference performance. To solve this problem, we propose a

Algorithm 1. Sequence warp with sliding window algorithm.
***
Require: *sequence_list*;
Ensure: *save_sequence_list*;
 1: sort *sequence_list* in decreasing order based on sequence length;
 2: $sn \leftarrow$ size of *sequence_list*;
 3: Create *saved_sequence_list* as lists of size sn;
 4: Create *states* as lists of size sn;
 5: Create *warp_lists* as lists of size sn;
 6: $states=0, warp\_lists=0,\ pk=0$;
 7: for $pk < sn - 1$ do
 8:   while $i < sn$ do
 9:     $j \leftarrow sn\text{-}1$;
10:    $if(states[i] == 0)$
11:      while($j¿i$ and $states[j]==0$) do
12:       Find the sum of pk sequences in the interval $[i, j]$ equal to *max_seq_length*;
13:       $j \leftarrow j\text{-}1$
14:       update *saved_sequence_list states_list warp_lists*
15:    *endif*
16:    $i \leftarrow i+1$
***

sequence warp method that packs several sequences whose length is less than *max_seq_length* into a longer one. In the inference processes of most transformer applications, the sequence is first preprocessed, the zero-padding operation is adopted when *seq_length* < *max_seq_length*, and the mainstream framework usually directly calculates the data of *max_seq_length* length now. Computing redundant invalid information increases the amount of computation and requires more GC.

Algorithm 2. Sequence warp with greedy algorithm.
***
Require: *sequence_list*;
Ensure: *save_sequence_list*;
 1: $i \leftarrow 0$;
 2: while $i¡\ sn$ do
 3:   $if(states[i] == 0)$
 4:    Find the sum of max *maxn* consecutive sequences less than *max_seq_length*;
 5:    update *saved_sequence_list,states_list,warp_lists*
 6:   *endif*
 7:   $i \leftarrow i+maxn$
***

The analysis of the calculation process shows that whether or not to calculate this part of the zero-padding data will not affect the final result. For the XW, Self-Output, and FFN parts, whether it is the input or output matrix, *seq_length* is only related to the dimension of the row. Taking matrix multiplication as an example, the row information of the output matrix is only related to the corresponding row information of the input matrix and the weights. In contrast, the weights are unrelated to seq_length. If the part of the input data after zero-padding is invalid, the corresponding part of the output data is also invalid. The same is true for other operators such as GELU and layernorm. Therefore, there is no need to calculate invalid information for the XW, SelfOutput, and FFN parts. However, when calculating QK^t in the SelfAttention part, the row dimension of the matrix Q and the column dimension of matrix K^t are related to seq_length. If not processed, it will affect the accumulation of the k dimension in matrix multiplication, thereby affecting the FFN part of the operation, resulting in uncontrollable errors. We hope that the invalid data of the intermediate result after softmax approaches zero so as not to affect the operator calculation of the FFN part. Moreover, we found that when the execution of QK^t is completed, the output will add attention_mask and apply the softmax operator to it, where attention_mask is related to the length of the sequence. When the seq_length does not exceed max_seq_length, the value of the attention_mask corresponding to the sequence is $-infinity$, the intermediate result add attention_mask is still -infinity, and $e^{-infinity}$ is close to 0 after applying softmax. Therefore, the result of the invalid part will be close to 0 and will not affect the result of subsequent parts.

To sum up, when seq_length is less than max_seq_length, although invalid data is not calculated to reduce computation, it still wastes some valuable memory space. To solve the problem, we propose the optimization method named sequence warp. We will replace the memory space required by invalid data in the input data and pack the valid information of multiple input data. It can reuse the weight and improve the overall inference efficiency.

The optimization method of sequence warp proposed in this paper mainly uses the sliding window algorithm and the greedy algorithm, as shown in Algorithms 1 and Algorithms 2. First, we collect all sequences after embedding named seq_length_list, and sort them in descending order according to the seq_length, then create three collections called $saved\_sequence\_list$, states $warp\_lists$, $saved\_sequence\_list$ as the final input to the acceleration engine, states to check if the sequence has been added to $saved\_sequence\_list$, $warp\_lists$ is used to record whether the sequence needs to be packed. Finally, store sequence pairs whose sum of $pk(pk > 0\&\&pk < sn - 1)$ equals max_seq_length in $saved\_sequence\_list$, and update states and $warp\_lists$. We use a greedy algorithm to find sequence pairs where the sum of seq_length of the remaining sequences does not exceed max_seq_length, and when the state in all sequences changes, it means that the rearrangement of all sequences has been completed. and stored in $saved\_sequence\_list$. Then send $saved\_sequence\_list$ to the acceleration engine to complete the transformer inference, and judge whether to perform sequence warp and calculation according to the value of $warp\_lists$. For example, there are eight input sequences with lengths of 384, 320, 64, 128, 128, 128, 256, and 64, and we first sort the data in descending order. When $max\_seq\_length = 384$, the sequence of length 384 directly forms a pack, and then uses the sliding window algorithm to pack the sequence pairs of lengths 320 and 64 and the sequence pairs of lengths 128, 128, and 128, and then uses the

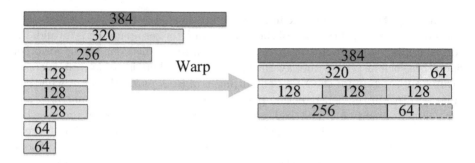

Fig. 7. An example of sequence warp for variable-length input when *max_seq_length*=384.

greedy algorithm to warp the lengths of 256 and 32, and finally form 4 packs, as shown in Fig. 7.

5   Experiment

In this section, we will show the benefits of optimization methods of our engine, our tests BERT(Base), BERT(Large), and ALBERT [13] models, and the models' parameters are as follows:

Table 1. Transformer model parameters

Model	Num_layer	Num_head	Hidden_size	Inter_size
BERT(Base)	12	12	768	3072
BERT(Large)	24	16	1024	4096
ALBERT	12	12	768	12288

All experiments were tested 10 times and averaged. We test the BERT(Large) model throughput for question answering applications based on the SQuAD-1.1 dataset on a GPU platform (NVIDIA GeForce RTX 3090) and our DSP. On the GPU platform, our tests are based on the PyTorch and the FasterTransformer, and the results are shown in Fig. 9. Our throughput is close to the throughput of NVIDIA GeForce RTX 3090 using PyTorch, and when the sequence length becomes longer, our throughput tends to be greater than PyTorch and the Faster-Transformer. It should be emphasized that the peak performance of the DSP is lower than that of the NVIDIA GeForce RTX 3090, but the memory used by NVIDIA GeForce RTX 3090 is GDDR6X, and the theoretical bandwidth exceeds **1 TB/s**. In contrast, the memory used by DSP is DDR4, and the theoretical bandwidth is only **43 GB/s**. We tested the performance before and after optimization on our engine. Figure 8 shows the overall benefit of our engine using the

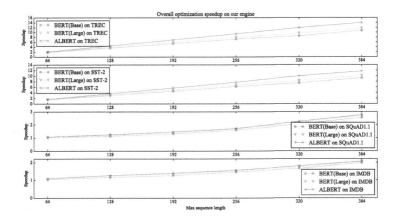

Fig. 8. Overall optimization speedup on our engine with fours datasets.

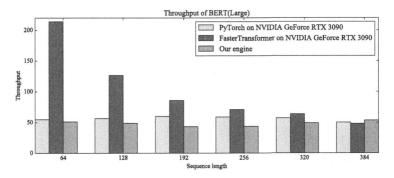

Fig. 9. Throughput of BERT(Large) with different library.

optimization method on the TREC, SST-2, SQuAD-1.1, and IMDB datasets. It can be seen that the speedup increases with the increase of sequence length. The maximum speedup of the BERT(Base), BERT(Large), and ALBERT models reaches 10.74x, 11.72x, and 13.98x on the TREC dataset, 9.28x, 10.11x, and 11.68x on SST-2 the dataset, 2.61x, 2.71x, and 2.75x on the SQuAD-1.1 dataset, and 1.97x, 2.05x, and 2.06x on the IMDB dataset, respectively.

Kernel Library. As mentioned before, GEMM takes up most of the computation in the transformer inference. Figure 10 shows the time proportion of each part of the operator on our engine before and after optimization, the time proportion of GEMM operation is 82.00% and 89.81%, respectively, and the benefits of this part mainly come from fine-grained task merging in the SelfAttention and FFN parts, which brings a 1.32x speedup. Not only that, but we have also optimized the edge operator, and the time proportion of each part has decreased.

The Benefits of Memory Management Strategies. We tested the benefits brought by our memory allocation optimization strategy. When using our task

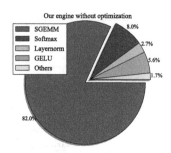
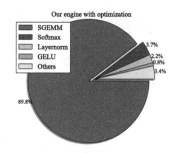

(a) Our engine without kernel opti- (b) Our engine with kernel optimiza-
mization   tion

Fig. 10. The proportion of operator time based on the BERT(Large) model with and without kernel optimization.

Table 2. Memory footprints savings(MB) based on BERT(Large) model

Model	Sequence length					
	64	128	192	256	320	384
BERT(Base)	8.81	21.75	38.81	60.00	85.31	114.75
BERT(Large)	19.13	49.50	91.13	144.00	208.13	283.50
ALBERT	11.81	29.25	52.31	81.00	115.31	155.25

merge strategy, the memory footprint savings used FP32 are shown in Table 2. Let the sequence length be *len*, the formula is shown in Eq. (2).

$$Saved_0 = \frac{((num\_head - 1) \times len + (inter\_size - hidden\_size)) \times len \times 4}{1024 \times 1024}$$

(2)

The memory management strategy reduces the memory footprint and makes our data flow better on GC. Figure 11 shows the latency benefits brought by the memory management strategy of the SelfAttention and the FFN parts. There is a small benefit when *seq_length* is small since the GC space is enough to put down the intermediate results. As *seq_length* increases, the overall trend is upward. The benefits mainly come from not needing to move data from GC to DDR. BERT(Large) has the highest benefit in the SelfAttention part because its heads_nums is larger, while ALBERT has the highest benefit in the FFN part because it's *inter_size* is larger, and the maximum speedup of BERT(Base), BERT(Large), and ALBERT models can reach 1.40x, 1.44x, and 1.48x.

The Benefits of Sequence Warp. We also test the throughput of three FP32 models based on the TREC, SST-2, SQuAD-1.1, and IMDB datasets when using sequence warp. Figure 12 shows the maximum speedup can reach 9.92x, 8.29x, 1.95x, and 1.58x compared to not using sequence warp, respectively, where the sequence lengths of the SST-2 and TREC datasets are smaller than the

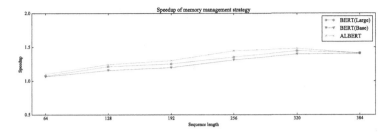

Fig. 11. Latency benefits speedup of three models by using memory management strategies.

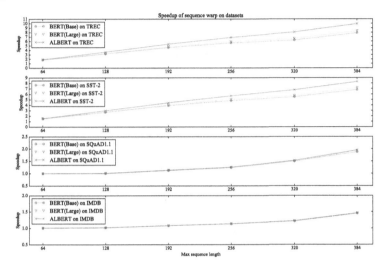

Fig. 12. Speedup of sequence warp on four datasets.

SQuAD-1.1 and the IMDB datasets. We can see from the figure that when the max sequence length is small because there are fewer sequence pairs that can be packed, the effect of using sequence warp is not apparent. When the max sequence length becomes larger, the throughput speedup of each dataset is improved, and the speedup of the SST-2 and TREC datasets is better than the SQuAD-1.1 and the IMDB datasets.

6 Conclusion

Our engine is designed to solve the huge computational load problem brought by the transformer model and the memory management problem caused by the variable length of the input sequence. It includes an efficient operator library, which optimizes the GEMM operators that take up most of the time, optimizes edge operators, and performs kernel fusion. These optimization methods support the efficiency of the operator library. It includes a reasonable software-managed memory optimization strategy. The maximum speedup ratio can reach 1.48x and save a lot of memory usage; It also includes a sequence warp method, which can bring a maximum speedup of 9.92x. The overall maximum speedup using the above method can reach 13.98x. By comparing it with GPU GeForce RTX 3090, it can be seen that our engine an achieve comparable performance to the GPU. It turns out that our engine can effectively increase throughput and achieve less memory footprints.

Acknowledgements. This work has been supported by the National Natural Science Foundation of China No.61872377 and Fund of PDL.

References

1. Abadi, M., et al.: Tensorflow: a system for large-scale machine learning. In: Proceedings of the 12th USENIX conference on Operating Systems Design and Implementation, pp. 265–283 (2016)
2. Carion, N., Massa, F., Synnaeve, G., Usunier, N., Kirillov, A., Zagoruyko, S.: End-to-end object detection with transformers. In: Vedaldi, A., Bischof, H., Brox, T., Frahm, J.-M. (eds.) ECCV 2020. LNCS, vol. 12346, pp. 213–229. Springer, Cham (2020). https://doi.org/10.1007/978-3-030-58452-8_13
3. Chen, T., et al.: TVM: an automated end-to-end optimizing compiler for deep learning. In: Proceedings of the 13th USENIX conference on Operating Systems Design and Implementation, pp. 579–594 (2018)
4. Cho, K., et al.: Learning phrase representations using RNN encoder-decoder for statistical machine translation. In: EMNLP (2014)
5. Dice, D., Kogan, A.: Optimizing inference performance of transformers on CPUs. arXiv preprint arXiv:2102.06621 (2021)
6. Dosovitskiy, A., et al.: An image is worth 16×16 words: transformers for image recognition at scale. In: International Conference on Learning Representations (2020)
7. Fang, J., Yu, Y., Zhao, C., Zhou, J.: Turbotransformers: an efficient gpu serving system for transformer models. In: Proceedings of the 26th ACM SIGPLAN Symposium on Principles and Practice of Parallel Programming, pp. 389–402 (2021)
8. Ganiev, A., Chapin, C., De Andrade, A., Liu, C.: An architecture for accelerated large-scale inference of transformer-based language models. In: Proceedings of the 2021 Conference of the North American Chapter of the Association for Computational Linguistics: Human Language Technologies: Industry Papers, pp. 163–169 (2021)
9. Han, K., Xiao, A., Wu, E., Guo, J., Xu, C., Wang, Y.: Transformer in transformer, vol. 34, pp. 15908–15919 (2021)
10. Hendrycks, D., Gimpel, K.: Gaussian error linear units (GELUs). arXiv preprint arXiv:1606.08415 (2016)
11. Hochreiter, S., Schmidhuber, J.: Long short-term memory. Neural Comput. **9**(8), 1735–1780 (1997)
12. Kenton, J.D.M.W.C., Toutanova, L.K.: BERT: pre-training of deep bidirectional transformers for language understanding. In: Proceedings of NAACL-HLT, pp. 4171–4186 (2019)

13. Lan, Z., Chen, M., Goodman, S., Gimpel, K., Sharma, P., Soricut, R.: Albert: a lite BERT for self-supervised learning of language representations. In: International Conference on Learning Representations (2019)
14. Li, B., et al.: Ftrans: energy-efficient acceleration of transformers using FPGA. In: Proceedings of the ACM/IEEE International Symposium on Low Power Electronics and Design, pp. 175–180 (2020)
15. li, G., et al.: Easy and efficient transformer: Scalable inference solution for large NLP mode. arXiv preprint arXiv:2104.12470 (2021)
16. Li, Z., et al.: Auto-ViT-Acc: An FPGA-aware automatic acceleration framework for vision transformer with mixed-scheme quantization. arXiv preprint arXiv:2208.05163 (2022)
17. Liu, Y., et al.: Roberta: a robustly optimized BERT pretraining approach. arXiv preprint arXiv:1907.11692 (2019)
18. Liu, Z., Li, G., Cheng, J.: Hardware acceleration of fully quantized BERT for efficient natural language processing. In: 2021 Design, Automation & Test in Europe Conference & Exhibition (DATE), pp. 513–516. IEEE (2021)
19. NVIDIA: Nvidia TensorRT (2020)
20. NVIDIA: Fastertransformer (2022)
21. Paszke, A., et al.: PyTorch: an imperative style, high-performance deep learning library, vol. 32 (2019)
22. Qi, P., Song, Y., Peng, H., Huang, S., Zhuge, Q., Sha, E.H.M.: Accommodating transformer onto FPGA: coupling the balanced model compression and FPGA-implementation optimization. In: Proceedings of the 2021 on Great Lakes Symposium on VLSI, pp. 163–168 (2021)
23. Vaswani, A., et al.: Attention is all you need, vol. 30 (2017)
24. Wang, X., Xiong, Y., Wei, Y., Wang, M., Li, L.: LightSeq: a high performance inference library for transformers. In: Proceedings of the 2021 Conference of the North American Chapter of the Association for Computational Linguistics: Human Language Technologies: Industry Papers, pp. 113–120 (2021)
25. Wang, Y., et al.: End-to-end video instance segmentation with transformers. In: Proceedings of the IEEE/CVF Conference on Computer Vision and Pattern Recognition, pp. 8741–8750 (2021)
26. Wang, Y., Wang, Q., Chu, X.: Energy-efficient inference service of transformer-based deep learning models on GPUs. In: 2020 International Conferences on Internet of Things (iThings) and IEEE Green Computing and Communications (GreenCom) and IEEE Cyber, Physical and Social Computing (CPSCom) and IEEE Smart Data (SmartData) and IEEE Congress on Cybermatics (Cybermatics), pp. 323–331. IEEE (2020)
27. Wu, S., Lv, T., Yuan, P., Zhao, P., Ye, J., Lin, H.: Optimization for BERT inference performance on CPU (2021)
28. Zhou, L., Zhou, Y., Corso, J.J., Socher, R., Xiong, C.: End-to-end dense video captioning with masked transformer. In: Proceedings of the IEEE conference on Computer Vision and Pattern Recognition, pp. 8739–8748 (2018)

GCNPart: Interference-Aware Resource Partitioning Framework with Graph Convolutional Neural Networks and Deep Reinforcement Learning

Ruobing Chen[1], Haosen Shi[2], Jinping Wu[1], Yusen Li[1(✉)], Xiaoguang Liu[1], and Gang Wang[1]

[1] NanKai University, Tianjin 300300, China
{chenrb,wujp,liyusen,liuxg,wgzwp}@nbjl.nankai.edu.cn
[2] Nanyang Technological University, Singapore, Singapore

Abstract. The clouding server providers usually take workload consolidation to maximize server utilization. For eliminating performance interference due to the competition among multiple shared resources, resource partitioning becomes an important problem in daily commercial servers scenario. However, partitioning the critical multiple resources coordinately is particularly challenging due to the complex contention behaviors and the large search space to be explored for finding the optimal solution.

In this paper, we propose GCNPart, which focuses on allocating the optimal shared compete resource partition for colocated applications to optimize system performance. The existing resource partitioning frameworks lack analysis and good modeling of applications, resulting in inefficiencies or lack of generality. We formulate the resource partitioning problem as a sequential decision problem. GCNPart builds an accurate application performance model based on graph convolutional neural networks (GCN) to learn the mapping relationships from multiple resources to applications, and then constructs deep reinforcement learning (DRL) model to consider temporal information for real-time resource partitioning decisions. The extensive experiments evaluate that compared with the existing resource partitioning frameworks, GCNPart improves system throughput by $5.35\% \sim 26.57\%$.

Keywords: Workload consolidation · Performance interference · Resource partitioning · Deep reinforcement learning · Graph neural network

1 Introduction

Huge data centers or cloud computing platforms usually colocate multiple applications on the same server to maximize the utilization of server resources. However, applications may suffer severe performance degradation due to the

© Springer Nature Switzerland AG 2023
W. Meng et al. (Eds.): ICA3PP 2022, LNCS 13777, pp. 568–589, 2023.
https://doi.org/10.1007/978-3-031-22677-9_30

competition for shared resources. The most critical shared resources that affect application performance are Last Level Cache (LLC) and memory bandwidth (MB) [25,35]. Considering that many modern applications support multi-process concurrency, CPU cores are also important and need to be partitioned reasonably [6].

Resource partitioning has become a popular approach to reduce the contention among the colocated applications [7,10,14,18,35]. By using the following resource isolation tools, i.e., Intel's Cache Allocation Technology (CAT) [21], Memory Bandwidth Allocation (MBA) [4] and *taskset*, each application can be allocated with dedicated resources and performance interference can be prevented or mitigated. Although the partitioning problem has been extensively studied, it's pretty tough to well tackle the resource partitioning problem due to several critical challenges.

- First, the solution space of the problem is prohibitively large. For a colocation of 6 jobs, the total number of resource partitioning configurations is up to 10^{21} when 10 CPU cores and 10 cache ways are considered [6].
- Second, the interactions among multiple applications and multiple resources is complex and non-linear (see Fig. 1). It is very difficult to establish an accurate performance model to guide the exploration of search space.
- Third, real commercial server environments often face rapid and unpredictable changes (i.e., phase change) as shown in Fig. 2, the method for resource partitioning problem should make decisions online and can quickly adapt to the new state.
- Forth, resource partitioning is a sequential decision problem. As shown in Fig. 3, at every time when the system changes the partitioning scheme, the application may suffer a performance loss (which we call *transition penalty*) because each application's running context and relevant data should be migrated among CPU cores.

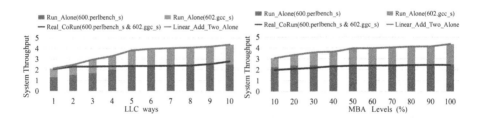

Fig. 1. Resource competition among applications. The left figure shows the system throughput (indicated by instruction per cycle (IPC)) of two applications (600.*perlbench_s* and 602.*gcc_s* from SPEC CPU2017 [3]) running alone and co-running at different LLC settings; the right figure shows the system throughput of two applications running alone and co-running at different MB settings. If resource competition is linear, the green line should be parallel to the yellow line, so resource competition among applications is non-linear. (Color figure online)

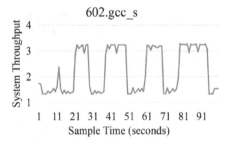

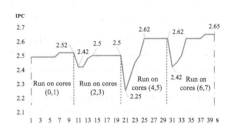

Fig. 2. Take benchmark 602.*gcc_s* as an example, applications usually have quick and unpredictable phase changes (indicated by IPC change).

Fig. 3. Performance loss of application 500.*perlbench_r* during partitioning scheme transitions. 500.*perlbench_r* originally runs on CPU cores (0, 1), and migrates to CPU cores (2, 3), (4, 5), (6, 7) respectively.

In theory, an optimal resource allocation strategy can be easily obtained if a full long-term profile is performed for each application or if there is user-generated resource information for a particular application. However, it is very expensive and difficult to implement as the numbers and types of applications continues to grow nowadays.

Therefore, previous work such as DICER [22], dCat [37], KPart [14], DCAPS [35] tried to build performance models to estimate the performance of colocated applications based on extensive domain knowledge, but these models can only handle a single resource and are not easily extended to multiple resources. Other methods have attempted to eliminate the dependence on performance models, either by directly ignoring the characteristics of the application and adjusting online through the black-box method like CLITE [25], or by simply analyzing the application characteristics and adaptively adjusting resource partitioning based on simple rules in a greedy manner such as Heracles [18], Quasar [11], PARTIES [7], CoPart [23]. However, the black-box methods are slowly to provide real-time resource partition and it is difficult to guarantee the quality of the solution when the number of applications increases due to the great resource partitioning decision search space. The approaches based on simple rules usually classify applications based on the resource sensitivity intuitively first [23], and then allocate the resources in a greedy manner [7,18,23] according to the real-time system state adaptively. However, the sensitivity or other instinctive threshold like QoS is set by experience and can only be applied to specific scenarios and optimization goals that researchers are familiar with. The state-of-the-art approach DRLPart [6] builds the relatively accurate performance model based on deep learning method without domain knowledge, but the model did not well learn the mapping relationships from multiple resources to applications. The accuracy of the performance model was not enough, which greatly affected the upper limit of performance improvement. Another disadvantage is that DRLPart just regards resource partitioning problem as a single decision problem and does not consider the impact of the transition penalty effect of the previous decision on the current decision.

So, without an accurate performance model, these solutions are limited by the scale of applications and resources; or cannot make multiple resources partition decision simultaneously; or cannot be used for more general scenarios. In addition, all of these methods do not take into account that online resource partitioning problem is a sequential decision problem, therefore they fail to explicitly consider the impact of the previous decision on the current decision, which leads to a decrease in performance improvement.

In the paper, we seek to solve the resource partitioning problem to maximize system throughput. We propose GCNPart, a resource management framework with a accurate performance model based on graph convolutional neural networks [34] and a resource partitioning decision making model based on deep reinforcement learning decision model [30]. The performance model estimates the performance of colocated applications under any resource partitioning schemes, and the decision making model decides multiple resources partitioning at the same time quickly in real-time. The main contributions of this paper include:

(1) Considering that the applications are always in phase change, GCNPart formulates the resource partitioning problem as an sequential decision problem. We extract the applications' characteristics at different time state as input features to establish a more realistic performance prediction model and a real-time resource partitioning decision model.
(2) GCNPart presents a GCN-based performance prediction model, which models the mapping relationships from resources to applications by abstracting them into graph structures to capture the nature of application interference and resource contention. GCNPart improves the learning efficiency and the performance of system throughput.
(3) GCNPart proposes a DRL-based partitioning decision making model to consider the transition penalty when making partitioning decision, which can cause significantly performance loss due to context switch and data migration among CPU cores and cache ways.

2 Motivation and Related Work

We motivate the need for new technology to solve the resource partitioning problem. Existing solutions for resource partitioning are inadequate to varying degrees, all of them do not take into account that online resource partitioning is a serialization decision problem. We divide the existing approaches into 4 categories for discussion.

Greedy Tunning based on Simple Rules at Runtime without Performance Model. The approaches like [7,11,18,23] do not rely on performance model to estimate the performance of partitioning schemes. Instead, they use greedy algorithms by simple rules to dynamically tune the partitioning scheme in real time. Basically, they solve this problem by repeating the process of reducing a unit of resource allocated to an application and assigning that resource to another application. For example, CoPart [23], whose goal is to ensure fairness among the colocated applications, repeatedly increases resource allocation for low IPC applications and decreases resource allocation for high IPC applications until all applications have the same IPC.

Advantage and Limitation. The greedy tuning approaches are simplicity with small overhead. However, they can only find sub-optimal solutions [25], because they explore only one resource and tune the resource in small steps for an application at a time. Besides, they need to design simple rules, which require domain knowledge and vary from expert to expert.

Black-box Methods based on Approximate Performance Model. The recent work CLITE [25] is the representation. CLITE samples a small number of partitioning schemes online based on Bayesian Optimization (BO) to build approximate performance model and then searches solutions guided by the model. CLITE updates the performance model with each search.

Advantage and Limitation. Even with not-accurate-enough model, CLITE can partition the multiple resources coordinately through the evaluation from the performance model, which solves the problems of the previous methods, and CLITE does not rely on domain knowledge. However, due to the insufficient accuracy of the model, CLITE can only find the near-optimal solution [25]. In addition, BO will lose effectiveness in higher dimensions [26], in our context, CLITE can only handle colocations of small sizes (less than 5-apps [6]).

Heuristic Search Guided by Domain Knowledge Performance Model. The representative approaches in this category include DCAPS [35], dCat [37], KPart [14], DICER [22] etc. These approaches generally slove the resource partitioning problem by building a performance model relying on extensive domain knowledge and find the optimal partitioning scheme based on handcrafted heuristic algorithms, where the quality of each scheme is evaluated by the performance model.

Advantage and Limitation. Thanks to the performance model, this kind of methods have the opportunity to expand the methods to partition multiple resources coordinately. However, they rely more heavily on domain knowledge while the experts have different experiences or intuitions to analyze resource contention behavior, which causes the model has bias and inaccuracy (e.g., DCAPS has a IPC prediction model with 80.1% accuracy). When new scenes are encountered, the heuristic algorithms need to be redesigned (at least the parameters of the algorithm must be adjusted carefully).

Deep Reinforcement Learning (DRL) Framework based On Neurons Networks Performance Model. The latest work DRLPart [6] is a representation of this category. DRLPart builds the relatively accurate performance model based on deep neurons networks to predict system throughput under any resource partitioning schemes, and constructs DRL model to make partition decisions online.

Advantage and Limitation. DRLPart takes easy-to-collect performance counters as the input features of neurons networks without the need of domain knowledge and handcrafted heuristics. In addition, DRLPart is strong robustness, the solving ability is not affected by high dimensions. However, in DRLPart, the mapping relationships from resources to applications are not well represented in the input features of the learning models, which requires the learning models to learn them from raw features implicitly. As with all previous methods, DRLPart makes partitioning decisions without considering the transition penalty, which can result in significantly performance loss due to context switch and data migration among CPU cores and cache ways.

Summary: We need a resource partitioning framework, which 1) can make multiple resource allocation decisions simultaneously; 2) is not limited by application scale and resource scale; 3) requires no expensive or limited domain knowledge. In the previous approaches, DRLPart [6] meets the above requirements, so we choose to design a more complete framework based on it. However, DRLPart has defects as we dicussed in the previous paragraph, in order to overcome these, we need to define the problem as a sequential decision problem first. And then we build a more accurate model that can directly learn the mapping relationships, and finally make real-time sequential resource partitioning decisions.

3   Problem Formulation

Given a set of applications which are colocating on the same server, our goal is to find the optimal partitioning scheme such that the system throughput is maximized. The system throughput particularly refers to the total (Instructions Per Cycle) IPCs of the applications. Moreover, the proposed framework can be easily extended to support other performance metrics. We consider the dynamic system where the applications have phase changes. Thus, the partitioning scheme should be updated adaptively.

   We formulate the resource partitioning problem as a sequential decision problem. This requires us to consider the influence of the decision of the previous time step and add temporal information into the modeling of the real environment.

   We focus on the partitioning of the most important resources affecting the application performance [6,25,35]: CPU cores, last level cache (LLC) and memory bandwidth (MB). The CPU is partitioned in core granularity. At least one CPU core will be allocated to each application. We isolate LLC resource according to Intel's Cache Allocation Technology (CAT) [21], where one unit of LLC is a cache way. CAT requests that the allocation of LLC for an application must be defined as a set of contiguous indexed cache ways, and a cache way is allowed to be shared by multiple applications (e.g., the allocation of LLC for two different applications can be {4,5,6} and {5,6}). MB is partitioned according to Intel's Memory Bandwidth Allocation (MBA) [4], where one unit of MB is 10% MBA level.

4   GCNPart: Design

The design of GCNPart follows three principles.

Principle I: The quality of every partitioning decision should be guaranteed.

Inaccurate performance models are used to evaluate any resource partitioning schemes, which can lead to exploration in the search space far away from optimal solutions because the model built does not learn the mapping relationships from resources to applications (i.e., application interference and resource contention).

Principle I intends to address the above issue and guarantees every partitioning decision's quality by learning the nature of the relationship and improving the accuracy of prediction.

Principle II: Modeling needs to be adaptable to phase change and low overhead when making online decisions.

Principle II requires that the proposed framework can make fast online decisions based on the real-time environment of the colocation.

Principle III: The proposed resource allocation framework can solve the sequential decision making problem, successive partitioning decisions should not be significantly different.

Principle III intends to minimize the *transition penalty* of the successive partitioning schemes, which refers to the sharp performance loss at every time when the system changes the partitioning scheme. The transition penalty is due to context switch and data migration, which could be significant (see the example in Fig. 3). Basically, the transition penalty is proportional to the amount of data migrated. So, in order to minimize the transition penalty, we need to reduce the data migration, meaning that successive partitioning decisions should be as close as possible.

In recent years, deep reinforcement learning (DRL) has been widely used in sequential decision making problems and achieved good results [28]. Compared with traditional methods, DRL methods do not require domain knowledge, can easily to partition the critical multiple resources coordinately, and the trained model can be easily migrated to new scenarios. So, GCNPart takes DRL algorithm to make resource partitioning decision.

4.1   Overview Design

The overview design of GCNPart is shown in Fig. 4, which consists of two components. The modeling component takes charge of collecting samples and training the GCN performance prediction model and the DRL decision making model offline. According to the real-time system state, the partitioning component generates new partition decisions periodically through DRL model, and applies the partitioning decisions to the actual environment.

The key technologies include: (1) to address *Principle I*, we propose the GCN-based performance prediction model, which uses graph struction to describe the

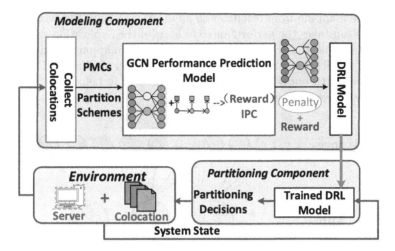

Fig. 4. The Overview of GNCPart Design.

mapping relationships from resources to applications with high accuracy; (2) to address *Principle II*, we propose a trained DRL based decision making model to make sequential decision, it interacts with the real environment to collect real-time state information and gives partitioning decisions in a short time; (3) to address *Principle III*, we add the impact of transition penalty to the reward for the DRL model to generate the final partitioning decision, which significantly reduces the transition penalty;

4.2   The GCN-based Performance Prediction Model

The performance model is designed to predict the system throughput (indicated by IPC) of any colocation under any resource partition scheme based on graph convolutional neural networks (GCN). Due to phase changes, we need to use colocation's real-time state information to evaluate partitioning schemes to make online decisions. That is, the input of the performance model should be real-time state information, which contains current application features and resource allocation. Inspired by DRLPart, the application real-time features can be represented by performance counters, because they can be collected quickly online with little cost and are not limited to specific applications.

Different from DRLPart, we first set up the mapping relationships from resources to applications as graph (see Fig. 5), and use the graph node aggregation based on GCN to learn the nature of interference and resource competition among applications. Then we explicitly express the temporal information into the neural networks (see Fig. 6).

Figure 5 shows how the graph is defined. The nodes in the middle row represent the applications, the nodes in the bottom row represent the cache ways, the nodes in the top row represent the CPU cores, and the edges between nodes represent the mapping from resources to applications. The node associated with each application takes the performance counters of the application as its feature. It is easy to see that the graph explicitly describes the mapping relationship from resources to applications. Each application information after mutual interference and resource partitioning are aggregated by nodes, it helps the performance model to learn relationships more directly.

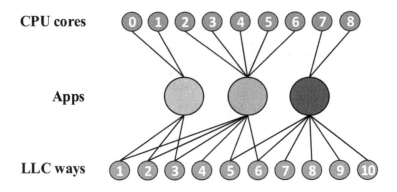

Fig. 5. The graph representing resource allocations.

Consider a colocation of N applications. We use a N-tuple $F_t = (f_t^1, \ldots, f_t^N)$ to denote the values of performance counters (PMCs) of applications at time step t, where f_t^i refers to the values of performance counters associated with the i-th application. The impact of the resources containing positional information on the application will vary from location to location, so they are the keys to learning the nature of resources-to-applications mappings. As shown in Fig. 5, only the resources containing positional information (that is, CPU cores and LLC) participate in the structure of the graph to perform node aggregation calculation. Because of the different position of the CPU cores on the motherboard, such as the distance from the fan or power supply, there is a slight performance difference among the cores. Position information should also be remembered for LLC resource, because a unit of LLC is allowed to be shared by multiple applications. For example, the throughput of allocating {1,2}, {2,3,4} to $app1$ and $app2$ is very different from the throughput of allocating {1,2}, {1,2,3} to $app1$ and $app2$, even though $app1$ and $app2$ are allocated to two and three cache ways consistently. So we use $P_t = (p_t^1, \ldots, p_t^N)$ to represent the allocation of resources with positional information at time step t, where p_t^i refers to the resources allocation for the i-th application and $p_t^i = (c_i, llc_i)$. In the tuple (c_i, llc_i), c_i is the number of allocated CPU cores and $llc_i = (llc_i^l, llc_i^r)$ denotes the number of allocated cache ways. And then we use a tuple $B_t = (b_t^1, \ldots, b_t^N)$ to represent the allocation of memory bandwidth, where b_t^i refers to the bandwidth level for the i-th application. So, we use $C_t = (P_t, B_t)$ to represent the total resource partitioning scheme at time step t.

Suppose a colocation of N-apps is at the real-time state $S = (F, C)$. We define the resource partition scheme A that we want to estimate performance as (P', B'), where P' denotes the allocation of CPU cores and LLC resource, B' denotes the allocation of MB resource. The input of the performance model is $I = (S, A)$, which is composed by the current application features F, the current resource partitioning scheme C, the resource partitioning scheme we want to estimate A. The output of the prediction model is the predicted system throughput of the colocation under A scheme. Let the N-tuple $IPC_{A|S} = (IPC_{A|S}^1, \ldots, IPC_{A|S}^N)$ denotes the IPCs of applications if A is applied to S, where $IPC_{A|S}^i$ refers to the IPC of the i-th application. Noted that, A is not really put into the real system, and the IPCs associated with action A is just prediction values.

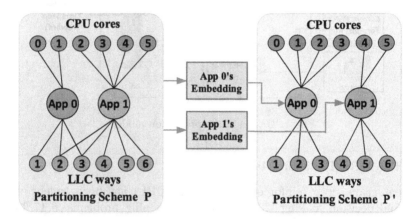

Fig. 6. The GCN representing P and P'.

In DRLPart, the input feature of the prediction model is the simple concatenation vector of F, C, and A. However, this representation requires the model to learn the mapping relationship of resources to applications from raw features implicitly. Moreover, the sequential relationship between $C = (P, B)$ and $A = (P', B')$ (A is the next partitioning scheme after C) is not indicated. To address this issue, we design the following neural networks. We combine P and P' in a single GCN which describes the mapping relationship explicitly. Figure 6 shows how the GCN is defined. As shown in Fig. 6, the left side of the GCN represents the partitioning scheme P, where the features of each application's node denoted by F. The right side of the GCN represents the partitioning scheme P', where the feature of each application's node is an embedding generated by the left side of the GCN. Unlike CPU cores and cache ways, memory bandwidth has no positional information, so we map B and B' to high-dimensional vector through a neural network layer (fully-connected (fc) embedding) that is different from other resources (GCN embedding).

Figure 7 shows the overall design of the prediction model. Both B and B' are mapped to high-dimension through a fc embedding layer. Then, three fc layers are used to encode the graph and the output of the embedding layers, and a multi-head attention module [32] is used to calculate the outputs of the fc layers. Through the multi-head attention module, the final output is generated, i.e. the IPCs of applications.

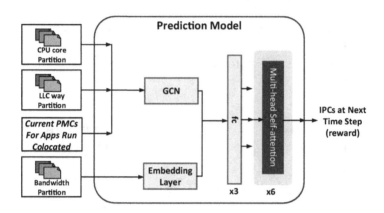

Fig. 7. Design of the prediction model.

4.3 The DRL Decision Making Model

In recent years, deep reinforcement learning (DRL) has been widely used in sequential decision making [28], resource partitioning problems [6,17,33] and achieved good results. So, GCNPart takes DRL algorithm to periodically generates new partitioning decision according to real-time system state, and then applies the decision to the real system.

RL is a method in which the agent selects an action according to the current policy by observing the current environment state, and updates the policy based on the feedback (i.e. the reward from the environment). Policy is learned through interactions with the environment by trial-and-error, with the goal of maximizing cumulative reward over time. Finding the optimal policy is not an easy task. Deep neural networks (DNN) has strong fitting ability to establish the mapping from input to output. It's popular to use DNN to approximate the policy, which we call Deep Reinforcement Learning (DRL). In addition, RL requires a large number of interactions between agent and environment to train the model, the cost of interactions is very expensive [30]. So we build the performance prediction model based on GCN, which can precisely predict the performance of applications under any given partitioning schemes. With the performance model, the DRL model can estimate the reward in the training processes without interacting with the real system, greatly reducing the training overhead.

We formally define the basic concepts (i.e., environment, state, action, policy and reward) of a DRL model in the context of resource partitioning.

Environment. The server is the environment, since we partition resources among applications which is colocating on a server.

State. The real system state of the observed colocation. In our context, the system state $S = (F, C)$, where F denotes the current application features (indicated by PMCs, more details can be found in Sect. 5), C represents the current resource partitioning scheme.

Action. In our context, the action is the resource partitioning decision. $A_t = \{a_t^1, \ldots, a_t^N\}$ denotes the action at time step t, where a_t^i refers to the resource allocation for the i-th application. Note that A_t is a random scheme when collecting data for the prediction model, where A_t is a partitioning decision generated by the DRL model when the colocation running at real environment.

Policy. Our DRL method uses GCN-based prediction model to approximate the policy model. The policy model maps the input (i.e., the system state S_t) to the output (i.e., the partitioning decision A_t). There are three key parts that should be carefully designed for the policy model: the representation of the input features, the GCN-based prediction model and the format of the output.

We represent the input features as a graph, which constructs the mapping relationships from resources to applications. The GCN-based prediction model helps DRL model to estimate the reward of a given action without expensive interactions with the real environment. The output is the real-time resource partitioning decision.

The policy model maps the input (i.e. the system state S_t) to the output (i.e. the partitioning decision A_t). Figure 8 presents the overall design of the DRL model. The DRL model uses the same typical encoder-decoder architecture as DRLPart, while GCNPart learns the policy through graph structure. The encoder takes charge of compositing the input. B_t is mapped to high-dimension through an embedding layer. Then, three fully-connected (fc) layers are used to encode the graph and the output from the embedding layers. The input is fed to the decoder network through an attention layer. The Gated Recurrent Unit (GRU) is commonly used for sequential decision, so the decoder network

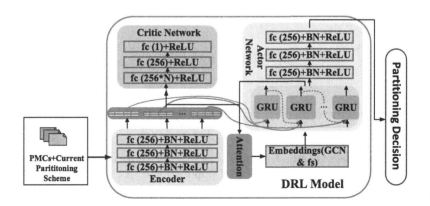

Fig. 8. Design of the DRL model.

adopts GRU to generate the partitioning decision. The policy model is trained by Actor-Critic algorithm.

Note that due to the transition penalty, successive partitioning decisions should not be significantly different. We use a greedy strategy to map the CPU cores to applications. The greedy strategy is guided by *Principle III*, which aims to keep the new allocation of CPU cores as close as possible to that in the current partitioning scheme for minimizing the transition penalty.

Algorithm 1 shows the details. For each application i from 1 to N, we use O_i' to denote the CPU cores allocated to application i, and O_i to denote the CPU cores to be allocated to application i in the partitioning decision. We classify the applications into two sets I and I' (lines 3 to 4), where I denotes the applications whose CPU cores will be decreased (i.e., $c_i < |O_i'|$) and I' denotes the applications whose CPU cores will be increased (i.e., $c_i > |O_i'|$). For each application $i \in I$, we randomly select c_i CPU cores from O_i', and recycle the remaining CPU cores in O_i' to a temporary set T (lines 5 to 8). After that, for each application $i \in I'$, we keep its original CPU cores (i.e., the CPU cores in O_i') and allocate another $c_i - |O_i'|$ CPU cores which are randomly chosen in T (lines 9 to 13).

Algorithm 1. CPU Cores Allocation Algorithm

Require: $O_i' \leftarrow$ the CPU cores allocated to the i-th application in the original partitioning scheme, $1 \le i \le N$
   $c_i \leftarrow$ the number of CPU cores allocated to the i-th application in the partitioning decision, $1 \le i \le N$
Ensure: O_i, the CPU cores allocated to the i-th application in the partitioning decision, $1 \le i \le N$
1: $T \leftarrow \emptyset$, a temporary set
2: $O_i \leftarrow \emptyset$, for $1 \le i \le N$
3: $I \leftarrow \{i | c_i < |O_i'|, 1 \le i \le N\}$
4: $I' \leftarrow \{i | c_i > |O_i'|, 1 \le i \le N\}$
5: **for** each $i \in I$ **do**
6:    randomly move c_i CPU cores from O_i' to O_i
7:    $T \leftarrow T \bigcup O_i'$
8: **end for**
9: **for** each $i \in I'$ **do**
10:    $O_i \leftarrow O_i \bigcup O_i'$
11:    randomly move $c_i - |O_i|$ CPU cores from T to O_i
12:    $T \leftarrow T \bigcup O_i'$
13: **end for**
14: **return** O_i, $1 \le i \le N$

Reward. The goal of resource partitioning is to maximize the system throughput (e.g., the total IPC of all the colocated applications). As mentioned earlier, the system throughput is not only determined by the partitioning scheme, but also affected by the transition penalty. So, the reward is defined as the weighted sum of the system throughput and the transition penalty. Specifically, let $IPC^i_{A_t|S_t}$ denote the IPC of the i-th application if A_t is applied to S_t. The reward for time step t is defined as

$$r_t = \sum_{i=1}^{N} IPC^i_{A_t|S_t} - \alpha Penalty_{A_t|S_t} \tag{1}$$

where $\sum_{i=1}^{N} IPC^i_{A_t|S_t}$ refers to the system throughput, $Penalty_{A_t|S_t}$ denotes the transition penalty and α is the weight of the penalty.

5   Implementation

This section gives the implementation details of the proposed framework.

Selection of the Performance Counters. As mentioned earlier, we use performance counters as the application features at real-time. DRLPart selects the 20 most important PMCs from over 400 PMCs according to their correlations to IPC under different resource partitioning schemes. For fair comparison, we use the same PMCs as it.

Implementation of the GCN-based Prediction Model. We adopt the varietal GCN [15] with Chebyshev filter of size 2 and a latent vector of dimension 257 to process the application features. The embedding layers are composed of neuros of size 3 for both memory bandwidth allocation and the numbers of threads. Three fc layers with neurons of sizes (512, 64, 1) are used to contact the embedding vectors from GCN and embedding layers. We use the rectified nonlinearity (ReLU) [20] as the activation function and add a dropout layer after each fc layer (with probability 0.5) to prevent over-fitting and enhance generalization. The hyperparameters of attention layers are set according to [32]. The model uses Adam optimizer [5] with a learning rate of 10^{-3}, takes *smooth_l1_loss* as the loss function, and is trained in batches with a batch size of 256.

Implementation of the DRL Decision Making Model. For the DRL model, we set the same parameters as [6]. And then we carefully tune the weight of transition penalty (i.e., the parameter α) in the reward, and find that $\alpha = 0.1$ achieves the best performance in our evaluations.

6   Evaluations

We conduct extensive experiments to evaluate the proposed framework and compare it with the state-of-the-art baselines. This section presents the details.

6.1   Experimental Settings

Platform. We implement and evaluate the proposed solution on a 2.20 GHz 10-core Intel® Xeon® Silver 4114 processor. The server has 128 GB memory and provides hardware support of LLC and memory bandwidth partitioning.

The server provides 11 *cache ways* (with 1 MB per cache way) and a total of 2666 MT/s memory bandwidth (10 levels for allocation, from 10% to 100%). The server runs on a CentOS 7.5 with Linux version 4.12.0. For all the experiments, the Hyper Threading and Turbo Boost features of the evaluated CPU are disabled.

Applications. We use the same 120 applications as DRLPart for evaluations, with the applications from SPEC CPU2017 [3], SPEC CPU2006 [2], and *pyperforamce* [1]. We consider an application *Resource Sensitivity* if its performance degradation exceeds 15% when a type of allocated resource are reduced from maximum to minimum when running alone. An application sensitive to only one resource, sensitive to multiple resources, and insensitive to any resources is respectively recorded as *single-sensitive* (Single-S), *multiple-sensitive* (Multi-S), *insensitive* (IN-S).

6.2   Baselines

We compare GCNPart with four state-of-the-art baselines. The first baseline NoPart simply consolidate multiple applications without considering resource partitioning. The second baseline DCAPS [35] considers partitioning LLC only, which determines a partitioning decision by a simulated-annealing-based search, where the performance of partitioning decisions is estimated by a performance model build based on domain knowledge. The third baseline CLITE [25] leverages Bayesian Optimization to build approximate performance model online and uses the performance model to guide searches for the near-optimal partitioning scheme. The last baseline is DRLPart [6], which maps relatively simple relationships from resources to applications for building a DRL-based model to partition resources.

6.3   Performance of the Prediction Model

We first show the performance of the proposed prediction model. We only compare the performance of prediction model with DRLPart, since the other baselines lack the prediction model for evaluating the performance of multi-resource partitioning schemes.

Table 1. Performance of the prediction models over different colocation sizes.

		4-apps	5-apps	6-apps	7-apps
DRLPart	Mean Accuracy	92.87%	95.43%	96.83%	93.52%
	RMSE	0.104	0.047	0.028	0.051
Our	Mean Accuracy	94.97%	97.83%	98.60%	97.53%
	RMSE	0.031	0.010	0.002	0.008

Table 1 compares the mean accuracy and RMSE (root-mean-square error) between the proposed prediction model and the one in DRLPart for different colocation sizes. The mean accuracy is defined by $\frac{1}{n}\sum_{i=1}^{n}|y_i - y_i'|/y_i$, where y_i is the actual observed value and y_i' is the predicted value. Both a higher Mean Accuracy and a smaller RMSE indicate a higher prediction accuracy.

We have two observations from the results. First, our GCN-based prediction model outperforms the one in DRLPart, which improves the mean accuracy by 1.8% (for 4-apps) to 4% (for 7-apps) and decreases the mean RMSE by 0.02 (for 6-app) to 0.05 (for 7-apps). For neural networks, the last 5% accuracy improvement is very difficult. The increase of the accuracy of the prediction model can significantly increase the upper limit of performance improvement. Intuitively, as shown in Fig. 9, GCNPart shows a 6% performance improvement over DRL-Part (9.65% $\rightarrow$ 15.65%). We attribute this to the adoption of GCN, which is more powerful to represent the mapping relationship from resources to applications. Second, the prediction accuracy for 4-apps and 7-apps is slightly worse than other colocation sizes for both models. This is because the colocations with small size have more partitioning schemes and thus more diverse performance, while the colocations with large size should face higher input dimensions and more complex relationships. The accuracy of the prediction model in DRLPart is especially low for small colocation size and large colocation size (only 92.87% and 93.52%), but GCNPart has obvious improvement compared with DRLPart in these two cases. This is because vectors are more affected by size changes than structures, and neural networks should focus on learning high-dimensional maps reflected by structures rather than vector lengths. Compared with taking graph structure as input, training neural network in simple vector form will vary greatly with colocation size, so it will be affected more by size change.

6.4   Overall Performance of the Partitioning Framework

We next show the overall performance of the proposed partitioning framework and other baselines. We randomly generate 400 colocations, with 100 colocations of 4-apps, 5-apps, 6-apps, and 7-apps respectively. The first row in the Table 2 shows the mean throughput of all the colocations achieved by each approach, and the second row shows the throughput improvement of our framework over each baseline.

Table 2. Overall performance of each approach over 400 colocations.

	NoPart	DCAPS	CLITE	DRLPart	Our
Avg. Throughput	7.94	8.25	8.52	9.54	10.05
Throughput Imp.	26.57%	21.81%	17.96%	5.35%	-

We have three observations. First, NoPart performs the worst among all the approaches, with performance loss up to 26.57% (compared to our approach), which confirms the necessity of resource partitioning. Second, our approach outperforms DCAPS, CLITE, with advantage of 21.81% and 17.96% respectively, which demonstrates the advantage of modeling for the resource partitioning problem. Our approach also outperforms DRLPart by 5.35%, which confirms the benefits of improving the accuracy of the prediction model and reducing the transition penalty. The improvement of 5.35% seems not much, because we use random colocations for the experiment, there are colocations that are difficult to improve the performance (such as the Type-D, Type-E, Type-F mentioned in Sect. 6.6).

Figure 9 breaks down the results according to different colocation sizes, where the y-axis represents the throughput improvement of each approach over NoPart. We have two observations from the results. First, our approach always outperforms the baselines, but the advantage is different across different colocation sizes. The proposed framework achieves the highest benefit for the colocation size of 5-apps (33.51%), and less benefit for both small colocation size (e.g., 22.06% for 4-apps) and large colocation size (e.g., 21.64% for 7-apps). The reason is the same as that the accuracy of prediction model is slightly different for different colocation sizes. Second, CLITE performs as bad as NoPart when the colocation size is larger than 5. This is because CLITE is a method based on BO, as the colocation size increases to 6, CLITE fails to make partitioning decision online.

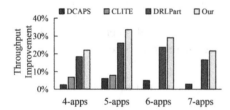

Fig. 9. Breakdown of performance over different colocation sizes.

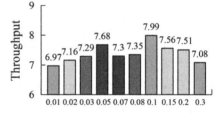

Fig. 10. System throughput for different weight of transition penalty (i.e., α).

6.5   Impact of Transition Penalty

We next show how the transition penalty affects the performance. To this end, we vary the weight (i.e., the parameter α) of the transition penalty in the reward of the DRL model. We randomly generate 30 colocations for each size from 4-apps to 7-apps. Figure 10 shows the average system performance of the 120 colocations for each value of α. We observe that the system achieves the highest throughput for $\alpha = 0.1$, while lower throughout for both small and large α. The results indicate the importance of an appropriate weight for the transition penalty. If the transition penalty is over-weighted (i.e., α is too large), the partitioning decision will be opt to minimizing data migration, which may not be optimal for maximizing system performance. In contrast, if the transition penalty is under-weighted (i.e., α is too small), the partitioning decision will ignore the impact of data migration, which may cause significant performance loss.

6.6   Impact of Resource Sensitivity

Colocations are composed by applications with different resource sensitivities, resulting in different performance improvement boundary from resource parti-tioning. Like DRLPart, colocations are classified into six classes based on the type of applications that colocation contains (see Sect. 6.1). We use the following tuples to indicate which applications each type of colocation contains: Type-A (Multi-S), Type-B (Multi-S, Single-S), Type-C (Multi-S, IN-S), Type-D (Single-S, IN-S), Type-E (Single-S), Type-F (In-S). We generate 100 colocations for each colocation sizes, each colocation is composed by random types and random numbers of applications.

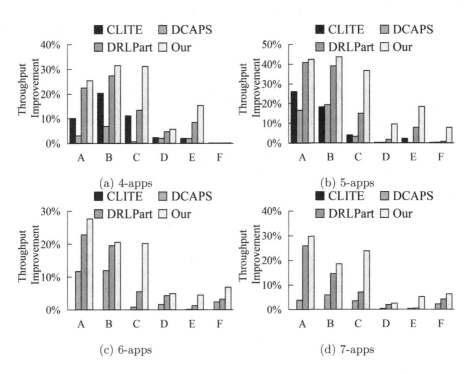

Fig. 11. The throughput improvement of each approach compared to NoPart over different colocation types.

We have several observations from the results in Fig. 11. First, the throughput improvement is more significant for colocations of Type-A, Type-B than other colocation types for most of the approaches. Performance improvements from Type-D and Type-F are always low. This is because the colocation has more sensitive applications is more likely to benefit from resource partitioning because of heavily resource contention. Second, compared to DRLPart, the proposed framework has more significant improvement on Type-C. We attribute this to that the applications in Type-C are significantly different (Multi-S vs. IN-S), so the impact of resource partitioning is more significantly and the partitioning decision should be made more carefully. Third, GCNPart always outperforms the baselines, which confirms that the proposed partitioning framework is more effective to handle complex situations.

7   Related Work

Traditional Resource Partitioning Methods. Resource partitioning for applications with optimization goals (e.g., throughput, fairness) has been extensively studied. Due to the lack of effective resource partitioning tools, the early work [16,27] was based on emulators to simulate the partitioning performance, which was far from the behaviors of the actual system. Recent approaches using Intel CAT and MBA technologies to isolate LLC and MB, generally give resource partitioning decisions based on the following two ways. The first is to adjust decisions online without performance model according to expert-designed rules or black-box methods. However, the experts can only make simple rules, which are expensive with poor portability, such as [7,9,22,36,37][?]. As the scale of resources and applications increases, black-box methods [25,29] such as BO often fail to make decisions. The second way [14,19,24,31] is to build a dedicated performance model and design heuristics to make decisions. However, such solutions basically rely heavily on experts and cannot easily be extended to multiple resources.

Machine Learning for Resource Management. Machine Learning has been applied to resource management problems in recent years. [17,33] use RL to decide the application placement on the cluster. [12] aims to maximize the net profit of cloud provider by building the DRL model to learn resource partitioning and pricing policy. However, the methods mentioned above fail to consider the performance interference. [8,13] which consider the performance interference construct machine learning models to predict the performance among colocated applications. However, resource partitioning is not considered in these approaches. DRLPart is the fist attempt to adopt DRL for multiple-resources partitioning problem.

8   Limitations

The limitation of the proposed framework is that it cannot be used in scenarios where the application is running for a short time (e.g., serverless services) and there are execution dependencies between the applications (e.g., loose-coupled microservices). This is because services such as serverless services usually can run within a minute, the benefit from resource partitioning cannot keep up with the speed at which the services run out. Loose-coupled microservices are composed of cascaded services, and the performance of the applications in the current layer is not known to be affected by the applications in the previous layer. This is not the focus of this paper, need to have another design.

9   Conclusion

In this paper, we propose a resource partitioning framework based on deep learning for improving system throughput on commodity servers. We solve the resource partitioning problem by formulating it as a sequential decision problem. First, we leverage GCN to construct an accurate performance prediction model to evaluate the resource partitioning schemes where the model learns application interference and resource contention directly and greatly assists in online partitioning decisions. Then, we propose a DRL partitioning decision making model, which takes temporal information into consideration and then generates optimal successive partitioning decisions. We conduct abundant experiments to evaluate the proposed framework and the results show that GCNPart is superior to the baselines. In the future, we would like to extend the framework to cover more scenarios and more optimization goals.

Acknowledgment. This work is supported by Key-Area Research and Development Program of Guangdong Province 2021B0101310002; State Key Laboratory of Computer Architecture, ICT, CAS, under Grant No. CARCHB202013; National Science Foundation of China (62141412, 61872201); Science and Technology Development Plan of Tianjin (20JCZDJC00610); Fundamental Research Funds for the Central Universities.

References

1. The python performance benchmark suite. https://pyperformance.readthedocs.io/ (2006)
2. The spec cpu®2006 benchmark suite. https://www.spec.org/cpu2006/ (2006)
3. The spec cpu®2017 benchmark suite. https://www.spec.org/cpu2017/ (2017)
4. Andrew, H., Abbasi, K.M., Marcel, C.: Introduction to memory bandwidth allocation. https://software.intel.com/en-us/articles/introduction-to-memory-bandwidth-allocation (2019)
5. Brownlee, J.: Gentle introduction to the adam optimization algorithm for deep learning. Machine Learning Mastery 3 (2017)
6. Chen, R., Wu, J., Shi, H., Li, Y., Liu, X., Wang, G.: DRLPart: a deep reinforcement learning framework for optimally efficient and robust resource partitioning on commodity servers. In: Proceedings of the 30th International Symposium on High-Performance Parallel and Distributed Computing, pp. 175–188. Association for Computing Machinery (2020)
7. Chen, S., Delimitrou, C., Martínez, F.J.: Parties: QoS-aware resource partitioning for multiple interactive services. In: Proceedings of the Twenty-Fourth International Conference on Architectural Support for Programming Languages and Operating Systems (ASPLOS), pp. 107–120 (2019)

8. Cheng, Y., Chen, W., Wang, Z., Xiang, Y.: Precise contention-aware performance prediction on virtualized multicore system. J. Syst. Archit. **72**, 42–50 (2017)
9. Delimitrou, C., Kozyrakis, C.: QoS-aware scheduling in heterogeneous datacenters with paragon
10. Delimitrou, C., Kozyrakis, C.: Paragon: QoS-aware scheduling for heterogeneous datacenters. In: Proceedings of the 18th International Conference on Architectural Support for Programming Languages and Operating Systems (ASPLOS). vol. 48, pp. 77–88. ACM (2013)
11. Delimitrou, C., Kozyrakis, C.: Quasar: resource-efficient and QoS-aware cluster management. ACM SIGPLAN Notices **49**(4), 127–144 (2014)
12. Du, B., Wu, C., Huang, Z.: Learning resource allocation and pricing for cloud profit maximization. In: The Thirty-Third AAAI Conference on Artificial Intelligence (AAAI-19) (2019)
13. Dublish, S., Nagarajan, V., Topham, N.: Poise: Balancing thread-level parallelism and memory system performance in GPUs using machine learning. In: 2019 IEEE International Symposium on High Performance Computer Architecture (HPCA), pp. 492–505 (2019)
14. El-Sayed, N., Mukkara, A., Tsai, P.A., Kasture, H., Ma, X., Sanchez, D.: Kpart: A hybrid cache partitioning-sharing technique for commodity multicores. In: 2018 IEEE International Symposium on High Performance Computer Architecture (HPCA), pp. 104–117. IEEE (2018)
15. Hammond, D.K., Vandergheynst, P., Gribonval, R.: Wavelets on graphs via spectral graph theory. Applied and Computational Harmonic Analysis **30**(2), 129–150 (2011). https://doi.org/10.1016/j.acha.2010.04.005, https://www.sciencedirect.com/science/article/pii/S1063520310000552
16. Kasture, H., Sanchez, D.: Ubik: efficient cache sharing with strict QoS for latency-critical workloads. In: Proceedings of the 19th international conference on Architectural support for programming languages and operating systems (ASPLOS), vol. 49, pp. 729–742 (2014)
17. Li, S., Wang, L., Wang, W., Yu, Y., Li, B.: George: Learning to place long-lived containers in large clusters with operation constraints. In: Proceedings of the ACM Symposium on Cloud Computing, pp. 258–272 (2021)
18. Lo, D., Cheng, L., Govindaraju, R., Ranganathan, P., Kozyrakis, C.: Heracles: Improving resource efficiency at scale. In: International Symposium on Computer Architecture (ISCA), vol. 43, pp. 450–462. ACM (2015)
19. Mars, J., Tang, L., Hundt, R., Skadron, K., Soffa, M.L.: Bubble-up: Increasing utilization in modern warehouse scale computers via sensible co-locations. In: Proceedings of the 44th annual IEEE/ACM International Symposium on Microarchitecture, pp. 248–259 (2011)
20. Nair, V., Hinton, G.E.: Rectified linear units improve restricted boltzmann machines. In: ICML (2010)
21. Nguyen, K.T.: Introduction to cache allocation technology in the intel® xeon® processor e5 v4 family. https://software.intel.com/en-us/articles/introduction-to-cache-allocation-technology/ (2019)
22. Nikas, K., Papadopoulou, N., Giantsidi, D., Karakostas, V., Goumas, G., Koziris, N.: Dicer: Diligent cache partitioning for efficient workload consolidation. In: Proceedings of the 48th International Conference on Parallel Processing, p. 15 (2019)
23. Park, J., Park, S., Baek, W.: Copart: Coordinated partitioning of last-level cache and memory bandwidth for fairness-aware workload consolidation on commodity servers. In: Proceedings of the Fourteenth EuroSys Conference 2019, pp. 1–10 (2019)

24. Park, J., Park, S., Han, M., Hyun, J., Baek, W.: Hypart: A hybrid technique for practical memory bandwidth partitioning on commodity servers. In: Proceedings of the 27th International Conference on Parallel Architectures and Compilation Techniques, pp. 1–14 (2018)
25. Patel, T., Tiwari, D.: Clite: Efficient and QoS-aware co-location of multiple latency-critical jobs for warehouse scale computers. In: 2020 IEEE International Symposium on High Performance Computer Architecture (HPCA), pp. 193–206 (2020). https://doi.org/10.1109/HPCA47549.2020.00025
26. Pelikan, M., Sastry, K., Goldberg, D.E.: Scalability of the Bayesian optimization algorithm. Int. J. Approximate Reasoning **31**(3), 221–258 (2002)
27. Qureshi, M.K., Patt, Y.N.: Utility-based cache partitioning: A low-overhead, high-performance, runtime mechanism to partition shared caches. In: Proceedings of the 39th Annual IEEE/ACM International Symposium on Microarchitecture, pp. 423–432 (2006)
28. Roijers, D.M., Vamplew, P., Whiteson, S., Dazeley, R.: A survey of multi-objective sequential decision-making. J. Artif. Intell. Res. **48**, 67–113 (2013)
29. Roy, R.B., Patel, T., Tiwari, D.: Satori: efficient and fair resource partitioning by sacrificing short-term benefits for long-term gains. In: 2021 ACM/IEEE 48th Annual International Symposium on Computer Architecture (ISCA), pp. 292–305. IEEE (2021)
30. Sutton, R.S., Barto, A.G.: Reinforcement learning: an introduction. MIT press (2018)
31. Tang, L., Mars, J., Vachharajani, N., Hundt, R., Soffa, M.L.: The impact of memory subsystem resource sharing on datacenter applications. In: 2011 38th Annual International Symposium on Computer Architecture (ISCA), pp. 283–294. IEEE (2011)
32. Vaswani, A., et al.: Attention is all you need. In: Advances in neural information processing systems, pp. 5998–6008 (2017)
33. Wang, L., Weng, Q., Wang, W., Chen, C., Li, B.: Metis: Learning to schedule long-running applications in shared container clusters at scale. In: SC20: International Conference for High Performance Computing, Networking, Storage and Analysis, pp. 1–17. IEEE (2020)
34. Wu, Z., Pan, S., Chen, F., Long, G., Yu, P.S.: A comprehensive survey on graph neural networks (2019)
35. Xiang, Y., Wang, X., Huang, Z., Wang, Z., Luo, Y., Wang, Z.: Dcaps: dynamic cache allocation with partial sharing. In: Proceedings of the Thirteenth EuroSys Conference 2018, p. 13 (2018)
36. Xiao, J., Pimentel, A.D., Liu, X.: CPPF: A prefetch aware LLC partitioning approach. In: Proceedings of the 48th International Conference on Parallel Processing, pp. 1–10 (2019)
37. Xu, C., Rajamani, K., Ferreira, A., Felter, W., Rubio, J., Li, Y.: DCAT: dynamic cache management for efficient, performance-sensitive infrastructure-as-a-service. In: Proceedings of the Thirteenth EuroSys Conference 2018, p. 14 (2018)

PipeFB: An Optimized Pipeline Parallelism Scheme to Reduce the Peak Memory Usage

Wei Jiang[✉], Bo Wang[✉], Sheng Ma[✉], Xiang Hou, Libo Huang, Yi Dai, and Jianbin Fang

National University of Defense Technology, Changsha, China
{jiangwei,bowang,masheng,houxiang,libohuang,daiyi,j.fang}@nudt.edu.cn

Abstract. Neural network models is developing toward deeper and wider to obtain higher accuracy and robustness. However, the limited physical memory capacity of existing hardware devices limits the scale of the neural network that can be trained, and the limited computing capacity resulting in excessively long training time. Therefore, the distributed parallelism scheme based on multi-accelerator machines becomes an effective method to training large-scale neural networks. The pipeline parallelism is one of the distributed parallelism scheme, which has large advantages in the training speed. But it also significantly increases the peak memory usage and communication overhead, because it needs to store multiply versions of activations. Our previous work has proposed a data transfer mechanism and applied it to the PipeDream design (a mature pipeline parallelism scheme), which offloads activations in the pipeline to other memory devices, such as the CPU memory. The data transfer mechanism greatly reduces the peak memory usage of the PipeDream, but it brings a large amount of communication, which makes the PipeDream lost a lot of training speed.

This paper proposes an optimized pipeline parallelism scheme, the PipeFB, for applying the data transfer mechanism. The PipeFB deploys the forward propagation and backward propagation of the neural network on different computing nodes, which is different from the traditional pipeline parallelism scheme. We implements the PipeFB and applies the data transfer mechanism to it. The experimental results shows that our design has the same peak memory usage as the PipeDream with the data transfer mechanism, but the training speed of our design is 1.48 to 2.27 times faster.

Keywords: Neural network training · Distributed parallelism · Pipeline parallelism · Data transferring mechanism

This work is supported in part by the National Key R&D Project No.2021YFB0300300, the NSFC (62172430, 61872374, 62272476), the NSF of Hunan Province (2021JJ10052, 2022JJ10064).

W. Jiang, B. Wang and S. Ma—Contribute equally to this work.

W. Meng et al. (Eds.): ICA3PP 2022, LNCS 13777, pp. 590–604, 2023.
https://doi.org/10.1007/978-3-031-22677-9_31

1   Introduction

Deep learning neural networks have been successfully applied in several fields such as the computer vision [11,19,21], speech recognition [6,9], natural language processing [3,7], recommendation system [2,18] etc. Since the DNN was proposed, a large number of new neural network models have been emerging, and these models are becoming deeper and wider. At the same time, the development of big data technology provides a large amount of data [8,25], which makes the scale of the dataset for machine learning increases rapidly. The increase in the size of network models and the dataset makes the neural network training becomes difficult. However, researchers are still willing to increase the depth of the network model to obtain higher accuracy and robustness, although it will increase training cost.

With the existing hardware technology [4,5,14], the limited physical memory capacity of the device limits the scale of the network model that can be trained [20], and the limited computing capacity leads to an excessively long training time [24]. Therefore, the distributed parallelism scheme becomes a commonly method for the large-scale neural network training. The distributed parallelism scheme deploys multiple accelerators on one machine or deploys multiple machines to form a cluster, which accommodates large-scale neural network models by gathering the physical memory capacity of multiple accelerators, and effectively speed up training by parallelizing the computation.

The pipeline parallelism scheme is one of the distributed parallelism schemes, which has obvious advantages in the training speed [10,12,26]. But it induces excessive communication overhead and peak memory usage, which limit its performance. Our previous work proposed a data transfer mechanism [13] and apply it to the PipeDream [10](a mature pipeline parallelism scheme). The data transfer mechanism offloads the activations in the pipeline to other memory devices, which reduces the peak memory usage of the PipeDream, but it also makes the PipeDream lost a lot of training speed. This is due to that applying the data transfer mechanism introduces a large amount of communication.

This paper analyzes the communication of the PipeDream and the data transfer mechanism, and proposes an optimized pipeline parallelism scheme: PipeFB. The PipeFB deploys the forward propagation and backward propagation of the training process on different computing nodes, which changes the communication behavior of the pipeline. And that's why we named it PipeFB. The PipeFB applies the data transfer mechanism by only inducing a small impact on training speed. In the experiment, we implements the PipeFB and applies the data transfer mechanism to it. The experimental results show that our design has the same peak memory usage as the PipeDream with the data transfer mechanism, but the training speed is 1.48 to 2.27 times faster.

2   Related Work

2.1   Memory Optimization on a Single Device

During the training process, the temporary data that needs to be used or generated is preferably placed in the memory device that is close to the computing core, which ensures the data supply match the throughput of the computing core. However, the memory capacity of existing hardware devices is usually limited. Previous researches have made several explorations to address this challenge.

The training process requires storing the activations of each layer and can not discard it until the backword propagation is finished. Based on this observation, some existing neural network frameworks (torch [15], tensorflow [1], etc.) are configured with an optional recomputation function. This function deletes the activations, then recomputes it in the backward propagation. This method significantly reduces the peak memory usage of training process, but recomputing activations incurs a large time overhead.

The vDNN [16] proposes a prefetching and offloading technique. It offloads the activations to the CPU memory and retrieves the data back when they are needed. This method reduces the peak memory usage, but it brings large amount of communications which slows down the training process. Therefore, Rhu et al. further proposes a CDMA compression engine [17]. The CDMA engine compresses the activations before offloading it to the CPU memory, which relieves the communication pressure.

The SuperNeurons [23] proposes a method that combines the data offloading and the recomputing function. It offloads the output of the layers which consume a large amount of computing resources (the Convolution layer etc.), and recomputes the output of other layers which consume less computing resources (the Pooling layer and the ReLU layer etc.).

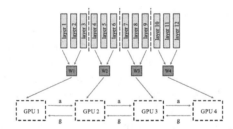

Fig. 1. The network model dividing and deploying process. The 'a' is activations and the 'g' is gradients. The 'w' is the parameter of network, i.e. weight.

2.2   Distributed Parallelism Scheme

The distributed Parallelism Scheme are suitable for training tasks which limited by memory capacity and computing capacity. One type of this scheme needs to divide the network model into multiply modules and deploy them to different computer nodes. Figure 1 displays the dividing and deploying process. A 12-layer network model is divided into 4 network modules, and then these modules are deployed to 4 GPUs respectively. Each GPU only needs to calculate its own module, and communicate with other GPUs.

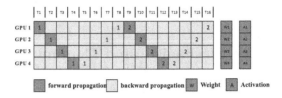

(a) The training process of the model parallelism scheme.

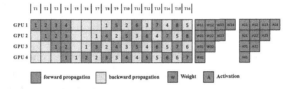

(b) The training process of the PipeDream.

Fig. 2. The blue square is forward propagation and the orange square is backpropagation. The number in the middle of the square is the ID of the mini-batch. (Color figure online)

Figure 2a displays the training process of the model parallelism scheme. The network model is divided and deployed according to the method of Fig. 1. In forward propagation, each GPU receives upstream output to compute its own module, then sends its output to the downstream GPU. And this operation is reversed in the backward propagation phase. The model parallelism scheme has the quite low memory usage because each GPU stores only one version of the weights and activations, and its training speed is quite slow because only one GPU is working at each moment.

The PipeDream [10] is a mature and representative work of pipeline parallelism schemes. Figure 2b displays the training process of the PipeDream. The PipeDream also adopts the network dividing and deploying method of Fig. 1. When each GPU completes the backward propagation of the first mini-batch, they enter a stable scheduling state of 1F1B(1 forward and 1 backward). In this state, each GPU strictly switches the forward and backward computation. If ignoring the communication delay, all GPUs are working at each moment, so the PipeDream has the high training speed.

Since multiple mini-batchs are performed in parallelism, the PipeDream introduces the weight stashing mechanism to avoid mismatching of weights and gradients. Under this mechanism, the corresponding weights and activations of each mini-batch that unfinished will be stored, which will be selected for computing gradient in backward propagation. Meanwhile, the interval between the forward and backward propagation of the front GPU is longer than that in the rear GPU, so the front GPU stores more versions of data. Therefore, The PipeDream not only has extremely high peak memory usage, but also has unbalanced memory usage among different GPUs. Even the PipeDream use the recomputation function, its peak memory usage is still high.

3   Data Transfer Mechanism and Communication Analysis

Our previous work proposes a data transfer mechanism which reduces the peak memory usage of the PipeDream [13]. But it makes the PipeDream lost a lot of training speed.

3.1   Data Transfer Mechanism

The data transfer mechanism offloads activations of the pipeline to other memory devices and retrieves the data back when it is needed, which reduces the peak memory usage. And our work only transfers the activations, because the memory usage of the activations is far more than the other data. There are two destinations for offloading, one is the free memory of the other GPUs in the pipeline (the memory usage of the rear GPU is much less than that of the front GPU), and the other is the CPU memory. The former is named as G-transfer and the latter is named as C-transfer.

G-transfer. Figure 3 displays the training process of the PipeDream with G-transfer. The G-transfer mechanism offloads the activations to the free memory of the rear GPU, and then retrieves the activations back in the backward propagation. Since the memory capacity of the rear GPU is limited, the G-transfer sets a constraint mechanism to prevent excessive transmission. When the memory usage of the rear GPU exceeds the front GPU, the G-transfer stops the new data transferring until the rear GPU sends some data back and releases new space. After the PipeDream applies the G-transfer, the amount of data in the front GPU is decreased, so the peak memory usage of the pipeline is decreased.

C-transfer. Figure 4 displays the training process of the PipeDream with C-transfer. The C-transfer offloads the activation to CPU memory, and then retrieves the activations back in the backward propagation. Due to the capacity of the CPU memory is large, all versions of activations can be offloaded. So each GPU immediately offloads the data to the CPU memory once they finish the forward propagation. After the PipeDream applies the C-transfer, the amount of versions of activations stored in each GPU is reduced to 1. Therefore, the peak memory usage of the pipeline is significantly decreased.

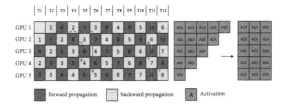

Fig. 3. Training process of the PipeDream with G-transfer.

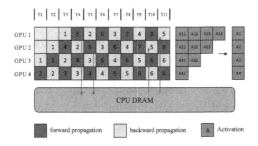

Fig. 4. Training process of the PipeDream with C-transfer.

3.2   Communication Analysis

Before analysis the communication of the PipeDream, there is a concept that needs to be declared. The pipeline parallelism and the model parallelism scheme involved in this paper use the recomputation function, so one version of activations actually only contains the input of the upper boundary layer and the output of the lower boundary layer of the network module deployed in the GPU. And the output of the upstream GPU is actually the input of the downstream GPU. The communication traffic of activations of one boundary layers is considered as 1a, and the communication traffic of gradient is considered as 1g.

Communication Analysis of the PipeDream. Figure 5 displays the communication of the PipeDream, which picks a complete training process of one mini-batch. Completing this process requires 4 times communications of activations and 4 times communications of gradient. Since the execution of different mini-batches is is parallelized, multiply GPUs needs communicate with others at the same time, which resulting in high pressure on the communication bandwidth.

Communication Analysis of the Pipedream with the G-transfer. Figure 6 displays the communication of the PipeDream with the G-transfer. The GPU 1 finishes the forward propagation at time T1 and immediately sends its output to the GPU 2. Then the GPU 1 offloads its output to the GPU 5 and GPU 4 simultaneously, because the output of GPU 1 is the input of GPU 2.

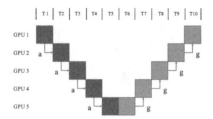

Fig. 5. Communication of the PipeDream.

So the added communication traffic of this process is 1a. The GPU 2 needs to offloads its output to the GPU 4 at time T4, and the added communication traffic is 1a. At this point both GPU 1 and GPU 2 have offloaded a complete activations. In the backward propagation, the GPU 1 and GPU 2 retrieve the complete activations, and the added communication traffic is 1a and 2a respectively. Therefore, the added communication traffic of the PipeDream applying the G-transfer is 5a.

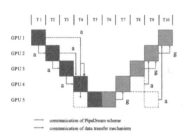

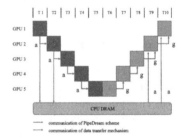

Fig. 6. Communication of the PipeDream with G-transfer.

Fig. 7. Communication of the PipeDream with C-transfer.

Communication Analysis of Pipedream Combined with C-transfer.
Figure 7 displays the communication of the PipeDream with the C-transfer. When the GPU 1 sends its output to the GPU 2, the data are sended to GPU 2 through the PCIe switch and the CPU memory, so it can be received by CPU memory in the same time. So this process is regarded as once communication, and the offloading process has no added communication traffic. Then the GPU 2 offloads its output in a same manner. The GPU 2 needn't to offload its input because its input is the output of GPU 1, and the GPU 1 had sended its output to the CPU memory. In backward propagation, the GPU 1 and GPU 2 retrieves the complete activations, and the added communication traffic is 1a and 2a respectively. Therefore, the added communication traffic of the PipeDream applying the C-transfer is 3a.

4 Design of the PipeFB

4.1 Network Dividing and Deploying Method of PipeFB

The PipeFB adopts the same network model dividing method as the PipeDream scheme, but it deploys the forward propagation and backward propagation of the network module on different GPUs. Figure 8 displays the dividing and deploying process of the PipeFB. In a 5-stage pipeline platform, the PipeFB divides the network model into 3 modules, and then deploys the forward propagation on the GPU 1, GPU 2 and GPU3; deploys the backward propagation on the GPU 3, GPU 4 and GPU5.

The GPU 1 and GPU 2 need to send its output to the downstream GPU, and send the complete activations to the GPU 4 and GPU 5 for the backward propagation. The GPU 4 and GPU 5 need to receive activation from the GPU 1 and GPU 2 to perform the backward propagation, and need to send the updated weights to GPU 1 and GPU 2.

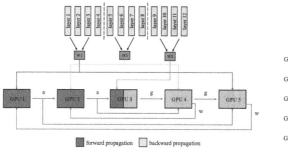

Fig. 8. The network dividing and deploying method of PipeFB. The 'a' is activations and the 'g' is gradients. The 'w' is the parameter of network, i.e. weight.

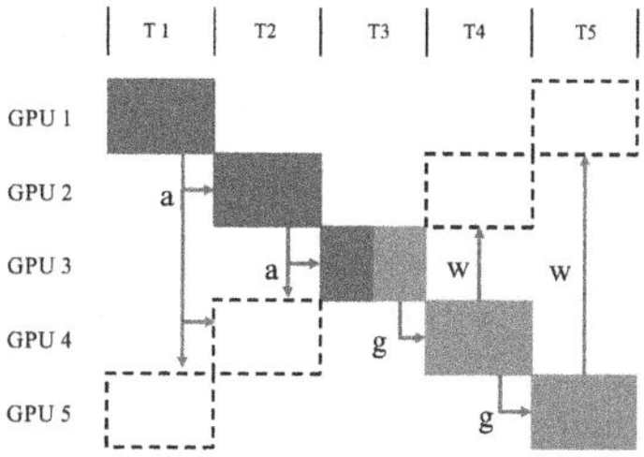

Fig. 9. Communication of the PipeFB.

4.2 Communication Analysis of PipeFB

The PipeFB also uses the recomputation function by default like the PipeDream, so the versions of activations of the PipeFB have the same characteristics as that of the PipeDream, as we reminded in Sect. 3.2. The communication traffic of activations of one boundary layers is considered as 1a, and the communication traffic of gradients and weights is considered as 1g and 1w.

Figure 9 displays the communication of the PipeFB. Taking the GPU 1 as an example, the GPU 1 sends its output to the GPU 2, GPU 4 and GPU 5, and the communication traffic is 1a. The GPU 1 sends its output to the GPU 4 because its output is the input of the GPU 2, so the GPU 2 needn't to send its input to the GPU 4 anymore. Then the GPU 2 sends its output to the GPU 4 and GPU 5, and the communication traffic is 1a. So the total communication traffic of activations in the PipeFB is 2a. Plus the communication of weights and gradients, the total communication traffic of the PipeFB is 2a+2w+2g.

4.3   Training Process of PipeFB

Figure 10 displays the training process of the PipeFB. Since the forward and backward propagation of the network modules are deployed separately, the training process can be arranged in a pipeline parallelism manner without using any scheduling method such as 1F1B.

Due to the GPU 4 and GPU 5 performs the backward propagation, they receives the activations from the GPU 1 and GPU 2 for computing gradients, and the received data will not be used until the backward propagation. Therefore, the GPU 4 and GPU 5 need to store multi-version of activations and weights. The GPU 1 and GPU 2 discard activations and weights are discarded after the forward propagation, so they needs to store only one version of data. The GPU 3 also needs to store only one version of data, because it performs backward propagation immediately after forward propagation. Therefore, the peak memory usage of the PipeFB usually occurs in the last GPU.

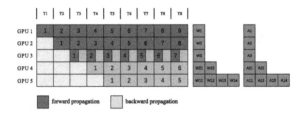

Fig. 10. Training process of the PipeFB. The blue square is forward propagation, and the orange square is backpropagation. The number in the middle of the square is the ID of the mini-batch. (Color figure online)

5   PipeFB with the Data Transfer Mechanism

5.1   PipeFB Applies the G-transfer

In the PipeFB scheme, the memory usage of the GPU deployed at the rear position is larger than the GPU deployed in front position, because the rear GPU stores more versions of activations and weights. However, the activations is generated in the front GPU. Therefore, the way the PipeFB applies G-transfer is actually by delaying the initiation time of the offloading to make some versions of activations stored in the front GPU.

Figure 11 displays the training process of the PipeFB with G-transfer. Taking the GPU 1 and GPU 5 as an example, the GPU 1 finishes the forward propagation at time T1, but sends its activations to the GPU 5 at time T3. Through controlling the initiation time of the offloading, at time T5, the GPU 1 stores two versions of activations, which belong to the mini-batch 3 and mini-batch 4; and the GPU 5 also stores two versions of activations, which belong to the mini-batch 1 and mini-batch 2. Since the GPU 4 stores only two versions of activations in the original PipeFB, there is no need to perform G-transfer between the GPU 2 and GPU 4. In such a 5-stage pipeline platform, the amount of versions of activations of the PipeFB is reduced from 4 to 2 after it applies the G-transfer, which reduces the peak memory usage.

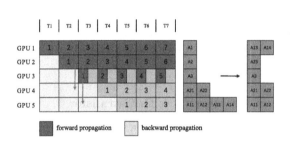

Fig. 11. Training process of the PipeFB with G-transfer.

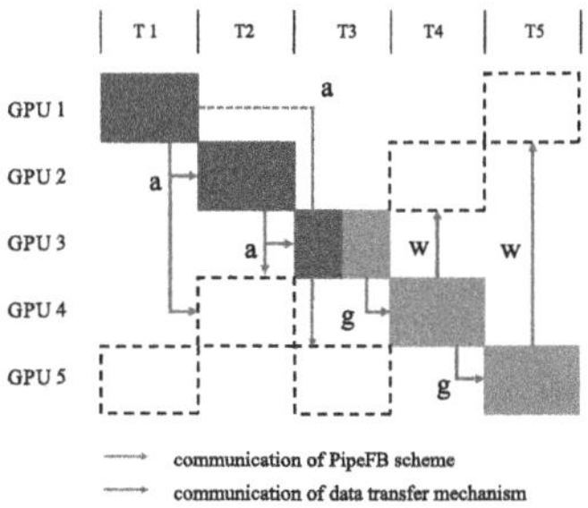

Fig. 12. Communication of the PipeFB with G-transfer.

5.2   Communication Analysis of the PipeFB with G-transfer

Figure 12 displays the communication of the PipeFB with G-transfer. The GPU 1 finishes the forward propagation at time T1, but sends its output to GPU 5 at time T3, and the added communication traffic is 1a. At this point the GPU 1 have offloaded its complete activations because the activations contains only the output of the lower boundary layer. Therefore, the PipeFB applies the G-transfer only increases the communication traffic of 1a, which is much less than the PipeDream applies the G-transfer(5a).

5.3   PipeFB Applyies the C-transfer

When the PipeFB applies the C-transfer, the front GPU offloads its activations to the CPU memory, then the rear GPU retrieves the activations from CPU memory. Figure 13 displays the training process of the PipeFB with the C-transfer. The GPU 1 and GPU 2 offload its activations to CPU memory. Then, the GPU 4 and GPU 5 retrieve the corresponding activations from the CPU memory to perform the backward propagation. In the 5-stage pipeline platform, the amount of versions of activations of the PipeFB is reduced from 4 to 1 after it applies the C-transfer, which significantly reduces peak memory usage.

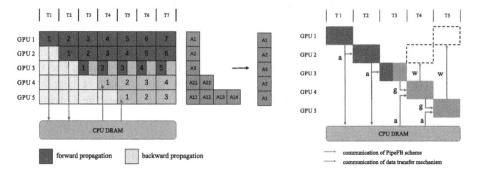

Fig. 13. Training process of the PipeFB with C-transfer.

Fig. 14. Communication of the PipeFB with C-transfer.

5.4 Communication Analysis of the PipeFB with C-transfer

Figure 14 displays the communication of the PipeFB with C-transfer. Taking the GPU 1 and GPU 5 as an example, when the GPU 1 sends its output to the GPU 2, the data are sended to GPU 2 through the PCIe switch and the CPU memory, so it can be received by CPU memory at the same time. This process is regarded as once communication, so it introduces no added communication traffic. At time T2, the GPU 2 sends its output to GPU 3 and CPU memory in same manner. The GPU 2 needn't to send its input, because its input is the output of GPU 1, and the GPU 1 had sended its output to CPU memory. Then the GPU 4 and GPU 5 retrieve the complete activations from the CPU memory, and the communication traffic is 1a and 2a respectively. Therefore, the total added communication traffic of the PipeFB applying C-transfer is 3a.

5.5 Summary

Table 1 summarizes the communication traffic of each scheme. The memory usage of the weights is quite small compared to activations and gradients, so the communication overhead of the weights can be ignored. Therefore, the PipeFB with the data transfer mechanism has far less communication overhead than the PipeDream with the data transfer mechanism.

Table 1. The communication traffic of each scheme.

		Original traffic	Added traffic	Total traffic
Pipedream	Pipedream	$4a + 4g$	0	$4a + 4g$
	G-transfer	$4a + 4g$	$5a$	$9a + 4g$
	C-transfer	$4a + 4g$	$2a$	$6a + 4g$
PipeFB	PipeFB	$2a + 2g + 2w$	0	$2a + 2g + 2w$
	G-transfer	$2a + 2g + 2w$	$1a$	$3a + 2g + 2w$
	C-transfer	$2a + 2g + 2w$	$3a$	$5a + 2g + 2w$

6 Evaluation

This paper establish a platform, which deploys 7 GPUs of RTX2070super. The GPUs communicate through the PCIe channel, and the PCIe bandwidth is 16GB/s. In the experiment, we select the AlexNet [22], VGG-16 [19] and ResNet-50 [11] as benchmark network, and we select 20 classes of Imagenet [8] as the benchmark dataset. We divide the network model into 5 modules when deploying the model parallelism scheme and the PipeDream scheme, and divide the network model into 3 modules when deploying the PipeFB scheme.

In the experiment, we apply the data transfer mechanism to the PipeFB and PipeDream scheme, and we call them PipeFB-G, PipeFB-C, PipeDream-G and PipeDream-C respectively.

6.1 Memory Usage Test

Figures 15, 16 and Fig. 17 display the memory usage of each scheme. Due to the problem of storing multiply versions of data, the peak memory usage of the PipeFB is high and close to that of the PipeDream. When the PipeFB applies the G-transfer and trains the three network models, its peak memory usage are reduced by 12.7%, 14.5%, and 19.6% respectively. The G-transfer has limited effect in reducing the peak memory usage because it only offloads partial versions of activations. In addition, the memory usage of GPU 1 and GPU 2 is increased because the G-transfer keeps some versions of activations in the front GPU.

When the PipeFB applies the C-transfer and trains the three network models, its peak memory usage are reduced by 22.0%, 26.5%, and 58.6% respectively, which is much less than that of the PipeFB-G. And the peak memory usage of the PipeFB-C is close to that of the model parallelism scheme. The C-transfer has significantly effect in reducing memory usage because it offloads all versions of activations.

Compared with the PipeDream-G and PipeDream-C, the PipeFB-G and PipeFB-C have the same low peak memory usage.

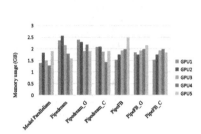

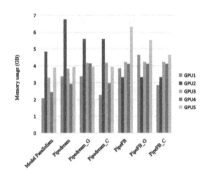

Fig. 15. Memory usage of each scheme when training AlexNet.

Fig. 16. Memory usage of each scheme when training VGG-16.

6.2   Training Speed Test

We evaluate training speed by testing the time that each schemes finish a fixed epoch. Figure 18 displays the training speed of each scheme. When the PipeFB applies the G-transfer and trains the three network models, its training speed loses 4.55%, 9.82% and 5.94% respectively. And when the PipeFB applies the C-transfer, its training speed loses 33.9%, 19.4% and 18.7%. The training speed lost caused by the G-transfer is less than the C-transfer, because the G-transfer introduces less communication overhead. When the PipeDream applies the data transfer mechanism, its training speed loss caused by G-transfer and C-transfer is at most 61.2% and 67.5% respectively. The experiment shows that the PipeFB applies the data transfer mechanism has a much lower cost than the PipeDream.

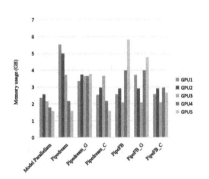

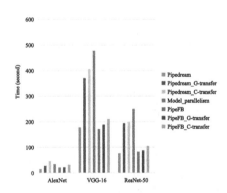

Fig. 17. Memory usage of each scheme when training ResNet-50.

Fig. 18. Training speed of each scheme.

The PipeFB-C has a large speed loss when trains the AlexNet. That's because the AlexNet's model is small, so its communication overhead is relatively large compared with its computation overhead. Therefore, the impact of added communication of the C-transfer in training speed is greater. However, in applications, there is no need to deploy the pipeline parallelism scheme to train small networks like the AlexNet. So we focus on the large scale network model such as the VGG-16 and ResNet-50, and we can see the PipeFB-G and PipeFB-C can still maintain most of the training speed of the PipeFB. The experiment shows that the PipeFB with the data transfer mechanism is more suitable for training the network model with a larger amount of computation.

When training the VGG-16 and ResNet-50, the PipeFB and PipeDream apply the data transfer mechanism have close effect on reducing the peak memory usage, but the former is 1.48 to 2.27 times faster than the latter. Especially, the PipeFB-C has the same low peak memory usage as the model parallelism scheme, but the PipeFB-C is 2.26 to 2.46 times faster, while the PipeDream-C is only 1.28 to 1.67 times faster. So the experiment shows that the PipeFB applies the data transfer mechanism can greatly reduce the memory usage and maintain the training speed advantage of the pipeline parallelism.

7   Conclusion

The traditional pipeline parallelism schemes apply the data transfer mechanism to reduces the peak memory usage will lost a lot of training speed. We propose an optimized pipeline parallelism scheme: PipeFB. The PipeFB applies the data transfer mechanism can greatly reduce the peak memory usage and maintain the training speed. This contribution enables the pipeline parallelism scheme to train more larger network models and keep its training speed advantage. Further work will explore how to optimize the communication such as utilizing the data compression.

References

1. Tensorflow: Large-scale machine learning on heterogeneous distributed systems (2016)
2. Abdollahi, B., Nasraoui, O.: Explainable restricted boltzmann machines for collaborative filtering (2016)
3. Athiwaratkun, B., Wilson, A.G.: Multimodal word distributions (2017)
4. Chen, T., et al.: DianNao: a small-footprint high-throughput accelerator for ubiquitous machine-learning. ACM Sigplan Notices 49(4), 269–284 (2014)
5. Chetlur, S., Woolley, C., Vandermersch, P., Cohen, J., Shelhamer, E.: cuDNN: efficient primitives for deep learning. Computer ENCE (2014)
6. Chung, Y.A., Belinkov, Y., Glass, J.: Similarity analysis of self-supervised speech representations. In: ICASSP 2021–2021 IEEE International Conference on Acoustics, Speech and Signal Processing (ICASSP) (2021)
7. Collobert, R., Weston, J., Bottou, L., Karlen, M., Kavukcuoglu, K., Kuksa, P.: Natural language processing (almost) from scratch. J. Mach. Learn. Res. 12(1), 2493–2537 (2011)
8. Deng, J., Dong, W., Socher, R., Li, L.-J., Li, K., Fei-Fei, L.: ImageNet: a large-scale hierarchical image database. In: 2009 IEEE Conference on Computer Vision and Pattern Recognition, pp. 248–255. IEEE (2009)

9. Graves, A., Schmidhuber, J.: Framewise phoneme classification with bidirectional LSTM and other neural network architectures. Neural Netw. **18**(5–6), 602–610 (2005)
10. Harlap, A., et al.: Pipedream: Fast and efficient pipeline parallel DNN training (2018)
11. He, K., Zhang, X., Ren, S., Sun, J.: Deep residual learning for image recognition. IEEE (2016)
12. Huang, Y., et al.: GPipe: efficient training of giant neural networks using pipeline parallelism. arXiv (2018)
13. Jiang, Xu, R., Ma, S., Wang, Q., Hou, X., Lu, H.: A memory saving mechanism based on data transferring for pipeline parallelism. In: 2021 IEEE International Conference on Parallel Distributed Processing with Applications, Big Data Cloud Computing, Sustainable Computing Communications, Social Computing Networking (ISPA/BDCloud/SocialCom/SustainCom), pp. 1230–1235 (2021)
14. Jouppi, N., Young, C., Patil, N., Patterson, D.: Motivation for and evaluation of the first tensor processing unit. IEEE Micro **38**(3), 10–19 (2018)
15. Paszke, A., Gross, S., Massa, F., Lerer, A., Chintala, S.: PyTorch: an imperative style, high-performance deep learning library (2019)
16. Rhu, M., Gimelshein, N., Clemons, J., Zulfiqar, A., Keckler, S.W.: VDNN: virtualized deep neural networks for scalable, memory-efficient neural network design. ACM (2016)
17. Rhu, M., O'Connor, M., Chatterjee, N., Pool, J., Keckler, S.W.: Compressing DMA engine: Leveraging activation sparsity for training deep neural networks. IEEE Computer Society (2017)
18. Sarwar, B.: Item-based collaborative filtering recommendation algorithms. In Proceedings of the 10th International World Wide Web Conference (WWW10), Hong Kong, May 1–5 (2001) (2001)
19. Simonyan, K., Zisserman, A.: Very deep convolutional networks for large-scale image recognition. Computer Science (2014)
20. Szegedy, C., Ioffe, S., Vanhoucke, V., Alemi, A.: Inception-v4, inception-resnet and the impact of residual connections on learning (2016)
21. Szegedy, C., Liu, W., Jia, Y., Sermanet, P., Rabinovich, A.: Going deeper with convolutions. IEEE Computer Society (2014)
22. Ts/Technicolor, and Sor Related. ImageNet classification with deep convolutional neural networks [50]
23. Wang, L., Ye, J., Zhao, Y., Wei, W., Kraska, T.: Superneurons: dynamic GPU memory management for training deep neural networks (2018)
24. You, Y., Zhang, Z., Demmel, J., Keutzer, K., Hsieh, C.J.: ImageNet training in 24 minutes (2017)
25. Zeng, W., et al.: Pangu-α: Large-scale autoregressive pretrained Chinese language models with auto-parallel computation (2021)
26. Zhang, J., Zhan, J., Li, J., Jin, J., Qian, L.: Optimizing execution for pipelined-based distributed deep learning in a heterogeneously networked GPU cluster. Concurrency and Computation Practice and Experience (2020)

Operator Placement for IoT Data Streaming Applications in Edge Computing Environment

Sixin Chen[1,2], Bing Tang[1,2], Qing Yang[3(✉)], and Yuanyuan Liu[1,2]

[1] School of Computer Science and Engineering, Hunan University of Science and Technology, Xiangtan 411201, China
[2] Hunan Key Laboratory for Service Computing and Novel Software Technology, Hunan University of Science and Technology, Xiangtan 411201, China
[3] School of Information and Communication Engineering, Guangzhou Maritime University, Guangzhou 510725, China
qyang@gzmtu.edu.cn

Abstract. With the rapid development of IoT applications, how to process large and continuous data streams in real time for IoT applications has become a challenge in recent years. This paper presents a model to predict the Maximum Sustainable Throughput (MST) of data streaming applications at the edge, and then proposes GACP, a constraint programming-base operator placement strategy to maximize MST using the genetic algorithm. We evaluated the proposed operator placement strategy in terms of MST, the number of edge servers in usage, and the percentage of communications within edge servers. Experimental results show that compared with the existing heuristic algorithms, the proposed GACP strategy can achieve better MST, which is 2–5 times higher than existing algorithms.

Keywords: Operator placement · Data streams · Edge computing · Genetic algorithm · IoT

1 Introduction

We are moving into a data-driven era, and it has become a challenge to process large and continuous data streams in real time. In the last decade, distributed computing systems, such as Hadoop and Hive, have been widely used and deployed to process big data. However, in recent years, a large number of IoT applications have emerged, such as network monitoring, telecom data management, sensor networks and so on. In these scenarios where real-time data flows must be analyzed swiftly and changes must be quickly responded to, batch processing model can no longer meet the requirements, which has the characteristics of slow response and high latency. Therefore, stream data processing has received extensive attention. In contrast to traditional databases, stream processing systems run continuous queries and analyze data in real time to provide continuous output [12]. Academia and industry have been working on data stream processing (DSP). Several programming architectures based on data streams, such as Apache Spark and Twitter's Storm, have been built.

© Springer Nature Switzerland AG 2023
W. Meng et al. (Eds.): ICA3PP 2022, LNCS 13777, pp. 605–619, 2023.
https://doi.org/10.1007/978-3-031-22677-9_32

Edge computing supports distributed computing to reduce latency and bandwidth bottlenecks by moving computations and storage to edge servers near end users. The shared aim of reducing latency in DSP and edge computing has led a constant increase in the deployment of stream processing applications in edge environments. As a result, substantial research has been done on placement techniques between edge servers [9] or across hybrid cloud and edge environment [11]. All of these research used the same measurements and optimization goals as prior attempts that dealt with resource heterogeneity in the cloud [10]. Their specific aims are to reduce latency or response time [9] as well as the overall data traffic among edge nodes [4].

However, in practice, the amount of the data input stream is not always constant. For existing deployments that minimizing latency and considering the network heterogeneity of the edge environment, it is difficult to change when the incoming data stream rate increased, especially when resources are limited in the edge environment. The amount of data that a stream processing system can receive while maintaining stable performance is called the Maximum Sustainable Throughput. When the data input rate exceeds MST, the data intake rate of the data stream processing system cannot keep up with the data input rate. As a result, data will be continuously piled up, which will have a huge negative impact on the performance of the data flow processing system [6]. MST is currently recognized as an important indicator for DSP system performance in the literatures [6,7]. Given the dynamics and volatility of data stream, we propose MST should be considered an essential metric and optimization objective for operator deployment in edge scenarios. Therefore, we propose a model for evaluating the deployment of operators in edge scenarios, and introduce a genetic algorithm based on constraint programming.

The main contributions of this paper are listed as follows:

(1) We proposed a constraint programming model to solve the deployment problem of data streaming applications in edge environment. The model can predict the MST under different operator deployment strategies and give the related constraints for the MST maximization problem.
(2) We proposed a genetic algorithm based on constrained programming. We can select the optimal operator deployment scheme aiming at maximizing MST by genetic algorithm.
(3) Comparing GACP with greedy algorithm [10] and graph partitioning algorithm [3], experimental results show that GACP can support MST 2–5 times higher than others.

2   Related Work

In a variety of data centers and the network's edge, IoT applications have been widely implemented. There are some solutions that placing some operators in micro data centers closer to where the data is generated. Gu et al., aiming at minimizing the communication cost of BDSP among geographically distributed data centers, modeled the deployment problem of flow processing applications as a mixed integer linear programming (MILP) problem, which was solved by multi-virtual machine placement algorithm (MVP) [4]. Fischer and Benoit et al. argued that the problem of deploying IoT applications on edge heterogeneous topologies is at least NP-hard [2,3].

Low latency is the goal of both data stream processing and edge computing. In [10], Peng et al. proposed the R-storm system. Different from the default Storm scheduling method, R-Storm considers edge node memory as a hard resource constraint, CPU and bandwidth utilization as soft resource constraints, and performs scheduling based on resource awareness to maximize throughput. A task-parallel distributed stream processing system scheduling method based on graph partitioning has been proposed [1]. Renart et al. proposed an IoT edge framework (R-Pulsar) in [11], which dynamically splits IoT applications and pushes partitions of them to the edge, reducing latency, data exchange volume, and communication costs between edge and cloud. Considering the location of IoT sensors, Happ et al. described the combined employment of brokers and operators on current edge, fog, and cloud resources as an optimization problem [5]. To solve the joint problem, a heuristic method is proposed. Lambert et al. proposed a throughput capacity model for DSP on cloud computing to solve the high latency and low processing throughput created by the edge computing paradigm [8].

Many work focused on operator placement strategies in edge environments, which mostly employ the same metrics and optimization goals as previous work dealing with resource heterogeneity in the cloud. Specifically, these studies usually take the system's throughput and ability to maintain low latency as indicators to evaluate the success of DSP deployment at the edge while ignoring MST. In this research, we suggest that it is particularly significant to use MST as an optimization metric for operator deployment in highly dynamic network environments. Therefore, on the basis of the above research work, we further propose an application deployment method with the goal of maximizing MST, namely the genetic algorithm based on constraint programming.

3   Operator Placement Strategy

3.1   System Overview

In this paper, the operator deployment of the IoT data streaming application refers to the mapping problem of each operator to the server nodes. We designed a scenario with four operators and three servers to illustrate the algorithm in this paper, as shown in Fig. 1. The operator layer is a Storm topology, that is, the logical dependencies of Spout and Bolt are given and the connection between operator instances is omitted. We define that each op operator contains multiple operator instances, assuming $OP = \{op_1, op_2, ..., op_m\}$, the number of instances of each operator is $I = \{I_1, I_2, ..., I_m\}$. For example, in the operator layer, for op_1, I_1 equals to 3. For any two server u, v, b_{uv} stands for their bandwidth. Each edge server has a fixed number of slots ,which is the maximum number of

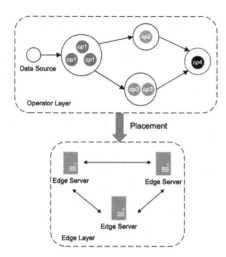

Fig. 1. Stream processing application deployment model in edge environment.

operator instances that can be placed. We expect to deploy the operator on a suitable edge server to maximize the MST of the entire system.

3.2   System Model

In this section, we propose a simple model designed to represent the bandwidth consumption of operator placement and how to infer estimates of MST from it. For simplicity, we will focus on communication, assuming that the CPU is not the bottleneck (operators are sufficiently replicated). For convenience, the main symbols in this paper are listed in Table 1.

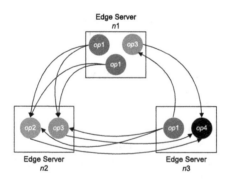

Fig. 2. Example of placement scheme.

$DAG(V_O, E_O, W_O)$ represents the application with its operators and their dependencies. V_O is the set of operator instances. Note that two instances of the same operator are two different vertices of V_O. E_O describes the data exchange

Table 1. Notations.

Symbol	Meaning
I_m	The number of operator instances of the mth operators
σ	Optimal placement $\sigma : V_O \rightarrow V_N$
D	System maximum input rate
$BU(\sigma, u, v)$	Actual bandwidth usage between nodes u, v
$\mu_{oo'}$	Corresponding communication coefficient on
$BE(\sigma, u, v)$	Bandwidth overflow
b_{uv}	Standard bandwidth between nodes u, v
S_v	Number of available slots on server node V_N
S_i	A set of all operator instances whose operator type is i
In_i	Total amount of data received at the ith stage
FS_i	Set of front stages with a path length of 1 from stage S_i
$C_{i,j}$	Output by $E_{i,j}$ accounts for the weight of output by S_i
α_i	The variation coefficient of a data stream related with S_i
r_i	Total number of operator instances in ith stage
$\beta_{i,j}$	Communication coefficient related D given by $E_{i,j}$
$x_{i,u}$	The number of operator instances in S_i placed on node u

between the two operator instances, and W_O describes the amount of data exchanged between the two operator instances. We assume that if V_x and V_v are different operator instances of the same kind of operator, and both have a dependency on V_z, then $W_{x,z} = W_{v,z}$. In $DAG(V_N, E_N)$, V_N is a set of edge server nodes, and E_N describes the data exchange between the two edge servers. Based on the relational dependency graph $DAG(V_O, E_O, W_O)$ of the operator instance and the server placement graph $DAG(V_N, E_N)$ given above, we present a placement scheme, as shown in Fig. 2.

In particular, if the operators with sequential dependencies are located on the same edge server, we believe that the transmission between them does not consume bandwidth. For example, op_1 and op_3 are deployed in edge server $n1$, where no bandwidth is consumed and the connection between them is omitted, as shown in Fig. 2. Note that there can be multiple instances of the same operator in the same server. We define that the amount of data transmission between the server node u and the server node v is equal to the accumulation of the weights between the operator instances with dependencies on the node u and the node v. Therefore, after matching all the operator instances in node u and node v, the actual bandwidth transmitted between nodes u, v can be obtained by accumulating W_O. For example, in Fig. 2, the actual transmission bandwidth of edge server $n1$ and edge server $n2$ is the sum of the corresponding weights of $E_{1,3}$ and $E_{3,4}$. From this, we derive the following formulas.

For placement scheme σ, we define the actual bandwidth usage from node u to node v as $BU(\sigma, u, v)$, which is calculated as

$$BU(\sigma, u, v) = \sum_{oo' \in E_O, \sigma(o)=u, \sigma(o')=v} W_O(oo') \tag{1}$$

where $W_O(oo') = \mu_{oo'} \times D$, and $oo' \in E_O$. W_O means the actual transmission bandwidth between operator instances o and o'. $\mu_{oo'}$ is a fixed multiplicative factor given by the edges in E_O (we assume that all communications changes linearly when the input rate changes). We define bandwidth overflow BE as the difference between the actual transmitted bandwidth and the standard bandwidth. Note that if the the difference is negative, BE is considered to be 0. More precisely, $BE(\sigma, u, v) = \max(0, BU(\sigma, u, v) - b_{uv})$. We define MST τ as the maximal input rate D if and only if $BE(\sigma) \leq 0$. Combine the above equations to get $\sum_{oo' \in E_O, \sigma(o)=u, \sigma(o')=v} \mu_{oo'} \times D \leq b_{uv}$,which is equivalent to $D \leq \frac{b_{uv}}{\sum_{oo' \in E_O, \sigma(o)=u, \sigma(o')=v} \mu_{oo'}}$. Then, we get the formula for τ as

$$\tau = \min_{u, v \in V_N^2} \frac{b_{uv}}{\sum_{oo' \in E_O, \sigma(o)=u, \sigma(o')=v} \mu_{oo'}} \tag{2}$$

Definition of MST-Maximization Problem. Given a dependency graph $DAG(V_O, E_O, W_O)$ between operator instances and a placement graph $DAG(V_N, E_N)$ of edge server nodes, MST-Maximization problem is to find the optimal placement $\sigma : V_O \to V_N$ of operator instances to maximize τ.

3.3   Constraint Programming Formulation

In the stage dependency graph $DAG(V_O, E_O, W_O)$, $V_O = \bigcup S_i$, E_O is used to describe the dependency between stages, and W_O is used to describe the amount of data exchanged and transmitted between the two stages. Let the data source be S_0 (the number of operator instances is 1), and the amount of data received in this stage is D. For stage S_i, the amount of data it accepts is the accumulation of the corresponding weights of all the edges that have dependencies on it. More precisely,

$$\begin{cases} In_0 = D \\ In_i = \sum_{j \in FS_i} \beta_{j,i} \times D \end{cases} \tag{3}$$

where FS_i represents the set of pre-stages with a path length of 1 from the stage S_i. For example, the set of pre-stages of S_4 is $FS_4 \{S_2, S_3\}$. For $W_{j,i}$, if S_j is the data source, the weight of the edge should be $W_{0,i} = D \times C_{0,i} \times \alpha_i$. If S_j is not the data source, $W_{j,i} = In_j \times C_{j,i} \times \alpha_i$. $C_{j,i}$ represents the weight of the data volume output by edge $E_{j,i}$ to the total output data volume of the stage S_j. For example, in Fig. 1, $W_{1,3} = D \times C_{1,3}$ and $C_{1,3} + C_{1,2} = 1$. From this we get a linear relationship between $W_{j,i}$ and D. We describe this linear relationship with the constant $\beta_{j,i}$ and give the following definition of β: β is a property of an edge. Suppose $E_{j,i}$ is the edge corresponding to S_j pointing to S_i, then the communication coefficient of this edge is $\beta_{j,i}$, and the data transmission amount corresponding to this edge is $W_{j,i} = \beta_{j,i} \times D$. More precisely,

$$\begin{cases} \beta_{0,i} = C_{0,i} \times \alpha_i & FS_i = \{0\} \\ \beta_{j,i} = (\sum_{x \in FS_j} \beta_{x,j}) \times C_{j,i} \times \alpha_i & else \end{cases} \tag{4}$$

Constraint programming (CP) is a linear programming approach, in which decision variables can be multiplied. We apply a constraint programming to the maximization problem of MST. We define the decision variable: $\forall i \in [0, N], \forall v \in V_N$, $x_{i,u}$ where $x_{i,u}$ represents the number of operators in stage S_i placed on the node u. The formulas for applying linear constraints to the MST-Maximization problem are as follows.

$$\forall i \in [0, N], \forall v \in V_N, x_{i,v} \geq 0 \tag{5}$$

$$\forall i \in [0, N], \sum_{v \in V_N} x_{i,v} = r_i \tag{6}$$

$$\forall v \in V_N, \sum_{i \in [0,N]} x_{i,v} \leq S_v \tag{7}$$

$$\forall u, v \in V_N, u \neq v \sum_{i \in [1,N], j \in FS_i} x_{i,u} x_{j,v} \frac{\beta_{j,i} \times D}{r_j \times r_i}$$

$$+ \sum_{j \in [1,N], i \in FS_j} x_{j,v} x_{i,u} \frac{\beta_{i,j} \times D}{r_i \times r_j} \leq b_{uv} \tag{8}$$

Equation (5) ensures that the number of instances of each operator deployed on each server is greater than or equal to 0. Equation (6) ensures that all operator instances in each stage are deployed to the server. Equation (7) ensures that the total number of operator instances deployed on the server is less than the number of slots. Equation (8) ensures that the actual bandwidth between any two edge servers does not exceed the standard bandwidth during actual transmission.

4   Proposed Algorithm

4.1   Genetic Algorithm Based on Constraint Programming

Because the genetic algorithm has a relatively complete mathematical model and theory, it has good performance in solving many NP-hard problems. Applying the genetic algorithm to the scenario of this paper and combining the constraints proposed above, we propose a genetic algorithm based on constraint programming called GACP.

4.2   Algorithm Description

First, we should initialize the population. The upper bounds UB and lower bounds LB of each gene variable are given according to the constraints presented above. We generate random numbers uniformly distributed between UB and LB of the variable to ensure that each generated chromosome is legitimate. More precisely, $m_{op_i,n_j} = LB(op_i) + (UB(op_i) - LB(op_i)) * rand$. After randomly generating an initial population of 5,000 legitimate candidate solutions, we replicate the chromosomes with good fitness performance in the original population and mutate the existing population to generate a new generation of population secondly. Iterate continuously until we reach our preset maximum evolutionary generation. In the iteration, we calculate MST as the optimization objective function, and use the objective function to find the maximum placement scheme of MST within the search range. Finally, the best fitness, and the best placement scheme are output, as shown in Algorithm 1.

Algorithm 1. Genetic Algorithm

Input: $DAG(op)$, $DAG(node)$
Output: $Answer_{Op_m, V_n}$, $BestFitness$
 1: Initialize $DAG(op)Weight$ array randomly
 2: Initialize $Bandwith$ array randomly
 3: Initialize $OpInstanceNum$ array randomly
 4: Initialize $Slot$ array $\leftarrow 8$
 5: Initialize $MaxGeneration \leftarrow 100$
 6: Initialize $PopulationSize \leftarrow 5000$
 7: Initialize $InitialPopulation$ array $\leftarrow$ Init($Papulationsize$)
 8: **for** i to $MaxGeneration$ **do**
 9:     Select($Papulation$)
10:     Cross($Papulation$)
11:     Mutation($Papulation$)
12:     Update $BestFitness$
13:     Update $Answer_{Op_m, V_n}$
14:     $i \leftarrow i + 1$
15: **end for**

---

5   Baseline Approaches

Inspired by R-Storm scheduler proposed by Peng [10], who uses resource-aware scheduling algorithm to improve system throughput, we design two Greedy strategies, namely GD-I and GD-II. Both of them aim to maximize the MST of the system by increasing intra-server node communication, that is, reducing communication between two server nodes.

5.1   Greedy Intra-node Communication (GD-I)

First, we number the operators in the operator dependency graph according to the DFS (depth-first search) rule. Second, we select the server node with the most available slots, assign the operator instance numbered 1 to this node, and select the operator instance that has a dependency on it and assign it to this node. Then select an operator that has a dependency on the operator just assigned and assign it to the node. Repeat the above operation until the number of slots in the node is used up, which is to make more operators within the node have dependencies. Using this assignment for each server node, we can get a set of unique solutions. Note that because the server nodes are connected in pairs, we assume there is no difference between the two servers. Finally, we output the matrix solution and its corresponding MST.

5.2 Greedy Improved Intra-node Communication (GD-II)

For the scenario where the number of operator instances of each operator is smaller than the number of server slots, we propose a more efficient strategy to improve intra-node communication. Compared with GD-I algorithm, GD-I algorithm only tends to assign all the instances of this operator to nodes (instead of only allocating one instance of this operator) every time an operator is allocated.

5.3 Graph Partitioning (GP)

The strategy we propose here is based on the graph partition problem. The goal is to divide the vertices of the operator instance dependency graph into n sets with the same cardinality, while minimizing the edge weight (referring to the weight of one set to another). More precisely, let $G = (V, E, W)$ be a graph with edge weights, $P = (p_1, p_2, ..., p_n)$ be a partition of V, i.e., $\cup P_i = V$, $\forall i \neq j, p_i \cap p_j = \emptyset$. The edge-cut of this partition are defined as $uv \in E_{cut}$ if and only if $u \in p_i, v \in p_j, i \neq j$. Graph partitioning is a well-known technique for reducing communication between processes. Applying it to this scenario, we define the weight between different sets as the amount of communication. In order to use as many server node resources as possible (more links to share the communication between nodes), we define n as the number of server nodes, and the cardinality value as the ratio of the total number of operator instances to n. Use the above GD-II strategy to reduce the edge cut weight, that is, the traffic between nodes (increase the proportion of traffic within nodes). Finally, we output the matrix solution and its corresponding MST.

5.4 Random Strategy (RS)

We randomly generated 500 reasonable placements and obtained their MST, intra-node communication, and the average number of server nodes used, and recorded the average value.

6 Experimental Results and Analysis

6.1 Experiment Configurations

Parameter Setting. We set up 8 slots per edge server. The weights of each edge in the operator dependence graph are random within the range of 0.1–0.9, and the weights of edges linked at the same starting node add up to 1. The proportion of actual received data of each operator α is random in $[1/3, 1]$ or $[1, 3]$. Bandwidth between edge server nodes is random in $[10\text{Mbps}, 100\text{Mbps}]$. We take MST, proportion of intra-node communication, and the number of server nodes used as the metrics of experimental evaluation.

In the experiment, we first took the number of edge servers as an independent variable, which is changed in the range of $[6, 13]$. For each operator Op_m, I_m is fixed to 4. Since some of the experimental variables were random, we did multiple experiments and recorded the average value of each metric when the independent variables obtained the same value. Subsequently, we took the total number of operator instances as independent variable, which changes in $[20, 40]$. It is worth mentioning that, when the independent variable changes, the number of operator types and dependence remain unchanged, but only the number of instances of each operator changes. The number of server nodes is fixed at 8. For each operator Op_m, I_m is randomly selected within the legal range, which is expressed by the following equation:

$$
\begin{cases}
I_m \geq 1 \\
I_m \leq IV - \sum_{t \in [1, m-1]} I_t
\end{cases}
\tag{9}
$$

where IV represents the current value of independent variable, that is, the total number of operator instances. For the accuracy of the experiment, we also conducted several tests and recorded the average value of each indicator under the five strategies.

6.2   Metrics

- **The average MST**. The maximum throughput of the system after the operator deployment is tested, and the average value is recorded after several experiments.
- **The average proportion of intra-node communication**. After the deployment of the operator, the proportion of intra-node traffic in the system to the total traffic is measured, and the average value is recorded after multiple experiments. It is worth mentioning that intra-node communication does not need to occupy transmission bandwidth.
- **The average number of edge servers used**. The number of servers used by the system after the deployment of operator is completed, where at least one operator instance is deployed on it. The average value is recorded after several experiments.

6.3   Results and Analysis

The Average MST. Figure 3 shows the changes of the average MST under different strategies with the increase of the total number of operator instances when the number of available edge servers is fixed to 8. Figure 4 shows the

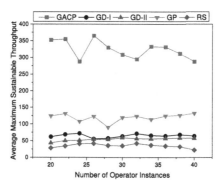

Fig. 3. Impact of total number of operator instances on average MST.

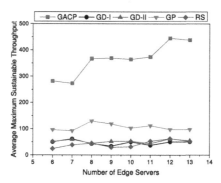

Fig. 4. Impact of the number of edge servers on average MST.

changes of the average MST under different strategies as the number of available edge servers increases when the number of instances of each operator is fixed to 4. It can be clearly seen from Fig. 3 and Fig. 4 that the algorithm GACP proposed in this paper can achieve the optimal MST, because the genetic algorithm can find a more comprehensive solution space and find the optimal deployment scheme. The average MST of GD-I and GD-II is much lower than that of GACP strategy, which is close to that of RS strategy. This is because under the greedy strategy, all operators are concentrated on fewer server nodes, which means that the system only uses a few links to communicate, resulting in some links easily reaching their maximum load and severely limiting the growth of MST. The performance of the GP strategy is second only to the GACP strategy. This is because the GP strategically selects the maximum number of available servers, which means that there are more links to undertake the communication, and strives to minimize the total traffic between edge nodes.

The Average Proportion of Intra-node Communication. In the experiment, the number of servers is fixed and the total number of operator instances is increased, and then operators are deployed according to different strategies

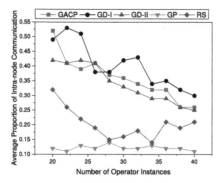

Fig. 5. Impact of the total number of operator instances on the average proportion of intra-node communication to total traffic.

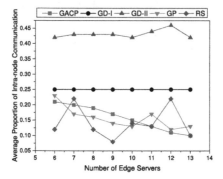

Fig. 6. Impact of the number of edge servers on the average proportion of intra-node communication to total traffic.

in edge environment. After the deployment, compare the average proportion of intra-node communication to the total traffic under different strategy, as shown in Fig. 5. It can be observed that the GACP strategy proposed in this paper is second only to the GD-II strategy, and the average proportion of intra-node communication of GP strategy is the worst or even lower than that of RS strategy. In subsequent experiments, we fixed the number of instances of each operator and successively increased the number of available edge servers. Figure 6 shows the average proportion of intra-node communication to the total traffic under different strategies in this experiment. In Fig. 6, we notice that the GACP strategy proposed in this paper has similar performance with GP strategy and RS strategy. They are lower than the two greedy strategies.

The Average Number of Edge Servers Used. Figure 7 shows the change of the average number of edge servers used under different strategies with the increase of the total number of operator instances when the fixed number of available edge servers is 8. Figure 8 shows the change of the average number of

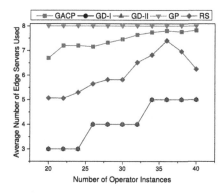

Fig. 7. Impact of the total number of operator instances on the average number of edge servers used.

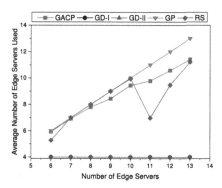

Fig. 8. Impact of the number of edge servers on the average number of edge servers used.

servers used under different strategies as the number of available edge servers increases when the number of instances of each operator is fixed to 4. We observe that the GACP strategy is second only to the GP strategy, which always selects the largest number of edge servers. The two greedy strategies selected the least number of servers or even lower than the random strategy, which severely limited the growth of MST. That's why the number of servers used by the optimal strategy GACP tends to grow as the number of available servers increases and is always at the forefront, as shown in Fig. 8.

At the same time, we note that the GACP strategy proposed in this paper performs best in the average MST metric, but is not always optimal in the other two metrics. The reasons are stated below. In the experiment with the number of available servers as the independent variable, we found that although GD-II significantly improved the proportion of intra-node communication compared with GD-I, the MST under the GD-II strategy still had little difference with that under the GD-I strategy, as shown in Fig. 6 and Fig. 4. That is to say, if the operator deployment strategy only increases the communication within the node but the number of servers used is still low, MST will almost never be promoted. Similarly, GP strategy adopts the maximum number of edge server nodes which is at the cost of sacrificing the communication ratio within the node, and MST under this strategy is also limited. Therefore, these two metrics, the ratio of communication within nodes and the number of edge servers used, are only of reference value. This is why the optimal operator deployment strategy GACP keeps them within reasonable limits rather than achieving extreme values. Furthermore, according to Eq. (2), we note that MST depends on the edge of the server topology with the smallest maximum load value which is closely related to the standard bandwidth of this edge. Therefore, we believe that an excellent operator deployment strategy aimed at maximizing MST must have excellent bandwidth awareness. Obviously, neither greedy algorithm nor graph partition algorithm has bandwidth awareness, while the algorithm in this paper, GACP, has strong bandwidth awareness because bandwidth is one of the constraints. This is why the algorithm GACP in this paper can achieve the optimal MST.

7   Conclusion

In an edge environment where network bandwidth and data stream are highly dynamic, we believe that MST should be used as an optimization target when deploying stream processing applications. This paper proposes a model to calculate and predict the maximum sustainable throughput of stream processing applications in an edge environment and model the stream application deployment as a constraint programming problem. By evaluating the MST, the number of servers used and the proportion of intra-node communication under different operator deployment strategies of system in edge environment, we believe that an excellent operator deployment strategy should have good bandwidth resource awareness. More importantly, the genetic algorithm strategy based on constraint programming proposed can achieve the optimal MST, which is 2–5 times higher than the baseline strategies.

However, we do not consider the influence of other network factors on the operator topology, that is, we assume that the dependencies between operators are static, which is different from the real application. In future work, we can obtain relevant data for practical application and implement our GACP strategy at Storm. In addition, we can also extend our model to consider other optimization goals, such as communication costs and latency.

Acknowledgments. This work is supported by National Key R&D Program of China under grant no. 2018YFB1402800, National Natural Science Foundation of China under grant no. 61872138 and 61602169, and Natural Science Foundation of Hunan Province under grant no. 2021JJ30278.

References

1. de Assunção, M.D., Veith, A.D.S., Buyya, R.: Distributed data stream processing and edge computing: a survey on resource elasticity and future directions. J. Netw. Comput. Appl. **103**, 1–17 (2018)
2. Benoit, A., Dobrila, A., Nicod, J., Philippe, L.: Scheduling linear chain streaming applications on heterogeneous systems with failures. Future Gener. Comput. Syst. **29**(5), 1140–1151 (2013)
3. Fischer, L., Bernstein, A.: Workload scheduling in distributed stream processors using graph partitioning. In: 2015 IEEE International Conference on Big Data (IEEE BigData 2015), Santa Clara, CA, USA, October 29 - November 1, 2015, pp. 124–133. IEEE Computer Society, USA (2015)
4. Gu, L., Zeng, D., Guo, S., Xiang, Y., Hu, J.: A general communication cost optimization framework for big data stream processing in geo-distributed data centers. IEEE Trans. Comput. **65**(1), 19–29 (2016)
5. Happ, D., Bayhan, S., Handziski, V.: JOI: joint placement of IoT analytics operators and pub/sub message brokers in fog-centric IoT platforms. Future Gener. Comput. Syst. **119**, 7–19 (2021)
6. Imai, S., Patterson, S., Varela, C.A.: Maximum sustainable throughput prediction for data stream processing over public clouds. In: Proceedings of the 17th IEEE/ACM International Symposium on Cluster, Cloud and Grid Computing, CCGRID 2017, Madrid, Spain, May 14–17, 2017, pp. 504–513. IEEE Computer Society/ACM, USA (2017)
7. Karimov, J., Rabl, T., Katsifodimos, A., Samarev, R., Heiskanen, H., Markl, V.: Benchmarking distributed stream data processing systems. In: 34th IEEE International Conference on Data Engineering, ICDE 2018, Paris, France, April 16-19, 2018, pp. 1507–1518. IEEE Computer Society, USA (2018)
8. Lambert, T., Guyon, D., Ibrahim, S.: Rethinking operators placement of stream data application in the edge. In: CIKM 2020: The 29th ACM International Conference on Information and Knowledge Management, Virtual Event, Ireland, October 19-23, 2020, pp. 2101–2104. ACM, USA (2020)
9. Nardelli, M., Cardellini, V., Grassi, V., Presti, F.L.: Efficient operator placement for distributed data stream processing applications. IEEE Trans. Parallel Distrib. Syst. **30**(8), 1753–1767 (2019)
10. Peng, B., Hosseini, M., Hong, Z., Farivar, R., Campbell, R.H.: R-storm: Resource-aware scheduling in storm. CoRR abs/1904.05456 (2019)
11. Renart, E.G., Veith, A.D.S., Balouek-Thomert, D., de Assunção, M.D., Lefèvre, L., Parashar, M.: Distributed operator placement for IoT data analytics across edge and cloud resources. In: 19th IEEE/ACM International Symposium on Cluster, Cloud and Grid Computing, CCGRID 2019, Larnaca, Cyprus, May 14-17, 2019, pp. 459–468. IEEE, USA (2019)
12. Tantalaki, N., Souravlas, S., Roumeliotis, M.: A review on big data real-time stream processing and its scheduling techniques. Int. J. Parallel Emergent Distrib. Syst. **35**(5), 571–601 (2020)

Makespan and Security-Aware Workflow Scheduling for Cloud Service Cost Minimization Using Firefly Optimizer

Chengliang Zhou[1], Tian Wang[1], Liying Li[1], Jin Sun[1], and Junlong Zhou[1,2,3(✉)]

[1] School of Computer Science and Engineering,
Nanjing University of Science and Technology, Nanjing 210094, China
{zhouchengliang,eclipse_wt,liyingli,sunj,jlzhou}@njust.edu.cn
[2] State Key Laboratory of Computer Architecture, Institute of Computing
Technology, Chinese Academy of Sciences, Beijing 100190, China
[3] National Trusted Embedded Software Engineering Technology Research Center,
East China Normal University, Shanghai 200062, China

Abstract. As efficient commercial information technology, cloud computing has attracted more and more users to submit their requests to the cloud platform and pay for them based on the amount and quality of services. One of the most important concerns of cloud service providers is to minimize the monetary cost for completing users' requests while meeting constraints on the quality of services such as makespan and security. To solve this concern, this paper proposes a makespan and security-aware workflow scheduling method based on an improved firefly optimizer that consists of a new solution initialization scheme, a firefly position updating scheme, a firefly-to-solution mapping operator, and two task-to-virtual machine assignment schemes. We carry out extensive simulation experiments on real-world workflows to validate our proposed workflow scheduling method. The results reveal that the monetary cost reduction achieved by our method can be up to 54.0% compared to a baseline and two state-of-the-art approaches.

Keywords: Cloud computing · Workflow scheduling · Cost minimization · Makespan and security · Firefly algorithm

1 Introduction

Cloud computing is an interactive business mode that is developed based on virtualization technology as well as parallel processing and distributed computing technologies [1,2]. It provides large-scale hardware, software, storage, and network resources as various services to cloud users in a "pay as you go" manner. Cloud users can purchase the services according to the characteristics and requirements of their requests. Infrastructure-as-a-Service (IaaS) is a very popular service mode provided by many cloud platforms such as Amazon EC2, IBM

Corresponding author: Junlong Zhou.

© Springer Nature Switzerland AG 2023
W. Meng et al. (Eds.): ICA3PP 2022, LNCS 13777, pp. 620–641, 2023.
https://doi.org/10.1007/978-3-031-22677-9_33

Blue Cloud and Sun Grid. It allows cloud providers to rent cloud computing resources to remote users in the form of various virtual machines (VMs) with different hardware configurations, quality of service (QoS), and price models.

Workflow has been widely used in describing data-intensive applications deployed on IaaS clouds, which contain a group of parallel tasks with data/control dependencies [3,4]. Such a workflow application can be represented as a directed acyclic graph (DAG) where nodes represent tasks and edges represent data/control dependencies. Cloud users purchase cloud services from IaaS service providers to execute the requests they submit, typically with a certain requirement on deadline and QoS. However, since users need to upload their applications (i.e., requests) to the cloud for processing, the applications may face various security threats such as sensitive data divulgence, eventually causing huge financial loss. More importantly, with the rapid development of computing technology, the amount of data uploaded to cloud has increased significantly, posing fundamental challenges to the construction of security-critical cloud computing systems [5]. Therefore, cloud servers must provide security services to protect sensitive data and maintain a high level of security. From the perspective of cloud providers, if multiple workflows are executed with deadline and security requirements specified by users, reducing the execution cost of tasks and shortening the completion time of tasks are the primary goals to maximize their profit. However, the two goals are contradictory since shortening task completion time often requires better computing capacity that in turn increases the execution cost.

To solve this conflict, we need to obtain the best trade-off between cost and makespan. To this end, this paper studies the workflow scheduling problem to minimize cost while meeting timing and security constraints. Considering that the firefly algorithm (FA) [6] is a classic meta-heuristic algorithm widely used in solving complex optimization problems and has the advantages of simple structure and fewer parameters, we propose an improved firefly algorithm (IFA) to solve the cost minimization problem without violating all the design constraints. Specifically, given a workflow application, the proposed IFA judiciously determines the sequence of tasks to be executed, the selection of security services for tasks, and the assignment of tasks to VMs. Extensive simulation experiments are carried out to validate the efficacy of IFA.

The remainder of this paper is organized as follows. Section 2 reviews related work and Sect. 3 describes system models. Section 4 defines the studied problem and gives an overview of the proposed methodology. The proposed IFA is detailedly introduced in Sect. 5. Section 6 presents the experimental results and Sect. 7 concludes the paper.

2   Related Work

Minimizing cost is a key concern in executing workflow applications in the cloud and it has attracted wide attention recently. Wen et al. [7] presented a new workflow management framework that dynamically partitions scientific workflows across federated cloud servers for minimizing financial cost and gracefully solving run-time failures. To minimize the cost and makespan of executing precedence-constrained tasks in workflow applications, Zhou et al. [8] designed a new heterogeneous earliest-finish-time algorithm that utilizes fuzzy dominance sort to find the optimal scheduling solution. Wu et al. [9] proposed an ant colony optimization based heuristic algorithm and a list scheduling based heuristic algorithm to schedule workflow applications in the cloud with the target of optimizing cost under the deadline constraint. To cope with the dynamics of multiple deadline-constrained workflows arriving randomly on the cloud, Arabnejad et al. [10] developed a dynamic workload scheduler. Based on the delay-aware Lyapunov optimization technique and greedy strategy, a dynamic cloud-edge heterogeneity-aware resource provisioning framework is proposed in [11] to achieve the best trade-off between timing performance and cost. All the aforementioned approaches are effective in reducing the cost of executing workflow applications, however, they do not consider the security issues.

Due to the connection to the Internet, running workflow applications on clouds may suffer various data privacy and security issues. Using cryptographic algorithm based security services provided by the cloud is an effective countermeasure to defend against attacks. Such security services are typically manufactured in advance and sold to users for protecting sensitive data and users need to pay for the use of security services depending on the efficacy. Xie et al. [12] firstly introduced the concept of quality of security to quantify the security level of tasks using security services and designed a task scheduling algorithm for independent tasks with security and deadline constraints. Jiang et al. [13] designed a genetic algorithm to address the security optimization of security-critical distributed real-time applications. Zhou et al. [14] presented an analysis-based two-stage scheme that decides the allocation of tasks to processors, the operating frequency of tasks, and the selection of security services for tasks, to solve the energy-constrained security optimization problem. However, these methods [12–14] are designed for either embedded systems or the Internet of Things. Unlike them, Nawrocki et al. [15] proposed security-aware task scheduling algorithms for cloud computing to improve cloud resource and service utilization. A new model checking based approach is introduced in [16] to analyze the security requirements of workflow applications. Although the security issues can be well solved by the above-mentioned methods, none of them considers the cost of task execution and data encryption.

3   System Model

This section presents system models used in this paper, including the application model, the cloud resource model, and the security model.

3.1 Application Model

Consider a workflow application which consists of numerous parallel tasks with dependencies. The workflow application can be modeled as a DAG, i.e., $G(\Gamma, E)$ where Γ is a group of tasks and E is a set of edges representing the dependencies between the tasks. Specifically, $\tau_i \in \Gamma = \{\tau_1, \tau_2, \cdots, \tau_N\}$ denotes the i-th task (i.e., the i-th node in the DAG). E is an $N \times N$ 0–1 matrix where $E(i, j) = 1$ indicates the precedence constraint between tasks τ_i and τ_j. The constraint requires that task τ_j can start its execution only after task τ_i has been finished. In other words, τ_i is an immediate predecessor of τ_j and τ_j is an immediate successor of τ_i. If $E(i, j) = 0$, indicating no dependency between τ_i and τ_j. Let $Pred_{\tau_i} = \{\tau_g | E(g, i) = 1\}$ and $Succ_{\tau_i} = \{\tau_j | E(i, j) = 1\}$ represent the set of predecessors and successors of task τ_i, respectively. If a task has no any predecessors (or successors), the task is called an entry task and defined as τ_{entry} (or an exit task and defined as τ_{exit}), which satisfies $Pred_{\tau_{\text{entry}}} = \phi$ (or $Succ_{\tau_{\text{exit}}} = \phi$). As an example, Fig. 1 shows the DAG of a workflow application that is composed of six dependent tasks.

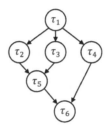

Fig. 1. Example of a DAG application.

3.2 Cloud Resource Model

IaaS providers offer a set of pre-configured VMs based on infrastructure resources for users to deploy workflow applications. Users are charged according to the usage or occupancy of resources. The charges to different VMs are not the same due to their different computing capacities and communication bandwidths, which also impact execution and communication time.

Denote the IaaS platform as a triple, i.e., $IaaS = \{V, R, PC\}$, where $V = \{V_1, V_2, \cdots, V_M\}$ is a set of VMs and used to execute/encrypt tasks. V_m ($m = 1, 2, \cdots, M) \in V$ is the VM created for task τ_i. $R = \{R_1, R_2, \cdots, R_Q\}$ is a set of the VM type, where R_q ($q = 1, 2, \cdots, Q) \in R$ is the type of V_m. $PC = \{PC_1, PC_2, \cdots, PC_Q\}$ is a set of the charge price for different VM types, where PC_q ($q = 1, 2, \cdots, Q) \in PC$ is the price of the VM of type R_q. Note that different VMs could be the same type, but each VM can only belong to one type. We use Z to represent the relationship of VMs and their types, which is an $M \times Q$

matrix. Taking V_m for an example, $z_{m,q} = 1$ indicates that V_m is the type R_q and $z_{m,q} = 0$ otherwise. Clearly, $\sum_{q=1}^{Q} z_{m,q} \leq 1$ holds. The tasks are assigned and executed onto proper VMs. We use X to represent the task assignment strategy, which can be formulated as an $N \times M$ matrix. In this matrix, $x_{i,m} = 1$ means that τ_i is assigned to V_m and $x_{i,m} = 0$ otherwise. Tasks are all indivisible such that they can only be assigned to one VM at a time, i.e., $\sum_{m=1}^{M} x_{i,m} = 1$. The concept of computing unit (CU) is used to describe the computing capacity of VMs. The larger the CU, the higher the computing performance of the VM. CU determines the execution time of tasks. For simplicity, we define the reference execution time of a task as the execution time served on the VM whose CU is 1. Let T^{ref} be a task's reference execution time, then the actual execution time T^{act} of task τ_i running on the VM of type R_q can be formulated as

$$T^{\mathrm{act}}_{\tau_i} = \frac{T^{\mathrm{ref}}_{\tau_i}}{CU_{R_q}}, \tag{1}$$

where $T^{\mathrm{ref}}_{\tau_i}$ is the reference execution time of τ_i and CU_{R_q} is the computing capacity of the VM of type R_q.

Due to the dependence between tasks, the communication overhead is non-negligible. The communication time between two tasks depends on the communication bandwidth of the VM and the size of the transferred data. It can be ignored only when two dependent tasks are served on the same VM. In general, the communication bandwidth of different types of VMs are different. Let BW be the communication bandwidth of a VM and $DATA$ be the size of transferred data of a task. Assume tasks τ_i and τ_j are assigned to VMs V_α and V_β, respectively. The communication time needed to transfer data from τ_i to τ_j is

$$T^{\mathrm{com}}_{\tau_i,\tau_j} = \begin{cases} \frac{DATA_{\tau_i}}{\min(BW_{R_\alpha}, BW_{R_\beta})}, & \text{if } V_\alpha \neq V_\beta, \\ 0, & \text{if } V_\alpha = V_\beta, \end{cases} \tag{2}$$

where R_α and R_β ($R_\alpha, R_\beta \in R$) are the VM types of V_α and V_β respectively and $DATA_{\tau_i}$ is the size of the transferred data of τ_i.

3.3   Security Model

To ensure security during data transmission, it is necessary to use security services to defend against threats. We assume that the system has provided multiple security services for VMs since various security protection mechanisms have been studied and developed in the literature. Users can readily adopt the security services to improve system quality of security under the cost constraint.

Let $S = \{S_1, S_2, \cdots, S_K\}$ be a security service set containing K different security services. Each security service is associated with an encryption algorithm, the time overhead, and the corresponding security level achieved by using the encryption algorithm. The encryption time overhead and the monetary cost are usually linearly and positively correlated with the achieved security level. Let

SC_k $(1 \leq k \leq K)$ be the charge price for encrypting each unit of data by using security service S_k. Assume task τ_i adopts S_k as its security service. After using S_k, the achieved security level of task τ_i is denoted by s_i. Let $T^{enc}_{\tau_i,s_i}$ be the time overhead by using service S_k to encrypt each unit of data. The data encryption starts after the task execution. The time overhead of encrypting unit data can be formulated as $T^{uni}_{s_i} = A_i \times s_i$, where A_i is a positive coefficient depending on the encryption algorithm adopted by task τ_i. The encryption time overhead is positively correlated with the size of data to be encrypted. It is expressed as

$$T^{enc}_{\tau_i,s_i} = T^{uni}_{s_i} \times \rho_i = A_i \times s_i \times \rho_i, \qquad (3)$$

where ρ_i is the size of data segment that needs to be encrypted in task τ_i.

The system quality of security is defined as the sum of security levels of all tasks in the workflow application. It is derived as

$$SecuLevel_{sys}(\Gamma) = \sum_{i=1}^{N} s_i, \qquad (4)$$

where s_i is the security level achieved by task τ_i.

4   Problem Formulation and Methodology Overview

This section formulates the problem to be solved in this paper and introduces our solution to the problem in brief.

4.1   Problem Definition

Our goal is to minimize the cost of scheduling workflows at the premise of meeting makespan and security constraints. The makespan and cost are calculated as follows. Let $T^{sta}_{\tau_i}$ and $T^{fin}_{\tau_i}$ represent the start time and finish time of task τ_i, respectively. The time required to complete a task consists of two parts: i) the time required to run on the VM and ii) the time demanded to use the security service for data protection. Hence, the task finish time $T^{fin}_{\tau_i}$ is calculated as

$$T^{fin}_{\tau_i} = T^{sta}_{\tau_i} + T^{act}_{\tau_i} + T^{enc}_{\tau_i,s_i} = \max\{T^{ava}_{V_m}, \max_{\tau_j \in Pred(\tau_i)} (T^{fin}_{\tau_j} + T^{com}_{\tau_i,\tau_j})\} + T^{act}_{\tau_i} + T^{enc}_{\tau_i,s_i}, \qquad (5)$$

where $T^{ava}_{V_m}$ is the available time of VM V_m that would be dynamically changed during the task allocation process. Clearly, the start time of entry task $T^{sta}_{\tau_{entry}}$ is 0. The makespan, defined as the latest finish time of all tasks, is expressed as

$$Makespan = \max_{\tau_i \in \Gamma} T^{fin}_{\tau_i}, \qquad (6)$$

where $T^{fin}_{\tau_i}$ is derived by Eq. (5).

Let $Cost_{VM}(V_m, R_q, PC_q)$ denote the monetary cost of using VM V_m whose type is R_q and price is PC_q. Let $Cost_{ser}(\tau_i, s_i, SC_k)$ denote the monetary cost of task τ_i when using security service S_k with price SC_k. Thus the total monetary cost is derived as

$$Cost_{tot} = \sum_{V_m \in \Psi} Cost_{VM}\left(V_m, R_q, PC_q\right) + \sum_{i=1}^{N} Cost_{ser}(\tau_i, s_i, SC_k), \qquad (7)$$

where Ψ is a VM set including the VMs that are selected to run tasks and s_i is the security level of task τ_i.

We define our optimization problem as follows. Given a workflow application, an IaaS platform and a group of security services, we aim at obtaining a task sequence and a task scheduling scheme for minimizing the cost of scheduling workflow tasks at the premise of meeting makespan and security constraints. The problem can be mathematically formulated as

$$
\begin{aligned}
\text{Minimize:} \quad & Cost_{tot} \\
\text{subject to:} \quad & Makespan \leq D \\
& SecuLevel_{sys}(\Gamma) \geq \mathcal{L}
\end{aligned}
\qquad (8)
$$

where $Cost_{tot}$ given in Eq. (7) is the total monetary cost spending for VMs and security services, $Makespan$ given in Eq. (6) is the latest finish time of all tasks, $SecuLevel_{sys}$ given in Eq. (4) is the system quality of security. The 1st constraint requires that all tasks should be finished before a common deadline D and the 2nd constraint ensures that system security level is no lower than a threshold $\mathcal{L}$.

4.2   Methodology Overview

The studied problem involves the decisions on i) the execution order of tasks, and ii) the assignment of tasks to VMs and the selection of security services. Considering the combinatorial nature of this problem, we propose IFA to solve it. IFA follows the rationale of traditional FA [6], which exploits the luminous characteristics of fireflies to attract other fireflies. Specifically, for any two fireflies, the attraction between them is determined by their brightness, also called light intensity. When two fireflies attract each other, the firefly with less brightness will move towards the firefly with more brightness. Inspired by this social behavior of fireflies, we define fireflies as the solutions to the studied problem and define the brightness of a firefly as the objective of a solution. According to the luminous characteristics, the firefly with a low objective value will move towards the firefly with a high objective value, such that all fireflies will eventually surround the firefly with the best objective value (i.e., the optimal solution). Unlike the traditional FA used in solving continuous optimization problems, our IFA uses a distance-based mapping operator that considers not only the distance between each firefly and the brightest one but also the current optimal solution. Figure 2 gives an overview of IFA, including solution representation and initialization, firefly updating, firefly mapping, and solution evaluation.

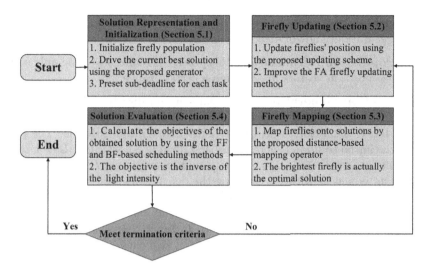

Fig. 2. The overview of the proposed IFA.

5   Proposed Improved Firefly Algorithm

Distinct from the traditional FA [6], our IFA improves the way of firefly updating by enabling each firefly to move towards the brightest one according to their distance. Specifically, we propose a new distance-based mapping operator to ensure that the corresponding solution of each firefly is inherited from the current optimal solution. To speed up the convergence process, we also design an initial heuristic algorithm to provide a good initial solution for IFA.

5.1   Solution Representation and Initialization

Representation: The solution of IFA is the rank of all tasks (i.e., the task sequence and denoted by ζ). As mentioned earlier, data dependency between tasks is considered in this paper. The dependency is broken if a task is prior to its predecessor in the sequence. Thus, a valid task sequence must follow data dependencies. For example, given three tasks τ_1, τ_2, τ_3, τ_1 is the predecessor of τ_2 and τ_3. Among the three permutations of these tasks, i.e., $\zeta_1 = (\tau_1, \tau_2, \tau_3)$, $\zeta_2 = (\tau_2, \tau_1, \tau_3)$, $\zeta_3 = (\tau_3, \tau_2, \tau_1)$, only ζ_1 is a valid task sequence. Let $\zeta_{\ell[i]}$ denote the i-th task in the ℓ-th solution, we have $\zeta_{1[2]} = \tau_2$. Supposing Ω is the population of fireflies, the position vector of the ℓ-th ($\ell = 1, 2, \cdots, |\Omega|$) firefly is denoted by $Y_\ell = \{Y_{\ell,1}, Y_{\ell,2}, \cdots, Y_{\ell,N}\}$ where $Y_{\ell,n} \in [DL, UL]$ ($n = 1, 2, \cdots, N$). DL and UL are the lower limit and the upper limit of the firefly domain, respectively. The position vector of a firefly can be mapped to a valid task sequence (i.e., solution), and the firefly's brightness is associated with the objective (i.e., cost) of this solution. Considering this, we define the intensity of the ℓ-th firefly I_ℓ as the reciprocal of its fitness function. That is, $I_\ell = 1/f(\zeta_\ell)$ where ζ_ℓ is the solution and f is the fitness function (i.e., the total monetary cost, $f(\zeta) = Cost_{\text{tot}}$).

Initialization: it consists of three parts: firefly population initialization, initial solution generation, and sub-deadline calculation.

Firefly Population Initialization: this process is realized by randomly setting the fireflies' position vectors in Ω within a certain range.

Initial Solution Generation: the initial solution directly affects the efficacy of IFA. To let IFA start with a good initial solution, we propose a composite heuristic based generator to provide a high-quality initial solution. The procedures of the initial solution generator are described in Algorithm 1. Line 1 creates three empty solutions $\zeta_{ISG}, \zeta_{ESM}, \zeta_{Temp}$, and an empty set R. Lines 2–7 generate random sequences without violating the dependencies of tasks in the DAG. Note that when all the predecessors of a task have been included in the initial sequence, the task is deemed as a ready task and can be added to the set R. Specifically, line 2 adds the entry tasks into R. Lines 3–4 randomly select a task from set R and add it to the end of the initial sequence ζ_{ISG} in each iteration until R is empty. In each iteration, lines 5–7 traverse the whole DAG graph to check whether there are ready tasks that are neither in the initial sequence nor in R. If so, line 7 adds these ready tasks into set R.

Lines 8–15 use an exchange-based search method to improve ζ_{ISG}. Specifically, line 8 sets solutions ζ_{ESM} and ζ_{Temp} to ζ_{ISG}. Line 11 exchanges the i-th task in ζ_{Temp} with its subsequent task τ_j to obtain a candidate solution. Lines 12–15 check the validity of this candidate solution and judge whether the solution is improved. If so, line 13 updates ζ_{ESM} to ζ_{Temp}. Otherwise, line 15 resets ζ_{Temp} to ζ_{ESM}. The algorithm repeats the above process until all tasks have been tried, and obtains ζ_{ESM} as the best candidate solution. Line 16 sets ζ^* to ζ_{ESM}. The generator finally outputs ζ^* as the initial solution.

Sub-deadline Calculation: We need to pre-set a sub-deadline for each task, to ensure that all the tasks can be completed before the common deadline while being assigned to the appropriate VM. To this end, we first sort the communication bandwidth and computing unit of Q different types of VMs in ascending order. To make full use of the given deadline and make the time left for each task as loose as possible, we consider allocating VMs with small BW_{R_q} and CU_{R_q} to tasks. Suppose the average execution time of tasks on different types of VMs is $AT_{\tau_i}^{act}$ and the average communication time is AT_{τ_i,τ_j}^{com}. The communication time here only considers the case that τ_i and τ_j are assigned to different VMs since the communication time between two tasks on the same VM is negligible. Let β and α ($1 \leq \alpha \leq \beta \leq Q$) be the upper and lower bounds of the range of selected VM types. To ensure the sub-deadline assigned to each task is only related to itself, we assume that each task is allocated to the same security service when meeting the security level requirement $\mathcal{L}$, i.e., $s_i = \lceil \frac{\mathcal{L}}{N} \rceil$. Therefore, the encryption time of each task can be calculated using Eq. (3). The procedure of calculating the sub-deadline of tasks is given in **Algorithm 2**. $SubD = \{SubD_1, SubD_2, \cdots, SubD_N\}$ is the set of tasks' sub-deadlines. The algorithm starts assignment from the VM type with the lowest bandwidth and computing capacity in line 1. Line 2 calculates s_i according to the security quality requirement $\mathcal{L}$. Lines 4–6 calculate the average execution time and the encryption time of tasks. Lines 7–12 iteratively derive the sub-deadline of tasks, starting

---

Algorithm 1: Initial Solution Generator

Input: Task set Γ;
Output: Initial solution ζ^*;

1 Create empty solutions ζ_{ISG}, ζ_{ESM}, ζ_{Temp}, and a set $R = \phi$;
2 Add τ_{entry} into R;
3 **while** $R \neq \phi$ **do**
4   Randomly select a task from set R and add it to the end of ζ_{ISG};
5   **for** $i = 1$ to N **do**
6   **if** τ_i is a ready task and not in R or ζ_{ISG} **then**
7   Add τ_i into set R;

8 Set $\zeta_{ESM} = \zeta_{ISG}$ and $\zeta_{Temp} = \zeta_{ISG}$;
9 **for** $i = 1$ to $N - 1$ **do**
10   **for** $j = i + 1$ to N **do**
11   Exchange task τ_i with τ_j in ζ_{Temp};
12   **if** ζ_{Temp} is valid and improved **then**
13              $\zeta_{ESM} = \zeta_{Temp}$;
14   **else**
15              $\zeta_{Temp} = \zeta_{ESM}$;

16 $\zeta^* = \zeta_{ESM}$;

---

from the exit task. Afterward, lines 13–16 reset α and β since bandwidth and

---

Algorithm 2: Sub-deadline Calculation

Input: Task set Γ; VM type Set R; security services set S; deadline D; security quality constraint $\mathcal{L}$;

Output: Set of tasks' sub-deadlines, $SubD = \{SubD_1, \cdots, SubD_N\}$;

1   Initialize $\alpha = 1$, $\beta = 1$;

2   Calculate $s_i = \lceil \frac{\mathcal{L}}{N} \rceil$;

3   **while** $SubD \leq 0$ **do**

4   **for** $i = 1$ to N **do**

5        $AT_{\tau_i}^{\mathrm{act}} = \frac{\sum_{q=\alpha}^{\beta} T_{\tau_i, R_q}^{\mathrm{act}}}{\beta - \alpha + 1}$ where $T_{\tau_i, R_q}^{\mathrm{act}}$ is derived by Eq. (1);

6   Calculate $T_{\tau_i, s_i}^{\mathrm{enc}}$ by Eq. (3);

7   **for** $i = N$ to 1 **do**

8   **if** τ_i has no successors **then**

9           $SubD_i = D$;

10   **else**

11           $AT_{\tau_i, \tau_j}^{\mathrm{com}} = \frac{\sum_{q=\alpha}^{\beta} T_{\tau_i, \tau_j, R_q}^{\mathrm{com}}}{\beta - \alpha + 1}$ where $\tau_j \in Succ(\tau_i)$ and $T_{\tau_i, \tau_j, R_q}^{\mathrm{com}}$ is derived by Eq. (2) ;

12           $SubD_i = \min(SubD_j - (AT_{\tau_i, \tau_j}^{\mathrm{com}} + AT_{\tau_i}^{\mathrm{act}} + T_{\tau_i, s_i}^{\mathrm{enc}}))$;

13   **if** $\beta = Q$ **then**

14        $\alpha = \alpha + 1$;

15   **else**

16        $\beta = \beta + 1$;

---

computing capacity may be too small to finish all tasks before deadline. If the sub-deadlines of all tasks are valid (i.e., positive), the algorithm outputs $SubD$.

5.2   The Improved Updating Scheme

The proposed updating scheme is an improved version of that in traditional FA [6]. In traditional FA [6], the ℓ-th firefly updates its position by the following equation when it is attracted by another brighter firefly.

$$Y_\ell = Y_\ell + \beta_0 e^{-\gamma r_{\ell,\hbar}^2}(Y_\hbar - Y_\ell) + \alpha(\varepsilon - \frac{1}{2}), \qquad (9)$$

where Y_ℓ is the ℓ-th firefly's current position. $\beta_0 e^{-\gamma r_{\ell,\hbar}^2}$ is the degree of attraction of the $\hbar$-th firefly to the ℓ-th firefly. $\alpha(\varepsilon - \frac{1}{2})$ is a random search. β_0 is the maximum attraction of the light source, varying in the range of $[0, 1]$. γ is the light intensity absorption coefficient and it usually takes a value from $[0.01, 100]$. α is a random step factor whose value is in the range of $[0, 1]$. ε is a random factor obeying uniform distribution on the interval $[0, 1]$. $r_{\ell,\hbar}$ is the Euclidean distance between the ℓ-th firefly and the $\hbar$-th firefly, which can be derived by

$$r_{\ell,\hbar} = \sqrt{\sum_{n=1}^{N}(Y_{\hbar,n} - Y_{\ell,n})^2}. \tag{10}$$

It can be observed from Eq. (9) that the random moving range of fireflies is $[-\frac{1}{2}\alpha, \frac{1}{2}\alpha]$ in the traditional FA. It means that once α is determined, the random moving range will be fixed and is independent of the distance between the firefly and the brightest one. However, we hope the firefly moves in a wider range when it is far from the brightest one. On the basis of this idea, we propose a new updating method that improves the position calculation by

$$Y_\ell = Y_\ell + \beta_0 e^{-\gamma r_{\ell,\hbar}^2}(Y_\hbar - Y_\ell) + \frac{r_\ell^*}{N}(\varepsilon - \frac{1}{2}), \tag{11}$$

where r_ℓ^* is the distance between the ℓ-th firefly and the brightest one. N is the dimension of the firefly's position. In our improved updating scheme, the range of the random moving range is related to the distance r_ℓ^*, which is in interval $[-\frac{1}{2}\frac{r_\ell^*}{N}, \frac{1}{2}\frac{r_\ell^*}{N}]$. In other words, with the increase of r_ℓ^*, the random moving range increases and vice versa. To prevent the firefly from frequently hitting the boundary during its movement, we divide its Euclidean distance by the dimension N to control its search range.

5.3 The Distance-Based Mapping Operator

To map the firefly to the corresponding solution, we propose a distance-based mapping operator considering both the distance r^* and the current optimal solution. The principle of mapping inherits the idea of the traditional FA, that is, each firefly approaches the brightest one in each iteration. In other words, the fireflies nearer to the brightest one have larger possibilities to be mapped onto a better solution. The process of the distance-based mapping operator is summarized in Algorithm 3.

Let ζ^* denote the current optimal solution and r_ℓ^* denote the distance between the ℓ-th firefly and the brightest one. Firstly, line 1 generates an empty solution ζ_ℓ and a set G. ζ_ℓ is used to store the resultant solution while G is used to store tasks that are not directly inherited. Lines 2–7 describe the inheritance step. It is assumed that the probability of each task directly being inherited into ζ_ℓ is $p = e^{-r_\ell^*}$. Since r_ℓ^* must be a non-negative number, the value of p is in the interval $(0, 1]$. Clearly, the smaller r_ℓ^*, the larger p. It indicates that the closer the ℓ-th firefly is to the brightest one, the larger possibility the corresponding solution will inherit tasks directly in the same position from the current optimal solution. Specifically, line 3 randomly generates a number δ in $(0, 1)$. Lines 4–7 determine whether tasks can be inherited to ζ_ℓ. If δ is smaller than p, line 5 adds $\zeta_{[i]}^*$ to ζ_ℓ in the same position. Otherwise, line 7 adds the $\zeta_{[i]}^*$ into G.

Lines 8–13 describe the random insertion step. Specifically, line 8 randomly sorts the remaining tasks in G. Lines 9–13 select the first task in G and insert it into the first empty position in ζ_ℓ. If all the predecessors of the task have been inserted before this position, line 12 inserts this task into ζ_ℓ and line 13 removes the task from G. Otherwise, it selects the second task in G, inserts the task into the first empty position in ζ_ℓ, and continues to judge in the same way until the insertion is successful. After successful insertion, the operator continues to insert the first task in G after updating, and repeats the above process until there is no task left in G. Finally, the operator outputs the solution ζ_ℓ and terminates.

However, since each solution originates from the current optimal solution ζ^*, we cannot get rid of the possibility that the solutions obtained are the same as ζ^*. If so, IFA will fall into the local optimum and stop looking for the global optimal solution. Thus, we propose a theorem and prove it below to discuss the possibility that the solution ζ_ℓ is the same as ζ^*.

Theorem 1. *For the ℓ-th firefly that is not the brightest, its corresponding solution ζ_ℓ generated by the mapping operator satisfies* $\lim_{N\to\infty} P(\zeta_\ell = \zeta^*) = 0$.

Proof. Two situations may cause $\zeta_\ell = \zeta^*$. The first is that in the inheritance step, ζ_ℓ inherits tasks directly in the same position from ζ^*. The second is that in the inheritance step, ζ_ℓ inherits some tasks directly in the same position from ζ^*, but in the random insertion step, the remaining tasks are accidentally inserted into the same positions as before. Supposing the possibilities of the two situations are P_a and P_b respectively, we have $P(\zeta_i = \zeta^*) = P_a + P_b$.

- In situation 1, since ζ_ℓ inherits all the tasks in the same position from ζ^*, P_a can be expressed as $P_a = p^N$.
- In situation 2, supposing $\mathcal{R}$ represents the number of the remaining tasks that have not been inserted into ζ_ℓ, and μ denotes the probability of the remaining tasks accidentally being inserted into ζ_ℓ at the same position, $0 < \mu < 1$ holds. Thus, P_b can be expressed as $P_b = \mu p^{N-\mathcal{R}}(1-p)^{\mathcal{R}}$.

Considering the two situations, $P(\zeta_\ell = \zeta^*)$ can be expressed as

$$P(\zeta_\ell = \zeta^*) = P_a + P_b = p^N + \mu p^{N-\mathcal{R}}(1-p)^{\mathcal{R}}. \tag{12}$$

Since the number N of tasks is assumed to be large enough, meaning that the number of the remaining tasks $\mathcal{R}$ is approximately equal to the mathematical expectation $N - N \cdot p$, we can derive $\lim_{N\to\infty} P(\zeta_i = \zeta^*) = \lim_{N\to\infty} p^N + \lim_{N\to\infty} \mu p^{N\cdot p}(1-p)^{N(1-p)}$. Since $r_\ell^* \neq 0$, we have $0 < p < 1$, $0 < p^p < 1$, and $0 < (1-p)^{1-p} < 1$. Thus, $\lim_{N\to\infty} p^N = 0$, $\lim_{N\to\infty} p^{N\cdot p} = \lim_{N\to\infty} (p^p)^N = 0$, and $\lim_{N\to\infty} (1-p)^{N(1-p)} = \lim_{N\to\infty} (1-p)^{(1-p)^N} = 0$. As each term in the formula tends to zero, we can draw the conclusion that $\lim_{N\to\infty} P(\zeta_\ell = \zeta^*) = 0$. ∎

From Theorem 1 we can conclude that for large-scale applications, the possibility of obtaining the same solution as ζ^* is approximately equal to 0 and it is independent of the probability p of each task directly being inherited into ζ_ℓ.

Algorithm 3: Distance-based Mapping Operator

Input: Current optimal solution ζ^*; distance between the ℓ-th firefly and the brightest one r_ℓ^*.

Output: Solution ζ_ℓ.

1 Generate an empty solution ζ_ℓ and a set $G = \phi$;

2 **for** $i = 1$ to N **do**

3 $\quad$ Randomly generate a number $\delta \in (0, 1)$;

4 $\quad$ **if** $\delta \le e^{-r_\ell^*}$ **then**

5 $\quad\quad$ $\zeta_{\ell[i]} = \zeta_{[i]}^*$;

6 $\quad$ **else**

7 $\quad\quad$ Add $\zeta_{[i]}^*$ into G;

8 Rank G randomly;

9 **while** $G \ne \phi$ **do**

10 $\quad$ **for** $i = 1$ to $|G|$ **do**

11 $\quad\quad$ **if** $G_{[i]}$'s predecessors have been added into ζ_ℓ **then**

12 $\quad\quad\quad$ Add $G_{[i]}$ into ζ_ℓ at the first empty position;

13 $\quad\quad\quad$ Remove the task $G_{[i]}$ from G;

5.4 Task Assignment Scheme

Given the corresponding task sequence of each firefly, we use a heuristic algorithm to schedule the tasks to VMs. Through the task-to-VM scheme, we can calculate the total cost and the corresponding light intensity to evaluate fireflies.

After obtaining the task sub-deadline set $SubD$, we first randomly allocate security services to tasks under the security constraint and then assign appropriate VMs to each task. The assignment problem is actually a packing problem. In this case, the VM is identical to the receiving box and its capacity is determined by the deadline while the task is identical to the item and it is loaded into the box. We need to find a way to load N items into as few boxes as possible, and make the items in each box not exceed its capacity. Therefore, we adopt two classic heuristic algorithms to solve the task assignment problem: First-Fit (FF) algorithm and Best-Fit (BF) algorithm.

- FF based assignment: its principle is that each time it assigns a new item to the box with the smallest index and increases the index successively until the item can be loaded. Otherwise, it assigns the item to an empty box. Thus, the FF based assignment algorithm assigns tasks to VMs in turn according to the input task sequence ζ^*, and gives priority to the VM with the smallest index.
- BF based assignment: its principle is that it assigns the item to the box with the smallest available space that can load the item. If the item cannot be loaded into any non-empty box, it will assign it to an empty box. Thus, the BF based task assignment algorithm will give priority to the VM whose available time is closest to the common deadline.

After task-to-VM assignment, the total cost $Cost_{tot}$ can be calculated as the sum of $Cost_{VM}$ required for the assignment and $Cost_{ser}$ required for the random security service selection. $Cost_{tot}$ is also used as the fitness function in IFA, which means $I = 1/f(\zeta) = 1/Cost_{tot}$.

5.5   The Detailed Procedures of IFA

The procedure of IFA can be divided into four steps. i) IFA initializes the population of fireflies, and employs the initial heuristic to obtain a current optimal solution. ii) IFA uses the distance-based mapping operator to map the fireflies onto their corresponding solutions and calculates the fitness of each firefly through the task assignment algorithm. After the assignment and evaluation, IFA can seek out the real brightest firefly. iii) The fireflies begin the movement towards the brightest one through the improved updating scheme in IFA. iv) IFA re-assigns all the fireflies obtained in the third step, calculates their fitnesses, and resets the brightest firefly and the optimal solution if a new optimal solution is discovered, then starts the next round until the number of iterations reaches the maximum.

The detailed procedures of IFA are described in Algorithm 4. Lines 1–2 set up the values of parameters in IFA, and initializes the firefly population. Line 3 calculates the brightness of fireflies. Algorithm 4 calls Algorithm 1 to obtain a current optimal solution in line 4, and calls Algorithm 2 to preset the sub-deadlines of all the tasks in line 5. Line 6 randomly selects a firefly from the initial population as the brightest firefly. The process of fireflies' evaluation is described in lines 7–13, aiming to find the real brightest firefly. If a new optimal solution is discovered, then both the brightest firefly and the optimal solution will be reset. Lines 14–25 give the procedures of firefly population updating. The ℓ-th firefly will move towards the $\hbar$-th firefly and updates its position by Eq. (10), if the brightness of the $\hbar$-th firefly is larger (lines 17–19). After the ℓ-th firefly's position updating, it will be mapped onto a new solution. If the objective of this solution is better than the current optimal solution, the brightest firefly and the optimal solution will be updated (lines 20–25). When the number of iterations reaches the upper bound, IFA stops and outputs the best solution's fitness $f(\zeta^*)$.

6   Simulation

This section validates our scheme through extensive simulation experiments. Four real-world workflows provided by Pegasus workflow management system, i.e., Inspiral, Montage, Sipht, and CyberShake [17] are adopted in the simulation. They are widely used in evaluating algorithm performance. All four workflows can be represented by DAGs, as shown in Fig. 3. Table 1 lists the characteristics of the four workflows. We adopt the pricing model of Amazon EC2 [18] and select the General Purpose VM group in the US East region. Table 2 presents the type, computing unit, bandwidth, and price of the selected VMs. A commonly accepted security service set [13] is used to enhance the security of tasks. The security services are developed based on RC4, RC5, BLOWFISH, IDEA, SKIPJACK,

---

Algorithm 4: Improved Firefly Algorithm (IFA)

Input: Task set Γ;
Output: Fitness of the best solution $f(\zeta^*)$;

1 Set the maximum iteration number M and the parameters β_0 and γ;
2 Initialize the population of fireflies $\Omega = \{Y_1, Y_2, \ldots, Y_{|\Omega|}\}$ randomly;
3 Calculate the brightness as $I_\ell = 1/f(\zeta_\ell)$;
4 Call **Algorithm 1** to obtain a current best solution ζ^*;
5 Call **Algorithm 2** to calculate the sub-deadline of each task.
6 Randomly set a firefly b from the initial population as the brightest one;
7 **for** $\ell = 1$ to $|\Omega|$ **do**
8   Calculate the distance r_ℓ^*;
9   Call **Algorithm 3** to obtain the solution ζ_ℓ using r_ℓ^* and ζ^*;
10   Derive the fitness $f(\zeta_\ell)$ using FF/BF-based task assignment;
11   Update I_ℓ;
12   **if** $f(\zeta_\ell) \leq f(\zeta^*)$ **then**
13       $b = \ell,\ \zeta^* = \zeta_\ell,\ f(\zeta^*) = f(\zeta_\ell)$;

14 **while** $t < M$ **do**
15   **for** $\ell = 1$ to $|\Omega|$ **do**
16   **for** $\hbar = 1$ to $|\Omega|$ **do**
17   **if** $I_\ell < I_\hbar$ **then**
18   Calculate the distance $r_{\ell\hbar}$ by Eq. (10);
19   Move the ℓ-th firefly towards the $\hbar$-th firefly and obtain its new position by Eq. (11);

20   Calculate the distance r_ℓ^*;
21   Call **Algorithm 3** to obtain the solution ζ_ℓ using r_ℓ^* and ζ^*;
22   Derive the fitness $f(\zeta_\ell)$ using FF/BF-based task assignment;
23   Update I_ℓ;
24   **if** $f(\zeta_\ell) \leq f(\zeta^*)$ **then**
25             $b = \ell,\ \zeta^* = \zeta_\ell,\ f(\zeta^*) = f(\zeta_\ell)$;

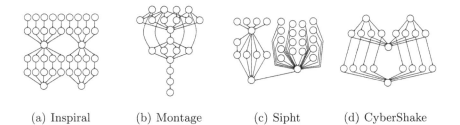

(a) Inspiral   (b) Montage   (c) Sipht   (d) CyberShake

Fig. 3. The structure of four real-world workflows.

and 3DES encryption algorithms. Their execution time, cost consumption, and security level are given in Table 3. The size of data to be encrypted for each task is varied from 1000 to 4000 KB.

Table 1. The characteristics of real-world workflow applications.

Workflow	Number of nodes	Number of edges	Average data size (MB)	Average task runtime (s)
Inspiral 30/50/100	30/50/100	95/160/319	9.00/9.16/8.93	206.78/226.19/206.12
Montage 25/50/100	25/50/100	95/206/433	3.43/3.36/3.23	8.44/9.78/10.58
Sipht 30/60/100	30/60/100	91/198/335	7.73/6.95/6.27	178.92/194.48/175.55
CyberShake 30/50/100	30/50/100	112/188/390	747.48/864.74/849.60	23.77/29.32/31.53

Table 2. Parameters of VMs in Amazon EC2.

VM type	Compute unit	Bandwidth (MB/s)	Price ($)
m3.medium	3	56.25	0.067
m3.large	6.5	56.25	0.133
m3.xlarge	13	62.5	0.266
m3.2xlarge	26	125	0.532
m4.large	6.5	56.25	0.120
m4.xlarge	13	93.75	0.239
m4.2xlarge	26	125	0.479
m4.4xlarge	53.5	250	0.958
m4.10xlarge	124.5	500	2.394

Table 3. Parameters of the security service set.

Security serverce	Cryptographic algorithm	Execution time (ms/KB)	Price ($/KB)	Security level
S_1	RC4	0.0063	$1.2682 * 10^{-5}$	1
S_2	RC5	0.0140	$2.2828 * 10^{-5}$	2
S_3	BLOWFISH	0.0231	$3.1129 * 10^{-5}$	3
S_4	IDEA	0.0336	$3.8046 * 10^{-5}$	4
S_5	SKIPJACK	0.0459	$4.3517 * 10^{-5}$	5
S_6	3DES	0.0591	$4.8698 * 10^{-5}$	6

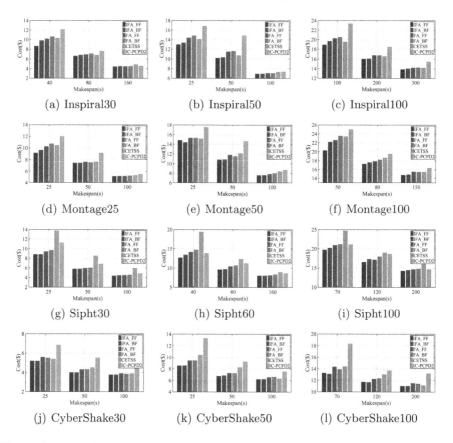

Fig. 4. Average cost on 10 experiments with varying timing constraint of 12 workflows.

IFA needs to decide two key parameters β_0 and γ. As aforementioned, β_0 is generally set varied in the range $[0, 1]$. When β_0 is set to 1, the brightest firefly uses its maximum brightness to attract other fireflies to move towards it, which means it will have a significant impact on the position of other fireflies. Since the mapping operator maps the firefly onto the solution according to the distance from the brightest firefly. The smaller the distance, the greater the probability of the firefly inheriting the optimal solution. Therefore, we hope the distance between the firefly and the brightest one can become smaller after movement every time, so we set β_0 to 1. The value of γ also has a great influence on the movement of fireflies. Generally, γ is set from 0.01 to 10. Based on simulation results, we empirically set γ to 4. As for α in traditional FA, we take the most common value of 0.5. We set the population size $|\Omega|$ as 30, the range of each dimension of each firefly as $[4, 4]$, and the maximum number of iterations in each round as 200. When the number of iterations exceeds 200, the algorithm terminates. For each test case, we conduct 10 experiments and record the cost/fitness.

Table 4. Average cost of 12 workflows using six algorithms.

Workflow	IFA-FF	IFA-BF	FA-FF	FA-BF	CETSS [19]	IC-PCPD2 [20]
Inspiral 30	6.5507	7.0210	7.1690	7.2269	7.3048	8.0870
Inspiral 50	10.0183	10.1969	10.9808	11.1597	10.7075	13.0077
Inspiral 100	16.2627	16.5899	17.0623	17.1490	16.7378	19.0938
Montage 25	6.8922	7.0313	7.6682	7.8002	7.7861	8.8675
Montage 50	11.0693	10.9403	11.6396	11.6003	11.8933	13.6203
Montage 100	17.4187	18.2111	18.6620	18.7245	19.1460	20.2915
Sipht 30	6.3218	6.3606	6.6162	6.7582	9.7345	7.6428
Sipht 60	10.0968	10.3795	10.8949	11.2612	13.5478	11.2272
Sipht 100	16.8466	17.3236	17.5809	17.9727	19.9092	18.1385
CyberShake30	4.3151	4.3138	4.5997	4.5569	4.5917	5.8885
CyberShake50	7.1566	7.2059	7.7517	7.7595	8.3179	10.0320
CyberShake100	12.0061	11.9388	12.7021	12.5593	12.8675	15.0782
Total Average	10.3874	10.6261	11.1106	11.2107	11.8787	12.5813

We compare our IFA with the baseline FA and two benchmarking approaches CETSS [19] and IC-PCPD2 [20] that are all applied to solve our problem.

- IFA-FF and IFA-BF are the combination of the proposed Improved Firefly Algorithm with First-Fit and Best-Fit task assignment, respectively.
- FA-FF and FA-BF are the combination of the baseline Firefly Algorithm with First-Fit and Best-Fit task assignment, respectively.
- CETSS [19] is a Cost-Efficient Task Scheduling Strategy that efficiently schedules all tasks to achieve optimal financial cost and system performance.
- IC-PCPD2 [20] is an IaaS Cloud-Partial Critical Path based on Deadline Distribution. It modifies the deadline distribution and the planning phases to adapt to the Cloud environment, and creates a schedule that minimizes the total execution cost based on their sub-deadlines.

Figure 4 compares the average costs of running 12 different workflows when using the proposed IFA-FF, IFA-BF, and benchmarking schemes FA-FF, FA-BF, CETSS [19], and IC-PCPD2 [20] under varying timing constraints (i.e., makespan) and the same security constraint. The results clearly show that the proposed IFA always outperforms FA, CETSS, and IC-PCPD2 in decreasing cost regardless of makespan and application scale. In most cases, the mean costs of IFA-FF are lower than those of IFA-BF. The reason is described as follows. As in sub-deadline calculation, given a task sequence, the sub-deadline of previous tasks will be relatively loose while the sub-deadline of subsequent tasks will be relatively tight. Thus, the computing capacities of VMs with small indexes are usually poor, and vice versa. In other words, in most cases, when assigning tasks, IFA-FF would give priority to VMs with poor computing capacity and leave the VMs with strong computing capacity to the subsequent tasks. In this way, the idle time of each VM can be fully utilized. However, in IFA-BF, some tasks may not be able to be assigned to the previous VMs with weak computing capacity due to the tight latest completion time, resulting in low utilization of these VMs.

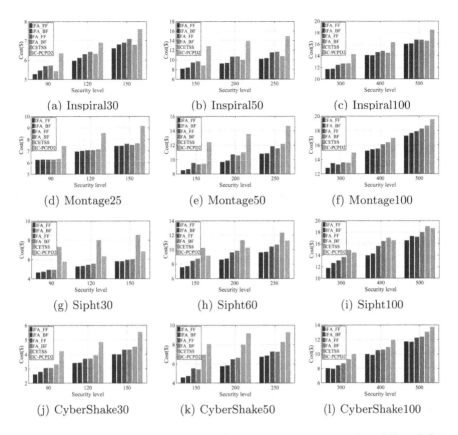

Fig. 5. Average cost on 10 experiments with varying security constraint of 12 workflows.

The results also indicate that the mean cost of IC-PCPD2 is always the worst and the mean cost of CETSS is close to those of FA-FF and FA-BF.

For better illustration, we also list the average cost of scheduling 12 workflows using IFA-FF, IFA-BF, FA-FF, FA-BF, CETSS [19], and IC-PCPD2 [20] in Table 4. We can find that in most cases, the mean costs of IFA-FF are about 0.5%–4% better than those of IFA-BF. Only in few workflows such as Montage50, CyberShake30, and CyberShake100, the mean costs of IFA-BF are slightly better than those of IFA-FF. Compared to IFA-BF, FA-FF, FA-BF, CETSS, and IC-PCPD2, the average reductions on mean costs realized by IFA-FF are 2.3%, 7.0%, 7.9%, 14.5%, and 21.7%, respectively. The maximum reduction achieved by IFA-FF can be up to 54.0% when compared to CETSS in the Sipht30 case.

We also compare the average costs of running 12 different workflows when using the proposed IFA-FF, IFA-BF, and benchmarking schemes FA-FF, FA-BF, CETSS [19], and IC-PCPD2 [20] under varying security constraints and the same makespan constraint. As shown in Fig. 5(a)–(l), the proposed IFA always outperforms FA, CETSS, and IC-PCPD2 in decreasing cost, indicating IFA also performs well in reducing cost using a random security service selection scheme.

7 Conclusion

To minimize the cost of executing precedence-constrained tasks of a workflow application under the deadline and security constraints, this paper proposes an improved firefly algorithm (IFA) that minimizes the total monetary cost spending for renting VMs and using security services. IFA consists of an initial solution generator to obtain the first current optimal solution, an improved updating scheme to update fireflies' positions, a distance-based mapping operator to map fireflies onto corresponding solutions, as well as a random security service selection scheme and two task assignment schemes to meet system security and deadline constraints. We evaluate our proposed IFA by comparing it with a baseline and two state-of-the-art approaches on scheduling tasks of 12 different real-world workflows. Experimental results show that the cost reduction achieved by our IFA can be up to 54.0%.

Acknowledgements. This work was supported in part by the National Natural Science Foundation of China under Grant No. 62172224, in part by the Natural Science Foundation of Jiangsu Province under Grant No. BK20220138, in part by the China Postdoctoral Science Foundation under Grant Nos. 2021T140327 and 2020M680068, in part by the Fundamental Research Funds for the Central Universities under Grant Nos. 30922010318 and 30922010406, in part by the Postdoctoral Science Foundation of Jiangsu Province under Grant No. 2021K066A, in part by the Open Research Fund of the State Key Laboratory of Computer Architecture, Institute of Computing Technology, Chinese Academy of Sciences under Grant No. CARCHA202105, in part by the Future Network Scientific Research Fund Project under Grant No. FNSRFP-2021-YB-6, and in part by the Open Research Fund of the National Trusted Embedded Software Engineering Technology Research Center (East China Normal University).

References

1. Cong, P., Zhang, Z., Zhou, J., Liu, X., Liu, Y., Wei, T.: Customer adaptive resource provisioning for long-term cloud profit maximization under constrained budget. IEEE Trans. Parallel Distrib. Syst. **33**(6), 1373–1392 (2022)
2. Dickinson, M., et al.: Multi-cloud performance and security driven federated workflow management. IEEE Trans. Cloud Comput. **9**(1), 240–257 (2021)
3. Zhou, J., Sun, J., Zhang, M., Ma, Y.: Dependable scheduling for real-time workflows on cyber-physical cloud systems. IEEE Trans. Industr. Inf. **17**(11), 7820–7829 (2021)
4. Casas, I., Taheri, J., Ranjan, R., Wang, L., Zomaya, A.Y.: A balanced scheduler with data reuse and replication for scientific workflows in cloud computing systems. Futur. Gener. Comput. Syst. **74**, 168–178 (2017)
5. Shaikh, F.B., Haider, S.: Security threats in cloud computing. In: International Conference for Internet Technology and Secured Transactions, pp. 214–219 (2011)
6. Yang, X.S.: Nature-Inspired Metaheuristic Algorithms. Luniver Press (2008)

7. Wen, Z., Qasha, R., Li, Z., Ranjan, R., Watson, P., Romanovsky, A.: Dynamically partitioning workflow over federated clouds for optimising the monetary cost and handling run-time failures. IEEE Trans. Cloud Comput. **8**(4), 1093–1107 (2020)
8. Zhou, X., Zhang, G., Sun, J., Zhou, J., Wei, T., Hu, S.: Minimizing cost and makespan for workflow scheduling in cloud using fuzzy dominance sort based HEFT. Futur. Gener. Comput. Syst. **93**, 278–289 (2019)
9. Wu, Q., Ishikawa, F., Zhu, Q., Xia, Y., Wen, J.: Deadline-constrained cost optimization approaches for workflow scheduling in clouds. IEEE Trans. Parallel Distrib. Syst. **28**(12), 3401–3412 (2017)
10. Arabnejad, V., Bubendorfer, K., Ng, B.: Dynamic multi-workflow scheduling: a deadline and cost-aware approach for commercial clouds. Futur. Gener. Comput. Syst. **100**, 98–108 (2019)
11. Zhou, Z., Yu, S., Chen, W., Chen, X.: CE-IoT: cost-effective cloud-edge resource provisioning for heterogeneous IoT applications. IEEE Internet Things J. **7**(9), 8600–8614 (2020)
12. Xie, T., Qin, X.: Improving security for periodic tasks in embedded systems through scheduling. ACM Trans. Embed. Comput. Syst. **6**(3) (2007)
13. Jiang, W., Zhang, X., Zhan, J., Ma, Y., Jiang, K.: Design optimization of secure message communication for energy-constrained distributed real-time systems. J. Parallel Distrib. Comput. **100**, 1–15 (2017)
14. Zhou, J., et al.: Security-critical energy-aware task scheduling for heterogeneous real-time MPSoCs in IoT. IEEE Trans. Serv. Comput. **13**(4), 745–758 (2020)
15. Nawrocki, P., Pajor, J., Sniezynski, B., Kolodziej, J.: Security-aware job allocation in mobile cloud computing. In: IEEE/ACM 21st International Symposium on Cluster, Cloud and Internet Computing, pp. 713–719 (2021)
16. Du, Y., Wang, Y., Yang, B., Hu, H.: Analyzing security requirements in timed workflow processes. IEEE Trans. Depend. Secure Comput. **19**(1), 190–207 (2022)
17. Bharathi, S., Chervenak, A., Deelman, E., Mehta, G., Su, M., Vahi, K.: Characterization of scientific workflows. In: 2008 Third Workshop on Workflows in Support of Large-Scale Science, pp. 1–10 (2008)
18. Amazon: Amazon Ec2 Pricing. http://aws.amazon.com/ec2/ pricing/
19. Tang, X., et al.: Cost-efficient workflow scheduling algorithm for applications with deadline constraint on heterogeneous clouds. IEEE Trans. Parallel Distrib. Syst. **33**(9), 2079–2092 (2022)
20. Abrishami, S., Naghibzadeh, M., Epema, D.: Deadline-constrained workflow scheduling algorithms for infrastructure as a service clouds. Futur. Gener. Comput. Syst. **29**(1), 158–169 (2013)

Efficient Multiple-Precision and Mixed-Precision Floating-Point Fused Multiply-Accumulate Unit for HPC and AI Applications

Hongbing Tan, Run Yan, Ling Yang, Libo Huang[(✉)], Liquan Xiao, and Qianming Yang[(✉)]

National University of Defense Technology, Changsha 410073, China
{tanhongbing,yanrun,yangling,libohuang,xiaoliquan,yqm21249}@nudt.edu.cn

Abstract. In this paper, a multiple-precision and mixed-precision floating-point fused multiply-accumulate (FMA) unit is proposed base on the practical requirements of high performance computing (HPC) and artificial intelligence (AI) applications. In addition to the double-precision and single-precision formats used in high performance computing, three types of low-precision formats, TensorFloat-32, BFloat16, and half-precision, dedicated to deep learning tasks are also supported by this FMA unit. The proposed FMA architecture can execute one double-precision operation, or two parallel single-precision operations, or four half-precision operations at each clock cycle. Moreover, the mixed-precision FMA operations are also supported by this proposed FMA, the products of two lower precision multiplications can be accumulated to a higher precision addend. One mixed-precision operation using single-precision multiplication and double-precision addition, or two parallel mixed-precision operations using low-precision (TensorFloat-32, BFloat16, or half-precision) multiplication and single-precision addition is performed every clock cycle. The presented FMA design uses both segmentation and reusing methods to trade off performance, such as throughput and latency, against area and power. The proposed FMA unit has only 17.0% larger area than a standard double-precision FMA implementation, but can support multiple-precision and mixed-precision operations. Compared to the state-of-the-art multiple-precision FMA design, the proposed FMA supports more types of precisions such as TensorFloat-32 and BFloat16 with less hardware overhead.

Keywords: High performance computing · Deep learning · Floating-point fused multiply-add · Multiple-precision · Mixed-precision

1 Introduction

Artificial intelligence(AI) has achieved great success in speech recognition [25], computer vision [10,15] and natural language processing [5], and trends to be

W. Meng et al. (Eds.): ICA3PP 2022, LNCS 13777, pp. 642–659, 2023.
https://doi.org/10.1007/978-3-031-22677-9_34

integrated with multi-disciplinary in recent years. The application of deep learning in high performance computing (HPC) tasks has been done in many research works, for example the climate prediction [16], drug screening [23], cosmology analysis [21] and so on. However, the data precisions is varied in the implementation of HPC and AI applications (HPC and AI) due to the dynamic range requirement in data processing, which caused extra cost and complexity in hardware design. In this paper, we will focus on the design of a novel arithmetic unit to make the HPC and AI hardware platform more efficient.

The fused multiply-add (FMA) unit is the basic component of the arithmetic unit, and various FMA architecture have been proposed for accelerating the HPC [11,20,26] and AI [27,28] applications in previous works. The FMA architectures support double-precision floating-point operations or single-precision floating-point operations are commonly used in HPC applications, while reducing precision operations during the training and inference of deep learning is proposed to lower the cost of hardware. In addition to single-precision, three types of low-precision formats, the TensorFloat-32, the BFloat16, and the half-precision float-point are proposed for deep learning tasks. In the deep learning training and inference, the single-precision operations offer sufficient data range and precision but at the cost of complexity and expensive overhead in architecture design. The half-precision operations can provide higher throughput with less resource cost but may result in error gradients during back propagation of deep learning training. The TensorFloat-32/BFloat16 directly truncates the mantissa of single-precision numbers from 23-bit to 10-bit/7-bit while reserves an 8-bit exponent, which can provide the same data range as that of single-precision. However if the mantissa bandwidth is not enough, the accuracy of the deep learning training will have a significant degradation by using TensorFloat-32 or BFloat16 format. In general, these above datatypes are suitable for different specific scenarios and achieved a good performance in deep learning training and inference. However, the arithmetic units proposed by these previous research works are aimed at HPC or AI workloads respectively, which can not meet the practical requirement of HPC-enabled AI scenarios.

In addition to normal FMA operations, mixed-precision FMA operations are also getting more popular recently. Mixed-precision FMA operation refers to using lower precision multiplication to improve the throughput while accumulating products in higher precision to maintain the large dynamic range. Both in the field of scientific calculation and deep learning, the mixed-precision methods are widely applied [2,8,18]. Compared to using high-precision operations to implement these tasks, hardware overhead can be saved by using mixed-precision.

In this paper, an efficient multiple-precision floating-point FMA architecture supports normal and mixed-precision operations is proposed, in which both segmentation and reusing methods are applied to trade off performance, such as throughput and latency, against area and power. In normal FMA operations, one double-precision operation, or two parallel single-precision operations, or four parallel half-precision operations are performed at each clock cycle. In mixed-precision FMA operations, one mixed-precision operation using single-precision multiplication and double-precision addition, or two parallel mixed-precision operations using low-precision (TensorFloat-32, BFloat16, or half-precision) multiplication and single-precision addition is performed every clock cycle. The presented FMA design uses both segmentation and reusing methods to trade off performance, such as throughput and latency, against area and power.

The remainder of this paper is organized as follows. Section 2 gives an overview of the related works. Section 2.1 introduces the supported data formats and a conventional implementation of FMA architecture. In Sect. 3, the architecture of the proposed multiple-precision and mixed-precision floating-point FMA unit is presented. Then the synthesis results, the analysis, and the comparison with baseline design are presented in Sect. 4. Finally, Sect. 5 gives the conclusion of the whole work.

2   Related Works

In recent years, the design of FMA architecture to reduce latency, area, and power consumption has aroused great interest from researchers, and various precisions FMA operations are supported in these works respectively [4,17,22]. In order to efficiently support multiple-precision and mixed-precision operations for different applications in a single architecture, some dual-mode FMA units [11,12,26] are proposed in the literature. The [12] proposed an FMA architecture that can support one double-precision or two parallel single-precision float-point FMA operations, and then extends the work to a low-cost SIMD binary128 [11] FMA design. In addition to one double-precision or two single-precision operations, the binary128 (quadruple-precision) FMA operation is supported by using two binary64 FMA units based on the iteration and combination methods with the cost of an extra clock cycle. The [26] design a multiple-precision and mixed-precision floating-point FMA architecture, which not only can support normal FMA operations that one quadruple-precision operation, or two parallel double-precision operations, or four parallel single-precision operations, or eight parallel half-precision operations at each clock cycle, but also supports mixed-precision FMA operation and mixed-precision 2-term dot-product operation for these precisions. Half-precision and double-precision mixed-precision operations are proposed in the work [8], which utilizes the half-precision Tensor Cores in GPUs to speed up iterative refinement solvers for HPC applications. Moreover, some specific datatypes for artificial intelligence neural network applications are proposed, for example, the study [13] introduces BFloat16 for deep learning training and achieves the same state-of-the-art (SOTA) results as FP32 do. The TensorFloat-32 format is applied in tensor core [7] of NVIDIA GPU A100 and H100 to accelerate the deep learning training.

The main contribution of this paper is proposing and evaluating a novel architecture for floating-point FMA unit which supports both multiple-precision and mixed-precision operations. The FMA architecture is achieved by modifying several basic modules of the conventional double-precision FMA unit, then multiple-precision and mixed-precision FMA operations are supported with no significant area and power overhead.

2.1   Basic FMA Architecture

The conventional FMA operation refers to $A \times B + C$, and the operands are of the same precision. Figure 1 illustrates the basic architecture of FMA implementation, which serves as the baseline for the proposed FMA unit. The datapath of the basic FMA architecture as follows:

- Firstly, the mantissa, $ManA$ and $ManB$, are multiplied by an unsigned multiplier, and then generating the carry-save format product.
- At the same time, the exponent difference between product $A \times B$ and C, the sign processing, the exponent prediction, and alignment for addend C based on the value of exponent difference are performed.
- Then, the aligned addend C and the mantissa product are added together through a carry save adder (CSA), and the normalization shifting amount is also predicted by a leading zero anticipator and counting (LZAC) unit at the same time.
- Lastly, normalization shifting and exponent adjustment are performed according to the leading zero amount, and then rounding to generate the mantissa. The FMA result is obtained after the combination of the processed sign, the adjusted exponent, and the rounded mantissa.

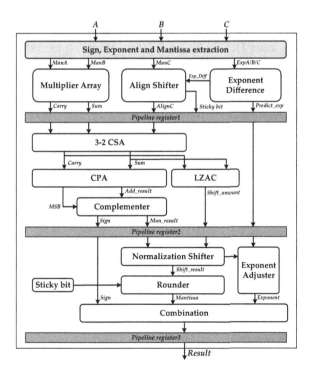

Fig. 1. Basic architecture of FMA unit.

In this paper, multiple-precision and mixed-precision operations are supported in the proposed FMA unit by modifying the basic FMA architecture. In order to evaluate the resource overhead introduced by the support of extra precisions and mixed-precision operations in the proposed FMA unit, the implementation of DP, SP, HP, TF32, and BF16 FMA units are designed based on the basic FMA architecture. The total resource consumption of these FMA units can be compared and evaluated for the proposed FMA architecture.

3   The Proposed FMA Architecture

A block diagram of the proposed FMA architecture, illustrating the details of the FMA datapath, is shown in Fig. 2. The proposed architecture is fully-pipelined, and multiple-precision and mixed-precision operations are implemented with the latency of three clock cycles. In the proposed FMA unit, the supported five precisions (DP, SP, HP, TF32 and BF16) are controlled by a 3-bit signal *prec*, and a 1-bit signal *mode* is applied to determine the selection of normal FMA operation or mixed FMA operation. Because of the requirement of parallel calculation for low-precision operations and low-power purposes, the 64-bit input and output operands are split into four 16-bit sections and enabled by a 4-bit signal *valid*.

In the proposed FMA unit, the multi-precision and mixed-precision operations are classified into three modes according to the addend precision. Specifically, the HP mode refers to the normal FMA operation in HP precision, while the SP mode includes the normal FMA operation in SP precision and the mixed FMA operation adopts HP, TF32, or BF16 as the low-precision formats. In DP mode, the DP and SP formats are employed in normal and mixed FMA operation, respectively, as same to SP mode.

The whole FMA datapath is split into three pipeline stages, and the grey thick lines represent the position of pipeline registers. In the first stage, the initial signs, exponents, and mantissa of three operands are extracted according to the value of the signals *prec* and *mode* at the input operand processing module, and then sent into the mantissa multiplier, alignment shifter, sign and exponent processing modules. The mantissa multiplier works parallelly with the alignment shifter which controlled by the exponent difference value. The second stage performs the mergence of the aligned C and product of $A \times B$ by a carry save adder, then sending the merged vectors to the LZAC unit to generate the leading zero amount. Together the merged vectors with the cin produced by the alignment shifter, the result is obtained through a carry select adder. Finally, the normalization, exponent adjustment and rounding of the result are performed, and then combined to output in the last pipeline stage. In the following sections, the main components of the proposed FMA architecture are discussed in more detail.

3.1   Input Operands Processing

In the proposed FMA architecture, the input operand can accommodate one DP number, two SP or TF32 numbers, or four HP or BF16 numbers according to the precision signal *prec*, and the sign, the exponent, and the mantissa of these numbers are extracted into unified formats in this module. Because of the support of parallel operation for low-precision formats, all the unified vectors are consist of four parts (*part0 ∼ part3*).

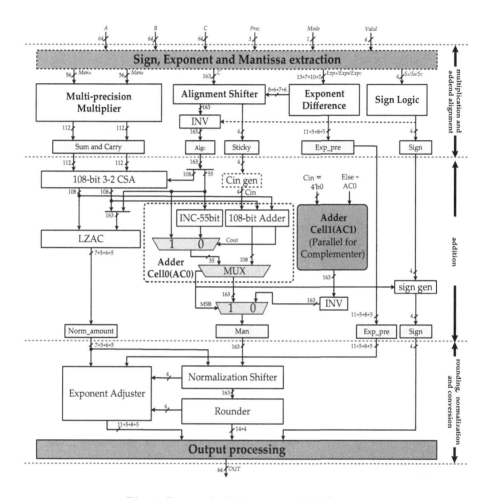

Fig. 2. Datapath of the proposed FMA unit.

The part0 and part2 are only used for HP mode, the part1 can be used for both HP mode and SP mode, while the part3 can be applied for all modes. These four parts are enabled by a 4-bit signal *valid*, if one bit in *valid* is zero, the corresponding part will be set to zeros, which can avoid invalid toggles of flip-flops to reduce power consumption. For the sign processing, the signs of each input operand are organized into a 4-bit signal S corresponding to the four numbers in HP mode. The exponents are also extracted and organized into a unified vector, but the wordlength of each parts of the unified vector is different.

Moreover, two extra bits added in all modes are used for indicators of negative result and overflow, so the wordlength of $part3 \sim part0$ is 13-bit, 7bit, 10-bit and 7bit, respectively. The mantissa is also processed into a unified format before sent to the multiple-precision multiplier, as shown in Fig. 3. The total bitwidth of the unified mantissa is set to 56-bit. For lower precisions, each of the mantissa is prefixed with zeros to fill the 56-bit bitwidth, as shown in the white region of Fig. 3.

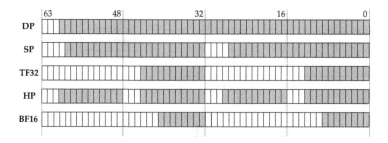

Fig. 3. Unified mantissa format for different precisions.

3.2 Multiple-Precision Multiplier

As mentioned in Fig. 3, the mantissa of the operand A and B has been organized into unified vectors, and then inputted into the mantissa multiplier. The 56-bit mantissa is split into four sections, so the mantissa multiplication can be represented as:

$$
\begin{aligned}
DP_{mode} &: \{a_3, a_2, a_1, a_0\} \times \{b_3, b_2, b_1, b_0\} \\
SP_{mode} &: \{a_3, a_2\} \times \{b_3, b_2\} + \{a_1, a_0\} \times \{b_1, b_0\} \\
HP_{mode} &: \{a_3, a_2, a_1, a_0\} \bullet \{b_3, b_2, b_1, b_0\}
\end{aligned}
\tag{1}
$$

where the a_i and b_i refer to one 14-bit section in the unified vectors, and "$\bullet$" means element-wise operation.

In order to meet the requirement of all supported precision operations, four parallel multiplications for HP mode, or two parallel multiplications for SP mode, or one multiplication for DP mode are implemented at each clock cycle. As shown in Eq. (1), the operations for mantissa vectors are differed in different precisions. So, we adopt a 14×14 multiplier as the basic unit for lower-precision (HP, TF32, and BF16) multiplication, and combined multiple units together for the implementation of higher precision multiplication in a recursive method.

In the proposed design, the radix-4 modified Booth multiplier [3] is applied to reduce the cost of the basic 14-bit multiplier. The 14-bit multiplier operand is padded with 1-bit zero after the least significant bit (LSB) and 2-bit zero before the most significant bit (MSB), then the resulting 17-bit vector is divided into eight 3-bit encode groups to generate eight partial products. These eight partial products are merged by two levels of 4-to-2 carry save adders, then generating the product $A_i \times B_i$.

In the proposed multiplier, sixteen products $A_i \times B_i$ have been generated and placed in specific locations, as shown in Fig. 4. For the implementation of low-precision multiplication, because of the bitwidth of their mantissa are less than 14-bit, only four 14×14 multipliers are enabled to perform the multiplication. The locations of these four multipliers are shown in Fig. 4, the $A_0 * B_0$, $A_1 * B_1$, $A_2 * B_2$, and $A_3 * B_3$. As for HP mode, the effective mantissa is 11-bit or 8-bit. Therefore, the product cannot be larger than 22-bit. As a result, the products can be found in the least significant 22-bit of every 28-bit.

In SP mode, results of four of the 14×14 multipliers need to be combined to generate one SP result, as shown in Eq. (1). These four products are accumulated using (4, 2)-compressors and two results are generated at the least significant 48-bit of each 56-bit. In DP mode, all products are merged through two levels (4, 2)-compressors, and the result can be extracted from the least significant 106-bit of the result.

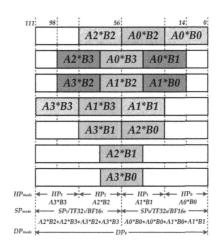

Fig. 4. The struct of multiple-precision multiplier.

3.3   Alignment Shifter

The alignment shifter works parallelly with the mantissa multiplier to reduce the latency of the FMA datapath. The alignment shifting method applied in the proposed design is similar to the previous FMA design [17]. The initial position and maximum alignment position of the processed mantissa of C operand and product $A \times B$ are shown in Fig. 5. The mantissa of C is placed 2-bit to the left of the carry save format product in the initial position, and the maximum alignment amount is reached when the MSB of C is placed 2-bit to the right of the LSB of the product. The bitwidth of mantissa C and mantissa A/B is M_q-bit and M_p-bit, respectively. In normal FMA operation, all operands in same precision,

$M_q = M_p$, so the bitwidth of alignment shifter is $(3 \times M_p + 4)$-bit. Specifically for DP, SP, and HP operations, a 163-bit, 76-bit, and 37-bit alignment shifter is required, respectively. For mixed-precision FMA operation, the precision of addend C is higher than multiplier operand A/B, the $M_q > 2 \times M_p$, so a $(2 \times M_q + 5)$-bit alignment shifter is required with the consideration of the heading one of product $A \times B$ located in the 1-bit to the right of MSB.

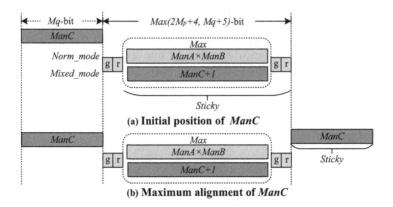

(a) **Initial position of ManC**

(b) **Maximum alignment of ManC**

Fig. 5. Alignment of C operand in the proposed FMA unit.

The mantissa of addend C is rearranged into the unified format to enable resource sharing among all precisions operations, as shown in Fig. 6. The mantissa of each precision is extended with zeros to fill the required shifting bitwidth. The unified vectors are right aligned, so that the bit shifted out of the shifter can be used to generate the partial sticky bit.

The implementation of the proposed alignment shifter is shown in Fig. 7, which is composed of eight levels of shifter cells. The shifter cell is a selector that received the input signals for the left and up cells, and generated the shifting results to the right and down cells. The shifting operations are controlled by the alignment shifting count (ASC) which calculated by the exponent difference module. If the corresponding bit of ASCs is one, the right shifting performed, otherwise select the input as the aligned result directly. According to the bitwidth of maximum alignment amount, the 8-bit, 7-bit, 6-bit shifting control signals are

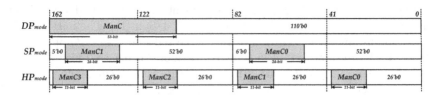

Fig. 6. Unified format of addend C in the proposed FMA unit.

generated for all supported precisions, respectively. The ASCs are divided into four parts as shown in Fig. 7 corresponding to the four small alignment shifters. In the *level0 ∼ level5*, four smaller alignment shifters run independently and generated four aligned results for HP mode. Then, the generated four aligned results are divided into two groups in the level6, and two aligned results for SP mode are generated by two larger shifter cells. Finally, one 163-bit shifter cell is placed which controlled by the 8-th bit of the ASC for DP mode in the last level.

Moreover, the shifted out bits in right of each shifter cell are used to generate the sticky bit. In the first five levels, partial sticky bits are generated by each shifter, and then generated a 4-bit sticky bit in level5, a 2-bit sticky bit in level6, and a 1-bit sticky bit in level7 for HP mode, SP mode, and DP mode, respectively.

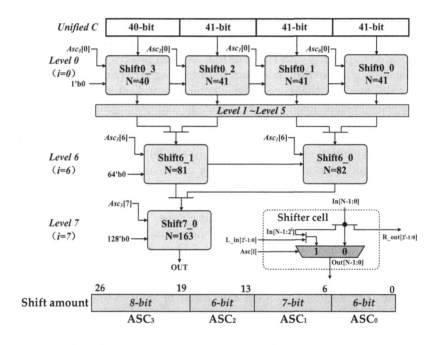

Fig. 7. The architecture of the proposed alignment shifter.

3.4 Adder

The alignment of addend C has been performed, and the generated 163-bit vectors need to be added with the products of mantissa multiplication $A \times B$. In order to reduce the cost of the adder, the addition is split into four parts. In DP mode, the 163-bit input vector is processed as a whole. For the most significant 55-bit, an incrementer is applied since only one of the two vectors contains useful data. For the less significant 108-bit, the input vectors need to be added using a carry propagate adder (CPA). The generated result of the incrementer and the initial input vector at the higher 55-bit are selected by the carry of the lower 108-bit CPA, and combined with the CPA result to generate the addition results.

In practical terms, the 163-bit adder is divided into four narrower width adders to support parallel operations for low-precision formats. These four narrower width adders run independently when implemented the HP mode, and generated carry of each adders will not be propagated. In SP mode, every two narrower width adders are combined and run parallelly to generated SP format results. In DP mode, all the narrower width adders are performed together, the carries in lower adders are propagated to generate the higher precision results.

The sign of the FMA result is determined by the sign of addition. Specifically, if the addition result is positive, the sign of product $A \times B$ is selected to be the sign of FMA result, otherwise the sign of addend C is selected.

3.5   Leading Zero Anticipator

In order to reduce the latency of FMA datapath, the leading zero anticipation is implemented in parallel with the addition. As both positive results and negative results can be generated by addition, both leading zeros and leading ones need to be anticipated. In this paper, the general case indicator presented in [24] is used.

The overall architecture of the leading zero anticipator and counting (LZAC) is shown in Fig. 8. The organization of the 163-bit input operands are same as the unified addend C, as shown in Fig. 6. In the DP mode, the higher or lower 108-bit of input operands are selected by the control signal $Bdry$ generated by the exponent difference module, and generated the input vector for LZACs. The 108-bit LZAC also consists of four 27-bit smaller LZAC units for parallel operation of low-precision, each LZAC unit consists of the encoding module and leading zero count (LZC) module. In HP mode, these four 27-bit LZAC units run independently, each of them generating a 5-bit normalization shifting amount and outputted directly. In SP mode, every two LZACs are grouped together to generate a 6-bit normalization shifting amount for the 54-bit addition. In a similar way, the leading zero prediction result of the 108-bit addition can also be obtained in DP mode.

3.6   Normalization

The normalization shifter is applied to remove the leading zeros of addition. The architecture of the proposed normalization shifter is similar to the alignment shifter, but simpler. Compared to alignment shifter, the normalization shifting is a left shifting, and the left shifted out bits can be discarded directly. In the proposed design, before sent to the normalization shifter, the 163-bit input vector generated by addition need be processed, a 108-bit processed vector is obtained after the selection controlled by the signal $Bdry$. In DP mode, the normalization shifting result is generated after seven levels left shifting, which is controlled by a 7-bit shifting amount signal generated by the LZA. One more final level

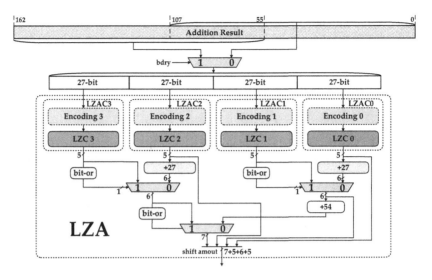

Fig. 8. The architecture of the leading zero anticipator and counting.

shifting is added to correct the error generated by the LZAC. If the leading bit is detected and when it is not one after seven levels shifting, 1-bit more left shifting is performed. In SP and HP modes, the shifting operation is split into multiple sections and runs independently similar to the alignment shifter, two or four normalized results are generated by these sections of normalization shifter.

3.7 Rounding and Exponent Adjustment

In the proposed design, roundTiesToEven, which is the default rounding mode in IEEE 754-2008 [6], is implemented. The rounding module also consists of four rounding cells, and the input vector generated by normalization shifter is rounded base on the FMA precisions. Except for the difference in bitwidth, the logics in each cell are similar, and the correlation between these four cells and FMA operations is mentioned in Sect. 3. In DP mode, the 163-bit input vector is rounded to a 53 bit mantissa, while split into two parts and rounded to two 24-bit mantissa in SP mode, or rounded to four 11-bit mantissa in HP mode. The Cin is also generated by rounding which means the FMA exponent needs to add one.

The exponent of FMA result is predicted by the comparison result between addend C and product $A \times B$, and the larger one will be selected as the exponent of FMA result in pipeline stage 1. However, the leading zeros caused by subtraction and the Cin generated by rounding need be considered, so the predicted exponent must be adjusted before output. Specifically, the leading zeros amount calculated by LZA need be subtracted and the Cin generated by mantissa rounding need be added by the predicted exponent.

After rounding and exponent adjustment, the rounded mantissa, the adjusted exponent, and the processed sign are combined together, and then the FMA results are generated.

4   Synthesis and Evaluation

In this paper, the model of the proposed FMA architecture is implemented using Verilog HDL. For the verification of standard floating-point format (DP, SP, and HP), extensive testing vectors are generated with the help of TestFloat [9]. The TF32 and BF16 formats are verified by a customized software model written in C language. In addition to the proposed FMA unit, single-mode FMA units based on the conventional FMA architecture corresponding to all supported precisions are designed for comparison purposes.

All these designs are synthesized in 28 nm CMOS technology with typical case parameters (1.00 V and 25 °C), and the dynamic power is measured by synthesis tools.

Firstly, each pipeline stage of the proposed FMA architecture is synthesized, and the area of pipeline stages and pipeline registers are shown in Table 1. The synthesis results are obtained under time constraint of 0.64 ns, which can make a tradeoff between area and performance. As shown in Table 1, the first pipeline stage consumes the most area (62%) due to the large mantissa multiplier and alignment shifter. Except the combinational logics designed for pipeline stages, the pipeline registers of these three stages consume 12% area.

Table 1. Synthesis results of each pipeline stage of the proposed FMA

Stage	Delay(ns)	Area (μm^2)	Percent
Multiplication and alignment	0.64	16429	62
Addition and LZAC	0.64	4050	18
Rounding and normalization	0.64	1855	7
Pipeline registers	0.64	3180	12

As the baseline design of this paper, the normal double-precision FMA unit (N-DP-FMA) is designed based on the conventional FMA architecture. By contrasting the overhead between the N-DP-FMA unit and the proposed FMA architecture, a straight forward evaluation for the cost of added functions in the proposed FMA unit is implemented. The parallel FMA operations for SP, HP, TF32, and BF16 precisions are also supported in the proposed design, so the normal single-precision FMA unit (N-SP-FMA) and normal half-precision

FMA unit (N-HP-FMA), the mixed-precision FMA unit, M-SP-FMA for SP and DB mixed-precision operations, M-TF-FMA for TF32 and SP mixed-precision operations, M-BF-FMA for BF16 and SP mixed-precision operations, and M-HP-FMA for HP and SP mixed-precision operations are also designed for comparison purposes.

Table 2. Area and energy comparison of the proposed FMA with baseline FMA design

Mode	Delay (ns)	Cycles	Area (μm^2)	Power (mW)
N-DP-FMA	0.60	3	22644	78.5
N-SP-FMA	0.41	3	9212	54.8
N-HP-FMA	0.25	3	2718	30.8
M-SP-FMA	0.45	3	13005	67.5
M-TF-FMA	0.35	3	4469	30.8
M-HP-FMA	0.35	3	4340	27.1
M-BF-FMA	0.35	3	3735	26.6
Proposed (Multi-mode)	0.64	3	26499	79.8

As shown in Table 2, the proposed FMA consumes only 17.0% more area and 1.7% more power compared to a conventional double-precision FMA unit. However, as discussed in previous sections, in addition to the double-precision FMA operation, parallel FMAs for both normal and mixed-precision operations are performed by the proposed design. The area overhead comes mainly from the multiplexers used to support multiple-precision data selection and the logic to support mixed-precision operations. On the other hand, in terms of functionality, we need 4 HP FMAs, 2 SP FMAs, 1 DP FMAs, and several other mixed-precision FMAs to realize the same functionality as the proposed FMA provides. For ease of comparison, the synthesis results of area and power are also graphed in Fig. 9. The proposed FMA is compared with the combination of single-mode FMA units for implementing same functionality by replicated methods. We can see that the proposed multiple-precision and mixed-precision FMA can save roughly 70.3% area than the combination of FMA units.

The comparison of the functionality, performance and overhead of the proposed FMA with previous works are shown in Table 3. Compared to other multiple-precision FMAs, the proposed FMA is specific for HPC and AI applications. Both normal and mixed-precision FMA operations for DP/SP/TF32/BF16/HP formats are supported. Since these previous designs are synthesized using different semiconductor technologies, in order to make a fair comparison, the equivalent area ($NAND2$ gate count) and equivalent delay ($FO4$ delay) for each design are calculated, and the throughput is compared in a unified method where op/FO4 is used.

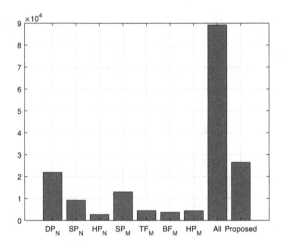

Fig. 9. Area comparison for different FMA configurations.

The comparison of the dual-mode FMA architecture [1, 12, 19] using the same bitwidth of operands as the proposed FMA is shown in the Table 3. Compared to the works [12, 19], both of them support one DP FMA operations or two parallel SP FMA operations. The proposed design can support multiple-precision and mixed-precision operations, and increase the throughput by 1.3/2.1x but has 5/2% smaller area than [12, 19], respectively. The design in [1] uses Karatsuba algorithm [14] to reduce the number of required multiplier. In addition, the design in [1]uses six pipeline stages for the mantissa multiplier. The timing constraints for each pipeline stage will be loose, which further helps to reduce the area during synthesis. Therefore, it has the smallest area among the three compared dual-mode designs. The critical path of the FMA is usually located in the mantissa multiplier. In the proposed design, the radix-4 Booth multiplier that has smaller critical path delay than the array multiplier is utilized which effectively reduces the critical path delay. Therefore, the proposed design requires five fewer pipeline stages than the design of [1].

The works [11, 20, 26] have wider bitwidth of operands, in which QP operation is supported. However, for the implementation of aimed applications in this paper, QP operation is not required. For example, SP and lower precisions operations can meet the requirements of DNN's training and inference in AI applications, and DP operation can provide enough accuracy in most of HPC applications.

The proposed FMA can provide high throughput and consume less area than [11, 20, 26], which has a smaller critical path delay (68–81% reduced) than these three FMA designs. The less delay comes from two aspects, on one hand, the radix-4 Booth multiplier used in the proposed design caused a reduction of critical path delay. On the other hand, the narrower bitwidth mantissa multiplexer has a shorter logic path.

Table 3. Comparison of the proposed FMA with previous works

Design	Function	Delay(ns)		C	Area		Throughput	
		ns	FO4		μm^2	NAND2	MOPS	op/FO4
[12]-180 nm	1DP/2SP FMA	3.4	34.3	3	708,590	58,081	294	29
[19]-130 nm	1DP/2SP FMA	3.43	52.7	3	286,766	56,228	291	18
[1]-130 nm	1DP/2SP FMA	3.24	49.8	8	149,000	29,215	308	20
[20]-65 nm	1QP/2DP/4SP FMA	3.41	110	3	672,046	420,028	293	9
[11]-90 nm	2DP/4SP FMA/MUL	2.15	47.7	3	718,725	163,346	465	21
	1QP ADD	2.15	47.7	3	718,725	163,346	465	21
	1QP FMA/MUL	2.15	47.7	4	718,725	163,346	232	10
[26]-90nm	1QP/2DP/4SP/8HP FMA	2	44.5	3	794,790	180,634	500	22
	1DP/2SP/4HP MIX-FMA	2	44.5	4	794,790	180,634	500	22
	1DP/2SP/4HP MIX Dot-Product	2	44.5	4	794,790	180,634	500	22
Prop-28 nm	1DP/2SP/4HP FMA	0.64	26.7	3	26,499	55,206	1,563	38
	1SP/2TF/2BF/2HP MIX-FMA	0.64	26.7	3	26,499	55,206	1,563	38

1 $FO4 \approx$ 24 ps, 1 $NAND2 \approx 0.48\,\mu m^2$@28 nm; 1 $FO4$ $\approx$ 31 ps, 1 $NAND2 \approx$ 1.44 μm^2@65 nm;
1 $FO4 \approx$ 45 ps, 1 $NAND2 \approx 4.4\mu m^2$@90 nm; 1 $FO4$ $\approx$ 65 ps, 1 $NAND2 \approx$ 5.1 μm^2@130 nm;
1 $FO4 \approx$ 99 ps, 1 $NAND2 \approx 12.2\,\mu m^2$@180 nm;
C: the cycles of FMA operation; $op/FO4$: (MOPS/FO4) $\times 10^{-3}$;

For the implementation of HPC applications, in which DP operations are most widely used. Two parallel DP operations are performed with a latency of three cycles by [20] and [11]. The proposed design can increase throughput by 2.1 with 87% less area than [20]. The [11] has a 1.1x throughput than the proposed design with the cost of 66% area overhead. Moreover, [20] and [11] can not support low-precision operations, so the AI applications, such as DNNs, are performed inefficiently by using high-precision operations.

In [26], normal FMA operations and mixed-precision FMA operations are performed with a latency of three and four cycles, respectively. In the proposed design, both normal and mixed-precision operations are performed with the latency of three cycles. The [26] has 1.1x throughput in performing normal operations than the proposed design. However, the cost of the larger throughput is more hardware overhead, the area of [26] is 3.3x than the proposed design. Moreover, more types of formats, TensorFloat-32 and BFloat16 specific for deep learning workloads are supported in the proposed work, which makes the implementation of DNN more efficient.

5   Conclusion

In this paper, a multiple-precision and mixed-precision floating-point FMA unit is designed for HPC and AI applications. The precisions and functions supported by the proposed FMA unit are based on the practical requirements of HPC and AI workloads. For normal FMA operations, the proposed FMA unit is capable of performing one SP, or two SP, or four HP standard FMA operations in parallel. For mixed-precision FMA operations, one mixed-precision FMA using SP multiplication and DP addition, or two mixed-precision FMA using low-precision (HP/TF32/BF16) multiplication and SP addition are performed. This design consumes significantly less area and power while achieving more functionalities than a conventional DP FMA unit. The proposed FMA architecture can be used in efficient processor designs or specialized hardware accelerators. The support of parallel low-precision and the mixed-precision operations makes the proposed design suitable for scientific computing and deep learning workloads.

Acknowledgements. This work is supported in part by NSFC (No. 61872374, 62090023, 62172430), NSFHN (No. 2022JJ10064, 2021JJ10052) and NKRDP (No. 2021YFB0300300).

References

1. Arunachalam, V., Raj, A.N.J., Hampannavar, N., Bidul, C.: Efficient dual-precision floating-point fused-multiply-add architecture. Microprocess. Microsyst. **57**, 23–31 (2018)
2. Baboulin, M., et al.: Accelerating scientific computations with mixed precision algorithms. Comput. Phys. Commun. **180**(12), 2526–2533 (2009)
3. Booth, A.D.: A signed binary multiplication technique. Q. J. Mech. Appl. Math. **4**(2), 236–240 (1951)
4. Bruguera, J.D., Lang, T.: Floating-point fused multiply-add: reduced latency for floating-point addition. In: 17th IEEE Symposium on Computer Arithmetic (ARITH 2005), pp. 42–51. IEEE (2005)
5. Chowdhary, K.: Natural language processing. In: Fundamentals of Artificial Intelligence, pp. 603–649 (2020)
6. Dan, Z., et al.: IEEE standard for floating-point arithmetic. IEEE Std 754-2008, pp. 1–70 (2008)
7. Fasi, M., Higham, N.J., Mikaitis, M., Pranesh, S.: Numerical behavior of NVIDIA tensor cores. PeerJ Comput. Sci. **7**, e330 (2021)
8. Haidar, A., Tomov, S., Dongarra, J., Higham, N.J.: Harnessing GPU tensor cores for fast FP16 arithmetic to speed up mixed-precision iterative refinement solvers. In: SC18: International Conference for High Performance Computing, Networking, Storage and Analysis, pp. 603–613. IEEE (2018)
9. Hauser, J.: Berkeley testfloat, June 2018. http://www.jhauser.us/arithmetic/TestFloat.html
10. He, K., Zhang, X., Ren, S., Sun, J.: Deep residual learning for image recognition. In: Proceedings of the IEEE Conference on Computer Vision and Pattern Recognition, pp. 770–778 (2016)
11. Huang, L., Ma, S., Shen, L., Wang, Z., Xiao, N.: Low-cost binary128 floating-point FMA unit design with SIMD support. IEEE Trans. Comput. **61**(5), 745–751 (2011)
12. Huang, L., Shen, L., Dai, K., Wang, Z.: A new architecture for multiple-precision floating-point multiply-add fused unit design. In: 18th IEEE Symposium on Computer Arithmetic (ARITH 2007), pp. 69–76. IEEE (2007)
13. Kalamkar, D., et al.: A study of BFLOAT16 for deep learning training. arXiv preprint arXiv:1905.12322 (2019)

14. Karatsuba, A.A., Ofman, Y.P.: Multiplication of many-digital numbers by automatic computers. In: Doklady Akademii Nauk, vol. 145, pp. 293–294. Russian Academy of Sciences (1962)
15. Krizhevsky, A., Sutskever, I., Hinton, G.E.: ImageNet classification with deep convolutional neural networks. In: Advances in Neural Information Processing Systems, vol. 25 (2012)
16. Kurth, T., et al.: Exascale deep learning for climate analytics. In: SC18: International Conference for High Performance Computing, Networking, Storage and Analysis, pp. 649–660. IEEE (2018)
17. Lang, T., Bruguera, J.D.: Floating-point multiply-add-fused with reduced latency. IEEE Trans. Comput. 53(8), 988–1003 (2004)
18. Langou, J., Langou, J., Luszczek, P., Kurzak, J., Buttari, A., Dongarra, J.: Exploiting the performance of 32 bit floating point arithmetic in obtaining 64 bit accuracy (revisiting iterative refinement for linear systems). In: SC 2006: Proceedings of the 2006 ACM/IEEE Conference on Supercomputing, pp. 50–50. IEEE (2006)
19. Manolopoulos, K., Reisis, D., Chouliaras, V.A.: An efficient dual-mode floating-point multiply-add fused unit. In: 2010 17th IEEE International Conference on Electronics, Circuits and Systems, pp. 5–8. IEEE (2010)
20. Manolopoulos, K., Reisis, D., Chouliaras, V.A.: An efficient multiple precision floating-point multiply-add fused unit. Microelectron. J. 49, 10–18 (2016)
21. Mathuriya, A., et al.: CosmoFlow: using deep learning to learn the universe at scale. In: SC18: International Conference for High Performance Computing, Networking, Storage and Analysis, pp. 819–829. IEEE (2018)
22. Quinnell, E., Swartzlander, E.E., Lemonds, C.: Bridge floating-point fused multiply-add design. IEEE Trans. Very Large Scale Integr. (VLSI) Syst. 16(12), 1727–1731 (2008)
23. Rifaioglu, A.S., Atas, H., Martin, M.J., Cetin-Atalay, R., Atalay, V., Doğan, T.: Recent applications of deep learning and machine intelligence on in silico drug discovery: methods, tools and databases. Brief. Bioinform. 20(5), 1878–1912 (2019)
24. Schmookler, M.S., Nowka, K.J.: Leading zero anticipation and detection-a comparison of methods. In: Proceedings 15th IEEE Symposium on Computer Arithmetic, ARITH-15 2001, pp. 7–12. IEEE (2001)
25. Yu, D., Deng, L.: Automatic Speech Recognition. SCT, Springer, London (2015). https://doi.org/10.1007/978-1-4471-5779-3
26. Zhang, H., Chen, D., Ko, S.B.: Efficient multiple-precision floating-point fused multiply-add with mixed-precision support. IEEE Trans. Comput. 68(7), 1035–1048 (2019)
27. Zhang, H., Chen, D., Ko, S.B.: New flexible multiple-precision multiply-accumulate unit for deep neural network training and inference. IEEE Trans. Comput. 69(1), 26–38 (2019)
28. Zhang, H., Lee, H.J., Ko, S.B.: Efficient fixed/floating-point merged mixed-precision multiply-accumulate unit for deep learning processors. In: 2018 IEEE International Symposium on Circuits and Systems (ISCAS), pp. 1–5. IEEE (2018)

Efficient-Secure k-means Clustering Guaranteeing Personalized Local Differential Privacy

Yuling Luo, Zhangrui Wang, Shunsheng Zhang$^{(\boxtimes)}$, and Junxiu Liu

School of Electronic and Information Engineering, Guangxi Normal University, Guilin, China
shunszhang@gxnu.edu.cn

Abstract. One highly discussed research topic is user privacy protection and the usability of models in data mining tasks. Currently, the most k-means clustering approach using differential privacy is based on trusted third-party servers. However, malicious servers exist in many applications and cause privacy leakages of user data. The Personalized Local Differential Privacy k-means algorithm (PLDP k-means) is proposed in this paper. To satisfy the PLDP mechanism, a perturbation mechanism is used to perturb the user data at the local side. Then clustering is completed by iteration between the local and server sides. The third-party server remains inaccessible to the real user data and considers the users' personalized privacy demands in the proposed algorithm. In addition, the iterative centroid perturbation algorithm is proposed in this paper for resisting inference attacks and improving the utility of clustering via a privacy budget allocation sequence. Theoretical analysis demonstrates the privacy of the proposed algorithm. Experimental results indicate that the proposed algorithm effectively preserves the utility of clustering while satisfying the PLDP mechanism.

Keywords: Cluster · k-means · Privacy protection · Personalized Local Differential Privacy

1 Introduction

The popularisation of smart devices and the development of big data analytics has led to tremendous growth in the generation, collection, and analysis of personal digital information. The useful information extracted from massive data can bring immeasurable value [1,2]. As a classical data analysis method, clustering is a type of unsupervised learning method. k-means is one of the most popular clustering methods due to its efficiency and simplicity [3]. Although the data analysis has great potential, it also has a risk of leakage of user privacy. Sensitive information such as medical, location, and financial data can directly lead to users' private information leakage. Traditional anonymization methods wipe out identifiers that cannot resist both differential and background knowledge attacks. An attacker can correlate or identify users' private information.

© Springer Nature Switzerland AG 2023
W. Meng et al. (Eds.): ICA3PP 2022, LNCS 13777, pp. 660–675, 2023.
https://doi.org/10.1007/978-3-031-22677-9_35

Therefore, ensuring there is no leakage of users' private information and maintaining a high level of utility in clustering becomes a problem that needs to be solved.

The Differential Privacy (DP) model is currently considered as a reliable model with rigorous and falsifiable privacy guarantees [4]. Compared with traditional protection models such as anonymity and random perturbation, differential privacy has significant advantages in privacy preservation in cluster analysis [5,6]. A differential privacy-based model for cluster analysis, which is referred to as Differential Privacy *k*-means Algorithm (DP *k*-means), has been widely applied for its efficiency and privacy preservation [7,8]. DPLloyd-Impr made an improvement on DPLloyd by introducing the concept of sphere packing [9]. DP-KCCM, as a novel algorithm, is effective when cluster merging and adaptive noise mechanisms are adopted to improve clustering utility [10]. The above work improves DP *k*-means from data pre-processing, cluster delineation, etc., and is based on trusted third-party servers. The servers can collect real user data, perform clustering and uniformly add noise. However, with the development of cloud computing and the diversification of data analysis demands, the assumption that all third-party servers are trustworthy is not valid, as malicious servers may steal and take advantage of users' private information.

Local Differential Privacy (LDP) [11] was proposed because third-party servers cannot be trusted. LDP has more stringent privacy requirements than DP. It requires users to perturb their data at the local side and sends it to an untrusted server. LDP has also been applied to practical cases to create feasible solutions [12,13]. A *k*-means algorithm based on LDP was proposed in [14] to protect location data through feature transformation and privacy budget allocation. Although LDP can effectively address the problem of privacy leakage on third-party servers, it still faces the challenge of reduced clustering utility due to excessive noise [15]. Owing to the perturbation of user data at the local side, the noise of LDP is larger compared to that of DP. The influence of noise is further amplified in the clustering iterations. Also, most research on LDP implicit assumption is that there is uniform protection of the private information of all users. However, different users and data often have different privacy requirements. To address the above issue, Personalized Local Differential Privacy (PLDP) was proposed in [16], which allows each user to set the privacy level of their data independently.

Based on the above discussions, the main issue that needs to be addressed is how to take into account the protection of users' private information and the utility of clustering in *k*-means clustering. A clustering framework based on the PLDP *k*-means algorithm is proposed in this paper. Firstly, the user can perturb sensitive data at the local side by the PLDP *k*-means algorithm and send it to the server, which performs high-quality *k*-means clustering on the perturbed data. Thus, the threat of malicious servers is eliminated while the users' personalized privacy demands are met. In addition, an iterative centroid perturbation algorithm is proposed, which prevents privacy leakage caused by inference attacks by perturbing the centroids in the iterative process. The proposed algorithm also reduces the impact of perturbation on the clustering utility by designing a privacy budget allocation sequence. The main contributions of this paper are as follows.

1) A clustering framework based on the PLDP k-means algorithm is proposed. In the framework, the server does not access users' private information while ensuring quality clustering and users' personalized privacy demands.
2) Iterative centroid perturbation algorithms are proposed to address the potential leakage of private information during iteration. They help prevent inference attacks and further protect users' private information.
3) Theoretical analysis demonstrates the privacy protection capability of the proposed mechanism, and extensive experiments show that the proposed algorithm has better or similar performance than existing DP k-means algorithms. To the best of our knowledge, this paper is the first attempt at adopting PLDP in k-means clustering.

The rest of this paper is organized as follows. The basic concepts required for this framework and the related technical foundation are introduced in Sect. 2. The proposed approach is present in Sect. 3. The experimental results and analysis are illustrated in Sect. 4. Finally, the paper is concluded in Sect. 5.

2   Preliminaries

In this paper, the concept of personalized local differential privacy is adopted. To make the paper more self-contained, some basics of LDP and PLDP are briefly introduced in this section.

Differential privacy is a privacy-preserving model widely used in data analysis, in which the real data of all users is protected by a trusted data collector. However, the prerequisite of a trusted data collector usually does not hold in real-world applications. LDP is an extension of DP that extends to the local settings. LDP implements data sanitization locally by designing random perturbation algorithms that comply with differential privacy requirements. This way, sensitive data information is protected without relying on trusted third-party collectors. The following is the formal definition of LDP.

Definition 1. *(ε-LDP). A randomized mechanism $F : D \to R$ satisfies ε-LDP iff for any possible output result t^* ($t^* \subseteq R$) on any two records t and t' ($t, t' \subseteq D$) that satisfies Eq. 1.*

$$Pr\left[F(t) = t^*\right] \le e^{\varepsilon} \times Pr\left[F\left(t'\right) = t^*\right]. \tag{1}$$

The parameter ε is the privacy budget, which is public and usually set in [0,2]. The value of ε determines the probability of outputting the same result t^* for any two input values t and t' of the algorithm F. Thus, stronger (weaker) privacy guarantees are provided by smaller (larger) values of ε.

The LDP provides a way to protect private data on the local side of the user, but different privacy protection requirements may exist for different users and data. Therefore, PLDP is adopted to satisfy different privacy requirements in this paper. Each user in PLDP has a set of optional parameters (G_i, ε_u), ε_u representing the desired strength of privacy protection for that user, i.e., the privacy budget. G_i represents a security range specified by the user containing his real data, where the user data is indistinguishable from other data.

Definition 2 *((G_i, ε_u)-PLDP). Given a set of privacy requirements (G_i, ε_u) to one user n, a randomized mechanism $F : D \to R$ satisfies (G_i, ε_u)-PLDP iff for any possible output result t^* ($t^* \subseteq R$) on any two records t and t' ($t, t' \subseteq G_i$) that satisfies Eq. 2.*

$$Pr\left[F(t) = t^*\right] \le e^{\varepsilon_u} \times Pr\left[F\left(t'\right) = t^*\right]. \tag{2}$$

when G_i is set to the domain D, and all users are unified ε, PLDP is equivalent to LDP.

Differential privacy has two important combinatorial properties: the sequential and parallel combinatorial properties, which are formally defined as follows.

Property 1 (sequence combinability). Given a dataset D and privacy algorithms $\boldsymbol{F} = \{F_1, F_2, \dots, F_n\}$, $F_i(1 \le i \le n)$ satisfies the ε_i-DP. Then the sequence combination of $\{F_1, F_2, \dots, F_n\}$ on D satisfies ε-DP, where $\varepsilon = \sum_{i-1}^{n} \varepsilon_i$.

Property 2 (parallel combinability). Given a dataset D, divide it into n disjoint subsets, $\boldsymbol{D} = \{D_1, \dots, D_n\}$, let F be any privacy algorithm that satisfies ε_i-DP, then the algorithm F satisfies ε_{max}-DP on D.

3   Proposed Approach

In this section, the PLDP k-means clustering algorithm is proposed, and its privacy is demonstrated. Existing privacy issues in clustering analysis are first analyzed. The overall flow of the proposed framework is then described, and the corresponding design of the perturbation mechanism based on PLDP theory is given. Finally, the privacy of the proposed overall system is proved theoretically.

3.1   Overview

The privacy issues faced by DP and LDP k-means clustering model and the solutions are analyzed in this subsection. A third-party data collector collects sensitive data (e.g., location, income, cases, etc.) from many users, processes it using the k-means algorithm, and shares or publishes the model results to partners or public platforms. When users are faced with third-party collectors (e.g., service providers, etc.) asking for their data, protecting their privacy becomes an issue that must be addressed. DP is considered an effective solution to this problem by perturbing the user's data on a third-party server so that neither the attacker nor the subsequent release can cause a leakage of the user's privacy. However, the attacker may be external, or the data collector may be malicious, knowing all the user's real data. LDP protects user data assuming that third-party servers are not trusted. The way solves the problem of malicious data collectors is that the data is perturbed by the LDP at the local side and then uploaded to the server. The new problem is that due to LDP properties, there are limitations in protecting user data, and the availability of perturbed data is generally considered inferior to that of DP. At the same time, the risk of privacy leakage cannot be completely avoided by simply perturbing the data in clustering. So the problem is to design a model that achieves a better utility of clustering while avoiding the influence of malicious collectors.

A clustering framework based on the PLDP k-means algorithm is proposed in this paper to address the issues mentioned above. A randomized perturbation algorithm satisfying PLDP is used to perturb the user's local data, eliminating the risk of malicious collectors while satisfying personalized privacy requirements and enhancing the utility of clustering. Meanwhile, an iterative clustering centroid perturbation algorithm perturbs the real clustering information locally to prevent privacy leakage due to inference attacks.

3.2 Proposed Framework

A framework based on PLDP k-means that can solve the above problem is proposed, and its overall framework is shown in Fig. 1. The clustering model has a user set $U = \{u_0, u_1, \ldots, u_{n-1}\}$, an attribute set $A = \{a_0, a_1, \ldots, a_{d-1}\}$. Each user has a d-dimensional data vector $S_i = \{s_0, s_1, \ldots, s_{d-1}\}$. where $0 < i < n$, $0 < j < d$ and $d = |S_i|$ is the number of attributes. s_j corresponds to a numerical value of a_j. The target of k-means is to classify the user data into k clusters $C = \{c_0, c_1, \ldots, c_{k-1}\}$.

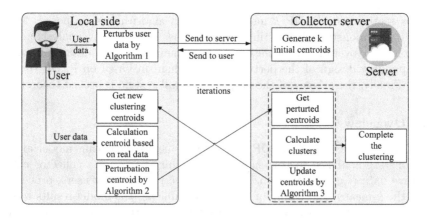

Fig. 1. Cluster privacy-preserving framework based on PLDP k-means.

As shown in Fig. 1, a clustering privacy-preserving framework based on PLDP is proposed. The proposed framework consists of two parts: the local side and the collector server. The local side describes how the user data is perturbed by the PLDP perturbation algorithm. The collector server describes how k-means is performed based on the perturbed data. The user data S_i is perturbed to get S_i^* by Algorithm 1 at the local side and then sent to the server. The server generates k initial centroids by the initial centroid selection algorithm and attribute set A, then sends them to the local side. The next clustering iteration is performed. The local side calculates the distance between the real user data S_i and each centroid received from the server to find the nearest centroid c_i and the corresponding clusters. The found centroid c_i is then perturbed to get c_i^* by Algorithm 2 and sent to the server. The server updates a new set of centroids based on the received C^* and the perturbed data S_i^* by Algorithm 3, then sends them to the local side. The iterative process is repeated until the results converge.

Local Side Method. As shown in Fig. 1, the local side consists of two core components, user data perturbation, and centroid perturbation.

User Data Perturbation. In contrast to the usual LDP k-means approach of converting the data into binary strings and then perturbing each dimension to obtain the perturbed results before aggregation, this paper normalizes the user data vector S_i to $[-1,1]$ through data pre-processing for the next perturbation process. Because each bit of the binary string has to be equally assigned privacy budget ε, which may cause excessive noise problems when the budget is small, or the number of bits in the string is large.

The Duchi solution [17] is a multidimensional data perturbation scheme based on LDP. Since S_i has already completed data pre-processing to obtain $S_i' = \{s_0', s_1', \ldots, s_{d-1}'\}$, the Duchi-based PLDP mechanism can be used to perturb user data. In the clustering model of this paper, a set of privacy parameters (G_i, ε_u) can be self-selected by each user. ε_u represents the user's selected privacy budget, i.e., the user's requirement for the strength of data protection. Averaging ε_u by user data dimension d to obtain $\varepsilon_d = \frac{\varepsilon_u}{d}$. $G_i = \{g_0, g_1, \ldots, g_{d-1}\}$ represents the user's acceptable security range, and $g_j (0 < j < d)$ represents the security range of the j-th dimensional data. e.g., a set of age data distributed between $[1,100]$. A user data is 25 years old, and after LDP perturbation, the perturbed data range is between $[1,100]$, representing the user's expectation that their age data is indistinguishable in the range $[1,100]$, a wide privacy requirement that is generally unnecessary. In PLDP, the user needs to choose a security range g_j. The range and size of g_j is user-defined, and the user's real data values must be included within the security range. For example, $g_j=[10,40]$ means that the age is indistinguishable within the range $[10,40]$ to satisfy the user's privacy demands. w_j and m_j are defined as the size and midpoint of g_j. Since a secure region symmetric about 0 needs to be obtained, each user moves the secure range, and the user data points within the range move to $s_j'' = s_j' - m_j$. After processing the $S_i'' = \{s_0'', s_1'', \ldots, s_{d-1}''\}$ representing S_i is obtained. The perturbation mechanism is defined by

$$\Pr\left(s_j^* = x \mid s_j''\right)$$

$$= \begin{cases} \dfrac{2 \cdot s_j'' \cdot (e^{\varepsilon}d - 1) + w_j \cdot (e^{\varepsilon}d + 1)}{2 \cdot w_j \cdot (e^{\varepsilon}d + 1)}, & \text{if } x = \dfrac{w_j}{2} \cdot \dfrac{e^{\varepsilon}d + 1}{e^{\varepsilon}u - 1} + m_j, \\[3mm] -\dfrac{2 \cdot s_j'' \cdot (e^{\varepsilon}d - 1) + w_j \cdot (e^{\varepsilon}d + 1)}{2 \cdot w_j \cdot (e^{\varepsilon}d + 1)}, & \text{if } x = -\dfrac{w_j}{2} \cdot \dfrac{e^{\varepsilon}d + 1}{e^{\varepsilon}d - 1} + m_j. \end{cases} \quad (3)$$

Since a range move was performed on S_i' before the perturbation, m_j is added to the perturbation result x in Eq. 3 to restore the data. After completing the perturbation, send S_j^* to the server, which gets all the perturbation data and calculates the mean value of each dimension of the data.

The overall process of user data perturbation is shown in Algorithm 1, where S_i^* is obtained according to Eq. 3 perturbation and then sent to the collector server. The privacy proof of the Algorithm 1 is described in Sect. 3.3.

Algorithm 1. User data perturbation.

Require: privacy budget ε_u, security range $G_i = \{g_0, g_1, \ldots, g_{d-1}\}$, user u_i data vector $S_i = \{s_0, s_1, \ldots, s_{d-1}\}, 0 < i < n, 0 < j < d$

Ensure: user u_i data vector after perturbation $S_i^* = \{s_0^*, s_1^*, \ldots, s_{d-1}^*\}$

1: S_i is normalized to obtain $S_i' = \{s_0', s_1', \ldots, s_{d-1}'\}$
2: S_i' range moves to obtain $S_i'' = \{s_0'', s_1'', \ldots, s_{d-1}''\}$
3: **for** $j \leftarrow 0 \ldots d - 1$ **do**
4:      $w_j = |g_j|$
5:      m_j is the centroid of g_j
6:      $p \leftarrow$ Bernoulli $\left(\dfrac{2 \cdot s_j'' \cdot (e^{\varepsilon}d - 1) + w_j \cdot (e^{\varepsilon}d + 1)}{2 \cdot w_j \cdot (e^{\varepsilon}d + 1)}\right)$
7:      **if** $p = 1$ **then**
8:          $s_j^* = \dfrac{w_j}{2} \cdot \dfrac{e^{\varepsilon}d + 1}{e^{\varepsilon}d + 1} + m_j$
9:      **else**
10:        $s_j^* = -\dfrac{w_j}{2} \cdot \dfrac{e^{\varepsilon}d + 1}{e^{\varepsilon}d + 1} + m_j$
11: **return** S_i^*

Centroid Perturbation. As shown in Fig. 1, the local side enters the iterative process after the user data perturbation is completed. The centroids from the server are first accepted, then iteration centroids are calculated based on the real user data. Although the server cannot infer privacy information from the user data, the clustering information of the user belonging to that cluster, i.e., the iteration centroids sent to the server in each iteration, may reveal user privacy. Because the clusters to which users belong are calculated from real data, over multiple iterations, the server can infer the approximate distribution or exact value of the user data as the clusters to which users belong change, and the iteration centroids are updated. For example, assuming the user data is two-dimensional location data, the user can be positioned in a circular region in each iteration. In multiple iterations, overlapping these circular regions will help the server locate the user's exact location or exact location range.

To address the problem that iterative centroids may cause user privacy leakage, the iterative centroid perturbation algorithm is proposed in this paper to generate perturbed iterative centroids using a random perturbation mechanism. Also, The centroids in the first few iterations of the clustering change greatly, while the centroids in the last few iterations change only a little. Suppose the privacy budget is distributed equally, i.e., given the same amount of noise in each round. In that case, it will cause the problem of poor clustering utility or failure to converge. A privacy budget allocation mechanism in which the privacy budget for each round is incremented with the number of iterations is proposed in this paper. i.e., a smaller privacy budget is used for the first few rounds to add a larger noise. As the number of iterations increases, the privacy budget is incremented, and the noise is gradually reduced. The iterative centroid perturbation algorithm is described in Algorithm 2.

Algorithm 2. Iterative centroid perturbation algorithm.

Require: privacy budget ε_u, user's clustering centroid c_i, cluster centroid set C, the maximum number of iterations L, number of current iterations l_c, number of centroids k

Ensure: centroid after perturbation c_i^*

1: Generate a privacy budget allocation sequence by $P(n) = 2 \cdot P(n - 1)$ $\left(2 < n < L, P(0) = P(1) = \frac{1}{2^{L-1}} \cdot \varepsilon_u\right)$

2: $\varepsilon_n = P(l_c)$

3: $p \leftarrow$ Bernoulli $\left(\frac{e^{\varepsilon_n}}{e^{\varepsilon_n} + k - 1}\right)$

4: **if** $p = 1$ **then**

5:     $c_i^* = c_i$

6: **else**

7:     $c_i^* \leftarrow$ random sample from $\{C/c_i\}$

8: **return** c_i^*

As shown in Algorithm 2, the K-Randomized Response (K-RR) is used to perturb the user clustering information. Since K-RR can be applied to multivariate perturbations, there is no need to encode the centroids. The privacy budget allocation algorithm is inspired by the Fibonacci sequence. Since the goal of budget allocation is to construct an allocation scheme that increase by degrees and sums to ε, a privacy budget allocation sequence is constructed in this paper. Assuming that there are L iterations and the recursive formula for the sequence is as follows, $P(n) = 2 \cdot P(n-1) \left(2 < n < L, P(0) = P(1) = \frac{1}{2^{L-1}} \cdot \varepsilon_u\right)$, e.g. $L=5$, then we have a privacy budget allocation sequence $P = \{\frac{1}{16} \cdot \varepsilon_u, \frac{1}{16} \cdot \varepsilon_u, \frac{1}{8} \cdot \varepsilon_u, \frac{1}{4} \cdot \varepsilon_u, \frac{1}{2} \cdot \varepsilon_u\}$, the privacy budget for the third iteration is $\varepsilon_3 = \frac{1}{8} \cdot \varepsilon_u$ and the sum is ε_u. The iteration centroid perturbation is shown in the following Eq. 4.

$$\Pr\left[c_i^* = c_i\right] = \begin{cases} p = \frac{e^{\varepsilon_n}}{e^{\varepsilon_n} + k - 1} & \text{if } c_i^* = c_i \\ q = \frac{1}{e^{\varepsilon_n} + k - 1} & \text{if } c_i^* \neq c_i \end{cases}. \tag{4}$$

where ε_n represents the privacy budget for the current number of iterative rounds, L is the maximum number of iterative rounds, k is the number of centroids and c_i^* represents the iteration centroid after perturbation. The detailed procedure for the iterative centroid perturbation algorithm is described in Algorithm 2.

Collector Server Method

Initial Centroid Selection. The server randomly generates k d-dimensional initial centroids C based on the S_i^* and sent them to the user.

Aggregation and Centroid Computation. The server groups the user perturbation data S_i^* according to the perturbation centroid $C^* = \{c_0^*, c_0^*, \ldots, c_{K-1}^*\}$ sent from the local side. In each cluster, the mean of each dimension of S_i^* is calculated separately, and the centroid C is updated in this way.

$$c_i = \frac{1}{|c_i^*|} \cdot \left\{ \sum_{S_i^* \in c_i^*} s_0^*, \sum_{S_i^* \in c_i^*} s_1^*, \ldots, \sum_{S_i^* \in c_i^*} s_{d-1}^* \right\} \tag{5}$$

where c_i is the new centroid updated by the calculation, $|c_i^*|$ is the number of user data belonging to c_i^*, and $\sum_{S_i^* \in c_i^*} s_j^*$ is the intra-class sum of the j-th dimensional data. Send the new centroid to the local side after the calculation is completed. Clustering iterations are performed as described above until the clustering is complete. The main steps of the centroid update are shown in Algorithm 3.

Algorithm 3. Centroid update algorithm.

Require: centroid after perturbation C^*, user u_i data vector after perturbation S_i^*, number of centroids k
Ensure: centroid after update C
1: **for** $i \leftarrow 0 \ldots k - 1$ **do**
2: $\quad c_i = \frac{1}{|c_i^*|} \cdot \left\{ \sum_{S_i^* \in c_i^*} s_0^*, \sum_{S_i^* \in c_i^*} s_1^*, \ldots, \sum_{S_i^* \in c_i^*} s_{d-1}^* \right\}$
3: **return** $C = \{c_0, c_1, \ldots, c_{k-1}\}$

3.3 Privacy Analysis

This section proves that Algorithms 1 and 2 satisfy the definition of differential privacy and further proves that the overall framework satisfies the definition of differential privacy.

Theorem 1. *Algorithm 1 provides (G_i, ε_u)-PLDP for each uesr u_i with (G_i, ε_u).*

Proof. For any two values $s_{j1}', s_{j2}' \in g_j$ and $s_j^* \in \{\frac{w_j}{2} \cdot \frac{e^{\varepsilon_u}+1}{e^{\varepsilon_u}-1} + m_j, -\frac{w_j}{2} \cdot \frac{e^{\varepsilon_u}+1}{e^{\varepsilon_u}-1} + m_j\}$, there is $s_{j1}'' = s_{j1}' - m_j$, $s_{j2}'' = s_{j2}' - m_j$. Then there is

$$\frac{\Pr\left(s_j^* \mid s_{j1}'\right)}{\Pr\left(s_j^* \mid s_{j2}'\right)} = \frac{\Pr\left(s_j^* \mid s_{j1}''\right)}{\Pr\left(s_j^* \mid s_{j2}''\right)}$$

$$= \frac{\frac{2 \cdot s_{j1}'' \cdot (e^{\varepsilon}d - 1) + w_j \cdot (e^{\varepsilon}d + 1)}{2 \cdot w_j \cdot (e^{\varepsilon}d + 1)}}{\frac{2 \cdot s_{j2}'' \cdot (e^{\varepsilon}d - 1) + w_j \cdot (e^{\varepsilon}d + 1)}{2 \cdot w_j \cdot (e^{\varepsilon}d + 1)}}. \tag{6}$$

or

$$\frac{\Pr\left(s_j^* \mid s_{j1}'\right)}{\Pr\left(s_j^* \mid s_{j2}'\right)} = \frac{-\frac{2 \cdot s_{j1}'' \cdot (e^{\varepsilon_d}-1)+w_j \cdot (e^{\varepsilon_d}+1)}{2 \cdot w_j \cdot (e^{\varepsilon_d}+1)}}{-\frac{2 \cdot s_{j2}'' \cdot (e^{\varepsilon_d}-1)+w_j \cdot (e^{\varepsilon_d}+1)}{2 \cdot w_j \cdot (e^{\varepsilon_d}+1)}}. \tag{7}$$

Using Eq. 6 as an example,

$$\frac{\Pr\left(s_j^* \mid s_{j1}'\right)}{\Pr\left(s_j^* \mid s_{j2}'\right)} = \frac{2 \cdot s_{j1}'' \cdot (e^{\varepsilon_d}-1)+w_j \cdot (e^{\varepsilon_d}+1)}{2 \cdot s_{j2}'' \cdot (e^{\varepsilon_d}-1)+w_j \cdot (e^{\varepsilon_d}+1)}. \tag{8}$$

It can be seen from Eq. 8 that when $s_{j1}'' = \frac{w_j}{2}, s_{j2}'' = -\frac{w_j}{2}$ $\left(s_{j1}'' = -\frac{w_j}{2}, s_{j2}'' = \frac{w_j}{2}\right)$, Eqs. 6 and 7 to obtain the maximum value,

$$\frac{\Pr\left(s_j^* \mid s_{j1}'\right)}{\Pr\left(s_j^* \mid s_{j2}'\right)} \leq e^{\varepsilon_d}. \tag{9}$$

Algorithm 1 satisfies (g_j, ε_d)-PLDP by Eq. 9. Since $S_i' = \left\{s_0', s_1', \ldots, s_{d-1}'\right\}$, $G_i = \{g_0, g_1, \ldots, g_{d-1}\}$, and $\varepsilon_d = \frac{\varepsilon_u}{d}$, $\sum_{j=0}^{d-1} \varepsilon_d = \varepsilon_u$. According to Property 1 of Sect. 2, differential privacy has the sequence combinability property. So for user u_i with (G_i, ε_u), Algorithm 1 satisfies (G_i, ε_u)-PLDP.

Theorem 2. *Algorithm 2 provides ε_u-LDP for each uesr u_i throughout the clustering process.*

Proof. For any two values $c_{i1}, c_{i2}, c_i^* \in C$ there is

$$\frac{\Pr\left[c_{i1} = c_i^*\right]}{\Pr\left[c_{i2} = c_i^*\right]} = \frac{\frac{e^{\varepsilon_n}}{e^{\varepsilon_n}+k-1}}{\frac{1}{e^{\varepsilon_n}+k-1}} \tag{10}$$

$$= e^{\varepsilon_n}.$$

Algorithm 2 satisfies ε_n-LDP. For all iterations, the Property 1 sequence combinability property of Sect. 2 is applied. Since $\sum_{l_c=1}^{L} \varepsilon_n = \varepsilon_u$, for the whole clustering process, Algorithm 2 satisfies ε_u-LDP.

4   Experimental Evaluation

In this section, experiments are designed to investigate the improvements in the proposed framework compared to the existing DP k-means algorithm and how the relevant parameters influence the utility of the proposed framework.

4.1   Experimental Environment and Datasets

The hardware platform for this experiment uses Intel Core i7-11700 CPU @ 2.50 GHz, and 32.00 GB RAM. The experimental platform uses python 3.7. Two databases from the UCI dataset were used for the experiments. The Blood dataset records 748 individual blood donations from the Blood Transfusion Service Centre in Hsinchu city. Each record has five attributes. The Adult dataset is a dataset extracted from the 1994 census database. There are 488,42 records with 14 attributes per record. In this paper, six numerical attributes are retained for each record.

4.2   Experimental Setup and Evaluation Metrics

This paper focuses on three aspects of experimenting with the proposed framework.

1) Compare the utility of clustering with existing algorithms [9,10] for uniform k values under different ε. To the best of our knowledge, this paper is the first attempt at adopting PLDP in k-means clustering, so the extant advanced DP k-means algorithm was selected for comparison with the algorithm proposed in this paper. The PLDP k-means algorithm proposed in this paper is compared with the DPLloyd-Impr algorithm [9], and the DP-KCCM algorithm [10]. The DPLloyd-Impr algorithm completes the initial centroid selection by an initial centroid selection algorithm and then adds the Laplace noise to each round on average. In the DP-KCCM algorithm, the privacy budget allocation algorithm and the cluster merging algorithm are combined to enhance the clustering utility, and noise is injected through the Laplace mechanism. It is worth noting that both of these algorithms are based on differential privacy mechanisms and do not prevent attacks by malicious servers.
2) Compare the effects of different setting on the utility of clustering. Two sets of experiments are set up to understand the impact of key mechanisms on the utility of clustering. Firstly, the effect of privacy budget allocation methods on clustering utility was explored. Secondly, experiments were conducted on the effect of the iterative centroid perturbation algorithm on the clustering model.
3) Comparing the effect of different parameter distributions on clustering utility. Users can set their privacy budget ε_u and the size of the security range w_j according to their privacy needs in PLDP. All users' privacy parameters cannot be the same in practical applications. To understand the effect of key parameters on clustering utility, three sets of experiments were set up to investigate the effect of different parameters and different distributions on clustering utility.

In this paper, the utility of clustering is assessed using the Normalised Intra-Cluster Variance (NICV) [9]. The essential goal of the k-means algorithm is to divide the data into k clusters based on minimizing the error function, with distance as the evaluation metric. Therefore NICV can directly reflect the utility of clustering, while the NICV value can also reasonably reflect the impact of privacy protection mechanisms on the utility of clustering. The smaller NICV value means the better utility of clustering. NICV is defined as follows,

$$NICV = \frac{1}{N} \sum_{i=1}^{k} \sum_{S_i' \in c_i} \left\| S_i' - c_i \right\|^2 \tag{11}$$

where N represents the total number of users, k represents the number of centroids, S_i' represents the user data S_i normalized to $[-1,1]$, and $S_i' \in c_i$ represents the centroid c_i is the closest centroid to S_i'.

4.3 Experimental Analysis

The results of the experiments are shown below. The first experiment explores the performance of two existing algorithms [9,10] and the PLDP k-means proposed in this paper under different privacy budgets ε. The data were normalized to $[-1,1]$, w_j was set to 0.1, and the maximum number of iterations was set to 12. For comparison purposes, this experiment will unify the privacy budget ε_u and w_j for users. As seen in Fig. 2, PLDP k-means performs better than DPLloyd-Impr [9] and performs similarly to DP-KCCM [10]. However, the algorithm proposed in this paper does not require a trusted third-party server, which means that the PLDP k-means algorithm can obtain a similar or better clustering utility while eliminating the risk of malicious servers.

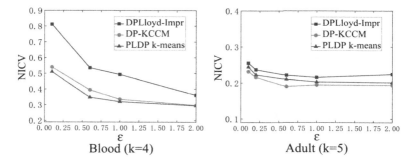

Fig. 2. Performance with respect to ε.

The second experiment explored the effect of different privacy budget allocation methods on the utility of clustering. A privacy budget allocation sequence is designed in this paper. Such that the allocation of privacy budgets in iterations presents a increase by degrees tendency. As shown in Fig. 3, the average privacy budget allocation method and the proposed allocation method were compared. It can be seen that the proposed method in this paper is significantly better than the average method. This demonstrates that the proposed privacy budget allocation algorithm in this paper can further improve the utility of clustering.

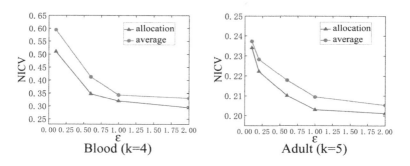

Fig. 3. Performance with respect to privacy budget allocation methods.

Iterative centroid perturbation algorithms are proposed to prevent privacy leakage caused by inference attacks. To evaluate the impact of this algorithm on the utility of clustering, a comparison experiment was conducted between using the iterative centroid perturbation algorithm and using real centroids directly. As shown in Fig. 4, the use of true centroids performed better than the use of the iterative centroid perturbation algorithm. This illustrates that some usability is sacrificed to improve privacy protection.

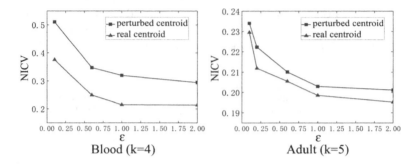

Fig. 4. Performance with respect to iterative centroid perturbation algorithm.

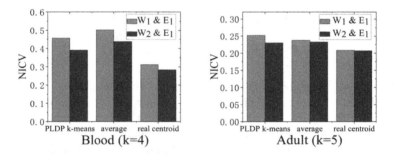

Fig. 5. Performance under the different W and the same E.

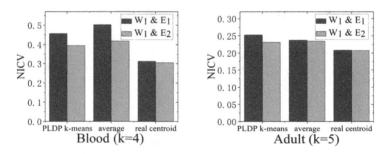

Fig. 6. Performance under the different E and the same W.

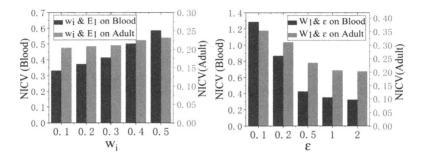

Fig. 7. Performance with respect to w_j and ε under the W_1,E_1.

The effect of the parameters is next explored. A fixed range is specified, $w_j \in [0.1,0.5]$, $\varepsilon_u \in [0.1,2]$. Each user can take their parameters from the range. Suppose the distributions of w_j, ε_u are uniform (W_1, E_1) or normal (W_2, E_2) respectively. W_1 and W_2, E_1 and E_2 have equal means. E_2 and W_2 have standard deviations of 0.3 and 0.1, respectively. PLDP k-means algorithm and the two variants of the algorithm based on this section discussed above, average, real centroid, were used for testing. Figure 5 (Fig. 6) shows the results of the three algorithms at different $W(E)$ and the same $E(W)$ on the two datasets. The control variables method shows that the results for W_2 and E_2 are better than those for W_1 and E_1, respectively. Although the means of the two distributions are equal, the normally distributed data are distributed with a high probability around the mean and a lower probability for smaller ε_u and larger w_j, which leads to better NICV values.

The effects of w_j and ε_u were further explored. The influence of varying w_j, ε_u on the utility of clustering was explored for the W_1,E_1 cases, respectively. As illustrated in Fig. 7, a larger w_j (ε_u) results in the poorer (better) utility of clustering.

Based on the experimental analysis above, the proposed algorithm in this paper improves the utility of clustering while ensuring the strength of privacy protection, and the experiments illustrate that the desired effect is achieved.

5   Conclusion

A clustering framework based on the PLDP k-means and an iterative centroid perturbation algorithms is proposed in this paper. This framework not required trusted third-party servers, and users are allowed to personalize their privacy requirements by the proposed PLDP k-means algorithm. An iterative centroid perturbation algorithm is also proposed that refines the privacy-preserving scheme by perturbing the centroids in the iterative process. Experimental results show that the proposed algorithm in this paper has better or similar performance than the extant DP k-means algorithm. Besides, the PLDP k-means algorithm requires only one upload of perturbation data, unlike the DP k-means algorithm, but the computational and communication costs during the iteration are still nonnegligible. Future work is to analyze and reduce the computational and communication costs of the PLDP k-means algorithm.

Acknowledgements. This research was supported by the National Natural Science Foundation of China under Grant 61801131, and Guangxi Natural Science Foundation under Grant 2022GXNSFAA035632.

References

1. Wang, X., Yang, L.T., Song, L., Wang, H., Ren, L., Deen, M.J.: A tensor-based multiattributes visual feature recognition method for industrial intelligence. IEEE Trans. Ind. Informatics **17**(3), 2231–2241 (2021)
2. Liu, Q., Tian, Y., Wu, J., Peng, T., Wang, G.: Enabling verifiable and dynamic ranked search over outsourced data. IEEE Trans. Serv. Comput. **15**(1), 69–82 (2022)
3. Wang, S., Sun, Y., Bao, Z.: On the efficiency of k-means clustering: evaluation, optimization, and algorithm selection. In: Proceedings of the VLDB Endowment, pp. 163–175 (2020)
4. Dwork, C.: Differential privacy. In: Bugliesi, M., Preneel, B., Sassone, V., Wegener, I. (eds.) ICALP 2006. LNCS, vol. 4052, pp. 1–12. Springer, Heidelberg (2006). https://doi.org/10.1007/11787006_1
5. Dwork, C.: Differential privacy: a survey of results. In: Agrawal, M., Du, D., Duan, Z., Li, A. (eds.) TAMC 2008. LNCS, vol. 4978, pp. 1–19. Springer, Heidelberg (2008). https://doi.org/10.1007/978-3-540-79228-4_1
6. Xiao, Y., Xiong, L.: Protecting locations with differential privacy under temporal correlations. In: Proceedings of the ACM Conference on Computer and Communications Security, pp. 1298–1309. ACM, Denver (2015)
7. Su, D., Cao, J., Li, N., Bertino, E., Lyu, M., Jin, H.: Differentially private k-means clustering and a hybrid approach to private optimization. ACM Trans. Priv. Secur. **20**(4), 1–33 (2017)
8. Nguyen, T.D., Gupta, S., Rana, S., Venkatesh, S.: Privacy aware K-means clustering with high utility. In: Bailey, J., Khan, L., Washio, T., Dobbie, G., Huang, J.Z., Wang, R. (eds.) PAKDD 2016. LNCS (LNAI), vol. 9652, pp. 388–400. Springer, Cham (2016). https://doi.org/10.1007/978-3-319-31750-2_31
9. Bertino, E.: Differentially private k-means clustering. In: Proceedings of the Sixth ACM Conference on Data and Application Security and Privacy, pp. 26–37. ACM, New Orleans (2016)
10. Ni, T., Qiao, M., Chen, Z., Zhang, S., Zhong, H.: Utility-efficient differentially private k-means clustering based on cluster merging. Neurocomputing **424**(1), 205–214 (2021)
11. Ye, Q.Q., Meng, X.F., Zhu, M.J., Huo, Z.: Survey on local differential privacy. J. Softw. **29**(7), 1981–2005 (2018)
12. Erlingsson, Ú., Pihur, V., Korolova, A.: RAPPOR: randomized aggregatable privacy-preserving ordinal response. In: Proceedings of the ACM Conference on Computer and Communications Security, pp. 1054–1067. ACM, Scottsdale (2014)
13. Cormode, G., Jha, S., Kulkarni, T., Li, N., Srivastava, D., Wang, T.: Privacy at scale: local differential privacy in practice. In: Proceedings of the ACM SIGMOD International Conference on Management of Data, pp. 1655–1658. ACM, Houston, TX, USA (2018)

14. Xia, C., Hua, J., Tong, W., Zhong, S.: Distributed k-means clustering guaranteeing local differential privacy. Comput. Secur. **90**(1), 1–11 (2020)
15. Gu, X., Li, M., Xiong, L., Cao, Y.: Providing input-discriminative protection for local differential privacy. In: International Conference on Data Engineering(ICDE), pp. 505–516. IEEE, Dallas, Texas (2016)
16. Chen, R., Li, H., Qin, A.K., Kasiviswanathan, S.P., Jin, H.: Private spatial data aggregation in the local setting. In: 2016 IEEE 32nd International Conference on Data Engineering, ICDE 2016, pp. 289–300. IEEE, Helsinki, Finland (2016)
17. Duchi, J.C., Jordan, M.I., Wainwright, M.J.: Minimax optimal procedures for locally private estimation. J. Am. Stat. Assoc. **113**(521), 182–201 (2018)

Optimizing Yinyang K-Means Algorithm on ARMv8 Many-Core CPUs

Tianyang Zhou[1,2], Qinglin Wang[1,2(✉)], Shangfei Yin[1,2], Ruochen Hao[1,2], and Jie Liu[1,2]

[1] Science and Technology on Parallel and Distributed Processing Laboratory, National University of Defense Technology, Changsha 410073, China
wangqinglin.thu@gmail.com

[2] School of Computer Science, National University of Defense Technology, Changsha 410073, China

Abstract. K-Means algorithm is one of the most common clustering algorithms widely applied in various data analysis applications. Yinyang K-Means algorithm is a popular enhanced K-Means algorithm that avoids most unnecessary calculations using triangle inequality. However, Yinyang K-Means algorithm is time-consuming when the problem size is large. Due to the influence of performance and energy-efficiency, ARM CPUs have appeared in high performance computing. Therefore, it is very interesting to accelerate Yinyang K-Means algorithm on ARM CPUs. In this paper, we propose an efficient parallel implementation of Yinyang K-Means algorithm on ARMv8 many-core CPUs by means of vectorization, NUMA affinity memory optimization and data layout optimization. The experiment on two ARMv8 many-core CPUs has shown that our implementation can achieve up to 5.6 times faster than the open-source multi-threaded one of Yinyang K-Means algorithm. To the best of our knowledge, this is the first work that studies the optimization of Yinyang K-Means algorithms on ARMv8 CPUs.

Keywords: K-Means · NUMA · Vectorization · ARMv8 · Performance optimization

1 Introduction

The classic K-Means algorithm [16] is one of the most important unsupervised learning algorithms that can be widely applied to data mining, document clustering, intrusion detection applications, etc. The algorithm consists of two steps: *assignment* and *rechosen*. The *assignment* step takes N points and K centroids as input, finds the closest centroid for each point and divides all points into K clusters. The *rechosen* step updates the centroid of each cluster by calculating the mean of all data points assigned to the cluster. These two steps are repeated

Supported by the National Natural Science Foundation of China under Grant No. 62002365.

W. Meng et al. (Eds.): ICA3PP 2022, LNCS 13777, pp. 676–690, 2023.
https://doi.org/10.1007/978-3-031-22677-9_36

until each centroid's location does not change, or the iteration reaches several times.

When the number of points or centroids is large, the classic K-Means algorithm often runs slowly. Many optimizations are proposed to accelerate the algorithm itself, such as initial location optimization of centroids [1], structural optimization [12,19], and triangle inequality optimization [5,7]. One of the most popular implementations based on triangle inequality optimization is Yinyang K-Means [4], an enhanced K-Means that can effectively avoid most unnecessary distance calculations using triangle inequality. The Yinyang K-Means algorithm introduces several distance bounds to form a three-level filter. The *global filter* screen out points whose cluster remains unchanged in the current iteration. The *group filter* identifies groups whose centroids in this group cannot be the closest centroid of point in the current iteration. The *local filter* excludes some centroids in the group, and these centroids cannot be the closest centroid for a point.

At the same time, many efforts have been made in the parallel optimization of K-Means algorithms to reduce their execution time. For instance, Wu et al. [25] achieved fine-grained SIMD parallelism by taking each dimension of all data points as a long vector and parallelizing the vectorized K-Means algorithm on Intel MIC architecture. Kwedlo et al. [14] proposed a hybrid MPI/OpenMP parallelization of four approaches: Drake's, Elkan's, Annulu's, and Yinyang algorithm. Zhao et al. [28] proposed a parallel K-Means clustering algorithm based on MapReduce, and the experimental results show that the MapReduce K-Means has good scalability and can efficiently process large datasets. Kumar et al. [13] parallel the K-Means clustering for quantitative ecoregion delineation using large data sets on a many-core supercomputer. Besides, existing research also tries to parallelize the K-Means algorithm using GPU [2,27], FPGA [3], and so forth. For example, Taylor et al. [22] optimized the implementation of Yinyang K-Means algorithm on GPU and achieved a speedup over the multi-core CPU of up to 8x on real-world datasets. However, there is little work on the optimization of K-Means algorithms on ARMv8 many-core CPUs.

In order to achieve a better balance between performance and energy-efficiency, ARM-based processors have been adopted in high performance computing field, such as A64FX in Fugaku supercomputer [17], ARM Cortex-A15 CPUs in Mont-Blanc prototype [20], and Phytium FT-2000+ in Tianhe-3 prototype [26]. Many algorithms and applications also have been parallelized and evaluated on ARM architectures, such as fast Fourier transform [15], deep learning [8,9,23,24], and Monte Carlo simulation [10]. Therefore, optimizing and evaluating K-Means algorithms on ARM CPUs is also enjoyable.

Although existing multi-threaded implementations of classical and optimized K-Means algorithms can directly work on ARM multi/many-core CPUs, they often perform sub-optimally because they do not utilize the vector processing units in ARM CPUs. Moreover, they also do not consider non-uniform memory access (NUMA) characteristics that are often found in many-core CPUs and may bring loss in performance. This paper mainly focuses on optimizing Yinyang K-Means algorithms on ARMv8 many-core processors. Leading optimization includes

vectorization and NUMA affinity memory optimization. A new memory data layout is proposed to support the optimization above. We design sets of experiments to compare the performance of our accelerated implementation with the
open source multi-threaded implementation [21] of Yinyang K-Means algorithm on
two ARMv8 many-core processors. The experiments show that the vectorization
achieved a maximum speedup of 4.6x, and the NUMA optimization achieved up to
1.5x speedup on real-world datasets. Our accelerated Yinyang K-Means with all
optimization techniques achieves a speedup of up to 5.6x over the native Yinyang
K-Means. We also carried out a set of experiments to demonstrate the parallel efficiency of our accelerated implementation. To the best of our knowledge, this is the
first work which optimizes and evaluates Yinyang K-Means algorithms on ARMv8
CPUs.

The structure of this paper is as follows. Section 2 introduces the Yinyang
K-Means algorithm, ARMv8 architecture and NUMA affinity. Section 3 analysis
the optimization opportunity on ARMv8 many-core CPUs. Section 4 describes
the optimization techniques in detail. The experimental results are presented in
Sect. 5. Section 6 gives the conclusion and future work.

2   Background

2.1   Yinyang Algorithm

Yinyang K-Means [4] is an enhanced K-Means that can generate the same result
as standard K-Means and produce significant speedup. The pseudocode of the
native Yinyang K-Means algorithm is described as Algorithm 1. The algorithm
randomly chooses K points as centroids, groups them into T groups, and initializes all of the N data point's assignment and distance bounds (lines 1–3). In
each iteration, the algorithm updates centroids first (line 5), then iterate over all
data points. The *global filter* in line 9 checks whether a point needs to change its
cluster with a single comparison, part of the points will be filtered and will not
be passed to the next filter. Lines 10–11 tighten the upper bound and recheck
the global filter condition to filter more points. For a point that goes through
the *global filter*, Lines 12–13 access all groups of centroids and labels each group
using the *group filter*. All centroids from groups that do not meet the group filter
condition will be filtered. If a group of centroids passes through the *group filter*,
the *local filter* further removes centroids in this group through another lemma,
as these centroids could not be the closest centroid. Finally, in lines 16–17, the
remaining points will compute the distance with the remaining centroids and find
the closest centroid for each point. The Yinyang K-Means algorithm computes
the Euclidean distance between points and centroids, which can be denoted as:

$$d(p_i^d, c_i^d) = \sqrt{\sum_{j=1}^{d}(p_{ij} - c_{ij})^2} \tag{1}$$

where $d(p_i^d, c_i^d)$ is the distance between point p_i and centroid c_i, both p_i and c_i
have d dimensions. We can also briefly summarize the whole filtering process of
the Yinyang K-Means algorithm in Fig. 1.

In this paper we removed the *local filter* as Newling and Fleuret [18] have shown that the *local filter* degrades performance.

Algorithm 1: Native multi-threaded implementation of Yinyang K-Means algorithms

---

    input : points$\{x_1, x_2, x_3, \ldots, x_n\}$
    output: centroids$\{c_1, c_2, c_3, \ldots, c_k\}$
1 Randomly choose K centroids
2 Group centroids into T groups
3 Initialize N points
4 **while** *Not converged* **do**
5   Update K centroids
6   #omp parallel for schedule(static)
7   **for** $i = 1 : 1 : N$ **do in parallel**
8   Update upper bound and group lower bounds for x_i
9   **if** *Global filter condition of x_i* **then**
10   Tighen the upper bound of x_i
11   Check the global filter condition for x_i again
12   **for** $l = 1$ *to* T **do** // Iterate over all groups
13   **if** *Group filter condition of G_l* **then**
                   /* Iterate over all centroids in a group   */
14   **for** $m = 1$ *to* K/T **do**
15   **if** *Local filter condition of C_m* **then**
16   Compute distance from x_i to c_m
17   Assign point x_i to its closest c_m

2.2 ARMv8 Architecture

ARMv8 is an ARM instruction set architecture that first introduced the 64-bit operating capabilities called *AArch64*. It maintains full compatibility with older ISA and introduces many enhancements, including cryptography extensions, enhanced barrier types, etc. ARMv8 incorporates 128-bit VFPs (vector processing units) and the Advanced SIMD (Single Instruction Multiple Data) architecture extension called Neon technology. With VFPs and additional instructions Neon provides, ARMv8 processor can parallel process two double-precision floating numbers or four single-precision floating numbers, thus obtaining better performance.

2.3 Non Uniform Memory Access

Figure 2 is a generic NUMA architecture. As the figure described, NUMA is a kind of memory architecture that consists of multiple nodes. Each node incorporates one or more cores and has its memory called local memory. In a NUMA architecture, any processor can access its local memory much faster than remote memory(memory of other processors). The memory access time depends on the memory location relative to the processor. Therefore reducing access to remote memory can significantly improve performance.

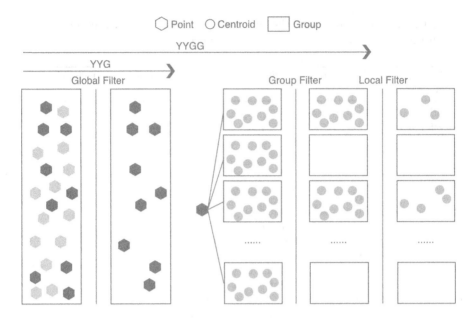

Fig. 1. A brief description of the Yinyang K-Means algorithm. YYG implies Yinyang K-Means with the *global filter* only, and YYGG implies Yinyang K-Means with the *global* and *group filter*.

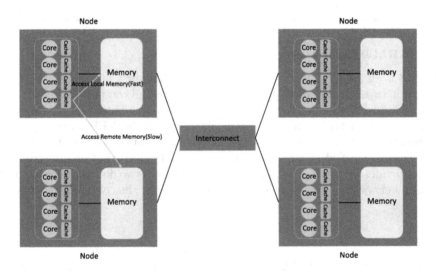

Fig. 2. A generic NUMA architecture

3   Analysis

The *assignment step* occupies most of the running time of Yinyang K-Means as it contains vast amounts of distance calculations. Existing paralleled implementations mainly focus on accelerating distance-computing using multi-threading, and it performs sub-optimal because it does not use the vector processing units to improve performance further. For vectorization of the Yinyang K-Means algorithm, we need to determine whether to vectorize points data or centroids data. In the first case, we treat all points data as a long vector and compute the distance between multiple points to a centroid simutaneously. Vectorize centroids data means we treat all centroids data as a long vector and compute the distance between multiple centroids to a point at once. Wu et al. [25] has shown that the vector must be sufficiently long if we want to gain good performance. Therefore, it is better to do vectorization on points data as points data size is much larger to generate a much longer vector for SIMD (Single Instruction Multiple Data) instructions. Second, we do vectorization in the distance calculation process and wherever it can be vectorized. For instance, we can check multiple points at once when checking the *global filter* condition. However, we must adjust the data memory layout to make it more suitable for vectorization and to obtain better data locality.

NUMA architecture is typical for supercomputers or servers as it can increase the bandwidth and bring more scalability. However, NUMA architecture has its natural drawbacks: high remote memory access costs. No researchers try to optimize Yinyang K-Means for NUMA architecture, so existing implementations may perform poorly when running on NUMA architecture processors, especially when there are many nodes in the NUMA architecture. So reducing the amount of remote memory access is an important issue. This problem can be solved through *thread binding, data distribution,* and *work distribution.*

4   Optimization Technique

4.1   Vectorization

Vectorization relies on the on-chip vector processing units of the core. ARMv8 architecture incorporates 32 128-bit registers per core and provides additional vector instructions so that can process two double-precision floating point numbers at once. So compared with the native Yinyang K-Means algorithm, which processes one point in a single for loop, the vectorized Yinyang K-Means algorithm can process two points simultaneously. So the algorithm can theoretically achieve a maximum speedup of 2x. As aforementioned in Analysis, we vectorize point data to compute the distance from multiple points to one centroid at once. As shown in Algorithm 2, we first do vectorization on the points initialization phase(line 5). Specifically, we put the exact dimension of two adjacent points into a vector and broadcast one dimension of a single centroid to another vector. Then we compute the euclidean distance of the two vectors using SIMD instructions. Then in a single iteration, we update the upper and lower bound for two points at once and check the *global filter* condition for two points simultaneously (lines 10–11). We can skip these two points if their centroid does not change in the current iteration. If any of the two meet the *global filter* condition, we must move on to tighten the upper bound of two points and recheck the *global filter* condition simultaneously. After that, from lines 15 to 17, we also do group and local filtering for two points. From lines 18 to 21, we do vectorization for distance computing as illustrated in the points initialization phase. Compared to the native Yinyang K-Means algorithm, our algorithm process two points in a single for loop; therefore, the number of iterations is halved. All of these vectorizations are implemented by ARM Neon intrinsic instructions.

4.2 NUMA-Aware Optimization

The executing characteristic of the Yinyang K-Means Algorithm indicates that points data can be processed independently by each core of NUMA nodes. In contrast, centroid data must be shared between each node, so if we put all of the point data in the memory of one single node. All of the memory access from the other nodes' cores are remote, bringing much more overhead, thus decreasing the performance. The ideal circumstance is that all the point data needed by the node are placed in its local memory in advance; therefore, all the memory access from each node to point data are fast and efficient [9].

According to the analysis of NUMA-Aware optimization, we implement the NUMA-Aware Yinyang K-Means algorithm in the following three steps:

(1) *Threads Binding:* in this step, we specify how threads are bound to processors. Fortunately, OpenMP 4.0 or above provides two environment variables called `OMP_PLACES` and `OMP_PROC_BIND`. These two environment variables are often used in conjunction with each other. `OMP_PLACES` specifies the places on the machine to which the threads are bound. `OMP_PROC_BIND` specifies the binding policy (thread affinity policy), which prescribes how the threads are assigned to places. In our implementation, we use the same number of OpenMP threads as cores of the processor and distribute OpenMP threads to all of the cores one by one. Each thread is bound to one single core (line 1 in Algorithm 2) so that the parallelism capability of the CPU is fully utilized.

(2) *Data Distribution:* after the *Threads Binding* process, we already know which threads are bound to the current node; thus, the points data needed by the node is explicit. OpenMP provides a data distribution approach among NUMA nodes: `First Touch Policy`. The First Touch Placement Policy allocates the data page in the memory closest to the thread accessing this page for the first time. So we need to parallelize access to all points data (line 2 in Algorithm 2) before the start of the Yinyang K-Means algorithm.

(3) *Workload Distribution:* we divide all the point data processing work into m parts and then distribute it to m OpenMP threads statically (line 8 in Algorithm 2). For now, every thread is bound to a core, and the point data needed by each thread are placed in the node's local memory to which the

core belongs. So that remote memory access to point data for each node will not occur.

Algorithm 2: Our accelerated implementation of Yinyang K-Means algorithms

---

    input : points$\{x_1, x_2, x_3, \ldots, x_n\}$
    output: centroids$\{c_1, c_2, c_3, \ldots, c_k\}$
1 Bind each thread to a different core
2 Parallelized accessing all of the points to distribute points data needed by each node
3 Randomly choose K centroids
4 Group centroids into T groups
5 Initialize N points using SIMD instructions
6 **while** *Not converged* **do**
7   Update K centroids
8   #omp parallel for schedule(static)
9   **for** $i = 1 : 2 : N$ **do in parallel**
10   Update upper bound and group lower bounds for x_i and x_{i+1}
11   **if** *Global filter condition of x_i and x_{i+1}* **then**
12   Tighen the upper bound of x_i and x_{i+1}
13   Check the global filter condition for x_i and x_{i+1} again
14   **for** $l = 1$ *to* T **do** // Iterate over all groups
15   **if** *Group filter condition of G_l* **then**
                    /* Iterate over all centroids in a group   */
16   **for** $m = 1$ *to* K/T **do**
17   **if** *Local filter condition of C_m* **then**
18   Put the same dimension of x_i, x_{i+1} in a vector
19   Broadcast one dimension of c_m to a vector
20   Compute vector distance from x_i, x_{i+1} to c_m
21   Assign point x_i and x_{i+1} to its closest c_m

4.3 Memory Layout Optimization

We assume there are n points, and each point has d dimensions. The most common memory data layout of these points can be presented in Fig. 3. Every point and every dimension of each point is stored sequentially. However, this memory layout has a significant drawback when doing vectorizations on points data. To compute the Euclidean distance of the two adjacent points to one centroid using the algorithm mentioned in Eq. 1, we need to access the exact dimension of two points to construct a vector. However, the span between two memory accesses is too large, which may cause plenty of cache misses, and the performance will degrade dramatically.

To make the memory access continuous when accessing the same dimension of two points, we can intuitively aggregate the same dimension of all points together, as we describe in Fig. 4. However, aggregated memory data layout brings the same problem as classic memory data layout when we access the next dimension of n points, and is not suitable for distributing points data to

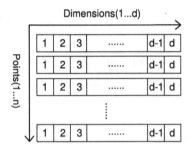

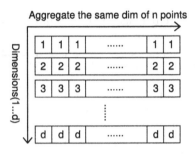

Fig. 3. Classic memory data layout of N points

Fig. 4. Aggregated memory data layout of N points

each node when doing NUMA-Aware optimization. We still need to adjust the memory data layout to improve the data locality.

We proposed a group aggregated memory data layout to solve the data locality problem, as shown in Fig. 5. Considering the 128-bit vector processing unit, we group the data of two points and use aggregated memory layout within the group. In this case, the memory access is entirely continuous, whether accessing the adjacent dimension of two points or the adjacent group of points. So the data locality is improved, and it is also more suitable for distributing points data to each NUMA node.

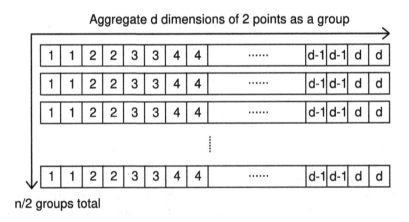

Fig. 5. Group aggregated memory data layout of N points

5 Experimental Result

5.1 Setup

To demonstrate the efficacy of our optimizing technique on the Yinyang K-Means algorithm. We use four large, real-world datasets, two are taken from the

UCI machine learning database [6] and the other two are from Kaggle [11]. The metrics of four datasets are described in Table 1.

we use the following two main implementations of Yinyang K-Means:

➤ **YYG:** Yinyang K-Means algorithm with *global filter* only.
➤ **YYGG:** Yinyang K-Means algorithm with *global* and *group filter*.

Table 1. Properties of the real-world datasets used in the experiments

Dataset	n(number of points)	d(dimension)	Ref
YearPrediction (YP)	515345	90	[6]
BotnetAttackDetection(BAD)	555932	115	[6]
WifiWithPCA (WWP)	258125	252	[11]
OGBNProducts (OP)	2449029	100	[11]

Besides, we also use three symbols to represent YYG(G) algorithm with different optimization technique.

➤ **YYG(G)-SV:** Open source multi-threaded CPU implementation [21] of scalar Yinyang K-Means algorithm.
➤ **YYG(G)-VV:** Multi-threaded Yinyang K-Means algorithm with vectorization.
➤ **YYG(G)-NUMA:** Multi-threaded Yinyang K-Means algorithm with vectorization and NUMA-Aware optimization.

All host code is written in C/C++ and compiled using GCC with the *-O3* optimization flag as we use Neon Intrinsic to implement vectorization. The convergence condition of the Yinyang algorithm is that the centroid of each cluster does not change or iteration number up to 1000. We performed experiments on four datasets for $k \in \{64, 128, 256, 512\}$. Each time measurements are averaged over three times trials. All data are stored as double-precision floating point values. All experiments are carried out on two kinds of ARM-based processors:

➤ **Phytium FT-2000+:** 8 NUMA nodes in a single processor. The processor has 64 cores and the working frequency of these cores is 2.2 GHz. Each core has one hardware thread.
➤ **Marvell ThunderX:** two processors constitute a NUMA system, each processor incorporates 48 2.0 GHz cores and each core has one hardware thread.

In order to prove the effect of vectorization, we perform several experiments for YYG(G)-SV and YYG(G)-VV. Both YYG(G)-SV and YYG(G)-VV are executed with the Linux command *numactl -interleave = all* to distribute all the data evenly to each node to obtain stable performance. Besides, we further optimized the YYG(G)-VV algorithm target NUMA architecture and compared it with YYG(G)-VV to demonstrate the performance improvements brought by NUMA-Aware optimization. Finally, we contrast YYG(G)-NUMA with YYG(G)-SV to get all the optimization techniques' overall speedup. Besides, we also performed some experiments on a single dataset to demonstrate our accelerated algorithm's scalability.

5.2 Comparison

Table 2 present the speedup of the YYG(G) vectorised version over the scalar version on Phytium FT-2000+. We only list the experimental results of vectorization on FT-2000+ for brevity, as the experimental results on the two platforms are similar. We describe the experimental results of vectorization on two platforms in words and list the key points as follows:

Table 2. The speedup of vectorized version of YYG(G) over scalar version on FT-2000+

k	Algorithm	YP	BAD	WWP	OP
64	YYG-VV vs YYG-SV	2.65	3.68	2.95	**3.70**
	YYGG-VV vs YYGG-SV	0.60	1.04	**1.04**	1
128	YYG-VV vs YYG-SV	2.67	**4.22**	3.24	3.66
	YYGG-VV vs YYGG-SV	0.57	**1.21**	1.20	0.89
256	YYG-VV vs YYG-SV	3.34	**4.54**	3.65	4.50
	YYGG-VV vs YYGG-SV	0.60	1.31	1.25	1.14
512	YYG-VV vs YYG-SV	3.47	**4.61**	3.90	3.93
	YYGG-VV vs YYGG-SV	0.63	1.33	**1.35**	1

1. On FT-2000+ and ThunderX, the Vectorized algorithm outperforms the scalar algorithm in most cases, yielding speedup up to 4.6x on FT-2000+ and 1.9x on ThunderX. A interesting result is that vectorized YYG has a more significant speedup than vectorized YYGG. We can explain it from two aspects: algorithm YYG has only one filter, thus bringing fewer logical statements; on the other hand, algorithm YYGG screens out more points data, thus distance calculations decrease. So vectorization is more efficient for YYG.
2. We observed that vectorized algorithm performs worse than the scalar algorithm on dataset YearPrediction. The main reason vectorization does not work in some cases is that the dimension of YearPrediction is relatively low, so the instruction pipeline emptying and loading accounted for too much of the total time. Therefore, vectorization is more suitable for datasets with greater dimensionality. From our experimental results, datasets whose dimensions more than 100 can achieve good performance after vectorization.
3. Vectorization theoretical speedup is 2x as we use the 128-bit vector processing unit. However, the experimental result shows that the speedup of vectorization on FT-2000+ is up to 4.6x, which is beyond our expectations. After

that, we performed experiments on a single node, and the speedup dropped to 1.x. Therefore, this indicates that the scalar algorithm is more influenced by NUMA architecture than the vectorized algorithm.

Table 3 shows the speedup of the YYG(G)-NUMA algorithm over the YYG(G)-VV algorithm on FT-2000+. The results show that the YYG(G)-NUMA algorithm consistently outperforms the YYG(G)-VV algorithm, the speedup spanning 1.1–1.5x; this demonstrates that remote memory access is effectively avoided through our NUMA-Aware optimization strategy. NUMA-Aware optimization on ThunderX is not as effective as FT-2000+ as ThunderX only has 2 NUMA nodes, so it benefits less from the optimization.

Table 3. The speedup of NUMA-Aware vectorized version of YYG(G) over vectorized version on FT-2000+

k	Algorithm	YP	BAD	WWP	OP
64	YYG-NUMA vs YYG-VV	**1.51**	1.42	1.44	1.29
	YYGG-NUMA vs YYGG-VV	1.38	1.44	**1.47**	1.24
128	YYG-NUMA vs YYG-VV	**1.51**	1.28	1.38	1.20
	YYGG-NUMA vs YYGG-VV	1.34	1.30	**1.36**	1.24
256	YYG-NUMA vs YYG-VV	**1.32**	1.20	1.29	1.11
	YYGG-NUMA vs YYGG-VV	1.34	1.20	1.29	1.14
512	YYG-NUMA vs YYG-VV	**1.27**	1.21	1.22	1.13
	YYGG-NUMA vs YYGG-VV	1.12	1.19	**1.22**	1.12

Combining NUMA-Aware optimization and vectorization, the YYG(G)-NUMA algorithm is much faster than the YYG(G)-SV algorithm. Tables 4 and 5 list the speedup on FT-2000+ and ThunderX. From these two tables, either FT-2000+ or ThunderX, we achieved practical performance improvements for the Yinyang K-Means algorithm on four high-dimension datasets in most cases.

Table 4. The overall speedup of NUMA-Aware vectorized version of YYG(G) over scalar version on FT-2000+

k	Algorithm	YP	BAD	WWP	OP
64	YYG-NUMA vs YYG-SV	3.99	**5.23**	4.24	4.78
	YYGG-NUMA vs YYGG-SV	0.82	1.50	**1.53**	1.24
128	YYG-NUMA vs YYG-SV	4.02	**5.38**	4.49	4.41
	YYGG-NUMA vs YYGG-SV	0.76	1.56	**1.63**	1.11
256	YYG-NUMA vs YYG-SV	4.42	**5.43**	4.72	5.00
	YYGG-NUMA vs YYGG-SV	0.81	1.58	**1.62**	1.17
512	YYG-NUMA vs YYG-SV	4.38	**5.59**	4.75	4.46
	YYGG-NUMA vs YYGG-SV	0.71	1.58	**1.64**	1.11

Table 5. The overall speedup of NUMA-Aware vectorized version of YYG(G) over scalar version on ThunderX

k	Algorithm	YP	BAD	WWP	OP
64	YYG-NUMA vs YYG-SV	1.20	**1.88**	1.50	1.33
	YYGG-NUMA vs YYGG-SV	1.00	**1.79**	1.45	1.24
128	YYG-NUMA vs YYG-SV	1.08	**1.94**	1.52	1.20
	YYGG-NUMA vs YYGG-SV	1.00	**1.86**	1.50	1.14
256	YYG-NUMA vs YYG-SV	1.19	**1.97**	1.55	1.36
	YYGG-NUMA vs YYGG-SV	0.96	**1.88**	1.50	1.20
512	YYG-NUMA vs YYG-SV	1.17	**2.00**	1.54	1.18
	YYGG-NUMA vs YYGG-SV	0.95	**1.87**	1.51	1.14

In addition, we also designed a set of experiments using the dataset Wifi-WithPCA on FT-2000+ to study the strong scaling of our accelerated Yinyang K-Means algorithm. We ran our accelerated Yinyang K-Means algorithm and native Yinyang K-Means algorithm on a single NUMA node and 8 NUMA nodes, respectively. The experimental results are described in Fig. 6 and Fig. 7. Figure 6 shows that both vectorization and NUMA-Aware optimization improve the parallel efficiency of YYG. The parallel efficiency of YYG-VV has increased from 30%+ to 60%+ after being vectorized and further increased to 85%+ after NUMA-Aware optimization. The parallel efficiency of YYGG-VV has reached 90%+. Vectorization reduces its efficiency, but NUMA-Aware optimization increases parallel efficiency to the same level it started. So we can briefly conclude that our optimization techniques can effectively increase the parallel efficiency for YYG and maintain the same parallel efficiency level as the original Yinyang K-Means for YYGG.

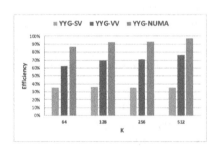

Fig. 6. Efficiency of YYG on dataset WifiWithPCA

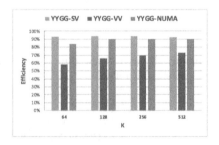

Fig. 7. Efficiency of YYGG on dataset WifiWithPCA

6   Conclusion and Future Work

This paper optimized the Yinyang K-Means algorithm on ARMv8 many-core CPU using several optimization techniques, including vectorization and NUMA-Aware optimization. We also proposed a new memory data layout to gain better data locality to be more suitable for vectorization. Experiments on FT-2000+ and ThunderX have shown that both vectorization and NUMA-Aware optimization can significantly boost performance in most cases. Besides, the scalability of our algorithm is at the same level as the native Yinyang K-Means algorithm. Therefore, we can conclude that we achieved comprehensive performance improvement for Yinyang K-Means on ARMv8 many-core CPUs.

In the future, we will utilize multiple ARMv8 nodes to further accelerate Yinyang K-Means algorithms.

References

1. Arthur, D., Vassilvitskii, S.: k-means++: the advantages of careful seeding. Technical report, Stanford (2006)
2. Bhimani, J., Leeser, M., Mi, N.: Accelerating k-means clustering with parallel implementations and GPU computing. In: 2015 IEEE High Performance Extreme Computing Conference (HPEC), pp. 1–6. IEEE (2015)
3. Dias, L.A., Ferreira, J.C., Fernandes, M.A.: Parallel implementation of k-means algorithm on FPGA. IEEE Access **8**, 41071–41084 (2020)
4. Ding, Y., Zhao, Y., Shen, X., Musuvathi, M., Mytkowicz, T.: Yinyang k-means: a drop-in replacement of the classic k-means with consistent speedup. In: International Conference on Machine Learning, pp. 579–587. PMLR (2015)
5. Drake, J., Hamerly, G.: Accelerated k-means with adaptive distance bounds. In: 5th NIPS Workshop on Optimization for Machine Learning, vol. 8 (2012)
6. Dua, D., Graff, C.: UCI machine learning repository (2017). http://archive.ics.uci.edu/ml
7. Hamerly, G.: Making k-means even faster. In: Proceedings of the 2010 SIAM International Conference on Data Mining, pp. 130–140. SIAM (2010)
8. Huang, X., Wang, Q., Lu, S., Hao, R., Mei, S., Liu, J.: Evaluating FFT-based algorithms for strided convolutions on ARMv8 architectures. Perform. Eval. **152**, 102248 (2021). https://www.sciencedirect.com/science/article/pii/S0166531621000651
9. Huang, X., Wang, Q., Lu, S., Hao, R., Mei, S., Liu, J.: NUMA-aware FFT-based convolution on ARMv8 many-core CPUs. In: 2021 IEEE International Conference on Parallel & Distributed Processing with Applications, Big Data & Cloud Computing, Sustainable Computing & Communications, Social Computing & Networking (ISPA/BDCloud/SocialCom/SustainCom), pp. 1019–1026. IEEE (2021)
10. Jin, C., Wang, Q., Zhao, Y., Dou, Y.: Parallelization of fast Monte Carlo dose calculation for radiotherapy treatment planning on the ARMv8 architecture. In: 2021 11th International Conference on Information Science and Technology (ICIST), pp. 261–265 (2021)
11. Kaggle: Kaggle datasets. https://www.kaggle.com/datasets. Accessed 18 Apr 2022
12. Kanungo, T., Mount, D.M., Netanyahu, N.S., Piatko, C.D., Silverman, R., Wu, A.Y.: An efficient k-means clustering algorithm: analysis and implementation. IEEE Trans. Pattern Anal. Mach. Intell. **24**(7), 881–892 (2002)

13. Kumar, J., Mills, R.T., Hoffman, F.M., Hargrove, W.W.: Parallel k-means clustering for quantitative ecoregion delineation using large data sets. Procedia Comput. Sci. **4**, 1602–1611 (2011)
14. Kwedlo, W., Czochanski, P.J.: A hybrid MPI/OpenMP parallelization of k-means algorithms accelerated using the triangle inequality. IEEE Access **7**, 42280–42297 (2019)
15. Li, Z., et al.: AutoFFT: a template-based FFT codes auto-generation framework for arm and x86 CPUs. In: Proceedings of the International Conference for High Performance Computing, Networking, Storage and Analysis, SC 2019. Association for Computing Machinery, New York, NY, USA (2019). https://doi.org/10.1145/3295500.3356138
16. Lloyd, S.: Least squares quantization in PCM. IEEE Trans. Inf. Theory **28**(2), 129–137 (1982)
17. Matsuoka, S.: Fugaku and A64FX: the first exascale supercomputer and its innovative arm CPU. In: 2021 Symposium on VLSI Circuits, pp. 1–3 (2021)
18. Newling, J., Fleuret, F.: Fast k-means with accurate bounds. In: International Conference on Machine Learning, pp. 936–944. PMLR (2016)
19. Pelleg, D., Moore, A.: Accelerating exact k-means algorithms with geometric reasoning. In: Proceedings of the Fifth ACM SIGKDD International Conference on Knowledge Discovery and Data Mining, pp. 277–281 (1999)
20. Rajovic, N., et al.: The mont-blanc prototype: an alternative approach for high-performance computing systems (2016)
21. Taylor: Scalar yinyang kmeans. https://github.com/ctaylor389/k_means_yinyang_gpu. Accessed 18 Apr 2022
22. Taylor, C., Gowanlock, M.: Accelerating the Yinyang k-means algorithm using the GPU. In: 2021 IEEE 37th International Conference on Data Engineering (ICDE), pp. 1835–1840. IEEE (2021)
23. Wang, Q., Li, D., Huang, X., Shen, S., Mei, S., Liu, J.: Optimizing FFT-based convolution on ARMv8 multi-core CPUs. In: Malawski, M., Rzadca, K. (eds.) Euro-Par 2020. LNCS, vol. 12247, pp. 248–262. Springer, Cham (2020). https://doi.org/10.1007/978-3-030-57675-2_16
24. Wang, Q., Mei, S., Liu, J., Gong, C.: Parallel convolution algorithm using implicit matrix multiplication on multi-core CPUs. In: 2019 International Joint Conference on Neural Networks (IJCNN), pp. 1–7. IEEE (2019)
25. Wu, F., Wu, Q., Tan, Y., Wei, L., Shao, L., Gao, L.: A vectorized K-means algorithm for Intel many integrated core architecture. In: Wu, C., Cohen, A. (eds.) APPT 2013. LNCS, vol. 8299, pp. 277–294. Springer, Heidelberg (2013). https://doi.org/10.1007/978-3-642-45293-2_21
26. You, X., Yang, H., Luan, Z., Liu, Y., Qian, D.: Performance evaluation and analysis of linear algebra kernels in the prototype Tianhe-3 cluster. In: Abramson, D., de Supinski, B.R. (eds.) SCFA 2019. LNCS, vol. 11416, pp. 86–105. Springer, Cham (2019). https://doi.org/10.1007/978-3-030-18645-6_6
27. Zechner, M., Granitzer, M.: Accelerating k-means on the graphics processor via CUDA. In: 2009 First International Conference on Intensive Applications and Services, pp. 7–15. IEEE (2009)
28. Zhao, W., Ma, H., He, Q.: Parallel K-means clustering based on MapReduce. In: Jaatun, M.G., Zhao, G., Rong, C. (eds.) CloudCom 2009. LNCS, vol. 5931, pp. 674–679. Springer, Heidelberg (2009). https://doi.org/10.1007/978-3-642-10665-1_71

Mining High-Value Patents Leveraging Massive Patent Data

Ruixiang Luo[1], Lijuan Weng[1], Junxiang Ji[1], Longbiao Chen[1],
and Longhui Zhang[2(✉)]

[1] Fujian Key Laboratory of Sensing and Computing for Smart City,
School of Informatics, Xiamen University, Xiamen 361021, Fujian, China
[2] ZFusion Technology Co., Ltd., Xiamen 361021, Fujian, China
`lzhan015@zfusion.cn`

Abstract. A patent is an inventor's way of protecting its intellectual property. In recent years, the trend of patent filings has become more prevalent than ever as commercial competition among firms has intensified. While patents have promoted our society forward, only a few patents have made significant contributions, and they are often referred to as high-value patents. However, there is no clear definition of high-value patents, so traditional mining methods often rely on expert reviews in related fields, which is usually labor-intensive and time-consuming. Although existing literatures have resorted to human-designed statistical features to identify high-value patents, they ignore potentially valuable text and images in patents. In this work, we propose a two-phase framework to effectively extract heterogeneous features from the multimodal text and image to mine high-value patents among the massive patents. In feature extraction phase, features are divided into three categories: statistical features, visual features, and textual features. Among them, statistical features are obtained according to a pretrained graph, textual features are extracted by a BERT-like language model, and a DenseNet-based network is used to extract visual features. In the multiview learning phase, we use heterogeneous features to train views, then concatenate their features to the final several layers to evaluate the value of a patent. The evaluation result shows that our method outperforms the baseline methods.

Keywords: Massive patent mining · Multi-view learning · Heterogeneous feature fusion

1 Introduction

Patents, dating back to the Middle Ages, are an important tool for protecting inventors' ideas. Nowadays, more and more organizations anticipate in competition for patent applications to protect individual intellectual property. According to World Intellectual Property Indicators 2020[1], the Chinese government

---

[1] https://www.wipo.int/publications/en/details.jsp?id=4526.

© Springer Nature Switzerland AG 2023
W. Meng et al. (Eds.): ICA3PP 2022, LNCS 13777, pp. 691–706, 2023.
https://doi.org/10.1007/978-3-031-22677-9_37

has adopted various measures to promote inventions, and the number of patent applications has grown rapidly over the past decade, reaching 1.4 million in 2019.

Have you ever thought every patent has great practical value? The truth is no. While all patents contribute to the development of our society, that doesn't mean they are all so important that they change our daily lives in a particular field. Therefore, when we want to understand the development of a field, it is necessary for us to figure out the patents that have a significant impact on our life from the vast number of patents, which are often called high-value patents.

How to evaluate whether a patent has high value? So far, there is no clear standard for the specific judgment method. Traditionally, this work is usually assigned to experts who have conducted extensive experiments in the field [8]. The biggest disadvantage of this method is that it is too subjective and cannot rely on a certain standard, because experts have their own standards. A method of collecting results from numerous experts has been proposed, and while the results may be more accurate, but requires more money and takes longer time.

Therefore, how to figure out high-value patents from large number of patents in a low cost? In tradition, it only depends on cited number, which means the high-cited patent is more important and high-value [2]. At present, more statistical indexes have been considered into criterion such as the number of inventors. Though the major standard is constructed, details are still decided by experts [13]. Therefore, Many companies have launched products about high-value patents mining. However, they haven't published how their system evaluates patents. Lots of researchers also devote themselves to mining patents in a specific field, but few researchers focus their attention on high-value patent mining. The common method in high-value patent mining only uses statistical features, which ignores the textual information and visual information of patents [2,4,13].

In order to better utilize patent meta-information and reduce time consumption, we build a model to fuse heterogeneous features, which includes statistics, text descriptions and design drawings. However, in order to establish a high-value patent mining model, the following issues have to be solved:

1. *A Large Amount of statistical Features.* Patents have many statistical features to describe content. However, not all statistical features are effective in determining whether a patent is of high value. Therefore, in order to save computational resources and computation time, it is necessary to estimate whether features are helpful for evaluation, and select the effective ones as statistical features.
2. *Multi-source Description about Patents.* Patents have a wide variety of text, such as title abstracts, claims, etc., that vary in length and subject. Therefore, it is important to select the appropriate patent text content for patent mining.
3. *Multi-angle Visualization about Patents.* When inventing a patent, inventors show the appearance of patents from multiple angles. Due to differences among ideas, some patents have numerous pictures, and some have a small number. Therefore, how to choose a picture to represent a patent is a confusing question.

4. *Fuse Heterogeneous Features.* Heterogeneous features present patents in comprehensive aspects. Therefore, we need to consider how to fuse them.

In order to solve above-mentioned problems, we proposed a two-phase framework incorporating a wide range of heterogeneous data for high-value patent mining. In the first phase, we extract heterogeneous features from patents materials. According to authoritative patent databases, we have established a patent-related graph, in which nodes include inventors, applicants, patents, and agents, and edges are composed of patent agents, patent applications, patented inventions, united applications, united inventions, and simple groups. Next, for each patent, we extract its internal attributes and edge features, such as the number of citations, the number of applicants, etc. Next, for the textual information of each patent, we select its abstract and use a Bert-like language model to extract its textual features. Finally, for each patent's image information, we use a DenseNet-based model to extract its image features. In the second stage, we adopt a multi-view learning approach, each view has its own features, and classify high-value patents by concatenating features in different views.

In summary, the main contributions of this paper include:

1. To reduce the cost of manpower and material source and improve accuracy, we propose a framework on fusing visual data, semantic data and structured data to figure out high-value patents in massive patent data.
2. We propose a collaborative classification based on heterogeneous features. First, we use various methods to select the valuable information relevant to high-value patents. then we use Bert to extract the deep semantics from patents' abstracts. Finally, we use multi-view learning to concatenate heterogeneous features to mine high-value patents in massive dataset.
3. We evaluate our framework using real-world patents. The result shows that the proposed framework can not only accurately figure out high-value patents, but also evaluate whether a patent is high-value. We have deployed our system on a company devoted to knowledge property, it performs well in reality.

The rest of this paper is illustrated as follows. We firstly review the related work in Sect. 2. Then we present an overview of the proposed framework in Sect. 3. In next two sections, we detail two phases of the framework: Feature Extraction in Sect. 4, Multi-view Learning in Sect. 5. Evaluation is reported in Sect. 6 to show effectiveness of the proposed framework. Finally, we conclude the paper and chart the future directions in Sect. 7.

2   Related Work

In this section, we review the related work in three parts. The first part is about high-value patent mining, the second part concentrates on heterogeneous features in various fields, and the third part states multi-view Learning.

2.1   Patent Mining

Patents bring benefits for organizations. It's an interesting question for researchers to mine the patents they need. Researchers made surveys about patent mining. Zhang et al. [26] introduced patent mining could be divided into many subtasks such as patent retrieval, patent visualization, patent valuation.

Patent Retrieval, searching highly correlative patent documents, is a brunch of Information Retrieval. Although the rapid development of techniques, various challenges still exist, which leads to low recall and accuracy. Walid et al. [20] proposed an interactive relevance feedback mechanism to query reformulation and term weighting. Zhang et al. [27] proposed a new integrated framework, which transforms patent application into an effective search query automatically.

Patent Visualization is an essential part when facing a bulk of patents. In origin, analysts use structured data such as citation to build a patent graph. Huang et al. [12] create a patent citation graph to analyze distinction and similarity on groups of companies. but it ignores text in analysis. Kim et al. [14] proposed a visualized method to combine structured and unstructured data, which clusters patent documents and form a semantic network of keywords.

Patent Valuation is an imperative section in practice. In recent years, Hsu et al. [10] test various natural language processing (NLP) methods to evaluate methods' predictive power. Liu et al. [19] proposed a Bayesian network-based model to predict the paths toward the realization of patent valuation.

2.2   Heterogeneous Feature Fusion

Information has various ways to be presented, such as image, voice. If evaluating objects in only one aspect, it would ignore useful heterogeneous features. Therefore, researchers propose methods to fuse heterogeneous features. In structured features, Yang et al. [25] proposed an incremental feature selection method to handle heterogeneous data with symbolic and real-valued features. In unstructured features. Cao et al. [5] proposed a machinery called Heterogeneous Feature Machine (HFM) to solve visual recognition tasks.

2.3   Multi-view Learning

Multi-view learning algorithms aim to fuse heterogeneous information, it has two types: consensus principle and complementary principle [15]. In complementary principle, Zheng et al. [1] proposed a new multi-view subspace clustering approach called Feature Concatenation Multi-view Subspace Clustering (FCMSC). Liu et al. [18] proposed Feature Concatenation for adversarial Domain Adaptation (FCDA) method to improve the discriminability. In complementary principle, Song et al. [21] presented a distance-to-model and adaptive clustering-based multi-view ensemble (DM-ACME) learning method for predicting default risk in P2P lending. Carissimi et al. [6] applied a approach to combine face-based deep features to avoid the weakness of feature concatenation.

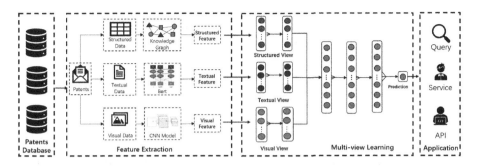

Fig. 1. Overview of high-value patent mining framework.

3   Framework

In this section, we provide preliminary knowledge of high-value patent mining and multi-view, then we illustrate framework of our method.

3.1   Preliminaries of High-value Patent Mining

Patents have kinds of metadata such as abstract and figures, and they presents as number, text, image and so on. The experts commonly divide them into two categories: structured data and unstructured data.

Structured data, such as patent ID, has a fixable form, which can be parsed into statistical features. Some can be directly considered as features, which are usually represented in statistical form. the others have to be parsed and restructured in an appropriate way. In order to realize patent mining, structured data is used as attributes to build a patent graph.

Unstructured data, including abstracts, figures, etc., have non-fixable forms. Some data are presented in multimedia form, and features can be extracted using computer vision models. The remaining unstructured data is text, we can try to extract textual features using a natural language processing model.

3.2   Preliminaries of Multi-view Learning

Multi-view learning is a method of combining heterogeneous features to output the most likely prediction. Multi-view learning has two types: consensus principle and complementary principle. Consensus principle requires many classifiers train their own views and vote for predictions. Complementary principle trains only one model by feature fusion.

3.3   Overview of Framework

In this subsection, we present the overview of framework. Shown in Fig. 1, the framework consists of two phases: Feature Extraction and Multi-view Learning.

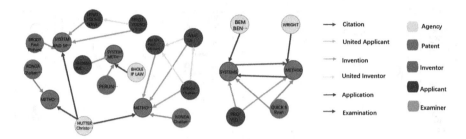

Fig. 2. Knowledge Graph of Patents. We build a patent graph to extract hidden structured features conveniently. It includes five-class nodes and six-class relationship. Five-class nodes are Agency, Applicant, Examiner, Inventor, and Patent. Six-class relationships includes Citation (between patents), United Inventor (between inventors), United Applicant (between applicants), Invention(between inventors and patents), Application (between applicants and patents), Examination (between examiner and patents).

Feature Extraction. Before fusing heterogeneous features, features need to be extracted from multi-source data. Therefore, we first divide data into two categories: structured data and unstructured data. Unstructured data can be divided into textual data and visual data. In order to process structured data, we build a knowledge graph based on massive patents, and then we extract structured features from the graph. Next, when it comes to text data, we use the pretrained BERT to extract text features. Finally, in the processing of visual data, we utilize DenseNet to extract visual features.

Multi-view Learning. In order to fuse heterogeneous features, we build a multi-view model to mine high-value patents. In this step, we provide each view with their own features and concatenate features in final several layers to evaluate high-value patents, so as to realize mining of high-value patents (Fig. 2).

4   Feature Extraction

In this section, our goal is to extract heterogeneous features from metadata of patents. However, there remains several challenges in practice: (1) Some structured data is a containment relationship, and some latent data requires researchers to mine from hidden relationships among patents. (2) Descriptions about patents are so rich that we have to select part of them as textual data for extracting semantic features. (3) The images of a patent shows different appearance details, but the number of images has a huge difference, so we have to consider how to select images to extract the visual features for massive patents.

To address above challenges, We first build a patent graph to figure out hidden relationships to determine structured features. Then we use the pretrained BERT to extract semantic features from textual data. Finally, in terms of visual data, we use DenseNet to extract visual features.

4.1 Structured Features Extraction Based on Patent Knowledge Graph

Structured features consist of part of metadata in a patent and the relationships hidden among patents. In order to mine hidden relationships among patents and figure out all structured features quickly, we build up a graph for patents.

Before we build up a patent graph, we filter out useless metadata in patents to keep the efficiency of the graph. Useless metadata consists of three-kind items: 1) blank information 2) duplicate information 3) irrelevant information. To eliminate blank information, we observe metadata of massive patents and find that the presentation of blank items is obvious: these items in almost patents are blank such as litigation date, expired date. Therefore, we filter out blank items manually. Filtering out duplicate information is a challenging task, since some items have an inclusive relationship, such as 5-year citation and 3-year citation. We consult experts and select most effective ones as the representative. Finally, in order to filter out irrelevant items, we use the chi-square test in the hypothesis test. We set P-Value to 0.05, and filter out irrelevant ones such as public year, application year, to ensure the relevance of features.

In a patent graph, there exists many roles such as inventor, applicant. Therefore, we perform roles splitting on the filtered metadata to obtain five entities: patent, applicant, inventor, examiner, and agency, and each entity has its own attributes, which are nodes in the graph. What's more, we discover six relationships among nodes, including Citation, United Inventor, United Applicant, Invention, Application, Examination, which are edges in our knowledge graph.

After building the graph, we consider to extract statistical features. For each patent, besides structured metadata, we extract other features from relationships and roles. Some features could be extracted from the number of edges such as citations, the number of inventors. The others could be extracted from relevant roles, such as the number of patents held by the applicant, the number of patents held by the inventors, and the number of patents held by the agencies. Finally, as shown in Table 1, we extract a 20-dimensional structured features (Fig. 3).

Table 1. Structured Data of Nodes. Each type of node has its own unique meta information, and some structured data have to be obtained by establishing edges.

Node	Structured Data
Agency	Patents, Agency Level
Applicant	Patents, Citations
Examiner	Patents
Inventor	Patents, Citations
Patent	Length of Abstract, Length of Title Family Members in PatSnap, Citations in PatSnap, Applicants, Inventors, References, Number of Figures, Citation by Others, Citation from Others, Simple Family Members Family Members in INPADOC, Simple Family Members in INPADOC

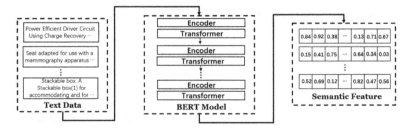

Fig. 3. Semantic Feature Extraction Framework. We concatenate the title and abstract of each patent and feed them into a BERT model to extract semantic features.

4.2   Semantic Features Extraction Based on BERT

Text is a way to convey individual minds. In order to introduce patents comprehensively, inventors tend to write lots of textual materials. Therefore, various texts exist in a patent. However, it is impossible to read all text carefully to evaluate a patent. Therefore, we leverage expert knowledge to select the text that contains rich semantics. Our scope of consideration is narrowed to three parts: title and abstract, independent claims, and claims. Independent claims and claims are relative items. When observing metadata, we discover that quite a few patents lack relevant descriptions in claims and independent claims, so we leverage title and abstract as textual data to extract semantic features.

In recent years, Natural Language Processing (NLP) has made a rapid development so that its application can be discovered everywhere. Among excellent models, BERT [7], proposed by Google, is a pre-training technique for Natural Language Processing and performs well on various text tasks. Therefore, we use BERT to extract semantic features from text of massive patents.

In this work, when text is sent to BERT, it is encoded as an input vector of fixed length 512, and if the length is longer than 512, we would truncate the head and tail parts to keep the effectiveness of semantic features [24]. In a input vector, it consists of three embedding features: 1) WordPiece [23], 2) Position embedding, 3) Segment embedding. It contains a token called CLS, indicating that the feature is used to implement classification. More importantly, its framework consists of a multi-layer transformer proposed in [22], which implements a series of encoding and decoding to transform the input text into possible predictions.

Due to the difficulty and resource consumption of training BERT, we use the pre-trained BERT to extract semantic features. Finally, we extract a 768-dimensional semantic features for each patent (Fig. 4).

4.3   Visual Features Extraction Based on DenseNet

Drawing is an essential part of patents, illustrating structure, so inventors draw relevant figures when submitting application materials to official departments. Due to differences between patents, the number of drawings among patents is in a wide range, which means we need to select a fixed number of figures.

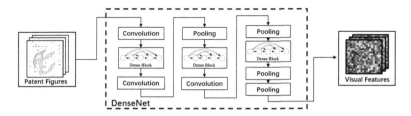

Fig. 4. Visual Features Extraction. We select schematic figures to represent patents and send them into DenseNet. DenseNet outputs visual features.

Each patent consists of a schematic figure and many detailed figures, and the number of detailed figures is in a wide range. If we select the number greater than one for each patent, we have to consider how to fuse them efficiently. However, no matter which way we use, it undoubtedly requires us to manually select detailed figures, which is a time-consuming and impractical work in reality. Therefore, we only select the schematic figure of each patent to extract visual features.

When it comes to computer vision, nobody can avoid mentioning Convolutional Neural Networks (CNN) [16,17]. In the network, the most crucial structure is convolutional kernels, which imitate animals' visual system, extracting features from each picture. With time goes by, the accuracy of object recognition models has been better than that of humans in some situations. DenseNet [11] is an outstanding representative in the field of object recognition.

In DenseNet, the crucial part is a feedforward structure called dense block, it views the outputs of all previous layers as the input of the current layer, which not only preserves the feature information, but also reduces the number of parameters. Furthermore, it also adds the residual block [9] to improve performance. We use the pretrained DenseNet121 to extract a 1024-dimensional visual features for each patent.

5   Multi-view Learning

In this section, our goal is to utilize heterogeneous features to evaluate value of a patent. In most studies, features of patents tend to be isomorphic because patents are described in the same view [2,4,8], though patents are composed of various meta-information. In our framework, we implement an algorithm called multi-view learning to fuse heterogeneous features. In multi-view learning, each view has its own contribution to final predictions, and each view can contribute under two principles: consensus principle and complementarity principle.

In the consensus principle, each view trains its own classifier to reach a consensus to output the final label. Co-training [3], a classic representative of the consensus principle, is a multi-learner semi-supervised learning algorithm. In co-training, two views train their own classifiers and make fake labels on unlabeled data. Then each classifier selects samples with high confidence and sends them to the other classifier to train. Although co-training is an efficient algorithm, creating views in practical applications is a challenging task.

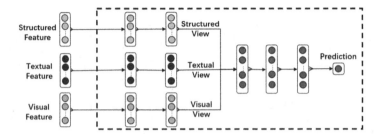

Fig. 5. Framework of Multi-view Learning. Heterogeneous features are from meta-information, we regard each of them as independent views. We train each view separately and concatenate them in final several fully connected layers to predict.

In the complementarity principle, each view extracts its own features and concatenate before being input to last layers. Therefore, it is inevitable to consider which type of layers could be chosen as last few layers. A obvious way is to use several fully connected layers directly. Like multi-layer perception, fully connected layers is concise and easy to understand. Traditionally, fully connected layers are frequently used to aggregate features and make predictions.

In our framework, we adopt complementarity principle to realize high-value patent mining. Specifically, we build a multi-view learning neural network to fuse heterogeneous features. For each view, we use two fully connected layers to produce the predicted vector in same size. Then, we concatenate the predicted vectors, and use a fully connected layer to predict value of patents. In addition, we add a dropout layer after each fully connected layer, which uses to avoid over-fitting. Meanwhile, we use ReLU as the activation function in each fully connected layer, and exploit Adam optimizer to train our model (Fig. 5).

6   Evaluation

In this section, we evaluate our framework on a real-world dataset. We introduce experiment settings including dataset description, metrics, and baselines, then present the mining result. Finally, we would conduct a series of case studies to demonstrate the effectiveness and deficiency of our method.

6.1   Dataset Description

In our dataset, it includes about 20,000 patents, each of which contains as detailed information as possible. We guarantee that each patent contains the meta-information required in our experiment. The dataset contains 1,988 high-value patents, and each patent is labeled by experts in the field of intellectual property.

Considering that the number of low-value patents is relatively large and low-value patents should be better classified, we also invite experts to classify low-value patents. Therefore, based on our dataset, three datasets, including three-class dataset, four-class dataset, and five-class dataset, are builded. In each dataset, each class contains 1,500 training samples and 500 testing samples.

6.2   Metrics on High-Value Patent Mining

In this work, we do not directly define the task of high-value patent mining as a binary classification task, we divide patents into multi-classes, so as to further realize patent classification in massive patent data. We compare predicted labels with the real-world data to evaluate our framework.

Detection Accuracy: A patent is predicted as a high-value patent and its label is high-value, we call it a *true positive(TP)*. And if its label and predicted label are not high-value, we call it a *true negative(TN)*. If its predicted label is a low-value but ground-truth is high-value, we call it a *false negative(FP)*. If it is predicted as a high-value but ground-truth label is low-value, we call it a *false negative(FN)*. Based on definition, precision and recall are calculated as follows:

$$Precision(P) = \frac{TP}{TP + FP} \tag{1}$$

$$Recall(R) = \frac{TP}{TP + FN} \tag{2}$$

$$F1 - score = \frac{2 * Precision * Recall}{Precision + Recall} \tag{3}$$

In order to observe comprehensive effectiveness of our model, F1-score is a great criteria to present. In addition, we would first implement multi-classifications, and then classify the class except the high-value patents into one class, to realize the mining of high-value patents.

6.3   Baselines

In order to present the effectiveness of our method, we compare our method with some representative baseline methods in high-value patent mining.

XGBoost. This method is essentially a tree model that uses gradient descent to update itself in time, and it supports distributed computing for faster training.

Random Forest (RF). This method consists of decision trees, each of which is different. Each tree uses different samples to train and vote for results.

Naive Bayes (NB). This method calculates the probability among different categories of samples, which assume that all feature conditions are independent.

K-Nearest Neighbors (KNN). In this method, if most k-nearest samples in feature space belong to a certain class, the sample also belongs to this category.

Linear Discriminant Analysis (LDA). This method projects high-dimensional pattern samples into optimal discriminant vector space to achieve the effect of extracting classification information and compressing dimension of feature space.

Mine-SV. This method concatenates structured features and visual features to build a patent mining model.

Mine-ST. This method concatenates structured features and textual features to build a patent mining model.

Mine-VT. This method concatenates visual features and textual features to build a patent mining model.

Mine-S. This method only uses structured features to build a mining model.

Mine-T. This method only uses textual features to build a mining model.

Mine-V. This method only uses visual features to build a mining model.

6.4   Results

In this subsection, we show a series of test results. Specifically, we first evaluate the performance of our framework on three datasets. Then we analyze high-value patents mining results. Finally, we show runtime performance of our model.

Multi-class Patent Classification Results. We present multi-class patent classification results in Table 2. It shows that the proposed method achieves the best performance in most situations. The Mine-V performs worst, since it merely consider visual features. Mine-V performs good in a way, which shows how traditional machine learning-based patent classification method performs. With regard to heterogeneous features, Mine-VT performs worse than Mine-ST and Mine-SV, since textual features and visual features could not fit well. Based on structure data, Mine-ST and Mine-SV perform well, which illustrates that heterogeneous features could describe a patent better. In traditional machine learning algorithms, XGBoost performs best since it enumerates several candidates that may become segmentation points according to the percentile method, and then calculates the best segmentation point from the candidates. Random Forest and Naive Bayes perform worst since they could not fit heterogeneous features and find which feature is crucial. In general, our method realize multi-class classification and achieves relatively high results.

Table 2. Patent evaluation results in three datasets

DatasetMethods	Three-class Dataset			Four-class Dataset			Five-class Dataset		
	P(%)	R(%)	F1-Score	P(%)	R(%)	F1-Score	P(%)	R(%)	F1-Score
XGBoost	**91.23**	89.00	0.901	86.91	**88.40**	**0.876**	**86.32**	83.80	0.850
RF	79.50	79.33	0.794	68.94	69.20	0.691	57.33	57.70	0.575
NB	65.96	64.73	0.654	54.86	54.90	0.549	45.35	46.00	0.457
KNN	84.49	85.53	0,856	80.13	79.90	0.800	79.33	79.10	0.792
LDA	86.35	86.33	0.863	72.64	72.10	0.724	69.18	69.20	0.692
Mine-SV	87.25	85.33	0.863	85.12	84.80	0.850	82.79	81.20	0.820
Mine-ST	86.92	88.16	0.875	84.90	84.33	0.846	83.01	82.66	0.828
Mine-VT	69.84	67.60	0.687	57.26	57.00	0.571	53.13	52.30	0.527
Mine-S	87.75	87.67	0.877	82.17	64.10	0.720	69.34	57.40	0.628
Mine-T	66.06	65.47	0.758	57.43	55.50	0.565	48.51	43.70	0.460
Mine-V	39.71	47.87	0.434	38.82	38.70	0.388	33.75	32.80	0.333
Ours	90.57	**89.80**	**0.902**	**87.09**	87.20	0.871	85.74	**84.40**	**0.851**

High-Value Patent Mining Result. We regard the highest value class of patents as high-value patents in the multi-classification task, and the remaining classes of patents as low-value patents, and the task becomes binary classification. At this point, we get high-value patent mining results in Table 3.

It shows that high-value patents are well mined on each dataset, which illustrates the effectiveness of our model. Among metrics, we pay more attention to recall, which indicates how well our model can mine all potentially high-value patents. We find that our model has a good recall on each dataset, which demonstrates our model is able to mine potentially high-value patents well.

Runtime Performance on High-Value Patent Mining. We implement our methods using Tensorflow. We deploy our framework on a server with an NVIDIA GeForce GTX 2080 graphic card and 11 GB RAM, and it takes an average of 20 s to estimate the value of a patent.

To speed up the processing of our method, we use parallel computing to deploy our model on a server with 4 NVIDIA GeForce GTX 2080 graphic cards with 64 GB RAM. Heterogeneous metadata in a patent is processed by their own GPUs at the same time, it shows that average time to evaluate a model is 11 s, which improved the efficiency of our model in a way.

6.5   Case Study

In this subsection, we would conduct case studies to evaluate the value of patents. We would compare high-value patents and low-value patents published in the same year, analyzing hidden factors of the case.

Structured Data Comparison. We compare structured data of two patents, we find that a high number of citations can represent high-value, which is the most intuitive evaluation method. The Higher number of cited other patents indicates richer knowledge in high-value patents. The greater number of figures shows higher importance attached to high-value patents. What's more, the longer length of abstract, the more detailed the description of high-value patents.

Textual Data Comparison. We compared titles and abstracts of two patents, and found that the description of the high-value patent is comprehensive and detailed, which appears a series of technical terms. Compared with high-value patents, the low-value one has short description and only uses common words to describe the patent.

Table 3. High-Value patent mining results

Dataset	Precision(%)	Recall(%)	F1-Score
Three-class	93.40	94.00	0.937
Four-class	86.00	93.00	0.894
Five-class	83.60	92.50	0.878

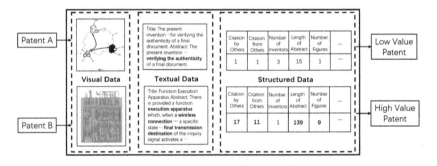

Fig. 6. Comparison between a High-value patent and a Low-value patent.

Visual Data Comparison. Comparing the schematic figure of two patents, we find that figures of the high-value patent have more details, and its design is more complicated, which is a time-consuming work. Compared to high-value patents, the low-value one has simple lines depicting the appearance, and its complexity is hard to discover from the image (Fig. 6).

7   Conclusion and Future Work

In this paper, we propose a two-phase framework to utilize metadata in patents to evaluate patents and mine high-value ones. First, we select items in patents, and divide them into three kinds: structured data, textual data and visual data. In order to extract features, we build a patent graph to extract structured features, use pretrained BERT to extract semantic features, and use pretrained DenseNet to extract visual features. Second, we build a multi-view learning model fusing heterogeneous features to evaluate patents and figure out high-value ones. We evaluate our framework on massive real-world patents. The result shows our framework outperforms than others and efficiently figure out high-value ones.

In the future, we plan to deepen and broaden this work in three directions. First, we consider to add more possibly relative items as features into our method. Second, we plan to improve some details in our method, such as redesigning feature fusion method in our method. Finally, we plan to implement our method in more fields to validate its effectiveness and efficiency.

References

1. Zheng, Q., Zhu, J., Li, Z., Pang, S., Wang, J., Li, Y.: Feature concatenation multi-view subspace clustering. Neurocomputing **379**, 89–102 (2020)
2. Abrams, D., Akcigit, U., Grennan, J.: Patent value and citations: Creative destruction or strategic disruption? Social Science Electronic Publishing (2013)
3. Blum: Combining labeled and unlabeled data with co-training. In: Proceedings of the Annual ACM Conference on Computational Learning Theory (2000)
4. Briinger-Weilandt, S., Geils, D.: Quality-key factor for high value in professional patent, technical and scientific information. World Patent Information (2011)
5. Cao, L., Luo, J., Liang, F., Huang, T.: Heterogeneous feature machines for visual recognition, pp. 1095–1102, November 2009
6. Carissimi, N.: A multi-view learning approach to deception detection. In: 2018 13th IEEE International Conference on Automatic Face Gesture Recognition (2018)
7. Devlin, J., Chang, M.W., Lee, K., Toutanova, K.: Bert: pre-training of deep bidirectional transformers for language understanding (2018)
8. Hall, B.H., Jaffe, A., Trajtenberg, M.: Market value and patent citations. Rand J. Econ. **36**(1), 16–38 (2005)
9. He, K., Zhang, X.: Deep residual learning for image recognition. In: 2016 IEEE Conference on Computer Vision and Pattern Recognition (CVPR) (2016)
10. Hsu, P.H., Lee, D., Tambe, P., Hsu, D.H.: Deep learning, text, and patent valuation. Social Science Electronic Publishing
11. Huang, G., Liu, Z.: Densely connected convolutional networks (2017)
12. Huang, M.H.: Constructing a patent citation map using bibliographic coupling: a study of taiwan's high-tech companies. Scientometrics (2003)
13. Jiayun, H.: Establishment and verification of patent value evaluation system applicable to the examination stage of medical and biological fields (2019)
14. Kim, Y.G., Suh, J.H., Park, S.C.: Visualization of patent analysis for emerging technology. Expert Syst. Appl. **34**(3), 1804–1812 (2008)
15. Kincaid, J., Fishburn, R., Chissom, B.: Derivation of new readability formulas for navy enlisted personnel, January 1975
16. Krizhevsky, A., Sutskever, I., Hinton, G.: Imagenet classification with deep convolutional neural networks, pp. 1097–1105, January 2012
17. Lecun, Y., Bottou, L., Bengio, Y., Haffner, P.: Gradient-based learning applied to document recognition. Proc. IEEE **86**, 2278–2324 (1998)

18. Li, J., Li, Z., Lü, S.: Feature concatenation for adversarial domain adaptation. Expert Syst. Appl. (2020)
19. Liu, W.: Discovering the realistic paths towards the realization of patent valuation from technical perspectives: defense, implementation or transfer. Neural Comput. Appl. (2021)
20. Shalaby, W., Zadrozny, W.: Toward an interactive patent retrieval framework based on distributed representations (2018)
21. Song, Y., Wang, Y.: Multi-view ensemble learning based on distance-to-model and adaptive clustering for imbalanced credit risk assessment in p2p lending (2020)
22. Vaswani, A., et al.: Attention is all you need (2017)
23. Wu, Y., Schuster, M., Chen, Z.: Google's neural machine translation system: bridging the gap between human and machine translation, September 2016
24. Sun, C., Qiu, X., Xu, Y., Huang, X.: How to fine-tune BERT for text classification? CoRR (2019). and machine translation syst BERT for text classification? CoRR (2019). and machine translation syst BERT for text classification? CoRR (2019). and machine translation syst
25. Yang, Y., Song, S., Chen, D., Zhang, X.: Discernible neighborhood counting based incremental feature selection for heterogeneous data (2020)
26. Zhang, L., Li, L., Li, T.: Patent mining: a survey. SIGKDD Explor. Newsl. **16**(2), 1–19 (2015). https://doi.org/10.1145/2783702.2783704
27. Zhang, L., Liu, Z., Li, L., Shen, C., Li, T.: PatSearch: an integrated framework for patentability retrieval. Knowl. Inf. Syst. (2018)

EasyNUSC: An Efficient Heterogeneous Computing Framework for Non-uniform Sampling Two-Dimensional Convolution Applications

Yu Lu[1], Ce Yu[1], Jian Xiao[1(⊠)], Hao Wang[1], Hao Fu[2], Shanjiang Tang[1], Bo Kang[2], and Gang Zheng[2]

[1] College of Intelligence and Computing, Tianjin University, Tianjin, China
xiaojian@tju.edu.cn
[2] National Supercomputer Center in Tianjin, Tianjin, China

Abstract. Non-uniform sampling two-dimensional convolution (NUSC for short) is a practical method in the field of 2D space image processing. NUSC maps sampling data of non-uniform distribution to a regular output grid through convolution. The growth rate of such data volume continues to increase, and the computational performance of NUSC is one of the key issues to be solved. Heterogeneous computing platforms provide advanced computing capabilities for accelerating NUSC performance. But heterogeneous programming and performance tuning are complex. A simple and efficient dedicated programming model and corresponding runtime framework can effectively solve such a problem.

This paper proposes a parallel programming model and framework for the development of NUSC applications in heterogeneous computing environments, named EasyNUSC. When developing NUSC applications, EasyNUSC can automatically parallelize NUSC applications and perform tedious work. Developers no longer need to pay attention to the details of algorithm parallelization and task scheduling. In terms of performance optimization, this paper proposes a series of strategies in vectorization, memory access, and data reuse. The experimental data shows that EasyNUSC achieves up to 339 times the performance of a serial program within a single node, while providing excellent scalability.

Keywords: Heterogeneous computing · NUSC · Programming model · Runtime framework

1 Introduction

Non-uniform sampling two-dimensional convolution (NUSC) is a practical technique for processing real-world 2D space image data in astronomy, remote sensing, medicine, and other fields [2,5,17]. Due to the non-uniform distribution of sampling data in space, it is hard to process these data by conventional convolution, which makes NUSC a key technique for processing such data. NUSC

© Springer Nature Switzerland AG 2023
W. Meng et al. (Eds.): ICA3PP 2022, LNCS 13777, pp. 707–721, 2023.
https://doi.org/10.1007/978-3-031-22677-9_38

resamples and reprojects the collected sampling data, and maps the irregular data to a regular grid with uniform intervals through convolution [11].

As the growth rate of the NUSC data volume keeps rising, traditional hardware architectures that only rely on multi-core CPUs have struggled to process data in an acceptable time [3]. Instead, heterogeneous computing platforms are used to accelerate NUSC applications. However, heterogeneous programming is complex and error-prone [12]. Programmers have to consider computing devices with different hardware architectures and storage levels [9,16]. Meanwhile, NUSC is a class of computing-intensive and memory-intensive application. These factors make programmers face great challenges when programming. Specifically, developing NUSC applications in a heterogeneous computing environment has the following key issues:

- Task mapping. There are a large number of processor cores in heterogeneous computing platforms and numerous tasks in NUSC applications. Reasonably mapping tasks to all computing resources is the first consideration.
- Memory access. NUSC applications read large amounts of data from memory frequently. The reading process is irregular and discontinuous. Proper handling of memory access is critical to performance improvement.
- Data reuse. In NUSC applications, repeated data access doubles the data volume that the program actually has to access. Increasing the data reuse rate can reduce the number of memory accesses and data transmissions.
- Scalability and vectorization. To solve large-scale problems, it is essential to develop a well-extended program. Additionally, vectorizing the computational process is an effective way to improve program performance [6].

Existing research on NUSC applications has focused on using GPUs to accelerate the convolution [7,13,17]. While program performance can be improved with the help of accelerators such as GPUs, it requires developers to have a deep understanding of the underlying devices and parallel programming techniques, and some of the performance issues inherent in NUSC applications have not been addressed. Also, most of the research is aimed at specific applications in specific fields, often lacking generality and universality. Therefore, this paper presents EasyNUSC, which can help users develop concise heterogeneous parallel programs. Specifically, this paper makes the following key contributions:

1) A programming model is proposed for NUSC applications. The model separates the specific application and parallel details for users.
2) Based on the programming model, the runtime framework is designed and implemented. The framework provides two interfaces for users, **findData()** and **compute()**. By implementing the two interfaces, users can easily develop NUSC applications in heterogeneous computing environments.
3) This paper analyzes the factors that restrict the NUSC performance. Accordingly, a series of strategies in vectorization, memory access, data reuse are proposed to improve the data processing efficiency of EasyNUSC.
4) The Gridding algorithm and the Geometric Correction algorithm are used as typical applications to illustrate the usage of EasyNUSC. Further, the

experiments are conducted to evaluate EasyNUSC in terms of simplicity, performance and scalability with the Gridding algorithm.

The rest of the paper is structured as follows. Section 2 introduces the heterogeneous programming model and the related research. Section 3 proposes the programming model. The implementation and optimization of the runtime framework is discussed in Sect. 4. Section 5 provides demo applications of how to use the framework. In Sect. 6, the experimental evaluation is reported. Section 7 talks about some conclusions and future work.

2   Related Work

2.1   Heterogeneous Programming Model

Heterogeneous programming model can be used as a bridge between applications and hardware platforms [15]. The various existing heterogeneous programming models can be divided into two types [19]:

One is to design a programming model for a specific heterogeneous architecture, such as the CPU+GPU architecture. Mainstream programming models include OpenCL and CUDA [14], which take the form of Host/Device. Programming in this model is close to the underlying hardware.

The other is a guided programming model that is extended based on the existing framework. Representative guided programming models include OpenACC, OpenMP [1]. This kind of model tells the compiler where parallel code regions are located by writing guidance statements on the source code. The compiler parallelizes the program based on the guidance statements.

2.2   Non-uniform Sampling Two-Dimensional Convolution

In order to illustrate NUSC, two forms of two-dimensional convolution are compared and analyzed here, namely conventional two-dimensional convolution and non-uniform sampling two-dimensional convolution.

Conventional two-dimensional convolution has been widely used in convolutional neural network [4]. The targets of the convolution are often regular matrix images [20]. For each pixel value of the matrix, the corresponding data can be found and computed in the input matrix according to a regular convolution kernel. This kind of convolution often has a strong regularity.

Non-uniform sampling two-dimensional convolution is often used in practical applications [11]. This kind of convolution usually needs to first establish a mapping relationship between the input and output data. Then, a convolution kernel is used to find the input sampling data required by the output pixels. The input data is often unevenly distributed in space so that the storage of data in the computer is discontinuous. The computation of this kind of convolution generally needs to be customized based on specific applications.

2.3 Parallelization Research of NUSC Applications

There are two typical NUSC applications mentioned in this paper, astronomy Gridding algorithm and remote sensing Geometric Correction algorithm.

The Gridding algorithm is one of the indispensable steps to process astronomical image data [18]. Gridding deals with sampling points that are unevenly distributed in a certain sky area. The current research is mainly based on the heterogeneous architecture of CPU+GPU [10,17]. The CPU sorts the sampling data and establishes the mapping relationship. The GPU is responsible for the convolution, which is the most time-consuming part of the program.

The Geometric Correction algorithm processes the original remote sensing image data collected on the satellite [2]. A related study is based on a cluster with CPU+GPU architecture. Besides, some work formulates different optimization strategies for images with different resolutions. At a finer granularity level, eliminating rotational error, extracting the control points and correcting geometric distortion for overlapping regions are proposed to further improve the program performance [8,13].

3 Programming Model

The computing mode of NUSC applications is shown in Fig. 1. The whole figure represents a complete output grid. Each small square indicates an output pixel in the grid. The scattered black dots denote the sampling points that are not uniformly distributed in space. The relative position of the dots to the output grid is determined by a predefined mapping relationship. As an example, to compute the value of the green output pixel, the convolution range is determined by the convolution kernel centered on the pixel, which is the interior of the dashed circle in the figure. Then, the value of the green output pixel is obtained by computing all the sampling point data inside the circle according to certain computing rules. Similarly, after the values of all the pixels in the grid are computed, the whole convolution computing is finished.

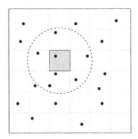

Fig. 1. An example of NUSC applications computing mode (Color figure online)

According to the computing mode, the programming model of EasyNUSC is shown in Fig. 2. The model shows a typical NUSC workflow: 1) Input, which contains multiple convolution tasks. 2) Tasks assignment, which assigns tasks to computing resources. 3) Convolution, which performs convolution computing in an accelerator. For each pixel, a single convolution process can be divided into two steps, data finding and convolution computing. This phase calls **findData()** and **compute()** to compute the value. 4) Results generation, which organizes the calculated data and generates the results. 5) Output, which presents the results to users in the form of file.

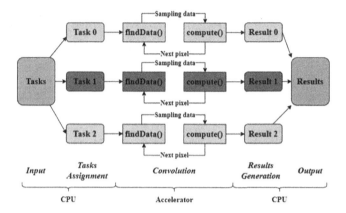

Fig. 2. Programming model of EasyNUSC

The programming model separates the parallel phase from the convolution phase. Users only need to focus on the implementation of the convolution. The significance of the model lies in that users can simplify programming with the help of the model. The model can automatically complete tasks in parallel, hiding the tedious parallelization work. Moreover, the model can be reused in other similar problems by simply changing the parameters and interfaces.

4   Runtime Framework

4.1   Programming Interfaces for Users

During the convolution computing, users are provided with **findData()** and **compute()**. The specific functions and usage of the two interfaces are as follows.

- **findData()**. The interface requires a mapping relationship between the input and output data. Based on the relationship, the program finds the data within the coverage of the convolution kernel.
- **compute()**. The interface computes the found data according to certain calculation rules, such as weighted summation.

Users are able to implement the two interfaces in a serial-like programming manner. This is the main coding task for users. The framework can automatically call the interfaces at the appropriate location without the user's involvement.

4.2   Framework Design and Implementation

There are four main modules in the design of the framework. As shown in Fig. 3, the input file contains multiple convolution tasks. The framework executes the following four modules in order to process the input data.

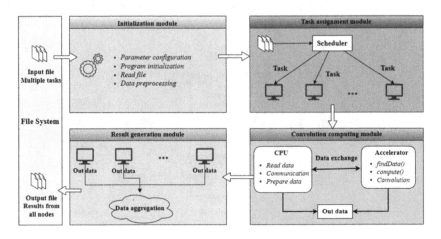

Fig. 3. Modules design for the framework of EasyNUSC

The initialization module. This module configures the parameters required to run the program, initializes the program and pre-processes the data.

The task assignment module. This module divides the tasks and assigns them to computing resources by a scheduler. The scheduler can schedule tasks based on the current available computing resources and ensure load balancing.

The convolution computing module. Within a node, the platform adopts the architecture of CPU+accelerator. The CPU is responsible for logic control and preparing for convolution. The accelerator parallelizes the process of convolution. The calculation of each pixel value depends on the user-implemented **findData()** and **compute()** interfaces. When the values of all output pixels are computed, the accelerator transfers the results back to the CPU.

The result generation module. After all nodes finish the tasks, the framework aggregates the results returned from all nodes and generates the output file.

4.3   Performance Optimization

Vectorization and Error-Fixed. Vectorization enables devices to process 2, 4, 8 or more copies of data with a single instruction. For NUSC applications, the multiple loops for the computation of sampling data can be vectorized. Several consecutive sampling data in memory is packed into a vector so that these data can be computed at once.

Vectorization also introduces an additional issue. The data of sampling points for a pixel is discontinuous in memory. Vectorization directly computes several consecutive data, which may lead to the participation of some data that should not be computed. This situation will lead to bias in the results. To address this issue, a data filtering method is shown in Fig. 4. The method computes the vector to be computed with a standard vector. The standard vector can determine whether a data needs to be computed or not, which can be set according to the convolution kernel. Thus, the vector can be used to filter out data that does not need to be computed.

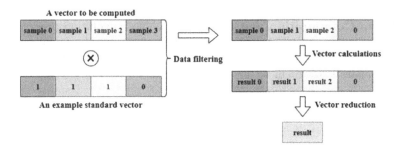

Fig. 4. Vectorized calculation of sampling data

Data Packing and Loading. To reduce data transfer frequency and increase bandwidth utilization, for one output pixel, the continuous sampling data are packed into a set. In this way, all the data the pixel requires is composed of discontinuous multiple sets of data in memory. The green, red and yellow parts in Fig. 5 represent different sets of data. An area in the on-chip memory (or a storage area closer to the chip such as shared memory) is used as a cache area.

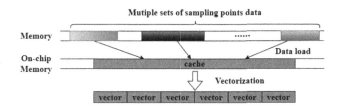

Fig. 5. Load packaged data into on-chip memory (Color figure online)

Once the program finds a set of contiguous sampling data, it loads the entire set of data from memory into the cache area. The method can load a chunk of data at one time via DMA. Moreover, with the vectorization, such a method is more convenient to the fast construction of vectors.

Intermediate Results Caching. For an output pixel, the sampling data usually cannot be found at one time. It is necessary to go through the cycle of "find part of the data - compute - update the intermediate results" several times. The situation may take hundreds of rounds of the above cycle to derive the value of a pixel. It is not wise to write the intermediate results back to memory for each round. Our approach is to create a buffer in on-chip memory, where the intermediate results computed in each round are recorded and updated. When the computing is completed, the final result is written back to memory only once.

Overlap of Computation and Load. The whole convolution process can be divided into four steps from the perspective of the computer: find, load, compute, and write back. There are dependencies between these four steps, making it difficult to parallelize them.

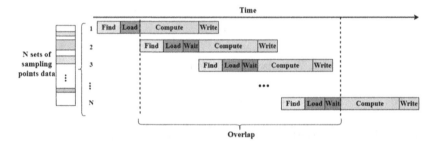

Fig. 6. The pipeline approach for convolution computing

Since the convolution process requires multiple rounds of the above four steps, the stages between rounds are relatively independent. The pipeline approach in Fig. 6 can hide a portion of time. For an output pixel, there are N sets of sampling data, which need to be computed in N rounds. First, the program finds and loads the first round of data from memory. Then, while the data of the first round is computed and written back, the data of the second round is found and loaded. While the data of the second round is being computed and written back, the data of the third round is found and loaded. And so on, until the last round of data is computed and written back.

Tiling Method for Data Reuse. There is an extremely high frequency of repeated data access in NUSC. Figure 7 serves as an example. The green and blue squares are the two pixels that are close to each other. The red dots are the sampling data that need to be computed for both pixels. Without any interference, these data are loaded and computed separately for each pixel. This situation leads to an exponential increase in the amount of data actually loaded.

The key to the problem is to make the sampling data loaded at one time available to multiple pixels. For this purpose, the tiling method divides the entire

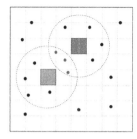

Fig. 7. An example of repeated data access (Color figure online)

output grid into many small tiles of fixed size blocks or lines. The left part of Fig. 8 shows an example of the two tiling methods.

Accordingly, the convolution range of a tile is determined by the range of individual pixels and the number of pixels in the tile. As shown in the right part of Fig. 8, inside the black circle is the convolution range of a pixel. The interior of the red circle or rectangle is the new convolution range of the tile. The new range covers the ranges of all pixels in the tile. By loading the data covered by the new range, the value of each pixel in the tile can then be computed from part of the data therein, data loaded once can be shared by all pixels in the tile.

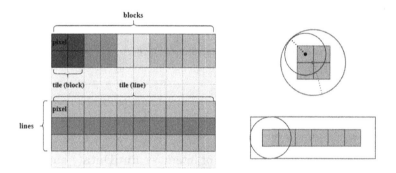

Fig. 8. The tiling method for data reuse (Color figure online)

5   Application Examples

5.1   Astronomy Gridding Algorithm

The Gridding algorithm transforms the observed raw data from an irregular sampling space to a regular grid space. Most of the implementations of the Gridding algorithm are based on the gather method. The key steps are as follows.

1) Divide the spatial plane into a regular output grid. Establish a spatial correspondence between the input sampling data and the output grid.
2) For each output pixel in the grid, centering on the coordinates of the pixel, find the input sampling points within the convolution range.
3) Weighted summation of all the data of sampling points in the range, resulting in the value of the output pixel.
4) Repeat steps 2),3) until all output pixels in the grid have been computed.

Algorithm 1. findData() and compute() for Gridding Algorithm

1: **procedure** FINDDATA
2:     Get current pixel coordinates l_c, b_c;
3:     Get kernel size ks;
4:     $up, down \leftarrow getUpDown(l_c, b_c, ks)$;
5:     **while** $up \leq down$ **do**
6:         $left, right \leftarrow getLeftRight(up)$;
7:         $data_l, data_r \leftarrow getData(left, right)$;
8:         Load data into cache from $data_l$ to $data_r$;
9:         $up = up + 1$;
10:     **end while**
11: **end procedure**
12:
13: **procedure** COMPUTE
14:     **for** each $data$ in cache **do**
15:         Get current pixel coordinates l_p, b_p;
16:         Get current sampling point coordinates l_s, b_s;
17:         $weight \leftarrow getWeight(dist)$;
18:         $pixel_v += data \times weight$;
19:     **end for**
20: **end procedure**

In this case, the key pseudo-code of interfaces **findData()** and **compute()** that users need to implement is shown in Algorithm 1.

5.2   Geometric Correction Algorithm for Remote Sensing Images

The Geometric Correction algorithm consists of two main parts, geometric position transformation and gray value computing. The geometric position transformation is to establish a mapping relationship between the input and output image space. The gray value computing is the calculation of pixel values using interpolation. In general, the key steps of the algorithm are as follows.

1) Establish the input and output image spaces, and the functional mapping relationships between them.

2) For each pixel, the coordinates of its mapping point in the input image are calculated according to the inverse mapping function. Then find the input data within a certain neighborhood of that mapping point.

3) An interpolation method is selected to compute the input data to obtain the gray values of the output pixel.

4) Repeat steps 2),3) until all output pixels in the output image are computed.

In this case, the key pseudo-code of interfaces **findData()** and **compute()** that users need to implement is shown in Algorithm 2.

Algorithm 2. findData() and **compute()** for Geometric Correction Algorithm

---

1: **procedure** FINDDATA
2:     Create forward mapping of input to output $(u, v) = f(x, y)$;
3:     Create inverse mapping of output to input $(x, y) = g(u, v)$;
4:     Get current pixel coordinates u_c, v_c;
5:     $x_c, y_c \leftarrow g(u_c, v_c)$;
6:     $nearList \leftarrow getNear(x_c, y_c)$;
7:     Load $nearList$ into cache;
8: **end procedure**
9:
10: **procedure** COMPUTE
11:     $pixel_v \leftarrow interpolation(nearList)$;
12: **end procedure**

---

6   Experiments and Evaluation

This section evaluates EasyNUSC framework in terms of simplicity, performance, and scalability. The experiments are performed with the Gridding algorithm. The DSP (Digital Signal Processor) is used as the accelerator in a heterogeneous computing environment. Also, the GPU is used as a comparison platform.

6.1   Simplification of Programming

One of the goals of EasyNUSC is to provide users with an easier way to develop efficient NUSC applications. The line of code is used to measure the simplicity. Table 1 compares the line of code for writing Gridding and Geometric Correction algorithm with EasyNUSC and writing the two algorithms directly.

The first two columns indicate the line of code for writing the two algorithms directly in C/C++ within a single node and across multiple nodes. The last column means the line of code required to write multi-node algorithms with EasyNUSC. Note that the results only count the line of code in the parallelization part and the key computation part.

Table 1. Comparison of line of code of two algorithms

Algorithm	Single-node	Multi-node	EasyNUSC
Gridding	289	368	95
Geometric Correction	138	172	69

6.2   Performance Evaluation Within a Node

Evaluation of Optimization Strategies. Subsection 4.3 proposes five single-node performance optimization strategies. For illustration, the five versions corresponding to the five strategies are named as *vec, load, cache, overlap, reuse*. Note that the five strategies are stackable, and the latter version is further optimized from the previous one. The final version *reuse* has the best performance because all the strategies are stacked together. The performance of different versions is shown in Fig. 9.

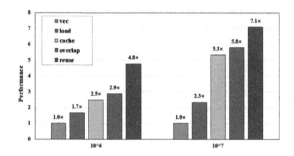

Fig. 9. Performance of optimized strategies

In this experiment, 10^6 and 10^7 denote the number of input sampling points. The performance of the parallelized version after vectorization *vec* is used as a baseline. The experimental data show that the performance is significantly improved with these strategies for both datasets. The final optimized version *reuse* achieves a 4.8 and 7.1 times compared to the base version *vec* for the two data sizes, respectively. At 10^7 data size, the program performance improvement is higher than at 10^6 data size. This proves that our proposed optimization strategies can better cope with the performance bottlenecks caused by data transfer and memory access.

Comparison of Different Platforms. Table 2 shows three platforms: CPU, GPU, DSP. The CPU and DSP are specially designed. For comparison, we run the serial program on CPU, and run the parallel program on GPU and DSP.

Figure 10 shows the results. There are three sizes of input data, 10^5, 10^6, and 10^7. The output grid size is 90×90. The figure shows the performance

Table 2. Computing resources of three platforms

Platform	Model name	The computing resources of a device
CPU	Specially designed	64 processor cores
GPU	NVIDIA V100	5120 CUDA units
DSP	Specially designed	96 integrated computing units

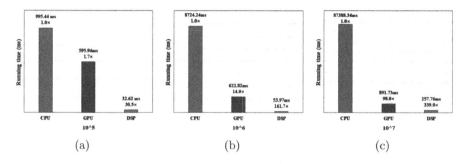

(a)   (b)   (c)

Fig. 10. Performance comparison of three platforms at three data sizes

improvement of the parallel program over the serial program is dramatic. The performance gap increases as the data size grows. At 10^7 data size, the GPU program achieves 98 times faster compared to CPU program, while the DSP program achieves a 339x performance boost.

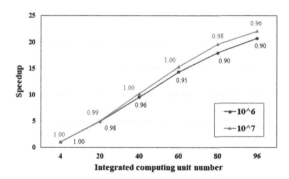

Fig. 11. Scalability within a single node

Scalability. There are 96 integrated computing units within a DSP node for parallelizing a single task. Figure 11 shows the scalability of the framework within a node. The sizes of input data are 10^6 and 10^7, the output pixels number is 900×900. The experiment keeps the task unchanged and increases the number of integrated computing units within a node. It can be seen that the framework scales well with both datasets. The performance grows almost linearly as the number of units increases, and the scaling efficiency remains over 90%.

7   Conclusion

NUSC applications have a stronger need for heterogeneous computing as the growth rate of data volumes keeps increasing. But heterogeneous programming and performance tuning are difficult for most programmers.

This paper proposes EasyNUSC. When users develop NUSC applications in heterogeneous computing environments, EasyNUSC can help them easily write high-performance parallel programs. The details of parallelization and performance optimization are handled by EasyNUSC. Users can write code in a serial-like manner. In terms of the performance and scalability, EasyNUSC is deployed in a DSP node. The experimental data show that EasyNUSC achieves up to 339x acceleration, obtaining ideal scalability.

In conclusion, our work is meaningful for theoretical studies and parallelization of NUSC applications. The performance optimization strategies can be simply ported to other similar platforms. Moreover, the experimental environment of this paper mainly adopts the heterogeneous architecture of CPU+DSP, which is valuable for the promotion of DSP-based heterogeneous computing platforms. In the future, we will extend EasyNUSC to larger scale heterogeneous computing platforms to solve real-world problems with more data volume.

Acknowledgments. The authors would like to thank all those who have helped to improve this paper. This work is supported by the National Natural Science Foundation of China (61972277).

References

1. Aldinucci, M., et al.: Practical parallelization of scientific applications with OpenMP, OpenACC and MPI. J. Parallel Distrib. Comput. **157**, 13–29 (2021)
2. Dave, C.P., Joshi, R., Srivastava, S.S.: Article: a survey on geometric correction of satellite imagery. Int. J. Comput. Appl. **116**(12), 24–27 (2015)
3. Feldmann, J., et al.: Publisher correction: parallel convolutional processing using an integrated photonic tensor core. Nature **591**(7849) (2021)
4. Georganas, E., et al.: Anatomy of high-performance deep learning convolutions on simd architectures. In: SC 2018 (2018)
5. Gu, Z., et al.: Ce-net: context encoder network for 2d medical image segmentation. IEEE Trans. Med. Imaging **38**(10), 2281–2292 (2019)
6. Hassan, S.A., Mahmoud, M.M., Hemeida, A., Saber, M.A.: Effective implementation of matrix-vector multiplication on intel's AVX multicore processor. Comput. Lang. Syst. Struct. **51**, 158–175 (2018)
7. Jordà, M., Valero-Lara, P., Peña, A.J.: cuConv: Cuda implementation of convolution for CNN inference. Clust. Comput. **25**(2), 1459–1473 (2022)

8. Li, Y., He, L., Ye, X., Guo, D.: Geometric correction algorithm of UAV remote sensing image for the emergency disaster. In: 2016 IEEE International Geoscience and Remote Sensing Symposium (IGARSS), pp. 6691–6694 (2016)

9. Liao, X.K., Yang, C.Q., Yi, T.T.H.Z., Wang, F., Wu, Q.: Jingling: OpenMC: towards simplifying programming for tianhe supercomputers. J. Comput. Sci. Technol. **29**(3), 532 (2014)

10. Luo, Q., et al.: HyGrid: a CPU-GPU hybrid convolution-based gridding algorithm in radio astronomy. In: Vaidya, J., Li, J. (eds.) ICA3PP 2018. LNCS, vol. 11334, pp. 621–635. Springer, Cham (2018). https://doi.org/10.1007/978-3-030-05051-1_43

11. Martinez, A., Gelb, A., Gutierrez, A.: Edge detection from non-uniform fourier data using the convolutional gridding algorithm. J. Sci. Comput. **61**(3), 490–512 (2014)

12. Mittal, S., Vetter, J.S.: A survey of CPU-GPU heterogeneous computing techniques. ACM Comput. Surv. **47**(4) (2015)

13. Paz, A., Plaza, A.: GPU implementation of target and anomaly detection algorithms for remotely sensed hyperspectral image analysis. In: Huang, B., Plaza, A.J., Serra-Sagristà, J., Lee, C., Li, Y., Qian, S.E. (eds.) Satellite Data Compression, Communications, and Processing VI. Society of Photo-Optical Instrumentation Engineers (SPIE) Conference Series, vol. 7810, p. 78100R, August 2010

14. Petrovič, F., et al.: A benchmark set of highly-efficient CUDA and OpenCL kernels and its dynamic autotuning with kernel tuning toolkit. Futur. Gener. Comput. Syst. **108**, 161–177 (2020)

15. Tang, S., et al.: Easypdp: an efficient parallel dynamic programming runtime system for computational biology. IEEE Trans. Parallel Distrib. Syst. **23**(5), 862–872 (2012)

16. Wang, C., Yu, C., Sun, J., Meng, X.: Dpx10: an efficient x10 framework for dynamic programming applications. In: 2015 44th International Conference on Parallel Processing, pp. 869–878 (2015)

17. Wang, H., Yu, C., Zhang, B., Xiao, J., Luo, Q.: HCGrid: a convolution-based gridding framework for radio astronomy in hybrid computing environments. MNRAS **501**(2), 2734–2744 (2021)

18. Winkel, B., Lenz, D., Flöer, L.: Cygrid: a fast Cython-powered convolution-based gridding module for python. A&A **591**, A12 (2016)

19. Xie, G., Zhang, Y.l.: A few of the most popular models for heterogeneous parallel programming. In: 2017 16th International Symposium on Distributed Computing and Applications to Business, Engineering and Science (DCABES), pp. 15–18 (2017)

20. Zhang, J.-Y., Guo, Y., Hu, X.: Parallel computing method for two-dimensional matrix convolution. J. ZheJiang Univ. (Eng. Sci.) **52**(3), 515 (2018)

DNNEmu: A Lightweight Performance Emulator for Distributed DNN Training

Jian Wang, Enda Yu, Dezun Dong[(✉)], and Zhengbin Pang

College of Computer, National University of Defense Technology, Changsha, China
{wjian,yuenda,dong,zhengbinpang}@nudt.edu.cn

Abstract. Distributed deep learning system usually leverages large-scale GPU clusters to speed up training. Therefore, for organizations lacking GPU resources temporarily, it is difficult to evaluate distributed communication optimization. Specifically, due to the complex interaction between computation and communication, accurately predicting the performance of distributed training is an almost impossible task. In this paper, we propose *DNNEmu*, a lightweight performance emulator for distributed DNN training to help ML developers design and optimize the communication strategies before target machines are available. Based on our key observation that the computation overhead could be predicted by input features and replaced by simulation programs, we use CPUs to emulate the communication and computation of distributed training. *DNNEmu* makes layer-wise predictions based on profiling traces collected by the layer-wise profiler, and emulates DNN training by simulating computation. *DNNEmu* contains three integrated modules: (i) the layer-wise profiler profiling operators with layer names; (ii) the performance predictor predicting the layer-wise operator runtime; and (iii) the computation simulator simulating the actual computation with the predicted runtime. *DNNEmu* is implemented over MXNet and requires no changes to the developers' models or inputs. We show that *DNNEmu* can emulate distributed training with an average estimation error of 7.2%.

Keywords: Distributed training · Communication optimization · Performance emulator · Layer-wise profiler

1 Introduction

Today, large-scale distributed training has increased the speed and efficiency of deep neural network (DNN) training. Popular deep learning frameworks, including MXNet [3], PyTorch [15] and TensorFlow [1], support distributed training using data parallelism or model parallelism techniques. Under the data parallelism, which is more common, the dataset is partitioned into each worker node. Each worker will have a local copy of the neural network. The results, such as gradients and updated weights, are communicated across these workers. It is a common belief that the communication cost limits the scalability of the distributed training and causes inefficient utilization of the computation resources since the communication involves significant amounts of data transfer.

© Springer Nature Switzerland AG 2023
W. Meng et al. (Eds.): ICA3PP 2022, LNCS 13777, pp. 722–736, 2023.
https://doi.org/10.1007/978-3-031-22677-9_39

To alleviate the above problem, there has been a surge of research from machine learning systems on addressing the communication challenges in recent years. These works are mainly focused on increasing communication efficiency and better overlap of computation and communication [23].

However, large-scale distributed training demands multiple machines, typically equipped with powerful GPUs. For developers studying communication optimizations, they are more interested in how much the performance has been improved with the communication optimizations. As a result, it is common for developers to ask this question:

What is the performance of communication strategy X in a large cluster of GPU Y?

Accurately answering the above question enables machine learning (ML) developers to evaluate communication optimization alternatives under various assumptions and ensure that the communication optimization can meet performance objectives. Besides, it can help ML developers optimize and evaluate communication strategies even when the target GPU cluster is unavailable.

However, since the execution time of DNN training is determined by the sequential computation time of each layer in the neural network, it is difficult to predict the performance of DNN training accurately. Due to the complex interaction between computation and communication in distributed training, the prediction accuracy may be severely affected if there is a significant error in the estimation of the computation or communication time. A lot of studies [16,24] have made efforts in this area, but the effect is still not satisfactory. Paleo [16] models the communication among multiple workers based on an analytical performance model, while it cannot predict the communication time of complex distributed optimizations. Daydream [24] simulates the DNN execution based on the dependency graph to predict the overall runtime, and can effectively model the most common DNN optimizations. However, with the rising of DNN models and optimization algorithm complexity, the accuracy of the above model-based approaches is becoming increasingly compromised. In addition, the existing works are not completely convincing since they do not run on actual machines and just simulate or predict.

To conclude, current approaches cannot accurately predict the performance of various communication-efficient optimizations for large-scale distributed training, especially for complex and new emerging hardware architecture and communication strategies.

To fill this gap, this paper presents a lightweight emulator for distributed DNN training named *DNNEmu*. It provides a desired feature for developers and cloud service providers when they have no available powerful GPUs for distributed training. DNNEmu can emulate distributed training across multiple powerful GPUs using CPUs. When implementing communication optimizations, developers can evaluate the efficacy of their work initially. *DNNEmu* contains three integrated modules. The core part of *DNNEmu* is the computation simulator module, modeling the actual computation with a performance predictor. The performance predictor module estimates DNN runtime based on DNN configuration using offline profiling or online gradient boosting decision tree (GBDT) [5]. We also implement layer-wise profiler based on MXNet profiler, which can profile operators with layer names. The layer-wise profiler can provide a real-world dataset for our performance predictor and help to compare experimental results more accurately. *DNNEmu* can be applied to not only a single device training but also distributed DNN training.

We implement *DNNEmu* based on the MXNet framework and evaluate it on five real-world representative models (GooglNet [20], MobileNetV2 [17], ResNet18 [7], ResNet50 [7], and VGG16 [18]) with two different distributed optimizations. We use *DNNEmu* to emulate DNN training under various configurations and find that it makes accurate predictions with an average estimation error of 7.2%, confirming the effectiveness of our proposed approach. The results also show that *DNNEmu* is robust to the choices of neural network architectures, communication optimization strategies, and hardware architectures.

In summary, we make the following key contributions:

- We systematically explore how the performance of DNN models is influenced.
- We present a performance predictor using pre-trained GBDT model.
- We propose and implement *DNNEmu*, a lightweight performance emulator, to predict the performance of distributed training on large-scale GPU clusters using CPUs.
- We perform comprehensive evaluations on a variety of DNN models and communication optimizations. The results show the effectiveness and robustness of *DNNEmu*.

The context of this paper is structured as follows: Sect. 2 describes the background and related work. Section 3 presents the design and implementation of *DNNEmu*. Our experimental results are presented and analyzed in Sect. 4. Finally, we conclude in Sect. 5.

2 Background and Related Work

2.1 Performance Measurement

Due to the complexity of DNN models, ML developers usually need additional profiling tools to analyze the performance. Popular deep learning frameworks have their own built-in profiling tools. In addition, hardware vendors provide profiling tools that enable detailed performance information. The profiling tools could be divided into kernel level profiling tools and operator level profiling tools.

Kernel Level Profiling Tools. On the kernel level, the profiling tools measure the information of low-level GPU kernels. For example, the NVProf [14] enables ML developers to understand and optimize the performance with information for each GPU kernel. It also provides a timeline that shows CPU and GPU activity that occurred at the kernel level. Using the Nsight [13] profiler, ML developers can capture detailed performance metrics, such as kernel name, latency, memory usage, etc.

Operator Level Profiling Tools. The operator level profiling tools are usually built-in to the deep learning frameworks. The operator name, time usage, total count, and memory allocation are captured by the framework profiler when it is executing in the training or inference. However, mainstream frameworks (e.g., MXNet, PyTorch, and TensorFlow) cannot extract per-layer runtime of operators. Although the PyTorch community provides TochProf [22], which is a layer-by-layer profiling tool. TorchProf only works well in forward propagation, and it does not work in backward propagation.

We do not favor kernel level profiling tools because they require precise knowledge of how each operator is implemented in frameworks using different kernels. Profiling is performed at the operator level, which could be more accurate in our simulation module without more processing. We implement a layer-wise profiler based on the MXNet profiler since the MXNet profiler cannot extract per-layer runtime of operators.

2.2   Performance Prediction

Prior works have shown that DNN training is a highly time-consuming process. Therefore, knowing the accurate runtime consumption of DNN models in advance is very important for ML developers. A runtime usage estimation tool is handy in this regard.

The architecture of the DNN models and the configuration of the hyperparameters would severely affect the accuracy of performance prediction. Meanwhile, the resulted elapsed time and throughput may depend heavily on the frameworks and platforms. A few AI component benchmarks like MLPerf [12] and AIBench [21] adopt real-world benchmarks to cover the feature space that impacts the performance. However, they do not consider each layer's runtime.

The DNN model consists of multiple neuron layers. It transforms the input data from the input layer through all connected layers into the output layer. To this end, prior works [2,6,8,16] build performance prediction models by collecting the profiling traces of the primary layers that are commonly used in DNN models. Then, they use machine learning models trained on profiling traces to predict the performance and runtime of DNN models.

However, these works cannot be directly applied to deep learning frameworks. So, we present a lightweight emulator for distributed DNN training named *DNNEmu* to help ML developers design and optimize distributed training even when the target GPU cluster is unavailable. Our key observation is that the computation overhead of distributed DNN training could be simulated by computation simulation programs. Such computation simulation is a performance predictor of DNN models, predicting performance based on input features. Then the computation simulation will replace the actual computation with the predicted overhead.

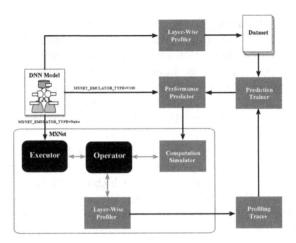

Fig. 1. *DNNEmu* architecture. Components of *DNNEmu* are in blue sharp-edged rect-angles. We use an environment variable `MXNET_EMULATOR_TYPE` to control emulation on different GPUs. (Color figure online)

3   System Design

In this paper, we propose an emulator for distributed training called *DNNEmu*. It predicts the performance of distributed training on large-scale GPU clusters without using any GPUs. In this section, we present the design overview about *DNNEmu*.

3.1   Overview of *DNNEmu*

Figure 1 shows the overview of the system design and implementation of *DNNEmu*, which has three main components: the layer-wise profiler module, the performance predictor module, and the computation simulator module.

The layer-wise profiler collects runtime traces from training execution with layer names, which are later fed to the performance predictor. We outline the details behind our layer-wise profiler and how it is implemented in Sect. 3.2.

The performance predictor predicts the runtime of DNN models via machine learning model trained on historical DNN profiling traces. As more types of GPU or DNN models are involved, the performance predictor could be adapted and incrementally improved. To make our performance predictor flexible enough to retrain the prediction model, we have made the layer-wise profiler and prediction trainer independent. Developers can add new types of GPU or DNN model features to improve our existing performance predictor constantly.

The computation simulation is the imitation of the operators of a real-world process in deep learning frameworks. In the emulation environment, the actual computation would be replaced by the simulation program. The simulated DNN training process will be similar to actual DNN training, except that the computation is simulated. With this computation simulator, developers can study communication optimizations without using any GPUs.

3.2   Layer-Wise Profiler

It is often helpful to check the execution time of each layer's operator in a neural network. We can then determine where to focus our effort to speed up model training or inference. In particular, it is difficult to use the MXNet profiler or the CUDA profiler because the profiling information of operators is not layer-wised (MXNet profiler), or it requires precise knowledge of how each kernel is implemented in operation (CUDA profiler). We implement our layer-wise profiler based on the MXNet profiler, a profiling tool compatible with Chrome's about:tracing trace event profiling viewer.

In order to compare the two methods, we use the MXNet profiler and our layer-wise profiler to profile each operator runtime of training MNIST [10] dataset on LeNet [11] model. Figure 2 presents the difference between MXNet profiler and our layer-wise profiler. We select the following operators as examples: convolution (*conv*), activation (*act*), pooling (*pool*), and fully-connected (*fc*). For MXNet profiler, it does not consider layer names when classifying operators. For example, the *conv* in Fig. 2a consists of *con0* and *con1* in Fig. 2b. To solve this problem, we provide our layer-wise profiler, which enables profiling operators with layer names. Layer-wise profiler helps to collect datasets and compare experimental results more accurately. The code of our layer-wise profiler is publicly available on GitHub[1].

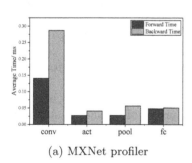

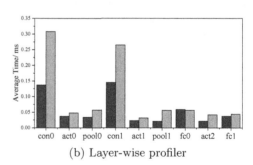

(a) MXNet profiler   (b) Layer-wise profiler

Fig. 2. The profiling traces collected by MXNet profiler (Fig. 2a) and our layer-wise profiler (Fig. 2b). Experiments are performed on MNIST [10] dataset using LeNet [11] model.

3.3   Performance Predictor

Architecture of Performance Predictor. Figure 3 illustrates the architecture of our performance predictor. For an individual operator, we use either

---

[1] https://github.com/Adnios/DNNEmu.

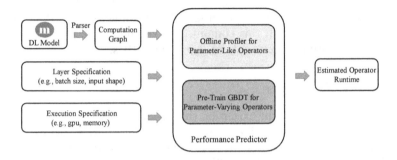

Fig. 3. Architecture of performance predictor.

offline profiling or pre-trained GBDT to make predictions. It accepts the computation graph, the operator specification, and the execution specification as the inputs and then reports the estimated execution time. The computation graph provides network structure. The operator specification includes operator names and hyper-parameter values (e.g., input image size and kernel size). The execution specification contains runtime information such as GPU type and memory capacity. Each of these inputs can contain an almost endless list of features. For convenience to establish a performance prediction model, we define a core subset of these features. However, other features could easily be added. We present input features in Table 1.

To handle various operators, *DNNEmu* makes predictions using either (i) offline profiling or (ii) pre-trained gradient boosting decision trees (GBDT). The choice of two different techniques will depend on whether the operator has various hyper-parameters. Offline profiling assumes that the runtime of a given DNN operator is the same on a given GPU (e.g., sgd_mom_update, sum_grad). However, some DNN operators are implemented using different hyper-parameters (e.g., convolution). We refer to these operators as *parameter-varying. DNNEmu* utilizes offline profiling for the rest of the operators, which we call *parameter-alike*.

We implement offline profiling for parameter-alike operators using our layer-wise profiler. In this paper, we assume that the runtime of parameter-alike operators is constant on a given GPU. The parameter-alike operators in *DNNEmu* include (i) sgd_mom_update, (ii) sum_grad, (iii) batchnorm, (iv) concat, (v) elemwise_add, and (vi) argmax.

For parameter-varying operators, *DNNEmu* makes predictions using pre-trained GBDT. We treat this process as a regression problem: using the input features of DNN models, layer specification, and the execution specification to predict the execution time of each operator. GBDT is widely used and works incredibly well for many real-world problems. In this paper, we leverage GBDT as the performance predictor for parameter-varying operators. As we learn a GBDT for all parameter-varying operators, *DNNEmu* supports: (i) convolution, (ii) pooling, (iii) fully-connected, and (iv) activation.

Table 1. Input features of our prediction model.

Name	Range	Operator
Batch Size	1–128	All
Image Size	1–512	Convolution, Pooling
Kernel Size	1–11	Convolution
Channel In	3–2048	Convolution, Pooling
Channel Out	16–2048	Convolution
Strides	1–4	Convolution, Pooling
Padding	0–3	Convolution, Pooling
Bias	0–1	Convolution, FullyConnect
Activation Type	ReLU/Sigmoid/Tanh Softmax/Softplus	Activation
Input vector	1–4096	FullyConnect
Output vector	1–4096	FullyConnect
Pooling Size	1–7	Pooling
GPU Type	K80/V100	All
Memory	24 GB/32 GB	All

GBDT: Data and Training. In the following section, we describe the details behind *DNNEmu*'s performance predictor: how we (i) collect training data, and (ii) train the performance prediction model based on GBDT.

For convenience to establish a performance prediction model, we define a core subset of input features. However, other features could be added easily. We present all input features in Table 1. We gather training data by measuring the forward and backward pass execution time of parameter-varying operators at randomly sampled input configurations. We use the predefined ranges for each feature to collect training data. During sampling, we ignore any configurations that result in invalid arguments (e.g., the kernel size larger than the image size). Profiling traces are collected on two GPU clusters listed in Sect. 4.1. We gather training data by measuring the execution time of each layer's operator, including forward and backward execution times using our layer-wise profiler.

We implement our gradient boosting decision tree (GBDT) using Light-GBM [9]. The training of GBDT aims to minimize the root-mean-square error (RMSE) between predicted runtime and target runtime:

$$RMSE = \sqrt{\frac{1}{n}\Sigma_{i=1}^{n}\left(Predicted_i - Target_i\right)^2}$$

Smaller error indicates better estimation accuracy.

GBDT is an effective machine learning algorithm and has quite a few popular implementations, such as LightGBM [9]. The performance of GBDT depends on hyper-parameters. An optimal set of hyper-parameters can help to achieve higher accuracy. Finding hyper-parameters manually is tedious and computationally expensive. Therefore, we use bayesian optimization [19] to automate hyper-parameters tuning.

The hyper-parameters optimization follows three steps: (i) define an objective function which takes hyper-parameters as inputs and gives a score as output, (ii) define a search space and narrow the parameter range in the optimization process, and (iii) run the bayesian optimization function and get the hyper-parameters that get the best score.

After we get the best optimization parameters found by bayesian optimization, we train the GBDT using LightGBM on our collected dataset until the training scores do not improve for 200 rounds. Finally, the model with the highest accuracy is selected as the final result. We assign 80% of our dataset to the training set and the rest to the test set. None of the configurations that we test in Sect. 4 appear in our training set.

3.4 Computation Simulator

The computation simulator module is the key part of *DNNEmu*, simulating the actual computation overhead predicted by our performance predictor for a given operator. In this paper, we only focus on operators used in computer vision (CV). In addition, our simulator supports various operators using offline profiler or pre-trained GBDT. We note that these operators are the most time-consuming in DNN models. Other operators are running in normal mode, as they are almost running on CPU, or the elapsed time could be ignored compared with those time-consuming operators. It would make the runtime of the computation simulation close to that of the actual computation environment.

In order to implement computation simulation, we add a computation simulator module before the operator module in MXNet (as shown in Fig. 1). The simulator module receives predicted execution time of each operator from performance predictor module and replaces the actual computation with computation simulation. We use the sleep function in C++ to implement the computation simulation.

We have added an environment variable named `MXNET_EMULATOR_TYPE` to help developers specify a different powerful GPU for emulation. Assuming we want to emulate the DNN training on the V100 GPU cluster, we only need to set the environment variable (`MXNET_EMULATOR_TYPE`) to the `V100`. With the environment variable, developers can control the emulation on different GPUs.

4 Experimental Results

DNNEmu is implemented based on MXNet v1.4.1. We also implement a layer-wise profiler based on MXNet profiler. Earlier sections of this paper introduce the motivation and design of *DNNEmu*. We now focus on an end-to-end evaluation that aims to answer the following questions:

– Can *DNNEmu* predict each layer's operator execution time accurately?

- How does the emulation of *DNNEmu* compare to the actual DNN training?
- Can *DNNEmu* emulate the efficacy of complex and new emerging communication optimizations on distributed training?

In this section, we will introduce our experimental settings and the performance of *DNNEmu* for different models and optimizations. At first, we show our performance predictor in DNN models. Secondly, we perform *DNNEmu* on distributed training. Besides, we evaluate the influence of different communication optimizations on *DNNEmu*.

4.1 Experimental Setup

Hardware. In our experiments, we use two different clusters connected with a 56 Gbps InfiniBand network. One installs four K80 Tesla GPUs and Xeon E5-2660 v3 (2.60 GHz) on each node, and the other is equipped with four V100 Tesla GPUs and Xeon Gold 6132 (2.60 GHz) on each node.

Runtime Environment. We use MXNet v1.4.1 for all experiments. The K80 GPU cluster provides Red Hat 4.8.3, CUDA v8.0, and cuDNN v6.0. The V100 GPU cluster is installed with Centos 7.6, CUDA v10.0, and cuDNN v7.4.1.

Models and Dataset. In this paper, we use existing common DNN models, such as GoogLeNet, MobileNetV2, ResNet18, ResNet50, and VGG16. All the experiments are based on ImageNet [4].

4.2 Runtime Prediction

To evaluate *DNNEmu*'s prediction accuracy, we apply it to predict the training time, including forward and backward pass for five DNN models on two GPU clusters. In this subsection, we evaluate the layer-wise prediction. Unlike prior works, which make the network-level runtime prediction by summing up each layer time, we use *DNNEmu* to emulate the DNN training process on a single node.

Layer-Wise Prediction. We compare our predicted runtime with actual runtime using our layer-wise profiler in VGG16 and ResNet18. Experiments run on the K80 and V100 clusters using a single node with a 32 batch size.

Figure 4 shows layer-by-layer compassion of forward and backward propagation with all layers included. Our performance predictor makes accurate layer-wise predictions since the average prediction error across all GPUs and DNN models is 3.25%. The average layer-wise prediction errors of VGG16 and ResNet18 are 3.86% and 3.69%, respectively.

When comparing Fig. 4a and Fig. 4c (or Fig. 4b and Fig. 4d), we can conclude that the V100 offers almost 10× faster training speedups than the K80. As a result, *DNNEmu* can accurately predict the layer-wise operator execution time.

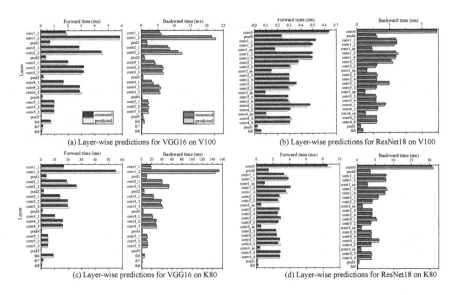

Fig. 4. Layer-wise runtime predictions for VGG16 and ResNet18 on V100 and K80.

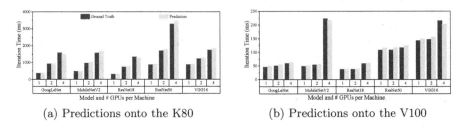

Fig. 5. DNN training emulation on a single node.

Network-Level Prediction. Having demonstrated the accuracy of our performance predictor at the layer-wise prediction, we try to get the runtime of the entire network. Prior works predict the network-level runtime by summing up each layer runtime. This method ignores many operators, which may lead to inaccuracy.

We use *DNNEmu* to emulate the DNN models training using a single node on two GPU clusters. Figure 5 shows the comparisons between runtime emulated by *DNNEmu* and the measured ground truth runtime. We use *DNNEmu* for three kinds of system configuration (1 GPU per machine, 2 GPUs per machine, and 4 GPUs per machine) on K80 and V100 GPU clusters and plot the emulated and measured iteration execution times. In our experiments, we apply *DNNEmu* to emulate the DNN training without using any GPUs.

DNNEmu makes accurate training emulation of DNN models since the average prediction error across all DNN models is 5.6%. The average emulation errors across all GoogLeNet, MobileNetV2, ResNet18, ResNet50, and VGG16 are 6.8%, 4.6%, 5.0%, 6.5%, and 5.0%, respectively.

We observe that *DNNEmu* is slower than the baseline in most cases. Since *DNNEmu* runs entirely on the CPU and there are significant architecture differences between CPU and GPU. Some operators on the GPU cannot be simulated by CPU. For instance, the copy operators (e.g., CopyCPU2CPU) on the CPU are usually more time-consuming than that on the GPU (e.g., CopyGPU2GPU). Even though, *DNNEmu* can emulate the DNN training in single machine training accurately.

4.3 Distributed Training

Next, we use *DNNEmu* to emulate distributed training using data parallelism. We train each DNN model using different number of nodes in a 56 Gbps InfiniBand network. In Fig. 6, we show the comparisons between the measured ground truth runtime and runtime emulated by *DNNEmu*, for each DNN model under different system configurations. In all of the configurations, *DNNEmu* emulates the distributed training with at most 10.9% error.

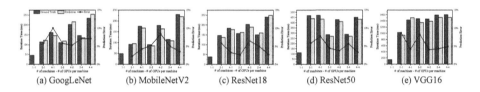

(a) GoogLeNet   (b) MobileNetV2   (c) ResNet18   (d) ResNet50   (e) VGG16

Fig. 6. Iteration execution time emulations for distributed training across five models.

When the model has more parameters, the speedups by distributed training, as compared to the training on a single node, may become more obvious. The communication-to-computation ratio of ResNet18, ResNet50, and VGG16 is much higher than that of GoogLeNet and MobileNetV2. Distributed training benefits more when the communication-to-computation ratio of the model is higher. Our prediction also fits this phenomenon, as described in Fig. 6.

We see that *DNNEmu* predicts the performance of distributed training accurately across all models. The training speed of *DNNEmu* in distributed training is much higher than the baseline in the distributed training. This is because the training of *DNNEmu* has fewer actual computation overhead and uses less memory, leaving more room for improvement with communication scheduling. In addition, we note that the error in GoogLeNet is much higher than the others. This is because the inception block in GoogLeNet consists of four parallel convolutional layers, leading to a higher probability of prediction errors.

4.4 Communication Optimization

We further examine the distributed training with different communication optimizations. We apply priority-based parameter propagation (P3) and 2-bit quantification to *DNNEmu*.

Priority-Based Parameter Propagation. We evaluate *DNNEmu*'s emulation accuracy for the optimization of P3 based on the MXNet in order to show
how well *DNNEmu* can predict the performance of various optimizations. We
train VGG16 with a 16 batch size and ResNet50 with a 32 batch size and each
node uses one GPU card. We conduct this experiment by using the V100 cluster
with four different node counts (2, 3, 4, and 5 nodes) over a 56 Gbps InfiniBand
network.

Figure 7 shows the training speed of multi-node training. P3 enables the
training to be faster in multi-node training. The emulation of *DNNEmu* can
represent the trend of P3 speedups when the number of training nodes increases.
The average prediction errors on VGG16 and ResNet50 are 8.5% and 7.2%,
respectively. *DNNEmu* can emulate the efficacy of communication optimizations
well.

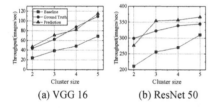

(a) VGG 16   (b) ResNet 50

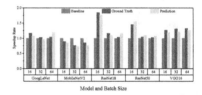

Model and Batch Size

Fig. 7. Priority-based parameter propagation – *DNNEmu*'s prediction of P3 in
multi-node training.

Fig. 8. 2-bit quantification – comparing baseline (FP32), ground truth with
2-bit quantification, and emulations by
DNNEmu.

2-Bit Quantification. We apply the 2-bit quantification to the five models
with three different batch size values (16, 32, and 64). In this experiment, we
use one GPU card per node on two V100 nodes. In order to compare the speedup
rate, we take the speed of conventional training (without 2-bit quantification)
as the baseline. Figure 8 shows the performance of 2-bit quantification and the
corresponding *DNNEmu*'s emulations. Our predictions have errors below 12.7%
for all the models.

2-bit quantification achieves a much higher speed than baseline on the models
except MobileNetV2. This phenomenon is caused by the powerful computation
of V100 GPU and MobileNetV2 has fewer parameters, leading to performance
degradation. However, even considering this expectation, 2-bit quantification still
significantly reduces the network communication time, as implied in Fig. 8. From
the compassion of each model in Fig. 8, 2-bit quantification benefits even more,
when the communication-to-computation ratio of DNN models is higher.

5   Conclusion

When implementing communication optimizations on distributed training system, developers often run into the situation where the powerful GPUs are unavailable because the cloud computing provider has an insufficient supply. Prior works have proposed DNN simulators to estimate the final runtime based on existing tracing information. However, they lack credibility for new optimization methods and cannot handle complex situations.

We have presented *DNNEmu*, a distributed training emulator that helps developers to evaluate the efficacy of the proposed communication optimizations. *DNNEmu* executes the emulation of distributed training accurately by embedding performance predictor and layer-wise profiler as part of the system modules. Our experiments show that *DNNEmu* can emulate the distributed training accurately with an average estimation error of 7.2%. *DNNEmu* is also effective and robust to the choices of communication optimizations, neural architectures, and system configurations.

Although we implement *DNNEmu* based on MXNet, the ideas of *DNNEmu* are also available in other frameworks (e.g., TensorFlow and PyTorch). For the future work, we aim to extend our current system to more frameworks and evaluate *DNNEmu* on larger computer clusters with various training configurations.

Acknowledgements. This work was supported by the National Key R&D Program of China under grant agreement 2018YFB0204300, the Excellent Youth Foundation of Hunan Province under grant number 2021JJ10050, and High-speed Interconnection Network Technology for Heterogeneous Intelligent Computing under grant number WDZC20205500112.

References

1. Abadi, M., et al.: Tensorflow: a system for large-scale machine learning. In: 12th USENIX Symposium on Operating Systems Design and Implementation (OSDI), pp. 265–283 (2016)
2. Cai, E., Juan, D.C., Stamoulis, D., Marculescu, D.: Neuralpower: predict and deploy energy-efficient convolutional neural networks. In: Asian Conference on Machine Learning, pp. 622–637. PMLR (2017)
3. Chen, T., et al.: MXNet: A Flexible and Efficient Machine Learning Library for Heterogeneous Distributed Systems. CoRR abs/1512.01274 (2015). http://arxiv.org/abs/1512.01274
4. Deng, J., Dong, W., Socher, R., Li, L.J., Li, K., Fei-Fei, L.: Imagenet: a large-scale hierarchical image database. In: 2009 IEEE Conference on Computer Vision and Pattern Recognition, pp. 248–255. IEEE (2009)
5. Friedman, J.H.: Greedy function approximation: a gradient boosting machine. Ann. Stat. 1189–1232 (2001)
6. Geoffrey, X.Y., Gao, Y., Golikov, P., Pekhimenko, G.: Habitat: a runtime-based computational performance predictor for deep neural network training. In: 2021 USENIX Annual Technical Conference (USENIX ATC 21), pp. 503–521 (2021)

7. He, K., Zhang, X., Ren, S., Sun, J.: Deep residual learning for image recognition. In: Proceedings of the IEEE Conference on Computer Vision and Pattern Recognition, pp. 770–778 (2016)

8. Justus, D., Brennan, J., Bonner, S., McGough, A.S.: Predicting the computational cost of deep learning models. In: 2018 IEEE International Conference on Big Data (Big Data), pp. 3873–3882. IEEE (2018)

9. Ke, G., et al.: Lightgbm: a highly efficient gradient boosting decision tree. Adv. Neural Inf. Process. Syst. **30**, 3146–3154 (2017)

10. LeCun, Y.: The mnist database of handwritten digits (1998). http://yann.lecun.com/exdb/mnist/

11. LeCun, Y., et al.: Backpropagation applied to handwritten zip code recognition. Neural Comput. **1**(4), 541–551 (1989)

12. Mattson, P., et al.: Mlperf training benchmark. arXiv preprint arXiv:1910.01500 (2019)

13. NVIDIA: NVIDIA Nsight. https://developer.nvidia.com/tools-overview

14. NVIDIA: NVIDIA Profiler. docs.nvidia.com/cuda/profiler-users-guide/index.html

15. Paszke, A., et al.: Pytorch: an imperative style, high-performance deep learning library. Adv. Neural Inf. Process. Syst. **32**, 8026–8037 (2019)

16. Qi, H., Sparks, E.R., Talwalkar, A.: Paleo: a performance model for deep neural networks. In: Proceedings of the International Conference on Learning Representations (2017)

17. Sandler, M., Howard, A., Zhu, M., Zhmoginov, A., Chen, L.C.: Mobilenetv 2: inverted residuals and linear bottlenecks. In: Proceedings of the IEEE Conference on Computer Vision and Pattern Recognition, pp. 4510–4520 (2018)

18. Simonyan, K., Zisserman, A.: Very deep convolutional networks for large-scale image recognition. arXiv preprint arXiv:1409.1556 (2014)

19. Snoek, J., Larochelle, H., Adams, R.P.: Practical bayesian optimization of machine learning algorithms. Adv. Neural Inf. Process. Syst. **25** (2012)

20. Szegedy, C., et al.: Going deeper with convolutions. In: Proceedings of the IEEE Conference on Computer Vision and Pattern Recognition, pp. 1–9 (2015)

21. Tang, F., et al.: Aibench training: balanced industry-standard AI training benchmarking. In: 2021 IEEE International Symposium on Performance Analysis of Systems and Software (ISPASS), pp. 24–35. IEEE (2021)

22. Wong, A.W.: TorchProf. https://github.com/awwong1/torchprof

23. Yu, E., Dong, D., Xu, Y., Ouyang, S., Liao, X.: CD-SGD: distributed stochastic gradient descent with compression and delay compensation. In: 50th International Conference on Parallel Processing, pp. 1–10 (2021)

24. Zhu, H., Phanishayee, A., Pekhimenko, G.: Daydream: accurately estimating the efficacy of optimizations for DNN training. In: 2020 USENIX Annual Technical Conference (USENIX ATC 20), pp. 337–352 (2020)

Ordis: A Dynamic Order-Dispatch Algorithm for Ridehailing and Ridesharing in a Large Region

Ming Jin[1,2], Juanjuan Zhao[1,2], Yang Wang[1,2(✉)], and Chengzhong Xu[3]

[1] Shenzhen Institute of Advanced Technology, CAS, Shenzhen, China
yang.wang1@siat.ac.cn
[2] University of Chinese Academy of Sciences, Beijing, China
[3] The State Key Laboratory of IoT for Smart City, University of Macau, Macau, China

Abstract. Online ridesourcing framework is often designed with a goal to achieve optimized matching between driver and passenger for not only minimizing passenger's travel time but also maximizing driver's revenue incomes. However, traditional order dispatching that materializes this matching is typically conducted on per pair of passenger and driver basis in a relatively small area, which often lead to suboptimal global matching rate. In this paper, we model the order dispatching as a distributed matching problem for a wide area based on a developed multi-queue model, each queue in charge of a region service. Based on this model, we propose a dispatching algorithm, called *Ordis*, by applying the network-flow theory to the multi-queues with an attempt to maximize the overall service revenue while improving the service efficiency and user experience for both ridehailing and ridesharing across multiple regions. To validate the effectiveness of the proposed approach, we developed an online taxi-hailing simulation system and compared it with some commonly used dispatch algorithms based on real trace data. We found that the proposed method is superior to those compared methods.

Keywords: Order dispatching · Ridehailing and ridesharing · Multi-queues model · Networkflow-based matching · Distributed algorithm

1 Introduction

With the rapid development of global positioning system (GPS), wireless communication and mobile device, all kinds of ridesourcing platforms and online applications have gradually substituted for traditional taxi services and become a novel way to transportation services on demand via mobile devices [1–3]. For example, Didi [4], Uber [5], Lyft [6] and other mobile e-hailing services are widely popular across the world, and greatly changing the way people daily travel.

This work was supported in part by Key-Area Research and Development Program of Guangdong Province (2020B010164002).

Order dispatching is a critical component to the online ridesourcing application, which typically serves the function to match drivers and passengers in forms of one-to-one ridehailing and one-to-many ridesharing services. As such, it not only affects the transportation capacity but also determines the customer satisfaction and the service income. In reality order dispatching often seeks the most suitable driver for each request made by passenger so that the match between them with the best pre-defined metrics can be achieved. With these in mind, the current order dispatching algorithms mostly either exploit some heuristic ideas to find the best driver to serve requesting passenger, such as greedy in distance [7–9], queuing in service order [10,11] or adopt some data-driven strategy, such as those machine learning-based algorithms [12,13], to optimize the dynamic matching.

Although these methods are effective in some cases, they are largely myopic to achieve good results only for each individual order in a relatively small area, lacking the notion of global optimality in real time for all the orders across different regions in a wide area since in these algorithms, it is highly likely that the local optimal match in a region may lead to sub-optimality in global match across multiple regions or even no match at all for either some driver or some passengers.

The goal of this paper is to desgin optimal order dispatching strategies for both ridehailing and ridesharing services in real time for all the drivers and passengers across different regions, here in our study, the ridehailing service is defined as an one-to-one service where a driver can select an order to pick up and serve an individual passenger while the ridesharing refers to the service that connects a driver with his/her multiple passengers, each with a similar destination and close departure times, but having different origins alone a particular route to the destination. With this design, the ridesouring system can not only achieve the best matching results for local region but also optimize dynamic taxi resource allocation for optimal global matching.

To this end, we partition the wide area into different regions, each being regulated by a driver-passenger queue where the local matching is conducted. As such, the order dispatching problem is formulated into a distributed matching problem across the multiple queues. Then, we propose a dispatching algorithm, called *Ordis* (Order dispatch), by applying the network-flow theory to the multi-queues with an attempt to maximize the overall service revenue while improving the service efficiency and user experience across multiple regions.

To validate the effectiveness of the proposed approach, we developed an online taxi-hailing simulation system and compared it with some commonly used dispatch algorithms based on real trace data. We found that the proposed method is superior to those compared methods.

The main contributions of this paper are summarized as follows:

– Propose a distributed multi-queue model to address the order dispatching in a wide area, where each region of the area is modeled as a queue to regulate the matching between the co-resident passengers and drivers.

- Develop a network-flow based dispatching algorithm by exploiting the distributed multi-queue model to obtain the optimal local match in each region.
- Build an online taxi-hailing simulation system and conduct trace-based studies to validate the effectiveness of the proposed algorithm by comparing with some commonly adopted task dispatching algorithms.

The organization of the paper is as follows: We introduce some related work regarding the order dispatching in Sect. 2, and then describe the formulation and notation of the order dispatching problem in Sect. 3 and build a distributed multi-queue model with the proposed algorithm in Sect. 4. We present the simulation studies to validate our methods in Sect. 5, followed by the conclusion of the paper in the last section.

2 Related Work

Order dispatching is a typical bilateral market, which matches the demand sent by passengers with the idle drivers provided by the ridesourcing platform, and as stated it is mainly designed to serve the ridehailing and ridesharing. The quality of order dispatching has a great impact on the overall performance and efficiency of online e-hailing service. A good dispatching method can not only provide better service for passengers, but also efficiently use fewer taxis to complete more orders.

In recent years, many experts and scholars have conducted a lot of research on order dispatching. Lee et al. [8] proposed a scheduling system to determine taxi scheduling according to real-time traffic conditions, which dispatches the taxi with the shortest time path to the passengers. Considering the randomness and dynamics of traffic conditions and future demand, Wong et al. [14] proposed a rolling horizon method for taxi scheduling optimization to find a taxi for passengers on the rolling horizon with minimum expected total waiting time. These methods only focus on an individual order. When the request appears, they immediately find the best match for it. However, for other orders, they may not be able to match the most suitable driver or no matching driver, resulting in poor effect of the system in the long term.

Non-immediate batch matching can solve the problem of long-term poor effect. At this point, the system will be subdivided multiple time windows, accumulate the order requests and idle taxis in each time window, and conduct two-way matching in batches. Santos et al. [15] studied the ridesharing problem with time window, and proposed a dispatching system composed of a client application and a server, which can maximize the matching rate and the total revenue of the system receiving orders. Akbarpour et al. [16] discussed the influence of the information related to batch matching in the dynamic matching market, and specified the condition that the local algorithm is close to the optimal, under which it can select the appropriate time for matching but does not use the global network structure.

However, these methods all use one processor for centralized processing. When the amount of data is very large, the problem of computing overload will occur, resulting in the decrease of dispatching efficiency. To solve this problem, some methods based on distributed and multi-agent reinforcement learning have emerged. Seow et al. [17] proposed a multi-agent taxi scheduling system TuCab, which realized the automatic scheduling of taxis in a distributed way, greatly reducing passengers' waiting time and cruising time of empty taxi. Ke et al. [18] proposed a two-stage framework, in which multi-agent reinforcement learning was used to determine the delay time of requests, and the combinatorial optimization model was used to perform optimal matching. However, these methods do not consider the dynamic balance of resources among multiprocessors, and the reinforcement learning methods require long-term and complex training.

Aiming at these problems, in this paper we comprehensively consider multiple influencing factors, use decentralized processing to improve the efficiency of the system, achieve a lightweight long-term optimal matching method, and realize the dynamic balance of global resources.

3   Problem Formulation

The order dispatching problem considered in this article is as follows. We assume that the map is subdivided into M regions, each region m is characterized by its P_m^t order requests and Q_m^t available vehicle in the t-th time window, then the p-th order request is expressed as r_{mp}^t, and the order requests appearing in this region are represented as vector $r_m^t \triangleq [r_{m1}^t, r_{m2}^t, \ldots, r_{mP}^t] \in R^{1 \times P}$ and the available drivers as vector $d_m^t \triangleq [d_{m1}^t, d_{m2}^t, \ldots, d_{mQ}^t] \in R^{1 \times Q}$. Note that the order request is a 4-tuple containing starting time of the order t_{st}, service duration t_{du}, starting coordinate $ST \in R^2$ and ending coordinate $DT \in R^2$. So we can get $r_{mp}^t = (t_{st}, t_{du}, ST, DT)$, where $ST = (x_s, y_s)$, $DT = (x_e, y_e)$. Unlike the order request, the vehicle information is simply a position $PD = (x_d, y_d)$.

In this paper, our research goal is to maximize the revenue of the system across all the drivers by improving the matching rate, and reducing drivers' cruising cost and passengers' waiting time. Suppose the position of driver is (x_d, y_d), source and destination coordinates of the order are (x_s, y_s) and (x_e, y_e) respectively, the driver's cost per distance unit (e.g., one kilometer) is α, the total charge passenger should pay the part of the travel distance less than two kilometers as ξ, and the charge per distance unit more than two kilometers is β. In order to simplify the study, we use the Euclidean distance $\gamma = \sqrt{(x_e - x_s)^2 + (y_e - y_s)^2}$ to calculate the driving distance. Thus, the cost of the driver's cruising for passenger pickup is

$$\text{cost}_1 = \alpha \times \frac{\sqrt{(x_s - x_d)^2 + (y_s - y_d)^2}}{1000}, \tag{1}$$

and the cost of the order service is

$$\text{cost}_2 = \alpha \times \frac{\sqrt{(x_e - x_s)^2 + (y_e - y_s)^2}}{1000}. \tag{2}$$

Thus, we can have the price of the order

$$\text{price} = \begin{cases} \xi & , \gamma \leq 2000 \\ \xi + \beta \times \frac{(\gamma - 2000)}{1000} & , \gamma > 2000 \end{cases} \tag{3}$$

At the same time, in order to prioritize orders that have been waiting for a long time, we put weight on them, which is set as the income per time unit when driver serves the order, thus, the drivers can get more rewards for accepting the orders that have been waiting for a long time (t_{wait}). Suppose the travel distance of a driver in a time window is δ, the reward value can be obtained as

$$\text{award} = \beta \times \frac{\delta}{1000} \times t_{\text{wait}}. \tag{4}$$

According to the above formula, a driver can obtain the profit when accepting an order, $profit = price - cost_1 - cost_2 + award$. The goal is to maximize the revenue of all the drivers receiving orders in the system.

4   Order Dispatch Algorithm

Given the problem formulation, in this section, we present our dynamic order-dispatch algorithm, called *Ordis*, to achieve our goal. To this end, we introduce a distributed multi-queue model to abstract the problem whereby a distributed matching algorithms for ridehailing and ridesharing are developed by exploiting the minimum-cost maximum-flow in network-flow theory.

4.1   Distributed Multi-queue Model

In our model, a queue is designed for each region to store idle drivers and unserved order information and a matching pool is employed to maintain the information of serving drivers and his/her orders. However, in actual scenario, if all the order requests and drivers in the whole map are put into the same queue for centralized matching, the performance will be degraded due to the large amount of computation and other control complexity. Therefore, we consider to subdivide the whole map into multiple regions according to the request density and build a distributed multi-queue model, one for each region as shown in Fig. 1, to share the computational loads for system efficiency as with this design, the orders and vehicles in each region could be isolated from each other and their matching can be computed independently. Our distributed multi-queue model enjoys the following features:

– The whole map is subdivided into multiple regions according to the request density, and each region has a queue to maintain the incoming requests (passengers) and ride-hailing vehicles (drivers) and a matching pool to store their matching pair results.
– The order requests and available drivers in a region will be put into the queue of this region for matching each other, Then the successfully matched pairs are put into the matching pool of this region.

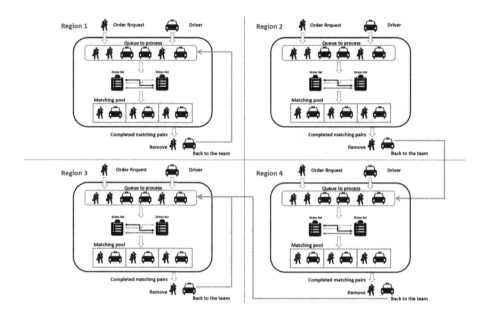

Fig. 1. Distributed multi-queue model

- The order requests in the queue will be removed if no driver picks up the orders after waiting for a predefined period of time.
- When the available drivers in the queue have no matching order after waiting for a predefined period of time, the system will prompt the drivers based on their positions and the request densities across the system to go to the regions with higher density and join the corresponding queues of those regions.
- After a driver in the matching pool completes his/her order, the matching pair will be removed from the matching pool. The driver will be re-added to the queue of this region if he/she is still available to this region; otherwise, he/she will be added to the queue of another region.

4.2   Order Dispatching Algorithms

Based on the distributed multi-queue model, we transform the order dispatching problem with respect to ridehailing and ridesharing into a network-flow problem for maximizing the flow with minimum-cost, and propose the Ordis algorithm for maximizing the matching rate to improve the overall revenue of the drivers while reducing the driver's cruising cost and passengers' waiting time.

For the problem of ridehailing, we set the driver nodes and order nodes as the middle layer and add a source node and a sink node when building the network flow diagram. Among them, there is a directed edge between the source node and each driver node, whose capacity is defined as 1 and cost as 0; there is also a directed edge between each driver node and the order node within its matching radius (the matching mode who's revenue less than or equal to 0 will

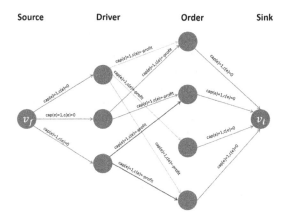

Fig. 2. Network-flow for ridehailing

not be considered), and the capacity of this edge is 1, and the cost is the opposite number of the revenue that the driver can get after serving the order; finally, a directed edge between each order node and the sink node is also defined with capacity being defined as 1 and cost as 0 as shown in Fig. 2.

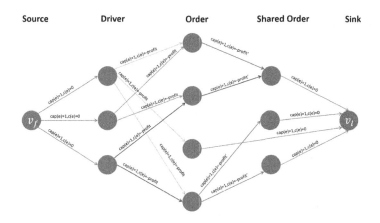

Fig. 3. Network-flow for ridesharing

As far as the ridesharing is concerned, the construction of network-flow diagram is similar to that in ridehailing—adding a source node and a sink node, setting the driver nodes as the second layer, the order nodes as the third layer, and the shared order nodes as the forth layer. Among them, there is a connected directed edge between the source node and each driver node, the capacity of which is defined as 1 and the cost as 0; there is also a connected directed edge between each driver node and order nodes within its matching radius, and the capacity of the edge is 1, the cost is the opposite number of the revenue of this order; if there is an order that can be served at the same time with an order (i.e., a shared order node, which has similar travel information with above orders), there is a connected directed edge between these nodes that can be served at the same time, and its capacity is 1, the cost is the opposite number of the revenue of the shared order; each shared order node has a directed edge connected with the sink node, whose capacity is 1 and cost is 0; for the order node without shared order point, it is directly connected with the sink node, and the edge's capacity is 1 and its cost is 0, as shown in Fig. 3.

Algorithm 1. Ordis algorithm

Require: orders, drivers
Ensure: tmpPool
 1: **Initialize** tmpPool, profits
 2: **if** It's a ridehailing problem **then**
 3:     build a network flow diagram G for ridehailing
 4: **else**
 5:     build a network flow diagram G for ridesharing
 6: **end if**
 7: build a cost network G' with the same structure of G
 8: look for a zero flow in graph G'
 9: **while** True **do**
10:     use SPFA algorithm to find a path with minimum cost in G'
11:     **if** not find path **then**
12:         break
13:     **end if**
14:     calculate maximum of flow that can pass on the found path in G
15:     **for** each edge on path **do**
16:         modify available flow of edge and reverse edge in G
17:         modify cost and direction of edge in G'
18:         **if** edge is between driver and order **then**
19:             **if** cost of edge < 0 **then**
20:                 put match into tmpPool
21:             **end if**
22:             delete edge in G and G'
23:         **end if**
24:         **if** It's a ridesharing problem **then**
25:             **if** edge is between order and sharedOrder **then**
26:                 **if** cost of edge < 0 **then**
27:                     add sharedOrder to driver's match in tmpPool
28:                 **end if**
29:                 delete edge in G and G'
30:             **end if**
31:         **end if**
32:     **end for**
33: **end while**
34: **return** tmpPool

We can see that maximizing the total profit of the system is equivalent to finding the minimum cost in the network-flow diagram while maximizing the matching rate is to find the maximum flow in the network-flow diagram, thus we propose the Ordis algorithm as shown in **Algorithm** 1 to achieve the best matching of local resources in each region by finding the minimum cost maximum flow in the network flow graph.

Algorithm: To this end, the algorithm first judges whether it is a ridehailing problem or a ridesharing problem (`Line1-6`), and then build a corresponding network-flow graph and define the cost network for it (`Line7`). After that, the algorithm tries to look for a zero flow in the graph (`Line8`) whereby the Shortest Path Faster Algorithm (SPFA) algorithm [19] is exploited to find a path from source to sink with minimum sum of the weights of all edges on the path. This procedure is repeatedly performed until it cannot find any path like this (`Line9-13`).

Given the case that such a path is found, the graph is incrementally updated by calculating the maximum of flow that can pass on the found path (`Line14`). It first modifies the amount of flow that can pass through each edge on the path in the network flow (`Line16`), and then updates the cost network according to the following rules (`Line17`):

1. when there is no flow through the edge, the flow direction remains unchanged and the cost is the original cost;
2. when the flow is equal to the maximum capacity of the edge, change the flow direction as well as the cost to the negative of the original cost;
3. when the flow is less than the maximum capacity of the edge, increase the same amount of reverse flow, and change the cost as the negative of the original cost.

In this process, we should notice that in the ridehailing problem, a driver can exclusively service one order, so we should delete the directed edge between the driver node and other order nodes on the path (`Line18-23`), while in the ridesharing problem, a driver can serve one order and one shared order at most at the same time, so we should delete the directed edges of the driver node and other ordering nodes on the path (`Line18-23`), as well as the directed edges of the order node and other shared nodes on the path (`Line24-31`).

Analysis: As the Ordis algorithm for ridehailing is built on top of the SPFA algorithm to find the least-cost augmented path. The time complexity of this process is thus known as $O(km)$. Since finding an augmented path needs to modify at most $O(n)$ edges, there are at most $O(fn)$ argmented paths where f is the maximum flow value, so the time complexity of the Ordis algorithm with respect to ridehailing is $O(fkmn^2)$ where m is the number of edges and $O(n)$ is the number of nodes.

Unlike the case in the ridehailiing, the Ordis algorithm for ridesharing needs to modify $O(m/2)$ edges when leveraging the SPFA algorithm to find a least-cost augmented path. As such, given the same number of argmented paths in the ridehailing case, its time complexity is increased to $O(fknm^2/2)$ where f is the maximum flow value, m the number of edges and $O(n)$ the number of nodes.

Although compared with some existing algorithms the Ordis algorithm proposed in this paper has a higher time complexity and a relatively larger overhead in practice, its impact on the system performance is fully controllable as the algorithm is only executed once in each time window whose size can be adjusted as a reaction to the actual situation.

5   Performance Evaluation

In this section, we first build an online ride-hailing simulation system to verify the effectiveness of the model and the proposed algorithm proposed. Then we introduce the data sources used in this experiment and related processing work. Finally, we compare the performance of the proposed method with some often-used task processing algorithms to show its superiority in terms of total order revenue, average order revenue, and average waiting time.

5.1   Simulation System

The online ride-hailing simulation system is composed of four main parts we describe below:

User Behavior Module: This module simulates the passengers' behavior in sending order request at a certain time. The order information mainly includes the time when the order appears, the time required to process the order, the source and destination of the trip, the waiting time of the passenger, the cost of receiving the order and the amount of the order, etc.

Driver Status Module: This module simulates the ride-hailing vehicle information that can be allocated in the system and dynamically updates the available vehicle status of the system in real time. The driver information mainly includes the driver's location, whether it is available, whether it can accept a shared order and order information it services.

Resource Allocation Module: According to the request densities across the whole map, this module reasonably subdivides the map into different regions, and build a distributed multi-queue model, to share the computational loads on among multiple nodes for high system efficiency.

Task Scheduling Module: This module uses the multi-queue model and the Ordis algorithm proposed to match the pending orders with the available drivers. The system completes the matching task between the orders and drivers in consideration of the overall income of drivers, the cost of cruising, the waiting time of passengers, the matching rate and other factors.

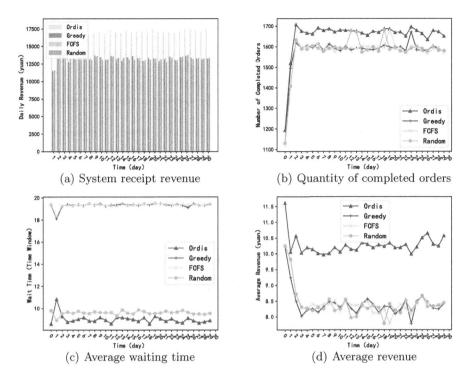

(a) System receipt revenue

(b) Quantity of completed orders

(c) Average waiting time

(d) Average revenue

Fig. 4. Comparison between Ordis and other algorithms

5.2   Dataset

The dataset used in this paper comes from Didi Gaia Data Opening Program [4], which provides the order information processed in Chengdu from November 1, 2016 to November 30, 2016, and the drivers and orders information in it are encrypted, desensitized and anonymous. This data set has a quantity of 663MB and a total of 7,065,937 transaction records. Each record contains information such as order ID, start billing time, end billing time, longitude and latitude of boarding position and disembarking position.

To simplify the experiments, we removed the data in remote areas, and restrict the data in latitude and longitude from (103.89325, 30.547255) to (104.20675, 30.852745). Since the coordinate system in the dataset is GCJ02, we change the GCJ02 coordinate system to the World Geodetic System 1984 coordinate system (WGS84). At the same time, we divided the time of the day into 1440 time windows and got rid of the data that lasted more than 60 time windows.

5.3   Results

Firstly, we compared the performance of the proposed algorithm with Greedy, FCFS and Random when the system is subdivided into four regions in terms of total revenue of the system per day, the quantity of completed orders per day, the average waiting time of each order and the average revenue of each order, as shown in Fig. 4.

In terms of total daily revenue, the average daily revenue obtained by the four algorithms were 16957.98 yuan, 13233.35 yuan, 13270.09 yuan and 13249.62 yuan, and daily revenue of the Ordis algorithm is 28.1%, 27.8% and 27.9% higher than greedy, FCFS and Random, respectively. Therefore, the Ordis algorithm proposed in this paper can significantly improve the total revenue of the system.

In terms of order response rate, the number of orders received daily of Ordis is higher than that of the other three algorithms, and the values of each algorithm within 30 days is 1653, 1577, 1575 and 1577. Therefore, the Ordis algorithm improves 4.8%, 5.0% and 4.8% compared with other algorithms.

In terms of average waiting time of passengers for each order, the time obtained by the four algorithms are 9.00, 19.33, 19.34 and 9.59 time windows respectively. It can be seen that the average waiting time of orders obtained by the Ordis algorithm is slightly lower than random, far lower than greedy and FCFS.

In terms of average revenue, the average revenue of each order obtained by the four methods were 10.27 yuan, 8.39 yuan, 8.43 yuan and 8.41 yuan, and the Ordis algorithm is 22.4%, 21.8% and 22.1% higher than the Greedy, FCFS and Random algorithm, respectively.

Therefore, compared with other algorithms, the comprehensive performance of Ordis algorithm is better.

In order to verify the superiority of the multi-queue model proposed in this paper, we compare the system daily revenue, the quantity of completed orders per day and the average waiting time of passengers when the system was subdivided into single region, two regions and four regions, as shown in Fig. 5.

In terms of daily revenue, compared with one region, the daily revenue is 28.7% higher when system is subdivided into two regions, and 40.1% higher when system is subdivided into four regions.

In terms of order response rate, compared with one region, the number of orders completed per day is 20.7% higher when system is subdivided into two regions, and 27.3% higher when system is subdivided into four regions.

In terms of average waiting time, compared with one region, the average waiting time for each order is 4.8% lower when system is subdivided into two regions, and 21.2% lower when system is subdivided into four regions.

In terms of average revenue, compared with one region, the average revenue is 6.7% higher when system is subdivided into two regions, and 10.1% higher when system is subdivided into four regions.

It can be seen that the multi-queue model based on regions can increase the revenue of system, improve the matching rate, reduce the idling cost of

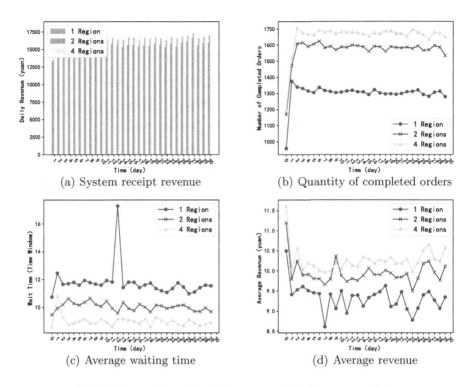

(a) System receipt revenue

(b) Quantity of completed orders

(c) Average waiting time

(d) Average revenue

Fig. 5. Comparison of multi-queue and single-queue models

receiving orders and reduce the waiting time of passengers. And in a range, when subdivided into more partitions, the performance of the system is better.

Then we compared the effects of order response rate every day, average daily revenue of one day and average waiting time of passengers per order on ridehailing and ridesharing, as shown in Fig. 6. It can be seen that, compared with ridehailing, the response rate of order in ridesharing increases by 41.3%, daily system revenue increases by 82.1%, average waiting time of passengers decreases by 61.3%, and average revenue increases by 27.4%. So we can know that conpared with ridehailing, ridesharing can improve the efficiency of order dispatching and increase the revenue of the system as well.

According to the foregoing results, we can know that, compared with the reference algorithms, the proposed algorithm can significantly improve the system's order receiving revenue, improve the matching rate of drivers and passengers, and reduce the waiting time of passengers. The distributed multi-queue model is better than the centralized single queue model in the above three indicators. At the same time, the effects on the above three indicators are better for ridesharing than for ridehailing.

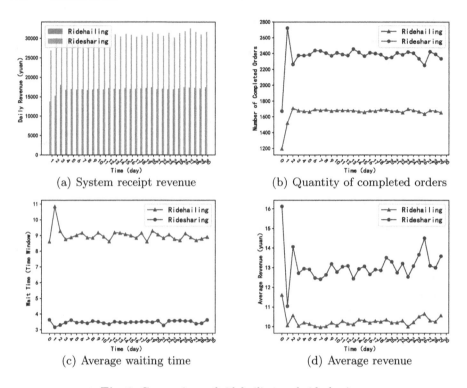

(a) System receipt revenue   (b) Quantity of completed orders

(c) Average waiting time   (d) Average revenue

Fig. 6. Comparison of ridehailing and ridesharing

6   Conclusion

In this paper, we comprehensively considered multiple factors affecting the effects on the matching of drivers and orders in ridehailing and ridesharing. To this end, we first established a distributed multi-queue model, each for a defined region, to realize a decentralized processing of the order matching for the overall system performance. Based on the multi-queue model, we further proposed a dynamic order dispatching algorithm, called Ordis, to achieve the local optimal matching between drivers and passengers in each region. Our simulation results validate the effectiveness of the proposed algorithm by comparing with some commonly adopted task dispatching algorithms. To further improve the algorithm, we will find the most appropriate guidance method as a immediately future work to minimize the moving cost of idle drivers and maximize the probability of matching orders.

References

1. Li, B., Zhang, D., Sun, L., et al.: Hunting or waiting? Discovering passenger-finding strategies from a large-scale real-world ride-hailing dataset. In: 2011 IEEE International Conference on Pervasive Computing and Communications Workshops (PERCOM Workshops), pp. 63–68. IEEE (2011)

2. Miao, F., Han, S., Lin, S., et al.: Taxi dispatch with real-time sensing data in metropolitan areas: a receding horizon control approach. IEEE Trans. Autom. Sci. Eng. **13**(2), 463–478 (2016)

3. Zhang, D., Sun, L., Li, B., et al.: Understanding taxi service strategies from taxi GPS traces. IEEE Trans. Intell. Transp. Syst. **16**(1), 123–135 (2014)

4. Chuxing, D.: http://www.didichuxing.com/

5. Uber. https://www.uber.com/

6. Lyft. https://www.lyft.com/

7. Chung, L.C.: GPS taxi dispatch system based on A* shortest path algorithm. Malausia University of Science and Technology, Kuala Lumpur, Malaysia (2005)

8. Lee, D.H., Wang, H., Cheu, R.L., et al.: Taxi dispatch system based on current demands and real-time traffic conditions. Transp. Res. Rec. **1882**(1), 193–200 (2004)

9. Kim, Y., Yoon, Y.: Zone-Agnostic greedy taxi dispatch algorithm based on contextual matching matrix for efficient maximization of revenue and profit. Electronics **10**(21), 2653 (2021)

10. Lees-Miller, J., Hammersley, J., Davenport, N.: Ride sharing in personal rapid transit capacity planning. Automated People Movers, pp. 321–332 (2009). Efficient Maximization of Revenue and Profit. Electronics, 2021, 10(21): 2653. Connecting People, Connecting Places, Connecting Modes.

11. Coltin, B.J., Veloso, M.: Towards ridesharing with passenger transfers. In: Proceedings of the 2013 International Conference on Autonomous Agents and Multi-agent Systems, pp. 1299–1300 (2013)

12. Wang, D., Cao, W., Li, J., et al.: DeepSD: supply-demand prediction for online car-hailing services using deep neural networks. In: 2017 IEEE 33rd International Conference on Data Engineering (ICDE), pp. 243–254. IEEE (2017)

13. Jindal, I., Qin, Z.T., Chen, X., et al.: Optimizing taxi carpool policies via reinforcement learning and spatio-temporal mining. In: 2018 IEEE International Conference on Big Data (Big Data), pp. 1417–1426. IEEE (2018)

14. Wong, K.I., Bell, M.G.H.: The optimal dispatching of taxis under congestion: a rolling horizon approach. J. Adv. Transp. **40**(2), 203–220 (2006)

15. Santos, D.O., Xavier, E.C.: Dynamic taxi and ridesharing: a framework and heuristics for the optimization problem. In: 23rd International Joint Conference on Artificial Intelligence (2013)

16. Akbarpour, M., Li, S., Gharan, S.O.: Thickness and information in dynamic matching markets. J. Polit. Econ. **128**(3), 783–815 (2020)

17. Seow, K.T., Dang, N.H., Lee, D.H.: A collaborative multiagent taxi-dispatch system. IEEE Trans. Autom. Sci. Eng. **7**(3), 607–616 (2009)

18. Ke, J., Xiao, F., Yang, H., et al.: Optimizing online matching for ride-sourcing services with multi-agent deep reinforcement learning. arXiv:1902.06228 (2019)

19. Fanding, D.: A faster algorithm for shortest-path-SPFA. J. Southwest Jiaotong Univ. **2**(9), 2 (1994)

20. Krishna, K., Murty, M.N.: Genetic K-means algorithm. IEEE Trans. Syst. Man Cybern. Part B (Cybern.) **29**(3), 433–439 (1999)

Multi-initial-Center Federated Learning with Data Distribution Similarity-Aware Constraint

Xiaoying Li[1,2], Xiaojun Chen[1(✉)], Shaopu Wang[1,2], Yangyang Ding[1], and Kaiyun Li[1,2]

[1] Institute of Information Engineering, Chinese Academy of Sciences, Beijing, China
{lixiaoying,chenxiaojun,wangshaopu,dingyangyang,likaiyun}@iie.ac.cn
[2] School of Cyber Security, University of Chinese Academy of Sciences, Beijing, China

Abstract. Federated Learning (FL) has recently attracted high attention since it allows clients to collaboratively train a model while the training data remains local. However, due to the inherent heterogeneity of local data distributions, the trained model usually fails to perform well on each client. Clustered FL has emerged to tackle this issue by clustering clients with similar data distributions. However, these model-dependent clustering methods tend to perform poorly and be costly. In this work, we propose a distribution similarity-based clustered federated learning framework FedDSMIC, which clusters clients by detecting the client-level underlying data distribution based on the model's memory of training data. Furthermore, we extend the assumption about data distribution to a more realistic cluster structure. The center models are learned as good initial points to obtain common data properties in the cluster. Each client in a cluster gets a more personalized model by performing one step of gradient descent from the initial point. The empirical evaluation on real-world datasets shows that FedDSMIC outperforms popular state-of-the-art federated learning algorithms while keeping the lowest communication overhead.

Keywords: Clustered federated learning · Kullback-Leibler divergence · Model-Agnostic Meta-Learning · Non-IID data

1 Introduction

Federated learning (FL) is a promising distributed machine learning framework that can collaboratively train a joint model while keeping the data on the client side [19]. Classical FL trains a unique global model for all clients [20, 22, 27, 33, 34]. However, such global collaboration always fails to achieve good performance for individual clients since the data statistical heterogeneity, which is known as non-i.i.d. data [19, 27, 38]. In practice, clients usually have varying preferences. Consider the scenario for mobile device keyboards, certain emojis are used by one

© Springer Nature Switzerland AG 2023
W. Meng et al. (Eds.): ICA3PP 2022, LNCS 13777, pp. 752–772, 2023.
https://doi.org/10.1007/978-3-031-22677-9_41

demographic but not others. Therefore, it is necessary to provide personalized models for each client in FL.

A variety of personalized approaches have been proposed to tackle data heterogeneity, mainly from two perspectives: global model personalization and personalized models learning. The former first trains a global model and then fine-tune the global model locally [29,41]. However, the local distribution may be fairly different from the global distribution in highly personalized scenarios. Consequently, the relevant global model does not exist, and these approaches downgrade to each client learning only locally [13,32]. While the latter directly learns multiple individual personalized models. MOCHA [39] frames FL personalization as an MTL problem by exploiting penalization terms to capture relationships among clients. Unfortunately, it is usually tricky to simultaneously optimize multiple non-convex objectives determined by large neural networks.

To address the lack of the above studies, clustered FL groups clients into clusters and trains a model for each cluster, providing a trade-off between a purely global and personalized model. Several methods [3,38,42] clusters clients at the server-side based on the cosine similarity or l_2 distance of local model weights. Unfortunately, due to the high dimensionality and permutation invariance of neural network (NN) parameters, these methods often fail to cluster clients correctly. Other approaches [14,29] performs the cluster identities estimation at the client sides. In particular, k global models are randomly initialized, representing k clusters, and each client selects the model with the lowest loss on its local data. Clients that select the same model are assigned to a cluster. The methods improve the clustering performance, however, increasing the communication and computation burden for receiving and running multiple global models.

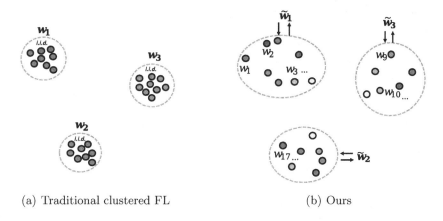

(a) Traditional clustered FL   (b) Ours

Fig. 1. Comparison of traditional clustered FL and ours.

Moreover, the existing clustered FL methods are limited by the ideal assumption that each client belongs to a cluster with a specific data distribution. However, data heterogeneity is usually severe in the cross-device scenario with massive clients. Clients in a group can share one learning task, e.g., animals or vehicles classification [4], but the data distributions are still different (e.g., covariate shift, concept drift, and so forth [19]). We regard it as a more realistic cluster structure that clients in the same cluster are more loosely separated. Figure 1 depicts a comparison between traditional clustered FL and ours. Under the complicated data distribution, the client's data distribution information is not fully exploited using traditional clustered FL, which affects the clustering accuracy more severely.

In this paper, we present a novel clustered multi-task federated learning framework named FedDSMIC. Under the assumption of a realistic cluster structure, FedDSMIC reformulates the problem as an alternating minimization (AM) approach in the distributed setting, which optimizes the cluster assignment and minimizes the loss functions of the models alternatively. Specifically, FedDSMIC clusters clients based on Kullback-Leibler divergence between models' probability output distribution with respect to indicator samples on the server, which accurately detects the similarity of client-level underlying data distributions. Inspired by Model-Agnostic Meta-Learning (MAML), the goal of FedDSMIC is to learn the cluster model as a good initial point shared between all clients in the cluster, which performs well after each client updates it with respect to its loss function. The current or new clients in the cluster can quickly get their personalized models by performing one or a few steps of gradient descent from the initial point. This approach keeps all the benefits of the clustered FL architecture and leads to more personalized models for each client.

We summarise our main contributions as:

- We propose a dynamic clustered federated learning framework, which clusters clients by detecting the client-level underlying distribution based on the model's parameter memory for the training data, improving the clustering accuracy in high data heterogeneity.
- We illustrate the limitation of sharing one model in the cluster and introduce a two-step learning method, which builds an initial center model to capture the intra-cluster common information and learns personalized models for each client to acquire unique features, improving the personalized model performance.
- Extensive experiments conducted on five real-world datasets demonstrate FedDSMIC outperforms other state-of-the-art methods with fewer communication rounds and computational consumption.

2   Related Work

Here, we mainly review the existing works from two aspects: classic federated learning and personalized federated learning.

2.1   Classic Federated Learning

The classic federated learning [33,40] trains a single global model to minimize an empirical risk function over the union of the data across all clients. However, various studies have shown that non-i.i.d. decentralized data leads to statistical challenges such as model weights divergence [44], data distribution biases [16], and a drifted global model that is slow to converge even unguaranteed convergence [27]. Li *et al.* [27] proposed FedProx, which adds a proximal term to the local objective function to reduce the gap between local and global models. SCAFFOLD [20] introduces control variates to correct the client drift in its local updates. FedGen [46] sets a generator on the server to ensemble client information and regulate local training using the learned knowledge. While the above work focus on building a robust global model across non-i.i.d. data, they do not directly address local model performance relevant to individual clients.

2.2   Personalized Federated Learning

Global Model Personalization. A natural approach for personalized FL is learning a global model and fine-tuning parameters on each client's local dataset [1,9,29,30,41]. The global model serves as a starting point for a few-shot adaptation for each client. Therefore, a class of algorithms referred to as meta-learning has been developed to train a more suitable global model for local customization [6,11,18,21]. Interpolation of global and local model [15,24,29] build personalized models for clients by combining the global model and the local model. A good global model is critical, as the personalization performance directly depends on the generalization performance of the global model. Unfortunately, it is difficult to obtain a good global model in high data heterogeneity.

Learning Personalized Models. Multi-Task federated learning methods treat clients as different tasks and train personalized models for each client. Simth *et al.* [39] proposed MOCHA that adds a penalization term to capture relationships between clients. However, it only learns simple models because of the complex penalization term. Other MTL-based approaches [17,26] are able to train more general models at the cost of considering simpler penalization terms. Therefore, it is tricky to optimize the complex objective function, and all of them lack statistical assumptions about local data distributions.

Clustered FL assumes that the clients can be partitioned into k clusters, representing k different distributions. CFL [38] recursively separate clients with incongruent optimization directions by the cosine similarity of the parameter updates. FedSEM [42] uses a l_2 distance-based stochastic expectation maximization (EM) algorithm, which ignores l_2 distance often suffer in high-dimension, low-sample-size (HDLSS) situation [37]. Briggs *et al.* [3] propose an agglomerative hierarchical clustering method named FL+HC, which relies on iterative calculating the pairwise distance between all clusters. The above parameter-based similarity measures always fail to cluster clients correctly because of the permutation invariance of NN parameters, i.e., for any given NN, many variants of it only differ in the ordering of parameters. To overcome the drawback, IFCA [14,29] divides the clients into clusters with a center model that can minimize their loss values while requiring each client to train all k global models per round. Therefore, the computational and communication efficiency will become bottlenecks when IFCA is applied to a large-scale FL system.

Our clustering method is similar to IFCA but allows clustering on the server for less communication. We focus on detecting the client's underlying data distribution without explicitly using model parameters. Finally, unlike previous work, we learn a personalization model for each client based on the center model to cope with more complicated heterogeneous data.

3   Preliminaries

Consider M clients, each client i has a private labeled dataset $\mathcal{Z} = \{z_i^{(n)} = (x_i^{(n)}, y_i^{(n)})_{n=1}^{n_i}\}$, where n_i is the training dataset size of client i. It is generated according to the local distribution $\mathcal{D}_i = \{\mathcal{X}_i, \mathcal{Y}_i\}$, where $\mathcal{X}_i$ and $\mathcal{Y}_i$ denote the input features and corresponding labels, respectively. Each private dataset $\mathcal{Z}_i$ will be used to train a local supervised learning model $w_i : \mathcal{X}_i \rightarrow \mathcal{Y}_i$. We define $f_i : \mathbb{R}^d \rightarrow \mathbb{R}$ as the expected loss over the data distribution with respect to client i, i.e.,

$$f_i(w) := \mathbb{E}_{(x,y) \sim \mathcal{D}_i}[l_i(w_i; x, y)] \tag{1}$$

where $w_i \in \mathbb{R}^d$ is the parameter space, $l_i(w_i; x, y)$ is the error of model w_i in predicting the true label $y \in \mathcal{Y}_i$ given the input $x \in \mathcal{X}_i$. The goal of vanilla FL (FedAvg) is to solve the objective function

$$\min_{w \in \mathbb{R}^d} F(w) := \sum_{i=1}^{M} \frac{n_i}{n} f_i(w). \tag{2}$$

where $n = \sum_{i=1}^{M} n_i$ is the total training dataset size. FedAvg optimizes (2) by the local updates of clients and the aggregation of the server alternately. At each communication round t, the server broadcasts the latest global model w^t to all clients and selects a random subset M_t of M clients to participate in this round. Client i optimizes the loss function based on the local data by its local solver (SGD) with several iterations or epochs and gets the updated local model w_i^{t+1}. Then, the server takes a weighted average of all local resulting model parameters $\{w_1^{t+1}, w_2^{t+1}, ..., w_{M_t}^{t+1}\}$ into a global one w^{t+1} and finish the current round. However, the different distributions of the local data $\mathcal{D}_i$ lead to different local model parameters, failing to converge to a stable optimal global solution w.

The existing clustered FL framework usually assumes that clients can be clustered into several groups to address the data heterogeneity. Besides, clients in the cluster share the same data distribution and optimization goal.

4   Framework

4.1   Problem Formulation

We assume a non-i.i.d. data distribution with a clustering structure: the data distribution of clients in a cluster is similar but still different, which we discussed in the Introduction. Under this assumption, we aim first to build several clusters and learn the initial center models to capture the intra-cluster common information, then learn personalized models for each client to discover knowledge different from others in the cluster. Specifically, we formulate a clustered multi-task federated learning problem as follows:

$$\min_{\{w_i\},\{\widetilde{w}_c\},\{u_i^c\}} \sum_{c=1}^{C} L_c(\widetilde{w}_c) - \sum_{c=1}^{C}\sum_{i=1}^{M} u_i^c S(w_i, \widetilde{w}_c) \tag{3}$$

$$L_c(\widetilde{w}_c) = \sum_{i=1}^{M_c}\sum_{n=1}^{n_i} l_i(w_i; \mathbf{x}_i^{(n)}, y_i^{(n)}), i \in G_c \tag{4}$$

where M is the number of total clients, M_c is the number of clients in cluster G_c, C is the number of clusters. $\widetilde{w}_c$ is the parameters of the center model for cluster G_c. In addition, $S(w_i, \widetilde{w}_c)$ denotes the similarity of local model w_i and the center model $\widetilde{w}_c$. $\{u_i^c\}$ denotes the cluster assignment, with $u_i^c = 1$ if the clients C_i belongs to cluster G_c and $u_i^c = 0$ otherwise.

In the above formulation, the first term (4) is the sum of loss functions of all center models, and the loss of each center model is given by the sum of empirical errors across all clients in this cluster. The second term is the sum of similarities between local models and center models, which can be seen as K-means clustering to maximize the intra-cluster similarity. Here we have three variables $\{w_i\}, \{\widetilde{w}_c\}, \{u_i^c\}$ to be solved under federated settings. Alternating minimization [2] is the general approach to solving such a non-convex optimization problem. Specifically, we minimize the loss functions based on w_i and $\widetilde{w}_c$, and estimate the cluster assignment u_i^c by alternatively fixing one and optimizing another until convergence.

We elaborate our alternating optimization with a formal shown in Algorithm 1. As shown in Fig. 2, FedDSMIC is a dynamic clustered federated learning with four main processes. FedDSMIC starts with C randomly initialized center models and M local models. At each communication round t, each participating client i updates locally and sends the local model w_i^{t+1} to the server. The server computes the similarity of clients based on Kullback-Leibler divergence between the predictions of local models $\{w_1^{t+1}, w_2^{t+1}, ..., w_{M_t}^{t+1}\}$ and center models $\{\widetilde{w}_1^t, ..., \widetilde{w}_c^t\}$ on "indicator samples". Then the server updates u_i^c and clusters clients to maximize the intra-cluster similarity of the models. Finally, each center model $\widetilde{w}_c^t$ is updated by the weighted average of local models in this cluster to $\widetilde{w}_c^{t+1}$ and sent to the intra-cluster clients. After training T rounds, the personalized models of clients are obtained by performing one or a few gradient descents from their corresponding center model. FedDSMIC also allows new clients to get their personalized models easily. In Sect. 4.2 and Sect. 4.3, we present the optimization of cluster structure and the optimization of the models, respectively.

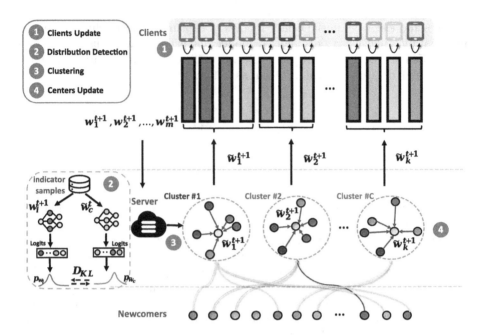

Fig. 2. An overview of FedDSMIC

4.2   Cluster Structure Optimization

Based on the guideline of FedDSMIC, we aim to first cluster the clients with similar data distribution into one group without access to the local data. When w_i and $\widetilde{w}_c$ is fixed, problem (3) w.r.t u_i^c can be seen as K-means clustering on the local's models. The crucial challenge is how to quantify the similarity of models for accurately clustering clients with similar underlying data distributions.

Similarity of Models. To tackle the challenge, we leverage the memory (learned parameters) of the model and get the similarity of models from the underlying data distribution on which it is trained. Knowledge distillation performs knowledge transfer by reducing the distance between the predicted output probability distribution of the student model and the teacher model on the same dataset [43]. Inspired by this, we set up some "indicator samples" on the server and then feed the samples into the model to get predictions to reflect the training data distribution of the model. The assumption for the distribution of "indicator samples" is independent and identically distributed. In the experiment, the samples are randomly sampled from the raw dataset (e.g., 10 samples per class) before partitioning the client data. In practice, these samples can be sampled from the relevant public datasets or a small sharing of datasets from clients under the premise of privacy protection. In addition, we will demonstrate the effect of indicator sample size on describing clients in Sect. 5.

Algorithm 1. FedDSMIC

1: **Input:** numbers of clusters C, initialize $\{\widetilde{w}_c\}_{c=1}^C$, $\{w_i\}_{i=1}^M$, number of communication rounds T
2: **Output:** $\{w_i\}_{i=1}^M, \{\widetilde{w}_c\}_{c=1}^C$
3: **for** $t = 0, ..., T$ **do**
4:     $M_t \leftarrow$ random subset of M clients
5:     **Clients:**
6:     **for** each client $i \in M_t$ **in parallel do**
7:         $w_i^{t+1} \leftarrow$ **ClientUpdate**(i, w_i^t)
8:     **end for**
9:     **Server:**
10:     **for** each cluster $c = 1, ..., C$ **do**
11:         Calculate $Dis(w_i^{t+1}, \widetilde{w}_c^t)$ as in (6)
12:         Update u_i^c using $Dis(w_i^{t+1}, \widetilde{w}_c^t)$ as in (7)
13:     **end for**
14:     Group devices into G_c using u_i^c
15:     Update $\widetilde{w}_c^{t+1}$ by $\widetilde{w}_c^{t+1} = \sum_{i=1}^{M_c} \frac{n_i}{n_c} w_i^{t+1}, i \in G_c$
16:     **for** each cluster $c = 1, ..., C$ **do**
17:         **for** $i \in$ cluster G_c **do**
18:             Send $\widetilde{w}_c^{t+1}$ to client i
19:         **end for**
20:     **end for**
21: **end for**

Algorithm 2. ClientUpdate

1: **Input:** the corresponding cluster center model from server $\widetilde{w}_c^t \rightarrow w_i^{t,0}$
2: **Output:** w_i^{t+1}
3: $\mathcal{B} \leftarrow$ split D_i into batches of size $\mathcal{B}$
4: **for** k: 1 to τ **do**
5:     Set $\widehat{w}_i^{t+1,k+1} = w_i^{t+1,k} - \eta\widetilde{\nabla}l_i\left(w_i^{t+1,k}, D_i^k\right)$
6:     Set $w_i^{t+1,k+1} = w_i^{t+1,k} - \varepsilon\widetilde{\nabla}l_i\left(\widehat{w}_i^{t+1,k+1}, D_i^{'k}\right)$
7: **end for**
8: $w_i^{t+1} = w_i^{t+1,\tau}$

Let p^k be the probability belonging to each class k for an input sample x given by a neural network w, which is computed as:

$$p_w^k(x) = \frac{\exp\left(z_1^k\right)}{\sum_{k=1}^K \exp\left(z_1^k\right)} \tag{5}$$

where the logit z^k is the output of the pre-softmax layer of model w on the data x. The final layer of a recognition model is a fully connected layer with a softmax non-linearity. Each neuron in this layer corresponds to a class k, and its activation value is treated as the probability that the model predicts for that class. The weights connecting the previous layer to this neuron w^k can be considered the template of the label k learned by the network [35]. The predicted label probability is proportional to the alignment of the pre-final layer's output with the template w^k. In other words, the value of trained weights w^k increases with the marginal density of label-k training data $p(y)^k$. Furthermore, the trained model has a higher probability of predicting the label-k sample as class k.

Therefore, we leverage the output probability distribution of the model to approximate the data distribution on which it was trained. To quantify the distance of the local model's and center model's predictions, we use the Kullback Leibler (KL) Divergence. The KL distance from p_{w_i} of the local model $\boldsymbol{w}_i$ to $p_{\widetilde{w}_c}$ of the center model $\widetilde{\boldsymbol{w}}_c$ is computed as:

$$
D_{\mathrm{KL}}[\sigma(f(\boldsymbol{w}_i, \boldsymbol{x}_o)), \sigma(f(\widetilde{\boldsymbol{w}}_c, \boldsymbol{x}_o))]
$$

$$
= \sum_{n_o=1}^{N_o} \sigma(f(\boldsymbol{w}_i, \boldsymbol{x}_o)) log \frac{\sigma(f(\boldsymbol{w}_i, \boldsymbol{x}_o))}{\sigma(f(\widetilde{\boldsymbol{w}}_c, \boldsymbol{x}_o))} \tag{6}
$$

$$
= \sum_{n_o=1}^{N_o} \sum_{k=1}^{K} p_{w_i}^k(\boldsymbol{x}_o) log \frac{p_{w_i}^k(\boldsymbol{x}_o)}{p_{\widetilde{w}_c}^k(\boldsymbol{x}_o)}
$$

where the logits $f(\boldsymbol{w}, \boldsymbol{x}_o)$ is the output of the pre-softmax layer of model $\boldsymbol{w}$ on the indicator samples $\boldsymbol{x}_o$. σ is the non-linear activation (usually the softmax function for multi-class classification) applied to such logits. N_o is the number of indicator samples, and K is the number of classes (labels).

Cluster Identity Estimation. The server computes the KL divergence between local models and center models by (6), and obtain a KL divergence matrix $Dis \in \mathbb{R}^{M \times C}$, with $Dis_{i,j} = D_{\mathrm{KL}}[\sigma(f(\boldsymbol{w}_i, \boldsymbol{x}_o)), \sigma(f(\widetilde{\boldsymbol{w}}_j, \boldsymbol{x}_o))]$. As the smaller $Dis_{i,j}$ corresponds to the greater similarity $S(\boldsymbol{w}_i, \widetilde{\boldsymbol{w}}_j)$ in (3), the server updates the cluster assignment vector $\boldsymbol{u}_i^c$ by (7).

$$
\boldsymbol{u}_i^c = \begin{cases} 1, & \text{if } c = \mathrm{argmin}_j \, Dis_{i,j} \\ 0, & \text{otherwise} \end{cases} \tag{7}
$$

The efficiency analysis of our clustering method is as follows. Suppose the time of model inference is t, the total number of parameters of the model is d.

- **Computation.** In FedDSMIC, the time to get the probability distributions is $(M+C)*t$. In IFCA, the time to estimate the cluster identities is $M*C*t$ (each client trains C global models locally). The time complexity of FedDSMIC constantly grows with the number of clients M, while IFCA grows linearly. Therefore, our method has lower computational complexity, especially when M is large.
- **Communication.** In FedDSMIC, the server sends the cluster model to the corresponding clients in this cluster and receives M local models, so the traffic per round is $(M+M)*d$. In IFCA, the server sends C cluster models to each client, so the traffic per round is $(C*M+M)*d$, which is $(1+C)/2$ times more than ours. As the modern neural network model grows, the communication consumption of IFCA will increase.

4.3   Model Weights Optimization

Now $\{u_i^c\}$ is fixed, the optimization of local models $\{w_i\}$ and center models $\{\widetilde{w}_c\}$ are as follows. The goal of FedDSMIC is to find a good initial cluster center model for representing the common information in this cluster. The cluster model performs well on all the clients in the cluster after each client updates it with respect to local data. We use one step of gradient descent from the initial model for computational efficiency. Therefore, the first term (4) in (3) can be rewritten as

$$L_c\left(\boldsymbol{w}\right) = \sum_{i=1}^{M_c} \sum_{n=1}^{n_i} l_i\left(\boldsymbol{w} - \alpha \nabla l_i\left(\boldsymbol{w}\right); \mathbf{x}_i^{(n)}, y_i^{(n)}\right) \tag{8}$$

for all $c \in C$. The optimal solution of $\boldsymbol{w}$ of $L_c\left(\boldsymbol{w}\right)$ is the learned cluster center model $\widetilde{w}_c$. Equation (8) maintains the advantages of clustered FL, and further captures the difference between the clients in the cluster. To solve (8), we redefined the local function of client C_i as

$$g_i(\boldsymbol{w}) := l_i\left(\boldsymbol{w} - \eta \nabla l_i(\boldsymbol{w})\right) \tag{9}$$

where η is the learning rate. The gradient of $g_i(\boldsymbol{w}_i)$ is computed as

$$\nabla g_i(\boldsymbol{w}) = \left(I - \eta \nabla^2 l_i(\boldsymbol{w})\right) \nabla l_i\left(\boldsymbol{w} - \eta \nabla l_i(\boldsymbol{w})\right) \tag{10}$$

For computationally efficient, we use the first-order approximations of (10), i.e., the second-order gradient $\nabla^2 l_i(\boldsymbol{w})$ is approximated to zero. Then Eq. (10) can be rewritten as

$$\nabla g_i(\boldsymbol{w}) = \nabla l_i\left(\boldsymbol{w} - \eta \nabla l_i(\boldsymbol{w})\right) \tag{11}$$

Similar to Stochastic Gradient Descent (SGD), we take a batch of data $\mathcal{D}_i$ to obtain the unbiased estimate $\widetilde{\nabla} l_i(\boldsymbol{w})$ of $\nabla l_i(\boldsymbol{w})$

$$\widetilde{\nabla} l_i\left(\boldsymbol{w}\right) := \frac{1}{|\mathcal{D}_i|} \sum_{(\boldsymbol{x}, y) \in \mathcal{D}_i} \nabla l_i(\boldsymbol{w}; \boldsymbol{x}, y). \tag{12}$$

At each communication round t, the server sends the cluster center model $\widetilde{w}_c^t$ to the corresponding clients in this cluster. Each client C_i in the cluster sets the initial parameters of the local model $\boldsymbol{w}_i^{t+1,0} = \widetilde{w}_c^t$. Then client C_i performs τ steps of stochastic gradient descent locally with respect to g_i. The number of local iterations is τ, then the local updates sequence $\left\{\boldsymbol{w}_i^{t+1,k}\right\}_{k=0}^{\tau}$ are updated by

$$\boldsymbol{w}_i^{t+1,k+1} = \boldsymbol{w}_i^{t+1,k} - \varepsilon \widetilde{\nabla} g_i\left(\boldsymbol{w}_i^{t+1,k}\right) \tag{13}$$

where ε is the local learning rate, $\widetilde{\nabla} g_i\left(\boldsymbol{w}_i^{t+1,k}\right)$ is an estimate of $\nabla g_i\left(\boldsymbol{w}_i^{t+1,k}\right)$ in (11). The stochastic gradient $\widetilde{\nabla} g_i\left(\boldsymbol{w}_i^{t+1,k}\right)$ for all local iterates is computed using independent batches $D_i^k, D_i'^k$ as follows

$$\widetilde{\nabla} g_i\left(\boldsymbol{w}_i^{t+1,k}\right) = \widetilde{\nabla} l_i\left(\boldsymbol{w}_i^{t+1,k} - \eta \widetilde{\nabla} l_i\left(\boldsymbol{w}_i^{t+1,k}, D_i^k\right), D_i'^k\right). \tag{14}$$

Actually, the updates in (13) can be implemented in two stages: first, we compute the first-order update value $\widehat{\boldsymbol{w}}_i^{t+1,k+1}$ as in (15), and then compute the final updated value $\boldsymbol{w}_i^{t+1,k+1}$ as in (16)

$$\widehat{\boldsymbol{w}}_i^{t+1,k+1} = \boldsymbol{w}_i^{t+1,k} - \eta \widetilde{\nabla} l_i \left(\boldsymbol{w}_i^{t+1,k}, D_i^k \right) \tag{15}$$

$$\boldsymbol{w}_i^{t+1,k+1} = \boldsymbol{w}_i^{t+1,k} - \varepsilon \widetilde{\nabla} l_i \left(\widehat{\boldsymbol{w}}_i^{t+1,k+1}, D_i^{'k} \right) \tag{16}$$

The steps of client local update are depicted in Algorithm 2. Our solution procedure follows the previous work [10–12] with convergence guarantees. After the local models are updated, each cluster model is obtained by the weighted average of the client models in this cluster as:

$$\widetilde{\boldsymbol{w}}_c^{t+1} = \sum_{i=1}^{M_c} \frac{n_i}{n_c} \boldsymbol{w}_i^{t+1}, i \in G_c \tag{17}$$

where n_c is the total data size of cluster G_c. Benefit from the properties of meta-learning [12], FedDSMIC allows an unseen client, i.e., a client $C_{new} \notin [M]$ arriving after the distributed training procedure, to easily learn its personalized model. Each new client simply first train on its local dataset for a few epochs and choose the most similar cluster center model through (6) and (7). Then the client obtains its personalized model by performing one or few steps with respect to its local data.

5   Experiments

5.1   Datasets and Baselines

Datasets and Models. We evaluate our algorithm on five federated benchmark datasets: handwritten digits recognition (MNIST [25]), handwritten characters recognition (EMNIST [7] and FEMNIST [5]), and image classification (CIFAR10 and CIFAR100 [23]). We train a convex multinomial logistic regression (MCLR) model on MNIST, a CNN in LEAF [5] on EMNIST and FEMNIST, and MobileNet-v2 [36] on CIFAR10 and CIFAR100. Table 1 summarizes datasets, models, and the number of clients. For all datasets, we randomly split each local dataset into training (80%) and test (20%) sets.

Table 1. Datasets and models setting

Dataset	Clients	Total samples	Model
MNIST [25]	100	70000	MCLR
EMNIST [7]	100	81415	2-layer CNN + 2-layer FFN
FEMNIST [5]	287	61049	2-layer CNN + 2-layer FFN
CIFAR10 [23]	80	30000	MobileNet-v2 [36]
CIFAR100 [23]	125	30000	MobileNet-v2 [36]

Baselines

- Local: To make the experiment more comprehensive, we report the performance of a naive personalized method named Local that trains only on the local dataset without collaboration.
- FedAvg [33]: the vanilla federated learning framework.
- FedProx [27]: a popular federated learning optimizer which adds a quadratic penalty term to the local objective.
- IFCA [14]: a hypothesis-based CFL framework that client selects the model with minimal empirical loss.
- FedSEM [42]: an l_2 distance-based CFL framework that minimizes the expectation of discrepancies between local models and center models stochastically.
- PerFedAvg [11]: a personalized method that finds one initial shared model for all clients.
- FedDS: clustering-only of our method that the clients in a cluster share the same model.

5.2   Experimental Setting

Client Heteroeneity. For FEMNIST, the raw data is naturally non-i.i.d distributed since writers who write the same words have different stroke widths. For MNIST, EMNIST, CIFAR10 and CIFAR100, similar to prior arts [17,31], we simulate a data distribution with a clustered structure that satisfies our assumption. First we divide all classes (labels) to C clusters, and then simulate a heterogeneous partition into M clients by sampling $p_c \sim Dir_I(\alpha)$ and allocating a $p_{c,i}$ proportion of the training instances of cluster c to local client i, in which a smaller α indicates higher data heterogeneity. The clients in the same cluster have relatively similar data distributions but are different from each other. We visualize the effects of adopting different α on the statistical heterogeneity for the MNIST dataset with M = 20 in Fig. 3.

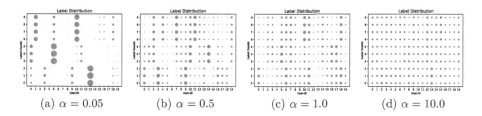

    (a) $\alpha = 0.05$ (b) $\alpha = 0.5$ (c) $\alpha = 1.0$ (d) $\alpha = 10.0$

Fig. 3. Visualization of a realistic cluster structure simulation among clients on MNIST dataset, where the x-axis indicates client IDs, the y-axis indicates class labels, and the size of scattered points indicates the number of training samples for a label available to that client.

Implementation. Unless otherwise mentioned, the number of clusters is 3 for all cluster-based methods, and all clients participate in each round, training occurred over 300 communication rounds for MNIST and FEMNIST, and 200 rounds for all other datasets. We use the learning rate 0.01, the mini-batch size $B = 32$, the local updating steps $\tau = 20$ and SGD with momentum $= 0.9$ for all algorithms. In addition, we extract a piece of data from each class of the dataset as indicator samples before assigning the data to the client.

Evaluation Metrics. Like previous research on personalized federated learning [11,39], we evaluate the performance of each personalized model on the local test dataset. In FedAvg and FedProx, we evaluate the global model based on the test set of all clients. In IFCA and FedSEM, we evaluate the cluster center model based on the test set of the clients in this cluster. Given the multiple accuracies of clients with different data sizes, we report the average weighted accuracy with weights proportional to local dataset sizes. Note that the heterogeneity will affect the convergence, resulting in more significant fluctuations in model accuracy during the training process. Therefore, we report the average of the top-5 test accuracy rates.

5.3 Effectiveness of Proposed Framework

Average Performance of Personalized Models. The comparison results with respect to the average performance of personalized models are shown in Table 2 and Fig. 4. We have the following findings from the results:

- Overall, FedDSMIC obtains the best performance across all datasets and has the most rapid learning curves. Notably, FedDSMIC improves test accuracy by around 3% to 5% on handwritten digit recognition tasks while improving accuracy more than by +10% on CIFAR10 and CIFAR100, which are more complex classification tasks. The results demonstrate the effectiveness of FedDSMIC, especially when the data distribution is highly complicated.
- As one of the most competitive baselines, IFCA can achieve similar performance to FedDS in specific settings, but the convergence is slower than FedDS. This result implies that our method fully leverages information about underlying data distribution, whose effect is more explicit.
- FedSEM performs worst in all settings compared with FedDSMIC and IFCA, which can be interpreted as failing to cluster clients correctly. FeSEM always clusters all clients into a group. Therefore, it has been downgraded to one optimization direction and behaves similarly to FedAvg.

Table 2. Average test accuracy across clients/bottom test accuracy under different settings. For MNIST and EMNIST, a smaller α indicates higher heterogeneity. For FEMNIST, r denotes the ratio between active users and total users. For CIFAR10 and CIFAR100, τ denotes the local training steps, E denotes the local training epochs.

Dataset	Setting	Local	FedAvg	FedProx	IFCA	FedSEM	PerFedAvg	FedDS	FedDSMIC
MNIST	$\alpha = 0.05$	94.0/65.5	89.7/76.7	89.6/76.7	92.8/75.3	90.6/72.1	92.0/77.4	92.5/75.0	**94.2/79.0**
	$\alpha = 0.5$	88.9/73.5	90.0/83.4	90.7/83.4	90.7/84.8	90.1/82.2	91.5/85.0	91.5/82.9	**92.5/86.0**
	$\alpha = 1.0$	87.5/68.3	90.4/84.2	90.3/84.0	90.7/83.1	90.4/84.1	91.8/**86.6**	90.7/84.2	**92.0**/85.4
EMNIST	$\alpha = 0.05$	90.1/48.4	86.6/76.5	85.7/81.3	92.3/72.7	84.6/77.0	92.0/84.1	92.7/82.1	**93.2/84.4**
	$\alpha = 0.5$	78.6/31.2	88.0/80.9	87.6/79.3	89.1/80.7	87.7/81.9	88.9/81.9	89.4/80.2	**90.7/83.0**
	$\alpha = 1.0$	75.2/55.9	87.6/82.5	87.0/81.7	87.1/80.8	87.5/82.5	88.2/**84.6**	88.9/83.9	**89.0**/84.1
FEMNIST	r = 0.2	69.2/50.8	81.7/64.2	81.5/63.1	**87.7/67.2**	79.8/63.8	83.8/72.3	87.2/65.7	87.4/67.1
	r = 0.5	69.4/47.7	84.0/53.8	82.5/48.1	87.1/67.5	83.4/59.4	86.8/67.4	87.0/62.3	**87.1/68.0**
	r = 1.0	69.5/48.6	83.9/51.0	82.3/45.1	87.0/67.3	84.1/56.0	86.8/67.9	87.0/62.5	**87.4/68.2**
CIFAR10	$\tau = 10$	36.8/18.0	70.5/44.3	69.1/47.0	73.1/49.7	64.4/38.9	73.4/53.4	75.3/**56.4**	**75.5**/55.6
	$\tau = 20$	35.7/17.9	72.3/47.5	70.5/45.3	73.5/44.8	66.2/42.4	72.5/52.6	75.6/52.1	**76.2/60.5**
CIFAR100	E = 3	13.8/3.2	40.9/10.0	39.1/10.9	42.7/9.6	39.9/7.0	41.1/6.2	42.7/7.8	**44.9/11.2**
	E = 6	13.1/4.5	41.8/10.8	36.6/10.5	43.9/10.5	40.5/8.9	40.9/3.4	43.7/9.2	**44.8/11.6**

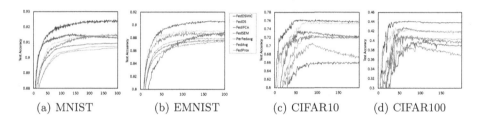

(a) MNIST   (b) EMNIST   (c) CIFAR10   (d) CIFAR100

Fig. 4. Average test accuracy vs. communication rounds on MNIST, EMNIST, CIFAR10, CIFAR100, $\alpha = 0.5$ for all datasets, $C = 3$ for FedDSMIC, FedDS, IFCA and FeSEM.

Fairness Across Clients. This work discusses heterogeneous data scenarios in horizontal federated learning, so we mainly focus on performance fairness, i.e., accuracy is evenly distributed among clients [45]. Unfair performance could result from learning excellent models for some clients at the expense of poor models for other clients [31]. Consequently, we show the average of the five worst accuracies called bottom accuracy in Table 2 (the minimum accuracy is particularly noisy when some local datasets are too small). FedDSMIC ensures that clients with the worst personalized model are better than other methods.

Generalization to Unseen Clients. Table 3 shows that FedDSMIC allows new clients to learn a personalized model and consistently outperforms other CFL-based methods. As discussed in Sect. 4.3, FedDSMIC allows new clients arriving after the distributed training to learn their personalized models quickly. To evaluate the quality of unseen clients' personalized models, we performed an experiment where only 80% of the clients participate to the training. The remaining 20% join the system after training and get their personalized model by our method.

Table 3. Average test accuracy across clients unseen at training

Dataset	FedAvg	IFCA	FedSEM	FedDMIC
MNIST	90.92	90.62	88.93	**91.52**
EMNIST	81.89	81.71	82.56	**86.18**
FEMNIST	73.84	74.76	72.94	**75.75**
CIFAR10	35.59	36.89	42.45	**57.74**
CIFAR100	13.8	14.37	10.26	**15.43**

Communication Consumption. As shown in Fig. 5, FedDSMIC has the lowest communication consumption and highest accuracy on different network structures. FedDSMIC and FedSEM perform cluster estimation on the server side without sending additional models, therefore having the same traffic as FedAvg. As discussed in Sect. 4.2, IFCA requires the server to send all center models to each client, thus consuming the most communication.

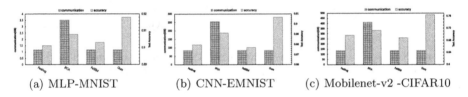

(a) MLP-MNIST   (b) CNN-EMNIST   (c) Mobilenet-v2 -CIFAR10

Fig. 5. Communication consumption of FL frameworks on different network structures for 300 rounds.

5.4   Sensitivity Analysis

Impacts of Data Heterogeneity. As shown in Fig. 6, FedDSMIC performs better than others under various data heterogeneity settings, and the gain of FedDSMIC is more notable when the data distributions are highly heterogeneous (with a small α). This result verifies our motivations since the advantage of FedDSMIC is building personalized models for each client based on its corresponding cluster model, which mitigates the data heterogeneity. This advantage is otherwise not obtained by other baselines. For MNIST, Per-FedAvg has the best performance at the i.i.d setting ($\alpha = 10$) because it may utilize information from more training data. For the more complex dataset EMNIST, the performance gain of our approach is consistently significant, which verifies the robustness of our method to fit complex distributions.

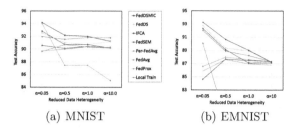

(a) MNIST

(b) EMNIST

Fig. 6. Performance w.r.t data heterogeneity.

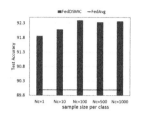

Fig. 7. Effects of indicator samples on MNIST with $\alpha = 0.5$.

Effects of the Indicator Sample Size. We test the effect of FedDSMIC with different indicator sample sizes on MNIST as in Fig. 7. N_c is the number of samples per class. The gain of FedDSMIC over FedAvg is consistently remarkable given different indicator sample sizes, whereas a sufficient number of indicator samples brings better performance. The model accuracy is high enough when $N_c = 1$, proving that it is acceptable to distinguish different customers despite the small sample size. When N_c reaches 100, the performance tends to stabilize.

Impacts of Straggler Clients. We explore different numbers of total clients versus active clients on FEMNIST, with active ratios of 0.2, 0.5, and 1.0, respectively. Figure 8 that FedDSMIC consistently outperforms all baselines under various active client settings. Combined with Fig. 8(a),(b), and (c), we can observe that our approach requires much fewer communication rounds to reach the same performance, regardless of the setting of straggler clients.

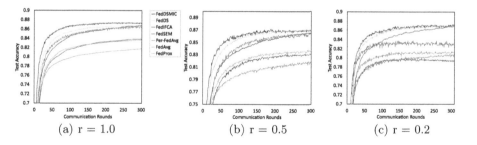

(a) r = 1.0

(b) r = 0.5

(c) r = 0.2

Fig. 8. Average test accuracy vs. communication rounds on FEMNIST w.r.t different ratio of straggler clients

Effects of Communication Frequency: We explore local updating steps τ and local epochs E for CIFAR10 and CIFAR100, respectively. The higher τ or E means longer communication delays before global communication. As shown in the last two rows of Table 2, our approach is robust against different levels of communication delays.

5.5   Ablation Results

We set up ablation experiments to explore the role of the two points. FedDS (clustering-only of our method) and FedDSMIC are shown in the last two columns of Table 2. The results indicate that FedDS is already better than other cluster FL methods, especially the faster convergence speed (Fig. 4 and Fig. 8), which demonstrates our similarity calculation method detects the data distribution to cluster accurately. FedDSMIC can further improve performance by building personalized models for clients, especially under complicated data distribution.

5.6   Discussion

Finally, we visualize the feature representations of the training data via client-side models on CIFAR10 obtained by Local, FedAvg, and FedDSMIC, respectively. There are two types of clients. One is shown in Fig. 9, which has enough local data to train its model. The performance of FedAvg degrades because the global model does not fit the local data distribution. In contrast, the client model obtained with FedDSMIC can benefit clients with similar data distributions. Therefore, the feature representation of the client model is looser than the local-trained model under the premise of ensuring good classification ability, i.e., the model's generalization will be more robust. The other is shown in Fig. 10, whose local data is insufficient to train a good model. Although FedAvg performs better than Local, the accuracy is still low due to heterogeneous data distribution. Whereas FedDSMIC can get an excellent personalized model that fits the data distribution nearly perfectly, leading to better generalization.

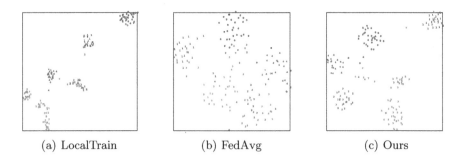

(a) LocalTrain   (b) FedAvg   (c) Ours

Fig. 9. The visualization of feature representations of 59-th local model with t-SNE for CIFAR10.

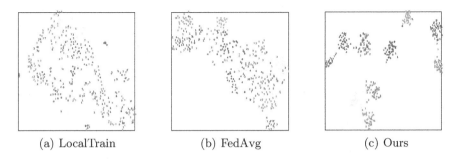

(a) LocalTrain   (b) FedAvg   (c) Ours

Fig. 10. The visualization of feature representations of 17-th local model with t-SNE for CIFAR10.

6   Conclusion

In this paper, we proposed a new clustered multi-task framework based on the assumption of a realistic cluster structure to address client heterogeneity. Our algorithm detected the local underlying data distribution by the trained model's memory to cluster similar clients. Furthermore, we learned personalized models for each client based on the initial cluster model to address the limitations of existing clustered FL. Extensive empirical evaluation has shown that our approach trained models with higher accuracy, fairness, and lower resource consumption than state-of-the-art FL algorithms, even for clients not present at training time.

Acknowledgments. This work is supported by The National Key Research and Development Program of China No. 2021YFB3101400 and the Strategic Priority Research Program of Chinese Academy of Sciences, Grant No. XDC02040400.

References

1. Ben-David, S., Blitzer, J., Crammer, K., Kulesza, A., Pereira, F., Vaughan, J.W.: A theory of learning from different domains. Mach. Learn. **79**(1), 151–175 (2010)
2. Bezdek, J.C., Hathaway, R.J.: Some notes on alternating optimization. In: Pal, N.R., Sugeno, M. (eds.) AFSS 2002. LNCS (LNAI), vol. 2275, pp. 288–300. Springer, Heidelberg (2002). https://doi.org/10.1007/3-540-45631-7_39
3. Briggs, C., Fan, Z., Andras, P.: Federated learning with hierarchical clustering of local updates to improve training on non-IID data. In: 2020 International Joint Conference on Neural Networks (IJCNN), pp. 1–9. IEEE (2020)
4. Caldarola, D., Mancini, M., Galasso, F., Ciccone, M., Rodolà, E., Caputo, B.: Cluster-driven graph federated learning over multiple domains. In: Proceedings of the IEEE/CVF Conference on Computer Vision and Pattern Recognition, pp. 2749–2758 (2021)
5. Caldas, S., et al.: Leaf: a benchmark for federated settings. arXiv preprint arXiv:1812.01097 (2018)

6. Chen, F., Luo, M., Dong, Z., Li, Z., He, X.: Federated meta-learning with fast convergence and efficient communication. arXiv preprint arXiv:1802.07876 (2018)
7. Cohen, G., Afshar, S., Tapson, J., Van Schaik, A.: EMNIST: extending MNIST to handwritten letters. In: 2017 International Joint Conference on Neural Networks (IJCNN), pp. 2921–2926. IEEE (2017)
8. Corinzia, L., Beuret, A., Buhmann, J.M.: Variational federated multi-task learning. arXiv preprint arXiv:1906.06268 (2019)
9. Cortes, C., Mohri, M.: Domain adaptation and sample bias correction theory and algorithm for regression. Theoret. Comput. Sci. **519**, 103–126 (2014)
10. Fallah, A., Mokhtari, A., Ozdaglar, A.: On the convergence theory of gradient-based model-agnostic meta-learning algorithms. In: International Conference on Artificial Intelligence and Statistics, pp. 1082–1092. PMLR (2020)
11. Fallah, A., Mokhtari, A., Ozdaglar, A.: Personalized federated learning with theoretical guarantees: a model-agnostic meta-learning approach. Adv. Neural. Inf. Process. Syst. **33**, 3557–3568 (2020)
12. Finn, C., Abbeel, P., Levine, S.: Model-agnostic meta-learning for fast adaptation of deep networks. In: International Conference on Machine Learning, pp. 1126–1135. PMLR (2017)
13. French, R.M.: Catastrophic forgetting in connectionist networks. Trends Cogn. Sci. **3**(4), 128–135 (1999)
14. Ghosh, A., Chung, J., Yin, D., Ramchandran, K.: An efficient framework for clustered federated learning. Adv. Neural Inf. Process. Syst. **33**, 19586–19597 (2020)
15. Hanzely, F., Richtárik, P.: Federated learning of a mixture of global and local models. arXiv preprint arXiv:2002.05516 (2020)
16. Hsieh, K., Phanishayee, A., Mutlu, O., Gibbons, P.: The non-IID data quagmire of decentralized machine learning. In: International Conference on Machine Learning, pp. 4387–4398. PMLR (2020)
17. Huang, Y., et al.: Personalized cross-silo federated learning on non-IID data. In: AAAI, pp. 7865–7873 (2021)
18. Jiang, Y., Konečný, J., Rush, K., Kannan, S.: Improving federated learning personalization via model agnostic meta learning. arXiv preprint arXiv:1909.12488 (2019)
19. Kairouz, P., et al.: Advances and open problems in federated learning. Found. Trends® Mach. Learn. **14**(1–2), 1–210 (2021)
20. Karimireddy, S.P., Kale, S., Mohri, M., Reddi, S., Stich, S., Suresh, A.T.: Scaffold: stochastic controlled averaging for federated learning. In: International Conference on Machine Learning, pp. 5132–5143. PMLR (2020)
21. Khodak, M., Balcan, M.F.F., Talwalkar, A.S.: Adaptive gradient-based meta-learning methods. In: Advances in Neural Information Processing Systems, vol. 32 (2019)
22. Konečný, J., McMahan, H.B., Yu, F.X., Richtárik, P., Suresh, A.T., Bacon, D.: Federated learning: strategies for improving communication efficiency. arXiv preprint arXiv:1610.05492 (2016)
23. Krizhevsky, A.: Learning multiple layers of features from tiny images. Master's thesis, University of Tront (2009)
24. Kulkarni, V., Kulkarni, M., Pant, A.: Survey of personalization techniques for federated learning. In: 2020 Fourth World Conference on Smart Trends in Systems, Security and Sustainability (WorldS4), pp. 794–797. IEEE (2020)

25. LeCun, Y., Bottou, L., Bengio, Y., Haffner, P.: Gradient-based learning applied to document recognition. Proc. IEEE **86**(11), 2278–2324 (1998)

26. Li, T., Hu, S., Beirami, A., Smith, V.: Ditto: fair and robust federated learning through personalization. In: International Conference on Machine Learning, pp. 6357–6368. PMLR (2021)

27. Li, T., Sahu, A.K., Talwalkar, A., Smith, V.: Federated learning: challenges, methods, and future directions. IEEE Sig. Process. Mag. **37**(3), 50–60 (2020)

28. Li, T., Sahu, A.K., Zaheer, M., Sanjabi, M., Talwalkar, A., Smith, V.: Federated optimization in heterogeneous networks. Proc. Mach. Learn. Syst. **2**, 429–450 (2020)

29. Mansour, Y., Mohri, M., Ro, J., Suresh, A.T.: Three approaches for personalization with applications to federated learning. arXiv preprint arXiv:2002.10619 (2020)

30. Mansour, Y., Mohri, M., Rostamizadeh, A.: Domain adaptation: learning bounds and algorithms. arXiv preprint arXiv:0902.3430 (2009)

31. Marfoq, O., Neglia, G., Bellet, A., Kameni, L., Vidal, R.: Federated multi-task learning under a mixture of distributions. In: Advances in Neural Information Processing Systems, vol. 34 (2021)

32. McCloskey, M., Cohen, N.J.: Catastrophic interference in connectionist networks: the sequential learning problem. In: Psychology of Learning and Motivation, vol. 24, pp. 109–165. Elsevier (1989)

33. McMahan, B., Moore, E., Ramage, D., Hampson, S., Arcas, B.A.: Communication-efficient learning of deep networks from decentralized data. In: Artificial intelligence and statistics, pp. 1273–1282. PMLR (2017)

34. Mohri, M., Sivek, G., Suresh, A.T.: Agnostic federated learning. In: International Conference on Machine Learning, pp. 4615–4625. PMLR (2019)

35. Nayak, G.K., Mopuri, K.R., Shaj, V., Radhakrishnan, V.B., Chakraborty, A.: Zero-shot knowledge distillation in deep networks. In: International Conference on Machine Learning, pp. 4743–4751. PMLR (2019)

36. Sandler, M., Howard, A., Zhu, M., Zhmoginov, A., Chen, L.C.: Mobilenetv 2: inverted residuals and linear bottlenecks. In: Proceedings of the IEEE Conference on Computer Vision and Pattern Recognition, pp. 4510–4520 (2018)

37. Sarkar, S., Ghosh, A.K.: On perfect clustering of high dimension, low sample size data. IEEE Trans. Pattern Anal. Mach. Intell. **42**(9), 2257–2272 (2019)

38. Sattler, F., Müller, K.R., Samek, W.: Clustered federated learning: model-agnostic distributed multitask optimization under privacy constraints. IEEE Trans. Neural Netw. Learn. Syst. **32**(8), 3710–3722 (2020)

39. Smith, V., Chiang, C.K., Sanjabi, M., Talwalkar, A.S.: Federated multi-task learning. In: Advances in Neural Information Processing Systems, vol. 30 (2017)

40. Wang, H., Yurochkin, M., Sun, Y., Papailiopoulos, D., Khazaeni, Y.: Federated learning with matched averaging. arXiv preprint arXiv:2002.06440 (2020)

41. Wang, K., Mathews, R., Kiddon, C., Eichner, H., Beaufays, F., Ramage, D.: Federated evaluation of on-device personalization. arXiv preprint arXiv:1910.10252 (2019)

42. Xie, M., et al.: Multi-center federated learning. arXiv preprint arXiv:2108.08647 (2021)

43. Zhang, Y., Xiang, T., Hospedales, T.M., Lu, H.: Deep mutual learning. In: Proceedings of the IEEE Conference on Computer Vision and Pattern Recognition, pp. 4320–4328 (2018)

44. Zhao, Y., Li, M., Lai, L., Suda, N., Civin, D., Chandra, V.: Federated learning with non-IID data. arXiv preprint arXiv:1806.00582 (2018)

45. Zhou, Z., Chu, L., Liu, C., Wang, L., Pei, J., Zhang, Y.: Towards fair federated learning. In: Proceedings of the 27th ACM SIGKDD Conference on Knowledge Discovery and Data Mining, pp. 4100–4101 (2021)
46. Zhu, Z., Hong, J., Zhou, J.: Data-free knowledge distillation for heterogeneous federated learning. In: International Conference on Machine Learning, pp. 12878–12889. PMLR (2021)

An Efficient Graph Accelerator with Distributed On-Chip Memory Hierarchy

Ran Zheng[1], Yingxin Jiang[1], Yibo Wang[1], Yongbo Su[1], Long Zheng[1,2(✉)], Pengcheng Yao[1,2], Xiaofei Liao[1], and Hai Jin[1]

[1] National Engineering Research Center for Big Data Technology and System/Services Computing Technology and System Lab/Cluster and Grid Computing Lab, School of Computer Science and Technology, Huazhong University of Science and Technology, Wuhan 430074, China
{zhraner,yxjiang,wyb,suyb,longzh,pcyao,xfliao,hjin}@hust.edu.cn
[2] Zhejiang Lab, Hangzhou 311121, China

Abstract. Graph processing has evolved and expanded swiftly with artificial intelligence and big data technology. *High-Bandwidth Memory* (HBM), which delivers terabyte-level memory bandwidth, has opened up new development possibilities for FPGA-based graph accelerators. However, despite the tremendous expansion of underlying hardware capabilities, existing graph accelerators have not benefited too much. In this paper, we observe that the uniformed on-chip memory hierarchy is the key to the low scalability of existing graph accelerators. We present a novel graph accelerator with a *distributed* on-chip memory hierarchy called GraphS. The on-chip memory of GraphS is divided into numerous tiny blocks, each of which is assigned to only one *Processing Element* (PE). Different PEs are connected through a scalable *network-on-chip* (NoC). For realistic graphs with power-law properties, a degree-aware preprocessing method is designed to balance the workload among different PEs. Our results with various graph algorithms demonstrate that GraphS can outperform state-of-the-art ForeGraph by up to 21.84×.

Keywords: Graph processing · Field-programmable gate array · High bandwidth memory

1 Introduction

For a variety of applications about graphs, such as route learning [1], social network analysis [2], autonomous driving [3], and machine learning [4], graph has been widely used to represent the connection relationship between different entities. With the continuous development of the Internet and cloud computing, the scale and complexity of graph data are expanding, which brings significant challenges to the performance and energy efficiency of modern graph processing systems [5].

© Springer Nature Switzerland AG 2023
W. Meng et al. (Eds.): ICA3PP 2022, LNCS 13777, pp. 773–787, 2023.
https://doi.org/10.1007/978-3-031-22677-9_42

At present, many algorithms [6,7] and systems [8,9] for graph computing have been proposed. However, some characteristics of large-scale graphs bring challenges. (1) **Load Unbalance.** The irregularity of the graph will lead to an extremely unbalanced load among different processing threads. (2) **Random Data Access Pattern.** The irregularity of the graph leads to unpredictable connections between vertices, which leads to a large number of random memory accesses. (3) **Heavy Data Conflicts.** When multiple vertices update a vertex simultaneously, it results in high-latency atomic update operations and heavy data conflicts. (4) **Lack of Scalability.** In large-scale graph processing, communication over PEs causes heavy hardware overhead. Thus, it becomes difficult to design a scalable graph accelerator.

Many approaches have been proposed in the past to address these issues. Most of them focus on addressing memory inefficiencies using sophisticated on-chip memory management strategies [10,11]. For example, Graphicionado [12] stores all data except edge data on-chip to eliminate all off-chip random accesses. These previous works achieve dozens of times improvement over traditional processors but do not consider the scalability of their on-chip memory hierarchy.

HBM has recently emerged, enabling terabytes per second memory bandwidth. However, the performance of graph accelerators has not kept pace with the rapid expansion of underlying hardware capabilities. The fundamental reason is that existing graph accelerators use an on-chip centralized memory hierarchy [13,14], which means that all PEs share the on-chip memory. A crossbar-like switch causes hardware overhead grows exponentially as the number of PEs grows. ScalaGraph [15] has experimented with existing graph accelerators. When the number of PEs reaches 128, Scalagraph found existing graph accelerators with the crossbar will see a severe frequency drop. Even worse, route failure will occur if the number of PEs surpasses 256.

This paper has made the following contributions:

(1) We build an efficient HBM-based graph accelerator called GraphS, which adopts the distributed memory design to build a dedicated graph processing architecture.
(2) We introduce the Omega network to reduce the hardware complexity of NoC significantly. The scalability of the accelerator is improved.
(3) We present a degree-aware preprocessing method to achieve load balance, with 1.3%–12.4% speedups against ForeGraph.

2   Background and Motivation

In this section, we first introduce the programming model of graph processing. Then we discuss the limitation of existing graph accelerators and finally introduce our approach.

2.1   Programming Model

The *Vertex-Centric Programming Model* (VCM) [16] is classic and most graph accelerators use it. Since there are extensive dependencies in graph data, it is

---

Algorithm 1 Vertex-Centric Programming Model

Input: The current iteration's active vertex set V_{active}, corresponding edges $E(v, u)$
Output: The next iteration's active vertex set V'_{active}
 1: **for** each *vertex* $v \in V_{active}$ **do**
 2: **for** each *edge* $E(v, u)$ *of active vertex* v **do**
 3:   $Res = \mathbf{Process}(E_{weight}, V_{prop}[v]);$
 4:   $V_{temp}[u] = \mathbf{Reduce}(V_{temp}[u], Res);$
 5: **end for**
 6: **end for**
 7: **for** each *vertex* v **do**
 8: $ApplyRes = \mathbf{Apply}(V_{prop}[v], V_{temp}[v], V_{const});$
 9: **if** $ApplyRes! = V_{prop}[v]$ **then**
10:   $V_{prop}[v] = ApplyRes;$
11:   $V'_{active}.push(u);$
12: **end if**
13: **end for**

---

essential to decouple these related dependencies by exploring the data characteristics around vertices or edges and designing a specific and compelling programming model.

Algorithm 1 shows a typical procedure using VCM. The whole process is divided into two stages: the scatter stage and the apply stage. In the scatter stage, the algorithm traverses all active points and their corresponding edges to update other vertices. In the apply stage, the algorithm traverses all vertices and updates their values one by one to generate active vertices.

2.2   Limitation of Existing Architecture

Figure 1(a) shows a typical architectural template of an existing FPGA-based graph accelerator [17]. The scheduler and the processor are divided into multiple *Scheduler Elements* (SEs) and *Processor Elements* (PEs) according to the number of pipelines. Due to the irregularity of the graph, the PE needs to transmit data with all on-chip *Memory Partitions* (MPs), which leads any two pairs of PE and MP to be connected. Existing graph accelerators often take on-chip and off-chip I/O efficiency as the focus of optimization. Thus, a fully connected NoC is often used as a switching structure, which minimizes the delay of on-chip message transfer. However, the uniformed memory hierarchy maintains high efficiency in on-chip memory access but does not consider its scalability.

Emerging 3D stacked memory offers at least an order of magnitude more memory bandwidth than the traditional DRAM. The significant increase in memory bandwidth provides an opportunity to develop a high throughput graph accelerator. However, the HBM subsystem of U280 supports up to 32 pseudo-channels, implying that at least 32 on-chip pipelines are required to utilize the HBM fully. Assuming that the PEs in the accelerator can process one edge per clock cycle, where one edge is represented by 4 bytes. An accelerator running at

250 MHz would require at least 460 PEs to utilize the aggregated bandwidth of 460 GB/s fully.

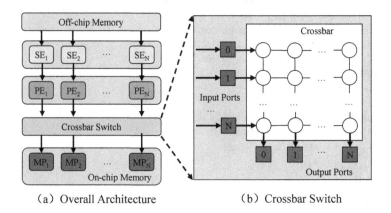

(a) Overall Architecture   (b) Crossbar Switch

Fig. 1. A typical graph accelerator architecture with uniformed on-chip memory interconnection

However, as the number of PEs grows, the hardware overhead of the fully connected NoC will quickly become the bottleneck of an accelerator. Figure 1(b) depicts a typical fully connected NoC, with the hardware complexity of $O(N^2)$. ScalaGraph [15] runs a series of comparative experiments on the FPGA-based accelerator Accugraph [14] to validate the impact of fully connected NoC in existing graph accelerators on scalability. The test environment is a Xilinx Avleo U280 FPGA card with a memory bandwidth of 425 GB/s. The test estimates the accelerator's performance by running a round of the PageRank algorithm. In the test, two versions of the accelerator are implemented with and without the crossbar.

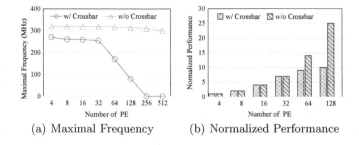

(a) Maximal Frequency   (b) Normalized Performance

Fig. 2. Performance of ForeGraph with a fully connected crossbar

The results in Fig. 2(a) show that when the number of PEs increases, the frequency of the version that implements the crossbar drops sharply until it cannot be synthesized, while another version can keep running at about 300 MHz.

Figure 2(b) shows the normalized performance results. The accelerator can achieve 10×–12× speedups when scaling from 4 to 64 PEs. However, scaling from 64 to 128 PEs results in a slight improvement or even a decrease in performance. Our observation is that the hardware complexity of the traditional crossbar is $O(N^2)$. Once the number of PE increases, the overhead of hardware resources increases exponentially, which seriously affects performance.

2.3   Distributed On-Chip Memory Hierarchy

The main bottleneck limiting the performance of massively parallel graph accelerators is on-chip memory scalability. Developing a highly scalable graph accelerator can avoid the aforementioned issues.

We propose a distributed on-chip memory hierarchy, where memory partitions are distributed and tied directly to the PE. The distributed model [18], is widely used in multiprocessors and distributed computing.

Challenges. However, it is difficult to implement such a distributed on-chip cache hierarchy. One challenge is dealing with the routing overhead introduced by the NoC. Most NoCs, in contrast to the fully connected crossbar, require multiple cycles to transmit loads, resulting in increased communication overhead. Furthermore, multiple data streams will compete for the same routing link at the same time, resulting in routing conflicts. Another challenge is dealing with the load imbalance problem caused by the irregularity of the graph. As a result, we must solve these issues through software and hardware co-design.

3   GraphS Architecture

In this section, we show the overall architecture of GraphS and describe the functions and workflow of each module in detail.

3.1   Hardware Design

As shown in Fig. 3, the overall architecture modularizes different stages of graph processing on the FPGA and executes operations in various stages of graph processing, respectively. The connection between other modules is in the form of the pipeline. The detailed design of each module of the architecture is as follows.

Prefetcher. The *Prefetcher* module is responsible for interacting with off-chip memory. The module consists of several sub-modules, the number of which depends on the number of pseudo-channels used. In each iteration of graph processing, the *Prefetcher* obtains the set of active vertex sent by the dispatcher and prefetches the attributes of the active vertex and the offset of the corresponding edge data in the off-chip HBM. After reading the offset data, the *Prefetcher* will prefetch the related edge data according to the obtained offset.

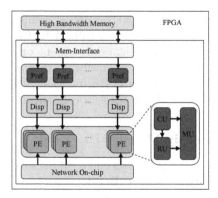

Fig. 3. The architecture of GraphS

Dispatcher. The *Dispatcher* module is responsible for the delivery of data and for controlling the start and end of iterations. Each *Dispatcher* module is divided into *Vertex Dispatcher* (VDU) and *Edge Dispatcher* (EDU). The VDU accepts the active vertex set from PE and sends it to the *Prefetcher*. At the same time, the EDU will receive edge data from *Prefetcher* and assign it to the corresponding *Processor* module.

PE. Each PE is divided into three modules: *Computing Unit* (CU), *Routing Unit* (RU), and *Memory Unit* (MU). The CU module receives the load from the EDU and processes it to generate an update request, deciding whether to send the request to the MU or the RU based on the hash value of the updated vertex. The RU is in charge of communicating between update requests and the on-chip interconnect network. The MU is part of the PE and comprises a portion of the on-chip memory, which is in charge of storing active vertex sets and properties.

NoC. We use an Omega network as a base NoC of GraphS. The Omega network has the following characteristics. First, the Omega network has relatively low hardware complexity compared to the fully connected network, which is $O(Nlog_2N)$. Second, even though the Omega network is a multi-stage crossbar, the structure of each Omega stage is the same, so the implementation is relatively simple. Finally, the routing rules of the Omega network are straightforward and do not introduce additional control overhead.

3.2   Workflow

Figure 4 depicts a VCM-based on-chip workflow pipeline. The on-chip pipeline is made up of various modules and small FIFO queues that connect the modules. The on-chip pipeline divides the stage into two steps: *Dispatch* and *Process*, representing the process of on-chip data transmission and on-chip logic calculation, respectively.

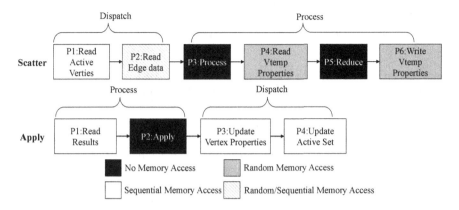

Fig. 4. The workflow of GraphS

Scatter Workflow. In stage P1, DU will read an active vertex and its properties. In stage P2, the corresponding edge of the active point will be accepted. Following that, DU will route workloads to the corresponding PEs. The GU will run the *Process* function in stage P3 to process the workload and send the results to the RU. The RU will determine whether to send workloads to the local SPD or the RU of another neighbor PEs through the NoC based on its destination vertex. The SPD will update V_{temp} in the stages P4–P6 by executing the *Reduce* function after receiving the local update request.

Apply Workflow. SPD will first read the V_{prop} and V_{temp} for each vertex stored locally before executing the *Apply* function. Second, in stage P3, SPD will compare the result to the old vertex property and update the vertex's properties. Finally, for the next iteration, SPD will update the active set in stage P4. The V_{prop} and V_{temp} represent the properties of the source vertex and destination vertex, respectively.

4 GraphS Optimizations

We propose three optimization methods based on the GraphS design in Sect. 3 to reduce the number of data transfers while fully utilizing PE.

4.1 Data Placement

On-chip memory is insufficient to accommodate all graph data when the scale of graph data grows. As a result, using off-chip memory to store part of the graph data is unavoidable. Because on-chip memory and off-chip memory have uneven access latency and bandwidth, how properly layout graph data is critical in determining accelerator efficiency.

For an input graph, data is mainly divided into vertex data and edge data. As shown in Algorithm 1, during the algorithm execution, the vertex data is frequently changed to track the status of vertices. On the contrary, the edge data never changes. GraphS employs different strategies to handle them.

Vertex Data. Vertex data mainly includes active vertex set and V_{temp}. Most vertex data will be changed frequently during the execution. Suppose vertex data is stored in the off-chip memory. It will lead to severe memory access overhead because the latency of reading and writing data from off-chip memory is very high. In addition, the size of vertex data in most graph algorithms is smaller than the width of the off-chip memory bus, which means that the utilization of off-chip memory is very low, which will seriously waste off-chip bandwidth. Further, if the currently written vertex data is the same as the next vertex data that needs to be updated, the long access delay of off-chip memory will cause the on-chip pipeline to stagnate.

For active vertex sets, GraphS defines two bitmaps, i.e., *current active-map* and *next active-map*, which save the active vertex set of the current iteration and the active vertex set of the next iteration. These two bitmaps are stored in the on-chip cache resources. Each node in the graph occupies a bit in the bitmap (and a vertex consumes 2 bits). The value of each bit in the bitmap represents whether the vertex is active with 1 for active and 0 for inactive. The bitmap approach conserves on-chip memory while lowering data access overhead. Furthermore, it provides excellent prefetching properties for active vertices access.

Edge Data. Edge data is much larger than vertex data in scale. Therefore, edge data inevitably has to be stored in the off-chip memory. Access to edge data has become one of the bottlenecks faced by most graph accelerators. How to store as much graph data as possible in a limited space and efficiently utilize off-chip bandwidth have become issues that need to be addressed when a graph accelerator is designed.

GraphS represents edge data with *Compressed Sparse Row* (CSR). CSR is derived from the adjacency matrix, which is efficient for sparse matrix storage. Figure 5 shows an example of CSR, in which Fig. 5(b) is the CSR representation corresponding to the example graph in Fig. 5(a). The compact layout of CSR enables better utilization of off-chip bandwidth.

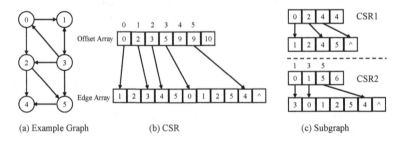

(a) Example Graph   (b) CSR   (c) Subgraph

Fig. 5. An example of CSR-based subgraph representation format

In GraphS, the number of external pseudo-channels determines the number of subgraphs. Thus, in the above example, if two PEs are connected to different pseudo-channels, the two subgraphs will be stored in different pseudo-channels instead of the same pseudo-channel.

4.2   Omega Network

After the PE generates an update request, it must be sent to other PEs through NoC. The most straightforward way to achieve this is to use the full $N \times N$ crossbar when there are N PEs. However, such a crossbar will consume N^2 FIFO resources, which an FPGA will struggle to satisfy when N scales to a large number.

GraphS proposes an approach to using Omega network for NoC to improve scalability. Omega network is a multi-stage crossbar, which means that a switch fabric of multiple stages connects PEs. Assume that the input of Omega network and output ports are N, where N must be a power of 2 because the number of stages is the logarithm of N concerning 2. In the shuffling mechanism, each port is randomly assigned an address from 0 to $N - 1$. Omega network connects the ports between different stages in a cyclic left-shift manner. Since N is a power of 2, each output port has a unique input port connected to it.

Regarding resource usage and efficiency, we will compare the two ways (full crossbar vs. Omega). A full $N \times N$ crossbar uses N^2 FIFOs, whereas an Omega equivalent uses $log_2N \times (N/2) \times 2 = Nlog_2N$ FIFOs. Omega consumes less FIFO than its counterpart $N \times N$ full crossbar, which is easy to demonstrate. The full crossbar requires $8 \times 8 = 64$ FIFOs, whereas the Omega only consumes $3 \times 4 \times 4 = 48$ FIFOs. The disparity in resource use will widen as the number of ports grows.

In terms of efficiency, the $N \times N$ full-crossbar achieves 1-hop message passing latency, but the equivalent Omega requires log_2N-hop message passing latency. Nevertheless, graph processing is a throughput-critical application. It is reasonable to exchange latency for the resource.

4.3   Degree-Aware Preprocessing Method

The power-law properties of the graph introduce a significant degree gap between different vertices. For unprocessed graph data, the degrees of other vertices are entirely random. Therefore, simply adopting the hash mapping method will likely cause serious load imbalance problems.

Based on this observation, we present a degree-aware preprocessing method to achieve load balance. As shown in Algorithm 2, the key idea is to sort each vertex according to the load quantization value. It mainly consists of the following three steps. First, the algorithm traverses the edge array of the input graph and counts the in-degree and out-degree numbers of different vertices. Second, the algorithm quantifies the workload for each vertex according to the number of in-degree and out-degree and saves it in the workload array. After sorting,

---

Algorithm 2 Degree-aware Preprocessing Method

Input: E_{set} - Original Edge Set
Output: E'_{set} - New Edge Set
1: **for** each $E(v,u)$ *of* E_{set} **do**
2:     Indegree[u]++;
3:     Outdegree[v]++;
4: **end for**
5: **for** each *Vertex* v **do**
6:     Workload[v] = **Calculate**(Indegree[v],Outdegree[v]);
7: **end for**
8: **Sort**(Workload);
9: **for** each $E(v,u)$ *of* E_{set} **do**
10:     $NewEdge = \{$sort(v),sort(u)$\}$;
11:     E'_{set}.push($NewEdge$);
12: **end for**

---

each vertex will get a new index according to its workload. Finally, the algorithm outputs the renumbered edge array according to the new and old index mapping relationship. Because graphs are mostly power-law and degree-aware preprocessing works is fit well for power-law graphs.

5   Evaluation

In this section, we will evaluate the performance of GraphS on different graph algorithms and datasets.

5.1   Experimental Settings

Evaluation Tools: Our accelerator is built on the Xilinx Alveo U280 accelerator card. The U280 has 9.072 MB BRAM, 34.56 MB URAM, and 1304K LUTs. The HBM subsystem on the U280 card has 32 pseudo-channels, 8 GB of storage capacity, and a theoretical aggregated memory bandwidth of up to 460 GB/s. Using Xilinx Vivado 2019, we verify the correctness of the accelerator and obtain the clock rate and resource utilization. We use DRAMSim3 [19] to simulate the cycle-accurate behavior of off-chip accesses.

Graph Algorithms: We implement three representative graph algorithms on our accelerator, including *Breadth First Search* (BFS), *Weakly Connected Components* (WCC), and *Single Source Shortest Path* (SSSP).

Graph Datasets: We choose four realistic graphs taken from [20] and two synthetic RMAT graphs shown in Table 1. The first number in the names of RMAT graphs represents the scale of the graph, and the second number represents the average degree.

Table 1. Graph datasets

Names	Vertices	Edges	Avg. Deg	Directed
DBLP	0.32 M	1.05 M	3.28	N
Youtube	1.13 M	2.99 M	2.64	N
Wiki	2.39 M	5.02 M	2.10	Y
LiveJournal	4.85 M	69.0 M	14.22	Y
RMAT20-30	1.0 M	30.0 M	30	Y
RMAT19-40	0.5 M	20.0 M	40	Y

Table 2. Resource utilization

	BFS	SSSP	WCC
LUT	25.5%	26.2%	26.4%
BRAM	38.1%	38.1%	38.1%
URAM	27.1%	54.2%	54.2%
Simulation Clock rate	200 MHz	200 MHz	200 MHz

5.2   Experimental Results

Resource Utilization: Table 2 shows the frequencies used by different algorithms and their resource usage when GraphS uses 32 pseudo-channels, and each pseudo-channel corresponds to 4 PEs. The resource usage is obtained by designing GraphS in Xilinx Vivado. The resource usage of different algorithms is different because the actual processing logic and data width corresponding to the three algorithms are different. Since GraphS stores all vertex data in the algorithm on-chip, the consumption of on-chip storage resources is relatively high.

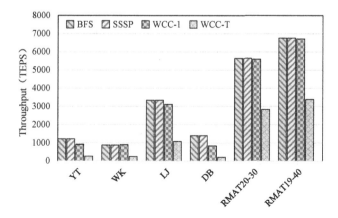

Fig. 6. Performance variation of GraphS configured with 32 HBM Pseudo-channels and 128 PEs

Throughput: Figure 6 shows the throughput performance of GraphS on various datasets and algorithms. Throughput is called the number of *traversed edges per second* (TEPS). Because the first iteration of WCC will traverse all vertices and their related edges, the throughput of the first iteration of WCC can be used to measure the graph accelerator's performance. The results show WCC-1 and WCC-T representing the throughput of the first iteration and the entire processing, respectively. As shown in Fig. 6, GraphS achieves 212 MTEPS–6757 MTEPS overall graph algorithms and datasets.

The accelerator performs poorly on sparse datasets, such as *Youtube*, *Wiki*, and *DBLP*. A low average degree results in the poor locality of edge data, making each access to edge data random. When dealing with relatively dense graph data, such as *LiveJournal*, the edge prefetching can fully use the high bandwidth of HBM. As shown in Fig. 6, the performance increases linearly when the average degree is less than 16.

Table 3. Performance comparison between GraphS and ForeGraph

Algorithms	Datasets	ForeGraph	GraphS
BFS	YT	299 MTEPS	1221 MTEPS
BFS	WK	100 MTEPS	888 MTEPS
BFS	LJ	153 MTEPS	3343 MTEPS
WCC	YT	187 MTEPS	261 MTEPS
WCC	WK	96.5 MTEPS	252 MTEPS
WCC	LJ	119.3 MTEPS	1080 MTEPS

Table 3 shows the performance comparison results with ForeGraph [10]. Table 3 shows that GraphS achieves 4.08×–21.84× speedups for BFS and 1.39×–9.05× speedups for WCC compared to ForeGraph. The speedup mainly comes from the high bandwidth of HBM. We can see that the speedup ratio on dense graphs is superior. The reason is that the high bandwidth of HBM has a good effect on edge prefetching of dense graphs.

According to comparison results, we can see that ForeGraph is limited by its limited off-chip bandwidth. Even though many mechanisms optimize data access patterns, the throughput is difficult to catch up with graph accelerators using HBM. It shows that with the rapid development of hardware performance, the main bottleneck of graph accelerators has changed from random accesses and data conflicts caused by graph irregularity to efficiently utilize the high bandwidth of new memory devices.

Normalized Performance: The performance indicator is referred to as TEPS. The normalized performance of Fig. 8 is similar.

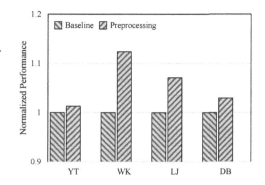

Fig. 7. Performance benefit from degree-aware preprocessing method

Benefits from Degree-Aware Preprocessing Method: As shown in Fig. 7, the degree-aware preprocessing method achieves 1.3%–12.4% speedups compared to the baseline. Overall, the more uneven the load on the input graph, the better performance the degree-aware preprocessing method can achieve. Conversely, if the degree between the vertices of the input graph itself is already averaged, it is difficult for this method to achieve significant results. So it is appropriate to trade some overhead for stable performance. Since the preprocessed graph data can be executed multiple times, the overhead is amortized in each execution.

5.3 Performance Scaling

For GraphS, there are two scaling directions: increasing the numbers of pseudo-channels and increasing the numbers of PEs.

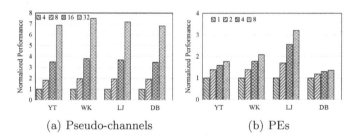

(a) Pseudo-channels   (b) PEs

Fig. 8. Performance characterization of GraphS by adopting different number of (a) Pseudo-channels and (b) PEs

Figure 8(a) presents the performance of GraphS configured with 4 PEs for each pseudo-channel and uses increasing numbers of pseudo-channel. From Fig. 8(a), we can observe that the performance speedups are almost linear according to the number of pseudo-channel. It demonstrates that in GraphS the decoupled design is effective on performance scaling in the direction of increasing pseudo-channels. Because the scaling of pseudo-channel means that the prefetcher can read more edge data from the off-chip memory per cycle. At constant frequency, the bandwidth between the FPGA and the off-chip memory will linearly increase as the number of channels increases. Therefore, it can achieve good performance improvement for both sparse and dense graphs.

Figure 8(b) presents the performance of GraphS that configures with varying PEs on 16 pseudo-channels. We can observe that the performance of GraphS rises with more PEs, and such performance gains are higher when the vertices of the input graph have higher average degrees. However, when the degree of most vertices is much smaller than the off-chip bus bandwidth, the accelerator wastes a lot of off-chip memory bandwidth.

Comparing Fig. 8(a) with Fig. 8(b), we can observe that although the number of PEs on the chip is the same, the speedup ratio of increasing the number of PEs corresponding to each pseudo-channel is smaller than that of increasing the number of pseudo-channels. Based on this, we can see that the accelerator should prioritize scaling the number of pseudo-channels rather than simply increasing the number of PEs when scaling.

6   Conclusion

We present GraphS, an efficient graph accelerator with distributed on-chip memory hierarchy. Compared to the fully connected crossbar, GraphS uses the Omega network for NoC, which improves scalability. To improve load imbalance, we propose software/hardware co-design. Our evaluation on a variety of graph algorithms shows that GraphS can achieve throughputs of up to 3.342 GTEPS on realistic graphs, with a speedup of up to 21.84 × compared to ForeGraph.

Acknowledgment. This work is supported by the NSFC (No. 62072195, 61825202, 61832006, and 61929103).

References

1. Katz, G., Kider, J.: All-pairs shortest-paths for large graphs on the GPU. In: Proceedings of the 23rd ACM SIGGRAPH/EUROGRAPHICS Symposium on Graphics Hardware, pp. 47–55. ACM (2008)
2. Jamshidi, K., Mahadasa, R., Vora, K.: Peregrine: a pattern-aware graph mining system. In: Proceedings of the 15th European Conference on Computer Systems, pp. 1–16. ACM (2020)
3. Paden, B., Cap, M., Yong, S.Z., Yershov, D., Frazzoli, E.: A survey of motion planning and control techniques for self-driving urban vehicles. IEEE Trans. Intell. Veh. **1**(1), 33–55 (2016)
4. Chong, Y., Ding, Y., Yan, Q., Pan, S.: Graph-based semi-supervised learning: a review. Neurocomputing **408**(1), 216–230 (2020)

5. Zhang, Y., Liao, X., Jin, H., He, B., Liu, H., Gu, L.: Digraph: an efficient path-based iterative directed graph processing system on multiple GPUs. In: Proceedings of the 24th International Conference on Architectural Support for Programming Languages and Operating Systems, pp. 601–614. ACM (2019)
6. Dhulipala, L., Blelloch, G.E., Shun, J.: Theoretically efficient parallel graph algorithms can be fast and scalable. ACM Trans. Parallel Comput. **8**(1), 1–70 (2021)
7. Shun, J.: Practical parallel hypergraph algorithms. In: Proceedings of the 25th ACM SIGPLAN Symposium on Principles and Practice of Parallel Programming, pp. 232–249. ACM (2020)
8. Gonzalez, J.E., Low, Y., Gu, H., Bickson, D., Guestrin, C.: Powergraph: distributed graph-parallel computation on natural graphs. In: Proceedings of the 10th USENIX Symposium on Operating Systems Design and Implementation, pp. 17–30. USENIX Association (2021)
9. Sabet, A.H.N., Zhao, Z., Gupta, R.: Subway: minimizing data transfer during out-of-GPU-memory graph processing. In: Proceedings of the 15th European Conference on Computer Systems, pp. 1–16. ACM (2020)
10. Dai, G., Huang, T., Chi, Y., Xu, N., Wang, Y., Yang, H.: Foregraph: exploring large-scale graph processing on multi-FPGA architecture. In: Proceedings of the 2017 ACM/SIGDA International Symposium on Field-programmable Gate Arrays, pp. 217–226. ACM (2017)
11. Ma, X., Zhang, D., Chiou, D.: FPGA-accelerated transactional execution of graph workloads. In: Proceedings of the 2017 ACM/SIGDA International Symposium on Field-programmable Gate Arrays, pp. 227–236. ACM (2017)
12. Ham, T.J., Wu, L., Sundaram, N., Satish, N., Martonosi, M.: Graphicionado: a high-performance and energy-efficient accelerator for graph analytics. In: Proceedings of the 49th Annual IEEE/ACM International Symposium on Microarchitecture, pp. 1–13. IEEE (2016)
13. Rahman, S., Abu-Ghazaleh, N., Gupta, R.: Graphpulse: an event-driven hardware accelerator for asynchronous graph processing. In: Proceedings of the 53rd Annual IEEE/ACM International Symposium on Microarchitecture, pp. 908–921. IEEE (2020)
14. Yao, P., Zheng, L., Liao, X., Jin, H., He, B.: An efficient graph accelerator with parallel data conflict management. In: Proceedings of the 27th International Conference on Parallel Architectures and Compilation Techniques, pp. 1–12. ACM (2018)
15. Yao, P., et al.: Scalagraph: a scalable accelerator for massively parallel graph processing. In: Proceedings of the 28th IEEE International Symposium on High-Performance Computer Architecture, pp. 1–13. IEEE (2022)
16. Malewicz, G., et al.: Pregel: a system for large-scale graph processing. In: Proceedings of the 2010 ACM SIGMOD International Conference on Management of Data, pp. 135–146. ACM (2010)
17. Abeydeera, M., Sanchez, D.: Chronos: efficient speculative parallelism for accelerators. In: Proceedings of the 25th International Conference on Architectural Support for Programming Languages and Operating Systems, pp. 1247–1262. ACM (2020)
18. Cybenko, G.: Dynamic load balancing for distributed memory multiprocessors. J. Parallel Distrib. Comput. **7**(2), 279–301 (1989)
19. Li, S., Yang, Z., Reddy, D., Srivastava, A., Jacob, B.: DRAMsim3: a cycle-accurate, thermal-capable DRAM simulator. IEEE Comput. Archit. Lett. **19**(2), 106–109 (2020)
20. Leskovec, J., Krevl, A.: SNAP datasets: Stanford large network dataset collection (2014). http://snap.stanford.edu/data

Routing Protocol Based on Mission-Oriented Opportunistic Networks

Yahui Cui[✉], Xinlian Zhou, Wei Liang, and Kuan-Ching Li

School of Computer Science and Engineering, Hunan University of Science and Technology, Xiangtan, China
Cyh2510@163.com

Abstract. Mission-oriented opportunistic networks are a new form of network. Its application background is to complete specific tasks. Its prominent feature is Mission-oriented mobility. This paper, based on the goal-driven mobility model of human nodes in the established Mission-oriented opportunistic networks, proposes a routing protocol based on multi-dimensional trust evaluation parameters (MTEPRP). Firstly, contact intimacy, delivery credibility and location intimacy are selected by the routing protocol as the direct-trusting multi-dimensional trust evaluation parameters to calculate the direct trust value of the nodes, and the weight coefficient of the direct trust value is adjusted by grey relational analysis algorithm. Then, contact intimacy and delivery credibility are selected to calculate the recommended-trusting multi-dimensional trust evaluation parameters, which uses the collaborative computing technology and joint multi-nodes to calculate the recommendation trust values. Finally, the total trust values of nodes are calculated by fusing direct trust values and recommendation trust values. This paper transforms a routing problem for dynamic moving and unstructured space is transformed into a routing problem for static and structured multi-dimensional trust evaluation parameter space by adopting the data forwarding strategy of comparing multi-dimensional trust evaluation parameters. Experimental results show that compared with Epidemic and Prophet routing protocol, the MTEPRP proposed in this paper has better performance in network transmission success rate, data transmission delay and routing overhead.

Keywords: Mission-oriented opportunistic networks · Routing protocol · Multi-dimensional trust evaluation parameters · Grey relational analysis · Collaborative computing

1 Introduction

With the rapid development of information technology, the trend of informationization, digitalization and networking of society is deepened. A large number of low-cost mobile devices with short-range communication interfaces are greatly changing day by day [1–3]. For example, smart phones with Wi-Fi and Bluetooth interfaces, Personal Digital Assistant (PDA) and vehicle-mounted wireless devices share data or collaborate to access the Internet in the form of ad hoc networks [4]. There are some extreme

© Springer Nature Switzerland AG 2023
W. Meng et al. (Eds.): ICA3PP 2022, LNCS 13777, pp. 788–800, 2023.
https://doi.org/10.1007/978-3-031-22677-9_43

environments in real life, such as typhoon, earthquake, flood and other natural disasters [5], in which there is no basic communication facility or the basic communication facility is seriously damaged. Therefore, it is necessary to establish a communication network with mobile nodes, wireless communication and easy self-organization to realize regional data transmission [6]. Therefore, the opportunistic networks have been to solve the network communication problem under extreme conditions in academic circles [7]. Opportunistic networks are a kind of self-organizing networks which do not need a complete path between the source node and the destination node, and realizes network communication by using the encounter opportunity brought by node movement [8–10]. Unlike traditional networks, the opportunistic networks are suitable for establishment without any additional infrastructure and can tolerate long delays during data communication [11]. What's more, they do not require end-to-end connections, but to realize inter-node communication in a "store-carry-forward" routing mode, which is of great significance to future pervasive computing [12, 13]. With the deepening of researches, it is found that most of the existing opportunistic networks routing protocol are impractical or mechanical, without considering that mobile communication devices are carried by human beings in real life [14]. It is easy to ignore that the movement of nodes is actually human's movement. And the previous routing protocol cannot reflect that human movement in the network is Mission-oriented [15]. Therefore, we focus on the Mission-oriented Opportunistic Networks (MOONs), which is the evolution of Opportunistic Networks (OPPNET). MOONs, based on the application background of completing a specific task, requires mobile nodes to use "opportunity" to forward data, and gradually achieve the goal of completing tasks in a dynamic and cooperative way.

MOONs is a new network form, focusing on its theory, technology and application, such as Mission-oriented human mobility model, node discovery and communication mechanism, data forwarding and routing strategy, privacy and security, etc. [16]. MOONs not only have the characteristics of general OPPNET, but also have the following three basic characteristics:

- Human participation. In MOONs, people who carry wireless communication devices (such as smart phones, PDA or wireless sensors) act as mobile nodes and become part of the network, and in a sense act as communication devices and data carriers."
- The movement of human nodes is purposeful. Because people are intelligent. They will make mobile decisions guided by task completion, which will play a positive role in task completion. This is essentially different from many published mobile models in which nodes move randomly "mechanically" [17].
- Network communication is "opportunistic". Two or more nodes can communicate and forward data only when they move to each other's communication range, and the data forwarding strategy is also based on whether it is beneficial to complete tasks. Otherwise, nodes can only save information in their buffers till new communication opportunities are found [18].

In MOONs, because there is no complete connection path between the two parties, the traditional routing strategy is not applicable here. Exploring the data forwarding strategy with high trust evaluation, designing routing protocol that reduce delay, and improving transmission success rate are the basis of other applications of MOONs. Therefore, studying efficient and credible routing protocol is one of the basic studies of MOONs applications. This paper proposes a routing protocol based on multi-dimensional trust evaluation parameters (MTEPRP). In this protocol, the direct trust value is calculated by grey relational analysis algorithm, and the recommendation trust value is calculated jointly by multiple nodes by collaborative computing technology. Finally, the total trust value of nodes is calculated by integrating the direct trust value and the recommendation trust value.

2 Related Work

In recent years, scholars at home and abroad have conducted extensive research on opportunistic networks and proposed many opportunistic networks routing protocol [19], but finding a high-performance opportunistic network routing protocol is still a huge challenge.

Boldrini et al. propose a context-based routing protocol (HiBOp). HiBOp provides a general framework for managing and using context to make forwarding decisions. It does not pay attention to the predefined context information set. Instead, it can describe its context with any information that users are willing to provide [20]. Gupta et al. based on cognitive-based routing protocol (CRPO), make intelligent decisions based on past experience and perceived input. It defines a neural network at each node, and understands the simulation environment over time in order to successfully deliver messages [21]. Kiranmayi et al. propose a propagation-based routing protocol (Epidemic), which is based on paired contact between nodes, in which nodes exchange digest vectors containing message lists stored on each node. Based on the digest vector received, each node requests a message that is not yet in its buffer. When the destination encounters a node hosting a message destined for the destination, the message is delivered to the destination [22]. Grasic et al. propose a probability-based routing protocol (Prophet), which introduces the concept of delivery predictability. Delivery predictability is the probability that a node meets a specific destination. Prophet routing protocol requests messages only when the receiving node delivers to the destination with greater predictability [23]. Magaia et al. propose a privacy-based routing protocol (PRIVO). PRIVO models DTN as a time-varying adjacency graph, where edges correspond to the adjacency relationship between pairs of nodes. PRIVO ensures privacy by protecting sensitive information on each node, even if that information must be processed elsewhere. In addition, nodes use Paillier homomorphic encryption scheme to compare their routing metrics in a private way [24]. Zhang et al. propose a replication-based routing protocol (FGAR), which is a routing protocol designed for mobile opportunistic networks. It utilizes fine-grained contact characteristics and adaptive message replication. In FGAR, the sliding window mechanism is used to describe the contact history in a fine-grained way, and the future contact is predicted based on the fine-grained contact information, so as to improve the accuracy of contact prediction [25].

Due to the intermittent and unstable connection between source and destination, message routing and forwarding in opportunistic networks have become a challenging and thorny problem in recent years [26]. Although some research achievements have been made on data routing protocol for opportunistic networks applications, it has promoted the implementation of some prototype systems, but the existing research still has some shortcomings. For the above MOONs, the corresponding data routing protocol is quite different from the published results, and the new data forwarding must reflect the comprehensive indicators such as human behavior orientation and purpose-driven in a specific environment. In addition, the research work of data routing protocol must fully consider the tradeoff among link usage "opportunity", delay tolerance and network load throughput efficiency.

3   Routing Protocol Based on Multi-dimensional Trust Evaluation Parameters

In this paper, we try to improve the data forwarding process by using the internal characteristics of each node in the network, and try to transform a frequently changing and unstructured routing problem into a static and structured routing problem in the trust evaluation parameter space by using the data forwarding strategy based on trust evaluation parameters. Based on this idea, in MOONs, we construct a multidimensional trust evaluation parameter set with the goal of completing the task, and calculate the reliability of node data forwarding to determine the selection of the next hop receiving node. In this paper, we propose a routing protocol based on multidimensional trust evaluation parameters routing protocol (MTEPRP). MTEPRP is divided into three modules: Trust computing module, direct trust computing module and recommendation trust computing module. Figure 1 shows the structure diagram of MTEPRP routing protocol.

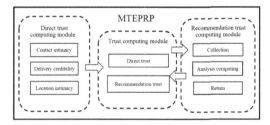

Fig. 1. MTEPRP routing protocol structure diagram

3.1   Multidimensional Trust Evaluation Parameters

Traditional single direct trust attribute cannot completely reflect the attributes of the network. The past routing protocol didn't take the influence of the internal relationship among trust attributes on trust value into consideration. In order to ensure data transmission to Sink nodes, on the basis of reducing node energy consumption, we find a method that can not only improve data transmission rate, but also shorten data transmission delay. We design multi-dimensional trust evaluation parameters according to the characteristics of Mission-oriented opportunistic networks and the mobility characteristics of nodes. This paper mainly studies data forwarding in opportunistic networks. Data forwarding is accomplished when nodes meet. We choose three important attributes in the encounter mode, and design three indexes as the calculation parameters of the routing protocol: contact intimacy, delivery credibility and position intimacy. They are introduced below:

- Contact intimacy: V_C represents the intimacy of direct contact between the current node and the Sink node. Sink node is the base station of opportunistic network model, and its communication range covers the whole area. In the opportunistic networks model of this paper, the goal of ordinary nodes is to deliver messages to Sink nodes. The higher the frequency of direct interaction between nodes and Sink nodes (the higher the contact intimacy), the higher the probability that nodes will send messages to Sink nodes, whereas the lower the probability that nodes will send messages to Sink nodes. The calculation formula is as follows:

$$V_C = \frac{C_S}{C} \tag{1}$$

C_S represents the number of contacts between nodes and Sink nodes. And C represents the number of contacts with all nodes in the network.

- Delivery credibility: V_D represents the credibility of nodes when transmitting messages. The high frequency of packet loss indicates the low delivery credibility, while the low frequency implies the high delivery credibility. Selfish nodes and malicious nodes mostly choose not to forward data, while normal nodes will forward the received data. Delivery credibility helps to distinguish normal nodes from selfish and malicious nodes. Its calculation is as follows:

$$V_D = \frac{C_P}{R_P} \tag{2}$$

C_P represents the number of packets forwarded by the node, and R_P represents the total number of packets received by the node.

- Location intimacy: V_L represents the location intimacy between the current node and the Sink node. The smaller the distance between the node and the Sink node, the greater the tendency of the node to close to the destination node, and the greater the probability of meeting the Sink node, the greater the probability of transmitting packets. Its calculation is as follows:

$$V_L = 1 - \frac{D_S}{S}. \tag{3}$$

D_S represents the distance between the node and the Sink node. And S represents the diameter or diagonal length of the whole communication range.

3.2 MTEPRP Routing Protocol

MTEPRP routing protocol uses direct trust and recommendation trust to calculate the total trust value of nodes. Its calculation method is to integrate direct trust value and recommendation trust value. The formula is shown in Eq. (4):

$$T_{i,j} = \theta_1 T_{i,j}^{direct} + \theta_2 T_{i,j}^{recom} \tag{4}$$

Assuming that node i is an evaluation node, and that node j is an evaluation node which i determines whether to forward data or not, $T_{i,j}$ is the total trust value, $T_{i,j}^{direct}$ represents the direct trust value of node i to j, and $T_{i,j}^{recom}$ represents the recommendation trust value calculated by node i to j. And θ_1 and θ_2 are the weight coefficients of direct trust and recommendation trust respectively, which represents the importance of direct trust calculation and recommendation trust calculation to the calculation of total trust value. In the opportunistic networks routing protocol, $\theta_1 = \theta_2 = 0.5$ is generally chosen as the weight coefficient of direct trust value and recommendation trust value. In this paper, $\theta_1 = \theta_2 = 0.5$.

The direct trust value is fused and calculated according to contact intimacy, delivery credibility and location intimacy. Multi-dimensional trust attributes are used to construct the basic parameters of direct trust, and multiple trust attributes affecting network performance are comprehensively considered, which ensures the overall stability and fairness of the network and exerts the advantages of multi-dimensional trust evaluation parameters. In a time period, the calculation formula of the direct trust value of node i to node j is shown in Eq. (5):

$$T_{i,j}^{direct} = \beta_1 V_C + \beta_2 V_D + \beta_3 V_L \tag{5}$$

Among them, β_1, β_2 and β_3 are respectively the weight coefficients of contact intimacy, delivery credibility and position intimacy, $\beta_1 + \beta_2 + \beta_3 = 1$. In MOONs, the neighbor nodes contacted during node movement change. In each time period, by calculating the proportion of each attribute in the direct trust calculation of the routing protocol, the direct trust value can be accurately calculated to express the trust degree in the process of direct contact with the evaluated nodes. Gray correlation analysis is a method to analyze and determine the degree of influence between contact intimacy, delivery credibility, and location intimacy or the contribution measure of factors to the main behavior of the system through gray correlation. The steps of grey relational analysis are as follows:

a. First, we should determine the reference sequence, which is the data sequence reflecting the behavior characteristics of opportunistic network routing protocol. In this paper, the constant sequence $x_0 = \{V_C^0, V_C^0, V_C^0\}$ is selected as the reference sequence. The selection of reference sequence should reflect the best state of the model. In the ideal state, when the value of reference sequence tends to $x_0 = \{1, 1, 1\}$, the data forwarding state of nodes in the network is the best, so $x_0 = \{1, 1, 1\}$ is selected as the reference sequence.

b. Determine the comparison sequence, which is the data sequence composed of factors affecting system behavior. And the time series of contact intimacy, delivery credibility and position intimacy as the reference sequence are selected.

$$\begin{cases} x_1 = \left\{ V_C^t, V_C^{t-1}, V_C^{t-2} \right\} \\ x_2 = \left\{ V_D^t, V_D^{t-1}, V_D^{t-2} \right\} \\ x_3 = \left\{ V_L^t, V_L^{t-1}, V_L^{t-2} \right\} \end{cases} \tag{6}$$

V_C^t, V_D^t and V_L^t are contact intimacy, delivery credibility and position intimacy at t moment. Because the parameters of the reference sequence are all percentages and the units are uniform, it is not necessary to carry out dimensionless treatment.

c. Calculate $\xi(x_i)$, the grey correlation coefficient of reference sequence and comparison sequence, and calculate the correlation coefficient of comparison sequence relative to reference sequence at each point of curve:

$$\xi_k = \frac{\Delta(min) + \rho\Delta(max)}{\Delta_{oi(k)} + \rho\Delta(max)} \tag{7}$$

ρ is the resolution coefficient generally between 0 and 1. The second-level minimum difference in the comparison sequence is marked as $\Delta(min)$. $\Delta(max)$ is the two-level maximum difference. The extreme difference is the difference between the maximum data and the minimum data in a group of data. The absolute difference between each point on the curve of the comparison sequence x_i ($i = 1, 2, 3$) and each point on the curve of the reference sequence X_0 is denoted as $\Delta_{oi(k)}$.

d. Find the correlation degree. The correlation coefficient is the correlation degree value between the comparison sequence and the reference sequence at each time (that is each point in the curve). The correlation degree is calculated as follows:

$$r_k = \frac{1}{N} \sum_{i=1}^{n} \xi_k(i) \tag{8}$$

e. Calculate the weight coefficient, β_1, β_2 and β_3, of each attribute in the direct trust value according to the correlation degree.

$$\beta_i = \frac{r_i}{r_1 + r_2 + r_3} \tag{9}$$

Finally, the direct trust value $T_{i,j}^{direct}$ is calculated according to the calculation formula (4) of direct trust. The grey relational degree reflects the influence of various factors in routing protocol on network performance, and improving the accuracy of direct tru.t value calculation.

For the false recommendations spread by selfish and malicious nodes in opportunistic networks, here designs a recommendation trust based on collaborative computing, including the collaborative computing of recommendation trust, the design of recommendation features and the introduction of algorithm computing steps. The routing protocol selects contact intimacy and delivery credibility as recommendation trust parameters, and proposes a collaborative computing recommendation trust filtering algorithm based on KNN, which considers the security requirements and efficiency requirements of opportunistic networks. Recommendation trust based on collaborative computing can effectively filter the false recommendation of recommendation trust information and improve the accuracy of recommendation trust calculation. The recommendation trust calculation formula based on collaborative computing is as follows:

$$T_{i,j}^{recom} = \frac{\sum_{m \in R}\left\{T_{i,m}(t) \times T_{m,j}(t)\right\}}{\sum_{m \in R} T_{i,m}(t)} \tag{10}$$

R is the set of recommend node, m is the set of random recommend node. Node m and i make collaborative decisions. $T_{i,m}(t)$ is a trust value evaluation node m of node i and $T_{m,j}(t)$ is a trust value evaluation node j of node m.

4 Experimental Evaluation

4.1 Simulation Environment Settings

In order to verify the effectiveness of MTEPRP routing protocol in improving network performance, we use ONE simulator to simulate the routing protocol. We compare MTEPRP routing protocol with Epidemic and Prophet routing protocol. It's found that the Epidemic routing protocol can maximize the success rate of packet transmission and reduce transmission delay, which can be used as a standard comparison between transmission rate and delay. Prophet routing protocol is an algorithm based on scheduling strategy, which can be used as a benchmark for predictive forwarding decision. This experiment simulates an opportunistic network consisting of a base station (Sink) and various mobile nodes within the communication range of the base station. The simulated area is 5 km\times 3 km, the node moving speed is general 1–5 m/s, and a new data is generated every 30–45 s. The total number of nodes set in the experiment is 400, 100 selfish nodes and malicious nodes are set, and 300 normal nodes verify the performance of MTEPRP in the network. The simulation parameters are set as shown in Table 1.

Table 1. Network simulation parameters

Parameters	Value
Number of normal nodes	400
Number of Sink Nodes	1
Scope of simulated area	5 km\times 3 km
Node moving speed	1 ~ 5 m/s
Transmission rate	250 KB/s
Cache size	5 MB
Message size	400 ~ 800 KB
Frequency of data generation	30 ~ 45 s
Communication radius of normal nodes	15 m
Communication radius of Sink	The communication covers the whole area

4.2 Analysis of Simulation Result

In order to verify the network performance of MTEPRP routing protocol in opportunistic networks, under the condition of different ratio between selfish, malicious node and normal node, through three aspects of data transmission success rate, transmission delay, routing overhead, the experiment makes a comparison between MTEPRP routing protocol and Epidemic, Prophet routing protocol to verify the effectiveness of the routing protocol.

There are totally 400 nodes in the experiment. Because the different density of selfish and malicious nodes have a great difference on the impact of the network, firstly, 50 selfish and malicious nodes and 350 normal nodes are set in the network to verify the performance of the routing protocol. As it shown in Fig. 2, with the running time progresses, resources are gradually consumed, and the transmission success rate of each routing protocol decreases overall. At the beginning, Epidemic has the highest transmission success rate, but the simulation time increases gradually, and the transmission success rate of Epidemic, which consumes the most resources, drops sharply. This is because Epidemic is at the expense of network resources to improve the transmission success rate. MTEPRP adopts multi-dimensional trust evaluation parameters, comprehensively considers all factors affecting node transmission in the network, realizes collaborative computing among nodes, and effectively resists attacks from selfish and malicious nodes. The transmission success rate of MTEPRP is higher than that of Prophet in the figure, and with the increase of time, the consumption of network resources and the decline rate of transmission success rate are relatively stable.

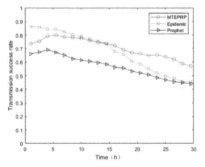

Fig. 2. Comparison chart of network transmission success rate (number of selfish and malicious nodes 50)

In Fig. 3, the average transmission delay of Epidemic is the smallest at the beginning of the experiment. But the average delay time increases obviously with the increase of simulation time. The average transmission delay of MTEPRP is smaller than that of Prophet. MTEPRP routing protocol combines the current routing table to calculate the trust value, which simplifies the decision-making process and has relatively small transmission delay.

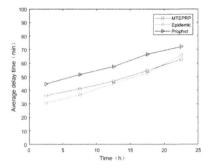

Fig. 3. Comparison chart of average delay time (number of selfish and malicious nodes 50)

Figure 4 shows the routing overhead of nodes. MTEPRP routing protocol eliminates most selfish nodes and malicious nodes in the selection of next hop nodes, and selects a small number of nodes with higher trust values as the next hop, which greatly reduces the routing overhead of the network. Epidemic uses a flooding algorithm. In the process of data transmission, nodes transmit data to all nodes in contact with them, and the routing overhead is the highest till the data is transmitted to the target node.

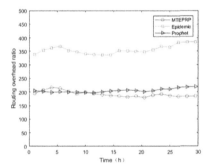

Fig. 4. Comparison chart of network routing overhead ratio (number of selfish and malicious nodes 50)

Next, consider the increase in the proportion of selfish nodes and malicious nodes. In the experiment, the number of selfish and malicious nodes is 100, and the number of normal nodes is 300. At this time, the threat to the opportunistic network will increase, and the overall performance will decline. As shown in Fig. 5, with the gradual progress of simulation time and the gradual consumption of network resources, the transmission success rate of all models or algorithms generally decreases. Among them, Epidemic has the highest transmission success rate and the fastest downward trend when the network starts to run. As can be seen from the figure, under the condition that the number of selfish and malicious nodes increases, the data transmission success rate of MTEPRP is high and stable.

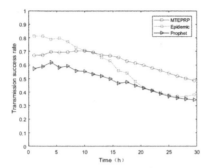

Fig. 5. Comparison chart of network transmission success rate (number of selfish and malicious nodes 100)

In Fig. 6, the average delay time of MTEPRP model at the beginning of simulation is only longer than that of Epidemic routing algorithm at each time, and smaller than that of Epidemic and Prophet in the later stage of simulation experiment.

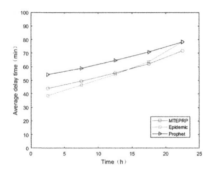

Fig. 6. Comparison chart of average delay time (number of selfish and malicious nodes 100)

Figure 7 shows the routing overhead ratio of each routing protocol, It can be seen that when the number of selfish nodes and malicious nodes increases, the routing overhead ratio of each routing mechanism increases, but relatively speaking, the routing overhead of MTEPRP is also the smallest, because MTEPRP routing protocol eliminates most selfish nodes and malicious nodes in design and greatly reduces the routing overhead of the network.

To sum up, compared with Epidemic and Prophet routing protocol, MTEPRP performs well in all aspects. It can achieve good performance in the harsh Mission-oriented opportunistic networks environment. After many times of the comparison of the experiments, MTEPRP routing protocol not only has good performance in improving the success rate of data transmission, but also controls the transmission delay and network overhead, so it is a routing protocol with strong comprehensive performance. Compared with other routing protocol, it can effectively defend against the bad influence of selfish and malicious nodes on the network performance.

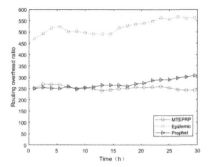

Fig. 7. Comparison chart of network routing overhead ratio (number of selfish and malicious nodes 100)

5 Conclusion

This paper proposes a routing protocol based on multidimensional trust evaluation parameters. Contact intimacy, delivery credibility and location intimacy are selected as multi-dimensional trust evaluation parameters of the routing protocol. By comparing the data forwarding strategy of multi-dimensional trust evaluation parameters, a routing problem for dynamic moving and unstructured space is transformed into a routing problem for static and structured multi-dimensional trust evaluation parameter space. The MTEPRP routing protocol combines the direct trust value and the recommendation trust value to calculate the total trust value of nodes. Simulation results show that compared with Epidemic and Prophet, MTEPRP has better performance in network transmission success rate, data transmission delay and routing overhead.

Acknowledgment. This research is supported in part by the Key Project of Hunan Education Department (No. 19A169), the National Natural Science Foundation of China (No. 61702180), the Hunan Natural Science Foundation of China (No. 2019JJ50167), and the Science Research Project of Hunan Education Department (No. 21C0324).

References

1. Li, X., Niu, J., Kumari, S., et al.: A robust biometrics based three-factor authentication scheme for global mobility networks in smart city. Futur. Gener. Comput. Syst. **83**, 607–618 (2018)
2. Jiang, L., Liu, J., Zhou, D., et al.: Predicting the evolution of hot topics: a solution based on the online opinion dynamics model in social network. IEEE Trans. Syst. Man Cybern.: Syst. **50**(10), 3828–3840 (2018)
3. Diao, C., Zhang, D., Liang, W., et al.: A Novel spatial-temporal multi-scale alignment graph neural network security model for vehicles prediction. IEEE Trans. Intell. Transp. Syst. (2022)
4. Yu, Y., Yu, J., Chen, Z., et al.: A universal routing algorithm based on intuitionistic fuzzy multi-attribute decision-making in opportunistic social networks. Symmetry **13**(4), 664 (2021)
5. Li, X., Peng, J., Niu, J., et al.: A robust and energy efficient authentication protocol for industrial internet of things. IEEE Internet Things J. **5**(3), 1606–1615 (2017)
6. Dong, Y., Chang, L., Luo, J., et al.: A routing query algorithm based on time-varying relationship group in opportunistic social networks. Electronics **10**(13), 1595 (2021)

7. Zou, P., Zhao, M., Wu, J., et al.: Routing algorithm based on trajectory prediction in opportunistic networks. Information **10**(2), 49 (2019)
8. Zhang, S., Li, X., Liu, H., et al.: A privacy-preserving friend recommendation scheme in online social networks. Sustain. Cities Soc. **38**, 275–285 (2018)
9. Li, X., Niu, J., Kumari, S., et al.: A three-factor anonymous authentication scheme for wireless sensor networks in internet of things environments. J. Netw. Comput. Appl. **103**, 194–204 (2018)
10. Zhang, S., Liu, Q., Lin, Y.: Anonymizing popularity in online social networks with full utility. Futur. Gener. Comput. Syst. **72**, 227–238 (2017)
11. Wang, T., Jia, W., Xing, G., et al.: Exploiting statistical mobility models for efficient Wi-Fi deployment. IEEE Trans. Veh. Technol. **62**(1), 360–373 (2012)
12. Akestoridis, D.G., Papapetrou, E.: A framework for the evaluation of routing protocols in opportunistic networks. Comput. Commun. **145**, 14–28 (2019)
13. Sharma, D.K., Dhurandher, S.K., Agarwal, D., et al.: kROp: k-Means clustering based routing protocol for opportunistic networks. J. Ambient. Intell. Humaniz. Comput. **10**(4), 1289–1306 (2019)
14. Wang, T., Wu, Q., Wen, S., et al.: Propagation modeling and defending of a mobile sensor worm in wireless sensor and actuator networks. Sensors **17**(1), 139 (2017)
15. Ciobanu, R.I., Reina, D.G., Dobre, C., et al.: Context-adaptive forwarding in mobile opportunistic networks. Ann. Telecommun. **73**(9), 559–575 (2018)
16. Wu, Y., Huang, H., Wu, N., et al.: An incentive-based protection and recovery strategy for secure big data in social networks. Inf. Sci. **508**, 79–91 (2020)
17. Zhao, R., Zhang, L., Wang, X., et al.: A novel energy-efficient probabilistic routing method for mobile opportunistic networks. EURASIP J. Wirel. Commun. Netw. **2018**(1), 1–15 (2018)
18. Borah, S.J., Dhurandher, S.K., Woungang, I., et al.: A multi-objectives based technique for optimized routing in opportunistic networks. J. Ambient. Intell. Humaniz. Comput. **9**(3), 655–666 (2018)
19. Liu, K., Chen, Z., Wu, J., et al.: Predict and forward: an efficient routing-delivery scheme based on node profile in opportunistic networks. Futur. Internet **10**(8), 74 (2018)
20. Boldrini, C., Conti, M., Jacopini, J., et al.: Hibop: a history based routing protocol for opportunistic networks. In: 2007 IEEE International Symposium on a World of Wireless, Mobile and Multimedia Networks. IEEE, pp. 1–12 (2007)
21. Gupta, A., Bansal, A., Naryani, D., et al.: CRPO: cognitive routing protocol for opportunistic networks. In: Proceedings of the International Conference on High Performance Compilation, Computing and Communications, pp. 121–125 (2017)
22. Kiranmayi, D.: Evaluation of epidemic routing protocol in delay tolerant networks. Int. J. Comput. Sci. Inf. Technol. **5**(3), 4736–4740 (2014)
23. Grasic, S., Davies, E., Lindgren, A., et al.: The evolution of a DTN routing protocol-PRoPHETv2[C]. In: Proceedings of the 6th ACM Workshop on Challenged Networks, pp. 27–30 (2011)
24. Magaia, N., Borrego, C., Pereira, P., et al.: PRIVO: a privacy-preserving opportunistic routing protocol for delay tolerant networks. In: 2017 IFIP Networking Conference (IFIP Networking) and Workshops. IEEE, pp. 1–9 (2017)
25. Zhang, H., Wan, L., Chen, Y., et al.: Adaptive message routing and replication in mobile opportunistic networks for connected communities. ACM Trans. Internet Technol. (TOIT) **18**(1), 1–22 (2017)
26. Yan, Y., Chen, Z., Wu, J., et al.: An effective data transmission algorithm based on social relationships in opportunistic mobile social networks. Algorithms **11**(8), 125 (2018)

Author Index

Printed in the United States
by Baker & Taylor Publisher Services